D1131849

The Corsini Encyclopedia of Psychology and Behavioral Science

Third Edition

The Corsini Encyclopedia of Psychology and Behavioral Science

Third Edition

VOLUME 3

Co-Editors

W. EDWARD CRAIGHEAD
University of Colorado
Boulder, CO

CHARLES B. NEMEROFF
Emory University School of Medicine
Atlanta, GA

Editorial Board

JOHN WILEY & SONS
New York • Chichester • Weinheim • Brisbane • Singapore • Toronto

ISBN 0-471-24096-6 (Volume 1)
ISBN 0-471-24097-4 (Volume 2)
ISBN 0-471-24098-2 (Volume 3)
ISBN 0-471-24099-0 (Volume 4)
ISBN 0-471-23949-6 (Four-volume set)

Printed in the United States of America
10 9 8 7 6 5 4 3 2 1

Preface

This revision of Raymond J. Corsini's successful *Encyclopedia of Psychology* is based on the need to update and expand the previous edition. Because of the advances in behavioral science and the relationship of those advances to psychology, this edition has been renamed to reflect the inclusion of those advances.

The major purpose of these volumes is to make the current knowledge in psychology and behavioral science available to the community at large. It is hoped that they will constitute a concise and handy reference for individuals interested in these topics. Each entry is designed to inform the reader on its particular topic; of necessity, however, an entry in an encyclopedia can be only a succinct summary of that topic. Cross-references are provided for the entries so that the reader can easily make his or her way to related topics for more detail.

In order to keep the encyclopedia to four volumes and still be inclusive of contemporary topics, several now-outdated topics were dropped from the prior edition. We updated about two-thirds of the prior edition, and replaced the remaining one-third with new topics. We have sought to keep the international flavor that Corsini had employed in the original encyclopedia; thus, we selected our contributors from an international list of scholars on the chosen topics.

Coordinating a publication of this magnitude is a formidable task, particularly when undertaken within the framework of one's regular job. Thus, we are extremely appreciative of those who have been so helpful in making this project possible. We are deeply grateful to the more than 1,000 authors who contributed to this encyclopedia; without them, these volumes would not have been. Our greatest appreciation is expressed to Alinne Barrera, Benjamin Page, and Fiona Vajk, who have served as managing editors for this project. We also express our gratitude to Nancy Grabowski (administrative assistant to W. Edward Craighead), who provided necessary support to the editors and managing editors. It is hard to imagine a better or more efficient working team than Kelly Franklin and Jennifer Simon at John Wiley & Sons. Even though many of us involved in this project have experienced numerous, and at times unbelievable, life events during the development and production of these volumes, the project has been brought to a successful and timely completion. We are happy and grateful to have been surrounded by such a fine group of wonderful and dedicated individuals.

In the final analysis, production of these volumes has allowed us to continue a warm friendship and professional collaboration begun about 15 years ago at Duke University Medical Center—a friendship and collaboration that have survived the selection, coordination, and editing of the contributions of well over 1,000 authors on more than 1,200 topics. We have treated patients together; we have conducted collaborative research; we have published together; we have presented together at professional meetings; and we have laughed and cried together in good times and bad. It has been a satisfying experience to edit these volumes together. We trust they will be useful to you, the reader.

W. Edward Craighead, PhD
Boulder, Colorado

Charles B. Nemeroff, MD, PhD
Atlanta, Georgia

112712

Contributors List

NORMAN ABELES
Michigan State University

L. Y. ABRAMSON
University of Wisconsin

ROSEMARY C. ADAM-TEREM
Kapiolani Medical Center, Honolulu, HI

HOWARD S. ADELMAN
University of California, Los Angeles

BERNARD W. AGRANOFF
University of Michigan

LEWIS R. AIKEN
Pepperdine University

ICEK AJZEN
University of Massachusetts

GEORGE W. ALBEE
Florida Mental Health Institute

LYNN E. ALDEN
University of British Columbia

THERON ALEXANDER
Temple University

MARY J. ALLEN
California State College

LAUREN B. ALLOY
Temple University

G. HUGH ALLRED
Brigham Young University

NANCY S. ANDERSON
Emory School of Medicine

JOHN L. ADREASSI
*City University of New York-Baruch
   College*

J. E. ALCOCK
The Australian National University

L. B. AMES

RICHARD S. ANDRULIS
Andrulis Associates, West Chester, PA

HYMIE ANISMAN
Carleton University, Ottawa

H. L. ANSBACHER

RUBEN ARDILA
National University of Colombia

E. Ö. ARNARSON
University of Iceland

MARK ARONOFF
State University of New York, Albany

RICHARD M. ASHBROOK
Capital University

J. WILLIAM ASHER
Purdue University

J. A. ASTIN
University of Maryland School of Medicine

CAROL SHAW AUSTAD

ROBERT M. DAVISON AVILES
Bradley University

K. W. BACK

ALBERT BANDURA
Stanford University

DAVID H. BARLOW
Boston University

AUGUSTINE BARÓN, JR.
University of Texas, Austin

DANIEL BAR-TAL
Tel Aviv University

S. HOWARD BARTLEY
Memphis State University

VALENTINA BASSAREO
University of Cagliari, Italy

B. M. BAUGHAN
University of Colorado, Boulder

ANDREW SLATER BAUM
University of Pittsburgh Cancer Institute

ALAN A. BAUMEISTER
Louisiana State University

RAMÓN BAYÉS SOPENA
Universidad Autónoma de Barcelona

STEVEN BEACH
University of Georgia

AARON T. BECK
*Beck Institute for Cognitive Therapy and
   Research*

GARY S. BELKIN
Brown University

ALAN S. BELLACK
University of Maryland

JOEL B. BENNETT
Texas Christian University

THOMAS S. BENNETT
*Brain Inquiry Recovery Program, Fort
   Collins, CO*

HEATHER A. E. BENSON
University of Manitoba

P. G. BENSON
New Mexico State University

SHERI A. BERENBAUM
Southern Illinois University

S. BERENTSEN

LEONARD BERGER
Clemson University

JOANNE BERGER-SWEENEY
Wellesly College

GREGORY S. BERNS
Emory University

G. G. BERNTSON
Ohio State University

MICHAEL D. BERZONSKY
State University of New York, Cortland

SIDNEY W. BIJOU
University of Nevada

AIDA BILALBEGOVIC
Tufts University, Medford, MA

JEFFREY R. BINDER
Medical College Of Wisconsin

JERRY M. BINDER
*Behavioral Health Consultant, Corona Del
   Mar*

NIELS BIRMBAUER
University of Tübingen, Germany

D. W. BLACK
University of Iowa

THEODORE H. BLAU

BERNARD L. BLOOM
University of Colorado

MILTON S. BLOOMBAUM
Southern Oregon University

JODI L. BODDY
Simon Fraser University, British Columbia

C. ALAN BONEAU
George Mason University

EDWARD S. BORDIN
University of Michigan

EDGAR F. BORGATTA
University of Washington

P. BOSE
University of Florida

DALE E. BOWEN
*Psychological Associates, Grand Junction,
   CO*

A. D. BRANSTETTER

C. REGINALD BRASINGTON
University of South Carolina

MARGARET BRENMAN-GIBSON
Harvard Medical School

RONAL BRENNER
St. John's Episcopal Hospital, Far Rockaway, NY

WARRICK J. BREWER
The University of Melbourne & Mental Health Research Institute of Victoria

SARA K. BRIDGES
Humboldt State University

ARTHUR P. BRIEF
Tulane University

R. W. BRISLIN
University of Hawaii

GILBERTO N. O. BRITO
Instituto Fernandes Figueira, Brazil

DONALD E. BROADBENT
University of Oxford

J. D. BROOKE
Northwestern University

FREDERICK GRAMM BROWN
Iowa State University

ROBERT TINDALL BROWN
University of North Carolina, Wilmington

SHELDON S. BROWN
North Shore Community College

J. BROZEK

MARTIN BRÜNE
Ruhr University, Germany

B. R. BUGELSKI
State University of New York, Buffalo

GRAHAM D. BURROWS
University of Melbourne

JAMES M. BUTCHER
University of Minnesota, Minneaplois

ANN B. BUTLER
George Mason University

REBECCA M. BUTZ
Tulane University

J. T. CACIOPPO
University of Chicago

SHAWN P. CAHILL
University of Pennsylvania

JOHN B. CAMPBELL
Franklin & Marshall College

N. A. CAMPBELL
Brown University

TYRONE D. CANNON
University of California, Los Angeles

SAMUEL S. CARDONE
Illinois Department of Mental Health, Chicago

BERNARDO J. CARDUCCI
Shyness Research Institute, Indiana University Southeast

MARK CARICH
Adler School of Professional Psychology

PETER A. CARICH
University of Missouri

JOHN G. CARLSON
University of Hawaii, Honolulu

J. DOUGLAS CARROLL
Rutgers University

GIOVANNI CASINI
Tuscia University, Italy

T. CASOLI
I.N.R.C.A., Italy

LOUIS G. CASTONGUAY
Pennsylvania State University

CARL ANDREW CASTRO
Walter Reed Army Institute of Research

FAIRFID M. CAUDLE
College of Staten Island

JOSEPH R. CAUTELA

STEPHEN J. CECI
Cornell University

JAE-HO CHA
Seoul National University

PAUL F. CHAPMAN
University of Minnesota, Minneaplois

U. CHARPA
Cologne University, Germany

GORDON J. CHELUNE
The Cleveland Clinic Foundation

GLYN CHIDLOW
University of Oxford

IRVIN L. CHILD
Yale University

MARGARET M. CLIFFORD
University of Iowa

RICHARD WELTON COAN
Retired, University of Arizona

KIMBERLY PEELE COCKERHAM
Allegheny Ophthalmic and Orbital Associates, Pittsburgh

MARK S. COE
DePaul University

NORMAN J. COHEN
Baylor State University

P. COHEN-KETTENIS
Utrecht University, The Netherlands

RAYMOND J. COLELLO
Virginia Commonwealth University

GARY R. COLLINS
Trinity Evangelical Divinity School

MARY BETH CONNOLLY
University of Pennsylvania

M. J. CONSTANTINO
Pennsylvania State University

GERALD COOKE
Plymouth Meeting, PA

JEREMY D. COPLAND
Columbia University College of Physicians and Surgeons

STANLEY COREN
University of British Columbia

GERALD F. COREY
California State University, Fullerton

JOHN F. CORSO
State University of New York, Cortland

ERMINIO COSTA
University of Illinois, Chicago

JOSEPH T. COYLE
Harvard University

BENJAMIN H. CRAIGHEAD
Medical College of Virginia

W. EDWARD CRAIGHEAD
University of Colorado

PAUL CRITS-CHRISTOPH
University of Pennsylvania

ARNOLD E. DAHLKE
Los Angeles, CA

JOHN G. DARLEY
University of Minnesota, Minneaplois

WILLIAM S. DAVIDSON II
Michigan State University

EDWARD L. DECI
University of Rochester

CRISTINA MARTA DEL-BEN
Universidade de São Paulo, Brazil

H. A. DEMAREE
Kessler Medical Rehabilitation Research and Education Corporation

FLORENCE L. DENMARK
Pace University, New York

M. RAY DENNY
Michigan State University

DONALD R. DENVER
Quebec, Montreal, Canada

NORMAN K. DENZIN
University of Illinois, Urbana

SARAH E. DEROSSETT

FRANCINE DEUTSCH
San Diego State University

DAVID L. DEVRIES
Kaplan DeVries Institute

DONALD ALLEN DEWSBURY
University of Florida

ESTHER E. DIAMOND

MILTON DIAMOND
University of Hawaii, Honolulu

R. DIAZ-GUERRERO
University of Mexico

MANFRED DIEHL
University of Colorado

VOLKER DIETZ
University Hospital Balgrist, Zurich

R. DILLON

RAYMOND DINGLEDINE
Emory University School of Medicine

JOHN W. DONAHOE
University of Massachusetts

NICK DONNELLY
University of Southampton, UK

SYLVAIN DORÉ
Johns Hopkins University

MICHAEL G. DOW
University of South Florida

PETER W. DOWRICK
University of Hawaii, Manoa

JURIS G. DRAGUNS
Pennsylvania State University

CLIFFORD J. DREW
University of Utah

D. A. DROSSMAN
University of North Carolina

PHILIP H. DUBOIS

HUBERT C. J. DUIJKER
University of Amsterdam

BRUCE R. DUNN
The University of West Florida

M. O. A. DUROJAIYE
University of Lagos, Nigeria

TERRY M. DWYER
University of Mississippi School of Medicine

G. D'YDEWALLE
University of Leuven, Belgium

BARRY A. EDELSTEIN
West Virginia University

THOMAS E. EDGAR
Idaho State University

WILLIAM E. EDMONSTON, JR.
Colgate University

C. L. EHLERS
University of California, San Diego

HOWARD EICHENBAUM
Boston University

ROGER E. ENFIELD
West Central Georgia Regional Hospital, Columbus, GA

JOHN WILLIAM ENGEL
University of Hawaii, Honolulu

FRANZ R. EPTING
University of Florida

ANGELICA ESCALONA
Nova Southeastern University

DAVID RICHARD EVANS
University of Western Ontario

FREDERICK J. EVANS
Reading Hospital

ROBERT B. EWEN
Miami, FL

CORA E. EZZELL
Medical University of South Carolina

CLARA C. FAURA-GINER
Universidad Miguel Hernandez, Spain

HERMAN FEIFEL
Veterans Administration Outpatient Clinic, Los Angeles

LAURIE B. FELDMAN
State University of New York, Albany

EVA DREIKURS FERGUSON
Southern Illinois University

JOSEPH R. FERRARI
Depaul University

MICHAEL A. FIEDLER
University of Alabama, Birmingham

FRANK W. FINGER
University of Virginia

S. FINGER
Washington University

HAROLD KENNETH FINK
Honolulu, HI

NORMAN J. FINKEL
Georgetown University

CHET H. FISCHER
Radford University

DAVID A. FISHBAIN
University of Miami

DENNIS F. FISHER
U.S. Army Human Engineering Laboratory

DOUGLAS A. FITTS
University of Washington

REIKO MAKI FITZSIMONDS
Yale School of Medicine

DEBRA A. FLEISCHMAN
Rush-Presbyterian St. Luke's Medical Center

EDNA B. FOA
University of Pennsylvania

JAMES L. FOBES
Army Research Institute for the Behavioral Sciences

JOHN P. FOREYT
Baylor College of Medicine

BARBARA L. FORISHA-KOVACH
University of Michigan

GEORGE FOURIEZOS
University of Ottawa

MARCI GITTES FOX
Beck Institute for Cognitive Therapy and Research

NATHAN A. FOX
University of Maryland

J. FRANKENHEIM
National Institutes of Health

CALVIN J. FREDERICK
University of California, Los Angeles

MATS FREDERICKSON
Uppsala University, Sweden

C. R. FREEMAN
McGill University

W. O. FRIESEN
University of Virginia

ROBERT H. FRIIS
California State University, Long Beach

KARL J. FRISTON
Institute of Neurology, UK

BENJAMIN FRUCHTER
University of Texas, Austin

ISAO FUKUNISHI
Tokyo Institute of Psychiatry

TOMAS FURMARK
Uppsala University, Sweden

PAUL A. GADE
U. S. Army Research Institute

SOL L. GARFIELD
Washington University

G. GASKELL
University of York, UK

STEVEN J. GARLOW
Emory School of Medicine

TIMOTHY L. GASPERONI
University of California, Los Angeles

JEAN S. GEARON
University of Maryland

NORI GEARY
Weill Medical College of Cornell University

K. F. GEISINGER
Le Moyne College

MARK S. GEORGE
Medical University of South Carolina

T. D. GIARGIARI
University of Colorado, Boulder

KAREN M. GIL
University of North Carolina, Chapel Hill

RITA T. GIUBILATO
Thomas Jefferson University

THOMAS A. GLASS
Honolulu, HI

WILLIAM GLASSER
The William Glasser Institute, Chatsworth, CA

J. M. GLOZMAN
Moscow University

CHARLES J. GOLDEN
Nova Southeastern University

ROBERT N. GOLDEN
University of North Carolina School of Medicine

ARNOLD P. GOLDSTEIN
Syracuse University

JEFFREY L. GOODIE
West Virginia University

G. KEN GOODRICK
University of Houston

LEONARD D. GOODSTEIN
Washington, DC

BERNARD S. GORMAN
Nassau Community College

GILBERT GOTTLIEB
University of North Carolina, Chapel Hill

DONALD L. GRANT
Roswell, CTA

J. W. GRAU
Texas A & M University

MARTIN S. GREENBERG
University of Pittsburgh

W. A. GREENE
Eastern Washington University

SHELLY F. GREENFIELD
McLean Hospital, Belmont, MA

JAMES LYNN GREENSTONE
Southwestern Academy of Crisis Interveners, Dallas

WILLIAM EDGAR GREGORY
University of the Pacific

SEBASTIAN P. GROSSMAN
University of Chicago

AMANDA J. GRUBER
McLean Hospital, Belmont, MA

ROBERT M. GUION
Bowling Green State University

LAURA GULI
University of Texas, Austin

G. GUTTMANN
University of Vienna

RUSSELL A. HABER
University of South Carolina

HAROLD V. HALL
Honolulu, HI

KATHERINE A. HALMI
Cornell University Medical Center

MARK B. HAMNER
Medical University of South Carolina

GREGORY R. HANCOCK
University of Maryland

FOREST W. HANSEN
Lake Forest College

J. M. HARPER
Brigham Young University

JOSEPH T. HART
University of Colorado

ALISHA B. HART
Kupat Holim Klalit, Tel Aviv

E. I. HARTLEY

SCOTT HARTMAN
Center for Marital and Family Studies, University of Denver

DAVID B. HATFIELD
Eastern Washington University

ELAINE HATFIELD
University of Hawaii, Manoa

ROBERT P. HAWKINS
West Virginia University

STEPHEN N. HAYNES
University of Hawaii, Manoa

N. A. HAYNIE

DONALD A. HECK
Iowa State

S. R. HEIDEMANN
Michigan State University

J. HEIMAN
University of Washington

LYNNE M. HENDERSON
The Shyness Institute, Stanford

GREGG HENRIQUES
University of Pennsylvania

P. P. HEPPNER
University of Missouri, Columbia

GREGORY M. HEREK
University of California, Davis

EDWIN L. HERR
Pennsylvania State University

ALLEN K. HESS
Auburn University

ERNEST R. HILGARD
Stanford University

JEANNE SWICKARD HOFFMAN
Honolulu, HI

RALPH E. HOFFMAN
Yale School of Medicine

CHRISTINE HOHMANN
Morgan State University

P. Y. HONG
University of Kansas

B. HOPKINS
Seattle University

RONALD R. HOLDEN
Queen's University, Ontario

DAVID L. HOLMES
The Eden Institute, Princeton

DAVID SHERIDAN HOLMES
University of Kansas

WAYNE H. HOLTZMAN
University of Texas, Austin

BURT HOPKINS
Seattle University

J. HOSKOVEC

ARTHUR C. HOUTS
University of Memphis

ROBERT H. HOWLAND
University of Pittsburgh School of Medicine

C. H. HUBER
New Mexico State University

BRADLEY E. HUITEMA
Western Michigan University

LLOYD G. HUMPHRIES
University of Illinois, Champaign

MAX L. HUTT

G. W. HYNDE
University of Georgia

JAMES ROBERT IBERG
Chicago, IL

S. S. ILARDI
University of Kansas

DANIEL R. ILGEN
Michigan State University

Y. IWAMURA
Toho University, Japan

I. JACKSON
Brown University

L. JANOSI
Exponential Biotherapies, Inc.

ARTHUR R. JENSEN
University of California, Berkeley

QICHENG JING
Chinese Academy of Sciences, Beijing

DAVID W. JOHNSON
University of Minnesota, Minneaplois

JAMES H. JOHNSON
University of Florida

ORVAL G. JOHNSON
Centennial BOCES, La Salle, CO

ROGER T. JOHNSON
University of Minnesota, Minneaplois

EVE S. JONES
Los Angeles City College

LASZLO JANOSI
Exponential Biotherapies, Inc.

JON H. KAAS
Vanderbilt University

ROBERT B. KAISER
Kaplan DeVries Institute

AKIRA KAJI
Exponential Biotherapies, Inc.

JAMES W. KALAT
North Carolina State University

P. W. KALIVAS
Medical University of South Carolina

TOMOE KANAYA
Cornell

SAUL KANE
Queens College, City University of New York

BARRY H. KANTOWITZ
Battelle Institute, Seattle

RICHARD PAUL KAPPENBERG
Hawaii Professional Psychology Group, Honolulu

WERNER KARLE
Corona Del Mar, CA

NADINE KASLOW
Emory School of Medicine

A. J. KASTIN
University of New Orleans

BOJE KATZENELSON
University of Aarhus, Denmark

TERENCE M. KEANE
Boston University

A. J. KEARNEY
Behavior Therapy Institute

E. JAMES KEHOE
University of New South Wales

TIMOTHY KEITH-LUCAS
The University of the South

SALLY KELLER
Adelphi University

THOMAS M. KELLEY
Wayne State University

CAROLIN S. KEUTZER
University of Oregon

GREGORY A. KIMBLE
Duke University

JAMES E. KING
University of Arizona

BRENDA J. KING
University of Tennessee

DANIEL N. KLEIN
State University of New York

WALTER G. KLOPFER

MAX J. KOBBERT
Hochschule for Beildende Künste, Münster

ALBERT T. KONDO
University of Houston

S. J. KORCHIN

WILLIAM J. KOROTITSCH
University of North Carolina, Greensboro

SURESH KOTAGAL
Mayo Clinic

G. KOVACS
Dalhousie University

LEONARD KRASNER
Stanford University School of Medicine

DAVID R. KRATHWOHL
Syracuse University

ALAN G. KRAUT
American Psychological Society, Washington, DC

STEFAN KRUEGER
Yale School of Medicine

STANLEY KRIPPNER
Saybrook Graduate School, San Francisco

SAMUEL E. KRUG
MetriTech, Inc., Campaign, IL

CAROL LANDAU
Brown University Division of Medicine

PHILIPPE LANDREVILLE
Laval, Sainte-Foy, Quebec

TED LANDSMAN
University of Florida

CHRISTOPH J. G. LANG
University of Erlangen-Buremberg, Germany

GEORGE M. LANGFORD
Dartmouth College

KEITH LANGLEY
University of Strasbourg, France

E. K. LANPHIER
Pennsylvania State University

V. W. LARACH
Univerdidad de Chile

DAVID G. LAVOND
University of Southern California

ARNOLD A. LAZARUS
Center for Multimodal Psychological Services, Princeton

RICHARD S. LAZARUS
University of California, Berkeley

THOMAS H. LEAHEY
Virginia Commonwealth University

ROBERT A. LEARK
Pacific Christian College

ARTHUR LERNER
Los Angeles City College

RICHARD M. LERNER
Tufts University

L. S. LEUNG
University of Western Ontario

ALLAN LEVEY
Emory University

HARRY LEVINSON
The Levinson Institute

SHARON C. LEVITON
Southwestern Academy of Crisis Interveners, Dallas

EUGENE E. LEVITT
Indiana University School of Medicine

P. M. LEWINSOHN
Oregon Research Institute, Eugene

RONALD T. LEY
State University of New York, Albany

ANDRE L'HOURS
World Health Organization, Geneva

KAREN Z. H. LI
Max Planck Institute for Human Development

SHU-CHEN LI
Max Planck Institute for Human Development

P. E. LICHTENSTEIN

CAROL SCHNEIDER LIDZ
Touro College

SCOTT O. LILIENFELD
Emory University

G. LIN
National Institutes of Health

HENRY CLAY LINDGREN
San Francisco State University

RONALD LIPPITT

MARK W. LIPSEY
Vanderbilt University

A. LLOYD

JOHN E. LOCHMAN
University of Alabama, Tuscaloosa

JOHN C. LOEHLIN
University of Texas, Austin

JANE LOEVINGER
Washington University

DONALD N. LOMBARDI
Seton Hall University

WOLF-EKKEHARD LÖNNIG
*Max Planck Institut fur
   Züchtungsforschung, Köln, Germany*

JOSEPH LOPICCOLO
University of Missouri

JEFFREY P. LORBERBAUM
Medical University of South Carolina

O. IVAR LOVAAS
University of California, Los Angeles

ROBERT E. LUBOW
Tel Aviv University

J. O. LUGO
Fullerton, CA

K. LUKATELA
Brown University

ROBERT W. LUNDIN
Wheaton, IL

DAVID T. LYKKEN
University of Minnesota, Minneapolis

BRETT V. MACFARLANE
University of Queensland

ROBIN M. MACKAR
*National Institute on Drug Abuse, Bethesda,
   MD*

S. MADHUSOODANAN
*St. John's Episcopal Hospital, Far
   Rockaway, NY*

MICHAEL P. MALONEY
Pasadena, CA

HOWARD MARKMAN
*Center for Marital and Family Studies,
   University of Denver*

RONALD R. MARTIN
West Virginia University

C. MARTINDALE
University of Maine

P. MARUFF
La Trobe University, Australia

ROBERT C. MARVIT
Honolulu, HI

MELVIN H. MARX
N. Hutchinson Island, FL

JOSEPH D. MATARAZZO
Oregon Health Sciences University

BARBARA B. MATES
City College, NY

RYAN K. MAY
The University of Memphis

FAUZIA SIMJEE MCCLURE
University of California, San Diego

BARBARA S. MCCRADY
Rutgers University

JANET L. MCDONALD
Louis State University

JENNIFER J. MCGRATH
Bowling Green State University

JOHN PAUL MCKINNEY
Michigan State University

KATHLEEN MCKINNEY
University of Wisconsin

C. M. MCCLEOD
University of Toronto

JAMES H. MCMILLAN
Virginia Commonwealth University

PATRICK MCNAMARA
Boston University

NEIL MCNAUGHTON
University of Otago, New Zealand

JANICE MCPHEE
Florida Gulf Coast University

PAUL W. MCREYNOLDS
University of Nevada

HEATHER MEGGERS
University of Missouri

RICHARD MEILI
University of Bern, Switzerland

RONALD MELZACK
McGill University, Montreal

P. F. MERENDA
University of Rhode Island

STANLEY B. MESSER
Rutgers University

CINDY M. MESTON
University of Texas, Austin

JAMIE L. METSALA
University of Maryland

ANDREW W. MEYERS
The University of Memphis

K. D. MICHEVA
Stanford University

DAVID J. MIKLOWITZ
University of Colorado

STANLEY MILGRAM

MARK W. MILLER
Boston University

NEAL ELGAR MILLER
Yale University

RALPH R. MILLER
State University of New York, Binghamton

THEODORE MILLON
University of Miami

HENRYK MISIAK
Fordham University

AKIRA MIYAKE
University of Colorado

TAE-IM MOON

STEWART MOORE
University of Windsor, Ontario

JAMES A. MORONE
Brown University

DANIEL G. MORROW
University of New Hampshire

F. MUELLER
*Forschungszentrum Juelich GmbH,
   Germany*

K. L. MULLER
Rutgers University

R. MURISON
University of Bergen, Norway

FRANK B. MURRAY
University of Delaware

ANNE MYERS
St. Jerome Convent, Philadelphia

FRANCIS A. NEELON
Duke University

ROBERT A. NEIMEYER
University of Memphis

J. NEISEWANDER
Arizona State University

A. NELSON

ROSEMARY O. NELSON-GRAY
University of North Carolina, Greensboro

CORY F. NEWMAN

DAVID G. NICKINOVICH
University of Washington

PHILIP T. NINAN
Emory School of Medicine

J. T. NOGA
Emory University

TREVOR R. NORMAN
University of Melbourne

M. S. NYSTUL

WILLIAM H. O'BRIEN
Bowling Green State University

WALTER EDWARD O'CONNELL
Natural High Center, Bastrop, TX

W. O'DONOHUE

K. DANIEL O'LEARY
State University of New York, Stony Brook

G. A. OLSON
University of New Orleans

R. D. OLSON
University of New Orleans

MARLENE OSCAR-BERMAN
Boston University

THOMAS M. OSTROM
Ohio State University

J. BRUCE OVERMIER
University of Bergen, Norway

B. D. OZAKI
Honolulu Waldorf School

DANIEL J. OZER
University of California, Riverside

K. PACAK
National Institutes of Health

DAVID C. PALMER
Smith College

EDWARD L. PALMER
Davidson College

LOREN D. PANKRATZ
Oregon Health Sciences University

C. PANTELIS
University of Melbourne, Australia

WILLIAM M. PARDRIDGE
University of California School of Medicine, Los Angeles

ALAN J. PARKIN
University of Sussex, England

E. J. PARKINS
Nottingham University, England

H. MCILVANIE PARSONS
Human Resources Research Organization, Alexandria, VA

R. PATUZZI

PAUL PAULI
University of Tübingen, Germany

V. PEČJAK

PAUL PEDERSON
University of Alabama, Birmingham

T. M. PENIX

HAROLD BRENNER PEPINSKY
Ohio State University

KATHERINE L. PETERS
University of Alberta

C. PETERSON
University of Michigan

DONALD R. PETERSON
Rutgers University

CHARLES S. PEYSER
The University of the South

E. JERRY PHARES
Kansas State University

D. PHILIP
University of Florida

JESSICA M. PIERCE
Boston University

AARON L. PINCUS
Pennsylvania State University

LUIGI PIZZAMIGLIO
Universita Degli Studi di Roma, Italy

J. POIRIER
University of Washington

R. E. POLAND
University of California, Los Angeles

H. G. POPE, JR.
McLean Hospital, Belmont, MA

R. M. POST
National Institute of Mental Health

BRUNO POUCET
Centre National de la Recherche Scientifique, France

A. R. PRATKANIS
University of California, Santa Cruz

ANN B. PRATT
Capital University, Columbus, OH

ROBERT ALAN PRENTKY
Justice Resource Institute, Bridgewater, MA

AINA PUCE
Swinburne University of Technology, Australia

S. J. QUALLS
University of Colorado

MARK QUIGG
University of Virginia

KAREN S. QUIGLEY
Pennsylvania State University

RÉMI QUIRION
Douglas Hospital Research Center, Canada

ALBERT ISRAEL RABIN
Michigan State University

M. K. RAINA
Sri Aurobindo Marg, India

K. RAMAKRISHNA RAO
Duke University

U. RAO
University of California, Los Angeles

J. RAPPAPORT
University of Illinois, Chicago

MARK D. RAPPORT
University of Central Florida

RICHARD L. RAPSON
University of Hawaii, Manoa

NATHANIEL J. RASKIN
Northwestern University Medical School

R. L. RASMUSSON
Allegheny University of Health Sciences

A. RAVIV
Tel Aviv University

W. J. RAY
Pennsylvania State University

HERB REICH

ANTHONY H. REINHARDT-RUTLAND
University of Ulster

J. M. REINISCH
Indiana University

DANIEL REISBERG
Reed College

MAURICE REUCHLIN
Institute Nationale D'Orientation Professionale, Paris

MARY E. REUDER

G. R. REYES

CECIL R. REYNOLDS
Texas A&M University

GEORGE F. RHOADES, JR.
Ola Hou Clinic, Aiea, HI

ALEXANDER RICH
University of South Florida

DAVID C. S. RICHARD
Southwest Missouri State University

EDWARD J. RICKERT
University of Alabama, Birmingham

L. RIES

Y. RINGEL
University of North Carolina

ARTHUR J. RIOPELLE
Louisiana State University

CHRISTIE RIZZO
New York State Psychiatric Institute

DONALD ROBBINS
Fordham University

GARY JEROME ROBERTSON
Wide Range, Inc., Tampa

GEORGE H. ROBINSON
University of North Alabama

RONALD ROESCH
Simon Fraser University, British Columbia

MICHAEL J. ROHRBAUGH
University of Arizona

STEVEN PAUL ROOSE
Columbia University

R. ROSENBERG
Sleep Disorders Center, Evanston, IL

ROBERT ROSENTHAL
University of California, Riverside

SAUL ROSENZWEIG
Washington University

HELEN WARREN ROSS
San Diego State University

WILLIAM H. ROSS
University of Wisconsin

J. S. ROSSI
University of Rhode Island

B. O. ROTHBAUM
Emory University

DONALD K. ROUTH
University of Miami

PETER ROY-BYRNE
Harborview Medical Center, Seattle

MARK A. RUIZ
Pennsylvania State University

ROGER WOLCOTT RUSSELL
University of California, Irvine

J. J. RYAN
Central Missouri State University

DEBORAH SADOWSKI
Tufts University

W. S. SAHAKIAN

WILLIAM SAMUEL
University of California, San Diego

T. SAND
Norwegian University of Science and Technology

WILLIAM C. SANDERSON
Rutgers University

JEROME SANES
Brown University

LAWRENCE J. SANNA
Washington State University

C. SANTERRE
University of Arizona

JOHN WYNNE SANTROCK
University of Texas-Dallas, Richardson

EDWARD P. SARAFINO
The College of New Jersey, Ewing

WILLIAM IRVIN SAUSER, JR.
Auburn University

ALICE D. SCHEUER
University of Hawaii, Honolulu

K. SCHMIDTKE
University of Frieberg, Germany

DAVID A SCHULDBERG
University of Montana

ALEXANDER JULIAN SCHUT
Pennsylvania State University

JULIE B. SCHWEITZER
Emory School of Medicine

D. L. SEGAL
University of Colorado

SAUL B. SELLS
Texas Christian University

J. SHANTEAU

D. H. SHAPIRO
University of California, Irvine

KENNETH JOEL SHAPIRO
Psychologists for the Ethical Treatment of Animals

S. L. SHAPIRO
University of Arizona

J. A. SHARPE
University of Toronto

Y. SHAULY
Allegheny University of Health Sciences

ROBERT A. SHAW
Brown University

GLENN D. SHEAN
College of William and Mary

STEVEN D. SHERRETS
Maine Head Trauma Center, Bangor

EDWIN S. SHNEIDMAN
University of California School of Medicine, Los Angeles

VARDA SHOHAM
University of Arizona, Tucson

BERNARD H. SHULMAN
Northwestern University Medical School

JULIE A. SHUMACHER
State University of New York, Stony Brook

M. SIGUAN
Barcelona, Spain

ELSA A. SIIPOLA
Smith College

ALCINO J. SILVA
University of California, Los Angeles

HIRSCH LAZAAR SILVERMAN

L. SILVERN
University of Colorado, Boulder

HERBERT A. SIMON
Carnegie Mellon University

ALAN SIMPKINS
University of Hawaii, Honolulu

M. BREWSTER SMITH
University of California, Santa Cruz

WILLIAM PAUL SMITH
Vanderbilt University

DAWN SOMMER
University of Texas, Austin

SUBHASH R. SONNAD
Western Michigan University

PETER W. SORRENSEN
University of Minnesota, St. Paul

JANET TAYLOR SPENCE
University of Texas, Austin

DANTE S. SPETTER
New England Medical Center, Boston

ROBERT P. SPRAFKIN
Veterans Administration Medical Center, Syracuse

SCOTT STANLEY
Center for Marital and Family Studies, University of Denver

KEVIN D. STARK
University of Texas, Austin

STEPHEN STARK
University of Illinois, Champaign

TIMOTHY STEENBERGH
The University of Memphis

ROBERT A. STEER
University of Medicine and Dentistry of New Jersey

A. STEIGER
Max Plank Institute of Psychiatry, Germany

ROBERT M. STELMACK
University of Ottawa

ROBERT H. STENSRUD
University of Northern Iowa

R. J. STERNBERG
Yale University

GERALD L. STONE
University of Iowa

WILLIAM S. STONE
Harvard University

HUGH A. STORROW
University of Kentucky

EZRA STOTLAND
University of Washington

GEORGE STRICKER
Adelphi University

RICHARD B. STUART
Weight Watchers International

D. I. SUCHMAN
University of Florida

ARTHUR SULLIVAN
Memorial University, Newfoundland

S. W. SUMERALL
William Jewell College

NORMAN D. SUNDBERG
University of Oregon

J. T. SUPER

ROBERT J. SUTHERLAND
University of New Mexico

H. A. SWADLOW
Brown University

SUSAN SWEARER
University of Texas, Austin

JULIAN I. TABER
Veterans Administration Medical Center, Reno

ANA TABOADA
University of Maryland

YASUMASA TANAKA
Gakushuin University, Tokyo

JAMES T. TEDESCHI
State University of New York

J. A. TESTA
University of Oklahoma

ALEXANDER THOMAS
New York University School of Medicine

S. M. THOMPSON
University of Maryland

BEVERLY E. THORN
University of Alabama, Tuscaloosa

B. MICHAEL THORNE
Mississippi State University

DAVID F. TOLIN
University of Pennsylvania

ELEANOR REARDON TOLSON
University of Washington

JOE TOMAKA
University of Texas, El Paso

LOUIS G. TORNATZKY
National Science Foundation, Washington, DC

DANIEL TRANEL
University of Iowa

FREDERICK TRAVIS
Maharishi University of Management, Fairfield, IA

WILLIAM T. TSUSHIMA
Straub Clinic and Hospital, Inc., Honolulu

LEONARD P. ULLMANN
Incline Valley, Nevada

E. ULVESTAD

RHODA KESLER UNGER
Montclair State College

SUSANA PATRICIA URBINA
University of Northern Florida

T. BEDIRHAN ÜSTÜN
World Health Organization, Geneva

A. L. VACARINO
University of New Orleans

P. VALDERRAMA-ITURBE
Mexico

P. VANDEL
Hospital Saint-Jacques, Bensancon, France

R. D. VANDERPLOEG
University of South Florida

KIRSTEN M. VANMEENAN
University of Maryland

ANTHONY J. VATTANO
University of Illinois, Champaign

FRANCES E. VAUGHAN
California Institute of Transpersonal Psychology, Menlo Park

P. E. VERNON

WILLIAM F. VITULLI
University of Southern Alabama

N. J. WADE
University of Dundee, Scotland

REX ALVON WADHAM
Brigham Young University

E. E. WAGNER
Forest Institute of Professional Psychology

RICHARD D. WALK
George Washington University

ARLENE S. WALKER-ANDREWS
Rutgers University

PATRICIA M. WALLACE
University of Maryland

ROGER N. WALSH
University of California, Irvine

ZHONG-MING WANG
Zhejiang University, China

WILSE B. WEBB
University of Florida

JOEL LEE WEINBERGER
Adelphi University

ARNOLD D. WELL
University of Massachusetts

W. W. WENRICH
University of North Texas

MICHAEL WERTHEIMER
University of Colorado

DONALD L. WERTLIEB
Tufts University

IAN Q. WHISHAW
University of Lethbridge, Alberta

M. A. WHISMAN
University of Colorado, Boulder

SARAH WHITTON
Center for Marital and Family Studies, University of Denver

ERIKA WICK
St. John's University

DELOS N. WICKENS
Ohio State University

RICHARD E. WILCOX
University of Texas, Austin

SABINE WILHELM
Massachusetts General Hospital, Charlestown

DOUGLAS A. WILLIAMS
University of Winnipeg

RICHARD H. WILLIS
University of Pittsburgh

J. WILSON
University of Minnesota, Duluth

MARGARET T. T. WONG-RILEY
Medical College of Wisconsin

MICHAEL L. WOODRUFF
East Tennessee State University

D. S. WOODRUFF-PAK
Temple University

MARGARET P. WOODS

T. E. WOODS
University of Wisconsin School of Medicine

ROBERT L. WOOLFOLK
Rutgers University

ANTHONY WRIGHT
University of Manitoba

TRISTAM D. WYATT
University of Minnesota, St. Paul

R. C. WYLIE

LARRY J. YOUNG
Emory University

L. M. YOUNGBLADE
University of Colorado

ZAHRA ZAKERI
Queens College, City University of New York

O. L. ZANGWILL
Cambridge, England

JOHANNES M. ZANKER
The Australian National University

PATRICIA A. ZAPF
University of Alabama

W. ZHANG
New York Medical College

DANIEL J. ZIEGLER
Villanova University

PHILIP G. ZIMBAROO
Stanford University

M. ZUCKERMAN
University of Delaware

FIONA VAJK: MANAGING EDITOR
BENJAMIN PAGE: MANAGING EDITOR
ALINNE BARRERA: MANAGER EDITOR

The Corsini Encyclopedia of Psychology and Behavioral Science

Third Edition

M

MacCORQUODALE, KENNETH (1919–1986)

Kenneth MacCorquodale received the BA at the University of Minnesota with the intention of pursuing a career in art. However, his interests turned to psychology, and he entered the Minnesota graduate school in that field. Among other distinguished professors, he studied with B. F. Skinner who had recently become an assistant professor there. He received the PhD at Minnesota after returning from military service in 1946. He remained a member of the Minnesota faculty until his retirement.

His career was intertwined with that of Paul Meehl in their combined work in the philosophy of science and learning theory, most notably that of E. C. Tolman. MacCorquodale and Meehl are well known for their joint article "On a distinction between hypothetical constructs and intervening variables." They also collaborated on Tolman's theory in Estes and colleagues *Modern Learning Theory.*

MacCorquodale published a retrospective review of Skinner's verbal behavior and a rebuttal to Chomsky's critical review of Skinner's book. Besides his scholarship, he was highly regarded as a teacher, receiving the Liberal Arts College's Distinguished Teaching Award.

R. W. LUNDIN
Wheaton, Illinois

MAHER, BRENDAN (1924–   )

Brendan Arnold Maher is the Edward C. Henderson Research Professor of Psychology at Harvard University. Born October 31, 1924 in Widnes, England, he served in the Royal Navy Volunteer Reserve as a Lieutenant, then continued his formal education at the university of Manchester, graduating in 1950 with First Class Honours in psychology.

Maher was awarded a Fulbright and an English-Speaking Union scholarship for graduate study in clinical psychology at Ohio State University, where he received his MA in 1951 and his PhD in 1954. Maher interned at the Illinois Neuropsychiatric Institute in Chicago, then returned to England and an appointment to the position of psychologist in Her Majesty's Prison in Yorkshire. In subsequent years he pursued teaching and research at Ohio State, Northwestern University, Louisiana State University, Harvard University, University of Wisconsin, Brandeis University, University of Copenhagen, New York University, and University of Utah. He has received numerous honors, including an honorary MA and Phi Beta Kappa, as well as a Geyser Fellowship, from Harvard; a PhD (honoris causa) from the University of Copenhagen; and the Zubin Award of the Society for Research in Psychopathology.

Maher served as both editor (1964–1971) and co-editor (1972–1989) of *Progress in Experimental Personality Research.* He edited the *Journal of Consulting and Clinical Psychology* from 1972 to 1978 and was elected charter president of the Society for Research in Psychopathology in 1986. Maher also co-chaired the National Research Council's committee to study research-doctoral programs in the United States. In 1995 he co-authored and edited *Research-Doctorate Programs in the United States: Continuity and Change,* which reported the findings of that study.

By the end of 1999 Maher had authored or co-authored 9 books and 190 papers or chapters in scientific and scholarly publications. His early work, from 1955 to 1966, was focused on the model of motivational conflict as the origin of neurotic behavior. This work was done within the then-contemporary interest in reconciling Freudian concepts with the findings of Pavlovian and neo-Pavlovian psychology.

His 1966 book *Principles of Psychopathology* was the first textbook to present the topic of abnormal psychology from the point of view of experimental psychology and biopsychology. It was republished in 1970 in an international edition for students, and was translated into Spanish (1970) and Japanese (1974). He emphasized the central necessity of an empirical and quantitative approach to the study of abnormal psychology, both in its development as a science and as a basis for clinical applications. The period following the publication of this book was characterized by the gradual decline of Freudian influence in psychopathology. The decline was due to several factors, such as the rise of pharmacological treatments for psychosis and the growing sophistication of the neurobiological sciences. In this respect, Maher's text was in tune with the beginning of the return of psychopathology to its scientific roots.

His own empirical research then turned to the nature of the language disturbances found in the schizophrenias. A series of studies beginning with the first computer-based analyses of spontaneous written utterances by psychotic patients, *Studies in Psychotic Language* (with McKean and McLaughlin, 1966) led to the development of a model in which the intrusion of hyperactive associational processes could be seen to account for many of the manifest clinical phenomena in these utterances. The model was presented and developed most clearly in two papers, "The Language of Schizophrenia: A Review and Interpretation" (1972) and "Towards a Tentative Theory of Schizophrenic Language" (1983). Continued interest in the problem of language in schizophrenia has led to a cumulative series of studies examining the relationship among inadequate development of lateral dominance, early onset, and anomalies of language and thought in these patients, leading Maher to develop more sensitive and quantifiable methods of measuring dominance in manual skilled performance.

In 1970, Maher wrote a seminal paper on the causes of delusions. In this paper, he demonstrated that the prevailing belief that delusions arise from a basic defect in reasoning was not consistent with the evidence from empirical studies of reasoning in patients and the normal population. Instead, he proposed that the underlying pathology was to be found in the aberrant experiences of the patient (sensory, motor, etc.) and that these experiences mostly arose from neuropsychopathology. The task facing the psychopathologist is to identify and quantify these experiences, and to find the correlated neuropsychopathology. This paper had a substantial impact on the subsequent work of others by setting a new agenda for research into delusions.

With his wife and colleague, Dr. Winifred B. Maher, he made a series of contributions to the literature of the history of psychopathology. The main emphases in these papers were on the distinction between myth and fact in history, and the necessity of understanding earlier concepts about and attitudes toward the mentally ill by setting them in the larger social and intellectual context from which they arose.

Maher's other incidental empirical investigations have included criminal behavior, eating disorders, effects of hemodialysis, carbon monoxide poisoning, and the genetics of personality traits.

STAFF

MAJOR DEPRESSIVE DISORDER: RECOVERY AND RECURRENCE

MAJOR DEPRESSIVE DISORDER

Major depressive disorder (MDD) is characterized by depressed mood or a lack of interest or pleasure in once-enjoyable activities, and associated symptoms (e.g., sleep disturbance; appetite/weight disturbance; difficulty concentrating; worthlessness or exaggerated guilt). To receive a diagnosis of MDD, at least five symptoms must be present most of the day, nearly every day, for at least 2 weeks (American Psychiatric Association (APA), 1994).

The lifetime and 12-month prevalence of MDD is higher than that of any other major psychiatric disorder (Kessler et al., 1994), and evidence suggests that the prevalence of MDD has been increasing in recent birth cohorts (Lewinsohn, Rohde, Seeley, & Fischer, 1993) while the age at first onset has been decreasing (Klerman & Weissman, 1989). Indeed, approximately 25% of entering college students have previously experienced an episode of MDD (Lewinsohn, Clarke, Seeley, & Rohde, 1994). Although episodes of MDD appear to be self-limiting, the disorder is typically episodic, with high rates of relapse/recurrence of the disorder.

REMISSION AND RECOVERY

Over the years, researchers have used various definitions of "remission" and "recovery" from MDD. Recently, guidelines have been published (Frank et al., 1991) which have increased consistency across studies. There is now some agreement that remission is a period during which full criteria for MDD are no longer met but there are still some significant symptoms (i.e., partial remission), or during which the individual experiences no more than minimal (e.g., two or fewer) symptoms for up to six months (i.e., full remission). Full recovery is defined as six months or longer with no more than two symptoms.

An episode of major depression appears to be self-limiting, in that most cases remit in approximately six to eight months, even if untreated. Recovery rates appear to be similar across children and adult samples. For example, Kessler and Walters (1998) found that, in a community sample of adolescents and young adults, the average length of the longest episode an individual had suffered was 32.5 weeks. Similarly, Kovacs and colleagues (1984a) reported a mean length of 32 weeks for a sample of depressed children. Within 1 year of onset of a major depressive episode, 78% of adults will have recovered (Keller, Lavori, Rice, Coryell, & Hirschfeld, 1986).

Despite the high rate of spontaneous remission of MDD, it must be noted that six to eight months is the average length of episode; therefore, a number of individuals suffer significantly longer episodes of depression. While 78% of depressed adults remit within 1 year of onset of MDD, 22% experience a more chronic course. The longer an individual suffers from an episode of MDD, the lower the probability of recovery from that episode. Thus, for individuals who have not recovered within one to two years of onset, the prognosis is relatively poor. The long-term prognosis for individuals who recover more quickly from MDD is also discouraging, in that a large proportion will go on to suffer a relapse or recurrence of the disorder.

RELAPSE AND RECURRENCE

Relapse is a return of symptoms such that the individual once again meets full criteria for MDD during the period of remission but before recovery; a recurrence, on the other hand, is a new episode of MDD with onset occurring after full recovery from the previous episode (Frank et al., 1991). Although these terms have been defined fairly consistently in recent research, much of the earlier research did not differentiate between relapse and recurrence; therefore, these terms will be used interchangeably here.

In a recent review of the literature, it was found that more than 50% of adults who recover from an episode of MDD again meet criteria for MDD within 3 years of the index episode (Hart, Craighead, & Craighead, 2000). More specifically, the recurrence rate in adult outpatient samples was found to be between 19% to 32% at 1-year follow-up, 36% to 38% after 18 months, 21% to 44% after two years, and 43% at 30-months follow-up. In adult samples comprised of both outpatients and inpatients, between 24% to 36% experienced a recurrence within six months of recovery, increasing to 37% to 40% after 10 to 12 months, 52% by 26-month follow-up, 57% at three years, and 71% in the five years postrecovery. The highest recurrence rates were reported for inpatient samples: Between 38% to 43% recurred within six months of recovery, a rate not achieved in outpatient samples until 18 months after recovery; 51% suffered a recurrence within nine months, 27% to 55% within one year (with only one study reporting a rate lower than 41%), and 54% to 68% within two years. Similar rates of relapse and recurrence have been found in children and adolescents with MDD (e.g., Kovacs, Feinberg, Crouse-Novak, Paulauskas, Pollack, & Finkelstein, 1984b).

It appears that each new MDD episode increases the risk of suffering yet another episode (APA, 1994); additionally, there is some evidence of increasing severity with each new MDD episode, as well as decreased well time between episodes. Given the high cost of depression, and the increasing severity of the disorder with each new episode, developing effective means of preventing the relapse and recurrence of MDD must become a national mental health priority.

REFERENCES

American Psychiatric Association. (1994). *Diagnostic and statistical manual of mental disorders* (4th ed.). Washington, DC: Author.

Frank., E., Prien, R. F., Jarrett, R. B., Keller, M. B., Kupfer, D. J., Lavori, P. W., Rush, A. J., & Weissman, M. M. (1991). Conceptualization and rationale for consensus definitions of terms in major depressive disorder. *Archives of General Psychiatry, 48,* 851–855.

Hart, A. B., Craighead, L. W., & Craighead, W. E. (2000). Relapse and recurrence of major depressive disorder: A decade later. Manuscript submitted for publication.

Keller, M. B., Lavori, P. W., Rice, J., Coryell, W., & Hirschfeld, R. M. A. (1986). The persistent risk of chronicity in recurrent episodes of nonbipolar major depressive disorder: A prospective follow-up. *American Journal of Psychiatry, 143,* 24–28.

Kessler, R. C., McGonagle, K. A., Zhao, S., Nelson, C. B., Hughes, M., Eshleman, S., Wittchen, H., & Kendler, K. S. (1994). Lifetime and 12-month prevalence of *DSM-III-R* psychiatric disorders in the United states. *Archives of General Psychiatry, 51,* 8–19.

Kessler, R. C., & Walters, E. E. (1998). Epidemiology of *DSM-III-R* major depression and minor depression among adolescents and young adults in the national comorbidity survey. *Depression and Anxiety, 7,* 3–14.

Klerman, G. L., & Weissman, M. M. (1989). Increasing rates of depression. *Journal of the American Medical Association, 261,* 2229–2235.

Kovacs, M., Feinberg, T. L., Crouse-Novak, M., Paulauskas, S. L., & Finkelstein, R. (1984a). Depressive disorders in childhood I: A longitudinal prospective study of characteristics and recovery. *Archives of General Psychiatry, 41,* 229–237.

Kovacs, M., Feinberg, T. L., Crouse-Novak, M., Paulauskas, S. L., Pollack, M., & Finkelstein, R. (1984b). Depressive disorders in childhood II: A longitudinal study of the risk for a subsequent major depression. *Archives of General Psychiatry, 41,* 643–649.

Lewinsohn, P. M., Clarke, G. N., Seeley, J. R., & Rohde, P. (1994). Major depression in community adolescents: Age at onset, episode duration, and time to recurrence. *Journal of the American Academy of Child and Adolescent Psychiatry, 33,* 809–818.

Lewinsohn, P. M., Rohde, P., Seeley, J. R., & Fischer, S. A. (1993). Age-cohort changes in the lifetime occurrence of depression and other mental disorders. *Journal of Abnormal Psychology, 102,* 110–120.

A. B. HART
University of Colorado, Boulder

DEPRESSION

MALE SEXUAL DYSFUNCTION

LOW SEXUAL DESIRE

Low sexual desire in men is an especially interesting dysfunction because it involves a male behaving in a manner that is inconsistent with our cultural sexual script for males. Perhaps because of our assumptions regarding the scripted male sexual role, there is a paucity of objective, empirical research on the syndrome of low sexual desire in men. In its place there exists primarily case studies and theories of etiology. These theories include family of origin perspectives, in which factors such as an incestuously eroticized relationship with a parent of the opposite sex and exposure to a highly conflicted relationship between the parents are stressed (Kaplan, 1979; Zilbergeld & Ellison, 1980); and relationship dynamic explanations in which the low drive is seen to have an adaptive value in the maintenance of relationship equilibrium (LoPiccolo & Friedman, 1988).

Low sexual desire has been seen with increasing frequency in clinical practice. In fact, complaints of attenuated desire are now the most common among patients seeking therapy (LoPiccolo & Friedman, 1988). Treatment for low sexual desire can be a complex issue, as people with low sexual desire often have even lower levels of desire for therapeutic intervention. Perhaps because of this, treatment outcome measures for low drive are relatively scarce. However, some studies have demonstrated good treatment results using a complex, cognitive-behavioral treatment program (LoPiccolo & Friedman, 1988) with a focus on low desire symptomology (Schover & LoPiccolo, 1982). This focus on specific symptoms is seen as imperative to the success of treatment of low desire, as standard sex therapy often fails to raise desire (Kaplan, 1979).

MALE ERECTILE DISORDERS

For the past two decades, the major focus of work on erectile dysfunction has been on differential diagnosis. Since Masters and Johnson claimed in 1970 that 95% of all erectile failure cases had purely psychogenic origins, the field of sex research and therapy has evolved to recognize that physiology and psychology combine in myriad ways to cause difficulties in achieving or sustaining an erection. Physiological problems, such as neurologic diseases, hormonal abnormalities, or failure of blood to flow to the penis, are involved in a considerable percentage of cases of erectile failure, with or without corresponding psychological origins (Tanagho, Lue, & McClure, 1988).

A number of diagnostic strategies have been proposed to elucidate the relative contributions of physiologic and psychologic processes in erectile failure. Due to the inability to reliably diagnose etiology with paper-and-pencil questionnaires (e.g., Melman & Redgield, 1981; Segraves, Schoenberg, Zarins, Knopf, & Karnic, 1981) several alternative methods based upon physiologic evaluation procedures have subsequently been developed and used. These methods have included evaluation of penile blood flow, evaluation of pelvic reflexes and sensory thresholds, and the recording of nocturnal penile tumescence (NPT). Although all of these measurement techniques have shown promise in the ability to detect organic impairment, they are not without problems (see Zorgniotti, 1984; Wasserman et al., 1980).

While evaluation for organic impairment is always necessary before undertaking behavioral treatment for erectile disorder, the presence of such impairment does not always negate the need for behavioral treatment. Using a behavioral treatment program in which two basic goals are attained (i.e., first ensuring that the patient is receiving adequate levels of psychological and physical stimulation from his partner, and second eliminating anxiety related to performance demands) can potentially eliminate psychological and behavioral difficulties related to the erectile failure. With the elimination of these difficulties, the patient's mildly impaired physiologic capacity may be sufficient to produce a functional erection (LoPiccolo, 1994).

PREMATURE EJACULATION

At the present time, there are no objective criteria for what constitutes premature ejaculation. Since Kinsey and colleagues (1948) reported that the average length of intercourse was 2 minutes, subsequent studies have found that this average has gradually increased to approximately 10 to 14 minutes (e.g., Hunt, 1974). However, duration, as a single criterion, seems an inadequate standard for determining the presence of a sexual disorder. Perhaps it is easier to describe what is not premature ejaculation: Both partners agree that the quality of their sexual activities is not negatively impacted by efforts to postpone ejaculation.

Definitive data on the etiology of premature ejaculation do not currently exist. Sociobiologists have theorized that it offers an evolutionary advantage and has been built into the human organism (Hong, 1984). However, this theory does not effectively deal with the large variability in duration of intercourse that has been observed across species. Another theory proposed by Kaplan (1974) postulates that these men are unable to accurately perceive their own level of arousal and thus do not engage in self-control procedures to avoid rapid ejaculation. One laboratory analogue indicates, however, that men with premature ejaculation were better able to perceive their own levels of sexual arousal when compared to controls (Spiess, Geer, & O'Donohue, 1984). Finally, it has been proposed that premature ejaculation is related to low frequency of sexual activity (Kinsey, Pomeroy, & Martin, 1948). While some research offers tentative support for this theory (e.g., Spiess et al., 1984), it is possible that *premature ejaculation causes low rates of sex,* as it makes sex an unpleasant failure experience.

The standard treatment for premature ejaculation involves the pause procedure developed by Semans (1956) and modified into the pause and squeeze technique by Masters and Johnson (1970). While there has not been a controlled experimental study of the relative effectiveness of the pause procedure versus the pause and squeeze technique, both appear to be effective. Success rates of 90% to 98% "cure" have been reported, and this success has been demonstrated in group and individual treatment as well as in self-help programs (Kilmann & Auerbach, 1979).

MALE ORGASMIC DISORDER

Male orgasmic disorder has received very little attention in the therapeutic literature. As initially reported by Masters and Johnson (1970), this remains a rare dysfunction, and etiology remains unclear. Clinical case studies suggest a variety of psychological factors as causes, but there is virtually no empirical support for these theories (Dow, 1981; Schull & Sprenkle, 1980). Male orgasmic disorder can, however, result from a number of physiological conditions, such as multiple sclerosis and damage to the hypothalamus. Finally, the inability to reach orgasm may be a side effect of several medications (Ban & Freyhan, 1980), especially selective-serotonin reuptake inhibitors.

Perhaps due to the ambiguity surrounding the etiology of male orgasmic disorder, relatively little has appeared in the literature regarding treatment. The standard sexual treatment strategies, involving elimination of performance anxiety and ensuring adequate stimulation, remain the preferred treatment approaches. Additional elements taken from the treatment program for female anorgasmia also seem to have some success in treating males (LoPiccolo, 1977). For cases caused by organic impairment, there is some success reported with the use of drugs that work to activate the sympathetic nervous system (Murphy & Lipshultz, 1988). In addition, behavior modification that leads to increased stimulation of the scrotal, perineal, and anal area also tends to trigger orgasm.

REFERENCES

Ban, T. A., & Freyhan, F. A. (1980). *Drug treatment of sexual dysfunction.* New York: Karger.

Dow, S. (1981). Retarded ejaculation. *Journal of Sex and Marital Therapy, 2,* 229–237.

Hong, L. K. (1984). Survival of the fastest. *Journal of Sex Research, 20,* 109–122.

Hunt, M. (1974). *Sexual behavior in the 1970s.* Chicago: Playboy.

Kaplan, H. S. (1974). *The new sex therapy.* New York: Brunner/ Mazel.

Kaplan, H. S. (1979). *Disorders of desire.* New York: Brunner/ Mazel.

Kilmann, P. R., & Auerbach, R. (1979). Treatments of premature ejaculation and psychogenic impotence: A critical review of the literature. *Archives of Sexual Behavior, 8,* 81–100.

Kinsey, A. C., Pomeroy, W. B., & Martin, C. E. (1948). *Sexual behavior in the human male.* Philadelphia: Saunders.

LoPiccolo, J. (1994) Sexual dysfunction. In L. W. Craighead, W. E. Craighead, A .E. Kazdin, & M. J. Mahoney (Eds.), *Cognitive and behavioral interventions: An empirical approach to mental health problems* (pp. 183–196). Boston: Allyn & Bacon, Inc.

LoPiccolo, J. (1977). Direct treatment of sexual dysfunction in the couple. In J. Money & H. Musaph (Eds.), *Handbook of sexology* (pp. 1227–1244). New York: Elsevier/ North Holland.

LoPiccolo, J., & Friedman, J. (1988). Sex therapy: An integrative model. In S. Lynn & J. Garske (Eds.), *Contemporary psychotherapies: Models and methods.* New York: Merrill.

Masters, W. H., & Johnson, V. E. (1970). *Human sexual inadequacy.* Boston: Little, Brown.

Melman, A., & Redgield, J. (1981). Evaluation of the DSFI as a test of organic impotence. *Sexuality and Disability, 4,* 108–114.

Murphy, J., & Lipshultz, L. (1988). Infertility in the paraplegic male. In E. Tanagho, T. Lue, & R. McClure (Eds.), *Contemporary management of impotence and infertility.* Baltimore, MD: Williams Wilkins.

Schover, L., & LoPiccolo, J. (1982). Treatment effectiveness for dysfunctions of sexual desire. *Journal of Sex and Marital Therapy, 8,* 179–197.

Schull, W., & Sprenkle, T. (1980). Retarded ejaculation. *Journal of Sex and Marital Therapy, 6,* 234–246.

Segraves, R. T., Schoenberg, H. W., Zarins, C. K., Knopf, J., & Carnic, P. (1981). Discrimination of organic versus psychological impotence with the DSFI: A failure to replicate. *Journal of Sex and Marital Therapy, 7,* 230–238.

Semans, J. H. (1956). Premature ejaculation: A new approach. *Southern Medical Journal, 49,* 353–357.

Spiess, W. F., Geer, J. H., & O'Donohue, W. T. (1984). Premature ejaculation: Investigation of factors in ejaculatory latency. *Journal of Abnormal Psychology, 93,* 242–245.

Tanagho, T., Lue, F., & McClure, R. (Eds.). (1988). *Contemporary management of impotence and infertility.* Baltimore: Williams & Wilkins.

Wasserman, M. D., Pollak, C. P., Spielman, A. J., & Weitzman, E. D. (1980). Theoretical and technical problems in the measurement of nocturnal penile tumescence for the differential diagnosis of impotence. *Psychosomatic Medicine, 42,* 575–585.

Zilbergeld, B., & Ellison, C. R. (1980). Desire discrepancies and arousal problems in sex therapy. In S. Leiblum & L. Pervin (Eds.), *Principles and practice of sex therapy* (pp. 29–64). New York: Guilford Press.

Zorgniotti, A. W. (1984). Practical diagnostic screening for impotence. *Urology, 23,* 98–102.

H. MEGGERS
J. LoPICCOLO
University of Missouri, Columbia

FEMALE SEXUAL DYSFUNCTION
SEX THERAPY
SEXUAL DYSFUNCTIONS

MALINGERING

The Diagnostic and Statistical Manual of Mental Disorders (Third Edition) states that the essential feature in malingering is the voluntary production and presentation of false or grossly exaggerated physical or psychological symptoms. These symptoms are produced for an obviously recognizable goal. The goal relates to the person's situational or circumstantial factors and is not a psychological or "dynamic" goal. Examples of such goals are avoidance of military duty, avoidance of work, financial compensation, evasion of criminal prosecution, or access to drugs.

Although numerous articles have been published on the general topic of malingering, few specific conclusions can be made. Research and publications in this area can be loosely organized into several different topic areas: military studies, simulation of psychosis, psychological tests in malingering, general simulation of medical disorders, and compensation cases.

The military studies were predominantly published during and immediately after World Wars I and II, most of them written by military psychiatrists and other medical officers during World War II. The literature of this period consists essentially of broad theoretical discussions of malingering or articles providing specific practical advice for detecting the malingerer. Studies also attempted to define malingering more accurately and to determine the rate of malingering in groups of persons conscripted for military duty.

The simulation of psychosis studies are a group of primarily anecdotal and case studies. In case study articles there has been little systematic research effort in this area. The majority of the studies were published by psychiatric centers or in cases relating to persons reigning psychosis to avoid criminal responsibility. While it is generally agreed that this is an extremely important issue for society in general, there is little consensus as to the rate of this type of malingering and no specific reliable method for determining it.

Malingering has been investigated in research studies with nearly all the major psychological tests. However, the total number of studies is relatively small; often, only five or six studies with a given test have been reported over several decades. These studies are usually done in relative isolation from one another. The literature can be organized into three issues: (a) intellectual incompetency; (b) organic impairment; and (c) psychological maladjustment. The most common tests used in these studies were the Bender Visual-Motor Gestalt Test, the Minnesota Multiphasic Personality Inventory, the Wechsler Adult Intelligence Scale, and the Rorschach Inkblot Test. Published studies in this area are so varied in terms of purpose and quality of methodology that no specific conclusions can be made. It does appear, however, that psychological tests can be useful in determining malingering on a case-by-case basis.

Studies related to the general simulation of medical disorders are probably more numerous than in any other subarea of malingering. The studies, however, are extremely varied, and hard empirical data are lacking. Most of these studies are case reports of attempts to detect the reigning of an illness by conducting certain types of medical examinations.

Increasing concern over the last few decades has focused on malingering in compensation cases. Compensation cases refer primarily to Workers' Compensation claims and personal injury claims. In both of these types of cases, an individual is alleging some type of physical or psychological impairment and is attempting to gain monetary compensation. Research in this area has been much more recent than in the previously-mentioned areas. This would seem to relate to the fact that civil laws relating to various types of compensation have broadened in the last few decades. There is an increasing professional concern in this area that appears to reflect an increasing societal problem. As in all areas of malingering, there is an urgent need for more exacting, better-designed research.

M. P. MALONEY
Pasadena, California

**FACTITIOUS DISORDERS
LEARNED HELPLESSNESS
LIE DETECTION**

MANAGED MENTAL HEALTH CARE

Managed health care has evolved so swiftly from the 1980s to the turn of the century that its definition must remain fluid. Broadly interpreted, managed care is any health care delivery method in which an entity other than the health care provider actively manages both financial and medical aspects of health care. It includes a wide variety of techniques that integrate the financing and the delivery of health care services to covered individuals. The term is applied to many products and services that range on a continuum from simple pre-authorization to provider-negotiated delivery systems, and encompasses a large variety of organizational arrangements.

Managed care was originally based on the premise that health providers will alter their practices in response to financial incentives. It was created to control the costs, use, and quality of health care by raising the cost consciousness of provider and patient, by increasing provider accountability to payers, by promoting competition among providers, and by stimulating practice standards. The rise of managed care has generated considerable controversy about its success in achieving these general goals (Austad, 1996; Callan & Yeager, 1991; Small & Barnhill, 1998). The most serious objections made about managed care are that earnings are valued over patient welfare through the use of egregious profit-oriented practices, such as denying and delaying access to necessary treatments and providers, awarding bonuses to providers for reducing referrals to specialists, delaying authorization of necessary treatments, and arbitrarily discharging providers who use too many resources (Ginzberg & Ostow, 1997). Accurate generalizations about managed care are difficult to confirm, since researching the effects of managed care on health care is complicated because its conditions vary widely. While well executed designs are needed, the controversies are based upon vague assertions, anecdotal evidence, exaggerated concerns, and inflated claims (Mechanic, 1996). Overall, the advent and rapid growth of managed behavioral health care reflects a convergence of multiple variables, such as diverse economic, political, regulatory, marketplace, professional, clinical, and humanitarian factors that reflect current problems of the American health care system (England, 1999).

Mental health and chemical dependency services have been grouped together under managed care and called behavioral health care. Managed behavioral services can coexist with or be delivered within general managed care health systems, or they can be separated from (carved out of) general health care plans and contracted to specialized providers who are responsible for utilization control, provider selection, finances, and quality assurance (Golan, 1992; Buck, Teich, Umland, & Stein, 1999).

HISTORY OF MANAGED MENTAL HEALTH CARE

The history of managed mental health care is intertwined with the history of managed health care, which is intricately linked with the history of prepaid health care (the provision of a set package of health care services for a preestablished fee; Nelson, 1987). Initially, the originators of managed care intended to deliver affordable and accessible care to poor and middle-class laborers and farmers who wanted to eliminate the threat of sudden, unexpected medical bills. For example, in 1929, physician Michael Shadid and farmers in Oklahoma arranged to provide and receive comprehensive health care for a fixed monthly fee. The lumbering, mining, water, and transport industries of the Northwest found doctors to treat employees on-site and to provide comprehensive health services for a prepaid monthly rate. Despite resistance and opposition from the traditional medical community, prepaid health care survived and evolved. These first-generation HMOs formed in various locations with the help of industry, city government, organized labor, and philanthropic organizations. The federal government became actively involved during the Nixon administration when Paul Ellwood advocated changing the incentives in the American health care system by supporting the growth of "health maintenance organizations" (Starr, 1986). The HMO Act of 1973 (Public Law 97–222) and its consequent amendments gave governmental support for this alternative form of health care delivery in the form of loans and grants to organizations willing to provide or arrange for comprehensive, specified inpatient or outpatient services; to serve a voluntarily enrolled population; to charge a fixed per capita fee that was not related to how much service would actually be used; and to assume some financial risk. While initial legislation provided that HMOs be organized according to one of three models—staff, group, or independent practice association—later legislation allowed providers to combine elements of these models, and variant models continue to emerge. In 1981, federal funding for HMOs stopped, and involvement of the private for-profit sector grew. The cost-reducing methods used in managed care to lower health costs for members are now being used as more efficient forms of management for the private sector. However, the cost of health care was not brought successfully under control through early managed care efforts. In the 1990s, complex business arrangements were created in response to market and regulatory forces. Major medical companies developed, bought, affiliated with, and merged with existing HMOs.

Mental health care became an integral part of the benefit package in managed care only with the passage of the HMO Act of 1973 and its consequent amendments. In order to be federally qualified, an HMO had to provide mental health/substance-abuse treatment in the form of short-term, outpatient mental health evaluation and crisis intervention services as well as 60 days of inpatient services. The mental health component of health care became a matter of grave concern to payers when costs began to rise at a rate greater than those of other health care services. Mandating mental health benefits into managed care has met reluctance on the part of payers because of the fear that if individuals are allowed to use mental health services freely, overutilization will result in out-of-control costs. Arguments against this concern of overutilization have been based upon the so-called medical offset effect showing that the use of mental health services leads to an eventual reduction in general medical health services (Cummings & Folette, 1968; Cummings, 1988). Such reductions have been found following specific types of mental health treatment for elderly medical inpatients, outpatients with somatic complaints, adult alcoholics, and some patients with major medical illnesses (Olfson, Sing, & Schlessinger, 1999).

The trend toward carving out behavioral health benefits and separating them from general health care grew rapidly. Exclusive provider arrangements and carve-outs of behavioral health care from medical benefits became more common during the 1980s and 1990s. Managed behavioral health care companies that subcontract the delivery of mental health care for a given population became dominant (Bennett, 1988; Buck, Teich, Umlan, & Stein, 1997). As of 1997, 75% of Americans with health insurance were enrolled in some type of behavioral health program, and the numbers continue to grow. Consolidation of managed behavioral organizations continues to concentrate benefit plans into the hands of fewer organizations (Wineburgh, 1998). Single organizations accountable for behavioral services are usually responsible for initial assessment, referral to an appropriate provider, precertification for inpatient care, triage to determine the appropriate course of treatment, treatment evaluation, and reevaluation.

FORMS OF MANAGED HEALTH CARE

Forms of managed health care can be defined according to structural characteristics, relationship of providers and patients to systems, and financial arrangements. In general, managed care organizations or managed care programs use an assortment of methods to reduce unnecessary health care costs, including methods for reviewing the medical necessity of specific services; intensive management of high-cost cases; regulation of inpatient admissions and length of stay; monetary incentives for providers and patients to select less costly forms of care; increased beneficiary cost sharing; cost sharing incentives for outpatient treatments; and selective contracting with health care providers. The lines between types of organizations have been blurred so that many mixed models or hybrids, which blend the characteristics of more than one model, are continually emerging (Boaz, 1988; Dacso & Dacso, 1995). Variation can also occur from diverse sets of local and regional requirements. Most states regulate companies that deal with health care and insurance under specific statutes and under different state departments. State regulatory concerns center around fiscal soundness, quality assurance standards, and adequacy of provider networks (Hastings, 1990). The major types of managed health care follow (Austad & Berman, 1991; Davis, 1990; Dacso & Dacso, 1995; Mechanic, 1999).

Utilization review and management

Utilization review and management are the simplest managed care methods devised to evaluate the medical necessity and appropri-

ateness of mental health services before, during, or after they are rendered. In prospective management, the necessity for inpatient or outpatient services is determined before the service is rendered (e.g., precertification and second-opinion programs). In concurrent review, treatment is monitored to assure that services continue to be appropriate. In retrospective review, services are evaluated to see whether treatment provided in the past was appropriate.

Staff Model Health Maintenance Organization (HMO)

This type of managed care offers necessary health services to a defined population for a fixed price. This method of financing is called capitation. Providers are salaried employees or contractors who usually work in specific locations and are expected to deliver cost effective care and to keep hospitalizations to a minimum. Patient freedom of choice of provider is limited to the staff of the HMO.

Independent Practice Association (IPA)

In an IPA, individual providers contract with an HMO to provide care in their own offices to HMO subscribers. Reimbursement may be fee-for-service on a prearranged fee schedule, capitated, or a percentage of the subscriber's premium. Contracts can be made between the provider and the IPA (direct contract model) or between the HMO and the IPA. When the contract is between the HMO and the IPA, the IPA establishes a risk pool into which each provider contributes, putting the provider at risk to cover excess expenses through a percentage holdback. IPA incentives to control utilization are diluted because cost sharing is diffuse. When retaining fee-for-service payment, cost sharing is spread across all providers involved.

Group Model HMO

Group model HMOs contract with groups of providers to provide services and to devote a specified percentage of their practice time to HMO subscribers on a salaried or a fixed capitated basis. Providers usually practice in a group in a central location. In a cost-sharing HMO, there are financial incentives for providers to deliver cost effective care because they share in the group's profit or loss. Individual providers are usually at risk for overruns or can share savings at the end of a fiscal period.

Preferred Provider Organization (PPO)

Caregivers in the PPO are theoretically selected because their treatment patterns are consistent with cost effective care. PPOs do not offer comprehensive health services. Providers are not at risk. They maintain an exclusive fee-for-service billing arrangement with a predetermined subscriber group. Payment for services is negotiated and includes either discounted rates or an agreement to accept a schedule of maximum payments in return for a certain number of referrals. While subscribers may be able to use non-participating providers, they are encouraged to use the PPO provider by being given greater financial incentives in the form of reduced copayments or deductibles. The financial benefit to all is that the purchaser buys services at a lower cost, the consumer pays less (or sometimes nothing) if a PPO provider is used, and the provider receives an increased flow of referrals. PPOs often use some form of review procedure to control utilization.

Exclusive Provider Organization (EPO)

The EPO is a form of PPO that pays for services by participating providers only. Exclusive provider organizations differ from HMOs in the manner in which they are regulated by state insurance. An EPO is similar to an HMO in that it is structured so that a limited provider panel of primary care physicians serve as gatekeepers.

Broker Model

In a broker model, independent brokers in specific geographic areas serve as liaisons between providers who want to sell and buyers who want to purchase services. The broker helps to establish and/or arrange a network of providers and sells the services to groups of individuals (small businesses, self-insured companies, guilds, etc.) who group together in order to purchase the services for specific, discounted rates.

Network Model

The network model is a hybrid plan that combines features of the IPA, group, and staff models, and contracts with an HMO to provide services. Providers can give care to non-members and do not provide exclusive care to HMO members.

Point-of-Service (Open-Ended) Plan

Under the point-of-service plan, reduced fees or increased benefits are offered to consumers to encourage the use of specific, network providers. Increased charges, copays, or deductibles may be charged if the patient uses out-of-network providers. This arrangement allows the consumer to have the comprehensive benefits of an HMO while still being able to use non-system providers of his or her own choice, even though there is a financial disincentive to use system providers. This plan replaces the unrestricted choice plan with the opportunity to use a managed care network (Golan, 1992).

Employee Assistance Program (EAP)

With an EAP, mental health services are provided to the employee either in the work place or off-site. The hope is that early intervention may help an employee to solve mental health or substance abuse problems that are diminishing the quality of his or her work performance. Employee assistance programs either employ personnel from the company to provide services or contract with outside providers, or both. Some EAPs add managed mental health programs so they can offer comprehensive mental health services (Pearson, 1992).

Social HMO

The range of services in a social HMO include not only comprehensive health services, but also social services such as assistance for shut-ins and the elderly. Although a few demonstration projects were run in the 1970s, little research or work is being done on developing this form of health care system at the present (Cummings & Dahl, 1989).

Integrated Delivery System (IDS)

"Integrated delivery system" is a generic term used to describe a variety of providers who work to deliver health care in an integrated fashion. For example, the system might consist of a management service entity, a medical foundation, a group provider practice, and a physician-hospital organization. Ideally, the IDS should provide coordinated, comprehensive care for patient needs, including acute inpatient, outpatient, and prevention services.

REFERENCES

Austad, Carol S. (1996). *Is long term psychotherapy unethical?* San Francisco: Jossey Bass.

Austad, C. S., & Berman, W. (1991). *Psychotherapy in managed health care: The optimal use of time and resources.* Washington, DC: American Psychological Association.

Bennett, M. J. (1988). The greening of the HMO: Implications for prepaid psychiatry. *American Journal of Psychiatry, 145*(12), 1544–1548.

Boaz, J. T. (1988). *Delivering mental health care: A guide for HMOs.* Chicago: Pluribus.

Buck, J. A., Teich, J. L., Umlan, B., & Stein, M. (1997). Behavioral health benefits in employer sponsored health plans—1997. *Health Affairs, 18,*(2), 67–78.

Callan, M. F., & Yeager, D. C. (1991). *Containing the health care cost spiral.* New York, McGraw Hill.

Cummings, N. A. (1988). The emergence of the mental health complex. *Professional Psychology, 19*(3), 323–335.

Cummings, N. A., & Dahl, L. D. (1989). The new delivery system. In L. Dahl & N. A. Cummings, (Eds.), *The future of mental health services: Coping with crises.* (pp. 85–99). New York: Springer.

Cummings, N. A., & Folette, W. (1968). Psychiatric services and medical utilization in a pre-paid health plan setting: Part II. *Medical Care, 6,* 31–41.

Dacso, S. T., & Dacso, C. C. (1995). *The managed care answer book.* New York: Aspen.

Davis, G. S. (1990). A managed health care primer. In D. A. Hastings, W. W. Krasner, J. L. Michael, & N. D. Rosenber (Eds.), *The insider's guide to managed care* (pp. 13–35). Washington, DC: The National Lawyers Association.

Dahl, L., & Cummings, N. A. (Eds.). (1989). *The future of mental health services: Coping with crises.* New York: Springer Publishing.

England, M. J. (1999, March–April). Capturing mental health cost offsets. *Health Affairs,* 91–93.

Feldman, S. (Ed.). (1992). *Managed mental health services.* Springfield, IL: Charles C. Thomas.

Ginzberg, E., & Ostow, M. (1997). Managed care: A look back and a look ahead. *The New England Journal of Medicine, 336*(14), 1017–1020.

Golan, M. J. (1992). Managed mental health and group insurance. In S. Feldman (Ed.), *Managed mental health services* (pp. 27–43). Springfield, IL: Charles C. Thomas.

Hastings, D. A. (1990). Legal and regulatory issues in managed mental health care. In D. A. Hastings, W. L. Krasner, J. L. Michael, & N. D. Rosenber, (Eds.), *The insider's guide to managed care.* Washington, DC: The National Lawyers Association.

Mechanic, D. (1996). Can research on managed care inform practice and policy decisions? In A. Lazarus (Ed.), *Controversies in managed mental health care* (pp. 197–211). Washington, DC: American Psychiatric Press.

Nelson, J. (1987). The history and spirit of the HMO movement. *HMO: Practice, 2*(1), 75–86.

Olfson, M., Sing, M., & Schlessinger, H. (1999, March–April). Mental health/medical care cost offsets: Opportunities for managed care. *Health Affairs,* 79–90.

Pearson, J. (1992). Managed mental health: The buyer's perspective. In S. Feldman (Ed.), *Managed mental health services* (pp. 27–43). Springfield, IL: Charles C. Thomas.

Small, R. F., & Barnhill, L. (1998). *Practicing in the new mental health marketplace.* Washington, DC: American Psychological Association.

Starr, P. (1986). *The social transformation of American medicine.* New York: Basic Books.

Wineburgh, M. (1998). Ethics, managed care and outpatient psychotherapy. *Clinical Social Work Journal,* 433–443.

C. S. AUSTAD

MANAGEMENT DECISION MAKING

A major concern in management has been to understand and improve decision making. Various approaches have been proposed by psychologists, most based on a divide-and-conquer strategy. This strategy, also labeled problem decomposition, involves breaking a large decision problem into smaller parts and working on the parts separately. The idea is not new: In his "Letter to Joseph Priestly" (1956), Benjamin Franklin was one of the first to describe a decision decomposition strategy. The theoretical justification for this approach was outlined by Simon (1957) in his account of bounded rationality. This concept says that cognitive processing limitations leave humans with little option but to construct simplified mental models of the world. According to Simon (p. 198) a person behaves rationally with respect to this model " . . . [although] such behavior is not even approximately optimal with respect to the real world." There have been two approaches to management decision making (Huber, 1980). The first is concerned with the development and application of normative decision rules based on formal logic from economics and statistics. The second involves descriptive accounts of how people actually go about making judgments, decisions, and choices.

NORMATIVE ANALYSES

As initially outlined by von Neumann and Morgenstern in *Theory of Games and Economic Behavior* (1947), a variety of techniques have been devised for making optimal decisions, often making a distinction between riskless choices (certain outcomes) and risky choices (uncertain outcomes). Two examples of each approach are summarized here.

Certain Outcomes

Multi-Attribute Utility   This approach, abbreviated MAU, applies to decisions made with more or less certain outcomes. As described by Gardiner and Edwards (1975), MAU is based on obtaining a utility value for each decision alternative and then selecting the alternative with the highest value. The utility for an alternative is derived from a weighted sum of the utilities of the separate parts for various attributes. The MAU approach has been successfully applied to management decisions such as new plant sitings, personnel selection, and zoning decisions.

Linear Models   Growing out of multiple-regression analyses, linear models have been used both to prescribe and to describe judgments under certainty. A major concern has been the weights assigned to the cue (or attribute) values. Research has shown that equal weights, or even random weights, often serve as well as optimal weights in many settings. The robustness of linear models has allowed their use in many applied tasks, such as graduate school admissions, clinical diagnosis, and medical care decisions (Goldberg, 1970).

Uncertain Outcomes

Decision-Tree Analysis   A decision tree is a graphical model that displays the sequence of decisions and the events that compose a (risky) sequential decision situation (Huber, 1980). The approach involves laying out choice alternatives, uncertain events, and outcome utilities as a series of branches (hence the name decision tree). For each alternative, an expected value (EV) is computed as the average outcome value over all possible events. The optimal choice is the alternative with the highest EV. Decision trees have been used to guide risky-decision making such as marketing strategy, plant expansion, and public policy planning. *Bayesian Networks.*   This approach combines elements of Bayesian probability theory, artificial intelligence, and graphical analysis into a decision analytic tool (Breese & Heckerman, 1999). Starting with a fully connected network, all possible cause-and-effect linkages between nodes for a problem space are described. Through a process of pruning using computer algorithms, the structure of the network is simplified to only the essential links between nodes. This results in an enormous reduction of problem complexity. The approach is being used to diagnose computer programming errors and to anticipate trouble spots around the world.

DESCRIPTIVE ANALYSES

Most, but not all, descriptive analyses of decision making were initially concerned with the discrepancies between normative rules (e.g., EV) and actual behavior. For instance, Edwards (1954) modified EV by substituting subjective probabilities for objective probabilities and psychological utilities for payoff amounts to produce subjectively expected utility (SEU). This model has become the starting point for descriptions of risky decision behavior. However, many other approaches have been offered by psychologists. A few of them are:

Social Judgment Theory (SJT)

Based on the Lens Model developed by Brunswik (1952), Hammond (1955) proposed a comprehensive perspective on judgment and decision making. By adapting procedures from multiple regression, this approach combines elements of both normative and descriptive analyses into a single framework. Central to SJT is the distinction between analytic and intuitive modes of cognition. The approach has been used to describe decisions by highway engineers and medical doctors (Cooksey, 1996).

Information Integration Theory (IIT)

Anderson (1996) has shown repeatedly that individuals use an averaging rule to combine information from multiple sources when making judgments. This rule is more descriptive than the adding or summing rule assumed by normative models (such as MAU). Through functional measurement, IIT allows the simultaneous evaluation of processing strategy and psychological values. The IIT approach has been applied to marketing decisions, family choices, and expert judgments (Phelps & Shanteau, 1978).

Image Theory

As described by Beach (1990), image theory holds that the decision maker possesses three distinct but related images, each of which constitutes a particular part of his or her decision-related knowledge. The value image consists of the decision maker's values, beliefs, and ethics, which collectively are labeled principles. The trajectory image consists of the decision maker's future agenda (or goals). The strategic image consists of various plans that have been adopted to achieve the goals. Using these concepts, image theory has been applied to auditing, childbearing, and political decisions.

Heuristics and Biases

Tversky and Kahneman (1974) argued that risky decisions are often made using psychological shortcuts, or heuristics. For instance, the representativeness heuristic refers to a tendency to base probability judgments on the similarity of an event to an underlying source; the greater the similarity, the higher the probability estimate. Although easy to perform psychologically, such heuristics often lead to biases in that relevant information, such as base rates, may be ignored. This approach has been used to account for suboptimal risky decisions in finance, accounting, management, and marketing.

Fast and Frugal Heuristics

Simon (1957) developed the concept of bounded rationality to deal with two interlocking components: the limitations of the human mind, and the structure of the environment in which humans operate. For instance, satisficing (selecting the first option that meets acceptable standards) is a cognitively simple, but often surprisingly efficient, decision strategy. These ideas have been extended by Gigerenzer and Todd (1999) to apply to various simple, fast and frugal heuristics that take advantage of environmental constraints. These heuristics have been applied to improve decision making in medicine and forecasting.

Naturalistic Decision Making

This perspective was developed by Klein, Orasanu, Calderwood, and Zsambok (1993) to account for on-line decision making by experts in time sensitive environments. In situations such as fire fighting, there is not enough time to apply normative choice rules. Instead, experienced decision makers frequently follow a recognition-primed decision making strategy; that is, they identify a single course of action through pattern matching. The NDM approach has been applied in many real-world decisions, ranging from military commands and intelligence analysis to medical diagnosis and accounting.

Expert Decision Making

Behind much of the advances in decision research has been the desire of psychologists to help professionals make better decisions. For instance, considerable effort has gone into studies of how clinical psychologists make decisions (Dawes, 1988). Although such analyses often reveal that experts are biased in their decisions, there are many domains in which surprisingly good decisions are observed. For example, Stewart, Roebber, and Bosart (1997) found that weather forecasters make reliable and valid short-term predictions of precipitation and temperature. Similarly, auditors were found by Krogstad, Ettenson, and Shanteau (1984) to have an effective grasp of what information to use.

CONCLUSIONS

Drawing on both normative and descriptive approaches, there have been many successful applications of behavioral decision theory in management, business, and other settings. In large part, these successes reflect the importance of Ben Franklin's original insight into problem decomposition: Decision making can usually be improved by breaking a problem into parts, working on the parts separately, and then combining them to make a final decision.

REFERENCES

Anderson, N. H. (1996). *A functional theory of cognition.* Mahwah, NJ: Erlbaum.

Beach, L. R. (1990). *Image theory: Decision making in personal and organizational contexts.* Chichester, UK: Wiley.

Breese, J. S., & Heckerman, D. (1999). Decision-theoretic troubleshooting: A framework for repair and experiment. In J. Shanteau, B. A. Mellers, & D. A. Schum (Eds.), *Decision science and technology: Reflections on the contributions of Ward Edwards* (pp. 271–287). Norwell, MA: Kluwer Academic Publishers.

Brunswik, E. (1952). *The conceptual framework of psychology.* Chicago: University of Chicago Press.

Cooksey, R. W. (1996). *Judgment analysis: Theory, methods, and applications.* San Diego: Academic Press.

Dawes, R. M. (1988). *Rational choice in an uncertain world.* San Diego: Harcourt, Brace, Jovanovich.

Edwards, W. (1954). The theory of decision making. *Psychological Bulletin* 1954, 380–417.

Franklin, B. (1956). Letter to Joseph Priestly. In *The Benjamin Franklin sampler.* New York: Fawcett.

Gardiner, P. C., & Edwards, W. (1975). Public values: Multiattribute-utility measurement for social decision making. In M. F. Kaplan & S. Schwartz (Eds.), *Human judgment and decision processes.* New York: Academic Press.

Gigerenzer, G., & Todd, P. M. (1999). *Simple heuristics that make us smart.* New York: Oxford University Press.

Goldberg, L. R. (1970). Man versus model of man: A rationale, plus some evidence for a method of improving on clinical inferences. *Psychological Bulletin, 73,* 422–432.

Hammond, K. R. (1955). Probabilistic functioning and the clinical method. *Psychological Review, 62,* 255–262.

Huber, G. P. (1980). *Managerial decision making.* Glenview, IL: Scott, Foresman and Co.

Klein, G., Orasanu, J., Calderwood, R., & Zsambok, C. E. (1993). *Decision making in action: Models and methods.* Norwood, NJ: Ablex.

Krogstad, J. L., Ettenson, R. T., & Shanteau, J. (1984). Context and experience in auditors materiality judgments. *Auditing: A Journal of Practice & Theory, 4,* 54–73.

Phelps, R. H., & Shanteau, J. (1978). Livestock judges: How much information can an expert use? *Organizational Behavior and Human Performance, 21,* 209–219.

Simon, H. A. (1957). *Models of man.* New York: Wiley.

Stewart, T. R., Roebber, P. J., & Bosart, L. F. (1997). The importance of the task in analyzing expert judgment. *Organizational Behavior and Human Decision Processes, 69,* 205–219.

Tversky, A., & Kahneman, D. (1974). Judgment under uncertainty: Heuristics and biases. *Science, 185,* 1124–1131.

von Neumann, J., & Morgenstern, O. (1947). *Theory of games and economic behavior.* Princeton, NJ: Princeton University Press.

SUGGESTED READING

Arkes, H. R., & Hammond, K. R. (Eds.). (1986). Judgment and decision making: An interdisciplinary reader. Cambridge, UK: Cambridge University Press.

Beach, L. R., Campbell, F. L., & Townes, B. D. (1979). Subjective expected utility and the prediction of birth planning decisions. *Organizational Behavior and Human Performance, 24,* 18–28.

Dawes, R. M., & Corrigan, B. (1974). Linear models in decision making. *Psychological Bulletin, 81,* 95–106.

Hammond, K. R., Hamm, R. M., Grassia, J., & Pearson, T. (1987). Direct comparison of the efficacy of intuitive and analytic cognition in expert judgment. *Transactions on Systems, Man, and Cybernetics, SMC-17, 5,* 753–770.

Kahneman, D., Slovic, P., & Tversky, A. (1982). *Judgment under uncertainty: Heuristics and biases.* Cambridge, UK: Cambridge University Press.

Keeney, R. L., & Raiffa, H. (1976). *Decisions with multiple objectives: Preferences and value tradeoffs.* London: Wiley.

Klein, G. (1998). *Sources of power: How people make decisions.* Cambridge, MA: MIT Press.

Payne, J. W., Bettman, J. R., & Johnson, E. J. (1993). *The adaptive decision maker.* Cambridge, UK: Cambridge University Press.

Shapira, Z. (Ed.). (1997). *Organizational decision making.* Cambridge, UK: Cambridge University Press.

von Winterfeldt, D., & Edwards, W. (1986). *Decision analysis and behavioral research.* Cambridge, UK: Cambridge University Press.

Wallsten, T. S. (Ed.). (1980). *Cognitive processes in choice and decision behavior.* Hillsdale, NJ: Erlbaum.

Yates, J. F. (1990). *Judgment and decision making.* Englewood Cliffs, NJ: Prentice Hall.

J. SHANTEAU

INDUSTRIAL PSYCHOLOGY
LEADERSHIP STYLES
WORK EFFICIENCY

MAO INHIBITORS

The MAO inhibitors comprise a category of psychotropic medication that has important historical, heuristic, and clinical value. Their name is derived from their primary pharmacological action: the inhibition of the activity of the enzyme monoamine oxidase (MAO), which is responsible for the metabolic degradation within neurons of several key neurotransmitters, including serotonin, norepinephrine, epinephrine, and dopamine.

The MAO inhibitors were among the very first compounds found to be effective in the treatment of depression. Serendipity played an important role in the discovery of the antidepressant properties of these medications. In the 1950s, intensive efforts were launched to develop antibiotic treatments for tuberculosis (TB). An early report of the clinical properties of one of these compounds, iproniazid, indicated that the medication appeared to possess mood-elevating properties when given to TB patients (Bloch, Doonief, Buchberg, & Spellman 1954). This fortuitous observation was soon confirmed in controlled trials (see Kline, 1984). Several years later, the putative mechanism of action was identified when Zeller (1963) reported that iproniazid inhibited the activity of MAO enzymes both in vivo and in vitro in the brain. When iproniazid was found to be associated with significant liver toxicity in a number of patients, its use as an antidepressant was discontinued. However, several other compounds with MAO inhibitory activity were then developed and shown to possess antidepressant efficacy.

Shortly after the widespread introduction of the MAO inhibitors into clinical practice, case reports began to emerge regarding severe, at times fatal, hypertensive crises in some patients. Blackwell, Marley, Price, & Taylor (1967) demonstrated that these reactions were due to the hypertensive effects of tyramine and related compounds in certain foods and beverages. Tyramine can provoke a dramatic elevation in blood pressure, but monoamine oxidase in the gut wall usually breaks it down before it can be absorbed into the body. However, the MAO inhibitors block this activity and can lead to sudden increases in blood pressure when patients receiving them ingest foodstuffs that are rich in tyramine. Once the physiological basis for these reactions was recognized, dietary guidelines were developed which allow for the safe use of the MAO inhibitors. In addition to foods that possess high tyramine content, several medications with sympathomimetic properties are contraindicated for patients receiving MAO inhibitors (see Figure 1). These restrictions, and the fear of a potentially-life threatening reaction, have substantially diminished the use of these medications, which have now been largely supplanted by the new generation of antidepressants such as the selective serotonin reuptake inhibitors.

The discovery that the signs and symptoms of clinical depression could be reversed by treatment with the MAO inhibitors had a profound effect on both the practice of clinical psychiatry and on neuroscience research. Coupled with the nearly concurrent discovery of other effective antidepressant (i.e., the tricyclics) and antipsychotic pharmacotherapies, the MAO inhibitors helped to launch the revolution of modern clinical psychopharmacology. Psychiatrists began to incorporate biological therapies into treatment approaches that previously had been dominated by psychodynamic psychotherapy. Also, the relative specificity of action of these medications (i.e., the effectiveness in treating major depression, but not adjustment disorders or normal bereavement) ultimately led to greater emphasis on reliable and valid diagnostic procedures and criteria. In the neurosciences, these medications focused attention on the potential role of the biogenic amine neurotransmitters in the pathophysiology of depression. By blocking the intraneuronal degradation of norepinephrine, serotonin, and dopamine, the MAO inhibitors led to the accumulation of these neurotransmitters and eventually the release of larger quantities into the synapse, leading to an enhancement in neurotransmission. These observations of the pharmacological actions of the MAO inhibitors, coupled with their clinical efficacy, were the basis of several theories that postulated that a functional deficit in one or more of these neurotransmitters was responsible for the development of clinical depression. More recently, it has been suggested that the clinical response to the MAO inhibitors may be linked to secondary adaptive changes in various neurotransmitter receptors, and thus their mechanism of action and the pathophysiology of depression remain unclear.

There are two types of monoamine oxidase in the human central nervous system and in some peripheral organs. The main sub-

Figure 1.   Partial Listing of Food and Medication Restrictions for MAOIs*

FOODS	MEDICATIONS
Cheese (except cream cheese)	Tricyclic antidepressants
Over-ripe fruit (especially banana peels)	Serotonin selective reuptake inhibitors
Fava beans	Meperidine
Sausages and preserved meats	Buspirone
Pickled fish and vegetables	Sympathomimetics (e.g., l-dopa, pseudoephedrine)
Chicken and beef liver	
Red wines, sherry, liquors	
Monosodium glutamate	

* Note: This is a partial, representative listing. Patients receiving treatment with an MAO inhibitor should check carefully with their physicians for a comprehensive list of prohibited foods and medications.

strates for MAO-A activity are the neurotransmitters dopamine, norepinephrine, epinephrine, and serotonin, while dopamine, phenylethylamine, phenylethanolamine, tyramine, and benzylamine are the main substrates for MAO-B. The classic MAO inhibitors (phenelzine, isocarboxazide, and tranylcypromine) irreversibly affect both MAO-A and MAO-B. Newer agents, including several that are not currently available in this country, target one of the specific forms of MAO (e.g., selegiline is an MAO-B–specific inhibitor) and/or have reversible effects (e.g., moclobemide is a reversible inhibitor of MAO-A).

The primary use of the MAO inhibitors is the treatment of depression. Several studies have suggested that these medications are especially effective in the treatment of atypical depression, in which the usual physical signs and symptoms of depression are reversed (i.e., hypersomnia rather than insomnia; increased appetite with weight gain rather than decreased appetite with weight loss) (Quitkin et al., 1990). There is also substantial research documenting the efficacy of MAO inhibitors in the treatment of panic disorder (Lydiard et al., 1989), although the SSRIs and high potency benzodiazepine derivatives are more widely used. Limited controlled trials have also supported the use of these medications in the treatment of social phobia and posttraumatic stress disorder (Versiani et al., 1992; Kosten, Frank, Dan, McDougle, & Giller, 1991).

Side effects are often more frequent and more severe with the use of MAO inhibitors than with other, newer antidepressants. The most frequent side effects include orthostatic hypotension, insomnia, dizziness, constipation, blurred vision, and weakness (Krishnan, 1998). Liver damage may occur in rare instances. These side effects, coupled with the inconvenience and concern regarding dietary and medication restrictions and the availability of the new generation of antidepressants, have led to considerable decrease in the use of the MAO inhibitors. However, they are still utilized by many clinicians in the treatment of refractory cases of depression. In the future, the development of more specific and reversible forms of MAO inhibitors may stimulate a resurgence in their use in clinical psychiatry.

REFERENCES

Blackwell, M., Marley, E., Price, J., & Taylor, D. (1967). Hypertensive interactions between monoamine oxidase inhibitors and food stuffs. *British Journal of Psychiatry, 113,* 349–365.

Bloch, R. G., Doonief, A. S., Buchberg, A. S., & Spellman, S. (1954). The clinical effect of isoniazid and iproniazid in the treatment of pulmonary tuberculosis. *Annals of Internal Medicine, 40,* 881–900.

Kosten, T. R., Frank, J. B., Dan, E., McDougle, C. J., & Giller, E. L., Jr. (1991). Pharmacotherapy for post-traumatic stress disorder using phenelzine or imipramine. *Journal of Nervous and Mental Disorders, 179,* 366–370.

Kline, N. S. (1984). Monoamine oxidase inhibitors: An unfinished picaresque tale. In F. J. Ayd & B. Blackwell (Eds.), *Discoveries in Biological Psychiatry* (pp. 194–204). Baltimore: Ayd Medical Communications.

Krishnan, K. R. R. K. (1998). Monoamine oxidase inhibitors. In A. F. Schatzberg & C. B. Nemeroff (Eds.), *The American Psychiatric Press textbook of psychopharmacology* (pp. 239–250) Washington, DC: American Psychiatric Press.

Lydiard, R. B., Laraia, M. T., Howell, E. F., Fossey, M. D., Reynolds, R. D., & Ballenger, J. C. (1989). Phenelzine treatment of panic disorder: Lack of effect on pyridoxal phosphate levels. *Journal of Clinical Psychopharmacology, 9,* 428–431.

Quitkin, F. M., McGrath, P. J., Stewart, J. W., Harrison, W., Tricamo, E., Wagner, S. G., Ocepek-Welikson, K., Nunes, E., Rabkin, J. G., & Klein, D. F. (1990). Atypical depression, panic attacks, and response to imipramine and phenelzine: A replication. *Archives of General Psychiatry, 47,* 935–941.

Versiani, M., Nardi, A. E., Mundim, F. D., Alves, A. B., Liebowitz, M. R., & Amrein, R. (1992). Pharmacotherapy of social phobia: A controlled study with meclobemide and phenelzine. *British Journal of Psychiatry, 161,* 353–360.

Zeller, E. A. (1963). Diamine oxidase. In P. D. Boyer, H. Lardy, & K. Myrback (Eds.), *The enzymes* (Vol. 8, 2nd ed.). London: Academic Press.

R. N. GOLDEN
University of North Carolina

ANTIDEPRESSANTS
DEPRESSION
PSYCHOPHARMOCOLOGY

MARIJUANA (CANNABIS)

Cannabis sativa, a plant containing the psychoactive compounds Δ^9- or Δ^9-trans-tetrahydrocannabinol (THC), has been used by humans for its psychotropic effects for thousands of years. After alcohol, cannabis is the most widely used intoxicating drug in the world. There are many types of cannabis preparations. When the upper leaves, flowering or fruited tops, and stems are dried and smoked, the preparation is most commonly called marijuana. When the resin is removed from the leaves of the plant and dried and smoked, the preparation is usually called hashish. Cannabis may also be ingested after being mixed with tea or food. The effects of cannabis after smoking occur within five to ten minutes and last up to three hours. After oral ingestion, the onset of effects occurs in 30 to 60 minutes, and effects may last up to 12 hours.

THC exerts its effects by binding to cannabinoid receptors, which are members of the family of G-protein-coupled receptors. Two types of cannabinoid receptors have been identified so far. CB1 receptors are found mainly in neurons, and they modulate adenylate cyclase activity and voltage-sensitive calcium channels when stimulated. CB2 receptors are found on cells in the immune system. An edogenous ligand, anandaminde, has been identified, which appears to have a modulatory effect on the dopaminergic neurotransmitter system. Dopamine is a neurotransmitter that has been shown to play a role in regulating mood, attention and cognitive processes, and movement. THC, probably through second order effects, has also been shown to affect other neurotransmitter systems, including the serotonergic, noradrenergic, and cholinergic systems.

During acute cannabis intoxication, users commonly report euphoria and perceptual distortions. Less commonly, users experience dysphoria, increased anxiety, paranoia, depersonalization, and derealization. All of these effects are transient and have not been shown to persist for prolonged periods after intoxication. However, impairment on various cognitive, perceptual, and psychomotor tasks has been demonstrated to persist in many users 24 to 48 hours after acute intoxication. There is some evidence that chronic use of cannabis may produce residual deficits in short-term memory and attention, possibly lasting for weeks after last use; whether any of these deficits can become permanent remains unknown. Physiologic effects include conjunctival injection, dry mouth, increased appetite, tachycardia, hypertension, bronchoconstriction followed by bronchodilation, decreased intraocular pressure, and increased cortisol secretion. Cannabis has been reported to effect sleep, alter brain activity as measured by EEG, and to possess analgesic and anti-emetic effects. Medical uses of marijuana include the treatment of glaucoma, vascular headache, decreased appetite associated with chronic illnesses, and nausea associated with chemotherapy.

Many long-term cannabis users report mild withdrawal symptoms after discontinuing use. These may include increased anxiety, irritability, and physical tension, decreased appetite, insomnia, headache, nausea, and chills. Withdrawal symptoms appear within the first few days and resolve approximately a week after stopping use. Although the symptoms are similar to those seen after discontinuation of heroin or alcohol, they may be slower to appear and less intense because, unlike these other drugs which leave the body rapidly, cannabis is fat-soluble and leaves the body more slowly over a longer period of time.

While a large percentage of the population, perhaps more than 50 percent in the United States, has tried marijuana, only a small percentage develop abuse or dependence syndromes. Environmental factors seem to be the greatest predictor of lifetime marijuana use, while genetic factors strongly predict the development of chronic marijuana use, marijuana abuse, and dependence. Reasons commonly given for long-term chronic marijuana use include relaxation, stress reduction, feeling "high", improving mood, increased creativity, and inducement of an altered state of consciousness. Some people appear to use marijuana for self-medication of depression, bipolar disorder, anxiety disorders, disorders of attention, and to control hyperaggressiveness.

Negative attributes commonly reported by chronic users are cost, loss of time spent stoned, chronic cough or shortness of breath when exercising, difficulty waking up in the morning, daytime fatigue, negative social stigma, and marijuana's illegal status. At some point in their lives, many people who have been chronic users of cannabis decide to stop. Reasons commonly given include the prevention of the negative effects described above, loss of peer group or source of cannabis, pregnancy, or changing work and family responsibilities. The majority of people who decide to stop are able to do so without help. However, some people find it difficult to stop because of withdrawal symptoms, or because they are using marijuana to help them with a psychiatric problem or as their primary means of dealing with life stress. Heavy cannabis users who are interested in discontinuing use are often helped by the knowledge that the physical withdrawal syndrome lasts only a week or so, and also by participation in self-help groups such as AA and SMART recovery. People using marijuana to self-medicate a psychiatric disorder, or as their main coping mechanism, may find it easier to stop if they receive treatment for their primary psychiatric disorder or if they are taught alternative techniques for dealing with stress and anxiety.

SUGGESTED READING

Felder, C. C., & Glass, M. (1998). Cannabinoid receptors and their endogenous agonists. *Annual Review of Pharmacology and Toxicology, 38,* 179–200.

Gruber, A. J., & Pope, H. G., Jr. (1996). Cannabis-related disorders. In A. Tasman, J. Kay, & J. A.Lieberman (Eds.), *Psychiatry* (pp. 795–806). Philadelphia: Saunders.

Kendler, K. S., & Prescott, C. A. (1988). Cannabis use, abuse, and dependence in a population-based sample of female twins. *American Journal of Psychiatry, 155*(8), 1016–1022.

A. J. GRUBER
H. G. POPE
McLean Hospital

HALLUCINOGENIC DRUGS
PSYCHOPHARMOCOLOGY
SUBSTANCE ABUSE

MARITAL DISCORD

The large volume of research on marital discord and the related constructs of marital conflict and marital dissatisfaction attest to the perceived importance of understanding the problems that sometimes arise in marriage. Of the various terms used in this area of inquiry, "marital satisfaction" is the best defined, referring to an evaluation of the relationship or the partner. Because of their clarity and brevity, measures of marital satisfaction play a prominent role in all areas of marital research. "Marital conflict" is a somewhat broader term than "marital satisfaction" and is used to refer to spousal perceptions, emotions, anticipations, and behavior in relation to some disagreement or area of differing interests. Marital conflict, however, is not inherently negative and may or may not be associated with marital dissatisfaction. In some cases marital conflict may set the stage for increases in relationship satisfaction, while in others it may be the harbinger of deterioration in the relationship. For this reason, the study of marital conflict is often considered distinct from the study of marital satisfaction, and researchers in this area place considerable importance on direct observation of marital interaction.

"Marital discord" is also a relatively broad term, referring to a state of marital dissatisfaction in conjunction with any of a number of problems that may beset couples and lead to long-standing marital conflict, loss of marital commitment, feelings of estrangement within marriage, or marital dissolution. Because the construct combines a variety of disparate features, measures of marital discord tend to be collections of heterogeneous items. The most comprehensive self-report instrument of marital discord is called the Marital Satisfaction Inventory. This inventory solves the problem of heterogeneous content by assessing each content area using a separate scale. Its primary disadvantage is its overall length of 150 items. Maintaining the distinctions between different terms used in the area has become increasingly important as research in the area of marital discord has developed. Of particular importance is the distinction between marital satisfaction and marital conflict, as these two constructs may often diverge in their implications. On the other hand, measures of marital satisfaction and measures of marital discord are often highly correlated, and the two terms are sometimes used interchangeably.

Inquiry into the causes, consequences, and correlates of marital discord is driven in part by the perceived importance of better understanding the effect of marital discord on numerous processes related to personal and family adjustment. Supporting this perception, much recent research suggests that marital discord and the related constructs of marital dissatisfaction and marital conflict play an important role in individual and family well-being. For example, marital dissatisfaction commonly co-occurs with depression, eating disorders, some types of alcoholism, as well as physical and psychological abuse of partners. In addition, marital discord and marital dissolution covary with problems of delinquency and may presage children's later problems with intimate communication. Similarly, marital discord is associated with poorer health and with specific physical illnesses such as cancer, cardiac disease, and chronic pain. Marital interaction studies suggest possible mechanisms that may account for these links showing, for example, that hostile behaviors during conflict relate to alterations in immunological, endocrine and cardiovascular functioning. Better understanding of marital discord therefore offers the potential for more effective treatment of certain types of individual psychopathology and family difficulty and can offer hope for better managing the patients' sequelae. In addition, increased understanding of marital discord may also prove useful in developing better health maintenance strategies and in the management of chronic health problems.

Inquiry regarding marital discord is also fueled by the perceived importance of developing harmonious marital relationships as an end in itself. Better understanding of marital discord is sought as a way to provide guidance to those attempting to develop interventions to relieve marital discord or to those developing programs to prevent marital distress and divorce. That is, understanding marital discord is potentially important because enhancing marital satisfaction and alleviating marital discord is a desirable goal in its own right.

Ongoing societal changes in the nature of marital discord provide a challenge to research that attempts to explicate the causes and consequences of marital discord. For example, in 1998, the most recent year for which statistics are available, the American divorce rate had declined for eight straight years. The decreasing divorce rate over this period is most probably explained by a concurrent sharp increase in the age at first marriage over this same period. As this example illustrates, the challenges confronting marriages and families continue to change. In addition, despite hopeful news regarding decreasing divorce rates, the rate of divorce remains high, with about half of all first marriages projected to end in permanent separation or divorce. Further, the average level of satisfaction in intact first marriages has declined since at least the mid-1970s

As these considerations suggest, there is good reason for continuing research on the topic of marital therapy and the development of prevention programs designed to prevent decline in marital satisfaction and the development of marital discord. Because of the need to control for various extraneous effects, randomized clinical trials of various marital therapy programs have been conducted. The results of these trials indicate that substantial benefit may be obtained from several types of marital therapy, including behavioral marital therapy, emotion-focused marital therapy, insight-oriented marital therapy, and cognitive-behavioral marital therapy. Similarly, promising results have been obtained for divorce prevention programs. However, because of the difficulty in conducting randomized clinical trials on preventative intervention, and the difficulty in reaching couples at greatest risk for developing marital discord and divorcing, many questions about the utility of preventative programs remain unanswered. Further, despite advances in treatment and prevention efforts, fewer than half of discordant couples receiving marital therapy remain maritally satisfied at long-term follow-up. Likewise, the majority of couples in need of prevention services do not seek them out. Accordingly, there is considerable room for progress in the development of marital interventions and divorce prevention programs.

Recent advances in social cognition suggest the potential for changes in our understanding of the structure of marital dissatisfaction, the factors that maintain and alleviate marital discord, and the nature of marital conflict. Efforts to bridge the gap between basic research of this sort and the applied context of marital discord are essential to fuel future progress in the area. Historically, advances in marital therapy and marital prevention have depended upon advances in basic research and advances in our understanding of the complex phenomena associated with marital discord.

SUGGESTED READING

Fincham, F. D., & Beach, S. R. H. (1999). Marital Conflict. *Annual Review of Psychology, 50,* 47–77.

Gottman, J. M. (1994). *What predicts divorce.* Hillsdale, NJ: Erlbaum.

Hahlweg, K., Markman, H. J., Thurmaier, F., Engl, J., & Eckert, V. (1998). Prevention of marital distress: Results of a German prospective longitudinal study. *Journal of Family Psychology, 12,* 543–556.

Markman, H., Stanley, S., & Blumberg, S. L. (1994). *Fighting for your marriage.* San Francisco: Jossey-Bass.

Weiss, R. L., & Heyman, R. E. (1997). A clinical-research overview of couple interactions. In W. K. Halford & H. Markman (Eds.), *The clinical handbook of marriage and couples interventions* (pp. 13–41). Brisbane: Wiley.

S. BEACH
University of Georgia

MARRIAGE COUNSELING

MARITAL INTERACTION STYLES

The style of relating that tends to form in marriage finds its pattern early in the dating period, possibly at the first meeting of a couple. As discussed by Dreikurs in *The Challenge of Marriage,* each dating partner, usually unconsciously, assesses the fit of personal values, attitudes, and behavior with the personal values and behavior of the other person. As both seek to define how they mesh, certain patterns of relating begin to occur repeatedly, almost as though a dance of interactional behavior were taking place. This interactional dancing has pattern and rhythm in which a couple discovers a comfortable fit and continues to repeat those ways of relating, thus establishing a pattern. Raush, Barry, Hertel, and Swain (1974) reported that such patterns of behavior continued for years into the marriage and sometimes remained unchanging during the entire marital life cycle. These repetitive ways of relating, called *marital interactional styles,* fall into different types.

Two of these styles, vertical and level interaction, have been identified in some detail by Allred (1976). The *vertical interaction style* is analogous to two people on a ladder who are climbing over each other in an effort to be superior, when there is only room for one person on each rung of the ladder. Often the patterns of relating in this type of relationship involve destructive criticisms. If only one person is critical, the other may respond by being placating or withdrawing. One might tell the other what to do and the other might then follow with blind compliance. If both are critical, they often resort to blaming, name-calling, or mutual withdrawal. Both could be terrified of making mistakes and thus want to appear to always be right even when at fault.

By contrast, a *level interactional style* is characterized by cooperation. In this type of marriage a spouse's place does not depend on making the other partner feel left out. This way of relating is free from demeaning, critical comments, and love and trust are expressed openly. Each person sees the other as a team member with whom to share life experiences rather than as an enemy who must be subdued. Each spouse can develop personal interests and activities with encouragement and help from the other. Their interaction involves statements that contain tentative elements communicating that the truth may be different from what each one is saying. Most couples have some degree of both vertical and level behavior, but a marital interactional style is determined by the predominance of one or the other.

Three styles of interaction—complementary, symmetrical, and parallel—were originally identified by Bateson (1928/1958) and have been researched by Harper, Scoresby, and Boyce (1977). In *complementary interaction* individuals exchange opposite behaviors. These exchanges might include dominant/submissive, talkative/quiet, sloppy/neat, cheerful/depressed, and all other opposing interactions. This kind of relationship is based on inequality of control, with one partner occupying a superior position and the other an inferior position. One person often initiates action and the other follows.

In *symmetrical interaction* each person tries to avoid losing control of the relationship. It becomes an "I am as good as you are" status struggle. Each person fights for the right to initiate action, criticize the other, offer advice, and so on. Anger might be exchanged for anger, depression for depression, and control attempts for control attempts. In *parallel interaction,* on the other hand, both partners know that neither will win at the expense of the other. In this relationship, one does not consistently elicit a particular behavior from the other. Instead, each person may employ similar or opposite behavior, but use it at the more appropriate and productive times.

Early family experiences have tremendous impact on these marital interaction styles. In the family, a child encounters unknown customs and rules. By evaluating responses of family members to the child's explorations, curiosity, and other behaviors, the child creates what Adler called a "blueprint for living" that will guide the child's actions throughout life. The combination of the family situation and the child's interpretation of it gives rise to the child's creation of a mental map of ways to belong and find importance. In determining a fit with a potential mate, this blueprint guides each partner, usually unconsciously.

When choosing mates, people actually know more about each other than they consciously realize. Dreikurs (1946) believed that acceptance or rejection of a possible marriage partner is based on much knowledge and agreement that entirely escapes awareness. Couples generally feel comfortable with each other because their lifestyles mesh, which means that with each other they can continue to live out their blueprints for living, including those blueprints resulting from birth order. There are no magic formulas for couples to use as they make the marital choice, but the identification of marital interaction styles can help them become more aware of their mutual behaviors. It is then possible to change ways of interacting to form more loving, lasting bonds.

REFERENCES

Allred, G. H. (1976). *How to strengthen your marriage and family.* Provo, UT: Brigham Young University Press.

Bateson, G. (1958). *Naven* (2nd ed.). Stanford, CA: Stanford University Press. (Original work published 1928)

Dreikurs, R. (1946). *The challenge of marriage.* New York: Duell, Sloan, & Pearce.

Harper, J. M., Scoresby, A. L., & Boyce, D. W. (1977). The logical levels of complementary, symmetrical, and parallel interaction classes in family dyads. *Family Process, 16,* 199–210.

Raush, H. L., Barry, W. A., Hertel, R. K., & Swain, M. A. (1974). *Communication, conflict, and marriage.* San Francisco: Jossey-Bass.

SUGGESTED READING

Ansbacher, H., & Ansbacher, R. R. (Eds.). (1956). *The individual psychology of Alfred Adler.* New York: Basic Books.

Eckstein, D. G., Baruth, L., & Mahrer, D. (1978). *Life style: What is it?* Dubuque, IA: Kendall/Hunt.

Hoopes, M. H., & Harper, J. M. (1981). Ordinal positions, family systems, and family therapy. In M. R. Textor (Ed.), *Theorie und praxis der familien-therapie.* Wurzburg, Germany: Paderborn.

Mosak, H. H. (1973). *Alfred Adler: His influence on psychology today.* Park Ridge, IL: Noyes Press.

Toman, W. (1976). *Family constellation* (3rd ed.). New York: Springer.

J. M. Harper
G. H. Allred
R. A. Wadham
Brigham Young University

PERSONALITY TYPES

MARRIAGE COUNSELING

Relationship difficulties are among the most common reasons people consult mental health professionals, and approximately 75% of health service providers report that they provide marital therapy (VandenBos & Stapp, 1983). As evidenced by recent narrative reviews (Baucom, Stroham, Mueser, Daiuto, & Stickle, 1998) and meta-analytic evaluations (e.g., Dunn & Schwebel, 1995; Shadish et al., 1993), there is considerable evidence that couple therapy is effective for treating relationship difficulties. For example, Shadish and colleagues reported a mean effect size of .71 across 16 marital therapy outcome studies evaluating the effect of marital therapy on global dissatisfaction. An effect size of .71 converts to a correlation coefficient of .33 (Hedges & Olkin, 1985, p. 77), which translates into a treatment success rate $(.50 \pm r/2;$ Rosenthal & Rubin, 1982) of approximately 67% for treated couples and .34% for control couples. This effect size is quite similar to those obtained for other interventions. For example, Smith and Glass

(1977) reported a mean effect size of .68 across 375 studies of the effectiveness of psychotherapy, and Lipsey and Wilson (1993) reported a mean effect size of .47 across 156 meta-analyses representing approximately 9,400 treatment outcome studies evaluating psychological, educational, and behavioral treatments. Thus, the efficacy of couple therapy is similar to that obtained by other psychosocial interventions.

There are several major theoretical approaches to conducting marital counseling. One of the most thoroughly researched approaches is behavioral marital therapy (Jacobson & Margolin, 1979), which focuses on increasing pleasing exchanges (i.e., caring behaviors) between partners, as well as improving communication and problem-solving skills. More recently, cognitive interventions that target dysfunctional unrealistic relationship beliefs and maladaptive causal and responsibility attributional styles have been added to this approach, and the treatment has been labeled cognitive-behavioral marital therapy (Baucom & Epstein, 1990). A second treatment approach is emotion-focused couples therapy (Greenberg & Johnson, 1988), which targets problems of adult attachment insecurity by modifying couples' interaction patterns and the emotional responses that evoke and are evoked by these interactions. A third approach is insight-oriented marital therapy (Snyder & Wills, 1989), which focuses on helping couples become aware of interaction patterns, relationship cognitions, and developmental issues that are either totally or partially beyond their conscious awareness. To date, there is little evidence to suggest that these different approaches yield different outcomes in terms of marital satisfaction (see Shadish et al., 1993). In addition to developing different theoretical approaches to working with couples, there has been a recent movement towards developing integrating approaches that cut across treatment modalities. For example, integrative marital therapy approaches have recently been advanced by Jacobson and Christensen (1996) and by Snyder (in press). Although there are several theoretical and integrative approaches to marital counseling, there are few empirically based guidelines to help match couples to types of treatments.

In addition to efforts devoted to enhancing outcome for relational problems, there have been efforts devoted to evaluating marital therapy as a treatment for psychiatric disorders. This movement is based on research findings that when couples have problems in their relationships, there is often co-occurring psychiatric dysfunction. For example, Whisman (in press) reported that marital dissatisfaction was associated with mood disorders, anxiety disorders, and substance-use disorders in a large, representative population-based sample. As reviewed by Baucom et al. (1998), marital therapy has been shown to be effective in treating depression, anxiety problems, and alcohol use disorders. Thus, there is evidence that marital therapy is effective in treating problems traditionally viewed as "individual" problems, as well as treating relationship difficulties.

Another important development in marital counseling has been seen in the prevention of relationship problems. As reviewed by Hahlweg and Markman (1988), several studies have found that behavioral approaches to premarital counseling are effective in improving satisfaction and reducing divorce rates, and that these gains are maintained for as long as five years after participation (Markman, Renick, Floyd, Stanley, & Clements, 1993). Efforts such as these are important in establishing that marital counseling is effective in preventing relationship difficulties, as well as effective in overcoming relationship problems once they exist.

Finally, a recent development in marital therapy outcome research has been evaluations of very brief interventions. For example, Halford, Osbargy, and Kelly (1996) reported that a 3-session approach to behavioral couples therapy yielded similar outcomes as those obtained following 12 to 15 sessions. Similarly, Davidson and Horvath (1997) found that three sessions of treatments resulted in positive impact on couples' relationships. Identifying the active components of marital therapy and distilling them into brief treatments holds particular promise for reaching people who might not otherwise seek marital counseling.

REFERENCES

Baucom, D. H., & Epstein, N. (1990). *Cognitive behavioral marital therapy.* New York: Brunner/Mazel.

Baucom, D. H., Shoham, V., Mueser, K. T., Daiuto, A. D., & Stickle, T. R. (1998). Empirically supported couple and family interventions for marital distress and adult mental health problems. *Journal of Consulting and Clinical Psychology, 66,* 53–88.

Davidson, G. N. S., & Horvath, A. O. (1997). Three sessions of brief couples therapy: A clinical trial. *Journal of Family Psychology, 11,* 422–435.

Dunn, R. L., & Schwebel, A. I. (1995). Meta-analytic review of marital therapy outcome research. *Journal of Family Psychology, 9,* 58–68.

Greenberg, L. S., & Johnson, S. M. (1988). *Emotionally focused therapy for couples.* New York: Guilford Press.

Hahlweg, K., & Markman, H. J. (1988). Effectiveness of behavioral marital therapy: Empirical status of behavioral techniques in preventing and alleviating marital distress. *Journal of Consulting and Clinical Psychology, 56,* 440–447.

Halford, W. K., Osbargy, S., & Kelly, A. (1996). Brief behavioural couples therapy: A preliminary evaluation. *Behavioural and Cognitive Psychotherapy, 24,* 263–273.

Hedges, L. V., & Olkin, I. (1985). *Statistical methods for meta-analysis.* Orlando, FL: Academic Press.

Jacobson, N. S., & Christensen, A. (1996). *Integrative couple therapy.* New York: Norton.

Jacobson, N. S., & Margolin, G. (1979). *Marital therapy: Strategies based on social learning and behavior exchange principles.* New York: Brunner/Mazel.

Lipsey, M. W., & Wilson, D. B. (1993). The efficacy of psychological, educational, and behavioral treatment: Confirmation from meta-analysis. *American Psychologist, 48,* 1181–1209.

Markman, H. J., Renick, M. J., Floyd, F. J., Stanley, S. M., & Clements, M. (1993). Preventing marital distress through communication and conflict management training: A 4- and 5-year follow-up. *Journal of Consulting and Clinical Psychology, 61,* 70–77.

Rosenthal, R., & Rubin, D. B. (1982). A simple, general purpose display of magnitude of experimental effect. *Journal of Educational Psychology, 74,* 166–169.

Shadish, W. R., Montgomery, L. M., Wilson, P., Wilson, M. R., Bright, I., & Okwumabua, T. (1993). Effects of family and marital psychotherapies: A meta-analysis. *Journal of Consulting and Clinical Psychology, 61,* 992–1002.

Smith, M. L., & Glass, G. V. (1977). Meta-analysis of psychotherapy outcome studies. *American Psychologist, 32,* 752–760.

Snyder, D. K. (in press). Affective reconstruction in the context of a pluralistic approach to couple therapy. *Clinical Psychology: Science and Practice.*

Snyder, D. K., & Willis, R. M. (1989). Behavioral versus insight-oriented marital therapy: Effects on individual and inter-spousal functioning. *Journal of Consulting and Clinical Psychology, 57,* 39–46.

VandenBos, G. R., & Stapp, J. (1983). Service providers in psychology: Results of the 1982 APA Human Resources Survey. *American Psychologist, 38,* 1330–1352.

Whisman, M. A. (in press). Marital distress and psychiatric disorders in a community sample: Results from the National Comorbidity Survey. *Journal of Abnormal Psychology.*

M. A. WHISMAN
University of Colorado, Boulder

COUNSELING

MARX, MELVIN H. (1919–   )

Melvin H. Marx was born on June 8, 1919. He received his AB, MA, and PhD degrees from Washington University (St. Louis) during the years 1940 to 1943. He has been married to Kathleen Kendall for over 50 years, with four children.

At the University of Missouri, Columbia (1944–1984) Marx served in positions from instructor through research professor, during which time he supervised 40 MA and 30 PhD students. Among the latter were Aaron Brownstein, Shinkuro Iwahara, and Reed Lawson (all now deceased), and Phil Dunham, Robert Goldbeck, Felix Goodson, Robert Henderson, W. A. Hillix, W. A. Pieper, Jo Tombaugh, and Tom Tombaugh. Marx's subsequent appointments were as senior research scientist at Georgia State University in Atlanta (1985–1989) and as distinguished visiting professor at Western Carolina University, in Cullowhee, North Carolina, from 1991 to the present. Temporary appointments included research scientist at the U.S. Air Force's HRRC laboratory at Lackland Field, Texas (1950–1951), psychometrist at a U.S. Army induction station (1942), and visiting distinguished professor, science faculty, at Monash University, Melbourne, Australia (1970).

Marx has authored, co-authored, and edited 13 textbooks, most notably *Psychological Theory* (1951), which was the first text on the topic, and, with W. A. Hillix, *Systems and Theories in Psychology* (1963, with revisions through 1987).

Among Marx's academic awards were election to Phi Eta Sigma (1937), Omicron Delta Kappa (1939), Phi Beta Kappa (1940), and Sigma Xi (1941, 1943). He received the University of Missouri Columbia Alumni Association Distinguished Faculty Award (1977), and the American Psychological Association (APA) Division One Hilgard Lifetime Contribution Award (1997). He served as chairman of the Missouri Academy of Science Psychology Section (and was organizer in 1965), and was president of the Missouri Psychological Association (1956) and the Midwestern Psychological Association (1964).

Among Marx's professional services were consulting and associative editorships for several journals (e.g., *Contemporary Psychology* [from its inception in 1956] for 17 years, the *Journal of Comparative and Physiological Psychology* for 8 years, *Psychological Abstracts,* 2 years, and *Psychological Reports,* since 1958). From 1974 to 1997 he wrote an annual review of psychology for the *Britannica Yearbook of Science and the Future,* and also two special reports for the *Britannica Medical and Health Annual.* He served as Missouri delegate to the Council of Representatives of APA, as a member of the executive council of the Missouri Psychological Association, and as a member of the executive council and chairman of the program committee of the Midwestern Psychological Association.

In 1945, Marx established an animal laboratory at the Columbia campus of the University of Missouri. In 1964 he applied for and received from the National Science Foundation (NSF) matching funds for a new animal laboratory building. His personal research support at Missouri totalled over $1.5 million, mainly from the National Institutes of Health (NIH, 14 years), NSF (7 years), the U.S. Army Research Institute (8 years), and the U.S. Air Force (6 years). For the last 20 years of his career at Missouri he received a salary stipend as a Research Career Award from the National Institute of Mental Health (NIMH).

Marx's research interests have generally focused on various problems in the fields of learning and cognition. For the first half of his career at Missouri he used mainly animal subjects (mostly laboratory rats); since then he has studied human subjects. The first research problems Marx attacked tended to be physiological experiments, such as the effects of dietary supplements on learning. Also included in this research program were experiments on topics such as audiogenic seizures and a series of empirical and theoretical studies on food-hoarding by rats. Marx's early years at Missouri also saw a continuation of the human error research he had done for his masters' research at Washington University, under the supervision of Marion Bunch. Special attention was paid to gradients of error repetition produced by reward (the phenomenon first reported by E. L. Thorndike as the "spread of effect").

More recently, Marx has attacked the problem of how human subjects are able to judge the frequencies with which events have occurred. He identified a response-strength factor (called "a feeling of familiarity" by many subjects) as a viable alternative to counting in the explanation of the surprisingly good ability of most subjects to recall such frequencies. This factor was found to be increasingly evident as a function of age, as determined from the retrospective reports obtained from the subjects. These results, which also showed significant improvements over age (up to college age), raised a serious question about the complete automaticity of this recall ability and its invariance over development, which had been generally assumed.

Most recently, Marx has called attention to the pervasiveness and the significance in everyday life of the inference process. Inferences have been relatively under-researched, except in the areas of formal logic and the comprehension of discourse. Marx's research has centered on how various biases in memory operate to facilitate the making of suggested inferences, even when instructions are used to encourage subjects to be careful in their recall. The making of suggested inferences was found to be a function of such factors as associated affect (e.g., children generally refrained from recalling negative actions of highly favored subjects, like puppies and kittens). With more neutral subjects, however, inferences were found to be consistently made at an error rate above 50% by elementary-school children of all ages, except for gifted ones (IQs above 130) in the sixth grade. In collaboration with Bruce Henderson, Marx is also investigating the role of associative inferences in the formation of "false memories," using the research paradigm popularized by Roediger and McDermott.

STAFF

MASLOW, ABRAHAM H. (1908–1970)

Abraham Maslow studied with two of the leading Gestalt psychologists, Max Wertheimer and Kurt Koffka, at the New School for Social Research. From these men he got the idea for a holistic psychology. He took all three of his academic degrees from the University of Wisconsin, receiving the PhD in 1934. Along with Carl Rogers, Rollo May, and Charlotte Buhler, Maslow was one of the founders of the American Association of Humanistic Psychology. His most important books, presenting his humanistic position, include *Motivation and Personality* and *Toward a Psychology of Being.*

Maslow considered his basic approach to psychology to fall within the broad range of humanistic psychology, which he characterized as the Third Force in American psychology (the other two being behaviorism and psychoanalysis). His main efforts were directed to the field of personality. He believed that psychology had dealt too much with human frailty and not enough with human strengths. In deploring the pessimism of so many psychologists—Freud, for example—Maslow looked to the more positive side of humanity. He believed human nature was essentially good. As personality unfolded through maturation, the creative powers manifested themselves ever more clearly. If humans were miserable or neurotic, it was the environment that made them so. Humans were not basically destructive or violent, but became so when their inner nature was twisted or frustrated.

Maslow proposed a theory of motivation which has become extremely popular in humanistic circles. Our basic needs or drives could be arranged in a hierarchy, often pictured as a pyramid. At the bottom were the basic physiological needs: hunger and thirst.

Next were safety needs: security from attack, avoidance of pain, freedom from invasion of privacy. On top of these were the needs for love and belonging. Higher up were the needs for self-esteem: feeling good, pride, confidence. At the top of the hierarchy was the need for self-actualization, a basic driving force for self-fulfillment. This emphasis on self-actualization is shared by many humanistic psychologists.

To understand human nature, Maslow felt it was more profitable to study people who have realized their potentiality rather than those who were crippled (psychologically) or neurotic. He selected a group of people, some from history, whom he felt had reached a considerable degree of self-actualization—such persons as Abraham Lincoln, Thomas Jefferson, Albert Einstein, and Eleanor Roosevelt. In studying them he found certain distinguishing characteristics, such as (a) a realistic orientation, (b) acceptance of themselves and others, (c) spontaneity of expression, (d) attitudes that were problem-centered rather than self-centered, (e) independence, (f) identification with humanity, (g) emotional depth, (h) democratic values, (i) a philosophic rather than a caustic sense of humor, (j) transcendence of the environment, and (k) creativity.

R. W. LUNDIN
Wheaton, Illinois

MASTURBATION

Masturbation is the term used to signify any type of autoerotic stimulation. Both males and females indulge in stimulation of the genitals for sexual gratification. The term is also applied to an infant's manipulation of the genitals, a common exploratory behavior in the early years. During adolescence, masturbation becomes one of the main sexual outlets, and remains so for many adults. Michael, Gagnon, Laumann, and Kolata (1994) found that among Americans, 60% of men and 40% of women report that they have masturbated during the past year. Twenty-five percent of men and 10% of women say they masturbate at least once a week. Estimates vary, depending on the studies cited and the specific approaches used in collecting the data.

Of all the areas of sexual behavior, masturbation appears to be subject to wide variation in reported frequency, owing no doubt to the privacy of this behavior, and the shame that has traditionally surrounded it. While in earlier historical periods masturbation was considered a sign of depravity or sinfulness, it is more generally accepted today as a common practice among adolescents and adults, both male and female.

REFERENCE

Michael, R. T., Gagnon, J. H., Laumann, E. O., & Kolata, G. (1994). *Sex in America: A Definitive Survey.* Boston: Little, Brown.

J. P. McKINNEY
Michigan State University

MATARAZZO, JOSEPH D. (1925–   )

Joseph D. Matarazzo was born on November 12, 1925, to U.S. citizens in Italy. In 1943, after completing his primary and secondary education in New York, he served on active duty in the U.S. Navy for six months before being selected for officer's training, which he completed in the Navy V-12 program at Columbia University and the Naval ROTC program at Brown University. Following his June, 1946, graduation with an AB in Naval Sciences and a commission as an ensign, Matarazzo served aboard a Navy tanker in the far east.

Although he had taken no psychology courses during officer's training, Matarazzo, after a year in the Pacific, reapplied to Brown and was accepted in the graduate program in psychology. The first year of graduate study he spent fulfilling the requirements for a bachelor's in psychology and working as a research assistant for Carl Pfaffman, who, along with Walter Hunter, Harold Shlosberg, Lorrin Riggs, and Gregory Kimble, was one of the country's outstanding teachers of experimental psychology. That first year of study would influence not only Matarazzo's choice of career—academic psychology—but also his personal life, as he met and in 1949 married Ruth Wood Gadbois, another psychology graduate student at Brown.

Because Brown did not offer clinical psychology in its PhD program, Matarazzo transferred in the fall of 1949 to Northwestern University. At Northwestern, William A. Hunt became Matarazzo's role model for the psychologist as scientist-practitioner, a role that at the Boulder Conference a year later would become the prototype for education and training in clinical psychology. At every opportunity Hunt impressed upon Matarazzo that a solid foundation in the scientific basis of psychology was a sine qua non for the clinical psychologist practitioner who wished to remain au courant throughout a lifelong career.

After two years at Northwestern, Matarazzo took an internship with Robert I. Watson and Ivan N. Mensh at the Washington University School of Medicine in St. Louis, and stayed on at the request of the dean of the medical school for his fourth year of PhD study in order to teach a required course in medical psychology to first-year medical students. Matarazzo taught at the Washington University School of Medicine from 1952 to 1955 and the Harvard Medical School from 1955 to 1957, then established and served as chairman for the first administratively autonomous department of medical psychology at the Oregon Health Sciences University (1957–1996). In 1996 he became a professor of behavioral neuroscience and stepped down from the chair position at OHSU.

Over the years Matarazzo has served as president of such organizations as the Academy of Behavioral Medicine Research, the International Council of Psychologists, the Western Psychological Association, the American Psychological Association (APA) Division of Health Psychology (Division 38), and the American Association of State Psychology Boards. He was one of the founders of the Council of Graduate Departments of Psychology (COGDOP) and was elected to its Charter Executive Committee; he also served as chairperson of the Board of Trustees of the Association for the Advancement of Psychology (AAP). He was elected to the APA Council of Representatives, served a three year term (1986–1989) as a member of the Board of Directors of the APA, and was elected President of the APA for the 1989 to 1990 term.

Matarazzo is a Diplomate of the American Board of Professional Psychology (ABPP) in both clinical psychology (1957) and clinical neuropsychology (1984), and has been in the active and continuous clinical practice of psychology concurrent with the full time position he has held in Oregon since 1957 as professor and, until 1996, chairman of the medical school's department of medical psychology.

He has served on National Institutes of Health (NIH), National Institute of Mental Health (NIMH), and National Science Foundation (NSF) training committees, advisory panels, and study sections, and served as the charter chairperson of the NIH Behavioral Medicine Study Section. He served for 20 years as the psychology editor for *Stedman's Medical Dictionary,* and currently serves on the editorial boards of three APA journals as well as on the editorial boards of 16 other scientific and professional journals. In 1991 he was appointed by the U.S. Secretary of Health and Human Services to a 4-year term on the NIMH National Mental Health Advisory Council.

Matarazzo's awards include the Annual Award for Contributions to Health Psychology (APA, Division 38), the Annual Distinguished Scientist Award (Division 12), the Annual Distinguished Service to the Profession of Psychology Award (ABPP), the American Psychiatric Association's Annual Research Award (Hofheimer Prize), and the APA's 1991 Annual Distinguished Professional Contributions Award (for Distinguished Professional Contributions to Knowledge).

His more than 200 research publications span three areas: (a) intellectual and neuropsychological functions, (b) nonverbal indices of empathy and related psychological processes, and (c) the role of lifestyle risk factors in health and illness. He also has written extensively on parity for psychologists as members of the medical staffs of hospitals, on licensing and credentialing, and on issues involved in the graduate education and training of future research, academic, and professional psychologists. He authored the 1972 *Fifth Edition of Wechsler's Measurement and Appraisal of Adult Intelligence;* co-authored a 1972 book on the interview and a 1978 book on nonverbal communication; and was editor-in-chief of the 1984 *Behavioral Health: A Handbook of Health Enhancement and Disease Prevention.*

Matarazzo is a Fellow of the APA (1959) and AAAS (1958), and a charter member of the Psychonomic Society.

STAFF

McCLELLAND, DAVID C. (1917–1991)

McClelland was known for his work in the field of motivation and especially in the area of the need for achievement. He received the BA degree from Wesleyan University and the MA from the University of Missouri. Yale conferred a PhD on him in 1941. For his accomplishments, he received a number of honorary degrees. After serving as an instructor at Wesleyan from 1941 to 1946, McClelland left for Harvard, where he was emeritus professor in the department of psychology.

Conceiving an early interest in social motivation, McClelland developed a method of measuring human needs through content analysis of imaginative thought. He researched extensively the role of the needs for achievement, power and affiliation in occupational success, economic and political development, health, and personal adjustment. Among McClelland's books are *Personality: The Achievement Motive* (with others); *The Achieving Society; Motivating Economic Achievement* (with D. Winter); *The Drinking Man* (with others); *Power: The Inner Experience;* and *Human Motivation.*

STAFF

McDOUGALL, WILLIAM (1871–1938)

William McDougall received his medical training at Cambridge and London. He then taught at Oxford and University College, London, from 1904 to 1920, except for an interruption during World War I, when he served in the British Medical Corps. His observations on mental patients during this period led to his writing the *Outline of Abnormal Psychology.* In 1920 he was called to Harvard to fill a chair once occupied by William James. In 1927 he accepted an invitation to become chairman of the Psychology Department at Duke University, where he remained until his death.

McDougall was much concerned with social psychology. *An Introduction to Social Psychology* (1908) set forth his theory of instincts to explain human behavior and, in particular, social behavior. McDougall antedated John Watson in defining psychology as the "science of conduct" (behavior). In this book he described an instinct as having three aspects: (a) a predisposition to notice certain stimuli; (b) a predisposition to make movements toward a goal; and (c) an emotional core that involved the energy that gave impetus to the activity, once a stimulus was presented to trigger an organism to action. McDougall's was a purposive psychology that was goal-directed. He called it "hormic," from the Greek *hormé,* meaning "urge."

In the first edition of *An Introduction to Social Psychology,* McDougall postulated 12 basic instincts. By 1932 the number had grown to 17, including hunger, sex, curiosity, escape, pugnacity, gregariousness, self-assertion, and acquisition. In the 1930s, as the term "instinct" was growing out of fashion, McDougall changed the name to "propensity," but the concept was the same. Often two or more instincts could combine to account for other behavior. For example, a man's love for his wife could be a combination of the sex and maternal instincts, which McDougall called sentiment.

In *Body and Mind* McDougall presented his doctrine of "soul." He believed there was a bit of soul in everything, even inorganic matter. This doctrine never became very popular at a time when psychology was fighting vigorously to cast off any theological implications. In addition, McDougall was a firm believer in psychic phenomena. He welcomed the research on extrasensory perception by J. B. Rhine at Duke University. This involved mental telepathy, clairvoyance, and other psychic phenomena.

Among the unpopular causes that McDougall supported was the Lamarckian hypothesis that characteristics acquired by one generation could be passed on to its offspring through the mechanisms of heredity. In one experiment—now generally discredited because of its lack of proper controls—he trained 23 generations of white rats to escape from a tank by one or two exits. If a rat attempted the wrong exit, it was given an electric shock. At the conclusion of the experiment those animals the ancestors of which had had the training performed in a superior way, as compared with those rats whose ancestors had never had any training in previous generations. However, the experiment has never been replicated.

Although, as far as human behavior is concerned, instinct doctrine is not generally accepted today (except by the Freudians), McDougall's ideas have led to a revival of interest in instincts among animal ethologists in particular, as seen in the work of Tinbergen and Lorenz. Furthermore, McDougall's idea of purposive or goal-directed behavior is still advocated by some contemporary psychologists.

R. W. LUNDIN
Wheaton, Illinois

McEWEN, BRUCE S.

Bruce S. McEwen received an AB in chemistry from Oberlin College, summa cum laude, in 1959, and a PhD in cell biology from The Rockefeller University in 1964. Wishing to go abroad and study the fledgling field of neurobiology, he went to Sweden to study in the laboratory of Holger Hyden and was a USPHS postdoctoral fellow in Goteborg, Sweden, from 1964 to 1965. After a brief sojourn at the University of Minnesota, McEwen returned to The Rockefeller University in 1966 to join the laboratory of Neal E. Miller as a cell biologist in a physiological psychology group. McEwen has remained at Rockefeller throughout his career. At present, he is the Alfred E. Mirksy Professor and head of the Harold and Margaret Milliken Hatch Laboratory of Neuroendocrinology at The Rockefeller University in New York City. A member of the National Academy of Sciences and the Institute of Medicine, he was president of the Society for Neuroscience from 1997 to 1998 and is a past president of the International Society of Neuroendocrinology.

As a neuroscientist and neuroendocrinologist, McEwen (and his laboratory) studies environmentally-regulated, variable gene expression in brain mediated by circulating steroid hormones and endogenous neurotransmitters in relation to brain sexual differentiation and the actions of sex, stress, and thyroid hormones on the adult brain. McEwen combines molecular, anatomical, pharmacological, physiological, and behavioral methodologies and makes an effort to relate his findings to human clinical information.

As a PhD student of the late Alfred E. Mirsky and Vincent G. Allfrey in the early 1960s, McEwen became fascinated with the notion of environmentally-regulated, variable gene expression and with the possibility that—in the brain—circulating steroid and thyroid hormones coordinate neural with body function by regulating the expression of nervous-system genes. Moreover, the notion that the brain regulates the endocrine system, and that the endocrine system, in turn, regulates brain function, provides a powerful model to understand how external events influence behavior and the plasticity of the brain over hours, days, and even years. Until recently, study of gene expression in the brain was not fashionable, and ion movements and neurotransmission were the main focus of neuroscience research.

When McEwen joined the Neal Miller laboratory in 1966, he set out to elucidate, in cellular and molecular terms, the basis for long-term effects of sex and stress hormones on the brain that were inferred from the classical work of Frank Beach, Daniel Lehrman, and W. C. Young, among others. He was one of the first investigators to look for, detect, and characterize receptors for steroid hormones in brain tissue in the late 1960s, and the work that has arisen from this has become one of the foundations of the growing intersection of neurobiology, endocrinology, and behavioral science.

In 1968, he found in the hippocampus receptors for adrenal steroid stress hormones that are transcription factors, a discovery that has triggered an ever-growing number of studies throughout the world on the neural effects of adrenal steroids and stress on the hippocampus in experimental animals and in human disorders, such as Major Depression, Post-Traumatic Stress Disorder, schizophrenia, Cushing's syndrome, and dementia. Recent work shows that adult hippocampal neurons undergo a range of structural changes that indicate how adaptable they are: stress-induced remodeling of dendrites of pyramidal neurons; neurogenesis in the dentate gyrus that is inhibited by stress and increased by an enriched environment; and biphasic stress hormone effects on long-term potentiation and parallel biphasic modulation of hippocampal-dependent spatial and declarative memory processes. With the use of magnetic resonance imaging, atrophy of the human hippocampus has been described in a number of disorders, and McEwen and others are involved in attempts to reverse or prevent such atrophy with pharmaceutical agents that interfere with the stress-induced structural changes in the animal models.

In their studies of the hippocampal formation, the McEwen laboratory found that estradiol induces formation of new synapses between nerve cells in the adult hippocampus. This form of plasticity, like the stress-related plasticity described previously, involves a significant participation of N-methyl-D-aspartate (NMDA) receptors along with circulating hormones. McEwen had previously studied the actions of ovarian hormones on the reproductive neuroendocrine axis of the brain. He described estrogen receptors in the developing brain and demonstrated the role of aromatization of testosterone in rat brain sexual differentiation, as well as key actions of estradiol on the hypothalamus that activate sexual behavior in adulthood. In addition, his laboratory found that estrogens regulate cholinergic neurons in the basal forebrain, a finding that provided the rationale for the first trial of estrogens for Alzheimer's disease in The Rockefeller University Hospital by Howard Fillit.

During the past 9 years, McEwen has worked with two networks of the John D. and Catherine T. MacArthur Foundation Health Program, applying concepts of stress neurobiology to understand how stressful experiences affect health. This involvement stimulated work in his laboratory on the effects of stress and stress hormones on the immune system. This work has revealed that acute stress enhances immune function by promoting immune cell movements to locations in the body where they are needed to fight an infection.

As an additional consequence of MacArthur involvement, McEwen examined the protective and damaging effects of the biological mediators of stress, initially with the collaboration of the late Eliot Stellar. They developed a concept called allostatic load, which refers to the cost to the body and brain of adaptation to chronic stress and other environmental challenges. Validation and measurement of allostatic load is presently underway in collaboration with clinical colleagues, and McEwen is involved in a MacArthur network in applying the allostatic load concept to understanding why gradients of health exist across the range of socioeconomic status and not merely at the extreme bottom of the scale. He is also involved in exploring the implications of these findings for public policy.

STAFF

McGAUGH, JAMES L.

James L. McGaugh was born in Long Beach, CA, on December 17, 1931. During his childhood he first lived in Southern Arizona and later in Southern California. As an undergraduate student at San Jose State University in California he studied drama, music, and psychology. He graduated with highest honors in 1953. He then studied physiological psychology at the University of California, Berkeley, where he received his PhD in 1959. At Berkeley his interests in learning and memory and their neural bases were shaped by his professors, E. C. Tolman, D. Krech, and M. Rosenzweig and his graduate student research colleague, L. Petrinovich. In 1957 McGaugh accepted a faculty position at San Jose State University. In 1961 he received a National Academy of Sciences/National Research Council postdoctoral fellowship that enabled him to do postdoctoral research in neuropharmacology with Nobel Laureate D. Bovet at the Istituto Superiore di Sanita in Rome, Italy. McGaugh subsequently joined the faculty of the department of psychology at the University of Oregon.

In 1964, McGaugh moved to the University of California, Irvine, where he was a founding faculty member and the founding chair of the department of neurobiology and behavior, the world's first department of neuroscience. At UCI, McGaugh subsequently served as dean of the School of Biological Sciences, academic vice chancellor and executive vice chancellor. In 1981 he became founding director of the Center for the Neurobiology of Learning and Memory, a position he has held for almost two decades. He is also a research professor in the department of neurobiology and behavior.

McGaugh was founding editor of the journal *Neurobiology of Learning and Memory,* and served as editor of that journal (and its precursors, *Behavioral Biology* and *Behavioral and Neural Biology*) for almost three decades. He also served on the editorial advisory boards of many other journals, including *Brain Research, Neuron, Journal of Neurobiology, Psychopharmacology, Behavioral Neuroscience,* and *Archives of Medical Research.*

McGaugh's many honors recognizing his distinguished research accomplishments include election as a member of the National Academy of Sciences, a fellow of the American Academy of Arts and Sciences, foreign member of the Brazilian Academy of Sciences, a fellow of the Society of Experimental Psychology, and a fellow of the World Academy of Arts and Science. He received the Distinguished Scientific Contribution Award from the American Psychological Association and the John P. McGovern Award from the American Association for the Advancement of Science.

He received an honorary doctorate of science from Southern Illinois University. He is a William James Fellow and past president of the American Psychological Society. He received the Distinguished Alumnus Award from San Jose State University. At UC Irvine McGaugh received the Distinguished Faculty Research Award, the Extraordinarious Award, and the UCI Medal. He was a Merit Award Recipient from the National Institute of Mental Health and served on the NIMH Advisory Council. Awards for excellence in students' research have been established in McGaugh's honor at both San Jose State University and UC Irvine.

McGaugh's extensive and seminal research contributions to understanding the neurobiology of learning and memory span over four decades. He first pioneered in investigations of memory consolidation and discovered that memory consolidation in animals can be enhanced by administration of stimulant drugs shortly after learning. These findings greatly influenced subsequent studies of memory consolidation in animal and human subjects. The use of posttraining drug administration provided a powerful methodology for differentiating drug effects on learning and performance. In subsequent work, McGaugh and his colleagues have used this methodology in examining the effects, on consolidation, of drugs affecting several neuromodulatory and neurotransmitter systems. Furthermore, by using microinfusions of drugs into specific brain regions, they have investigated the involvement of brain systems in memory consolidation.

Extensive work in McGaugh's laboratory has revealed that memory consolidation is influenced by drugs affecting noradrenergic, GABAergic, opioid peptidergic, and cholinergic systems. Moreover, findings indicate that all of these actions involve the release of norepinephrine in the amygdala. The basolateral nucleus of the amygdala is particularly critical. Other important findings of research by McGaugh and his colleagues indicate that adrenal stress hormones, including epinephrine and corticosterone (or cortisol in humans) modulate consolidation and that, as with other neuromodulators, the effects are mediated by noradrenergic activation of the basolateral amygdala. Additional critical findings indicate that the amygdala is not the neural locus of long-term memory, but rather serves to modulate the memory consolidation in other brain regions. In studies of human memory conducted in collaboration with colleagues at UC Irvine, McGaugh and his laboratory group have confirmed that strong memories induced by emotional arousal involve activation of adrenergic systems and the amygdala. This process by which stress hormones released by experiences influence brain processes that regulate memory consolidation is highly adaptive in that it serves to insure that significant experiences will be well-remembered.

STAFF

McGUIRE, WILLIAM J. (1925–   )

William J. McGuire was born to parents of modest means on the East Side of New York on February 17, 1925. He attended elementary and high schools taught by Marist Brothers until, in 1943 at age 17, he volunteered for the US Army. He served for three years, the last in the European Theater of Operations. He was demobilized in 1946 with G.I. Bill entitlement to 48 months of university tuition and subsistence stipend.

This financial support enabled him to attend Fordham University at whose rigorous Jesuit College he majored in Aristotelian/Thomistic philosophy and minored in experimental psychology (B.A., 1949). He went on to Fordham's graduate school in 1949–50, receiving an MA in 1950 in experimental psychology with a thesis that investigated the extent to which one learns the order of a series of items by interitem associations versus by associating each item with its ordinal position. In the same academic year he served as instructor in Fordham's philosophy department, teaching natural theology and rational psychology. These inquiries intensified his interest in phenomenology, which led him to spend the following academic year (1950–51) at the Katholieke Universiteit te Leuven in Belgium as a Fulbright scholar in the Institut Supérieur de Philosophie with psychologists A. Michotte and J. Nuttin.

The year at Leuven University strengthened McGuire's interest in experimental psychology, so he applied successfully for doctoral programs in leading US universities. Because earlier at Fordham his imagination had been gripped by a Clark Hull book, *Mathematico-Deductive Theory of Rote Learning,* he chose Yale (whose admissions committee may have been amused by his stated plan to join Hull in applying symbolic logic to behavioral theory, a line of research which Hull had dropped over a decade earlier). During McGuire's three years of doctoral studies at Yale (1951–1954), his teaching-by-films assistantship inaugurated work on vicarious learning, demonstrating that vicarious reinforcement of the actor in a film derives its teaching efficacy from spaced practice as well as from assimilated hedonic gratification. McGuire's PhD (1954) dissertation showed that paired associate learning involves three subprocesses: discriminating the stimulus elements, integrating the response elements, and establishing the designated connections between the two. Also at Yale he began work on his probabilogical model of thought systems. In his last graduate year at Yale, a tutorial with L. Doob enhanced his interest in social psychology, so he obtained a Social Science Research Council postdoctoral fellowship in 1954–55, sponsored by L. Festinger at the University of Minnesota. McGuire had intended to apply Hullian behavioristic theorizing to group processes, but instead he worked on a probabilogical model of thinking more closely related to the dissonance theory research to which Festinger's interests had turned. During this Minnesota postdoctoral year, he and Claire Vernick married and began their long collaboration.

After his postdoctoral year, Yale invited McGuire back as an instructor, along with a batch of bright young social psychologists mostly from Michigan—A. R. Cohen, I. Sarnoff, M. J. Rosenberg, J. Brehm, and others. He worked on thought processes and on attitude change, not in the Yale model of persuasion by presenting new information from an outside source, but by using Socratic questioning to manipulate the salience of information already in the person's cognitive system. After three years at Yale he moved to the University of Illinois, joining valued colleagues like C. Osgood and P. Tannenbaum for three years (1958–1961). There an NSF grant facilitated his research on immunization against persuasion.

After these Illinois years, McGuire returned to New York City with Claire, their three children, Jim, Anne, and Steve, and his NSF grants to join the faculty at Columbia University (to whose dining halls he and his father before him had delivered milk in the old days). He worked for six years at Columbia, including a year's leave at the Center for Advanced Study in the Behavioral Sciences as a member of the cutting-edge group on cognitive consistency. At Columbia his research focused on personality correlates of persuadability, resistance to persuasion, anticipatory belief changes, and the self-concept. He also wrote numerous review articles (*Handbook of Social Psychology, Handbook of Personality, Encyclopedia Britannica,* and so on) and served as a Stakhanovite writer of manuscript critiques and proposals for many journals and funding agencies, including the National Science Foundation's peer review committee.

The McGuires then moved to LaJolla for three years (1967–1970), when William joined the faculty at the new University of California, San Diego, followed by a 1970–1971 year as a Guggenheim/NIMH fellow at the London School of Economics. At San Diego, McGuire's research focused on the self-concept and the operation of thought systems. He also worked extensively on the research of others as editor of the *Journal of Personality and Social Psychology* and as a member of the National Institute of Mental Health and other peer review panels.

McGuire returned to Yale for a third time in 1971 and stayed there (except for frequent triennial leaves usually spent working in London or Paris) with his research continuing to be supported by grants, first from the National Science Foundation and then from the National Institutes of Health. Several lines of his research are relevant to health psychology and other domains of application as well as to basic research topics like theories of attitude change. He published research during this third Yale period focused on such topics as trait salience in the self-concept, contrasts between self- versus other-perception, effects of context on the sense of self, organizational principles of thought systems, word-order primacy, and positivity asymmetries in thought systems. McGuire also contributed to the psychology of science by developing a "perspectivist" approach describing how researchers do and should develop psychological knowledge. He also described creative heuristics for generating hypotheses and wrote histories of several fields of psychology.

McGuire's work has received a variety of recognitions including fellowships (Fulbright, Social Science Research Council, Guggenheim, National Institutes of Health, Center for Advanced Study in the Behavioral Sciences) and awards (Annual Socio-Psychological Award by the American Association for the Advancement of Science, 1963; Distinguished Scientific Contribution Award by the American Psychological Association, 1988; the Distinguished Scientist Award by the Society of Experimental Social Psychology, 1992; the Annual Award for Distinguished Scientific Contribution to Political Psychology by the International Society of Political Psychology, 1999). He received an honorary doctorate from the Eötvös Loránd University in Budapest, 1990. Several lines of McGuire's life and works are reviewed in his book, *Constructing Social Psychology: Creative and Critical Processes.*

STAFF

McKEACHIE, WILBERT J. (1921–   )

Wilbert J. McKeachie was born in 1921 in Clarkston, Michigan. The son of a teacher, he was fascinated by psychology and was religiously motivated from mid-adolescence onward—a convergence of values and perspectives that was to shape his work for decades to come. He enrolled in Michigan State Normal College with plans of teaching high school. In addition to his interest in mathematics, English, and history, McKeachie became interested in psychology, taking the three courses the college had to offer.

After completing his BA at Michigan State Normal College in 1942, McKeachie served briefly as a Methodist minister in rural Upper Peninsula Michigan. He married Virginia Mack (whom he'd met as a senior in college) one day before he entered the Navy, and served during most of World War II as a radar and communications officer on a Pacific destroyer. Although he continued to hold religious services on board the ship, he settled on entering the field of psychology as a graduate student upon finishing military service.

In the fall of 1945, McKeachie entered the University of Michigan in the MA program in clinical psychology, and soon shifted into the doctoral program. A crucial formative experience at Michigan was his participation as a teaching fellow in introductory psychology under Harold Guetzkow, who, with McKeachie and other teaching fellows, hashed out issues of teaching goals, methods, and pragmatics, and who pressed them toward empirical answers to questions of teaching effectiveness. McKeachie's interest in research in teaching was heightened by his work as coordinator for the introductory course's research projects, and extended into his doctoral research on social-psychological factors in the classroom. When McKeachie was invited to remain at Michigan upon completion of his PhD in 1949 to assume the responsibility for introductory psychology, he understood that his major field would be social psychology. In his interactions with the Research Center for Group Dynamics, he posed what would be a career-long argument that it does make a difference what persons (personal characteristics) were inside each of the empty circles representing group members in the group dynamics research. Meanwhile, alongside his burgeoning teaching research program, he accepted major responsibilities for improving Michigan's undergraduate and graduate curricula in coordination with national reviews of psychology curricula under APA auspices.

McKeachie remained at Michigan, where he has been a full professor since 1960, continuing his devotion to exceptional teaching and engaging in productive programs of research to explore student motivation, the interaction of personality variables and teaching methods, the cognitive and learning analyses of classroom teaching, students' perceptions of teachers and teaching, and the evaluation of teaching effectiveness. As chair of the psychology department from 1961 to 1971, he guided its development as one of the nation's premier departments. In the late 1950s he obtained National Science Foundation grants for conferences and summer Research Participation Institutes for teachers in small colleges. Participants from traditionally Black colleges were helpful during his chairmanship, when Pat Gurin led a vigorous program to recruit African-American doctoral students.

In 1964, McKeachie brought Dick Mann from Harvard to

Michigan to head an introductory psychology program. Shortly thereafter, Mann and a group of teaching fellows developed a unique proposal for replacing the fourth hour of the 4-hour introductory course with 3 to 5 hours of experiential or service learning in settings such as a state mental hospital, a residential treatment center for psychologically disturbed children, or a school. McKeachie negotiated for university approval of this departure from the tradition of an hour in the classroom for each hour of credit; later, when the experience proved a positive contribution to the students' education, he negotiated for its designation as a separate credit course. Project Outreach was one of the country's first service learning courses.

McKeachie has devoted much of his work to the understanding and improvement of educational practice. He has made myriad contributions through the direct teaching of thousands of undergraduate psychology students; through his successful introductory text; and through the introduction and facilitation of widely adopted innovations in undergraduate curricula, as well as his key participation in APA's initial reports on undergraduate psychology curricula. Generations of predoctoral psychologists have benefited from what has come to be his well known "Teaching of Psychology Seminar," and from his *Teaching Tips,* which has seen 10 editions and has been translated into Chinese, Portuguese, Japanese, Arabic, and Spanish. McKeachie has pioneered research in the psychology of classroom teaching and learning, and his work in instructional psychology is internationally recognized. He has played an inspiring role as a force for the full recognition and reward of teaching excellence.

McKeachie's awards from his own and other universities for distinguished teaching and research give an incomplete picture of this psychologist. McKeachie has served on numerous national boards and committees, and has been an officer or on at least one committee of APA or its Divisions continuously for the past 45 years. He was Secretary of APA at the 1970 Miami convention, at which women psychologists presented a list of 63 "demands" to the Board of Directors. McKeachie was asked by the Board to negotiate with the women psychologists; as a result The Board accepted a number of the proposals and also agreed to develop a task force (with McKeachie continuing as Board Liaison) to consider the remaining demands. He was President of APA in 1975–76.

STAFF

MEAD, GEORGE H. (1863–1931)

George H. Mead was educated at Harvard, where he became acquainted with William James. He joined the Philosophy Department at the University of Chicago in the same year as John Dewey (1894) and remained there until his death.

At Chicago Mead came under the influence of the functionalist movement as well as that of early behaviorism. He has been called by some a social behaviorist. He is best known for his concept of the self and has become one of the most important of the self theorists of the 20th century. His most important book, *Mind, Self and Society,* was a combination of notes taken by his students from his lectures and published posthumously in 1934. Mead himself never wrote books.

For Mead, the self was an object of awareness rather than a system of processes. At birth there is no self because a person cannot enter his own experiences directly. However, as a result of experiences received from the outside world, one learns to think of oneself as an object and develops attitudes and feelings about oneself; hence, the development of self-consciousness. Important to the development of the self is the social setting in which social communication occurs. Mead believed that one becomes a "self" to the degree that one can take the attitudes of others and act toward oneself as others act.

Actually, as we develop we can acquire many selves, each of which represents a separate set of responses acquired from different social groups. For example, there may be a family self, a school self, or a self developed from other groups with which one interacts. Incorporated into the conception of the self is the "I" and the "me." The "me" is the social self or one of the social selves, developed through role taking. The "I" is the unique individual who has never existed as an object of consciousness.

Mead's concept of the self has some implications for current self theories to be found in contemporary humanistic psychology—in particular, for the person-centered theory of Carl Rogers.

R. W. LUNDIN
Wheaton, Illinois

MEAD, MARGARET (1901–1978)

Margaret Mead received the BA from Barnard College, where she became acquainted with two famous anthropologists, Franz Boas and Ruth Benedict. She received the MA in psychology and the PhD in anthropology (1929) from Columbia. She then became associated with the American Museum of Natural History from 1926 to 1959.

Mead was one of the foremost anthropologists of her time. She pioneered in research methods that helped to turn cultural anthropology into a major science. Her anthropological expeditions included trips to Samoa, New Guinea, Bali, and other parts of the South Pacific.

Her first book, *Coming of Age in Samoa,* was a result of her study of female adolescents in that society. In it she pointed out that the storm and stress of adolescence found in America was rare in Samoa. She discovered no conflict or revolt among girls of that age group, for their status was determined by their age; as far as their rights and privileges were concerned, they progressed according to their age and nothing else. In *Sex and Temperament in Three Primitive Societies,* Mead studied three contrasting tribes in New Guinea. There she found sex roles and temperament to be a function of each particular culture. Males or females were aggressive or passive in terms of what the culture dictated. Likewise, in *Male and Female* (1949) she attributed the differences in behavior between the sexes to the kind of upbringing, particularly by the mother.

Throughout her career Mead promoted the importance of environmental influences, women's rights, and racial harmony.

R. W. LUNDIN
Wheaton, Illinois

MEASUREMENT

Psychological research focuses on the relationship among observable variables. Psychological theory is concerned with the relationship among constructs. These theoretical constructs are generally operationally defined by observable variables. In both theory and research these relationships are expressed most accurately and precisely when they are in quantitative terms. But if a relationship is to be expressed quantitatively, the variables also must be given quantitative values. In the most general sense, this is the purpose of measurement: to provide quantitative descriptions of the characteristics of objects or individuals.

A characteristic can be measured only if: (1) it can be defined (at least tentatively); (2) it is manifested in observable behavior; and (3) it occurs in differing degrees. If these three requirements are not met, measurement is not possible.

Note that what is measured are the characteristics of individuals. Psychologists also assign quantitative values to stimuli and/or responses—a process usually called scaling. Although measurement and scaling use similar procedures, this article will focus on measurement of the characteristics of individuals rather than on the scaling of stimuli and responses.

MEASUREMENT DEFINED

There are various definitions of measurement. The most commonly used states that measurement is the process of assigning numerals to objects or events according to rules. In psychology the "objects or events" are individuals, and what is measured are the characteristics (attributes) of individuals. Thus psychological measurement is the assignment of numerals to the characteristics or attributes of individuals according to rules.

This definition implies that three sets of factors are involved in measurement: the characteristics of individuals, the numerical values assigned, and the rules and procedures for relating the numerals assigned to the characteristics of the individuals. The measurement process can be viewed as a mapping operation, where numerical values are mapped onto individual characteristics (using specified rules and procedures). The goal is to produce an isomorphic relationship—one where the numerical representation (the scale values assigned) accurately corresponds to differences in the levels of the characteristic among individuals (the empirical "reality").

The use of quantitative descriptions has several advantages over qualitative descriptions. Quantitative descriptions are more precise (they are finer and more accurate), are more objective (there is greater agreement between observers), facilitate communication, and are more economical (a set of data or a relationship can be expressed by one or a small number of quantitative values).

The Measurement Process

There are three basic elements in the measurement process: a dimension, a set of rules and procedures, and a scale. The dimension describes what property (or properties) is to be measured. The rules and procedures indicate how the measurement occurs—the conditions under which the measurement is obtained, the procedures used, and the mathematical model applied. The scale is the units in which the results are expressed.

To illustrate: to measure the length (the dimension) of a book requires using certain procedures and rules (e.g., place a ruler parallel to the long side of the book with the zero point at one end of the book) which result in a quantitative value expressed in defined scale units (e.g., nine inches). Similarly, to measure the intelligence of a child requires defining what is meant by intelligence (the dimension), establishing specified rules for the measurement (e.g., administering a particular set of items or tasks under specified conditions), and expressing performance on a defined scale (the IQ).

The meaning of any measurement depends on the relations between these three elements. The relations between the operations and the scale determine the scale properties. The relations between the dimensions and the procedures, and between the dimension and the scale, determine the validity of the measurement.

What is Measured?

Because the constructs used in psychological theories are often intangible or only vaguely defined, in empirical studies certain observable characteristics are used to operationally define these constructs. These attributes are what are measured. To be useful, any measured attribute should be defined precisely and in such a way as to differentiate it from other attributes.

More precisely, what is measured is the indicants of attributes rather than attributes per se. For example, mathematical ability (an attribute) cannot be measured directly; rather, one observes responses to certain items or problems presumed to reflect mathematical ability. These specific responses are used as indicants of the attribute.

As a consequence, psychological measurement always involves inferences. In all cases the attribute is inferred from its indicants. When dealing with theoretical constructs there is yet another level of inference: from the attribute to the construct. Unless there is empirical evidence or a logical reason to believe that the indicants actually reflect the attribute, and/or that the attribute is a good reflection of the theoretical construct, these inferences will be in error, thus making the measurement less valid and useful.

Rules and Procedures

Although certain standards apply to all types of measurement (e.g., the procedures should be clearly specified, standardized, and replicable), the exact procedures used will vary, depending on the characteristic being measured. Thus for example, different procedures may be used for maximal performance measures such as ability and achievement tests, than for typical performance measures such as personality inventories. The definition of the attribute often suggests appropriate measurement procedures. Conversely, results obtained from (different) measuring procedures may suggest needed alterations in the definition of the attribute. In all cases, the rules and procedures used must be consistent with the purpose of the measurement and the definition of the attribute.

In psychological measurement the procedures usually indicate magnitude (the degree to which an individual exhibits the attribute); however, there are also measures of proximity (how similar two individuals are). In physical measurement the process is usually direct; in contrast, in psychological measurement characteristics are usually inferred from their effects (e.g., learning is inferred from performance on an achievement test rather than measured directly). The scores obtained may be for a single attribute or expressed as the relationship between two or more attributes. And a given attribute may reflect a single construct or some combination of constructs. (The latter approach, where attributes are "pure" measures of constructs, has certain obvious advantages when determining the meaning of scores.) Variations on these dimensions will result in different sets of rules being appropriate.

One other situation is frequently encountered in psychological measurement: a given characteristic can be measured by several different methods. For example, anxiety can be measured by a self-report inventory, by observers' ratings, or by physiological measures. Whether these various methods produce similar results, and thus can be used interchangeably, is an empirical question.

The Scale
The result of any measurement is a set of quantitative scale values representing the level of the attribute in each individual measured. In physical measurement, scale units are usually intuitively meaningful because of their widespread use and their clear correspondence with the properties of the object measured. (Inches is a widely used scale, and differences in the lengths of objects closely parallel our perceptions of their size.) With a few possible exceptions (like the IQ), psychological measurement does not have such widely accepted and clearly defined measurement scales.

In empirical studies this is often not a critical problem: clearly defined scales obtained by using standardized, replicable procedures will usually suffice to establish a relationship. When scores are used to describe individuals, the need for meaningful units becomes more apparent. Psychologists have usually sidestepped this problem by expressing performance in terms of relative position in a comparison group (norm-referenced measurement) or in comparison to a standard of minimal proficiency or content mastery (content-referenced or criterion-referenced measurement), rather than on scales that have meaning in and by themselves.

Types of Errors
In psychological measurement, scores are not consistent over time, situations, or sample of items. These inconsistencies are called measurement errors and result from variations in conditions (ones not completely specified by the measurement rules) or from fluctuations within the individual. The extent of these measurement errors determines the reliability of the measure.

Systematic errors are also important in measurement. These result from measuring characteristics that are stable facets of an individual's personality but which are irrelevant to the purpose of a particular measurement (e.g., writing skill on an essay examina-

tion, the social desirability response set). Systematic errors reduce the validity of a measure.

Summary
Measurement involves developing a set of rules and procedures for assigning quantitative values to characteristics of individuals. These procedures should be selected so that the differences in the assigned numerals parallel the differences in the amount of the characteristic that individuals exhibit. No single set of rules and procedures is applicable to all types of measurement. In any specific situation the rules and procedures must be chosen to fit the nature of the characteristic measured and the purpose of the measurement.

TYPES OF MEASUREMENT SCALES
Because different sets of rules and procedures can be used to make a measurement, different types of measurement scales can be derived. These scales can be distinguished on several bases: the empirical operations used to construct the scale, their mathematical postulates, or their permissible transformations. The last is the most common basis of differentiation. Permissible transformations refer to the mathematical operations that can be performed on the scale scores without changing the relations among the scores.

Stevens' Scale Types
In "Mathematics, Measurement, and Psychophysics," S. S. Stevens distinguished between four basic types of measurement scales. In ascending order they are nominal, ordinal, interval, and ratio scales. These scales are hierarchical: the higher level scales have all the properties of the lower order scales plus additional ones.

A *nominal scale* involves classification of objects into qualitatively different and independent categories. All objects in a given category share certain features in common. Numerals can be assigned to the categories for identification, with each category being assigned a different numeral. Scores on a nominal scale can be subjected to any transformation $[x' = f(x)]$ as long as a different numeral is used for each category.

An *ordinal scale* involves classification and magnitude (greater or less); that is, objects can be ranked in order by the amount of the characteristic they possess. The numerals assigned represent the individuals' rank-order position in a particular group. Nothing is specified or assumed about the distances between adjacent positions; these differences may be large or small, and will not necessarily be the same between all pairs of positions. Values on an ordinal scale can be transformed by any order-preserving monotonic transformation $[x' = \text{monotonic } f(x)]$.

An *interval scale* involves classification, magnitude, and equal-sized intervals. When interval sizes are equal, a difference of, say, 5 points will represent the same amount of difference at any region of the score scale (e.g., the difference between scores of 5 and 10 will be equivalent to the difference between scores of 45 and 50). On an interval scale only a linear transformation $[x' = ax + b,$ where a and b are constants and greater than zero] is permissible.

In addition to indicating classification and magnitude and having equal-sized intervals, a *ratio scale* has a definable absolute zero point. On ratio scales the only permissible transformation is a linear transformation through the zero point [$x' = ax$].

These are not the only types of scales. Other examples include log-interval scales, which involve power transformations; ordered interval scales, where the intervals differ in size but the relative size of the intervals is known; summated scales, which involve combining items having nominal or ordinal properties to form a scale approximating interval properties; and absolute scales, which involve only counting.

Issues

Several questions arise from the fact that different levels of measurement can exist. Which types of scales should be considered? In a broad sense, all the scales discussed represent measurement, as all involve the assignment of numerals to characteristics of individuals. Yet many writers (e.g., Nunnally, 1978/1967) claim that only procedures that involve magnitude are truly measurement and that nominal scales should not be considered such. Yet others (e.g., Jones, 1971) would require that measurement scales have fixed units; thus only interval and ratio scales would properly be called measurement.

Others (Allen & Yen, 1979) have pointed out that, while one can assume that certain measurement procedures attain a given level of measurement, there is no empirical evidence that they do. And Clyde Coombs and others (*Mathematical Psychology*) have stated that no measurement model fits the assessment of certain abilities such as intelligence.

However, procedures that do not meet a particular definition of measurement may still produce valid and useful scores. For example, scores on most ability and achievement tests are assigned by definition, rather than to fit some specified measurement model. Yet there is ample evidence that these scores can be valid predictors of a variety of socially important criteria and can be used as operational definitions of constructs in psychological theories.

A related question concerns the scale level attained by psychological measurement. There are examples of measurement procedures that result in interval or ratio scales—for example, latent trait and item characteristic curve test models and certain psychophysical scaling methods. Many psychologists believe, however, that test scores usually represent only ordinal measurement. Yet test scores are generally interpreted as if they were on an interval scale. Support for this seemingly contradictory behavior has been supplied by Paul Gardner (1975), who has persuasively argued that many test scores are best viewed as a summated scale. Gardner suggested that although specific items or observations may only have the properties of a nominal or ordinal scale, combining a large number of items or observations into a composite results in a scale whose properties closely approach those of an interval scale.

Another heatedly debated question is the relationship between scale properties and the use of statistics to analyze data. Some psychologists have argued that the choice of a statistic is dictated by the nature of the measurement scale on which the empirical data is expressed. This argument has been refuted by Norman Anderson (1961) and others, who have pointed out that most statistical methods made no assumptions about measurement scale levels, thus decisions about appropriate statistical methods can be made without considering the measurement scale level.

Although statistical methods do not make assumptions about measurement scale levels, the two are not unrelated. To illustrate, suppose a psychologist is interested in comparing the effectiveness of two training methods, and that the same 50-item test is used as a pre-test and post-test. Suppose also that the average scores of the two training groups are 10 and 15 on the pre-test and 35 and 45 on the post-test, and that the group by time interaction is statistically significant. Is the post-test difference greater than the pre-test difference? Psychologists who take measuring scales seriously would say it depends on whether scores are on an interval scale. If they are, the conclusion that there is a larger difference after training is valid. If the scale intervals cannot be demonstrated to be equal, the difference may reflect a true difference or a difference in scale units at different regions of the scale. Thus, although the nature of the measurement scale does not dictate what statistical methods must be used to analyze the data, it must be considered when interpreting the data.

CRITERIA OF GOOD MEASUREMENT

As various sets of measurement operations can be used, how can one differentiate between good and poor measurement procedures or determine which of several alternative measurement models is best?

One set of criteria is internal: good measurement models have clearly specified and replicable procedures which are internally consistent and parsimonious, and result in reliable scores. A second set of criteria are external and concern the empirical validity of the measurement model. Here one is concerned with such questions as whether the model helps: (a) explain the construct or phenomena being measured; (b) predict relations with other variables and external criteria; and (c) discover empirical or theoretical laws. Third, a good measurement model is generalizable: it can be used with different samples of people and in a variety of situations. Finally, the best measurement procedure is the one that is most practical, least costly, and most efficient.

Viewed from the approach of traditional test theory, a good measurement model has standardized procedures and produces reliable, valid, and interpretable scores.

SUMMARY

Psychological measurement involves the assignment of numerals to the characteristics of individuals. It should be considered as a model or a tool, rather than as an end in itself. Any set of rules can be used to measure any dimension that an investigator can define. The only restriction is that the rules should be internally consistent and produce replicable results.

Psychological measurement has both practical and theoretical uses. In theoretical studies it provides the basis for measuring the attributes and characteristics used as the operational definitions of theoretical constructs. Its practical uses include providing broad, general descriptions of the characteristics of individuals, or of groups of individuals, and to measure attributes that can be used in decision-making situations such as selection, placement, determining proficiency, and evaluating treatments and programs.

Measurement in psychology has several important characteristics that must be kept in mind when interpreting scores. First, it is descriptive: it indicates a person's current status on the dimension measured, but not how the person attained this status. To determine how a person attained this status requires knowledge of the person's developmental history and the nature of the characteristic measured. Second, as there are few intuitively meaningful scales or scales with true zero points, most psychological measurement is relative. Scores are thus interpreted as a relative ranking in a designated comparison group or in relation to some arbitrarily defined standard. Third, psychological measurement is indirect. Attributes are always inferred from their indicants, and constructs are inferred from their attributes. Usually there is no direct method to empirically demonstrate that the measurement procedures do, in fact, tap the attribute or construct of concern. Thus psychologists are always faced with the question: Am I measuring what I want to measure and only what I want to measure? This question can be answered only by a continual accumulation of relevant data that will either support or argue against use of a particular measurement model.

The usefulness of any measurement model depends on its external validity—whether it makes accurate predictions about empirical data and leads to the development of theoretical laws and principles. Thus, as Irving Lorge (1951) has stated, "The primary concern of measurement . . . should be *for* an understanding of [a] field of knowledge rather than *with* statistical or mathematical manipulations upon observations."

REFERENCES

Allen, M., & Yen, W. (1979). *Introduction to measurement theory.* Monterey, CA: Brooks/Cole.

Anderson, N. H. (1961). Scales and statistics: Parametric and nonparametric. *Psychological Bulletin, 58,* 305–316.

Coombs, C. H., Dawes, R. M., & Tversky, A. (1969/1970/1981). *Mathematical psychology, an elementary introduction.* Englewood Cliffs, NJ: Prentice-Hall.

Gardner, P. (1975). Scales and statistics. *Review of Educational Research, 45,* 43–57.

Jones, L. V. (1971). The nature of measurement. In R. L. Thorndike (Ed.), *Educational measurement* (2nd ed.). Washington, DC: American Council on Education.

Lorge, I. (1951). The fundamental nature of measurement. In E. F. Lindquist (Ed.), *Educational measurement.* Washington, DC: American Council on Education.

Nunnally, J. (1978/1967). *Psychometric theory.* New York: McGraw-Hill.

SUGGESTED READING

Baird, J. C., & Noma, E. (1978). *Fundamentals of scaling and psychophysics.* New York: Wiley.

Coombs, C. H. (1976/1964). A *theory of data.* New York: Wiley.

Ghiselli, E. E., Campbell, J. P., & Zedeck, S. (1981). *Measurement theory for the behavioral sciences.* San Francisco: Freeman.

Kerlinger, F. N. (1973). *Foundations of behavioral research* (2nd ed.). New York: Holt, Rinehart & Winston.

Krantz, D. H., Luce, R. D., & Tversky, A. (1971). *Foundations of measurement. I. Additive and polynomial representations.* New York: Academic.

Suppes, P., & Zinnes, J. L. (1963). Basic measurement theory. In R. D. Luce, R. R. Bush, & E. Galanter (Eds.), *Handbook of mathematical psychology* (Vol. 1). New York: Wiley.

Traub, R. (Ed.). (1979). Methodological developments. [entire issue] *New Directions for Testing and Measurement, 4.*

Wolins, L. (1978). Interval measurement: Physics, psychophysics, and metaphysics. *Educational and Psychological Measurement, 38,* 1–9.

F. G. BROWN
Iowa State University

OBSERVATIONAL METHODS
PSYCHOMETRICS
STATISTICS IN PSYCHOLOGY

MEDICAL MODEL OF PSYCHOTHERAPY

The medical model of physical illness rests on the assumption that the etiology of a disease can ultimately be traced to the disruption of internal physiological processes. Further, it is often posited that this disruption is caused by specific pathogens such as viruses, bacteria, toxins, genetic abnormalities, or cellular abnormalities. To relieve symptoms of an illness and bring the patient back to a state of health, the medical model requires that the practitioner correctly diagnose the disorder, identify the underlying pathology, and provide an intervention that removes, inactivates, or reverses the action of the internal pathogen.

Applied to psychiatric illness, the medical model presupposes that a patient's report of disturbed mood, problematic thoughts, and/or aberrant behavior are caused by the disruption of internal physiological processes such as neurochemical abnormalities or central nervous system damage. Operating from this perspective, a practitioner will attempt to treat the underlying pathology by prescribing or supporting the use of medications, surgical interventions, or electroshock therapy.

The medical model of psychotherapy is based on a set of assumptions similar to those described above. That is, persons who support the medical model of psychotherapy argue that the primary causes of behavior problems can be traced to dysregulation of internal processes. Unlike the medical model of illness, however, the medical model of psychotherapy substitutes biological pathogens with what can be described as "*intrapsychic pathogens*"—dysfunctional internal psychological processes that give rise to problematic behavior. Many examples of intrapsychic pathogens have been reported in the psychoanalytic and psychodynamic literature, including unconscious conflicts, poor ego development, psychosexual fixations, unconscious defenses, childhood traumas, and impaired object relations (Fenichel, 1945; Freud, 1933/1964; London, 1986; Luborsky, 1984; Luborsky, Barber, & Crits-Christoph, 1990). Because practitioners endorsing the medical model of psychotherapy view intrapsychic factors as the primary cause of behavior problems, assessment and treatment procedures target presumed internal psychological processes as opposed to external (e.g., situational) processes.

EVALUATION OF THE MEDICAL MODEL OF PSYCHOTHERAPY

Several criticisms of the medical model of psychotherapy have been articulated by authors who endorse a scientifically-based cognitive-behavioral approach to assessment and therapy (e.g., Barrios, 1988; Hawkins, 1986; Haynes & O'Brien, 1999). First, because internal, unobservable, and hence unmeasurable intrapsychic processes are cited as the primary causes of behavior, nonscientific and untestable explanations of behavior disorders are often relied upon by persons who endorse the medical model of psychotherapy. Second, there is very little scientific evidence supporting two critical assumptions underlying the medical model of psychotherapy, namely: (a) intrapsychic factors are the primary cause of disordered behavior, and (b) treatments that target intrapsychic factors, relative to interventions that target external factors (e.g., behavioral approaches), yield better client outcomes. In fact, several meta-analytic reviews suggest that psychoanalytic and psychodynamic interventions typically produce outcomes that are inferior to empirically-based interventions such as cognitive-behavioral techniques (e.g., Svartberg & Stiles, 1991; Weisz, Weiss, Han, Granger, et al., 1995).

A third criticism is related to patient diagnosis and labeling. Specifically, the medical model tends to locate the cause of disordered behavior within the individual as opposed to finding its source in external, situational factors. Thus, practitioners who endorse this view appear to be more apt to believe that their clients have longstanding and less treatable personality-based problems (Brehm & Smith, 1986).

Recent changes in mental health care have also adversely affected the acceptance and use of the medical model of psychotherapy. Specifically, because practitioners are now required to demonstrate more clearly that their treatments yield cost-effective outcomes, scientifically supported treatments are increasingly being used to treat a wide array of psychological disorders (Chambless & Hollon, 1998; Geraty, 1995). Moreover, because there are limited scientific data supporting the use of interventions that target intrapsychic factors, techniques based on the medical model of psychotherapy are less frequently being used in clinical practice (Altshuler, 1990). To address declining use and the changing health care environment, medical psychotherapy is broadening to include more scientifically supported procedures and interdisciplinary techniques (Gabbard, 1994; Weissman, 1994).

SUMMARY

The medical model approach to psychotherapy, like the medical model of illness, rests on the assumption that problematic behavior arises from disruption of internal pathogenic processes. As a result,

assessment and treatment emphasize measurement and modification of presumed intrapsychic determinants of behavior. Criticisms of the medical model combined with changes in mental health care have caused this approach to become less well accepted and less frequently used in clinical settings. Adherents of the medical model are calling for changes that will permit inclusion of scientifically-based assessment and treatment procedures. This broadening of the medical model will be needed if it is to survive as an approach to psychotherapy.

REFERENCES

Altshuler, K. Z. (1990). Whatever happened to intensive psychotherapy? *The American Journal of Psychiatry, 147,* 428–430.

Barrios, B. A. (1988). On the changing nature of behavioral assessment. In A. S. Bellack & M. Hersen (Eds.), *Behavioral assessment: A practical handbook* (3rd ed., pp. 3–41). New York: Pergamon.

Brehm, S. S., & Smith T. W. (1986). Social psychological approaches to behavior therapy and behavior change. In S. L. Garfield & A. E. Bergin (Eds.), *Handbook of psychotherapy and behavior change* (3rd ed., pp. 69–115). New York: Wiley.

Chambless, D., & Hollon, S. (1998). Defining empirically supported therapies. *Journal of Consulting and Clinical Psychology, 66,* 7–18.

Fenichel, O. (1945). *Psychoanalytic theory of neurosis.* New York: Norton.

Freud, S. (1964). New introductory lectures in psychoanalysis. In J. Strachey (Ed.), *The standard edition of the complete psychological works of Sigmund Freud* (pp. 7–184). London: Hogarth. (Original publication date 1933)

Gabbard, G. O. (1994). Mind and brain in psychiatric treatment. *Bulletin of the Menninger Clinic, 58,* 427–446.

Geraty, R. D. (1995). General hospital psychiatry and the new behavioral health care delivery system. *General Hospital Psychiatry, 17,* 245–250.

Hawkins, R. P. (1986). Selection of target behaviors. In R. O. Nelson & S. C. Hayes (Eds.), *Conceptual foundations of behavioral assessment* (pp. 331–385). New York: Guilford.

Haynes, S. N., & O'Brien, W. H. (1999). *Behavioral assessment: Principles and practice.* New York: Plenum.

London, P. (1986). *The modes and morals of psychotherapy* (2nd ed.). New York: Hemisphere.

Luborsky, L. (1984). *Principles of psychoanalytic psychotherapy: A manual for supportive expressive treatment.* New York: Basic Books.

Luborsky, L., Barber, J. P., & Crits-Christoph, P. (1990). Theory-based research for understanding the process of dynamic psychotherapy. *Journal of Consulting and Clinical Psychology, 58,* 281–287.

Svartberg, M., & Stiles, T. (1991). Comparative effects of short-term psychodynamic psychotherapy: A meta-analysis. *Journal of Consulting and Clinical Psychology, 59,* 704–714.

Weissman, S. (1994). American psychiatry in the 21st century: The discipline, its practice, and its workforce. *Bulletin of the Menninger Clinic, 58,* 503–518.

Weisz, J. R., Weiss, B., Han, S. S., Granger, D. A., et al. (1995). Effects of psychotherapy with children and adolescents revisited: A meta-analysis of treatment outcome studies. *Psychological Bulletin, 117,* 450–468.

W. H. O'BRIEN
J. J. McGRATH
Bowling Green State University

ANATABUSE
NEUROCHEMISTRY
PHYSIOLOGICAL PSYCHOLOGY
SOMATOPHYSICS

MEDITATION

Throughout the more than 2,500 years that meditation has been practiced, it has been largely a part of Eastern religions. Its recent popularity in the West has occurred primarily as a result of two developments: (a) the widespread practice of transcendental meditation (TM); and (b) the scientific interest in meditation and objective verification of the physiological benefits it confers in combatting the widely experienced ill effects of stress in modern life. Adoration of meditation as a panacea, and cynical regard of it as an occult fad, have marked the two extreme reactions.

Because meditation is practiced in many different forms, it is recommended that beginners familiarize themselves with the variety of techniques and preferably obtain a qualified teacher before initiating a serious program of practice. The differential selection of the best program for each person is important. Psychotherapists who use meditation as an adjunct to treatment with clients are wise to use it in their own lives first so as to alleviate stress reactions, offset burnout, understand client reactions to meditation training, and facilitate more productive interviews.

In *The Varieties of the Meditative Experience,* Goleman has distilled certain invariant ingredients in every system of meditation: concentration, retraining attention, mindfulness, "one-pointed attention to one object to the exclusion of all other thoughts," and an altered state of consciousness. These common experiences and goals, however, are achieved through different techniques in different systems of meditation: by the silent chanting of a mantra; by gazing at an object such as a candle flame; by counting one's breaths; and by dealing with the inevitable distractions of life by striving for a one-pointedness that brings a sense of self-control and inner calm. Customarily the meditator sets aside at least two periods a day, morning and evening, of 10 to 30 minutes each, and sits or lies in a quiet, comfortable environment while going through whatever procedures the particular system requires.

Benson, in researching TM and other major meditational systems, has demonstrated in *The Relaxation Response* that one need not study an exclusive or exotic system of meditation, nor obtain a secret mantra, but only follow four essential steps in order to reap the beneficial physiological and psychological results that his research has disclosed: to meditate in a quiet place, free of distractions; to use a mental device such as the word "one" to focus one's attention, saying it silently to oneself with every breath; to take a passive let-it-happen attitude rather than striving for success; and to sit or lie in a comfortable manner. Sitting is the preferred position; lying down, one might go to sleep and miss meditation's awareness benefits. Benson found that the word "one" is as effective as any secret mantra. The physiological benefits indicate lowered levels of tension: slower heart rate, decreased blood pressure, lower oxygen consumption, and increased alpha brain wave production. The benefits experienced in 20 minutes of meditation exceed those of deep sleep, thus indicating the regenerative power of meditation and the saving of wear and tear on the body.

Cautions and contraindications must be observed in the psychotherapeutic use of meditation, and careful supervision by the therapist is ordinarily essential, although some people embark upon a self-managed program with highly beneficial results. Extremely anxious clients may drive themselves instead of relaxing; similar caution is needed with depressed clients and active psychotics.

The maximum benefits of meditation, of course, are realized not simply in the morning and evening meditation periods, but in transferring the learning to the daily world of stress, remaining relaxed and controlled in the midst of anxiety-producing stimuli. Such voluntary control of the involuntary nervous system was considered impossible 15 years ago. Paradoxically, the control is achieved not by striving to attain it, but by faithfully putting in the twice-daily periods of meditation and then simply letting it happen.

The introduction of meditation in its current popular appeal has been largely as a means of coping with stress and as an adjunct to some programs of psychotherapy. Le Shan in his *How to Meditate* provides a guide to the basic types of meditation, details benefits and cautions, and emphasizes meditation as much more than a problem-solving approach. The many paths of meditation can lead the serious follower to a realization of untapped potential that is difficult to reach in other ways. One can accomplish this not by withdrawal or renunciation as in Eastern meditative traditions, but by a renewed ability to cope with the fight-or-flight stress of daily living in a serene and creatively individual way.

REFERENCES

Benson, H. (1975). *The relaxation response.* New York: Morrow.

Goleman, D. (1977). *The varieties of the meditative experience.* New York: Dutton.

Le Shan, L. (1974). *How to meditate.* Boston: Little, Brown.

SUGGESTED READING

Bloomfield, H. H., Cain, M. P., & Jaffe, D. T. (1975). *TM, discovering inner energy and overcoming stress.* New York: Delacorte.

Carrington, P. (1977). *Freedom in meditation.* New York: Anchor/Doubleday.

Goleman, D., & Schwartz, G. E. (1976). Meditation as an intervention in stress reactivity. *Journal of Consulting and Clinical Psychology, 44*, 456–466.

Johnston, W. (1976). *Silent music: The science of meditation.* San Francisco: Harper & Row.

Naranjo, C., & Ornstein, R. (1971). *On the psychology of meditation.* New York: Viking.

Pelletier, K. (1977). *Mind as healer, mind as slayer: A holistic approach to preventing stress disorders.* New York: Dell.

Ornstein, R. (1980). *The psychology of consciousness.* Harmondsworth, England: Penguin.

Pelletier, K., & Garfield, C. (1976). *Consciousness: East and west.* New York: Harper & Row.

Robbins, J., & Fisher, D. (1972). *Tranquility without pills.* New York: Wyden.

Stoyva, J., & Budzynski, T. (1973). Cultivated low arousal—An anti-stress response? In L. DiCara, *Recent advances in limbic and autonomic nervous system research.* New York: Plenum.

Wallace, R. K. (1970). Physiological effects of transcendental meditation. *Science, 167,* 1751–1754.

Wallace, R. K., & Benson, H. (1972). The physiology of meditation. *Scientific American, 226,* 84–90.

S. MOORE
University of Windsor

MEEHL, PAUL E. (1920–   )

Paul Everett Meehl was born in 1920 in Minneapolis, Minnesota. He attended public schools there and received his PhD in clinical psychology from the University of Minnesota in 1945. Among the teachers at Minnesota who shaped his thinking were psychologists D. G. Paterson, William T. Heron, B. F. Skinner, and his advisor, Starke R. Hathaway; philosopher Herbert Feigl; and statisticians A. Treloar and P. O. Johnson.

He became interested in psychoanalysis by reading Karl Menninger's *The Human Mind* and much of Freud in his teens; but the Minnesota psychology department was behavioristic, statistical, and anti-Freudian. The resulting cognitive conflict led Meehl to try to answer questions in "soft" psychology with rigorous methodological approaches, as is reflected in his work on clinical versus actuarial prediction, his criticism of the misuse of null hypothesis testing in psychology, and his development of new statistical techniques to deal with the problem of classification.

Meehl published, with K. MacCorquodale, animal research on latent learning; and he co-authored, with W. K. Estes and others, *Modern Learning Theory* (1954), summarizing the Dartmouth Conference on learning theory, which many believe signalled the closing phase of grand general theories of learning. The MacCorquodale and Meehl article "On a distinction between hypothetical constructs and intervening variables" (1948, *Psychological Review*) is considered a classic. A philosophically related classic paper (with L. J. Cronbach) was "Construct validity in psychological tests" (1955, *Psychological Bulletin*).

His early writings and colloquium lectures on the Minnesota Multiphasic Personality Inventory (MMPI) forced clinicians to take the MMPI seriously; this work included the first analysis of profile patterns, the first theoretical exposition, the first use of an actuarial approach to MMPI interpretation, and identification of the K-factor.

His training analyst, B. C. Glueck, interested him in Rado's theory of schizotypy, and J. C. McKinley taught him that many schizophrenes have neurological aberrations. This clinical knowledge greatly influenced his theory of schizotypy, that it is a result of genetic hypokrisia at the neural synapse conjoined with social learning regimes, schizophrenia being its clinical decompensation in a small minority of schizotypes.

In order to test any theory of schizophrenia, Meehl realized that new statistical procedures for classification were needed. This led him to invent a taxometric method, coherent cut kinetics, which is a collection of specific taxometric procedures that provide consistency tests of the underlying coherence of data to tell whether the latent situation is purely dimensional or taxonic. Its importance and application is general, not confined to detecting schizotypy.

Meehl's work has ranged widely; he has published in animal behavior, learning theory, psychopathology, interview assessment, psychometrics, MMPI scale development and validation, methods of actuarial interpretation, forensic psychology, political behavior, behavior genetics, and philosophy of science. His books include the *Atlas for Clinical Interpretation of the MMPI* (1951, co-authored with S. R. Hathaway), *Clinical vs. Statistical Prediction* (1954), *Psychodiagnosis: Selected Papers* (1973), *Selected Philosophical and Methodological Papers* (1991; edited by C. A. Anderson and K. Gunderson), and *Multivariate Taxometric Procedures: Distinguishing Types from Continua* (1998, co-authored with N. G. Waller).

Meehl served as chairman of the psychology department at Minnesota from 1951 to 1957. He was a co-founder, with Herbert Feigl and Wilfred Sellars, of the Minnesota Center for Philosophy of Science, the prototype for such centers around the world. Until his retirement, he engaged part-time in the practice of psychotherapy (psychoanalytic and, later, rational-emotive). He has served as an expert witness in civil and criminal trials and as advisor to the Minnesota legislature. He is a diplomate (clinical) of the American Board of Professional Psychology and the first non-grandfather to serve on the board. He is a member (and in 1962 served as president) of the American Psychological Association (APA); he is a member of the National Academy of Sciences, and a fellow of the American Academy of Arts and Sciences. He has received APA's Distinguished Scientific Contributor Award, Award for Distinguished Professional Contributions to Knowledge, and Award for Outstanding Lifetime Contribution to Psychology; the APA Clinical Division's Distinguished Contributor Award and its 1996 Centennial Award; the APA Division of Experimental Clinical Psychology's Distinguished Scientist Award; the APA, Division 5 award for Distinguished Lifetime Contribution to Evaluation, Measurement, and Statistics; the Bruno Klopfer Distinguished Contribution Award from the Society for Personality Assessment; the

American Board of Professional Psychology's Award for Distinguished Service and Outstanding Contributions to the Profession; the American Psychological Foundation Gold Medal Award for Life Achievement in the Application of Psychology; the Joseph P. Zubin Award for Distinguished Contributions in Psychopathology; the Educational Testing Service Award for Distinguished Service to Measurement; and the Lifetime Achievement Award in Basic and Applied Research in Psychology from the American Association of Applied and Preventive Psychology. He is a William James Fellow of the American Psychological Society and has received its James McKeen Cattell Fellow award.

Meehl is now Regents' Professor of Psychology, Emeritus, and Member, Emeritus, of the Center for Philosophy of Science. Since his retirement in 1990, he has been concerned with taxometrics, having the coherent cut kinetics method refined, tested, and published in full; with metatheoretical issues (e.g., what path analysis can prove about causality, what can replace the weak use of significance testing in the social sciences); and with cliometric metatheory, formulating psychometric approaches to empirical, history-based philosophy of science (e.g., how we can numerify a theory's empirical track record).

STAFF

MELZAK, RONALD

Ronald Melzack was born and raised in Montreal, where he studied psychology at McGill University. After he received his PhD in 1954, under the supervision of D. O. Hebb, he spent five years carrying out physiological research at the University of Oregon Medical School, University College London, England, and the University of Pisa, Italy.

In 1959, Melzack was appointed to the faculty at the Massachusetts Institute of Technology. There he met Patrick Wall, and their discussions led to the innovative gate control theory of pain published in 1965. The gate control theory stated that pain signals are not carried passively in a straight-through pathway but are modulated by other sensory inputs and by psychological factors during their transmission to the brain. It provided a plausible physiological mechanism for the phenomena of pain and showed how physiological processes, mental states, and social beliefs interacted in the determination of pain experience. The gate control theory has had an enormous impact on the field of pain research and therapy. Many experiments by Melzack and others subsequently examined the neural, pharmacological, and psychological mechanisms that underlie the inhibition of pain-signaling nerve impulses.

In 1963, Melzack returned to McGill, where he continued his research on pain. As part of a research program on prolonged brain activity, Melzack and postdoctoral student Kenneth Casey produced a theoretical model of pain processing in the brain, which involved widely distributed, parallel neural networks, and Melzack subsequently carried out major research programs to reveal the neural areas and pharmacological mechanisms involved in pain. This model is now widely accepted and has given rise to important research on every dimension of pain.

Concurrently with this work, Melzack also developed the McGill Pain Questionnaire (MPQ) to obtain measures of the multiple dimensions of subjective pain experience. The MPQ is a carefully planned set of verbal descriptors to help patient and physician communicate more clearly with one another about the experience of pain. It also provides numerical information that permits research on every type of pain and on the relative effectiveness of different forms of therapy. The McGill Pain Questionnaire has been translated into numerous languages and has become the most widely used instrument in research on pain in humans. Melzack's other research at this time used the MPQ to investigate the physiological and psychological mechanisms of morphine analgesia in cancer patients.

In addition to more than 200 papers on research and theory, Melzack wrote *The Puzzle of Pain,* which has been translated into seven languages. He and Patrick Wall later wrote *The Challenge of Pain,* translated into five languages. Wall and Melzack have also edited the *Textbook of Pain* (1984; 4th edition, 1999). In 1983, Melzack edited *Pain Measurement and Assessment,* which firmly established the field of pain measurement and his major role in it. In 1993, he and Dennis Turk edited the *Handbook of Pain Assessment,* which is now the premier book in the field.

Phantom limb pain has held a special fascination for Melzack because it provides a strong argument that central neural mechanisms, rather than peripheral fibers, generate the nerve impulse patterns that produce pain. He wrote an important paper in 1971 that proposed a central neural mechanism as the basis of phantom limb pain. He suggested that the loss of input to a central biasing mechanism produces a decrease in descending inhibitory control, so that deafferented spinal cells fire at abnormally high rates to produce pain. In the attempt to understand phantom limbs, Melzack and colleague Philip Bromage carried out studies of experimental phantoms after anesthetic blocks of the brachial plexus or spinal cord. Melzack was invited to talk about phantom limb pain at a meeting at which the International Association for the Study of Pain was founded by John Bonica. There, Melzack met John Loeser, a neurosurgeon who specializes in pain problems; the two brought together case histories of paraplegic patients who suffered severe pain below the level of known total spinal cord sections. They argued that a pattern-generating mechanism above the level of the spinal break produces the pattern that evokes pain.

During the past decade, Melzack has developed a new model of brain function, in which the concept of a widespread neural network—or neuromatrix—plays a major role in explaining phantom limb pain. The model extends the scope of pain research and theory by incorporating stress-regulation mechanisms as an integral part of the pain process. Prolonged stressors, psychological as well as physical, may produce a variety of disorders, and thereby produce the basis for prolonged, chronic pain. This neuromatrix model has stimulated substantial research in many laboratories internationally, and provides a new way of understanding the remarkable capacity of the brain to create perceptions, emotions, and thoughts.

Not only is Melzack an outstanding research psychologist, but he is also a superb teacher, and the many students who have taken his classes at McGill invariably laud his efforts. In 1996 he received

McGill's David Thomson Award for Excellence in Graduate Supervision and Teaching.

Melzack's work has received national and international recognition. In 1982, he was elected a fellow of the Royal Society of Canada, and in 1985, he received the Molson Prize from the Canada council. He was elected president of the International Association for the Study of Pain (IASP) from 1984 to 1987 and was honorary president of the Canadian Psychological Association in from 1988 to 1989. In 1986, he was appointed to the E. P. Taylor Chair of Psychology at McGill University, and in 1992, he received an honorary doctorate (LittD) from the University of Waterloo. In 1994, he received the Prix du Québec (Prix Marie-Victorin) for pure and applied sciences, and in 1995 he was appointed an officer of the Order of Canada.

STAFF

MEMORY

Memory is usually thought of as a faculty or a capacity by which past experiences can be brought up, thought about, or described at the present time. Thus when a 75-year-old man talks about events of his childhood, he is presumed to be "using" his memory, relying upon it, or somehow activating and searching it, to provide some basis for his remarks. Usually in such cases one cannot be certain that the report corresponds in any way to the actual happenings. Many people often lie. Others may believe they are telling the truth and still be wrong. Whatever else memory may be, it is not a tape recorder that has recorded all the sights, sounds, experiences, and so on that we might remember under appropriate circumstances. Some writers on the subject believe something very close to this. Penfield (1958), a Montreal neurosurgeon, has reported detailed recall of past experiences from people whose brains he was able to stimulate with an electric probe while they were on the operating table. As there was no attempt made to verify the truth of the recalls, the reports must be accepted with some reservations. Even if the reports were accurate, they would not be proof that everything previously experienced had been "stored" in the brain.

Memory is also thought of as something that can be "exercised" or strengthened by practice. There seems to be no evidence that one can improve one's memory by repeated memorizing, although one can learn to use more effective methods of learning. Mnemonic devices may help. People who fail to remember some items might complain about having a "poor memory," but probably they only learned something poorly and should not have expected to remember it. More likely, there is no such thing as a good or poor memory, although good and poor learners are common enough.

It is sometimes thought that "memorizing" amounts to using the memory, but memorizing something by repetition or rehearsal is only engaging in learning trials. We say people have memorized something when they are letter-perfect in a recitation. It is thought that they now possess something in some way. The problem, however, is that after some time has passed those individuals are no longer letter-perfect or as efficient as they were at the end of the learning trials. We then say they have forgotten the material, so that

memory and forgetting become the same problem. It is easier to deal with learning and forgetting without talking about memory, because we do learn and forget, but whether we possess and use a memory may be scientifically doubtful. No one can study a memory, as it cannot be seen or manipulated in any way. It might just be a noun form of talking about remembering.

Sometimes forgetting happens all at once, without the passage of time, as when an accident to the head leaves one stunned or unconscious. Upon recovery from the trauma we might not remember events that happened just before the blow. Patients who undergo electroconvulsive shocks commonly do not remember the immediately preceding events. Such amnesia may be permanent or temporary. Children sometimes seem to show amazing retention of events or situations. Such detailed recall is especially astonishing to adults because, as we grow older, we seem to lose the ability to recall many events and kinds of information. Old people sometimes seem unable to remember contemporary events, while having allegedly firm recalls of childhood experiences. It should be observed that the recall of childhood experiences might be strengthened by frequent rehearsals and retellings, or even constitute quite distorted recollections made to sound reasonable by confabulation and extraneous knowledge.

The failure of retention of recent events might be due to a lack of interest and failure to learn or observe. In laboratory studies, when old people are motivated to learn to the same criteria as young people, they frequently remember as well as the young learners.

KINDS OF MEMORY

The reference to memory of current events suggests that memory can be divided according to how long ago something happened. If a list of nine numbers is read to you, for example, at a rate of one per second, and you try to report on them immediately, we are dealing with what some psychologists call *short-term memory* or *STM*. Whether this is a proper categorization of memory is debatable; it might more properly be called "attention span" or "repetition span." In experiments on short-term memory a person is shown or told something—say, three letters like KRB—and is told to start subtracting by threes from some large number for the next 30 seconds or so. In such studies it is found that a person cannot recall all three letters even after only 18 seconds of subtraction. Whatever can be remembered in such tests of novel material presented once, followed by a distracting task to prevent rehearsal, is attributed to short-term memory. Without distraction a person might remember from five to nine items in a test of immediate recall. Telephone numbers—generally seven digits in two groups (three and four)—are usually retained long enough to be dialed or tapped out on a phone; but if they have been looked up only once, they are quickly forgotten.

Short-term memory might better be regarded as the results of a first learning trial. Hebb (1961) demonstrated that when many strings of digits are repeatedly presented, subjects will recall more and more of particular strings of nine digits, even though they do not recognize them as having been presented on earlier trials. The more often something is rehearsed, the more of it will be retained, and the longer. Researchers in short-term memory usually refer to anything remembered after 30 seconds as the function of *long-term memory* or *LTM,* but as that is the only kind of retention that concerns most people, the term LTM becomes too general to be of any descriptive value.

Tulving (1972) has described what he calls "episodic" and "semantic" memories. *Episodic memory* is the retention of specific events or particulars like names of different people. *Semantic memory* refers to general knowledge—for instance, the ability to speak English or to multiply. We may not remember when and where we learned to multiply fractions, for example, but we may remember how to do so. It is probable that semantic memory is acquired in so many different situations that interference (see below) occurs and prevents specific recall. On the other hand, we might remember what we ate at a particular restaurant in some vacation town we visited once long ago, as nothing may interfere with that recall.

PROCEDURES FOR ASSESSING MEMORY

In the laboratory, retention is usually measured in one of three ways: recall, recognition, and relearning.

Recall

In recall studies persons are asked to report on what they have just seen or heard either after each trial or after several trials. They may be asked to report verbatim (in order or sequence), or "freely"— that is, to report anything they think of in any order at all (free recall). Usually the recallers try to follow the original sequence of events. If they have had but one exposure to the material, they will report more material under free recall conditions unless the material is rather short. Any report cannot be considered a complete or total disclosure of the material recalled, as the subject may think of some material and not report it because it may be out of sequence, or because the subject may judge it to be incorrect. Even if subjects report nothing, it does not mean that they do not remember or recall something; there are no completely blank minds. The subjects may not wish to disclose something, or if they think it is wrong, they may hesitate to appear unintelligent. Sometimes a first recall is not as complete as a later subsequent recall. In such instances the term *reminiscence* is employed to describe the additional recall. Because the term has other ordinary references it is probably not well chosen, but no better term has been coined to refer to improved recall following a rest. When persons are unable to recall all the material presented on their own, they can frequently be guided, aided, or cued with associated stimuli and report more material. If they forgot that the word "cat" was in a list, they might remember if they were asked if any animals were mentioned. Such operations are called *cued recall.*

Recognition

A more direct method of prompting is to present the person with the original material embedded in a collection that includes material not originally seen. If a list of 20 words was used as the original material, the subject might be asked to pick out those 20 words from a new list of 40 words. The new words are called "distractors." Depending upon the nature of the distractors, the subject may recognize all—or perhaps none—of the original words. Thus if the new words are in a foreign language, the subject would have no difficulty. On the other hand, if they are all close synonyms, the difficulty might be great. It is commonly found that under fair conditions of distraction, subjects can recognize much more than they can recall. It is a familiar experience of most people that they can recognize a forgotten name they were unable to recall, if is mentioned either alone or in a short list of other names.

Relearning

It has been found in learning studies that material once learned and now forgotten can be relearned in a fraction of the original learning time. The difference in the two learning times, called a *savings score,* was originally described by the first psychologist to study learning experimentally—Hermann Ebbinghaus, in 1885. The savings-score finding has stood up for 100 years. The fact that there is a savings in almost any situation tested has led to the generalization that one never really forgets something that has been learned—at least, not completely. Some residue of the original learning persists and can be taken advantage of. Thus high school French can be relearned by a 50-year-old person in a short time, at least to the level originally covered. If long periods intervene, a person might improve learning skills and learn, in a fraction of the original time, material that had been lost completely. But savings scores are discovered in short-term periods where a subject shows no recall or recognition of the original material. Such situations are readily arranged when subjects learn 40 or 50 lists of nonsense syllables. By the 50th list they no longer recognize the first list as something previously learned, yet they relearn it in a few trials relative to the original learning. It pays to go to school, even if sometimes it appears that all that was learned has evaporated after the examination period.

THEORIES OF MEMORY

The prominent current theories of memory or forgetting are: (a) the theories of disuse or decay; and (b) the theory of interference, which may not be completely contradictory. Both are based on the passage of time.

Disuse Theory

The disuse theory is commonly accepted by laymen as intuitively correct. With the passage of time material things corrode, weaken, or disappear. It might be the same for memory, as it is commonly observed that events of the past begin to appear dim and fade with time and are less well recalled. Just as our sense organs and muscles weaken with age, so might our memories, when viewed as some kind of organ that also suffers deterioration. If material is to be retained it must be practiced, as witness piano performances by aging virtuosos. The disuse theory, like its competitor, suffers from lack of physiological support and is usually opposed on the grounds that time, by itself, accomplishes nothing. It is what happens during the passage of time that is important. Iron does not rust because of time, but because an oxidation process operates. Such logical arguments encourage support for the interference theory.

Interference Theory

In the interference theory it is assumed that if something is learned to any criterion it will be retained to that criterion, unless something else either previously or newly learned interferes with the particular experience under consideration. In behavioral terms, if something is learned, it amounts to an association between a stimulus and a response. Thus if stimulus A is associated with response A, that association should be retained indefinitely. However, stimulus A may later become associated with response B to a stronger degree; subsequently, stimulus A will tend to evoke response B instead of A, and response A will then be forgotten. According to the interference theorists, it is not forgotten so much as unavailable or inaccessible. It becomes a case of "we don't forget; we just don't remember." For example, if you learn to open a certain lock by turning a key to the right, and the lock is then changed so that it now requires a turn to the left, you will at first tend to turn right, but finally overcome the original habit and turn left consistently. You will have forgotten to turn to the right. Note that the second learning—turning to the left—will suffer some little interference at first, because of the original learning to turn to the right. This illustration introduces two strong research areas in the field of forgetting, those involving retroactive and proactive inhibition, or RI and PI.

Retroactive Inhibition

In retroactive inhibition studies, a group of subjects first learns some material, say a list of words, or material A. They then learn another list, material B. Subsequently they are tested for recall of A and it is regularly found that if material B is somewhat similar to material A, there will be a drop in retention over that of a control group that learns only material A and is tested after the same interval.

Proactive Inhibition

If material B is similar to material A, the learners will have more trouble learning B than a control group that has not learned A. This is called proactive inhibition. If you learn one thing and one thing only, you will not forget it, nor can it impede you in the future, as you are not going to learn anything else. But such a situation is impossible, since we all keep learning new things. Hence, because of past experience, we have some unnecessary or uncalled-for trouble in learning new things, as well as trouble in retaining what we learned before. These remarks apply only to situations where we have trouble learning new things because of past experience, and trouble retaining old learning because of new. In many instances past experience *helps* us to learn new things (perhaps at the expense of some retention of the old), and many new learnings are so unrelated to old experience that no interference can occur.

Retroactive and proactive inhibition apply only to situations where two sets of materials or habits have interference potential; such potential usually resides in the similarities of the two habits or materials. It sometimes appears that the more we learn or know, the more we forget. Our past experience is cumulative, and much of it may contain similar elements to materials or operations in new learning. Proactive inhibition is therefore more likely than retroactive inhibition to be a source of interference. Such has been found to be the case (Underwood, 1948).

SUMMARY

We cannot make progress in memory research by regarding memory as some kind of thing-in-itself, a faculty, or organ, or some mechanism. Such thinking is sometimes fostered by regarding brains as computers. Computers are said to have *memory banks,* whereas they of course have no such things. They only have prearranged electrical connections that can be brought into play or action by certain electrical signals. While the language is analogical, the memory of a computer is not like that of a human being. The computer, for example, never forgets anything at all to the slightest degree. Its memory can also be erased completely by one switch setting, without other damage to the computer. Our memories are erased completely only when we are dead.

Memory might best be thought of as a change in the ability of an individual to react in some particular way to some stimulus or a signal. Because of growth and development and constantly changing experiences, our bodies—in particular, our nervous systems—must undergo changes, too. When we do not know something, it is because our nervous systems are not able to process some stimulus input with a particular output. When we have learned whatever is concerned, we have been changed so that we now produce the appropriate response. With other changes we may be unable to respond in the desired way: again, we have changed so that the stimuli are not processed as they formerly were. When some responses or skills are practiced over a long time period, we become quite resistant to change. Even an amnesiac who has forgotten his name and address will remember to speak English when telling you that he cannot remember. When the amnesiac tells us that he cannot remember his name, we are forced to assume that something is preventing his nervous system from operating in a normal way. He may of course be lying. Many of the memories of all of us can be described as lies—albeit not deliberate but because of the changes we undergo in our experience of life.

REFERENCES

Hebb, D. O. (1961). Distinctive features of learning in the higher animal. In J. F. Delafresnay (Ed.), *Brain mechanisms and learning.* London, New York: Oxford University Press.

Penfield, W. (1958). *The excitable cortex in conscious man.* Springfield, IL: Thomas.

Tulving, E. (1972). Episodic and semantic memory. In E. Tulving & W. Donaldson (Eds.), *Organization of memory.* New York: Academic.

Underwood, B. J. (1948). Retroactive and proactive inhibitions after 5 and 48 hours. *Journal of Experimental Psychology, 38,* 29–35.

SUGGESTED READING

Wickelgren, W. A. (1977). *Learning and memory.* Englewood Cliffs, NJ: Prentice-Hall.

B. R. BUGELSKI
State University of New York

INFORMATION PROCESSING THEORY

MENTAL ILLNESS: ATTITUDES TOWARD

Korchin, in *Modern Clinical Psychology,* has observed that attitudes toward mental illness were more directly related to the observing of severe abnormalities. In earlier centuries the afflicted were thought to be possessed by demons and so were incarcerated and tortured. During the Roman Empire, physicians advocated a more scientific view combined with humane treatment, but after Rome's demise, the belief in possession revived, lasting until the Enlightenment. Weyer was the only notable figure during this period who tried to counter the cruel treatment of the insane by having them considered ill. There was no change until the French and the American revolutions.

In 1801 Pinel removed his patients' shackles and treated them as sick people. In his *Treatise on Insanity* (1801/1962) he spoke against punishment and advocated treatment by direct confrontation, scientific study, and the use of case records and life histories. He even suggested that some conditions may have psychogenic origins. Unfortunately, public and professional opinion lagged far behind. In fact, even though American and British hospitals emphasized moral treatment in the 19th century, the abuses exposed by people like Dix and Beers showed society's continued readiness to mistreat the mentally ill. Prior to the first half of the 20th century, the mentally ill were still viewed for the most part as simply mad. The insane continued to capture people's imaginations, and it was not uncommon to see so-called crazy people on display in circuses and freak shows.

An important influence on attitudes toward mental illness was the emergence of the medical model, which removed mental illness from the realm of witchcraft and placed it in the field of medical study and treatment. The following characteristics of the medical model have been noted by Korchin: Mental illnesses are diseases having etiology, course, and outcome; they have organic bases; like physical ailments, there is an underlying state with surface symptoms; cure depends primarily on medical intervention; and the disease process is within the person.

Szasz has shown in *The Manufacture of Madness* that the medical model gained strength in the early 1950s with the introduction of the major tranquilizers. However, he has also been one of the major critics of the model. In *The Myth of Mental Illness,* Szasz stated that mental illness symptoms cannot be related to nervous system lesions, but should be viewed as communications by the patients concerning their beliefs about themselves and the world. This sociopsychological point of view represents the other important force that has helped to shape prevailing attitudes toward mental illness.

Korchin (1976) quoted the psychological model as evolving with the discovery that behaviors could be driven by unconscious processes and psychological determinants. Mesmer's demonstrations of animal magnetism provided some of the initial evidence for this phenomenon, and the work of the early French psychiatrists and finally Sigmund Freud firmly established the psychological approach. Since these beginnings, psychologists and other researchers have shown that mental illnesses can be learned social responses and are treatable by various psychotherapy approaches. Like the medical model, the psychological model has had significant impact on public attitudes toward mental illnesses.

The prevailing public attitude toward the mentally ill in the second half of the 20th century is that they are sick people deserving treatment and humane care. Rabkin (1974), tracing attitudes through 1960, concluded that mental patients were dimly viewed and that public acceptance of the medical model was weak. In the last third of this century, people have become better informed, though still repelled by the notion of mental illness. Crocetti and his colleagues (1972) observed that the public has become more accepting of the medical model, more willing to agree that the mentally ill are in need of care, and more optimistic about prognosis.

As more ailments have come under the purview of the mental health practitioner, there has been a tendency to evaluate complaints in the direction of illness. Sattin (1980) has written that a professional's perception of the presence of mental illness is high when expectancy is high. This observation has led to recommendations from other researchers for the development of more refined evaluation methods that, in effect, give a person an opportunity to be found free of illness. Bowden and his colleagues (1980) showed that patients sometimes also had detrimental attitudes. Those with harsh and pessimistic views about mental illness had more severe psychopathology and tended to do less well. Expectation of medication was strongly associated with lower education, greater illness severity, lower treatment satisfaction, more treatment dropouts, and less improvement. Those with more benign views tended to move in the opposite direction.

In general, Korchin (1976) has noted a growing awareness of psychology among the public and a reduced stigma associated with getting help. There has been a shift in emphasis from psychological illness to psychological health. The mentally ill, who used to be treated in insane asylums, are now being cared for in psychiatric hospitals and mental health centers, and even as outpatients.

Changing attitudes have produced a variety of effects. Brockman and Darcy (1978) have noticed a reduced social distance between the public and the mentally ill. Korchin (1976) has seen a significant increase in the number of conditions falling within the realm of abnormal psychology and a subsequent increase in the range of the clinician's work. However, Szasz (1970) noted that social stigma is an unfortunate by-product of the label "mental illness" and that an individual's good qualities tend to be ignored. His assertion has gathered support from various studies such as Nuehring's (1979), which demonstrated that even 6 months after discharge former patients still were experienced as a stigma and burden.

Modern attitudes toward mental illness have also produced many legislative changes. Efforts have been made to produce a patients' bill of rights to ensure proper treatment. Laws have been established to safeguard dangerous individuals from themselves and to protect those around them. The mentally ill are no longer held automatically responsible for acts committed during an illness. Sanity must be established as part of the legal proceedings, though it remains a hotly contested issue. Various studies have shown how different treatment methods yield attitude changes about mental illness. Fieve (1977) suggested that pharmacological outpatient treatment has enhanced positive attitudes toward the mentally ill because of a reduced need for inpatient care. Educational seminars designed to demythologize mental illness successfully reduce fears about it, as reported by Morrison and Teta (1980) and by Janus and his colleagues (1980).

Korchin (1976) has identified two major goals of a public education program: to improve care for the mentally ill and to foster prevention. He mentioned that the most effective educational programs with attitude change as a goal are those in which learners actively participate. Whether education methods involve mass media or seminars, Korchin has identified three target groups: those vulnerable to emotional disorder, those holding power in the community, and those with care-giving functions. Korchin has emphasized that correct information reduces fears and reassures people, provides standards for self-evaluation, and inoculates against oncoming stress.

REFERENCES

Bowden, C. L., Schoenfeld, L. S., & Adams, L. (1980). Mental health attitudes and treatment expectations as treatment variables. *Journal of Clinical Psychology, 36,* 653–657.

Brockman, J., & Darcy, C. (1978). Correlates of attitudinal social distance toward the mentally ill: A review and re-survey. *Social Psychiatry, 13,* 69–77.

Crocetti, G. M., Spiro, H. R., Lemkau, P. V., & Siassi, I. (1972). Multiple models and mental illnesses: A rejoinder to failure of a moral enterprise: Attitudes of the public toward mental illness, by T. R. Sarbin & J. C. Mancuso. *Journal of Consulting and Clinical Psychology, 39*(1), 1–5.

Fieve, R. R. (1977). The revolution defined: It is pharmacologic. *Psychiatric Annals, 7*(10), 10–18.

Janus, S. S., Bess, B. E., Cadden, J. J., & Greenwald, H. (1980). Training police officers to distinguish mental illness. *American Journal of Psychiatry, 137*(2), 228–229.

Korchin, S. J. (1976). *Modern clinical psychology.* New York: Basic Books.

Morrison, J. K., & Teta, D. C. (1980). Reducing students' fear of mental illness by means of seminar-induced belief change. *Journal of Clinical Psychology, 36*(1), 275–276.

Nuehring, E. M. (1979). Stigma and state hospital patients. *American Journal of Orthopsychiatry, 49*(4), 626–633.

Pinel, P. (1962). *Treatise on insanity.* New York: Hafner. (Original work published 1801)

Rabkin, J. (1974). Public attitudes toward mental illness: A review of the literature. *Schizophrenia Bulletin, 10,* 9–33.

Sattin, D. (1980). Possible sources of error in the evaluation of psychopathology. *Journal of Clinical Psychology, 36*(1), 99–105.

Szasz, T. S. (1970). *The manufacture of madness.* New York: Harper & Row.

Szasz, T. S. (1974). *The myth of mental illness: Foundations of a theory of personal conduct.* New York: Harper & Row. (Original work published 1961)

W. KARLE
J. BINDER
Corona Del Mar, California

MENTAL ILLNESS: EARLY HISTORY

HIPPOCRATES

Hippocrates (c. 460–c. 377 B.C.), the towering figure of ancient medicine, first introduced mental aberrations into medical literature. His writings on psychopathology were as polemical and provocative as they were original. In his writings on the "sacred disease" (epilepsy), Hippocrates decried current ignorance: "It thus appears to me to be in no way more divine, nor more sacred than other diseases, but has a natural cause from which it originates like other affections" (Zilboorg, 1941, pp. 43–44).

Hippocrates is noted primarily for his shrewd clinical observations, his rational biomedical approach, and his forthright, stoical presentation of his views. He believed that disease resulted from an imbalance of the humors, a notion first encountered in the writings of Empedocles (493–433 B.C.), who had combined the basic elements advanced by Thales (water), Anaximenes (air), Heraclitus (fire), and Xenophanes (earth). Empedocles' writings became the basis for Hippocratic humoral and Aristotelian chemical theorizing.

Zilboorg (1941) reports that Hippocrates was once asked to observe the great philosopher Democritos, whose friends considered him to be mentally ill. Hippocrates apparently concurred with lay opinion and prescribed hellebore. Hippocrates cured the king of Macedonia of what had been diagnosed as phthisis (a progressive, deteriorative condition) but which Hippocrates recognized as psychological in origin. Lyons and Petrucelli (1978) sum up Hippocrates' contribution to the understanding of mental illness thus: "Concerning the emotional state of the patient and mental illness in general, the writings are especially astute and accurate in terms of modern understanding. Assignment of the brain as organ of thought and sensation is an important indication of a high state of understanding" (p. 214).

SOCRATES AND PLATO

Hippocrates was deeply committed to natural philosophy (science). However, the Zeitgeist favored Hippocrates' contemporary, Socrates (470–399 B.C.). In view of Socrates' devotion to ethics and epistemology, rather than rational science, it is not surprising that Socrates was said to attribute his own inspirations to demons (Becker, 1978; Gibson, 1889). Zilboorg (1941) conjectured that Socrates' demons may have been auditory hallucinations and the man himself schizophrenic. Socrates' pupil Plato (429–347 B.C.) adopted a system of psychopathology that was, in many respects, Hippocratic and set forth the first clear body-soul dualism. According to Plato, the soul is made up of three parts. The rational part of the soul is immortal and divine. The irrational soul is mortal and includes the whole gamut of affect (anger, fear, pain, pleasure, etc.). Emotions such as anger and fear reside in the heart, while appetites such as passion and desire lie in the upper abdomen. The rational soul presides over the irrational soul. When the irrational soul becomes disturbed it falls out of the rational soul's control. The result is madness, of which there are three forms: melancholia, mania, and dementia. Hence, any excess of affect (e.g., too sad or too happy) spells a lack of rationality and thus madness. Plato adhered to Hippocrates' humoral theory. When morbid humors contacted any part of the irrational soul, the result was madness.

ARISTOTLE

Aristotle (384–322 B.C.) was a student in Plato's Academy for some 20 years until Plato's death, but was in no sense a disciple of Plato. A rational philosopher of natural (principally biological) and mathematical interests, he rejected mysticism and is regarded by many as the founder of scientific psychology. Certainly a pioneer in sensation and perception, he held that we perceive and hence comprehend our physical world through our senses. Plato did not trust the senses, concluding that ultimate truths must derive from inspiration. Aristotle rejected inspiration but recognized that the senses were often an unreliable source of objective data. Hence, Aristotle devised logic to comprehend a reality that, while not mystical, often defied mortal understanding.

Aristotle divided the human soul into the rational, including wisdom, logic, reason, and discretion, and the irrational, comprising virtues such as self-control, dispassion, morality, and courage. Unlike Plato, Aristotle held that the various ingredients constituting the soul are inseparable and function in concert. Human behavior is not an isolated event but the consequence of integration.

According to Aristotelian psychology, mental illnesses have organic etiologies. No afflictions are entirely psychological. Illnesses may lead to mental aberrations, hence the origin is physical. Furthermore, reason exists independent of mortal beings and is thus immune to the deteriorative effects of illness. Since reason is both creative and insulated from the effects of illness, illness may coexist with creativity. Aristotle noted the frequent occurrence of hypnagogic imagery among normal people and concluded that some mental disturbances may actually enhance creativity. He stated: "Those who have become eminent in philosophy, politics, poetry, and the arts have all had tendencies toward melancholia." Also attributed to Aristotle is the remark that "no excellent soul is exempt from a mixture of madness." Aristotle's chain of logic led to the conclusion that mental illness was of physical origin and was peculiar to the human species.

CELSUS AND THE ROMAN EMPIRE

There appear to have been three significant peaks in the development of ancient medicine: the era of Hippocrates in the third century before Christ; Celsus around the time of Christ; and Galen in the second century after Christ.

Aulus Aurelius Cornelius Celsus (30 B.C.–50 A.D.) was primarily a scholar, chronicler, and historian of medicine. Since he was not a practitioner of medicine, his voluminous writings were mostly ignored by his contemporaries. His medical writings spanned a wide range of topics, including mental illness. Included in his writings on

mental illness were therapeutic measures for treating phrenitus (delirium).

A contemporary of Celsus is Gaius Plinius Cecilius Secundus, or Pliny the Elder (23–79 A.D.). He was a Roman scholar of note, whose imaginative writings were influential in his day. If there is one theme throughout his writings, it is the Greek teleological notion that everything has a purpose. Pliny believed there would be a cure for all diseases (Gordon, 1949).

Pliny was not a physician and was highly suspicious of medicine. Gordon states that "he was against physicians and particularly those of Greece, whom he accused of all sorts of ethical violations and moral weakness" (1949, p. 671). Yet Pliny influenced the next several hundred years of medicine by pointing out the cathartic effects of the torpedo fish in relieving labor pains in pregnant women. (Parenthetically, when electroshock therapy was formally introduced into medical practice some 1700 years later, it was by two Roman physicians—Cerletti and Bini.) Pliny's ideas, though often far-fetched, were not inconsistent with those of his contemporaries. Indeed, many of his convictions can be found in writings over the next 16 centuries.

Scribonius Largus, a contemporary of Pliny, used torpedo fish to alleviate headaches around 45 A.D. Largus placed a fish across the patient's brow and caused it to discharge. While it is not clear what size fish were used in these treatments, the large Mediterranean torpedo electricus develops potentials of 100 to 150 volts at a high amperage.

GALEN

Another advocate of the use of torpedo fish was Claudius Galen of Pergamum (129–199 A.D.), who after Hippocrates was the most famous of the ancient physicians and probably the most influential writer on medical topics of all time (Lyons & Petrucelli, 1978). Galen's physiology was based, in good measure, upon Hippocrates' humoral theory. When the four elements of the blood were in correct proportion, the organism was healthy. There were also three spirits, one of them responsible for growth (natural), one for generation and dissipation of heat (vital), and one for sensation and movement (animal). If Galenic physiology is couched in modern terms, it can be seen as a most significant contribution to Hippocratic medicine. Talbott (1970) suggested that the vital spirit might be interpreted as oxygen and the animal spirit as electrical potential or neuronal conduction. Galen's physiology was at variance with Aristotle's cardiocentric notions, and he invested considerable energy in refuting Aristotle (Clarke & O'Malley, 1968). Most of Galen's knowledge was based upon clinical and experimental contact with infrahumans (primarily the Barbary ape), hence he necessarily made many mistakes. But Lyons and Petrucelli (1978), point out that "in spite of Galen's mistakes and misconceptions, one is astonished at the wealth of accurate detail in his writings" (p. 254)

Galen, like Pliny, held strong anthropocentric convictions. Everything in the universe was made by God for a particular reason or purpose. To Aristotle's remark that "Nature does nothing without a purpose," Galen would rejoin that he understood the purpose. Such a view held that any plant or animal that did not serve a useful function for humans (such as food, clothing, or medicine) existed only to teach a moral lesson. While Galen's teleology was not in the Hippocratic tradition, his treatment certainly was, assisting nature in the healing process with diet, rest, and exercise. He was particularly sensitive to and concerned with the effect of emotional states on bodily symptoms. Galenic medicine was unquestionably a monumental forward step that influenced the next 15 centuries of treatment. Even the eminent Vesalius, who often disagreed with "the dogmas of Galen," "did not dare to swerve a nail's breadth from the doctrines of the Prince of Medicine" (Foster, 1901, p. 14).

THE MIDDLE AGES

There were few substantive improvements in the treatment of mental illness until about the 10th century. One interesting figure, however, was the fifth-century physician Caelius Aurelianus, who translated Soranus of Ephesus, a revered Greek physician, into Latin. Soranus' writings were organized by Aurelianus into "Acute diseases" and "Chronic diseases." The writings of Soranus/Aurelianus provide excellent insights into current thinking on the diagnosis and treatment of mental illness. The following excerpts from Soranus' *Chronic Diseases* are reported by Goshen (1967, pp. 30–31).

Some hold that the patient should be made drunk. But the fact is that madness and insanity are often the result of drunkenness. Some say he should be flogged, apparently so that he may regain his sanity by a kind of whipping of his reason. But the raining of blows upon the inflamed parts will only aggravate these parts; and, when the attack is over and the patient recovers his senses, he will still be assailed by the pain from these blows. . . .

Some physicians prescribe the opening of an artery; but this treatment causes injury to the head without any advantage.

And so the treatment of insanity is marked by all these futile and haphazard procedures.

As may be apparent from the last comment, Soranus and Aurelianus vigorously opposed the then-popular ways of treating mental illness. As an alternative to restraint by chains, violence, and starvation, Aurelianus recommended irritant injections in the ear.

Perhaps the greatest of all medieval physicians was Abu (Ali al-Husayn ibn Abdullah ibn Sina, or Avicenna), born in Bukhara in Central Asia in 980. In the hierarchy of great philosophers, Talbott (1970) places Avicenna just below Aristotle. His extraordinary intellect ranged over diverse areas of knowledge from metaphysics, theology, and verse to astronomy, natural philosophy, and medicine. His theory that mental illness was attributable to physical disturbances in the brain was as novel—and as ignored—as the heliocentric hypothesis of Aristarchus around 300 B.C.

There were two noteworthy figures of the 11th century. The recipient of Avicenna's medical, if not geographic, mantle was Abu Imran Musa ibn Maimun ibn Abd Allah, or Rabbi Moses Ben Maimon, known as Maimonides (1135–1204), a Jewish-Arabian physician born in Cordova, Spain. His writings clearly reflected Hippocrates, Galen, and Avicenna, though he himself exerted considerable influence upon European medicine (Talbott, 1970).

Maimonides discussed the problem of mental illness in his *Ethics,* classifying "psychic dispositions" among "moral imperfections" (Goshen, 1967, p. 36). He roundly and energetically condemned mystical, superstitious, and divine attributions, holding instead that when behavior inclines toward one of two extremes ("inordinate passion and insensibility"), the soul becomes diseased (Goshen, 1967, p. 37).

A little-known figure is Roger Frugardi, who developed the technique of trephination around 1150. This, the first attempt at psychosurgical intervention, involved placing burr holes in the cranium to allow demons or spirits to escape. The operation was performed for minor problems such as headaches as well as major ones such as mania and melancholia.

Another landmark in the treatment of the mentally ill was the establishment of the first mental institution at Valencia, Spain, in 1410. The first three asylums were all in Spain, the second being at Saragossa (1435) and the third at Granada (1452). Spain's progress in this regard is probably attributable to King Ferdinand and Queen Isabella. Another hundred years passed before the Bethlehem Royal Hospital in London was established (1547), the institution that came to be known as Bedlam.

PARACELSUS AND THE REBIRTH

One of the most extraordinary figures in medical history, as well as a seminal figure in psychiatry, was the Swiss physician and alchemist Philippus Theophrastus Bombastus von Hohenheim (1493–1541), known as Paracelsus ("better than Celsus"), who marked the beginning of a gradual transition from iatrochemistry (alchemy) to chemistry. A committed mystic and astrologer, he also believed in the four elements of the Greeks and the three elements of the Arabs (mercury, sulfur, and salt) and spent much of his life in search of the philosopher's stone. He was a rebel in the tradition of Rabelais and Luther and in fact was called "the Luther of medicine" by Sir William Osler. The prevailing view of his time was solidly entrenched in Galenism. Mental illness was still considered a subject of theological or demonological inquiry, and there was precious little empirical data to support any contrary theoretical viewpoint. The opposition of Paracelsus to Galenic medicine fell in three general categories: (a) It was too inflexible and systematized, adhering to a rigid biogenic model; (b) it precluded all psychological aspects of the individual, relying instead on the unassailable influence of the humors; and (c) it represented the conservative vested interests and the respectability of the professional establishment (Zilboorg, 1941).

The authoritative text on mental illness in Paracelsus' time was the *Malleus Maleficarum* (Witches' Hammer). Written in 1484 by Heinrich Kramer and James Sprenger, monks of the Dominican Order, the *Malleus Maleficarum* was essentially the product of a papal bull of Innocent VIII (Veith, 1965). This textbook, which laid the groundwork for persecution, torture, and death, had as its premise that "many persons of both sexes . . . have abandoned themselves to devils, incubi and succubi. . . . These wretches furthermore afflict and torment men and women . . . with terrible and piteous pains and sore diseases, both internal and external; they hinder men from performing the sexual act and women from conceiving, when husbands cannot know their wives nor wives receive their husbands" (Veith, 1965, pp. 59–60). According to the monks, cooperation of the devil and a witch could occur only through indulgence "in every kind of carnal lust with Incubi or Succubi and all manner of filthy delights" (Veith, 1965, p. 61). The *Malleus Maleficarum* appeared throughout Europe in 30 editions over a period of 200 years, flourishing during the Renaissance, a period otherwise characterized by a rebirth and blossoming of the arts and sciences. Veith (1965) notes that "a careful study of this fantastic document reveals beyond doubt that many, if not most, of the witches as well as a great number of their victims described therein were simply hysterics who suffered from partial anesthesia, mutism, blindness, and convulsions, and, above all, from a variety of sexual delusions" (p. 61).

In 1526 Paracelsus wrote *The diseases that deprive man of his reason, such as St. Vitus dance, falling sickness, melancholy, and insanity, and their correct treatment.* In the preface of this tour de force, Paracelsus advised (Sigerist, 1941):

In nature there are not only diseases which afflict our body and our health, but many others which deprive us of sound reason, and these are the most serious. While speaking about the natural diseases and observing to what extent and how seriously they afflict various parts of our body, we must not forget to explain the origin of the diseases which deprive man of reason, as we know from experience that they develop out of man's disposition. The present-day clergy of Europe attribute such diseases to ghostly beings and three-fold spirits; we are not inclined to believe them. For nature proves that such statements by earthly gods are quite incorrect and, as we shall explain in these chapters, nature is the sole origin of diseases. (p. 142)

As Sigerist notes, Paracelsus determined that health and disease were accountable to five spheres: *ens astrale* (the stars or passage of time—diseases that are fatal today may be prevented tomorrow); *ens veneni* (the environment, providing food that nourishes as well as poisons that kill); *ens naturale* (the individual nature or personality); *ens spirituale* (the spiritual sphere or psyche, which may lead to or protect from mental illness); and *ens Dei* (the sphere of God).

Paracelsus revolutionized psychiatry by providing the first descriptive observational approach to the understanding of mental illness. He associated head injury with paralysis, cretinism with thyroid dysfunction, and sexuality with hysteria. He dismissed the divine intervention of St. Vitus in the etiology of epilepsy and was probably the first to recognize the role of unconscious forces (*unwüssende*) in illness. He distinguished between natural (physical) illness and psychological (*spiritus vitae*) illness. In his discussion of *suffocatio intellectus,* he points out that the most profound disturbance of the intellect (reason) may be secondary to a psychological disturbance. His writings on the clinical manifestations of mania and hysteria remained unsurpassed for several hundred years. Apparently he was the first to conceive the notion of individual personality, a concept not formally developed until the mid-19th century. Only some 300 years later would his clinical, descriptive methodology be fully incorporated into medical practice (Zilboorg, 1941). Paracelsus can be remembered as much for his novel and revolutionary approach to mental illness as for his unrelenting battle to bring about the demise of cosmologic and astrologic medicine.

REFERENCES

Becker, G. (1978). *The mad genius controversy.* Beverly Hills, CA: Sage.

Clarke, E., & O'Malley, C. D. (1968). *The human brain and spinal cord.* Berkeley, CA: University of California Press.

Foster, M. (1901). *Lectures on the history of physiology during the sixteenth, seventeenth and eighteenth centuries.* Cambridge, UK: University Press.

Gibson, C. (1889). *The characteristics of genius: A popular essay.* London: Scott.

Gordon, B. L. (1949). *Medicine throughout antiquity.* Philadelphia, PA: Davis.

Goshen, C. E. (1967). *Documentary history of psychiatry.* New York: Philosophical Library.

Lyons, A. S., & Petrucelli, R. J. (1978). *Medicine: An illustrated history.* New York: Abrams.

Sigerist, H. E. (Ed.). (1941). *Four treatises of Theophrastus von Hohenheim called Paracelsus.* Baltimore: Johns Hopkins University Press.

Talbott, J. H. (1970). *A biographical history of medicine.* New York: Grune & Stratton.

Veith, I. (1965). *Hysteria. The history of a disease.* Chicago: The University of Chicago Press.

Zilboorg, G. (1941). Ambulatory schizophrenia. *Psychiatry, 4,* 149–155.

R. A. PRENTKY
Justice Resource Institute

BEHAVIORAL MEDICINE
EMPIRICISM
PSYCHOLOGY: HISTORY
PSYCHOLOGICAL HEALTH
PSYCHOTHERAPY
SUPERSTITION

MENTAL MEASUREMENTS YEARBOOKS (MMY)

Originating in 1938, the various mental measurements yearbooks published over a span of 40 years have provided an invaluable service to a broad array of test consumers. The success of the MMY series is due entirely to the commitment and foresight of Oscar K. Buros, originator and editor, and his wife, Luella Buros.

According to Buros, the objectives of the MMYs were: (a) to provide a current bibliography of all tests available in English-speaking countries; (b) to provide a comprehensive and accurate bibliography for specific tests; and (c) to provide critical test reviews by qualified reviewers to help test consumers select suitable tests for specific purposes. Other goals cited by Buros include exerting pressure on test publishers to produce fewer tests, but of greater quality, and to provide more complete information about published tests. It was also hoped that test users would become more discriminating consumers of standardized tests (Buros, 1968).

The monumental effort required to prepare an MMY is evident in the statistical summary for the 1978 *Eighth Mental Measurements Yearbook.* The two volumes of that MMY contain a listing of 1,184 tests. There are 898 test reviews by 484 reviewers and 140 test reviews excerpted from 29 journals. The total number of references for specific tests is 17,481 (Buros, 1978). A total of 24 separate works were published by the Buros Institute of Mental Measurements. Upon the death of Buros in 1972, the Institute was transferred to the University of Nebraska at Lincoln.

REFERENCES

Buros, O. K. (1968). The story behind the mental measurements yearbooks. *Measurement and Evaluation in Guidance, 1*(2), 86–95.

Buros, O. K. (Ed.). (1978). *The eighth mental measurements yearbook.* Highland Park, NJ: Gryphon.

G. J. ROBERTSON
Wide Range, Inc.

PSYCHOMETRICS: NORMS, RELIABILITY, VALIDITY, AND ITEM ANALYSIS
TESTING METHODS

MENTAL RETARDATION

HISTORY OF THE CONCEPT

The concept of mental retardation is relatively new, having first appeared in the mid-19th century. Formerly, there was little awareness of individual differences with respect to intelligence. What awareness existed appears to have been a recognition of gross deviance, and in this regard, mental retardation was typically confused with mental illness or associated with gross physical abnormality and deformity. By the late 17th century, observers had begun to perceive a basic difference between the mentally ill and the mentally deficient. Not until 1838 was a formal, scientific explanation offered. The French scientist Esquirol postulated that the essential difference between mental retardation and madness lay in the developmental character of the former. In *Mental Maladies* (1845) he suggested that mental retardation or "idiocy" is "not a disease, but a condition in which the mental faculties . . . have never been developed sufficiently" (p. 446). Esquirol proposed the first classification system for the retarded which roughly corresponds to the modern day profound, severe, and moderate levels of mental retardation.

In the early 20th century, the French Ministry of Public Education commissioned Binet to develop a method to determine which children could not profit from public education. Binet's method, developed as a screening device for mental retardation, became the first test of intelligence. Binet believed that intelligence consisted of a wide variety of complex mental processes such as memory, reasoning, and judgment. His test, developed in collaboration with Théodore Simon, constituted an attempt to measure these faculties. The first Binet–Simon scale was published in 1905. The 1908 revision introduced the concept of "mental age." Test items were ordered by increasing difficulty and were grouped according to the age at which children generally passed or failed. Mental age was determined by assessing at what level an individual performed. For example, a child who passed all items up to and including those passed by the majority of 6-year-olds would have a mental age of 6, regardless of the child's chronological age. The use of mental age was helpful in comparing children with their age peers and was enthusiastically received.

Terman at Stanford University revised and translated the Binet–Simon Scale and published the Stanford–Binet Intelligence Scale in 1916. Herein was introduced the "intelligence quotient," or IQ: the ratio of the individual's mental age (MA) divided by chronological age (CA) and multiplied by 100 (IQ = MA ÷ CA × 100). Individual comparisons of intelligence were thus made technically quite simple.

The importance of this early work in intelligence testing cannot be overestimated. First, it produced a concrete, reliable, practical method for evaluating a person's mental functioning. Second, this method allowed for the quantitative determination of differences among individuals. Binet's test concretely demonstrated both the existence and extent of individual differences in intelligence. Furthermore, as Kanner (1964) noted, "It became evident that intellectual inadequacy was not an absolute, all-or-none attribute, as had been previously assumed. There were graduations from the slightest deviations to the most profound state of deficiency" (p. 122). Third, the fine graduations made possible by the use of the IQ test indicated that there were many people whose intelligence fell between the severely retarded and average. Graduation of mental retardation was thus officially discovered and recognized.

Once the concept of mental retardation as a distinctive phenomenon had been accepted by the scientific community, speculation began regarding the nature and etiology of the condition. Several studies conducted in the late 19th and early 20th centuries suggested that mental retardation was related to genetic factors. In 1877, for example, Dugdale published his study of the Jukes family. Over a period of 75 years this family had cost their state more than a million dollars in welfare and various types of institutional care. In 1916, Estabrook located 1,258 members of the family and estimated that one-half of them were "feeble minded."

In the 1930s and 1940s a debate began regarding the causes of mental retardation. A long series of "twin studies"—comparing the intellectual abilities of identical and fraternal twins or of identical twins raised apart—together with the work of such earlier researchers as Dugdale and others, suggested that heredity was the dominant factor. Other researchers, such as Bayley and Spitz concluded that IQ is not fixed or constant and that one's environment may have a profound impact on the development of intelligence. By the 1950s, the debate had subsided and an interactionist position was generally accepted. In other words, intellectual ability was believed to be a product of the interaction between one's genetic endowment and one's environment. In 1961 Hunt published *Intelligence and Experience,* which emphasized the critical role of experience in the development of intelligence. This work further solidified the interactionist-environmentalist position, which by the mid-1960s was dominant in scientific thinking regarding mental deficiency.

THE CONCEPT OF MENTAL RETARDATION

According to the American Association of Mental Deficiency (AAMD; Grossman, 1977), mental retardation refers to "significantly subaverage general intellectual functioning existing concurrently with deficits in adaptive behavior, and manifested during the developmental period." In its basic form, this definition has also been accepted and utilized by the World Health Organization. The AAMD definition of mental retardation consists of three criteria, all of which must be present before a diagnosis of mental retardation can be made.

Significantly subaverage general intellectual functioning. This first requirement relates to the person's level of general intelligence. This level is defined and measured by performance on an individually administered standardized test of intelligence. The upper cutoff for mental retardation is usually an IQ of 70: All persons with IQs below this cutoff point satisfy the first requirement for a diagnosis of mental retardation. The most commonly used accepted tests for making this determination are the Stanford–Binet and the various Wechsler scales (Wechsler Adult Intelligence Scale–Revised; Wechsler Intelligence Scale for Children–Revised; Wechsler Preschool and Primary Scale of Intelligence).

Deficits in adaptive behavior. Adaptive behavior is defined as the degree to which one meets the standards of personal independence and social responsibility expected for one's age and cultural group. Since those standards are age-related and culturally variable, this criterion is difficult to satisfy and measure reliably. Fortunately, fairly good normative developmental data are available and, generally speaking, there is an expectation for increasing independence, self-mastery, and conformity to societal demands and conventions as the person progresses from one developmental level to the next. The mere presence of deficits at any age level, however, does not by itself imply mental retardation. Such deficits can occur for a variety of reasons (e.g., situational or emotional problems). Only when these deficits are manifested by a person with an IQ below 70 do they constitute criteria for mental retardation. At that point the adaptive impairment is considered to be related to the intellectual deficit.

Manifestation during the developmental period. This third requirement is included primarily to distinguish mental retardation from a variety of other disorders in which low IQ and adaptive deficits are present. These disorders include such conditions as brain damage, resulting from stroke or trauma, and emotional disorders. It is important to distinguish between persons who had ability but lost it and those who never really developed it. The "development period" refers to the time during which the growth of intelligence is presumed to occur. This is usually considered to be between birth and 16 to 18 years of age. Thus, the current concept of mental retardation stresses the notion of "developmental disability." Persons who develop intellectual and adaptive deficits as adults are not mentally retarded because their condition did not originate or exist in the developmental period; presumably, they developed in a normal fashion.

The AAMD definition of mental retardation has several important implications. First, this definition refers only to performance at a given time and does not explicitly imply irreversibility. Second, mental retardation is not defined solely in terms of a score on an IQ test. The two-dimensional definition (low intelligence and adaptive deficit) is important because it precludes diagnosing a socially competent individual as retarded simply because he or she performs poorly on an IQ test. Lastly, the AAMD definition is developmental and emphasizes the assessment of a person in terms of success with developmental tasks appropriate for that individual's age group.

LEVELS OF MENTAL RETARDATION

Since the advent of the intelligence test, the classification of mental retardation has been based almost exclusively on IQ levels. Grossman (1977) has developed a universally recognized system that employs the terminology "mild," "moderate," "severe," and "profound." The *mildly* retarded individual's IQ falls between 55 and 69. These persons usually look and act normal and display no overt, obvious signs of retardation. As adults they are frequently able to find and keep a semiskilled job, but often need supervision in social and financial affairs. They are generally able to care for themselves adequately and to travel about familiar locales with ease. Intellectually they are at the level of a fourth- or fifth-grade child. Mildly retarded persons are vulnerable to occupational displacement due to adverse economic conditions or automation. Motor slowness and poor reading skills make competitive employment difficult for them. One of the common problems with mildly retarded adults is their inability to handle leisure time.

The *moderately* retarded person has an IQ of 40 to 54, with an approximate mental age of 6 to 8 years. These people frequently look as though something is wrong with them. The chief focus of training is on self-care and other practical skills, and the majority become fairly proficient in such skills as dressing, toileting, eating, and grooming. Although the moderately retarded may be able to recognize some written words or even read some simple sentences, essentially they are functionally illiterate. Very few marry or become independent. They have few friends outside the immediate family, and any employment they obtain is usually of a repetitive, unskilled nature, perhaps in a sheltered setting where income is not dependent on production.

Severely retarded persons have an IQ of 25 to 39, with a mental age of about 3 years, 9 months to 6 years. Although neurological damage is common in this group, they tend to be ambulatory. Special training can teach them to talk and care for simple personal needs. Academic training, however, is not effective. The focus of training is on self-care skills, and little independent behavior occurs. These individuals need constant supervision and care. They are apt to be openly friendly in the manner of small children and attach themselves to persons with whom they come in contact.

Profoundly retarded persons have an IQ below 25, with an estimated adult mental age of 3 years, 8 months or less. The probability of concomitant neurological damage is high and many are non-ambulatory. They are often multiply handicapped. They may learn to walk and to speak a few words. Until recently, most of these persons were unable to feed and toilet themselves, but the widespread use of behavior modification techniques has increased the number who have such skills. For this group total supervision is necessary, usually in an institutionalized setting.

PREVALENCE AND CAUSATIVE FACTORS

Allman and Jaffe (1978) estimate that approximately 7 million persons in the United States may be classified as mentally retarded. Presently, less than 10% of these persons are in institutions, and most of those institutionalized are severely or profoundly retarded. The remainder, consisting primarily of the mildly or moderately retarded, live in the community. The vast majority of these live at home and are integrated members of their families, often performing useful functions in the home and, not infrequently, working productively in external settings ranging from sheltered workshops to independent employment.

Less than 15% of the cases of mental retardation have a known organic or medical cause (Smith, 1971). Thus, for most persons diagnosed as mentally retarded, no specific reason for their deficits can be identified. Most cases of mental retardation with a known cause, or etiology, fall in the severe or profound range. Organic causative factors include genetic abnormalities such as Down syndrome; maternal infections or disorders during pregnancy such as rubella or drug ingestion; birth difficulties that deprive the fetus of oxygen; or postnatal factors such as infections (e.g., encephalitis or meningitis), head injury, asphyxiation, or toxins (e.g., poisoning). The remaining 85% of the cases are idiopathic: A specific cause cannot be determined. These persons are likely to be moderately or mildly retarded. It is generally believed that low intelligence for the most part is a result of an interaction between mediocre or poor genetic or neurological heritage and a mediocre or poor environment (e.g., one characterized by infant neglect, poor stimulation, or lack of learning experiences).

REFERENCES

Allman, L., & Jaffe, K. (1978). *Abnormal psychology in the life cycle.* New York: Harper & Row.

Dugdale, R. L., (1877). *The Jukes: A study in crime, pauperism, disease and heredity.* New York: Putnam.

Esquirol, J. E. D. (1845). *Mental maladies.* Philadelphia, PA: Lea & Blanchard.

Estabrook, A. H. (1916). *The Jukes in 1915.* Washington, DC: Carnegie Institute.

Grossman, H. J. (1977). *Manual on terminology and classification in mental retardation* (1977 revision). American Association on Mental Deficiency. Baltimore: Garamond/Pridemark.

Hunt, J. M. (1961). *Intelligence and experience.* New York: Ronald.

Kanner, L. A. (1964). *A history of the care and study of the mentally retarded.* Springfield, IL: Thomas.

Smith, R. M. (1971). *An introduction to mental retardation.* New York: McGraw-Hill.

SUGGESTED READING

Maloney, M. P., & Ward, M. P. (1979). *Mental retardation and modern society.* New York: Oxford University Press.

M. P. MALONEY
Pasadena, California

CHROMOSOME DISORDERS
HUMAN DEVELOPMENT
IDIOT SAVANT (SAVANT SYNDROME)
INDIVIDUAL DIFFERENCES
SPEECH DEVELOPMENT

MERRILL–PALMER SCALES

Two editions of the Merrill–Palmer Scales are currently available: the Merrill–Palmer Scale of Mental Tests (Stutsman, 1931/1948), the original version published in 1931; and the Extended Merrill–Palmer Scale (Ball, Merrifield, & Statt, 1978), a revised version. The original edition was designed for use with children aged 18 months to 6 years; the revision is restricted to ages 3, 4, and 5. Both scales were designed to provide a broader assessment of the preschool child's abilities than a conventional intelligence scale such as the Stanford–Binet.

The Merrill–Palmer Scale of Mental Tests consists of 93 tasks grouped into nine 6-month age groups, beginning with ages 18 to 23 months. Four broad clusters of tests are cited: Language, All-or-None, Form Board and Picture, and Motor Coordination (Stutsman, 1931/1948). Content is heavily weighted with gross and fine motor tasks and with perceptual-motor items. Total point scores may be converted to mental ages and within-age percentile ranks. Ratio IQs may be computed. Norms were derived during the 1920s.

The Extended Merrill–Palmer Scale consists of 16 tasks, four for each of four dimensions: Semantic Production, Figural Production, Semantic Evaluation, and Figural Evaluation. Grouping of content into the four dimensions was based on four factor-analytic studies of 25 tasks with more than 1,200 children. Guilford's Structure of Intellect Model provided a taxonomy for structuring the content. The first descriptor for each dimension defines the type of content (semantic or figural), while the second term describes the process (production or evaluation). The authors advocate the separate interpretation of each dimension; norms consist of within-age percentile ranks, based on a sample of 1,124 children, aged 3 to 5. There are no battery composite or mental age scores, because the authors are opposed to the general intelligence construct (Ball et al., 1978).

REFERENCES

Ball, R. S., Merrifield, P., & Statt, L. H. (1978). *The extended Merrill–Palmer scale, instruction manual.* Chicago: Stoelting.

Stutsman, R. (1948). *Guide for administering the Merrill–Palmer scale of mental tests.* New York: Harcourt Brace Jovanovich. (Original work published 1931)

G. J. ROBERTSON
Wide Range, Inc.

INTELLIGENCE MEASURES

MESMER, FRANZ ANTON (1734–1815)

Franz Anton Mesmer, despite the controversies about him as a person, is commonly recognized as the founding father of modern hypnosis. His own position he called animal magnetism, but even if that theory was misguided, he had evidence that *something* was happening in his encounters with his patients.

For his doctoral dissertation on the influence of the planets on human behavior (1766), he relied heavily upon a book by Isaac Newton's friend Richard Mead, who had published on the influence of the planets on human beings in 1704. Thus he was attempting to build upon the rock of Newtonian ideas to find some basis for understanding human illness and cures. Perhaps there were physiological tides that ebbed and flowed with the moon in the body, as ocean tides did around the world.

Mesmer's marriage to a wealthy widow in Vienna permitted him to live well while carrying on his practice. He was a patron of the arts, and one of Mozart's operas was performed for the first time in his private theater. He was also involved in the development of the glass harmonica, still used to this day. He had access to prominent people, and his ideas became popular for a time. He began experimenting with magnets, a practice that had entered medicine with Paracelsus (1493–1541) and been revived at intervals thereafter by Van Helmont and others. A local Jesuit astronomer, Maximilian Hell, had been fashioning magnets, and some of Mesmer's first cures were done with one of his magnets, starting in 1774. By 1775 he was well enough known to be called upon to defy a Catholic priest, Johann Gassner, who had been curing people by casting out demons. Mesmer showed that he could produce and cure the same symptoms by his method of animal magnetism, and won what was the only successful empirical contest of his career. However, he got into trouble in Vienna, and moved to Paris in 1778, where he attained the height of his success.

During the years of popularity he had a fashionable clientele of prominent citizens who would gather about his *baquet* in order to be cured of their troubles. The baquet consisted of a tank in which there were iron filings and other magnetized materials, and bottles of water magnetized by Mesmer, to which each of the seated patients was connected by means of an iron rod so as to share in the magnetic properties. As Mesmer moved from one to another in his fancy robe, one responsive patient after another would go into a crisis and be removed to a recovery room, where, on recovery, the person would be free of symptoms. The medical profession was skeptical throughout, and a Royal Commission—of which Benjamin Franklin, the American ambassador, was the nominal chair-

man—was established to investigate. Their negative verdict, along with other attacks, put an end to Mesmer's welcome in Paris; in 1784 he left for Switzerland. His disciples continued his practices, particularly under the Marquis de Puységur, and only after many years was animal magnetism given up in favor of hypnotism. Hypnotism did not become fully respectable medically in France until J. M. Charcot's presentation before the Academy of Sciences in 1882.

Mesmer returned to Paris briefly between 1798 and 1802, but then moved back to his childhood village in Switzerland, where he spent his last years in retirement.

The character of Mesmer was such as to leave an ambiguous impression: He was part showman, part serious scientist trying to make the best of the inadequate knowledge of psychological disease and its treatment at the time. His names lives on, however, in the term "mesmerism" (with a lower-case "m"), still heard occasionally as a name for hypnosis.

E. R. HILGARD
Stanford University

META-ANALYSIS

The fundamental problem addressed by meta-analytic procedures is the cumulation of evidence. There has long been a pessimistic feeling in the social, behavioral, and biological sciences that our progress has been exceedingly slow, at least when compared to the progress of "harder" sciences, such as physics and chemistry. In particular, it has seemed that the "softer" (and newer) sciences do not show the orderly progress and development of the harder (and older) sciences. In other words, the more recent work of the harder sciences seems to build directly upon the older work of those sciences, whereas the more recent work of the softer sciences seems often to be starting from scratch.

CUMULATING SCIENTIFIC EVIDENCE

Those who have looked closely at the issue of cumulation in the physical sciences have pointed out that these disciplines have ample problems of their own (Collins, 1985; Hedges, 1987; Mann, 1990; Pool, 1988). Nonetheless, in the matter of cumulating evidence, the softer sciences have much to be modest about.

Poor cumulation does not seem to be due primarily to lack of replication, or to the failure to recognize the need for replication. There are many areas of the softer sciences for which we have the results of numerous studies, all addressing essentially the same question. Our summaries of the results of these sets of studies, however, have not been nearly as informative as they might have been, either with respect to summarized significance levels or with respect to summarized effect magnitudes. Even the best reviews of research by the most sophisticated writers have rarely told us much more about each study in a set of studies than the direction of the relationship between the variables investigated, and whether or not a given significance level was attained. However, this state of affairs is beginning to change. More and more reviews of the literature are moving from the traditional literary approach to quantitative approaches to the research synthesis described in an increasing number of textbooks of meta-analysis (Cooper, 1989; Cooper & Hedges, 1994; Glass, McGaw, & Smith, 1981; Hedges & Olkin, 1985; Hunter & Schmidt, 1990; Light & Pillemer, 1984; Rosenthal, 1991). The goals of these quantitative approaches of meta-analysis are to help us discover what we have learned from the results of the studies conducted, and to help us discover what we have not yet learned.

Defining Research Results

Before we can consider various issues and procedures in the cumulation of research results, we must be quite explicit about the meaning of the concept "results of a study." It is easiest to begin with what we do not mean. We do not mean the prose *conclusion* drawn by the investigator and reported in the abstract, the results, or the discussion section of the research report. We also do not mean the results of an omnibus F test with $df > 1$ in the numerator or an omnibus χ^2 test with $df > 1$. (These omnibus tests address vague questions that are rarely, if ever, of scientific interest.)

What we do mean is the answer to the question: What is the relationship between any variable X and any variable Y? The variables X and Y are chosen with only the constraint that their relationship be of interest to us. The answer to this question should normally come in two parts: (a) the estimate of the magnitude of the relationship (the effect size); and (b) an indication of the accuracy, precision, or stability of the estimated effect size (as in a confidence interval placed around the effect size estimate). An alternative to the second part of the answer is one not intrinsically more useful, but one more consistent with the existing practices of researchers; that is, the examination of the significance level of the difference between the obtained effect size and the effect size expected under the null hypothesis (usually an effect size of zero). If the significance level is employed, it should always be reported accurately, and never as "significant" or "not significant" (Wilkinson & the Task Force on Statistical Inference, 1999).

Because a complete reporting of the results of a study requires the report of both the effect size and level of statistical significance, it is useful to make explicit the relationship between these quantities. The general relationship is given by:

$$\text{Test of Significance} = \text{Size of Effect} \times \text{Size of Study}$$

In other words, the larger the study in terms of the number of sampling units, the more significant the results will be. This is true unless the size of the effect is truly zero, in which case a larger study will not produce a result that is any more significant than a smaller study. However, effect magnitudes of zero are not encountered very often.

A Brief Historical Note

We are inclined to think of meta-analysis as a recent development, but it is older than the t test, which dates back to 1908 (Gosset, 1908)! We can simultaneously describe the early history of meta-analysis and provide a classic illustration of the meta-analytic enterprise. In 1904, Karl Pearson (1904) collected correlation coeffi-

cients (rs); there were six of them with values of .58, .58, .60, .63, .66, and .77. The weighted mean r of these six correlation coefficients was .64, the unweighted mean r was .63, and the median r was .61.

Karl Pearson was collecting correlation coefficients because he wanted to know the degree to which inoculation against smallpox saved lives. His own rough-and-ready summary of his meta-analysis of six studies was that there was a .6 correlation between inoculation and survival—a truly huge effect. An r of that magnitude can be thought of as the effects of inoculation changing the proportion of people surviving from 20% to 80% (Rosenthal & Rubin, 1982; Rosenthal, 1991).

When Karl Pearson quantitatively summarized six studies of the effects of smallpox inoculation, a meta-analysis was an unusual thing to do. It is unusual no longer. Indeed, there is an explosion of meta-analytic research syntheses such that a rapidly increasing proportion of all reviews of the literature are in the form of quantitative reviews. The trajectory is such that within just a few years, virtually all reviews of the literature in the serious scientific journals of our fields will be quantitative reviews—meta-analyses.

REFERENCES

Collins, H. M. (1985). *Changing order: Replication and induction in scientific practice.* Beverly Hills, CA: Sage.

Cooper, H. M. (1989). *Integrating research: A guide to literature reviews* (2nd ed.). Newbury Park, CA: Sage.

Cooper, H., & Hedges, L. V. (Eds.). (1994). *Handbook of research synthesis.* New York: Russell Sage.

Glass, G. V., McGaw, B., & Smith, M. L. (1981). *Meta-analysis in social research.* Beverly Hills, CA: Sage.

Gosset, W. S. (Student) (1908). The probable error of a mean. *Biometrika, 6,* 1–25.

Hedges, L. V. (1987). How hard is hard science, how soft is soft science? *American Psychologist, 42,* 443–455.

Hedges, L. V., & Olkin, I. (1985). *Statistical methods for meta-analysis.* New York: Academic.

Hunter, J. E., & Schmidt, F. L. (1990). *Methods of meta-analysis: Correcting error and bias in research findings.* Newbury Park, CA: Sage.

Light, R. J., & Pillemer, D. B. (1984). *Summing up: The science of reviewing research.* Cambridge, MA: Harvard University Press.

Mann, C. (1990). Meta-analysis in the breech. *Science, 249,* 476–480.

Pearson, K. (1904, Nov. 5). Report on certain enteric fever inoculation statistics. *British Medical Journal,* 1243–1246.

Pool, R. (1988). Similar experiments, dissimilar results. *Science, 242,* 192–193.

Rosenthal, R. (1991). *Meta-analytic procedures for social research* (rev. ed.). Newbury Park, CA: Sage.

Rosenthal, R., & Rubin, D. B. (1982). A simple, general purpose display of magnitude of experimental effect. *Journal of Educational Psychology, 74,* 166–169.

Wilkinson, L., & the Task Force on Statistical Inference, APA Board of Scientific Affairs. (1999). Statistical methods in psychology journals. *American Psychologist, 54,* 594–604.

R. ROSENTHAL
University of California, Riverside

CHI-SQUARE TEST
CORRELATION METHODS
INFORMATION PROCESSING
STRUCTURAL EQUATION MODELING
TIME-SERIES ANALYSIS

MEXICO, PSYCHOLOGY IN

The Aztecs of Mexico were aware of the importance of behavior and cognition for mood and personality. The Tlamatinime, the fundamental counselors in the society, who had a clearly psychotherapeutic role (Portilia, 1979), were known to use such instructions as to ask someone who was depressed to participate in a festival. This is almost the same as the old Mexican dictum: "El que canta las penas espanta" (He who sings scares suffering away). But aside from the educated members of religious orders, and people such as Benito Diaz de Gamarra, Antonio Rubio, and Fray Alonso de la Vera Cruz (who, in addition to a description of the behavioral effects of mushrooms in the local population, wrote an Aristotelian *De Anima*), little can be said about psychology during the Spanish Colonial days (1521–1821). An exception is Jose Ignacio Bartolache. In the 1770s, he was systematically dissecting human bodies and he accurately described hysteria (Robles, 1952).

INDEPENDENT MEXICO

By about 1835, phrenology became widely debated. In 1884, Rafael Serrano published his *Optic Psychiatry.* Robles (1952) considers him one of the great thinkers in psychiatry and psychology in early Mexico. Porfirio Parra, who wrote on cerebral localization and a taxonomy of sensibility; Jose Olvera, on hysteria and the relationships among embriology, psychology, and religion; and Juan Cordero, with his book *La Vida Psiquica* were the major figures to emerge around the end of the 19th and the beginning of the 20th century.

The Reform

Of particular importance in the history of Mexico was the event known as "The Reform." When Benito Juarez, an Oaxacan Indian, took over the government of Mexico in 1867, his liberalism and coincidence in time with Gabino Barreda, a disciple of Auguste Comte, were to produce many changes in Mexico's educational system. The Ley Organica de Instruccion Publica (the Organic Law of Public Instruction) of 1867 and of 1869, inspired by liberals and positivists (Solana et al., 1981), provided the basis for pragmatic, secular, and scientific teaching. Liberal education was even supported by Emperor Maximilian, to the dismay of the conservatives. In this climate, the first psychology course was inaugurated.

Its instigator and teacher, beginning in 1896, was Ezequiel Chavez, an enthusiastic and capable lawyer and philosopher and a self-educated psychologist, who was strongly influenced by Herbert Spencer, Théodule Ribot, William James, Edward B. Titchener, William J. McDougall, James Mark Baldwin, and Pierre Janet. In 1904, Chavez translated Titchener's *Elements of Psychology* into Spanish. In 1928, he published his *Ensayo de Psicologia de la Adolescencia,* probably the first book on the psychology of adolescence by a Spanish-speaking author. He is also well known for the first essay on the psychology of the Mexican (Chavez, 1901).

The Mexican Revolution of 1910

Positivism, which had been strongly supported during Porfirio Diaz's dictatorship, was widely attacked. Hernandez (1953) provides a good description of the philosophical ideas and attitudes toward education of the individuals who elaborated on the Mexican constitution of 1917. Those changes had a strongly anticlerical bias. Just prior to that time, Enrique O. Aragon had founded (in 1916) the first psychological laboratory at the National University of Mexico. It was a Wundtian laboratory with a psychiatrist as its leader. Jose Curiel (1962) states that this laboratory remained active for 30 years, and Miguel Cevallos (1953) reports that research was undertaken there on manual work, fatigue, and plethysmography. It is said that Pablo Boder, a disciple of Ivan Pavlov, conducted some studies in this laboratory in 1925.

Aragon, who wrote prolifically, died in 1942. He was preparing to publish his *Obras Completas* in ten volumes at the time, two of which appeared posthumously: *Trabajos de Neurologia y Psiquiatria* and *Historia del Alma.*

For many years, Aragon, Chavez, Roberto Solis Quiroga, and others made strenuous efforts to develop psychology as a major field of study in the Facultad de Filosofia y Letras of the National University of Mexico. In the meantime, as a result of the Second Mexican Congress of the Child in 1923, the Secretariat of Education became aware of the importance of psychology in education and a Department of Psychopedagogy and Hygiene was established. Later, in 1935, the Instituto Nacional de Psicopedagogia came into being, and much later, in 1971, it became the Instituto Nacional de Investigacion Educativa. Many capable teachers and psychologists labored there in the development and standardization of vocational and intelligence tests (Solana et al., 1981).

PSYCHOLOGY AS A CAREER

In 1937, a three-year course of study in psychology leading to the master's degree was established at the University of Mexico. But its psychological laboratory was still "brass instrumented." In 1939, Pascual Del Roncal (an expert on the Rorschach test), Jose Gaos and David Garcia Bacca (favorite disciples of Ortega y Gasset), and Eugenio Imaz, Eduardo Nicol, Juan Roura-Parella, and Joaquin Xirau (Spanish refugees), imported to Mexico Robin G. Coilingwood, Wilhelm Dilthey, Martin Heidegger, Edmund G. Husserl, Friedrich Schiller, Eduard Spranger, and Gestalt psychology.

In 1945, Fernando Ocaranza, a research physiologist, created the first autonomous Department of Psychology at the University of Mexico. In 1952, a PhD in psychology was instituted by Guillermo Davila, Robles, Del Roncal, and Jose Luis Curiel. In 1959, a four-year course leading to a professional psychology degree was approved. During the 1940s and 1950s, psychiatrists, psychoanalysts, lawyers, and philosophers on the faculty taught fundamental clinical, educational, phenomenological, and some industrial and statistical psychology. Among distinguished teachers during these decades were G. Davila, S. Ramirez, A. Fortes, M. Lopez Chaparro, R. Macias, R. Gonzalez Enriquez, E. Buentello, R. Herrera y Montes, J. Gomez Robleda, J. Peinado Altable, L. Vera, R. Solis Quiroga, A. Escobar, G. Herrera, C. Hereford, J. McGregor, A. Shore, and A. Zaar Vergara (Curiel, 1962).

In 1951, Robles, Werner Wolff, Manuel Falcon, and Rogelio Diaz-Guerrero founded the Interamerican Society of Psychology (SIP) in Mexico City. The Sociedad Mexicana de Psicologia (SMP) began simultaneously as a branch of the SIP. The SMP held congresses beginning in 1953 in Santo Domingo; and its 20th congress was scheduled for Quito, Ecuador, in 1983. The SIP is now the National Society of Psychology.

The 1960s and 1970s saw dramatic changes in the teaching, research, and practice of psychology in Mexico. Psychologists from the University of Texas and Mexican psychiatrists and psychologists from the National University of Mexico (UNAM) initiated a series of meetings in 1955. From 1959 well into the 1970s, groups of up to 100 Mexican psychology students visited the University of Texas departments of psychology and educational psychology for three to four weeks, to interact and attend classes, conferences, and seminars in many different fields of theoretical, experimental, and applied psychology (Holtzman et al., 1964; Holtzman, 1970).

In 1966, there was an internal academic revolution in the Colegio de Psicologia (UNAM). Younger teachers, many veterans of visits to the University of Texas, and active local students demanded radical changes in the outdated curriculum. An ambitious 4½-year program leading to a professional degree in psychology was instituted. In 1971, after further student and teacher visits to the University of Texas, and with the help of postgraduate students returning from Europe and the United States with advanced degrees, an equally ambitious, but better balanced program was inaugurated. Masters' and doctors' degrees were made available to selected students with interests in academic and research pursuits in clinical, experimental, and social psychology and the experimental analysis of behavior, and a paper defending advanced degrees was written by Lafarga (1975). Advanced professional specializations were offered in child development, clinical psychology, and group psychotherapy in institutions (Facultad de Psicologia, 1979–1980). The student population seeking the professional degree mushroomed from 200 in 1956 to 2,680 in 1972 and to more than 4,000 by 1982 (UNAM). Since 1960, more than 40 professional psychology degree programs have been inaugurated in Mexico (Polo & Iñesta, 1977). In 1973, the Colegio de Psicologia became an independent faculty of psychology.

The 1970s

Several events were notable in the 1970s. They included: (1) the return to Mexico of young graduates from the United States, Canada, and Europe, most holding the PhD degree, and sophisticated about psychology; (2) the receipt of the local doctoral degree by several mature, experienced teachers and/or researchers who had become so immersed in local activities that they did not seek the degree until many years after the termination of their studies; (3) the attainment of medium or, occasionally, high status in governmental and private enterprise by several graduates; (4) the greater importance placed by both state and private institutions on the technologies of psychology; (5) the granting by the International Society of Scientific Psychology (IUPsyS) to the SMP of responsibility for the organization of the 23rd International Congress of Psychology in 1984.

As a result, a veritable explosion of application, research, and teaching occurred. Not all of it was positive. Some, particularly small private institutions, inaugurated psychological programs without even moderately well-trained teaching personnel. The Consejo Nacional de la Enseñanza e Investigacion en Psicologia (CNEIP), with some internal problems of its own, became particularly preoccupied in arresting this unruly, not very professional, and even less scientific growth. Concurrently there was some disillusionment among psychologists about the relevance of psychology to social and economic problems. Finally, political ideologies sometimes induced exaggerated doubts, and even hostility, about the most common scientific methodologies and psychological techniques.

Among Mexican authors who have published about psychology in Mexico are Alvarez and Ramirez (1979), Cevallos (1953), Colotla and Gallegos (1978), Diaz-Guerrero (1966, 1974, 1976, 1979, 1981), Gallegos (1980), Meneses (1976), Ribes Iñesta (1968, 1975), and Rodriguez de Arizmendi (1971–1972).

Three surveys are pertinent to the psychological profession. The first, which surveyed 108 psychologists, was conducted in 1964 (Diaz-Guerrero, 1974). It showed that 70% of the psychologists had more than one place of employment. The main employment categories reported were counseling (40%), clinical psychology (25%), teaching of psychology (12%), research in psychology (9%), and industrial psychology (7%). In a survey carried out by Covarrubias de Levy in 1970, it was found that in the Federal District, 31% of the schools and 18% of the industries employed psychologists, while 36% of the schools and 25% of the industries consulted them. It was also found that the work done by psychologists in the schools was 81% counseling and 13% teaching, and that work in industry was 75% in personnel selection and 25% in general consulting services. In both Diaz-Guerrero's and Covarrubias de Levi's (1970) surveys, the income reported would place psychologists in the low middle class, for those who had only one place of employment or in the upper middle class for psychologists with more than one employer.

In Velasco Hernandez's (1978) survey of schools in Mexico, 68% of the schools were found to have eclectic teaching, 16% psychodynamic, 12% behavioral, and 4% humanistic. As for the preferred areas in the teaching of psychology, clinical psychology was number one, followed by educational, social, industrial, and developmental.

RESEARCH

As recently as 1973, most research in Mexico had been carried out through the efforts of two groups and their leaders, one in the field of neuropsychology and the other in the field of personality development and cross-cultural research. The first leader was Raul Hernandez Peon, who did research on sleep and dreaming, sensory-evoked potentials, and wakefulness and attention (Morgane, 1970). Another group formed around Diaz-Guerrero. A good part of this group's cross-cultural research dealt with child development, style of coping, and affective meaning. The group began in 1959, when four Mexican graduate students, led by Diaz-Guerrero, spent several months at the University of Texas, working closely with American psychologists on the problems of conducting research on personality in the two countries. In 1963, the Centro de Investigaciones en Ciencias del Comportamiento (CICC), at the Computer Center of UNAM, was founded by Diaz-Guerrero. In 1973, the CICC decentralized from the National University and became INCCAPAC (the Institute for Behavioral Sciences and Public Opinion, AC), a nonprofit research organization. Many books and articles have been published as a result of the efforts of INCCAPAC; for example, *Personality Development in Two Cultures, a Cross-Cultural Longitudinal Study of School Children in Mexico and in the United States,* by W. Holtzman and colleagues. Further details may be found in an article on INCCAPAC (Diaz-Guerrero, 1981).

The group began its cross-cultural studies with an awareness of the numerous side benefits (Diaz-Guerrero, 1964, 1969): (a) the opportunity to train hundreds of students in field work; (b) to provide data for theses; (c) to develop local and adapt foreign instruments for sociopsychological research and program evaluation in Mexico; (d) to develop baselines for many groups in the Mexican population; and (e) to begin building hypotheses and theory in harmony with the data and the people.

Another group participating in early behavioral research was formed by Guillermo Davila, Alfonso Millan, Michael Maccoby, and Erich Fromm. This group's major product was a volume by Fromm and Maccoby entitled *Social Character in a Mexican Village.*

Hernandez Peon, Diaz-Guerrero, and the Frommian group were all given fundamental support for their work by the Foundations' Fund for Research in Psychiatry. Much of the credit for the initial development of behavioral research in Mexico should go to the three groups of researchers, the Foundations' Fund for Research in Psychiatry, and the University of Texas. Several of the Texas researchers, particularly W. H. Holtzman, R. Peck, C. Hereford, P. Worchel, C. McGuire, and the Hogg Foundation for Mental Health, helped with consultation and advice.

Recent developments in psychological research are more difficult to assess. In the following, the researchers are classified in alphabetical order and by the broad psychological areas in which they are doing their work.

1. *Physiological psychology, neuropsychology, and psychopharmacology.* Victor Alcaraz, H. Brust, Luis Castro, Victor Colotla, Augusto Fernandez Guardiola, Jacobo Grinberg, Hector Lara Tapia, Armando Nava Rivera, Cesar Perez de Francisco, A. Salgado, and Rene Truker Colin.

2. *Action research, educational and social program evaluation.* Eduardo Almeida, Hector Ayala, Hector Manuel Cappello, Cathy Chism, Silvia Lara, Angeles Mata, Maria Teresa Patto, Horacio Quiroga, and Isabel Reyes Lagunes.

3. *Community psychology and mental health.* Ameida, Ayala, Victor Castillo Vales, Jose Cueli, Luis Antonio Gamiochipi, Maria Teresa Lartigue, Horacio Quiroga, and Rebeca Zimmerman.

4. *Criminological psychology and prisons' captive communities.* Benjamin Dominguez, Luis Antonio Gamiochipi, and Victor Garcia.

5. *Social psychology.* Almeida, Yolanda Avila, Cappello, Rolando Diaz Loving, Gilda Gomez Perez-Mitre, Sofia Liberman, Jose Medina Pichardo, Susana Pick de Leonard, Lucy Reidl, and Graciela Rodriguez de Arizmendi.

6. *Educational psychology.* Javier Aguilar, Roberto Alvarado, Blanca Alvarez, Victor Arrendondo, Fernando Garcia, Olga Loredo, Jorge Martinez Stack, Jorge Molina, Dolores Mercado, Ely Rayek, Isabel Reyes Lagnnes, and Juan Jose Sanchez Sosa.

7. *Clinical psychology and personality research.* Blanca Chavez, Jacqueline Fortes, Juan Lafarga, Tapia, Jose Lichtszajn, Raymundo Macias, Roberto Navarro, Ezequiel Nieto Cardoso, and Rafael Nuñez.

8. *Experimental analysis of behavior and applied experimental analysis of behavior.* Ayala, Arturo Bouzas, Luis Lara Tapia, Florente Lopez, Stack, Jorge Peralta, Rayek, and Emilio Ribes Iñesta.

9. *Cognition.* Jesus Figueroa, Serafin Mercado Domenech, and Araceli Otero.

10. *Child development.* Elda Alicia Alba Canto, Trinidad Berrum, S. Cram, Vincente Garcia, Isabel Reyes Lagunes, Alicia Marisela Velazquez Medina, and Zimmerman.

11. *Labor, industrial and organizational psychology.* Fernando Arias Galicia, Mauro Cardenas, Darvelio Castaño, Carlos Gomez Robledo, Rodolfo Gutierrez, German Herrera, Silvia Macotela, and Graciela Sanchez Bedoya.

TRAINING AND PRACTICE

Occasionally accounts have appeared dealing with a specific area of psychology (Ortega & Lopez, 1953; Nuñez, 1962; Castaño & Bedoya, 1978). Papers assessing the state of development of psychology in Latin America or the world, including Mexico, have been presented at the international level. It is likely that the earliest was by Carl Hereford (1966); others were by Ruben Ardila (1968, 1969, 1971a, 1971b), and by Morton Bertin (1974). Monographs and books have also appeared at the international level, including Henry David (1964) on *Clinical Psychology Around the World;* Ira Iscoe's *Mental Health in the Americas* (1972); and *A Bibliography of Psychology in Latin America* by Ruben Ardila and Gordon Finley (1975). This account of psychology in Mexico would be incomplete without mentioning the Chicano outgrowth (Padilla, 1980). The *Hispanic Journal of Behavioral Sciences* reports much of the product of Chicano psychology which is often relevant to psychology in Mexico. Trillas has published in Mexico, beginning in 1965, more than 200 translations, or originals in Spanish, updating psychology.

Mexican psychologists generally are not joiners. Nevertheless the SMP has maintained several hundred members and publishes a bulletin (*Boletin de la SMP*). There are several specialized psychological societies in Mexico, including the Society of Clinical Psychology, the Society of Behavioral Psychology, the Society of Industrial Psychology, and the Society of Psychologists in the Service of the Government. The CNEIP (Consejo Nacional para la Enseñanza e Investigacion en Psicologia) deserves special mention. It has 28 institutional members—mostly universities or institutes with departments or professional schools of psychology. Its editorial wing is responsible for the publication of *Enseñanza e Investigacion en Psicologia*. Several journals presenting psychological material began, and then disappeared after several issues. Among these were *Revista Psicologia, Medicina Psicosomatica, Hipnosis y Sofrologia, Journal de Psicologia, Revista Mexicana de la Investigacion Psicologica, Anuario de Psicologia,* and the *Revista Mexicana de Psicologia,* which, by 1971, had published five volumes. A journal called *Psicologia,* sold in bookstores, had a circulation of 7,000 copies in 1982. The Instituto Mexicano de Psiquiatria publishes *Salud Mental,* of interest to psychiatrists and clinical psychologists. Recently the Facultad de Psicologia of UNAM started to publish the *Acta Psicologica Mexicana,* and the Associacion Latinoamericana de Psicologia Social began its *Revista.*

Finally, the following lists departments or schools of psychology in Mexico: Department of Psychology, Universidad de las Americas; Escuela de Psicologia, Universidad Anahuac; Escuela de Psicologia, Universidad Autonoma de Coahuila; Escuela Libre de Psicologia, Universidad Autonoma de Chihuahua; Facultad de Ciencias de la Conducta, Universidad Autonoma del Estado de Mexico; Escuela de Psicologia, Universidad Autonoma del Estado de Morelos; Escuela de Psicologia; Escuela de Psicologia, Universidad Autonoma de Guadalajara; Departamento de Sociologia, Area de Psicologia Social, Universidad Autonoma Metropolitana—Unidad Ixtapalapa; Division de Ciencias Sociales y Humanidades, Carrera de Psicologia, Universidad Autonoma Metropolitana—Unidad Xochimilco; Area de Psicologia, Universidad Autonoma del Noreste; Facultad de Psicologia, Universidad Autonoma de Nuevo Leon; Escuela de Psicologia, Universidad Autonoma de Puebla; and Escuela de Psicologia, Universidad Autonoma de Queretaro.

Also: Departamento de Psicologia, Universidad Iberoamericana; Escuela de Psicologia, Universidad Intercontinental; Departamento de Psicologia, Universidad de Monterrey; Facultad de Psicologia, Universidad Nacional Autonoma de Mexico; Carrera de Psicologia, Escuela Nacional de Estudios Profesionales, Unidad Zaragoza, UNAM; Escuela de Psicologia, Universidad del Noreste; Escuela de Psicologia, Universidad Regiomontana; Facultad de Psicologia, Universidad Veracruzana; Escuela de Psicologia, Centro Universitario de Mazatlan; Departamento de Psicologia, Instituto Technologico y de Estudios Superiores de Monterrey, Unidad Estado de Mexico; Escuela de Psicologia, Instituto Technologico y de Estudios Superiores de Occidente; Departamento de Psicologia, Instituto Technologico de Sonora; Area de Psicologia, Instituto Universitario de Ciencias de la Educacion; and Escuela de Psicologia, Universidad de Yucatan.

Psychology in Mexico has undergone a veritable explosion since 1980. Rivera-Sierra and Urbina-Soria (1989), in a comprehensive statistical study, report that in 1964 only 5 deparments or schools of psychology were offering the licenciate (professional degree), 14 in 1970, and more than 20 in 1973, but there were 82 in 1987, with a total registration of 28,866 students. The licenciate in psychology demands nine semesters—six of basic subjects and three of specialization in one or another branch of psychology—and a dissertation. There is, however, little information regarding the policy and qualifications of the staff of the nonuniversity-affiliated private schools of psychology.

From various sources (Galindo, 1988; Montiel-Marques et al., 1989), it is clear that publication in psychology and research is done mostly in Mexico City, with the lion's share belonging to researchers at the National University of Mexico. To the many areas of research enumerated in the previous edition of this encyclopedia, the following can be added:

12. *History of Psychology.*   German Alvarez, Edgar Galindo, S. Jurado-Cardenas, Jorge Molina, Fermin Rivero del Pozo, Jesus Nieto, and particularly Pablo Valderrama-Iturbe.

13. *Ecological Psychology.*   German Alvarez, Serafin Mercado-Domenech, Maria E. Montero, Patricia Ortega-Andeane, and Javier Urbina-Soria.

14. *Health Psychology.*   Health psychology is an area soaring with activity (systematic information may be obtained from Graciela Rodriguez, Facultad de Psicologia, UNAM, Ciudad Universitaria, Mexico 20, D.F. and Maria Elena Medina-Mora, Instituto Mexicano de Psiquiatria, Antiguo Camino a Xochimilco #101, Mexico 21, D.F.). Alcaraz, Diaz-Loving, Maria E. Medina-Mora, Jorge Palacios-Venegas, Susana Pick de Weiss (erroneously called "de Leonard" in the first edition), the pioneer Graciela Rodriguez, and Sanchez-Sosa.

15. *Instructional Psychology.*   Original research is being done by Sandra Castanedo and Miguel Lopez and their colleagues and students.

The social impact of psychology in Mexico became prominent through therapeutic and rehabilitation efforts in the aftermath of the brutal 1985 earthquake. The journal *Revista Mexicana de Analisis de la Conducta* has appeared consistently for many years. The recent journals are *Revista Mexicana de Psicologia,* and *Revista de Psicologia Social y Personalidad.*

Many, if not most, cognitive, personality, and social psychology research psychologists in Mexico are conscious that the results of their studies are idiosyncratic. Articles by Diaz-Guerrero (1989; 1991) and Diaz-Guerrero and Diaz-Loving (1990) provide a conceptualization, the data, and some of the applications of a systematic ethnopsychology of cognition and personality. Beginning in the mid-1980s, a number of researchers actively contributed to this area, including, in alphabetical order, Laura Acuna, Patricia Andrade Palos, Rocio Avendano-Sandoval, Carlos A. Bruner, Mirta Flores-Galez, Celina Inmaculada Girardi, Luis Lara-Tapia, Jorge La Rosa, Susana Pick de Weiss, Isabel Reyes-Lagunes, Sofia Rivera-Aragon, Rosario Silva, and Jose Luis Valdez.

If there is one book that will demonstrate the excitement and preoccupation of Mexican psychologists with their science, it is

Urbina-Soria's edited book *El Psicologo, Formacion, Ejercicio Profesional, Prospectiva* (1989) (*The Psychologist, Profesional Practice, and prospective*). It illustrates in more than 60 articles the concerns of the leaders in Mexican psychology about their discipline and profession and the many ways they are trying to develop congruence between training and practice. Thus, although the student population of psychology has mushroomed across Mexico, its leaders are highly concerned about the future of their science and profession.

REFERENCES

Alvarez, G., & Ramirez, M. (1979). En busca del tiempo perdido. *Enseñanza e Investigacion en Psicologia, 5,* 386–391.

Ardila, R. (1968). Psychology in Latin America. *American Psychologist, 23,* 567–574.

Ardila, R. (1969). Desarrollo de la psicologia Latinoamericana. *Revista Latinoamericana de Psicologia, 1,* 63–71.

Ardila, R. (1971). A contecimientos importantes en la historia de la psicologia Latinoamericana. *Revista Interamericana de Psicologia, 5,* 1–11.

Ardila, R. (1971). *Los pioneros de la psicologia.* Buenos Aires: Paidos.

Ardila, R., & Finley, G. (1975). Psychology in Latin America: A bibliography [Special issue]. *Interamerican Journal of Psychology, 9.*

Bertin, M. A. (1974). *An overview of psychology in Latin America.* Department of the Navy, Office of Naval Research, Arlington, VA, ONR-35.

Castaño, D. A., & Sanchez Bedoya, G. (1978). Problemas de la importacion tecnologico-psicolaboral en los paises en desarrollo. *Revista Latinoamericana de Psicologia, 10,* 71–82.

Cevallos, M. A. (1953). La psicologia en Mexico en los ultimos cincuenta años. In Universidad Naciona Autonoma de Mexico (Ed.), *Memoria del Congreso Científico Mexicano,* Ciencias de la Educacion, Psicologia-Filosofia (Vol. 15, pp. 563–569). Mexico, D.F.

Chavez, E. A. (1901). Ensayo sobre los rasgos distintivos de la sensibilidad como factor del caracter mexicano. *Revista Positiva, 1,* 81–90.

Colotla, V. A., & Gallegos, X. (1978). La psicologia en Mexico. In R. Ardila (Ed.), *La profesion del psicologo.* Mexico, D.F.: Editorial Trillas.

Covarrubias de Levy, A. C. (1970). La realidad del psicologo mexicano. Estudio del mercado de trabajo de la psicologia en la industria y en escuelas del Distrito Federal. *Journal de Psicologia, 4,* 3–8.

Curiel, J. L. (1962). *El psicologo.* Mexico, D.F.: Libreria Porrua y Hnos.

David, H. P. (1964). *International resources in clinical psychology.* New York: McGraw-Hill.

Diaz-Guerrero, R. (1964). A research proposal submitted to the Foundations' Fund for Research in Psychiatry. *Anuario de Psicologia,* (Vol. III, 100–109). Universidad Nacional Autonoma de Mexico.

Diaz-Guerrero, R. (1966). Mexico. In S. Ross, I. Alexander, H. Basowitz, M. Werber, & P. O. Nicholas (Eds.), *International opportunities for advanced training and research in psychology.* Washington, DC: American Psychological Association.

Diaz-Guerrero, R. (1969). La enseñanza de la investigacion psicologica en Latinoamerica. Un paradigma. *Revista Latinoamericana de Psicologia, 3,* 5–36.

Diaz-Guerrero, R. (1974). El psicologo mexicano, ayer, hoy y mañana. *Memorias del Primer Congreso Mexicano de Psicologia.* Mexico, D.F.: Imprenta Universitaria, Universidad Nacional Autonoma de Mexico.

Diaz-Guerrero, R. (1976). Mexico. In V. S. Sexton & H. Misiak (Eds.), *Psychology around the world.* Monterey, CA: Brooks/-Cole.

Diaz-Guerrero, R. (1979). Mexico. In B. B. Wolman (Ed.), *International directory of psychology.* New York & London: Plenum.

Diaz-Guerrero, R. (1981). Momentos culminantes de la historia de la psicologia en Mexico. *Revista de Historia de la Psicologia* (Spain), *2,* 125–142.

Diaz-Guerrero, R. (1989). Una etnopsicologia mexicana. *Ciencia v Desarrollo, 15*(86), 69–85.

Diaz-Guerrero, R. (1991, February) *Mexican ethnopsychology: Pictures in an exhibition.* Lecture presented at the 20th annual meeting of the Society for Cross Cultural Research, Isla Verde, Puerto Rico.

Diaz-Guerrero, R., & Diaz-Loving, R. (1990). Interpretation in cross-cultural personality assessment. In C. R. Reynolds & R. W. Kamphaus (Eds.), *Handbook of psychological and educational assessment of children: Personality, behavior, and context* (pp. 491–523). New York: Guilford.

Diaz-Guerrero, R., & Diaz-Loving R. (1990). *La etnopsicologia Mexicana. El centro de la corriente.* Revista de pivulgacion y culture psicologica, Universidad Nacional Autonoma de Mexico.

Galindo, E. (1988). La psicologia Mexicana a traves de sus obras, 1959–1987. *Revista Mexicans de Psicologia, 5*(2), 183–202.

Gallegos, X. (1980). James M. Baldwin's visits to Mexico. *American Psychologist, 35,* 772–773.

Hereford, C. F. (1966). Current status of psychology in Latin America. *Latin American Research Review, 1,* 97–108.

Hernandez, O. A. (1953). Las ideas sociales, politicas y juridicas del constituyente de 1917 en materia educativa. In Universidad Nacional Autonoma de Mexico (Ed.), *Memoria del Congreso Científico Mexicano* (Vol. 15). Mexico, D.F.: Ciencias de la Educacion, Psicologia-Filosofia.

Holtzman, W. H. (1970). Los seminarios internacionales de Texas. Un experimento continuo de intercambio transcultural en psicologia. *Revista Interamericana de Psicologia, 4,* 279–282.

Holtzman, W. H., Iscoe, I., & Ned, J. W. (1964). Final report—Mexican Psychology Students Seminar, January 5–25, 1964. Austin, TX: University of Texas Press.

Iscoe, I. (1972). Mental health in the Americas [Special issue]. *Interamerican Journal of Psychology, 6,* 1–2.

Lafarga, J. (1975). ¿Por que programas de grado en psicologia en Mexico? *Enseñanza e Investigacion en Psicologia, 1,* 77–84.

Meneses, E. (1976). Veinticinco años de enseñanza de la psicologia en la Universidad Iberoamericana 1950–1975. *Enseñanza e Investigacion en Psicologia, 2,* 122–127.

Montiel-Marquez, M., Colotia-Espinosa, V., & Escalante-Davila, E. (1989). El posgrado y la investigacion en psicologia en Mexico. In J. Urbina-Soria (Ed.), *El psicologo, formacion, ejercicio profesional, prospective.* Mexico City: UNAM.

Morgane, P. J. (1970). Raul Hernandez Peon (1924–1968). *Physiology and Behavior, 5,* 379–388.

Núñez, R. (1962). *Problemas psicosociales de la prolesion de la psicologia clinica en Mexico.* Mexico, D.F.: Núñez.

Ortega, P., & Lopez, M. (1953). La medición psicologica en México. In Universidad Nacional Autonoma de México (Ed.), *Memoria del Congreso Cientifico Méxicano,* Ciencias de la Educación, Psicologia, Fifosofia (Vol. 15). Mexico, D.F.

Padilla, A. M. (1980). Notes on the history of Hispanic psychology. *Hispanic Journal of the Behavioral Sciences, 2*(2), 109–128.

Ribes-Iñesta, E. (1968). Psychology in Mexico. *American Psychologist, 23,* 565–566.

Ribes-Iñesta, E. (1975). Some recent developments in psychology in Mexico. *American Psychologist, 30,* 774–776.

Robles, O. (1952). Panorama de la psicologiá en México, pasado y presente. *Filosofiá y Letras, 23,* 239–263.

Rodriguez de Arizmendi, G. (1971/1972). L'enseignement universitaire de la psychologie au Mexique. *Bulletin de Psychologie, 294,* 25, 38–44.

Solana, F., Cardiel Reyes, R., & Bolaños Martinez, R. (Eds.). (1981). *Historia de la educacion publica en Mexico.* Mexico, D.F.: Fondo de Cultura Economica.

Urbina-Sorbia, J. (1989). *El Psicologo, formacion, ejercicio profesional, prospective.* Mexico City: Universidad Nacional Autonoma de Mexico.

R. Diaz-Guerrero
University of Mexico at Mexico City

MEYER, ADOLF (1866–1950)

Adolf Meyer attended medical school in Zurich. Unable to find a university position in Europe, he emigrated to the United States and took a position as pathologist at the state hospital in Kankakee, Illinois, in 1893. He later became professor of psychiatry at Cornell Medical College in New York City. In 1909 he was invited by G. Stanley Hall to participate in the celebration of the 20th anniversary of the founding of Clark University, along with Freud and Jung. The remainder of his career was spent at the Phipps Clinic in Baltimore.

Meyer is best known for his theory of psychobiology, which emphasized the importance of a biographical study in understanding an individual's personality in all its aspects. He considered each person a biological unit that always functioned, whether alone or in a group. Because of the complexity of the human personality, the psychiatrist must study the individual from various aspects: medical, biographical, artistic, and educational. He stressed an objective approach to the understanding of a person based on biological, social, and psychological forces. Furthermore, the psychiatrist must study both normal and abnormal behavior from these various perspectives. Meyer opposed those theories of personality which made use of abstract and fictional constructs in favor of a common-sense approach.

In making a psychiatric diagnosis, argued Meyer, the physician must examine the patient's life history (biographical approach) and his present personality traits as well as his physical, neurological, and genetic conditions, in order to formulate a plan for therapy. Psychobiological therapy started with an evaluation of the person's assets and liabilities. This involved an examination of the life history. The psychiatrist started by examining a patient's better self. The general aim of the entire therapy was to help a person, hampered by abnormal conditions, to make the best adjustment possible to life and change. Rather than stressing unconscious processes as Freud had done, Meyer felt that a person's problems should be approached at the conscious level. This involved a face-to-face contact to implement the psychiatrist's efforts to focus on the current situation and reactions to everyday difficulties, as well as the patient's long-term life adjustment. In the process of therapy the person was led to modify unhealthy adjustments. Meyer called this habit training. It involved the use of guidance, suggestion and reeducation.

Meyer remained for 32 years at the Phipps Clinic, which became a world-renowned center for the training of psychiatrists. While at the clinic he became acquainted with John B. Watson, who was director of the psychological laboratory from 1913 to 1920, and 10 years later with W. Horsley Gantt, who established the Pavlovian laboratory there.

R. W. Lundin
Wheaton, Illinois

MILGRAM, STANLEY (1933–1984)

Stanley Milgram received the PhD in social psychology from Harvard in 1960. Using an auditory judgment task rather than the visual judgment task of the original Solomon Asch studies, Milgram compared the conformity levels of Norwegians and Frenchmen and found Norwegians to be the more conforming.

His best-known studies were on the dynamics of obedience to authority. In these studies, a subject was commanded to give increasingly higher voltages of electric shock to a learner, every time the latter gave a wrong answer on a verbal-learning task. The learner was an actor who feigned increasingly intense suffering with increases in shock levels. Milgram found an unexpectedly high rate of obedience. Milgram conducted more than 20 variations of this basic experiment. A full report of his research program on obedience to authority is found in *Obedience to Authority: An Experimental View,* which has been translated into 11 languages.

From the beginning, the obedience studies were embroiled in controversy—praised by some, vilified by others. Much of the controversy had to do with the ethics of deceiving participants into believing that they may have harmed an innocent human being (e.g., Baumrind, 1964; Kelman, 1967; Milgram, 1964, 1977b). For an exploration of ethical issues raised by these experiments, see Miller (1986).

The obedience work became one of the best-known pieces of research in the social sciences. The 1963 report became a citation classic in 1981 (Milgram, 1981) and has been reprinted in dozens of anthologies.

Milgram went on to make a number of other original contributions. The following are brief summaries of the principal ones: In 1970 Milgram published the article "The experience of living in cities," in which he introduced the concept of overload as a way to understand urban/rural differences in social behavior. In 1965, Milgram and colleagues (Milgram, 1969; Milgram, Mann, & Harter, 1965) introduced an unobtrusive way of measuring community attitudes and opinions. They scattered 400 "lost letters" throughout New Haven—on sidewalks, in phone booths, on car windshields. One hundred each were addressed to Friends of the Nazi Party, Friends of the Communist Party, Medical Research Associates, and a Mr. Walter Carnap. While a majority of the latter two were mailed, only a minority of the first two were. This technique is the most widely used nonreactive measure of attitudes.

In 1967, Milgram introduced a technique for studying the small-world phenomenon, the not-uncommon situation of meeting someone in, say, San Francisco who happens to know one's first cousin in Toronto. In the small-world method, a sample of starters are each given a packet that needs to reach a designated stranger, the target person, in another city, with the limitation that each person can send it to only someone he or she knows on a first-name basis. Milgram found that among completed chains it typically required only a small number of intermediaries—averages ranged from 4.4 to 5.9—for the mailing to reach the target. The technique is an important tool of social-network researchers (Kadushin, 1989).

An integrative review of the whole corpus of Milgram's work can be found in Blass (1992). An updated version of most of Milgram's published writings has been published (Sabini & Silver, 1992). A symposium exploring Milgram's contributions to social psychology was conducted at the annual convention of the American Psychological Association in Boston in 1990 (Blass, 1990).

STAFF

MILITARY PSYCHOLOGY

Military psychology is generally defined as the application of psychological principles and methods to military needs. That is, military psychology is not so much a separate field of psychology, but rather is defined by its area of application: military personnel and organizations. Military psychologists may be uniformed service members serving on active duty, civilian employees of the Department of Defense (DoD) or the military services, or civilian contractors hired by the DoD or military services. Military psychologists work in a variety of settings. Some are uniformed clinical psychologists who work in hospitals or are assigned to military units. Other uniformed psychologists are researchers and/or teachers at one of the military academies. Civilian military psychologists are typically researchers who are employed by one of the major DoD or specific service laboratories or are contractors who do business with those laboratories. Military psychologists, both uniformed and civilian, are often called upon to assist military policy makers by providing information about the behavioral consequences of the decisions they may wish to make.

A BRIEF HISTORY

Most scholars agree that military psychology began during World War I. Robert M. Yerkes, then the president of the American Psychological Association, organized the leading psychologists of the day to assist with the war effort. Under his direction, a massive selection program was developed to screen millions of men for military service based on their mental suitability. The Army Examinations Alpha (for those who could read English) and Beta (for those who were not literate in English) developed for this purpose were the forerunners of the group paper-and-pencil mental testing that flourished in American psychology following the war. During WWII, most of American psychology was consumed with the war effort, and military psychology expanded its assessment and selection programs and moved into new areas such as training and ergonomics as well.

ASSESSMENT, SELECTION, AND ASSIGNMENT

Since WWI, military psychology has led the way in developing mass assessment and assignment technology. Continued development of assessment technology during WWII and afterward laid the groundwork for the postwar development of civilian assessment programs and organizations in education and industry such as the Educational Testing Service. Assessment is still the strong suit of military psychology today. The U.S. Army's "Project A/ Building the Career Force" has produced new tests that measure psychomotor and motivational attributes as well as general cognitive ability, thereby permitting the military services to select and assign people to more nearly optimize their performance on military jobs.

The U.S. Navy's pioneering research on computerized adaptive testing during the last three decades has led the way in measuring these attributes more accurately, making the selection and assignment process far more efficient. For example, it is now possible for military recruiters to estimate accurately a potential recruit's general cognitive suitability for military service in about ten minutes or less, using the Computerized Adaptive Screening Test (CAST). By comparison, the paper and pencil version of this screening test takes about 40 minutes to administer, not including the time necessary to hand-score the answer sheet.

TRAINING AND SIMULATION

Prior to WWII, military training was conducted according to the apprenticeship model. During the war, military psychologists developed systematic training and training effectiveness evaluation methods. Since then, military psychology has made major innovations and contributions to instructional systems design, the teaching of basic skills (e.g., mathematics) and military/technical skills (e.g., flight training and electronics), distance learning technology, and the integration of simulators into the training process. Today, the Army's Simulation, Training, and Instrumentation Command is devoted to the development of highly realistic, simulation based training for individuals and teams through the use of computer-simulated operational scenarios and technologies such as virtual reality. In addition to providing realistic training, determining the frequency of refresher training needed to optimize skill retention is a major area of investigation for military psychologists. Based on this research, military psychologists were able to tell policy makers how frequently critical tasks, such as mine detection, would need to be retrained during recent operations in Bosnia and Kosovo. Because the military conducts its operations in units, collective training is a key area of research, development, and application for military psychologists.

The military services constantly seek new ways to improve human performance by identifying new skills and developing new training techniques. Military psychologists must carefully evaluate the validity of such new approaches. For example, the U.S. Army, through a contract with the National Research Council (NRC), asked prominent behavioral scientists to determine the potential of popularized New Age techniques, such as neural linguistic programming and paranormal phenomena, for enhancing human performance. After carefully studying the issues over several years, the panel of experts concluded that many of these New Age techniques had little or no value for training or otherwise enhancing human performance.

HUMAN FACTORS AND ERGONOMICS

Human factors/ergonomics concerns the interrelationships between people and their machines and environments. The human factors/ergonomics area within military psychology began primarily with the study and design of person-machine interfaces, particularly with respect to cockpits and information displays. Since the mid-1970s, through such formal programs as the U.S. Army's MANPRINT, military psychologists have incorporated a consideration of human characteristics and abilities in designing, developing, and operating military equipment.

MILITARY SOCIAL PSYCHOLOGY

By studying the military as a unique social organization within its parent society, military psychologists have informed debates on several military-social issues in the United States, Canada, and some European countries as well. For example, military psychologists provided information on how attitudes, beliefs, and likely behaviors might effect the acceptance of homosexual individuals in the military services of the United States, Canada, and the Netherlands. Similarly, military psychologists have investigated attitudes and beliefs surrounding the integration of women into the U.S. military, particularly in combat roles, and they have conducted experiments in gender-integrated basic military training that demonstrated the feasibility of such training. More recently, military psychologists have played a significant role in studying the incidence of and potential causes for sexual harassment within the U.S. military services.

MILITARY CLINICAL PSYCHOLOGY

Like their civilian counterparts, military clinical psychologists provide a variety of clinical services to service members and their families. However, unlike civilian psychologists, a military clinical psychologist is first and foremost a military service member whose primary obligation is to ensure that service members are fit to perform their military duties. Military psychologists are often called upon to diagnose problem individuals, who are referred by a commanding officer, to determine their fitness for continued service. They may also participate as part of a team of evaluators in determining the suitability of service members for certain types of assignments or training, such as Special Forces. They may serve as part of a team in a large medical center or as part of a deployed unit to deal with stress and other mental health issues, or may help develop psychological profiles of world leaders as part of an intelligence-gathering unit.

Military psychologists also counsel service members for self-referred adjustment problems. Being a service member can produce ethical dilemmas for the military clinical psychologist conducting such counseling. For example, if a service member client reveals, in the course of counseling, that he or she has violated military regulations or laws, the military psychologist is obliged as a military officer to report such behavior. In so doing, the military psychologist will violate the professional ethic that demands confidentiality and may be censured by the American Psychological Association.

Military psychology has also become the testing ground for innovative ideas in clinical psychology, such as permitting specially trained military clinical psychologists to prescribe psychotropic drugs. An estimated 20 to 30% of combat casualties require psychological interventions. About 75% of those casualties can be returned to duty within about three days if properly treated with appropriate psychological interventions, including drugs such as sedatives. Because of this, the Department of Defense was ordered by the U.S. Congress to conduct a test training program for psychologists to prepare them to prescribe such drugs. This test was known as the Psychopharmacology Demonstration Project (PDP). Only a few psychologists were selected for and completed the training and, although the program was a success, the General Accounting Office felt that such a training program would not be cost effective. However, the success of the PDP paved the way for similar training programs for clinical psychologists in the civilian realm, where such training is likely to be more cost effective.

LEADERSHIP AND ORGANIZATIONAL PSYCHOLOGY

Leadership continues to be a prime interest and research focus for military psychologists. Social-demographic and geopolitical changes in the world together with the technological revolution of the information age have produced new demands on leadership skills. Modern military leaders must lead in distributed electronic communications environments, often without face-to-face contact with those they lead. They must be politically sensitive and able to deal effectively with an electronic medium that watches over their shoulders as they perform politically sensitive peacekeeping or dangerous combat missions. Military psychology must grapple with how best to develop such leaders.

Military psychologists must also deal with related organizational issues such as commitment, cohesion, morale, and increasingly, military families. Military cohesion, the emotional bonding among members of a military unit, has been shown to affect group and individual performance, job and military satisfaction, retention, well-being, readiness, and discipline. Family well-being and its influence on soldier performance and retention has become a focus for research and interventions by military psychologists in many countries. Such issues have become particularly important as many of the world's military services move from conscription to volunteer systems. In peace, as in war, military psychology continues to provide vital services to society and to the men, women, and families who serve in the world's military services.

SUGGESTED READING

Cronin, C. (1998). *Military psychology: An introduction.* Needham Heights, MA: Simon & Schuster.

Driskell, J. E., & Olmstead, B. (1989). Psychology and the military: Research applications and trends. *American Psychologist, 44,* 43–54.

Gal, R., & Mangelsdorf, A. D. (1991). *Handbook of military psychology.* New York: Wiley.

Jeffrey, T. B., Rankin, R. J., & Jeffrey, L. K. (1992). In service of two masters: The ethical-legal dilemma faced by military psychologists. *Professional Psychology: Research and Practice, 23,* 91–95.

Mangelsdorf, A. D. (1999). Military cohesion [Special issue]. *Military Psychology, 11,* 1–128.

Sands, W. A., Waters, B. K., & McBride, J. R. (1997). *Computerized adaptive testing: From inquiry to operation.* Washington, DC: American Psychological Association.

Stouffer, S. A., Lumsdaine, A. A., Lumsdaine, M. H., Williams, R. M., Jr., Smith, M. B., Janis, I. L., Star, S. A., & Cottrell, L. S., Jr. (1949). *The American soldier: Volume 2. Combat and its aftermath.* Princeton, NJ: Princeton University Press.

Swets, J. A., & Bjork, R. A. (1990). Enhancing human performance: An evaluation of "new age" techniques considered by the U.S. Army. *Psychological Science, 1,* 85–96.

P. A. GADE
U.S. Army Research Institute

APPLIED RESEARCH
LEADERSHIP TRAINING

AUTHOR NOTE
The views, opinions, and/or findings contained in this article are solely those of the author and should not be construed as an official Department of the Army or Department of Defense position, policy, or decision, unless so designated by other official documentation.

MILLER ANALOGIES TEST

The Miller Analogies Test consists of 100 verbal analogy items (A:B::C:D) drawn from a wide range of academic areas. It is a highly regarded test, with reasonably substantial prediction of the academic success of potential students in a variety of departments in graduate schools. It measures verbal and reasoning ability and has the technical characteristics of being able to differentiate among high-ability students of varying potential. The test has been shown to predict graduate school grades in a broad range of areas, and seems to serve this purpose as well as any predictor available except for those fields involving considerable quantitative material. This test has been the subject of considerable research to support its claims. The Miller Analogies Test was carefully constructed, and access to it is strictly controlled. It has a high level of difficulty, and good aids to help users interpret the scores on the test.

J. W. ASHER
Purdue University

INTELLIGENCE MEASURES

MILLER, NEAL E. (1909–   )

Neal Elgar Miller (born in Milwaukee, WI, August 3, 1909), professor emeritus of Rockefeller University since 1981 and research affiliate at Yale University since 1985, was the first psychologist to receive the National Medal of Science, the nation's highest award for scientific achievement. On February 8, 1965, President L. Johnson presented Miller with the medal, citing him: "For sustained and imaginative research on principles of learning and motivation and illuminating behavioral analysis of the effects of direct electrical stimulation of the brain."

After receiving his MA at Stanford University in 1932, Miller came to the Institute of Human Relations at Yale University where he got involved in applications of experimental psychology techniques to the study of psychiatric patients. At Yale he was also strongly influenced by C. L. Hull, applying principles of Pavlov's conditioning to Thorndike's trial-and-error learning. In 1935 he received his Yale PhD and became interested in the process of the acquisition of neuroses and psychotherapy as phenomena of learning. Miller went through psychoanalytical training in Vienna in 1935–36 in Freud's laboratory and later visited Pavlov's laboratory in the USSR in order to test the different hypotheses experimentally; he became an active proponent of a Pavlovian approach toward the study of higher nervous functions.

During World War II Miller served as an officer in charge of psychological research for the Army Air Corps, where his unit was responsible for developing some of the first tests for the selection of pilots and objective measures of flying skill.

In 1950, when Miller became full professor of psychology at Yale, his interest shifted to the use of a variety of behavioral, physiological, and pharmacological techniques to study mechanisms of motivation and reward. In 1953, with W. Roberts and J. Delgado, Miller performed the first experiments to demonstrate trial-and-error learning, or operant conditioning, motivated by direct stimulation of the brain. With other coworkers he studied electrical brain stimulation, eliciting eating and drinking and displaying motivational properties of a drive such as hunger or thirst. In other experiments they had shown that eating could be elicited by adrenergic stimulation and drinking by cholinergic stimulation.

Investigating whether visceral responses, such as salivation, heart rate, and blood pressure, could be modified by operant conditioning, Miller started a new chapter in the study of visceral conditioning and stress which became a fundamental problem of his new Laboratory of Physiological Psychology at The Rockefeller University, to which he moved in 1966. The general goal of the Miller lab was to coalesce recent advances in the behavioral sciences, neurophysiology, and molecular biology into a unified approach in order to understand how the brain controls behavior. In this direction his laboratory made a crucial contribution toward clinical psychophysiology and biofeedback research, and Miller became senior member of the group which founded the Society for Neuroscience, currently an organization of over 28,000 biomedical scientists and researchers.

In an article in *Science* (July, 1980) describing the emergence of behavioral medicine, it is written that "the most direct precursor of behavioral medicine is psychosomatic medicine, a field based on psychoanalytic theories about disease etiology which grew up in the 1950s and 1960s" and that "schism developed in the field between those who were psychoanalytically oriented and the basic scientists whose roots were in psychobiology. It was the latter group that broke off to define the field of behavioral medicine." This development also mirrors the evolution of Miller's attitudes toward psychogenic and neurogenic pathogenesis of neuroses and some somatic diseases. Miller pioneered the application of learning theory to behavioral therapy and the use of chemical and electrical stimulation to analyze the brain's mechanisms of behavior, homeostasis, and reinforcement.

Miller has won many awards and held outstanding offices and advisory posts. President of the APA in 1960–61, he was elected the second president of the Society for Neuroscience (1971–72), and then became the first president of the Academy of Behavioral Medicine Research (1979–80) and of the Biofeedback Society of America (1980–81).

In 1961 Miller was appointed by President J. F. Kennedy to serve as chairman of the Behavioral Sciences section in the Life Sciences Panel of the President's Science Advisory Committee. This panel produced a paper on research and science policy which was widely distributed and influential.

Earlier, in 1959, the APA honored Miller with its Distinguished Scientific Contribution Award, citing him as follows: "For his sustained and imaginative research on the basic principles of learning. Through brilliantly conceived and skillfully executed experiments, he and his students have served as a major spearhead in the current breakthrough in the area of motivation and learning. The importance of his research in extending knowledge is matched by its importance in stimulating the research of others. His influence has been greatly enhanced by his clear reports and reviews, in which he is never afraid to point out the broad implications of his results. In every respect, he is a fortunate model to set before budding young psychologists."

In the field of applied psychophysiology and biofeedback, Miller's early work with animals did more than any other single factor to arouse the interest and focus the attention of the scientific community on the new field of biofeedback. In the late 1960s Miller conducted a series of studies in which he taught curarized rats to control such visceral responses of the autonomic nervous system as blood flow, heartbeat, and stomach contractions. Miller believed that if visceral responses could be made "visible", it would be possible to apply instrumental learning to control and modify them. His dramatic research on the self-regulatory control of blood pressure in quadriplegic patients, with B. Brucker, rendered it highly probable that autonomic response systems in human beings could be controlled through biofeedback or operant conditioning without the mediating of the somatic musculature. In 1972, Miller's work was the subject of a two-part *New Yorker* magazine profile by Gerald Jonas, later published as a book, *Visceral Learning: Toward a Science of Self-Control.*

A member of the National Academy of Sciences since 1958, Miller was elected to senior membership in its Institute of Medicine in 1983. He is a fellow of the American Philosophical Society and of the New York Academy of Sciences, which elected him an honorary life member in 1976, and an honorary fellow of the British Psychological Society and the Spanish Psychological Society, among others.

Miller has served on the editorial boards of *Science* and a number of other journals and is the author of over 260 scholarly papers, coauthor of the volumes *Frustration and Aggression* (1939), *Social Learning and Imitation* (1941), and *Personality and Psychotherapy* (1950), and the author of *Graphic Communications and the Crisis in Education* (1957), and of *Selected Papers* (1971).

Miller has been awarded honorary Doctor of Science degrees at numerous universities, including the University of Uppsala, Sweden (1977), where he was presented in front of the king as part of the celebration of the university's 500th year.

Miller has also been a great teacher of his craft; a number of his students have gone on to make significant contributions to the fields of behavioral medicine and biofeedback. For example, J. Weiss has shown clearly that digestive system lesions can be produced by stress in rats; P. Cowings has developed a biofeedback technique for the control of the nausea associated with motion sickness; and B. Brucker has carried out significant work in the use of biofeedback for the rehabilitation of movement after injury to the central nervous system.

STAFF

MILLON CLINICAL MULTIAXIAL INVENTORY (MCMI)

This inventory, developed by Theodore Millon in 1977, utilized as its model the Minnesota Multiphasic Personality Inventory (MMPI), seeking to improve upon its forerunner by minimizing its limitations and introducing theoretical advances and modern psychometric innovations (Butcher & Owen, 1978; Korchin & Schuldberg, 1981).

Including 175 self-descriptive statements, it is linked both to the clinical theory presented in Millon's *Modern Psychopathology and Disorders of Personality,* and to the *Diagnostic and Statistical Manual of Mental Disorders (Third Edition).* A special effort was made to distinguish the more enduring personality pattern of a patient, recorded on Axis II of the *DSM,* from the patient's more acute clinical syndrome, noted on Axis I in a *DSM-III* diagnosis.

The 20 clinical scales, composed of 16 to 47 overlapping items, fall into four major categories: Basic Personality Patterns (Axis II); Pathological Personality Syndromes (Axis II); Moderate Clinical Syndromes (Axis I); and Severe Clinical Syndromes (Axis I).

Validation was an integral element of construction. In addition to programs for rapid machine scoring of answer forms, a computer-synthesized interpretive report that integrates both personological and symptomatic features of the patient is available. In line with current psychodiagnostic thinking, the interpretive report follows a multiaxial framework of assessment.

REFERENCES

Butcher, J. N., & Owen, P. L. (1978). Objective personality inventories. In B. B. Wolman (Ed.), *Clinical diagnosis of mental disorders.* New York: Plenum.

Korchin, S. J., & Schuldberg, D. (1981). The future of clinical assessment. *American Psychologist, 36,* 1147–1158.

Millon, T. (1977). *Millon clinical multiaxial inventory manual.* Minneapolis, MN: National Computer Systems.

T. MILLON
University of Miami

MINNESOTA MULTIPHASIC PERSONALITY INVENTORY (MMPI)
PERSONALITY ASSESSMENT

MILNER, BRENDA L. (1918–   )

Brenda L. Milner, née Langford, attended Withington Girls' School and Newnham College, Cambridge. While at Cambridge, she studied experimental psychology under Oliver Zangwill, whom she credits with inspiring her interest in human brain function.

The outbreak of World War II found Milner at Newnham College, doing graduate work. As the work of the Cambridge Psychological Laboratory shifted to applied research in the war effort, Milner became involved in designing tests to be used in the selection of air crew members, and later in examining and evaluating different methods of radar display and control.

After her marriage to Peter Milner in 1944 she moved to Montreal and, because of her ability to speak French fluently, obtained a teaching position at the University of Montreal. Milner's influence was felt immediately by the newly formed Institut de Psychologie, where she taught comparative and experimental psychology in its formative years. While maintaining this position, she began PhD studies at McGill University and obtained the PhD in 1952.

Milner's doctoral thesis explored the intellectual effects of temporal lobe damage in humans, and was the beginning of a gradually expanding study of memory disorders. More recently, her work has explored the effect of brain lesions or injury on cerebral organizations. In 1971–1972 Milner returned to Cambridge for a year and earned the ScD degree. Presently, she holds the position of professor of psychology in the Department of Neurology and Neurosurgery at McGill.

STAFF

MIND/BODY PROBLEM

For centuries, scholars have struggled to define the nature of the human being. One of the key questions in this struggle deals with mind, body, and the relationship between them.

There is general agreement that the term "body" refers to the material, physical characteristics of the organism, the activities of which can be studied by the traditional empirical methods of science. There is also general agreement that having a body is at least a part of the nature of being human.

It is the mind (psyche, soul)—the question of whether such an entity exists, and how to define it—that is the crux of the mind/body problem. For some thinkers, the immediate experience of self-awareness constitutes evidence that mind is qualitatively different from the physiological body. At one extreme, the term "mind" or "mental" has been defined as a non-physical, non-corporeal entity. Such an entity would not necessarily function according to the same laws as would matter. Its existence would thus logically permit acknowledgment of the possibilities of life after death, extrasensory perception, and other non-material phenomena.

Being non-material and non-physical, the mind cannot be verified or studied by means of input from the physical senses. This feature of mind causes the mind-body problem for those who would study human behavior by empirical methods.

In the interest of solving this dilemma, scholars have made three major approaches to defining mind in a different manner. The first is one of extreme reductionism. From this viewpoint, mind per se does not exist: It is simply a label for a particular level of biological functioning—specifically, the activity of the brain and nervous system.

The second approach tries in some way to relate the qualitatively unlike mind and body by learning about the former from empirical knowledge of the latter. This approach is typically illustrated by inferences concerning the nature of mental activities by observing and correlating characteristics of externally observable behavior. Such an approach, however, leaves the psychologist with the problem of evolving a means for relating the internal activity of the mind to the physically observable behavior of the body.

The third approach is in some ways similar to reductionism, but is not as simplistic. In this perspective, neither mind nor body is viewed as being an independent entity. Instead, the human being is viewed as a single composite of mind and body, neither of which has existence without the other. Such viewpoints have come to be called "double aspect."

The defining characteristic of this attempt to solve the mind-body problem depends upon whether the particular definition of the mind aspect best lends itself to study of the mind by the method of rationalism, the method of empiricism, or some combination of the two. Thus, the necessity for interpreting psychological and be-havioral data in terms of their correlates with the laws of physics and biology (instead of by independent laws of their own) will de-pend upon the nature of mind and its relationship, if any, to body.

Without being explicit as to their particular philosophical posi-tions on the mind-body problem, neuropsychologists collectively tend to use methodology by which they correlate either brain ac-tivity, loci, or patterns with observable behavior, verbal or other-wise. The phenomenal scope of development of modern technol-ogy (including MRI, CT scan, etc.) has broadened the range and complexity of behavior comprising the study of neuropsychology.

M. E. REUDER

PSYCHOLOGY AND PHILOSOPHY

MINNESOTA MULTIPHASIC PERSONALITY INVENTORY (MMPI-2)

The most widely researched and used clinical assessment instru-ment is the Minnesota Multiphasic Personality Inventory (MMPI-2). The MMPI was originally published in the 1940s to assess men-tal health problems in psychiatric and medical settings, and it rapidly became a standard personality instrument in a wide variety of settings (Hathaway and McKinley, 1940). The popularity of the true-false personality inventory was due in large part to its easy-to-use format and to the fact that the scales have well established validity in assessing clinical symptoms and syndromes (Butcher, 1999). The MMPI underwent a major revision in the 1980s, result-ing in two forms of the test—an adult version, the MMPI-2 (Butcher et al., 1989) and an adolescent form, MMPI-A, (Butcher et al., 1992). The MMPI-2 is a 567-item inventory comprised of symptoms, beliefs, and attitudes in adults above age 18. The MMPI-A is a 467-item version that is used for assessing young people from ages 14 to 18. This discussion will only address the MMPI-2.

ASSESSING PROTOCOL VALIDITY

Some people in some settings, when taking psychological tests, are motivated to present themselves in ways that do not disclose accu-rate information about themselves. For example, in cases where a person is being tested to determine sanity in a pretrial criminal evaluation, the person might be exaggerating symptoms. The ini-tial step in MMPI-2 profile interpretation is the important one of determining whether the client has cooperated with the testing and responded in a frank, open manner. A number of indices are avail-able on the MMPI-2 to aid the clinician in determining whether the client's item responses provide key personality information, or whether they are simply reflecting response sets or deceptive moti-vational patterns that disguise the true feelings and motivations of the client (Baer, Wetter, Nichols, Greene, & Berry, 1995). Several validity scales have been developed to evaluate the client's ap-proach to the test. Four of these assessment strategies will be de-scribed here.

The L Scale

The L scale is a measure of the client's willingness to acknowledge personal faults or problems. Individuals who score high on this scale are presenting an overly favorable picture of themselves. High scorers are claiming virtue not found among people in general. The L scale is particularly valuable in situations like personnel screen-ing or some types of court cases, because people in those settings try to put their best foot forward and present themselves as "bet-ter" adjusted than they really are.

The K Scale

The K scale was developed to assess test defensiveness or the ten-dency to minimize problems. This scale, in addition to serving as an index of defensiveness, serves also as a correction factor to com-pensate for the tendency of some people to deny problems.

The F Scale

The F scale was developed to assess the tendency of some people to exaggerate their problems or "fake" the test by overresponding to extreme items. The items on this scale are very rare or bizarre symptoms. Individuals who endorse a lot of these items tend to ex-aggerate symptoms on the MMPI-2, perhaps as a way of trying to convince professionals that they need psychological services. As noted earlier, this motivational pattern is also found among indi-viduals with a need to claim problems in order to influence the court in forensic cases. The F scale can be elevated for several pos-sible reasons. The profile could be invalid because the client be-came confused or disoriented or responded in a random manner. High F scores are also found among clients who are malingering or producing exaggerated responses in order to falsely claim mental illness (Graham, Watts, & Timbrook, 1991).

TRIN and VRIN scales

Two inconsistency scales for determining profile validity have been developed in the MMPI-2. These scales are based on the analysis of the individual's response to the items in a consistent or inconsis-tent manner. The scales are comprised of item pairs that involve re-sponses that are semantically inconsistent; for example, a pair of items that contain contradictory content that cannot logically be answered in the same direction if the subject is responding consis-tently to the content.

ASSESSING CLINICAL SYMPTOM PATTERNS

The assessment of clinical problems is approached in several ways through the self-reported symptoms and behaviors. We will examine three types of scales that comprise the MMPI-2's problem measures: the traditional clinical scales and profile codes, the MMPI-2 content scales, and the specific problems or supplemental scales. A scale is a group of items from the MMPI-2 item pool that have been shown to measure certain symptom patterns or personality traits. Each item cluster or scale is "normed" on a population of normal individuals. This normative group serves as the reference point to which all profiles are compared.

The MMPI-2 Clinical Scales

The authors of the original MMPI developed the clinical scales to empirically group patients into clinical problem types. For example, they developed scales to assess hypochondriasis (The Hs scale), depression (the D scale), hysteria (the Hy scale), psychopathic deviation (the Pd scale), paranoid thinking (the Pa scale), psychasthenia (the Pt scale), schizophrenia (the Sc scale), and mania (the Ma scale). In addition, two other scales were included on the clinical profile to address problems of sex role identification (the Mf scale) and social introversion and extraversion (the Si scale). In addition to interpretation of single clinical scales, elevations on certain scale patterns or configurations of scores (referred to as profile or code types) are interpreted. These profile types result from clients endorsing two or more of the clinical scales.

Content-based Scales

The MMPI-2 contains a number of scales that assesses the content themes an individual endorses in the item pool. The content scales are homogeneous item clusters that assess unitary themes and represent clear communications about problems to the practitioner. There are 15 content scales measuring different symptom areas and problems; examples include Antisocial Practices (ASP), Bizarre Mentation (BIZ), and Family Problems (FAM).

Special Scales

Several supplemental scales have been developed to assess specific problems, such as the potential to develop problems of addiction (the MacAndrew Addiction Scale or MAC-R, and the Addiction Potential Scale or APS) and whether or not the individual acknowledges having problems with drugs or alcohol. The Marital Distress Scale assesses clients' attitudes toward their marital relationship. These special scales allow the practitioner to assess specific problems that are not addressed in the clinical or content scales.

HOW THE MMPI-2 IS USED

There are many diverse, current applications for the MMPI-2 for evaluating individuals across a wide variety of settings. Contemporary uses include: evaluating clients who are being admitted to an inpatient psychiatric facility; understanding problems and possible treatment resistance of clients entering psychotherapy; providing personality information for therapists to employ in giving the client feedback in psychotherapy; assessing possible personality prob-

lems of students applying for a graduate clinical psychology program; measuring behavior problems and symptoms in neuropsychological evaluation of a client with severe head injury; appraising personality factors and psychological adjustment in applicants for an airline pilot position; examining persons who are being tried for murder and are claiming to be not guilty by reason of insanity; and using the test as a research instrument to evaluate the psychological changes in a drug trial. There have been over 25 translations and adaptations of the MMPI-2 for use in other countries. The items and scales have shown remarkable robustness when used in other languages and cultures (Butcher, 1996).

In summary, the MMPI-2 is a self-report personality inventory that provides the test user with scores on a number of scales. These scales assess response attitudes, mental health symptoms and personality traits, and special problems that the client might be experiencing. The MMPI-2 has been widely validated and is used in numerous settings around the world.

REFERENCES

Baer, R. A., Wetter, M. W., Nichols, D., Greene, R., & Berry, D. T. (1995). Sensitivity of MMPI-2 validity scales to underreporting of symptoms. *Psychological Assessment, 7,* 419–423.

Butcher, J. N. (1999). *The MMPI-2: A beginner's guide.* Washington, DC: American Psychological Association.

Butcher, J. N. (1996). *International adaptations of the MMPI-2.* Minneapolis: University of Minnesota Press.

Butcher, J. N., Dahlstrom, W. G., Graham, J. R., Tellegen, A. M., & Kaemmer, B. (1989). *Minnesota Multiphasic Personality Inventory-2 (MMPI-2): Manual for administration and scoring.* Minneapolis: University of Minnesota Press.

Butcher, J. N., Williams, C. L., Graham, J. R., Tellegen, A., Ben-Porath, Y. S., Archer, R. P., & Kaemmer, B. (1992). *Manual for administration, scoring, and interpretation of the Minnesota Multiphasic Personality Inventory for Adolescents: MMPI-A.* Minneapolis: University of Minnesota Press.

Graham, J. R., Watts, D., & Timbrook, R. (1991). Detecting fake-good and fake-bad MMPI-2 profiles. *Journal of Personality Assessment, 57,* 264–277.

Hathaway, S. R., & McKinley, J. C. (1940). A multiphasic personality schedule (Minnesota): 1. Construction of the schedule. *Journal of Psychology, 10,* 249–254.

J. M. BUTCHER
University of Minnesota

MISCHEL, WALTER (1930–   )

Walter Mischel was born February 22, 1930, in Vienna, Austria; his family was forced to flee their home (ironically, near Sigmund Freud's office) to escape the Nazis when Mischel was 8 years old. After much wandering in Europe and the United States, his family settled in 1940 in Brooklyn, where Mischel attended public schools and received a BA in psychology from New York University in

1951. While also working as a social worker with young children and older adults in settlement houses of New York City's lower east side, he obtained an MA in clinical psychology from City College of New York in 1953, with Gardner Murphy as his thesis advisor. Mischel studied clinical psychology under the mentorship of Julian B. Rotter and George Kelly at Ohio State University, where he received a PhD in 1956.

Mischel's academic appointments began as an assistant professor at the University of Colorado (1956–1958), followed by 4 years as assistant professor and lecturer at Harvard University's Department of Social Relations. From 1962 to 1983 he was in Stanford University's psychology department, where he became a professor and (twice) chairman. Wishing to return to New York City, he joined the psychology department at Columbia University in 1983, and served as its chairman from 1988 to 1991. He became the Robert Johnston Niven Professor of Humane Letters in Psychology at Columbia in 1994, and currently holds that endowed chair. He was elected editor of the *Psychological Review,* the field's flagship theory journal, for the 2000 to 2005 term.

Mischel's scientific contributions to psychology have been recognized widely. In 1982 he won the field's highest scientific honor, the Distinguished Scientific Contribution Award of the American Psychological Association (APA). The award cited Mischel for " . . . outstanding contributions to personality theory and assessment. His critical analyses of personality trait conceptions, and the case he has made for the cross-situational discriminativeness of behavior have had landmark effects. He has shown that the perception and organization of personality consistencies may depend more on the temporal stability of prototypical features than on the observation of behavioral consistency across dissimilar situations. He has led the way in linking modern cognitive psychology to the study of personality. His studies on delay of gratification have elucidated the psychological mechanisms of self-control. . . ."

Other awards and honors include the Distinguished Scientist Award of the APA's Division of Clinical Psychology (1978), and in 2000, the Distinguished Scientist Award of the Society of Experimental Social Psychologists. His long-term research program received a Merit Award from the National Institute of Mental Health (NIMH, 1989–1999) and another in 2000. In 1997 his alma mater, Ohio State University, awarded him an honorary Doctor of Science degree, citing him as the "acknowledged leader and innovator in the field of personality."

Mischel was elected a fellow of the American Academy of Arts and Sciences (1991), a William James Fellow of the American Psychological Society (1990), and a fellow of the Society of Experimental Psychologists (1999); he was also a fellow at the Center for Advanced Study in the Behavioral Sciences (1976–1977). Mischel served as president of APA's Division of Personality and Social Psychology in 1985, and president of its Division of Clinical Psychology (Section III) in 1971. From 1983 to 1994 he served on the scientific advisory board of the Max-Planck Gesellschaft in Berlin, and was on the Social Sciences Commission of the Max-Planck Gesellschaft from 1981 to 1990. Mischel also served for more than 8 years on review committees for NIMH, and was a trustee of the Association for the Advancement of Psychology (1982–1986). From 1989 to 1995 he was on the publication board of APA.

Mischel's early research combined field observation methods from anthropology with clinical assessment techniques to study the links between fantasy and behavior within Shango religious celebrations in Trinidad. In the same setting he also began his cross-cultural studies of self-control patterns and the ability to delay gratification, which remained a life-long theme in his research.

His greatest impact on the field, however, began with his 1968 monograph, *Personality and Assessment.* This penetrating critique of the state of personality theory, assessment, and findings identified what became known as the basic personality paradox— namely, that consistency across situations is much less than our intuitions predict, and that the situation or context plays a crucial role in the regulation and structure of behavioral consistency. The seemingly intuitively evident core assumption of personality psychology had been that personality characteristics are stable and broadly consistent across diverse contexts. For example, a conscientious person is expected to behave conscientiously across many different situations. The evidence from diverse research over many years, however, indicated that these consistencies were much more modest than had been assumed, and allowed surprisingly limited predictions of what a particular individual was likely to actually do in particular types of situations. While such evidence before had been dismissed as due to error in the research, Mischel's thesis was that the evidence reflected error in the theoretical assumption. The monograph shocked the field and produced a paradigm crisis the repercussions of which still persist. Three decades later, this now-classic work and the reactions that followed have reoriented much of the field and reset its agenda, still influencing its current directions.

After precipitating the paradigm crisis, for the next 3 decades Mischel's research and theory-building were directed at trying to resolve it. The cognitive-social learning approach to personality he developed shifted the unit of personality study from global traits inferred from behavioral signs to the individual's cognitions, affect, and actions assessed in relation to the particular psychological conditions in which they occur. The focus thus changed from describing situation-free individuals with broad trait adjectives to analyzing the interactions between conditions and the cognitions, feeling states, and behaviors of interest. The theoretical model he developed incorporated social, cognitive, and emotional processes and variables into the conceptualization of personality, taking systematic account of the role of the situation in interaction with the characteristics of the person, into the expressions of behavioral consistency.

The theoretical model was supported by research observing and analyzing the structure and organization of the individual's social behavior as it unfolds across situations and over time. In collaboration with Shoda and others, Mischel discovered that a key expression of personality stability was in the form of the individual's characteristic patterns of variability, which form characteristic, stable signatures of "if . . . then . . . , situation-behavior relations" (e.g., she X when A but Y when B). Further, these signatures reflect, and provide a route to understanding, the beliefs, motivations, conflicts, and goals that underlie and generate them.

While showing the importance of the situation in the structure and functioning of personality, Mischel also clarified the processes that enable individuals to exert willpower and overcome the pressures and temptations of the immediate situation in the light of delayed but more important outcomes. This research on goal-directed delay of gratification showed how individuals become able to persist in pursuit of long-term difficult goals even in the face of potent barriers and temptations along the route.

Mischel also influenced the field by teaching and working with many students who have made significant contributions in their own right.

STAFF

MNEMONIC SYSTEMS

The typical individual prefers not to learn by rote and usually learns by making materials meaningful. In using an available association or past learning to help learn new material (positive transfer), the individual finds that this strategy can qualify as a memory aid or mnemonic. For example, when one is learning a list of paired associates, the nonsense syllable pair *ros-lac* might be transformed into *rose-lake*, which might be a real place that is familiar to the learner. Or to facilitate learning and recall of the word pair *fox-sled*, one might conjure up the image of a fox coasting down a snowy hill on a sled.

There are several special mnemonic devices. One is the *pegword* method for memorizing lists of items or events. An individual first memorizes a rhyme for, say, 20 integers: One is a bun, two is a shoe, three is a tree, four is a door, five is a hive, and so on. The individual then associates one item on the list, say, *sugar,* with bun (e.g., an image of sugar heavily sprinkled all over the bun). For the next item, the individual might imagine two *bananas* sticking out of a shoe, and so on through the list. The images can be as bizarre as the individual chooses, but it is not clear that bizarre images are always superior mnemonic devices. Later, when the individual recites the rhyme, each cue word triggers a correct item on the list. The pegword method permits one to recall any item by its position in the list, such as the 3rd or 10th, as well as items in their original order.

In general, concocting mental images to aid in the learning of arbitrary verbal associations facilitates memory by a sizable amount. Paivio and Okovita (1971) found that concrete nouns can elicit more memorable visual images than do abstract nouns, which are more or less devoid of imagery. Perhaps this is due to the dual coding of concrete words, which have both a verbal representation and an image. This redundancy doubles one's access to these words in the future and could thereby increase the chances of recall.

The method of *loci,* used in ancient Greece, resembles the pegword method and is especially useful for recalling a long sequence of words or digits. It exploits one's familiarity with an itinerary or a well-traveled route that contains many distinctive loci, or landmarks. For example, a high school student memorized and recalled a list of 40 digits by this method, using the daily walk to school as the learned sequence of loci. Opening the front door to leave for school was the first cue and was associated in imagery with the first item to be remembered; the fire hydrant in front of the house was the second cue and was associated with the second item; the hill to climb to reach the main street was next; then came the radio store on the corner, and so on. (Note: Almost 60 years later the images are still pretty vivid to that individual). To recall the list, one simply runs through the route in imagery, and each locus cue triggers the correct digit. One learns only single, isolated associations. There is no information overload or span limitation; the task is relatively simple.

The learning of foreign language vocabulary is facilitated by using the *keyword* method devised by Atkinson and Raugh (1975). A keyword is an English word that sounds like some part of the foreign word. For example, the Russian word *zvonok* means "bell." The last syllable is emphasized and sounds like *oak.* Using *oak* as the keyword, the memorizer erects some imagery to connect the two English words—for example, a transparent bell with an oak leaf–shaped clapper hanging inside. When confronted with either the Russian word or its English equivalent the appropriate response is elicited. When Atkinson and Raugh evaluated the method's effectiveness they found about 50% superiority for the keyword method, which persisted over 6 weeks.

Some mnemonics are effective for remembering how to differentiate between two similar terms, such as the *abscissa* and *ordinate* of a graph, or between *stalactites* and *stalagmites.* To distinguish between the two geological terms, remember that the stalactite that hangs from the ceiling of a cave contains the letter *c,* the same as the initial letter for ceiling, and the stalagmite that protrudes from the ground contains the letter *g.* Some appreciate this mnemonic for remembering abscissa as the horizontal axis and ordinate as the vertical: When one says *ordinate* aloud, one's lips extend in a vertical direction, whereas when one says *abscissa* one's lips remain practically horizontal.

Signalers in the U.S. Navy have been taught the phonetic alphabet (e.g., Alpha for *a* and Bravo for *b*) and the Morse code together, using a mnemonic of appropriate visual stimuli that elicit both the phonetic letter and the corresponding Morse code symbol. For example, a simple line drawing of a building with four dots (windows) in a row represents both the phonetic symbol (a hotel) and the Morse code symbol (four dots in a row) for the letter *h.* Later, the letter simply elicits the visual image that cues the correct phonetic and Morse code response. All of the images used are adequately straightforward.

Frequently, when introduced to a stranger, individuals have trouble later in recalling the stranger's name. Typically, this is because the name was not learned in the first place. A new name must be rehearsed and related to names already known (or to something the name suggests from experience) in order to be remembered. The name may be related to the person it signifies based on what is unusual or distinctive about his or her manner, appearance, or resemblance to someone else. Meaningful procedures such as these are not time-consuming but are remarkably effective.

REFERENCES

Atkinson, R. C., & Raugh, M. R. (1975). An application of the mnemonic keywork method to the acquisition of a Russian vocabulary. *Journal of Experimental Psychology: Human Learning and Memory, 104,* 126–133.

Paivio, A., & Okovita, H. W. (1971). Word imagery modalities and associative learning in blind and sighted subjects. *Journal of Verbal Learning and Verbal Behavior, 10,* 506–510.

M. R. DENNY
Michigan State University

IMPRESSION FORMATION
MEMORY
MNEMONIC SYSTEMS
SOCIAL COGNITION

MOB PSYCHOLOGY

Crowds are defined as "co-acting, shoulder-to-shoulder, anonymous, casual, temporary, and unorganized collectivities" (Brown, 1954, p. 840). Crowds can be further subdivided according to whether they are active or passive, the former being a *mob* and the latter an *audience.* Mobs, in turn, are further classified according to the dominant behavior of the participants (a) aggressive, (b) escape, (c) acquisitive, or (d) expressive. *Aggressive* mobs, which include riot and lynch mobs, involve a display of aggression toward persons or objects. The dominant behavior of *escape* mobs is one of panic, as during a fire in a theater; orderly escape is not panic. According to Brown (1954), "Panic is emotional and irrational. The escape behavior of the fear-driven mob must either be maladaptive from the point of view of the individual, or, if personally adaptive, the behavior must ruthlessly sacrifice the interests of others who also seek to escape" (p. 858). *Acquisitive* mobs are similar to escape mobs in that both involve a competition for some object that is in short supply—tickets to the theater in the case of the acquisitive mob, and exits from the theater in the case of the escape mob. *Expressive* mobs represent a wastebasket category that includes all mobs not in the first three categories. Included here is behavior that can best be described by the obsolete word "revelous" which denotes behavior that might be displayed at religious revivals, sporting events, and rock music concerts.

Although there is no universal agreement among theorists, certain features tend to be attributed to mobs, including like-mindedness or "mental homogeneity," and emotionality. Gustav Le Bon (1903), in his classic work, *The crowd,* explained the mental homogeneity of mobs in terms of contagion—a mechanical, disease-like spreading of affect from one member to another. More recent research (Hatfield, Cacioppo, & Rapson, 1994) suggests that contagion is not mechanical, but rather, is dependent on a number of conditions. Milgram and Toch (1969) suggest that the mechanism of convergence may also account for the seeming mental homogeneity of mobs: Like-minded individuals tend to converge and join mobs. Thus, homogeneity precedes rather than follows from membership in the mob. Brown (1954) questioned the homogeneity of aggressive mobs and suggested that the composition of such mobs could be ordered in terms of mob members' readiness to deviate from conventional norms of society. He identified five types of participants, ranging from the "lawless" whose actions "trigger" the mob, to those "supportive onlookers" who stand on the fringes shouting encouragement.

A central issue in the study of mob behavior is determining why restraints that lead to conventional behavior break down when individuals find themselves in a crowd. Two important mechanisms that account for the violation of conventional behavior in crowds are: (a) the loss of responsibility through anonymity, and (b) the impression of universality. Both mechanisms are enhanced by the size of the crowd. Le Bon (1903) and many others have pointed out that aggressive mob members find it easier to act out their impulses because of the difficulty legal authorities have in singling them out and holding them responsible for their actions. Mob participants will feel safer from legal reprisals in large crowds because the sheer size of the crowd will pose impediments to identification and apprehension by the authorities. Allport (1924) and, more recently, Turner and Killian (1957) have contended that an individual is swayed by the mob because of a belief that if everyone else is acting in a certain way, the actions cannot be wrong—the mob simply redefines the norm for correct behavior. In their "emergent norm theory," Turner and Killian (1957) take issue with the causal role of emotional contagion, and argue instead that people act the way they do in crowds because the crowd helps to define the situation and the appropriate behavior. In the crowd context, the less anonymous one is to coacting peers, the greater the conformity to crowd norms. The greater the number of crowd participants, the stronger the impression of universality. Crowd size has different implications for aggressive as opposed to acquisitive and escape mobs. Whereas in aggressive mobs a larger number of crowd members enhances beliefs in anonymity and impressions of universality, in acquisitive and escape mobs, a large number of crowd members increases the competition for scarce resources (e.g., theater tickets, escape exits), thereby amplifying crowd responses.

Mob psychology has attracted little attention from social psychologists in recent years, owing in part to methodological difficulties in studying such phenomena. The last edition of the *Handbook of Social Psychology* to feature a chapter on mob psychology was in 1969. Similarly, recent social psychology textbooks no longer include a chapter on mob psychology. The last text to do so was one written by Roger Brown in 1965.

REFERENCES

Allport, F. H. (1924). *Social psychology.* Boston: Houghton Mifflin.

Brown, R. (1954). Mass phenomena. In G. Lindzey (Ed.), *Handbook of social psychology* (Vol. 2, pp. 833–876). Cambridge, MA: Addison-Wesley.

Brown, R. (1965). *Social psychology.* New York: The Free Press.

Hatfield, E., Cacioppo, J. T., & Rapson, R. L. (1994). *Emotional contagion.* New York: Cambridge University Press.

Le Bon, G. (1903). *The crowd.* London: Unwin.

Milgram, S., & Toch, H. (1969). Collective behavior: Crowds and social movements. In G. Lindzey, & E. Aronson (Eds.), *Handbook of social psychology* (2nd ed., Vol. 4, pp. 507–610). Reading, MA: Addison-Wesley.

Turner, R. H., & Killian, L. M. (1957). *Collective behavior.* Englewood Cliffs, NJ: Prentice-Hall.

M. S. GREENBERG
University of Pittsburgh

EMOTIONAL CONTAGION

MODELING

Psychological theories have traditionally emphasized learning through the rewarding and punishing effects that actions produce. Yet, if knowledge and competencies could be acquired only by direct experience, human development would be severely retarded, not to mention unmercifully tedious and perilous. A given culture could never transmit the complexities of its language, mores, social practices, and essential competencies if they had to be shaped laboriously in each new member solely by response consequences, without the benefit of models to exemplify the cultural patterns. Trial-and-error experience can be a tough teacher; errors can be highly costly and some missteps are deadly. The abbreviation of the acquisition process is, therefore, vital for survival as well as for successful human development. Moreover, the constraints of time, resources, and mobility impose severe limits on the situations and activities that can be directly explored for the acquisition of knowledge and competencies.

Humans have evolved an advanced capacity for learning by observation that enables them to develop their knowledge and competencies from information conveyed by modeling influences. Indeed, virtually all types of behavioral, cognitive, and affective learning resulting from direct experience can be achieved vicariously by observing people's behavior and its consequences for them (Bandura, 1986; Rosenthal & Zimmerman, 1978).

Much human learning occurs either deliberately or inadvertently by observance of the actual behavior of others in one's social environment and the consequences they experience. However, a great deal of information about human values, styles of thinking, behavior patterns, and sociostructural opportunities and constraints is gained from modeled styles of behavior portrayed symbolically through the electronic mass media. The growing importance of symbolic modeling lies in its tremendous scope and multiplicative power. A single model can transmit new ways of thinking and behaving to multitudes of people in widely dispersed locales simultaneously. The accelerated development of electronic technologies has vastly expanded the range of models to which members of society are exposed day in and day out. These electronic systems, feeding off telecommunications satellites, have become the dominant vehicle for disseminating symbolic environments. By drawing on these modeled patterns of thought and action, observers transcend the bounds of their immediate environment.

Not only are social practices being widely diffused within societies, but ideas, values, and styles of conduct are being modeled worldwide. The electronic media are coming to play an increasingly influential role in transcultural and sociopolitical change (Bandura, 1997; Braithwaite, 1994). Because the electronic media occupy a large part of people's lives, the study of acculturation in the present electronic age must be broadened to include electronic acculturation.

MECHANISMS OF OBSERVATIONAL LEARNING

Observational learning is governed by four component subfunctions. *Attentional processes* determine what people selectively observe in the profusion of modeling influences and what information they extract from ongoing modeled events. Observers' preconceptions, cognitive development, interests, and value preferences influence what they explore and how they perceive what is modeled in the social and symbolic environment.

People cannot be much influenced by modeled events if they do not remember them. A second subfunction concerns *cognitive representational processes.* Retention involves an active process of transforming and restructuring information about modeled events into rules and conceptions for generating new patterns of behavior. In the third subfunction in observational learning—*the behavioral production process*—symbolic conceptions are transformed into appropriate courses of action. Skills are usually perfected through a conception-matching process. Conceptions guide the construction and execution of behavior patterns and the behavior is modified as necessary to achieve close correspondence between conception and action.

The fourth major subfunction concerns *motivational processes.* People do not perform everything they learn. Performance of styles of behavior acquired through modeling are influenced by three types of incentive motivators—direct, vicarious, and self-produced. People are more likely to perform observationally-learned behavior if it results in valued outcomes for them, than if it has unrewarding or punishing effects. The observed detriments and benefits experienced by others influence the performance of modeled patterns in much the same way as do directly experienced consequences. People are motivated by the successes of others who are similar to themselves, but discouraged from pursuing courses of behavior that they have seen often result in adverse consequences. Personal standards of conduct provide a further source of incentive motivation. People pursue activities they find self-satisfying and that give them a sense of self-worth but reject those of which they personally disapprove.

ABSTRACT MODELING

Social modeling is not merely a process of behavioral mimicry. Highly functional patterns of behavior, which constitute the proven skills and established customs of a culture, may be adopted in essentially the same form as they are exemplified. There is little leeway for improvisation on how to drive automobiles. However, in many activities, subskills must be improvised to suit different situations. Modeling influences can convey rules for generative and innovative behavior as well. For example, an individual may see others confront moral conflicts involving different matters yet apply the same moral standard to each of them. In abstract modeling, observers extract the rules or standards governing specific judgments differing in content but embodying the same underlying rule. Once people extract the rules, they can use them to judge things and generate new courses of behavior that fit the prototype but go beyond the examples they have seen or heard. Evidence that generative rules of thought and behavior can be created through abstract modeling attests to the broad scope of observational learning (Bandura, 1986; Rosenthal & Zimmerman, 1978).

Modeling can contribute to creativeness in several ways. Originality largely involves synthesizing experiences into new ways of thinking and doing things. When exposed to models of differing styles of thinking and behaving, observers often vary in what they adopt from the different sources and thereby create new blends of personal characteristics that differ from the individual models. Modeling influences that exemplify new perspectives and innovative styles of thinking also foster creativity by weakening conventional mind sets.

MOTIVATIONAL, EMOTIONAL AND VALUATIONAL EFFECTS

In addition to cultivating competencies, modeling influences can alter incentive motivation (Bandura, 1986). Seeing others achieve desired outcomes by their efforts can instill motivating outcome expectations in observers that they can secure similar benefits for comparable performances. These motivational effects rest on observers' judgments that they have the efficacy to produce the modeled attainments and that comparable accomplishments will bring them similar beneficial outcomes. By the same token, seeing others punished for engaging in certain activities can instill negative outcome expectations that serve as disincentives.

People are easily aroused by the emotional expressions of others. What gives significance to vicarious emotional influence is that observers can acquire lasting attitudes and emotional and behavioral proclivities toward persons, places, or things that have been associated with modeled emotional experiences. They learn to fear the things that frightened models, to dislike what repulsed them, and to like what gratified them (Bandura, 1992). Fears and intractable phobias are ameliorated by modeling influences that convey information about coping strategies for exercising control over the things that are feared (Bandura, 1997; Williams, 1992). Values can similarly be developed and altered vicariously by repeated exposure to modeled preferences. The actions of models can also serve as social prompts that activate, channel, and support previously learned behavior. Thus, the types of models that prevail within a social milieu partly determine which human qualities, from among many alternatives, are selectively encouraged.

During the course of their daily lives, people have direct contact with only a small sector of the physical and social environment. In their daily routines, they travel the same routes, visit the same familiar places, and see the same group of friends and associates. As a result, their conceptions of social reality are greatly influenced by modeled representations of society in the mass media (Gerbner, 1972). The more their conceptions of the world around them depend on portrayals in the media's symbolic environment, the greater the media's social impact (Ball-Rokeach & DeFleur, 1976).

SOCIAL DIFFUSION THROUGH SYMBOLIC MODELING

Much of the preceding discussion has been concerned mainly with modeling at the individual level. As previously noted, the electronic media are coming to play an increasingly powerful role in transcultural change. In this broader function, symbolic modeling usually serves as the principal conveyer of innovations to widely dispersed areas, especially in early phases of diffusion. Modeling instructs people in new ideas and social practices and designates their functional value.

A number of factors, including perceived self-efficacy to execute the modeled patterns, possession of necessary resources, outcome expectations concerning the costs and benefits of the new styles of behavior in the new milieu, and perceived opportunities and impediments, determine whether people will adopt and put into practice what they have learned observationally (Bandura, 1986; 1997).

People are enmeshed in networks of relationship. They are linked, not only directly, by personal relationships. Because acquaintanceships overlap different network clusters, people become linked to each other indirectly by interconnected ties. These multilinked social networks provide diffusion paths for the spread of new ideas, lifestyle patterns, and social practices (Granovetter, 1983; Rogers & Kincaid, 1981).

REFERENCES

Bandura, A. (1986). *Social foundations of thought and action: A social cognitive theory.* Englewood Cliffs, NJ: Prentice-Hall.

Bandura, A. (1992). Exercise of personal agency through the self-efficacy mechanism. In R. Schwarzer (Ed.), *Self-efficacy: Thought control of action* (pp. 3–38). Washington, DC: Hemisphere.

Bandura, A. (1997). *Self-efficacy: The exercise of control.* New York: Freeman.

Bandura, A., Ross, D., & Ross, S. A. (1963). Imitation of film-mediated aggressive models. *Journal of Abnormal and Social Psychology, 66,* 3–11.

Braithwaite, J. (1994). A sociology of modeling and the politics of empowerment. *British Journal of Sociology, 45,* 445–479.

Gerbner, G. (1972). Communication and social environment. *Scientific American, 227,* 153–160.

Granovetter, M. (1983). The strength of weak ties—A network theory revisited. In R. Collins (Ed.), *Sociological theory 1983* (pp. 201–233). San Francisco: Jossey-Bass.

Rogers, E. M., & Kincaid, D. L. (1981). *Communication networks: Toward a new paradigm for research.* New York: Free Press.

Rosenthal, T. L., & Zimmerman, B. J. (1978). *Social learning and cognition.* New York: Academic Press.

Williams, S. L. (1992). Perceived self-efficacy and phobic disability. In R. Schwarzer (Ed.), *Self-efficacy: Thought control of action* (pp. 149–176). Washington, DC: Hemisphere.

A. Bandura
Stanford University

MONISM/DUALISM

Monism-dualism refers to a traditional classification of the various types of solutions proposed for the mind-body problem. Such solutions assume that the human being comprises either a single, unified entity (monism) or two qualitatively different, independent entities (dualism). Adherents of each type of solution also tend to differ in epistemology. Monists tend to view empiricism as the primary (even the only) acceptable method of knowledge. Dualists, on the other hand, accept empiricism and rationalism as equally appropriate and valid, each in its own sphere.

Because monists tend to equate knowledge with empiricism, all of their definitions try in one way or another to equate or reduce mind (or mental functions) to the activity of the brain and nervous system. Thus, in effect, mind and body become one. Mind is defined as being of the materialistic order of things. In the field of psychology, this position gives neuroscience a central locus of importance in the understanding and explanation of behavior. Many neuropsychologists thus view the study of the brain and nervous system as the primary approach to understanding human behavior.

Dualists, in contrast, are faced with the problem of relating the activities of the nonmaterial mind and the material body. Two primary patterns of dualism have appeared to prevail throughout history. The first are the interactionist theories, of which the views of Descartes are considered classic. Modern dualists have not had much success in replacing Descartes's explanation in terms of modern neurological knowledge.

A form of dualism that avoids the difficulty of explaining an interaction is psychophysical parallelism. Mind and body are viewed as acting in concert such that events that affect the one, affect the other; thus, knowledge of the one provides information about the other. The isomorphism of mental activity and brain functions, as well as the applications of the concepts of topology and field theory by Gestalt psychology, represent a modern version of psychophysical parallelism in present-day thinking.

A key element of dualistic positions as they affect psychology is that when the mind is defined as being a totally separate entity from the materialistic body, conceptualizations of the activity of the mind are not constrained by the laws of materialism. Thus, although mental activity may parallel physiological (or physical) activity, there is no necessity for it to do so. Laws unique to mental activity become acceptable and appropriate. The study of cognitive activity without concern or consideration of any underlying nervous system activity has led to many attempts to develop such laws of behavior.

Although it is self-evident that the relating of psychological, especially cognitive, behavior to physiological activity implies the taking of a position on the monism-dualism problem, few neuropsychologists (either clinical or research) ever explicitly state a position on the problem. However, since the days when Watsonian behaviorism made its great impact, American psychology has been heavily monistic, and the monistic position still prevails in this discipline, although the rise in popularity of existentialism, human-

ism, and other self-oriented philosophies and their effects on the thinking of psychologists, particularly psychotherapists, have led to revived interest in problems that logically require dualistic positions. Such areas of concern as imageless thought, life after death, and mental telepathy have aroused the interest of serious scientists. Concomitantly, there has arisen new interest in dualism.

M. E. REUDER

MONTESSORI, MARIA (1870–1952)

Following her graduation from medical school in Italy, Maria Montessori attacked exploitation of child labor and championed the cause of working women. Her practice as a physician brought her into contact with retarded children. She helped establish and directed a state orthophrenic school in Rome. That school became her training grounds for learning about retarded children whom she taught to read and write. For 2 years, she studied the children, and they became Montessori's teachers. This experience had a profound influence on her, which resulted in a career change from medicine to education.

She returned subsequently to the university classroom to register formally for courses in psychology and philosophy. There she was able to transfer her training and knowledge of the retarded to normal children. She began to formulate her own theories of child growth and developed a philosophy of education. Montessori used her scientific background to create universal principles and special methods and materials for a new pedagogy. In 1909, she published the first book on the Montessori method, which became an instant success, translated into over 20 foreign languages. Other books followed: *The Secret of Childhood, What You Should Know About Your Child,* and *To Educate the Human Potential.*

For more than 40 years, Montessori labored to impart her novel ideas through writing, lecturing, and teacher training. She was described as a lecturer par excellence. Demand for her lectures came not only from Italy but also from other European countries and the United States. She initiated a number of schools and trained as many as 5,000 teachers from every part of the globe.

A Montessori society arose in Rome and others followed. The American Montessori Society was organized under the presidency of Alexander Graham Bell, but did not follow the European model. Montessori presided at eight international Montessori congresses.

Among her accolades were the French medal Legion d'Honneur, the Dutch Officer of the Order of Orange-Nassau, and an honorary doctorate from the University of Amsterdam. According to Montessori, "Work is necessary. It can be nothing less than a passion. A person is happy only in accomplishment."

S. S. BROWN
North Shore Community College

MONTESSORI METHOD

At the turn of the century a new and revolutionary educational method swept across Europe: the Montessori method, based on the original ideas of Maria Montessori (1870–1952), the first woman physician of Italy. Her love for teaching began while she was educating retarded children and later unmanageable children at her first school, the Casa dei Bambini, in the San Lorenzo slum district of Rome.

Though not formally trained as a pedagogue, Montessori studied children from infancy through adolescence. Observing children at close range gave her insights into their development. She viewed the central problem in education as the need to establish a new and better relationship between the child and adults during the various stages of the child's development (Standing, 1962). She recognized the rights of children long before it became fashionable and respected them as human beings having a sense of personal dignity. The job of the teacher, she explained, was to facilitate the pupil–teacher relationship. This was accomplished by manipulating the classroom setting and by introducing materials that captivated the children and enabled them to teach themselves at their own rates. The teacher became the directress and the classroom the prepared environment. The school building became the Children's House, complete with child-sized furniture and equipment specially built to meet the intellectual and physical needs of youngsters.

The prepared environment of the typical Montessori school provides a variety of materials to pique the natural curiosity of 3- to 6-year olds. Montessori discovered that "things are the best teachers" (Ahlfeld, 1970). Children have the freedom to select any materials to which they are spontaneously attracted. Each learner's choices reveal the child's unique potentialities. The children may work independently or in groups. The class is ungraded, and rules are intended to encourage mutual cooperation instead of competition. Pupils are responsible for maintaining cleanliness and order. In this environment the children are said to prefer work to play and find working with educational devices intrinsically rewarding (Standing, 1962). Since children become absorbed in their work, they do not have time for mischief. Instead, they acquire self-discipline.

Montessori materials are designed to provide the preschooler with practical life experiences, sensory activities, and language and school skills. Practical life experiences include exercises in personal grooming and dressing, housekeeping, and manners. These exercises are meant to help the child acquire self-discipline, love of order, and muscular coordination. Sensory materials enable the children to visually discriminate colors and properties of physical objects, discriminate among various sounds and music, discriminate fabrics by touch and trace geometric shapes, and balance themselves. Language skills are enhanced through vocabulary enrichment. Writing is introduced before reading by tracing sandpaper letters. By age 4 or 5, Montessori children burst spontaneously into writing. Spelling is learned with a movable alphabet.

To round out the curriculum, science, history, geography, geometry, and arithmetic are explored. Arithmetic, for instance, is learned with sandpaper numbers, beads, and other concrete objects that are used to understand abstract number concepts. To see a tot playing with a square-root board is not unusual. The curriculum is based on the finding that preschool children can solve problems and can accomplish a great amount of intellectual work before entering formal schooling. Montessori referred to the absorbent mind from birth to 6 (Montessori, 1949).

The role of the directress is to encourage and support the children. She is expected to eliminate any obstacle that halts their progress and also not to interfere with their spontaneous interests and concentration. The directress's reward is to see the learner freely turn away from the didactic materials and approach her (directress) as a resource for further knowledge. Thus, a new and better relationship emerges between child and adult.

Along with the climate of American education in the 1960s stressing the teaching of basic skills came the proliferation of Montessori nursery schools. Organizations that promote the Montessori movement are the American Montessori Society of New York City and the Washington Montessori Institute of Washington, DC.

REFERENCES

Ahlfeld, K. (1970). The Montessori revival: How far will it go? *Nation's Schools.*

Montessori, M. (1949). *The absorbent mind.* Madras, India: Theosophical Publishing House.

Standing, E. M. (1962). *The Montessori method: A revolution in education.* Fresno, CA: Academy Guild Press.

SUGGESTED READING

Edelson, K., & Orem, R. C. (1970). *The Children's House parent–teacher guide to Montessori.* New York: Capricorn Books.

Gitter, L. (1967). The promise of Montessori for special education. *The Journal of Special Education, 2,* 5–13.

Montessori, M. (1964). *Dr. Montessori's own handbook.* Cambridge, MA: Bentley.

Montessori, M. (1976). *Education for human development: Understanding Montessori.* New York: Schocken.

S. S. Brown
North Shore Community College

MONTESSORI, MARIA

MORAL DEVELOPMENT

Moral development deals with the process by which individuals internalize socially approved rules and restrictions and orient their behavior using those rules. Research and theory have focused on three distinguishable aspects of this developmental process: moral judgment (how one reasons about moral situations), moral behavior (how one acts), and moral emotions (what one feels).

MORAL JUDGMENT

Since early in the 20th century, psychologists like Baldwin in *Social and Ethical Interpretations in Mental Development* and McDougall in *An Introduction to Social Psychology* have studied the process of moral development. The seminal investigations of Piaget published in *The Moral Judgment of the Child* have, however, inspired most contemporary research. Piaget's cognitive-developmental account postulated a two-stage progression from a heteronomous morality of constraint to an autonomous morality of cooperation. Although the stages differ on a number of dimensions—including employment of expiatory punishment versus restitution, belief in immanent justice, and unilateral obedience to authority—most research has examined whether moral judgments are based on objective consequences or subjective intentions. A story-pair paradigm is typically used. In one story, negligible objective consequences occur despite the actor's "bad" intentions—for instance, breaking a small cup while "snitching" a cookie. In the second, "good" intentions covary with considerable damage—for example, breaking four plates while helping to wash the dishes. Research supports a general age-related shift from an objective to a more subjective (intentional) conception of responsibility. Piaget offered a referential interpretation of this finding; young children fail to differentiate between subjective (mental) and objective phenomena and consequently rely on concrete referents when reasoning about moral situations. Research indicates, however, that other developmental variables—comprehension, memory, integration of information, and so on—may be implicated.

In 1958, Kohlberg proffered a six-stage theory of moral reasoning that has since served as the framework for considerable research and theorizing. Extending Piaget's structural view, Kohlberg hypothesized that progressive internalization of moral rules and principles continues throughout adolescence and into adulthood. Moral development is considered to be hierarchical in nature; each stage reorganizes and integrates preceding ones, providing an increasingly more comprehensive basis for moral decisions. Although the theory postulates an invariant, universally-ordered progression of stages, interindividual differences in the rate and final level of development may occur. Kohlberg assumes a justice orientation to morality; thus, moral situations involve a conflict of interests and rational principles of justice are used to resolve moral conflicts and protect individual rights. The theory is comprised of three general levels of moral reasoning—preconventional, conventional, and postconventional morality—each of which is divided into two specific stages.

Moral decisions at the preconventional level are externally oriented. At Stage 1, heteronomous, punishment orientation, what is right is defined by avoiding punishment and obeying authority. At Stage 2, individualistic and instrumental orientation, what is right is defined in terms of hedonistic acts that satisfy personal needs and self-interest.

Moral decisions at the conventional level are mediated by internalized rules, expectations, and values. At Stage 3, mutual interpersonal expectations and interpersonal conformity, what is right is defined as adherence to rules and expectations in order to please and gain approval from significant others. At Stage 4, social system and law and order, what is right is defined as doing one's duty, obeying the law, and maintaining the existing social order.

At the postconventional level, people strive to differentiate themselves from concrete rules and expectations by personally selecting moral principles that have applicability and validity independent from a specific authority or social order. At Stage 5, social contract and individual rights, what is right is defined in terms of a personal obligation to abide by contractual commitments, including implicit societal contracts. People understand the relativistic nature of rules and laws, but realize the need for contractual agreements to protect individual rights. Concerns about public welfare and equal justice make contractual laws binding and obligatory in the present. Rational considerations about social utility, however, may necessitate subsequent changes and revisions of existing laws: They are not viewed as being eternally fixed and inviolate. At Stage 6, universal ethical principles, right is defined in terms of self-selected rational ethical principles considered to be universally valid. (Because so few people have been found to reason at Stage 6, it has been retained mainly as a theoretical construct rather than an empirically viable category; see Colby, Kohlberg, Gibbs, & Lieberman, 1983).

A series of hypothetical dilemmas is the basis for stage assignments. In the most familiar example, Heinz and the drug dilemma, a man is confronted with a choice between passively letting his wife die or actively stealing a newly discovered drug that will cure her. The crux of the dilemma is that the husband has exhausted all legal methods of raising the necessary money, and the druggist refuses to lower the cost or give him credit. In Kohlberg's structural view, the explanations people offer are more important than the content (to steal or not to steal) of their response.

The central tenet of Kohlberg's formulation (namely, a fixed moral developmental sequence) has been supported by empirical investigations, especially the supposition that preconventional morality is a prerequisite for conventional reasoning and both must precede the development of postconventional morality (Colby et al., 1984). However, the highest level may not necessarily be found in all samples of adolescents or adults, especially Stage 6, which has been deleted in the revised scoring method (Colby & Kohlberg, 1987).

Gilligan (1982) has argued that Kohlberg's model reflects a male bias. She maintains that women emphasize a care orientation (the needs of others) when dealing with moral conflicts, whereas men rely on a justice orientation (the rights of others). Research, however, has not revealed reliable sex differences on Kohlbergian moral dilemmas (Walker, 1984). Moreover, a justice orientation to morality seems to imply caring about others as ends-in-themselves. Critics have also underscored the role that sociocultural factors may play in promoting postconventional reasoning, especially experiences within the context of a jurisprudence system of justice. Although Kohlberg's model may not provide the universal view of a moral person, it does seem to be relevant to people living in countries with constitutionally based legal systems.

MORAL BEHAVIOR

The empirical link between moral cognition and action has been elusive. People can exhibit the same behavior for different reasons, and individuals at the same level of moral reasoning may act in different ways. Although some linkages have been reported, relationships between moral reasoning and behavior are typically not linear (e.g., Hann, Smith, & Block, 1968). This is not a surprising finding because levels of moral reasoning reflect characteristic ways of framing and interpreting moral conflicts, rather than modes of behavior. If moral behavior is mediated by moral reasoning, it may be necessary to focus on intraindividual variation over time and situations. Knowing that people are conventional moral reasoners may not be sufficient to accurately predict their behavior; the specific normative expectations or rules that particular people hold need to be identified. Other relevant factors may include knowing how personally committed people are to translating their reasoning into action and the extent to which they possess the self-regulatory resources to do so.

In the 1920s, Hartshorne and May addressed a more fundamental issue of moral behavior in their Three-volume classic *Studies in the Nature of Character: Do individuals demonstrate intraindividual consistency in their moral behavior?* They devised numerous behavioral indices of the extent to which participants would resist the temptation to lie, cheat, and steal in experimental settings. Correlational analyses provided little evidence for a general personality trait of honesty; they advanced the position that moral behavior was situation-specific. Research has continued to support the situation-specificity doctrine of moral behavior (Bersoff, 1999). Of course, not all people yield when confronted by situational temptations and external pressures. Research underscores the role that individual differences in self-regulatory resources play in impulse control, temptation resistance, and self-restraint.

MORAL EMOTION

The psychoanalytic theory of guilt-motivated morality was presented by Freud in *The Passing of the Oedipus Complex.* Children are said to experience an intense love attraction to their opposite-sexed parent. A boy, for instance, experiences Oedipal feelings; he is erotically attracted to his mother and, consequently, he resents his father, his major rival for the mother's affection. Anxiety experienced about anticipated punishment (castration) results in the repression of Oedipal feelings. More important, the boy's fear of paternal retaliation prompts an introjection of the father's rules and prohibitions; thus, the superego or conscience is formed. In subsequent situations, according to Freud, the child experiences self-punishment or guilt when he is tempted to violate these internalized rules. Research indicates, however, that power-assertive parental practices are associated with an externalized morality: Children comply with normative standards because they fear detection and punishment (Hoffman, 1994). A more internalized morality results when discipline is coupled with parental explanations about the harmful consequences of the child's behavior for

others, termed "other-oriented inductive techniques." Such inductions may contribute to moral development by enhancing children's tendencies to anticipate the consequences of their actions and to experience another person's emotional state empathically (Hoffman, 1994).

The development of postconventional moral reasoning and internalized moral responding are both associated with principles and explanations that emphasize individual rights and the negative impact that misdeeds have on others. Knowing that people are postconventional moral reasoners may not, however, be sufficient for predicting how they will behave in moral situations. The particular principles to which they are personally committed, their motivation to implement them, and whether or not they have sufficient self-regulatory resources to do so must also be taken into account.

REFERENCES

Bersoff, D. (1999). Why good people sometimes do bad things: Motivated reasoning and unethical behavior. *Personality and Social Psychology Bulletin, 25,* 28–38.

Colby, A., & Kohlberg, L. (1987). *The measurement of moral judgment* (Vols. 1–2). New York: Cambridge University Press.

Colby, A., Kohlberg, L., Gibbs, J., & Lieberman, M. (1983). A longitudinal study of moral judgment. *Monographs of the Society for Research in Child Development, 48* (1–2, Serial No. 200).

Freud, S. (1950/1925). The passing of the Oedipus complex. In *Collected papers* (Vol. 2). London: Hogarth.

Gilligan, C. (1982). *In a different voice: Psychological theory and women's development.* Cambridge: Harvard University Press.

Hann, N., Smith, B., & Block, J. (1968). Moral reasoning of young adults. *Journal of Personality and Social Psychology, 10,* 183–201.

Hoffman, M. L. (1994). Discipline and internalization. *Developmental Psychology, 30,* 26–28.

Kohlberg, L. (1958). *The development of modes of moral thinking and choice in the years 10 to 16.* Unpublished doctoral dissertation, University of Chicago.

Piaget, J. (1965/1932). *The moral judgment of the child.* New York: Free Press.

Walker, L. J. (1984). Sex differences in the development of moral reasoning: A critical review. *Child Development, 55,* 677–916.

M. D. Berzonsky
State University of New York, Cortland

INTERNALIZATION

MODELING

MORENO, JACOB L. (1892–1974)

Jacob L. Moreno received his MD in Vienna in 1917 and worked there until coming to the United States in the early 1930s. During his early years in the United States he developed a methodology for social psychology called sociometry and founded a journal by that name. He was also involved in prison reform.

Moreno is best known as the developer of psychodrama. This technique had its roots in the early 1920s in Vienna, where Moreno was involved with the Theater of Spontaneity. He objected to the Freudian approach as being an artificial world of dreams and words occurring in offices. Instead, he emphasized acts or behaviors in natural surroundings, including role-training methods. In the several years before Moreno came to the United States, this became known as Impromptu Theater with publications in *Impromptu Magazine.* In the group setting it was important to have a genuine two-way cohesion that he called *tele.* More than simple transference and empathy, it involved cognitions, wishes, desires, choices, and behaviors. Moreno was a European pioneer in group psychotherapy.

In the United States Moreno developed the technique further and published *Psychodrama.* The technique involves time, reality, space, and warming up. As regards *time,* problems can occur in the past, the present, or the future. The past should be dealt with, but not overemphasized as in Freud. One needs to anticipate the future to be better prepared for it. The encounter itself occurs in the here-and-now; for purposes of the technique, all problems are transferred to the present. Although one can deal with actual *reality* or a limited portion of it, most often it is useful to deal with the "surplus" reality of role playing (including role reversal), auxiliary ego, or bodily contact (within ethical limits). As for *space,* psychodrama occurs in an action-centered stage, not in the limited, language-centered restrictions of a professional office. Just as athletes, singers, and engines require *warming up* for best performance, the first phase is the critical phase-in. The psychodrama then proceeds to the action phase and finally to the post-action sharing.

Various psychodrama techniques may be used. In *therapeutic soliloquy* the patient acts out feelings in the current situation. Since in reality the other characters could not observe these feelings, they do not react to this portion of the patient's behavior. In *multiple double* several others take the role of the patient, but at different periods in the patient's life. Perhaps one will play the patient of now, another the patient of 5 years ago, and still another the patient during a particular life crisis. In *mirror* the patient joins the group and observes someone else taking the patient's role.

Moreno claimed to obtain more catharsis or emotional reliving that at least partially solved the psychological problem with his psychodrama than Freud did by just talking with the client. For Moreno, action was the key to realism.

C. S. PEYSER
The University of the South

MORITA, SHOMA (1874–1938)

Shoma Morita was a professor of psychiatry at the Tokoyo Jikeikai School of Medicine. At the time, Japanese psychiatry was very much dominated by theories of Emil Kraepelin that suggested that behavior disorders were caused by biological and constitutional

disturbances. Morita took a new approach not only to the causes of disorders but the ways in which they should be treated. His important books include *Theory of Nervosity and Neurasthenia* and *Nature and Theory of Nervosity.*

His main contribution to psychiatry and psychology was the development of a new form of psychotherapy, generally known as Morita Therapy. Apparently he suffered from a variety of neurotic symptoms from the time of his adolescence, and is reported to have entered the field of psychiatry in an attempt to understand his own personality difficulties. He contended that neurotic disorders were not due to constitutional or body conditions but the result of intense attention paid to them by the patient. The more attention given, the more severe the symptoms became. Thus a vicious circle arose that Morita termed "to be caught." The most successful way of treating these symptoms was to gain insight. Morita's method combined psychotherapy and Zen Buddhism. To gain insight, the patient must be in harmony with the universe. One should not challenge nature but accept it and, in so doing, live in peace with it. According to Morita, nature was the therapist and the task of the psychotherapist was merely to assist the patient in gaining insight. In the process of Morita therapy, the patient went through various stages, of which the first was bed rest. During this period, isolation might intensify the symptoms. In the next stages a diary was kept and the therapist's function was to comment on and interpret what was written. The last stage involved "taking things as they are": learning to be natural and comfortable with oneself.

R. W. LUNDIN
Wheaton, Illinois

MORPHEMES

Morphemes are the meaningful elements that comprise the internal or sublexical structure of words. Work on the role of sound structure in language processing is common, but only recently have psychologists begun to examine morphemes as units of sublexical processing. Much of the work on morphemes (morphology) focuses on how language users store and understand words composed of more than one morpheme (complex words) and how they create new ones. Compare the English words "indent," "indented," and "indenture." There is no way to break down the word "indent" into smaller meaningful parts, but "indented" and "indenture" each consists of the base morpheme "indent" and an affix, either "-ed" or "-ure." Most complex words can be described in terms of rules for combining components. In the case at hand, the rules generate a past tense or a nominal from the base morpheme. However, not all complex words can be easily described in these terms. For example, we can tell that the word "forget" consists of the prefix "for" and the base "get," because "forget" has the same irregular past tense form as "get": "got." Yet there is no rule in modern English forming "forgot" from "get."

The final component of "fullness" is the suffix "-ness." Its function is to form a noun. It is joined together with the first component, the base adjective "full," to form a noun with the predictable meaning "condition of being full." The same suffix occurs in many other nouns derived from adjectives (e.g. "fondness, fussiness") and can also be used to form novel words like "nerdiness" or "emotiveness" whose meanings are understood easily by speakers of English. The fact that nouns like "walkness" or "tableness" are awkward also tells us that there are restrictions on how morphemes combine. Morphemes that appear before or after the base morpheme are called affixes (viz., prefixes and suffixes, respectively). Affixes may vary quite widely in their productivity (the likelihood that they will be used to create new words). Compare the two English suffixes "-ure" and "-ness," both of which form nouns from adjectives (e.g., "indenture" and "sadness"). The first suffix is completely unproductive in modern English; no new word with this suffix has been added to the language in centuries. The second is highly productive: Innovations are common.

Languages differ greatly in the prevalence of complex words and in the way in which morphemes combine to make complex words. Some languages (e.g., Chinese) have very little in the way of combining morphology. Others (e.g., Turkish) are famous for their complex morphology, combining many morphemes within a single word. Rules for combining morphemes also vary across languages. In Serbian or English, for example, morphemes are linked linearly (e.g., un+forget+ful+ness). In Hebrew, morphemes can be interleaved with one another (e.g., "N-F-L" combines with "-a-a" to form "NaFaL," meaning "he fell," and with "-o-e" to form "NoFeL," meaning "he falls").

Suffixes such as "-ure" and "-ness" are examples of derivational affixes, whereas "-ed" is an inflectional morpheme. Adding a derivational affix forms a new word and often changes the word class of the base morpheme as in the preceding "indent-indenture" example. Derivational formations tend to be semantically unpredictable, as is true with "indent-indenture." Compare, for example, the relation of "confess-confession" to "profess-profession." Inflectional morphology is concerned with the different forms that a word may take, depending on its role in a sentence. English is quite poor inflectionally, but in many other languages (e.g., Serbian or Swahili) each noun, verb, and adjective will have a large number of inflected forms.

Words that are morphologically related tend to have similar orthographic and phonological forms as well as similar meanings. Knowledge about words comprises the mental lexicon. A major research question for psycholinguists is whether morphological knowledge is explicitly represented in the mental lexicon or whether it falls out of the conjoint similarity of form and meaning. Among theorists who think that morphology is explicitly represented, some describe morphological knowledge in terms of lexical representations that are decomposed into constituent morphemes. Others describe morphological knowledge in terms of a principle of lexical organization among full forms that are related. Another point of discussion is whether all word forms, or only those forms that are irregular in either form or meaning, are stored as wholes in the mental lexicon. When regularity is defined with respect to form, we can ask whether words that undergo a change, such as "forget-forgot," are represented differently than are words such as "forfeit," whose past tense form ("forfeited") is regular. When regularity is defined in terms of meaning, we can ask whether the meaning of the base morpheme must be semantically transparent with re-

spect to the complex form in order to be represented in the lexicon in terms of its morphological structure. Similarly, we can ask whether inflected and derived forms are represented in the same manner.

In the psycholinguistic literature, a classical task for exploring morphological knowledge is the lexical decision task. Letter strings are presented visually, and skilled readers must decide whether each is a real word. Words are usually presented in pairs: a prime and then a target. Sometimes prime and target are presented in immediate succession. Other times there are intervening items. Decision latencies to the target as a function of the type of prime that preceded it are measured.

Whether reduced similarity in spelling or pronunciation between "forget-forgot"-type relatives diminishes the magnitude of facilitation to targets relative to "indent-indented"-type pairs appears to depend on the timing relation between them. Results in Hebrew, Dutch, and Serbian have shown morphological facilitation with semantically opaque as well as transparent morphological relatives. However, when prime and target are presented in immediate succession, there is some evidence that at long—but not at shorter—time intervals, morphological facilitation is greater following semantically transparent morphological relatives as compared with those that are semantically more opaque. Similarly, facilitation for targets tends to be greater following inflectional than following derivational relatives.

The segment shifting task, modeled after the reordering of morphemic segments that occurs in spontaneous speech errors, also provides evidence of morphological processing. In this task, subjects segment and shift a sequence of letters ("en") from a source word to a target word ("bright") and then name the product aloud ("brighten"). Letter sequences come from morphologically complex source words such as "harden" and their morphologically simple controls such as "garden." Naming latencies are faster following "harden"-type words than following "garden"-type controls. Effects of productivity have been demonstrated for suffixes as well as for bases that enter into many or few combinations to form words. Similar results have been observed for English, in which the morphemic status of the shifted sequence was varied and sequences were appended after the base morpheme, and for Hebrew, in which one morpheme was interleaved with another.

Morphemes and their properties play a critical role in word recognition. Morphology cannot be expressed in terms of similarity of form or meaning alone, although facilitation among morphological relatives is sensitive to similarity of form and meaning. Psychologists study morphology for what it reveals about how the components of words (sublexical structure) contribute to word identification and production.

SUGGESTED READING

Aronoff, M. (1994). *Morphology by itself.* Cambridge, MA: MIT Press.

Bauer, L. (1983). *English word-formation.* Cambridge: Cambridge University Press.

Booij, G., & van Marle, J. (1991). *Yearbook of morphology.* Dordrecht: Kluwer.

Feldman, L. B. (Ed.). (1995). *Morphological aspects of language processing.* Hillsdale, NJ: Lawrence Erlbaum.

Matthews, P. H. (1991). *Morphology* (2nd ed.). Cambridge: Cambridge University Press.

Sandra, D., & Taft, M. (Eds.). (1994). *Morphological structure, lexical representation and lexical access.* Hove, UK: Lawrence Erlbaum.

Spencer, A. (1991). *Morphological theory.* Oxford: Blackwell.

Zwicky, A., & Spencer, A. (Eds.). (1997). *Handbook of morphology.* Oxford: Blackwell.

L. B. FELDMAN
M. ARONOFF
State University of New York, Albany

COMPLEX WORDS
DECISION LATENCIES
DECOMPOSED REPRESENTATIONS
DEPRIVATIONAL MORPHOLOGY
INFLECTIONAL MORPHOLOGY
LEXICAL DECISION TASK

MORPHINE

Morphine is the principal alkaloid of opium, and is used for the control of moderate to severe pain. The word "opium," itself, is derived from the Greek name for "juice," the drug being obtained from the juice of the poppy, *Papaver somniferum.* Opium contains more than 20 distinct alkaloids. In 1806, Setürner reported the isolation of an opium alkaloid that he named morphine, after Morpheus, the Greek god of dreams.

Morphine and other morphine-like drugs (heroin, codeine, or methadone) produce analgesia primarily through their interaction with opioid receptors located in the central nervous system and periphery. The existence of multiple opioid receptors was proposed in 1977 and confirmed by various studies. Soon after the demonstration of these opioid receptors, three classes of endogenous opioid peptides were isolated and identified: the enkephalins, the endorphins, and the dynorphins. (Reisine & Pasternak, 1996).

Although there are now many compounds with pharmacological properties similar to those produced by morphine, this old drug remains the most useful in clinical settings. However, in spite of its efficacy, morphine treatment has some associated problems. Side effects such as nausea, vomiting, constipation, drowsiness, confusion, and variability in analgesic response among patients are common clinical problems during morphine therapy, with respiratory depression being a less-frequent but more serious side effect (Martindale, 1996). Although the development of dependence and/or tolerance is not generally a problem when morphine is used in patients with opioid-sensitive pain, the possibility of tolerance and dependence with long-term use may complicate its clinical utilization. In fact, the development of tolerance and physical depend-

ence with repeated use is a characteristic feature of all the opioid drugs. Tolerance can be defined as a loss of potency of a drug after its repeated administration, so that doses must be increased to achieve the same effect. Drug dependence of the morphine type is a state arising from repeated administration of morphine or morphine-like drugs (heroin, pethidine, etc.); it is characterized both by an overwhelming need to continue taking the drug or one with similar properties, and by a tendency to increase the dose owing to the development of tolerance. Abrupt withdrawal of morphine and morphine-like drugs from individuals physically dependent on them precipitates a withdrawal syndrome, the severity of which depends on different factors such as the individual, the drug used, and the intensity and duration of the treatment (Martindale, 1996). However, it is important to note that when morphine and morphine-like drugs are used correctly in appropriate doses to treat morphine-sensitive pain, tolerance, dependence, and severe side effects are not a clinical problem (McQuay, 1989).

During morphine treatment, common side effects such as nausea, constipation, and drowsiness are usually controlled by appropriate measures. What complicates morphine use in the clinical setting is the variability among patients' pharmacological responses. Careful evaluation of the morphine dose required to alleviate the pain is needed, because the effective dose varies not only from patient to patient but also from time to time (because of disease progression and/or tolerance). The correct dose for the patient is that which gives good pain relief during the interval between doses, without producing unacceptable side effects. Another fact that complicates morphine pharmacology is its pharmacokinetics: what the body does to the drug. Pharmacokinetics deals with absorption of the drug from the site of administration (oral, rectal, intramuscular), its distribution into the body, its biotransformation, and its elimination from the body. Morphine is a very versatile drug because it can be administered by many different routes (oral, parenteral, spinal). When administered by the oral route, it undergoes extensive biotransformation or metabolism, mainly in the liver. Biotransformation of morphine also occurs when it is administered by other routes, but to a lesser extent. For this reason oral doses must be much larger than parenteral doses to achieve the equivalent effect. The biotransformation of morphine produces two major and important metabolites, morphine-3-glucuronide (M3G) and morphine-6-glucuronide (M6G). These metabolites are found in the plasma and cerebrospinal fluid after administration of morphine. M6G has pharmacological activity and a more potent antinociceptive effect than morphine. The other metabolite, M3G, produces stimulatory effects but is devoid of analgesic activity. There are, however, conflicting reports of its effects (antagonism) on morphine and M6G analgesia (Smith, Watt, & Cramond, 1990; Suzuki, Kalso, & Rosenberg, 1993; Faura, Olaso, Garcia Cabanes, & Horga (1996). It has been suggested that these metabolites may contribute to the global effects of morphine, but the pharmacological activity and real contribution of morphine metabolites remains intriguing despite many years' investigation (Faura et al., 1998).

Given the pharmacological activity of the morphine metabolites and their possible contribution to the global effects of morphine, it is important to specify the factors that can modify the morphine-metabolite relationship. Age of the patient, presence of renal impairment, and route of administration are important factors in the kinetics of morphine and its metabolites. There is evidence that newborn children produce morphine metabolites at a lower rate than do older children or adults, mainly because of their functional immaturity. Morphine metabolites are eliminated from the body mainly via the kidneys, which is why the presence of renal impairment results in their high plasma concentrations. No evidence of kinetic changes has been observed in association with liver disease. Intravenous, intramuscular, and rectal administration of morphine result in lower metabolite production than does oral administration (Faura et al., 1998). Although some factors affecting the kinetics of morphine and its metabolites have been determined, the cause for variation in the pharmacological response of morphine remains unknown (Bowsher, 1993).

The available information on morphine confirms that despite the relative ignorance about its pharmacology, this old drug is still the standard against which other analgesic drugs are compared. Its efficacy and safety when properly used make morphine the drug of choice for moderate to severe opioid-sensitive pain.

REFERENCES

Bowsher, D. (1993). Paradoxical pain. *British Medical Journal, 306,* 473–474.

Faura, C. C., Olaso, M. J., Garcia Cabanes, C., & Horga, J. F. (1996). Lack of morphine-6-glucuronide antinociception after morphine treatment: Is morphine-3-glucuronide involved? *Pain, 65,* 25–30.

Faura, C. C., Collins, S. L., Moore, R. A., & McQuay, H. J. (1998). Systematic review of factors affecting the ratios of morphine and its major metabolites. *Pain, 74,* 43–53.

Martindale, J. E. F. (1996). *The extra pharmacopoeia* (31st ed. pp. 63–79). London: Royal Pharmaceutical Society.

McQuay, H. J. (1989). Opioids in chronic pain. *British Journal of Anaesthesia, 63,* 213–226.

Reisine, T., & Pasternak, G. (1996). Opioid analgesics and antagonists. In J. G. Hardman & L. L. Limbird (Eds.), *The pharmacological basis of therapeutics* (9th ed., pp. 521–555). New York: McGraw-Hill.

Smith, M. T., Watt, J. A., & Cramond, T. (1990). Morphine-3-glucuronide a potent agonist of morphine analgesia. *Life Sciences, 47,* 579–585.

Suzuki, N., Kalso, E., & Rosenberg, P. H. (1993). Intrathecal morphine-3-glucuronide does not antagonize spinal antinociception by morphine or morphine-6-glucuronide in rats. *European Journal of Pharmacology, 249,* 247–250.

C. C. Faura-Giner
Universidad Miguel Hernández, Spain

OPIOD RECEPTORS

OPIUM, OPIODS, AND OPIATES

MOTION DETECTION

THE SIGNIFICANCE OF MOTION DETECTION

Because we live in a world in which objects (living or man-made) constantly move, the image on our retina is never still. To make things worse, we ourselves move rather frequently—we walk or drive, we turn our head or shift our gaze. Visual motion therefore is ubiquitous, but unless we have to solve specific problems, such as catching a ball or assessing the approach of a vehicle, we rarely are aware of it. So it is not surprising that motion perception has a long tradition as a research topic (Wade, 1998), starting with classical observations of the waterfall illusion: After prolonged exposure to visual motion, as when watching a stream of water, human observers perceive static objects as moving in the opposite direction to the motion they have just been observing (also referred to as motion after-effect). Manifold attempts to create sensations of movement from still images, which eventually led to practical applications like motion pictures, form part of this tradition. The study of phenomena analogous to human motion perception in animal systems, from insects to primates, has provided valuable clues to the neural basis of motion processing, and has suggested computational models that are increasingly relevant for machine vision. Thus, motion vision can be regarded as an exemplar for the understanding of the brain mechanisms underlying perception.

BASIC PROCESSING STEPS

In the late 19th century, experiments by psychologist and physiologist S. Exner took a fundamental step toward the functional understanding of motion perception. He first presented electric sparks, either synchronously at two locations that could not be separated, or at a single location while minimizing the time intervals between consecutive sparks until they appeared as continuous light. By then presenting the sparks in the same rapid succession but alternating between the two locations, he elicited the sensation of apparent motion and thus established motion vision as an independent perceptual quality. Importantly, this experiment also indicates the crucial components of a minimum motion stimulus as well as the basic components of a fundamental mechanism to detect visual motion. However, it was to be half a century, during which time real and apparent motion stimuli were studied mainly in the framework of a Gestalt psychology seeking to define the crucial attributes that constitute a particular motion percept, before low-level mechanisms returned to the center of attention. An elementary motion detector (EMD), based on analysis of the insect visual system, was proposed for and turned out to be rather successful in describing the function of a variety of visual systems. The EMD (sketched in the center of Figure 1) consists of four fundamental operations: (a) two input elements, separated by the sampling base $\Delta\varphi$, pick up luminance signals from neighboring locations in the visual scene; (b) temporal filters shift the input signals with a time constant τ; (c) the original signal from one location interacts with the temporally filtered signal from the other location (e.g., by means of multiplication); (d) the outputs of two antisymmetric subunits are subtracted in an opponency stage (indicated by Δ). The amplitude of the final EMD output depends on the speed,

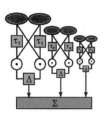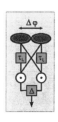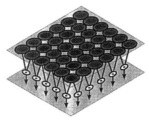

Figure 1   Models of Motion Perception: Elementary Motion Detector (EMD, Middle), and Two-dimensional arrays (Right), Spatiotemporal Pooling (Left)

contrast, and spatial properties of the luminance profile moving across the input elements; the sign of the output clearly reflects the direction of motion (Borst & Egelhaaf, 1989). Thus, motion is detected with a small number of simple operations, all of which can be easily realized with neural processing elements.

PROPERTIES OF LOCAL MOTION DETECTION
A number of quantitative predictions can be derived from this model that represents a class of correlation or motion energy models. The specific spatial and temporal tuning of the EMD, related to $\Delta\varphi$ and τ, is often used as the fingerprint of this mechanism. For example, moving patterns with different spatial structure (spatial frequency) will elicit a maximum response at different speeds, implying a constant rate of light changes (i.e., a temporal frequency optimum). This and other predictions from the EMD model are consistent with behavioral and physiological evidence from a wide range of animal species. In particular, the dependence on temporal frequency of motion detection and motion direction discrimination, as well as the strength of motion after-effects, suggests that EMD design principles are implemented in human vision. Another even more obvious prediction derived from the EMD model is the existence of displacement limits for motion detection—that is, the movement of a pattern will no longer be detected once it is displaced beyond the sampling base of the EMD. This is exactly what was found in a number of experiments in which stimuli were generated from randomly distributed dots. Such stimuli do not allow the identification of objects without motion's being detected in the first place. Based on the displacement limits for such Random Dot Kinematograms, a short-range process that relies on spatiotemporal correlation is distinguished from a long-range process that identifies and tracks objects during a motion sequence (Braddick, 1980).

INTEGRATION OF MOTION INFORMATION
The basic motion detection mechanism, and the EMD model, form only the starting point for a cascade of processing steps in which local filters are combined in various ways:

- Spatial or temporal pooling helps to reduce noise, which is inherent to neural processing and is ambient in natural scenes. Noise is often used in psychophysical experiments to probe the sensitivity of the visual system.

- Movements of the observer generate characteristic flowfields (Gibson, 1979), and two-dimensional arrays of motion detectors (right part of Figure 1) are required to analyze such complex motion-signal distributions. Segmenting regions of different directions or speed is crucial to detect camouflaged objects and to extract depth information from motion parallax.

- For speed estimation it is necessary to integrate the outputs from EMDs, which are tuned to different spatiotemporal frequencies (by variation of $\Delta\varphi$ and τ; see left part of Figure 1). This integration is important for a number of motor control tasks, and can also lead to the reduction of noise.

- Motion detectors may operate on a variety of inputs, such as luminance, color, texture, or motion itself. Additional nonlinear processing steps give rise to first- and second-order motion detection, finally leading to a parallel and hierarchical processing system able to extract a wide variety of motion cues (Cavanagh & Mather, 1989).

The complexity indicated by this brief list of the processing interactions possible among local motion detectors reflects the scope and significance of tasks the visual system faces when it comes to making sense of the immense flow of visual information entering the eyes in everyday life.

REFERENCES
Borst, A., & Egelhaaf, M. (1989). Principles of visual motion detection. *Trends in Neuroscience, 12,* 297–306.

Braddick, O. J. (1980). Low-level and high-level processes in apparent motion. *Philosophical Transactions of the Royal Society London, 290,* 137–151.

Cavanagh, P., & Mather, G. (1989). Motion: The long and short of it. *Spatial Vision, 4,* 103–129.

Gibson, J. J. (1979). *The ecological approach to visual perception.* Hillsdale, NJ: Erlbaum.

Wade, N. J. (1998). *A natural history of vision.* Cambridge, MA: MIT Press.

J. M. ZANKER
Australian National University

MOTION PARALLAX

MOTION PARALLAX
Various types of information contribute to the visual perception of depth. Examples include binocular disparity—difference between the retinal images due to the separation of the eyes—and pictorial cues such as relative size and interposition. The observer's motion also generates depth information. "Motion parallax" refers to the visual motions elicited at the moving observer's eye by static objects. The direction of visual motion is opposite to that of the observer's motion for objects in front of fixation, and in the same di-

rection for objects behind fixation; rates of visual motion increase with increasing distance from fixation. An elaboration of motion parallax applies to a surface slanted in depth: The visual geometry transforms with the observer's motion, according to the degree of slant. Motion information has been emphasized in ecological treatises and computational modeling of depth perception (Simpson, 1993).

The best evidence that motion parallax is important in depth perception comes from depth-from-motion simulations, an analog of Julesz's (1971) anaglyphs for demonstrating the importance of binocular disparity. The observer rests his or her head on a movable chin-support, while viewing monocularly a random array of computer-generated dots. When the observer is stationary, the dots appear to be in the plane of the computer screen. However, when the observer's head moves from side to side, that motion causes, via the chin-support, systematic motions across the array, simulating motion parallax. Even minimal head motion elicits a compelling perception that the display consists of surfaces varying in distance from the observer, suggesting that motion parallax is as effective as binocular disparity (Rogers & Graham, 1982).

Researchers need to know, however, whether the conclusions drawn from simulations apply to real stimuli. Real stimuli convey pictorial information based, for example, on their believed physical sizes and shapes. One study employed an Ames' distorted-room stimulus, which is rich in misleading pictorial information: The stimulus is constructed from trapezoidal surfaces to appear as the interior of a cube when viewed from a peephole in the front surface. Gehringer and Engel (1986) tested a belief that the illusion is destroyed if the front surface is removed to permit head motions of about 120 cm in range. Moving-monocular judgments were more veridical than static-monocular judgments—but only by about 10%; that is, the illusion remained largely intact, even for moving subjects. Other studies employed single trapezoidal or rectangular surfaces differing in their slant-in-depth (Reinhardt-Rutland, 1995), and objects at different distances—the physical sizes of the objects varied to take into account the pictorial cue of relative visual size (Hell, 1978). Again, motion parallax was not particularly effective. Furthermore, Reinhardt-Rutland (1996) had observers judge the slant-in-depth of untextured triangular surfaces conveying limited pictorial information: Observers made veridical judgments only at the greatest extent of motion (30 cm). While the previous studies were dependent on side-to-side head motion, similar results are reported if observers walk towards and away from stimuli (Eriksson, 1974).

How can the conflicting evidence from simulations and real stimuli be reconciled? One point is that visual motion is ambiguous: The moving observer may be viewing static objects, the static observer may be viewing moving objects, or the moving observer may be viewing moving objects (Reinhardt-Rutland, 1988). To resolve this ambiguity, it seems that effective motion parallax requires cumulative processing over a period of time. In contrast, most other depth information is available for immediate processing: Pictorial information can be obtained instantaneously, while binocular disparity relies on simultaneous comparison of the retinal images. Since studies of real stimuli entail competition between motion and pictorial information, it is likely that the latter is

more important if rapid judgment is required. Indeed, this can apply in a motion-rich activity such as driving; when depth judgments are made rapidly, pictorial information based on the believed sizes of vehicles and pedestrians can play a major role (Stewart, Cudworth, & Lishman, 1993).

That depth-from-motion simulations are successful maybe because the systematic motion of the dots introduces information that would normally be conveyed pictorially. For example, an edge is a powerful cue for a difference in depth between surfaces—the surface lying to one side of the edge is at a different distance than is the surface lying to the other side of the edge. Edges are normally specified pictorially, even by something as simple as a line in a pen and ink drawing, but may also be defined by a spatial discontinuity in a depth-from-motion simulation. However, an edge does not convey which surface is the closer; other information is required. Rogers and Rogers (1992) suggested that earlier simulation studies had inadvertently included in the display information that allowed the observer to decide which parts of the array of dots appeared closer and which parts appeared further away. When this additional information was eliminated, they found that the depth relationships became ambiguous, confirm that the information conveyed by motion in simulations may generally be restricted to specifying edges.

Another form of pictorial information—interposition—may be enhanced by motion; "interposition" refers to the fact that a closer object may occlude a more distant object. If we consider the objects as they are viewed by a moving observer, the pattern of interposition changes. At one point in the observer's motion both objects may be fully visible. At another point the more distant object may become partially or totally occluded. The changing pattern of occlusion varies systematically with the observer's motion, providing unambiguous information for relative order in depth.

To conclude, motion parallax has a role in depth perception, but it is perhaps not as important as some have asserted. Its limitation is that it requires time-consuming cumulative processing, while other sources of depth information are in principle available for immediate processing. The observer's motion, however, generates other information that enhances pictorial information, and it is this that may make the observer's motion particularly important in depth perception.

REFERENCES

Eriksson, E. S. (1974). Movement parallax during locomotion. *Perception and Psychophysics, 16,* 197–200.

Foley, J. M. (1978). Primary depth cues. In R. Held, H. W. Leibowitz, & H. L. Teuber (Eds.), *Handbook of Sensory Physiology. Vol. 8: Perception* (pp. 181–213). Berlin: Springer.

Gehringer, W. L. & Engel, E. (1986). Effect of ecological viewing conditions on the Ames' distorted room illusion. *Journal of Experimental Psychology: Human Perception and Performance, 12,* 181–185.

Hell, W. (1978). Movement parallax: An asymptotic function of amplitude and velocity of head motion. *Vision Research, 18,* 629–63 5.

Julesz, B. (1971). *Foundations of cyclopean perception.* Chicago: Chicago University Press.

Reinhardt-Rutland, A. H. (1988). Induced in the visual modality: An overview. *Psychological Bulletin, 103,* 57–72.

Reinhardt-Rutland, A. H. (1995). Perceiving the orientation in depth of real surfaces: Background pattern affects motion and pictorial information. *Perception, 24,* 405–414.

Reinhardt-Rutland, A. H. (1996). Depth judgments of triangular surfaces during moving monocular viewing. *Perception, 25,* 27–35.

Rogers, B., & Graham, M. (1982). Similarities between motion parallax and stereopsis in human depth perception. *Vision Research, 22, 261–270.*

Rogers, S., & Rogers, B. (1992). Visual and nonvisual information disambiguate surfaces specified by motion parallax. *Perception and Psychophysics, 52,* 446–452.

Simpson, W. A. (1993). Optic flow and depth perception. *Spatial Vision, 7,* 35–75.

Stewart, D., Cudworth, C. J., & Lishman, J. R. (1993). Misperception of time-to-collision by drivers in pedestrian accidents. *Perception, 22,* 1227–1244.

A. H. REINHARDT-RUTLAND
University of Ulster, Ireland

DEPTH PERCEPTION

MOTIVATED FORGETTING

All of us forget to remember, at least occasionally. Whether it is the name of a relative, an item to purchase at the store, or, more rarely, entire events from our lives, we have all experienced the phenomenon of forgetting. Unlike a computer hard drive, the human memory system does not lay down tracks of data and retrieve them in a mechanical fashion. Only a portion of what is available to our senses is stored in memory, and only a portion of what is stored is available at any given moment to be retrieved. As will be seen, there are both conscious and unconscious bases for our failures to remember.

Many different types of forgetting have been identified by researchers and clinicians. The simplest type involves the difficulty we have in accessing some memories as they fade with the passage of time or become lost amid myriad other memories that interfere with their retrieval. For example, if memories are not exercised regularly, we may have trouble retrieving them because their trace in memory needs to be rehearsed enough times to become durable before it fades away. This is the reason most of us forget phone numbers we do not call regularly. It also becomes increasingly more difficult to recall former memories as we commit new experiences to memory, because the latter memories interfere with the retrievability of the former ones. This form of forgetting is called retroactive interference. (This process works in reverse, as well, since former memories can interfere with the accessibility of more recently acquired memories—so-called proactive interference). These are all common forms of memory failure. They have in common the fact that we are unable to recollect information despite energetic efforts to do so.

A less prosaic type of forgetting, however, is labeled "motivated," and it has nothing to do with the sheer passage of time or interference by subsequent experiences. And, unlike the unconscious forms of forgetting and interference described previously, this form of forgetting has at its root a conscious desire to forget or suppress events. Indeed, some individuals can train themselves to suppress an unpleasant event immediately after it occurs (i.e., before it has faded or been interfered with) by redirecting their conscious thinking away from it. This is often claimed to be true of victims of traumatic experiences. Unlike so-called deep repression, in which memories are claimed to be unavailable even if the individual tries very hard to recall them, motivated forgetting or suppression is associated with the ability to recall unpleasant experiences when we consciously attempt to do so. They are only temporarily out of consciousness as a result of a desire to avoid thinking of them. "Thus, when we say that we suppressed an experience, we mean that we have consciously elected not to dwell on it because it is too unpleasant, embarrassing, or threatening" (Ceci & Bruck, 1995, p. 194). Frequently writers mix these two types of memory failure (repression and motivated forgetting):

There are a range of hypotheses concerning the effects of trauma on memory. At one extreme is the hypothesis that trauma blanks out painful memories in order to protect the individual from the pain. According to some people, this is an unconscious process and is called repression; according to others, it is a conscious process called *motivated forgetting.* (Thompson, Morton, & Fraser, 1997, p. 616)

A concept that is closely related to motivated forgetting is called directed forgetting or thought suppression. Both directed forgetting and thought suppression are defined as "avoiding consciousness of a thought" (Wegner, 1989, p. 9), but the term "directed forgetting" is used almost exclusively to refer to forgetting words, whereas the term "thought suppression" is employed to deal with the forgetting of discrete objects, events, or sequences of events.

An example of thought suppression is to ask someone to try not to think of food when he or she is dieting. Ideally, the individual will actively engage in experiences that are distracting, such as watching TV or reading a book. Another example comes from desensitization therapy: If someone wants to not think about the possibility of a plane crash while boarding a plane, he or she could try to imagine how his or her family would cope and survive without him (Wegner, 1989). And, of course, if an individual experienced a traumatic or embarrassing event, he or she would try to distract his or her thoughts away from this particular event and engage in more pleasant thoughts.

One irony about motivated forgetting and thought suppression is that these techniques "create a monitoring process that ironically increases the automatic activation of the very thought that is to be suppressed" (Wegner, Quillian, & Houston, 1996, p. 680). Therefore, by consciously trying to forget a word/event, one often becomes more likely to remember it! This observation has led researchers to remark that "people often continue to remember items they have been asked intentionally to forget" (Wegner et al., p. 681).

One final aspect of conscious forgetting techniques deserves mention. When a subject is motivated to forget a film he or she has watched, even though his or her overall memory of the film is unimpaired, the subject is nevertheless *less* able to retrieve the sequence of events in the film than subjects who were told to think about the film or subjects who were not given any instructions (Wegner et al., 1996). This finding has an interesting implication with regard to thought suppression of traumatic events, since such events are often recollected in a fragmentary, nonsequential manner.

REFERENCES

Ceci & Bruck, (1995). *Jeopardy in the courtroom: A scientific analysis of children's testimony.* Washington DC: American Psychological Association.

Thompson, J., Morton, J., & Fraser, L. (1997). Memories for the marchioness. *Memory, 5,* 615–638.

Wegner, D. M. (1989). *White bears and other unwanted thoughts: Suppression, obsession and psychology of mental control.* New York: Viking.

Wegner, D. M., Quillian, F., & Houston, C. E. (1996). Memories out of order: Thought suppression and the disturbance of sequence memory. *Journal of Personality and Social Psychology, 71,* 680–691.

S. J. CECI
Cornell University

T. KANAYA
Cornell University

FORGETTING
MEMORY

MOTIVATION

Motivation, simply stated, refers to internal energizing states of animals and humans. Motivation leads to the instigation, persistence, energy, and direction of behavior. Direction is provided by environmental cues and by the individual's goals. Motivation *disposition* differs from motivation *arousal.* One may become fearful or anxious as a motivational disposition, but being actually aroused (that is, *motivated*) occurs only in a given moment or situation.

Motivation may refer to internal states experienced by animals of all species, such as hunger, or it may be uniquely human, such as the striving for achievement and excellence. Psychologists study many internal variables (personality, thinking, learning, and intelligence), and these variables often interface with that of motivation. For example, a number of personality theories are primarily motivational theories, in that they speak of the development and manifestation of life-pattern attitudes and behaviors in motivational terms. These are psychodynamic theories of personality, such as the theories of Adler and Freud. Learning and motivation are closely related, and motivation involves many learned aspects. Cognition, problem solving, and information processing—that is, symbolic events and thought—are closely related to motivation, especially in the case of humans. Although these internal variables are interrelated, they require independent scientific scrutiny and definition (Ferguson, 2000).

DIFFERENT KINDS OF MOTIVATIONS: SPECIFICITY AND DIRECTION

Motivation leads to goal-directed behavior. Thirsty animals look for water, or a person in a stressful job tries to escape from an unpleasant work situation. One way of describing goals is as objective events, that is, as tangible environmental outcomes. Animal behaviorists have referred to a "goal box," with a thirsty rat obtaining water in a goal box after running a maze. In this example, water is defined as a goal in an objective, environmental sense.

The second way of describing goals is as an internal representation or abstraction rather than an objective external event. This is an internal cognition occurring in any given moment as a representation of an event the person anticipates in the future. The motivation and the goal as here-and-now internal processes exist regardless of whether or not the goal is objectively (environmentally) reached. For example, when one is motivated to leave a stressful work situation, the goal of finding a less stressful job is a thought a person has about future events. The goal of finding another place of employment is directing and steering, in that behavior follows specific response alternatives. In moving towards a goal, the person makes certain responses rather than others, and the motivation is internal. If a parent sets a standard for a child, or an employee's supervisor has an expectation of work accomplishment, neither of these external goal events are motivating unless the person internally self-sets such a goal.

Motivation can be directional in terms of specific antecedent events, not merely in terms of outcomes (actual or cognitively representational outcomes). The motivation of thirst is specific not only in terms of water-seeking goal orientation, but also because it results from specific prior events such as the animal or person having been deprived of water, or having eaten unusually salty food, or in other ways having become dehydrated. Various antecedent events lead to different kinds of motivational states, and very often the behavior of the individual differs according to what specific antecedents have occurred.

INTENSITY

Motivation differs not only in kind, such as an individual being thirsty rather than fearful, but also in intensity. We can speak of being more or less thirsty, more or less fearful. Intensity has been described with terms such as "dynamogenic" or arousing, which refer to the energizing aspect of motivation. It is generally agreed that motivation excites or energizes, but theories differ as to how.

Different simultaneous sources of motivation may have a compounding effect on behavior. For example, an individual who is concurrently hungry, thirsty, fearful, and highly achievement-motivated can be said to be under more total motivational excitation than an individual who is only hungry or only fearful. Thus, heightened motivational arousal may occur as a result of increased intensity in any one kind of motivation or as a function of the combination of different sources of motivation. Behavioral manifestations of such heightened total motivation can be seen by increased responsivity, more startle to loud noises, and general "jumpiness." The energizing effect of heightened motivational intensity can be observed by means of physiological measures as well as overt responses.

A variety of physiological measures reflect different intensities of motivational arousal. Measures of brain waves, skin conductance, heart rate, and muscle tension can identify the intensity dimension of motivation. Under conditions of drowsiness and low excitation, electroencephalographic recordings generally show slow and large brain waves with a regular pattern, while under excited alertness the pattern is one of fast, low, irregular waves. When aroused or excited, individuals also tend to show increases in muscle potential, as measured by electromyographic recordings, and decreases in skin resistance. Individual differences lead to variation in physiological responses under arousal.

Animals generally run, turn wheels, and press bars at a faster rate when they have an increased level of motivation. Overall, organisms, especially naive ones, are more active when they are motivated. For animals and humans, heightened motivation tends to increase effort, persistence, and responsivity.

The energizing aspect of motivation can also be seen by increased stimulus generalization. Stimulus generalization refers to a broadening in the range of stimuli to which an organism responds. For example, if a person is conditioned to lift his finger or a dog to lift her paw to a certain tone, similar tones will also elicit the finger or the paw lifting, even if the subject has never previously learned to respond to these tones. Jenkins, Pascal, and Walker (1958) trained pigeons to peck at an illuminated circle 1.4 cm in diameter, and then tested the pigeons with larger and smaller circles. The animals that were trained and tested under strong hunger motivation, under 70% of body weight, gave responses to test stimuli that were further removed in size from the training stimulus than did the pigeons trained and tested under less hunger, that is, 90% of body weight.

Although at one time the reticular activating system (RAS) was cited as a physiological explanation for the diffusely energizing effects of increased motivation, considerable controversy exists regarding the processes involved in arousal. Some contemporary theorists (e.g., Steriade, 1996) have found cortical desynchronization to be associated with the firing of specific neurons and with signs of behavioral arousal, but a full understanding of arousal processes is not yet available.

DIFFERENCES BETWEEN PSYCHOLOGICAL AND PHYSIOLOGICAL NEED

Studies with a variety of mammals, and especially with nonhuman primates, have shown that psychological and physiological survival needs are very complex, and they also differ in numerous ways. Rhesus monkeys have been shown to require opportunities

for exploration and manipulation, and the need for loving relationships in young monkeys has been documented. Both in nonhuman species and in humans, social animals of all kinds require a wide variety of social satisfaction for optimum adaptation and effective coping. Psychological variables can influence physiology, and physiological variables can influence psychological processes. Motivation has been shown by health psychologists to affect immunological functioning, and in many ways, motivational states have a strong impact on the total health of the individual.

Psychological needs may be independent of physiological needs, and the reverse can be true. Many toxic effects which create physiological needs fail to relate to psychological needs. Physiological and psychological states also differ in the motivation of hunger. For human beings an important distinction exists between a physiological need for food for health and survival and a psychological need for food. Problems of obesity as well as anorexia nervosa have become more prevalent in current society. People can crave food when they are bored or anxious but not in a state of food deprivation, and people can find food aversive and abstain from eating even when there is a strong tissue need for nourishment (Capaldi, 1996). Overall, particularly for humans, although physiological needs may be powerful sources of motivation, they are neither necessary nor sufficient as the basis for motivation.

DIFFERENCES BETWEEN BEHAVIOR AND MOTIVATION

One cannot infer the existence of a motivation merely by the presence of certain behaviors. It is a tautology and not scientifically useful to say, for example, that because someone is aggressive this necessarily points to a motivation or drive for aggression. Behavior may be due to many factors. A person may eat and not be hungry, crouch in a manner suggesting fear and not be fearful, attain achievement and not be motivated by the "need to achieve." Because motivation is an intervening variable, that is, a state inferred to occur within an individual, how such a variable relates to behavior requires careful observation. Without adequate operational definitions people can conclude erroneously that "I couldn't have been hungry, because I didn't eat," or "I engage in sexual behavior because I'm under a high sexual drive." Evidence has shown that people can eat when feeling unloved, and individuals may refrain from eating when motivated to seek social approval, obtain a job, or participate in a political hunger strike. Sexual behavior may occur when individuals seek power, prestige, or social approval rather than sexual gratification related to sexual arousal (McClelland, 1973).

Rewards and reward pathways in the brain have been studied to gauge the ways they affect motivation and behavior, especially in addiction. Addiction to a wide range of substances in animals and humans has been found to be related to neurophysiological processes characterized as "rewarding." Incentives of all types have been shown to affect motivation, but how the motivation translates into behavior depends on a very large range of additional factors.

FEAR AND ANXIETY

From many kinds of studies it is evident that early life experiences and learning shape the way animals and humans respond to stressful and fear-arousing events. What situations arouse motivation of fear and anxiety depends on the species and on the individual's prior experiences. Research has focused on how these motivations are learned, what kinds of situations induce them, and how these motivations affect behavior. A wide variety of animal and human behaviors occur toward painful or fear-arousing stimuli, such as attack, "freezing," crouching, running, and fleeing, and some of these behaviors follow species-specific patterns. Stimuli associated with pain come to evoke fear. Fear occurs when painful stimulation is anticipated. Fear is associated with specific events or contexts while anxiety tends to be more generalized and nonspecific. In humans, painful events are often symbolic and not merely physical, and researchers have explored conceptual processes such as "fear of failure" (Atkinson, 1964).

If a painful stimulation can be terminated (escape) or prevented (avoidance), an animal or a person can learn new behavior that leads to such escape or avoidance. Behavior acquired through avoidance learning is typically acquired more slowly and persists longer than behavior acquired through escape learning. Dogs in shuttle boxes, for example, have been found to maintain shuttling behavior for very long periods of time in a situation in which painful shock had been previously given but was no longer being administered. Human anxiety has been thought to maintain avoidant behaviors in a comparable way. That is, persons behave defensively as if an aversive event might happen, without ever verifying whether or not the pain or danger actually occurs.

That anxiety has far more negative than positive consequences was noted long ago by Freud, who postulated that human neurosis has its roots in anxiety. Clinical, field, and laboratory findings have demonstrated that defensive motivations like fear and anxiety are likely to lead to behaviors that interfere with effective task performance and creative problem solving. Under mild anxiety concerning an upcoming exam, a student may spend time studying rather than going to movie, yet under severe anxiety that same student may withdraw into sleep, drug use, or other forms of task-irrelevant behavior. Task-oriented anxiety is likely to focus on task mastery, while self-oriented anxiety is likely to engender thoughts that indicate preoccupation with self-worth or with personal safety. Such thoughts may interfere with problem solving and limit the amount of attention given to task demands. A fear of failure may lead to behaviors directed toward preventing failure rather than behaviors directed toward attaining task success.

Anxiety can lead to stress-induced illness and lower immune system activity, and is associated with lowered productive energy. Memory, attentional control, and retrieval efficiency tend to suffer when an individual is anxious. State and trait anxiety have wide-ranging consequences, many of which have a spiral effect. That is, high trait anxious people are more pessimistic and more prone to take note of threatening information than are persons with low anxiety (Eysenck, 1991).

Anxiety can be measured as both a trait and a state. Usually, but not always, the two show a strong positive correlation. In certain situations persons who have a disposition to be anxious (high trait anxiety) may have low state anxiety, and likewise, under specific circumstances persons of low trait anxiety may be very high in state anxiety. Anxiety and fear not only affect behavior but may themselves result from a person's actions, so that a two-way rather than

unidirectional relationship exists between motivation and behavior. In one experiment, highly anxious college students learned word lists made up of pairs of associated words, like "adept-skillful" and "frigid-arctic," more rapidly than did their less anxious peers. In two other experiments, rather than anxiety altering performance, the reverse occurred: Subjects who performed poorly became anxious, while those who performed well had low anxiety after the learning task (Ferguson, 1983). Thus, not only can anxiety affect performance, but it can also rise or fall according to how well the person performs on a task.

A person's prior skill and the level of task difficulty are two factors that affect task performance. Thus, if the barrier to successful performance is lack of adequate comprehension or skill, the person should focus on acquiring the necessary comprehension or skill rather than on merely heightening motivation and increasing the amount of effort on the task. Anxiety can be reduced when the skills necessary to perform a task are improved. However, some individuals maintain high anxiety in spite of requisite skills and high performance.

Although anxiety and fear can rise in response to aversive external events, in human beings these motivations and allied emotions can also be self-generated. According to Adlerian theory and clinical evidence (Adler, 1927/1957; Dreikurs, 1967), emotions are linked with motivation, and they serve a goal and are generated for a purpose. For example, a child may develop strong anxiety to get her parents to cater to her whims, or a husband can display marked anxiety as a means of getting his wife to pamper him and provide him with constant service. In this way emotions which typically disrupt a person's performance or adaptive behavior can also be used as a vehicle for behavioral control. The complexity of human motivation is well-illustrated by anxiety, which can be facilitating as well as debilitating, can alter performance as well as be altered by it, and can serve a variety of interpersonal goals.

EXPECTANCY, CONTROL, AND APPROACH MOTIVATION

Cognitions and beliefs play a dominant role in human motivation. Beliefs are involved in values, expectation of future outcomes, and apperception of environmental events. Human motivation has been studied in terms of many kinds of cognitive processes. For example, literature on the achievement motive indicates that people who have a strong need to achieve learn to strive for excellence in performance at an early age. Such individuals are not readily discouraged by failure experiences and anticipate successful performance in optimistic ways (in terms of expectancies of probability of success). Self-reliance is a key aspect of their motivational disposition (Atkinson, 1964).

Many theorists have postulated that people function effectively when they believe that positive outcomes are possible and when they believe that they have control over the nature of events that happen to them. An early theory that emphasized the importance of teaching children self-reliance and courage (willingness to try new things and to expend effort even when success is not guaranteed) was that of Alfred Adler. He emphasized the importance of children learning to identify with fellow human beings and learning to strive to contribute to the welfare of human society (Adler, 1927/1959). The literature on the locus of control of reinforcement

(Rotter, 1966) indicates that people who believe they have little control over events that happen to them are more anxious and are less likely to behave in ways that lead to positive outcomes, compared with individuals who believe their actions alter external events and consequences. Children trained with encouragement and self-reliance rather than with praise and rewards are more likely to maintain socially constructive behaviors (Dreikurs, Grunwald, & Pepper, 1999). Laboratory studies with children and adults have shown that intrinsic motivation and self-direction maintain behavior more effectively than do extrinsic motivation and externally administered rewards (Deci, 1975).

Social motivation, expectancy, effort, and performance interrelate in a wide variety of settings. One study of sibling pairs found that, when children heard how their sibling performed on a task, those siblings who were allied in their relationship set different levels of expectation than did siblings who were competitive in their relationship (Ferguson, 1958). Realistic and moderately high goal-setting has been found to occur in children with a high need to achieve, and moderately high goal-setting also leads to improved workplace performance in adults. People who fear failure, moreover, tend to set unrealistic goals that are either too high or too low. Social motivation and task motivation alter individuals' expectancies and behavior in a very wide range of circumstances.

Predictability for negative as well as positive outcomes has far-reaching effects on behavior and motivation in animals as well as humans. Self-direction and symbolic processes are fundamental in determining motivation and its effects on behavior. Altruism and prosocial motivation enable humans to establish long-term emotional bonding, to overcome adversity, and to engage in cooperation and creative problem solving. Situational factors as well as intrinsic motivation shape people's cooperative or competitive actions and attitudes. External incentives and internal motive dispositions combine to shape the energizing and directive effects of motivation. Societal and personal values, prior experiences and learning, and situational variables all shape motivation and its effect on behavior.

REFERENCES

Adler, A. (1927/1959). *The practice and theory of individual psychology.* Paterson, NJ: Littlefield, Adams.

Atkinson, J. W. *An introduction to motivation.* New York: Van Nostrand, 1964.

Capaldi, E. D. (1996). Introduction. In E. D. Capaldi (Ed.), *Why we eat what we eat: The psychology of eating* (pp. 3–9). Washington, DC: American Psychological Association.

Deci, E. L. (1975). *Intrinsic motivation.* New York: Plenum.

Dreikurs, R. (1967). The function of emotions. In R. Dreikurs (Ed.), *Psychodynamics, psychotherapy, and counseling* (pp. 205–217). Chicago: Adler School of Professional Psychology.

Dreikurs, R., Grunwald, B. B., & Pepper, F. C. (1999). *Maintaining sanity in the classroom: Classroom management techniques* (2nd ed.). Philadelphia: Taylor & Francis.

Eysenck, M. W. (1991). Trait anxiety and cognition. In C. D. Spielberger, I. G. Sarason, Z. Kulcsar, & G. L. Van Heck (Eds.), *Stress and emotion: Anxiety, anger and curiosity* (Vol. 14; pp. 77–84). New York: Hemisphere.

Ferguson, E. D. (1958). The effect of sibling competition and alliance on level of aspiration, expectation, and performance. *Journal of Abnormal and Social Psychology, 56,* 213–222.

Ferguson, E. D. (1983). The effect of motivation and word characteristics on recognition. *American Journal of Psychology, 96,* 253–266.

Ferguson, E. D. (2000). *Motivation: A biosocial and cognitive integration of motivation and emotion.* New York: Oxford University Press.

Jenkins, W. O., Pascal, G. R., & Walker, R. W., Jr. (1958). Deprivation and generalization. *Journal of Experimental Psychology, 56,* 274–277.

McClelland, D. C. (1973). The two faces of power. In D. C. McClelland & R. S. Steele (Eds.), *Human motivation: A book of readings* (pp. 300–316). Morristown, NJ: General Learning Press.

Rotter, J. B. (1966,). Generalized expectancies for internal versus external control of reinforcement. *Psychological Monographs, 80* (1, Whole No. 609).

Steriade, M. (1996, April 12). Arousal: Revisiting the reticular activating system. *Science, 272,* No. 5259, 225–226.

SUGGESTED READING

Cohen, S., & Herbert, T. B. (1996). Health psychology: Psychological factors and physical disease from the perspective of human psychoneuroimmunology. *Annual Review of Psychology, 47,* 113–142.

Dreikurs, R., & Soltz, V. (1999). *Children: The challenge.* New York: Penguin.

Harlow, H. F. (1971). *Learning to love.* San Francisco: Albion.

Locke, E. A., & Latham, G. P. (1990). *A theory of goal setting and task performance.* Englewood Cliffs, NJ: Prentice-Hall.

McClelland, D. C. (1958). Risk taking in children with high and low need for achievement. In J. W. Atkinson (Ed.), *Motives in fantasy, action, and society* (pp. 309–318). New York: Van Nostrand.

Thayer, R. E. (1989). *The biopsychology of mood and arousal.* New York: Oxford University Press.

E. D. FERGUSON
Edwardsville, IL

INTRINSIC MOTIVATION
REWARDS AND INTRINSIC INTEREST

MOWRER, O. HOBART (1907–1982)

O. Hobart Mowrer first published a series of 19 papers concerning vestibulo-ocular reflexes and spatial orientation that, while not often cited in psychological literature, were well received in otology and sensory physiology. They also served, somewhat paradoxically, to gain him an appointment (1934–1940) at Yale's Institute of Human Relations. There he developed theoretical and research interests in the psychology of learning, language, psychopathology, certain cognitive processes, and interpersonal relations, which importantly influenced his subsequent professional career.

During his tenure at the Harvard Graduate School of Education (1940–1948), Mowrer had a courtesy appointment in the Department of Psychology and was associated with Talcott Parsons, Clyde Kluckhohn, Gordon Allport, and Henry Murray in the establishment of the Department of Social Relations. During the latter part of this period he was editor of the *Harvard Educational Review* and was instrumental in the ultimate transfer of all editorial responsibility to a student board.

In 1948 Mowrer was appointed research professor of psychology at the University of Illinois, a position he held until his retirement in 1975. From 1953 to 1954 he was president of the American Psychological Association, and served on the editorial panel of several professional journals. His best-known and probably most enduring practical contribution is a means of treating noctural enuresis known as the bell-and-pad method. His more substantive contributions are in learning, language, and interpersonal psychology.

Mowrer's complete bibliography contains some 235 items, a dozen of which are books. His major publications include *Abnormal Reactions or Actions; Learning Theory and Personality Dynamics;* Chapter 11 in the *History of Psychology in Autobiography; Learning Theory and Behavior; Leaves from Many Seasons; Selected Papers;* and *Learning Theory and Symbolic Processes.*

STAFF

MULTICULTURAL COUNSELING

Multicultural counseling assumes that each person's identity has been shaped by a great number of cultures and that different cultural identities become salient at different times, places, and circumstances. Multiculturalism has emerged as a social, political, economic, educational, and cultural movement during the last two decades, and has a significant influence on counseling and other applications of psychology. The term "multicultural" implies a wide range of special interest groups without grading, comparing, or ranking them as better or worse than one another, and without denying the distinct, complementary, or even contradictory perspectives that each group brings with it. Multicultural counseling recognizes that each individual belongs to many different cultures at the same time. Within-group differences as well as between-group differences are important in the multicultural perspective (Pedersen, 1997).

SOURCES OF MULTICULTURALISM

Interest in multicultural counseling grew out of the civil rights and feminist movements. The militancy of civil rights movements in the 1950s, combined with the community mental health movement of the 1960s, affirmed that mental health care was the right of all cit-

izens. Issues of feminism and the popular dissent against the Vietnam War promoted discontent wherever the media accepted and encouraged protest against inequity. By the 1970s, underuse of mental health services by minorities had become a serious issue. By the 1980s, large numbers of refugees demonstrated the importance of a multicultural global perspective in counseling, and by the 1990s, the rapidly changing demographic balance predicted that one third or more of the nation's school students would be nonwhite by the turn of the century, further highlighting the need for multicultural counseling.

Many minority writers have contributed to and shaped the multicultural perspective, which initially was focused on the oppression of minorities by the majority culture. Sue and Sue (1999) and Pedersen, Draguns, Lonner, and Trimble (1996) have documented the ways that the counseling profession has protected the status quo of the dominant culture's values. Wrenn (1962) described how cultural encapsulation of counselors has occurred through ethnocentrism ("mine is best") or through relativism ("to each his or her own"). Encapsulation results from defining reality according to dominant culture assumptions, being insensitive to cultural variations in society, protecting the status quo against change, and relying on a technique-oriented job definition.

Multiculturalism combines the alternatives of universalism and relativism by explaining behavior in terms of both those culturally-learned perspectives that are unique and those that provide common ground across cultures. Although the melting pot overemphasized similarities and neglected the culturally unique identity of each individual, the diversity perspective sometimes overemphasizes culturally unique perspectives while neglecting common-ground universals across cultures, which deprives individuals of the basis for working together in harmony. A multicultural perspective emphasizes both similarities and differences at the same time.

MULTICULTURALISM AS A FOURTH FORCE

Counseling is moving toward a generic theory of multiculturalism that recognizes the psychological consequences of each cultural context in which behaviors are learned and displayed. The notion of multiculturalism as a fourth force—supplementing the psychodynamic, behavioral, and humanist perspectives—emphasizes that all counseling is multicultural. Making culture central and generic rather than exotic or marginal adds meaning to other psychological theories, just as the fourth dimension of time adds metaphoric meaning to three-dimensional space (Pedersen, 1998).

Whether multiculturalism actually emerges as a fourth force on a global scale remains unclear. Much will depend on how closely the globalized paradigm shift in psychology toward a postmodern and constructivist perspective increases our awareness of cultural factors. Other facts that may be influential including the following:

1. While the term "multiculturalism" has been influential within different countries in describing the interaction of minorities with majority cultures, it has not yet received as much attention across cultures and countries on a global scale.

2. In some countries, such as South Africa, multiculturalism was used to justify an oppressive practice of apartheid, giving the

term a very different and more negative meaning than it has in most other countries.

3. While multiculturalism may become a generic fourth force, there is some question about whether the multicultural movement has achieved global status at this stage of its development.

4. Multiculturalism has been grounded in the values of a North American culture in which the collectivistic perspectives of minorities are minimized and the individualistic perspectives of the dominant culture are emphasized.

5. If multiculturalism is defined broadly to include gender, disability, age, lifestyle, and other affiliations, then the pervasiveness of multiculturalism becomes more obvious than if it is limited to ethnic and national factors.

6. Youth culture defines an identity that cuts across the other boundaries of culture and provides a means of classifying social trends, movements, and affiliations across cultural groups, if the broad definition of multiculturalism is applied.

7. The multicultural perspective will change not only the content of our thinking but even the process of thinking itself as we move away from social homogeneity toward cultural heterogeneity.

8. To the extent that all counseling occurs in a multicultural context (broadly defined) the term "multiculturalism" is likely to have generic applications.

CONTROVERSIES OF MULTICULTURAL COUNSELING

There has been some controversy between those supporting cross-cultural perspectives and those supporting cultural, transcultural, multicultural, or intercultural psychological descriptors. A recent attempt to synthesize these alternatives has resulted in a multicultural counseling theory (MCT) (Sue, Ivey, & Pedersen, 1996). Multicultural counseling theory is based on six major propositions about counseling theories as worldviews to develop a multicultural metatheory: (a) each western or nonwestern theory represents a different world view; (b) the totality and interrelationships of client-counselor experiences and contexts must be the focus of counseling; (c) a counselor's or client's cultural identity will influence how problems are defined and will dictate or define appropriate counseling goals or processes; (d) the ultimate goal of MCT is to expand the repertoire of helping-responses available to counselors; (e) conventional roles of counseling are only some of many alternative helping roles available in other cultural contexts; and (f) MCT emphasizes the importance of expanding personal, family, group, and organizational consciousness in a contextual orientation.

Multiculturalism has promoted research on racial and ethnic identity development Ponterotto, Casas, Suzuki and Alexander (1995) describe scales of ethnic identity for American Indians, Blacks, Hispanics, Whites and other populations; these scales generally include five stages. The first stage, pre-encounter, is the level of least awareness, followed by a second stage of encounter, in which a crisis occurs. Next is the immersion-emersion stage, in which cultural identity becomes more explicit, followed by the internalization stage, in which these new insights are internalized. Fifth and last is the internalization-commitment stage, which is the highest level of racial/ethnic awareness. These categories of increased awareness are important for counselors to use in assessing their own competencies and for defining constructive growth among clients from different cultural backgrounds.

SUPPORT FOR A MULTICULTURAL PERSPECTIVE

Support for multicultural issues in counseling has only recently been reflected in the counseling profession. The Basic Behavioral Sciences Task Force of the National Advisory Mental Health Council (1996) has identified specific examples in which (a) social and cultural beliefs influence diagnosis and treatment; (b) diagnosis differs across cultures; (c) symptoms are expressed differently across cultures; (d) diagnostic categories reflect majority values, and (e) most providers are from the majority cultures while most clients are from minority cultures.

Members of the American Psychological Association's Division 17 (Counseling) Education and Training Committee developed a position paper (Sue et al., 1982) of competencies for multicultural counseling divided into competencies emphasizing awareness, knowledge, and skill. The awareness competencies are the need for counselors to become aware of their own personal cultural heritage while valuing and respecting differences, to be aware of how their own values may affect culturally different clients, to become comfortable with differences in race and belief between clients and counselors, and to know when a minority client should be referred elsewhere. The four knowledge competencies are to have a good understanding of the sociopolitical dynamics between minority and majority cultures; to have specific knowledge and information about the client's particular culture; to have a clear and explicit knowledge of generic and traditional counseling theory and practice; and to be aware of institutional barriers that prevent minorities from using mental health services. The three skill competencies are that all culturally-skilled counselors should be able to generate a wide variety of verbal and nonverbal responses appropriate to the cultural setting and skill level; that counselors should be able to send and receive both verbal and nonverbal messages accurately and appropriately in each culturally different context; and that counselors should be able to advocate for or change the system or institution appropriately, when those changes are necessary, on behalf of their culturally different clients. These competencies have been adopted by the American Psychological Association and the American Counseling Association for professional standards of counseling (Sue et al., 1998).

REFERENCES

Basic Behavioral Science Task Force of the National Advisory Mental Health Council (1996). Basic behavioral science research for mental health Sociocultural and environmental processes. *American Psychologist, 51,* 722–731.

Pedersen, P. (1997). *Culture-centered counseling interventions.* Thousand Oaks, CA: Sage.

Pedersen, P. (1998). *Multiculturalism as a fourth force.* Philadelphia: Brunner/Mazel.

Pedersen, P., Draguns, J., Lonner, W., & Trimble, J. (1996). *Counseling across cultures: Fourth edition*. Thousand Oaks, CA: Sage.

Ponterotto, J. G., Casas, J. M., Suzuki, L. A., & Alexander, C. M. (1995). *Handbook of multicultural counseling*. Thousand Oaks, CA: Sage.

Sue, D. W., Bernier, J. E., Durran, A., Fineberg, L., Pedersen, P., Smith, C. J., & Vasquez-Nuttall, G. (1982). Cross-cultural counseling competencies. *The Counseling Psychologist, 19*(2), 45–52.

Sue, D. W., Carter, R. T., Casas, J. M., Fouad, N. A., Ivey, A. E., Jensen, M., LaFromboise, T., Manese, J. E., Ponterotto, J. G., & Vasquez-Nuttall, E. (1998). *Multicultural counseling competencies*. Thousand Oaks, CA: Sage.

Sue, D. W., Ivey, A. E., & Pedersen, P. B. (1997). *A theory of multicultural counseling and therapy*. Pacific Grove, CA: Brooks/Cole.

Sue, D. W., & Sue, D. (1999). *Counseling the culturally different: Theory and practice* (3rd ed.). New York: Wiley Interscience.

Wrenn, G. (1962). The culturally encapsulated counselor. *Harvard Educational Review, 32,* 444–449.

P. PEDERSEN
University of Alabama at Birmingham

MULTIDIMENSIONAL SCALING (MDS)

Multidimensional scaling (MDS) most typically refers to a family of models and associated methods for representing data on similarities or dissimilarities of stimulus objects or other entities (called "stimuli" hereafter) in terms of a spatial model. Essentially the aim of MDS, in the narrower meaning assumed in this article, is to simplify a complex, large set of observations by devising a spatial representation that will show the relationships among the stimuli. In such a spatial model, the *proximities* data (similarities, dissimilarities, association indices, or other measures of closeness or proximity) are assumed to relate in a simple and straightforward way to *distances* between pairs of stimuli. If the data are similarities, for example, the assumption is that the more similar a pair of stimuli are, the closer the points representing those stimuli should be in the spatial representation. The object of MDS is to construct a spatial map so that a simple relationship (usually linear or monotonic) between the proximities data and distances in that spatial map is, to the extent possible, obtained. Of course with real data, subject to error and systematic distortion, a perfect relationship will not generally be possible.

The spatial map that is sought to represent the stimuli may be only one-dimensional (corresponding to arraying the stimuli along a straight line), although more typically it is in two, three, or more dimensions. In a two-dimensional representation, the stimuli are represented simply as points in a plane. With the possible exception of the even simpler one-dimensional representation, such a two-dimensional map is by far the easiest to understand, since it can be easily inspected by standard graphical procedures. The two-dimensional map most nearly corresponds to our intuitive conception of a map, which is almost always two-dimensional.

One example frequently used to illustrate MDS, however, reverses the standard process of reading distances from a map of cities, so as to reconstruct the map knowing only the distances among the cities. In fact, in some forms of MDS—the *nonmetric* MDS procedures described in a moment—only the *rank order* of the intercity distances need be known to reconstruct the map. In one such example, the map of 10 U.S. cities was reconstructed so well, using the rank orders of distances from a table of airline distances among them, that the map could be almost perfectly superimposed on a standard map of the United States, once the scale factor was adjusted appropriately, and a rigid rotation was applied to the MDS map to align its coordinates with the north-south and east-west coordinates of the standard map.

The rotation of coordinates just mentioned is not a trivial issue in MDS, but an important one in practical applications. The object of MDS is not merely to construct the spatial map or representation of the stimuli, but to interpret it in terms of meaningful psychological (or other) dimensions. These dimensions correspond to the coordinates of the map. Whereas a standard map (of cities, say) could be described in terms of a northwest-southeast and northeast-southwest set of coordinates, the more standard north-south and east-west coordinate system gives a more understandable (or interpretable) account of the geographical relations of the cities. It is also true in psychological applications that certain coordinate systems correspond to natural or easily interpretable psychological dimensions, whereas others do not. The particular coordinate system provided by an MDS computer program may be highly arbitrary and require rotation for reasonable interpretability. With regard to individual differences, we shall later discuss how three–way MDS, and the INDSCAL approach in particular, may help solve this rotational problem.

Instead of constructing a geographical map of cities based on their physical distances, we could have constructed a psychological map based on their perceived psychological distances or dissimilarities. Wish, Deutsch, and Biener (1970) used MDS to do this, using nations rather than cities as stimuli. Two dimensions of nations found to be very salient for their subjects were: (a) "political alignment and ideology," contrasting communist with noncommunist nations; and (b) "economic development," contrasting highly developed industrialized countries (the United States, Russia, Western European countries, etc.) with underdeveloped or developing countries (e.g., Zaïre, India, Cuba). Mainland China fell more or less in the middle of the economic dimension and at the "communist" end of the political one. If these two dimensions were rotated differently, the two resulting dimensions might not be so readily interpretable. A good and fairly nontechnical treatment of the entire field of multidimensional scaling is provided by the SAGE monograph on this topic by Kruskal and Wish (1978).

We shall now focus on what, in the taxonomy proposed by Carroll and Arabie (1980), are called MDS models and methods for one-mode (e.g., stimuli), two-way (i.e., pairwise) proximities data. These proximities data can arise from direct human judgments of similarity or dissimilarity, from such data as confusability of pairs of stimuli, or from various types of derived measures of similarity or dissimilarity (e.g., a profile dissimilarity measure computed between stimuli over rating scales or various measures of similarity derived from word association tasks). In some cases matrices of correlations can be used as measures of similarity (of variables, people, stimuli, or other entities), so that MDS, when used this way, can be viewed as an alternative to factor analysis for deriving multidimensional structure from correlational data.

Once defined, the proximities can be thought of as comprising a two-way square table (or matrix) whose general entry is δ_{jk}—the proximity of stimuli (or other objects) j and k. This table will usually (but not always) be symmetrical. The model assumed for these proximities can be expressed as follows:

$$\hat{d}_{jk} = F(\delta_{jk}) \cong d_{jk} \qquad (1)$$

where F is some function (e.g., linear, some specified nonlinear function, or in the case of nonmetric MDS, a merely monotonic function); $\cong$ can be interpreted as meaning "approximately equals" (or equals, except for error terms which will not be further specified in this article); and d_{jk} is the distance between points representing j and k in an R dimensional multidimensional space. The distance d_{jk} is usually defined by the Euclidean distance formula as follows:

$$d_{jk} = \sqrt{\sum_{r=1}^{R} (x_{jr} - x_{kr})^2} \qquad (2)$$

where x_{jr} is the coordinate of the point representing the jth stimulus or other object on the rth dimension, while r ranges from 1 to R, the dimensionality of the space. The objective of MDS is, given the δ's, to solve for the coordinates x_{jr} of the R dimensional space, so that these distances match the δ's as much as possible in some specified sense.

An important distinction frequently made is between metric and nonmetric approaches to MDS. Essentially, this distinction comes down to the form assumed for the function F in equation (1) above. In the *metric* approaches F is generally assumed to be linear, although in some metric approaches F is some well-defined nonlinear function (e.g., exponential, polynomial, or a power function). Another way of stating this is that, in the metric approaches, the proximities are assumed to be measured on at least an *interval scale*. In *nonmetric* MDS, the function F is typically assumed only to be monotonic, or order-preserving. Thus, nonmetric scaling assumes proximities measured only on an *ordinal scale*. The classical metric approach to MDS, in which F is assumed to be linear, is discussed by Torgerson (1958). Other approaches can be implemented

by using appropriate options in many computer programs designed primarily for nonmetric MDS.

NONMETRIC MDS

Nonmetric MDS was first proposed by Coombs (1950, 1964/1976), whose methods for implementing nonmetric MDS were heuristic, however, and not readily applicable to practical data analytic situations. The first effective practical algorithm for nonmetric MDS was proposed by Shepard (1962a, b), who called them "analysis of proximities." Kruskal (1964a, b) then proposed a mathematically more rigorous and numerically more efficient approach, which has become the prototype of all subsequent approaches to nonmetric MDS, as for instance those of Guttman (1968), McGee (1966), and Roskam and Lingoes (1970), or the two-way approach of Takane, Young, and deLeeuw (1977). Although it is a metric rather than a nonmetric approach, and it is based on a rather different criterion of fit than the others, Ramsay's maximum likelihood approach (1977) also utilizes a numerical algorithm that has much in common with the approach first taken by Kruskal. While the details of the approach are too complex to describe adequately here, suffice it to say that Kruskal proposed using an explicit numerical method (the method of gradients, or steepest descent) to solve simultaneously for the matrix of coordinates x_{jr} of the n points in R dimensions ($j = 1,2, \ldots, n; r = 1,2, \ldots, R$), *and* for the merely monotonic function F (nonincreasing or nondecreasing, depending on whether δ is a dissimilarity or a similarity measure), so that F and x_{jr} ($j = 1,2,3, \ldots, n; r = 1,2, \ldots, R$) together optimize (minimize) a measure Kruskal called stress. *Stress* (in its original, and still most popular, definition), is defined thus:

$$\text{Stress} = \sqrt{\frac{\sum_{j}\sum_{k}(d_{jk} - \hat{d}_{jk})^2}{\sum_{j}\sum_{k} d_{jk}^2}} \qquad (3)$$

This general approach has also been adopted by Kruskal and others to provide alternatives to the classical approach to metric MDS described earlier.

AN ILLUSTRATIVE APPLICATION OF TWO-WAY NONMETRIC MDS

To illustrate the use of MDS, we borrow a now classical illustration from Shepard (1963) involving analysis of some data on confusions of Morse code symbols due to Rothkopf (1957). The confusability matrix for the 36 Morse code symbols is shown in Figure 1. (Note that this is a nonsymmetric proximities matrix.)

Shepard applied nonmetric MDS to this matrix, assuming the confusabilities to be measures of similarity of the stimuli (i.e., the more easily confused two stimuli are, the closer or more similar they are assumed to be psychologically). He found that two dimensions provided a generally good representation. The resulting two-dimensional configuration, with a curvilinear coordinate system (provided by Shepard) superimposed for purposes of aiding interpretation of this solution, is shown in Figure 2. The curvilinearity of Shepard's coordinate grid may indicate greater confusability

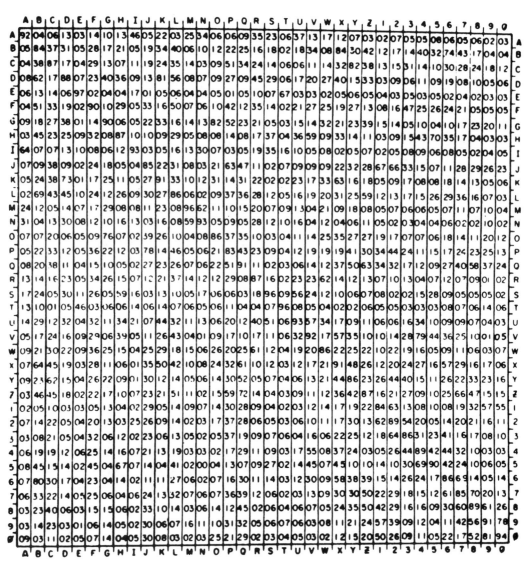

Figure 1.   Matrix of confusabilities of 36 Morse code signals (data from Rothkopf, 1957). From "Analysis of proximities as a technique for the study of information processing in man," by R. N. Shepard, 1963, *Human Factors, 5,* 38. Copyright 1963 by The Human Factors Society, Inc., and reproduced by permission.

of signals involving different numbers of dots than those with different numbers of dashes.

The power of MDS techniques can be easily discerned by comparing the information derived from inspection of the original 36×36 matrix of confusabilities to that conveyed by the two-dimensional representation Shepard found by use of MDS. To most of us, the data matrix just provides a headache combined with what James referred to as a "blooming, buzzing confusion"—appropriate, perhaps, for *confusions* data. While the two dimensions shown here may not account for all the structure in this matrix, they certainly do account for a very major portion of it. By simple inspection we see that the two dimensions can be called "number of components" (going systematically from the one-component to the five-component signals as we move vertically up the two dimensional diagram), and "dots versus dashes" (or dot-dash ratio, as it is sometimes called), contrasting signals on the left composed of all or mostly dots with those on the right made up of all or mostly dashes, with a relatively smooth transition between. These

two dimensions account for the major features of the original confusability matrix. To confirm this, one can note, by comparing the two-dimensional configuration with the confusions data, that those signals most often confused are indeed generally those that are closest in this configuration, although that correspondence is far from perfect. The monotonic function (not shown here) relating the original data (percent "same" judgments) to the interpoint distances appears to be very nearly a negative exponential or so-called exponential decay function, which there is good theoretical reason to expect for confusions data.

In two-way MDS, it is important to keep in mind that, while the data are sufficient to determine the configuration of points, they do not in general determine the appropriate orientation of coordinate axes. This is because Euclidean distances are invariant under rigid rotation of the coordinate system (i.e., the particular coordinate system we use is convenient for interpretation of the map, but the distances remain unchanged when we effect such a change in coordinates). Shepard, in fact, had first to rotate the essentially arbi-

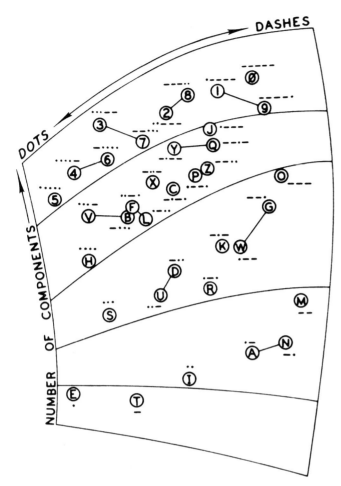

Figure 2. Two-dimensional configuration resulting from multidimensional scaling analysis of Rothkopf's Morse code confusabilities (analysis by Shepard, 1963). From "Analysis of proximities as a technique for the study of information processing in man," R. N. Shepard, 1963, *Human Factors, 5,* 39. Copyright 1963 by The Human Factors Society, Inc., and reproduced by permission.

trary coordinate system in terms of which the solution emerged from the computer, before drawing the slightly curved coordinate grid in terms of which he interpreted the solution. This process of rotating coordinates to effect optimal interpretability is relatively straightforward in two dimensions (where, after all, one can see precisely what is going on), but in 3, 4, 9, or 10 dimensions, this becomes very hard indeed (often prohibitively so). In fact, it is very likely the difficulty of finding the optimal rotation of coordinates in high-dimensional representations that has produced a strong bias in favor of small-dimensional solutions (usually two- or three-dimensional) in two-way MDS applications. We shall now see how effective use of individual differences among subjects (or subgroups of subjects, or other data sources) can be used to overcome this often insuperable problem by uniquely orienting the coordinate system.

INDIVIDUAL DIFFERENCES MULTIDIMENSIONAL SCALING

The first approach to individual differences multidimensional scaling was the points of view approach proposed by Tucker and Messick (1963). This was soon followed by the now dominant ap-

proach, generally called INDSCAL, for *IN*dividual *D*ifferences multidimensional *SCAL*ing (Bloxom, 1968; Horan, 1969; Carroll & Chang, 1970). INDSCAL accounts for individual differences in proximities data in terms of a model assuming a common set of dimensions underlying the stimuli (or other objects), while assuming that different subjects (or other data sources) have different patterns of saliences or importance weights for these common dimensions. Assuming for now that the three-way proximities data correspond to similarity judgments by different human subjects, the model makes the quite plausible assumption that each subject simply has a different set of scale factors (which can be thought of as amplifications or attenuations) applied to a set of fundamental psychological stimulus dimensions common to all individuals. It is as if each individual subject has a set of gain controls, one for each of the fundamental stimulus dimensions, and that these are differently adjusted for each subject. The different settings of these subjective gain controls (to continue the metaphor) might be due to genetic differences (as in the case of individual differences in color perception of subjects with normal and anomalous color vision, to be discussed below), to environmental factors related to different experiential histories, or most likely, to a combination of nature (genetics) and nurture (environment).

One strength of this model for individual differences in perception, as will be seen, is that the psychological dimensions assumed for the stimuli are uniquely determined by the similarities judgments of the subjects (based on the patterns of individual differences in similarities judgments). A second, equally important, advantage is that the saliences, or perceptual importance weights, can provide quite useful individual difference measures for the subjects. In the Wish and colleagues (1970) study of nations discussed earlier, the fundamental dimensions described above were in fact found by using the INDSCAL approach and relying on its property, sometimes called dimensional uniqueness, of uniquely orienting the coordinate axis. The subject saliences were also found to relate closely to a measure (independently derived) of political attitude of their subjects vis-à-vis the Vietnam war (then a pertinent issue). Doves put much more weight on the economic development dimension than on the political alignment and ideology (or communist-noncommunist) dimension, while hawks reversed this pattern. Moderates put about equal weight on the two dimensions.

The data for individual differences MDS generally comprise a number of symmetric proximities matrices, one for each subject (or other data source). Such data are generally designated as two-mode (stimuli and subjects) but three-way (stimuli × stimuli × subjects; Carroll & Arabie, 1980). A *mode* is a specific set of entities (e.g., the stimulus mode). The number of *ways* can be thought of as the number of directions in the data table (e.g., rows, columns, and what we might call slices for a three-way table, even though both rows *and* columns may correspond to the stimulus mode, while slices correspond to the subjects mode). In contrast, recall that a single proximities matrix is called one-mode, but two-way data.

Mathematically, the INDSCAL model can be expressed as follows:

$$F_i(\delta_{jk}^i) \cong d_{jk}^i = \sqrt{\sum_{r=1}^{R} w_{ir}(x_{jr} - x_{kr})^2} \qquad (4)$$

Here δ^i_{jk} is the similarity or dissimilarity judgment of subject i for stimuli j and k. F_i is a function transforming δ^i_{jk} approximately into a distance d^i_{jk} between the points representing stimuli j and k for that same subject (i), where that distance is expressed as a *weighted* Euclidean distance given by the formula on the right. F_i will generally be linear in metric approaches to INDSCAL and monotonic in nonmetric approaches. Comparing this equation for d^i_{jk} with equation (2) for Euclidean distance reveals that this formula differs only by the introduction of the *subject weights* w_{ir}. The stimulus coordinates (x_{jr} being the coordinate of stimulus j on the rth stimulus dimension) are the same for all subjects, only the weights for the R dimensions differ from subject to subject. The purpose of INDSCAL analysis is, given the three-way proximities data, to solve simultaneously for the stimulus coordinates (x_{jr}) and the subject weights (w_{ir}) so as to optimize the fit of the INDSCAL model to the (transformed) proximities data.

AN ILLUSTRATIVE APPLICATION OF INDSCAL TO SOME COLOR DISSIMILARITIES

We now illustrate in Figure 3 the INDSCAL model by an example that entails a reanalysis of some data on color perception collected by Helm (1964). Helm and Tucker (1962) had previously analyzed these data via a points of view analysis and found approximately 10 points of view necessary to account adequately for all the individual differences. Our analysis in terms of the INDSCAL model has quite nicely accounted for the individual differences among the 14 subjects in terms of a single two-dimensional solution. Moreover, the unique dimensions from the INDSCAL analysis shown in Figure 3 were interpretable without rotation of axes. Dimension 1 corresponds essentially to a "blue vs. yellow" (or more accurately, perhaps, a "purple-blue vs. green-yellow") factor, and dimension 2 to a "red versus green" (or "purple-red vs. blue-green") factor. This accords very well with physiological and psychophysical evidence, strongly suggesting the existence of blue-yellow and red-green receptors.

Included among Helm's subjects were four who were deficient, to varying degrees, in red-green color vision. In the INDSCAL analysis this deficiency is reflected in the fact that these subjects all have lower weights for the red-green factor (dimension 2) than do any of the normal subjects. The effect of these differential weights can be seen in Figure 2 by comparing the private perceptual spaces for the color-deficient subjects with those for the normals. The spaces for the color-deficient subjects are compressed in the red-green direction, relative to the spaces for the normals, reflecting the fact that red and green (for example) are much more similar to each other for these subjects than they are for the normals.

The inspection of the private spaces provides insight into the way in which INDSCAL uses individual differences in perception to determine a unique orientation of the coordinate axes. If the coordinate axes were oriented in a different way (say, by a 45° rotation of the axes of the group stimulus space), the private spaces for color deficient subjects could not be compressed along a line from red to green, but would have to be compressed in some other direction.

The INDSCAL method, as described in Carroll and Chang (1970), makes metric assumptions (i.e., it assumes that all the functions F_i in Equation (1) are linear) and entails a kind of three-way

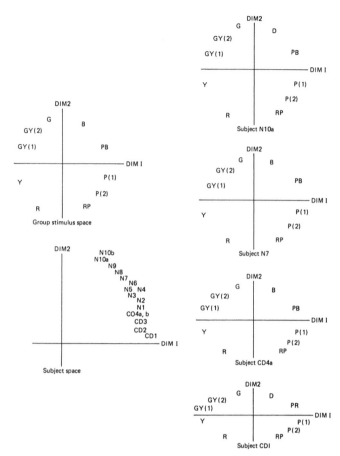

Figure 3.   The INDSCAL analysis of Helm's data on color perception produced the "group stimulus space," which conforms quite well with the standard representation of the color circle, and the "subject space." The coding of the stimuli is as follows: R = red; Y = yellow; GY(1) = green yellow; GY(2) = green yellow containing more green than GY(1); G = green; B = blue; PB = purple blue; P(1) = purple; P(2) = a purple containing more red than P(1); RP = red purple. In the subject space, CD1 through CD4 are four color-deficient subjects (CD4a and CD4b being two replications of one subject), while N1 through N10 are 10 normal subjects (N10a and N10b are replications by the same subject). On the right are shown the private perceptual spaces for four of the subjects, two red-green color deficient and two normal. These private perceptual spaces are generated from the group stimulus space and the subject space by applying (square roots of) the appropriate weights from the latter, as stretching or shrinking factors, to the dimensions of the former. From "An overview of multidimensional scaling methods emphasizing recently developed models for handling individual differences," by J. D. Carroll, 1971. In C. W. King and D. Tigert (Eds.), *Attitude research reaches new heights* (Chicago: The American Marketing Association). Reproduced by permission.

generalization of the "classical" method for two-way MDS described by Torgerson (1958). The most efficient approach for implementing this analysis is provided by a program called SINDSCAL offered by Pruzansky (1975). Recently, various alternative nonmetric and metric algorithms have been developed for fitting the INDSCAL model. Most prominent are Takane, Young, and de Leeuw's ALSCAL (with its three-way implementation; 1977), and Ramsay's MULTISCALE procedure (1977), which provides alternative methods for fitting the INDSCAL model, based on a maximum likelihood criterion. For a general discussion and comparison of computer programs for both two-way and three-way MDS, see Schiffman, Reynolds, and Young (1981) or Coxon (1982).

For discussion of other models and related methods, see Carroll and Arabie (1980) or Carroll and Wish (1974). Of particular interest among these alternative models and methods is one usually called Three-Mode Scaling proposed by Tucker (1972), which is an adaptation of Tucker's three-mode factor analysis model and method (1964) to the case of three-way proximities data.

BROAD DEFINITION OF MDS

In its broadest definition, multidimensional scaling (MDS) includes a wide variety of geometric models for representation of psychological or other behavioral science data. Such models can include *discrete* geometric models such as tree structures (typically associated with hierarchical clustering), overlapping or nonoverlapping cluster structures, or other network models. More typically, however, MDS is associated with continuous spatial models for representation of data. In the broad definition of MDS such spatial models can include—in addition to the distance model for proximities data discussed above—other geometric structures such as what are called the vector model, or the unfolding model for representation of individual differences in preference (or other dominance) data, or even the factor analysis model. For discussion of some of the models and associated methods included in this broad definition of MDS, see Carroll (1980); Carroll and Arabie (1980); Carroll and Pruzansky (1980); Shepard (1980); Arabie (1991); Arabie, Carroll and DeSarbo (1987); Carroll (1972, 1976, 1980); Carroll and Arabie (1980, 1998); Carroll and Chaturvedi (1995); Carroll and Klauer (1998); Carroll and Pruzansky (1980); Carroll and Winsberg (1995); Carroll and Wish (1974b); Coxon (1982); De-Soete and Carroll (1992, 1996); DeSoete, Carroll and Chaturvedi (1993); Heiser and de Leeuw (1979); Hubert, Arabie, and Hesson-Mcinnis (1992); Hutchinson (1989); Klauer and Carroll (1989, 1995); Meulman (1992); Shepard (1978, 1980); Winsberg and Carroll (1989); and Wish and Carroll (1974).

REFERENCES

Arabie, P. (1991). Was Euclid an unnecessarily sophisticated psychologist? *Psychometrika, 56,* 567–587.

Arabie, P., Carroll, J. D., & DeSarbo, W. S. (1987). *Three-way scaling and clustering.* Newbury Park, CA: Sage.

Bloxom, B. (1968). *Individual differences in multidimensional scaling* (Research Bulletin 68-45). Princeton, NJ: Educational Testing Service.

Carroll, J. D. (1971). An overview of multidimensional scaling methods emphasizing recently developed models for handling individual differences. In C. W. King & D. Tigert (Eds.), *Attitude research reaches new heights.* Chicago: American Marketing Association.

Carroll, J. D. (1972). Individual differences and multidimensional scaling. In R. N. Shepard, A. K. Romney, & S. B. Nerlove (Eds.), *Multidimensional scaling: Theory and applications in the behavioral sciences* (Vol. 1). New York: Seminar.

Carroll, J. D. (1976). Spatial, non-spatial, and hybrid models for scaling. *Psychometrika, 41,* 439–463.

Carroll, J. D. (1980). Models and methods for multidimensional analysis of preferential choice (or other dominance) data. In E. D. Lantermann & H. Feger (Eds.), *Similarity and choice.* Bern & Stuttgart, Germany: Huber.

Carroll, J. D., & Arabie, P. (1980). Multidimensional scaling. *Annual Review of Psychology, 31,* 607–649.

Carroll, J. D., & Arabie, P. (1998). Multidimensional scaling. In M. H. Birnbaum (Ed.), *Handbook of perception and cognition* (Vol. 3). San Diego, CA: Academic.

Carroll, J. D., & Chang, J. J. (1970). Analysis of individual differences in multidimensional scaling via an N-way generalization of Eckart-Young decomposition. *Psychometrika, 35,* 283–319.

Carroll, J. D., & Chaturvedi, A. (1995). A general approach to clustering and multidimensional scaling of two-way, three-way, or higher-way data. In R. D. Luce, M. D'Zmura, D. D. Hoffman, G. Iverson, & A. K. Romney (Eds.), *Geometric representations of perceptual phenomena.* Mahwah, NJ: Erlbaum.

Carroll, J. D., & Klauer, K. C. (1998). INDNET: An individual-differences method for representing three-way proximity data by graphs. In K. C. Klauer & H. Westmeyer (Eds.), *Psychologische methoden und soziale prozesse* (*Psychological methods and social processes*). Lengerich, Germany: Pabst Science Publishers.

Carroll, J. D., & Pruzansky, S. (1980). Discrete and hybrid scaling models. In E. D. Lantermann & H. Feger (Eds.), *Similarity and choice.* Bern & Stuttgart, Germany: Huber.

Carroll, J. D., & Winsberg, S. (1995). Fitting an extended INDSCAL model to three-way proximity data. *Journal of Classification, 12,* 57–71.

Carroll, J. D., & Wish, M. (1974a). Models and methods for three-way multidimensional scaling. In D. H. Krantz, R. C. Atkinson, R. D. Luce, & P. Suppes (Eds.), *Contemporary developments in mathematical psychology* (Vol. 2). San Francisco: Freeman.

Carroll, J. D., & Wish, M. (1974b). Multidimensional perceptual models and measurement methods. In E. C. Carterette & M. P. Friedman (Eds.), *Handbook of perception* (Vol. 2). New York: Academic.

Coombs, C. H. (1950). Psychological scaling without a unit of measurement. *Psychological Review, 57,* 148–158.

Coombs, C. H. (1976). *A theory of data.* New York: Wiley. (Original work published 1964)

Coxon, A. P. M. (1982). *The user's guide to multidimensional scaling.* Portsmouth, NH: Heinemann.

De Soete, G., & Carroll, J. D. (1992). Probabilistic multidimensional models of pairwise choice data. In F. G. Ashby (Ed.), *Multidimensional models of perception and cognition.* Mahwah, NJ: Erlbaum.

De Soete, G., & Carroll, J. D. (1996). Tree and other network models for representing proximity data. In P. Arabie, L. Hubert, &

G. De Soete (Eds.), *Clustering and classification*. River Edge, NJ: World Scientific.

De Soete, G., Carroll, J. D., & Chaturvedi, A. (1993). A modified CANDECOMP method for fitting the extended INDSCAL model. *Journal of Classification, 10,* 75–92.

Heiser, W. J., & de Leeuw, J. (1979). *How to use SMACOF-III* (Research report). Leiden, Netherlands: Department of Data Theory.

Guttman, L. (1968). A general nonmetric technique for finding the smallest coordinate space for a configuration of points. *Psychometrika, 33,* 465–506.

Helm, C. E. (1964). Multidimensional ratio scaling analysis of perceived color relations. *Journal of the Optical Society of America, 54,* 256–262.

Helm, C. E., & Tucker, L. R. (1962). Individual differences in the structure of color perception. *American Journal of Psychology, 75,* 437–444.

Horan, C. B. (1969). Multidimensional scaling: Combining observations when individuals have different perceptual structures. *Psychometrika, 34,* 139–165.

Hubert, L. J., Arabie, P., & Hesson-Mcinnis, M. (1992). Multidimensional scaling in the city-block metric: A combinatorial approach. *Journal of Classification, 9,* 211–236.

Hutchinson, J. W. (1989). NETSCAL: A network scaling algorithm for nonsymmetric proximity data. *Psychometrika, 54,* 24–51.

King C. W., & Tigert, D. (1971). *Attitude research reaches new heights*. Chicago: American Marketing Association.

Klauer, K. C., & Carroll, J. D. (1989). A mathematical programming approach to fitting general graphs. *Journal of Classification, 6,* 247–270.

Klauer, K. C., & Carroll, J. D. (1995). Network models for scaling proximity data. In R. D. Luce, M. D'Zmura, D. D. Hoffman, G. Iverson, & A. K. Romney (Eds.), *Geometric representations of perceptual phenomena*. Mahwah, NJ: Erlbaum.

Kruskal, J. B. (1964a). Multidimensional scaling by optimizing goodness of fit to a nonmetric hypothesis. *Psychometrika, 29,* 1–27.

Kruskal, J. B. (1964b). Nonmetric multidimensional scaling: A numerical method. *Psychometrika, 29,* 115–129.

Kruskal, J. B., & Wish, M. (1978). *Multidimensional scaling*. Newbury Park, CA: Sage.

McGee, V. E. (1966). The multidimensional analysis of "elastic" distances. *British Journal of Mathematical and Statistical Psychology, 19,* 181–196.

Meulman, J. J. (1992). The integration of multidimensional scaling and multivariate analysis with optimal transformations. *Psychometrika, 57,* 539–565.

Pruzansky, S. (1975). *How to use SINDSCAL: A computer program for individual differences in multidimensional scaling*. Unpublished manuscript. Murray Hill, NJ: AT&T Bell Laboratories.

Ramsay, J. O. (1977). Maximum likelihood estimation in multidimensional scaling. *Psychometrika, 42,* 241–266.

Roskam, E. E., & Lingoes, J. C. (1970). MINISSA–I: A Fortran IV (G) program for the smallest space analysis of square symmetric matrices. *Behavioral Science, 15,* 204–205.

Rothkopf, E. Z. (1957). A measure of stimulus similarity and errors in some paired-associate learning tasks. *Journal of Experimental Psychology, 53,* 94–101.

Schiffman, S. S., Reynolds, M. L., & Young, F. W. (1981). *Introduction to multidimensional scaling: Theory methods, and applications*. New York: Academic.

Shepard, R. N. (1962a). The analysis of proximities: Multidimensional scaling with an unknown distance function, part I. *Psychometrika, 27*(2), 125–140.

Shepard, R. N. (1962b). The analysis of proximities: Multidimensional scaling with an unknown distance function, part II. *Psychometrika, 27*(3), 219–246.

Shepard, R. N. (1963). Analysis of proximities as a technique for the study of information processing in man. *Human Factors, 35,* 33–48.

Shepard, R. N. (1978). The circumplex and related topological manifolds in the study of perception. In S. Shye (Ed.), *Theory construction and data analysis in the behavioral sciences*. San Francisco: Jossey-Bass.

Shepard, R. N. (1980). Multidimensional scaling, tree-fitting and clustering. *Science, 210,* 390–398.

Takane, Y., Young, F. W., & de Leeuw, J. (1977). Nonmetric individual differences multidimensional scaling: An alternating least squares method with optimal scaling features. *Psychometrika, 42,* 7–67.

Torgerson, W. S. (1958). *Theory and methods of scaling*. New York: Wiley.

Tucker, L. R. (1964). The extension of factor analysis to three-dimensional matrices. In N. Frederiksen & H. Gulliksen (Eds.), *Contributions to mathematical psychology*. New York: Holt, Rinehart & Winston.

Tucker, L. R. (1972). Relations between multidimensional scaling and three-mode factor analysis. *Psychometrika, 37,* 3–27.

Tucker, L. R., & Messick, S. J. (1963). An individual difference model for multidimensional scaling. *Psychometrika, 28,* 333–367.

Winsberg, S., & Carroll, J. D. (1989). A quasi-nonmetric method of multidimensional scaling via an extended Euclidean model. *Psychometrika, 54,* 217–229.

Wish, M., & Carroll, J. D. (1974). Applications of individual differences scaling to studies of human perception and judgement. In E. C. Carterette & M. P. Friedman (Eds.), *Handbook of perception* (Vol. 2). New York: Academic.

Wish, M., Deutsch, M., & Biener, L. (1970). Differences in conceptual structures of nations: An exploratory study. *Journal of Personality and Social Psychology, 16,* 361–373.

J. D. CARROLL
Rutgers University

PSYCHOMETRICS: NORMS, RELIABILITY, VALIDITY, AND ITEM ANALYSIS

STATISTICS IN PSYCHOLOGY

MULTIMODAL THERAPY

Multimodal therapy (MMT) provides an integrative assessment and treatment plan that considers the whole person in his or her social network. Multimodal therapy places most of its theoretical underpinnings within a broad-based social and cognitive learning theory, but draws on effective techniques from many disciplines without necessarily subscribing to their particular suppositions (i.e., it espouses technical eclecticism). In MMT one endeavors to use, whenever possible and applicable, empirically supported methods. Thus, its practitioners are at the cutting edge of the field, drawing on scientific and clinical findings from all credible sources.

This technically eclectic outlook is central and pivotal to MMT. It is important to understand that the MMT approach sees *theoretical* eclecticism, or any attempt to integrate different theories in the hopes of producing a more robust technique, as futile and misguided (see Lazarus, 1992, 1997).

Multimodal therapy is predicated on the assumptions that most psychological problems are multifaceted, multi-determined, and multilayered, and that comprehensive therapy calls for a careful assessment of seven parameters or modalities—Behavior, Affect, Sensation, Imagery, Cognition, Interpersonal relationships, and Biological processes. The most common biological intervention is the use of psychotropic Drugs. The first letters from the seven modalities yield the convenient acronym BASIC I.D.—although it must be remembered that the "D" represents not only the drugs commonly used for biological intervention, but for the entire panoply of medical and biological factors.

It is assumed that the more a patient learns in therapy, the less likely he or she is to relapse. In other words, therapeutic breadth is emphasized. Over many years, my follow-ups have revealed more-durable treatment outcomes when the entire BASIC I.D. is assessed, and when significant problems in each modality are remedied. Multimodal therapy uses several distinct assessment procedures that tend to facilitate treatment outcomes.

Second-order BASIC I.D. assessments may be conducted when therapy falters. For example, an unassertive person who is not responding to the usual social skills and assertiveness training methods may be asked to spell out the specific consequences that an assertive modus vivendi might have on his or her behaviors, affective reactions, sensory responses, imagery, and cognitive processes. The interpersonal repercussions would also be examined, and if relevant, biological factors would be determined (e.g., "If I start expressing my feelings I may become less anxious and require fewer tranquilizers"). Quite often, this procedure brings to light reasons behind such factors as noncompliance and poor progress. A typical case in point concerns a man who was not responding to role-playing and other assertiveness training procedures. During a second-order BASIC I.D. assessment, he revealed a central cognitive schemata to the effect that he was not entitled to be confident, positive, and in better control of his life, because these qualities would show up his profoundly reticent and inadequate father. Consequently, the treatment focus shifted to a thorough examination of his entitlements.

A 35-item *Structural Profile Inventory* (SPI) yields a quantitative BASIC I.D. diagram depicting a person's degree of activity, emotionality, sensory awareness, imagery potential, cognitive propensities, interpersonal leanings, and biological considerations (see Lazarus, 1997). The SPI is particularly useful in couples therapy where differences in the specific ratings reflect potential areas of friction. Discussion of these disparities with clients can result in constructive steps to understand and remedy them.

A method called *tracking* may be employed when clients are puzzled by affective reactions. "I don't know why I feel this way." "I don't know where these feelings are coming from." The client is asked to recount the latest untoward event or incident. He or she is then asked to consider what behaviors, affective responses, images, sensations, and cognitions come to mind.

One client who reported having panic attacks for no apparent reason was able to put together the following string of events. She had initially become aware that her heart was beating faster than usual. This brought to mind an episode in which she had passed out after drinking too much alcohol at a party. This memory or image still occasioned a strong sense of shame. She started thinking that she was going to pass out again, and as she dwelled on her sensations, the cognition only intensified, culminating in her feelings of panic. Thus, she exhibited an S-I-C-S-C-A pattern (Sensation, Imagery, Cognition, Sensation, Cognition, Affect). Thereafter, she was asked to note carefully whether any subsequent anxiety or panic attacks followed what might be called a similar firing order. She subsequently confirmed that her two trigger points were usually sensation and imagery. This alerted the therapist to focus on sensory training techniques (e.g., diaphragmatic breathing and deep muscle relaxation) followed immediately by imagery training (e.g., the use of coping imagery and the selection of mental pictures that evoked profound feelings of calm).

The BASIC I.D. lends itself to other assessment and treatment tactics that keep the clinician on track and enable him or her to address issues that might otherwise have been glossed over. Lazarus (1997) presents these methods in some detail.

Research findings on overall effectiveness of MMT have been conducted by Kwee (1984), a Dutch psychologist, who obtained encouraging results when conducting a controlled-outcome study using MMT with severe obsessive-compulsive patients, and with a group of extremely phobic individuals. Williams (1988), a Scottish psychologist, in a careful controlled-outcome study, compared MMT with other treatments in helping children with learning disabilities. He emerged with clear data pointing to the efficacy of MMT in comparison to the other methods studied.

In essence, it should be understood that MMT is a broad-spectrum orientation, extremely flexible, with which the therapist may match the best and most effective methods with the appropriate treatment style for each individual. It is both brief and comprehensive (Lazarus, 1997).

REFERENCES

Kwee, M. G. T. (1984). *Klinishe multimodale gedragtstherapie.* Lisse, Holland: Swets & Zeitlinger.

Lazarus, A. A. (1992). Multimodal therapy: Technical eclecticism with minimal integration. In J. C. Norcross & M. R. Goldfried (Eds.), *Handbook of psychotherapy integration* (pp. 231–263). New York: Basic Books.

Lazarus, A. A. (1997). *Brief but comprehensive psychotherapy: The multimodal way.* New York: Springer.

Williams, T. (1988). *A multimodal approach to assessment and intervention with children with learning disabilities.* Unpublished doctoral dissertation, Department of Psychology, University of Glasgow.

A. A. Lazarus
Center for Multimodal Psychological Services

PSYCHOTHERAPY

MULTIPLE CORRELATION

Multiple correlation is a multivariate analysis method widely used in psychology and other behavioral sciences. It can be considered an extension of bivariate correlation, and indicates the degree of association between one variable and an optimally weighted combination of several other variables. The weights are usually determined by the principle of least squares so as to minimize the residual, or unrelated, variance. A formula for the multiple correlation (R) of one variable (Y) with k weighted variables (X), in terms of the bivariate correlations and the standard partial regression ("beta") weights, is

$$R_{Y \cdot X_1 X_2 \cdots X_k} = \sqrt{\beta_{X_1 Y} r_{X_1 Y} + \beta_{X_2 Y} r_{X_2 Y} + \ldots + \beta_{X_k Y}}$$

The multiple correlation ranges in value from one to minus one, and is interpreted similarly to a bivariate correlation, if rectilinearity and the other assumptions of the bivariate intercorrelations from which the multiple correlation is computed are reasonable.

In psychology, the squared multiple correlation (R^2) frequently is used to estimate the proportion of variance in a dependent variable that is related to a set of independent variables. A related method, multiple regression, is used for predicting a dependent (or criterion) variable from a set of independent (or predictor) variables.

Many textbooks on multivariate and statistical methods describe the procedures and uses of multiple correlation, including interpretation, tests of significance (when it is used as an inferential statistic), cross-validation, and computer programs.

SUGGESTED READING

Cohen, J., & Cohen, P. (1983). *Applied multiple regression/correlation analysis for the behavioral sciences.*

Ezekiel, M., & Fox, K. A. (1959). *Methods of correlation and regression analysis.*

Guilford, J. P., & Fruchter, B. (1977). *Fundamental statistics in psychology and education.*

Stevens, J. P. (1999). *Intermediate statistics.*

B. Fruchter
University of Texas, Austin

CORRELATION METHODS
MULTIPLE REGRESSION
STATISTICS IN PSYCHOLOGY

MULTIPLE REGRESSION

Multiple regression is a multivariate analysis method that relates a dependent (or criterion) variable (Y) to a set of independent (or predictor) variables (X) by a linear equation, such as:

$$Y' = a + b_1 X_1 + b_2 X_2 + \ldots + b_k X_k$$

The regression or b weights are usually determined by the principle of least squares, so as to minimize the sum of the squared deviations of the dependent (or observed) values from the corresponding predicted values—that is, to minimize $\Sigma(Y - Y')^2$. Multiple correlation (R), a related method, is sometimes defined as $R = r_{YY'}$.

In a "stepwise" approach, variables are added (or removed) one at a time from the independent variable set until there is a nonsignificant change in the value of R. Also, sets of variables may be added (or removed) to evaluate their contribution to the multiple correlation, and an F-test done to determine if their effect is statistically significant. Nonlinear relationships may be evaluated by including higher order terms (e.g., X_1^2) and/or multiplicative terms (e.g., $X_1 X_2$) on the right-hand side of the equation.

Some common uses for multiple regression are:

1. To obtain the best linear prediction equation.

2. To control for confounding variables.

3. To evaluate the contribution of a specific set of variables.

4. To account for seemingly complex multivariate interrelationships.

5. To perform analysis of variance and covariance by coding the levels of the independent variables.

SUGGESTED READING

Cohen, J., & Cohen, P. (1983). *Applied multiple regression/correlation analysis for the behavioral sciences.* Mahway, NJ: Erlbaum.

Ezekiel, M., & Fox, K. A. (1959). *Methods of correlation and regression analysis.* New York: Wiley.

Guilford, J. P., & Fruchter, B. (1977). *Fundamental statistics in psychology and education.* New York: McGraw-Hill.

Pedhazur, E. J. (1982). *Multiple regression in behavioral research: Explanation and prediction* (2nd ed). New York: Holt, Rinehart, & Winston.

Stevens, J. P. (1999). *Intermediate statistics.* Mahway, NJ: Erlbaum.

B. FRUCHTER
University of Texas, Austin

MULTIPLE CORRELATION

MUNCHAUSEN SYNDROME BY PROXY

Munchausen syndrome by proxy (MSP), a potentially fatal form of child abuse in which parents feign or create illnesses in their children and then present the children to medical personnel for assessment and treatment, was first described by Meadow (1977). This syndrome is considered difficult to diagnose or treat, involving health care professionals in the perpetuation of abuse, that is, unneeded, extensive care of nonexistent illnesses.

Typically, the syndrome involves mothers as perpetrators. Common features are repeated efforts by mothers to secure medical treatment for children in several medical settings, mothers' perceptions of their children as vulnerable, mothers' willingness for their children to undergo diagnostic procedures and medical treatment of an invasive nature, and mothers inducing laboratory findings.

In an individual case, the child's medical history as related by the mother is long, detailed, and dramatic. The mother may present herself as anxious, angry, or paranoid and is not reassured by a negative finding. It is not uncommon for the mother to mishear findings or to draw illogical conclusions from information given. The mother also generally appears to be an exemplary caretaker.

The warning signs of MSP include:

1. Unexplained or unusual persistent or recurrent illnesses.
2. Discrepancies between clinical findings and history.
3. Signs and symptoms that do not make clinical sense.
4. Laboratory results at variance with apparent health of the child.
5. The working diagnosis is "a rare disorder."
6. An experienced physician states, "Never seen a case like it."
7. Signs and symptoms do not occur in the mother's absence.
8. An extremely attentive mother who refuses to leave the child alone and may offer to take over some of the medical care of the child, including obtaining vital signs or laboratory samples.
9. Unusual or repeated treatment intolerance.
10. Mother's level of concern discordant with medical personnel's.
11. Seizures or apnea spells only witnessed by mother.
12. Atypical cases of sudden infant death syndrome (SIDS) or near SIDS.
13. Mother with previous medical or nursing experience.
14. Mother with a history of Munchausen's syndrome or victimization in MSP.
15. Mother relates a history of personal illness similar to the child's (Guandolo, 1985; Richardson, 1987).

Several variants of MSP have been identified. Excluded from the diagnosis are *help seekers,* that is, mothers whose primary motivation appears to be a need for outside intervention obtained through a sick child. These nonpathological mothers typically react with relief and cooperation when confronted or help is offered.

Active inducers (Libow & Scheier, 1986) are considered prototypical MSP in which there are active and direct efforts by mothers to induce dramatic symptoms of illness in their children. Typically, the victims are infants or young children. The mothers are believed to gain attention through being perceived as excellent mothers, by "fooling" the "powerful" medical system and by nurturance received as the mother of an ill child. *Doctor addicts* are obsessed with obtaining medical treatment for nonexistent illnesses for their children. Mothers remain convinced of illness despite repeated negative evidence. These mothers also report false history and symptoms, but the victims typically are school age or adolescent children. Such mothers may appear to be outwardly angry and distrustful, occasionally paranoid in regard to the medical system. *Illness exaggerators* (Masterson, Dunworth, & Williams, 1988) differ from doctor addicts in that there is some documented but mild illness in the child. In the latter two types, there is likely to be a conflictual relationship between the mother and the medical staff.

Detection of MSP is extremely difficult and requires coordination of care, good communication systems, and careful documentation. The diagnosis may be met with disbelief by other members of the care system. Close observation of the mother with the child is necessary, with some advocating surreptitious videotaping and searching of mother's belongings (Epstein, Markowitz, Gallo, Holmes, & Gryboski, 1987). All agree that laboratory samples must be protected and the mother not allowed to obtain or come into contact with the samples (Meadow, 1982; Zitelli, Seltman, & Shannon, 1987). Toxicological screening and sophisticated knowledge of pharmacokinetics may be required. Most important, however, is clear, thorough, and detailed documentation. Managed health care systems and tertiary care systems may be particularly vulnerable to being drawn into this abuse (Krener & Adelman, 1988; Sullivan, Francis, Bain, & Hartz, 1991). Legal intervention is usually required but difficult to obtain. Serial abuse of other children in the family is not unusual, but may not provide adequate evidence for legal intervention. Removal of the child from the home or required approval for medical care are effective in prevention of future abuse (Rosenberg, 1987).

Perpetrators are resistent to treatment. Many remove their child from the particular medical system and repeat the abuse in a different setting. Psychotherapy for the mother is always indicated but seldom successful. MSP results in psychological trauma to the victim, with resulting morbidity ranging from separation and feeding disorders in infants to development of Munchausen's syndrome in adolescents (McGuire & Feldman, 1989).

REFERENCES

Epstein, M. A., Markowitz, R. L., Gallo, D. M., Holmes, J. W., & Gryboski, J. D. (1987). Munchausen syndrome by proxy: Considerations in diagnosis and confirmation by video surveillance. *Pediatrics, 80,* 220–224.

Guandolo, V. L. (1985). Munchausen syndrome by proxy: An outpatient challenge. *Pediatrics, 75,* 526–530.

Krener, P., & Adelman, R. (1988). Parent salvage and parent sabotage in the care of chronically ill children. *American Journal of Diseases of Children, 142,* 945–951.

Libow, J. A., & Schreier, H. A. (1986). Three forms of factitious illness in children: When is it Munchausen syndrome by proxy? *American Journal of Orthopsychiatry, 56,* 602–611.

Masterson, J., Dunworth, R., & Williams, N. (1988). Extreme illness exaggeration in pediatric patients: A variant of Munchausen's by proxy? *American Journal of Orthopsychiatry, 58,* 188–195.

McGuire, T. L., & Feldman, K. W. (1989). Psychologic morbidity of children subjected to Munchausen syndrome by proxy. *Pediatrics, 83,* 289–292.

Meadow, R. (1977). Munchausen syndrome by proxy: The hinterland of child abuse. *Lancet, 2,* 342–345.

Richardson, G. F. (1987). Munchausen syndrome by proxy. *American Family Physician, 16,* 119–123.

Sullivan, C. A., Francis, G. L., Bain, M. W., & Hartz, J. (1991). Munchausen syndrome by proxy: 1990. A portent for problems? *Clinical Pediatrics, 30,* 112–116.

Zitelli, B. J., Seltman, M. F., & Shannon, M. R. (1987). Munchausen's syndrome by proxy and its professional participants. *American Journal of Diseases of Children, 141,* 1099–1102.

SUGGESTED READING

Rosenberg, D. A. (1987). Web of deceit: A literature review of Munchausen syndrome by proxy. *Child Abuse and Neglect, 11,* 547–563.

J. S. HOFFMAN
Honolulu, Hawaii

CHILD ABUSE
DIAGNOSIS
FACTITIOUS DISORDERS

MURPHY, GARDNER (1895–1979)

Gardner Murphy's formal schooling included the Hotchkiss School, Yale, Harvard, and Columbia (1919–1923). In 1926 he married Lois Barclay, who later became a psychologist known worldwide for her innovative work in child psychology; they collaborated on a number of books. Murphy held the Richard Hodgson Fellowship in Psychical Research at Harvard University (1922–1925); taught at Columbia (1920–1940) and at the City College of New York (1940–1952); was director of research at the Menninger Foundation (1952–1968); and after retirement was a visiting professor (emeritus) at George Washington University (until 1973).

Murphy formulated the biosocial approach to psychology that by the 1950s was recognized as one of the most vital and influential movements in the field. Though there has not been a formal school nor any significant identifiable group of disciples, in K. E. Clark's 1957 survey of American psychologists Murphy ranked second only to Sigmund Freud in frequency of listing as the individual most influential in leading the respondents into work in psychology. As a teacher, he was superb. Class after class of graduating seniors at the City College of New York voted him "best liked teacher."

Murphy was elegantly discriminating and creatively eclectic in organizing and reorganizing material from an extraordinarily wide range of sources to create an integrated, holistic, functional system. He believed firmly that the study of origins and evolution was important for the understanding of phenomena; that the separation of psychology from either the biological or the social sciences is arbitrary and likely to be harmful; that psychology studies the whole individual and would have to include both internal (subjective) and external (objective) phenomena; that behavioral studies are good and behavioristic beliefs are bad for science; that if the findings are suggestive and helpful in developing a comprehensive perspective, many primitive groping efforts must be encouraged, though they may be far from achieving the status of science at present. Though his biosocial eclectic approach necessarily overlapped with the presentations of others, Murphy's systematization included a number of core ideas that were essentially his. His discussions of biological facets of motivation include, for example, an unusual emphasis on sensory and activity needs; he saw curiosity as reflecting a brain drive. The following concepts represent major recurring emphases in his writings: (a) *autism:* cognitive processes tend to move in the direction of need satisfaction; (b) *canalization:* needs tend to become more specific in consequence of being satisfied in specific ways; (c) a *three-phase developmental theory:* all reality tends to move from an undifferentiated, homogeneous condition through a differentiated, heterogeneous reality to an integrated, structured reality; (d) *feedback:* information from outside provides a basis for reality testing and a mode of escape from autistic self-deception; and (e) *field theory:* the human personality is conceived as "a nodal region, an organized field within a larger field, a region of perceptual interaction, a reciprocity of outgoing and incoming energies" (Murphy, 1947).

The esteem in which Murphy was held by his colleagues in psychology is reflected, in part, by the professional honors accorded him. He was elected to the presidency of the American Psychological Association, the Eastern Psychological Association, the

Southwestern Psychological Association, the Society for the Psychological Study of Social Issues, the London Society for Psychical Research, and the American Society for Psychical Research. He was awarded the Butler Medal by Columbia University in 1932, and the Gold Medal Award of the American Psychological Foundation in 1972. Honorary doctorates were given him by the City University of New York and the University of Hamburg, Germany. His publications included about 25 books and well over 100 articles.

E. L. HARTLEY

MURRAY, HENRY A. (1893–1988)

Henry A. Murray received the BA degree from Harvard and later the MA and then the MD degree from Columbia University. He completed a residency in surgery at Columbia Presbyterian Hospital. During his residency, he had the unusual experience of helping to care for the future president of the United States, Franklin D. Roosevelt. Following this, he spent 4 years at the Rockefeller Institute studying embryology. In 1927 he received the PhD from Cambridge University in England. While there he became acquainted with the writings of Carl Jung, whose *Psychological Types* had recently been translated into English.

This apparently contributed to a change in his interest from the biological sciences to psychology. Upon returning to the United States, he was invited to be Morton Prince's assistant at the newly formed psychological clinic at Harvard University. Over the objections of some, he succeeded Prince as its director. His interests began to turn more toward the Freudian approach to psychology. In 1928 he helped form the Boston Psychoanalytic Association and in 1933 he became a member of the American Psychoanalytic Association.

His interests continued in the direction of personality. By 1938, he embarked on the research published in *Explorations in Personality*. In this work he developed his taxonomy of needs and presses to characterize people's directions in their lives and activities. Thus he developed a systematic and dynamic approach to personality. Out of these studies there developed the Thematic Apperception Test (TAT) a projective technique consisting of semivague pictures in which the subject was asked to tell a story about each. The responses were analyzed in terms of Murray's system. The test is still widely used as a clinical diagnostic tool.

During World War II, Murray served in the Army Medical Corps. After the war, he returned to Harvard, where he was instrumental in establishing the Harvard interdisciplinary department of social relations. His association with Clyde Kluckhohn resulted in the classic work *Personality in Nature Society and Culture*.

In 1961 the American Psychological Association honored him with its Distinguished Contribution Award. He received in 1969 the Gold Medal Award of the American Psychological Foundation for lifelong significant contributions to psychology. Murray had hoped to foster a more comprehensive and systematic approach to personality as well as to complete an analysis of the writings of Herman Melville, but failing health prevented the completion of these efforts. He died of pneumonia at the age of 95. He goes down in history as one of the most important personality theorists of this century.

R. W. LUNDIN
Wheaton, Illinois

MUSCARINIC RECEPTORS

The multitudinous effects of the neurotransmitter acetylcholine are mediated by activation of two structurally unrelated classes of receptor known as the nicotinic and muscarinic cholinergic receptors. The word "muscarinic" is derived from muscarine, an alkaloid compound from the mushroom *Amanita muscaria* first extracted in 1869 and shown to mimic the effects of parasympathetic nerve discharge. Muscarinic receptors belong to the superfamily of metabotropic receptors, which elicit their physiological responses by interacting with GTP-binding regulatory proteins (G proteins). Members of this G protein–coupled receptor superfamily are characterized by a single protein subunit that spans the plasma membrane seven times, resulting in seven hydrophobic transmembrane helices connected by three extracellular and three intracellular hydrophilic loops. The seven transmembrane domains are tightly packed in a ring-like structure, the outer half of which is known to be the ligand recognition site. Agonist (e.g., acetylcholine) binding leads to a conformational change of the muscarinic receptor, thereby facilitating an interaction with associated heterotrimeric G proteins. Activated G proteins dissociate into their respective GTP binding α-subunits and βγ-subunit complexes, which can then alter the activity of effector molecules involved in signal transduction pathways. In addition to the classical ligand binding site, muscarinic receptors possess a site for allosteric regulation by compounds that can modify the binding and behavior of cholinergic ligands. Several allosteric ligands have been described, the majority of which exhibit negative cooperativity with agonists.

Heterogeneity among muscarinic receptors was first indicated by the differential selectivity of muscarinic receptors in certain tissues for ligands such as gallamine and pirenzipine. Although pharmacological/physiological tools revealed the existence of at least three subclasses of muscarinic receptors, it has been only since the application of molecular biological techniques to muscarinic receptor research that detailed information concerning the structure and signal transduction pathways of individual subtypes has become available. Molecular cloning has demonstrated that there are five subtypes of muscarinic receptors in humans (M_1–M_5) encoded by distinct genes. These five structural variants can be grouped into two broad functional categories based on their differential coupling properties: The odd-numbered muscarinic receptors (M_1, M_3, M_5) preferentially couple to G proteins of the G_q/G_{11} family, resulting in the stimulation of different isoforms of phospholipase Cβ and the breakdown of phosphatidylinositol lipids. Conversely, the M_2 and M_4 receptors are efficiently linked to G proteins of the G_i/G_o class, which are sensitive to pertussis toxin and mediate the inhibition of adenylate cyclase. The five receptor subtypes display a high degree of sequence identity, sharing about 145 amino acids, and this homology is most noticeable in the membrane-spanning regions. Nevertheless, a characteristic of muscarinic receptors is the very large third intracellular loop, which displays a clear sequence divergence between the $M_1/M_3/M_5$ subtypes and the M_2/M_4 subtypes. Mutational studies and chimeric receptors have shown that it is this region of the receptor that is particularly important for coupling to G proteins.

The majority of muscarinic receptors in the central nervous system (CNS) are located postsynaptically. However, a proportion are presynaptic receptors that exist either as autoreceptors of the cholinergic cell, or as heteroreceptors on GABA, glutamate, or aspartate neurons. Stimulation of presynaptic muscarinic autoreceptors results in the inhibition of acetylcholine release, and these receptors play a key role in the modulation of cholinergic transmission in structures such as the basal forebrain and hippocampus. Activation of presynaptic heteroreceptors results in inhibition of neurotransmitter release and enables the cholinergic system to selectively modulate the activity of other neurotransmitters. Early work suggested that the odd-numbered muscarinic receptors were located postsynaptically and mediated the excitatory effects of acetylcholine, while the M_2/M_4 subtypes were exclusively presynaptic and thus inhibitory in nature. However, such a view is overly simplistic, and populations of postsynaptic M_2 receptors and presynaptic M_3 receptors are found in the hippocampus.

Muscarinic receptors are widely distributed in the body. They are expressed by neurons of the central and peripheral nervous systems, cardiac and smooth muscle, and a variety of exocrine glands. In the brain, overall receptor density is highest in the telencephalon with a decreasing concentration of receptors found as one proceeds caudally through the diencephalon and mesencephalon to the metencephalon. Target fields innervated by cholinergic fibers—for example, the hippocampal formation—express high levels of muscarinic receptors. However, considerable regional and laminar heterogeneity is displayed by the various receptor subtypes. The M_1 receptor is the most abundant muscarinic subtype within the forebrain, comprising between 35 and 50% of all muscarinic receptors in the cortex and hippocampus. Levels of M_1 are dramatically lower in midbrain regions such as the thalamus and hindbrain structures including the pons/medulla and cerebellum, where the subtype forms only 5 to 15% of total muscarinic receptors. In contrast, hindbrain, brainstem, and midbrain regions are very enriched in the M_2 subtype, and although the absolute M_2 receptor density changes little across the brain, M_2 receptors make up only about 15% of muscarinic receptors in the forebrain. M_3 receptor density shows a similar pattern to the M_1 subtype, with highest amounts found rostrally and fewer receptors located in the midbrain and hindbrain. The M_4 subtype is particularly prevalent in the telencephalon as a whole and the striatum and olfactory tubercle in particular, but less numerous in the more caudal regions of the brain. Until recently, considerable doubt has existed as to the functional relevance of the M_5 molecular entity. The receptor is expressed only in very low quantities in the brain. Structurally, the M_5 subtype is most like the M_3 receptor, and localisation studies have shown the receptors to have overlapping but distinct patterns of expression, with highest densities of M_5 labelling seen in the outer cortex, caudate putamen, and olfactory tubercle. In common with the other subtypes, M_5 labelling can be detected in the hippocampus.

Muscarinic receptors play a key role in the functioning of the CNS, where they are involved in complex processes such as learning, memory acquisition and retention, arousal and control of movement. For example, in animal models, administration of muscarinic receptor antagonists leads to deficits in memory and attention. Cholinergic defects have been implicated in the etiology of a number of neurological disorders, most notably Alzheimer's disease, but also Parkinson's disease and Down syndrome. In Alzheimer's disease, loss of basal forebrain cholinergic neurons that project to the hippocampus and cortex leads to decreased levels of acetylcholine in these target areas and consequently to reduced activation of muscarinic receptors. In addition, there are reports of impaired muscarinic receptor-mediated signal transduction in the Alzheimer's brain, which further diminishes the physiological impact of cholinergic nerve stimulation. Progress has recently been made connecting M_1 and M_3 receptor signalling to control of amyloid precursor proteins, which have been shown to deposit progressively in patients with Alzheimer's disease. In addition, the activation of odd-numbered muscarinic receptors has been shown to attenuate the release of amyloid β-protein. However, elucidation of the roles played by particular muscarinic receptor subtypes has been hampered by a lack of selective pharmacological tools, and the ongoing development of agonists and antagonists for each of the subtypes should aid the development of therapeutic drugs for conditions such as Alzheimer's disease.

SUGGESTED READING

International Union of Pharmacology. XVII. (1998). Classification of muscarinic acetylcholine receptors. *Pharmacological Reviews, 50,* 279–290.

Ashkenazi, A., & Peralta, E. G. (1994). Muscarinic acetylcholine receptors. In S. J. Peroutka (Ed.), *Handbook of receptors and channels. G protein-coupled receptors* (pp. 1–27). Boca Raton, FL: CRC Press.

Felder, C. C. (1995). Muscarinic acetylcholine receptors: Signal transduction through multiple effectors. *FASEB Journal, 9,* 619–625.

Rouse, S. T., Marino, M. J., Potter, L. T., Conn, P. J., & Levy, A. I. (1999). Muscarinic receptor subtypes involved in hippocampal circuits. *Life Sciences, 64,* 501–509.

G. CHIDLOW
University of Oxford

ACETYLCHOLINE

MUSSEN, PAUL HENRY (1922–   )

Paul Henry Mussen received the BA (1942) and MA (1943) from Stanford University, and the PhD from Yale (1949). He has taught at the University of Wisconsin, Ohio State University, and the University of California at Berkeley.

He is best known for his research and writings in developmental psychology. His revision of *Carmichael's Manual of Child Psychology* (1970) is a standard reference work in the field. He is the senior author of a widely used text, *Child Development and Personality,* in collaboration with John Conger and Jerome Kagan. This work traces in a longitudinal manner behavioral development from the prenatal period through adolescence. Another work, *Psychological Development: A Life-Span Approach* in collaboration with Conger, Kagan, and James Gewitz, stresses development from childhood through adolescence, early adulthood, the middle years, and old age.

Mussen's experimental research has involved the study of developmental processes in preschool children, generosity in children of nursery school age, and the impact of television cartoons on children's aggressive behavior.

STAFF

MYELINATION

The speed at which neurons can convey sensory information to the brain and motor information to the muscles is dependent upon two critical features of its axon: its diameter and the presence of a myelin sheath. By increasing the diameter of an axon, a strategy used in the nervous systems of both invertebrates and vertebrates, the conduction velocity of a fiber increases as a result of a lower axolemma resistance to the flow of current. However, the limits to which the brain can expand in size as a result of this adaptation has prompted a second strategy to evolve that increases the speed of action potential propagation with little axon diameter growth (Hildebrand, Remahl, Persson, & Bjartmer, 1993). This strategy, called myelination, results from a complex interaction between neurons and either oligodendrocytes in the central nervous system (CNS) or Schwann cells in the peripheral nervous system (PNS). These two glial cell types are capable of synthesizing a membrane structure, called myelin, which is elaborated into a sheath and wrapped, in a concentric fashion, around an axon (Figure 1). This sheath of myelin is not continuous along the length of an axon but is laid down as segments of myelin (internodes) that are interrupted, at regular intervals, by areas devoid of myelin. These regions are termed the nodes of Ranvier (Figure 2). Moreover, sodium channels are concentrated at these nodes but virtually absent from regions of axon membrane covered by a myelin sheath. Therefore, when an action potential is triggered, the insulating properties of the myelin sheath and the enrichment of sodium channels at the nodes allows the current to be swiftly funneled by passive spread to the next node. This movement of the action potential from node to node is termed "saltatory conduction," and enables myelinated axons with a diameter of 4 μm to convey information at the same speed of unmyelinated axons with a diameter of 500 μm. Therefore, axon myelination provides the means by which the nervous system can convey electrical impulses at high speeds in a confined manner. Conversely, any loss of axon myelination, as seen in demyelinating diseases or nervous system trauma, disrupts action potential propagation, resulting in devastating consequences to normal motor and sensory functions (Compston, Scolding, Wren, & Noble, 1991).

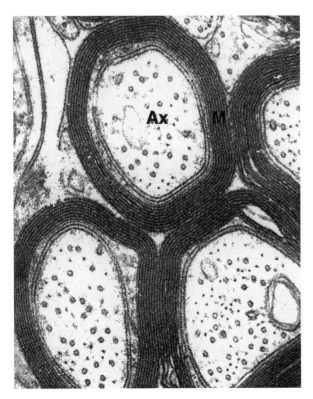

Figure 1.   Electron micrograph showing central nervous system axons (Ax) ensheathed with myelin (M) produced by oligodendrocytes.

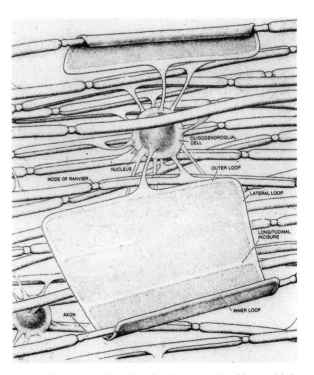

Figure 2.   Illustration of an oligodendrocyte ensheathing multiple axons with internodes of myelin.

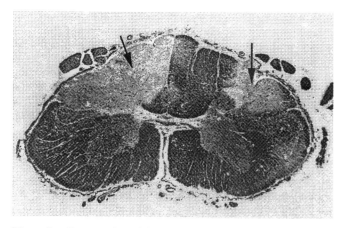

Figure 3.   Cross-section of the spinal cord of a patient who had multiple sclerosis, showing the loss of myelin (black stain) in fiber tracts of the spinal cord (arrows) responsible for conveying sensory impulses and voluntary movement.

Although the interactions that occur between neurons and either Schwann cells or oligodendrocytes produce the same outcome (i.e., an axon ensheathed in myelin), myelination in the PNS and CNS differ in a number of ways (Colello & Pott, 1997). In particular, it has been estimated that a single oligodendrocyte can ensheath 20 to 50 axons with an internode of myelin, whereas a single Schwann cell will ensheath only one axon with myelin. Consequently, the destruction of one oligodendrocyte will have a larger impact on motor or sensory function than will the destruction of one Schwann cell. Moreover, it has been shown that the types of myelin produced from oligodendrocytes and Schwann cells differ to some degree in their biochemical makeup of lipids and proteins (Snipes & Suter, 1995; Campagnoni, 1998). This may explain why some myelin diseases preferentially target either the CNS or PNS. Regardless of these differences, myelination in both systems can be regarded as the culmination of events that begin with the differentiation of glial cells from mitotically active, migratory precursor cells. Upon becoming postmitotic, these cells proceed to transcribe and translate the genes that make up myelin. The elaboration of myelin into a sheath by the processes of glial cells and the subsequent recognition of target axons are further distinct steps along the pathway leading to myelination. Finally, the initiation of axon ensheathment and the subsequent compaction of the myelin sheath around the axon complete the stages of myelination.

Although the process of myelination enables axons to propagate action potentials quickly and in a compact manner, the complexity of this neuron/glia interaction results in an increased vulnerability of the nervous system to disease. Indeed, a large number of pathological conditions that primarily target myelin have been identified (Hopkins, 1993). These diseases, which can lead to the destruction of the myelin sheath, are categorized as either acquired (e.g., multiple sclerosis) or hereditary diseases (e.g., leukodystrophies). Multiple sclerosis, which is the most common human demyelinating disease, is characterized by the formation of plaques—areas of demyelinated axons that can develop virtually anywhere in the CNS (Figure 3). Although axons in these plaque regions can survive, action potential conduction is slowed down or blocked, re-

sulting in a corresponding deficit in sensory or motor function. Due to the prevalence of plaque formation to regions within the brain stem, spinal cord, and optic nerve, the predominant symptoms of multiple sclerosis include weakness, lack of coordination, and visual impairment. These behavior deficits illustrate the crucial importance of myelination to how we perceive and act on information derived from our environment.

REFERENCES

Campagnoni, A. T. (1998). Molecular biology of myelin proteins from the central nervous system. *Journal of Neurochemistry, 51,* 1–14.

Colello, R. J., & Pott, U. (1997). Signals that initiate myelination in the developing mammalian nervous system. *Molecular Neurobiology, 15,* 83–100.

Compston, A., Scolding, N., Wren, D., & Noble, M. (1991). The pathogenesis of demyelinating disease: Insights from cell biology. *Trends in Neuroscience, 14,* 175–182.

Hildebrand, C., Remahl, S., Persson, H., & Bjartmer, C. (1993). Myelinated nerve fibers in the CNS. *Progress in Neurobiology, 40,* 319–384.

Hopkins, A. (1993). *Clinical neurology: a modern approach.* Oxford, UK: Oxford University Press.

Snipes, G. J., & Suter, U. (1995). Molecular anatomy and genetics of myelin proteins in the peripheral nervous system. *Journal of Anatomy, 186,* 483–494.

R. J. COLELLO
Virginia Commonwealth University

CENTRAL NERVOUS SYSTEM

MYERS–BRIGGS TYPE INDICATOR (MBTI)

The Myers–Briggs Type Indicator is a personality assessment measure the purpose of which is to ascertain how individuals perceive and judge. The instrument was devised to implement Jung's theory of type as expressed in *Psychological Types.* Specifically, the Myers–Briggs Type Indicator was developed to measure four bipolar dimensions (Myers, 1962):

1. *Extroversion versus introversion:* whether a person's attention is directed to people and things or to ideas.

2. *Sensing versus intuition:* whether a person prefers to perceive information by the senses or by intuition.

3. *Thinking versus feeling:* whether an individual prefers to use logic and analytic thinking or feelings in making judgments.

4. *Judgment versus perception:* whether an individual uses judgment or perception as a way of life. That is, does the individual evaluate events in terms of a set of standards or simply experience them?

The value of the Myers–Briggs Type Indicator lies in the integration of the four bipolar dimensions to yield 16 combinations, each reflecting the unique and individual character of the score pattern. These 16 interpretations have been subjected to numerous formal and informal research studies which, for example, have related the type which reflects the individual characteristics to labor turnover rates (Laney, 1949).

Other studies have established significant relationships of the individual's type with personality (Myers, 1962), interest (Stricker & Ross, 1962), and measures of scholastic performance for college students (Myers, 1962). Still other studies have explored the relationship of the individual's type with creativity among incumbents in a variety of occupations (Myers, 1962; MacKinnon, 1961).

The Myers–Briggs Type Indicator is a pencil-and-paper inventory with no time limit. About one hour is needed to complete the inventory. Scoring may be done by machine or manually. Norms for the instrument's results are based upon college, noncollege, and high school prep students, with appropriate breakdowns by sex and college major. Split half reliabilities range from 0.66 to 0.91 for males and from 0.74 to 0.93 for females on six samples of 100 students each (Myers, 1962).

REFERENCES

Laney, A. R. (1949). *Occupational implications of the Jungian personality function types as identified by the Briggs–Myers type indicator.* Unpublished master's thesis, George Washington University.

MacKinnon, D. W. (1961). *The personality correlates of creativity: A study of American architects.* Berkeley, CA: Institute of Personality Assessment and Research.

Myers, I. (1962). *The Myers–Briggs type indicator manual and test.* Palo Alto, CA: Consulting Psychologists Press.

R. S. ANDRULIS
Andrulis Associates

ANALYTICAL PSYCHOLOGY
PERSONALITY ASSESSMENT

N

NAKANISHI, SHIGETADA (1942–   )

Shigetada Nakanishi was born on January 3, 1942, in Ogaki, Japan. He received his MD and PhD from Kyoto University, in 1966 and 1971, respectively. He is professor in the Department of Biological Sciences of the Kyoto University Faculty of Medicine. From 1971 to 1974 he was a visiting associate at the Laboratory of Molecular Biology at the U.S. National Cancer Institute. He has received the following awards for his research: Bristol-Myers Squibb Award for Distinguished Achievement in Neuroscience Research (1995); Foreign Honorary Member of the American Academy of Arts and Sciences (1995); Keio Award (1996); Imperial Award/Japan Academy Award (1997), and Foreign Associate of the National Academy of Sciences (2000).

Nakanishi and his colleagues developed a novel cloning strategy to isolate receptors and ion channels by combining electrophysiology and the Xenopus oocyte expression system. They applied this strategy to the molecular cloning of glutamate receptors and reported the first molecular elucidation of NMDA receptor and metabotropic receptor (mGluR) of the glutamate receptor family. They showed that both groups of receptors are more diversified than previously envisioned, on the basis of comprehensive analyses of the structure, function, and expression of diverse members of the NMDA receptor and mGluR family. They provided evidence that different glutamate receptors have specialized functions in various brain regions. They also showed that specific glutamate receptors play a critical role in segregation of visual transmission and in the regulation of synaptic transmission and plasticity responsible for specific olfactory memory formation, hippocampal function, and cerebellar motor coordination. They have also developed a new technique to conditionally eliminate specific neuronal cell types in the functional neural network and indicated that synaptic modification mediated by NMDA receptors is critical for compensation of brain dysfunction.

In addition to these studies of glutamate receptors, Nakanishi and colleagues elucidated the molecular nature of neuropeptide and vasoactive peptide receptors, including receptors for substance P, substance K, endothelin, and neurotensin. The molecular elucidation of substance K receptor was the first indication of peptide receptors, which provided direct evidence that peptide receptors belong to the G protein-coupled receptor family.

STAFF

NARCISSISTIC PERSONALITY

The *Diagnostic and Statistical Manual of Mental Disorders* (*DSM-III*) describes this personality as possessing a grandiose sense of self-importance. Notable are the individual's exhibitionism and desire to gain attention and admiration from others. Abilities or achievements are unrealistically exaggerated and there is a tendency toward extreme self-absorption. A sense of entitlement—the expectation that others will bestow special favors and considerations without assuming reciprocal responsibilities—is also characteristic of the narcissist. This special status for self is taken for granted; there is little awareness that exploitative behavior is inconsiderate and presumptuous. Achievement deficits and social irresponsibilities are justified by a boastful arrogance, expansive fantasies, facile rationalizations, and frank prevarications. Marked rebuffs to self-esteem may provoke serious disruptions in the more characteristic unruffled composure. And despite the insouciant air of indifference and imperturbability, the individual is often quite preoccupied with how well he or she is regarded. When faced with criticism or failure, there is either an attitude of cool disdain or feelings of intense rage, humiliation, or emptiness.

Havelock Ellis, in his 1898 paper on auto-eroticism, first gave psychological significance to the term "narcissism." Sigmund Freud's major contribution, "On narcissism" (1914), was devoted exclusively to development and pathology. He suggested that in cases of "perversion" and homosexuality libidinal development the individual has suffered disturbances which lead him to avoid the mother as the primary love object and to substitute himself instead. Another early and significant formulation from a psychoanalytic perspective was furnished by Wilhelm Reich in *Charakteranalyse* (1933). Among the major features of what he termed the "phallic-narcissistic" type, he included such characteristics as being self-assured, arrogant, impressive in bearing, disdainful, and displaying airs of dignity and superiority.

More recent analytic conceptions include those of Otto Kernberg and Heinz Kohut. In *Borderline Conditions and Pathological Narcissism* (1975) Kernberg characterizes narcissistics as possessing an "unusual degree of self-reference in their interactions," as well as a great need to be admired, a shallow emotional life, and an exploitative and sometime parasitic relationship with others. Kohut's presentation of the narcissistic structure in *The Analysis of the Self* (1971) depicts the disorder primarily following serious incursions into self-esteem; thus he stresses features such as hypochondriasis, depression, and feelings of emptiness and deadness.

In a social-learning formulation that avoids psychoanalytic concepts, Millon (1969) presented the following criteria for review by the committee developing the *DSM-III.* It served as the basis for the manual's diagnostic description and criteria for the narcissistic personality.

1. Inflated self-image (e.g., displays pretentious self-assurance and exaggerates achievements; is seen by others as egotistic, haughty, and arrogant).

2. Interpersonal exploitativeness (e.g., takes others for granted and uses them to enhance self and indulge desires; expects special favors without assuming reciprocal responsibilities).

3. Cognitive expansiveness (e.g., exhibits immature fantasies and an undisciplined imagination; is minimally constrained by objective reality, takes liberties with facts, and often lies to redeem self-illusions).

4. Insouciant temperament (e.g., manifests a general air of nonchalance and imperturbability; appears coolly unimpressionable or buoyantly optimistic, except when narcissistic confidence is shaken).

5. Deficient social conscience (e.g., flouts conventional rules of shared social living, viewing them as naive or inapplicable to self; reveals a careless disregard for personal integrity and an indifference to the rights of others).

REFERENCES

Freud, S. (1957/1914). On narcissism: An introduction. In *The standard edition of the complete psychological works of Sigmund Freud* (Vol. 14). London: Hogarth.

Kernberg, O. F. (1975). *Borderline conditions and pathological narcissism.* New York: Aronson.

Kohut, H. (1971). *The analysis of the self.* New York: International Universities Press.

Millon, T. (1969). *Modern psychopathology: A biosocial approach to maladaptive learning and functioning.* Philadelphia: Saunders.

Reich, W. (1949/1933). *Charakteranalyse.* Leipzig, Germany: Sexpol Verlag.

T. MILLON
University of Miami

DIAGNOSTIC AND STATISTICAL MANUAL OF MENTAL DISORDERS (DSM-IV)
PERSONALITY DISORDERS

NARCOLEPSY

Narcolepsy is a life-long neurological disorder of REM or dream sleep in which the affected individual has attacks of irresistible daytime sleepiness, cataplexy (sudden loss of muscle control in the legs or neck in response to emotional triggers such as laughter, fright, or rage, leading to the patient's falling down or to his or her head's dropping) hypnagogic hallucinations (vivid and often terrifying dreams at sleep onset), and sleep paralysis (a momentary inability to move as one is drifting off to sleep). Cataplexy, sleep paralysis, and hypnagogic hallucinations are all manifestations of intrusion of fragments of REM sleep onto wakefulness. The entire set of symptoms is often not present initially, but may evolve gradually over a period of 5 to 10 years. Daytime sleepiness and cataplexy are the two most consistent diagnostic features. The daytime sleepiness frequently leads to automatic behavior of which the subject is unaware, impairment of memory and concentration, and emotional problems. Nighttime sleep is also disturbed, with frequent awakenings. The prevalence of narcolepsy varies from 1 in 600 in Japan, 1

in 10,000 in the United States, to 1 in 500,000 in Israel. It is not modified by specific geographic or socioeconomic factors.

The onset of symptoms can take place at any time between the first and fifth decades of life. A pooled study of 235 patients, derived from three research studies in which the age of onset was known, indicated that 34% of narcoleptic adults experienced onset of symptoms before the age of 15 years, 16% before the age of 10 years, and 4.5% before the age of 5 years. Patients frequently report a lag period of 5 to 10 years between the onset of clinical symptoms and actual confirmation of the diagnosis, reflecting of a lack of awareness of narcolepsy among health professionals.

About 15 breeds of dogs, cats, miniature horses, quarter horses, and Brahman bulls with narcolepsy have been described, with a confirmed inherited pattern (autosomal recessive) in Doberman pinschers and Labrador retrievers. [Canine narcolepsy is caused by a mutation in the hypocretin (orexin) receptor gene.] Feline narcolepsy is a useful model for the study of cataplexy and the associated chemical imbalances in the brain—cataplectic behavior can be induced in narcoleptic cats following the injection of carbachol (an acetylcholine-like substance) into the pontine reticular formation that is located in the brainstem. Microscopic examination of the brain fails to disclose any abnormalities, however. The presence of the histocompatibility antigens DQB1*0602 or DQA1*0102 in close to 100% of human narcolepsy patients (as compared to a 25% prevalence in the general population) also confirms the genetic susceptibility. Human narcolepsy does not have autosomal recessive inheritance, but is rather best explained on the basis of a two-threshold hypothesis, with an interplay between genetic susceptibility and environmental factors. This interplay triggers an imbalance between the brainstem cholinergic and catecholaminergic systems with an overall net excess of cholinergic activity in the brainstem that provokes cataplexy. Low levels of the catecholamines noradrenaline and dopamine decrease brain arousal activity and predispose the patient to sleepiness.

The diagnosis of narcolepsy is made on the basis of the patient's typical sleep-wake history along with the nocturnal polysomnogram and multiple sleep latency test. The nocturnal polysomnogram is a test in which activity of multiple physiological functions such as the electroencephalogram (EEG), eye movements, chin electromyogram, nasal airflow, respiratory effort, and oxygen saturation are recorded simultaneously on a strip of moving graph paper or a computer system. The test helps exclude disorders such as obstructive sleep apnea, periodic limb movement disorder, and idiopathic hypersomnia, which can also lead to daytime sleepiness and mimic narcolepsy. On the morning following the nocturnal polysomnogram, the patient undergoes a multiple sleep latency test (MSLT), during which four brief nap opportunities are provided in a darkened, quiet room at 2-hr intervals (e.g., at 1000, 1200, 1400, and 1600 hours) with simultaneous monitoring of polygraphic data. The MSLT provides quantitative and qualitative information about the transition from wakefulness into sleep. The time interval between lights-out and sleep onset observed on the EEG during the MSLT is termed "sleep latency"; a mean sleep latency is calculated by adding the sleep latencies of all naps and dividing the sum by the number of naps. The mean sleep latency is markedly shortened to less than 5 min in narcoleptics (in controls,

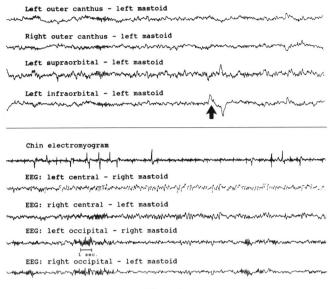

Left outer canthus - left mastoid

Right outer canthus - left mastoid

Left supraorbital - left mastoid

Left infraorbital - left mastoid

Chin electromyogram

EEG: left central - right mastoid

EEG: right central - left mastoid

EEG: left occipital - right mastoid

1 sec.

EEG: right occipital - left mastoid

Figure 1.

12–15 min). Furthermore, unaffected individuals show a transition from wakefulness first into non–REM sleep, with REM sleep appearing 75 to 120 minutes later; narcoleptic subjects tend to shift from wakefulness directly into REM sleep (sleep-onset REM; Figure 1). These diagnostic features are not consistently present in the early stages of the disorder in children and young adults, and sometimes necessitate serial sleep studies in order to establish a definitive diagnosis.

Narcolepsy requires life-long treatment. Daytime sleepiness is countered with stimulants such as pemoline, methyphenidate, or dextroamphetamine. The side effects of these agents include loss of appetite, nervousness, tics, and insomnia. Modafinil (Provigil), a drug with an unspecified mode of action, recently has also been reported to be effective in enhancing alertness and improving psychomotor performance. Its side effects include headache, nervousness, anxiety, and nausea. Because cholinergic pathways in the brainstem mediate cataplexy, drugs with anticholinergic activity, such as protryptiline and clompiramine, have been used for its control. One to three planned naps per day of 10 to 60 min each also help enhance daytime alertness and improve psychomotor performance. Some clinical trials are currently trying to determine the effectiveness of gamma hydroxybutyrate in the treatment of cataplexy, hypnagogic hallucinations, and sleep paralysis. Supportive psychotherapy and fluoxetine (Prozac) might also be indicated if patients develop emotional and behavioral problems. The Narcolepsy Network (tel. (973) 276–0115; E-mail narnet@aol.com) is a useful private, nonprofit resource for patients, families, and health professionals. Because of the increased risk of accidents from sleepiness, patients should be cautioned against driving long distances and working near sharp, moving machinery.

SUGGESTED READING

Challamel, M. J., Mazzola, M. E., Nevsimalova, S., Cannard, C., Louis, J., Revol, M. (1994). Narcolepsy in children. *Sleep, 17S*, 17–20.

Kotagal, S. (1996). Narcolepsy in children. *Seminars In Pediatric Neurology, 3*(1), 36–43.

Mignot, E., Young, T., Lin, L., & Fin, L. (1999). Nocturnal sleep and daytime sleepiness in normal subjects with HLA-DQB1*0602. *Sleep, 22,* 347–352.

Guilleminault, C., Heinzer, R., Mignot, E., & Black, J. (1998). Investigations into the neurologic basis of narcolepsy. *Neurology, 50*(Suppl. 1), S8–S15.

Carskadon, M. A., Dement, W. C., Mitler, M. M., Roth, T., Westbrook, P. R., Keenan, S. (1986). Guidelines for the multiple sleep latency test (MSLT): A standard measure of sleepiness. *Sleep, 9,* 519–524.

Lin, L., Faraco, J., Li, R., Kadatoni, H., Rogers, W., Lin, X., Oiu, X., de Jong, P. J., Nishino, S., Mignot, E. (1999). The sleep disorder canine narcolepsy is caused by a mutation in the hypocretin (orexin) receptor 2 gene. *Cell, 98,* 365–376.

S. KOTAGAL
Mayo Clinic

RAPID EYE MOVEMENT (REM) SLEEP
See SLEEP

NATHAN, PETER E.

Born and raised in St. Louis, Missouri, Peter E. Nathan received the AB in social relations, with honors, from Harvard College in 1957 and the PhD in clinical psychology from Washington University in 1962. During seven years (1962–1969) on the faculty of Harvard Medical School, most of which were spent as a clinical psychologist in the Psychiatry Service at Boston City Hospital, Nathan launched a program of research on basic psychosocial variables associated with alcoholism that has continued to the present.

On moving to Rutgers University in 1969 to become professor and director of clinical psychology training in the Department of Psychology, Nathan established the Alcohol Behavior Research Laboratory, which remained at Rutgers until he left in 1990. In 1974, Nathan was appointed chair of the Department of Clinical Psychology in Rutgers' Graduate School of Applied and Professional Psychology. He was named Henry and Anna Starr Professor of Psychology and assumed the directorship of Rutgers' Center of Alcohol Studies in 1983. In 1987, he began a partial leave of absence from Rutgers to serve as senior Health Program Officer for the MacArthur Foundation in Chicago. On January 1, 1990, he became Vice President for Academic Affairs, Dean of Faculties, and University of Iowa Foundation Distinguished Professor of Psychology at the University of Iowa. On July 1, 1993, he became provost, and on July 1, 1995, he became acting president of the University. On January 1, 1996, he stepped down from the acting presidency to return to the Department of Psychology.

Nathan has served as member and chair of the NIAAA's Alcoholism and Alcohol Problems Review Committee, as a member of the National Institute of Mental Health's (NIMH) Psychological Sciences Fellowship Review Committee, and as a member of the Veterans Administration's Behavioral Sciences Research Evaluation Committee. In 1988, he became a member of both the Work Group to consider changes in the diagnostic criteria for the Substance Use Disorders for *DSM-IV*, and the core *DSM-IV* Task Force itself. In 1990, he was appointed to a 4-yr term on the National Advisory Council on Alcohol Abuse and Alcoholism of the National Institutes of Health (NIH). He has written or edited more than 20 books and more than 200 journal articles and book chapters, dealing with such diverse issues as alcohol abuse and dependence, syndromal diagnosis, and psychotherapy outcomes. He has spoken and consulted widely on these issues, and has also served on many journal editorial boards, including 21 years as associate editor of the *Journal of Clinical Psychology,* 8 years as associate editor of *American Psychologist,* 7 years as executive editor of the *Journal of Studies on Alcohol,* 6 years as associate editor of *Contemporary Psychology,* and a current term as associate editor of *Prevention and Treatment.* In 1989, Nathan was the recipient of the Board of Trustees Award for Excellence in Research from Rutgers, The State University; in 1992, he received the Alfred M. Wellner Memorial Award from the National Register of Health Service Providers in Psychology; in 1996, he delivered the American Psychological Foundation Rosalee G. Weiss Lecture; and in 1999, he received the APA Award for Distinguished Professional Contributions to Knowledge. Nathan is a past president of APA's Division of Clinical Psychology and the current president of the National Register of Health Service Providers in Psychology.

STAFF

NATIONAL INSTITUTE ON DRUG ABUSE

The National Institute on Drug Abuse (NIDA) at the National Institutes of Health supports over 85% of the world's research on the health aspects of drug abuse and addiction. The mission of NIDA is to bring the full power of science to bear on the problems of drug abuse and addiction by generating scientific facts about the nature, prevention, and treatment of drug abuse and addiction, and ensuring the rapid dissemination and use of those findings to improve the health of the public. NIDA's research portfolio is devoted to increasing our understanding of the causes and consequences of drug abuse and addiction and to reducing or eliminating drug use, abuse, and their sequelae. NIDA accomplishes this goal through support of research projects that improve and refine methods for the assessment, treatment, and prevention of drug abuse and addiction. The scientific studies include research on individual differences among drug abusers and those at risk for abusing drugs, fundamental biological mechanisms of action of abused drugs, behavioral and/or pharmacological treatments for addiction, health services delivery strategies, community-based epidemiologic studies, and the epidemiology and prevention of HIV and other infectious diseases among drug abusers.

NIDA'S NEUROSCIENCE PORTFOLIO

The National Institute on Drug Abuse's investment in neuroscience research has led to important breakthroughs in such diverse fields as neuroimaging, genetics, and addiction treatment. These scientific advancements have led to an even greater understanding of neurotransmitters and neural pathways, and especially of how brain mechanisms work both under normal conditions and when affected by drugs of abuse. NIDA-supported research has led to the conclusion that drug use is a preventable behavior and drug addiction a treatable disease. Research supported by NIDA provides the scientific bases for the development of effective biomedical, behavioral, and psychosocial approaches to the prevention and treatment of drug abuse. Some areas being researched under NIDA's broad neuroscience portfolio are discussed below.

BEHAVIORAL SCIENCE OF ADDICTION

NIDA's neuroscience portfolio includes a strong foundation of basic behavioral research. All drugs of abuse act in the brain by altering normal neurobiological processes, which in turn cause changes in behavior and thinking patterns. Understanding the relationship between the brain mechanisms that underlie behavior and the changes in these mechanisms that are caused by drugs is critical to developing effective treatment and prevention programs. NIDA's behavioral researchers examine how behavioral factors such as impulsivity, cognitive processes of learning and memory, or judgment and decision making cause high-risk behavior leading to drug abuse or relapse to drug abuse. They also focus on behavioral and cognitive consequences or sequelae of drug addiction as well as state of the art behavioral treatments.

MAPPING THE BRAIN CIRCUITS OF DRUG ABUSE AND ADDICTION

Although much has been learned about the reward circuit at the base of the brain, less attention has been paid to the brain circuits and mechanisms involved in higher order cognitive and emotional processing of initial drug experiences and the role these brain circuits play in the complex processes of addiction. NIDA researchers are using neuroanatomical and functional imaging research to map the brain circuits controlling all aspects of drug abuse and addiction.

UNDERSTANDING AND PREVENTING RELAPSE TO DRUG USE

With the advent of new animal model systems, research is progressing rapidly to reveal the behavioral and biological mechanisms responsible for stress or environmental cues that trigger relapse. Understanding and clarifying the role of these mechanisms of relapse to drug use after periods of abstinence will be helpful in developing new and improved addiction treatment approaches.

VULNERABILITY TO DRUG ADDICTION

Current research suggests that there may be certain predisposing factors that account for individual differences in drug preference, tolerance, sensitization, abstinence signs, reinforcing efficacy, rate of acquisition of drug taking, maintenance, resistance to extinction, and reinstatement of drug taking. One of the vulnerability factors of interest to NIDA is the genetic influence, which might be involved in the reinforcing efficacy of drugs and the sensitivity to toxic consequences of drug taking, such as seizures, cognitive decline, or neurotoxicity. NIDA is also examining environmental factors that make individuals more or less susceptible to becoming addicted.

DRUGS AND LEARNING, MEMORY AND COGNITION

The role of learning and memory in drug tolerance, sensitization, dependence, and relapse is an emerging area of study. Stimuli that become associated with the drug experience are thought to elicit drug craving, yet little information is available concerning the neural mediators of the associative processes involved. NIDA is broadening its research in this important area.

ANIMAL MODELS TO STUDY THE NEUROBIOLOGY OF ADDICTION

The drug self-administration paradigm has been a mainstay in research on the behavioral neurobiology of drug abuse and addiction. From that paradigm has evolved the brain reward hypothesis of addiction. A need exists to expand that model to include the functional role of brain structures beyond the nucleus accumbens.

For more information about neuroscience research at NIDA, contact Roger M. Brown, PhD, Chief, Neuropsychopharmacology, Division of Basic Research, *rb99w@nih.gov,* 6001 Executive Boulevard, Room 4282, MSC 9555.

R. M. MACKAR
National Institute on Drug Abuse

SUBSTANCE ABUSE

NATIVISM

The United States is a nation of immigrants. The celebrated inscription on the Statue of Liberty announces an open door to the world's people: "Give me your tired, your poor / Your huddled masses yearning to breathe free." Many Americans celebrate their nation as a melting pot of race, nationality, and ethnicity.

At the same time, however, a powerful anti-immigrant sentiment runs through American history. The attack on immigrants is known as *nativism,* and the impulse toward it should be understood as both a cultural and a political phenomenon.

THE CULTURE OF NATIVISM

Immigrants arrived in the United States in a series of great waves. Nativist agitation begins with a fear that the latest newcomers threaten the nation because they do not share or appreciate its values. Benjamin Franklin expressed an early version of this fear two decades before the American Revolution (although Franklin soon recanted).

This will in a few years be a German colony. Instead of their learning our language, we must learn theirs, or live as in a foreign country. Already the

English begin to quit particular Neighborhoods, surrounded by Dutch, being made uneasy by the Disagreeableness of Dissonant Manners; and in Time, Numbers will probably quit the Province. . . . Besides, the Dutch under-live, and are thereby enabled to under-work and under-sell the English; who are thereby extremely incommoded, and consequently disgusted, so there can be no cordial Affection or Unity . . . between the two Nations. (Morone, 1996, p. 428)

Franklin's pessimism about the Dutch strangers touches points that remain tender to the present day: apprehension over the American language, anxiety about cultural inundation, the uneasy sense of racial difference, allegations of laziness (violating the all-American gospel of hard work), and social division articulated as middle-class flight. Beneath the specific complaints lurk the essential questions about shared culture: Can we be a single people? With *them?* Or will they ruin us?

Future generations would be more explicit about the "dissonant manners" that so disgusted the English neighbors. In the early 19th century, for example, some newcomers were Catholics—an alarming idea for many Americans who believed the United States and Protestantism both sprang from revolts against centralized authority. Citizenship and faith reinforced one another. In contrast, Catholics were ruled by a foreign Pope, they deferred to their clergy, they were incapable of independent (much less republican) thought. Their priests kept convents full of unmarried women, which true American mobs occasionally burned to the ground (Abinder, 1992).

The litany against foreigners went on, across time, race, and ethnicity: The Chinese were "cruel, cunning and savage," as social reformer Jacob Riis put it (1890, p. 97); they posed "a constant and terrible menace to society" (p. 102). Jews were "moral cripples with dwarfed souls" (Ross, 1907, p. 154); Italians were "gross little aliens" who lacked "the power to take rational care of themselves" (Ross, 1907, 101, 113). By the end of the 19th century, religious fears had been replaced by confused quasi-scientific notions about so-called inferior races that would debase the American stock.

The most celebrated recent nativist statement came from Patrick Buchanan during the 1992 Republican convention. Buchanan articulated a quite standard clarion call to "take back" American culture. Referring to recent riots in Los Angeles, Buchanan rallied his followers, saying, "As those boys . . . of the 18th Cav . . . took back the streets of Los Angeles, block by block, my friends, we must take back our cities and take back our culture, and take back our country" (1992).

Nativist fears generally arise when the structure of American society appears to be in flux: moments of large immigration, broad economic dislocation, or shifting social relations (like changing racial or gender patterns). Under such unsettling circumstances, nativists begin to warn their countrymen of the threat. Many of the alleged dangers are remarkably similar from one generation to the next: The immigrants resist assimilation, they cling to their alien ways, they do not share our values, and—always the bottom line—they threaten America with national decline.

THE POLITICS OF NATIVISM

Early American nativists did not try to curtail immigration. Rather, they focused on restricting the newcomers' political activities. In 1798, the Federalist Congress passed Alien Acts that changed the residency requirement for American citizenship from 5 to 14 years and added other barriers to political participation. The Federalists denounced the immigrants as "wild Irishmen and French refugees," although their real objection was the support the new arrivals gave Thomas Jefferson and his Democratic-Republican Party (Morone, 1998).

In the 1840s and 1850s, a very large number of immigrants from Ireland and Germany generated a new backlash. This time, the anti-immigrant urge grew into a political movement that shot briefly and brilliantly across the American political scene. The nativists formed the American party, a secret organization that defined the United States as a moral, Protestant nation. When asked about the party, members said they knew nothing, earning the party the nickname "Know-Nothings." The centerpiece of their political strategy involved a 21-year waiting period before immigrants could be naturalized (Abinder, 1992).

The Know-Nothings came from nowhere and met astonishing political success. In 1854, they carried the entire Massachusetts Congressional delegation and almost all 400 Assembly seats. They won 9 of 11 Congressional districts in Indiana, 11 in New York, and up to 17 out of 25 in Pennsylvania. The Know-Nothings grabbed majorities in a half-dozen state legislatures and ran strong in a dozen others. Contemporaries began to speculate about a Know-Nothing Congressional majority or President in the next election. This was the most successful nativist organization in American history—and one of the most successful third parties.

However, the Know-Nothing tide ran out as fast as it had come in. The party was swamped by an even greater American identity crisis: the question of slavery. Within a decade the Know-Nothings were gone.

In the 1880s, another nativist movement rose up and pursued a new political strategy: excluding all so-called undesirable immigrants. Congress banned Chinese immigrants in 1882 (a ban that would last almost a century); President Theodore Roosevelt later excluded the Japanese. By the turn of the century, nativist sentiment was also running strong against people thought of as inferior races from Eastern and Southern Europe.

After World War I, the apprehension about allegedly inferior people was amplified by a great red scare. A crusade very much like Joseph McCarthy's campaign of the 1950s imagined foreign Bolsheviks infiltrating American society. A broad anti-immigrant coalition gathered. It spanned the political spectrum—from labor unions (worried about wages) to the Ku Klux Klan (worried about Jews and Catholics). The outcry helped secure the National Origins Act (in 1924), which almost entirely shut the door to immigration from non–Anglo-Saxon nations.

The tight bans on most immigration remained in place until 1965. They were finally lifted during Lyndon Johnson's Great Society. The unanticipated result was another great immigration—this time largely from Latin America and Asia.

Today, many Americans are once again alarmed about the fast rising number of foreign born people living in the United States—roughly one in ten residents was born abroad. Immigration raises complex and legitimate policy questions about the optimal size of the American population and the wages offered to low-income workers. However, beneath the policy debates lurk more troubling questions: Will nativism grow along with immigration and become a powerful political force in the 21st century? Or will Americans welcome this generation of immigrants as the latest additions to a richly diverse and multicultural society?

REFERENCES

Abinder, T. (1992). New York: Oxford University Press.

Buchanan, P. (1992, August). *The election is about who we are: Taking back the country.* Speech delivered at the Republican National Convention, Houston, TX.

Morone, J. A. (1996). The struggle for American culture. *PS: Political Science and Politics, 29*(3), 425–430.

Morone, J. A. (1998). *The democratic wish: Popular participation and the limits of American government.* New Haven, CT: Yale University Press.

Riis, J. (1890). *How the other half lives.* New York: Scribner.

Ross, E. A. (1913). *The old world in the new.* New York: Century.

J. A. MORONE
Brown University

NATURAL SELECTION

With a growing number of distinguished evolutionists—including Ernst Mayr, Edward O. Wilson, and Francisco Ayala—I believe that Darwinism is more than just a scientific theory. It is the basis for a full world view, a Weltanschauung.

Michael Ruse (1986), p. 513.

NATURAL SELECTION: A DEFINITION

A typical definition of the term "natural selection" reads as follows (Parker, 1997, p. 312): "Darwin's theory of evolution, according to which organisms tend to produce progeny far above the means of subsistence; in the struggle for existence that ensues, only those progeny with favorable variations survive; the favorable variations accumulate through subsequent generations, and descendants diverge from their ancestors." A definition concentrating on evolution by "differential survival and reproduction of the members of a population" (Catania, 1994) deviates in an important point from that just given. The progeny which differentially survives is not necessarily the fittest, a point best illustrated by island populations endangered by more or less closely related intruders worldwide.

AREA OF APPLICATION: STRONGLY DIFFERENT OPINIONS AMONG SCIENTISTS

Apart from a few exceptions (Lima-de-Faria, 1988; Chauvin, 1997), most contemporary biologists and other scholars accept natural selection as a real process in nature. However, as to the extent of the effects of natural selection on the differentiation and the origin of new species and higher systematic categories, the differences of opinion are enormous; see, for example, Bell (1997), Catania (1994), Cziko (1995), Dawkins (1986, 1995, 1987/1996, 1998), Dennett (1995), Mayr (1997, 1998), Ruse (1996), versus Behe (1996), Berlinski (1996), Dembski (1998a), Junker and Scherer (1998), Lönnig and Saedler (1997), ReMine (1993), and Schützenberger (1996). The first group of authors firmly believes that natural selection is the key process for the origin of all life forms on earth, whereas most scientists of the second group are entirely convinced that the action of natural selection is only of limited significance and that it is largely incompetent to explain the origin of life's major features from biochemistry to systematics, especially the origin of higher systematic categories. Both groups claim that scientific reasons are the basis of their position in biology. "Missing links" representing nearly all possible shades between the views of these two groups may also be found; see, for instance, Chandebois (1993), Denton (1985, 1998), Gould (1996, 1997), Ho and Saunders (1984), Kauffman (1993), Prothero (1998), and Stanley (1998).

SOME BASIC PROBLEMS

The Reproductive Powers of Living Beings and the Survival of the Fittest

Dobzhansky's 1937 work *Genetics and the Origin of Species* is generally viewed as the crystallization point for the origin and growth of the modern synthesis or neo-Darwinian theory of evolution (Lönnig, 1999a). There is hardly a better example to illustrate the key message (and, at the same time, the weaknesses) of the modern theory of natural selection than the following quotation from this pioneering work of Dobzhansky (p. 149):

With consummate mastery Darwin shows natural selection to be a direct consequence of the appallingly great reproductive powers of living beings. A single individual of the fungus *Lycoperdon bovista* produces 7×10^{11} spores; *Sisymbrium sophia* and *Nicotiana tabacum*, respectively, 730,000 and 360,000 seed; salmon, 28,000,000 eggs per season; and the American oyster up to 114,000,000 eggs in a single spawning. Even the slowest breeding forms produce more offspring than can survive if the population is to remain numerically stationary. Death and destruction of a majority of the individuals produced undoubtedly takes place. If, then, the population is composed of a mixture of hereditary types, some of which are more and others less well adapted to the environment, a greater proportion of the former than of the latter would be expected to survive. In modern language this means that, among the survivors, a greater frequency of carriers of certain genes or chromosome structures would be present than among the ancestors. . . .

For agreement on and further documentation of the principle of natural selection, see the group of authors cited above, beginning with Bell (1997). However, in the 1950s, French biologists, such as Cuénot, Tetry, and Chauvin, who did not follow the modern synthesis, raised the following objection to this kind of reasoning (according to Litynski, 1961, p. 63):

Out of 120,000 fertilized eggs of the green frog only two individuals survive. Are we to conclude that these two frogs out of 120,000 were selected by nature because they were the fittest ones; or rather as Cuénot said that natural selection is nothing but blind mortality which selects nothing at all?

Similar questions may be raised for the 700 billion spores of *Lycoperdon*, the 114 million eggs multiplied with the number of spawning seasons of the American oyster, for the 28 million eggs of salmon, and so on. King Solomon wrote around 1000 BC: "I returned, and saw under the sun, that the race is not to the swift, nor the battle to the strong, . . . but time and chance happeneth to all of them" (KJV 1611).

If only a few out of millions and even billions of individuals are to survive and reproduce, then there is some difficulty believing that it should really be the fittest who would do so. Strongly different abilities and varying environmental conditions can turn up during different phases of ontogenesis. Hiding places of predator and prey, the distances between them, local differences of biotopes and geographical circumstances, weather conditions, and microclimates all belong to the repertoire of infinitely varying parameters. Coincidences, accidents, and chance occurrences are strongly significant in the lives of all individuals and species. Moreover, the effects of modifications, which are nonheritable by definition, may be much more powerful than the effects of mutations which have only "slight or even invisible effects on the phenotype" (Mayr 1970, p. 169, similarly 1976/1997; see also Dawkins, 1995, 1998), specifying that kind of mutational effects most strongly favored for natural selection and evolution by the neo-Darwinian school. Confronting the enormous numbers of descendants and the neverending changes of various environmental parameters, it seems to be much more probable that instead of the very rare "fittest" of the mutants or recombinants, the average ones will survive and reproduce.

Natural Selection, Population Genetics, and the Neutral Theory

Despite the impossibility to produce a strictly deterministic model for natural selection in the face of myriad varying parameters, there have been several attempts to quantitatively assess this problem. Fisher, perhaps the most important forerunner of the neo-Darwinian theory, has calculated (1930) that new alleles with even 1% selective advantage (i.e., more than is usually expected by neo-Darwinian theorists), will routinely be lost in natural populations. According to these calculations, the likelihood of losing a new allele with 1% advantage or no advantage is more than 90% in the next 31 generations (Fisher, 1930/1958; Dobzhansky, 1951; Schmidt, 1985; see also ReMine, 1993; Futuyma, 1998; Maynard Smith, 1998). Considering genetic drift (random fluctuations of gene frequencies in populations) Griffith and colleagues state in agreement with these authors (1999, p. 564):

Even a new mutation that is slightly favorable will usually be lost in the first few generations after it appears in the population, a victim of genetic drift. If a new mutation has a selective advantage of S in the heterozygote in which it appears, then the chance is only $2S$ that the mutation will ever succeed in taking over the population. So a mutation that is 1 percent better in fitness than the standard allele in the population will be lost 98 percent of the time by genetic drift.

Nevertheless, it appears that if such a mutation occurred at a constant rate in a large population, it would have a fair chance to become established after an average occurrence of about 50 times.

However, such estimates are made on exceedingly imperfect assumptions biased in favor of the modern synthesis. Note that the basis of these calculations are dominant mutant alleles with 1% fitness increase in the *heterozygous* state. In the plant kingdom, however, more than 98% of all the mutations are recessive and more than 99.99% of the dominant (as well as homozygous recessive) mutants in the plant and animal kingdoms are lowering fitness. Modifications, juvenile stages, and the endlessly varying environmental parameters are not (and hardly can be) taken into account, nor is the objection of the French biologists quoted above addressed Dobzhansky's "death and destruction of a majority of the individuals" occurs mainly before sexual maturity—as can be seen, for instance, each spring when billions of tree-seedlings appear, of which only an extremely low minority will ever become adult or full-grown trees: Obviously the environment is far more relevant than a 1% genetic advantage.

Most importantly, the calculations are invalid for small populations where most of the evolutionary novelties are said to have arisen according to the neo-Darwinian theory of evolution and punctuated equilibrium alike (Gould & Eldredge, 1993; Mayr, 1976/1997, 1998; Stanley, 1999). In a small population, the rate of advantageous mutations is extremely low (if they appear at all; aeons of time are needed to obtain the average 50 identical advantageous dominant mutations for one success) and genetic drift is almost totally substituting natural selection. Also, it is not possible in nature to raise mutation rates indefinitely since error catastrophe occurs when the mutation rate is too high, thereby terminating the existence of the population.

Neutral, slightly deleterious, and moderately favorable alleles all have nearly equal chances to spread in diploid populations, as the neutral theory of population genetics has definitely shown (Kimura, 1983; ReMine, 1993; Fisher, 1958). The neutral theory "contends that at the molecular level the majority of evolutionary changes and much of the variability within species are caused neither by positive selection of advantageous alleles nor by balancing selection, but by random genetic drift of mutant alleles that are selectively neutral or nearly so" (Li, 1997, p. 55). Hence, the net result of larger numbers of gene mutations can mean overall degeneration of a species instead of "upward" evolution. Moreover, the costs of the many substitutions necessary for neo-Darwinian evolution to function successfully in large populations can quickly surpass the adaptive possibilities of a species (see the discussions of *Haldane's Dilemma* by Dobzhansky et al., 1977 and especially ReMine, 1993).

Selection and Neutral Structures on the Morphological Level

On the morphological and anatomical level, there are many structures in nature for which no selective advantages can be found. For example, what could be the selective advantage of a plant displaying leaves with entire margins compared to one having dentate leaves or a plant with dentate leaves compared to one with serrate or doubly serrate leaves? A caterpillar would probably be quite happy finding more starting and attachment points for eating such leaves, which could be a decisive selective disadvantage for the plant. Also, many hypertrophic structures have appeared in the history of life (as in the cases of the enormous canine teeth of saber-toothed tigers, the burden of weighty antlers in prehistoric deer)

which seem to have led to the extinction of the affected species. Why did natural selection not select genes that would in time diminish such structures? Sexual selection will hardly solve these problems but constitutes a problem of its own (Lönnig, 1993).

DOES NATURAL SELECTION EXIST AT ALL?

The remarks made so far, however, do not refute the occurrence of natural selection. In spite of the problems just mentioned, it is self-evident that physiologically, anatomically, and ethologically damaged mutants and recombinants (to speak again in the contemporary genetic language of these individuals) will be at a disadvantage in many situations (lame prey in relation to their predators and *vice versa*). It is only on islands with loss or diminution of stabilizing selection that processes of degeneration may occur quickly (for further discussion of the topic, see Lönnig 1993, 1998; Kunze et al., 1997). Furthermore, survival of the fittest evidently takes place, for example, in cases of alleles and plasmids with strongly selective advantages, as in the cases of multiple resistance in bacteria and resistance to DDT in many insect species. After pointing out that Darwin knew hardly any cases of natural selection, Mayr asserts (1998, p. 191): "Now, there are hundreds, if not thousands, of well-established proofs, including such well-known instances as insecticide resistance of agricultural pests, antibiotic resistance of bacteria, industrial melanism, the attenuation of the myxomatosis virus in Australia, the sickle-cell gene and other blood genes and malaria, to mention only a few spectacular cases."

THE EVOLUTIONARY POTENTIALS AND LIMITS OF NATURAL SELECTION

According to the first group of authors mentioned earlier, there are hardly any evolutionary limits for natural selection. The assertion that "through billions of years of blind mutations pressing against the shifting walls of their environment, microbes finally emerged as men" by H. J. Muller (who was awarded the Nobel prize for his work in mutation genetics) may illustrate this conviction in the near omnipotent potentials of mutation and natural selection. Avire states (1999, p. 83) that "natural selection comes close to omnipotence." The second group of authors, however, point to several investigations which are at odds with this view (see discussion in the next paragraphs).

The Law of Recurrent Variation and Selection Limits

Mutations are thought to be the ultimate basis for evolution by natural selection. So let's have a look at the question of whether mutations could have provided the raw materials for natural selection for the origin of all species and life forms of the earth. Having investigated the question for about 35 years now including the work with collections of mutants of two model plant species (the pea and the snapdragon—more than 1 million plants), I have come to a conclusion strongly differing from the modern synthesis concerning the potential of mutagenesis. The results I have summed up in "the law of recurrent variation" (Lönnig, 1993, 1995; Kunze et al., 1997). This law specifies that, for any case thoroughly examined (from pea to man), mutants occur in a large but nevertheless limited spectrum of phenotypes which—in accordance with all the experiences of mutation research of the 20th century taken together—cannot transform the original species into an entirely new one. These results are in agreement with the statements of several renowned evolutionary geneticists, two of whom are quoted here. Stubbe wrote after a lifetime spent in mutation research (1966, p. 154):

The improved knowledge of mutants in *Antirrhinum* has provided some essential experience. During the years each new large mutation trial showed that the number of really new mutants recognized for the first time was steadily diminishing, so that the majority of the genetic changes was already known.

And Gottschalk stated in 1994, p. 180, "The larger the mutant collections are, the more difficult it is to extend them by new mutation types. Mutants preferentially arise that already exist."

To understand these observations one must clearly distinguish between two levels: first, the level of the phenotypes, and second, the DNA level. On the latter, the potential of missense and nonsense mutations and other sequence deviations is nearly infinite. However, the spectrum of the resulting different phenotypes is not, because the space of functionally valid sequences within a given system of tightly matching regulatory and target genes and correspondingly coordinated functions involved in the formation of the finely balanced whole of an organism cannot infinitely be stretched by chance mutations.

To take a crude illustration: Drop your computer from the desk or take a screwdriver and a hammer, open the casing, shut your eyes and then forcefully operate in the innards! Depending on the number of computers and how often and for how long one proceeds to act this way, one may collect a nearly endless number of *non-functional* changes. Yet—with much luck—one may also select a few operationally diminished, but nevertheless still working, systems. Thus, one may demolish a computer in a thousand and more different ways by some accidental procedures. However, the resulting still more or less *functional states* (the functional phenotypes), will be limited. The hope to secure a Pentium III from a 486 by this method would be very bold indeed.—Of course, the situation in biology is more complex than in engineering, because organisms are, for instance, reactive entities. Nevertheless, limits to selection have repeatedly been found in several areas of biological research.

The limits of selection due to the absence of hoped-for positive mutations were most severely felt in mutation breeding at the end of the 1970s and in the 1980s after some 40 years of worldwide mutation research with cultivated plants as maize, rice, barley, peas, and others. Mutation induction was originally thought to revolutionize plant breeding and substitute the costly and time-consuming "old" recombination method on a global scale. By mutation genetics, three time-lapse methods were available to the breeders: (a) raising the numbers of mutations so enormously in a few years, that nature would have needed millions of years to produce similar amounts of hereditary changes; (b) well-aimed and careful selection and conservation of promising genotypes, which often would have been lost in nature; and (c) well-aimed recombination of rare genotypes for which the chance to ever meet and mate in nature would again be very small.

After the neo-Darwinian school of biologists had taught plant breeders that mutation, recombination, and natural selection were responsible for the origination of all life forms and structures on earth, the possibility of the threefold time-lapse method led to a previously unknown euphoria among geneticists in order to revolutionize plant breeding. Literally billions of mutations were induced by different mutagenic agents in many plant species. However, relatively few useful mutants were obtained, mostly loss-of-function mutants loosing undesirable features like toxic constituents, shattering of fruits, spininess, and so on. Due to the limits summarized by the law of recurrent variation (also pertinent to the processes in nature, i.e., for natural selection), these efforts ended in a worldwide collapse of mutation breeding some forty years later. It is self-evident that selection, whether artificial or natural, cannot select structures and capabilities which were hoped or believed to arise, but never did (Lönnig, 1993, 1998). Thus, qualitative limits in generating positive mutations point to the limits of natural selection.

Selection Limits in Population Genetics and their Relevance for Natural Selection

The situation in population genetics, where selection limits have been found and described in many papers, has been summarized by Hartl and Jones as follows (1998, p. 686):

Population improvement by means of artificial selection cannot continue indefinitely. A population may respond to selection until its mean is many standard deviations different from the mean of the original population, but eventually the population reaches a selection limit at which successive generations show no further improvement.

Although often the qualitative differences between artificial and natural selection are stressed by many evolutionary biologists to avoid the inference to selection limits for the latter, there are no scientifically valid reasons to believe that natural selection is limitless. The plasticity of the genome is not infinite, irrespective of the kind of selection pressure exercised upon a population (Lönnig, 1993).

Natural Selection and the Origin of New Genes

The observations summarized in the law of recurrent variation directly lead to the question of the origins of new genes. The probability of obtaining an entirely new functional DNA sequence (necessary, for example, for the origin of the more than five thousand extant different gene families of today's living organisms) due to gene duplications with subsequent nucleotide substitutions by point and other mutations has been calculated by several authors to be less than 1 in 10^{50}, even granting billions of years for natural selection working on random mutations (ReMine, 1993; Kunze et al., 1997). The result is, simply put, that the probability is so low that no reasonable person would expect to obtain a target or goal in any other area of life by such small chances. Due to the factual absence of completely new functional DNA sequences in mutagenesis experiments, as well as the low likelihood referenced above, the origin of new genes and gene families cannot be explained by natural selection. Additionally, the necessity of genetic engineering for organism transformation simultaneously exemplifies the fact that induced mutations in the host organism cannot substitute for the task. This is not only true for slow-breeding organisms, but also for the fastest; for instance, bacteria like *Escherichia coli,* where thousands of generations with trillions of individuals per generation can be cultivated in the relatively short time of a few years (3,500 generations in 1 year; 1 gram of *E. coli* cells contains about 10^{13} individuals).

Natural Selection and the Origin of "Irreducibly Complex Structures"

Behe defines irreducible complexity (1998, p. 178) as follows: "An irreducible complex system is one that requires several closely matched parts in order to function and where removal of one of the components effectively causes the system to cease functioning." His mousetrap example illustrates the point: "The function of the mouse trap requires all the pieces: you cannot catch a few mice with just a platform, add a spring and catch a few more mice, add a holding bar and catch a few more. All the components have to be in place before any mice are caught." Concerning the significance of the principle of irreducible complexity for natural selection, Behe explains (p. 179):

Closely matched, irreducible complex systems are huge stumbling blocks for Darwinian evolution because they cannot be put together directly by improving a given function over many steps, as Darwinian gradualism would have it. The only possible recourse of a gradualist is to speculate that an irreducibly complex system might have come together through an indirect route—perhaps the mousetrap started out as a washing board, was changed into an orange crate, and somehow ended up as a mousetrap. One can never completely rule out such an indirect scenario, which is tantamount to trying to prove the negative. However, the more complex the system, the more difficult it becomes to envision such scenarios, and the more examples of irreducible complexity we meet, the less and less persuasive such indirect scenarios become.

In his 1996 book, *Darwin's Black Box,* Behe discusses several examples of biological irreducible complexity, among them the cilium, the bacterial flagellum with filament, hook, and motor embedded in the membranes and cell wall, and the biochemistry of blood clotting in man. The open questions of the different positions of Dawkins and Hitching on the famous example of the origin of the eye are discussed at some length, especially the problems of natural selection for the biochemistry of vision in the introductory chapter. He sums up his analysis as follows (1996, pp. 38–39):

Hitching's argument is vulnerable because he mistakes an integrated system of systems for a single system, and Dawkins rightly points out the separability of the components. Dawkins, however, merely adds complex systems to complex systems and calls that an explanation. This can be compared to answering the question "How is a stereo system made?" with the words "By plugging a set of speakers into an amplifier, and adding a CD player, radio receiver, and tape deck." Either Darwinian theory can account for the assembly of the speakers and amplifier, or it can't.

For a detailed anatomical and developmental study of the genesis of the eye, specifying Darwin's and Dawkins's fallacies of natural selection and gradualistic evolution under full quotation of the relevant passages (see Lönnig, 1989). Also, several important points (as the improbability to derive a *reflecting* eye from a *refracting* one) have been discussed by Denton (1998).

Since the origin of irreducibly complex systems or subsystems necessitates the concerted origin of many new gene functions, the odds against natural selection of undirected mutations as the final source of these genes and structures are rising correspondingly.

NATURAL SELECTION AS METAPHYSICS AND AS SCIENCE

Popper's Critique and Recantation

Another kind of objection that was launched on the concept of natural selection originated with scholars interested in the logical structure of scientific explanations. There is a long tradition among these scholars to view the concept of natural selection to be a tautology (MacBride, 1929; Waddington, 1960; Mahner & Bunge, 1997—excellent reviews on the debate between some 50 scientists and philosophers have been given by Bird, 1989; ReMine, 1993; and Chauvin, 1997). Waddington commented that natural selection "states that the fittest individuals in a population (defined as those which leave the most offspring) will leave the most offspring" (Waddington, 1960, p. 385), and

Natural selection is survival of the fittest, and the tautology hinges on the word *fittest.* When the fittest are identified by their survival then there is a tautology. We ask, who are the fittest? We are told, the survivors. We ask, who will survive? We are told, the fittest. Natural selection is then 'the survival of the survivors.' It is a tautology" (ReMine, 1993, p. 98)

This objection has been strongly attacked by neo-Darwinians and punctuationists alike, arguing that fitness can scientifically be defined and tested, and that the tautology argument has conclusively been disproved by many biologists and philosophers (Mayr, 1991, 1997).

Perhaps the most renowned case of a criticism and later recantation concerning the metaphysics/tautology-problem of natural selection by a philosopher was Sir Karl Popper's comment that "Darwinism is not a testable scientific theory but a *metaphysical research program,"* that is, natural selection was seen to be "almost tautologous" and at best only "a possible framework for testable scientific theories" (1974, p. 134; italics in original). In a time of rising creationism, these often quoted statements led to an unusual amount of criticism and pressure of the evolutionary community for Popper to check, extend, and reformulate his views on natural selection.

To back up his recantation four years later that "the theory of natural selection may be so formulated that it is far from tautological" (1978, p. 339), he mentioned as evidence the famous textbook example of "industrial melanism" of the peppered moth (*Biston betularia*) asserting that here "we can observe natural selection happening under our very eyes, as it were." In this case the majority of the light-colored form was believed to have been replaced by a dark type better adapted to sooty trees in the wake of the industrial revolution—an example of natural selection probably well-known to every student who ever attended a course on evolutionary biology at school or university all over the world.

Popper's Case of the Peppered Moth: Still More Metaphysics than Science

Looking at the famous case of industrial melanism more than twenty years later, we have to point to the surprising fact that the case has recently been found wanting (Sargent et al., 1998; Majerus, 1998; Coyne, 1998). Hence, we may conclude that Popper's partial retraction of his views was not necessary, at least not because of the example of the peppered moth.

After summarizing Kettlewell's presentation of the *Biston betularia* instance, Coyne (1998) states the main points of the critical recent observations as follows: (a) The peppered moth normally doesn't rest on tree trunks (where Kettlewell had directly placed them for documentation); (b) The moths usually choose their resting places during the night, not during the day (the latter being implied in the usual evolutionary textbook illustrations); (c) The return of the variegated form of the peppered moth occurred independently of the lichens "that supposedly played such an important role" (Coyne); and (d) Kettlewell's behavioral experiments have not been replicated in later investigations. Additionally, there are important points to be added from the original papers, as (e) differences of vision between man and birds and (f) the pollution-*in*dependent decrease of melanic morphs.

So Popper's case of the peppered moth as an observation against his own criticism of natural selection as a metaphysical research program consists, nonetheless, mostly of metaphysics. It may be asked: How is it possible that cases of insufficient or even false evidence for natural selection can be bolstered and presented in such a way that it appears to be so convincing and entirely compelling that even the best minds of the world can be grossly misled—even to the point of modifying a published evaluation on this topic?

For another renowned textbook example of natural selection which was pointed out recently to consist more of a metaphysical explanation than a scientifically valid case, see Gould for the origin of the neck of the giraffe (1996). Concerning the inherent limitations of one of the best examples for natural selection, the sickle cell allele and malaria resistance, see ReMine (1993). Moreover, one may ask whether Mayr's first four instances for natural selection mentioned above ("insecticide resistance of agricultural pests, antibiotic resistance of bacteria, industrial melanism, the attenuation of the myxomatosis virus in Australia") are really cases of natural selection or more "man-made" or "man-caused" selection.

NATURAL SELECTION AND THE LIMITED GEOGRAPHICAL DISTRIBUTION OF SPECIES

The main problem regarding natural selection and limited geographical distribution of species has aptly been summarized by the evolutionary biologist Futuyma (1998, p. 535):

(R)ange limits pose an evolutionary problem that has not been solved. A species has adapted to the temperature, salt levels, or other conditions that prevail just short of the edge of its range. Why, then, can it not become adapted to the slightly more stressful conditions that prevail just beyond its present border, and extend its range slightly? And if it did so, why could it not then become adapted to still more demanding conditions, and so expand its geographic range (or its altitudinal or habit distribution) indefinitely over the course of time? These questions pose starkly the problem of what limits the extent of adaptive evolution, and we do not know the answers. We will discuss several hypotheses, citing little evidence because little exists (Hoffmann and Blows, 1994; Bradshaw, 1991).

Part of the answer is the inherent limit of variation specified by the law of recurrent variation, that is, the intrinsic restriction of the ac-

tion of chance mutations to generate functionally new genetic material, either for one new gene or many of them indispensable for the origin of irreducibly complex structures. The absence of such "positive mutations" results in limits for natural selection.

NATURAL SELECTION AND LIVING FOSSILS

Living fossils have been totally unexpected for a theory according to which everything is in a state of permanent flux and evolution (Lönnig, 1999b). In the wording of Eldredge (1989, p. 108), "Living fossils are something of an embarrassment to the expectation that evolutionary change is inevitable as time goes by." Darwin admitted, "When I see that species even in a state of nature do vary little and seeing how much they vary when domesticated, I look with astonishment at a species which has existed since one of the earlier Tertiary periods. . . . This fixity of character is marvellous" (Darwin, 1852, quoted in Ospovat, 1995, p. 201). The general explanation by neo-Darwinians is that certain species are fixed because they are adapted to nonchanging environments. This explanation is doubtful for the following reasons: (a) There are hardly any constant environments over longer geologic time periods; (b) Most living fossils are found in permanently changing environments with high competition factors (Storch & Welsch, 1989); and (c) According to the modern synthesis, even in constant environments the endless generation of new advantageous mutations plus selection pressures within the species should lead to the permanent substitution of primitive structures and species by more advanced ones. So, in spite of billions of mutations in the long history of living fossils and in defiance of natural selection during millions of years, species did not diverge (see definition of natural selection at the beginning of the article). Therefore, the rich array of living fossils constitutes another serious problem for the neo-Darwinian school.

NATURAL SELECTION AND EARTH HISTORY

One of the major setbacks for the idea of a pervasive and history-of-life-dominating process of natural selection has been the rise of what neo-Darwinians derogatorily call "neocatastrophism" (Hsü, 1986; Alvarez, 1998; Prothero, 1998). Darwin "postulated a single process, the biotic struggle of natural selection, that was uniform over all the time on the earth, proceeded always at the same rate, on a planet that ceaselessly changed in detail but never abruptly changed state" (Hsü, p. 47). Today, Darwin's view is generally rejected by all informed scientists. The current question is not whether catastrophes have repeatedly interrupted natural selection worldwide, but which kinds of catastrophes are the most important ones in earth history.

THE QUEST FOR AN ALTERNATIVE

Although in this article alternatives for the origin of species cannot be discussed at length, a few points should be mentioned. As a first step into the direction of a realistic alternative to the doubtful hypothesis of the nearly omnipotent natural selection, let us shortly turn our attention to Behe's arguments again. He writes, "Closely matched, irreducibly complex systems not only are tall problems for Darwinism but also are the hallmarks of intelligent design.

What is design? In my definition, design is simply the purposeful arrangement of parts" (1998, p. 179). However, does this inference to intelligent design not lead us directly back into the realm of metaphysics in Popper's sense? Not necessarily. A thoroughly epistemological study to clearly distinguish between the three basic parameters for any explanation in science and other areas of life in terms of either law, chance, or design (and in special cases to discover the proportions in a combination of two or even all three of them) has recently been performed and published by Dembski (1998a, 1998b). In his "explanatory filter" the object of explanation is an event called E. The first question is whether E is a highly probable event. If it is certain that E occurs under a set of standard conditions, E is probably due to deterministic or nondeterministic natural laws. If this first prerequisite is denied, it must be determined whether E is an event of intermediate probability, that is, an event which one can commonly anticipate to happen by chance in normal situations of life. If an event has the probability of 1 in 10 million, it will happen 100 times in 1 billion corresponding situations. Concerning intelligent design, Dembski further explains (1998b, pp. 101–102).

But suppose that E is neither a high probability (HP) nor an intermediate (IP) event. By a process of elimination E will therefore make it all the way to the third and final decision node. In this case E is an event of small probability, or what I am calling an SP event. Our naive intuition is that SP events are so unlikely as not to occur by chance. To take an example, consider the possibility of a thermodynamic accident whereby a loaded gun (say a perfect replica of a .357 Magnum, complete with bullets) materializes in your hand, gets aimed at your favorite enemy, fires and kills him. Strictly speaking the laws of physics do not preclude such an event from happening by chance. Nevertheless, a court will surely convict you of willful homicide. Why does a court refuse to exonerate you by attributing such an event to chance? How would a jury respond to a defense that argues the gun simply materialized?

. . . Yet we cannot deny that exceedingly improbable events (i.e., SP events) happen by chance all the time. To resolve the paradox we need to introduce an extraprobabilistic notion, a notion I referred to as specification. If a probabilistic set-up, like tossing a coin 1,000 times, entails that an SP event will occur, then necessarily some extremely improbable event will occur. If, however, independently of the event we are able to specify it, then we are justified in eliminating chance as the proper mode of explanation. It is the specified SP events (abbreviated sp/SP) that cannot properly be attributed to chance.

For the details and a mathematical treatment of these insights see Dembski, 1998a, 1998b; for further information on a testable (that is, 'non-metaphysical') theory of intelligent design, see also ReMine, 1993 and Lönnig, 1998. In contrast, the modern synthesis with its main pillars of natural selection and random mutations has scientifically failed to explain the origin and history of the living world.

REFERENCES

Alvarez, W. (1998). *T. rex and the crater, of doom.* London: Penguin Books.

Avire, J. C. as quoted by E. J. Larson and L. Witham (1999). Scientists and Religion in America. Scientific American 281, 78–83.

Behe, M. (1996). *Darwin's black box: The biochemical challenge to evolution.* New York: Free Press.

Behe, M. (1998). Intelligent design theory as a tool for analyzing biochemical systems. In W.-A. Dembski (Ed.), *Mere Creation* (pp.177–194). Downers Grove, IL: InterVarsity Press.

Bell, G. (1997). *Selection: The mechanism of evolution.* New York: Chapman & Hall, International Thompson Publishing.

Berlinski, D. (1996, September). *The deniable Darwin Commentary 101,* 19–29. (And Denying Darwin David Berlinski and Critics. Letters from readers & Berlinski's answers: Commentary 102, September 1996).

Bird, W. R. (1989). *The origin of species revisited: The theories of evolution and abrupt appearance* (Vol. 2). New York: Philosophical Library.

Catania, A. C. (1994). Natural selection. In Corsini (Ed.), *Encyclopedia of Psychology* (2nd ed.). New York: Wiley.

Chandebois, R. (1993). *Pour en finir avec le Darwinisme: Une nouvelle logique du vivant.* Montpellier, VT: Editions Espaces.

Chauvin, R. (1997). *Le Darwinisme ou la fin d'un mythe.* Monaco: Éditions du Rocher.

Coyne, J. A. (1998). Not black and white (review of the book of Majerus, M. E. N., 1998, Melanism. *Nature, 396,* 35–36).

Cziko, G. (1995). *Without miracles: Universal selection theory and the second Darwinian revolution.* Cambridge, MA: The MIT Press.

Dawkins, R. (1986). *The Selfish Gene.* Oxford, UK: Oxford University Press.

Dawkins, R. (1995). *River out of Eden.* New York: BasicBooks.

Dawkins, R. (1987/1996). *The blind watchmaker: Why the evidence of evolution reveals a universe without design.* New York: W. W. Norton & Company.

Dawkins, R. (1997). *Climbing mount improbable.* New York: W. W. Norton & Company.

Dawkins, R. (1998). *Unweaving the Rainbow.* London: Penguin Books.

Dembski, W.-A. (1998a). *The design inference: Eliminating chance through small probabilities.* Cambridge, UK: Cambridge University Press.

Dembski, W.-A. (1998b). Redesigning Science. In W.-A. Dembski (Ed.), *Mere Creation* (pp. 93–112). Downers Grove, IL: InterVarsity Press.

Dennett, D. (1995). *Darwin's dangerous idea.* New York: Simon & Schuster.

Denton, M. (1985). *Evolution: A theory in crisis.* Bethesda, MD: Adler & Adler Publishers.

Denton, M. (1998). *Nature's destiny.* New York: Free Press.

Dobzhansky, T. (1937/1951). *Genetics and the origin of species* (3rd ed.). New York: Columbia University Press.

Dobzhansky, T., Ayala, F. J., Stebbins, G. L., Valentine, J. W. (1977). *Evolution.* San Francisco: Freeman.

Eldredge, N. (1987). *Life pulse: Episodes from the story of the fossil record.* London: Penguin Books.

Fisher, R. A. (1930/1958). *The genetical theory of natural selection.* New York: Dover Publications, Inc.

Futuyma, D. J. (1998). *Evolutionary biology* (3rd ed.). Sunderland, MA: Sinauer Associates.

Gottschalk, W. (1994). *Allgemeine Genetik 4 Aufl.* Stuttgart, Germany: Georg Thieme Verlag.

Gould, S. J. (1996). The tallest tale: Is the textbook version of the giraffe evolution a bit of a stretch? *Natural History* 5/96, 18–23 and 54–57.

Gould, S. J. (1997). The exaptive excellence of spandrels as a term and prototype. *Proceedings of the National Academy of Science 94,* 10750–10755.

Gould, S. J., and Eldredge, N. (1993). Punctuated equilibrium comes of age. *Nature 366,* 223–227.

Griffths, A. J. F., Miller, J. H., Suzuki, D. T., Lewontin, R. C., & Gelbart, W. M. (1996). *An introduction to genetic analysis* (6th ed.). New York: Freeman.

Griffths, A. J. F., Gelbart, W. M., Miller, J. H., Lewontin, R. C. (1999). *Modern genetic analysis.* New York: Freeman.

Hartl, D. L., & Jones, E. W. (1998). *Genetics: Principles and analysis* (4th ed.). Sudbury, MA: Jones and Bartlett Publishers.

Ho, M. W., Saunders, P. T.: *Beyond neo-Darwinism: An introduction to the new evolutionary paradigm.* London: Academic Press.

Hsü, K. J. (1986). *The great dying: Cosmic catastrophe, dinosaurs and the theory of evolution.* San Diego, CA: Harcourt Brace Jovanovich, Publishers.

Junker, R., & Scherer, S. (1998). *Evolution.* Ein kritisches Lehrbuch Gießen: Weyel Lehrmittelverlag.

Kauffman, S. A. (1993). *The origin of order: Self-organization and selection in evolution.* New York: Oxford University Press.

Kimura, M. (1983). *The neutral theory of molecular evolution.* Cambridge, UK: Cambridge University Press.

Kunze, R., Saedler, H., Lönnig, W.-E. (1997). Plant transposable elements. *Advances in Botanical Research 27,* 331–470.

Li, W.-H. (1997). *Molecular evolution.* Sunderland, MA: Sinauer Associates, Inc.

Lima-de-Faria, A. (1988). *Evolution without selection.* Amsterdam: Elsevier.

Litynski, Z. (1961). Should we burn Darwin? *Science Digest, 51,* 61–63.

Lönnig, W.-E. (1989). *Auge-widerlegt Zufalls-evolution, Ein paar Fakten und Zitate zur widerlegung des neodarwinismus und zum Beweis der Schöpfungslehre.* Köln, Germany: Naturwissenschaftlicher Verlag.

Lönnig, W.-E. (1993). *Artbegiff, evolution und Schöpfung* (3rd ed). Köln, Germany: Naturwissenschaftlicher Verlag.

Lönnig, W.-E. (1995). Mutationen: Das Gesetz der rekurrenten variation. In J. Mey, R. Schmidt und S. Zibulla (Eds.), *Streitfall Evolution* (pp. 149–165). Universitas, Stuttgart, Germany: Wissenschaftliche Verlagsgesellschaft.

Lönnig, W.-E. (1998). *Kann der Neodarwinismus durch biologische Tatsachen widerlegt werden?* (2nd Ed.). Köln, Germany: Naturwissenschaftlicher Verlag.

Lönnig, W.-E. (1999a). *Johann Gregor Mendel: Why his discoveries were ignored for 35 (72) years.* Köln, Germany: Naturwissenschaftlicher Verlag and http://www.mpiz.mpg.de/~loennig/mendel/mendel.
htm (In German with English Summary and Note on Mendel's Integrity).

Lönnig, W.-E. (1999b). http://www.mpiz-koeln.mpg.de/~loennig/mendel/mendel20.htm.

Lönnig, W.-E., & Saedler, H. (1997). Plant transposons: Contributors to evolution? *Gene, 205,* 245–253.

MacBride, E. W. (1929). Mimicry. *Nature, 123,* 712–713.

Mahner, M., & Bunge, M. (1997). *Foundations of biophilosophy.* Berlin, Germany: Springer Verlag.

Majerus, M. E. N. (1998). *Melanism: Evolution in action.* Oxford, UK: Oxford University Press.

Maynard Smith, J. (1998). *Evolutionary genetics* (2nd ed.). Oxford, UK: Oxford University Press.

Mayr, E. (1970). *Populations, species and evolution.* Cambridge, MA: The Belknap Press of Harvard University Press.

Mayr, E. (1988). *Toward a new philosophy of biology.* Cambridge, MA: The Belknap Press of Harvard University Press.

Mayr, E. (1976/1997). *Evolution and the diversity of life.* Selected essays (4th ed.). Cambridge, MA: The Belknap Press of Harvard University Press.

Mayr, E. (1997/1998). *This is biology: The science of the living world.* (6th ed.). Cambridge, MA: The Belknap Press of Harvard University Press.

Muller, H. J. (1960). The guidance of human evolution. In *Evolution after Darwin: Vol. II. Evolution of man* (pp. 423–462). Chicago: University of Chicago Press.

Ospovat, D. (1995). *The development of Darwin's theory.* Cambridge, UK: Cambridge University Press.

Parker, S. P. (Ed.). (1997). *McGraw-Hill Dictionary of Bioscience.* New York: McGraw-Hill.

Popper, K. (1978). Natural selection and the emergence of mind. *Dialectica, 32,* 339–355.

Prothero, D. R. (1998). *Bringing fossils to life: An introduction to paleobiology.* Boston: WCB/McGraw-Hill.

ReMine, W. J. (1993). *The biotic message: Evolution versus message theory.* St. Paul, MN: St. Paul Science Publishers.

Ruse, M. (1986). Darwin as a Hollywood epic. *Quarterly Review of Biology, 61,* 509–515.

Ruse, M. (1996). *Monad to man: The concept of progress in evolutionary biology.* Cambridge, MA: Harvard University Press.

Sargent, T. D., Millar, C. D., Lambert, D. M. (1998). The "classical" explanation of industrial melanism: Assessing the evidence. *Evolutionary Biology, 30,* 299–322.

Salomon (c. 1000 B. C.). *Ecclesiastes* (quotation from chapter 9:11). King James Version.

Schlipp, P. A. (1974) (Ed.). *The philosophy of Karl Popper.* La Salle, IL: Open Court.

Schmidt, F. (1985). *Grundlagen der kybernetischen evolution.* Krefeld, Germany: Goecke & Evers.

Schützenberger (1996, January). Les failles du darwinisme. "Les théories actuelles n'expliquent pas les miracles de l'évolution." *La Recherche,* 87–92.

Stanley, S. M. (1999). *Earth system history.* New York: Freeman.

Storch, V., & Welsch, U. (1989). *Evolution: Tatsachen und Probleme der Abstammungslehre.* München, Germany: Deutscher Taschenbuch Verlag.

Stubbe, H. (1966). *Genetik und Zytologie von Antirrhinum L. Sect Antirrhinum.* Jena, Germany: Gustav Fischer Verlag.

Waddington, C. H. (1960). Evolutionary adaptations. In S. Tax (Ed.), *Evolution after Darwin* (Vol. 1, pp. 381–402). Chicago: University of Chicago Press.

SUGGESTED READING

Behe, M. (1996). *Darwin's black box: The biochemical challenge to evolution.* New York: Free Press.

Dembski, W. A. (1998a). *The design inference: Eliminating chance through small probabilities.* Cambridge, UK: Cambridge University Press.

Lönnig, W.-E. (1995). Mutationen: Das Gesetz der rekurrenten variation. In J. Mey, R. Schmidt & S. Zibulla (Eds.), *Streitfall Evolution* (pp. 149–165). Universitas Stuttgart, Germany: Wissenschaftliche Verlagsgesellschaft.

Lönnig, W.-E. (1998). *Kann der Neodarwinismus durch biologische Tatsachen widerlegt werden?* (2nd ed.). Köln, Germany: Naturwissenschaftlicher Verlag.

ReMine, W. J. (1993). *The biotic messages: Evolution versus message theory.* St. Paul, MN: St. Paul Science.

W.-E. Lönnig
Max-Planck-Institut für Züchtungsforschung

EVOLUTION
HUMAN DEVELOPMENT
SOCIOBIOLOGY

NATURALISTIC OBSERVATION

Naturalistic observation refers to the unobtrusive and nonreactive study of organisms in their native habitats or environment, devoid of manipulation or control by the researcher. Naturalistic observation methods are intended to avoid manipulation of antecedent conditions or imposition of constraints on outputs, such as occurs in the case of experiments. The naturalness of the environment of the study is to be interpreted as a continuum rather than as a dichotomy (Dane, 1994), as all observation implies participation in the environment being studied. Fieldwork and qualitative research are examples of techniques sometimes identified incorrectly or used interchangeably with naturalistic observation. Naturalistic observation methods are a subcategory of a broader group of research methods and perspectives, referred to in the literature variously as field work, qualitative research, naturalistic research, naturalistic perspectives, naturalistic paradigms, and naturalistic inquiry.

The scope of studies using naturalistic observation methods extends from a single entity or a small unit to entire cultures. Dian Fossey's study of the mountain gorillas in their natural habitat in Kabara located within the Parc des Virungas of Zaire (1983), Jane Goodall's study of chimpanzees in their natural habitats of the forests of Gombe (1986), and Schaller's study of the gorillas in Zaire, the pandas in China, and wildlife in the Tibetan steppe (1963, 1993, 1998) are examples of recent naturalistic observation studies. Each of these examples is drawn from ethological studies. In addition to their use in animal ethology, which can be described as a new branch of biology and psychology, naturalistic observation techniques have been widely used in psychology and anthropology to study both human beings and animals, and have been adopted in education and sociology (e.g., to study school children, small groups, communities, or subcultures). The range, variety, and heterogeneity of naturalistic observation studies in different disciplines in the context of distinct social, cultural, and physical settings is reflected in the diversity of topics studied and the richness of the findings. Because naturalistic observation studies cover both animals and human beings, there are many similarities and differences in the two methods and approaches. A large number of topics are studied in the human and animal communities using naturalistic observation techniques, including instinctive behavior, imprinting, parental behavior, play, stimuli, communication and signals, feeding, hunting, predators and prey, learning, memory, adaptation, social groups and relationships, organizations, attraction, courtship and mating, reproductive processes, cooperation, competition, dominance, learning, migration, emigration, environment, depression, mental illness, children at play, and ecology.

The development of naturalistic observation may be roughly divided into three periods: (a) prior to 1900; (b) 1920 to 1950; and (c) after the 1950s. The first period dates back to antiquity. Though systematic use of naturalistic observation is rather recent, it is one of the oldest methodologies in science; its origins can be traced back to prehistoric times and are rooted in oral traditions and observable in cave paintings. Sumerian clay tablets that date back more than 5,000 years bear pictures of birds and fish. Recorded observations such as those by Herodotus comparing people from Greece with people from other countries go back to the fifth century BC (Wax, 1971). Similarly, during the fourth century BC, Aristotle classified and described characteristics of many animals based on his own observations and descriptions of travelers. Many explorers, travelers, journalists, and literary figures have also contributed observational accounts of societies. During the 19th century, naturalists carried out more systematic fieldwork and produced faithful accounts of animal life. The work of Darwin belongs to this period, and evolutionary perspectives continue to be one of the major facets of naturalistic observation of behavior.

The period between 1920 and 1950 includes what has been described as the classical period of ethology (Crist, 1999). This period witnessed comprehensive changes in naturalistic observation research that continue to evolve. Theoretical perspectives were introduced during the latter part of this period in order to understand and explain animal behavior.

The last period extends from the 1950s to the present. Ecological perspectives and human ethology were introduced after the 1950s (Willems & Raush, 1969); in addition, sociobiological perspectives, evolutionary psychological approaches, and the area of cognitive ethology have been recently introduced into the study of animal behavior. Behavior therapists have used direct observation in collecting specific behavioral data in natural settings (Hutt & Hutt, 1970; Johnson & Bolstad, 1973; Mash & Terdal, 1976). Clinicians extended the scope of their observations from individuals to the study of organizations. Naturalistic observation methods have been gradually adopted in the fields of educational psychology and educational program evaluation (Brandt, 1972; Hammersley, 1992).

The original techniques developed in naturalistic observation have sometimes been modified or extended in order to facilitate the study of human behavior. For example, the book *Unobtrusive Measures* (Webb, Campbell, Schwartz, & Sechrest, 1966) can be viewed as an interesting (though limited) extension of naturalistic observation techniques for application in psychology and the social sciences. The works of Lorenz, Tinbergen, and von Frisch were awarded the Nobel prize in 1973, and the prize provided a prestigious acknowledgement of the contributions of ethology (Tinbergen, 1985). In addition, ideas from other disciplines dealing with human behavior, such as game theory and optimality theory from economics and handicap principles from sports, have been borrowed to study animal behavior. For example, animal behavior in the context of competing demands for food and safety have been analyzed with the use of optimality theory, and game theory has been used to explain competitive behavior.

Technology has significantly impacted the methodology in recent years. The availability of versatile audio equipment, two- and three-dimensional video equipment, and digital equipment for recording observations, as well as computer equipment for analysis, has extended the range and scope of observation and has made the dissemination of the findings to larger audiences possible. Such records can be submitted to other researchers as well for their interpretations. These technological tools have radically altered the roles of researchers. Thus, observers are no longer the sole instruments of observation, nor are they necessarily the sole authors of data interpretations.

CONDUCTING NATURALISTIC OBSERVATION STUDIES

Though the naturalistic paradigm may be shared by different disciplines, the observation techniques vary significantly in different fields such as biology, psychology, anthropology, education, and sociology (Arrington, 1943; Denzin & Lincoln, 1994; Dewsbury, 1985; Lincoln & Guba, 1985; Malinowski, 1953; Pelto & Pelto, 1978; Taylor & Bogdan, 1984; Weick, 1985). There have been two

distinctive trends and developments related to studies using naturalistic observation methods and techniques.

The first group of researchers, consisting of ethologists, animal psychologists, and physical anthropologists working with animals, have commonly addressed four basic questions in their studies. The questions usually refer to the function, evolution and adaptation, causation, and development of behavior. Behavior is classified into different functional categories, such as cooperation among members of the group and the intended or unintended purpose of that behavior. The purpose is not necessarily a conscious act on the part of the animal. Evolution and adaptation raise the further question as to what extent the behavior is adaptive given the environmental factors and to what extent it contributes to the evolutionary process of the species. Causation would include establishing ecological, physiological, chemical, biological, instinctual, and systemic reasons for the different types of behavior of the organisms. Different types of behavior such as running are observed in detail whether it is a gallop or running interspersed with jumping. An ethogram of the behavior may be used or the behavior may be documented through videos in order to analyze the extensive repertoire of behavior. The study of stages of development of the individual organisms is yet another type of data collected by the researchers. Comparative studies are often preferred, since they address the four questions listed earlier.

In the conduct of studies of human societies from cultural anthropological and sociological perspectives, efforts to minimize the impact of observation on cultures, including access, entry, and role negotiation, often become necessary initial steps (unless one is already a member of the group to be studied). Interestingly enough, the same procedures must be followed by ethologists when they plan to study animal behavior within different national locations. The next phase consists of observation, recording, coding, interpreting, analyzing, and reporting, all of which are affected by the researcher's goals, techniques, and theoretical stance (Liebow, 1967).

The complexity of human beings and their social structures makes it necessary to use additional techniques to understand their behaviors. Thus, the use of naturalistic observational methods in social and behavioral sciences is usually supplemented by a large number of other tools such as laboratory studies. In the study of human beings, naturalistic observation is further supplemented by interviews, projective techniques, multi-site studies, use of informants, and content analysis. Clinical psychologists favor using a multidimensional approach such as rating scales and interviews in addition to observation of human behavior. In the case of animals, laboratory studies can be used to study other facets, such as physiology, neural control of behavior, and genetic composition of animals that are not affected by the captivity or the artificiality of the laboratory situation.

METHODOLOGICAL CONTROVERSY

At varying periods of time, naturalistic observation methods have been subjected to controversy and criticism about their importance, methodology, utility, and interpretation of behavior in the study of animals and human beings. The controversy was more extensive, prolonged, and divisive in the fields of education, sociology, and cultural anthropological sciences in the context of the study of human groups, societies, and cultures. Naturalistic methods in education and the social sciences adhere to a combination of diverse philosophical and research perspectives (e.g., phenomenology, feminist perspectives, postmodernism, and humanism) that explain and justify knowledge as a subjective process and interpret it in a contingent relationship to the environment, as opposed to the logical positivistic views about the duality of the observer and the observed and the assumption of a single reality as a given. In addition, the researcher, for example, is an intrusive factor, likely to affect the observed and their behavior. While ethologists and other naturalistic observers acknowledge that the problem of human intrusion is likely to initially affect the behavior of the animals being observed, they prefer to observe the animals openly if possible, as they expect the animals, children, and so forth that are being observed to become habituated.

Interpretation of another culture or of the behavior of animals by researchers who have their own personal and cultural lenses is another type of concern. The work of Darwin, for example, has been analyzed for its anthropomorphism by a social scientist (Crist, 1999). Should divergent interpretations be interpreted as lack of reliability and validity, or should they be regarded as contributions to a more complete understanding of the phenomena under study? Often, a time sample of the behavior of a group is taken for observational purposes, since it is not possible to observe the totality of their behavior. The questions raised by Arrington more than 50 years ago about the representativeness of the samples and the assessment of reliability are relevant even today.

Naturalistic observers in education and the social sciences accept such discrepancies because psychological interactions and social events are subject to varied interpretations. It is now generally recognized that social and behavioral sciences are not always devoid of researcher selectivity and bias (Haraway, 1989). For example, differential research emphases in the studies of monkeys of Arashiyama reflect the distinctive values and beliefs held by Japanese and Western researchers (Asquith, 1991). Naturalistic observation studies have been criticized for their lack of replicability and validity as well as their limited generalizability to other animal or human groups or cultures, which limits their use. A response to this criticism has been that a naturalistic observer is in search of understanding, rather than of universal laws. Naturalistic observation has made use of both deductive and inductive research procedures tested in the context of the animal group being studied. Naturalistic observation as an inductive method is engaged in generalizations based on a study of individual units or single groups. Comparative studies allow for inductive generalization and new interpretations of animal behavior, more adequate specification of existing theories, or development of new models and theories (e.g., imprinting). Similarly, hypothesis and theory testing have been routinely used in studies employing naturalistic observation methods.

TRENDS

It is clear that naturalistic observation methods have gained legitimacy among academicians and the academic disciplines. The search for naturalistic conditions or environments even in the context of experimental designs indicates an awareness of the special significance of natural environments in research studies of animals and human beings (Gibbons et al., 1994). The products and results of such studies have gained wide acceptance and following from outside academia as well, due to popularization and exposure by television programs and the popularity of books, written by ethologists, that are based on naturalistic observation. Names of researchers such as Goodall and Fossey are now widely known outside their own fields. The recent discoveries and recognition of the closeness of and similarities between the animal kingdom and human beings have provided an economic rationale for such studies. With the introduction of important newer topics such as ecology, and the controversial topic of cognitive ethology, the techniques of naturalistic observation are likely to be used more widely from biology to psychology.

REFERENCES

Arrington, R. E. (1943). Time sampling in studies of social behavior: A critical review of techniques and results with research suggestions. *Psychological Bulletin, 40*(2), 81–124.

Asquith, P. (1991). Primate research groups in Japan: Orientation and East-West differences. In L. M. Fedigan & P. J. Asquith (Eds.), *The monkeys of Arashiyama.* Albany, NY: State University of New York Press.

Brandt, R. M. (1972). *Studying behavior in natural settings.* New York: Holt, Rinehart & Winston.

Crist, E. (1999). *Images of animals, anthropomorphism and the animal mind.* Philadelphia: Temple University Press.

Dane, F. C. (1994). Survey methods, naturalistic observations and case studies. In A. M. Coleman (Ed.), *Companion encyclopedia of sociology.* London: Routledge.

Denzin, N. K., & Lincoln, Y. S. (1994). *Handbook of qualitative research.* Thousand Oaks, CA: Sage.

Dewsbury, D. A. (Ed). (1985). *Studying animal behavior: Autobiographies of the founders.* Chicago: University of Chicago Press.

Fossey, D. (1983). *Gorillas in the mist.* Boston: Houghton Mifflin.

Gibbons, E. F., Jr., Wyers, E. J., Waters, E., & Menzel, E. W. (Eds.). (1994). *Naturalistic environments in captivity for animal behavior research.* Albany: State University of New York Press.

Goodall, J. (1986). *The chimpanzees of Gombe: Patterns of behavior.* Cambridge, MA: Belknap.

Hammersley, M. (1992). *What's wrong with ethnography?* New York: Routledge.

Haraway, D. (1989). *Primate visions: Gender, race, and nature in the world of modern science.* New York: Routledge.

Hutt, S. J., & Hutt, C. (1970). *Direct observation and measurement of behavior.* Springfield, IL: Charles C. Thomas.

Johnson, S. M., & Bolstad, O. D. (1973). Methodological issues in naturalistic observations: Some problems and solutions for field research. In L. A. Hamerlynck, L. C. Handy, & E. J. Mash (Eds.), *Behavior change: Methodology, concepts, and practice.* Champaign, IL: Research Press.

Liebow, E. (1967). *Tally's corner: A study of negro street corner men.* Boston: Little, Brown.

Lincoln, Y., & Guba, E. (1985). *Naturalistic inquiry.* Beverly Hills, CA: Sage.

Malinowski, B. (1953). *Argonauts of the western Pacific: An account of native enterprise and adventure in the archipelagoes of Melanesian New Guinea.* New York: Dutton.

Mash, E. J., & Terdal, L. G. (Eds). (1976). *Behavior-therapy assessment: Diagnosis, design, and evaluation.* New York: Springer.

Pelto, P. J., & Pelto, G. H. (1978). *Anthropological research: The structure of inquiry.* (2nd ed.). Cambridge: Cambridge University Press.

Schaller, G. B. (1963). *The mountain gorilla: Ecology and behavior.* Chicago: University of Chicago Press.

Schaller, G. B. (1993). *The last panda.* Chicago: University of Chicago Press.

Schaller, G. B. (1998). *The wildlife of the Tibetan steppe.* Chicago: University of Chicago Press.

Taylor, S. J., & Bogdan, R. (1984). *Introduction to qualitative research methods: The search for meanings.* New York: Wiley.

Tinbergen, N. (1985). Watching and wondering. In D. A. Dewsbury (Ed.), *Studying animal behavior: Autobiographies of the founders* (p. 45). Chicago: University of Chicago Press.

Wax, R. H. (1971). *Doing fieldwork: Warnings and advice.* Chicago: University of Chicago Press.

Webb, E. J., Campbell, D. T., Schwartz, R. D., & Sechrest, L. (1966). *Unobtrusive measures: Nonreactive research in the social sciences.* Chicago: Rand McNally.

Weick, K. E. (1985). Systematic observational methods. In E. Aronson & G. Lindzay (Eds.), *Handbook of social psychology* (3rd ed., pp. 567–634). New York: Random House.

Willems, E. P., & Raush, H. L. (Eds.). (1969). *Naturalistic viewpoints in psychological research.* New York: Holt, Rinehart & Winston.

S. R. SONNAD
Western Michigan University

APPLIED RESEARCH
CROSS-CULTURAL PSYCHOLOGY
ENVIRONMENTAL PSYCHOLOGY
RESEARCH METHODOLOGY
SAMPLING
SOCIAL CLIMATE RESEARCH

NATURE–NURTURE CONTROVERSY

The so-called "nature–nurture controversy" is really a family of controversies about the relative roles of heredity (nature) and environment (nurture) in shaping human characteristics. These controversies exist not so much because the scientific questions involved are difficult—although many are—but because the proposed alternative solutions are perceived as having profound implications for cherished beliefs (often with religious or political overtones) concerning such matters as human equality, social justice, and individual responsibility.

The several controversies subsumed under the general heading of the nature–nurture controversy may be differentiated in various ways. One is by the aspect of behavior involved. Some controversies, such as that over instinct, have largely focused on drives or motives, while others such as the IQ controversy have dealt mainly with abilities. Another way of distinguishing among nature–nurture controversies is by whether the emphasis is on individual, group, or species characteristics. One can ask whether the variation among human individuals of the same race and sex on some trait is mainly due to heredity or environment. One can ask whether differences among races or between sexes are due to different experiences or different genes. Or one can argue about the origins of differences between humans and other species. These are separable questions. The history of the nature–nurture controversy has involved irregular shifts in emphasis among these from time to time, often without a very clear sense of the distinctions.

While precursors of the nature–nurture controversy may be found in the writings of the ancient Greeks, its modern form can be traced back fairly directly to Locke (1632–1704) on one hand and Darwin (1809–1882) on the other. Galton (1822–1911) was instrumental in focusing the conflict on specifically psychological issues. It was he who popularized the catchwords *nature* and *nurture* to epitomize the controversy, as in his *English Men of Science: Their Nature and Nurture* (1874). He probably took the words from Shakespeare's *The Tempest* (Act IV, Scene I) in which Prospero calls Caliban "A devil, a born devil on whose nature nurture can never stick." Key figures at the peak of the controversy within psychology in the early part of the twentieth century were the psychologists McDougall (1871–1938), Yerkes (1876–1956), Terman (1877–1957), and Watson (1878–1958). Recent flareups of the controversy have been in response to works by the psychologists Jensen (b. 1923), Herrnstein (1930–1994), and Rushton (b. 1943), and the zoologist E. O. Wilson (b. 1929).

Locke, seventeenth-century English philosopher and political theorist, may be considered the chief ideological father of the nurture side of the controversy. In *An Essay Concerning Human Understanding* (1690), Locke invoked the metaphor of the mind as a blank sheet of paper on which all of knowledge is written by the hand of experience. His political view that all men are by nature equal and independent and that society is a mutual contract entered into for the common good had an immense influence via Jefferson, Voltaire, Rousseau, and the other theorists of the American and French revolutions. Indeed, one simple way to view the successive episodes of the nature–nurture controversy is as a series of perceived challenges to the prevailing Lockean position, with those steeped in this tradition rising indignantly to battle what they saw as threats to inalienable human rights to life, liberty, and the pursuit of happiness.

In Locke's own view, human political equality was not inconsistent with an inborn diversity of human tendencies and capabilities. In *Some Thoughts Concerning Education* (§101) he wrote

"Some men by the unalterable frame of their constitutions are stout, others timorous, some confident, others modest, tractable, or obstinate, curious, or careless, quick or slow. There are not more differences in men's faces, and the outward lineaments of their bodies, than there are in the makes and tempers of their minds." Nevertheless, despite acknowledging the presence of innate constitutional tendencies, Locke judged the bulk of human variation to be the result of differences in experience (§1): "I think I may say, that of all the men we meet with, nine parts of ten are what they are, good or evil, useful or not, by their education."

Locke's successors in the English liberal intellectual tradition have tended to emphasize the latter view. Thus J. S. Mill (1806–1873) wrote in his *Autobiography:*

I have long felt that the prevailing tendency to regard all the marked distinctions of human character as innate, and in the main indelible, and to ignore the irresistible proofs that by far the greater part of these differences, whether between individuals, races, or sexes, are such as not only might but naturally would be produced by differences in circumstances, is one of the chief hindrances to the rational treatment of great social questions. and one of the great stumbling blocks to human improvement (p. 192).

Darwin, a contemporary of Mill's, gave the nature side of the controversy its modern form by placing the human mind solidly in the framework of biological evolution. In such works as *The Descent of Man* (1871) and *The Expression of the Emotions in Man and Animals* (1872), Darwin made it clear that human behavior shared common ancestry with the behavior of other animal forms and that behavioral as well as physical characters were subject to the basic evolutionary mechanism of hereditary variation followed by natural selection of the variants most successful in their environments.

Darwin's own writings stayed pretty close to biology, but others were quick to derive social and political implications from Darwin's theory of evolution. The English philosopher Herbert Spencer (1820–1903) found it easy to assimilate Darwin's views into his own developing theory of social evolution and may be considered the first of the so-called Social Darwinists, who argued that the successful and unsuccessful in society represented the fit and the unfit in a Darwinian framework.

Galton, a younger cousin of Darwin's, enthusiastically extended the latter's ideas of genetic variation and natural selection to the interpretation of human variability. Galton may be considered the founder of differential psychology. In his book *Hereditary Genius* (1869), Galton explored the tendency of eminence to run in families among such disparate groups as English judges, military commanders, poets, divines, oarsmen, and North Country wrestlers. Obviously, such familial resemblances are potentially explainable by either heredity or environment, but Galton believed them to be largely hereditary. He also discussed racial differences, concluding in a chapter called "The Comparative Worth of Different Races" that contemporary Englishmen averaged about two grades higher than African blacks on a scale that placed the Englishmen about two grades below the Athenians of ancient Greece. Galton believed these racial differences also to be largely hereditary. Galton saw clearly the social implications of his theories and founded the eugenics movement, which aimed to improve human-

ity by encouraging the more able to have larger families and the less able to have smaller ones.

Galton's emphasis on individual and racial differences burgeoned in the United States in the mental testing movement. The psychologists Terman and Yerkes were important figures whose own beliefs, on the whole, lay toward the nature side of the controversy. Yerkes organized the large-scale intelligence testing for military selection purposes in World War I. Blacks and immigrants from Southern Europe tended to do poorly on these tests, facts that C. C. Brigham made the basis of a hereditarian and controversial book, *A Study of American Intelligence.* Critics were quick to point out that these same data could readily be given cultural interpretations. Terman worked with Yerkes on the Army testing, having just finished revising and standardizing the intelligence scale of Binet and Simon as the Stanford-Binet IQ test. Later he organized a massive study of genius. Genius was identified by a high IQ, which Terman assumed to be a fairly direct measure of inborn intelligence. All this was in the best Galtonian tradition.

Another aspect of the Darwinian continuity of humans with lower animals was emphasized by the psychologist McDougall and others in the early part of the twentieth century. McDougall developed a social psychology around the doctrine of instincts, the idea that "the human mind has certain innate or inherited tendencies which are the essential springs or motive powers of all thought and action"(*An Introduction to Social Psychology,* p. 20). Examples of such inherited tendencies cited by McDougall were the instincts of gregariousness, self-assertion, curiosity, flight, repulsion, pugnacity, acquisition, construction, parental care, and reproduction.

McDougall's instinct doctrine, with its emphasis on the importance of inherited tendencies in shaping human social life, aroused vigorous opposition among psychologists, sociologists, anthropologists, and others in the Lockean tradition. Both McDougall's instinct doctrine and the Galtonian notion of inherited individual differences in capacities were vigorously rejected in the radical behaviorism of the psychologist J. B. Watson, who in 1925 issued his famous challenge:

Give me a dozen healthy infants, well-formed, and my own specified world to bring them up in and I'll guarantee to take any one at random and train him to become any type of specialist I might select—doctor, lawyer, artist, merchant-chief, and, yes, even beggar-man and thief, regardless of his talents, penchants, tendencies, abilities, vocations, and race of his ancestors. (*Behaviorism,* p. 82)

Significant events in the nature–nurture controversy in the United States were the publication in 1928 and 1940 of the *Twenty-Seventh Yearbook* and *Thirty-Ninth Yearbook* of the National Society for the Study of Education. These lengthy two-part volumes were respectively titled *Nature and Nurture* and *Intelligence: Its Nature and Nurture.* Although both still contained plenty of controversy, on the whole they signaled a shift from rhetoric to research. The first yearbook contained, among other things, the primary reports of two major IQ studies based on adoptions; a study by Burks emphasizing the effects of nature; and one by Freeman, Holzinger, and Mitchell stressing the role of nurture. The second contained reports from a half-dozen major ongoing studies of longitudinal development, family resemblance, and the effects of stimulating environments on IQ.

The next few decades were marked by a gradually decreasing salience of the nature–nurture controversy in psychology, although it never dropped entirely out of view. Concurrently, there was an increasing accumulation of relevant empirical studies with identical and fraternal twins, adoptive families, orphans, and so on, in both the United States and Europe. These studies, based on research designs that to some extent were able to separate genetic from environmental factors, were mainly focused on individual variation in ability, particularly the ubiquitous IQ, but they dealt to some extent with personality traits as well. An active research literature also developed on psychopathological conditions, such as neurosis, psychosis, criminality, and mental deficiency. A few instances were found of conditions following simple Mendelian lines of inheritance, hence clearly genetic in origin, or of conditions with simple, clear-cut environmental induction, such as mental defect from lead poisoning. All such cases are in some broad sense both genetic and environmental, because all behaviors involve both organism and environment, but the fact that one particular individual has the condition whereas another does not can be chiefly attributed to genetic or environmental factors affecting the one but not the other.

Most cases are not so clear-cut. Hebb (1966) suggested that asking about the relative contributions of heredity and environment to human intelligence is like asking about the relative contributions of width and length to the area of a field. Inasmuch as neither can contribute anything by itself, such a question, for one person or for one field, is meaningless. However, the situation changes when discussing a population. It is perfectly sensible to ask to what extent the areas of a particular group of fields depend on differences in their widths or on differences in their lengths. If the fields are all of nearly the same length, for example, most of the differences in area will be due to their variation in width. Likewise, it is quite feasible to estimate the relative contributions of the genes and the environment to the variation of a behavioral trait in a human population, via studies using identical and fraternal twins, adoptive families, and other informative groups. Many such empirical estimates have been made by behavior geneticists. Because such estimates have often been made using fairly small samples, and because methods of measuring psychological traits sometimes leave a good deal to be desired, the estimates can vary from study to study even in similar populations, leaving scope for persistence of the nature–nurture controversy in a quantitative sense.

One answer seemed obvious: better measures and larger samples to narrow the gap of uncertainty. Another was to get on with the question *how*—to investigate the specific mechanisms by which genes and environments have their effects (Anastasi, 1958). A broad and eloquent review of the nature–nurture question was made in Dobzhansky's 1959 Silliman Lectures at Yale, published in 1962 as *Mankind Evolving.* Dobzhansky elegantly integrated Darwinian concepts with an appreciation of the role of culture in human evolution and Lockean democratic ideals. By 1960, with the publication of the textbook *Behavior Genetics* by Fuller, a biologist, and Thompson, a psychologist, it appeared that the controversy might at last be becoming ordinary science.

The calm was illusory. In 1969, just a century after Galton's *Hereditary Genius,* the educational psychologist A. R. Jensen published a long article in the *Harvard Educational Review* titled "How Much can We Boost IQ and Scholastic Achievement?" Jensen surveyed various lines of evidence, and took a fairly strong hereditarian position, estimating about 80% of individual variation in IQ to be genetic. Moreover, he conjectured that at least part of the persistent disadvantage of U.S. blacks in IQ test performance was also genetic in origin. A furor arose in academic circles and the popular press—a furor exacerbated in 1971 by the publication of an article titled "IQ" in the *Atlantic Monthly* by psychologist R. J. Herrnstein. This article emphasized genetic differences arising among social classes in a mobile society, a theme introduced earlier by the British psychologist Cyril Burt.

A strong counterattack was launched against these new perceived threats to Lockean ideals, with perhaps the most extreme environmentalist position being taken by Leon Kamin in the book *The Science and Politics of IQ* (1974), which featured an attack on Burt but spread to a broad assault on human behavior genetics and its political uses. A more moderate critique was that of Jencks and his colleagues in *Inequality* (1972). Then in 1975, warfare opened up on a new front, with the publication by zoologist E. O. Wilson of *Sociobiology,* which outlined a modern population-genetic basis for the notion that biological instincts might play a central role in human affairs.

More attacks and counterattacks followed. The earlier participants brought out further works: Jensen's *Educability and Group Differences* (1973), *Bias in Mental Testing* (1980), and *The g Factor* (1998); Herrnstein's *IQ in the Meritocracy* (1973) and, with Charles Murray, *The Bell Curve* (1994). The last surprisingly became a bestseller, and provoked a spate of counterattacks, one of the more reasonable of which was Fischer and colleagues, *Inequality by Design* (1996).

Meanwhile, S. J. Gould blasted away at hereditarians and IQ testing in *The Mismeasure of Man* (1981), and in Britain, Eysenck represented the nature side with *The Inequality of Man* (1973), arguing directly with Kamin in *The Intelligence Controversy* (1981). Not all of the action was genteel academic debate—tires were slashed and speakers assaulted. Pearson (1991) gives an account of some of the goings-on. Many of Kamin's suspicions about the trustworthiness of Burt's data appeared to be substantiated in Hearnshaw's biography *Cyril Burt, Psychologist* (1979), but an interpretation more favorable to Burt was presented in Joynson's *The Burt Affair* (1989).

The topic of race differences in IQ provoked a small bookshelf, including Flynn's *Race, IQ, and Jensen* (1980), Ehrlich and Feldman's *The Race Bomb* (1977), Loehlin, Lindzey, and Spuhler's *Race Differences in Intelligence* (1975), and Jencks and Phillips' *The Black-White Test Score Gap* (1998). A new round of controversy on racial differences was generated by Rushton's *Race, Evolution, and Behavior* (1995), which suggested that for evolutionary reasons Negroid and Mongoloid races differ on a variety of dimensions of ability, character, physique, and personality, with Caucasoids intermediate.

Rowe's book *The Limits of Family Influence* (1994) questioned the potency of the family in shaping the characteristics of children, and Lynn's *Dysgenics* (1996) reasserted Galtonian eugenic views. A popular recent theme on the nurture side of the controversy is the so called "Flynn effect," an apparent general rise in IQ test scores during the present century, presumably nongenetic in origin (Neisser, 1998). Works in sociobiology, pro and con, have been multiplying rapidly. Well over 150 books on the topic appeared between 1975 and 1999, including further entries by Wilson himself: *On Human Nature* (1978) and, with Lumsden, *Genes, Mind and Culture* (1981). Thus, at the end of the twentieth century, with cloning and the sequencing of the human genome in the air, it appears that the modern eruptions of the nature–nurture controversy have by no means run their course.

It would not do to conclude, however, from the fact that the controversy is still active, that no progress has been made since the days of Darwin and Spencer and Mill. Modern views of biological evolution, while deriving from Darwin, are more complex, differentiated, and mathematical than his, and incorporate a much more adequate genetics. Modern psychology takes—in its better moments—a vastly more sophisticated view of the organism-environment interplay than did the instinct lists of McDougall or the behavioristic battle cries of Watson. Finally, nature–nurture controversialists must accommodate their prejudices to a much larger body of established fact nowadays. Even though nature–nurture controversies continue, they themselves also evolve.

REFERENCES

Buss, D. M. (1999). *Evolutionary psychology: The new science of the mind.* Needham Heights, MA: Allyn & Bacon.

Fischer, C. S., Hout, M., Jankowski, M. S., Lucas, S. R., Swidler, A., & Voss, K. (1996). *Inequality by design: Cracking the Bell Curve myth.* Princeton, NJ: Princeton University Press.

Herrnstein, R. J., & Murray, C. (1994). *The bell curve: Intelligence and class structure in American life.* New York: Free Press.

Hunt, M. (1999). *The new know-nothings: The political foes of the scientific study of human behavior.* New Brunswick, NJ: Transaction Publishers.

Jencks, C., & Phillips, M. (Eds.). (1998). *The black-white test score gap.* Washington, DC: Brookings.

Jensen, A. R. (1998). *The g factor: The science of mental ability.* Westport, CT: Praeger.

Loehlin, J. C. (1992). *Genes and environment in personality development.* Newbury Park, CA: Sage.

Lynn, R. (1996). *Dysgenics: Genetic deterioration in modern populations.* Wesport, CT: Praeger.

Neisser, U. (Ed.). (1998). *The rising curve: Long-term gains in IQ and related measures.* Washington, DC: American Psychological Association.

Plomin, R., DeFries, J. C., McClearn, G. E., & Rutter, M. (1997). *Behavioral genetics* (3rd ed.). New York: Freeman.

Rowe, D. C. (1994). *The limits of family influence: Genes, experience, and behavior.* New York: Guilford.

Rushton, J. P. (1995). *Race, evolution, and behavior: A life history perspective.* New Brunswick, NJ: Transaction Publishers.

SUGGESTED READING

Brody, N. *Intelligence.*

Buss, D. M. *Evolutionary psychology: The new science of the mind.*

Cravens, H. *The triumph of evolution: American scientists and the heredity-environment controversy 1900–1941.*

Cronbach, L. J. *Five decades of public controversy over mental testing.*

Degler, C. N. *In search of human nature: The decline and revival of Darwinism in American social thought.*

Willerman, L. *The psychology of individual and group differences.*

J. C. LOEHLIN
University of Texas at Austin

CULTURAL BIASES IN TESTING

HUMAN INTELLIGENCE

NEMEROFF, CHARLES B. (1949–   )

Charles B. Nemeroff was born in New York City in 1949 and educated in the New York City public school system. After graduating from the City College of New York in 1970, an interest in neuroscience led him to a research assistant position at McLean Hospital in Belmont, Massachusetts. He simultaneously enrolled in graduate school at Northeastern University and received an MS in biology in 1973. He then relocated to North Carolina and enrolled in the PhD program in neurobiology at the University of North Carolina, and, after a year of postdoctoral training in neurochemistry, enrolled in the medical school there. After his residency training in psychiatry (conducted at both the University of North Carolina and Duke University), he joined the faculty of Duke University Medical Center, where he was professor of psychiatry and pharmacology and chief of the Division of Biological Psychiatry. In 1991 he relocated to Emory University School of Medicine in Atlanta, Georgia, where he currently is the Reunette W. Harris Professor and chairman of the Department of Psychiatry and Behavioral Sciences. His research has concentrated on the biological bases of the major neuropsychiatric disorders, including affective disorders, Alzheimer's disease, schizophrenia, and anxiety disorders.

Nemeroff has received numerous honors during his career, including the A. E. Bennett Award from the Society of Biological Psychiatry (1979), the Curt P. Richter Award from the International Society of Psychoneuroendocrinology (1985), the Judith Silver Memorial Young Scientist Award from the National Alliance for the Mentally Ill (1989), the Kempf Award in Psychobiology (1989), the Samuel Hibbs Award (1990), the Gold Medal Award from the Society of Biological Psychiatry, and the Research Prize (1996) from the American Psychiatric Association. In 1993 he was given the Edward J. Sachar Award from Columbia University College of Physicians and Surgeons and the Edward A. Strecker Award from The Institute of Pennsylvania Hospital. In 1997, he was the recipient of the Gerald Klerman Award from the National Depressive and Manic-Depressive Disorders Association and the Selo Prize from the National Alliance for Research in Schizophrenia and Depression. In 1998, he was the recipient of the Research Award in Mood Disorders from the American College of Psychiatrists, and in 1999 he received the Bowis Award from the same organization.

The American College of Physicians named the Willam C. Menninger Awardee in 2000 for excellence of research in psychiatry. Nemeroff serves on the editorial boards of numerous journals, including the *Biological Psychiatry,* and is co-editor-in-chief of both *Critical Reviews in Neurobiology* and *Depression and Anxiety.* With Alan F. Schatzberg he is co-editor of the *Textbook of Psychopharmacology* published by the APA Press. He is a past president of the American College of Neuropsychopharmacology and president-elect of The American College of Psychiatrists. He serves on the Mental Health Advisory Council overseeing the activities of the Natural Institute of Mental Health as well as the Biomedical Research Council of NASA. He is currently the recipient of several research grants from the National Institutes of Health and has published more than 600 research reports and reviews. He is a member of the Board of Directors on Scientific Advisory Board of three patient advocacy groups: The National Depressive and Manic-Depressive Disorders Association (NDMDA), The American Foundation for Suicide Prevention (AFSP) and The Anxiety Disorders Association of America (ADAA).

STAFF

NEOBEHAVIORISM

Beginning in the 1930s, the psychologists who built on J. B. Watson's views, as well as those of A. P. Weiss, revised their behavioristic position to make it more sophisticated and elaborate; the prominent neobehaviorists were E. C. Tolman, C. L. Hull, E. R. Guthrie, B. F. Skinner, and K. W. Spence. Skinner, who eventually became the most prominent, was the last one to die. Their followers or students, to name only a few, were B. F. Ritchie and H. E. Gleitman (Tolman), N. E. Miller and O. H. Mowrer (Hull), F. D. Sheffield and N. E. Miller (Guthrie), M. Sidman and A. S. Catania (Skinner), and F. A. Logan and A. Amsel (Spence); they also made substantial contributions to neobehaviorism. J. R. Kantor, with his theory of interbehaviorism in which the response determines the stimulus as well as the other way around, should also be mentioned. Although Kantor's following has been small, it is still quite viable.

Neobehaviorism is often seen as allied with the philosophy of science school of logical positivism, or operationism, and this is especially true of Spence's writings with Bergmann (1941) who was his colleague at Iowa. That psychology as a natural science had to be empirical and objective was the main philosophical point for all neobehaviorists, but beyond that few were completely in sympathy with the logical positivism of Rudolf Carnap, H. Feigl, and C. G.

Hempel. However, Sigmund Koch, a severe early critic of neobehaviorism, considered them closely related. And because of the demise of logical positivism, according to Koch (1964), behaviorism was also dead or dying. From another perspective, behaviorism had just changed its clothes and taken a new name.

The learning theories of the neobehaviorists differ in certain respects, mainly with reference to the concept of reinforcement and the use of intervening variable concepts. Many other apparent internal differences are terminological. In the broadest and least controversial sense, stimulus and response are basic concepts in all these theories. Although Tolman emphasized the learning of S-S relations instead of S-R associations, these "what leads to what," or sign-significate, cognitions directed—at least intuitively—what a reasonable organism would do or where it would go. And although Skinner eschewed the concept of eliciting stimuli, his concept of a discriminative stimulus (S°) still controls emitted behavior. Skinner's definitions of stimulus and response are functional, which means that like all the other neobehaviorists he was chiefly concerned with molar behavior rather than specific movements. This he labeled *operant behavior,* while Guthrie termed it *acts* and Tolman, Hull, and Spence simply called it *molar behavior.*

Tolman, Hull, and Spence were the main proponents of the intervening variable approach to learning theories of behavior, while Skinner abandoned his early use of them in favor of a straightforward description of events. Tolman, as well, eventually criticized intervening variables for containing excess meaning—meaning beyond their operational definitions. That is, they were too much like hypothetical constructs that referred to hypothetical states or events going on inside the organism. Guthrie, Hull, Spence, and Skinner all employed hypothetical constructs even though they usually tried to avoid them—for example, Guthrie's movement-produced stimuli, Hull's little g or fractional anticipatory goal response, Spence's concept of emotional state as contributing to drive, and Skinner's notion of private events. In other words, Skinner's Black Box theory was not as black as many people maintained.

The Hull-Spence theory, as a hypotheticodeductive system, supplied hypotheses for testing the postulates of the theory and was constructed before much of the data were collected. Whereas for Skinner, theory came after data collection and was useful for application to behavioral control problems. Skinner's theory, as many view it, is incomplete. Pavlovian conditioning and all that it entails is essentially ignored in his emphasis on operant conditioning and behavioral consequences. This is too narrow a perspective for psychology. Skinner's approach, currently called experimental analysis of behavior, may represent the most valuable legacy of neobehaviorism.

REFERENCES

Bergman, G., & Spence, K. W. (1941). Operationism and theory in psychology. *Psychological Review, 48,* 1–14.

Koch, S. (1964). Psychology and emerging conceptions of knowledge as unitary. In T. W. Wann (Ed.), *Behaviorism and phenomenology: Contrasting bases for modern psychology.* Chicago: University of Chicago Press.

SUGGESTED READING

Zuriff, G. E. (1985). *Behaviorism: A conceptual reconstruction.* New York: Columbia University Press.

M. R. DENNY
Michigan State University

BEHAVIORISM
CLASSICAL CONDITIONING
COVERT CONDITIONING
LEARNING THEORIES
OPERANT CONDITIONING

NEOCORTEX

The two cerebral hemispheres mark the most anterior and prominent portion of the mammalian brain. In humans, most of the surface of these hemispheres is covered by a highly convoluted layer of tissue called neocortex ("cortex" is derived from Greek, meaning bark or covering). Neocortex (new cortex) is differentiated from evolutionarily older types of cortical tissue (archicortex, allocortex, paleocortex) by the number of its layers (usually six) that may be discerned. Birds and reptiles have no neocortex at all, but do have the older types of cortex. These older regions are also present in mammals, but the amount of neocortex increases greatly with behavioral complexity and intelligence. In humans, the neocortex reaches a peak of development and occupies about 80% of the total brain mass. In humans, neocortex is essential for rational thought, language, sensory perception, and goal-directed behavior, many of the characteristics that help to define our species. The neocortex may be thought of as the crown jewel of mammalian evolution, having shown the greatest expansion of any brain region during the past 65 million years. This increase in the cortical area has resulted in a highly convoluted cortical surface (gyri and sulci); these foldings represent a clever geometric solution to the problem of how to fit more of the two-dimensional neocortical sheet into a braincase without unduly increasing the size of the head. Not all mammals have a convoluted neocortex, and in primitive mammals, such as rodents, the neocortex is smooth. As the neocortex has evolved and increased in size, it has taken over many of the functions of lower sub-cortical brain centers. Humans, for example, are completely blind following destruction of the visual neocortex, but rats show much less disability following such loss.

STRUCTURAL AND FUNCTIONAL COMPONENTS

The neuron is the cellular unit of the nervous system. Each cortical neuron can be divided into several components: (a) the cell body, which houses the nucleus; (b) the dendrites, processes that branch off the cell body and are specialized for receiving synaptic input from other neurons; and (c) the axon, generally a single elongated process that originates at the cell body and, after branching, may extend great distances to make contact with other neurons. Each axonal branch ends in an enlargement, the terminal button, which houses the machinery of chemical synaptic transmission (the primary means by which neurons communicate with one another). Electrochemical impulses (action potentials) are generated near the cell body and rapidly travel along the axon until they reach the terminal button, where synaptic transmitter substance is released.

Cortical neurons may be divided into two general functional classes based on whether their synaptic contacts excite or inhibit their targets. About 80% of cortical neurons excite their targets, and most of these neurons are shaped like a pyramid (pyramidal neurons), with the apex aimed at the surface of the cortex. From this apex extends a thick apical dendrite, which branches repeatedly into a dense, tree-like pattern and usually extends to the surface of the cortex. Such neurons may receive 10,000 to 20,000 synaptic contacts from other neurons. The axon of the pyramidal neuron branches repeatedly in the vicinity of the cell body, but also sends a major branch to excite distant targets within the brain. The second major functional class of cortical neuron consists of neurons that inhibit their synaptic targets. Each of these generally projects its axon quite locally. Proper functioning of the neocortex (and all brain regions) depends on a delicate balance of excitation and inhibition. Excessive excitation, for example, can cause atypical firing of nerve cells that results in seizure activity (epilepsy).

Electron microscopic studies of the neocortex reveal a remarkable complexity (e.g., Braitenberg & Schuz, 1991; White, 1989). For example, in the mouse, each cubic millimeter of neocortex contains a total length of about 2.5 miles of axons and nearly a billion synapses. Extrapolating these figures to the human brain, which has nearly one million mm³ of cortical tissue, we can roughly estimate that our brain contains about 2.5 million miles of axonal wiring and a million billion (10^{15}) synapses. Since cortical neurons generally fire action potentials at rates of about 1/sec, we can estimate that each second we are alive, impulses conducting along the axons of our neocortex travel an astounding 2.5 million miles!

CORTICAL LAYERING AND COLUMNAR ORGANIZATION

Most of the neocortex is made up of six distinct layers of cell bodies and processes. The six layers (numbered I through VI, starting at the surface) differ from one another in the sizes and densities of their cell bodies and in their relative proportions of neurons of different types. The main properties of each layer are as follows:

- *Layer I*—few cell bodies, many synapses onto apical dendrites of pyramidal neurons
- *Layers II and III*—small-to-medium size pyramidal neurons
- *Layer IV*—especially prominent in sensory cortex, many densely packed small stellate cells
- *Layer V*—large, sparsely packed pyramidal neurons
- *Layer VI*—medium-sized pyramidal neurons

The functional operations of the neocortex may divided into three general components: (a) reception of neural information from subcortical and cortical brain regions (via synaptic inputs), (b) integration of this information, and (c) organization of output signals, which are sent to many different regions of the brain and to the spinal cord. The lamination pattern of the neocortex is related to these basic functions. For example, layer IV of sensory cortical areas is specialized for reception of information from lower sensory structures. This information is then integrated, and synaptic excitation flows upward and downward to superficial layers (II and III) and deeper layers (V and VI) of the cortex. Finally, pyramidal neurons within these various layers further integrate this information and project the results of this processing (in the form of trains of action potentials) to both subcortical and cortical targets.

This vertical spread of activation reflects the organization of the cortex into functional columns or modules, which have been described in many regions of neocortex (e.g., Hubel & Wiesel, 1979). Thus, the cortical column is thought to represent a basic circuit or functional processing unit of the neocortex, consisting of thousands of neurons that span the six cortical layers. The entire neocortex is thought to consist of hundreds of thousands of such functional columns, each performing similar operations on their inputs and projecting the results of their processing to their multiple targets. The power of the mammalian neocortex as an engine of information processing is thought to reside, in part, from the simultaneous, parallel operation of thousands of such cortical columns on inputs provided by external (sensory) and internal sources.

ORGANIZATION OF THE NEOCORTEX INTO SPECIALIZED REGIONS

Many different systems have been suggested for dividing the neocortex into subregions. Some of these systems are based exclusively on anatomical (structural) differences and some on functional differences among the cortical areas. A basic system for dividing the neocortex is based on large anatomical markers such as fissures and gyri. The two major landmarks on the lateral surface of each hemisphere are the central fissure and the lateral fissure. These fissures divide each hemisphere into four major lobes: the frontal, parietal, occipital, and temporal lobes. A somewhat more refined anatomical system is based on cytoarchitectonics (cellular architecture). Here, distinctions are based on the microscopic similarities and differences in the cell types and on the processes that constitute the various layers. The Brodmann map (named after its creator), for example, divides the neocortex into 52 distinct areas.

Functionally, cortical areas can be divided into three types: sensory areas, motor areas, and association areas. Each sensory modality (e.g., visual, auditory) has multiple representations, each with its own separate neocortical area. Neurobiologists have shown that the multiple representations of a given sensory modality have different functions, and are often organized in a hierarchical manner. In the visual system, for example, the primary visual cortex (in the occipital lobe) performs the initial cortical processing of visual information (Hubel & Wiesel, 1979). The visual cortex then passes on the results of its processing to higher visual areas, which specialize in analyzing color, motion, or other functional aspects of vision. These areas then project the results of their analyses to one of the highest visual areas, the inferotemporal cortex, which is necessary for object recognition. Thus, whereas the primary visual cortex is essential for visual sensation, the inferotemporal cortex is essential for visual perception. Other sensory

modalities are organized in a similar manner. Motor areas may also be organized in a hierarchical manner. The primary motor cortex is located in the precentral gyrus of the frontal lobe. This region is involved in the fine motor control of the body's muscle. Parts of the neocortex that cannot be divided into sensory or motor areas are called association cortex. There are many such areas, and some of these regions support the highest cognitive abilities such as language, foresight, and abstract reasoning. Association areas have been subdivided based on the specific cognitive deficits that result following lesions. Thus, language areas (Broca's and Wernicke's areas) are found in the temporal and parietal lobes, and areas involved in planning actions and forethought are found in the frontal lobe (prefrontal cortex).

Functions of the Major Cortical Lobes

The occipital lobes are the hindmost portion of the cortex and contain regions that are important in visual perception and processing. The very posterior pole of the occipital lobes is known as the primary visual cortex. Lesions of the occipital lobes can produce loss of vision for parts of the visual field. The location of the damage determines which part of the visual field will become blind (e.g., damage to the primary visual cortex in the right hemisphere will cause blindness in the left visual field). Blindness from occipital lobe damage is called cortical blindness. More specific visual disorders result when brain damage also includes the neighboring temporal and/or parietal lobe. For example, lesions to occipitotemporal regions can produce visual agnosias (agnosia means a loss or lack of knowledge), such as a deficit in recognizing objects, colors, or faces, despite otherwise normal vision. One remarkable case study of visual agnosia is told in *The Man Who Mistook His Wife for a Hat and Other Clinical Tales* (Sacks, 1985).

The parietal lobes constitute the dorsal and lateral area of each hemisphere and mediate somatosensory information from the body, including touch, pain, temperature, and limb position. The parietal lobes also play an important role in higher visual processing and in attending and integrating sensory information from different modalities. Parietal lobe lesions can often cause a striking deficit called unilateral neglect, in which a patient ignores visual, auditory, and somatosensory information coming from the side of the body opposite the brain lesion.

The temporal lobes contain areas of cortex involved in auditory and higher-order visual processing as well as structures crucial for learning, memory, higher multimodal integration, and emotion. Lesions to the temporal lobes' primary auditory area can cause partial or complete deafness. Lesions further down the auditory pathways can cause more selective hearing deficits. For example, temporal lobe lesions in the left hemisphere are often associated with disorders of speech perception, while lesions to the symmetrical areas in the right hemisphere can produce deficits in music perception. Within the temporal lobes are structures that are part of the limbic system, which is distinct from and phylogenetically older than the neocortex. These structures are crucial for forming long-term memories and for emotional behavior.

The frontal lobes constitute almost 50% of the volume of each cerebral hemisphere in humans. Phylogenetically and developmentally, these lobes are the last to develop. The frontal lobes play a major role in motor activity (control of body movements); participate in language functions; and are important for higher integrative functions, personality traits, emotionality, and executive control (the translation of thought into action). Damage to the primary motor area of a particular cerebral hemisphere can cause paralysis on the opposite side of the body. Fluent production of language (speech) has been associated with an area in the left frontal lobe called Broca's area. A large portion of the frontal lobes, called the prefrontal cortex, is involved in a variety of functions dedicated to integrating multimodal sensory and motor information, and to enhancing complex cognitive functions such as problem solving, planning action toward a goal, and using information flexibly.

HEMISPHERIC DIFFERENCES

The cerebral hemispheres, like much of the body, show a great deal of bilateral symmetry in both structure and function. Thus, for example, the left and right primary visual areas have similar structure and function, and deal only with visual information from opposite sides of the visual field. Some regions of the human neocortex, however, show considerable structural and functional asymmetry. The left hemisphere of almost all right-handed and most left-handed people is necessary for many language related functions. Injuries to the specific areas of the left hemisphere often result in language related disabilities (generally known as aphasia), such as Broca's aphasia (difficulty with speech production), Wernicke's aphasia (difficulty with comprehension), agraphia (inability to write), and alexia (inability to read). In contrast, the right hemisphere is superior for expressive speech intonation (prosody), appreciation of humor, and visuospatial integration such as recognition of objects and faces. According to some theorists, the left hemisphere is better at analyzing information analytically and in a piecemeal, detailed, and successive fashion, while the right hemisphere is better in analyzing information in a holistic, gestalt, and visuo-spatial manner.

The corpus callosum is a massive fiber tract that connects the two hemispheres. Although the two hemispheres perform different functions, we maintain a unified sense of consciousness because of constant communication through the corpus callosum. When the corpus callosum is surgically destroyed (this is sometimes done as a last resort to prevent the interhemispheric transmission of epileptic seizure activity) the two hemispheres may begin to act independently. The careful study of such so-called split-brain patients has led to many remarkable insights into hemispheric specialization and into how the two hemispheres are normally unified (e.g., Sperry, 1985).

CORTICAL DYSFUNCTION

Unfortunately, the enormous complexity of the neocortex makes it susceptible to many disease states (e.g., head injury, stroke, tumors, epilepsy, dementia). Some of these illnesses involve well defined, focal lesions that are associated with specific neuropsychological syndromes. Stroke results in focal lesions defined by the vascular territory of the blood vessel affected, and in particular neurological symptoms and syndromes (e.g., left hemisphere frontal lobe strokes can cause both paralysis on the right side of the body and Broca's aphasia). Other illnesses, such as Alzheimer's dementia or head injury, involve more diffuse damage, and may cause multiple cognitive deficits. Another common disorder, epilepsy, can result from any condition that heightens the excitability of brain tissue (e.g., head injury, stroke, tumor) and can result in either focal or generalized seizure activity.

REFERENCES

Braitenberg, V., & Schuz, A. (1991). *Anatomy of the cortex: Statistics and geometry.* New York: Springer-Verlag.

Hubel, D. H., & Wiesel, T. N. (1979). Brain mechanisms of vision. *Scientific American, 241,* 150–162.

Sacks, O. (1985). *The man who mistook his wife for a hat and other clinical tales.* New York: Summit.

Sperry, R. W. (1985). Consciousness, personal identity and the divided brain. In D. F. Benson & E. Zaidel (Eds.), *The dual brain: Hemispheric specialization in humans.* New York: Guilford.

White, E. (1989). *Cortical circuits.* Boston: Birkhauser.

SUGGESTED READING

Heilman, K. M., & Valenstein, E. (1993). *Clinical neuropsychology.* Oxford: Oxford University Press.

K. LUKATELA
Brown University Medical School

H. A. SWADLOW
University of Connecticut

BRAIN
CEREBRAL LOCALIZATION
NEUROPSYCHOLOGY

NEOPSYCHOANALYTIC SCHOOL

Seven theorists originally influenced by Sigmund Freud developed a number of basic differences with the orthodox psychoanalytic approach. Some broke away from Freud because of these differences. Each modified and in some way extended psychoanalysis as it had been conceived by Freud. At times some of these seven theorists have been called "neo-Freudians," but it is an oversimplification to place them in such a general category. Each of them went beyond Freud in certain ways, discarding parts of orthodox psychoanalysis, modifying other aspects, extending certain basic concepts, and developing new concepts in personality theory and psychotherapy. The seven theorists form a historical link between Freud and certain contemporary personality/psychotherapy theorists.

The first five—Carl Jung, Alfred Adler, Karen Horney, Erich Fromm, and Harry Stack Sullivan—shared views that separated them from Freud's orthodox psychoanalytic view. They agreed that social and cultural factors were of great significance in shaping personality, and reacted against what they considered to be Freud's narrow insistence on the biological determinants of personality, especially the role of sex and aggression. They also gave less emphasis than Freud to unconscious factors as a determinant of human personality and behavior. While most of them accepted the notion that early childhood experiences play a significant role in one's current psychological functioning and development, they rejected the notion that personality is fixed and determined by earlier experiences. They gave attention to critical factors during the entire life span of an individual.

A central feature of Carl Jung's analytic theory and view of the person was his emphasis on the role of purpose and goals. According to Jung, people are influenced not only by what they experienced as children, but also by what they aspire to in the future. Jung focused on the optimistic or creative side of humanity, the striving for completeness, and the role of living for purpose and meaning. Jung also broadened the Freudian notion of the unconscious, describing unconscious forces as both creative and destructive. More than being merely the sum of repressed childhood experiences, the unconscious is the wellspring of creativity and the source of finding direction in life.

A central feature of Alfred Adler's individual psychology is emphasis on the social determinants of personality. For Adler, humans are primarily motivated by social urges. He stressed that behavior is purposeful and goal-directed, and that humans are pushed by the need to overcome feelings of inferiority and pulled by strivings for superiority. Thus humans attempt to overcome basic feelings of helplessness by compensating—that is, by developing a unique lifestyle aimed at finding success.

Karen Horney's central idea was *basic anxiety,* the child's feeling of being isolated in a potentially hostile world. Her theory of personality focused on the role of anxiety that grows out of disturbed parent-child relationships. For her, the striving for security is a critical factor in human behavior.

Erich Fromm contended that humans shape social forces themselves and thus create their own natures. In his writings, Fromm stressed an existential view of humans which included dealing with loneliness, isolation, a sense of belonging, and the meaning of life. His basic theme is that humans have been separated from nature and from others and thus experience alienation. People can either unite themselves with others by learning how to love, or they can find some security by conforming their will to an authoritarian society.

Harry Stack Sullivan developed a theory of personality that emphasized interpersonal relations and the study of humans in relationship with significant others. The unit of study is the interpersonal situation, not the individual alone. As applied to psychotherapy, Sullivan saw the therapist as a participant/observer bringing objective and subjective reactions to the client.

Erik Erikson, identified as an ego psychologist, has developed an approach to personality that moves considerably beyond Freud's. Erikson's theory of development holds that psychosexual and psychosocial growth occur together, and that each stage of life is characterized by a crisis or major turning point at which individuals either achieve or fail to achieve successful resolutions. To a large extent, our lives are the result of the choices we make at each of these stages.

Wilhelm Reich pioneered body-oriented psychotherapy by putting the body at the center of psychology. While greatly influenced by Freud, Reich broke away from this orthodox tradition to develop the idea of character armor and develop techniques for loosening the muscular armor. His central idea was that emotions are an expression of the movement of body energy, and that chronic muscle tensions block this flow of energy and thus block the expression of emotions such as rage, fear, pain, joy, and anxiety. Reichian body-oriented techniques focus on loosening and dissolving the character armor, along with analytic work on psychological issues associated with restricted bodies. Heinz Kohut concentrated on self-esteem in his systematic position known as self psychology. Early difficulties in mother-child relationships make a person vulnerable to personality disorders.

SUGGESTED READING

Corey, G. (1982/1977). *Theory and practice of counseling and psychotherapy* (2nd ed.). Monterey, CA: Brooks/Cole.

Hall, C. S., & Lindzey, G. (Eds.). (1978/1957). *Theories of personality* (3rd ed.). New York: Wiley.

Schultz, D. (1981). *Theories of personality* (2nd ed.). Monterey, CA: Brooks/Cole.

G. F. COREY
California State University

ADLERIAN PSYCHOTHERAPY
ANALYTICAL PSYCHOLOGY
HORNEY'S THEORY
PSYCHOANALYSIS
SULLIVAN'S INTERPERSONAL THEORY

NERNST EQUATION

The Nernst equation is a simple but very important formula derived by the great German physical chemist Walther Hermann Nernst (1864–1941) from thermodynamic considerations, for which he was awarded the Nobel Prize in chemistry in 1920. It is the basic equation for study of cell membrane transport and potential, playing an extremely important role in neurophysiology.

The Nernst equation, which defines the thermal balance of chemical and electrical forces across a membrane, expresses the equilibrium condition quantitatively and makes it possible to calculate the theoretical resting membrane potential if the ratio of internal to external ion concentrations is known. In essence, it embodies the fact that (under conditions of uniform temperature and pressure) only two driving forces influence the diffusion of charged particles: a force arising from concentration differences and a force arising from electrical potential differences. When solutions having different concentrations of the same dissociable salt are placed on opposite sides of a barrier that is impermeable to one of the dissociation products, there will be no net movement of salt across the barrier despite the concentration difference. Net movement of the permeate ion is prevented by the development of an electrical potential difference across the barrier, the magnitude and orientation of which are such that they exactly cancel the driving force arising from the chemical concentration difference across the barrier. The Nernst equation (also referred to under these conditions as the Nernst potential or the Nernst equilibrium potential) is used to express the concentration gradient in electrical terms. The Nernst equation is a measure of the amount of work that can be done by an ion diffusing down its concentration gradient. It is the electrical equivalent of the energy (in mV) in the concentration gradient, and is expressed as $E_i = (RT/zF)\ln(C_i^o/C_i^i)$, where E_i = electrical potential (mV), R = natural gas constant, T = absolute temperature (°K), z = the valence of the ion, F = Faraday's constant (96,500 coulombs/mol), ln = natural logarithm, and C_i^o and C_i^i = the concentration of the ion (mmol/L) outside and inside the cell. When the Nernst equation is used to calculate the diffusion of electrolytes, such as Na^+ and K^+, it can be simplified by substituting for the constants (R, T, and F) and converting to common logarithms, yielding $E_i = 60\log(C_i^o/C_i^i)$, where E_i = the equilibrium potential (mV) for a particular ion, and C_i^o and C_i^i = the extracellular and intracellular concentrations of that ion. The valence is omitted because it is +1 for both Na^+ and K^+.

APPLICATION

Forces Acting on Ions

All biologic membranes are characterized by transmembrane electrical potential differences, which are produced by the movement of ions across the plasma membrane. The electrical potential difference arising from the diffusion of ions derived from a dissociable salt from a region of higher concentration to one of lower concentration is referred to as diffusion potential. Application of the Nernst equation permits us to determine whether the distribution of any inert solute across a cell membrane is passive or active. Using the Nernst equation, we can determine whether the ratio of the concentrations (activities) of ion across the membrane can be attributed entirely to thermal (passive) forces or whether additional (active) forces are necessary. At 37°C, if $V_m = E_i = (60/z)\log(C_i^o/C_i^i)$, the steady-state distribution of i across the membrane can be considered passive. If this equality does not hold, then forces in addition to thermal energy must be involved in establishing the observed distribution ratio of i. Thus, if we know V_m and the extracellular concentration of solute i, C_i^o, we can predict the intracellular concentration C_i^i that would be consistent with a passive distribution of i across the membrane and then compare that predicted value with the actual measured value. For example, if a cell is in a plasma-like solution, where C_{Cl}^o = 120 mmol/L, the intracellular concentration of Cl^- is determined to be 12 mmol/L and the electrical potential difference across this membrane is determined to be –60 mV. Using the Nernst equation, we obtain the predicted value for C_{Cl}^i to be $0.1C_{Cl}^o$ or 12 mmol/L. This agrees with the actually measured value so that the distribution of Cl^- across the cell membrane is the result of passive transport processes that do not require an investment of energy on the part of the cell.

Ionic Mechanisms of the Resting Potential

An electrical potential (voltage) difference exists between the inside and outside of all cells; this is called the resting membrane potential. In almost all instances, the transmembrane electrical potential difference is oriented so that the cell interior is electrically negative with respect to the extracellular compartment. The size of the electrical (membrane) potential difference, V_m, ranges from –10 mV to as high as about –100 mV. Furthermore, in a number of cell types, V_m is variable, and this variation is responsible for the propagation of signals by nerve tissue, contraction of muscle, and stimulus-secretion coupling in exocrine and endocrine secretory cells. The resting potential is approximately –80 mV in excitable cells (e.g., nerve cells and muscle cells) and approximately –20 to –40 mV in nonexcitable cells (e.g., red blood cells and epithelial cells). When excitable cells are stimulated, an action potential is generated, during which the membrane potential changes from –80 mV to about +45 mV and then returns to the resting potential. The magnitude of the resting potential depends on (a) The concentration gradient for each ion to which the membrane is permeable; and (b) The relative permeability (or conductance) of the membrane for each ion.

Concentration differences are maintained across the cell surface membrane even though it allows permeation of the major ions, by balancing of the force arising from a concentration gradient against the opposing force arising from the electrical gradient. As an ion species moves across the membrane and its concentration gradient diminishes, the transmembrane charge gradient is enhanced. At steady state, when there is no further net movement of ion, according Nernst equation it can be determined as $E^{ion} = -(60/z)\log$(concentration inside/concentration outside).

The resting potential of nerve and muscle is determined by the concentration gradients and membrane permeability (conductances) for Na^+ and K^+. K^+ is much more abundant in the intracellular fluid (ICF) than in extracellular fluid (ECF), whereas Na^+ is more abundant in the ECF than in the ICF. To preserve electroneutrality, the intracellular and extracellular cations must be balanced with anions. The primary anions of ECF are HCO_3^- and Cl^- and the primary anions of ICF are proteins and organic and inorganic acids. Na^+ leaks into, but K^+ leaks out of, the cell down their concentration gradients. The concentration gradients for these ions are established and maintained by the Na^+–K^+ pump, which keeps the concentration gradients for Na^+ and K^+ from changing by pumping Na^+ out of and K^+ into the cell. Because the permeability of the resting membrane to K^+ is so much higher than it is to Na^+, the value of the resting membrane potential can be approximated by the equilibrium potential for K^+. Extracellular K^+ concentration affects the resting membrane potential. Increases in extracellular K^+, which make the equilibrium potential for K^+ more positive, cause the resting membrane potential to depolarize, whereas decreases in extracellular K^+ cause it to hyperpolarize. Using the Nernst equation, we can determine the membrane potential (V_m) by calculating the K^+ equilibrium potential (E^K): $V_m \approx E_k = 60\log([K^+]o/[K^+]i)$ mV.

Because the plasma membrane of a real cell is not exclusively permeable to K^+ and Cl^-, the actual resting membrane potential is usually not exactly equal to that predicated by the Nernst equation for K^+ or Cl^-. If a membrane is permeable to more than one cation, the Nernst equation cannot be used to predict the resultant membrane potential. In such a case, the Goldman equation, $V_m = 60 \log\{([K^+]o + a[Na^+]o)/(K^+]i + a[Na^+]i)\}$ mV, can be used.

W. ZHANG
New York Medical College

ACTION POTENTIAL

NESTLER, ERIC J.

Eric J. Nestler received his BA in 1976 from Yale University, with a major in molecular biophysics and biochemistry. He graduated summa cum laude and was elected to Phi Beta Kappa. He then entered the MD-PhD program, also at Yale. He was awarded a PhD in 1982 in neuropharmacology. His graduate dissertation research was carried out in the laboratory of Paul Greengard, where Nestler studied regulation of protein phosphorylation by physiological and pharmacological stimuli. This work was the first to demonstrate activation of protein phosphorylation cascades in response to nerve impulse conduction. Nestler received his MD in 1983, and was elected to Alpha Omega Alpha, the national medical honor society. After completing residency training in psychiatry at McLean Hospital and Yale in 1987, he joined the Yale faculty, where until recently he was the Elizabeth Mears and House Jameson Professor of Psychiatry and Neurobiology and director of the Abraham Ribicoff Research Facilities and of the Division of Molecular Psychiatry. In 2000, Nestler joined the University of Texas Southwestern Medical Center in Dallas as Chairman of the Department of Psychiatry and the Lou and Ellen McGinley Distinguished Professor of Psychiatry.

Nestler is the recipient of numerous awards and honors, including the Pfizer Scholars Award (1987), Sloan Research Fellowship (1987), McKnight Scholar Award (1989), Efron Award of the American College of Neuropsychopharmacology (1994), and Pasarow Foundation Award for Neuropsychiatric Research (1998). He chairs the board of scientific counselors of the National Institute on Drug Abuse, and serves on the scientific advisory boards of the National Alliance for Research in Schizophrenia and Depression and of the National Alliance for Autism Research. Nestler was elected to the Institute of Medicine of the National Academy of Sciences in 1998. He serves on the editorial boards of several prominent neurobiology and psychiatry journals and is the author of five books and over 215 other publications.

The goal of Nestler's research is to better understand the ways in which the brain responds and adapts to repeated perturbations under both normal and pathological conditions. A major focus of his research is drug addiction, with related work underway in the areas of depression, psychosis, and stress.

With respect to addiction, the challenge is to identify molecular changes that drugs of abuse produce in the brain to cause addiction, and to characterize the genetic and environmental factors that determine individual differences in the ability of the drugs to produce these changes. Nestler's laboratory has discovered several molecular and cellular adaptations that occur in specific brain regions in response to chronic drug exposure, and has provided evidence that these adaptations are responsible for certain behavioral features of addiction. One example is upregulation of the cyclic AMP second messenger and protein phosphorylation system, which occurs in many types of neurons and appears to be a common mechanism of addiction for most, and possibly all, drugs of abuse. Another example is drug regulation of specific transcription factors (nuclear proteins that bind to the regulatory regions of certain genes and thereby increase or decrease the rate at which those genes are transcribed). Nestler and his colleagues have discovered a novel transcription factor, termed deltaFosB, which is induced in specific regions of brain in response to chronic, but not acute, exposure to many drugs of abuse. Once induced, this transcription factor persists in the brain for long periods due to its extraordinary stability. As a result, deltaFosB could function as a type of sustained molecular switch that mediates some of the long-lasting adaptations in the brain that underlie a state of addiction. Overall, Nestler's research is based on a strict medical-model view of addiction, namely, that a greater knowledge of the neurobiological basis of drug addiction will lead to more effective treatments and eventually preventive measures.

More generally, one of the major contributions of the Nestler laboratory has been advancing the field's ability to relate specific molecular and cellular adaptations to complex behavior. This has involved applying novel methods of viral-mediated gene transfer and inducible, tissue-specific genetic mutations in mice to the field of neuropsychiatry. This work has established experimental paradigms for relating alterations in individual genes and gene products to altered functioning of neurons in which those genes are expressed, and ultimately to altered behaviors that are mediated by those neurons.

STAFF

NETHERLANDS, PSYCHOLOGY IN

To a large extent, the cultural and scientific development of the Netherlands has been determined by its geographical position. Its western boundary is formed by the North Sea, which provides, for a maritime nation, the opportunity for close relations (in the past not always friendly) with Great Britain, and for two centuries, with the United States. On the south, it faces France, and the east, Germany. The days are long past when the Dutch Republic (a kingdom since 1815) was a major power, holding its own against Spain, France, and England, and having colonies all over the world. However, the old tradition of political, commercial, and cultural contacts still persists.

The Dutch language, in its various forms, is spoken by about 20 million people: the population of the Netherlands and of (roughly) the northern part of Belgium. This is a small number, compared with the surrounding language areas. However, because of the importance of international contacts, practically all Dutch people in leading or academic positions are able at least to read English, French, and German, the rudiments of which are taught in most secondary schools.

In the Netherlands, psychology, like the other sciences, is and always has been internationally oriented. For a time, in fact until the Nazis took over, the influence of German psychology was dominant. But during the Hitler régime, nearly all German psychologists emigrated or were forced to keep silent, or were imprisoned or murdered. Partly because of this, psychology's "center of gravity" moved to the United States, and the influence of North American psychology now is correspondingly great. It should be mentioned that the Fulbright program, which enabled many American psychologists to work in Dutch universities, not only was effective in extending knowledge of developments in American psychology, but in many cases also fostered enduring personal and scientific contacts.

In accordance with the European, particularly the German, tradition, Dutch academic psychology was—during the first part of the 20th century—closely connected with philosophy. As a matter of fact, until the end of World War II, the final examination in psychology was a variant of the final examination in philosophy.

Furthermore, theology has always been a dominant factor in Dutch social life, partly as a consequence of the fact that national independence was attained, during the 16th and 17th centuries, in a long war with Spain and its allies—a war generally depicted as a struggle for religious freedom. Religion and *Weltanschauung* were important factors in Dutch society, with the Netherlands sometimes described as a "confederation of ideologies."

At the present time, the ostensible influence of religion and philosophy on Dutch psychology has diminished; whether they still affect psychological thought and action in more subtle ways is a difficult question. It is answered in the affirmative by some (Marxist) critics and by some feminists.

Partly as a consequence of the European tradition, "orthodox" behaviorism has never been dominant, or even important, in the Netherlands. Both its naive realism and its curious taboo on self-report were unacceptable to the large majority of Dutch psychologists. On the other hand, "cognitive" psychology, which has had a large following in the United States since about 1960, has been welcomed enthusiastically. It gave scientific respectability to topics that were once, at least in the United States, considered suspect at best, and at worst unmentionable in academically "decent" company.

More or less complementary to the cognitive approach, with its emphasis on mental activities, is a growing interest in psychobiological (including psychophysiological and psychopharmacological) research. To a certain extent, this has been stimulated by the important contributions to ethology by several Dutch biologists (one of whom, N. Tinbergen, was awarded a Nobel prize). Sociobiology, on the other hand, is still very controversial, not only because of its tendency to sweeping generalizations, but also because of its (real or merely apparent) implications for politics.

In short, one may venture the statement that the psychological climate in the Netherlands is not very different from that in the United States.

LEGAL STATUS AND ORGANIZATION

In the Netherlands, the professional use of the title "psychologist" is restricted to those who have passed the final (doctoral) examination in psychology. Seven universities offer the programs required for this examination. The program contents are, in broad outline, prescribed by the central government (the Minister of Education) and the subjects (disciplines) that should be studied are listed in the "academic statute." The implementation, however, of these guidelines may differ considerably from university to university.

The program officially takes four years to complete. For some categories of students, the universities provide postdoctoral programs, admission to which is strictly limited.

A person who has passed the final (doctoral) examination is called a *doctorandus* (Drs). The degree of doctorandus in psychology (as in many other disciplines) is officially recognized as a qualification for professional activities. The universities also may confer the title of *doctor* (Dr), practically the equivalent of the Ph.D. in the United States. For this, the writing of a special thesis is required. However, in the Netherlands, the Dr degree is purely a scientific distinction, and implies no professional qualifications whatsoever.

The Dutch equivalent of the American Psychological Association (APA) is the Netherland Institute of Psychologists (NIP), founded in 1938. Membership is not obligatory; only about 50% of the 6,000 qualified psychologists are members of the NIP. Through the NIP, the Netherlands is represented in the International Union of Scientific Psychology. The NIP has a number of sections, comparable to the divisions of APA.

Another important organization is the Dutch Psychonomic Foundation, whose membership is open not only to psychologists, but to scientists from other fields as well. In addition, there are several other research associations—for social, educational, industrial, and developmental psychology. The common interest that brings and holds these groups together is not purely theoretical; it is also hoped that, by coordinated efforts, the chances of obtaining (additional) research funds will be increased.

There are at least seven psychological journals in the Netherlands. Nearly all of them are Dutch-language journals, although English summaries often are provided. The exception is *Acta Psychologica,* which is published in English, and is edited by the Psychonomic Foundation. Founded in 1933, it is the second oldest of the Dutch psychological journals. The oldest is the *Dutch Journal of Psychology,* dating from 1932. All Dutch universities and other research institutions, as well as many individual psychologists, subscribe to one or (usually) several U.S. journals.

The number of Dutch-language books on psychology (scientific or otherwise) is quite considerable. Only a tiny fraction of these books appear in English; for this reason, most Dutch contributions to psychology remain inaccessible to the rest of the world. The doctorate theses are required to include a summary in English.

There is a well-functioning center for information and documentation in the social sciences, operating under the auspices of the Royal Netherlands Academy of Science (SWIDOC). It provides, on request, information about psychological literature, in particular, about the contents of journals and the so-called "gray" literature—mimeographed research reports, and so on. It also contains the Steinmetz archive, where original research data (mainly, but not exclusively, from surveys, etc.) are stored, and which has connections with similar organizations in the United States and elsewhere.

CURRENT ACTIVITIES

It is difficult to enumerate all the activities that are considered "psychological," or all activities in which psychologists are engaged professionally. These activities are variegated and numerous in the Netherlands, as well as in other Western countries. About 5% of the qualified psychologists are involved in research; all others are practitioners. Clinical psychology, with a large variety of specialization (among which psychotherapy is prominent), is the largest field. Developmental and educational psychology are second, closely followed by industrial and organizational psychology. Examples of the many other fields in applied psychology include psychology of traffic, environmental psychology, psychology of collective behavior (mass psychology, surveys, media, advertising), gerontopsychology, economic psychology, forensic psychology, occupational guidance, and rehabilitation.

There is a great diversity of problems and approaches in applied, as well as in theoretical psychology. As far as scientific research is concerned, the situation may be summarized as follows: it is very unlikely that a U.S. colleague from any specialization who visited the Netherlands would not find at least one person (or group) studying a similar problem. A complete list of psychological research in the Netherlands would be neither feasible nor instructive; it would look like a small issue of *Psychological Abstracts*. Instead the following indicates some of the areas in which Dutch psychology meets high standards, and is internationally recognized as contributing significantly to present-day theoretical developments:

Psycholinguistics. The Max Planck Institute for Psycholinguistics (in Nijmegen) is an important center. Here research on a variety of psycholinguistic problems is being carried out by an international team under the direction of W. J. M. Levelt.

Methodology. This discipline includes mathematical psychology, data theory, and psychometrics. The groups at Nijmegen (Th. G. G. Bezembinder, E. E. C. I. Roskam), Leiden (J. P. van de Geer), the Free University (P. J. D. Drenth), and Amsterdam (G. J. Mellenbergh, R. F. van Naerssen) should be mentioned in particular in relation to this discipline, although it is an important field in all Dutch universities. To a large extent, this is attributable to the seminal work of A. D. de Groot, formerly of Amsterdam and now at Groningen.

Cognitive functions. Important work on perception is being done at Nijmegen (visual perception—E. Leeuwenberg, H. F. J. M. Buffart), Utrecht (chemical senses—E. P. Köster), as well as at the Institute for Sensory Physiology at Soesterberg (R. Plomp, W. A. Wagenaar) and the Institute for Perception Research at Eindhoven (M. A. Bouma, S. G. Nooteboom). Research on the psychology of thinking is also an important topic, mainly inspired by de Groot, whose book on the psychology of chess has been translated into English. The work of J. J. Elshout and N. H.

Frijda, both of the University of Amsterdam, also should be mentioned. At Nijmegen, G. A. M. Kempen is engaged in the study of artificial intelligence, and C. Wegman has made an impressive attempt to formalize certain key concepts and relations in Freud's earlier theories. In Groningen, J. A. Michon is working on time perception and on traffic psychology.

Human learning. In particular, the work of C. F. van Parreren (Utrecht) deserves mention. He not only has done important work on the specific characteristics of human learning, but also on the application of learning theories in classroom situations. He also played a major role in introducing the results of Russian (educational) psychology in the Netherlands.

Social psychology. Group dynamics became a subject of interest in the Netherlands immediately after World War II, and since has been an important area. J. M. Rabbie (Utrecht), H. Wilke (Groningen), and J. M. F. Jaspars (formerly Nijmegen, now Oxford) have been among the most productive researchers. H. C. J. Duijker (Amsterdam) has argued that social psychology gradually is transforming itself into a general theory of behavior on a situational basis.

In addition to those mentioned in this brief outline, there are many others in the Netherlands who have done interesting theoretical work in psychology. The inaccessibility of the majority of Dutch publications to a worldwide audience has already been noted. Perhaps the international community of psychologists should become aware of this state of affairs, and show its inventiveness by providing an adequate solution.

H. C. J. DUIJKER
University of Amsterdam, The Netherlands

NEURAL MECHANISMS OF LEARNING

Packed within about 1 kg of mass in the brain are thousands of billions of computing elements, connected to each other in a manner seemingly random. Each element converts thousands of chemical signals into electrical signals every second, compares their value, and then reconverts them into chemical signals. From all of these computations comes the richness of human behavior: thoughts, actions, and emotions.

The function of these computing elements changes with experience, so that humans are not constrained to perform the stereotyped behaviors they were capable of at birth. Learned behaviors are what make humans unique in the animal kingdom.

Neural mechanisms of learning and memory most likely involve changes at many levels. The electrical activity of an individual neuron, the chemical communication between pairs of neurons, and the behavior of interconnected networks of neurons, all change in some way as a result of an organism's experiences. Understanding what changes take place, where the changes are occurring, and how they affect behavior require analysis of each of these levels, individually and in combination.

Research in this area makes extensive use of model systems—examinations of either relatively simple behaviors or relatively simple nervous systems (or both). In addition, clinical literature from people whose brains have been damaged by accident or illness has provided insight into which parts of the human brain are involved in learning and memory. The combination of these approaches is beginning to reveal what, where, and how the brain changes when learning occurs.

EFFECTS OF BRAIN DAMAGE IN HUMANS AND MONKEYS

Examining the behavioral deficits of human subjects who have experienced brain damage has increased understanding of how behavioral functions are localized in the central nervous system. Since the first evidence that even higher functions are localized to specific parts of the brain, it has been apparent that understanding the mechanisms of learning and memory will require knowledge of where these changes are to be found. Several prominent clinical case studies of individuals who sustained brain damage as a result of surgical intervention or accidents as well as experimental studies on monkeys suggest that there are two important learning and memory systems in the primate brain: one in the medial temporal lobes of the cerebral cortex and one in the diencephalon, near the midline of the brain.

Effects of Damage to the Medial Temporal Lobes

The importance of the structures in the medial temporal lobe (including the hippocampus, amygdala, and surrounding neocortex) was demonstrated dramatically in the case of H. M., an individual of above normal intelligence who received a bilateral medial temporal lobectomy in 1954 to relieve intractable epilepsy. Following the surgery, H. M. exhibited a severe deficit in the ability to learn new information about facts or events, which has not shown any improvement for nearly 40 years (Squire, 1992). This anterograde amnesia (a memory deficit for the period of time after brain damage) exists in the absence of any other changes in H. M.'s personality or general intelligence (he scored slightly higher on IQ tests after the surgery, in spite of the amnesia).

As a result of H. M.'s surgery and subsequent amnesia, attention was focused on the medial temporal lobes and, in particular, on the hippocampus. The role of the hippocampus in the formation of long-term memories has been tested extensively in monkeys. Initially, lesion studies by Mishkin (1978) suggested that lesions of the hippocampus alone were not sufficient to produce an animal model of H. M.'s anterograde amnesia. When the amygdala was damaged along with the hippocampus, however, the resulting memory deficits were greater than those seen with lesions to either the hippocampus or the amygdala alone and were qualitatively similar to H. M.'s deficits. More recently, work by Zola-Morgan and Squire (1992) suggests that although the amygdala plays little or no role in the type of memory in which H. M. is deficient, the hippocampus contributes to the formation of new memories, as does the surrounding neocortex. These results in monkeys are consistent with those of patient R. B., who sustained relatively specific damage to the hippocampus after a temporary interruption of blood flow to the brain. R. B. showed a memory deficit similar to H. M.'s, although considerably less severe (Squire, 1992).

Effects of Damage to the Midline Diencephalon

Destruction of parts of the diencephalon (thalamus and hypothalamus) also can cause severe anterograde amnesia. Patient N. A. suffered damage to his thalamus when a miniature fencing foil was accidentally thrust into his brain through his nose. Subsequent to the injury, N. A. demonstrated an anterograde amnesia similar to that of H. M.

Other cases of damage to the midline diencephalon, especially the dorsomedial and anterior thalamus, and the mammillary bodies of the hypothalamus have been studied in individuals who have suffered injury to one of the blood vessels supplying this part of the brain or who have developed Korsakoff's disease, a degenerative disease caused by a vitamin deficiency seen principally in chronic alcoholics. It involves damage to the mammillary bodies, the thalamus, and other parts of the brain, including prefrontal cortex. Although the specific nature of the amnesia varies among the different causes of diencephalic damage and between individuals, the pattern of memory deficits is similar to that seen with medial temporal lobe lesions and suggests that the two structures may play related roles in the formation of new memories. Experimental evidence from both nonhuman primates and rodents supports this conclusion (Squire, 1992).

ANALYSIS OF SIMPLE LEARNING IN VERTEBRATES

Human case studies and lesion experiments in monkeys have provided invaluable information about the role of some brain structures in learning and memory and the nature of human memory. Much of the data are difficult to interpret, however, in terms of defining a specific role for any part of the human brain in the learning process or identifying which neurons or synapses within these structures are the most likely to change as a result of experience. The difficulty is intrinsic to the fact that both the neural circuitry and the behaviors involved in these studies are quite complex. For this reason, many researchers in the field have chosen to study simpler forms of learning and memory in mammals that are likely to involve relatively less complex neural circuits.

Pavlov (1928/1983) was the first researcher to develop a physiologically based theory of learning and memory. Pavlov proposed that the cerebral cortex, particularly well developed in humans, was the site of interactions between associable stimuli and thus the part of the brain in which learned responses were initiated. Lashley (1950) conducted a long and detailed study of the effects of cerebral cortical lesions on the ability of rats to learn and remember complex mazes. Based on his observations, Lashley concluded that learning could not be localized to any one part of the cerebral cortex, because sufficiently large ablations of any part of the cortex produced equivalent deficits on mazes of equal difficulty. More recently, however, studies that have employed lesions restricted to brain regions other than neocortex, examining a variety of different behaviors, have begun to suggest that investigations into the cellular and molecular basis of learning will be most productive if they focus on some especially important parts of the brain.

The Role of the Hippocampus in Rapid Learning

Experimental data derived from lesion studies are in general agreement with the clinical literature cited above; the hippocampus appears to play an important role in learning and memory. Although the exact nature of this role is a matter of debate, lesion of the hippocampus disrupts the learning or remembering of several different behavioral tasks, in rodents as well as primates.

One type of behavior disrupted by hippocampal lesions are those that appear to require animals to use spatial information (O'Keefe & Nadel, 1978). For rats, this means using navigational cues to locate either food (in appetitively motivated tasks) or a means of escape (in aversive tasks). Two widely used examples of this behavior are the radial maze and the water maze.

In the radial maze, the rat is placed in the center platform from which a number of arms (usually between 6 and 12) radiate out. The animal finds a food reward at the end of these arms; in some cases, only some of the arms are baited on each trial (e.g., 4 of 8), whereas in others, all arms are baited. An entry into either an unbaited arm, or reentry into a baited arm, are counted as errors. Rats with hippocampal lesions are impaired on either one of these tasks, provided they are required to use only cues outside the maze (e.g., features of the room surrounding the maze) to find the reward (Jarrard, 1986).

The water maze consists of a circular pool with sheer walls, filled with opaqued water. Hidden beneath the surface of the water is a platform on which the animal can stand. Having found the platform, the animal is removed from the pool. The platform remains in the same location from trial to trial for each animal, so after it has been found once, the animal need only remember where the platform is located, by using cues in the room, outside the maze. The paradigm is conceptually similar to the radial maze, except that the animal works to escape from a mildly aversive situation, rather than working for a food reward. This task also is exquisitely sensitive to lesions of the hippocampus (Morris, Garrud, Rawlins, & O'Keefe, 1982).

Most of the literature on the effect of hippocampal lesions in rats relates to its hypothesized role in spatial learning. There has been, however, a considerable amount of research into the role of the hippocampus in other forms of learning, some of which relate more directly to the amnesic syndrome seen in humans with medial temporal lobe damage, and to experimental lesion effects in monkeys. Many of these studies suggest a role for the hippocampus in either short-term memory or in the relatively short-term storage of information required for the establishment of long-term memory (Sutherland & Rudy, 1989; Zola-Morgan & Squire, 1990).

In addition to the evidence from lesion experiments implicating a role for the hippocampus in learning and memory, recordings of the electrical activity of hippocampal neurons also suggest that the structure is particularly active during behaviors associated with learning, e.g., the exploration of novel or complex environments or the repeated pairings of discrete sensory stimuli (Otto, Eichenbaum, Wiener, & Wible, 1991; Skelton, Scarth, Wilkie, Miller, & Phillips, 1987). Although the precise role of the hippocampus in learning and memory remains elusive, the accumulated evidence suggests that it will be an important structure in which to test theories of the biological mechanisms of learning.

The Role of the Amygdala in Conditioned Emotional Responses

The amygdala is another important medial temporal lobe structure. Historically, it has been credited with a critical role in the generation of emotional behavior. This theory dates back to the pioneering work of Klüver and Bucy (1937), who found that temporal lobe lesions (later restricted to amygdala) in monkeys produced a syndrome of bizarre behaviors all associated with inappropriate processing of emotional stimuli. More recently, research efforts have focused on the extent to which emotional behavior is learned, and there is a growing consensus that the amygdala is critically involved in emotional learning.

Lesions to the amygdala produce profound deficits in conditioned emotional responses (Davis, 1992). Normally, when an animal receives a signal that an aversive event is about to occur, it responds with changes in both the autonomic nervous system (heart rate, blood pressure, and respiration rate) and with one of several behavioral changes, including freezing and the enhancement of an acoustic startle response. Lesions to the amygdala apparently make it impossible for animals to appreciate the importance of these signals, as they abolish both the autonomic and behavioral aspects of the fear response (LeDoux, 1988).

Investigations into the function of the amygdala in primates has also supported a role for this structure in learning and memory (Aggleton, 1992). While some of these have confirmed a role for the amygdala in the detection of novelty of stimulus significance, others have proposed that by virtue of its anatomical connections, it is well designed to serve as an integrator of information from different sensory modalities. Indeed, lesions of the amygdala in monkeys severely impair the ability of the animals to learn a short-term recognition task that involves choosing an object by sight that they have never seen before, but have touched in the dark (Murray & Mishkin, 1985). As with the hippocampus, the precise role of the amygdala awaits definition, as does its importance in neural circuits, including other medial temporal and midline diencephalic structures.

The Role of the Cerebellum and Brainstem in Conditioned Motor Responses

Since the early 1960s, the conditioned nictitating membrane response (NMR) in the rabbit has served as an effective model system for studying the neural mechanisms of simple learned motor responses. The study of simple forms of learning offers the advantage of allowing more precise quantification of the learned response and (theoretically) a reduction in the complexity of brain circuitry required to perform it. Once the neural mechanisms of simple learning have been elucidated, it will be possible to determine whether more complex forms of learning are elaborations of these basic, elemental changes.

The behavioral procedure, first described in rabbits by Gormezano Schneiderman, Deaux, and Fuentes (1962), consists of presentations of a neutral stimulus (the conditioned stimulus, or CS, which is usually a brief tone) with a puff of air directed at the cornea (the unconditioned stimulus, or US). The US produces an eyeblink, which causes the passive extension of the nictitating membrane, a "third" eyelid. After repeated presentations of the CS and US, the animal begins to blink when presented with the tone alone. This represents a form of classic Pavlovian conditioning, in which the learning consists of the modification of a simple reflex response. Because the response itself is simple and because confounding factors such as the animal's motivational state play only a minor role in the acquisition of the learned response, the conditioned NMR has become an important model system for exploring the neural mechanisms of learning.

The results of a series of experiments have suggested that a neural circuit consisting of brainstem nuclei and the cerebellum may be necessary and sufficient for producing learned eyeblink responses (Thompson, 1990). Lesions restricted to the deep nuclei of the cerebellum produce complete, irreversible impairment of the conditioned NMR. Moreover, recording the electrical activity of neurons in the cerebellum indicates that at least some significant percentage of these cells change their pattern of activity during the learning of the conditioned NMR. Electrical stimulation of brainstem structures that send information to the cerebellum also can produce conditioned NMR, in the absence of any other stimuli.

As is the case with the investigations into the nature of hippocampal and amygdaloid involvement in learning and memory cited above, studies of NMR circuitry have given us an exciting glimpse of *where* learning might occur, but not yet *how* it might occur. Two different lines of research have provided evidence of what changes might occur between neurons during learning. One of these lines has used an even simpler form of learning in a much simpler organism. The other has concentrated on the mechanisms of change in the nervous system that occur during activation of the brain without consideration of their behavioral relevance.

LEARNING AND NEURONAL PLASTICITY IN AN INVERTEBRATE

Some of the most impressive advances in the field have come from examinations of conditioned defensive responses in the marine mollusk *Aplysia*. Eric Kandel and associates at Columbia University have examined the cellular and molecular correlates of the conditioned gill and siphon withdrawal in *Aplysia* for more than 20 years. They have described an elegant system whereby learned increases in reflex responding produce increases in the strength of synaptic communication between identified neurons, whereas decreases in responding are associated with weakened synaptic communication (Hawkins, Clark, & Kandel, 1988).

The Behavioral Responses of Aplysia

The learned responses are, of necessity, simple. *Aplysia* have a defensive reaction to tactile stimulation that involves the retraction of a fleshy spout (called the siphon) and the gill, both of which are used by the animal for respiration. The reflex shows both nonassociative and associative modulation. If the siphon is repeatedly stimulated mechanically (by a jet of seawater), the withdrawal reflex will habituate, so that after approximately 10 such stimuli, the Aplysia will no longer show any response to the tactile stimulus. If, in contrast, the tail is shocked, the animal will show both sensitization (by increasing the duration of a nonhabituated withdrawal) and dishabituation (the reinstatement of a habituated response). Furthermore, if the tail shock is repeatedly presented immediately after siphon stimulation (a Pavlovian conditioning paradigm),

Aplysia will show an increase in the duration of the withdrawal response to siphon stimulation that is greater than that seen in sensitization. In other words, this incredibly simple animal, with only about 1,000 neurons in its central nervous system, is capable of habituation, sensitization, and associative Pavlovian conditioning.

Changes in Neuronal Communication in Aplysia

Due in large part to the relative simplicity of *Aplysia*'s central nervous system, it has proven possible to determine the nature of the changes that occur during learning, in identified neurons known to participate in generating learned responses. Sensory neurons in the siphon form synaptic contacts with motor neurons responsible for siphon and gill withdrawal, i.e., activation of these sensory neurons causes them to release a chemical neurotransmitter, which is received by the motor neuron, and causes it to fire an action potential, which in turn causes its target muscles to contract. Kandel has presented strong evidence that the sensory neuron to motor neuron contacts are modified during learning.

When habituation occurs, the strength of the response in the motor neuron elicited by activation of the sensory neuron decreases. In other words, the same stimulus given to the siphon produces the same response in the sensory neuron that, due to a decrease in the amount of neurotransmitter released, becomes unable to affect the motor neuron after repeated activation. By contrast, sensitization is associated with an increase in transmitter release from the sensory neuron, as a result of the modulatory action of the neurotransmitter serotonin, released by facilitatory interneurons by the sensitizing tail shock.

The neural mechanism for associative conditioning appears to be an elaboration of the mechanism for sensitization. Behaviorally, the difference between the two procedures is that a touch to the siphon precedes the tail shock only in the Pavlovian procedure. At the neuronal level, this means that siphon sensory neurons are active just before the release of serotonin by facilitatory interneurons. The result is an amplification of the mechanism by which sensitization enhances reflex responding to tactile stimulation.

LONG-TERM POTENTIATION: CHANGING THE STRENGTH OF NEURON-TO-NEURON COMMUNICATION

Is a change in the strength of synaptic connections the mechanism whereby learning occurs in mammals as well as in Aplysia? The question is difficult to answer, because researchers do not have access to identified neurons that are unquestionably part of a neural circuit responsible for learning. The accumulated evidence does suggest, however, that certain brain regions are important for at least some forms of learning. A strategy that has shown great promise is to examine the mechanisms by which synapses change in these structures and then attempt to exploit that information to make inferences about the mechanisms of learning.

Long-term Potentiation

The most widely investigated form of use-dependent change in synaptic strength was conducted by Bliss and Lømo (1973), who found a long-lasting increase in the size of a synaptic response, resulting from brief, high-frequency activation of that synapse. Long-term potentiation (LTP) and learning share many common features, providing circumstantial evidence that LTP or an LTP-like phenomenon could be the basis of behavioral plasticity (Baudry & Davis, 1991). Both LTP and learning can be rapidly induced. Learning can occur in a single trial, such as when one touches a hot stove. LTP is induced by stimulation as brief as 250 milliseconds. Furthermore, one touch to a hot stove is sufficient to last a lifetime; learning is long lasting. Although there is some debate as to how long it is possible to accurately record LTP, it can last for months in some cases. Another important feature is that LTP cannot be induced in every part of the central nervous system, but the structures that do show the most robust LTP correspond to those that appear to be involved in rapid learning, especially the hippocampus.

LTP and Learning

Evidence supporting the hypothesis that long-term potentiation is the mechanism of learning in mammals goes beyond surface similarities and comes in two categories. First, measurements made during several behavioral tasks indicate that increases in synaptic response size correlate with learning (Skelton et al., 1987). Moreover, the decay of LTP of a period of weeks is highly correlated with forgetting, suggesting that LTP lasts as long as learning does (Doyere & Laroche, 1992). Second, pharmacological or genetic manipulations that block or attenuate LTP also block or attenuate learning (Morris, Anderson, Lynch, & Baudry, 1986; Silva, Paylor, Wehner, & Tonegawa, 1992; Silva, Stevens, Tonegawa, & Wang, 1992). This does not prove a common mechanism, but as further investigations reveal more treatments that affect LTP and learning identically, the case becomes stronger.

Researchers are still a long way from developing a complete understanding of how experience changes the adult brain. Data from invertebrates, rodents, monkeys, and humans are, however, converging. These data suggest that learning and memory are processes that result from activity in specialized parts of the nervous system. Moreover, alterations in the strength of synaptic communication within networks of connected neurons can be induced, and this synaptic plasticity remains the best candidate of a mechanism for learning.

REFERENCES

Baudry, M., & Davis, J. L. (Eds.). (1991). *Long-term potentiation: A debate of current issues.* Cambridge, MA: MIT Press.

Bliss, T. V. P., & Lomo, T. (1973). Long-lasting potentiation of synaptic transmission in the dentate area of anesthetized rabbit following stimulation of the perforant path. *Journal of Physiology, 232,* 331-356.

Doyere, V., & Laroche, S. (1992). Linear relationship between the maintenance of hippocampal long-term potentiation and retention of an associative memory. *Hippocampus, 2*(1), 39–48.

Gormezano, I., Scheiderman, N., Deaux, E. B., & Fuentes, I. (1962). Nictitating membrane: Classical conditioning and extinction in the albino rabbit. *Science, 138,* 33–34.

Hawkins, R. D., Clark, G. A., & Kandel, E. R. (1988). Cell biological studies of learning in simple vertebrate and invertebrate systems. In F. Plum & V. Mountcastle (Eds.), *Handbook of physiology. The nervous system V* (pp. 25–83). Bethesda, MD: American Physiological Society.

Kluver, H., & Bucy, P. C. (1937). "Psychic blindness" and other symptoms following bilateral temporal lobectomy in rhesus monkeys. *American Journal of Physiology, 119,* 352–353.

Lashley, K. S. (1950). In search of the engram. *Symposia of the Society for Experimental Biology, 4,* 454–482.

LeDoux, J. E. (1988). Emotion. In F. Plum & V. Mountcastle (Eds.), *Handbook of physiology. The nervous system V: Higher Functions* (pp. 419–459). Bethesda, MD: American Physiological Society.

Mishkin, M. (1978). Memory in monkeys severely impaired by combined but not be separate removal of amygdala and hippocampus. *Nature, 273,* 297–298.

Morris, R. G. M., Anderson, E., Lynch, G. S., & Baudry, M. (1986). Selective impairment of learning and blockade of long-term potentiation by an *N*-methy-*d*-aspartate receptor antagonist, AP5. *Nature, 319,* 774–776.

Morris, R. G. M., Garrud, R., Rawlins, J. N. P., & O'Keefe, J. (1982). Place-navigation impaired in rats with hippocampal lesions. *Nature, 297,* 681–683.

Murray, E. A., & Mishkin, M. (1985). Amygdalectomy impairs crossmodal association in monkeys. *Science, 228,* 604–606.

O'Keefe, J., & Nadel, L. (1978). *The hippocampus as a cognitive map.* Oxford, UK: Clarendon.

Otto, T., Eichenbaum, H. Wiener, S. I., & Wible, C. G. (1991). Learning-related patterns of CA1 spike trains parallel stimulation parameters optimal for inducing hippocampal long-term potentiation. *Hippocampus, 1,* 181–192.

Pavlov, I. (1983/1928). *Twenty-five years of objective study of the higher nervous activity (behavior) of animals.* Dover, NH: Pinter.

Silva, A. J., Paylor, R., Wehner, J. M., & Tonegawa, S. (1992). Impaired spatial learning in a-calcium calmodulin kinase II mutant mice. *Science, 257,* 206–211.

Silva, A. J., Stevens, C. F., Tonegawa, S., & Wang, Y. (1992). Deficient hippocampal long-term potentiation in a-calcium-colmodulin kinase II mutant mice. *Science, 257,* 201–206.

Skelton, R. W., Scarth, A. S., Wilkie, D. M., Miller, J. J., & Phillips, A. G. (1987). Long-term increases in dentate granule cell responsibility accompany operant conditioning. *Journal of Neuroscience, 7*(10), 3081–3087.

Squire, L. R. (1992). Memory and the hippocampus: A synthesis from findings with rats, monkeys, and humans. *Psychological Review, 99*(2), 195–231.

Sutherland, R. W., & Rudy, J. W. (1989). Configural association theory: The role of the hippocampal formation in learning, memory and amnesia. *Psychobiology, 17,* 129–144.

Thompson, R. F. (1990). Neural mechanisms of classical conditioning in mammals. *Philosophical Transactions of the Royal Society of London. Ser. B: Biological Sciences, 329*(12153), 161–170.

Zola-Morgan, S. M., & Squire, L. R. (1990). The primate hippocampal formation: Evidence for a time-limited role in memory storage. *Science, 250,* 288–290.

P. F. CHAPMAN
University of Minnesota

ACTION POTENTIAL
ANIMAL MODELS
BRAIN INJURIES
CLASSICAL CONDITIONING
FORGETTING
HABITUATION
HYPOTHALAMUS
NEUROSURGERY
PSYCHOSURGERY
RETICULAR ACTIVATING SYSTEM
SPLIT BRAIN RESEARCH

NEURAL MECHANISMS OF SLEEP

Sleep in mammals consists of two very different states: NREM sleep and REM sleep. Each of these states is nearly as different from the other as both are distinct from wakefulness. Traditionally, three physiological measures are employed to define the sleep states (and determine wakefulness); they are the EEG (electroencephalogram), the EOG (electrooculogram), and the EMG (electromyogram).

NREM sleep is divided into four stages. REM sleep usually is not subdivided into stages; however, tonic and phasic aspects of REM sleep are often distinguished. Tonic REM sleep events are persistent (e.g., there is an activated EEG and striated [voluntary] muscle inhibition); phasic REM sleep events are intermittent (e.g., there are brief periods of rapid eye movements and muscle twitches).

An examination of the neural control of sleep (NREM and REM) involves: (a) an exploration of the control of the major physiological concomitants of these states (i.e., the EEG, the EOG, and the EMG); and (b) a description of the executive mechanisms that initiate and coordinate the physiological processes that constitute NREM and REM sleep. Consequently, the neural bases for the EEG, EOG, and EMG of NREM sleep and REM sleep will be described; an overview of the integrative mechanisms that sustain each of these sleep states is then presented.

THE ELECTROENCEPHALOGRAM (EEG)

The state of NREM sleep is easily distinguishable from both wakefulness and REM sleep by high-amplitude, slow EEG waves. These waves are dependent upon the activity of large neuronal populations that generate the temporal and spatial summation of synaptic potentials. In turn, these synaptic potentials are dependent upon internal thalamic processes that interact with neocortical mechanisms (Steriade & McCarley, 1990).

Within the thalamus are GABAergic cells that produce rhythmic inhibitory postsynaptic potentials (IPSPs) in thalamocortical neurons. This results in a complex pattern of thalamic discharge that generates excitatory postsynaptic potentials (EPSPs) in cortical cells whose activity, recorded as the EEG, contributes to the synchronized pattern of the EEG.

Another slow oscillation appears during later NREM sleep stages; it consists of one component that is dependent upon the thalamus and another that is intrinsically cortical in nature. The cortical component lies in the delta band (1–4 Hz). The other part of the slow oscillation is a stereotyped, clock-like component that is generated in the thalamus and that results from the hyperpolarization-activated interplay between two intrinsic currents of thalamocortical (relay) neurons.

The cortical EEG of REM sleep closely resembles the EEG of active wakefulness, and in some species they are virtually indistinguishable. (This is a surprising finding, considering that these two states are so dramatically different from a behavioral point of view.) During REM sleep, the high-amplitude EEG waves of NREM sleep are replaced by low-frequency oscillations consisting of fast rhythms of low amplitude. Thus, the EEG pattern of REM sleep consists of fast (20–50 Hz) oscillations that are present in intracortical, intrathalamic, and corticothalamic neuronal networks. These fast oscillations depend upon interactions between thalamic and cortical neurons.

THE ELECTROOCULOGRAM (EOG)

The term "rapid eye movement sleep" (REM sleep) highlights the rapid eye movement as one of the defining features of the physiology of this sleep state. These movements contrast with the occasional slow, rolling eye movements of NREM sleep.

The mechanisms that control the eye-movement pattern of sleep are unknown. However, it is expected that they involve those complex brain systems that mediate waking eye movements, although it is thought that lower centers, especially those involving the vestibular nuclei of the brainstem, may be the ones that are primarily activated during REM sleep. Neural activity in the pons is especially intense in REM sleep, and the eye movements of this state occur even when forebrain structures are lesioned. The pons is also the site controlling horizontal eye movements, which predominate during REM sleep.

During REM sleep, there is also a special type of activity in the pons, geniculate nucleus, and occipital cortex: the so-called PGO (ponto-geniculate occipital) waves. PGO waves are sharp field potentials that often appear in clusters of up to six waves. They are usually related closely to the time of occurrence of rapid eye movements. PGO waves are generated by cholinergic neurons in the peribrachial region, which project rostrally; they are inhibited by serotonergic neurons of the raphe system.

THE ELECTROMYOGRAM (EMG)

The EMG exhibits dramatic changes during the sleep states. The passage from wakefulness to sleep, in humans, is accompanied by a decrease in the contraction of muscle fibers, and consequently, a decrease in muscle tone (Chase & Morales, 1990). Atonia, or the lack of tone of certain somatic muscles, occurs during the state of REM sleep. In addition, from time to time during REM sleep, even though there is a suppression of the activity of motoneurons, there occurs phasic excitation of motoneurons, whose discharge results in myoclonic twitches and jerks. Paradoxically, during these events there is a concommitant increase in the suppression of the excitability of the motoneurons.

Postsynaptic inhibition that is mediated by the inhibitory neurotransmitter glycine is the principal, and probably sufficient, mechanism responsible for atonia of the somatic musculature during REM sleep. How, then, could there be twitches and jerks of the eyes and limbs during rapid eye movement periods? The answer is simple: Most rapid eye movement periods are accompanied not only by increased motoneuron inhibition, but also by strikingly potent motor excitatory drives, which take the form of depolarizing and spike potentials and impinge on motoneurons during REM sleep. These patterns of activation probably reflect descending excitatory activity emanating from supraspinal systems.

Thus, from the perspective of motoneurons, REM sleep can be characterized as a state abundant in the availability of strikingly potent patterns of postsynaptic inhibition and, during rapid eye movements, by enhanced excitation and enhanced inhibition.

THE CONTROL OF NREM AND REM STATES

NREM sleep is thought to be dependent on the activity of different structures in the basal forebrain and hypothalamus. There are also rich interconnections, many involving GABA and histaminergic systems, between hypothalamic areas and sites in the brain stem that are involved in the generation of NREM sleep. The region of the nucleus of the solitary tract (NTS) in the lower brainstem may also constitute a second center for the regulation of NREM sleep. However, on the balance there has been relatively little research dealing with this area, and the evidence for an NTS role in NREM sleep control is weaker than that for a basal forebrain region role.

Cholinergic neurons have an important role in the generation of REM sleep (Siegel, 1994). These neurons are located in the laterodorsal tegmental nucleus and the pedunculopontine nucleus of the pons. They project directly or indirectly to three regions important for REM sleep: the thalamus, a region involved in EEG activation during REM sleep; the pontine reticular formation, a region in and within the vicinity of the nucleus pontis oralis (NPO) where administration of cholinomimetic agents readily induce REM sleep; and the medulla, a region important in the production of muscle atonia during REM sleep.

NEW PERSPECTIVES

A critical structure that appears to lie at the crossroads of the pathways involved in the generation and/or maintenance of REM sleep is the nucleus pontis oralis (NPO), located in the rostral portion of the pontine reticular tegmentum (Chase & Morales, 1990). For example, studies of the NPO have shown that it is central to the phenomenon of reticular response-reversal (Chase & Morales, 1990). This is a phenomenon wherein stimulation of the NPO in the pontine reticular formation results in somatic reflex activation when an animal is awake, and yet, remarkably, the identical stimulus during REM sleep yields potent postsynaptic inhibition of the same somatic reflexes. It is hypothesized that a neuronal mechanism in the pons is responsible for switching the stimulus directive from somatomotor excitation to somatomotor inhibition, simply according to in which state the animal happens to be at the time that the stimulus is applied.

Recent studies have begun exploring the interactions between the classic reticular activating system via-à-vis its role in the promotion of wakefulness, and the REM sleep system, whose control mechanisms also appear to be located in the same general pontine region (i.e., in and/or in the vicinity of the NPO). The authors have suggested the existence of a neuronal switch that functions to change an animal's state between wakefulness and sleep (REM sleep); this switch is based on the hypothesis that GABAergic neurons suppress the activity of REM sleep neurons in the NPO, thus allowing wakefulness to occur (Xi, Morales, & Chase, 1999).

In support of this hypothesis, the pontine microinjection of the inhibitory neurotransmitter GABA and its agonist have been shown to induce prolonged periods of wakefulness in unanesthetized, chronic cats. Conversely, the application of bicuculline, a $GABA_A$ antagonist, results in the occurrence of episodes of REM sleep of long duration. It was therefore concluded that the pontine GABAergic system plays a critical role in the control of the activity of NPO neurons, which in turn are responsible for the generation of sleep (REM sleep in particular). Because sleep and wakefulness are mutually exclusive states, as are NREM and REM sleep, there must be a mechanism that initiates and/or suppresses each state for the others to take place; the authors hypothesize that a GABAergic switch may perform this function.

In summary, although there are literally thousands of unanswered questions regarding the neural mechanisms of sleep, some of the most interesting that will be addressed and hopefully answered in the 21st century will likely involve the switches and/or mechanisms that determine the occurrence of either sleep or wakefulness, NREM or REM sleep.

REFERENCES

Chase, M. H., & Morales, F. R. (1990). The atonia and myoclonia of active (REM) sleep. *Annual Review of Psychology, 41,* 557–584.

Siegel, J. M. (1994). Brainstem mechanisms generating REM sleep. In M. H. Kryger, T. Roth, & W. C. Dement (Eds.), *Principles and practice of sleep medicine* (pp. 125–144). Philadelphia: WB Saunders.

Steriade, M., & McCarley, R. W. (1990). *Brainstem control of wakefulness and sleep.* New York: Plenum.

Xi, M., Morales, F. R., & Chase, M. H. (1999). A GABAergic pontine reticular system is involved in the control of wakefulness and sleep [12 paragraphs]. *Sleep Research Online* [On-line serial], *2*(2). Available http://www.sro.org/1999/Xi/43/

F. R. MORALES

M. H. CHASE
University of California, Los Angeles

RAPID EYE MOVEMENT (REM) SLEEP
SLEEP
SLEEP CYCLE

NEURAL NETWORK MODELS

Models containing networks of neuron-like elements have become prominent in psychology, neuroscience, and cognitive science. Such models have also appeared under the titles "connectionism," "parallel distributed processing," and "spreading activation." In psychology, neural networks have been used to explain phenomena as diverse as word recognition, categorization, visual pattern perception, coordinated motor action, neurological disorders, clinical disorders, and even social interaction. Neural network models represent a dramatic departure from older theories that assume grammar-like manipulations of symbolic information (Gluck & Bower, 1988; Rumelhart & McClelland, 1986). The nongrammatic and nonsymbolic features of neural networks, however, have made them suitable for explaining more basic behavioral phenomena, such as classical conditioning, and their neural underpinnings. Thus, neural network models are helping to integrate research areas within psychology, and to integrate psychology with neuroscience (Gabriel & Moore, 1990; Quinlan, 1998).

As the name implies, neural networks have been inspired by the fine structure of the brain. Yet, most neural network models in psychology have been constrained only weakly by the known architecture and functioning of real brains. For example, dendritic branching, the variety of synaptic connections, and frequency encoding are usually treated in a highly simplified manner. Stripped of its surplus meaning, the neural network model in psychology is a type of quantitative model, subject to the conventional criteria for testing any model. In neuroscience, however, neural network models are becoming more faithful to the chemical, electrical, and structural features of the brain (e.g., Pennartz, 1997; Stettner, Lang, & Obermayer, 1998; Webster & Ungerleider, 1998; Weinberger et al., 1990).

BASED FEATURES OF NETWORK ELEMENTS

The elements of a neural network model can be described by two equations: an *activation rule* and a *learning rule*. The activation rule combines inputs to an element and generates an output, also called an activation level. The computations of a network entail the transmission of activation levels from one element to other elements. The learning rule alters the transmission of activation levels from

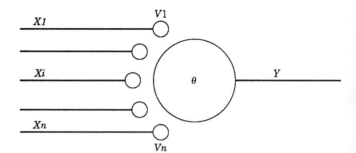

Figure 1. Threshold logic unit, in which Xi denotes input activation levels, Vi denotes connection weights, Q denotes the threshold value, and Y denotes the output activation level.

one element to another via variables called connection weights. Positive connection weights roughly duplicate the role of excitatory positive postsynaptic potentials (EPSPs) in real neurons, and negative connection weights capture the role of inhibitory postsynaptic potentials (IPSPs).

Activation Rules

Threshold logic unit   Activation rules originated in the work of McCulloch and Pitts (1943) concerning the ability of neurons to act as logic gates. Figure 1 depicts a generalized threshold logic unit. On the left side of the element are the input variables that are characterized as input activation levels (X_i) and their connection weights (V_i). Activation levels are often assumed to be binary ($X_i = 0, 1$), and the weights are often assumed to fall between -1 and $+1$. The total input level at any moment of time is the sum of the active input weights [$\Sigma(X_i V_i)$]. Like the input activations, the output of the unit is assumed to be binary ($Y = 0, 1$). Activation of the output is determined by a comparison of the total input level with a threshold value (Θ) according to the following formula:

$$Y = 1 \text{ if } \Sigma [X_i V_i] > \Theta, \text{ otherwise } Y = 0.$$

By manipulation of the connection weights and/or the threshold values, it is possible to produce common logic functions. For example, an AND gate can be constructed in the following fashion. Assume that an element has two inputs (X_1, X_2), each with a connection weight of .50 ($V_1 = .50$, $V_2 = .50$), and that the element's threshold is .75 ($\Theta = .75$). If only one of the inputs (X_1 or X_2) is active, the total input level will be only .50, which is less than the threshold value and hence too low to trigger an output. Hence, the value of Y would remain at 0. If, however, both inputs were active, the total input level would be 1.0, thus exceeding the threshold and thereby triggering the output ($Y = 1$). The same element can be converted to an OR gate by lowering the threshold to a value less than .50 or by raising the input weights to values greater than .75.

For a complete logic system, a NOT operator can be constructed using the unit shown in Figure 1 in the following fashion. First, assume that the X_1 input is permanently active and that its connection weight (V_1) is greater than the threshold value of .75, for example, $V_1 = 1$. Accordingly, the unit's output would normally be active ($Y = 1$). Second, assume that the connection weight for the other input has a large negative value, say, $V_2 = -1$. If the input

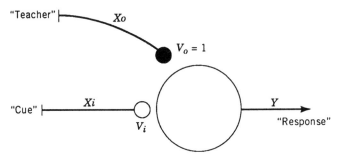

Figure 2. Hebbian adaptive unit, in which Xi denotes the cue input level, Vi denotes an adaptive connection weight, Xo denotes the teacher input level, Vo denotes the fixed connection weight, and Y denotes the response output level.

level for the second input were then activated ($X_2 = 1$), the sum of the two inputs would be zero [$\Sigma(X_i V_i) = 0$] and would fall below the threshold value, thus turning off the otherwise active output of the unit. Thus, by using a negative connection weight and mimicking an inhibitory synapse, the activation level for the second input would be inverted. That is, when $X_2 = 1$, then $Y = 0$.

Analog Intergrator Rules Whereas the threshold logic unit yields a binary output that corresponds to a single action potential, an analog integrator yields a graded output that corresponds to the frequency of action potentials over a few milliseconds. Analog integrators originated in an analysis of the firing frequency of retinal neurons in the horseshoe crab (Knight, 1972). In its basic form, a linear integrator produces a straight-line increase in activation level as a function of the intensity of the input stimulus. In a more generic form, integrator rules can produce S-shaped functions that relate activation level to input levels. If the slope is very steep, such functions closely approximate the all-or-nothing activation of the threshold logic unit (Anderson, 1995).

Learning Rules

Hebbian rules Learning rules for networks originated in ideas sketched by James (1892/1984) and Hebb (1949). In brief, they applied the ancient law of contiguity at a neural level; they contended that synaptic transmission would undergo a gain in efficiency whenever presynaptic activity was contiguous with postsynaptic activity. Figure 2 shows an example of a Hebbian element. This Hebbian element has two input connections. One input, here called the cue input (X_i), has no initial connection weight and thus is unable to trigger the element. The other input (X_o), commonly called a teacher input, has a fixed, large weight ($V_o = 1$) that is capable of triggering the element and producing the response output. If there are simultaneous inputs, then the cue input will provide the presynaptic activity (X_i) and the teacher input will induce postsynaptic activity (Y). In mathematical terms, the change in connection weight (ΔV_i) is represented as a product of the two levels of activity. This learning rule can be written as $\Delta V_i = c X_i Y$, where c is the learning rate ($0 < c < 1$) (Sutton & Barto, 1981).

Error correction rules While learning under the Hebbian rule depends strictly on the contiguity of activation levels, other rules as-

sume that learning depends on a mismatch between the cue's input weight and the teacher's input (Pennartz, 1997). An important example of an error correction rule is known variously as the delta rule (Rumelhart, Hinton, & Williams, 1986), the Rescorla-Wagner rule (Rescorla & Wagner, 1972), and the least-mean squares rule (Gluck & Bower, 1988). Where there are multiple, simultaneous cue inputs, this rule can be written as $\Delta V_i = c X_i [X_o V_o - \Sigma - (X_i V_i)]$. When the total input ($\Sigma [X_i V_i]$) differs greatly from the activation induced by the teacher input [$X_o V_o$], then the connection weight of each eligible input (V_i) will change dramatically. Conversely, when the difference is small, the change will be small.

An error-correction rule is more complex than a Hebbian rule but has three key advantages in simulating associative learning:

1. *Self-limiting increments.* Whereas a Hebbian rule produces connection weights that grow linearly, the error-correction rule is self limiting. This feature reproduces the negative acceleration seen in most learning curves.

2. *Reversibility.* The contiguity rule produces only increments in learning, but an error-correction rule produces both increments and decrements. Specifically, in a Hebbian rule, the absence of the teacher input (X_o) precludes any increments but has no decremental effect. However, for an error-correction rule, the absence of the teacher input means that the difference term becomes negative [$0 - \Sigma(X_i V_i)$], thus producing a decrement in the connection weight ($\Delta V_i < 0$). In this way, an error-correction rule can track changes in the predictive value of a cue for the teacher input. Under certain circumstances, this rule can even yield negative connection weights, thus capturing the behavioral phenomena of inhibitory learning.

3. *Selectivity and configural processing.* Where there are multiple cues, a Hebbian rule is applied independently to each input. In contrast, an error correction rule presupposes that the change in associative strength for each input depends on the net error based on all the active inputs. For example, if several active inputs each had a modest positive weight, their sum would be substantial and the difference term [$X_o V_o - \Sigma(X_i V_i)$] would be near zero. This near-zero value would prevent the connection weight of any new input from gaining strength. In this way, redundant cues would effectively be ignored; thus, an error correction rule captures a key feature of selective attention. By the same token, where no one cue has a preexisting advantage, the total connection weight will be spread across the concurrent cues. In this way, an element can be tuned so that it will be triggered by only a certain configuration of inputs rather than by any single input.

BASIC ARCHITECTURES OF NETWORKS

Although the individual elements provide the building blocks for a neural network, the architecture of their interconnections determines many of the emergent features of a network. There are two basic architectures: networks that contain multiple layers of elements, and networks that feed their outputs back as inputs to the network.

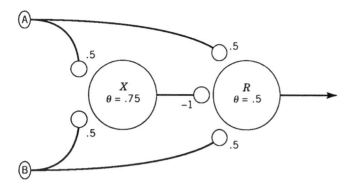

Figure 3. A layered network configured to obey the XOR rule.

Layered Networks

Figure 3 shows an example of a simple layered network. The network has two inputs (A, B), each of which project to two elements (H, R). The H element that intervenes between the input events and the output element is known as a hidden element. This small network contains five modifiable connections, namely, A-H, A-R, B-H, B-R, and H-R.

Layered networks have been proven crucial in resolving issues of stimulus representation and concept formation that have been intractable to conventional psychological theories and to single-layered network models. In particular, layered networks provide a basis for learning arbitrary mappings from stimulus input patterns to response output patterns. The key issue has been nonlinear mappings. In such mappings, the desired response to a combination of inputs is not an additive function of the responses to the separate inputs. For example, the simplest nonlinear mapping is the exclusive-OR (XOR) problem. The solution to the XOR problem requires a response to each of two inputs presented separately but not to their joint occurrence (Rumelhart, Hinton, & Williams, 1986). For example, many people show XOR-behavior in their taste preferences. A person may like potatoes and like licorice but refuse to eat licorice-flavored potatoes. If the separate stimulus-response mappings were strictly additive, licorice-flavored potatoes would be eaten with gusto.

It is possible to convert a nonlinear problem into a linear problem by postulating a special input for each combination of the basic stimulus inputs (Gluck & Bower, 1988; Rescorla & Wagner, 1972). However, where there is more than a handful of inputs, this tactic creates an explosion of special inputs. A more general solution is a learning mechanism that forms specialized encodings of combined inputs as the need arises. Layered networks have this ability. In brief, establishment of appropriate connection weights from the stimulus inputs to the hidden elements yields units that are specialized for a particular combination of inputs. The connections between the hidden elements and the output elements provide the mapping of the specialized units to the appropriate response outputs.

The small network shown in Figure 3 is configured to display XOR behavior. In this configuration, the A input by itself cannot trigger the H element, because the A-H connection weight is less than the threshold of H, but the A input can trigger the R element, because its threshold is just low enough for the A-R connection to be effective. Likewise, the B input can trigger only the R unit. Thus, the separate A and B inputs can each trigger the output of the network. However, as required by the XOR rule, the A and B inputs together will suppress an output. This is because the summed connection weights of the A and B inputs will trigger the H unit, and the H unit has a large negative connection with the R element. Consequently, the joint occurrence of the A and B inputs cancels their individual positive connections with the R element.

Autoassociative Networks

Figure 4 shows an example of a small autoassociative network. Each of five elements (A, B, C, D, E) receives one external input (a, b, c, d, e). These external inputs have fixed connections that are each capable of triggering an output from their respective elements. Furthermore, each element receives five recurrent inputs, one from each element's output including its own. For example, as shown in Figure 4, the C element has five connections, designated as Ac, Bc, Cc, Dc, and Ec. These connections are modifiable and operate according to the same learning rules as any other network. In brief, whenever an output and an input are both active, a positive connection weight can grow at their intersection.

Among other things, autoassociative networks can perform three functions that are of particular interest in psychology:

1. *Pattern completion.* If a set of interconnections have been well established in an autoassociative network, then only a portion of the original inputs can retrieve the entire set of outputs. For example, suppose that, for the network in Figure 4, the inputs a and e had been repeatedly presented. As a consequence, four interconnections would be established, namely Aa, Ae, Ea, and Ee, which are located in the four corners of the matrix of intersections. Subsequently, the a input by itself would trigger both the A and E outputs via the Aa and Ae connections. Likewise, the e input would trigger both outputs via the Ea and Ee connections.

2. *Noise tolerance.* Autoassociative networks can tolerate substantial noise (i.e., variation in the set of inputs). Provided that successive sets of inputs are not entirely random, the pattern of the interconnections will reflect any underlying prototypic set, even if that particular set is never presented to the network. Thus, by the same mechanism as seen in pattern completion, a new set of inputs that is similar to the prototypic set will tend to retrieve the prototypic pattern. This feature of autoassociative networks allows them to be used as models for phenomena ranging from stimulus generalization to pattern recognition to categorization.

3. *Superimposed storage.* Autoassociative networks can store a large number of input sets. This feature allows for the retrieval of both the prototypic pattern and specific, frequent exemplars. A network can also store multiple prototypic patterns and their common exemplars. For example, McClelland and Rumelhart (1985) showed that a network with 24 units and 552 potential interconnections could store and reliably retrieve three different prototypical patterns, each based on 50 different exemplars. They also showed that the pattern for at least one particular exemplar could also be retrieved when the net-

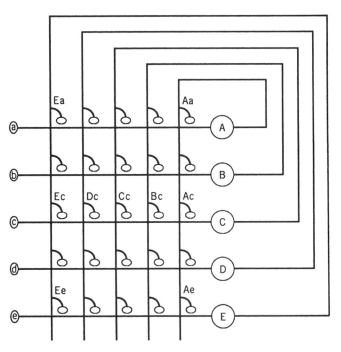

Figure 4. An autoassociative.

work was presented with a subset of inputs corresponding to the exemplar's name tag. In a similar fashion, Kohonen (1984) demonstrated that a network containing 3,024 elements could store and retrieve the digitized photographs of 100 different faces in a reasonably recognizable form. However, for exact reconstruction of an input pattern, a simple associative network has severe limits (Anderson, 1995).

ISSUES IN MODEL BUILDING

Researchers like models that are simple to understand, but rich enough to yield surprising, testable predictions. Although the basic operations of neural networks are simple, the multiplication of these operations in large networks requires considerable computer power to discern the overall behavior of the system. Even then, the resulting patterns of connection weights usually offer little insight. To prevent neural network modelling from becoming an exercise in curve-fitting, the following strategies have been used to turn neural networks into useful heuristic devices.

Single-Unit Models

One of the theoretical breakthroughs that reinvigorated the use of neural networks in the early 1980s was a landmark paper by Sutton and Barto (1981). Their paper focused on the importance of each unit's learning rule in the operation of networks. Among other things, Sutton and Barto showed that error-correction rules had widespread applicability. While their insight has been influential in the implementation of error-correction rules in large networks, Sutton and Barto were primarily concerned with the functioning of single elements on a moment-by-moment basis.

Sutton and Barto's work provided the basis for understanding the acquisition and timing of responses that anticipate their outcome, and, more generally, the mechanism of expectancy, particularly in classical conditioning. In turn, this research has helped in understanding the fine architecture and functioning of the neural pathways that subserve classical conditioning. For example, there are now several neural-level models aimed at explaining how an error-correction rule would be implemented in the cerebellum (Buonomano & Mauk, 1994; Moore & Desmond, 1992). As a consequence, otherwise mysterious projections from the efferent pathways for a conditioned response back to the afferent pathways for an unconditioned stimulus have been recognized as one possible neural basis for computing the all-important difference term in error-correction rules (e.g., Rosenfield & Moore, 1995; Sears & Steinmetz, 1990).

Minimalist Models

Although networks containing hundreds or thousands of elements seem to be required to explain cognitive activity or the neural activity of important brain structures, insights into these phenomena have been achieved by the use of networks containing a handful of elements. For example, there are now several models aimed at understanding the functioning of the hippocampus in learning, including lesion effects (Myers, Ermita, Hasselmo, & Gluck, 1998; Rolls, 1996). At the extreme, the simplest layered network containing only two elements has helped to explain how learning is protected during extinction training so that a completely-extinguished response can be rapidly reacquired when reinforced training is reinstated (Kehoe, 1988).

Superpower

A major feature of neural networks is their large number of free parameters. Each element possesses at least one parameter for its activation rule and at least one parameter for its learning rule. Moreover, each connection weight is also a free parameter. All these variable quantities make neural networks, especially layered networks, very powerful search engines, capable of fitting almost any given set of data (Massaro, 1988). This feature of neural networks has been used to advantage as a tool for data analysis similar to the more familiar techniques of multiple regression and factor analysis. For example, neural networks have been applied to the classification of action potentials (Stitt, Gaumond, Frazier, & Hanson, 1998), EEG activity (Gaetz, Weinberg, Rzempoluck, & Jantzen, 1998), abstract word meanings (Weimar-Hastings, 1998), the content of student essays (McKnight & Walberg, 1998), and personnel suitable for flight training (Griffin, 1998).

At the same time, the large number of free parameters has made any particular network difficult to test in experimentation. In order to test large network models, two tactics have been used by researchers. First, the scope of a particular model can be tested by determining whether a single set of parameter values can be used to fit several distinct sets of data. Second, models can be tested on a within-subjects basis by determining whether the parameters fitted for one phase of performance can predict performance in a later phase of the study.

APPRAISAL

In neuroscience, there has been a long-standing synergy between empirical research and neural network modelling. For example, the neuroanatomy of retinal projections to the superior colliculus influenced Pitts and McCulloch's (1947) work concerning the computational capabilities of networks of simple elements. Models that attempt to identify the key anatomical relationships and the flow of activity in real neural systems have remained a prominent feature in neuroscience (e.g., T'oth & Crunelli, 1998; Van Essen, Anderson, & Fellerman, 1992). Conversely, abstract neural network models are increasingly contributing to understanding how pathways in structures such as the cerebellum and hippocampus subserve learning and memory. Similarly, applications of abstract neural networks to understanding patterns of brain activity have begun to appear (Sanger, 1998; Stettner et al., 1998). Finally, neural networks have also been used to tackle the mind-body problem, specifically the emergence of consciousness from brain activity (Rolls, 1997; Taylor, 1998).

Within psychology, the growth of neural network modelling has been fueled by the development of error-correction learning rules and a recognition of the potential for layered architectures to acquire any arbitrary mapping of inputs to outputs. Neural network models have found natural homes in theories of perception (Chey, Grossberg, & Mingolla, 1998; Douglas, Phillips, & Sekuler, 1986; Kim & Francis, 1998; Rosenblatt, 1958) and conditioning (e.g., Commons, Grossberg, & Staddon, 1991; Klopf, Morgan, & Weaver, 1993; Sutton & Barto, 1981). Despite the divergence of neural network models from older theories that assume grammar-like manipulations of symbolic information, neural network models have become widespread in cognitive psychology (Bullinaria, 1997; Grainger & Jacobs, 1998; Jones, Wills, & McLaren, 1998). Moreover, they have begun to appear in other major areas of research, including clinical psychology (Kehoe & Macrae, 1997; Tryon, 1998) and social psychology (Read & Miller, 1998; Smith & DeCoster, 1998).

REFERENCES

Anderson, J. A. (1995). *An introduction to neural networks.* Cambridge, MA: MIT Press.

Bullinaria, J. A. (1997). Modeling reading, spelling, and past tense learning with artificial neural networks. *Brain and Language, 59,* 236–266.

Buonomano, D. V., & Mauk, M. D. (1994). Neural network model of the cerebellum: Temporal discrimination and the timing of motor responses. *Neural Computation, 6,* 38–55.

Chey, J., Grossberg, S., & Mingolla, E. (1998). Neural dynamics of motion processing and speed discrimination. *Vision Research, 38,* 2769–2786.

Commons, M. L., Grossberg, S., & Staddon, J. E. R. (1991). *Neural network models of conditioning and action.* Hillsdale, NJ: Erlbaum.

Douglas, W., Phillips, G., & Sekuler, R. (1986). Hysteresis in the perception of motion direction as evidence for neural cooperativity. *Nature, 324,* 253–255.

Gabriel, M., & Moore, J. W. (Eds.). (1990). *Learning and computational neuroscience: Foundations of adaptive networks.* Cambridge, MA: MIT Press.

Gaetz, M., Weinberg, H., Rzempoluck, E., & Jantzen, K. J. (1998). Neural network classification and correlation analysis of EEG and MEG activity accompanying spontaneous reversals of the Necker cube. *Cognitive Brain Research, 6,* 335–346.

Gluck, M. A., & Bower, G. H. (1988). Evaluating an adaptive network model of human learning. *Journal of Memory and Language, 27,* 166–195.

Grainger, J., & Jacobs, A. M. (Eds.). (1998). *Localist connectionist approaches to human cognition.* Mahwah, NJ: Erlbaum.

Griffin, G. R. (1998). Predicting naval aviator flight training performance using multiple regression and an artificial neural network. *International Journal of Aviation Psychology, 8,* 121–135.

Hebb, D. O. (1949). *The organization of behavior.* New York: Wiley.

James, W. (1984). *Briefer psychology.* Cambridge, MA: Harvard University Press. (Original work published 1892)

Jones, F. W., Wills, A. J., & McLaren, I. P. (1998). Perceptual categorization: Connectionist modelling and decision rules. *The Quarterly Journal of Experimental Psychology, 51B,* 33–58.

Kehoe, E. J. (1988). A layered network model of associative learning: Learning-to-learn and configuration. *Psychological Review, 95,* 411–433.

Kehoe, E. J., & Macrae, M. (1997). Savings in animal learning: Implications for relapse and maintenance after therapy. *Behavior Therapy, 28,* 141–155.

Kim, H., & Francis, G. (1998). A computational and perceptual account of motion lines. *Perception, 27,* 785–797.

Klopf, A. H., Morgan, J. S., & Weaver, S. E. (1993). Hierarchical network of control systems that learn: Modeling nervous system function during classical and instrumental conditioning. *Adaptive Behavior, 1,* 263–319.

Knight, B. (1972). Dynamics of encoding in a population of neurons. *Journal of General Physiology, 59,* 734–766.

Kohonen, T. (1984). *Self-organization and associative memory.* Berlin: Springer-Verlag.

Massaro, D. W. (1988). Some criticisms of connectionist models of human performance. *Journal of Memory and Language, 27,* 213–234.

McClelland, J. L., & Rumelhart, D. E. (1985). Distributed memory and the representation of general and specific information. *Journal of Experimental Psychology: General, 114,* 159–188.

McCulloch, W. S., & Pitts, W. (1943). A logical calculus of the ideas immanent in nervous activity. *Bulletin of Mathematical Biophysics, 5,* 115–133.

McKnight, K. S., & Walberg, H. J. (1998). Neural network analysis of student essays. *Journal of Research and Development in Education, 32,* 26–31.

Moore, J. W., & Desmond, J. E. (1992). A cerebellar neural network implementation of a temporally adaptive conditioned response. In I. Gormezano (Ed.), *Learning and memory: The biological substrates* (pp. 347–368). Hillsdale, NJ: Erlbaum.

Myers, C. E., Ermita, B. R., Hasselmo, M., & Gluck, M. (1998). Further implications of a computational model of septohippocampal cholinergic modulation in eyeblink conditioning. *Psychobiology, 26,* 1–20.

Pennartz, C. M. (1997). Reinforcement learning by Hebbian synapses with adaptive thresholds. *Neuroscience, 81,* 303–319.

Pitts, W., & McCulloch, W. S. (1947). How we know universals: The perception of auditory and visual forms. *Bulletin of Mathematical Biophysics, 9,* 127–147.

Quinlan, P. T. (1998). Structual change and development in real and artificial neural networks. *Neural Networks, 11,* 577–599.

Read, S. J., & Miller, L. C. (Eds.). (1998). *Connectionist models of social reasoning and social behavior.* Mahwah, NJ: Erlbaum.

Rescorla, R. A., & Wagner, A. R. (1972). A theory of Pavlovian conditioning: Variations in the effectiveness of reinforcement and nonreinforcement. In A. H. Black & W. F. Prokasy (Eds.), *Classical conditioning II* (pp. 64–99). New York: Appleton-Century-Crofts.

Rolls, E. T. (1996). A theory of hippocampal function in memory. *Hippocampus, 6,* 601–620.

Rolls, E. T. (1997). Consciousness in neural networks? *Neural Networks, 10,* 1227–1240.

Rosenblatt, F. (1958). The perceptron: A probabilistic model for information storage and organization in the brain. *Psychological Review, 65,* 386–408.

Rosenfield, M. E., & Moore, J. W. (1995). Connections in cerebellar cortex (Larsell's HVI) in the rabbit: A WGA-HRP study with implications for classical eyeblink conditioning. *Behavioural Neuroscience, 109,* 1106–1118.

Rumelhart, D. E., Hinton, G. E., & Williams, R. J. (1986). Learning internal representations by error propagation. In D. E. Rumelhart et al. (Eds.), *Parallel distributed processing: Explorations in the microstructures of cognition* (pp. 318–362). Cambridge, MA: MIT Press.

Rumelhart, D. E., & McClelland, J. L. (Eds.). (1986). *Parallel distributed processing: Vol. 1. Foundations.* Cambridge, MA: MIT Press.

Sanger, T. D. (1998). Probability density methods for smooth function approximation and learning in populations of tuned spiking neurons. *Neural Computation, 106,* 1567–1586.

Sears, L. L., & Steinmetz, J. E. (1990). Acquisition of classical conditioned-related activity in the hippocampus is affected by lesions of the cerebellar interpositus nucleus. *Behavioral Neuroscience, 104,* 681–692.

Smith, E. R., & DeCoster, J. (1998). Knowledge acquisition, accessibility, and use in person perception and stereotyping: Simulation with a recurrent connectionist network. *Journal of Personality and Social Psychology, 74,* 21–35.

Stettner, M., Lang, E. W., & Obermayer, K. (1998). Unspecific long-term potentiation can evoke functional segregation in a model of area 17. *Neuroreport: An International Journal for the Rapid Communication of Research in Neuroscience, 9,* 2697–2702.

Stitt, J. P., Gaumond, R. P., Frazier, J. L., & Hanson, F. E. (1998). Action potential classifiers: A functional comparison of template matching, principal components analysis, and an artificial neural network. *Chemical Senses, 23,* 531–539.

Sutton, R. S., & Barto, A. G. (1981). Toward a modern theory of adaptive networks: Expectation and prediction. *Psychological Review, 88,* 135–171.

T'oth, T. I., & Crunelli, V. (1998). Effects of tapering geometry and inhomogeneous ion channel distributions in a neuron model. *Neuroscience, 84,* 1223–1232.

Taylor, J. G. (1998). Cortical activity and the explanatory gap. *Consciousness and Cognition: An International Journal, 7,* 109–148.

Tryon, W. W. (1998). A neural network explanation of posttraumatic stress disorder. *Journal of Anxiety Disorders, 12,* 373–385.

Van Essen, D. C., Anderson, C. H., & Fellerman, D. J. (1992). Information processing in the primate visual system: An integrated systems perspective. *Science, 225,* 419–423.

Webster, M. J., & Ungerleider, L. G. (1998). Neuroanatomy of visual attention. In R. Parasuraman (Ed.), *The attentive brain* (pp. 19–34). Cambridge, MA: MIT Press.

Weimar-Hastings, K. (1998). Abstract noun classification: Using a neural network to match word context and word meaning. *Behavior Research Methods, Instrumentation, and Computers, 30,* 264–271.

Weinberger, N. M., Ashe, J. H., Metherate, R., McKenna, T. M., Diamond, D. M., Bakin, J. S., Lennartz, R. C., & Cassady, J. M. (1990). Neural adaptive information processing: A preliminary model of receptive-field plasticity in auditory cortex during Pavlovian conditioning. In M. Gabriel & J. W. Moore (Eds.), *Learning and computational neuroscience: Foundations of adaptive networks* (pp. 91–138). Cambridge, MA: MIT Press.

E. J. KEHOE
University of New South Wales

CONNECTIONISM
LEARNING
MEMORY
MODELS
NEURAL MECHANISMS OF LEARNING
NEURAL NETWORKS
PARALLEL DISTRIBUTED PROCESSING
SPREADING ACTIVATION

NEUROCHEMISTRY

A chemical approach to understanding the nervous system had its origins in the late 19th century. Early neurochemists found that mammalian brains contained large amounts of fatty substances (lipids), many of which were found to be unique to the nervous system. The human brain contains about 10% lipids, 10% protein, and 78% water, with the remaining 2% represented by DNA, RNA, electrolytes, and other small molecules. The gray matter contains mainly neuronal cell bodies and astroglia, generally regarded as support cells that are often interposed between cerebral blood vessels and neurons. White matter contains nerve axons, which are ensheathed in multilayers of lipid-rich membranes (myelin) produced by oligodendroglia. Brain lipids contain long, highly unsaturated fatty acids incorporated into phospholipids, as well as glycolipids, and little or no free cholesterol or triglyceride (conventional dietary fat, also found in adipose tissue).

The human brain weighs about 1,400 grams, or 2% of total body weight. Its pale appearance belies the fact that about 20% of the total cardiac output is required to supply it with glucose and oxygen, and to remove metabolic waste, principally carbon dioxide. The brain is efficient in this process and thus accounts for an even greater portion of the total resting basal metabolic rate, about 25%. Each molecule of glucose requires 6 molecules of oxygen for its oxidation, yielding 6 molecules of carbon dioxide. In the process, chemical energy for the working of the brain is generated and stored in the form of 38 molecules of ATP (adenosine triphosphate).

By injecting carbon-14-labeled 2-deoxyglucose, a nonmetabolized glucose analogue, it can be demonstrated that brain regions in animals can be selectively activated behaviorally (e.g., by visual stimulation), evidenced by increased glucose utilization. Regional cerebral blood flow (rCBF) is also increased. These approaches have been adapted for noninvasive studies in human subjects, employing positron emitting tracers such as fluorine-18 and positron emission tomography (PET). Changes in rCBF can also be studied in the absence of radioactivity by means of functional magnetic resonance imaging (fMRI) by the BOLD (blood oxygen level dependent) imaging method.

The brain and spinal cord are separated from the rest of the body by the "blood-brain barrier" (BBB). This term refers to the observation that while most small molecules readily diffuse from the blood into body organs, if they bear an ionic charge or are hydrophilic, they are excluded from the central nervous system, unless a special transport system exists, such as for glucose, vitamins, and essential amino and fatty acids. While this exclusion undoubtedly protects the brain, it necessitates molecular legerdemain and ingenuity in designing neuropharmacological agents.

The high energy needs of the adult brain reflect the enormous volume of information it handles at great speed: sensory input, central processing, storage and retrieval, and output of electrically and chemically coded messages. There is considerable evidence that this is all accomplished by neurons in the form of coded messages in the form of electrical impulses (neural conduction) and chemical messengers (synaptic transmission), whereby neurons communicate with one another. In neurotransmission, action potentials, originating in dendrites or in the neuronal cell body, generally move as a rapid depolarization wave down the axon to the presynaptic region. The electrical potential is generated by the efflux of neuronal potassium and influx of sodium. Ultimately, the ionically based electrical gradients must be regenerated by neuronal sodium extrusion and potassium influx. The chemical work to restore the gradient requires the enzyme Na$^+$ K$^+$ATPase, which cleaves ATP in the process. While the direction of information flow in neurons is unidirectional—from dendrite to cell body to axon—the supply of critical materials within the neuron is centrifugal: from the cell body out to the farthest reaches of its dendrites and axons. This is important because transcription and translation take place in the cell body, and cytoskeletal elements (microtubules, neurofilaments, actin, and so on) and organelles (mitochondria, vesicles, and so on) migrate centrifugally to the cell extremities via anterograde axonal transport, under the influence of "molecular motor" proteins, the kinesins. There is also a centripetal, or retrograde, flow process mediated by a dynein motor and thought to transmit messages from the synapse to the nucleus; for example, to make more neurotransmitters or to initiate the repair of a damaged nerve.

At the synapse, nerves communicate by a rapid chemically mediated process. The arrival of the axonal depolarization wave at the presynaptic nerve ending causes the release of a neurotransmitter, a chemical messenger molecule unique to the neuron, which traverses the synaptic cleft and binds to a specific receptor on the postsynaptic membrane of the postsynaptic neuron. Examples of known neurotransmitters are acetylcholine, glutamate, gamma-aminobutyric acid, glycine, norepinephrine, dopamine, and serotonin. They are released in packets, by the fusion of synaptic vesicles with the presynaptic membrane in a process of exocytosis, releasing the neurotransmitters into the synaptic cleft. The empty vesicles reform by a process of endocytosis and are recycled. The steps leading from the depolarization wave to presynaptic neurotransmitter release involve many specialized proteins. A number of naturally occurring toxic agents, such as black widow spider venom and botulinum toxin, exert their action by disrupting the presynaptic synaptic vesicle cycle.

The cellular process that completes the process of synaptic transmission is termed signal transduction. The released neurotransmitter serves as a ligand that binds to a highly specific membrane-spanning protein receptor molecule, the conformation of which is altered when its receptor site is occupied, usually by a guanine nucleotide binding protein (G-protein), which is coupled to the activation or block of an intracellular second messenger system. The most prominent second messenger systems are mediated by the formation of cAMP (adenosine 3′, 5′-cyclic monophosphate) or by the cleavage of the lipid phosphatidylinositol bisphosphate into inositol trisphosphate and diacylglycerol. These various second messenger molecules increase intracellular calcium, and activate various kinase cascades and nuclear transcription factors that lead to the final step in the original neuronal signal, such as continuation of the initial presynaptic depolarization signal, hyperpolarization, secretion, contraction, or induction of mRNA formation. It should be noted that the neurotransmitter itself does not enter the post-synaptic cell and must be removed from the synaptic cleft quickly. This removal is the "off" signal in signal transduction and can be accomplished by neurotransmitter metabolism or uptake by astroglia or by presynaptic reuptake. The entire process of synaptic transmission onset and termination can occur in a few milliseconds. The actions of neuroactive drugs, including stimulants, sedatives, anxiolytics, antipsychotic agents, as well as illicit addictive substances, can be traced to one or more steps in pre- or postsynaptic transmission.

Neurochemical studies on memory formation in a number of invertebrate and vertebrate species have led to the conclusion that long-term, but not short-term, memory formation requires ongoing protein synthesis. Such conclusions, initially based on the effects of antibiotic blocking agents, have been further documented by genetic mutant, transgenic, and "knockout" studies, primarily in fruit flies and in mice. Our improved understanding of neuroscience at the molecular level has led to a better understanding of drug action and the rational design of new ones. For example, administration of DOPA, a precursor of dopamine that can penetrate the BBB, alleviates the symptoms of Parkinson's disease resulting from a dopamine deficiency. Inhibitors of acetylcholinesterase address a known deficit in acetylcholine in Alzheimer's disease. By blocking the presynaptic reuptake of serotonin, fluoxetine relieves depression. An inborn error that has resulted in mental retardation, phenylketonuria (PKU) results from a defect in the ability of the liver to convert the amino acid phenylalanine to tyrosine. It can be treated successfully by a diet low in phenylalanine. Hundreds of genetic defects have been identified in recent years, and in many instances, the biochemical phenotypes, such as a defective protein, have been identified as well, an important next step in the eventual discovery of effective therapeutic strategies.

SUGGESTED READING

Cooper, J. R., Bloom, F. E., & Roth, R. H. (1996). *The Biochemical Basis of Neuropsychopharmacology,* 7th ed. New York: Oxford University Press.

Siegel, G. J., Agranoff, B. W., Albers, R. W., Fisher, S. K., & Uhler, M. D. (Eds.). (1999). *Basic Neurochemistry,* 6th ed. New York: Lippincott-Raven.

B. W. AGRANOFF
University of Michigan

BRAIN
CENTRAL NERVOUS SYSTEM
ENDORPHINS/ENKEPHALINS
PSYCHOPHARMACOLOGY

NEUROETHOLOGY

Neuroethology is the study of the neural basis of behavior, or how a certain coordinated pattern of movements (behavior) is planned and produced in response to a key stimulus by the integrated activity of different parts of the nervous system. The term *neuroethology* first came into use in the 1960s. This field emerged out of traditional ethology, or the study of animal behavior in a natural setting, when ethologists in collaboration with physiologists and anatomists began to investigate the relations between brain structure and functions and observed behaviors. Aims and features of neuroethology have been broadly discussed (Ewert, 1980; Ingle,

1985; Spiro & White, 1998) pointing to the multidisciplinary and comparative nature of neuroethological studies. Indeed, to study the structure and function of an animal's nervous system in relation to a species-typical behavior, different approaches are necessary and may include participation of disciplines such as ethology, neuroanatomy, neurophysiology, neuropharmacology, neuroendocrinology, and neuropsychology. In addition, the comparative approach helps identify neural circuits that may represent basic principles of organization for the neural correlates of behavior.

THE NEUROETHOLOGICAL APPROACH

It is known from ethology that species-specific, adaptive behaviors are often elicited by key stimuli in the animal's environment that release a stereotyped behavioral response (fixed action pattern) when the internal or motivational state of the animal is appropriate. This is supposed to be an innate program and it is known as "innate releasing mechanism," although strong influences of learning have been recognized in behavioral responses. According to Tinbergen (1951), one can identify at least seven different levels of investigation for a comprehensive analysis of the neural bases of behavior. These are 1), identification of the receptors and of the sensory processes for identification of key stimuli in the animal's environment; 2), study of the neuronal mechanisms for the localization of key stimuli; 3), elucidation of processes for the acquisition, retention, and recall of sensory information; 4), investigation of the neural correlates of motivational states; 5), experimental analysis of how sensory afferent information is processed to provide an organized motor output (analysis of the sensory-motor interface); 6), identification of the neural circuits providing coordinated motor patterns; and 7), analysis of the ontogenesis and maturation of the structure and of the functional properties of neural elements involved in such processes.

The key stimulus is likely to be detected by a population of specialized sensory neurons which eventually lead to the activation of appropriate populations of motor neurons whose function results in a stereotyped behavioral output. In general, sensory systems are characterized by both anatomical and functional specializations for the detection and localization of the key stimuli (Capranica, 1983). In addition, central sensory pathways, at least in vertebrates, are organized in a hierarchical fashion so that key stimuli can be "extracted" through a series of increasing levels of analysis. In the brain, sensory systems are generally organized in the form of topographic maps representing the animal's sensory space (for instance, visual maps, somatosensory maps, and so on). On the other hand, motor systems are also topographically organized as maps representing the animal's body plan. Therefore, the sensory-motor interface, allowing the transfer of sensory information from the key stimulus to motor areas of the brain, includes brain mechanisms for communication between sensory and motor maps (Scheich, 1983). The coordinated activity of motor neurons resulting in the behavioral output (fixed action pattern) is likely to be determined genetically and stored in neural motor networks (Ewert, 1980). Finally, the flow of information from the processing of key stimuli to the motor organization of the behavioral output is modulated by the activity of neural structures which are responsible for the animal's motivational state. For instance, hypothalamic nuclei are known to modulate aggressive (Anderson & Silver, 1998) or reproductive behaviors (Adler, 1983).

Classical studies in neuroethology have been devoted to the understanding of brain-behavior relationships in a variety of experimental animals that are highly specialized in specific behaviors. These include, for instance, electrolocation (fish; Heiligenberg, 1991), echolocation (bats; Simmons, 1989), sound localization (owls; Knudsen, 1987), vocal learning (songbirds; Bottjer & Johnson, 1997), navigation and spatial learning (homing pigeons; Casini, Fontanesi, Bingman, Jones, Gagliardo, Ioale, & Bagnoli, 1997), and prey-catching behavior (toads; Ewert, 1997).

GENETIC APPROACHES IN NEUROETHOLOGY

The genetic approach may help neuroethological research, especially in organisms such as *Drosophila* that constitute classic experimental models for genetic manipulations (Heisenberg, 1997). Indeed, identified genetic variants may reveal new properties of neurons and can provide useful tools for interpretation of neuronal circuitries and their roles in complex behavioral systems.

DEVELOPMENTAL NEUROETHOLOGY

In recent years, the term *developmental neuroethology* has gained a distinctive identity in defining the science which is specifically devoted to investigating the ontogeny of naturally occurring behaviors in terms of underlying neural mechanisms (Stehouwer, 1992). Issues in developmental neuroethology include, for instance, the roles played by hormones in the ontogeny of neural circuits subserving species-specific behaviors, transient appearance of neural circuits of behavioral relevance that are not retained in mature animals, organization of behavioral sequences during ontogeny, neural plasticity, and learning in behavioral ontogeny.

COMPUTATIONAL NEUROETHOLOGY

Adaptive behavior is classically regarded as the result of, mainly, the integrated activity of neural circuits. However, recent investigations strongly suggest that adaptive behavior does not depend solely on brain activity, but instead requires a continuous feedback between the nervous system, the body, and the environment. To understand these interactions, a new methodology called computational neuroethology has begun to be employed (Chiel & Beer, 1997). It is based on creating joint models of the relevant parts of an animal's nervous system, body, and environment. Using these models, one can study the contributions of the components to adaptive behavior and the new phenomena that may emerge from their interactions.

REFERENCES

Adler, N. T. (1983). The neuroethology of reproduction. In *Advances in vertebrate neuroethology,* J. P. Ewert, R. R. Capranica, & D. J. Ingle (eds.), pp. 1033–1065. New York: Plenum.

Anderson, K., & Silver, J. M. (1998). Modulation of anger and aggression. *Seminars in Clinical Neuropsychiatry, 3,* 232–242.

Bottjer, S. W., & Johnson, F. (1997). Circuits, hormones, and learning: Vocal behavior in songbirds. *Journal of Neurobiology, 33,* 602–618.

Capranica, R. R. (1983). Sensory processes of key stimuli. In *Advances in vertebrate neuroethology,* J. P. Ewert, R. R. Capranica, & D. J. Ingle (eds.), pp. 3–6. New York: Plenum.

Casini, G., Fontanesi, G., Bingman, V., Jones, T.-J., Gagliardo, A., Ioale, P., & Bagnoli, P. (1997). The neuroethology of cognitive maps: Contributions from research on the hippocampal formation and homing pigeon navigation. *Archives of Italian Biology, 135:*73–92.

Chiel, H. J., & Beer, R. D. (1997). The brain has a body: Adaptive behavior emerges from interactions of nervous system, body and environment. *Trends in Neuroscience 20:*553–557.

Ewert, J.-P. (1980). *Neuroethology: An introduction to the neurophysiological fundamentals of behavior.* Berlin: Springer-Verlag.

Ewert, J.-P. (1997). Neural correlates of key stimulus and releasing mechanism: A case study and two concepts. *Trends in Neuroscience 20:*332–339.

Heiligenberg, W. (1991). *Neural Nets in Electric Fish.* Cambridge, MA: MIT Press.

Heisenberg, M. (1997). Genetic approaches to neuroethology. *Bioessays 19:*1065–1073.

Ingle, D. (1985). Vertebrate neuroethology: definitions and paradigms. *Annual Review of Neuroscience 8:*457–494.

Knudsen, E. I. (1987). Neural derivation of sound source location in the barn owl: An example of a computational map. *Annual New York Academy of Science 510:*33–38.

Scheich, H. (1983). Sensorimotor interfacing. In *Advances in vertebrate neuroethology,* J. P. Ewert, R. R. Capranica and D. J. Ingle (eds.), pp. 7–14. New York: Plenum.

Simmons, J. A. (1989). A view of the world through the bat's ear: The formation of acoustic images in echolocation. *Cognition 33:*155–199.

Spiro, J. E., & White, S. A. (1998). Neuroethology: A meeting of brain and behavior. *Neuron 21:*981–989.

Stehouwer, D. J. (1992). The emergence of developmental neuroethology. *Journal of Neurobiology 23:*1353–1354.

Tinbergen, N. (1951). *The study of instinct* Oxford, U.K.: Clarendon.

G. CASINI
Tuscia University
Viterbo, Italy

NEUROIMAGING

Neuroimaging is the use of a variety of different techniques to map the location of different structural and functional regions within the living brain. It can be used clinically, as in identifying the location of a brain tumor, or in research, as in visualizing brain regions involved in complex behaviors or emotional states. The field of neurosciences is undergoing a radical acceleration in knowledge due to the use of these techniques and their potential for expanding our understanding of the brain correlates of cognition, behavior, and emotions.

Structural neuroimaging techniques include methods that generate anatomic images of brain structures (e.g., computed tomography and magnetic resonance imaging), while functional neuroimaging techniques generate data that relate to the functioning of the brain, including measures of neuronal activity, cerebral metabolism, or neuroreceptor characteristics (e.g., positron emission tomography or functional magnetic resonance imaging). The structural and functional techniques are often used in conjunction as each technique provides different data. Selection of the specific structural or functional tool to be employed typically varies depending on whether the information will be used for clinical or research purposes, the practitioner's accessibility to the tool, the cost of the imaging procedure, the age of the person being studied, and the time available for analyzing the imaging data.

All imaging procedures quantify a parameter for a unit of three-dimensional space within the brain. In computed tomography (CT or CAT), quantification techniques attempt to measure the capacity of organic tissue to absorb X rays in proportion to tissue density; magnetic resonance imaging (MRI) techniques measure radio waves emitted by hydrogen atoms in water molecules; and SPECT and PET measure the amount of radiation emitted by radioactive isotopes linked to particular tracers.

The measures of three-dimensional space acquired in the imaging techniques are called "voxels." Through quantification the values of the voxels are then arranged in an array to represent their spatial relationship within the living brain. These data are then typically transformed into an image displayed as a plane in two-dimensional space. Each unit within the image is identified as a "pixel." These images can be viewed on a computer monitor and printed on film or paper. The images are often initially presented in "gray scale," in which variations of gray reflect a relationship with signal intensity in the tissue. Researchers often use color in their images to indicate statistically significant findings and to emphasize their findings to a wider audience.

NEUROIMAGING TECHNIQUES

Computed Tomography

Modern brain imaging was revolutionized in the 1970s with the introduction of computerized X-ray tomography (CT). This was one of the first widely practiced and accessible neuroimaging techniques to be used that allowed investigation of the living brain. In CT, multiple X-ray beams of radiation are projected through the object of interest (e.g., the brain) and the intensity of the emerging radiation is measured by detectors. Each slice through the brain requires multiple readings from multiple projections of beams. Intravenous contrast agents may be used with CT to increase its sensitivity in detecting pathology in disruption of the blood-brain barrier. CT is particularly good at detecting abnormalities in the bone, calcifications, and acute bleeding. Limitations include expo-

sure to radiation, poor differentiation between soft-tissue densities, and circumscribed views of the person being scanned. CT is used in clinical settings when indicated; however, its use in research has declined with the availability of newer neuroimaging techniques.

Magnetic Resonance Imaging (MRI)

In magnetic resonance imaging (MRI), focused radio waves target the organ of interest centered in a magnetic field with the signals absorbed and re-emitted in proportion to the hydrogen ion concentration in the tissue. The absorbed energy, when it is re-emitted, is detected by a radio receiver. MRI has evolved rapidly and is increasingly used for both clinical and research applications into general cognitive functioning and pathology. The technique is preferred by many because it is noninvasive (e.g., does not expose one to ionizing radiation), produces images with excellent spatial and temporal resolution, and is less expensive than some other imaging techniques. The lack of ionizing radiation enables researchers to acquire repeated images within subjects and to test children. Structural MRI of the brain produces images of brain anatomy and functional MRI (fMRI) produces indirect measures of brain activity through the study of changes in blood flow and blood oxygenation. fMRI uses standard MRI scanners with fast imaging techniques, and it works on the principle that focal changes in neuronal activity tend to be coupled with changes in brain blood flow and blood volume. The majority of research using fMRI has focused on language, memory, and motor tasks. This list of applications is quickly expanding, however, as fMRI is the fastest growing neuroimaging tool due to its wide availability and relatively low cost. Limitations of fMRI include its relatively poor detection of changes in blood flow and problematic confounds due to subject movement and anatomic constraints (e.g., images near large brain cavities tend to be poor). Additional limitations to MRI include occasional claustrophobia, the loud noise produced by the machine, and prohibitive use of patients with metal implants.

Positron Emission Tomography (PET) and Single Photon Emission Computed Tomography (SPECT or SPET)

In both PET and SPECT a radioactive tracer is injected or inhaled into the blood stream. The tracer is distributed in the brain in relation to blood flow, metabolism, or receptor binding and emits a photon that is detected by a scanner as it is decaying. The techniques measure the regional distribution of radioactive counts and the number of counts corresponds to local blood flow. Blood flow is used as a measure of neural activity. A variety of tracers are available in PET with each measuring different parameters (e.g., regional cerebral blood flow, glucose metabolism, or receptor distribution). PET is increasingly used as an advanced technique to identify pathology (e.g., tumors). Water containing oxygen 15 (O^{15} water), a positron emitter, is considered the optimal PET tracer for cognitive studies in imaging because its short half-life (approximately 2 minutes) allows research subjects to be scanned several times at one study. In all PET and SPECT imaging there is an overall limit to how many scans per year can be acquired in an individual to minimize radiation exposure. Currently, the O^{15} water PET technique emits the lowest radiation of the PET and SPECT techniques available. For many years, PET was considered the standard for imaging brain function due to its high resolution throughout the brain and ability to characterize receptor functioning. Its main limitations include exposure to radiation and expense in producing the tracers.

Future Directions in Neuroimaging

Several other techniques show promise in revealing information on how the brain works. Many of these techniques will be used with those described above. Magnetoencephalography (MEG) and electroencephalography (EEG) are tools that can measure neuronal function with submillisecond temporal resolution—which is preferable for studying many cognitive processes. MEG is particularly promising because it can be used to visualize the time course of regions of activation as they become activated during a task. MEG measures signals proportional to electroencephalographic waves emanating from brain electrical activity. Finally, transcranial magnetic stimulation is a tool for the noninvasive manipulation of brain activity that may be combined with traditional imaging tools to help determine if a particular region is critical for performing a cognitive or motor operation.

SUGGESTED READING

Lewis, S., & Higgins, N. (1996). *Brain imaging in psychiatry.* Cambridge, MA: Blackwell Science.

J. B. SCHWEITZER
Emory University

BRAIN
ELECTROENCPHALOGRAPHY
NEUROPSYCHOLOGICAL ASSESSMENT

THE NEURONAL CELL BODY

As a single cell, the neuron is highly specialized in the extent of its regionalization, that is, its structural and functional compartmentalization. Three distinct regions or compartments can be identified in a typical neuron: dendrites, cell body, and axons. The cell body plays two principal roles in the life a neuron, supporting most of its macromolecular synthesis and serving as the site at which input signals are integrated to determine output signals.

The cell body, also called the neuronal soma, is defined as the compartment of the neuron containing the cell nucleus. In addition to the nucleus, the cell body is the compartment most like a typical animal cell in that it also contains ribosomes, endoplasmic reticulum, the Golgi apparatus, and the other cellular organelles involved in the synthesis, processing, and delivery of macromolecules throughout the cell, for example, proteins and membrane components. Axons (see entry for Axon) and dendrites (see entry for Dendrite) are both narrow extensions of cytoplasm that grow from the cell body during early embryonic development. The synthetic capacity of these other compartments is much reduced compared to the cell body and, in the case of axons, nearly absent. In addition to lacking synthetic machinery, the extreme length of many neural axons means that this compartment typically has the majority of the cytoplasmic mass of the cell. Thus, the axon grows and is maintained only by being supplied with proteins and membrane components from the relatively smaller mass of its cell body. Disruption in the synthesis, degradation, processing, or subsequent delivery to the axon of macromolecules underlies a variety of neuronal pathologies. In Alzheimer's disease, for example, inappropriate processing of a normal integral membrane protein of brain neurons produces short protein fragments that aggregate to form an insoluble precipitate. This, in turn, leads to neuronal cell death and progressive loss of cognitive function.

In addition to their differences in synthetic function, the three compartments of a neuron also differ in their electrical signalling functions as part of a system of neurons. Dendrites are the "input" side of neurons, receiving various chemical information from other cells, typically other neurons, and converting it into local electrical signals (see entry for Synapse). The cell body receives this electrical input, both stimulatory and inhibitory, from its entire dendritic arbor and integrates it to produce a net stimulus. This overall stimulus within the cell body then determines the informational electrical "output" of the neuron (see entry for Action Potential), which propagates along the very long and narrow axonal projection. The classic view of this process of integration is that the cell body is the site of essentially passive summing of the various inhibitory and stimulatory inputs to arrive at a net stimulation or inhibition of output, that is, initiation or suppression of action potentials. More recent evidence suggests that the cell body may actively amplify or decrease input signals as part of its integration function determining output.

Structurally, the cell body of neurons is usually a compact, rounded mass of cytoplasm that contrasts with the narrow tapering arbor of dendritic branches, and with the exceptionally elongated axonal process. In general, neuronal cell bodies tend to occur in identifiable aggregates within the nervous system at which neuron-to-neuron signalling occurs. In other words, cell bodies and their associated synapses tend to occur in clumps. In the brain, a region with a large number of cell bodies is called a *nucleus*. For example, the lateral geniculate nucleus is the brain region in which visual processing first occurs after the eyes. Outside the brain and spinal cord, aggregates of neuronal cell bodies are called *ganglia*. For example, dorsal root ganglia are found just outside the spinal cord and are aggregates of the cell bodies of sensory neurons from the skin and muscle that relay information about these peripheral tissues to the central nervous system.

S. R. HEIDEMANN
Michigan State University

NEUROPSYCHOLOGICAL ASSESSMENT

Neuropsychological evaluation is the assessment of the various psychological functions governed by the brain (Reitan & Wolfson, 1985). As with all psychological evaluations, neuropsychological assessment involves a process of answering clinical questions and responding to unique clinical situations that vary somewhat from patient to patient and across practice settings.

OVERVIEW

A wide variety of cognitive and intellectual abilities are typically assessed during a neuropsychological evaluation. Attention and concentration; learning and memory; sensory–perceptual abilities; speech and language abilities (sometimes including academic skills such as reading, spelling, and math); visuospatial and visuoconstructional skills; overal intelligence; and executive functions (such as abstraction; reasoning; problem solving; behavioral self-monitoring; response discrimination, selection, and inhibition; and mental-processing efficiency and flexibility). In addition psychomotor speed, strength, and coordination all would be addressed in some fashion. Included are measures of sensory–perceptual input, the two principal central processing systems (verbal–language and nonverbal–visuospatial), executive organization and planning, and response output (motor abilities). Underlying them all are attention, concentration, arousal, and motivation. Although this list of cognitive functions might be organized or labeled differently by different neuropsychological schools of thought, these behaviors would generally be evaluated in most comprehensive neuropsychological evaluations. Frequently, aspects of psychological functioning (psychopathology, behavioral adjustment, and interpersonal issues) are also included in a neuropsychological evaluation.

Neuropsychological evaluations differs from other neurodiagnostic procedures such as computer tomography (CT) or magnetic resonance imaging (MRI) scans that examine the anatomical structure of the brain. With a neuropsychological evaluation, cognitive capabilities, from which inferences about the brain and its function can be derived, are examined. In this regard it is similar to neurodiagnostic tests that assess other functional capabilities of the brain. For example, the electroencephalogram (EEG) and event-related potentials (ERPs) measure the electrical activity of the brain while the positron-emission tomography (PET) scans or single-photon–emission tomography (SPECT) scans assess anatomical patterns of cerebral blood flow or metabolic activity. Among these, the neuropsychological evaluation is the only neurodiagnostic procedure that can evaluate how a person cognitively and behaviorally functions in real life.

Neuropsychologists must be aware of the anatomic considerations and behavioral sequelae associated with various etiological conditions in the evaluation and interpretation of data. For example, some cognitive functions depend on well-defined anatomic structures (e.g., lower-level sensory–motor skills and even higher-level perception such as recognition of familiar faces located in the sensory-motor strip and bilateral basal occipital–temporal regions, respectively). Other abilities (e.g., new learning, abstract reasoning, and speed of information processing) are diffusely organized or rely on complex interacting cortical and subcortical networks. The effects of brain injury can result not only in deficits in various cognitive abilities but also in the emergence of new behaviors or symptoms such as perseverations, unilateral neglect, or confabulations (Goodglass & Kaplan, 1979).

Lezak (1983) has suggested that mastery of four areas is essential to competent neuropsychological practice: (a) clinical psychotherapeutic and assessment skills; (b) psychometrics; (c) neuroanatomy and functional neuroanatomy; and (d) neuropathologies and their behavioral effects. A fifth essential knowledge area is a theoretical understanding of how these four areas interrelate and interact. This latter knowledge base might best be viewed as a overarching model or knowledge of brain–behavior relationships that is applicable across settings and diagnoses. It is only within this conceptual framework that the neuropsychologist can integrate the historical information, medical material, and current cognitive abilities; provide an accurate description of a person's cognitive strengths and deficits; arrive at correct diagnoses (etiological conditions and anatomic localization); outline the implications of the results for that person's functional living potential; formulate prognostications; and make clinically useful recommendations.

THE EVALUATION PROCESS

There are three general reasons for conducting a neuropsychological evaluation: differential diagnosis, patient care, and research (Lezak, 1983). The first step in the assessment process is defining the questions that need to be answered to meet particular clinical needs. Next, the neuropsychologist must determine what information is required and how best to obtain it. Neuropsychological testing might be only one of several methods used. In fact, a psychological test is simply a sample of behavior obtained under controlled or standardized conditions (Anastasi, 1988; Maloney & Ward, 1976). Other methods of obtaining information about a person's past and present behavioral capabilities include the case history, clinical interview, mental status examination, direct behavioral observations, and reports of other people who are involved with the patient (spouse, children, friends, employer, and other professionals such as nursing staff). If testing is to be conducted, then test selection must be competently addressed. Structuring the testing session, administration procedures, scoring, and clerical issues also are important factors in the overall competent completion of the data-collection phase of the evaluation process. Following data collection come the interpretation and application phases of the evaluation process.

There are several neuropsychological schools of thought with somewhat differing approaches to the neuropsychological assessment process. Differences arise along two continuums: fixed versus flexible battery approaches to data collection and quantitative–normative-based versus qualitative–process-based approaches to data interpretation. The traditional Halstead–Reitan would be an example of a fixed battery, quantitative–normative approach. On the other end of both continua would be clinicians using a process approach, that is, a flexible battery with qualitative–process analyses of the results. In a recent survey of randomly selected neuropsychologists, 34% of respondents described their theoretical orientation as eclectic; many of these also checked "other orientations." A total of 31% affirmed a hypothesis-testing approach; 25%, a process approach; 20%, a Halstead–Reitan approach; 3%, a Benton orientation; and 2%, a Luria orientation (Butler, Retzlaff, & Vanderploeg, 1991).

There are two major fixed batteries employed in current clinical neuropsychological assessment practice, the Halstead–Reitan Neuropsychological Test Battery and the Luria–Nebraska Neuropsychological Test Battery. In a fixed battery approach the issue of test selection is moot, because the set of tests is predetermined. The philosophy is to use a set of tests that has previously been developed, organized, and validated to assess the clinically important or relevant aspects of brain-related behaviors. Fixed battery approaches are typically psychometrically and quantitatively oriented. Their advantage is that they are comprehensive and standardized. However, they are generally quite time-consuming and inflexible, which makes them inappropriate for some patients. Furthermore, fixed battery approaches are incapable of being easily adapted as new knowledge emerges regarding brain–behavior relationships and cognitive functions.

Flexible battery approaches to assessment are more numerous and varied. Neuropsychologists variously describe themselves as clinically oriented, flexible–adjustive, hypothesis testing, or process oriented. However, underlying all such distinctions is the philosophy that assessments should be designed uniquely for each patient (or type of patient) and should answer particular referral questions. Although quantitative information is certainly used, an emphasis also is placed on qualitative information, such as how patients pass or fail particular tasks (process approach). The advantages of this approach are that assessments are more focused and relevant to individual patients and particular clinical questions and, consequently, are less time-consuming. New knowledge and better designed or normed tests can easily be incorporated into the assessment. However, with a flexible approach, evaluations are not standardized across patients, assessments, or facilities. Specific problems or deficits may be missed because they were not a focus of the evaluation.

PRACTICE SETTINGS

As the field of clinical neuropsychology has grown, practice settings have diversified. Neuropsychological evaluations historically have been used to help determine lesion location in neurology and neurosurgical settings. That function has decreased in importance with the advent of such neuroradiological procedures as the CT and MRI scans. However, evaluations remain a frequently requested procedure to help identify the pattern and severity of deficits associated with various brain lesions or neurological conditions. They also play an important role in diagnosis of conditions such as Alzheimer's disease or AIDS dementia complex. Neuropsychological evaluations are often an important factor in helping medical staff, patients, and families make decisions about treatment issues and placement after hospitalization.

In rehabilitation centers, the neuropsychologist is called on to help identify deficits that would be amenable to treatment and behavioral capacities that remain relatively intact and potentially useful in a compensatory fashion for other impaired cognitive functions. In educational as in rehabilitation settings neuropsychological evaluations can be important in identifying different learning disabilities, serve as an important ingredient in designing treatment and/or educational plans and in setting realistic goals, and help evaluate the effectiveness of various interventions.

Neuropsychological evaluations also continue to play an important role in the differential diagnosis between neurological and psychiatric conditions that may appear clinically similar (e.g., dementia versus a pseudodementia secondary to depression or anxiety) but that have different prognostic implications and require divergent treatments. Finally, neuropsychological evaluations are appearing with increasing frequency in forensic settings where they are used to help document the presence or absence of behavioral impairments secondary to injuries (personal injury or medical malpractice cases) or in helping to evaluate issues of diminished capacity and competency.

SUMMARY

The field of clinical neuropsychology has become increasingly prominent over the past several decades, with the neuropsychological evaluation as its core. The unique contribution of the neuropsychological evaluation is that it is the only available diagnostic procedure that can assess brain–behavior relationships in terms of real-life behaviors.

Various approaches to assessment have been espoused and evaluations are being requested in a wide variety of settings to meet a spectrum of clinical needs. Evaluations are useful in differential diagnosis among similarly appearing neurologic disorders or between psychiatric and neurologic conditions. Neuropsychological assessments often serve as the nucleus of rehabilitation and educational intervention plans and are instrumental in the evaluation of their effectiveness.

REFERENCES

Anastasi, A. (1988). *Psychological testing* (6th ed.). New York: Macmillan.

Butler, M., Retzlaff, P., & Vanderploeg, R. (1991). Neuropsychological test usage. *Professional Psychology: Research and Practice, 22,* 510–512.

Goodglass, H., & Kaplan, E. (1979). Assessment of cognitive deficit in the brain-injured patient. In M. S. Gazzaniga (Ed.), *Handbook of behavioral neurobiology* (Vol. 2, pp. 3–22). New York: Plenum.

Lezak, M. D. (1983). *Neuropsychological assessment* (2nd ed.). New York: Oxford University Press.

Maloney, M. P., & Ward, M. P. (1976). *Psychological assessment: A conceptual approach.* New York: Oxford University Press.

Reitan, R. M., & Wolfson, D. (1985). *The Halstead-Reitan neuropsychological test battery: Theory and clinical interpretation.* Tucson, AZ: Neuropsychology.

SUGGESTED READING

Grant, I., & Adams, K. M. (Eds.). (1986). *Neuropsychological assessment of neuropsychiatric disorders.* New York: Oxford University Press.

Heilman, K. M., & Valenstein, E. (Eds.). (1979). *Clinical neuropsychology.* New York: Oxford University Press.

R. D. VANDERPLOEG
University of South Florida

ALZHEIMER'S DISEASE
DEMENTIA
ELECTROENCEPHALOGRAPHY
NEUROTRANSMITTER RELEASE

NEUROPSYCHOLOGICAL DEVELOPMENT

The initial lure of developmental neuropsychology was the belief that children are neurologically simpler than adults and would provide clearer data as to the relationship between brain function and behavior. This turned out to be a somewhat simplistic view, and the study of the developing nervous system quickly raised a number of important new questions. These included, "Why does the young brain appear to be so flexible in compensating for injury?", "How do environmental factors influence the developing brain?", and "How do functional and structural asymmetries develop, and what are the behavioral implications of these?" Before such questions can be answered, however, it is important to get an overview of the neural developmental process.

NEURAL DEVELOPMENT

The growth of the brain and nervous system can be described as if it were a series of changes that occur at particular ages. While some changes are rapid and dramatic, others are more gradual. Regardless of the rapidity of change, however, these changes occur in a generally fixed sequence. The first of these stages of brain development is cell migration, during which nerve cells are formed in the inner or ventricular lining of the brain. After formation they migrate from the inner lining through the layers that already exist, to eventually form a new outer layer. This means that structures such as the cortex actually mature from the inner to the outer surfaces.

During the cell migration stage, axonal growth manifests itself, as axons begin to sprout from the migrating cells. Axons are the elongated neural processes that carry information away from the cell body to be received by other cells down the line. Each axon has a specific target that it must reach if the neuron is to be functional. How each axon locates its target is still an unsolved question, although electrical or chemical gradients, or preexisting physical structures may provide the needed map or blueprint to guide this targeted growth process. The growth of dendrites is the next major change in the system. This growth doesn't start until after the cell reaches its final location after migration. The process of dendritic growth is much slower than axonal growth and involves much more branching and elaboration. At some stages of dendritic growth there appears to be an overabundance of dendritic branches. Some of these excess or unused branches are eventually lost in a process referred to as "pruning."

The time course of synapse formation has been mapped in detail for primates. Synapses begin to form about two months before birth and grow rapidly for several months after parturition. In humans synaptic growth is known to continue for at least 2 years after birth. There is some suggestion that experience may affect the survival of synapses. This is based upon the fact that, between about 2 and 16 years of age, there is actually a loss of about 50% of the synapses. One speculation is that only the regularly used synapses survive, with unused synapses disappearing through a process sometimes referred to as "shedding."

Axons are surrounded by a sheath called myelin, which is made up of fatty insulating cells. The degree of myelination is sometimes used an index of the degree to which the neural system has matured. Based upon this index we would say that the neocortex matures relatively early during gestation, while the sensory and motor areas begin to mature just before birth. Some areas of the cortex involved in higher-level processing (the so-called secondary or tertiary areas) continue to mature for 4 or more months after birth.

While most people tend to think that neural development has finished after about 2 years of age, growth continues well beyond this point. There is even some suggestion that brain growth occurs at irregular intervals which are called "growth spurts" (Banich, 1997). Such spurts occur at around 3 to 18 months, 2 to 4 years, 6 to 8 years, 10 to 12 years, and 14 to 16 years. Except for the first (rather long) spurt, during which brain weight increases by about 30%, each subsequent growth spurt increases brain mass by 5% to 10%. It is tempting to try to correlate these growth spurts with overt changes in development. It may be significant that the first four episodes of rapid brain growth seem to coincide with the four principal stages of cognitive development according to Piaget (Kolb & Wishaw, 1990).

Other changes in the neural system continue far beyond adolescence. Thus, although myelination begins prenatally and is well advanced by 15 years of age, myelin continues to develop as late as age 60. However, all of the later changes are not associated with growth. An important factor in the later stages of neuropsychological development is cell loss. For instance, the area of the occipital cortex, which receives projections from the fovea of the eye, contains about 46 million neurons per gram of tissue in a 20-year-old. In an 80-year-old, however, the neuronal density is reduced by nearly one-half, to only 24 million neurons per gram of tissue. This cell loss is believed to account for some of the loss of visual acuity in older individuals (Coren, Ward, & Enns, 1999). Similar losses in other areas of the brain might be expected to also affect normal functioning.

ENVIRONMENTAL AND EXPERIENTIAL EFFECTS

The nervous system does not develop in isolation. It is affected by the environment and also the activities of the developing organism. The general principle which describes the interaction between the environment and the developing nervous system is functional validation. According to this principle, some form of stimulation or neural activity is needed to validate the usefulness of sections of the nervous system. In the absence of such validation, these units will cease to function and will not continue their growth and maturation. We have already seen this process in action when we noted that unused synapses seem to disappear with age.

Features as simple as the size and mass of the brain can be affected by experience. Exposure to a stimulus-rich environment seems to increase brain size, especially in the neocortex, presumably by validating the functionality of many additional pathways. Such enriched stimulus exposure seems to increase the number of dendrites and synapses, especially if the enriched stimulus is experienced early in life. Furthermore, animals with these larger brains, through more varied experience, seem to perform better on a number of behavioral tasks, including those involving memory and learning.

Experimentally, the easiest way to observe how stimulation and activity affect brain function involves variation of an animal's sensory experience followed by direct monitoring of changes in the cortical areas that are used to process information from that sensory modality. For instance, a number of studies have looked at the effects of restricting visual experience upon the growth of the occipital cortex which is the primary processing site for visual information. In a classic series of studies, Hubel and Wiesel (1963) showed that, in very young kittens whose eyes had not yet opened, the general response patterns of the cells of the occipital cortex were similar to those of the adult (although somewhat sluggish and easily fatigued). They next showed that for the cells to continue in their normal functioning they needed stimulation (functional validation). They next reared cats for several months without any patterned visual stimulation. While they found that there was no effect upon the retina or lower visual centers, the occipital cortex showed massive disturbances. Many of the neural cells in this region showed disturbed or abnormal functions. Anatomically they have fewer and shorter dendrites and 70% fewer synapses than found in normally reared cats. Some of these abnormalities do correct themselves over time, when the animals are restored to normal visual stimulation. The ability of restricted experience to disrupt normal function is reduced in older animals. If an animal has normal visual experience during the first few months of life, and then is reared for the same amount of time without visual stimulation, the degree of abnormality observed is much less. This suggests that there is some critical period during which stimulation is needed for normal and continuing neural development of the affected areas of the brain. More recent experiments suggest that we can generalize these results from vision to other sensory systems and hence to other areas of the brain. From these results were are led to the conclusion that, although the basic functional pattern is innately determined and available early in the developmental process, adequate stimulation of the appropriate neural systems is necessary for normal function to be maintained (Coren, Ward, & Enns, 1999).

Environmental effects, in the form of traumas which affect the developing fetus (which might include the influence of toxic agents, mechanical injury, or chemical imbalances), can cause dramatic disturbances in neural development. Some of the readily visible abnormalities involve incomplete development of brain structures. The most severe of these is anencephaly, which is the absence of

cerebral hemispheres, diencephalon, and the midbrain. With this condition survival is unlikely. Slightly less drastic is microencephaly, where the brain development is stunted and rudimentary, and mental retardation is the most common behavioral result. Other developmental disturbances involve disruption of the normal pattern of brain structures. For instance, agenesis of the corpus callosum is the absence of the corpus callosum, which is the major connector between the two cerebral hemispheres. Another pattern of aberrant development is holoprosencephaly. In this condition, the cortex forms as a single unit, rather than dividing into the left and right cerebral hemispheres.

Contrasted to these clearly visible disruptions in neural development, we have less pronounced pathological conditions which only show up in terms of behavioral changes, such as learning disabilities, reduced intelligence, personality disturbances, motor insufficiencies, and so forth. Many of these behavioral indicators of disrupted neuropsychological development are quite subtle. In these instances atypical behaviors may serve as soft signs, which are nonphysiological indicators of disturbed neuropsychological development.

ASYMMETRY AND NEUROPSYCHOLOGICAL DEVELOPMENT

One way to illustrate the nature of neuropsychological development is to focus upon a specific research area. As an example of how developmental issues and neuropsychological issues interact, we will deal with functional asymmetries between the left and right sides of the body.

The differences in the functional properties of the two cerebral hemispheres are well known (e.g., language function is located predominantly in the left hemisphere and spatial functions predominantly in the right hemisphere). These differences may come about because of differences in the rate of development of the two hemispheres. One suggestion is that there is a left-to-right maturational gradient during development (e.g., Gazzaniga, 1998). This means that the left hemisphere develops earlier than the right, at least during the time when language functions are being acquired, while the right hemisphere catches up later. According to this theory, the left hemisphere gains control over language functions, not because it is intrinsically specialized for them, but simply because it is the more developed and dominant when language is learned. In addition, there is the suggestion that if the left hemisphere is damaged, there is enough plasticity for the right hemisphere to take over language function, but only if this situation occurs early in development. If the right hemisphere has developed beyond some critical stage for language acquisition, this form of compensation would not be possible.

One persistent idea in neuropsychology is that the functional properties of the nervous system become more fixed and specialized over time. In the context of cerebral asymmetry, this means that we should expect more evidence of lateralization with increasing age. This prediction has some experimental support, but the situation is complex. In general, research on the development of speech functioning after damage to the left hemisphere suggests that there are three critical age ranges: less than 1 year, 1 to 5 years, and older than 5 years. If the damage occurs before 1 year, disruption of speech is quite extensive. If damage occurs between 1 and 5 years, the recovery of speech is usually possible, with the right hemisphere reorganizing to take over most of the functions lost by the left. Injuries to the left hemisphere after 5 years of age, however, show no recovery of function (see Kolb, 1995). Presumably, all of the right hemisphere functions are now set and fixed, and there is not enough plasticity left to replace the functions lost by the other hemisphere.

In the example above, we noted how an observable function (language) changed as we monitored visible damage to specific regions of the brain. In some cases, changes in function (soft signs) are used to determine the likelihood that there is some form of damage or disruption in neurological development which can not be specifically seen in physiological examinations, but must be inferred from behavioral changes. One such soft sign which has been singled out for this purpose is left-handedness. It has been argued (e.g., Coren, 1992) that all human beings are genetically programmed to be right-handed. According to this notion, left-handedness comes about if the relevant neural pathways or brain centers are damaged during development or if normal maturational processes go awry. Evidence supporting this relationship comes from the fact that individuals who are born from a difficult pregnancy or a stressed birth are twice as likely to be left-handed than are normally born individuals. Furthermore, left-handers seem to mature more slowly and suffer from a variety of behavioral and physiological problems to a greater degree than do right-handers.

As is the case of many aspects of neuropsychological development, in the case of handedness there are indications that a bias toward a particular functional pattern exists quite early in development. There is also evidence that there is a gradual loss of plasticity with age, with a greater degree of specialization or asymmetry in older individuals (Coren, 1992). At birth there are indications that there is functional asymmetry which is correlated with handedness. This can be seen, for example, in the tonic neck reflex in infants, in which the head is turned to one side and the arm and leg on that side are extended. This reflex, which is limited to infants less than 20 weeks of age, shows a strong bias to the right side for the majority of subjects tested. This demonstrates an early functional bias toward the right.

Hand preference continues to evolve with age. For tasks such as reaching, handedness is not reliable before 6 months of age, and gradually becomes more stable and consistent up to about the age of 8 years. Thus, handedness is much more variable in preschool-aged individuals than in adolescents or young adults (Coren, Porac, & Duncan, 1981). Attempts to change handedness demonstrate the loss of plasticity of function with increasing age. Although the success of changing handedness is not very high at any age, there is a precipitous drop in the number of successful changes of handedness after about age 9 (Porac, Coren, & Searleman, 1986).

In the above example handedness is viewed as a typical function dependent upon the usual sequence of events found in neuropsychological development. Notice that the general pattern that emerges begins with an innate or early predisposition toward a particular behavioral pattern (in our example toward right-handedness). Disruption of the normal developmental pattern can cause changes in the observed behavior (the emergence of left-handedness). The functional specificity becomes more set with chronological age (consistent handedness begins to emerge) and there is a gradual loss in functional plasticity (handedness becomes set and relatively unchangeable). This same sequence of stages (initial developmental predisposition, period of environmental vulnerability, period of plasticity, and finally fixed functional properties) appears in neuropsychological development, whether we are looking at neurological structures, complex patterns of cerebral organization, or functional manifestations of behavior.

REFERENCES

Banich, M. T. (1997). *Neuropsychology: The neural bases of mental functioning.* Boston: Houghton-Mifflin.

Coren, S. (1992). *The left-hander syndrome: The causes and consequences of left-handedness.* New York: Free Press.

Coren, S., Ward, L. M., & Enns, J. T. (1989). *Sensation and perception* (5th ed.). San Diego: Harcourt Brace Jovanovich.

Coren, S., Porac, C., & Duncan, P. (1981). Lateral behaviors preference in pre-school children and young adults. *Child Development, 52,* 443–450.

Gazzaniga, M. S. (1998). *The mind's past.* Berkeley: University of California Press.

Hubel, D. H., & Wiesel, T. N. (1963). Receptive fields of cells in striate cortex of very young, visually inexperienced kittens. *Journal of Neurophysiology, 26,* 994–1002.

Kolb, B. (1995). *Brain plasticity and behavior.* Mahwah, NJ: Erlebaum.

Kolb, B., & Wishaw, I. Q. (1990). *Fundamentals of human neuropsychology.* New York: Freeman.

Porac, C., Coren, S., & Searleman, A. (1986). Environmental factors in hand preference: Evidence from attempts to switch the preferred hand. *Behavior Genetics, 16,* 251–261.

SUGGESTED READING

Banich, M. T. (1997). *Neuropsychology: The neural basis of mental functioning.* Boston: Houghton-Mifflin.

Martin, G. M. (1997). *Human neuropsychology.* New York: Prentice Hall.

S. COREN
Psychology Department, University of British Columbia

BRAIN INJURIES
BRAIN LATERALITY
HANDEDNESS
NEURAL NETWORK MODELS
NEUROCHEMISTRY
SPEECH-DISORDERS
SPLIT-BRAIN RESEARCH

NEUROPSYCHOLOGY

ORIGINS OF THE TERM NEUROPSYCHOLOGY

Historically, the field of neuropsychology was derived not only from the discipline of psychology, but also from the various related disciplines within the traditional professions of medicine, education, and law (Meier, 1997). The term *neuropsychology* is a combination of the word *neurology,* which is defined as a branch of medicine that deals with the nervous system and its disorders, and *psychology,* which is defined as the study of behavior or the mind. Neuropsychology today is used to describe a field of psychology that principally encompasses the identification, quantification, and description of changes in behavior that relate to the structural and cognitive integrity of the brain (Golden, Zillmer, & Spiers, 1992).

THE NEUROPSYCHOLOGIST AS A PROFESSIONAL

Most individuals who call themselves neuropsychologists are professionals involved with assessing and treating human patients (i.e., clinical neuropsychology). A majority of neuropsychologists in practice work with either psychiatric or neuropsychological populations in a variety of settings: private practice, university-based medical centers, psychiatric hospitals, general community hospitals, mental health centers, university psychology departments, prisons, and many other similar settings. Furthermore, neuropsychologists as clinicians have also become more involved in specifying the nature of brain-related disorders and applying this information to rehabilitation and education.

In order to achieve these goals, the clinical neuropsychologist is required to establish a comprehensive database of historical and current general medical, surgical, neurological, pharmacological, developmental, and psychosocial factors underlying the presenting problem (Meier, 1997). The database also includes a compilation of specialized neural diagnostic procedures such as neural imagining, electroencephalography, and brain mapping techniques. All this information is gathered so that the neuropsychologist can determine a diagnosis, perform the appropriate neuropsychological assessments, examine the effects of treatment, and design rehabilitation programs for a patient.

DIAGNOSIS IN NEUROPSYCHOLOGY

One of the major questions facing neuropsychologists in many settings is how to differentiate brain damage from the major psychiatric disorders. The reason for the difficulty in differentiation lies in the overlap between cognitive and personality symptoms that may be seen in the broad range of psychiatric disorders, and those seen in neurological disorders, as well as the increasing recognition that many psychiatric disorders may have a neuropsychological rather than psychological etiology.

The area of diagnosis may be subdivided into three subareas. The first involves the identification of the presence of a brain injury or related disorder, in which a differentiation must be made between disorders caused by emotional problems and those caused by injury to the function of the brain. The second involves the specification of the nature of the deficit caused by brain damage, including localizing the injury to specific areas of the brain. The third includes identifying or helping to identify the cause of the brain injury (the underlying process).

NEUROPSYCHOLOGICAL ASSESSMENT

The primary goal of assessment in neuropsychology is to address the relevant neurobehavioral aspects of higher psychological functioning that are considered to be central to understanding the cognitive strengths and deficits of the individual (Meier, 1997). This goal is based on the assumption that the brain is the organ of behavior, and can thus be evaluated through the use of behavioral measures (Goldstein, 1998).

In neurodiagnostic settings, the emphasis of neuropsychological assessment has traditionally been on deficit measurement rather than on strengths. There is also an emphasis on the search for dysfunctional aspects of an individual's cognition and behavior; this aids in diagnosis of a particular lesion, disease, syndrome, or condition, since neuropsychological exams provide additional and valuable information in difficult or unclear cases (Golden, Zillmer, & Spiers, 1992). Furthermore, neuropsychological assessments can also serve as a baseline for a patient's abilities, so that a course of recovery or decline in a patient can be evaluated (Golden, Zillmer, & Spiers, 1992).

Neuropsychological assessments are typically organized into standardized or flexible batteries. Standardized batteries are those in which patients take all tests in a given battery. Some examples of standardized neuropsychological batteries include the Halstead-Reitan (Reitan & Wolfson, 1993) and the Luria-Nebraska (Golden, Purisch, & Hammeke, 1985) test batteries. Both batteries are composed of an established set of tests that assess those neurocognitive functions that are susceptible to disruption from neurologic impairment, including that sustained after head injury.

Flexible neuropsychological batteries are those in which the neuropsychologist creates a customized battery of specific tests or modifies a basic battery based on individual patient issues and history (Smith et al., 1998). Some examples include Lezak's Hypothesis-Testing Approach and the Boston Process Approach (Kaplan, 1990). In many cases, these two approaches are melded together to produce a more useful evaluation of the client (Golden, Zillmer, & Spiers, 1992).

Regardless of the approach to testing employed, it is important that any neuropsychological examination be sufficiently comprehensive so that the major skill areas controlled by the brain are evaluated. Exams that are not sufficiently comprehensive may misdiagnose the presence or type of brain injury. An adequate exam will cover such areas as motor and tactile skills, nonverbal auditory skills, receptive language, expressive language, visual and visual-spatial skills, reading, writing, arithmetic, verbal and nonverbal memory, intelligence, and personality. The emphasis on a specific area within the evaluation may vary depending on the setting in which the testing is completed and the specific diagnostic problems under consideration.

NEUROPSYCHOLOGICAL APPROACH TO TREATMENT

Another area of interest to the neuropsychologist is the examination of the effects of treatment for a patient. Because most patients seen by neuropsychologists suffer from brain injuries or dementias that are not reversible, the neuropsychologist is concerned with approaching treatment by teaching the patient to work around his/her deficits in order to lead a more effective life. This behavioral treatment or behavioral modification approach centers around the altering of environmental contingencies so that desirable behaviors are systematically reinforced and increased, thus enhancing the emotional and cognitive functioning of the patient. This allows other treatments to be effectively delivered (Schefft, Malec, Lehr, & Kanfer, 1997).

Another form of treatment of interest to neuropsychologists is the assessment of drug effects. In assessing drug effects, the neuropsychologist frequently evaluates whether a particular drug makes a patient better or worse in terms of neuropsychological functioning. For instance, Goldberg, Gerstman, Mattis, Hughes, Bilder, and Sirio (1982) found significant increases on the Wechsler Memory Scale and the Selective Reminding Test in response to physostigmine treatment of a patient with Posttraumatic Anterograde Amnesia.

This study, as well as many others, reflects the need to document the effects and value of treatment. As the field of neuropsychology becomes more sophisticated, the documentation of the effects and value of treatment has become important because it allows clinicians to determine which treatment approach is successful, as well as which programs of approaches deserve funding from limited rehabilitation resources.

REHABILITATION

In conjunction with diagnosis and treatment, the neuropsychologist is also involved in the design of rehabilitation programs. The primary objective of neuropsychological rehabilitation is to improve the quality of life of individuals who have sustained neurological insult, which may involve cognitive, behavioral, emotional, and social factors (Hanlon, 1994). Neuropsychological assessment can serve as a first step in developing a rehabilitation program for a patient, because it allows the clinician to document fully the details of the patient's strengths and weaknesses. Documentation integrated with an understanding of brain function allows the clinician to understand the behavioral, cognitive, and emotional effects of an injury (Golden, Zillmer, & Spiers, 1992).

Hanlon (1994) described four primary approaches to cognitive rehabilitation that are currently being practiced. The first approach is the general stimulation or direct retraining approach, which includes the use of repetitive drills and exercises. The second approach is the substitution-transfer model, in which visual imagery is used to facilitate verbal retention and verbal mediation. Other treatments include elaboration to compensate for visual memory dysfunction and Melodic Intonation Therapy for nonfluent aphasia.

The third approach is the functional compensation and adaptation model, which involves the use of any and all strategies, tech-

niques, devices, and adaptive equipment (i.e., computers, visual communications systems) available to increase functional performance and enable the patient to perform tasks that can no longer be performed in a conventional manner. The fourth approach to cognitive rehabilitation is the behavioral approach, which is based on principles of learning theory and behavior modification similar to those discussed in the previous section.

FUTURE TRENDS IN NEUROPSYCHOLOGY

Neuropsychology is a field that continues to expand. Some issues affecting the future of neuropsychology stem from the use of computers in neuropsychological assessment. Kay and Starbuck (1997) noted that the relatively low cost of personal computers and the potential of having computers perform labor-intensive scoring and test administration procedures may explain the popularity of computer applications in neuropsychological assessment. However, they also add that computerized testing appears to have had only minimal impact on the field of neuropsychology; this is probably because of a general resistance to novel methods or to the lack of human-to-human contact.

REFERENCES

Goldberg, E., Gerstman, L.J., Mattis, S., Hughes, J.E.O., Bilder, R.M., & Sirio, C.A. (1982). Effects of cholinergic treatment of posttraumatic anterograde amnesia. *Archives of Neurology (Chicago), 39,* 581.

Golden, C.J., Purisch, A., & Hammeke, T. (1985). *Manual for the Luria-Nebraska neuropsychological battery.* Los Angeles: Western Psychological Services.

Golden, C.J., Zillmer, E., & Spiers, M. (1992). *Neuropsychological assessment and intervention.* Springfield, IL: Charles Thomas.

Goldstein, G. (1998). Introduction to neuropsychological assessment. In G. Goldstein, P.D. Nussbaum, & S.R. Beers (Eds.), *Neuropsychology* (pp. 1–5). New York: Plenum.

Hanlon, R. (1994). Neuropsychological rehabilitation. In Zaidel, D.W. (ed) *Neuropsychology.* San Diego, CA: Academic Press.

Kay, G.G., & Starbuck, V.N. (1997). Computerized neuropsychological assessment. In M.E. Maruish & J.A. Moses, Jr. (Eds.), *Clinical neuropsychology: Theoretical foundations for practitioners* (pp. 143–161). Mahwah, NJ: Erlbaum.

Meier, M.J. (1997). The establishment of clinical neuropsychology as a psychological specialty. In M.E. Maruish & J.A. Moses, Jr. (Eds.), *Clinical neuropsychology: Theoretical foundations for practitioners* (pp. 1–31). Mahwah, NJ: Erlbaum.

Reitan, R.M., & Wolfson, D. (1993). *The Halstead-Reitan neuropsychological test battery: Theory and clinical interpretation.* Tucson, AZ: Neuropsychology Press.

Schefft, B.K., Malec, J.F., Lehr, B.K., & Kanfer, F.H. (1997). The role of self-regulation therapy with the brain-injured patient. In M.E. Maruish & J.A. Moses, Jr. (Eds.), *Clinical neuropsychol-*

ogy: Theoretical foundations for practitioners (pp. 237–282). Mahwah, NJ: Erlbaum.

A. Escalona
C. J. Golden
Nova Southeastern University

NEUROPSYCHOLOGICAL DEVELOPMENT
U.S.S.R.: NEUROPSYCHOLOGY (IN THE FORMER)

NEUROSURGERY

Archaeological ruins offer ancient evidence of therapeutic intervention aimed at the nervous system. Trephining—the boring and scraping of the skull to release "evil spirits"—in fact relieved intracranial pressure caused by tumors, hemorrhages and skull fractures. In a craniotomy, an extension of trephining, a flap of skull is entirely removed, exposing the fibrous coverings of the brain (meninges) overlying the outermost brain structures (cerebral cortex), enabling visual examination of cortical structures and excision of pathological tissue. In 1947 the first stereotaxic device for humans was developed, allowing neurosurgery on deeper brain structures without serious damage to outer structures. This device locates hidden brain structures by using three-dimensional anatomical maps (atlases) and X-rayed reference points in the brain (such as the pineal gland or cerebral ventricles). The stereotax can be used for electrical stimulation at various tissue levels to test function before removing tissue, for testing the effect of temporarily halting tissue activity, and for facilitating circumscribed lesioning with electrolytic or radiofrequency currents.

Several procedures are available for diagnostic use before surgery, including X-rays of the skull (radiograph), of blood supply in the brain or spinal cord (angiograph, venograph), of ventricles in the brain (pneumoencephalograph, ventriculograph), or of spaces in and around the spinal cord (myelograph). Spinal (lumbar) punctures permit the collection of cerebrospinal fluid (CSF), evaluation of intracerebral pressure, and injection of contrast medium, and are necessary for one or more of the above techniques. These procedures may be painful or risky. Computerized axial tomographic scanning (CAT scan), a two-minute procedure with little risk or discomfort, reduces the need for more perilous tests. An X-ray tube and detector encircle the patient's head, measuring the amount of radiation getting through the tissue, while a computer plots a picture of the horizontal section of the brain. Other techniques, assessing cerebral blood flow and glucose utilization, provide access to ongoing regional brain function. In positron emission tomography (PET) the brain absorbs and utilizes radioactively tagged glucose which emits particles (positrons) affecting the passage of X-rays from a scanning device. A computer determines in which regions and to what degree the brain takes up the glucose. Biochemical changes can be observed over time. Ongoing recordings of electrical brain and neuromuscular activity are also used as diagnostic aids. The electroencephalogram produces waveforms from greatly amplified signals of electrical activity generated by neural firing in the cortex; abnormal waveforms indicate dysfunction and possible cellular pathology.

Most neurosurgery is for treatment of pathological conditions such as removal of tumors, arteriosclerotic plaque, blood clots, epileptogenic scars, or repair of aneurysm (thinning and stretching of blood vessel walls). Neurosurgery performed to ameliorate symptoms where no pathology is found is called functional. Functional neurosurgery is controversial and includes surgery for epilepsy with no apparent scar tissue, alleviation of motor disturbances with no manifest pathology, interruption of pain transmission, and surgery to control behavior and emotion. In seizure disorders, spots in the brain (epileptogenic foci) which irritate other brain structures generate the seizures; treatment involves removing the epileptic focus. When no foci or multiple foci are found, neurosurgery may involve removal of one anterior temporal lobe (removing both may cause severe memory loss and emotional disturbance), the severing of connections between the hemispheres (commissurotomy), removal of an entire hemisphere (usually performed in children with extremely severe epilepsy), or discrete stereotaxic lesions aimed at multiple foci. Movement disorders (rigidity, tremors, hemiballism) assumed to be caused by imbalance between excitation and inhibition of motor control systems, may be treated by lesioning the thalamus, presumably to destroy the dominant system and thus correct the imbalance. Neurosurgery to relieve chronic pain involves removing the sensory nerve that conducts the pain signal (nerve alvulsion, rhizotomy), interfering with spinal-to-brain pain signal transmission (anterolateral spinal cordotomy, anterior spinal commissurotomy, spinothalamic tractotomy), or removing parts of the limbic system of the brain, an area thought to control affective components of pain (removal of frontal lobe or cingulum).

Techniques used in psychosurgery (damage to nonpathological brain tissue to alter behavior or emotion) developed from animal experiments, observations of people with head injuries, and results of brain operations to control seizures and pain. The first frontal lobotomy, performed by Almeida Lima and Egas Moniz, was inspired by reports at a scientific meeting of an irascible chimpanzee rendered docile by surgical removal of the frontal lobe. Use of psychosurgery peaked in the 1950s and was performed throughout the world. Since then its popularity has declined, although removal of circumscribed nuclei in the brain is still performed.

SUGGESTED READING

Smith, R. R. (1980). *Essentials of neurosurgery.* Philadelphia, PA: Lippincott.

Valenstein, E. S. (1973). *Brain control: A critical examination of brain stimulation and psychosurgery.* New York: Wiley.

Valenstein, E. S. (Ed.). (1980). *The psychosurgery debate: Scientific, legal and ethical perspectives.* San Francisco: Freeman.

B. E. Thorn
University of Alabama

BRAIN INJURIES
PSYCHOSURGERY
SPLIT-BRAIN RESEARCH

NEUROTRANSMITTER RELEASE

Neurons can communicate by direct ion fluxes at "electrical synapses" resembling "gap junctions," but more commonly communicate indirectly with each other, or with muscle or endocrine cells, by the release of chemical messengers called neurotransmitters at "chemical synapses" situated at their terminals or at axonal varicosities. Transmitter molecules in neurons are either synthesized locally in presynaptic nerve terminals or transported from cell bodies and packaged into either secretory vesicles about 50nm in diameter or larger organelles with dense cores, from which they are released, in response to appropriate signals, into the synaptic cleft. They evoke a response in neighboring postsynaptic neurons or nonneuronal cells by binding to membrane receptors, which determine the nature of the elicited effect. They are subsequently eliminated by diffusion, enzymatic degradation, or by high-affinity uptake into presynaptic terminals or neighboring glial cells. Katz and his collaborators in the early 1950s were the first to recognize that the end-plate potential recorded at neuromuscular junctions was the sum of many "miniature" end-plate potentials produced simultaneously, each of which represented the release of a single quantum of the neurotransmitter acetylcholine, comprised of several hundred molecules enclosed within a synaptic vesicle. Since that time, a considerable number of molecules have been recognized to fulfill the four essential criteria of neurotransmitters:

1. synthesis in the neuron
2. presence in the axon terminal
3. release from terminals in response to stimulation
4. production of a biological effect when applied exogenously to synapses

Specific biological actions are generally ascribed to given neurotransmitters, but each may be involved in several functional pathways. Neurotransmitters can be classified according to their chemical structure:

- biogenic amines, principally acetylcholine, ACh, and monoamines, which can be subdivided into the indolamine, serotonin (5-hydroxytryptamine), and the catecholamines, dopamine, noradrenaline, and adrenaline
- amino-acids, the most common of which are GABA (γ aminobutyric acid), glutamic acid, and glycine
- neuroactive peptides, such as the endogenous opioids
- neurotransmitters with no chemical similarities, such as nitric oxide and adenosine

Neurotransmitters are released from neurons or from related endocrine cells in response to the arrival of an action potential or the interaction of specific ligands with membrane receptor proteins. These trigger the opening of voltage-dependent Ca^{2+} channels, allowing Ca^{2+} influx into the nerve terminal or endocrine cell. However, the release kinetics and Ca^{2+} requirements vary considerably between different types of neurons, between neurons and endocrine cells, and also between different types of neurotransmitters. Thus, exocytosis of small synaptic vesicles in neurons occurs less than a millisecond after stimulation, while in cultured pheochromocytoma cells the delay can be 200 ms and this increases to up to one second for adrenaline and noradrenaline secretion from large (2–500nm diameter) secretory granules in adrenal chromaffin cells. Apart from cell-type variations, neurotransmitters can be "fast" (e.g., ACh, GABA, etc.) compared to the "slow" peptides. Not only are peptides released more slowly, but they can act over long periods distant from their release sites because they are not rapidly eliminated. In addition to these differences, neurotransmitter release from synapses can be modified locally. Thus Ca^{2+} influx at a terminal can be modulated by presynaptic membrane receptors, such as GABA receptors, which can regulate Ca^{2+} channels.

Three principle hypotheses propose a molecular basis for neurotransmitter release, which is generally considered to occur via a multistep process:

- translocation of neurotransmitter storage vesicles to synaptic membrane
- docking at active sites
- exocytosis of vesicle contents into the extracellular space, initiated by Ca^{2+}-triggered fusion of the vesicle membrane with the terminal plasma membrane
- vesicle endocytosis involving clathrin-coated vesicles

Synaptic vesicles first accumulate in the distal cytoplasm of resting presynaptic terminals in a reserve pool, linked to F-actin by the protein synapsin, but a large population is already predocked (i.e., situated close to active sites on the synaptic membrane). Translocation of vesicles from the reserve pool towards active sites is thought to involve synapsin phosphorylation by PKC or Ca^{2+}/calmodulin-dependent kinase II, provoked by the rise in Ca^{2+} concentration near Ca^{2+} channels. This permits vesicles to dissociate from the cytoskeleton and migrate to the plasma membrane. The docking process itself is widely thought to be mediated by protein-protein interactions according to the SNARE hypothesis, in which certain highly conserved proteins also implicated in constitutive secretion and intracellular trafficking participate. These include soluble cytosolic NSF (N-ethylmaleimide Soluble Factor) proteins and Soluble NSF Attachment Proteins (SNAPs) interacting with target (t-) and vesicular (v-) membranes through t- and v-SNARE (Soluble NSF Attachment Receptor) proteins. The proteins synaptobrevin and synaptotagmin have been identified as v-SNAREs on the secretory vesicles and SNAP-25 and syntaxin have been identified as t-SNAREs on the plasma membrane. This docking process, involving GTP and the small G-protein rab3, requires the formation of NSF/SNAP/SNARE multimeric complexes. Subsequent Ca^{2+}-dependent ATP hydrolysis enables synaptotagmin and synaptobrevin to dissociate from the complex, permitting the vesicle to move closer to the membrane and thus initiating the fusion step. This Ca^{2+}-dependent step involves opening of a fusion pore, in which the vesicle membrane protein synaptophysin may participate, allowing the neurotransmitter inside the vesicle to diffuse into the synaptic cleft. Other synaptic vesicle proteins, such as cysteine string proteins and syntaxin, may aid vesicles to associate with Ca^{2+} channels, thus helping to prime the transmitter release cascade.

Two alternative models have been proposed for neurotransmitter release. The first, the "kiss and run" theory, is a variation on the above theme in which secretory organelles undergo rapid and reversible interactions with the membrane which stop short of complete fusion but allow variable amounts of neurotransmitter to leak out. This mechanism thus involves the transient formation of a gate with channel properties, which is equivalent to the initial step in complete fusion between synaptic vesicle and terminal membrane. A contrasting hypothesis completely abandons the notion that release involves vesicle fusion and suggests that a 200 kDa "gate" protein, termed a "mediatophore," located in the cholinergic nerve terminal membrane, is alone sufficient for the Ca^{2+}-dependent release step. It estimates that the brief opening of around ten gate proteins would allow quantal release of ACh and at the same time generate miniature end-plate potentials.

It seems unlikely that neurotransmitters are released by an identical mechanism in all neurons and related cells, since not all proteins considered to be implicated in exocytosis are expressed in all neurons. The markedly different release kinetics for neuroendocrine cells and neurons, and even for different types of synapses, also suggest that regulation differs between cell types. Photoreceptor retinal bipolar cells and hair cells of the inner ear illustrate this dramatically. They possess unusual structures called ribbon synapses specifically adapted to rapid, almost continuous firing, in contrast to the action potential-triggered periodic bursts of activity from conventional synapses. These release neurotransmitters from vesicles according to a graded response dependent upon the extent of their membrane depolarization. In such synapses, Ca^{2+} channel types differ from those in other neurons by their resistance to inactivation; and translocation of vesicles to their active zones is not controlled by synapsins, as in conventional terminals, but by a more efficient mechanism to satisfy their high firing rate.

K. LANGLEY
University of Strasbourg, France

ACETYLCHOLINE (ACH)
AMINO ACID NEUROTRANSMITTERS
DOPAMINE (DA)
GABA RECEPTORS
NEURONAL CELL BODY
SEROTONIN (5-HYDROXYTRYPTAMINE, 5-HT)

NEUROTRANSMITTERS

A neurotransmitter is a chemical substance that carries a "message" from the terminal bouton of one nerve cell or neuron across a tiny gap (synapse) to receptor sites on another neuron. Neurotransmitters are synthesized in the neuron's cell body and stored in tiny sacs called synaptic vesicles, or synthesized within the nerve terminal.

Nobel Prize winner Otto Loewi is credited with demonstrating synaptic transmission's chemical nature in 1920. Loewi isolated a frog heart with an attached vagus nerve. Stimulating the nerve caused the heart's rate to decrease; when Loewi extracted some of the fluid around the heart and applied it to an unstimulated second heart, the second heart's rate slowed as well. Loewi concluded that stimulating the nerve to the first heart had released a chemical at the synapse between the vagus and the heart, and this chemical had transported the message to the heart to slow down. Because he had stimulated the vagus nerve, Loewi called the mysterious chemical *Vagusstoff*. He later learned that *Vagusstoff* was really acetylcholine (ACh).

When a neurotransmitter such as ACh diffuses across the synapse, it contacts postsynaptic receptors to produce either a local excitatory effect or an inhibitory effect. Whether the postsynaptic neuron passes on the message by producing an action potential depends on the sum of the influences on it from presynaptic neurons.

A neurotransmitter that remained in the synapse for any length of time would limit the number of messages that could be passed from one neuron to another. Thus, the neurotransmitter is being inactivated almost from the moment of its release. The most common method of inactivation is called reuptake, which behaves just like it sounds—the neurotransmitter is taken back into the presynaptic neuron from which it came.

The second major inactivation mechanism is used on ACh and neuropeptides and is called enzymatic degradation. In this case, acetylcholinesterase (AChE) breaks the ACh molecule into two parts, neither of which produces the effect of ACh.

The brain uses dozens of neurotransmitters. For many years, it was believed that each neuron released only one particular neurotransmitter from all its nerve terminals. We now know that most neurons release two or three transmitters, and some may release as many as five or six.

The three major categories of neurotransmitters are biogenic amines, amino acids, and peptides. One biogenic amine—ACh—is found in the brain and spinal cord; it is also the chemical that carries messages from the motor nerves to the skeletal muscles. Other important biogenic amines include dopamine, norepinephrine, and serotonin.

Dopamine is importantly implicated in two major brain disorders: schizophrenia and Parkinson's disease. In Parkinson's disease, cells die in a brain area called the substantia nigra (Latin for "black substance"). In the course of the disease, the "black substance" actually becomes white because of the loss of dopamine-producing cells. Nigral cells normally send dopamine to a part of the brain controlling motor activities. Without this neurotransmitter, the afflicted individual begins to develop characteristic symptoms, such as tremor at rest and a lack of movement. Replacement therapy—supplying drugs to increase the amount of dopamine in the brain (e.g., L-dopa)—may work temporarily, but unfortunately, the disease is progressive.

Schizophrenia is also believed to be caused by a defect in the dopamine system, in this case by increased activity at certain dopamine receptors. Major antipsychotic drugs such as chlorpromazine (Thorazine) block dopamine receptors.

Norepinephrine (also called noradrenalin) is the neurotransmitter at the neuromuscular junctions in the sympathetic (fight or flight) nervous system and is also found at many places in the brain. Decreased norepinephrine and/or serotonin activity in the brain are thought to be responsible for depression. Drugs used to treat depression increase the release of norepinephrine, serotonin, or both.

Gamma-aminobutyric acid (GABA) is an example of an amino acid neurotransmitter. GABA is the most common inhibitory neurotransmitter in the brain, and the destruction of GABA neurons in a major motor system (the basal ganglia) is responsible for Huntington's disease. Symptoms of Huntington's disease include involuntary movements. Antianxiety drugs such as diazepam (Valium®) and alprazolam (Xanax®) act by stimulating GABA receptors.

The peptide neurotransmitters include all of the substances summarized by the generic term "endorphin," which stands for "endogenous morphine-like substance," as well as others. Because opiates such as morphine and heroin are so addictive, brain researchers suspected that there were receptors for the opiates in the brain. In 1973, such receptors were found, and their discovery led to the further discovery of naturally occurring neurotransmitters with the opiate-like properties of analgesia and euphoria. Some functions in which the endogenous opiates have been implicated include the placebo effect, runner's high, and pain relief from acupuncture (but not from hypnotically induced analgesia).

B. M. THORNE
Mississippi State University

DOWN REGULATION
NEURONAL CELL BODY
NEUROTRANSMITTER RELEASE

NEWCOMB, THEODORE M. (1903–1984)

Theodore M. Newcomb was among the first psychologists to identify himself with social psychology, a field scarcely known until the 1940s. Before that, there had been two social psychologies—one psychological and one sociological—and the twain rarely met. Newcomb's *Social Psychology* (1950) took pains to show how intrapersonal (psychological) and interpersonal (sociological) events are interdependent, each being an essential aspect of the socialization process that influences the other.

Newcomb's research is typically longitudinal and carried out in the field rather than in the laboratory. His first well-known study (1943), involving changes in attitudes toward public affairs on the part of all students in Bennington College over a four-year period, showed that individuals' characteristics and their group memberships interacted to influence attitude change—both over four years

or less in college and over 15 years after leaving college. A study (1961) of interpersonal attraction within 17-person groups of students, replicated in two successive years, supported Heider's theories of the relationship between perceived agreement with fellow members and liking (attraction) of individual fellow members.

Particularly during and after World War II, Newcomb was active in affairs of the American Psychological Association. He was president of the Society for the Psychological Study of Social Issues (1946), of the Division of Personality and Social Psychology (1950), and of the American Psychological Association (1955–1956). In 1981 he received the APA's annual gold medal award.

STAFF

NICOTINE

Nicotine is a pale yellow, highly toxic liquid contained in the leaves of several species of plants. Commercially, nicotine is extracted from dried *Nicotiana tabacum* leaves and used for making insecticides (nicotine sulfate) or tobacco products (Benowitz, 1998). Nicotine is extremely poisonous and can cause respiratory failure, convulsions, nervous system paralysis, and death if consumed in a single dose of 50 mg or more.

Nicotine is typically found in tobacco products such as cigarettes, cigars, snuff, chew, and pipes as well as in insecticides such as Black Leaf (40% nicotine sulfate; Benowitz, 1998). Most tobacco products, such as cigarettes, contain 10 milligrams or more of nicotine content (American Cancer Society, 1997). However, when smoked, a single cigarette delivers approximately 1 to 3 mg of nicotine, as well as 4,000 other chemicals, to the nose, mouth, and primarily to the lungs, where nicotine can quickly be assimilated through cell membranes into the pulmonary capillary blood flow (Grunberg, 1999). After inhaling, nicotine is transferred to the brain within approximately 10 seconds from the first puff (National Institute on Drug Abuse, 1998). With smokeless tobacco products, such as chew, snuff, pipes, or cigars, nicotine is more slowly absorbed through the membranes of the mouth.

Because smoking so quickly transports nicotine to the brain, cigarettes provide an efficient and consistent "drug-delivery system" (NIDA, 1998; Hurt & Robertson, 1998). Researchers are studying the complex neurochemical process of nicotine dependency in the brain (Stephenson, 1996). Nicotine effects the mesolimbic system, or the pleasure center of the brain, creating increased levels of dopamine, a neurotransmitter essential to the functioning of the central nervous system and emotion regulation. (Brauthar, 1995; Pich, Pagliusi, & Tessari, 1997). An increase of dopamine elicits feelings of euphoria and has been linked to the addictive process. Nicotine also elicits pleasurable feelings, such as relaxation, stimulation, and increased attention, reinforcing continued use (Corrigall, Franklin, Coen, & Clarke, 1992; Hurt & Robertson, 1998; Ovid & Pomerleau, 1992).

The discontinuation of tobacco use leads to severe withdrawal symptoms such as depressed mood, insomnia, irritability, difficulty concentrating, and decreased sensitivity to pleasure (Centers for

Disease Control and Prevention, 1995). These symptoms are most acute during the first two weeks, when nicotine is slowly leaving the body. Because of the pleasure associated with smoking and the withdrawal symptoms associated with discontinuation, tobacco use is very difficult to stop. Of an estimated 60 million current smokers (United States Department of Health and Human Services, 1998), nearly 35 million make a serious attempt to quit each year. Most relapse within the first few days of a quit-attempt. Less than 7% achieve more than a year of abstinence, with long-term abstinence rates at only 10% to 30% (e.g., Rose, 1996; Lichtenstein & Glasgow, 1992; Shiffman, 1993).

Because nicotine is so addictive, as well as toxic, tobacco use is a primary health concern. Cigarette smoking contributes to approximately 400,000 deaths annually in the United States and the majority of these deaths are directly attributable to cancer (ACS, 1999; Peto, Lopez, Boreham, Thun, & Heath, 1992). Nicotine stimulates the division of small cell carcinomas, a cancer cell line, by several hundred percent. As a result, tobacco use is associated with many types of cancers such as lung, larynx, esophageal, bladder, pancreatic, kidney, and colon cancers (ACS, 1996; CDC, 1993a, 1993b). Tobacco use also leads to an increase in heart disease as well as respiratory diseases such as emphysema and chronic bronchitis (CDC, 1993a). Additionally, women who smoke during pregnancy have increased risk of spontaneous abortion, preterm birth rates, low birth weights, and fetal or infant death (DiFranza & Lew, 1995; Slotkin, 1998).

Identifying those at risk for nicotine dependence, including effective prevention and treatment approaches, will help decrease the prevalence and mortality rate of smoking. Since young people vastly underestimate the addictive nature of nicotine, adolescence proves to be the most significant time for experimentation and initiation (Chassin, Presson, Rose, & Sherman, 1996). More than 6,000 persons under the age of 18 try their first cigarette each day (CDC, 1993b). At least 4.1 million adolescents between the ages of 12 to 17 become regular cigarette smokers, and these rates continue to climb, particularly among African-American and Hispanic adolescents (CDC, 1998). Approximately 70% of adolescent smokers report wishing they had never started smoking. Many factors, such as availability, sophisticated advertising techniques by tobacco companies, and minimal legal consequences for using tobacco help engage initial users and reinforce continued use. Public policy programs that target each of these factors will likely aid in the prevention of adolescent nicotine dependence and subsequent long-term health costs.

Effective methods to assist people in quitting smoking can clearly reduce the risk of cancer and health hazards from smoking (CDC, 1993a). Recent advances in the treatment of nicotine dependence offer a variety of options such as behavior modification programs, antidepressants (Zyban), nicotine replacement therapies such as the patch (Nicoderm CQ, Nicotrol, Habitrol, and so on) or nicotine gum (Nicorette), as well as nasal spray (Nicotrol NS; Henningfield, 1995; Rose, 1996). Different smoking-cessation therapies are more appropriate for certain individuals. A personal physician can assist individuals in tailoring treatments to meet their needs.

Scientists are currently investigating factors that influence the predisposition toward nicotine addiction, such as biological and genetic mechanisms of nicotine dependence. It is hoped that a more refined understanding of the biological, genetic, and behavioral mechanisms of nicotine dependence may lead to the development of interventions that will improve treatment outcome, and ultimately, the mortality and morbidity associated with smoking and cancer.

REFERENCES

American Cancer Society. (1996). *Cancer facts and figures, 1996.* Atlanta, GA: Author.

American Cancer Society. (1997). *Cigarette nicotine disclosure report, 1997.* Atlanta, GA: Author.

American Cancer Society. (1999). *Surveillance research: Vital statistics of the United States, 1998.* Atlanta, GA: Author.

Benowitz, N. L. (1998). *Nicotine safety and toxicity.* New York: Oxford University Press.

Brauthar, N. (1995). Direct effects of nicotine on the brain: Evidence for chemical addiction. *Archives of Environmental Health, 50*(4), 263–267.

Chassin, L., Presson, C. C., Rose, J. S., & Sherman, S. J. (1996). The natural history of cigarette smoking from adolescence to adulthood: Demographic predictors of continuity and change. *Health Psychology, 15,* 478–484.

Centers for Disease Control and Prevention. (1993a). Mortality trends for selected smoking-related and breast cancer–United States, 1950–1990. *Morbidity and Mortality Weekly Report, 42*(44), 857, 863–866.

Centers for Disease Control and Prevention. (1993b). Reasons for tobacco use and symptoms of nicotine withdrawal among adolescent and young adult tobacco users–United States, 1993. *Morbidity and Mortality Weekly Reports, 48*(19), 398–401.

Centers for Disease Control and Prevention. (1995). Symptoms of substance dependence associated with use of cigarettes, alcohol and illicit drugs, 1991–1992. *Morbidity and Mortality Weekly Reports, 44*(44), 830–831.

Corrigall, W. A., Franklin, K. B. J., Coen, K. M., & Clarke, P. B. S. (1992). The mesolimbic dopaminergic system is implicated in the reinforcing effects of nicotine. *Psychopharmacology, 107,* 285–89.

DiFranza, J. R., & Lew, R. A. (1995). Effect of maternal cigarette smoking on pregnancy complications and sudden infant death syndrome. *Journal of Family Practice, 40,* 385–394.

Grunberg, N. (1999). Understanding the facts about nicotine addiction. *Brown University Digest of Addiction Theory and Application, 18,* 6, S1.

Henningfield, J. (1995). Nicotine medications for smoking cessation. *New England Medicine, 333,* 1196–1203.

Hurt, R. D., & Robertson, C. R. (1998). Prying open the door to the tobacco industry's secret about nicotine: The Minnesota tobacco trial. *Journal of the American Medical Association, 280*(13), 1173–81.

Lichtenstein, E., & Glasgow, R. E. (1992). Smoking cessation: What have we learned over the past decade? *Journal of Consulting and Clinical Psychology, 60,* 518–527.

National Institute on Drug Abuse (1998). Nicotine addiction. *National Institute on Drug Abuse* (NIH Publication 98–4342). Washington, DC: US Government Printing Office.

Ovid, E. F., & Pomerleau, C. S. (1992). Nicotine in the central nervous system: Behavioral effects of cigarette smoking. *American Journal of Medicine, 93:* 1a–7s.

Rose, J. E. (1996). Nicotine addiction and treatment. *Annual Review of Medicine, 47,* 493–507.

Peto, R., Lopez, A. D., Boreham, J., Thun, M., & Heath, C. (1992). Mortality from tobacco in developed countries: Indirect estimation from national vital statistics. *Lancet, 339,* 1268–1278.

Pich, E. M., Pagliusi, S. R., & Tessari, M. (1997). Common neural substrates for the addictive properties of nicotine and cocaine. *Science, 275,* 83–86.

Shiffman, S. (1993). Smoking cessation treatment: Any progress? *Journal of Consulting and Clinical Psychology, 61,* 718–722.

Slotkin, T. A. (1998). The impact of fetal nicotine exposure on nervous system development and its role in sudden infant death syndrome. *Nicotine Safety and Toxicity.* New York: Oxford University Press.

Stephenson, J. (1996). Clues found to tobacco addiction. *Journal of the American Medical Association, 275,* 1217–1218.

United States Department of Health and Human Services. (1998). *National Household Survey on Drug Abuse, 1998.* Atlanta, GA: Centers for Chronic Disease Prevention and Health Promotion Research.

H. LaChance
K. Hutchison
University of Colorado, Boulder

ADDICTION

NIETZSCHE, FRIEDRICH WILHELM (1844–1900)

Friedrich Wilhelm Nietzsche was a German philosopher of the last century whose ideas have had a powerful influence on the attitudes and philosophies of the twentieth century. He attended the University of Leipzig and received his doctorate in classical philology in 1869. He took an appointment at the University of Basel from 1869 to 1879 teaching classical philology. He spent much of his life in the mountains of Switzerland and in Italy for reasons of health.

Nietzsche felt a need to devise a completely new system of values to account for the advances in the scientific field, particularly in biology and psychology. The human-individual was now considered as a biological specimen, a member of the animal kingdom;

the old idealism of humanity had lost its meaning. Charles Darwin had promoted the idea of life as a struggle for survival; Nietzsche redefined this life force as a creative, active surge. He taught that the human expression of this life force is the *will to power,* based on the biologic urge to excellence and equilibrium. The will to power was the motive force in the human evolutionary process (Edman & Schneider, 1941). Nietzsche was convinced that psychology should consider the will to power as the primary human motive.

Nietzsche influenced many important European writers, philosophers, and psychologists, Sigmund Freud among them. Freud's theories of the unconscious and of the instinctual nature of man were similar to Nietzsche's. Nietzsche taught that human motives are found in our instincts and drives, not in thoughts and reason; consciousness and conscious acts are done in service to untamed drives.

In another respect, Nietzsche foreshadowed the humanistic movement in psychology by criticizing the elemental approach of the experimental psychologists and by calling for "a psychology 'in the grand style' that would consider the entirety of a man's psyche" (Zuane, 1975, p. 196).

N. A. HAYNIE

NIGHTMARES

Nightmares are defined as disturbing dreams associated with anxiety or fear that cause an awakening from sleep. Generally, the sufferer quickly becomes alert after awakening and readily recalls the details of the dream. Nightmares are often confused with night terrors, which represent a clinically distinct entity. Night terrors involve an incomplete awakening from deep NREM sleep and are associated with disorientation, severe distress, and prominent autonomic arousal. During the night terror, the sufferer, most typically a young child, is difficult to awaken. Following complete awakening, the sufferer usually has no (or only vague) recall of dream mentation. Night terrors usually occur in the first hours of sleep when NREM slow-wave sleep stages are prominent. In contrast, nightmares occur predominantly in REM sleep, and involve often complex and elaborate imagery that can be easily recalled. Nightmares have been less frequently associated with light stages of NREM sleep and in this context may have a more linear, organized narrative structure than the often bizarre and nonlinear material from REM nightmares. However, there is only limited empirical support for this qualitative distinction. Nightmares typically occur in the last hours of sleep when REM sleep activity is more intense. Dream recall is also known to improve as a function of time elapsed since sleep onset irrespective of sleep stage (Rosenlicht, Maloney, & Feinberg, 1994). Thus, nightmares experienced at the end of the sleep period will be associated with better recall than those occurring early in the sleep period.

Nightmares are a universal human experience and have engendered much literary attention but only limited empirical research. One aspect of dreams and nightmares that makes them difficult to study is the simple fact that they cannot be directly observed.

Dreams can be recalled only after awakening, and the fidelity of recall is not known. For example, it is possible that dream-recall is limited to dream events occurring in the immediate period prior to arousal. Further, dream recall is subject to retrieval biases in which the subject will impose order on what can be chaotic mental experience.

While nightmares are experienced universally at some point, the experience of frequent nightmares is considerably less common. The *Diagnostic and Statistical Manual of Mental Disorders-Fourth Edition* (American Psychiatric Association [APA], 1994) include the diagnosis of Nightmare Disorder, which was formerly referred to as Dream Anxiety Disorder. The criteria for this disorder include repeated awakenings from sleep with recall of frightening dreams that leads to significant impairment. While the precise epidemiology of this disorder is yet to be characterized, the available data suggest that it occurs in 10 to 50% of children (APA, 1994), with a peak incidence between the ages of 3 and 6 (Leung & Robson, 1993), and a decline in frequency with age (Hartmann, 1984). Nightmares occur with less frequency in adults and can be associated with alcohol withdrawal, dopamine stimulating medications, or withdrawal of REM suppressing medication. Surveys have found that 10 to 29% of college students report having a nightmare once or more per month (Feldman & Hersen 1967; Belicky & Belicky, 1982). A survey of 1,006 adults, ages 18 to 80 years, in Los Angeles found that 5.3% of respondents reported that frightening dreams were a current problem (Bixler, Kales, & Soldatos, 1979). This and other surveys (Coren, 1994) have reported a higher prevalence of frightening dreams in women. Unfortunately, little polysomnography data are available in adults with Nightmare Disorder, in part because nightmares are rarely captured in the sleep laboratory. Further, survey data are limited by the fact that subjects are often confused about the difference between night terrors and nightmares (Hartmann, 1984).

There has long been an interest in the relationship between trauma exposure and nightmares (Freud, 1920; Kardiner & Spiegel, 1947; Horowitz, 1976; Brett & Ostroff, 1985; Ross, Ball, Sullivan, & Caroff, 1989). Subjectively, the experience of the nightmare feels as distressing as a traumatic experience feels during waking life. The nightmare is associated with the full sensory perception of an autonomic fear response. Because nightmares frequently occur during REM sleep, during which skeletal muscles are atonic, the sufferer will frequently experience a sense of paralysis and an inability to escape. Hartmann in his studies of frequent nightmare sufferers found that adult exposure to violent assault increased nightmare frequency, though he was not able to find a history of early childhood trauma (1984). He and others obtained data from frequent nightmare sufferers and suggested that frequent nightmare sufferers were distrustful, schizoid, and alienated, but not psychotic (Hartmann, Russ, van der Kolk, Falke, & Oldfield, 1981; Kales et al., 1980). Kales and colleagues (1980) also found that the onset of nightmares was preceded by major life events. The National Co-morbidity Survey reports a lifetime prevalence of Posttraumatic Stress Disorder (PTSD) of 10.4% in women and 5.0% in men (Kessler, Sonnega, Bromet, Hughes, & Nelson, 1995), similar to the gender ratio reported in frequent nightmare sufferers.

At present there are insufficient data to validate the diagnosis of Nightmare Disorder as a separate nosologic entity apart from PTSD. One large study of combat veterans found that frequent nightmares were virtually specific for those diagnosed with PTSD at the time of the survey (Neylan et al., 1998). In this study, combat exposure was highly associated with nightmares, moderately associated with sleep onset insomnia, and only weakly related to sleep maintenance insomnia. These relationships are consistent with the results of the combat veteran twin study (True et al., 1993), which showed that combat exposure was highly correlated with reports of dreams and nightmares and only weakly associated with sleep maintenance insomnia. These observations are also consistent with several other studies that show a low to moderate correlation between nightmares and other domains of sleep disturbance. (Coren, 1994; Krakow, Tandberg, Scriggins, & Barey, 1995). Thus, the nightmare appears to be the primary domain of sleep disturbance related to exposure to traumatic stress.

There is no standardized treatment for frequent nightmares. There are a number of small-scale, open-label trials using sedating antidepressants, cyproheptadine, benzodiazepine, clonidine, and guanfacine. None of these has been systematically studied in large, randomized, controlled trials. One novel treatment for repetitive nightmares is dream rehearsal therapy. Nightmare sufferers describe their nightmares in the context of group psychotherapy; they then repetitively rehearse alternate and non-traumatic outcomes to their nightmare narratives. This technique has been found to reduce the frequency and intensity of recurrent nightmares (Krakow, Kellner, Pathak, & Lambert, 1995).

REFERENCES

American Psychiatric Association. (1994). *Diagnostic and Statistical Manual of Mental Disorders* (4th ed.). Washington, DC: Author.

Belicky, D., & Belicky, K. (1982). Nightmares in a university population. *Sleep Research, 11,* 116.

Bixler, E. O., Kales, A., Soldatos, C. R., et al. (1979). Prevalence of sleep disorders in the Los Angeles metropolitan area. *American Journal of Psychiatry, 136,* 1257–1262.

Brett, E. A., & Ostroff, R. (1985). Imagery and posttraumatic stress disorder: An overview. *American Journal of Psychiatry, 142,* 417–424.

Coren, S. (1994). The prevalence of self-reported sleep disturbances in young adults. *International Journal of Neuroscience, 79,* 67–73.

Feldman, M. J., & Hersen, M. (1967). Attitudes toward death in nightmare subjects. *Journal of Abnormal Psychology, 72,* 421–425.

Freud, S. (1920). Beyond the pleasure principle. In *Complete psychological works* (Vol. 18). London: Hogarth.

Hartmann, E. (1984). *The nightmare: The psychology and biology of terrifying dreams.* New York: Basic Books.

Hartmann, E., Russ, D., van der Kolk, B., Falke, R., & Oldfield, M. (1981). A preliminary study of the personality of the nightmare sufferer: Relationship to schizophrenia and creativity? *American Journal of Psychiatry, 138,* 794–797.

Horowitz, M. J. (1976). *Stress response syndromes.* New York: Jason Aronson.

Kales, A., Soldatos, C. R., Caldwell, A. B., Charney, D. S., Kales, J. D., Markel, D., & Cadieux, R. (1980). Nightmares: Clinical characteristics and personality patterns. *American Journal of Psychiatry, 137,* 1197–1201.

Kardiner, A., & Spiegel, H. (1947). *War stress and neurotic illness.* New York: Paul B. Hoeber.

Kessler, R. C., Sonnega, A., Bromet, E., Hughes, M., & Nelson, C. B. (1995). Posttraumatic stress disorder in the National Comorbidity Survey. *Archives of General Psychiatry, 52,* 1048–1060.

Krakow, B., Kellner, R., Pathak, D., & Lambert, L. (1995). Imagery rehearsal treatment for chronic nightmares. *Behaviour Research and Therapy, 33,* 837–843.

Krakow, B., Tandberg, D., Scriggins, L., & Barey, M. (1995). A controlled comparison of self-rated sleep complaints in acute and chronic nightmare sufferers. *Journal of Nervous and Mental Disease, 183,* 623–627.

Leung, A. K., & Robson, W. L. (1993). Nightmares. *Journal of the National Medical Association, 85*(3), 233–235.

Neylan, T. C., Marmar, C. R., Metzler, T. J., Weiss, D. S., Zatzick, D. F., Delucchi, K. L., Wu, R. M., & Schoenfeld, F. B. (1998). Sleep disturbances in the Vietnam generation: An analysis of sleep measures from the National Vietnam Veteran Readjustment Study. *American Journal of Psychiatry, 155,* 929–933.

Rosenlicht, N., Maloney, T., & Feinberg, I. (1994). Dream report length is more dependent on arousal level than prior REM duration. *Brain Research Bulletin, 34,* 99–101.

Ross, R. J., Ball, W. A., Sullivan, K. A., & Caroff, S. N. (1989). Sleep disturbance as the hallmark of posttraumatic stress disorder. *American Journal of Psychiatry, 146,* 697–707.

True, W. R., Rice, J., Eisen, S. A., Heath, A. C., Goldberg, J., Lyons, M. J., & Nowak, J. (1993). A twin study of genetic and environmental contributions to liability for posttraumatic stress symptoms. *Archives of General Psychiatry, 50,* 257–264.

T. C. NEYLAN

ANXIETY
FEAR
SLEEP DISORDERS

NONASSOCIATIVE LEARNING

From a biological viewpoint, learning is the process of acquiring new knowledge about the environment and the self that is necessary for the survival of the species. Two major classes of learning can be distinguished: nonassociative and associative. In nonassociative learning, the subject learns about a stimulus by being repeatedly exposed to it. Three forms of nonassociative learning are distinguished: habituation, dishabituation, and sensitization. Habituation consists of a reduced response upon repeated presentation of the stimulus. For example, when a loud noise is repeatedly presented to a subject, the startle response rapidly diminishes. Dishabituation is the recovery from habituation to a given stimulus upon presentation of a new salient stimulus. Sensitization is an increased response to a stimulus upon its repeated presentation. An example of sensitization is an increased pain or fear response to a mild tactile stimulus after a painful pinch.

Habituation has been studied extensively in the marine mollusk Aplysia. In these studies habituation was found to be due to a decrease in synaptic transmission between sensory neurons, interneurons, and motor neurons. Aplysia has some defensive reflexes for withdrawing its tail, gill (respiratory organ), and siphon (used to expel seawater). When a tactile stimulus is delivered to the siphon, withdrawal of the siphon and the gill takes place; a mild tactile stimulus to the tail elicits tail withdrawal. When this stimulus is repeatedly presented, these withdrawal reflexes habituate. When the tactile stimulus is novel, sensory neurons innervating the siphon generate excitatory synaptic potentials in the interneurons and motor cells, and the gill is withdrawn. With repeated stimulation, the synaptic potential generated by sensory neurons on interneurons and motor cells becomes progressively smaller because the amount of transmitter released into the synaptic cleft is decreased. After these modifications, the reflex response is reduced. The decrease of synaptic transmission in the sensory neurons is due to a decrease of chemical transmitter released by each action potential from the presynaptic terminal. This decrease of synaptic transmission originates from an inactivation of an N-type Ca^{2+} channel in the presynaptic terminal. In this way, less Ca^{2+} enters into the terminals and, consequently, less transmitter is released. During habituation there is a decrease in the mobilization of transmitter vesicles into the active zone and the number of vesicles available for release. This reduction in the synaptic transmission can last for many minutes. Changes in the synaptic connections between several interneurons and motor neurons represent the components of the storage process for the short-term memory for habituation. This memory storage depends on plastic changes in the strength of preexisting connections. Habituation does not depend on specialized memory neurons which store information, but rather it depends on neurons that are integral components of a normal reflex pathway. Different types of experiences may be stored in different cells that have many functions other than storing information. In control animals, 90% of sensory neurons establish detectable connections with motor neurons, while in habituated animals these connections are reduced to 30%. This low incidence persists for one week and does not completely recover for three weeks. The duration of the habituation depends on the extent of training: A single training session of ten stimuli in Aplysia produces a short-term habituation lasting a few minutes, but four training sessions produce a long-term change that may last up to three weeks.

Habituation takes place also in the central nervous system of mammals. By monitoring the release of dopamine in different brain areas of rats by the microdialysis technique in vivo, it has been found that dopamine in the nucleus accumbens shell is also involved in the habituation phenomenon. Thus, when rats are fed an unusually palatable food, Fonzies, extracellular dopamine increases in the nucleus accumbens shell, but a second meal of the same food given after either two hours, one day, or three days fails to activate dopaminergic transmission. Recovery of responsiveness takes place after five days from the last meal. In contrast, feeding of Fonzies increases the extracellular dopamine in the prefrontal cortex; of about 100% and a second Fonzies feeding after 2h is able to again stimulate dopaminergic transmission in the prefrontal cortex, in fact, extracellular dopamine increases about 130%. Therefore, in the prefrontal cortex, in contrast to the nucleus accumbens, dopamine does not undergo habituation.

Sensitization is a more complex form of nonassociative learning, and it has been extensively studied in the gill-withdrawal reflex in Aplysia. A single stimulus can produce a reflex enhancement that lasts minutes (short-term sensitization), and later it can produce an enhancement that lasts days or weeks (long-term sensitization). Short-term sensitization is produced following a single noxious stimulus to the head or tail. Synapses made by the sensory neurons on interneurons and motor neurons become modified. After the sensitizing stimulus, a group of facilitating interneurons that synapse on the sensory neurons (some of which are serotoninergic) become activated. There is an enhanced transmitter release from the sensory neurons and a larger postsynaptic potential in the motor neurons. The consequence is an enhanced activation of interneurons and motor neurons and thus is an enhanced behavioral response. Serotonin binds receptors that are coupled with a GTP-binding protein (G_s), which activates adenylyl ciclase and increases the concentration of cAMP-dependent protein kinase. The protein kinase phosphorylates a K^+ channel protein, reducing a component of the K^+ current that normally repolarizes the action potential. There is a prolonged action potential and a prolonged activation of the N-type Ca^{2+} channels. More Ca^{2+} enters into the terminals and enhances transmitter release. Serotonin and cAMP enhance the Ca^{2+} through the L-type Ca^{2+} channel, increasing the availability of transmitter vesicles. Serotonin also binds another class of receptors coupled with diacylglycerol (DAG), the second messager that activates protein kinase C which facilitates the mobilization of vesicles and regulates a nifedipine-sensitive Ca^{2+} channel and the delayed K^+ channel. After these modifications, more transmitter is available for release than normal and thus more transmitter is released from the sensory neurons.

In long-term sensitization there are similar, but more extended, modifications than the short-term process at the same locus: the connections between the sensory neurons and motor neurons of the gill withdrawal reflex. In both short and long-term sensitization there is an increase in synaptic strength due to the enhanced transmitter release, but long-term facilitation requires the synthesis of new protein and mRNA. Repeated training prolongs activation of protein kinase A that phosphorylates nuclear regulatory proteins. These proteins affect the regulatory regions of DNA, increasing the transcription of RNA and the synthesis of specific proteins. One of the newly synthetized proteins initiates the internalization and degradation of neuronal cell adhesion molecules, allowing the restructuring of the axon arbor. With this process, sensory neurons can form other connections with the same motor neurons or make new connections with other cells. Other proteins also contribute to these processes. Prolonged activation of PKA is due to a decreased level of PKA regulatory subunits that depends on prolonged stimulation and increased level of cAMP. In this way the catalytic subunits are active for long time and contribute to long-term facilitation of transmitter release. Both in short-term and long-term sensitization, the enhanced responses of the animal to test stimuli depend on enhanced release of transmitters from sensory neurons to interneurons or to motor neurons at the level of preexisting synapses, but increases in axonal arborization and synaptic contacts are exclusive of long-term sensitization. The enhanced and prolonged activation of interneurons and motor cells depends on more synaptic connections with sensory neurons.

Studies about feeding show that dopamine transmission is activated by unpredicted food consumption in a different manner in the two compartments of the nucleus accumbens: the medioventral shell and the laterodorsal core. In fact, while dopamine transmission is activated by Fonzies feeding to a larger extent in the shell than in the core, preexposure to food consumption inhibits the dopamine response in the shell but potentiates it in the core. The response properties of dopamine transmission in the nucleus accumbens core, while different from those of the nucleus accumbens shell, are similar to those of the prefrontal cortex. So the response of the prefrontal cortex to Fonzies feeding is not inhibited by preexposure to appetitive stimuli. The responsiveness of dopamine transmission to consummatory stimuli in the nucleus accumbens compartments seems to differ in its adaptive properties. While the dopaminergic responsiveness to feeding in the nucleus accumbens core is sensitized by preexposure to Fonzies feeding, responsiveness in the shell is inhibited. Physically released dopamine in the nucleus accumbens shell might enable the association between the stimuli generated by food consumption and the biological consequences of feeding. By this mechanism, gustatory stimuli are attributed a motivational valence which determines the specific consummatory response to be emitted by the subject upon further encounter of the same food. The potentiation of dopaminergic transmission in the nucleus accumbens core by preexposure to Fonzies feeding is consistent with an activational role of dopamine in the nucleus accumbens and with the possibility that release of dopamine in the nucleus accumbens core facilitates the motor expression of motivated behavior.

REFERENCES

Bassareo, V., & Di Chiara, G. (1997). Differential influence of associative and nonassociative learning mechanisms on the responsiveness of prefrontal and accumbal dopamine transmission to food stimuli in rats fed ad libitum. *Journal of Neuroscience, 17*(2), 851–861.

Bassareo, V., & Di Chiara, G. (1999). Differential responsiveness of dopamine transmission to food-stimuli in nucleus accumbens shell/core compartments. *Neuroscience, 3,* 637–641.

Beggs, J. M., Brown, T. H., Byrne, J. H., Crow, T., LeDoux, J. E., LeBar, K., & Thompson, R. F. (1999). Learning and memory:

Basic mechanisms. In M. J. Zigmond, F. E. Bloom, S. C. Lands, J. L. Roberts, & L. R. Squire (Eds.), *Fundamental neuroscience* (pp. 1411–1454). San Diego, CA: Academic Press.

Eichenbaum, H. B., Cahill, L. F., Gluck, M. A., Hasselmo, M. E., Keil, F. C., Martin, A. J., McGaugh, J. L., Murre, J., Myers, C., Petrides, M., Roozendaal, B., Schachter, D. L., Simons, D. J., Smith, W. C., & Williams, C. L. (1999). Learning and memory: Systems analysis. In M. J. Zigmond, F. E. Bloom, S. C. Lands, J. L. Roberts, & L. R. Squire (Eds.), *Fundamental neuroscience* (pp. 1455–1486). San Diego, CA: Academic Press.

Kandel, E. R. (1985). Cellular mechanisms of learning and the biological basis of individuality. In E. R. Kandel (Ed.), *Principles of neural science* (pp. 1009–1031). Amsterdam: Elsevier.

Kaplan, H. I., Sadock, B. J., & Grebb, J. A. (1994). Contributions of the psychosocial sciences to human behavior. In Kaplan, H. I., & Sadock, B. J. (Ed.), *Synopsis of psychiatry* (pp. 157–220). Baltimore: Williams & Wilkins.

Kupfermann, I. (1985). Learning and memory. In E. R. Kandel (Ed.), *Principles of neural science* (pp. 997–1008). Amsterdam: Elsevier.

Moruzzi, G. (1975). Attività innate e attività acquisite. In UTET (Unione Topografico Editrice Torinese), Torino (Ed.), *Fisiologia della vita di relazione*.

V. BASSAREO
University of Cagliari, Italy

LEARNING
NEURAL MECHANISMS OF LEARNING

NONPARAMETRIC STATISTICAL TESTS

Nonparametric statistical methods are based on weaker assumptions than standard parametric procedures such as the *t* test, analysis of variance, and inferential procedures associated with the Pearson correlation coefficient. For example, the *t* test for two independent groups assumes that the scores in the groups are independent and are randomly sampled from normally distributed populations with equal variances. In contrast, nonparametric or distribution-free tests do not make such strong assumptions about the populations.

Although there is agreement that many standard parametric tests are fairly robust with regard to type 1 error when the assumption of normality is violated, the power of these tests may be severely reduced when the populations are not normally distributed. Severe losses of power may occur when the underlying populations are *heavy-tailed;* that is, when there are more scores in the extremes of the distributions (outliers) than would be expected for a normal distribution. In contrast, there does not seem to be a large effect on power if the underlying distributions are *light-tailed* (i.e., have rel-

atively fewer scores in the tails). In certain cases, it may be shown that certain nonparametric tests have considerably more power than the corresponding parametric tests. However, the nonparametric tests are not completely free of assumptions, and unless certain conditions are met, they do not test the same null hypotheses as the corresponding parametric tests. For example, the Wilcoxon-Mann-Whitney test based on ranks is a commonly used "nonparametric" analog of the independent-groups *t* test. The null hypothesis of the *t* test is that the population means of the two groups are equal. If one does not wish to make assumptions about the underlying populations but wants to make inferences about measures of location such as the mean or median, one must make the assumption (the so-called "shift" assumption) that, whatever their characteristics, the populations are identical except for their locations. Only in this case do the *t* and Wilcoxon-Mann-Whitney tests both address the same null hypothesis.

RATIONALES FOR SOME CLASSES OF NONPARAMETRIC TESTS AND SOME EXAMPLES

In most nonparametric tests, the original scores or observations are replaced by other variables that contain less information, so that the statistical tests that are used are less influenced by extreme scores. An important class of tests uses the ordinal properties of the data. The original observations are first replaced by the ranks from 1 to *n*, and subsequent operations are performed only on the ranks. Some of these procedures (but certainly not all) are computationally simple because the means and variances of the first *n* integers are easily obtained. It has been shown that some of these procedures are equivalent to what would be obtained by first converting the scores to ranks, then performing the standard parametric tests on these ranks.

If equality of population distributions except for location can be assumed, both the Wilcoxon-Mann-Whitney procedure mentioned above, and the Kruskal-Wallis procedure (the generalization to more than two conditions) test hypotheses about location with more power than their parametric analogues when the underlying distributions are heavy-tailed. If identical distributions cannot be assumed but homogeneity of the variances of the ranks can be assumed, Vargha and Delaney (1998) have shown that what is tested is whether there is a general tendency for scores in at least one of the populations to be larger (or smaller) than those in all of the remaining populations, taken together. If this holistic hypothesis is of interest in situations in which homogeneity of variance or ranks cannot be assumed, alternatives to the *t* and ANOVA procedures (such as the Welch test) performed on the ranks are recommended.

Another important class of tests employs only information about whether an observation is above or below some value such as the median. All values above the median might be assigned a "plus" and those below it a "minus," so that, in effect, they are replaced by a new variable that can take on only two values.

A number of nonparametric analogs exist for repeated-measures ANOVAs and matched-group *t* tests. One approach is simply to rank all of the scores, then perform a repeated-measures ANOVA on the ranks. This test is less powerful than the corresponding ANOVA performed on the original scores if the underlying populations have normal distributions. However, when the distributions are heavy-tailed, the ANOVA on the ranks can be more powerful. This approach is recommended when samples come from populations that are heavy-tailed and symmetric. If the distributions are skewed and the average correlation is not close to zero, the Friedman chi-square test, which involves ranking the scores separately for each subject, will tend to be more powerful.

A very different approach does not depend on the idea of the usual population model of inference—in which inferences are made about parent populations from which the available data have been randomly sampled. Rather, the ways in which a sample of scores, however acquired, is distributed across two or more treatment conditions is considered by permutation tests. If the scores are distributed in ways that would be unusual had they simply been randomly assigned to conditions, a treatment effect is indicated.

Yet another class of tests is based on the frequency with which "runs" occur in the data. A run is a series of events of one type occurring together as part of an ordered sequence of events. The ordering can occur temporally or could be based on the magnitudes of the scores. For example, assume that a fair coin is tossed 10 times and that on each toss, a head (H) or tail (T) randomly occurs. The sequence of outcomes

H H T H T T T H H T

has six runs (HH, T, H, TTT, HH, and T), whereas the sequence

H H H H H T T T T T

has the same numbers of heads and tails but only two runs. It is possible to generate the distribution of the number of runs that will occur if the coin is fair and the sequence of events is truly random. A study of the obtained runs can be helpful in deciding about the randomness of a sequence of observations.

REFERENCES

Vargha, A., & Delaney, H. D. (1998). The Kruskal-Wallis test and stochastic homogeneity. *Journal of Educational and Behavioral Statistics, 23,* 170–192.

SUGGESTED READING

Kepner, J. L., & Robinson, D. H. (1988). Nonparametric methods for detecting treatment effects in repeated-measures designs. *Journal of the American Statistical Association, 83,* 456–461.

Siegel, S., & Castellan, N. J. (1988). *Nonparametric statistics for the behavioral sciences.* New York: McGraw-Hill.

Zimmerman, D. W., & Zumbo, B. D. (1993). The relative power of parametric and nonparametric statistical methods. In G. Keren & C. Lewis (Eds.), *A handbook for data analysis in the behavioral sciences: Methodological issues.* Hillsdale, NJ: Erlbaum.

A. D. WELL
University of Massachusetts, Amherst

PARAMETRIC STATISTICAL TEST STATISTICS IN PSYCHOLOGY

NONVERBAL COMMUNICATION

Nonverbal communication is nonlinguistic transmission of information through visual, auditory, tactile, and kinesthetic channels. Like other types of communication, nonverbal communication involves encoding and decoding processes. Encoding is the act of generating the information; decoding is the act of interpreting the information. Nonverbal encoding processes include facial expressions, gestures, posture, tone of voice, tactile stimulation (such as touch), and body movements (such as moving closer or farther away from a person or object). Decoding processes involve the use of received sensations combined with previous experience in interpreting and understanding the information. Although nonverbal communication may refer to mass communication such as television, art products, and multimedia productions, in this discussion the emphasis is on interpersonal communication, whether face-to-face or indirect (e.g., by telephone or electronic mail).

Culture has a significant impact on nonverbal communication. For instance, the ways in which people use gestures are specific from culture to culture. People in the western world nod their heads to signal agreement, but people in countries like India and Bangladesh often move their heads from side to side to convey a similar meaning. Most Asians use gestures such as bowing to show their respect to other people. Many Asians are silent when they are disappointed, and continue using their usual tone of voice and smiling face even though they are in an emotional state such as anger, embarrassment, fear, or sadness. Most Americans seem more comfortable in using nonverbal communication to encode their emotional states than do Asians.

Scientists and practitioners have long been aware of the importance of the relationship between nonverbal communication and emotion. In 1872 Charles Darwin published *The Expression of the Emotions in Man and Animals.* In 1905 Sigmund Freud observed, "He that has eyes to see and ears to hear may convince himself that no mortal can keep a secret. If his lips are silent, he chatters with his finger-tips; betrayal oozes out of him at every pore" (Freud, 1905/1953, pp. 77–78). By the 1970s and 1980s researchers had started to develop refined procedures and technology for measuring the encoding and decoding processes of nonverbal communication (Feldman & Rimé 1991; Harper, Wiens, & Matarazzo, 1978). The methods vary from social to physiological and from descriptive to experimental studies. They have generated general laws and measures of individual differences about transmission of cognitive and affective information.

The relationship between facial expression and emotion has been extensively studied by Ekman (1993). He began studying facial expression and emotion in 1965 with a single question: Are they universal or culture-specific? When he could not find a simple answer, his research ran into "many new and challenging questions." With Friesen, Ekman originated the Facial Action Coding System (FACS) in 1978. The FACS is a reliable rating technique, using photographs or a video for encoding and decoding basic emotions such as anger, disgust, fear, happiness, sadness, and surprise. Matsumoto & Ekman (1992) developed the Japanese And Caucasian Facial Expressions of Emotion (JACFEE) and the Japanese And Caucasian Neutral Faces (JACNeuF). This instrument has been widely used around the world, and results have shown it to be reliable for studying emotions accurately. Reviewing Ekman's and others' studies on facial expressions of emotion and personal adjustment, Keltner, Kring, & Bonanno (1999) concluded that there is a correlation and proposed further study of the process of how facial expression has a significant role in personal adjustment.

Another nonverbal cue to the emotions experienced by another person is voice. Bachorowski (1999) summarizes vocal characteristics, sometimes called speech acoustics, such as pitch and jitter. Banse and Scherer (1996) found that vocal profiles not only show the degree of specific intensity for different emotions but also differentiate valence (pleasantness) and quality aspects. Raters use vocal cues to identify the speaker's emotional state from vocal information. During a psychoanalytic process, verbal and nonverbal messages are explored because they have both conscious and unconscious aspects (Sackler, 1998). Hall, Harrigan, and Rosenthal (1995) note the important role of nonverbal communication in the interaction between a clinician and a client. They claim that perceived quality of interaction depends mostly upon how a clinician uses nonverbal communication with his or her client. The clinician's facial expressions, voice tones, and gestures will create like and dislike in clients; and the success of therapy depends on the consistencies between the clinician's verbal and nonverbal communication.

Using vocal cues (sometimes called paralinguistics or prosody) Sundberg (1966) developed a Test of Implied Meanings (TIM) using judgments of the real meanings of sentences spoken by actors. Test results showed that skilled therapists were mostly accurate in judging the real meaning than others and females were better interpreter than males. The most developed and researched paralinguistic test is the Profile of Nonverbal Sensitivity (PONS) developed by Rosenthal, Hall, DiMatteo, Rogers, and Archer (1979). The PONS includes visual and auditory stimuli. One of its findings is that facial expression is superior in decoding accuracy as compared to other channels.

Intimacy may be detected from proxemics (the use of space in gestures, postures, and touching). The more intimate a relationship between individuals, the more nonverbal communication is observed (Patterson, 1990). Proxemics between the individuals is closer; they do more hugging and touching (although the amount and manner of this is related to culture). Hall and Veccia (1990) studied touching between the sexes. They found that both men and women touched each other on purpose with the same frequency. The difference was that males tended to put their arms on the females' shoulders, but females put their arms on the males' arms (perhaps related to differences in height).

The expression and perception of mental states are complex phenomena present in all people. How sincere and truthful is a person? How intensely does a companion feel? Is facial expression of emotion universal or culture-specific? How do people use gestures, tones of voice, and other nonverbal cues influence individuals perceptions of emotional states in others? Will increasing contact in a globalizing world require and lead to greater ability to encode and decode mental states in others? These are only a few of many questions that remain to be answered. The advancement of theory and research in nonverbal communication is important for improving the understanding of basic processes in human interaction.

REFERENCES

Bachorowski, J. A. (1999). Vocal expression and perception of emotion. *Current Directions in Psychological Science, 8,* 53–57.

Banse, R. & Scherer, K. R. (1996). Acoustic profiles in vocal emotion expression. *Journal of Personality and Social Psychology, 70*(3), 614–636.

Ekman, P. (1993). Facial expression and emotion. *American Psychologist, 48,* (4), 384–392.

Ekman, P. & Friesen, W. V. (1978). *Facial action coding system.* Palo Alto, CA: Consulting Psychologists Press.

Feldman, R. S. & Rimé, B. (Eds.). (1991). *Fundamentals of nonverbal behavior.* Cambridge: Cambridge University Press.

Freud, S. (1953). Fragment of an analysis of a case of hysteria. In *The standard edition of the complete psychological works of Sigmund Freud* (Vol. 7). London: Hogarth. (Original work published 1905.)

Hall, J. A., Harrigan, J. A., & Rosenthal, R. (1995). Nonverbal behavior in clinician-patient interaction. *Applied & Preventive Psychology, 4,* 21–37.

Hall, J. A. & Veccia, E. M. (1990). More "touching" observations: new insights on men, women, and interpersonal touch. *Journal of Personality and Social Psychology, 59*(6), 1155–1162.

Harper, R. G., Wiens, A. N. & Matarazzo, J. D. (1978). *Nonverbal communication: The state of the art.* New York: Wiley.

Keltner, D., Kring, A. M., & Bonanno, G. A. (1999). Fleeting signs of the course of life: Facial expression and personal adjustment. *Current Directions in Psychological Science, 8,* (1), 18–22.

Matsumoto, D. & Ekman, P. (1992). American-Japanese cultural differences in the recognition of universal facial expressions. *Journal of Cross-Cultural Psychology, 23,* 72–84.

Patterson, M. L. (1990). Function of nonverbal behavior in social interaction. In H. Giles & W. P. Robinson (Eds.), *Handbook of language and social psychology (pp. 101–120).* New York: Wiley.

Rosenthal, R., Hall, J. A., DiMatteo, M. R., Rogers, P. L. & Archer, D. (1979). *Sensitivity to nonverbal communication: The PONS test.* Baltimore: Johns Hopkins University Press.

Sackler, M. L. (1998). The unspoken message. *Modern Psychoanalysis, 23,* (1), 53–62.

Sundberg, N. D. (1966). A method for studying sensitivity to implied meanings. *Gawein 15,* 1–8.

SUGGESTED READINGS

Anderson, P. A. & Guerro, L. K. (Eds.). (1998). *Handbook of communication and emotion: Research, theory, applications, and contexts.* San Diego: Academic Press.

Darwin, C. (1965). *The expression of the emotions in man and animals.* Chicago: University of Chicago Press. (Reprint of same title, 1872, London: John Murray)

Guerro, L. K., De Vito, J. A., & Hecht, M. L. (Eds.). (1999). *The nonverbal communication reader: Classic and contemporary readings (2nd ed.).* Prospect Heights, Il.: Waveland Press.

Knapp, M. L. & Hall, J. A. (1992). *Nonverbal communication in human interaction (3rd. ed.).* New York: Holt, Rinehart, and Winston.

Russell, J. A. (1999). Emotion communicates. *Contemporary Psychology APA Review of Books, 44,* (1), 26–27.

J. E. P. Hadiyono
Gadjah Mada University, Yogyakarta, Indonesia

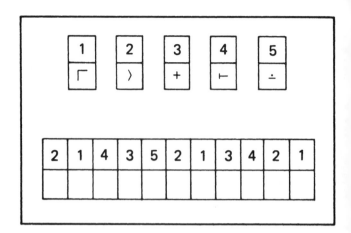

Figure 1.   Digit symbol task from the Wechsler Performance subtests, as adapted by L. J. Cronbach (1970), p. 210. © 1955 by The Psychological Corporation. Reproduced by permission.

NONVERBAL INTELLIGENCE TESTS

These are tests presenting nonlanguage tasks, and/or administered with minimal or no use of language, and presumably measuring intellectual capacity. Names and limitations of specific tests are found in Anastasi, *Psychological Testing* (1982, ch. 10, 16), and Cronbach, *Essentials of Psychological Testing* (1983/1970).

TERMS AND ILLUSTRATIVE TASKS

The term *nonverbal* is closely related to other test labels (Anastasi, 1982). A *performance* test connotes manipulation tasks such as block design or assembling objects, rather than paper and pencil tests. A *nonlanguage* test requires no use of oral or written language by examinee or tester. A *nonreading* test requires no reading or writing by examinee, but may require some verbal comprehension such as understanding oral directions to identify a picture. The distinction *verbal* versus *nonverbal* connotes language-laden, especially education-dependent tasks versus tasks lifted out of a verbal-educational context. The difference should not be confused with the *verbal* versus *quantitative* distinction, since many quantitative tests sample school-acquired skills (e.g., computing prices of products). Certain cognitive tests yielding verbal, quantitative, and nonverbal subscores attempt to tap these different (but not wholly independent) abilities.

The terms just reviewed are only roughly reflected in the names of tests or in the structure of nonverbal items. Substituting symbols for digits may be called a "performance" measure, for example, although it is a paper-and-pencil task (see Figure 1), while a figure-analogies task (see Figure 2) may combine nonverbal content with instructions the examinee must read. In addition to types of questions already named here, tasks typically called "nonverbal" have included picture arrangement, picture completion, drawing persons or animals, embedded figures (finding a geometric pattern in a larger pattern field), and matrices (see Figure 3). In the present discussion, *nonverbal* (NV) will refer to task content—a somewhat improper convenience, since psychometricians use that term and related labels technically, to refer both to content and to conditions of administration.

Figure 2.   Figure analogies item from the Cognitive Abilities Test. Reproduced by permission of R. L. Thorndike and E. P. Hagen.

Developmental tests are a category of measures related to NV tests, since infant and preschool testing must eliminate or control the role of language. Developmental tests often sample sensory, motor, attentional, perceptual, and manipulatory capabilities as well as cognitive functions. Piagetian scales assess qualitative functions such as imitation and the purposeful use of objects (Anastasi, 1982; Cronbach, 1970).

RELATION TO THEORY OF INTELLECT

The idea of a "pure," context-free ability to discern abstract relationships—distinct from schooled abilities and pervading performance on diverse intellectual tasks—goes back to Charles Spearman, who named this analytical talent *g.* NV tests have been significant in theoretical work on intelligence because tasks such as figure analogies, matrices, and embedded figures (all of which can range vastly in difficulty) have been considered good measures of a *g*-like ability. In the United States, theories of intellect departed from Spearman to stress separate abilities rather than a pervasive general ability, but "analytical" ability remained of interest. The evolution of this theory through the late 1960s, described by Cronbach (1970), had several phases. After about 1940, when tests yielding both verbal (V) and NV or performance (P) subscores become available, the conception of a "performance IQ" gained popularity. Bilingual children and mild retardates, for example, were found to score better on P measures than on V-loaded tests. (P subscores, however, came to be overinterpreted by some users, who thought of P as indicating the "true" IQ of a subject with V lower than P.) The V-P distinction lost credibility on empirical grounds, and was supplanted by the idea of an ability continuum with "crystallized" (education-dependent) abilities at one end, "fluid" (analytical)

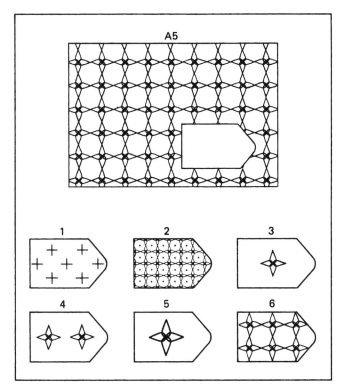

Figure 3.   Item from Raven Standard Progressive Matrices, a test given with oral instructions. From J. C. Raven, *Guide to the Standard Progressive Matrices* (London: H. K. Lewis & Co., 1960). Reprinted by permission of J. C. Raven Limited.

abilities at the other, and mixed cognitive tasks in between. Analytical ability was also theorized to be similar to Piaget's formal-operations level of intellect. Subsequent and/or more complex theories of intellect, often relying on factor analysis and contributing to practical multiple-aptitude measurement, are not of chief concern here, but functions important to NV performance have been clarified by this work. For instance, matrices performance seems to require perceptual, inductive, and spatial aptitudes (Anastasi, 1982; Cronbach, 1970). During the 1960s and 1970s, when both concern for fair test use and interest in cross-cultural testing increasingly dominated the U.S. testing scene, NV test tasks were drawn into the design of tests intended to be unlinked, or somehow "fairly" linked, to culture and subculture.

USES

Performance, nonlanguage, and nonreading measures have contributed to evaluation work with special populations, such as infants and preschoolers, the retarded, the handicapped, and nonreaders. Demonstration, pantomime, and translation are among the means used to construct or adapt tasks so as to minimize the role of language, education, or culture in test performance. Some NV measures first designed to be "culture-fair" came to be helpful in clinical testing. For discussions of special and clinical uses, see Anastasi (1982, ch. 10, 16).

The effort to use NV tasks in the search for "culture-free" tests, then for "culture-fair" tests, met with much less success than had been hoped (Anastasi, 1982). From the 1950s into the 1980s, re-

search usually showed that: (a) NV scores rise with socioeconomic level, as do V scores; (b) tests standardized on members of a culture or subculture favor persons of similar background; and (c) in a given cultural milieu, predictive validity of a test drops as cultural loading drops. NV tests sometimes have their applied uses when testers wish to minimize language-related advantages of some subjects over others, because NV performance depends less on verbal-educational shaping than V performance does. No test performance, however, is independent of culture; NV tasks cannot measure some "real" intellectual ability unrelated to experience in a human community.

REFERENCES

Anastasi, A. (1982). *Psychological testing* (5th ed.). New York: Macmillan.

Cronbach, L. J. (1983/1970). *Essentials of psychological testing.* New York: Harper & Row.

Raven, J. C. (1960). *Guide to the standard progressive matrices.* London: Lewis.

Thorndike, R. L., & Hagen, E. P. (1978). *Manual for the cognitive abilities test.* Iowa City, IA: Riverside Press.

SUGGESTED READING

Buros, O. K. (1949). *Mental measurements yearbook.* Highland Park, NJ: Gryphon Press.

A. B. PRATT
Capital University

CULTURAL BIAS IN TESTS
INTELLIGENCE MEASURES
MEASUREMENT

NONVERBAL THERAPIES

Nonverbal therapies are therapies whose effects are produced without a primary focus on verbal exchange between the therapist and client. Intended to produce emotional relief, personality growth and development, and the elimination of neurotic and psychotic symptomatology, they include art therapy (dance, drawing, music, painting, and sculpture); biofeedback training; breathing awareness techniques (yoga, Zen, and rebirthing); diet and megavitamin therapies; emotional release techniques (aqua-energetics, bioenergetics, LSD treatment, neo-Reichian, orgone, primal, and radix); energy-balancing techniques (acupressure, polarity, reflexology, shiatsu, and Touch for Health); massage and deep tissue work (postural integration, Rolfing, and Tragar); movement awareness techniques (Aikido, tai chi, and Feldenkrais); perception training; and sensory deprivation and sleep therapies.

Such nonverbal therapies are based on the nondualistic philosophy maintaining that body and mind are one, and thus any emotional suffering which was not relieved by open display at the time of occurrence and which has not been released since then, is represented not only mentally and emotionally but also physically. Thus a technique which liberates or corrects or develops the body also can be expected to liberate, correct, or develop the mind. Most nonverbal techniques conceptualize a block in the free energy flow throughout the tissues of the body part involved in the original suffering—a block caused by holding on to the tension, rather than relieving it by appropriate emotional display. Such blocks may promote further discomfort and malfunctioning in the body, as the body seeks to compensate for the poor functioning of the part originally damaged. Such blocks may also prevent further mental or physical development from proceeding healthfully. Any of these blocks, which may have originated in infancy or childhood, may be perpetuated despite extensive psychotherapy, if structural or functional changes are not produced by direct effects on the parts blocked.

Many nonverbal techniques have been originated by, and are taught to and practiced by, people whose background and training are outside the mental health professions. This may account for the relative absence of methodically collected data, the few control studies, and the almost total lack of presentations through the ordinary avenues of professional journals and conferences. These factors in turn alienate the academic and professional worlds from the world of "New Age Consciousness," and perpetuate their doubts about the validity of these techniques. Most validity claims depend on anecdotal reports from satisfied clients—reports typically presented by the practitioners themselves without any control over the halo effects involved. The overall effectiveness of these nonverbal techniques is usually represented as being significantly higher than that of traditional psychotherapies. In many cases the technique is claimed to be effective in more than 90% of cases—claims that further disenchant the academic world.

ART THERAPY

Prior to the 1960s, art therapy was generally regarded as an adjunct to verbal-process psychotherapy in the traditional mental health treatment facility. Music, dance, the graphic arts, and sculpture were used primarily to produce specific effects in the mood and behavior of the patient, especially inmates who did not readily engage in verbal exchange. The patients passively experienced works of art which were generally selected for their appreciation by caretakers whose primary training was in either occupational or recreational therapy or in the arts.

As the value of art productions by patients for diagnostic purposes was substantiated, the use of art in the treatment setting expanded. Art therapy has now gradually emerged as a primary treatment mode in its own right: art therapists are specialized mental health professionals whose education usually includes graduate training in psychology and supervised clinical practice. The patient is encouraged to produce art-works as active, creative expressions of personality dynamics and problem solutions.

Patients seen by psychotherapists in private practice are generally not specifically encouraged to participate in any particular art form; when such patients do seek to sublimate through an art form,

their activities are generally not interpreted by art therapists, but instead serve primarily as forms of catharsis. With the progressive decentralization of mental health care, changes in the use of art therapy can be anticipated.

BIOFEEDBACK TRAINING

Evidence of the beneficial effects of training the autonomic nervous system responses first appeared in scientific journals during the 1960s, although similar training had been carried out for more than 6,000 years in the guise of yogic training. The major advance made possible by modern biofeedback training is the use of an external visual or auditory signal to inform the subject that specific bodily changes are being produced. Initially, such signals were used primarily to train patients with psychosomatic diseases such as hypertension or gastric ulcers to curtail activities that contributed to their ailments, frequently by entering voluntarily into particular brainwave states. Also, they are increasingly in use to facilitate control over neurotic symptoms such as anxiety or depression, and to promote the detailed learning of optimal mental and physical sets, as in training an athlete to keep certain muscles relaxed. Breathing awareness techniques, movement awareness techniques, and perception training (as well as sex therapy) are all specific forms of biofeedback, but without the sophisticated electronic equipment to alert subjects to the quality of their performance.

BREATHING AWARENESS TECHNIQUES

Such techniques are described in detail in the ancient scriptures of Hinduism and Buddhism, where they are known as *Pranayama*, the science of the breath. Particular patterns of breathing involving measured lengths of inhalations, pauses, and exhalations have been in use for 6,000 years to produce particular energy flows and mind states associated with healing. Lifelong practice of the disciplined breathing was generally regarded as necessary for gaining yogic breath mastery. Such techniques were brought into use in the United States for specific therapeutic purposes as Zen therapy emerged in the 1940s. They utilized relaxed slow breathing to counter-condition neurotic symptom states.

Another breathing pattern in which the inhalations and exhalations are constantly connected, without any pauses, serves as the practice producing the Rebirthing phenomenon, a technique developed during the 1970s.

DIET AND MEGAVITAMIN THERAPIES

Also referred to as aspects of orthomolecular psychiatry, nutritional approaches to healing neurosis, psychosis, and character disorders came to the public's attention late in the 1960s. They are based in part on the theory that the brain can be allergic to or intoxicated by various substances which are part of the ordinary diet, and also on the theory that the brain may not receive appropriate nutrition when the body is coping with such commonly ingested substances as refined carbohydrates, caffeine, and nicotine. The basic premise of these therapies is that the brain's functions of healthy feeling and thinking can be accomplished only if the brain is receiving the nutrition it needs; if intoxicating substances are present in the diet or as metabolic products, extremely large doses of vitamins and minerals may be needed to help the body eliminate such toxins.

Hoffer's work with Megavitamins (1966) indicates that the vast majority of first-time admissions to state mental health hospitals can regain normal mental functions within six weeks to six months by taking doses of ascorbic acid and niacin in excess of 2,000 milligrams per day. Combined with a diet free of refined carbohydrates and high in natural fiber foods and high proteins, the Megavitamin approach has become widely used in private-practice psychiatry and is recommended for the public at large by health food advisers. Studies within penal institutions and schools also support the usefulness of the no-refined-carbohydrate diet approach for the hyperactive child and the adult offender.

EMOTIONAL RELEASE TECHNIQUES

Throughout the 1960s and 1970s, many techniques were developed which originally aimed at overcoming the resistance and defenses of the patient to verbal psychotherapy. Practitioners discovered that therapeutic effects were produced simply by release phenomena, leading to the use of such techniques to create a womblike setting and establish highly vulnerable body positions so as to promote open emotional release without verbal interaction. These techniques were based on the premise that emotional disturbance is directly related to the depth of repression of old emotional reactions. At times, the techniques are referred to as "scream" therapy.

Outlawed during the late 1960s for use by psychotherapists, LSD had previously been widely used to produce a synesthetic and emotionally labile state which was reported to be highly therapeutic with alcoholics and suicidally depressed and highly anxious people, including the terminally ill. It has been used illicitly to promote emotional release.

ENERGY-BALANCING TECHNIQUES

These techniques are based on ancient Oriental concepts of channels, called meridians, through which life energy is constantly traveling. Illness of every sort, including emotional disorders, is caused by blockage in such channels or by overemphasis of certain channels and underemphasis of others. Stimulation of certain points along appropriate meridians tunes and balances the energy patterns, with concomitant relief of both physical pain and psychological disturbance. Unlike acupuncture, which utilizes needles to stimulate such points, modern techniques like acupressure, polarity, reflexology, shiatsu, and Touch for Health use only finger massage. Some people believe them to be effective in treatment of opiate and amphetamine addictions as well as obesity, depression, and hyperactivity.

MASSAGE AND DEEP TISSUE WORK

These techniques are designed to lengthen fascial coverings of skeletal muscles which have been held in neurotic contraction, and to loosen fascial adhesions between muscles which have caused them to react as a group rather than independently. Deep tissue work is often accompanied by spontaneous emotional release, but this is regarded as secondary to the main aim of freeing the body armor and restoring the body's healthful alignment with the forces of gravity. Some believe these techniques to be effective for learning problems as well as common emotional disorders.

MOVEMENT AWARENESS TECHNIQUES

These procedures are often combined with regulated breathing patterns. Aikido and tai chi, the best known of the nonmartial Oriental practices, trace their beginnings to ancient disciplines originally designed to allow monks and prisoners to maintain good mental and physical health even if confined to very small spaces for long periods. As in dance therapy, the discipline requires specific emotional expression for proper performance.

Within the Western scientific tradition, Moishe Feldenkrais developed his technique from extended study of the way the body is structured and allowed to move when stressed and when functioning optimally. Emotional reactions to the technique are reported as profound and intense, but the technique is designed primarily as a learned correction of faulty movement habits, and is usually sought by people with skeletal-muscular pain or disability.

PERCEPTION TRAINING

This kind of training operates on the premise that healthy personality development, including healthy learning capacity, is based on healthy perceptual development that, in turn, is founded on development of healthy balance and movement skills. These skills can be taught effectively to both schoolchildren and adults, not only to release inherent good learning capacities but also to bring profound changes in personality, including major personality problems. The similarity between the behavior, especially on diagnostic tests, of the individual regarded as having a learning problem and the individual regarded as primarily disturbed psychologically, confounds the distinction between the two types of patients, and confounds as well the issue of which sort of therapy is recommended: psychotherapy or visual-perceptual training. Tests of binocularity and laterality—though available since the early 1900s and easy and quick to perform—are not routinely used within most psychodiagnostic settings; thus, visual-perceptual training is generally recommended only for schoolchildren.

SENSORY DEPRIVATION AND SLEEP THERAPIES

These therapies are based on the clinical finding that many emotionally disturbed people respond favorably to the lessening or elimination of daily stimulation, however routine, and are further supported by evidence that basic belief systems associated with limbic system values change in the absence of stimulation. Prolonged bed rest and sleep produced by sedatives have been recommended as treatment for neurotic and psychotic patients, but are difficult to manage medically, and so have lost favor to shorter periods of total sensory deprivation. Commercially produced tanks, called Samadhi tanks, are available for hourly rental without any specialized supervision and are reported to be extremely refreshing and therapeutic. The Japanese system of Morita therapy is in this genre.

SUGGESTED READING

Aguado, O., & Zucker, D. (1978). *Gravity, the netherside of paradise.* South Laguna, CA: School of the Form.

Andreev, B. F. (1960). *Sleep therapy in neuroses.* New York: Plenum.

Bernstein, P. (Ed.). (1979). *Eight theoretical approaches in dance-movement therapy.* Dubuque, IA: Kendall/Hunt.

Bonny, H., & Savary, L. M. (1973). *Music and your mind.* New York: Harper & Row.

Connelly, D. (1975). *Traditional acupuncture, the law of the five elements.* Columbia, MD: Center for Traditional Acupuncture.

Delacato, K. H. (1970). *A new start for the old with reading problems.* New York: Van Reese Press.

Feldenkrais, M. (1972). *Awareness through movement.* New York: Harper & Row.

Gantt, L., & Schmal, M. S. (1974). *Art therapy—A bibliography, January 1940—June 1973.* Bethesda, MD: National Institute of Mental Health.

Gordon, R. (1972). *Your healing hands.* Marina del Rey, CA: DeVorss.

Grof, S. (1980). *LSD psychotherapy.* Pomona, CA: Hunter House.

Harris, H. (1979). A handbook for aqua-energetics. Master's thesis, California State University, Northridge.

Hawkins, D., & Pauling, L. (1973). *Orthmolecular psychiatry—Treatment of schizophrenia.* San Francisco: Freeman.

Janov, A. (1970). *The primal scream.* New York: Vintage Books.

Jou, T. H. (1981). *The tao of tai-chi.* Rutland, VT: Tuttle.

Lesser, M. (1980). *Nutrition and vitamin therapy.* New York: Bantam.

Lilly, J. (1977). *The deep self.* New York: Warner Books.

Lowen, A. (1975). *Bioenergetics.* New York: Coward, McCann & Geoghegan.

Masunaga, S., & Ohashi, W. (1977). *Shiatsu.* Tokyo: Japan Publications.

Namikoshi, T. (1969). *Shiatsu.* Tokyo: Japan Publications.

Orem, R. C. (1971). *Learning to see—Seeing to learn.* Johnstown, PA: Fax.

Orr, L., & Ray, S. (1977). *Rebirthing in the new age.* Millbrae, CA: Celestial Arts.

Raknes, O. (1970). *Wilhelm Reich and orgonomy.* New York: St. Martin's Press.

Reich, W. (1972/1945). *Character analysis* (3rd ed.). New York: Orgone Institute Press.

Rolf, I. (1977). *Rolfing: Integration of human structures.* Santa Monica, CA: Dennis-Landman.

Segal, M. (1976). *Reflexology.* Hollywood, Calif.: Wilshire Books.

Shioda, G. (1968). *Dynamic akido.* Tokyo, New York, San Francisco: Kodamsha.

Thie, J. (1979). *Touch for health.* Marina del Rey, CA: DeVorss.

Vishnudevananda. (1960). *The complete illustrated book of yoga.* New York: Pocket Books.

Wold, R. M. (Ed.). (1969). *Visual and perceptual aspects for the achieving and underachieving child.* Seattle, WA: Special Child Publications.

E. S. JONES
Los Angeles City College

NOREPINEPHRINE

Norepinephrine is the main neurotransmitter released from noradrenergic (sympathetic) nerve terminals. The noradrenergic neurons occur in both the central and the peripheral autonomic nervous systems. Central noradrenergic fibers arise in neurons located in the brainstem, mainly in the ventrolateral and the dorsomedial medulla oblongata, the locus ceruleus, and the subceruleus area. In the peripheral autonomic nervous system, noradrenergic neurons are located in the para- and prevertebral sympathetic ganglia from which postganglionic fibers originate and supply various organs and blood vessels.

Chemically, norepinephrine is a catecholamine; "catechol" refers to compounds containing an aromatic benzene ring with two adjacent hydroxyl groups (Kopin, 1985; Pacak et al., 1995). Catechol itself (1,2 dihydroxybenzene) does not occur as an endogenous compound in animals. Endogenous catechols include the catecholamine precursor, dihydroxyphenylalanine, its amine products (dopamine, norepinephrine, and epinephrine) and their deaminated metabolites.

The first and rate-limiting enzymatic step in norepinephrine biosynthesis is hydroxylation of tyrosine to form dihydroxyphenylalanine (Figure 1). This reaction is catalyzed by tyrosine hydroxylase and requires tetrahydrobiopterin as a cofactor. Free dopamine and norepinephrine in the cytoplasm of dopaminergic and noradrenergic neurons inhibit tyrosine hydroxylase and thereby regu-

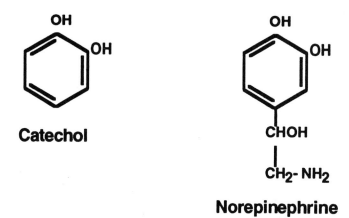

Figure 1.   Chemical sructure of catechol and nonrepinephrine.

late their own synthesis. Hydroxylation of tyrosine is followed by decarboxylation of dihydroxyphenylalanine by L-aromatic amino acid decarboxylase, and this reaction occurs in the cytoplasm of neuronal and nonneuronal cells to yield dopamine (Kagedal & Goldstein, 1988; Kopin, 1985; Pacak et al., 1995).

Dopamine is transported via a nonspecific amine transporter into vesicles found in noradrenergic terminals. In the vesicles hydroxylation of dopamine occurs by dopamine-β-hydroxylase to yield norepinephrine (Kagedal & Goldstein, 1988). In the brain and some peripheral tissues, especially adrenal medulla, norepinephrine is converted to epinephrine by phenylethanolamine-N-methyltransferase.

Upon nerve stimulation, a soluble vesicular content including norepinephrine and other cotransmitters such as chromogranins, neuropeptide Y, dopamine-β-hydroxylase, adenosine triphosphate, and enkephalins are released during noradrenergic nerve terminal depolarization. Sodium and calcium entering nerve terminals during depolarization are thought to evoke exocytosis. In contrast, chloride ions may exert an inhibitory presynaptic effect.

The metabolic disposition of norepinephrine differs in neurons and in nonneuronal cells. Neurons contain monoamine oxidase (a mitochondrial enzyme) but little if any catechol-O-methyl transferase. Axoplasmic norepinephrine is metabolized mainly by deamination in neurons, whereas nonneuronal cells contain catechol-O-methyl transferase as well as monoamine oxidase (Kopin, 1985). The product of norepinephrine deamination, 3,4 dihydroxyphenylglycolaldehyde, is reduced to form 3,4 dihydroxyphenylglycol. Most (60%–80%) of the dihydroxyphenylglycol formed in sympathetic nerve terminals is derived from vesicular norepinephrine. In subjects at rest, plasma dihydroxyphenylglycol levels are determined mainly by vesicular turnover, rather than by reuptake of released norepinephrine. Dihydroxyphenylglycol diffuses freely and rapidly across cell membranes and reaches extraneuronal cells, extracellular fluid, and plasma.

Norepinephrine released from peripheral nerve terminals is removed extensively by reuptake (90%, Uptake-1) and to a lesser degree by extraneuronal uptake (Uptake-2; Kopin, 1985; Pacak et al., 1985). In the brain, the relative roles of these modes of inactivation are poorly understood. Norepinephrine that enters the neurons is largely taken up into vesicles (Table 1). A portion of this norepinephrine (the exact amount of the portion is unknown in brain noradrenergic terminals) is thought to leak out of the vesicles and undergo metabolism in the axoplasm.

Norepinephrine and dihydroxyphenylglycol that enter extraneuronal cells, which, as indicated above, contain catechol-O-methyltransferase as well as monoamine oxidase, are O-methylated to form normetanephrine and further metabolized to methoxyhydroxyphenylglycol. Methoxyhydroxyphenylglycol is also formed from dihydroxyphenylglycol. Plasma normetanephrine accounts for a relatively small proportion (less than 10%) of the total norepinephrine metabolized in the body and is derived mainly from norepinephrine metabolized before entry into plasma and the remainder (45%) from norepinephrine after it enters plasma (Eisenhofer et al., 1995). The extent of nonneuronal metabolism of norepinephrine in the brain is poorly understood. Metoxyhydroxyphenylglycol in plasma is derived mainly either from dihydroxy-

Table 1.   Effects of some drugs on noradrenergic neurotransmission

Drug	Inhibitory effect	Stimulatory effect
Acetylcholine (nicotine receptor)	—	NE release
Acetylcholine	NE release	—
ACTH	—	NE release
Adenosine	NE release	—
Angiotensin II	—	NE release
Clorgyline	Monoamine oxidase-A	—
Cocaine	Uptake-1	—
Desimipramine	Uptake-1	—
Epinephrine (presynaptic β₂-adrenoreceptors)	—	NE release
GABA (GABA$_A$ receptor)	—	NE release
GABA	NE release	—
Glucocorticoids	Uptake-2	—
Lithium	Uptake-1	—
Opioids	NE release	—
Ouabain	Uptake-1	Na$^+$-mediated efflux
Pargyline	Monoamine oxidase-B	—
Phenoxybenzamine	Uptake-1	—
Prostaglandins E	NE release	—
Reserpine	Vesicular uptake	—
Tricyclic antidepressants	Uptake-1	—
Tyramine	—	Vesicular release
α-Methyldopa	Dopa decarboxylase	—

Abbreviations: ACTH: adrenocorticotropin; NE: norepinephrine; GABA: gamma-amino butyric acid.

phenylglycol formed in tissues or from normetanephrine formed in extraneuronal tissues before its entry into plasma. Thus, simultaneous measurements of norepinephrine and its metabolites provide a comprehensive picture of norepinephrine synthesis, turnover, and metabolism in brain and peripheral tissues.

In contrast to sympathetic nerve terminals where norepinephrine is released into the synaptic cleft and acts locally (only a small portion of norepinephrine can reach the bloodstream) via alpha and beta adrenergic receptors, epinephrine and norepinephrine (approximately 20% of the total body amount) released from the adrenal medulla are secreted directly into the adrenal vein and in very short time reach all sites in the body except for most brain regions (catecholamines do not cross the blood-brain barrier).

Norepinephrine released from noradrenergic terminals exerts its effect via adrenoceptors (e.g., α_1: blood vessel constriction, uterus, sphincters of gastrointestinal tract and urinary bladder contractions; α_2: feedback inhibition of norepinephrine release; β_1: heart rate increase; β_2: relaxation of blood vessels, bronchi, sphincters of gastrointestinal tract and urinary bladder dilation).

Distinct patterns of sympathoneuronal activation during exposure to different situations have been demonstrated. Orthostasis, hyperthermia, and cold exposure evoke selective norepinephrine release, whereas hypoglycemia evokes large epinephrine responses.

The availability of simultaneous measurements of norepinephrine and its metabolites introduced a novel application of clinical catecholamine neurochemistry: the delineation of neurochemical patterns associated with specific genetic abnormalities (Goldstein

NORADRENERGIC NERVE TERMINAL   EXTRANEURONAL COMPARTMENT

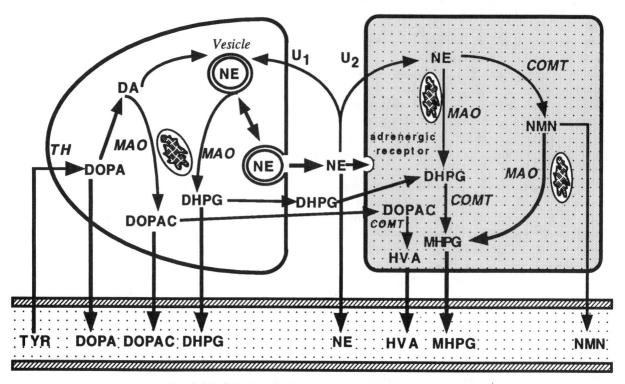

BLOODSTREAM OR EXTRACELLULAR FLUID

Figure 2.   Diagram showing the synthesis, release, uptake, and metabolism of norepinephrine (NE). Abbreviations: COMT: catechol-*O*-methyltransferase, DA: dopamine, DHPG: dihydroxyphenylglycol, DOPA: dihydroxyphenylalanine, DOPAC: dihydroxyphenylacetic acid, HVA: homovanillic acid, MAO: monoamine hydroxylase, NMN: normetanephrine, TH: tyrosine hydroxylase.

et al., 1996). Such abnormalities are seen in phenylketonuria (abnormal phenylalanine and tyrosine hydroxylation), Menkes disease and some forms of orthostatic hypotension (dopamine-β-hydroxylase deficiency or decreased activity), Norrie's disease and aggressive behavior (monoamine oxidase deficiency), and velo-cardio-facil syndrome and DiGeorge syndrome (decreased catechol-O-methyl transferase activity).

REFERENCES

Eisenhofer, G., Rundquist, B., Aneman, A., Friberg, P., Dakak, N., Kopin, I. J., Jacobs, M-C., & Lenders, J. W. M. (1995). Regional release and removal of catecholamines and extraneuronal metabolism to metanephrines. *Journal of Clinical Endocrinology and Metabolism, 80,* 3009–3017.

Goldstein, D. S., Lenders, J. W. M., Kaler, S. G., & Eisenhofer, G. (1996). Catecholamine phenotyping: Clues to the diagnosis, treatment, and pathophysiology of neurogenetic disorders. *Journal of Neurochemistry, 67,* 1781–1790.

Kagedal, B., & Goldstein, D. S. (1988). Catecholamines and their metabolites. *Journal of Chromatography, 429,* 177–233.

Kopin, I. J. (1985). Catecholamine metabolism: Basic aspects and clinical significance. *Pharmacology Review, 37,* 333–364.

Pacak, K., Palkovits, M., Kopin, I. J., & Goldstein, D. S. (1995). Stress-induced norepinephrine release in the hypothalamic paraventricular nucleus and pituitary-adrenocortical and sympathoadrenal activity: In vivo microdialysis studies. *Frontiers in Neuroendocrinology, 16,* 89–150.

K. PACAK
National Institutes of Health

R. MCCARTY
American Psychological Association

NEUROTRANSMITTERS

OBEDIENCE

Obedience is said to occur when a person does what he is told to do. Obedience is thus, by definition, a sociopsychological concept rooted in the relationship between two or more persons, one of whom prescribes a line of action that the other carries out. The psychological character of obedience varies, depending on the nature of the relationship between the subordinate and superordinate figures. The obedience of a child to its parent differs from that of a soldier to a superior. Obedience, however, refers specifically to the overt act of compliance. From one situation to the next, different psychological processes may animate the obedient act.

Obedience may be willingly given or compelled by coercion. Often, voluntary obedience and coercion subtly coexist. In advanced forms of social life, coercion is typically replaced by compliance to legitimate authority: that is, the source issuing the orders is recognized by the actor, and by society, as having the right to prescribe behavior. Thus obedience is given not simply to a person, but to a position or office. Or obedience may be owed to the products of authority, such as traffic lights and systems of law. Force is the ultimate sanction available to society to assure obedience, but in a harmoniously functioning social system it is never wholly the fear of such force which motivates obedience, but rather the obeyer's belief that those issuing commands have the right to do so, that they possess *legitimacy.* Obedience is ordinarily mediated through the assumption of roles that are mutually related in hierarchical terms and that constitute, in Parsons' terminology (1951), "a social system."

SOCIALIZATION

The inculcation of obedience begins in the earliest years. Born into a state of biological dependency, the child is confronted with numerous parental demands, enforced with greater or lesser degrees of discipline. Students of child development have long recognized that "the first social relationship is that of recognizing and complying with the suggestions of authority" (English, 1961). A further phase of socialization for obedience occurs in the school, where children are exposed to an institutional system of authority in which compliance is learned not only to specific persons, but to an impersonal organizational framework.

Such learning is generally deemed essential for mature functioning within the hierarchical systems that characterize the adult social world. Across this experience with authority there is continual exposure to a reinforcement structure in which compliance is rewarded and deviance punished.

THEORIES

In *Group Psychology and Analysis of the Ego* (1923), Freud argued that obedience is rooted in libidinal bonds that develop between members of a group and its leader. These are not reciprocated because the leader cannot love all members with total love. Since the object choice of members is to this extent frustrated, their libidinal ties with the leader come to be based on the more primitive process of identification. This involves introjection of the love object in place of the ego ideal: under the leader's influence, each member of the group renounces his or her own superego, allowing the leader to function as conscience. The leader acquires the same relationship to the followers as the hypnotizer to the hypnotized. The leader thus takes charge of the followers' critical faculties and they regress to a state of childlike dependence.

Erich Fromm's neo-Freudian treatment of obedience emphasizes the interplay between psychodynamic and sociohistorical factors. In *Escape from Freedom* (1941), Fromm argues that the primitive human was submerged in the group and lacked full differentiation as an individual. With increasing self-awareness man released himself from primitive group ties, but experienced corresponding terror at his isolation. Security was conferred by a stable social order which in the Middle Ages gave each individual a clearly defined place in society, though only a limited degree of personal freedom. The erosion of security-conferring structures in modern times leaves the individual anxious and isolated; as one solution to this problem, individuals escape into totalitarian submission, renouncing the insecurities of freedom.

RECENT APPROACHES

In *Obedience to Authority,* Stanley Milgram reported an experimental study on the conflict between conscience and authority. In this study (Milgram, 1963, 1974), persons came to the laboratory and were told to give increasingly severe electric shocks to another person (who was really an actor who did not receive any shocks). The experimenter told the subject to continue stepping up the shock level, even to the point of reaching a level marked *Danger: Severe Shock.* The purpose of the experiment was to see how far the naive subject would proceed before refusing to comply with the experimenter's instructions. The results of the experiment showed that it was far more difficult to defy the experimenter's authority than was generally supposed, and that a substantial proportion of the participants administered the highest shocks on the generator to a protesting victim.

The crux of Milgram's inquiry is a set of experimental variations which examine the variables which increase or diminish obedience. Among other things, his studies found the following: (a) closeness of the victim leads to diminished obedience—a finding explained by the increase in strain which proximity engenders; (b) group forces, depending on whether they support or oppose the experimenter's commands, create widely varying levels of disobedience; and (c) incoherence in the authority structure (as when two experimenters issue contradictory commands) eliminates all obedience. Thus these studies demonstrate the dependence of obedience on the precise arrangement of factors in the situation.

Kelman (1973) approaches the problem of destructive obedience with a tripartite analysis, focusing on factors that remove inhibitions against violence. In his system, *authorization* legitimates a set of destructive actions toward others; *routinization* reduces the destructive procedure to a set of mechanical and administrative routines which discourage the introduction of moral considerations; and *dehumanization* facilitates action against the victim by depriving the victim of personhood.

The significance of obedience for society cannot be overstated; it is the means whereby autonomously functioning individuals are integrated into larger systems of coordination and control. It is thus a key concept in linking the psychological processes of the individual to the social structures of the larger world.

REFERENCES

English, H. B. (1961). *Dynamics of child development.* New York: Holt, Rinehart & Winston.

Freud, S. (1960/1921). *Group psychology and the analysis of the ego.* New York: Bantam Books.

Fromm, E. (1965). *Escape from freedom.* New York: Avon Books. (Original work published 1941)

Kelman, H. (1973). Violence without moral restraint. *Journal of Social Issues, 29,* 25–61.

Milgram, S. (1963). Behavioral study of obedience. *Journal of Abnormal and Social Psychology, 67,* 371–378.

Milgram, S. (1974). Obedience to authority: *An experimental view.* New York: Harper & Row.

Parsons, T. (1951). *The social system.* Glencoe, IL: Free Press.

S. MILGRAM

ACCULTURATION
ALTRUISM
BYSTANDER INVOLVEMENT
DEINDIVIDUATION
MOB PSYCHOLOGY
PEER INFLUENCES
VIOLENCE

OBESITY

Jourard (1963, p. 129) considers obesity the primary appearance problem in the United States: "America is the only country . . . where overweight is a public health problem—where food is abundant, yet a slender body is a cultural value?" Ullman and Krasner (1969) state that overeating can symbolize progressive suicide. Kiev (1974) adds that obesity can hide depression. According to Moore, Stunkard, and Srole (1962), people of the lower economic classes more readily become obese than middle-class individuals, who in turn are more apt to be overweight than wealthier people, who can afford a better-quality, balanced diet. Obese individuals were found to be more immature, and had more psychological problems and poor impulse control.

In the American lifestyle much time is spent in *passive* occupations. Affluence and a short work week contribute to obesity. Overweight people are exploited by promoters of useless gadgets, often dangerous diets, and pills which have serious side effects. Myths persist, such as the necessity of "three full meals a day," breakfast as "the most important meal" with "all day to work it off," and eating by the clock instead of a self-demand schedule of five to six *tiny* meals to maintain blood sugar level. Only two factors lead to normal weight loss: reduced food intake of low calorie foods, avoiding the excess carbohydrates, and exercise sufficient to cause loss of breath.

Eating is a function of: (a) physiological signals ("hunger"); and (b) attractive food (Schachter, 1968). The overeating of obese individuals is governed almost entirely by the enticing appearance of food. Fear liberates sucrose from the liver, so there is no need to eat in a crisis, but in an experiment (Schachter, 1968), frightened obese students with full stomachs ate anyway, and ate more than normals when a laboratory clock falsely implied "dinnertime" (6:00 P.M.). Since a higher level of satiation is needed for them to feel satisfied, obese subjects eat even without hunger. Oversensitivity to environmental stimuli prompts them to eat without physiological need.

According to Lindgren and Byrne (1971), eating tends to make fat people hungry. They eat because the food is there, ignoring signs of satiety or recent consumption. According to Stunkard and Koch (1964), stomach churning does not decrease the eating of fat subjects. Schachter (1967) found that fat students eat more than needed because they ignore internal cues; they eat more as their environment improves, but are discouraged when eating is difficult, as through a tube, proving they need less food than they take in.

Fishbein (1959) emphasized that obese individuals eat without regard to appetite, "to overcome fear or social maladjustments." Calm people gain more, are relaxed and slow, worry less, and sleep longer. Although the main "fat depots" are the breasts, belly, and hips, fat later can invade organs. Excess weight causes shortness of breath and fatigue, joint trouble, high blood pressure and heart attacks, organ damage, and greater risk of diabetes.

Children's weights correlate with those of their parents. According to Eden (1975), the appestat (at the base of the brain, controlling appetite) is possibly "set" higher genetically in some people, or they inherit more fat cells. Children of one obese parent are six times, and children of two such parents 13 times, more likely to become overweight, although parental influence could explain this as well as heredity.

Fat children suffer more respiratory and orthopedic problems, and are more clumsy and accident-prone. Obesity stresses *all* organs, causing indigestion, nervous and dizzy spells, palpitations, rashes, menstrual disorders, and premature aging. The medical consensus is that only about 5% of obesity cases are glandular. People on a high-fat, low-fiber diet have more breast, prostate, and colon cancer, their major surgery risk being two to four times that of normals. Insurance companies advise that, to decrease infant mortality, women should slim down *before* conception, since fat cells multiply in the last three months of pregnancy. An eight-pound baby has three times more chance of becoming overweight than a seven-and-a-half-pound baby. The fat child reaches adulthood with three to four times the normal number of fat cells. Dieting shrinks but never destroys fat cells. Obese mothers have a more difficult labor, afterbirth complications, and more premature infants. The Metropolitan Life Insurance Company states that overweight men have a 50%, and overweight women a 47%, higher death rate.

Skovholt, Resnick, and Dewey (1979) list some secondary "gains" of overeating: (a) one can remain mother-dependent; (b) people expect less from fat people; (c) obesity can express defiance; (d) obesity can be a "chastity belt" for those who fear sex.

The disadvantages of overweight are numerous: (a) fat people are sicker, more accident-prone, and die younger; (b) the obese child is the last to be chosen for a school team, and the chances for college, following an interview, are reduced; (c) fat makes it harder to get an executive job, and fat executives earn less and advance more slowly; (d) fat individuals have fewer marital choices; and (e) the overweight sufferer has more problems in sports, in buying and wearing clothes, and in gaining respect and admiration.

A woman's fat insulates her from exhibitionistic tendencies and masculine approach. Her exaggerated curves may unconsciously deny lesbian interests. The "happy fat person" is a myth that masks frustration. Fat individuals may blame failures on appearance, robbing themselves of desire to resolve them. Masochism may add to the obese individual's self-contempt, and passivity may remove that individual from threatening competition. For many people, food is a tranquilizer. Some women patients use fatness—rather than their own hostile attitude—as an excuse for lacking dates and so feel safe from rejection. Orbach (1973) believes that women may use overweight to rebel against a male-dominated society which wants women to be slim, perfect, feminine, passive sex goddesses.

American mealtimes are social occasions for overeating, the most glaring example being the Thanksgiving binge. Going to fancy restaurants with family or clients symbolizes success. Overeating may start in infancy because of a nervous mother, or during a long convalescence. Fat parents are embarrassed by skinny children, and immigrants push their children to eat, since food has symbolized security and survival. The poor eat more starch, which is cheaper than vegetables and fruits. Boredom, loneliness, frustration, and feeling unloved contribute to food indulgence, as do TV ads and food store displays. Fat people overfeed their pets because food means love. Other fat family members sabotage one's efforts to get and stay thin, since they are jealous of one's possible success where they have failed. Overweight husbands escape chores and sex, and find emotional stability in their impregnable fortress of flab. Nisbett (1968) observed obese students who ate whatever was in front of them, but were too lazy to get up to get more from a refrigerator in the next room.

Eating is inhibited by the ventromedial region of the hypothalamus, and encouraged by the lateral section. The hypothalamus may contain glucoreceptors sensitive to blood sugar. Joliffe (1952) coined the term *appestat* for the hypothalamic appetite regulator. When people get used to overeating, they no longer feel satisfied with a sufficient amount. People overeat because of habit, to stop mother's pressure to be plump, or to compensate for social, financial, or sexual problems. The individual, through intense, persistent will power, has to "set" the appestat "lower" by eating less.

The newborn associates safety, comfort, love, and pleasure with

suckling, but bottle feeding tempts the mother to make her baby finish the bottle. Stuffing children through adolescence establishes a lifelong habit. According to Fishbein (1959), the neurotic mother prefers a "nice, quiet boy" who avoids "rough fellows" and athletics. Her daughter is a "sweet girl who plays house with other nice quiet girls." Such children may experience enuresis and bowel problems and, as infants, demand the bottle long after normal weaning time, and be too lazy to chew their food. They do not do things for themselves and without encouragement to develop motor skills, they remain dependent. Fat children may be brought to a physician because they no longer overeat, which worries the parents if they see plumpness as natural and desirable. Physical development and bone growth may be accelerated in obese children. Rewarding them through sweets worsens the problem. The fat babies studied by Mayer and Harris (1970) ate the same or less than thin babies, but were more inactive. The thin babies moved three times as much as the fat ones. Bruch (1948) concluded that overeating is mostly caused by: (a) a response to tension; (b) a substitute gratification in frightening situations; (c) emotional illness; and (d) food addiction.

Fat children usually have ineffective fathers and fat, dominating mothers who live out their fantasies through their offspring. The child is the mother's prize possession—she overprotects it to keep it dependent, thus making it feel inadequate and helpless. Guilt about holding the child too close makes her resent it, motivating her to fuss all the more. Irritated at the amount of care the child requires, her hostility and guilt push her to bribe it with more goodies—an endless, vicious cycle. Although the neurotic mother gains prestige from having a well-fed baby, she later nags it for its greed, putting it on a succession of sabotaged diets. Many overweight patients were "force-fed" in childhood ("Clean your plate; think of the starving Chinese") by mothers unable to give love. Food compensated for inferiority feelings and lack of love in the Depression, when parents worked long, hard hours to survive, and had little time for their children.

Ultrasensitive fat people are unable to stand much physical and emotional pain. Bruch (1948) notes that fat individuals cannot tolerate frustration or postpone satisfaction. To the timid child, physical bulk represents safety and strength, a defense against the world and its responsibilities. Since exercise and social contacts appear dangerous, the fat child generally lacks sources of satisfaction outside food.

REFERENCES

Bruch, H. (1948). Psychological aspects of obesity. *Bulletin of the New York Academy of Medicine, 24,* 73–86.

Eden, A. (1975). Fat-proof your child. *Reader's Digest,* December.

Fishbein, M. (1959). *Illustrated medical and health encyclopedia* (pp. 1492–1501). New York: Stuttman.

Joliffe, N. (1952). *Reduce and stay reduced.* New York: Simon & Schuster.

Jourad, S. M. (1968/1963). *Personal adjustment: An approach through the study of healthy personality.* New York: Macmillan.

Kiev, A. (1974). *Somatic manifestations of depressive disorders.* Princeton, NJ: Excerpta Medica.

Lindgren, H. C., & Byrne, D. (1971). *Psychology* (3rd ed.). New York: Wiley.

Mayer, J., & Harris, T. G. (1970, January). Affluence: The fifth horseman of the apocalypse. *Psychology Today, 43.*

Moore, M. E., Stunkard, A., & Srole, L. (1962). Obesity, social class, and mental illness. *Journal of the American Medical Association, 181,* 962–966.

Nisbett, R. E. (1968). Determinants of food intake in obesity. *Science, 159,* 1254–1255.

Orbach, S. (1978). Social dimensions in compulsive eating in women. *Psychotherapy: Theory, Research, and Practice, 15,* 186–189.

Schachter, S. (1967). Cognitive effects on bodily functioning: Studies of obesity and eating. In D. C. Glass (Ed.), *Biology and behavior: Neurophysiology and emotion.* New York: Rockefeller University Press.

Schachter, S. (1968). Obesity and eating. *Science, 161,* 751–756.

Skovholt, T. M., Resnick, J. L., & Dewey, C. R. (1979). Weight treatment: A group approach to weight control. *Psychotherapy: Theory, Research, and Practice, 16,* 121.

Stunkard, A. J., & Koch, C. (1964). The interpretation of gastric motility: Apparent bias in the report of hunger by obese persons. *Archives of General Psychology, 11,* 74–82.

Ullmann, L. P., & Krasner, L. A. (1975/1969). *A psychological approach to abnormal behavior.* Englewood Cliffs, NJ: Prentice-Hall.

H. K. FINK
Honolulu, Hawaii

APPETITE DISORDERS
EATING DISORDERS
PSYCHOPHYSIOLOGY

OBESITY TREATMENTS

Obesity, the presence of excessive adipose tissue, is a problem for millions in our world today. In the United States, for example, the Metropolitan Life Insurance Company has estimated that 30% of males and 40% of females between the ages of 19 and 40 are obese. The problem is not limited to the United States: many of the industrialized nations around the world show similar statistics.

Because of the physical, psychological, and social disadvantages of obesity, it has become the target for substantial treatment effort. Attempts to solve this problem have included dietary regimens, gastric bypass operations, mouth wiring, pharmacologic interventions, and exercise programs. All these approaches have either limited effectiveness, or applicability to only highly select populations. Two major contributions from psychology to the understanding and treatment of this refractory condition are psychoanalysis and behavior modification. The remainder of this discussion will focus upon these approaches.

PSYCHOANALYSIS

Psychoanalysis has contributed substantially to our present knowledge of the psychological factors associated with obesity. Much of the early work in this area was done by Hilde Bruch. Her clinical observations of obese children in the early 1940s were pioneering studies that formed the foundation for much of our understanding today. A perspective of Bruch's work can be gained by reading two of her books on obesity: *The Importance of Overweight* (1957) and *Eating Disorders: Obesity, Anorexia Nervosa, and the Person Within* (1973). The classical psychoanalytic view of obesity is that this condition is a product of dysfunctions occurring during the oral stage of development. This period of infancy is noted by the child's preoccupation with bodily pleasures, oral gratification being the most prominent among them. For the infant, ingestion and its associated processes are thought to be sources not only of pleasure but also of security and comfort. The latter qualities are presumed to derive from maternal closeness during the feeding experience. If inappropriate feeding occurs during this critical phase of development, the foundation for later adulthood obesity may be laid. For example, if the mother utilizes food to pacify the infant for reasons other than those associated with hunger, a relationship may be established between food and the alleviation of uncomfortable emotional states.

Myron L. Gluckman (1972) indicated that inappropriate eating patterns may find their derivation in a post-oral phase of development. From his clinical work and the reports of others, he noted a number of psychoanalytic phenomena associated with problems of eating: Oedipal conflicts, sibling rivalry, sexual inhibitions, affect reduction, and interpersonal manipulations. Further, Gluckman emphasized the complexity of these problems and the limitations of the purely psychoanalytic perspective. The psychoanalytic treatment of obesity is, in general, an indirect one. That is, the presenting symptom of obesity is not the problem upon which treatment is focused. Instead, attention is given to the underlying psychological conflicts. Presumably, when these conflicts are understood and resolved, the client's difficulties with overeating and overweight will subside.

At this time, little is known of the clinical applications of psychoanalysis in the treatment of obesity, including methods, results, and extent of use. This deficiency has been somewhat rectified by the research conducted by Rand and Stunkard (1978). They surveyed 72 members of the American Academy of Psychoanalysis who reported data on 84 of their obese clients. At the completion of the 42-month observation period, it was found that 47% of the clients had lost more than 9 kg and 19% had lost more than 18 kg. These results compared favorably with those achieved through behavior modification. The surprisingly good outcomes reported in this survey led Rand and Stunkard to suggest that psychoanalysis apparently was effective as an indirect treatment of obesity. Additionally, they found that clients undergoing this treatment decreased in their feelings of body disparagement. Interestingly, improved body image was not found to be related to weight loss.

Further studies may help determine whether these results are replicable, and may more accurately determine the overall effectiveness of this method.

BEHAVIOR MODIFICATION

The use of behavior modification in the treatment of obesity has been a relatively new occurrence. Its theoretical foundation was laid by Ferster, Nurnberger, and Levitt in "The control of eating" (1962). In 1967 Richard Stuart, using the ideas of Ferster and his colleagues, reported that eight outpatients lost an average of 17 kg over a one-year period, a heretofore unheard-of loss using psychological techniques. Stuart's phenomenal success provided the impetus for the rapid growth and development of behavior modification as a weight control treatment. Today it is the most widely used method of treating mild to moderate obesity. The behavioral treatment of obesity has taken many forms since its beginning. However, the basis of this approach still lies in the integrated application of four elements: stimulus control, eating management, contingency management, and self-monitoring.

Stimulus Control

Environmental cues often play a role in promoting inappropriate eating. Removing or making innocuous these cues is the objective of stimulus control procedures. Examples of this approach include removing food from view and easy accessibility, restricting food consumption to specific times and locations, and shopping from prepared lists.

Eating Management

Physiological evidence suggests that the feeling of satiation lags behind the ingestion of food. When individuals eat slowly, sufficient time is allowed for the awareness of satiation to occur, and the tendency to overeat lessens. Eating management is a method of slowing the pace of eating. Typical suggestions given to achieve this objective include putting utensils down between bites, taking smaller quantities per forkful, and chewing each morsel thoroughly and completely.

Contingency Management

In operant conditioning it is suggested that behaviors are highly influenced by their consequences. Behaviors that are rewarded tend to be reinforced, whereas those that are punished tend to be extinguished. Contingency management is an application of this principle to weight control. In programs of treatment, contingency management has been used for the achievement of weight loss goals and performance behaviors. Examples of the latter are completion of self-monitoring forms, maintenance of an exercise regimen, and eating meals over a prescribed period of time. The rewards or punishments may be administered by the therapist, significant others, or by the clients themselves.

Self-Monitoring

Self-monitoring is an essential element of most behaviorally oriented weight control programs. It is the pencil-and-paper process by which clients record their daily dietary intake and the pertinent factors associated with each eating event, including thoughts and feelings, individuals present, location, and time of day. Information obtained in this manner can be used to determine faulty dietary patterns and behaviors, as well as for monitoring progress.

Stimulus control, eating management, contingency management, and self-monitoring have generally formed the "core" of most behaviorally based weight control therapies, because of their assumed efficacy. In recent years, however, research findings have placed the former assumptions in doubt. The possibility that these components of behavioral treatment are not particularly effective may help explain the limited weight losses obtained through this approach.

While the application of behavior modification to obesity treatment has been lauded as a substantial improvement over most traditional methods, its results are nevertheless quite modest. Wilson and Brownell (1980) reviewed long-term weight loss outcome studies and found that participants averaged a loss of 4.7 kg by the end of treatment. Similarly, Foreyt, Goodrick, and Gotto (1981) reviewed 16 behavioral treatment programs in which one-year posttreatment follow-up data were available. Their data indicated an average weight loss of 6.1 kg at the end of one year. In their analysis of the results, the reviewers suggested that the modest losses demonstrated could be attributed to the possible ineffectiveness of the components of treatment, the difficulty in maintaining newly learned eating behaviors, the time-limited nature (usually between 8 to 12 weeks) of treatment, or the dissatisfaction of many clients with their slow rate of weight loss.

The ultimate objective of any weight control therapy is to produce substantial weight losses and to have those losses maintained. Behavior modification has not been highly successful in achieving either of these objectives. Considerable research effort has been engendered to find a more successful "formula."

Recent trends in the behavioral treatment of obesity derive primarily from the growing appreciation of the complexity of this problem. Few today assume that obesity is a simple disorder resulting solely from excessive caloric intake, or that obese people are substantially different from normal weight people in their eating behaviors. Obesity is a problem of numerous dimensions; its origins can be psychological, physical, social, and cultural. Behavior therapists have begun to recognize the complexity of this problem and have attempted to make the basic behavior modification to weight control more sophisticated. Recent research has examined the influence of various additions to the treatment. These additions include the use of very low calorie diets, social support, pharmacotherapy, relapse-prevention strategies, exercise, and cognitive interventions. Extensive empirical information regarding these approaches is still sparse and judgments regarding their efficacy cannot be made at this time.

Other research is being conducted to examine the issues of structure and format. Studies have questioned the efficacy of such behavioral treatment components as the 8-to-12-week duration of most treatment, once-a-week meetings, large group formats, standardized sessions given to all clients, and—as mentioned earlier—even the content of the treatment. Searching for the optimal treatment, behavioral researchers are going beyond incremental changes to explore the very foundations of previous assumptions.

CONCLUSION

Psychoanalysis and behavior modification have made major contributions to our understanding of obesity, but both are limited in their ability to help clients achieve and maintain significant weight loss. Both approaches are at a critical crossroads: to continue doing more of the same with mediocre results, or to make fundamental changes in theory and practice in the hope of achieving substantially better outcomes.

It is doubtful whether either treatment modality will find the satisfactory results it desires by remaining static. In the past few decades both have gained an appreciation of the complexity of the obesity problem. Such complexity does not appear to respond well to interventions of singular orientation. The future direction of weight control treatment seems to lie in a multidisciplinary approach commensurate with the complexity of the problem.

The extreme difficulty of losing weight in adulthood also suggests the logic of interventions that prevent rather than cure. The target of such prevention efforts should be children, a group much neglected in obesity research even though substantial evidence suggests that much of adult obesity begins in childhood. A concerted effort with this group and their parents might prevent many of the problems of obesity in later life. Prevention efforts should also extend to developing an environment that promotes a healthy way of life. Nutrition, exercise, and stress management can be promoted in schools, workplaces, and communities. By so doing, we can assist in the maintenance of normal weight as well as the achievement of overall health. In such an effort, psychoanalysts and behavior therapists can play major functions in the multidisciplinary teams that plan and implement the intervention programs.

REFERENCES

Bruch, H. (1979/1973). *Eating disorders: Obesity, anorexia nervosa, and the person within.* New York: Basic Books.

Bruch, H. (1957). *The importance of overweight.* New York: Norton.

Ferster, C. B., Nurnberger, J. I., & Levitt, E. B. (1962). The control of eating. *Journal of Mathetics, 1,* 87–109.

Foreyt, J. P., Goodrick, G. K., & Gotto, A. M. (1981). Limitations of behavioral treatment of obesity: Review and analysis. *Journal of Behavioral Medicine, 4,* 159–174.

Gluckman, M. L. (1972). Psychiatric observations on obesity. *Advances in Psychosomatic Medicine, 7,* 194–216.

Rand, C. S. W. (1978). Treatment of obese patients in psychoanalysis. *Psychiatric Clinics of North America, 1,* 661–672.

Wilson, G. T., & Brownell, K. D. (1980). Behavior therapy for obesity: An evaluation of treatment outcome. *Advances in Behavior Research and Therapy, 3,* 49–86.

SUGGESTED READING

Allon, N. (1975). The stigma of overweight in everyday life. In G. A. Bray (Ed.), *Obesity in perspective,* Vol. 2, Part 2 (DHEW Publication No. 75-708, National Institutes of Health). Washington, DC: U.S. Government Printing Office.

Bray, G. A. (1976). *The obese patient.* Philadelphia, PA: Saunders.

Mann, G. V. (1974). The influence of obesity in health. *New England Journal of Medicine, 291,* 178–185, 226–232.

Stunkard, A. J., & Mahoney, M. J. (1976). Behavioral treatment of eating disorders. In H. Leitenberg (Ed.), *The handbook of behavior modification and behavior therapy.* Englewood Cliffs, NJ: Prentice-Hall.

Wooley, S. C., Wooley, O. W., & Dyrenforth, S. R. (1979). Theoretical, practical, and social issues in behavioral treatments of obesity. *Journal of Applied Behavioral Analysts, 12,* 3–25.

J. P. FOREYT
Baylor College of Medicine

A. T. KONDO
University of Houston

BEHAVIOR THERAPY
OBESITY
PSYCHOANALYSIS

OBSERVATIONAL METHODS

Observation, whether formal or informal, consists of taking note of events or occurrences and making a record of what is observed. Observation is basic to all science, and special methods have been devised to make observations of behavior objective and reliable. Observational data may be obtained in numerous research and practical situations and recorded by a variety of instruments and procedures. The utility of such data depend not only on how, when, and where they are collected, but also on the interpretations placed upon them and their generalizability beyond the immediate situation.

In controlled observation, a situation is prearranged or contrived to study the responses of people or animals to certain stimuli or circumstances. For example, a psychologist may use a one-way mirror or a closed-circuit television monitor to observe the interaction between a mother and child under certain conditions. By remaining unseen, the psychologist attempts to minimize the effects of his or her own presence on the behavior of the performers. This is similar to the situational testing procedure that has been employed in military and other organizational contexts to evaluate candidates for certain jobs. In situational testing, a person is placed in a contrived, prearranged situation to determine how she or he performs specified tasks under stressful conditions.

Because controlled observation involves special procedures, uncontrolled observation, in which the observer exerts no control over the situation and merely takes note of behavior *in situ*, is more common. Illustrative of uncontrolled observation are naturalistic observations of children on a playground and the nest-building behavior of birds. Regardless of the degree of control an observer may exert over the situation, alert, well-trained observers of other people note a variety of details in the appearance and behavior of the individual(s) being observed. These include not only what the person looks like and says, but also how he or she sits, stands, moves, shakes hands, looks at the observer and other people, as well as facial expressions, tone of voice, and other nonverbal behaviors.

Much of what is known about the dynamics of personality and mental disorders is the result of observations made by people in clinical settings. The clinical method is not completely objective or controlled; not only does the therapist-observer affect the patient's behavior, but the patient also influences the responses of the therapist. Consequently, the accuracy of clinical observations and the interpretations placed upon them should be carefully checked by other observers and procedures. But whatever the observational situation may be, observers must try to remain objective. They should not let their biases and expectations influence what they observe, and should separate what is observed from how it is interpreted. For example, in making an anecdotal record of significant events in a child's everyday life, descriptions of the child's behavior should be kept separate from conclusions concerning its meaning.

People find it difficult to behave naturally when they know they are being observed, often acting as if they were on stage or otherwise engaging in role playing. Consequently, in scientific research it is considered important for observers to remain as unobtrusive as possible; in general, they should not be actively engaged with the individuals who are being observed. On the other hand, if the researcher elects to become a part of the observational situation and be a participant observer, the effects of his or her presence on the behavior of the performers needs to be considered in interpreting the research findings. Participant observation is commonly employed by cultural anthropologists, who maintain that active involvement in a social situation provides insights into behavior that are unattainable by other means.

Because people are rarely objective in describing their own thoughts, feelings, and behaviors, self-observation would seem to be even more biased than observations of oneself made by other people. With proper training, however, people can learn to make more objective, systematic observations of themselves. In short, they can learn to distinguish between experience and interpretation—between what actually occurred and what it means to them. A written record of one's experiences, actions, and thoughts may be kept in a daily log and subsequently reflected upon or analyzed by oneself and others. Content analysis of self-observations recorded in diaries, letters, and other personal documents can provide explanations for and insight into an individual's actions and personality.

An important first step in improving the accuracy of observations is to train the observers. Observers must be made aware of the effects of their own biases, conduct, and appearance on what is being observed, and of the tendency to confuse fact with interpretation. Training should also stress the importance of taking into account the influence of the situational context in which observations are made in interpreting the results. Recordings and interpretations made by novice observers, and to some extent even by those who have had some experience, should be checked frequently by observers who have had substantial experience in the observational situation.

Obtaining meaningful results from an observational study also demands that the sample of observed behavior be representative. Special data-sampling procedures may be employed to reduce the time, expense, and volume of data obtained from continuous observations of behavior. In incident sampling, only specified behavioral incidents—for example, of aggression—are noted and recorded. A second procedure, time sampling, involves making a series of observations lasting only a few minutes each over a period of a day or so. Finally, the use of an observational schedule, such as a rating scale or checklist filled out during or shortly after the behavioral occurrence, can improve the reliability of observations. Because memory is reconstructive rather than exact, it is important to record behavioral observations as soon as possible after they are made.

L. R. AIKEN
Pepperdine University

FIELD RESEARCH
PSYCHOLOGICAL RESEARCH

OBSESSIONS

Obsessions are described in the fourth edition of the *Diagnostic and Statistical Manual of Mental Disorders* (*DSM-IV;* American Psychiatric Association, 1994) as recurrent intrusive thoughts, impulses, or images, that produce anxiety or discomfort. Individuals with Obsessive-Compulsive Disorder (OCD) usually try to suppress or neutralize such obsessions with other thoughts or actions. Typical themes for obsessions are harming, sexuality, contamination, concerns with disease, religion, superstition, or otherwise neutral thoughts ("What if I cannot stop thinking about my breathing?"). Normally the thoughts are egodystonic and individuals with OCD know that the obsessions originate in their own mind and are not coming from the outside.

Although pure obsessions (i.e., obsessions without overt compulsions) have traditionally been assumed to be infrequent, treatment centers worldwide have reported anywhere between 1.5% and 44% of OCD patients who report no overt compulsions (median = 20%; for a detailed review see Freeston & Ladouceur, 1997). Moreover, epidemiologic studies have found that in the community, the percentage of individuals with OCD suffering from pure obsessions may be as high as 60%.

Several theories have attempted to explain the development of obessional problems and related compulsions. For example, Mowrer (1960) described a two-stage theory, stating that a fear of specific stimuli is first learned through classical conditioning—in stage 1, for example the patient feels anxious after thinking a blasphemous thought—and then maintained by operant conditioning in stage 2, as the individual learns to engage in ritualistic behavior to decrease anxiety (e.g., the patient may compulsively pray). Thus, rituals are preserved by reinforcing the properties of anxiety reduction, and since reinforced behaviors will occur more often in the future, the frequency of rituals increases. Rituals or avoidance behavior maintain the fear response because the sufferer does not stay in contact with the stimulus long enough for the anxiety to extinguish. This theory has led to the development of a treatment called exposure and response prevention (ERP; i.e., extended exposure to situations that trigger OCD symptoms combined with prevention of rituals during exposure and thereafter). Exposure and response prevention can be conducted in real-life or imagined situations to decrease the fear response to obsessions by the classical conditioning process of extinction (for reviews, see Abramowitz, 1996).

More recent theories for the development of obsessional problems have suggested information-processing biases and deficits with respect to decision making, failures of inhibition, and memory (for a detailed review see Steketee, Frost, Rheaume, & Wilhelm, 1998). For example, Enright and Beech (1993) showed that OCD patients had difficulty inhibiting the processing of irrelevant, emotionally neutral material. This difficulty may account for the frequency of intrusive thoughts in OCD. The evidence for memory deficits underlying obsessional problems is inconclusive: Several studies failed to find deficits but did find a lack of confidence in the sufferers' recall of their own actions (e.g., McNally & Kohlbeck, 1993).

Current cognitive models of OCD characterize intrusive thoughts as normal events that most people experience, indistinguishable from obsessional thoughts with respect to their content. Rachman and DeSilva (1978) found that those intrusive thoughts were reported by almost 90% of a nonclinical sample. Intrusive thoughts develop into obsessions not because of their content but because of the meaning individuals attribute to them. Nonobsessional individuals disregard intrusions and do not evaluate them as important, whereas people with OCD attend to them believing that they are meaningful. The appraisal of the intrusion is assumed to depend on underlying beliefs or assumptions acquired in a religious, cultural, or family context. People who appraise the intrusions in a maladaptive way experience negative emotions (e.g., guilt, anxiety) and fear negative consequences. Thus, in seeking ways to reduce discomfort they often engage in neutralizing strategies such as overt compulsions, mental rituals, avoidance behaviors, and attempts to suppress thoughts. However, a series of thought suppression experiments suggested that efforts to suppress specific thoughts resulted in an increase rather than a decrease of those thoughts (Wegner, 1989).

Faulty interpretations of intrusive thoughts have been categorized in several domains (for a detailed review see Steketee et al., 1998) and include: Overimportance of Thoughts and the Need to Control Thoughts, Overestimation of Threat, Intolerance of Uncertainty, Perfectionism, and Excessive Responsibility.

Many OCD sufferers attach too much importance to the content and presence of their thoughts, and erroneously believe that other people do not have intrusive thoughts. They may believe that simply because a thought occurs, it is meaningful or indicates that they will act on it. Extreme beliefs about the importance and meaning of thoughts can lead to beliefs about having to exert control over them. For example, if an individual interprets an intrusive thought as indicating "I am evil and insane" the feeling is likely to be followed by emotional discomfort and by attempts to remove

the intrusion. Like other anxiety disorder sufferers, OCD patients often overestimate both the probability and the severity of threat, harm, or negative outcomes; as a result they may interpret situations as dangerous until proven safe, whereas most people evaluate a situation as safe unless there is an indication of threat. The need for certainty in OCD patients or intolerance of uncertainty is another frequently noted feature of OCD. The tendency of OCD patients to overestimate danger may be related to their difficulties with ambiguous situations, and with making decisions. Theories of OCD have linked intolerance of ambiguous situations to perfectionism. For example, OCD patients may feel uncertain about the efficacy of their efforts to minimize harm when a perfect solution cannot be determined. The domain of Excessive Responsibility has received the most attention in recent studies and refers to the assumption that one has the pivotal power to generate or avert unwanted outcomes (e.g., Salkovskis, 1985). Excessive responsibility can induce guilt, which is then reduced by compulsions. Recent studies have tested cognitive treatments that address those cognitive domains (see Steketee et al., 1998).

In summary, several theories have been introduced for the development of obessional problems. Behavioral, biological, and other theories examining the cognitive aspects for the development of obessional problems have been proposed. Current cognitive research suggests that obsessional problems are the result of maladaptive interpretations of intrusive thoughts. A better understanding of obessional problems may result from an integration of these different areas of research.

REFERENCES

Abramowitz, J. S. (1996). Variants of exposure and response prevention in the treatment of obsessive-compulsive disorder: A meta-analysis. *Behavior Therapy, 27,* 583–600.

American Psychiatric Association. (1994). *Diagnostic and statistical manual of mental disorders* (4th ed.). Washington, DC: Author.

Enright, S. J., & Beech, A. R. (1993). Reduced cognitive inhibition in obsessive-compulsive disorder. *British Journal of Clinical Psychology, 32,* 67–74.

Freeston, M. H., & Ladouceur, R. (1997). *The cognitive behavioral treatment of obsessions: A treatment manual.* Unpublished manuscript.

McNally, R. J., & Kohlbeck, P. A. (1993). Reality monitoring in obsessive-compulsive disorder. *Behaviour Research and Therapy, 31,* 249–253.

Mowrer, O. H. (1960). *Learning theory and behavior.* New York: Wiley.

Rachman, S., & DeSilva, P. (1978). Abnormal and normal obsessions. *Behaviour Research and Therapy, 16,* 233–248.

Salkovskis, P. M. (1985). Obsessional-compulsive problems: A cognitive-behavioral analysis. *Behaviour Research and Therapy, 23,* 571–584.

Steketee, G., Frost, R. O., Rheaume, J., & Wilhelm, S. (1998). Cognitive theory and treatment of obsessive-compulsive disorder.

In M. A. Jenike, L. Baer, & W. E. Minichiello (Eds.), *Obsessive-compulsive disorder: Theory and management* (3rd ed., pp. 368–399). Chicago: Mosby.

Wegner, D. M. (1989). *White bears and other unwanted thoughts.* New York: Viking.

S. WILHELM
Massachusetts General Hospital

ANXIETY
COMPULSIONS
OBSESSIVE-COMPULSIVE PERSONALITY

OBSESSIVE-COMPULSIVE PERSONALITY

From Sigmund Freud's description of the anal character in *Character and Anal Eroticism* to the twentieth-century problem of workaholism, the obsessive-compulsive personality—also referred to as the anankastic personality—has posed a dilemma for mental health professionals. The characteristics of this disorder are troublesome, yet are often highly valued in our society.

The *Diagnostic and Statistical Manual of Mental Disorders* (*DSM-III*) recommended the term "compulsive personality disorder" for the syndrome which has been called the obsessive-compulsive personality. The diagnostic criteria include a limited ability to express warm emotions, perfectionism, a rigid insistence on one's plans, excessive commitment to work to the detriment of personal relationships, and indecisiveness.

The overcontrolled adherence to unrealistic standards, combined with an inability to make decisions, leads to chronic unhappiness in the obsessive-compulsive personality. The disorder is more common to men than women. Family members and colleagues often initiate psychological treatment for the obsessive-compulsive personality because of difficulties of living and working with such individuals. Mollinger (1980) described the style and the predicament as "full of ambivalence, opposites." For example, the idealization of a friend can be discarded quickly and replaced with complete rejection after an argument. Just as such contradictions impair the personal relationships of persons with an obsessive-compulsive personality, so psychotherapy can be extremely difficult for them.

Psychoanalytic explanations of etiology emphasize disordered development in the anal stage. Theoretically, then, the defense mechanisms of isolation, undoing, and reaction formation are necessary in order to defend against anal-sadistic impulses. Yet Pollak (1979) found little evidence supporting the psychoanalytic beliefs concerning etiology.

With respect to differential diagnosis, the obsessive-compulsive personality can be distinguished from the obsessive compulsive disorder by the absence of obsessions (recurrent unwanted thoughts) and compulsions (repetitive behaviors which are driven, but not pleasurable). It has not been demonstrated that the obsessive-compulsive personality style leads to the disabling symptoms of the obsessive-compulsive disorder.

In *The Obsessive Personality,* Salzman suggested that this is the most prevalent character style in American culture, and that much of society's order and progress is the work of obsessive-compulsive personalities. Yet as Berghner (1981) has pointed out, the obsessive-compulsive personality can be seen as a "harsh dictator over himself" and others.

REFERENCES

Berghner, R. M. (1981). The overseer regime: A descriptive and practical study of the obsessive-compulsive personality style. *Advances in Descriptive Psychology, 1,* 245–271.

Mollinger, R. N. (1980). Antithesis and the obsessive compulsive. *The Psychoanalytic Review, 4,* 456–477.

Pollak, J. M. (1979). Obsessive-compulsive personality: A review. *Psychological Bulletin,* 225–239.

Salzman, L. (1968). *The obsessive personality: Origins, dynamics and therapy.* New York: Aronson.

SUGGESTED READING

Freedman, A. M., Kaplan, H. I., & Sadock, B. J. (Eds.). (1980). *Comprehensive textbook of psychiatry* (Vol. III) Baltimore: Williams & Wilkins.

C. LANDAU
Brown University Division of Medicine

OPTIMAL FUNCTIONING
PERSONALITY TYPES
RIGIDITY

OCCUPATIONAL ADJUSTMENT

Occupational adjustment is concerned with the psychological processes and environmental influences that affect adult career development. Specifically, the individual progresses through a series of stages in her or his career development, with specific tasks to be mastered at each stage (Osipow & Fitzgerald, 1996). Selection and implementation of an occupation serve as a preamble to the vocational adjustments that occur within each of the stages of career development that follow entry into the workplace. Campbell and Heffernan (1983) suggest that most developmental career theories posit three general career stages: establishment, maintenance, and retirement. The central goals for each stage are:

- *Establishment:* to demonstrate the ability to function effectively in an occupation
- *Maintenance:* to reach and sustain a desired level of functioning
- *Retirement:* to leave full-time employment while maximizing personal options

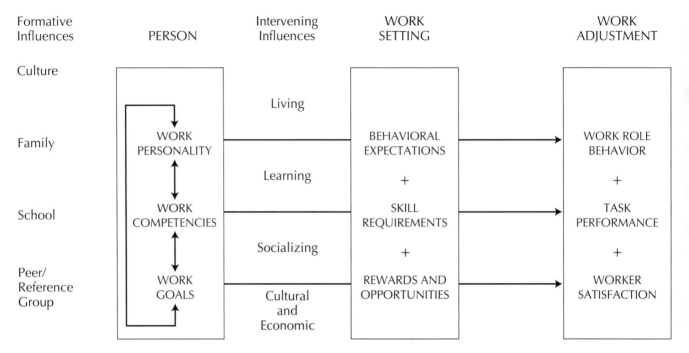

Figure 1. Elements to consider in counseling for work adjustment.

Within each of these stages are hypothesized criteria for adaptive vocational behaviors that are, essentially, work adjustments between an individual and his or her occupational circumstances.

Thus, occupational adjustment or vocational adjustment may be defined as "the state or condition of the individual in relation to the world of work at any given moment after he (or she) has entered an occupation" (Crites, 1969, p. 325). A related definition of occupational adjustment is provided by Dawis and Lofquist (1984) in their trait/factor-based Theory of Work Adjustment (TWA) as "a continuous and dynamic process by which a worker seeks to achieve and maintain a correspondence with a work environment" (p. 237).

The foundational aspects of vocational adjustment include the relationships between person and occupation, person and occupational environment(s), and the fit between personal needs and the reinforcing systems present in the occupational setting (Peterson & González, 2000). Implied is a process of (more or less) optimal alignment of a person's vocational behavior, her or his career development goals, and the occupational circumstances in which the person finds him or herself. The Theory of Work Adjustment recognizes such an alignment as correspondence with the occupational environment (Dawis & Lofquist, 1984).

Dawis and Lofquist outlined 18 propositions and corollaries in their Theory of Work Adjustment, which Peterson and González (2000) summarized into four basic principles: (a) The personality of the worker and the work environment must be in basic agreement; (b) The individual's needs are the primary concern for how he or she will fit into the work environment; (c) To achieve stability and tenure the individual's needs must correspond to the reinforcing system of the work environment; and (d) Job placement works most effectively when the worker's traits match the requirements of the work environment.

The criteria by which work adjustment is evaluated are vocational satisfactoriness (or success) and satisfaction (Osipow & Fitzgerald, 1996; Peterson & González, 2000). Vocational success refers to the employer and whether the employee is meeting the needs of the work environment, for example, work productivity, supervisor ratings, morale, and absenteeism. Satisfaction is a worker-centered, positive reaction to the vocational environment. It may be general (overall contentment) or specific (satisfaction with coworkers, salary, and tasks). Satisfaction may be assessed using the Minnesota Satisfaction Questionnaire (Weiss, Dawis, England, & Lofquist, 1967) or the Job Descriptive Index (Smith, Kendall, & Hulin, 1969).

Hershenson (1993) presented a more recent, systems-based vocational adjustment model (Figure 1). In his Model of Work Adjustment, Hershenson explicates three major areas of vocational adjustment: person[al], work setting, and work adjustment. Within the personal area are three interacting sub-systems: work personality (e.g., motivation, needs, self-concept), work competencies (e.g., work habits, interpersonal, cognitive, and physical skills), and work goals (e.g., development in moving from school to work). Hershenson also describes moderating factors that influence work adjustment as formative influences and intervening influences. Formative influences are contextual and include family, culture, school, and reference group. The interdependencies among Hershenson's formative influences coupled with the growth-oriented intervening influences describe a dynamic model of vocational adjustment that may be especially applicable in an increasingly diverse world of work.

REFERENCES

Campbell, R. E., & Heffernan, J. M. (1983). Adult vocational behavior. In W. B. Walsh & S. H. Osipow (Eds.), *Handbook of vocational psychology* (Vol. I). Hillsdale, NJ: Lawrence Erlbaum.

Crites, J. O. (1969). *Vocational psychology.* New York: McGraw-Hill.

Dawis, R., & Lofquist, L. (1984). *A psychological theory of work adjustment: An individual differences model and its applications.* Minneapolis: University of Minnesota Press.

Hershenson, D. (1993). Work adjustment: A neglected area in career counseling. *Journal of Counseling and Development, 74,* 442–446.

Osipow, S. H., & Fitzgerald, L. F. (1996). *Theories of career development (4th ed.).* Boston: Allyn & Bacon.

Peterson, N., & González, R. C. (2000). *The role of work in people's lives.* Belmont, CA: Brooks/Cole.

Smith, P. C., Kendall, L. N., & Hulin, C. L. (1969). *The measurement of satisfaction in work and retirement.* Chicago: Rand McNally.

Weiss, D. J., Dawis, R. V., England, G. W., & Lofquist, L. H. (1967). *Manual for the Minnesota Satisfaction Questionnaire.* Minneapolis, MN: Minnesota Studies in Vocational Rehabilitation, XXII.

R. M. Davison-Aviles
Bradley University, Peoria, Illinois

CAREER DEVELOPMENT
INDUSTRIAL PSYCHOLOGY
JOB SATISFACTION

OCCUPATIONAL COUNSELING

Occupational counseling, or career counseling, refers to "any treatment or effort intended to enhance an individual's career development or to enable the person to make better career-related decisions" (Spokane, 1991, p. 22). Recent conceptualizations of the career counseling process have expanded it beyond the traditional counselor-client dyad to include group interventions and alternative treatments such as workshops, job clubs, and computer-guided and self-directed activities (Osipow & Fitzgerald, 1996; Spokane, 1991). Discussions about the differences between occupational counseling and psychotherapy are ongoing, with an emerging body of literature distinguishing career counseling as a unique profession (Spokane, 1991). The professions have some shared attributes—for example, both involve a helping relationship between a help-seeker and help-giver, and both may involve individual or group counseling in a context of trust and acceptance. However, there is increasing evidence that career counseling is not a subset of psychotherapy, but a professional specialty with its own theories, tools, and techniques (Osipow & Fitzgerald, 1996). Some fundamental differences include the career-related concepts of person-environment fit, necessary adaptation to social forces influencing career development, specialized intervention technology that is independent of theory, and continuous and discontinuous career development. Interestingly, there is some evidence that career counseling alone has beneficial mental health effects (Spokane, 1991; Spokane et al., 1993).

Occupation counseling in the United States has its historical roots in the work of Frank Parsons and the Vocations Bureau (Reardon, Lentz, Sampson, & Pearson, 2000). Through the Bureau, Parsons (1909) sought to help individuals make wise vocational decisions via a three-step process that included: (a) self-assessment of interests, skills, and goals; (b) careful study of available educational and training options, such as school, vocational training, employment, and occupational experiences; and (c) making best choice based upon information gathered in the first two steps. While modern methods include computer-assisted options, distance-learning, and a wide variety of traditional and nontraditional educational opportunities, career counseling still centers around the Parsonian process of helping an individual identify interests, select from several occupational alternatives, and then enter and function effectively in a career.

The difference between Parson's time and the current world of work is that today's worker may go through several iterations of the occupation selection process. Moreover, the basic character of work is changing; there is no typical career development. Individuals now have to deal with a global economy that determines, in part, a worker's relative cost and benefit to the employer. New, flexible working hours, trimmed benefits plans, and telecommuting all demand an increased ability to cope with complexity in career planning. In addition, the impact of women's entry into the workforce is changing the way families organize their lives and the way employers define occupations (Reardon, Lentz, Sampson, & Pearson, 2000).

As rapidly changing social and economic realities cause persons planning their careers to reach out for help, school, college, and organizational career counselors also have a rapidly expanding practice and research base from which to draw appropriate strategies and techniques. There are several ways such a process can take place, usually involving (but not limited to) some combination of information-gathering, motivational strategies, assessment, self-directed behaviors, peer support, community support, and individual and group counseling. A comprehensive career intervention model (Table 1) was presented by Spokane (1991), who described three major phases (beginning, activation, and termination) and eight sub-phases (opening, aspiring, loosening, assessment, inquiry, commitment, execution, and follow-through). Within each subphase, Spokane provides descriptors defining therapeutic tasks, counselor process and techniques, and expected client reaction.

To help clients sustain the often challenging task of persisting in their career development efforts, Spokane also offers 10 career-focused guidelines:

- *Anticipate non-adherence.* Life circumstances will compete with your client's attention to career-related behaviors.

Table 1. Phases, Subphases, and Counselor and Client Processes in Individual and Group Career Intervention

Phases and subphases	Principal therapeutic task	Counselor process	Counselor technique	Client reaction
Beginning				
Opening	Establishment of therapeutic context	Set expectation	Structure, acceptance	Relief
Aspiring	Client rehearsal of aspirations	Activate hope	Fantasy	Excitement
Loosening	Perception of incongruity	Identify conflicts	Reflection, clarification	Anxiety
Activation				
Assessment	Acquisition of cognitive structure	Generate hypothesis	Testing, interpretation	Progress, insight
Inquiry	Mobilization of constructive behavior	Test hypothesis	Probing, leading	Self-efficacy, control, exploration
Commitment	Management of anxiety	Share hypothesis	Reassurance	Compromise
Completion				
Execution	Persistent search	Resolve conflicts	Reinforcement	Withdrawal, adherence
Follow-through	Consolidation of gain	Achieve closure	Periodic recontact	Satisfaction, certainty

- *Consider counseling from the client's perspective.* Personal beliefs and feelings influence a client's behaviors during the counseling process.

- *Collaborate and negotiate.* Client time and energy commitments need to be addressed directly via mutual agreement and assent.

- *Be client oriented.* Reinforce client behaviors toward their goals.

- *Customize treatment.* Meet your client's specialized needs—for example, stage or videotape mock interviews to reduce anxiety.

- *Enlist family support.* If appropriate, family support can be especially helpful during the beginning phase.

- *Provide a system of continuity and accessibility.* Success in career counseling often rests on facilitating client access to the tools and support they need (e.g., telephones, computers, counselor availability).

- *Use other career personnel and community resources.* Expand the client's support base.

- *Repeat everything.* Reminders done appropriately help motivate clients.

- *Don't give up.* Hopeless scenarios test both counselor and client—adjust and move forward.

Finally, there exist several sociocultural factors that influence the process and outcome of career counseling. These factors are social class or socioeconomic status (SES), race/ethnicity, gender, and sexual orientation (Osipow & Fitzgerald, 1996). Although not an exhaustive list, these factors serve to remind counselors to exercise caution when generalizing and applying interventions from research based on middle-class white male individuals. Conversely, counselors can access a growing body of culture-specific and culture-general information on the career development and vocational behaviors of diverse populations (Leong, 1995).

REFERENCES

Leong, F. T. L. (1995). Introduction and overview. In F. T. L. Leong (Ed.), *Career development and vocational behavior of racial and ethnic minorities* (pp. 1–4). Mahwah, NJ: Earlbaum.

Osipow, S. H., & Fitzgerald, L. F. (1996). *Theories of career development* (4th ed.). Boston: Allyn and Bacon.

Parsons, F. (1909). *Choosing a vocation.* Boston: Houghton Mifflin.

Reardon, R. C., Lentz, J. G., Sampson, J. P., & Pearson, G. W. (2000). *Career development and planning: A comprehensive approach.* Belmont, CA: Brooks/Cole.

Spokane, A. R. (1991). *Career intervention.* Englewood Cliffs, NJ: Prentice Hall.

Spokane, A. R., Fretz, B. R., Hoffman, M., Nagel, D., Davison Avilés, R. M., & Jashik-Herman, M. (1993). Forty cases: A framework for examining the interface between career and personal issues in counseling. *Journal of Career Assessment, 1,* 118–129.

R. M. Davison Avilés
Bradley University, Peoria, Illinois

CAREER DEVELOPMENT
COUNSELING
INDUSTRIAL PSYCHOLOGY

OEDIPUS COMPLEX

A fundamental concept in the psychoanalytic theory of personality developed by Freud is the Oedipus complex. It derives its name from the legendary Greek king who, unknowingly, killed his father and married his mother.

MALES

The young boy's Oedipus complex consists of a double set of attitudes toward both parents: (a) An intense love and yearning for his mother coupled with a powerful jealousy of and rage toward his father. This set is usually the stronger one; (b) He feels affection for his father, together with jealousy toward his mother. This occurs because all human beings are inherently bisexual (therefore the boy also behaves to some extent like a girl), and may become dominant if there exists an unusually strong constitutional tendency toward femininity.

The Oedipus complex may well be the most intense emotional

experience of one's life, and includes all the characteristics of a true love affair: heights of passion, jealous rages, and desperate yearnings. It begins at about age 2 to 3 years, when the boy learns to produce pleasurable sensations by manually stimulating his penis. His powerful attachment to his mother now acquires genital properties, and he tries to impress her by showing her the male organ he is proud to own. In addition, his father becomes a rival whom he would like to get rid of in order to enjoy sole possession of his mother.

Ultimately, however, the Oedipus complex leads to severe conflicts. The boy fears that his illicit wishes will cost him his father's love and protection, which Freud characterizes as a child's strongest need. The boy also inevitably learns of the physical differences between the sexes, concludes that girls originally possessed a penis but had it taken away as punishment, and fears that his seemingly all-powerful father will exact a similar penalty if the Oedipal wishes persist. To alleviate this intense castration anxiety, the boy eventually surrenders his conscious Oedipal strivings. At about age 5 to 6 years, he intensifies his identification with his father, seeking now to be like him rather than to replace him. The boy also develops internal prohibitions against doing certain things that his father does (such as enjoying special privileges with his mother), thereby learning to defer to authority. These identifications and prohibitions are incorporated into the component of personality which Freud called the superego, and help to bring about its formation. Since the boy's Oedipal wishes remain a powerful (albeit unconscious) part of his personality, the most important (albeit also unconscious) function of the superego is to prevent a recurrence of these incestuous and hostile strivings.

The whole Oedipal experience is so frightening that it is thoroughly repressed, and cannot be recalled without the aid of psychoanalytic therapy. Its effects may well become obvious, however, as when a man marries a woman who closely resembles his mother.

FEMALES

Like the boy, the girl forms a powerful attachment to her mother during infancy. At about age 2 to 3 years, however, her discovery that she lacks a penis evokes strong feelings of inferiority and jealousy (penis envy). She responds by intensifying the envious attachment to her father, who possesses the desired organ; and by resenting the mother who shares her apparent defect, who allowed her to be born in this condition, and who now looms as a rival for her father's affection. Thus, while the girl is also inherently bisexual and has twofold attitudes (love and jealousy) toward both parents, her complex (sometimes called the Elektra complex) typically takes the form of desire for her father and hostility toward her mother. (However, the reverse attitudes may become dominant if there exists an unusually strong constitutional tendency toward masculinity.)

The girl eventually seeks to compensate for her supposed physical deficiency by having her father's baby, preferably a boy baby who will bring the longed-for penis with him. Because the girl lacks the immediate and vital threat of castration anxiety, she remains Oedipal longer than the boy, and the superego that forms as a result of her less traumatic Oedipus complex is weaker than the boy's.

Thus the girl has greater difficulty in sublimating her illicit strivings, and is more likely to become neurotic.

Whereas Freud regarded the Oedipus complex as a monumental discovery, this evaluation finds little support today outside of orthodox psychoanalytic circles. In particular, Freud's views about the relative inferiority of women have been roundly rejected by most psychologists. Freud's family consisted of a beautiful, indulgent mother and a cold and indifferent father, and hence his conception may have been overly influenced by the experiences of his own childhood. The Oedipus complex cannot be counted among the numerous brilliant Freudian ideas that have found their way into the mainstream of modern psychology.

SUGGESTED READING

Brenner, C. (1974/1973). *An elementary textbook of psychoanalysis* (Rev. ed.). New York: Anchor Books.

Freud, S. (1961/1925). Some psychological consequences of the anatomical distinction between the sexes. In *The standard edition of the complete psychological works of Sigmund Freud* (Vol. 19). London: Hogarth.

Freud, S. (1964). New introductory lectures on psychoanalysis. In J. Strachey (Ed.), *The standard edition of the complete psychological works of Sigmund Freud* (pp. 7–184). London: Hogarth. (Original work published 1933)

Freud, S. (1969/1940). *An outline of psychoanalysis* (Rev. ed.). New York: Norton.

Freud, S. (1974/1924). The dissolution of the Oedipus complex. In *The standard edition of the complete psychological works of Sigmund Freud* (Vol. 19). London: Hogarth.

R. B. EWEN
Miami, Florida

PSYCHOANALYSIS
SEXUAL DEVIATIONS

OLDS, JAMES (1922–1976)

James Olds obtained his graduate degrees from Harvard University, the MA and the PhD in 1952. His undergraduate degree was earned at Amherst College. During 1952–1953, he was a lecturer and research associate at the Laboratory of Social Relations at Harvard, and from 1953 to 1955, a postdoctoral fellow at McGill University. It was at McGill that he met Peter Milner, the psychologist who collaborated with him in his work on mapping pleasure centers in the brain. In 1957, Olds joined the University of Michigan, but left in 1969 to assume a post as professor at the California Institute of Technology. His premature death occurred on August 21, 1976.

In 1954, Olds and Milner were able, by chance, to produce pleasurable effects by electrically stimulating the brain. This led them to assume a "reward mechanism" in the brain, which serves as a motivational apparatus. Their contentions, however, were the subject of constant debate, forcing them to make certain concessions. They reported their findings in a paper entitled "Positive reinforcement produced by electrical stimulation of septal area and other regions of rat brain."

W. S. SAHAKIAN

O'LEARY, K. DANIEL

K. Daniel O'Leary is a Distinguished Professor of Psychology at the State University of New York at Stony Brook. He is a clinical psychologist who received his PhD from the University of Illinois at Urbana-Champaign in 1967. He accepted a position at SUNY Stony Brook immediately thereafter, becoming a professor in 1973 and department chair in 1978.

O'Leary was born in West Chester, Pennsylvania. After his father, a biochemistry professor from Philadelphia, and his mother, a music teacher, divorced, his brother and he were reared primarily by their mother in rural Chester County, Pennsylvania. O'Leary graduated Phi Beta Kappa from Pennsylvania State University.

His early research demonstrated that behavior therapy procedures could be used by parents and teachers to change the aggressive and hyperactive behavior of children. More specifically, he showed that praise, soft reprimands, classroom rules, and structure were effective in reducing inappropriate behavior of children. For children who were not responsive to such interventions, he demonstrated that a token reinforcement program pairing stars and positive ratings for completion of academic work with classroom privileges and rewards markedly reduced disruptive behavior. Later, the children were taught to evaluate their own social and academic behavior, thereby showing how a system of external rewards can be faded to one that relies on self-evaluation. The token reinforcement research was discussed in a *Psychological Bulletin* article with Drabman in 1971, and the general approach was summarized in two editions of a book authored by O'Leary and his wife, Susan O'Leary (*Classroom Management: The Successful Use of Behavior Modification,* 1972 & 1977). While studying children in natural settings with teachers and parents, he conducted a number of studies with Kent on observational methodology, especially on factors that influenced the reliability of the observations.

With another colleague (Wilson), O'Leary wrote two books on the application of a behavior therapy approach to all major clinical problems. (*Behavior Therapy: Application and Outcome,* 1975 & 1987) and *Principles of Behavior Therapy* (1980). These books were among the first to illustrate how a behavior therapy approach could be applied to the assessment and treatment of a wide variety of clinical problems of both children and adults.

Based largely on the previous work, O'Leary was reported by *American Psychologist* as being among the top 100 cited psychologists in the English-speaking word in 1978. The behavior therapy procedures described by O'Leary and O'Leary in *Classroom Management* are now routinely used in many classes for children with emotional and behavioral problems. Additionally, O'Leary's work with hyperactive and attention-deficit children was a significant basis for a National Institute of Mental Health (NIMH) multisite outcome study comparing psychostimulant medication and behavior therapy treatments.

In the 1980s, O'Leary became interested in how marital discord affected children, and in particular, how marital discord mitigated the treatment success of behavior therapy consultation programs for parents and teachers of children with behavior problems. In turn, he began developing marital therapy treatments. His book with Beach and Sandeen, *Depression in Marriage* (1990), illustrated how marital problems can lead to depression; and his research with Beach showed that marital therapy, for clinically depressed and maritally discordant women, leads both to increases in marital satisfaction and to decreases in depression. For this work, O'Leary and Beach received the research award of the Marital and Family Therapy Association, and their marital therapy treatment is recognized by the American Psychiatric Association as a treatment that should be considered whenever an individual is depressed and experiences marital discord. Most recently with graduate students Cano and Christian-Herman, O'Leary has provided strong evidence that negative events in marriage, such as infidelity or separation, quickly lead to clinical depression in 40 to 70% of women.

Since the 1980s, O'Leary has investigated risk factors, causes, and treatments for men and women in physically aggressive relationships. He elucidated a psychological model of physical abuse, and has been assessing the relative contribution of factors to physical aggression, such as violence in the family of origin, personality styles such as aggression and impulsivity, marital discord, alcohol abuse, and psychological aggression. In studying physical aggression in a longitudinal sample of young engaged couples, O'Leary and his colleagues found that physical aggression occurred in almost half of a large sample of community couples. Furthermore, both men and women engaged in such aggression. These findings promted O'Leary to become interested in types of physical aggression in relationships and to argue for the need to evaluate and differentially intervene in cases of partner aggression. depending upon the length, severity, and risk factors associated with the aggression. In 1999, with Heyman and Neideg, O'Leary showed how gender-specific and couple-based treatments may lead to reductions in physical and psychological aggression.

O'Leary was editor of the *Journal of Applied Behavior Analysis* from 1978 to 1980 and associate editor of the *Journal of Abnormal Child Psychology.* He is or has been on the editorial boards of several other journals, including *Journal of Consulting and Clinical Psychology, Behavioral Therapy, Behavioral Assessment, Journal of Interpersonal Violence, Journal of Family Violence,* and *Journal of Family Psychology.* He is a past president of Division 12, Section III (Experimental-Clinical) of the American Psychology Association (APA) and is a fellow of APA Divisions 7, 12, and 25 (Developmental, Clinical, and Experimental Analysis of Behavior, respectively). He received the Distinguished Scientist Award from Division 12, Section III of APA in 1985. He was also president of the American Association fro the Advancement of Behavior Therapy from 1982 to 1983.

Because of the large number of his graduate students who obtained positions in research universities, O'Leary was asked to write an article for *Clinical Psychologist* (1993) on mentioning doctoral students, In 1993, he was awarded the Distinguished Scientist Award from Division 12 (Clinical) of APA. He served three terms as a member of research review panels at NIMH; he now serves on a research review panel for the National Center for Injury Prevention and Control of Violence Prevention, Center for Disease Control.

O'Leary has been in private practice since 1969 and was installed to the National Academies of Practice in psychology as a Distinguished Practitioner in 1986. In his private practice, he specializes in marital and abuse issues. Finally, he has conducted forensic evaluations in child custody cases for numerous judges in supreme and family court cases in Suffolk County, New York, for more than 10 years.

STAFF

OLFACTION

Olfaction means the act of smelling or the sense of smell. For various reasons, less is known about olfaction than about the other major senses. First, the olfactory receptors are tiny and are located deep in the head, where they are difficult to study. Also, it is technically difficult to present a known quantity of an odorant to the receptors, both because of the aerodynamics of the nasal cavity and the nature of the stimulus itself. Although efforts have been made to define primary odors, researchers have not successfully identified a limited number of categories into which all odorants can be placed.

Olfaction is important for the behavior of a variety of animals including mammals. For example, olfaction is often involved in predator-prey relationships. A predator may use olfaction to detect its prey, and prey animals may rely on their sense of smell to avoid predation. The mating behavior of many species is guided at least partially by olfactory cues, and this is also true for parental behaviors. By contrast, olfaction is usually not considered as important for humans as it is for many other mammalian species.

This does not mean that olfaction has no importance in humans. Without olfaction, most food would taste the same; almost everyone has experienced the blandness of taste caused by an upper respiratory ailment. Although it is difficult to recall smells or to name them, particular odors can trigger memories of specific times and places, and the memories are often accompanied by strong emotional feelings. In addition, humans spend millions of dollars annually to alter their odor to conform to cultural dictates.

OLFACTORY STIMULI

Odorant stimuli are airborne molecules of volatile substances—substances that have a gaseous state at normal temperatures—because air currents transport the molecules to the olfactory receptors. Although greater volatility generally means more odor, there are important exceptions. One is distilled water, which is highly volatile but has no detectable odor. Another exception is musk (a

secretion from deer and some other mammals), which has a powerful scent despite its low volatility.

There are several properties of odorant molecules that may be related to their smell. Two of the possibilities are the shape of the molecule and its vibration frequency (movement of atoms in the molecule). In 1964, Amoore, Johnston, and Rubin proposed that the shape of the odorant molecule (stereochemical or lock-and-key theory) determines its odor quality. Amoore and colleagues identified seven primary odors for humans, each associated with a particular molecular shape. For example, the odor camphoraceous, typical of mothballs, is produced by a spherical-shaped molecule, whereas a floral odor, exemplified by a rose, is elicited by a key-shaped molecule. The vibration theory states that an odor molecule breaks certain chemical bonds in the cell membrane of the receptor. The vibration frequency of the molecule determines which bonds are broken and thus the neural coding of the odor (Wright, 1977).

STRUCTURE OF THE OLFACTORY SYSTEM

The receptor cells for olfaction are located in the olfactory epithelium (literally "smell skin"), which is at the top of the nasal cavity. The roof of the nasal cavity is formed by bone called the cribriform plate. Openings in this structure permit the passage of the olfactory nerve, which is composed of axons of the receptor cells. The olfactory nerve passing through the cribriform plate is quite vulnerable to shearing forces generated by sudden changes in the movement or position of the head, which might be experienced in an automobile accident. Thus, many persons with head injuries of this sort lose their sense of smell. The olfactory nerve ends in the olfactory bulb, a neural structure at the base of the brain. Figure 1 is a schematic view of the human olfactory system.

Hairlike structures called cilia are located at the other end (away from the axon) of each receptor cell. The cilia are embedded in mucous and are probably the initial points of contact with the olfac-

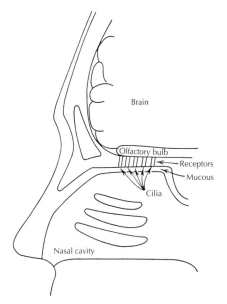

Figure 1. Schematic drawing of the anatomy of the peripheral olfactory system

tory stimulus. The sensitivity of an organism's olfactory system seems to be related to both the total number of receptor cells and to the number of cilia per receptor. By this measure, humans are low on the scale of sensitivity. For example, a dog may have up to 20 times as many receptor cells as a person, with each cell having more than 10 times as many cilia.

After leaving the olfactory bulbs, the olfactory pathways affect several structures in an area of the brain called the rhinencephalon (literally "nose brain"). Some key neural structures receiving olfactory input are the amygdala, the hippocampus, the pyriform cortex (located at the base of the temporal lobes), and the hypothalamus.

OLFACTORY PHENOMENA

The perceived intensity of an odor is greatly affected by adaptation, with only a brief exposure needed to render an odor undetectable. Although this rapid adaptation may be beneficial to workers in an animal laboratory, it is maladaptive to coal miners who might need to detect an increase in the intensity of a potentially lethal gas.

Adaptation occurs both to the stimulus to which you are exposed (self-adaptation) and to similar stimuli (cross-adaptation). The amount of cross-adaptation depends on the similarity between the adapting odor and other stimulus odor; the more similar the stimuli, the greater the cross-adaptation.

Olfactory cues are important for recognition of kin in a variety of mammals including humans. For example, Porter and Moore (1981) found that children were able to recognize the odors of their siblings when compared to the odors of unfamiliar children. Additionally, mothers were able to differentiate between odors of their own and other children, and both mothers and fathers were able to distinguish between their own children using olfactory cues.

Studies have demonstrated that people can select a T-shirt they have worn for several days from a group of T-shirts worn by others (e.g., Lord & Kasprzak, 1989). In addition, when people are asked to rate the pleasantness/unpleasantness of odors and to describe the characteristics of someone whose odor they are smelling, the ratings and descriptions tend to be remarkably consistent. In general, individuals described as having unpleasant odors are also perceived to have socially undesirable characteristics such as ugliness, obesity, and stupidity. Pleasant odors tend to be associated with more desirable social traits (McBurney, Levine, & Cavanaugh, 1977).

In addition, people seem to be able to discriminate the gender of an odor donor reliably, and they typically correctly attribute the more unpleasant (and stronger) odors to men and the nicer odors to women (e.g., Doty, Green, Ram, & Yankell, 1982). In general, females are better at this type of discrimination than males, and, in fact, are better at odor identification overall (e.g., Lord & Kasprzak, 1989). Extensive experience with an odor and its source seem to be necessary for accurate odor identification, at least in adults (e.g., Rabin, 1988).

REFERENCES

Amoore, J. D., Johnston, J. W., & Rubin, M. (1964). The stereochemical theory of olfaction. *Scientific American, 210,* 42–49.

Doty, R. L., Green, P. A., Ram, C., & Yankell, S. L. (1982). Communication of gender from human breath odors: Relationship to perceived intensity and pleasantness. *Hormones and Behavior, 16,* 13–22.

Lord, T., & Kasprzak, M. (1989). Identification of self through olfaction. *Perceptual and Motor Skills, 69,* 219–224.

McBurney, D. H., Levine, J. M., & Cavanaugh, P. H. (1977). Psychophysical and social ratings of human body odor. *Personality and Social Psychology Bulletin, 3,* 135–138.

Porter, R. H., & Moore, J. D. (1981). Human kin recognition by olfactory cues. *Physiology and Behavior, 27,* 493–495.

Rabin, M. D. (1988). Experience facilitates olfactory quality discrimination. *Perception & Psychophysics, 44,* 532–540.

Wright, R. H. (1977). Odor and molecular vibration: Neural coding of olfactory information. *Journal of Theoretical Biology, 64,* 473–502.

B. M. THORNE
Mississippi State University

ACCOMODATION
OLFACTORY CORTEX
TASTE PERCEPTION

OLFACTORY CORTEX

One of the most evocative of senses, olfaction produces powerful responses in humans and is used as a primitive but potent form of communication among animals. It is important to sexual attraction and, therefore, to fecundity. It is used to identify chemical messages among and between species and may provide an early alarm signal of potential danger. Disgusting smells may also signal the presence of putrid or contaminated material and thereby prevent contact between the organism and such material, reducing the risk of disease or illness. Our understanding of the brain mechanisms underlying olfactory ability has markedly improved in recent years, and brain areas subserving various olfactory abilities have been identified. Olfactory function can be broadly divided into acuity, identification ability, and olfactory memory. Each of these may be subserved by interrelated cerebral systems, which may be differentially affected in various neurological and neuropsychiatric disorders. We briefly discuss the functional neuroanatomy of olfaction, and then summarize the findings in various neurological and psychiatric disorders.

NEUROANATOMY OF OLFACTION

Olfactory perception begins in receptors located in the mucous-lined olfactory epithelium. The epithelium of each nasal cavity contains approximately 50 million receptor cells, which are bipolar neurons having a short peripheral process (dendritic) and a long central process (axonal). The short dendritic process connects to the mucosal surface, where it ends in an expanded olfactory knob, from which extends a dense mat of cilia. It is these cilia that interact with odorants introduced into the nasal cavity. The long axonal processes pass through the cribriform plate of the skull to the ipsilateral olfactory bulb, thereby carrying olfactory information centrally. The olfactory bulbs are situated directly beneath the orbitofrontal cortical surface (see Adams & Victor, 1981).

Olfactory bulb neurons project to allocortical and paralimbic (mesocortical) areas centrally. Importantly, unlike most sensory systems, there is no direct projection to neocortex. The allocortical area includes the hippocampus (archicortex) and pyriform or primary olfactory cortex (paleocortex), while the paralimbic structures include orbitofrontal cortex, insula, temporal pole, parahippocampal gyrus, and cingulate complex, and can be divided into olfactocentric and hippocampocentric groups. The olfactory pyriform cortex provides the allocortical focal point for orbitofrontal, insular, and temporo-polar paralimbic areas, while the hippocampus provides the allocortical focus for cingulate and parahippocampal components (see Mesulam, 1988).

Olfactory information from each olfactory bulb has five important projections (Adams & Victor, 1981). Each bulb has projections (medial stria) to the contralateral anterior olfactory nucleus (situated along the olfactory tract) via the anterior commissure (Powell, Cowan, & Raisman, 1965), suggesting there is some integration of olfactory information at an early stage of processing. Intermediate stria axons pass from the olfactory bulb to the ventral striatum (olfactory tubercle), which then projects to the orbitofrontal cortex via the medial dorsal nucleus of the thalamus (Potter & Nauta, 1979; Powell et al., 1965), whose functional significance is thought to be the conscious appreciation of odor and its identification (Staubli, Schottler, & Nejat-Bina, 1987). Further, these frontal connections may be relevant to cognitive aspects of smell (Potter & Butters, 1980), as well as to integration with other sensory modalities, including taste (Harrison & Pearson, 1989; Sobel, Prakhakaran, Desmond, Glover, Goode, Sullivan, & Gabrielli, 1998; Francis, Rolls, Bowtell, McGlone, O'Doherty, Browning, Clare & Smith, 1999).

Lateral stria axons from the olfactory tract have a number of projections, including radiations ipsilaterally to the anterior perforated substance, and terminate in the medial and cortical nuclei of the amygdaloid complex, which then relays information to the hypothalamus and tegmentum of the midbrain (Mesulam, 1988). Links to the hypothalamus are considered relevant to eating and reproduction (see Harrison & Pearson, 1989). Projections from the lateral stria axons also radiate to the pyriform cortex, which is located at the anterior end of the hippocampal gyrus and uncus and is thought to be the main olfactory discrimination region (see Harrison & Pearson, 1989; Staubli et al., 1987) and, therefore, is important to odor recognition and discrimination. The pyriform cortex has further projections to the amygdala and the entorhinal cortex (Adams & Victor, 1981). Lateral stria axons also have direct projections to the entorhinal cortex. The latter receives olfactory and other sensory information, unimodally as well as polymodally, and then conveys this polysensory information to the hippocampus by way of the perforant path (Van Hoesen & Pandya, 1975), indicating that these regions provide an interface for other sensory information with that of olfaction. The limbic projections of the lateral stria axons are thought to be relevant to the affective associations of odors and to olfactory memory (Staubli, Roman, & Lynch, 1984). In addition, evidence from lesion studies and neuro-

logical patients (see below) also implicates these areas as relevant to detecting odors (i.e., olfactory acuity; Rausch & Serafitinides, 1975; Jones-Gotman & Zatorre, 1988; Potter & Butters, 1980). The olfactory bulbs also receive efferent fibers from the brain, including those from the uncus, locus ceruleus, and raphe nuclei (Switzer, de Olmos, & Heimer, 1985), so that peripheral appreciation of olfactory stimuli may be modulated by central mechanisms (Martzke, Kopala, & Good, 1997).

The functional significance of the components of the olfactory cortex have been determined from experiments in animals, human lesion studies, and neurological disorders, and more recently, from work using newer brain imaging techniques, such as positron emission tomography (PET) and both structural and functional magnetic resonance imaging (MRI and fMRI). Early studies using PET and fMRI indicated that both pleasant and unpleasant odors activated expected regions of the entorhinal cortex and orbitofrontal cortex (OFC) and the amygdala, although odors also activated additional areas in the medial prefrontal cortex including the anterior cingulate gyrus (Zald, Donndelinger, & Pardo, 1998). This involvement of areas not regarded to be part of the olfactory system may have reflected the attachment of meaning to the odors used. Interestingly, the act of sniffing in anticipation of any odor also activated piriform cortex in the temporal lobe as well as the medial and posterior aspects of the orbitofrontal gyri (Sobel et al., 1998). This suggests that even the anticipation of odor will activate olfactory processing networks. The same study found that detection of the odor moved the focus of activation in the OFC to the lateral and anterior aspects of the orbitofrontal gyrus. This suggests that sniffing in anticipation of detecting an odor and smelling that odor are represented differently in the frontal cortex. However, cortical activation associated with the detection of odors is part of some supramodal system that attaches meaning to any sensory stimuli as pleasant-smells activated regions in the OFC, which were different from those activated by pleasant tastes and pleasant touches (Francis et al., 1999). Interestingly, when patients with hyposmia who are able to detect but not recognize odors perform the same olfactory task there is no activation of medial frontal, anterior cingulate, orbitofrontal, or temporal lobe areas (Levy, Henkin, Lin, & Finley, 1999).

In humans, the most informative data derive from neurological and neuropsychiatric disorders. While knowledge of the pathological processes in neurological disorders has informed our understanding of the olfactory system, we can also employ such knowledge to inform our understanding of neuropsychiatric disorders in which pathology is often ill-defined (e.g., schizophrenia and Obsessive-Compulsive Disorder).

ASSESSMENT OF OLFACTION

The assessment of olfactory function is usually undertaken using various odorants. Identification ability is usually assessed using scratch-and-sniff suprathreshold fragrances that are microencapsulated and embedded in plastic capsules that are coated onto labels. The only standardised identification task available is the University of Pennsylvania Smell Identification Task (UPSIT; Doty, Shaman, & Dann, 1984). Olfactory acuity, which refers to the ability to detect an odor, has often been assessed by forced choice method utilizing graded concentrations of selected odorants. Assessment of acuity is complicated by the choice of odorant, some of which may be noxious and trigger a trigeminal nerve response, while some may not be detectable by a significant proportion of the population (e.g., steroidal vs. nonsteroidal substances). The ability to discriminate among odors involves assessment of whether odors are the same or different but does not require identification. Odor recognition is the ability to ascertain whether the odor has ever been experienced, while for odor memory subjects are required to choose a target odorant from a series of odors (Martzke et al., 1997). Assessment of olfaction in females should also take account of changes in olfactory ability related to different stages of the menstrual cycle.

PERIPHERAL CAUSES OF OLFACTORY DEFICITS

The nasal diseases most frequently responsible for hyposmia and anosmia are those in which hypertrophy and hyperaemia of nasal mucosa block olfactory stimuli from contact with receptor cells, such as allergic, infective, or vasomotor rhinitis. In allergic rhinitis, sensory epithelial cells are present, but cilia are shortened and deformed, and hidden under other mucosal cells (Adams & Victor, 1981). Epithelial disorders involving the sensory cells are most often caused by viral infection (influenza-anosmia) or toxic destruction of the sensory epithelium (solvents or gases), which can affect acuity. The most common causes of permanent loss of smell are influenza and upper respiratory tract infection. Congestion and swelling of mucous membranes may also result from metabolic and hormonal disorders (Adams & Victor, 1981).

OLFACTION IN NEUROLOGY AND NEUROPSYCHIATRY

Independence of function of olfactory abilities has been suggested by studies in neurological patients with lesions in various parts of the olfactory system. Potter and Butters (1980) demonstrated a profound olfactory identification impairment in patients with lesions of the OFC, while odor detection was not impaired. Such dissociation of olfactory function is also observed in Korsakoff's amnestic syndrome (discussed later). Potter and Butters (1980) suggest a hierarchical organization of olfactory processing, passing from the medio-dorsal nucleus of the thalamus to the entorhinal cortex, and then to the lateral posterior OFC. They suggest that prefrontal lesions produce more dramatic olfactory impairment than does damage to midline structures, such as the thalamus. Further, Jones-Gotmann and Zatorre (1988) found that olfactory identification ability was significantly impaired following a unilateral excision in the temporal lobe or the OFC on either side, but not after a frontal lobe excision sparing the OFC. Greater deficits in identification were associated with lesions of the OFC than with lesions of the temporal area. Thresholds (measures of acuity) in both groups of lesioned patients were normal. Overall, if the orbital regions are spared, identification ability is maintained, and if they are not, deficits in identification, but not acuity, are present. Projections to the dorsal thalamus and the frontal cortex are the major neocortical representations involved in odor discrimination, and thus involvement of either is inferred in identification deficits (Kopala & Clark, 1990).

AGING

The available normative data suggest that olfactory threshold and identification ability decrease with age (Doty, 1989). Smell loss occurs with normal aging due to viral insult, cumulated exposure to toxins, head trauma, and calcification of the cribriform plate. Although it is tempting to assume that alterations in threshold function reflect peripheral dysfunction and that identification reflects central olfactory function (e.g., Koss, Weiffenbach, Haxby, & Freidland, 1988), there is little empirical support for such a simple dichotomy (Doty, 1989).

ALZHEIMER'S DISEASE & CORTICAL DEMENTIAS

Studies in Alzheimer's disease (AD) have identified impairments in olfaction (Doty, 1991) including difficulties in the ability to identify odors, suggesting that central mechanisms are involved, although most studies have also found deficits in the ability even to detect odors (see Harrison & Pearson, 1989). While the latter finding has been interpreted as implicating peripheral mechanisms, central mechanisms may also be involved (Doty, 1989). These findings are consistent with neuropathological evidence for typical AD changes in the anterior olfactory nucleus and olfactory bulb, as well as in those olfactory areas described above (amygdala, entorhinal and pyriform cortices, and hippocampi; see Harrison & Pearson, 1989). In keeping with these changes in limbic and paralimbic areas, olfactory memory deficits may also occur early in the course of AD (Nordin & Murphy, 1996). Further, olfactory identification deficits may be an early feature of AD, in the presence of intact threshold to detect odors (Koss et al., 1988), though not all studies have confirmed this finding (e.g., Doty, Reyes, & Gregor, 1987; Thompson, Knee, & Golden, 1998). Deficits in olfactory function may also discriminate AD from multi-infarct or other dementias, though the available reports are inconclusive (Thompson et al., 1998).

TEMPORAL LOBE EPILEPSY

The literature on olfaction in temporal lobe epilepsy (TLE) is extensive, with methodological inconsistencies. The better controlled studies using standard nonsteroidal odorants, which do not trigger a trigeminal nerve response, have assessed monorhinal function to investigate lateralized abnormalities, and have assessed function pre- and post-surgery. Such studies have found reductions in olfactory acuity in patients with right temporal lobectomies (Martinez, Cain, de Wijk, Spencer, Novelly, & Sass, 1993), while olfactory recognition, discrimination, and short-term memory ability were also impaired in patients pre-surgery, particularly on the right (Carrol, Richardson, & Thompson, 1993; Jones-Gotman, Zatorre, Cendes, Olivier, Andermann, McMackin, Staunton, Seigal, & Weiser, 1997; Martinez et al., 1993). Further, discrimination and Short Term Memory (STM) deficits are worse after temporal lobectomy (Martinez et al., 1993). These functions implicate the ipsilateral involvement of secondary pathways extending from primary olfactory cortex via the Dorso-medial Nucleus (DMN) of the thalamus to entorhinal cortex. Olfactory identification deficits are generally not apparent in TLE patients pre-surgery; however, lobectomized patients may manifest such deficits ipsilaterally when lesions involve the OFC (Jones-Gotman & Zatorre, 1988, 1997).

SUBCORTICAL DISORDERS

Parkinson's Disease and Related Disorders

In a recent meta-analysis of 43 studies that examined patients with AD and those with Parkinson's disease (PD) in comparison with controls (Mesholam, Moberg, Mahr, & Doty, 1998) found severe and similar deficits in both patient groups, including olfactory identification, recognition, and detection. The results of this analysis suggested that these patient groups could not be differentiated based on these tasks. However, Hawkes, Shephard, Geddes, Body, and Martin (1998) found that olfactory identification deficits or abnormal olfactory-evoked potentials were apparent in the majority of patients with established PD, and that these patients were more severely impaired than patients with AD, multiple sclerosis, or motor neuron disease. The potential diagnostic utility of olfactory function in parkinsonism is suggested by findings that, while severe olfactory dysfunction is found in idiopathic PD, such deficits are not apparent or are mild in atypical parkinsonian syndromes, including multisystem atrophy, corticobasal degeneration, and progressive supranuclear palsy (Wenning, Shephard, Hawkes, Petruckevitch, Lees, & Quinn, 1995; Doty, Golbe, McKeown, Stern, Lehrach, & Crawford, 1993). Olfactory deficits are also apparent early in the course of idiopathic PD and may provide an early diagnostic marker (Doty, Stern, Pfeiffer, Gollomp, & Hurtig 1992), particularly as these deficits are independent of age, sex, medication, and degree of neurological impairment (Doty, Deems, & Stellar, 1988). The changes in PD have been linked to neuronal loss and the presence of Lewy bodies in the olfactory bulb and tract and in the anterior olfactory nucleus (Pearce, Hawkes, & Daniel, 1995). The observed deficits also implicate the involvement of the orbitofrontal cortex (Mayberg, Starkstein, Peyser, Brandt, Dannals, & Folstein, 1992). It has been postulated that the observed deficits result from hypodopaminergia, which is the major neurochemical deficit in PD. This may involve dopamine (DA) loss in the olfactory tubercle (Quinn, Rossor, & Marsden, 1987) or the olfactory bulb (Zucco, Zaglis, & Wambsganns, 1991), or may be associated with depletion of DA in some limbic areas (Ward, Hess, & Calne, 1983). In contrast, Doty, Stern, Pfeiffer, Gollomp, and Hurtig (1992) suggest that peripheral mechanisms involving breakdown of the nasal mucosa may be involved.

Huntington's Disease

Of the few available studies in Huntington's disease (HD), olfactory deficits have been demonstrated, with identification ability being most impaired. Nordin, Paulsen, and Murphy (1995) found a raised threshold for olfactory detection, impaired ability to discriminate smells, and olfactory identification deficits in HD, while odor-recognition memory was intact. Tests of olfaction do not appear to be good indicators of at-risk offspring of HD patients (Moberg & Doty, 1997), nor of asymptomatic gene carriers (Bylsma, Moberg, Doty, & Brandt, 1997). However, olfactory dysfunction, including impaired olfactory recognition memory, may be a reliable early marker of HD after illness onset (Moberg, Pearl-

son, Speedie, Lipsey, Strauss, & Folstein, 1987; Doty, 1991). It has been suggested that involvement of frontal-striatal-thalamic circuits, particularly those involving the OFC, caudate, and DMN of the thalamus may underlie these deficits, particularly in identification ability.

Human Immunodeficiency Virus (HIV)

Deficits in threshold and identification ability in HIV-infected persons have been consistently reported (see Graham, Graham, Bartlett, Heald, & Schiffman, 1995; Razani, Murphy, Davidson, Grant, & McCutchan, 1996). Brody, Serby, Etienne, and Kalkstein (1991) reported clinically impaired olfaction in three groups of HIV-infected patients. Asymptomatic patients and patients with clinical evidence of immune compromise showed mild impairments in odor identification ability, whereas dementing patients showed deficits within the moderate range. These authors suggested that mild impairment in olfactory function might be an early indicator of the onset of immune suppression and/or of neurologic disease. While these results received some support from Westervelt and McCaffrey (1997) in their longitudinal study of at-risk, HIV-negative volunteers and asymptomatic and symptomatic HIV-infected patients, this study did not identify olfactory deficits in asymptomatic HIV individuals. Further, these studies did not assess acuity and were not able to exclude the possible contribution of peripheral nerve damage and/or other effects related to treatments, such as azidothymidine (AZT). Indeed, Hornung and colleagues (1998) identified nasal pathology as the main cause for variability in olfactory acuity in HIV-positive patients, which may partly affect more central olfactory functions. Neuropathological studies have identified AIDS virus receptor clusters in limbic system structures, including hippocampus, amygdala, and hypothalamus, and in cortical areas, including OFC (Pert, Ruff, Ruscetti, Farrar, & Hill, 1988; Ketzler, Weis, Haug, & Budka, 1990; Weis, Haug, & Budka, 1993) as well as in olfactory nerve fascicles, tracts, and bulbs (Lima & Vital, 1994).

CHRONIC ALCOHOLISM AND KORSAKOFF'S PSYCHOSIS

Evidence suggests that individuals with chronic alcohol abuse show deficits in olfactory match-to-sample tests, but not on smell identification (Kesslak, Profitt, & Criswell, 1991). Odor identification was also found to be intact in alcoholic dementia (Serby, Corwin, Conrad, & Rotrosen, 1985), while Ditraglia and colleagues (1991) observed olfactory identification deficits in detoxified chronic alcoholics. However, the contribution of general learning and memory deficits to olfactory function in these patients has not been excluded. Korsakoff syndrome patients, in contrast, show relatively intact acuity, while identification ability is impaired (Potter & Butters, 1980; Doty et al., 1984; Jones-Gotman & Zatorre, 1988). This may result from the observed degeneration of the mediodorsal thalamic nucleus together with atrophy in the prefrontal areas to which it projects (Jones, Butters, Moskowitz, & Montgomery, 1978; Potter & Butters, 1980). Further, the volume of the thalamus has been found to be a significant unique predictor of UPSIT score (Shear, Butters, Jernigan, DiTraglia, Win, Schukit, & Cermak, 1992).

OTHER NEUROLOGICAL DISORDERS

Olfactory identification deficits have been reported in patients with motor neuron disease (MND; Hawkes et al., 1998). Few studies have reported olfactory abnormalities in patients with multiple sclerosis (MS; Hawkes, Shephard, & Kobal, 1997; Doty, Li, Mannon, & Yousem, 1998), which has been associated with plaque numbers in inferior frontal and temporal lobes (Doty et al., 1998). Patients with Down syndrome demonstrate olfactory deficits related to the onset of Alzheimer-type dementia (McKeown, Doty, Perl, Frye, Simms, & Mester, 1996).

SOLVENTS

Mild impairments in odor identification have been reported with low exposure to solvents (Sandmark, Broms, Lofgren, & Ohlson, 1989). Chronic exposure to cadmium fumes impairs odor detection but not identification (Rose, Heywood, & Costanzo, 1992). Cacosmia (headaches, nausea, and subjective distress when exposed to neutral environmental odors) secondary to organic solvent exposure has been related to impaired verbal learning and visual memory (Ryan, Morrow, & Hodgson, 1988). As well as acting on the CNS, solvents may act peripherally on nasal mucosa and epithelium to interfere with odor detection (Schwartz, Ford, Bolla, Agnew, & Bleeker, 1991).

TRAUMATIC BRAIN INJURY

Smell deficits may be found after traumatic brain injury (TBI), particularly when areas involving the olfactory centers are structurally damaged. Doty and colleagues (1997) reported a high proportion of anosmia (66.8%) in patients with head trauma, though frontal impacts produced less olfactory dysfunction than did back or side impacts. These posttraumatic olfactory deficits generally signify orbitofrontal damage and/or shearing of the olfactory bulbs and are usually permanent. Often, anosmia is caused by damage to the delicate filaments of receptor cells as they pass through the cribriform plate (Adams & Victor, 1981), or from damage to the olfactory bulbs or tracts (Jones, Moskowitz, & Butters, 1975).

PSYCHIATRIC DISORDERS

Depression

Results from the few available studies of olfaction in depressed patients are conflicting because of differences in treatment status, use of nonstandard odorants, or use of irritating odorants (which cause trigeminal nerve activation). Serby, Larson, and Kalkstein (1990) found intact olfactory acuity in patients with Major Depressive Disorder (MDD), while Suffin and Gitlin (1986) reported higher olfactory threshold with greater severity of depression. Moberg, Pearlson, Speedie, Lipsey, and DePaulo (1986) reported decreased performance in MDD patients on an odor recognition test. Gross-Isseroff and colleagues (1994) demonstrated a significant increase in sensitivity to isoamyl acetate (a traditional odorant with a low propensity to trigger a trigeminal aversive reaction, used to assess olfactory acuity) after initiation of antidepressant drug therapy in patients with MDD, suggesting that olfactory deficits may be state rather than trait. While Serby and colleagues

(1990) found decreased odor identification in MDD, two studies found no impairment (Amsterdam et al., 1987; Warner, Peabody, & Csernansky, 1990). Further, Solomon, Petrie, Hart, and Brackin (1998) found intact olfactory identification ability in elderly depressed patients, and that the presence of such deficits correctly discriminated Alzheimer's disease patients from those with MDD. Overall, these studies suggest that olfactory deficits are not a prominent feature of depression. This is perhaps not surprising as PET studies in MDD have demonstrated involvement of lateral prefrontal rather than orbitofrontal cortex (Baxter, 1991; Rogers, Bradshaw, & Pantelis, 1998).

Obsessive-Compulsive Disorder

Few studies have examined olfactory function in patients with Obsessive-Compulsive Disorder (OCD), despite the suggestion that orbitofrontal cortex and subcortical nuclei are involved in this condition (Rauch, Savage, Alpert, Dougherty, Kendrick, Curran, Brown, Manzo, Fischman, & Jenike, 1997). Gross-Isseroff and colleagues (1994) found no impairment in olfactory acuity in 14 patients with OCD, while there are no studies of olfactory memory. In contrast, the two available studies have found impaired olfactory identification ability (Goldberg, Goldberg, & Vannopen, 1991; Barnett, Maruff, Purcell, Wainwright, Kyrios, Brewer, & Pantelis, 1999). Barnett and colleagues (1999), in their comparison of 20 patients with OCD with 23 age- and education-matched controls, found that 70% of the OCD patients were microsmic. The findings from these studies suggest a specific impairment of olfactory identification ability, which implicates OFC involvement in this disorder.

SCHIZOPHRENIA

A meta-analysis of olfactory function in schizophrenia examined studies of olfactory identification (18 studies), detection threshold (4 studies), discrimination (2 studies) and recognition memory (1 study; Moberg, et al., 1999). Moderator variables including age, gender, smoking, and medication status were also examined. Very large effect sizes were found for deficits in olfactory identification and olfactory recognition memory. Significant effects for elevated olfactory detection thresholds were also identified. Inconsistent results for odor discrimination were perhaps related to the different types of odors used in different studies. No differential gender effects were found for odor identification or acuity, while insufficient data were available to examine this for the other domains. Further, no medication-related effects were found for all four olfactory domains, and there was no significant effect of smoking on odor identification. The lack of gender effect is surprising, given evidence from other neurobiological studies of schizophrenia for gender-specific effects (e.g., Castle & Murray, 1991). The impact of illness chronicity was not examined in this meta-analysis. However, recent studies have assessed first-episode patients (Kopala, Clark, & Hurwitz, 1992; Brewer, Pantelis, Anderson, Velakoulis, Singh, Copolov, & McGorry, in press). These confirm the presence of olfactory identification deficits at this early stage of the illness, in the presence of intact olfactory acuity. Further, a follow-up study in this patient group found that these deficits were stable and did not change with changes in symptomatology (Brewer et al., in press), while the only study that has examined individuals at high risk for psychosis prior to illness onset reports the presence of olfactory identification deficits (Brewer, Francey, Yung, Velakoulis, Anderson, McGorry, Singh, Copolov, & Pantelis, 1998). These recent studies suggest that such deficits may be trait markers of the illness.

The robust olfactory identification deficits in schizophrenia provide evidence for involvement of orbitofrontal circuits (Pantelis & Brewer, 1995, 1996). Deficits in other olfactory domains are less consistent but may implicate neuronal systems involved in olfactory acuity, discrimination, and memory, including entorhinal cortex, as suggested by studies of neurological patients in which olfactory disturbances were dissociated (Potter & Butters, 1980).

SUMMARY

Olfactory deficits are observed in a number of neurological and psychiatric disorders. Such deficits involve different aspects of olfactory function, depending on the nature and extent of neurological involvement. There is evidence to suggest that olfactory functions may be dissociable, with the most profound deficits seen in higher-order function involving the ability to identify odors, which implicates OFC involvement. Examination of olfactory disturbances may provide early markers of impending neurological or psychiatric illness and, in some psychiatric disorders including schizophrenia, may be trait markers of the condition.

REFERENCES

Adams, K. M., & Victor, M. (1981). *Principles of neurology.* New York: McGraw-Hill.

Amsterdam, J. D., Settle, R. G., Doty, R. L., Abelman, E., et al. (1987). Taste and smell perception in depression. *Biological Psychiatry, 22*(12), 1481–1485.

Barnett, R., Maruff, P., Purcell, R., Wainwright, K., Kyrios, M.,

Brewer, W. & Pantelis, C. (1999). Olfactory identification deficits in obsessive compulsive disorder. *Psychological Medicine, 29,* 1227–1233.

Baxter, L. R. (1991). PET studies of cerebral function in major depression and obsessive compulsive disorder: The emerging prefrontal cortex consensus. *Annals of Clinical Psychiatry, 3*(2), 103–109.

Brewer, W. J., Pantelis, C., Anderson, V., Velakoulis, D., Singh, B., Copolov, D. L., & McGorry, P. D. (in press). Stability of olfactory identification deficits in neuroleptic-naïve patients with first-episode psychosis. *American Journal of Psychiatry.*

Brewer, W., Francey, S., Yung, A., Velakoulis, D., Anderson, V., McGorry, P., Singh, B., Copolov, D., & Pantelis, C. (1998). Cognitive and olfactory deficits: Course from high risk to first-episode psychosis. Abstract presented at the 9th Biennial Winter Workshop on Schizophrenia 7–13th February, Davos, Switzerland. *Schizophrenia Research 29,* 1–2.

Brody, D., Serby, M., Etienne, N., Kalkstein, D. S. (1991). Olfactory identification deficits in HIV infection. *American Journal of Psychiatry, 148,* 248–250.

Bylsma, F. W., Moberg, P. J., Doty, R. L., Brandt, J. (1997). Odor identification in Huntington's disease patients and asymptomatic gene carriers. *The Journal of Neuropsychiatry and Clinical Neurosciences, 9,* 598–600.

Carrol, B., Richardson, J. T. E., & Thompson, P. (1993). Olfactory information processing and temporal lobe epilepsy. *Brain and Cognition, 22,* 230–243.

Castle, D. J., & Murray, R. M. (1991). The neurodevelopmental basis of sex differences in schizophrenia. *Psychological Medicine, 21,* 565–575.

Doty, R. L. (1989). Influence of age and age-related diseases on olfactory function. *Annals of the New York Academy of Sciences, 561,* 76–86.

Doty, R. L. (1991). Olfactory dysfunction in neurodegenerative disorders. In T. V. Getchell, R. L. Doty, L. M. Bartoshuk, (Eds.), *Smell and taste in health and disease* (pp. 735–751). New York: Raven.

Doty, R. L., Deems, D. A., Stellar, S. (1988). Olfactory dysfunction in parkinsonism: A general deficit unrelated to neurologic signs, disease stage, or disease duration. *Neurology, 38*(8), 1237–1244.

Doty, R. L., Golbe, L. I., McKeown, D. A., Stern, M. B., Lehrach, C. M., Crawford, D. (1993). Olfactory testing differentiates between progressive supranuclear palsy and idiopathic Parkinson's disease. *Neurology, 43*(5), 962–965.

Doty, R. L., Gregor, T. P., & Settle, R. G. (1986). Influence of intertrial and sniff-bottle volume on phenyl ethyl alcohol odor detection thresholds. *Chemical Senses, 11,* 259–264.

Doty, R. L., Li, C., Mannon, L. J., Yousem, D. M. (1998). Olfactory dysfunction in multiple sclerosis. Relation to plaque load in inferior frontal and temporal lobes. *Annals of the New York Academy of Sciences, 30*(855), 781–786.

Doty, R. L., Reyes, P. F., & Gregor, T. (1987). Presence of both odor identification and detection deficits in Alzheimer's disease. *Brain Research Bulletin, 18,* 597–600.

Doty, R. L., Shaman, P., & Dann, W. (1984). Development of the University of Pennsylvania Smell Test: Standardised micro-encapsulated test of olfactory function. *Physiological Behavior, 32,* 489–502.

Doty, R. L., Stern, M. B., Pfeiffer, C., Gollomp, S. M., Hurtig, H. I. (1992). Bilateral olfactory dysfunction in early stage treated and untreated idiopathic Parkinson's disease. *Journal of Neurology, Neurosurgery and Psychiatry, 55*(2), 138–142.

Doty, R. L., Yousem, D. M., Pham, L. T., Kreshak, A. A., Geckle, R., Lee, W. W. (1997). Olfactory dysfunction in patients with head trauma. *Archives of Neurology, 54*(9), 1131–1140.

Francis, S., Rolls, E. T., Bowtell, R., McGlone, F., O'Doherty, J., Browning, A., Clare, S., Smith, E. (1999). The representation of pleasant touch in the brain and its relationship with taste and olfactory areas. *Neuroreport, 10,* 453–459.

Graham, C. S., Graham, B. G., Bartlett, J. A., Heald, A. E., & Schiffman, S. (1995). Taste and smell losses in HIV infected inpatients. *Physiology and Behavior, 58*(2), 287–293.

Gross-Isseroff, R., Luca-Haimovici, K., Sasson, Y., Kindler, S., Kotler, M., Zohar. (1994). Olfactory sensitivity in major depressive disorder and obsessive compulsive disorder. *Biological Psychiatry, 35,* 798–802.

Harrison, P. J., & Pearson, R. C. A. (1989). Olfaction and psychiatry. *British Journal of Psychiatry, 155,* 822–828.

Hawkes, C. H., Shephard, B. C., Geddes, J. F., Body, G. D., & Martin, J. E. (1998). Olfactory disorder in motor neuron disease. *Experimental Neurology, 150*(2), 248–253.

Hawkes, C. H., Shephard, B. C., & Kobal, G. (1997). Assessment of olfaction in multiple sclerosis: Evidence of dysfunction by olfactory evoked response and identification tests. *Journal of Neurology, Neurosurgery and Psychiatry, 63*(9), 145–151.

Hornung, D. E., Kurtz, D. B., Bradshaw, C. B., Seipel, D. M., Kent, P. F., Blair, D. C., & Emko, P. (1998). The olfactory loss that accompanies an HIV infection. *Physiological Behavior, 64*(4), 549–556.

Jones, B. P., Butters, N., Moskowitz, H. R., Montgomery (1978). Olfactory and gustatory capacities of alcoholic Korsakoff patients. *Neuropsychologia, 16,* 323–337.

Jones, B. P., Moskowitz, H. R., & Butters, N. (1975). Olfactory discrimination in alcoholic Korsakoff patients. *Neuropsychologia, 13,* 173–179.

Jones-Gotman, M., & Zatorre, R. J. (1988). Olfactory identification deficits in patients with focal cerebral excision. *Neuropsychologia, 26,* 387–400.

Jones-Gotman, M., Zatorre, R. J., Cendes, F., Olivier, A., Andermann, F., McMackin, D., Staunton, H., Seigal, A. M., & Weiser, H. G. (1997). Contribution of medial versus lateral temporal-lobe structures to human odor identification. *Brain, 120,* 1845–1856.

Kesslak, J. P., Profitt, B. F., & Criswell, P. (1991). Olfactory function in chronic alcoholics. *Perceptual and Motor Skills, 73,* 551–554.

Ketzler, S., Weis, S., Haug, H., & Budka, H. (1990). Loss of neurons in the frontal cortex in AIDS brains. *Acta Neuropathologica Berlina, 80*(1), 92–94.

Kopala, L., Clark C., Hurwitz, T. A. (1992). Olfactory deficits in neuroleptic naive patients with schizophrenia. *Schizophrenia Research, 8,* 245–250.

Kopala, L., & Clark, C. (1990). Implications of olfactory agnosia for understanding sex differences in schizophrenia. *Schizophrenia Bulletin, 16,* 255–261.

Koss, E., Weiffenbach, J. M., Haxby, J. V., & Freidland, R. P. (1988). Olfactory detection and identification performance are associated in early Alzheimer's disease. *Neurology, 38,* 1228–1232.

Levy, L. M., Henkin, R. I., Lin, C. S., & Finley, A. (1999). Rapid imaging of olfaction by functional MRI (fMRI): Identification of presence and type of hyposmia Source. *Journal of Computer Assisted Tomography, 23,* 767–775.

Lima, C., & Vital, J. P. (1994). Olfactory pathways in three patients with cryptococcal meningitis and acquired immune deficiency syndrome. *Neurological Science, 123*(1–2), 195–199.

Martinez, B. A., Cain, W. S., de Wijk, R. A., Spencer, D. D., Novelly, R. A., & Sass, K. J. (1993). Olfactory functioning before and after temporal lobe resection for intractable seizures. *Neuropsychology, 7,* 351–363.

Martzke, J. S., Kopala, L. C., & Good, K. P. (1997). Olfactory dysfunction in neuropsychiatric disorders: Review and methodological considerations. *Biological Psychiatry, 42,* 721–732.

Mayberg, H. S., Starkstein, S. E., Peyser, C. E., Brandt, J., Dannals, R. F., & Folstein, S. E. (1992). Paralimbic frontal lobe hypometabolism in depression associated with Huntington's disease. *Neurology, 42*(9), 1791–1797.

McKeown, D. A., Doty, R. L., Perl, D. P., Frye, R. E., Simms, I., & Mester, A. (1996). Olfactory dysfunction in young adolescents with Down's syndrome. *Journal of Neurology, Neurosurgery and Psychiatry, 61*(4), 412–414.

Mesholam, R. I., Moberg, P. J., Mahr, R. N., & Doty, R. L. (1998). Olfaction in neurodegenerative disease: A meta-analysis of olfactory functioning in Alzheimer's and Parkinson's diseases. *Archives of Neurology, 55*(1), 84–90.

Mesulam, M. M. (1988). *Principles of behavioral neurology.* Philadelphia: FA Davis.

Meyer, M., & Allison, A. C. (1949). Experimental investigation of the connexions of the olfactory tubercle in the monkey. *Journal of Neurology, Neurosurgery & Psychiatry, 12,* 274–286.

Moberg, P. J., Agrin, R., Gur, R. E., Gur, R. C., Turetsky, B. I., & Doty, R. L. (1999). Olfactory dysfunction in schizophrenia: A qualitative and quantitative review. *Neuropsychopharmacology, 21,* 325–340.

Moberg, P. J., & Doty, R. L. (1997). Olfactory function in Huntington's disease patients and at-risk offspring. *International Journal of Neuroscience, 89,* 133–139.

Moberg, P. J., Pearlson, G. D., Speedie, L. J., Lipsey, J. R., & DePaulo, J. R. (1986). Olfactory recognition and mood in major depression. In *Abstracts of the American Psychiatry Association Meeting* (87), Washington, DC: American Psychiatry Press.

Moberg, P. J., Pearlson, G. D., Speedie, L. J., Lipsey, J. R., Strauss, M. E., & Folstein, S. E. (1987). Olfactory recognition: Differential impairments in early and late Huntington's and Alzheimer's diseases. *Journal of Clinical and Experimental Neuropsychology, 9,* 650–664.

Nordin, S., Murphy, C. (1996). Impaired sensory and cognitive olfactory function in questionable Alzheimer's disease. *Neuropsychology, 10*(1), 113–119.

Nordin, S., Paulsen, J. S., & Murphy, C. (1995). Sensory- and memory-mediated olfactory dysfunction in Huntington's disease. *Journal of the International Neuropsychological Society, 1*(3), 281–290.

Pantelis, C., & Brewer, W. J. (1995). Neuropsychological and olfactory dysfunction in schizophrenia: Relationship of frontal syndromes to syndromes of schizophrenia. *Schizophrenia Research, 17,* 35–45.

Pantelis, C., & Brewer, W. J. (1996). Neurocognitive and neurobehavioral patterns and the syndromes of schizophrenia: Role of frontal-subcortical networks. In C. Pantelis, H. E. Nelson, & T. R. E. Barnes (Eds.), *Schizophrenia: A neuropsychological perspective* (pp. 317–343). Chichester: Wiley.

Pearce, R. K., Hawkes, C. H., & Daniel, S. E. (1995). The anterior olfactory nucleus in Parkinson's disease. *Movement Disorders, 10*(3), 283–287.

Pert, C. B., Ruff, M. R., Ruscetti, F., Farrar, W. L., & Hill, J. M. (1988). HIV receptor in brain and deduced peptides that block viral infectivity. In T. Bridge, A. F. Mirsky, & F. K. Goodwin (Eds.), *Psychological, neuropsychiatric and substance abuse aspects of AIDS: Advances in biochemical pharmacology* (Vol. 44). New York: Raven. pp. 73–84.

Potter, H., & Butters, N. (1980). An assessment of olfactory deficits in patients with damage to prefrontal cortex. *Neuropsychologia, 18,* 621–628.

Potter, H., & Nauta, W. J. H. (1979). A note on the problem of olfactory associations of the orbitofrontal cortex in the monkey. *Neuroscience, 4,* 361–367.

Powell, T. P. S., Cowan, W. M., Raisman, G. (1965). The central olfactory connections. *Journal of Anatomy, 99,* 791–813.

Quinn, N. P., Rossor, M. N., Marsden, C. D. (1987). Olfactory threshold in Parkinson's disease. *Journal of Neurology, Neurosurgery and Psychiatry, 50*(1), 88–89.

Rauch, S. L., Savage, C. R., Alpert, N. M., Dougherty, D., Kendrick, A., Curran, T., Brown, H. D., Manzo, P., Fischman, A. J., & Jenike, M. A. (1997). Probing striatal function in obsessive-compulsive disorder: A PET study of implicit sequence learning. *Journal of Neuropsychiatry & Clinical Neurosciences* vol. 9(4); 568-573.

Rausch, R., & Serafitinides, E. A. (1975). Specific alterations of olfactory functioning in humans with temporal lobe lesions. *Nature, 255,* 557–558.

Razani, J., Murphy, C., Davidson, T. M., Grant, I., & McCutchan, A. (1996). *Physiological Behavior, 59*(4–5), 877–881.

Rogers, M., Bradshaw, J., & Pantelis, C. (1998). Fronto-striatal deficits in major depression. *Brain Research Bulletin, 47,* 297–310.

Rose, C. S., Heywood, P. G., & Costanzo, R. M. (1992). Olfactory impairment after chronic occupational cadmium exposure. *Journal of Occupational Medicine, 34,* 600–605.

Ryan, C. M., Morrow, L. A., & Hodgson, M. (1988). Cacosmia and neurobehavioral dysfunction associated with occupational exposure to mixtures of organic solvents. *American Journal of Psychiatry, 145,* 1442–1445.

Sandmark, B., Broms, I., Lofgren, L., & Ohlson, C. G. (1989). Olfactory function in painters exposed to organic solvents. *Scandinavian Journal of Work and Environmental Health, 15,* 60–63.

Schwartz, B. S., Ford, D. P., Bolla, K. I., Agnew, J., & Bleeker, M. L. (1991). Solvent associated olfactory dysfunction: Not a predictor of deficits in learning and memory. *American Journal of Psychiatry, 148,* 751–756.

Serby, M., Corwin, J., Conrad, P., & Rotrosen, J. (1985). Olfactory dysfunction in Alzheimer's disease and Parkinson's disease. *American Journal of Psychiatry, 142,* 781–782.

Serby, M., Larson, P., & Kalkstein, D. (1990). Olfactory sense in psychoses. *Biological Psychiatry, 28,* 829–830.

Shear, P. K., Butters, N. M., Jernigan, T. L., DiTraglia, G. M., Win, M., Schukit, M. A., & Cermak, L. F. (1992). Olfactory loss in alcoholics: Correlations with cortical and subcortical MRI indices. *Alcohol, 9*(3), 247–255.

Sobel, N., Prakhakaran, V., Desmond, J. E., Glover, G. H., Goode, E. L., Sullivan, E. V., & Gabrielli, J. D. E. (1998). Sniffing and smelling—separate subsystems in the human olfactory cortex. *Nature, 392,* 282–286.

Solomon, G. S., Petrie, W. M., Hart, J. R., & Brackin, H. B. (1998). Olfactory dysfunction discriminates Alzheimer's dementia from major depression. *Journal of Neuropsychiatry and Clinical Neurosciences, 10,* 64–67.

Staubli, U., Roman, F., & Lynch, G. (1984). Hippocampal denervation causes rapid forgetting of olfactory information in rats. *Proceedings of the National Academy of Sciences USA, 81,* 5885–5887.

Staubli, U., Schottler, F., & Nejat-Bina, D. (1987). Role of dorsomeidal thalamic nucleus and piriform cortex in processing olfactory information. *Behavioral Brain Research, 25,* 117–129.

Suffin, S. C., & Gitlin, M. (1986). Olfaction in depression and recovery: A new marker. *Abstracts of the American Psychiatry Association Meeting* (p. 87). Washington DC: American Psychiatry Press.

Switzer, R. C., de Olmos, J., & Heimer, L. (1985). Olfactory systems. In G. Paxinos (Ed.), *The rat nervous system: Vol. 1. Forebrain and midbrain* (pp. 1–36). Sydney, Australia: Academic Press.

Thompson, M. D., Knee, K., & Golden, C. J. (1998). Olfaction in persons with Alzheimer's disease. *Neuropsychology Review, 8*(1), 11–23.

Van Hoesen, G. W., & Pandya, D. N. (1975). Some connections of the entorhinal (area 28) and perirhinal (area 35) cortices of the rhesus monkey: I. Temporal lobe afferents. *Brain Research, 95,* 1–24.

Ward, C. D., Hess, W. A., & Calne, D. B. (1983). Olfactory impairment in Parkinson's disease. *Neurology, 33*(7), 943–946.

Warner, M. D., Peabody, C. A., & Csernansky, J. G. (1990). Olfactory functioning in schizophrenia and depression. *Biological Psychiatry, 27,* 457–467.

Weis, S., Haug, & Budka, H. (1993). Neuronal damage in the cerebral cortex of AIDS brains: A morphometric study. *Acta Neuropathologica Berl, 85*(2), 185–189.

Wenning, G. K., Shephard, B., Hawkes, C., Petruckevitch, Lees, A., & Quinn, N. (1995). Olfactory function in atypical parkinsonian syndromes. *Acta Neurologica Scandinavica, 91*(4), 247–250.

Westervelt, H. J., & McCaffrey, R. J. (1997). Longitudinal analysis of olfactory deficits in HIV infection. *Archives of Clinical Neuropsychology, 12*(6), 557–565.

Zald, D. H., Donndelinger, M. J., & Pardo, J. V. (1998). Elucidating dynamic brain interactions with across subjects correlational analyses of positron emission tomographic data—The functional connectivity of the amygdala and orbitofrontal cortex during olfactory tasks. *Journal of Cerebral Blood Flow & Metabolism, 18*(8), 896–905.

Zucco, G. M., Zaglis, D., & Wambsganns, C. S. (1991). Olfactory deficits in elderly subjects and Parkinson patients. *Perceptual and Motor Skills, 73*(3), 895–898.

C. PANTELIS
W. J. BREWER
*University of Melbourne & the Mental Health Research
Institute of Victoria, Australia*

P. MARUFF
*La Trobe University & the Mental Health Research
Institute of Victoria, Australia*

BRAIN
OLFACTION

OPERANT BEHAVIOR

Psychologists who study learning usually divide behavior into two types—operant and respondent—based on how the behavior is influenced. Operant (also called instrumental) behavior is called by that name because of the fact that what influences the future probability of the behavior is the operation that it performs on the environment, its effects, its consequences. That is, operant behavior is behavior whose subsequent probability—when similar circumstances exist—depends on the consequences that immediately follow the behavior. If the immediate consequences make the behavior more probable in the future, when similar tasks or situations arise, they are said to have reinforced the behavior. The behavior can be said to have been selected (for repetition) by the consequences that it produces.

Often it is obvious to an observer that the consequences that are reinforcing an operant behavior are favorable ones. For example, when a person asks for a glass of water, it is obvious that the water is a favorable consequence for the operant behavior of asking, and when a cat meows by the door, it is obvious that access to the outdoors is a favorable consequence for the meowing. Other times it is not obvious to an observer why the consequences serve to reinforce the operant behavior that produces them, as when someone makes a remark (an operant behavior) that produces an apparently unfavorable consequence of hurting another person's feelings.

A simple example of an operant behavior (or simply, "operant") would be a person's twisting the lid of a jar counterclockwise, which is usually followed by the lid's coming loose. If the lid's coming loose is a reinforcing event for that person at that time, the stimulus feedback of the lid's coming loose will reinforce the movements that the person just made in twisting the lid. In the future, when having the lid off a jar would be a favorable consequence and such a jar is available, the person is more likely to make those same movements or ones very like them.

Most of the behaviors we observe routinely in ourselves, other persons, our pets, and other animals are probably operants. When we speak of "work," "performance," "skills," "accomplishments," and "knowledge," we are usually referring to the operants exhibited by a person in certain situations. Operants are also often called voluntary behavior, because we can often decide (which is also operant behavior) whether to exhibit them or not. Examples of the thousands of operants exhibited daily by most of us would be putting on one's shoes, scratching an itch, walking to the bathroom, making coffee, buying a newspaper, driving a car, thinking about a present to buy, speaking, writing, reading, recalling a friend's face, and pondering whether to redecorate the kitchen.

Of course, the stimuli that follow an operant are not always favorable. If having a jar open would currently be a favorable consequence and the person twists the lid clockwise, no consequence will follow—the jar will not open. That behavior will become less probable and, after a few more tries, the person may never exhibit that particular operant again. The behavior is said to have "extinguished," to have become improbable for lack of reinforcement. This is true even if the behavior was previously reinforced. For example, if a person dials a particular telephone number that previously led to a friend's answering, but now no one ever answers, the person will eventually stop dialing that number. Other examples of the extinction of an operant are an infant's tantrums' eventually ceasing if they never get the child what he or she wants, or a man's eventually stopping using a key to open a door that refuses to open with that key.

Some operants lead immediately to painful or otherwise unfavorable consequences. As in the case of extinction, those behaviors become less likely to occur when that situation arises again. Usually that effect is rapid. For example, if twisting the lid of a jar makes its contents spill on the floor, the particular movements producing that consequence will rapidly become less likely to recur. Unfavorable consequences are the reason that we seldom touch a steaming kettle or drop heavy objects on our toes, but there are many examples that are much more subtle.

One of the tasks of the mental health professional is often to discover why a client exhibits operant behaviors that quite obviously (at least to the professional) yield unfavorable consequences. One client may start arguments with her husband, to the detriment of their relationship. Another may expose his genitals in public, even though this leads to being jailed. Yet another ingests drugs that eventually impair his or her physical health, relationships, financial status, and more. In most cases, the analysis of such self-defeating behavior is that the more immediate consequences—those occurring within seconds of the behavior—are favorable to the client, given the client's learning history. The more delayed the consequences, the less direct effect they can have on the behavior. This is why the great majority of caucasians have been sunburned numerous times; the painful consequences are too delayed to directly affect the probability of going out in the sun and staying. We gain self control only through certain extensive and complex learning experiences that make it possible for our behavior to be more influenced, albeit only indirectly and often uncertainly, by the delayed consequences than the immediate ones.

The second class of behavior—respondent or classically-conditioned behavior—includes many of our reflexes and similar responses. The salivation that Pavlov studied is one example. Respondent behavior is considered a different class because it appears to be conditioned by the pairing of stimuli that *precede* it instead of the stimuli that follow it. Respondent behavior is always involved in emotional responses and even milder feelings, although operant behavior usually is as well.

Respondent behaviors are not readily controlled voluntarily. We do not decide to contract the pupils of our eyes, blush with embarrassment, salivate, shake with fear, or get "butterflies" in our stomachs. Those respondent behaviors simply occur and our operant behavior of deciding to exhibit them or not exhibit them usually has little effect on them.

R. P. HAWKINS
West Virginia University

BEHAVIORISM
BEHAVIOR MODIFICATION
CLASSICAL CONDITIONING
THORNDIKE'S LAWS OF LEARNING

OPERANT CONDITIONING

Operant conditioning, a term coined by B. F. Skinner in 1937, has several shades of meaning. It is both an experimental procedure and a behavioral process, a characteristic interaction of an organism and its environment observed in species with complex nervous systems. In the latter sense, it is a biological adaptation with a plausible evolutionary interpretation. The study of operant conditioning and related phenomena comprises a substantial research paradigm within psychology in both laboratory and applied settings. This paradigm endorses tightly controlled experiments to discover behavioral principles; the direct extension of those principles to behavior therapy, education, organizational behavior, and other applications; and the use of the principles as interpretive tools for understanding complex human behavior such as language, memory, and problem solving.

THE OPERANT CONDITIONING PROCEDURE

In an operant conditioning procedure, a consequence is made contingent upon a behavior; specifically, the experimenter arranges a contingency in which a stimulus is presented if and only if a target behavior has just occurred. For example, an apparatus might be arranged so that, whenever a rat presses a lever, a drop of water drips into a dish from which the rat can drink. If the rat has recently been denied access to water, the strength of the target behavior will change; among other effects, the rate of pressing the lever will increase in that setting and in similar settings. If replications and suitable control conditions demonstrate that this change in strength is in fact due to the contingency, and is not a coincidence, the procedure is an instance of positive reinforcement, and water is called a reinforcing stimulus. If the rat has not been deprived of water, the procedure might have no effect on behavior. Under these conditions, if the rat were forced to drink by squirting water in its mouth, for example, we would expect the rate of lever-pressing to decrease relative to a baseline condition. We then speak of a punishment contingency and of water as a punishing stimulus. Thus both reinforcement and punishment are defined, not by procedures or by the nature of particular stimuli, but by their effects on the probability of behavior under given conditions.

Thorndike (1898) was the first researcher to study operant conditioning systematically, but Skinner is recognized for developing the framework and much of the experimental foundation for modern operant theory. He designed most of his own apparatus, including the now-standard experimental chamber that bears his name. Skinner was the first to discover that the rate of behavior in freely moving organisms was highly sensitive to a wide variety of independent variables. In experiments using Skinner's methodology, the demonstration of operant principles has been found to be highly reliable in many species. Single-subject designs are preferred, since the behavioral principles of interest are revealed in the detailed interactions of organism and environment and may be obscured by averaging cases. Skinner recognized that appropriate units of analysis in psychology should not be defined in advance by the experimenter, but should be determined empirically, by looking for orderly relationships between the organism and its environment. The units that emerge from such an analysis are three-term contingencies of environment, behavior, and consequence, and no one term can be understood in isolation.

OPERANT CONDITIONING AS A BEHAVIORAL PROCESS

Operant conditioning procedures have revealed that behavior changes in strength or probability when it is followed by biologically important consequences such as access to food, water, sexual activity, or escape from painful stimuli, cold, or excessive heat. Activities that tend to promote survival and reproduction become more frequent, while those that bring harm are reduced or eliminated. Operant conditioning is thus an important evolutionary advance enabling an organism to adapt to variable environments where nourishment, comfort, potential mates, and danger are not ubiquitous but must be searched out, fought for, or avoided.

Food, water, and sexual contact are all examples of unconditioned reinforcers, stimuli that are innately reinforcing under relevant motivating conditions, presumably because organisms for whom they functioned as such were more likely to have offspring than those for whom they did not function. However, neutral stimuli can acquire a reinforcing function if they are frequently paired with unconditioned reinforcers. Thus we learn to respond to the dinner bell, to hunt for a water bubbler, and to approach a member of the opposite sex who smiles at us. In humans, money, fame, and prestige are particularly effective conditioned reinforcers only indirectly related to survival and differential reproduction.

The strengthening of adaptive behavior and the weakening of ineffective behavior is a selection process, analogous in many respects to natural selection. Behavior is variable; even a highly practiced behavior will vary somewhat from one instance to the next. By differentially reinforcing responses with some property (relatively forceful lever presses, for example), an experimenter can effect a change in the distribution of responses. More and more forceful lever presses occur to the point that the typical response is wholly unrepresentative of the original distribution of behavior. When organisms are exposed to such programs of gradually changing contingencies—a process called shaping—behavior can evolve and become highly differentiated over the lifetime of the individual, much as the morphology of organisms changes over evolutionary time. The repertoires of the skillful juggler, rock climber, and gymnast have presumably been shaped mainly by programs of intrinsic contingencies, but the repertoires of the seeing-eye dog, the race horse, the mathematician, the engineer, and the historian are likely to have been shaped mainly by programs of contingencies explicitly arranged by trainers or educators.

THE DOMAIN OF OPERANT CONDITIONING

Some response systems, such as respiration, circulation, and digestion, serve a narrow function in the economy of the organism, and for them to vary substantially with arbitrary contingencies of reinforcement would not be adaptive. In contrast, the orientation of receptors and responses mediated by skeletal muscles, such as the vocal apparatus, limbs, digits, and other effectors, can be recruited for a wide variety of functions with some variability from one species to another. Operant conditioning can most easily be demonstrated in the latter class of response systems.

It is characteristic of students of operant conditioning to confine their experimental analyses to objective, measurable variables. However, in any experiment some part of the behavior of an organism is always below the threshold of observability. Since this threshold depends upon the tools of the investigator and is not an intrinsic property of behavior, it must be assumed that the principles of operant conditioning apply not only to behavior that can be observed, but also to covert behavior as well. The psychologist's understanding of covert behavior is necessarily interpretive rather than experimental. The principle of reinforcement has been useful in such interpretations since the terms of the analysis have been well-established in single subjects under analogous conditions in the laboratory. However, the extent to which operant conditioning and other principles of learning provide a sufficient foundation for an interpretation of such phenomena as language, recall, covert problem solving, imagery, and perception remains controversial. In most adult humans, verbal rules (e.g., "Turn right at the second traffic light") can have effects on behavior comparable to those of direct exposure to relevant operant conditioning procedures. Be-

haviorists argue that such examples of rule-governed behavior do not require appeals to new principles but can be derived from established principles of learning. From this perspective, operant conditioning is the primary principle underlying all adaptive complexity in behavior.

SUGGESTED READING

Catania, A. C. (1998). *Learning.* Upper Saddle River, NJ: Prentice-Hall.

Donahoe, J. W., & Palmer, D. C. (1994). *Learning and complex behavior.* Boston: Allyn & Bacon.

Iverson, I. H., & Lattal, K. A. (1991). *Experimental analysis of behavior.* New York: Elsevier.

Skinner, B. F. (1938). *The behavior of organisms: An experimental analysis.* New York: Appleton-Century-Crofts.

Skinner, B. F. (1953). *Science and human behavior.* New York: Macmillan.

Sidman, M. (1960). *Tactics of scientific research.* New York: Basic Books.

Thorndike, E. L. (1898). Animal intelligence: An experimental study of the associative processes in animals. *Psychological Review Monograph Supplements, 2* (4, Whole No. 8).

D. C. PALMER
Smith College

BEHAVIORISM
BEHAVIOR MODIFICATION
CLASSICAL CONDITIONING
LEARNING THEORIES
OPERANT BEHAVIOR
REINFORCEMENT SCHEDULES

OPERATIONAL DEFINITION

Few topics in the area of scientific communication have been as troublesome as that of operational definition. Psychologists have done their share both to clarify and to muddy the waters on this problem, and this article outlines some of the principal facets they need to consider.

OPERATIONISM

The movement called operationism, in which the operational definition was the centerpiece, was initiated by Harvard University physicist Bridgman (1927). Bridgman had reviewed the history of definitions of fundamental physical concepts like length, space, and time as they were used before Einstein to learn why they required such drastic revisions in Einstein's revolutionary theorizing. Bridgman concluded that the traditional Newtonian definitions had contained substantial amounts of meaning not related to their actual physical measurements (e.g., the assumption of an absolute scale for time); it was this kind of excess meaning that was responsible for Einstein's need to make radical reformulations in these concepts.

Bridgman suggested that to avoid similar roadblocks in the development of physical theory in the future it would be necessary to impose more stringent requirements on the making of definitions. His proposal was that concepts should be defined strictly in terms of the operations used to measure them. As he put it, "The concept is synonymous with the corresponding set of operations" (Bridgman, 1927, p. 5).

Bridgman found, as he got into more of the nitty-gritty of operationism as a scientific methodology, that nothing was quite as simple and straightforward as it had seemed at first. He subsequently made some strategic retreats from his initially monolithic position, such as acknowledging at least the temporary admissibility of paper-and-pencil operations and accepting the usefulness of abstract concepts (Bridgman, 1952). Extended disputation on these secondary but important issues tended to impede acceptance of the more important basic notion that in scientific communication researchers are obligated to tell their listeners and readers what they mean, or intend to mean, as unambiguously as possible.

The idea that the meaning of all concepts should be restricted to the necessary operations underlying them had an immediate appeal for psychologists. Operationism was early promulgated within psychology by Harvard University psychologist Stevens (1935). Stevens was careful to point out that, on the one hand, operationism was no panacea but that, on the other hand, the operational-definition movement was simply a formalization of the methodology that had always been used by effective scientists, including psychologists.

Unfortunately, the balanced position advanced by Stevens did not quite prove to be the norm. Probably the single most important negative factor was the overselling of the operational ideal, especially as applied to situations in which perfectly operational definitions of psychological concepts were clearly not even approximately feasible. Also, there was the continuing persistence of the more grandly conceived operationism, and the consequent overloading of what should have been merely a fundamental methodological principle with essentially less relevant substantive issues of one kind or another. The net result over the past half century has been that far too little attention has been paid to the central principle.

A good example of the communication difficulties that await the unwary user or reader is afforded by the word *frustration*. Quite apart from the further complications of theoretical nuances, this word is used in at least three distinct ways, which are usually but by no means always kept clearly separated: (a) as a kind of blocking operation that prevents a motivated organism from obtaining a goal or persisting in goal-directed behavior; (b) as the kind of behavior that appears when such a goal-oriented organism is thus blocked; and (c) as some hypothetical inner process that is assumed to be responsible for the overt behavioral responses to the blocking operation. Needless to say, this last category of implicit process is most susceptible to ambiguity in definition and is, therefore, most in need of explicit operational definition.

None of the secondary and tertiary disputes over operationism

can eliminate the fact that psychologists all too often are simply failing to communicate adequately with each other because they continue to use key terms in a variety of loosely defined and highly ambiguous ways. Some basic considerations need to be emphasized. First, operational definitions are not all-or-none achievements, rather there is a continuum of operational clarity in definitions, i.e., in the degree to which ambiguity and excess meanings have been eliminated. Second, full operational clarity needs to be an objective kept clearly in mind throughout all phases of theoretical and empirical research; acceptance of ambiguity must be regarded in many situations as a necessary but, it is hoped, not a permanent condition, and it is important that scientific communicators explicitly recognize this state of affairs rather than simply ignore it and gloss over the problem. Third, substantive issues involving defined concepts must not be allowed to intrude on and confuse the primarily methodological criteria associated with operational definitions. Fourth, it would be nice if recognition of the importance of these desiderata serves as a spur to improve definitional clarity and ultimately to help make improvements in theoretical development. Taking this kind of positive approach to the definitional problem should also serve to help free psychologists from the semantic quagmires in which so many of the key concepts are still entangled.

REFERENCES

Bridgman, P. W. (1927). *The logic of modern physics.* New York: Macmillan.

Bridgman, P. W. (1952). *The nature of some of our physical concepts.* New York: Philosophical Library.

Stevens, S. S. (1935). The operational basis of psychology. *American Journal of Psychology, 47,* 323–330.

Stevens, S. S. (1935). The operational definition of psychological concepts. *Psychological Review, 42,* 517–527.

M. H. MARX
North Hutchinson Island, Florida

LOGICAL POSITIVISM

OPERATIONALISM

Operationalism is the demand that theoretical terms in science—that is, those that do not refer to something directly observable—be given operational definitions. Operational definition was proposed independently by the physicist Percy Bridgman (who named it) and by the logical positivists, who called it "explicit definition." It was introduced to psychology by S. S. Stevens in 1935, and played an important role in behaviorism. The goal of operationalism was to eliminate from science any concepts that were metaphysical, and to positivists meaningless, ensuring that science would ask only questions that had empirical answers, and would have theories that referred only to meaningful entities.

As empiricists, operationists assume that we can never be in doubt when talking about things we can observe. Thus, the meaning of an observational term such as "red" is unproblematic because it refers to a publicly observable attribute of objects. Uncertainty arises for theoretical terms such as "mass," "drive," "anxiety," and "superego." None of these is publicly observable, even though we have all experienced anxiety or hunger, while two terms, "mass" and "superego", may turn out not to refer to anything at all. Nevertheless, science needs theories and theoretical terms, and operationalists sought to guarantee the cognitive significance of theoretical terms by giving each an operational definition. In an operational definition, we define a theoretical term by linking it to some publicly verifiable operation—a measurement or a manipulation—we can perform on the environment. "Mass" becomes the weighing of an object at sea level, "drive" the withholding of food from an animal for some number of hours, and "anxiety" the score of a subject on the Taylor Manifest Anxiety Test.

The operationalist contends that the operational definition supplies the full meaning of a concept by linking it to unproblematic observation terms; anything more is unscientific surplus meaning. Moreover, operationalists question the scientific legitimacy of any term not operationally definable. Thus, the Freudian concept of the superego might be challenged as hopelessly unscientific, as there is no clear way of defining it in terms of something observable.

Operationalism gained wide assent in psychology, and, despite the death of logical positivism, psychologists continue to use operational definitions for theoretical terms that otherwise might have only mental, nonpublic, and therefore, psychologists fear, nonscientific meanings. Nevertheless, operationalism has been controversial. It has proved difficult, if not impossible, to operationalize all the terms even of physics, leading positivists themselves gradually to abandon operationalism. In psychology, operationalism has been criticized for unduly narrowing psychology's focus, making behaviorism the only acceptable psychology by methodological fiat rather than by superiority of results. That terms be operationalized remains, however, a common requirement of psychological theory.

SUGGESTED READING

Hempel, C. (1965). *Aspects of scientific explanation.* New York: Free Press.

Leahey, T. H. (1980). The myth of operationism. *Journal of Mind and Behavior, 1,* 127–43.

Suppe, F. (1972). Theories, their formulations, and the operational imperative. *Synthese, 25,* 129–64.

T. H. LEAHEY
Virginia Commonwealth University

EMPIRICISM
LOGICAL POSITIVISM
POSITIVISM
SCIENTIFIC METHOD

OPINION POLLS

A distinction may be made between two varieties of public opinion polls—in one, the accuracy of the poll can be ascertained by a subsequent event; in the other, views are assayed but the results can be checked only by internal consistency or by another poll. Forecasting elections is the prime example of the first type; investigating current thinking on such issues as taxation, abortion, limitation of nuclear weaponry, and control of immigration is of the second type.

The prediction of the outcome of an election is of interest to candidates (who may or may not modify their campaigns in the light of the findings) and to voters (who seem unlikely to modify their choices on learning the results of a poll, although this is debatable).

Exploring popular thinking on major issues has consequences that are potentially far more important than predicting election outcomes. In U.S. elections the personal characteristics of candidates carry much weight with voters, often greater than the views they espouse. Elections are sometimes considered as referenda on controversial matters, but most national elections, and many on lower levels, involve multiple issues and candidates are not necessarily identified with clear-cut positions on the issues. As far as possible, successful politicians avoid campaign statements that might alienate a block of potential supporters. Only occasionally is there a formal referendum on any public issue. This means that polls in which respondents take clear-cut positions on matters of concern provide legislators with an important means of learning the views and wishes of their constituents.

The public opinion poll probably has its greatest social justification as an antidote to the influence of pressure groups. In connection with various activities, there are "watchdog" organizations poised to alert their members whenever legislation is contemplated that could affect their special interest. Members then flood legislators with urgent messages that sometimes are mistaken as representing the opinions of constituents generally. A far better evaluation of public sentiment can be found from a scientifically conducted poll.

The modern poll began to take shape in the early 1930s. Pioneers included George Gallup, Elmo Roper, and Archibald Crossley, all of whom used somewhat similar methods that emphasized small, carefully selected samples. The best known of the earlier polls was conducted by a popular magazine called the *Literary Digest.* In polls on presidential elections, millions of ballots were mailed out to automobile owners and telephone subscribers. The large numbers of respondents were impressive, and in four successive presidential elections, from 1920 through 1932, the outcome was correctly predicted. In 1936 the *Literary Digest* prophesized that Franklin Delano Roosevelt would receive 42.9% of the majority party vote, but the actual percentage turned out to be 62.5%. In that same year, three polls, using new methods and conducted independently by Gallup, Roper, and Crossley, correctly predicted the Roosevelt victory and provided generally accepted evidence that the innovations in procedures had demonstrated their effectiveness and that the *Literary Digest* type of poll was obsolete. Mass mailings of ballots ended; groups of respondents were reduced from millions to hundreds, or at most a few thousand;

samples were carefully designed and selected to represent a defined population; and, as time went on, attention was given to factors that might distort results—wording of questions, modes of inquiry and response, and familiarity of respondents with the subject matter.

The crucial principle, first recognized by innovators in the 1930s, was that better deductions about what would happen in an election could be drawn from a small sample with defined characteristics than from a large sample with unknown characteristics. Current methods of the construction of samples are by no means uniform, but essentially there are three phases:

1. Clearly defining the group about which the prediction is to be made (this group is technically known as the "population").

2. Deciding on the size of the sample to be studied.

3. Devising a scheme by which every person in the population has equal probability of being included in the sample.

When dealing with a large and scattered population such as Americans eligible to vote, a truly random sample theoretically can be constructed from a complete list arranged in alphabetical order (or better still a completely nonsystematic arrangement) and finding each name at the interval of N/n, N being the size of the population and n being the desired size of the sample. This method is impractical; the list does not exist, and, even if it did, the time and travel required of the poll takers to make contacts would be excessive. Methods have been worked out, however, that yield good approximations to random samples. The Gallup organization has successfully used a three-tier randomization. First there is a random selection of election districts; then within each election district there is a random selection of households; and finally within each household there is a random selection of the individual to be interviewed. Samples developed by this method tend to be both representative of the population and reasonably accessible to interviewers. In addition to views on candidates or issues, interviewers record demographic data, observed or in reply to questions regarding: sex, age, education, occupation, income level, race, religious preference, and, when pertinent, political affiliation and vote in a recent election.

The use of modern computers permits adjustment of findings within an observed sample to what would probably be observed in the population, using statistics collected in the current population surveys of the U.S. Census Bureau. The demographic characteristics of the sample are compared with those of the population, and shortages or overages can be compensated for in predicting voting behavior or measuring sentiment on a public issue. Other adjustments may be made, such as screening out individuals ineligible or unlikely to vote.

Quota sampling is an alternative to the quasi-random procedure described above. Desired characteristics of the sample are determined in advance and quotas are established for men and women; for high, medium, and low rental areas; for race; for age groups; and for other factors related to the outcome under investigation. While quota sampling was often used from the early 1930s to the late 1940s, its chief defect soon became apparent: bias was introduced by the fact that, even while meeting assigned quotas, interviewers tend to seek out those respondents who are easiest to contact and to interview. Such individuals tend to have better education and higher income, together with related values.

When the group of individuals questioned in a poll closely approximates a truly random sample of the population under investigation, it need not be large. The Gallup organization has often used samples of only 1,500, a size that can be shown to be accurate within 2 or 3 percentage points in 95 out of 100 times (Gallup, 1972). When studying the reactions of minority groups that constitute only a small proportion of any random sample, results from successive surveys are often combined to develop a subsample of the population with stable characteristics.

Two kinds of questions are used in polling: the open-ended or free-response variety in which the respondent formulates the answer in his or her own words, and the structured-answer type in which the interviewee chooses from two or more suggested answers. Both classifications are useful. The open-ended question is essential when exploring respondents' knowledge in an area, overall opinions, and reasons for their views. The "objective" item, involving a choice of stated alternatives, is useful in predicting elections, in ascertaining divisions on public issues, and in following trends.

Polling organizations committed to the use of the scientific method give much attention to the selection of the questions and to their precise wording. Not only is the "stem," or principal working component studied to see that its meaning is clear, but the alternatives are examined to see that they are mutually exclusive and cover the range of opinion. Analysis by expert opinion is supplemented by testing on individuals considered to be similar to the population. When a stem or alternative is misinterpreted, it is modified or replaced.

Many public opinion polls are supported by newspapers and broadcasting organizations, which subscribe to a service that provides periodic reports on matters of current concern. Candidates and holders of public office sometimes commission opinion polls in about the same way commercial organizations commission market surveys, and with much the same motivation: Both are concerned with product acceptance.

Some office holders conduct opinion surveys by mailing questionnaires to a sample of voters in their constituency. If a list of eligible voters is available, sampling is not difficult. Sometimes a 100% sample is used. There may be problems in wording the questions and tabulating the results. The use of reply cards that can be read and tabulated by machine greatly reduces the cost of such surveys.

Another method of polling is by telephone. In some cases, the telephone numbers of individuals in a defined group can be ascertained and contacts made. However, some bias may be introduced in the sample because, for various reasons, the numbers at which some individuals may be reached are not in the telephone directory. There exists a computer-based dialing system by which a completely random selection of residential telephones (including unlisted numbers) in any desired area code can be contacted. Where the defined population is that of households having telephones, the procedure is useful. In some areas of study, such as smoking habits, the percentage of refusals to be interviewed has been found to be small and pertinent information is readily elicited.

As a tool in social science research, polling is limited only by the ingenuity of the investigator. Polling can use attitude measurement to study changes in perceptions and readiness for action correlated with varieties of events.

The better polls buttress their credibility with precise descriptions of the sample, when and how it was contacted, the exact wording of the questions, and how the survey was sponsored.

Polls are not always correct. All were wrong in 1948 when the predictions were that Thomas Dewey, rather than Harry Truman, would be elected to the presidency. But each time a major error occurs, the scientific poll managers review their methods, identify sources of the error, make new plans, and hope for more accurate results next time.

REFERENCES

Gallup, G. (1972). *The sophisticated poll watcher's guide.* Princeton, NJ: Princeton Opinion Press.

P. H. DuBois
Washington University at St. Louis

ATTITUDES
CONTROL GROUPS

OPIOID RECEPTORS

The effects of opiates, such as heroin or morphine, are consequences of the interactions of these drugs with opioid receptors. Opioid receptors, like receptors for other neurotransmitters, are cell surface proteins that (a) detect the presence of specific neurotransmitter or drug molecules in the extracellular environment, and (b) initiate biochemical changes that alter cellular processes in response to neurotransmitter or drug binding to the receptors. The activation of opioid receptors results in hyperpolarization, reduced neuronal excitability and the blockade of neurotransmitter release in cells bearing the receptors.

The existence of receptors that specifically bind opiate drugs was demonstrated in 1973, and endogenous opioid peptides that bind with these receptors were subsequently purified from brain (Pert & Snyder, 1973; Akil et al., 1984). There are three major families of endogenous opioid peptides: the endorphins, the enkephalins, and the dynorphins. The terminals of neurons containing endogenous opioid peptides are distributed in the same areas of the nervous system where there are high densities of opioid receptors, and it is believed that the endogenous opioid peptides function as the neurotransmitters or neuromodulators that utilize the opioid receptors. While the specific functions of endogenous opioid peptides are incompletely understood, they have been implicated in a variety of central nervous system functions including nociception, homeostatic function, mood regulation, and reward.

There are three subtypes of opioid receptor, referred to as mu, delta, and kappa receptors. The subtypes are distinguished by their distinct binding selectivities such that a given drug or opioid peptide may bind with high affinity to one receptor subtype but bind only weakly to another subtype. The opioid receptor subtypes also show distinct patterns of distribution in brain and spinal cord and have different functional properties. Opioid receptor subtypes can be further categorized (mu_{1+2}, $delta_{1+2}$, $kappa_{1-3}$) on the basis of binding selectivities, distribution, and function (Table 1).

Opioid receptors belong to the superfamily of G protein–coupled receptors. They transduce signals in response to receptor activation by mechanisms involving G proteins (proteins that are regulated by the binding of guanine nucleotides). All members of the G protein–coupled receptor family are associated with G proteins in such a way that the G proteins become functionally activated in response to receptor activation (e.g., by the binding of neurotransmitters). Activated G proteins can initiate functional changes by directly influencing effector proteins such as ion channels, and they can also induce changes in biochemical messenger systems that result in the indirect regulation of the function of effector proteins. Opioid receptors couple both to G proteins that directly influence ion channels and to G proteins that regulate intracellular messengers.

The most studied messenger system associated with opioid receptors is the inhibition of the adenylyl cyclase enzyme, which mediates the synthesis of cyclic adenosine -3', 5'-monophosphate (cAMP) from adenosine triphosphate (ATP). cAMP acts as a biochemical messenger that activates cAMP-dependent protein kinase (PKA). PKA is an enzyme that adds phosphate groups to (phosphorylates) a variety of types of cellular proteins, thus altering their size, charge, and functional capabilities. All three subtypes of opioid receptor can activate an inhibitory G protein (G_i), which inhibits AC activity and cAMP formation and consequently decreases substrate phosphorylation by PKA. Substrates for PKA include neurotransmitter receptors, synaptic proteins, and neurotransmitter synthetic enzymes, all of which can modify neuronal excitability. Functional consequences of opiate regulation of the cAMP pathway are not well elucidated, however, progress has been made in work on chronic opiate administration. Altered excitability of neurons in the locus coeruleus in the brain stem has been shown to be associated with opiate regulation of the cAMP pathway, and has been related to functional changes that occur during opiate withdrawal (Nestler & Aghajanian, 1997).

Opioid receptors are also coupled to G proteins that can directly regulate ion channel activity and therefore cellular excitability, independently of second messenger intervention. Opioid receptors regulate ion channels controlling K^+ and Ca^{++} currents though direct coupling with G proteins. The results of opioid receptor activation are increased K^+ outflow resulting in hyperpolarization of the membrane potential, and reduced Ca^{++} entry into cells (Duggan & North, 1983). These mechanisms are thought to be important to the opioid blockade of neurotransmitter release, which may be the primary mechanism whereby opiate drugs reduce transmission within pain pathways and produce analgesia.

Opioid receptors of each subtype have been cloned and sequenced in animals and humans (Knapp, Malatynska, Collins, Fang, Wang, Hruby, Roeske & Yamamura, 1995). The amino acid sequences indicate that they all contain the 7 hydrophobic mem-

Table 1.   Types of Opioid Receptors, Their Prototypic Ligands, and Their Most Important Physiological Effects

Receptor	Type	Ligands Endogenous	Exogenous	Major Effects
Mu				
	mu_1	β-endorphin	morphine hydromorphone etonitazene	supraspinal analgesia euphoria prolactin release miosis
	mu_2	β-endorphin(dynorphin?)	morphine	spinal analgesia inhibition of intestinal motility respiratory depression
Kappa				
	$kappa_1$	dynorphin	ethylketocyclazocine pentazocine trifluadom	hypothermia? miosis (weak) sedation spinal analgesia
	$kappa_{2+3}$		halorphine ethylketocyclazocine bremazocine	supraspinal analgesis dysphoria hallucinations
Delta				
	$delta_1$	met-enkephalin	etorphine D-Pen^2-D-Pen^5-enkephalin	spinal analgesia inhibition of smooth muscle
	$delta_2$		D-Ala^2-Glu^4-deltorphin D-Ser^2·Leu^5-enkephalin-Thr^6	spinal analgesia

From *Principles of Medical Pharmacology* (6th ed.), edited by Harold Kalant and W. Roschlau. Copyright © 1998 by Oxford University Press, Inc. Used by permission of Oxford University Press, Inc.

brane spanning domains characteristic of the G protein–coupled receptor superfamily (Figure 1). The sequences show significant homology (approximately 60%) overall, with the greatest homology in the transmembrane regions and in the intracellular regions that connect them. The extracellular regions show greater sequence divergence.

The three opioid receptor subtypes show distinct patterns of distribution in the nervous system (Mansour, Khachaturian, Lewis, Akil, & Watson, 1988). Mu receptors are found in regions that regulate functions altered by morphine—for example, the dorsal horn of the spinal cord, the spinal trigeminal nucleus, periaquaductal gray, and medial thalamus, consistent with a role in morphine-induced analgesia. Mu receptors are also found in brain-stem nuclei (nucleus of the solitary tract, area postrema, and others), which are involved in morphine depression of respiration and stimulation of nausea and vomiting. Mu receptors in the nucleus accumbens, hippocampus, and amygdala are important to morphine effects on mood and reward. Delta opioid receptors are more restricted in their distribution and are found mainly in forebrain structures (e.g., neocortex, caudate-putamen, and amygdala) and the spinal cord and are thought to participate in analgesia. Kappa receptor distribution also indicates a role for this subtype in analgesia. Additionally, kappa receptors are located in the hypothalamus, where they may regulate neuroendocrine function. Kappa receptors are also located in amygdala, hippocampus, and nucleus accumbens, and in contrast to mu-mediated effects, kappa receptor stimulation can produce dysphoria and psychotomimetic effects.

The diversity of opioid receptors and the complexity of the endogenous opioid peptide systems that utilize these receptors sug-

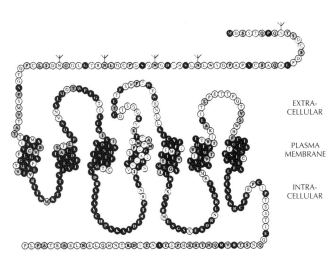

Figure 1. Proposed model for membrane topography of the rat mu-opioid receptor. Amino acid residues of mu-opioid receptor conserved in both delta- and kappa-receptors, in either delta- or kappa-receptors and in neither delta- nor kappa-receptor are shown by black, gray and white circles respectively. Branched structures show the potential N-linked glycosylation sites. (Reprinted from Neuroscience Research, vol. 23, Minami, M. and Satoh, M., Molecular biology of the opioid receptors: structures, functions and distributions, pp. 121–145, 1995, with permission from Elsevier Science).

gest that there is much to be learned regarding the nature of interactions between receptor subtypes, endogenous peptides and their functional significance. A greater understanding of the opioid system will guide the development of new pharmacological strategies in medicine as well as assist in our understanding of the addictive process.

REFERENCES

Akil, H., Watson, S. J., Young, E., Lewis, M. E., Khachaturian, H., & Walker, J. M. (1984). Endogenous opioids: Biology and function. *Annual Review of Neuroscience, 7,* 223–255.

Duggan, A. W., & North, R. A. (1983). Electrophysiology of opioids. *Pharmacology Review, 35,* 219–282.

Kalant, H. (1998). Opioid analgesics and antagonists. In H. Kalant & W. H. E. Roschlau (Eds.), *Principles of medical pharmacology* (6th ed., pp. 262–277). NY: Oxford University Press.

Knapp, R. J., Malatynska, E., & Collins, N. (1995). Molecular biology and pharmacology of cloned opioid receptors. *FASEB Journal, 9,* 516–525.

Mansour, A., Khachaturian, H., Lewis, M. E., Akil, H., & Watson, S. J. (1988). Anatomy of CNS opioid receptors. *Trends in Neuroscience, 11*(7), 308–314.

Minami, M., & Satoh, M. (1995). Molecular biology of the opioid receptors: Structures, functions, and distributions. *Neuroscience Research, 23,* 121–145.

Nestler, E. J., & Aghajanian, G. K. (1997). Molecular and cellular basis of addiction. *Science, 278,* 58–63.

Pert, C. B., & Snyder, S. H. (1973). Properties of opiate receptor binding in rat brain. *Proceedings of the National Academy of Science, U.S.A., 70,* 2243–2247.

C. H. Duman
Yale University

MORPHINE
OPIUM, OPIODS, AND OPIATES

OPIUM, OPIOIDS, AND OPIATES

Opium (from poppies) and the other opiates have been used for centuries to produce feelings of well-being and euphoria. The first recorded use of an opiate for reduction of pain was by the 2nd-century Roman physician Galen, and ever since, analgesia has been the primary legal use of opiates. Today most individuals have heard of endogenous opiates, especially endorphins, which have been thought to mediate the so-called runner's high and acupuncture. The original intention to use the term "opiate" to refer to effects of exogenous substances and the term "opioid" to refer to endogenous peptides with opiate activity has largely been abandoned, with both words now referring to the same drugs. There is, therefore, little point in using the more obscure "opioid," since "opiate" is clearly understood by all.

The endogenous opiate system was unknown until events of the early 1970s brought it to light. The ability of exogenous opiates to modulate the function of the central nervous system suggested there might be specialized receptors for those substances. Simultaneously but independently in laboratories around the world, including those of Goldstein, Hughes, Terenius, and Pert and Snyder,

such receptors were discovered in the brain, with particularly intense concentrations found in those areas associated with the perception of pain. Subsequently distinct classes of receptors were identified, with the main types being μ, κ, and δ, suggesting that they might modulate behaviors other than pain. In addition, there are subtypes of each of those, as well as the less–well understood σ, ε, and ξ receptors.

It followed logically that if there were receptors, there would also be endogenous ligands for those receptors, and the search expanded to look for them. In 1975, Hughes discovered such a ligand that acted in the same way as morphine on the receptors, and identified the amino acid sequence of enkephalin. Shortly thereafter, the sequence for β-endorphin, a larger 31–amino acid sequence peptide, was found by Li and Chung. A number of endogenous opiates are now known, as well as many more synthetic ones.

In general, it is assumed that the opiates are neuromodulators, although some may act as neurotransmitters. They are best known for their mediation of pain. Preceding the discovery of endogenous opiate systems, Reynolds (1969) and Mayer, Wolfe, Akil, Carder, and Liebeskind (1971) reported that focal electrical brain stimulation could elicit potent analgesia. After the identification of the endogenous opiates, the role of the opiates in activating these endogenous analgesic systems was determined. A number of sites within the nervous system associated with pain modulation also have high concentrations of opiate peptides and receptors, including midbrain periaqueductal gray and spinal cord dorsal horns. Both endogenous and exogenous opiates act at specific receptors in the spinal cord and brain to suppress pain, and may mediate analgesia produced by some forms of environmental stressors, focal electrical stimulation of the brain, transcutaneous electrical nerve stimulation (TENS), and placebo responses.

Another well-known property of the opiates is their relatively rapid development of tolerance and dependence. Although tolerance does not occur to miosis and constipation, it develops to the other effects of the opiates, including the endogenous ones. Dependence on opiates is manifested by the appearance of withdrawal symptoms after cessation of the drug or when an opiate antagonist, such as naloxone, is administered. The development of tolerance and dependence is receptor-specific, as cross-tolerance and cross-dependence occur only between opiates that act at the same receptor type or subtype. The mechanisms by which opiates produce tolerance and dependence are related to several physiological factors, including increased metabolic activity and cellular changes produced by the opiates. In addition, behavioral factors, such as classical conditioning, influence the development of tolerance and dependence.

It is not likely that the opiates evolved just to be ready for action in case of injury. It was reasoned that they probably had other functions, perhaps even more significant than antinociception. They do, in fact, modulate a number of physiological responses, although they may not be primarily responsible for the activities and may interact with other substances to produce their effects. A common response to the administration of opiates is inhibition of gastrointestinal activity, resulting in constipation when the drugs are used as analgesics. Similarly, suppression of respiratory function often occurs with opiates, and is the most frequent cause of death from overdoses. Opiate effects on cardiovascular responses, however, are inconsistent, depending on the particular opiate used and the conditions under which measurements occur. Frequently, hypotension occurs, but enough exceptions have been seen that generalizations are difficult to make. Heart rate and thermoregulation are even more variable in response to opiates, with a number of other factors influencing the outcome. Biological rhythms, from circadian to annual, including hibernation, are also influenced by the endogenous opiate system. In addition, specialized opiate growth factors have been found, primarily associated with the little-known ξ receptors, and opiates modify both prenatal and postnatal physiological and psychological development. Furthermore, recent work has shown that the opiates modulate the function of the immune system, suppressing it in some situations and stimulating it in others, suggesting exciting possible future applications for them.

At the molar level, the first demonstration of the behavioral effects of the opiates was by Kastin, Scollan, King, Schally, and Coy (1976), indicating facilitation of learning a Warden maze in mice. Subsequently, it has become clear that the opiates are mostly amnestic agents, although some types facilitate learning in certain paradigms. Many of the peptides have rewarding properties, which can be used for reinforcing or making associations or for altering mood, although at specified doses or in some circumstances, some have aversive qualities. Depression or schizophrenia may result from a dysfunction of the opiate system, although the specifics remain elusive due to the complexities of the disorders. Stress produces an activation of the opiate system, further complicating the issue. Some investigators believe that the primary function of the opiates is modulation of eating and drinking, with the opiates typically encouraging those behaviors and the opiate antagonists inhibiting them. Opiate antagonists also tend to inhibit intake of alcohol, and they are being used in the treatment of alcoholism. Activity levels are influenced by the opiates, with small amounts or initial effects showing activation and larger amounts or late-occurring effects suppressing activity. Specific behaviors, such as social play or aggression, are also mediated by opiates.

Both exogenous and endogenous opiates modulate a wide variety of functions and behaviors, the specifics of which are only beginning to be clarified. Knowledge has come a long way since the discovery of opiate receptors and opiate peptides less than 30 years ago, and a great amount of research in the area continues, since much is left to unravel. For more detailed information, the interested reader is referred to the annual reviews on endogenous opiates and behavior by the authors (e.g., Olson, Olson, Vaccarino, & Kastin, 1998).

REFERENCES

Kastin, A., Scollan, E., King, M., Schally, A., & Coy, D. (1976). Enkephalin and a potent analog facilitate maze performance after intraperitoneal administration in rats. *Pharmacology, Biochemistry, Behavior, 5,* 691–695.

Mayer, D., Wolfe, T., Akil, H., Carder, B., & Liebeskind, J. (1971). Analgesia from electrical stimulation in the brainstem of the rat. *Science, 174,* 1351–1354.

Olson, G. A., Olson, R. D., Vaccarino, A. L., & Kastin, A. J. (1998). Endogenous opiates: 1997. *Peptides, 19,* 1791–1843.

Reynolds, D. (1969). Surgery in the rat during electrical analgesia induced by focal brain stimulation. *Science, 164,* 444–445.

G. A. OLSON
R. D. OLSON
A. L. VACCARINO
A. J. KASTIN
University of New Orleans

OPOID RECEPTORS

OPPONENT-PROCESS THEORY OF EMOTION

The opponent-process theory of emotion was initially proposed by Solomon in 1970 as a general theory of motivation that focuses on the temporal pattern of changes in the qualitative nature and intensity of emotional/affective states (responses) evoked by sensory events (stimuli). Following an exemplary model developed by Hurwich and Jameson (1957) in their theory of color vision (especially complementary color afterimages), Solomon (1980; Solomon & Corbit, 1974) applied the opponent-process system in a parsimoniously elegant form to account for a broad range of psychological phenomena, chief among them addiction and aversion.

A description of the pattern of the affective dynamics underlying the theory begins with the introduction (onset) of either a pleasurable or aversive stimulus which evokes an affective/hedonic reaction (A State) that rises quickly to a peak; the intensity of the hedonic A State (affect/emotion/tone/feeling/mood) then declines to a steady level where it remains as long as the stimulus quality and intensity are maintained. Immediately following the termination of the stimulus, its affective reaction ends and is replaced by a different affective after-reaction (B State) which is opposite that of the initial hedonic state; that is, the B State is the opponent of the A State. This after-state (B State) reaches its peak at a slower rate than that of A State, then decays at a relatively slow rate until the initial neutral affective baseline is eventually re-established.

An everyday example of the phases of the affective dynamics in the case of a hedonically positive A State (which implies a negative B State) and the events that evoke them might be as follows. News (stimulus) that a long-absent loved one will soon return evokes a positive hedonic state (A State) of joy or happiness (response). If the subject hears subsequent news that plans for the return of the loved one have been canceled, the positive A State will end abruptly and be replaced with a negative hedonic B State of sorrow or unhappiness which will gradually decay until the neutral hedonic state extant prior to the positive news is re-established. An example of the affective dynamics in the case of a hedonically negative A State might be one in which news (stimulus) that a loved one is seriously ill evokes a negative hedonic A State of sorrow or unhappiness (response). If subsequent news announces that the diagnosis had been in error, the negative A State ends abruptly and is replaced with a positive hedonic B State of joy or happiness which decays gradually until the prior hedonically neutral state returns.

Beyond typical hedonic theories that assume events arouse positive or negative states, the opponent-process theory of emotion proposes that hedonic (affective/emotional) states are automatically opposed by self-regulatory negative feedback loops within the central nervous system (i.e., opponent *processes* which reduce the intensity of their respective hedonic *states*). If the A State is positive, its underlying *a* process is opposed by a negative *b* process, and if the A State is negative, its underlying *a* process is opposed by a positive *b* process. Thus, in addition to the "baseline-A-B-baseline" sequence of emotional states illustrated above, the theory posits that each emotional state is accompanied by underlying opponent processes. The intensity and duration of affective states is determined through an analysis of these underlying affective processes. Arousal of the *a* process is accompanied by arousal of its opponent *b* process, a slave process that is slow to rise and slow to decay. The difference between these two processes determines the hedonic quality of emotional experience (If *a* > *b*, then the organism is in the A State; and if *b* > *a*, the organism is in the B State). Because the *a* process ends abruptly with the termination of the stimulus for the A State, and because the *b* process is slow to decay, the termination of the stimulus for the A State will give rise to an opposite or opponent affective state. With frequent arousal of the A State, the *b* process will increase in magnitude and duration, thereby diminishing the intensity of the A State proportionately.

Although the theory does not depend on assumptions of associative learning to account for positive and negative reinforcement effects often applied in theories of addiction, the affective A and B States are subject to Pavlovian/classical conditioning. Thus, the theory accounts for addictive behavior in the absence of any apparent current pleasurable consequences of the addictive substance by pointing to the increase in intensity of the negative B State that accompanies withdrawal from the addictive substance (stimulus for A State) and by pointing to the conditionality of both the A State and the B State. According to the theory, associative processes, though present in cases of acquired motivation, are neither necessary nor sufficient to produce related behaviors. Addictive behaviors are representative of most acquired motives in social contexts. In acquired motivation, affective processes are inevitably involved: namely, contrast, habituation, symptoms of withdrawal, and opposition between states characteristic of the presence or absence of the stimuli.

In the study of addiction, a critical assumption of the theory lies in the effects of frequency of stimulus occurrence (use of addictive substance) and latency between doses on the changes in the intensity and duration of B States (and their underlying *b* processes) relative to A States (and their underlying *a* processes). According to the theory, the opponent process *b* is strengthened by use and weakened by disuse, whereas the primary affective process *a* is not significantly affected by use. As such, with frequent elicitation, the *b* processes will show a shorter latency of response, sharper rise time, greater asymptote, and slower decay time than *a* processes. The effect on hedonic response rate after many stimulations will be a lower peak of the A State (labeled A'), and a more intense, longer-lasting B State (labeled B'). Because the theory is nonassociative, a major implication of the postulation of opponent-processes is that physiological stress can be caused by pleasurable as well as aversive stimulation. Thus, a clinician should look for disorders of adaptation to types of stresses due to correlated physiological side effects of long duration and often-elicited intense *b* processes.

The theory provides a unique model for understanding a broad range of emotional/motivational phenomena; it is a singular contribution to the behavioral sciences, especially psychology, psychiatry, and psychophysiology. For examples of how the opponent-process theory has been applied in clinical respiratory psychophysiology to account for the anxiolytic effects of single inhalations of large concentrations of carbon dioxide (Wolpe, 1987) and amyl nitrite (Wolpe, 1990), see Ley (1994).

REFERENCES

Hurwich, L. M., & Jameson, D. (1957). An opponent-process of color vision. *Psychological Review, 64,* 384–404.

Ley, R. (1994). An opponent-process interpretation of the anxiolytic effects of single inhalations of large concentrations of carbon dioxide. *Journal of Behavior Therapy and Experimental Psychiatry, 25,* 301–309.

Solomon, R. L. (1980). The opponent-process theory of motivation: The costs of pleasure and the benefits of pain. *American Psychologist, 35,* 691–712.

Solomon, R. L., & Corbit, J. D. (1974). An opponent-process theory of motivation: I. Temporal dynamics of affect. *Psychological Review, 81,* 119–145.

Wolpe, J. (1987). Carbon dioxide inhalation treatments of neurotic anxiety: An overview. *Journal of Nervous and Mental Disorders, 175,* 129–133.

Wolpe, J. (1990). *The practice of behavior therapy* (4th ed.). New York: Pergamon.

R. LEY
State University of New York at Albany

EMOTION

OPTIC NERVE

The sensory visual system begins with light stimulation of the retinal photoreceptors. The information is then transmitted to the retinal ganglion cells and then transits the orbit and the optic canal as the optic nerve. The information then crosses in the optic chiasm, synapses in the lateral geniculate, and projects to the striate cortex. The optic nerve is a tract that is myelinated by oligodendrocytes, and therefore is considered part of the central nervous system. The one million axons not only transmit information about light, contrast, and color but also participate in setting circadian rhythms via projections to the hypothalamus. An intact anterior visual pathway is essential for normal visual function and pupillary reaction.

ANATOMY OF THE RETINAL GANGLION CELLS

The photoreceptors—the rods and cones—sense light and initiate the neuroelectrical signal, which is processed by the 12 retinal layers. The processed information is then transmitted to individual retinal ganglion cells. Each retinal ganglion cell then sends a myelinated axon to converge at the optic disc (the optic nerve head visible on retinoscopy). Ganglion cells in the macular region provide central vision and send their axons directly from the fovea to the temporal optic disc (the papillomacular bundle). Fibers from the peripheral nasal retina enter the nasal optic disc, while the temporal retinal fibers enter the superior and inferior aspects of the optic disc (superior and inferior arcuate bundles). The ganglion cell axons comprise the nerve fiber layer, which can be viewed with a direct ophthalmoscope. These fibers are best appreciated through a dilated pupil using green illumination. The surface nerve fiber layer derives its vascular supply from the central retinal artery and its branches. Pathologic states of the retina or optic nerve may result in nerve fiber layer loss (ganglion cell axon death) that allows a clearer view of the retinal vessels.

ANATOMY OF THE OPTIC NERVE HEAD

The optic nerve head is divided into three regions: retinal (prelaminar), choroidal (laminar), and scleral (retrolaminar). The lamina cribrosa is a grouping of perforations in the choroid and sclera through which the retinal ganglion cells exit. Although there are regional density differences, the connective tissue forms a tight seal that prevents leaking except under very high pressure.

The optic nerve head is composed of ganglion cell axons and a laminar matrix of astrocytes, capillaries, and fibroblasts. The axons account for 90% of the optic nerve head. The size and exit angle of the scleral canal varies from individual to individual. It lies approximately 3 mm nasal to the fovea and is an optically blind region due to the lack of photoreceptors. This blind spot is present on all visual fields, covers at least 5 degrees of visual space and lies 15 degrees temporal to fixation. The central retinal artery is a branch of the ophthalmic artery and pierces the optic nerve sheath inferiorly at 10 to 12 mm behind the globe, then emerges at the center of the disc.

The prelaminar region of the optic nerve head receives blood supply from the four short posterior ciliary vessels. In contrast, the short posterior ciliary, peripapillary choroidal vessels and pial arterial network (the incomplete circle of Zinn-Haller) perfuse the laminar aspect of the nerve.

ANATOMY OF THE OPTIC NERVE

The optic nerve has three meningeal layers: the dura, the arachnoid, and the pia. The subarachnoid space is filled with cerebrospinal fluid that is continuous with the central subarachnoid space.

The optic nerve is 50 mm but individual variation is common. In addition to the one millimeter intraocular component (the optic nerve head), the optic nerve has three other portions: intraorbital, intracanalicular, and intracranial. The intraorbital optic nerve segment is the longest and is often serpiginous. The ophthalmic artery,

a branch of the internal carotid artery just as it exits the cavernous sinus, perfuses the orbital portion. The intracanalicular portion lies within the optic canal formed by the lesser wing of the sphenoid bone, and receives perfusion from the ophthalmic and internal carotid arteries. The intracranial portion of the optic nerve continues as the optic chiasm and then the optic tracts. The intracranial aspect of the optic nerve has multiple vascular sources, including the internal carotid, anterior cerebral, anterior communicating, and ophthalmic arteries.

The orbital optic nerve is myelinated posterior to the lamina cribrosa and, by definition, extends from the globe to the optic canal. The 20 to 30 mm segment has a redundancy that allows marked proptosis (usually at least 9 mm) prior to tethering of the optic nerve, which may be visualized on neuroimaging. Just prior to entering the optic canal, the optic nerve is enveloped in the annulus of Zinn—a condensation of the tendonous insertions of the recti muscles.

The optic canal runs posterior and medial and has approximate dimensions of 10 mm long by 5 mm wide. The canal is thinnest medially where the optic nerve travels adjacent to the sphenoid sinus and posterior ethmoid cells. In addition to the optic nerve, the canal contains the ophthalmic artery and a sympathetic plexus. The periosteums of the sphenoid bone and the dura of the optic nerve are fused within the canal. The intracanalicular optic nerve is thereby tethered and prone to compression by any space-occupying lesions.

As the optic nerve exits the optic canal it ascends and converges posteromedially to form the optic chiasm. A majority (53%) of ganglion cell axons from the nasal retina cross in the chiasm and join the uncrossed temporal contralateral fibers. These fibers then continue hemi-decussated in the optic tract. The optic chiasm is adjacent to the floor of the third ventricle and inferior to the pituitary gland.

Most ganglion cell axons terminate in one of the six layers of the lateral geniculate, where information is processed and then projected to visual cortex via the optic radiations. These axons contain visual and pupillomotor information, and some fibers ascend to the hypothalamus and contribute to circadian control of diurnal rhythms.

COMMON PATHOLOGIC STATES OF THE OPTIC NERVE

Optic nerve function can be impaired by changes in its blood supply, or by inflammation, demyelination, or compression. The hallmark of optic nerve dysfunction is the afferent pupillary defect (Marcus Gunn pupil). The involved optic nerve is not transmitting as much light to the visual pathways as does the optic nerve on the normal side, so the involved pupil does not constrict as briskly and redilates more readily. Other findings include impaired color vision, central visual acuity, and a visual field defect. The optic nerve head may be normal, edematous, or pale.

Acute ischemic optic neuropathy occurs in the patient's fifth or sixth decade, and characteristically presents with acute, painless, unilateral loss of vision that is noticed upon awakening. The optic nerve typically has sectoral edema and the most common visual field defect is inferior altitutudinal loss. Most patients do not re-gain normal visual function. Aspirin should be prescribed to pre-vent contralateral involvement. A sedimentation rate should be obtained to rule out temporal arteritis. If systemic symptoms of malaise, weight loss, or temporal pain are present, a temporal ar-tery biopsy should be performed.

Optic neuritis typically occurs in women in their second or third decade. The visual loss is acute and accompanied by pain that is exacerbated with eye movement. The optic nerve head is often nor-mal, but the visual field is abnormal. An afferent pupillary defect is present unless the contralateral side has been previously damaged. Most patients begin to improve in six weeks and regain near-normal visual function. Recurrent bouts of optic neuritis or mag-netic resonance imaging evidence of multifocal periventricular de-myelination make the diagnosis of multiple sclerosis likely. Acute visual loss should be treated with a 3-day course of intravenous Methylprednisolone followed by an oral Prednisone taper. Oral cortico-steroids alone are contraindicated because they increase the risk of subsequent episodes.

Compressive optic neuropathy may occur from intra-orbital tu-mors, optic nerve tumors, intracranial expansions of the sphenoid wing, or increased intracranial pressure. Enlargement of the ex-traocular muscles—as seen in thyroid-associated ophthalmop-athy—can also compress the optic nerve at the orbital apex. The most common orbital tumor in adults is the cavernous heman-gioma—other less common masses include schwannomas, neu-rofibromas, lymphomas, and hemangiopericytomas. Optic nerve meningiomas typically occur in middle-aged women, while optic nerve gliomas present in the first decade without a gender predilec-tion. Sphenoid wing meningiomas are much more common than either of these primary optic nerve tumors. Intervention should be considered when proptosis (globe protrusion due to tumor growth) is dramatic or visual function is significantly impaired. Intra-orbital tumors can be surgically excised allowing preservation of vision. Optic nerve tumors, in contrast, can not be removed with-out resulting in complete visual loss. Sphenoid wing meningiomas are approached intracranially, but complete surgical excision is difficult. External beam radiation is useful for lymphomas, op-tic nerve meningiomas, and incompletely-excised sphenoid wing meningiomas.

Thyroid-associated ophthalmopathy presents with proptosis, double vision, and periorbital swelling. In less than 10% of cases, the optic nerve becomes compressed by the enlarged extraocular muscles. Intravenous corticosteroids, external beam radiation, and orbital decompression have all been successfully used to relieve the pressure on the optic nerve.

Pseudotumor cerebri (intra-cranial hypertension) characteristi-cally presents in young, obese women. Transient visual loss, double vision, and headaches precede visual loss. Bilateral optic nerve edema is present in most cases. Neuroimaging should be per-formed to rule out an intracranial tumor; a lumbar puncture is then performed to confirm elevated intracranial pressure. Diamox (1–2 g/day) is effective in controlling the symptoms and preventing vi-sual loss. A Lumboperitoneal shunt or optic nerve sheath fenes-tration should be performed if medical management is inadequate.

SUGGESTED READING

Bill, A. (1993). Vascular physiology of the optic nerve. In R. Varma & G. L. Spaeth (Eds.), *The optic nerve in glaucoma* (pp. 37–50). Philadelphia: JB Lippincott.

Beck, R. W., & Clearly, P. A. (1993). Optic neuritis treatment trial. *Archives of Ophthalmology, 111,* 773–775.

Hayreh, S. S. (1974). Anatomy and physiology of the optic nerve head. *Transactions of the American Academy of Ophthalmology & Otolaryngology, 78,* 240–254.

Jonas, J. B., & Naumann, G. O. (1993). Optic nerve: Its embryol-ogy, histology, and morphology. In R. Varma & G. L. Spaeth (Eds.), *The optic nerve in glaucoma* (pp. 3–26). Philadelphia: JB Lippincott.

Kupersmith, M. J., Frohman, L., Sanderson, M., Jacobs, J., Hirschfeld, J., Ku, C., & Warren, F. A. (1997). Aspirin reduces the incidence of second eye NAION: A retrospective study. *Journal of Neuro-ophthalmology, 17*(40), 250–253.

Pollock, S. C., & Miller, N. R. (1986). The retinal nerve fiber layer. *International Ophthalmology Clinic, 26,* 8811 201–221.

Rizzo, J. F., & Lessell, S. (1991). Optic neuritis and ischemic optic neuropathy. *Archives of Ophthalmology, 109,* 1668–1672.

Sadun, A. A. (1998). Anatomy and physiology of the optic nerve. In N. R. Miller & N. J. Newman (Eds.), *Walsh and Hoyt's clini-cal neuro-ophthalmology* (pp. 57–83). Baltimore: Williams & Wilkins.

K. P. COCKERHAM
Allegheny Opthalmic and Orbital Associates, Pittsburgh

OPTIMAL FUNCTIONING

The area of optimal functioning was introduced into modern sci-entific psychology by Jahoda. Those contributing most heavily to the area of optimal functioning are humanistic psychologists who see optimal functioning as qualitatively different from normality or lack of pathology.

Simply stated, this area of psychology is a scientific investiga-tion of what the person is capable of becoming, of the best the per-son can be, and of the way the person can realize any number of personal potentials. That some people are exceptional in the ways they have developed their own lives and have promoted the devel-opment of those around them, and that we all have particular times when we function extraordinarily well, has been long recognized in psychology. It has been the task of workers in this area to examine these phenomena in systematic and scientific ways.

SELF-ACTUALIZATION

Abraham Maslow's (1971) empirical and theoretical investigation of optimal functioning asserts that there are two basic realms of human need. One, called the D or deficiency realm, is composed of the things we need to be functioning persons. These include the physiological needs for food, water, and other biological requirements; the safety needs to be protected from chaos; the love and belongingness needs to be included in a family or friendship group to protect us from loneliness; and our esteem needs for self-respect, self-esteem, and for a sense of accomplishment and worth. These needs are states of deficiency that must be met for us to be minimally adequate as human beings.

The B needs represent the needs that enable us to be self-actualizing human beings—our needs for self-actualization and our aesthetic needs. Maslow posited that these B-level needs, or meta-needs, are just as necessary as the D-level needs. If D needs are not met, one becomes ill physiologically and psychologically. If the B-level need is not met, one develops meta-pathologies. Following Maslow's lead, Shostrom (1962, 1975) developed two inventories (the Personal Orientation Inventory and Personal Orientation Dimension) to measure self-actualization. Building directly on Shostrom's work, Jones and Crandall (1986, 1991) developed a short (15 item) index. In contrast, Summerlin and Bundrick (1996) developed a brief index by going back to Maslow's concept of needs hierarchy.

For Maslow, self-actualized persons are aided in their development by intense moments of ecstasy, joy, and insight called peak experiences. There are moments of transcendence that take a person beyond self-actualization to what Maslow called the Z realm, a realm beyond the self that transcends both space and time. Recently, Csikszentmihalyi (1997, 1996) has expanded the notion of peak experience in his concept of "flow."

BEAUTIFUL AND NOBLE PERSONS

Working within the tradition of Maslow's approach, Landsman (1974) developed a system for describing and empirically investigating the optimal functioning person, "the Beautiful and Noble Person," who is aided by having had significant positive experiences in life. Landsman describes his Beautiful and Noble Person as a self that proceeds from: (a) the passionate self, a self-expressive, self-enjoying state; to (b) the environment-loving self, where the person cares deeply for the physical environment and the tasks to be accomplished in the world; and finally (c) to the compassionate self, which enables the person to be loving and caring toward other persons. Working within the Landsman tradition, Privette (1989, 1997) has studied positive, peak, and transcended experiences in the area of sports and athletic performance.

FULLY FUNCTIONING PERSON

Rogers (1959, 1980) described what he considered to be the optimally functioning or, in his terms, the "fully functioning" person. In contrast to Maslow's approach, Rogers emphasized the process of being fully functioning as it occurs moment by moment in every person's life, rather than being primarily concerned with describing characteristics of persons. Rogers' emphasis is on process, rather than structural components of the optimally functioning person. His work has been of the greatest influence in the field of psychotherapy, with less attention being devoted to formal research investigation of healthy persons outside the therapy situation.

Rogers starts with the assumption that every person has the ca-

pacity to actualize or complete his or her own inner nature. The key to this is for the person to remain in contact with his or her deepest feelings, which Rogers called organismic experiences (experiences of the organism). These direct and deeper feelings can be symbolized accurately in the person's awareness or they can be distorted. Optimal functioning is promoted when the person is able to know in awareness exactly what is happening at this deeper, direct organismic level. The person must be able to develop the kind of self or self structure that is able to be congruent or in harmony with the person's own deep feelings or experiences.

PSYCHOLOGY OF OPTIMAL PERSONS

Another formulation of optimal functioning centering on the concept of process which emphasizes constant change is Kelly's (1980) formulation of the psychology of an optimal person. The unit of analysis is the personal construct, a meaning dimension or conviction a person might hold, such as seeing people as loving versus rejecting. The personality of the individual is made up of a number of these personal construct dimensions. Kelly's system of optimal functioning requires that each individual use his or her system of personal meaning in order to complete what he termed "full cycles of experiences." By this, he meant that each individual must create his or her own conceptions of the world in such a way that these conceptions are continually tested and re-evaluated. The goal of a full cycle of experience is that the total system of personal constructs will continue to change and develop so that a person can keep pace with an ever-changing world. In this way, people are truly changed by the nature of their experience and are kept in a continual mode of orderly change. The work within this framework has centered on ways to evaluate each of the steps and to promote a progression through these steps as elaborated by Epting and Amerikaner (1980). The concern in construct theory is more with the way in which people invent or create themselves rather than their uncovering or discerning an inner self.

OPTIMAL PERSONALITY TRAITS

Coan (1977) undertook a multivariate study of optimal functioning persons, and later elaborated the theoretical implications of this work. In this empirical approach, Coan employed a battery of tests that took university students six hours to complete. This battery included measures pertaining to phenomenal consistency, cognitive efficiency, perceptual organization, the experience of control, the scope of awareness, openness to experience, independence, the experience of time, reality contact, self-insight, logical consistency of the attitude-belief system, and various other aspects of attitudes, beliefs, and adjustments. The final factor analysis yielded 19 obliquely rotated factors. Of primary importance was the fact that no single general factor was found that could represent a global personality trait of self-actualization. Coan suggests, from his own factor analysis and from his reading of Eastern and Western theories of optimal functioning, that five basic characteristics can be isolated that characterize the ideal human condition: efficiency, creativity, inner harmony, relatedness, and transcendency.

OTHER SIGNIFICANT CONTRIBUTIONS

For the serious student of optimal functioning, special attention should be given to a number of other important systems of thought. These include Jung's concept of individuation, Fromm's productive character, Allport's conception of propriate functioning, Erickson's conception of maturity, Adler's formation of Social Interest, Horney's sense of a real self and self-alienation, Reich's notion of the genital character with self-regulation, Jourard's concept of self-disclosure, White's concern with competence, and Ziller's notion of the transcendent personality.

REFERENCES

Coan, R. W. (1977). *Hero, artist, sage, or saint.* New York: Columbia University Press.

Crandall, R., & Jones, A. (1991). Issues in self-actualization measurement. *Journal of Social Behavior and Personality, 6,* 339–344.

Csikszentmihalyi, M. (1996). *Creativity: Flow and the psychology of discovery and invention.* New York: Harper Collins.

Csikszentmihalyi, M. (1997). *Finding flow: The psychology of engagement with everyday life.* New York: Basic.

Epting, F., & Amerikaner, M. (1980). Optimal functioning: A personal construct approach. In A. W. Landfield & L. M. Leitner (Eds.), *Personal construct psychology: Psychotherapy and personality.* New York: Wiley.

Jones, A., & Crandall, R. (1986). Validation of a short index of self-actualization. *Personality and Social Psychology Bulletin, 12,* 63–73.

Kelly, G. A. (1980). A psychology of the optimal man. In A. W. Landfield & L. M. Leitner (Eds.), *Personal construct psychology: Psychotherapy and personality.* New York: Wiley.

Landsman, T. (1974). The humanizer. *American Journal of Orthopsychiatry, 44,* 345–352.

Maslow, A. H. (1971). *The farther reaches of human nature.* New York: Viking.

Privette, G. (1989). Effects of triggering activity on construct events: Peak performance, peak experience, flow, average events, misery, and failure. *Journal of Social Behavior and Personality, 4*(3), 299–306.

Privette, G. (1997). Psychological processes of peak, average, and failing performance in sport. *International Journal of Sports Psychology, 28*(4), 323–334.

Rogers, C. A. (1959). A theory of interpersonal relationships, as developed in the client-centered framework. In S. Koch (Ed.), *Psychology: A study of a science: Vol. III. Formulations of the person and the social context.* New York: McGraw-Hill.

Rogers, C. A. (1980). *A way of being.* Boston: Houghton Mifflin.

Shostrom, E. L. (1962). *Manual for the Personal Orientation Inventory (POI): An inventory for the measurement of self-actualization.* San Diego, CA: Educational and Industrial Testing Service.

Shostrom, E. L. (1975). *Personal Orientation Dimension (POD).* San Diego: Educational and Industrial Testing Service.

Summerlin, J. R., & Bundrick, C. M. (1996). Brief index of self-actualization: A measure of Maslow's model. *Journal of Social Behavior and Personality, 11*(2), 253–271.

SUGGESTED READING

Csikszentmihalyi, M. (1990). *Flow: The psychology of optimal experience.* New York: Harper & Row.

Mittleman, W. (1991). Maslow's study of self-actualization: A reinterpretation. *Journal of Humanistic Psychology, 31*(1), 114–135.

F. R. Epting
D. I. Suchman
D. Philip
University of Florida

EGO DEVELOPMENT
PEAK EXPERIENCES

ORGANIC PSYCHOSES

The term *organic psychoses* encompasses a host of disorders that have in common the fact that the particular etiology interferes with the individual's general mental functioning. Labeling some psychoses as organic and others as functional does not imply that there is no organic basis for the latter, but rather that a known and specifiable organic disorder is associated with the former.

Organic psychoses can be associated with any of a number of organic changes that directly or indirectly affect brain functioning: endogenous or exogenous toxic substances (alcohol, drugs, heavy metals, etc.), infections (paresis, meningitis, encephalitis, etc.), primary convulsive disorders (epilepsy), head trauma (concussions and resulting subdural hematoma), intracranial neoplasm (tumors), arteriosclerosis and cerebrovascular disorders, nutritional deficits (niacin, thiamine—Wernicke's syndrome), endocrine disorders (e.g., myxedema), and senile and presenile disturbances (e.g., Alzheimer's disease, Pick's disease, Huntington's chorea).

Symptomatically many of the organic psychoses begin mildly enough with symptoms of fatigue, headache, moodiness, drowsiness, and distractability and complaints of the inability to concentrate. Occasionally insidious personality changes take place, along with disturbances of sleep, and the appearance of increasing irritability and a loss of inhibitions, leading to behavioral changes such as increasing aggression, restlessness, and impulsiveness. Depending upon the particular etiology and its time course, aphasia, apraxia, hemiparesis, emotional instability, depression, disorientation, perceptual disturbance, hallucinations, memory disturbances, delirium, dementia, and even convulsions, may ensue. A number of patients, particularly those who have suffered trauma, will display a "catastrophic reaction" in which the patient becomes very agitated, anxious, and upset when faced with a difficult problem.

Treatment of the organic psychoses will depend upon the specific etiology. It is important, therefore, to establish the correct diagnosis as early as possible so that appropriate medical and/or surgical treatment can be initiated. For example, although the symptom patterns of delirium tremens and impending hepatic coma are quite different, treatment based on a confusion of one for the other could be fatal to the patient. In general, the treatment of the organic cause of the organic psychosis precedes treatment of the mental disturbance, because in a number of cases the latter will clear with treatment of the organic etiology.

SUGGESTED READING

Kolb, L. C. (1977). *Modern clinical psychiatry* (9th ed.). Philadelphia, PA: Saunders.

W. E. EDMONSTON, JR.
Colgate University

ALZHEIMER'S DISEASE
See NEUROPSYCHOLOGY

ORGANIZATIONAL DIAGNOSIS

Organizations may be viewed as agglomerations of people, as groups of groups, as interrelated boxes, as hierarchies of power and authority, as information-processing or decision-making systems, or as bureaucracies. Whatever the view, when a consultant undertakes to help an organization change, there is a need to understand the organization as an organic system, adaptive and capable of change with a life of its own that transcends that of the people in it, and with the capacity to perpetuate itself. Building on an open-system model, organizations may be seen as being made up of sub-systems.

All organizations strive toward some goal. They mobilize the energies of their people, and their financial, production, and technical resources. In the service of attaining that goal, they attack their respective environments and seek advantage in competition with other organizations. They also strive toward a stable regularity. These patterns of organizational behavior are consistent and observable.

PATTERNS OF BEHAVIOR

Value System

All organizations have a history, a culture, and a tradition. They strive toward some ideal, some standard of performance. They have rules, regulations, policies, procedures, norms of behavior, codes of conduct, and methods for monitoring all of those standards and controls. Much of an organization's activity is an outgrowth of the manner in which its leadership has constructed it, the kinds of people who have been attracted to it, and what it has done before, particularly its ways of having adapted to its unique crises.

History

All organizations, as a product of their history, culture, and traditions, also evolve a folklore. They have legendary heroes, recall certain competitive victories, develop certain repetitive ways of producing or selling or serving that characterize them and differentiate them from other organizations in the same field. Much of what an organization does is either rationalized or inexplicable, as verified by, "That's the way we've always done it." There is a powerful momentum of the past into the present, of which organization members often are unaware but which is nevertheless powerful and discoverable.

Information

All organizations must obtain, process, and act on information. They must sense their socioeconomic realities. They get information both from within themselves and from the marketplace, as well as the broader world, more or less systematically, which they then process and integrate into their ongoing activities. They act more or less effectively on that information, and may or may not understand its implications for them. There is an organizational memory. There is a history of how the organization mobilizes its skills, knowledge, and capacities to solve various problems. There is a pattern to how it acts on them. It has a certain posture or stance toward the outside world, toward its competitors, toward its communities, and even toward itself.

Communications

Organizations have methods of internal communication and modes of communicating with the outside. Organization communications patterns are akin to the nervous system of an individual. They are the devices by which messages are sent to all parts of the organization and action by those parts is stimulated. The communication system, together with the accounting control system, constitute what might be called the sensory and motor aspects of the organization, its way of enervating and controlling itself.

Power

All organizations have leadership, which in turn exercises power and distributes it to the rest of the organization. The components of the organization may have their own power either because they possess knowledge or resources or organizational advantages. In those cases, the leadership must often interact with other power centers. The leadership must also interact with various constituencies outside the organization.

Key Figures

All organizations have, in addition to leadership, key figures who possess certain knowledge or social power and who interact in certain ways. The interaction of these key figures has a significant impact on the way the rest of the organization operates.

Groups

All organizations are comprised of varied groups. These may be functional groups such as sales, accounting, manufacturing, engineering; or they may be disciplinary groups such as physicians and nurses, or teachers and principals; or they may be task groups such as different production and service facilities. These groups have relationships with each other and are continuously engaged in intergroup and intragroup adaptation as each seeks to achieve its own more limited goals and act in keeping with its own more limited values.

Adaptation

All organizations adapt in certain consistent ways. These may be more or less successful, but they tend to be characteristic. Adaptation patterns may change with an infusion of new and different leadership, or new and different organization membership, or changes in product or service orientation. But, by and large, barring such radical change, the adaptation processes are evolutionary and discernible.

THE DIAGNOSIS

Anyone who is to change any organization must have an understanding of the manner in which each of these systems (and different consultants may differentiate different systems) operates and how they interact with each other and with the whole, and the whole with its external environment. From that understanding the consultant may derive inferences concerning the disclosed gaps and inefficiencies and their effects. The consultant then uses his or her own discipline (sociology, psychology) and theory (social learning, psychoanalysis) to arrive at the meaning of the inferences. Proceeding from facts to inference to interpretation, the consultant may then come to a logical understanding of the organization and formulate a specific mode of action for dealing with its problem. That change effort then should be uniquely appropriate to a given problem, in a unique organization, under defined conditions, at a specific point in time.

Taken together, this process constitutes organizational diagnosis. All diagnosis is hypothesis. It is a definition of what the diagnostician thinks the problem is and with such a hypothesis the consultant is able to return continuously to the information on which the hypothesis is based if the diagnosis proves incorrect or inadequate or if the mode of intervention fails to produce the anticipated results.

The formulation of a diagnosis also requires the formulation of a prognosis. Anyone who would change an organization should assess what changes are possible for this organization, given its leadership, its resources, the kinds of people who are part of it, its history, its success or lack thereof, its level of sophistication, and the limits of competence and time of the consultant. A prognosis enables the consultant to put boundaries around his or her work and to arrive at realistic expectations.

In sum, organizational diagnosis is a systematic method for trying to understand the complexities of an organization in its context, and the problems that arise because of the unique configuration of forces operating within the organization and interacting with those from the outside. Organizational diagnosis is a method to explicate the data that reflect all of these forces, to validate those data, and to establish a solid data base to which one can return when inferences or interpretations prove inadequate. A consultant may modify such a data base repeatedly as the organization

changes. Organizational diagnosis calls the attention of the consultant to the range of data which he or she should have available as a basis for decision making and action. The integration of a plethora of complex data into a systematic whole provides the consultant with a solid basis for his or her work. It is otherwise difficult to maintain a grasp of a multitude of items of information to integrate them into a configuration that will serve as a basis for action. Organizational diagnosis avoids the part diagnoses of limited methods that tap only one or another aspect of the organization but are unable to take the whole into account.

A comprehensive diagnostic method enables an organizational consultant to use many different modes of gathering information. Such a data-gathering and data-organizing device also enables the same method to be used by consultants with a wide variety of orientations.

SUGGESTED READING

Argyris, C. (1970). *Intervention theory and method.* Reading, MA: Addison-Wesley.

Beckhard, R., & Harris, R. T. (1977). *Organizational transitions: Managing complex change.* Reading, MA: Addison-Wesley.

Kotter, J. P. (1978). *Organizational dynamics: Diagnosis and intervention.* Reading, MA: Addison-Wesley.

Lawrence, P. R., & Lorseh, J. W. (1969). *Developing organizations: Diagnosis and action.* Reading, MA: Addison-Wesley.

Levinson, H. (1972). *Organizational diagnosis.* Cambridge, MA: Harvard University Press.

Lippitt, G. L. (1982/1969). *Organization renewal.* Englewood Cliffs, NJ: Prentice-Hall.

Weisbord, M. W. (1978). *Organizational diagnosis.* Reading, MA: Addison-Wesley.

H. LEVINSON
The Levinson Institute, Boston

JOB ANALYSIS
MANAGEMENT DECISION MAKING

ORGANIZATIONAL PSYCHOLOGY

Organizational psychology aims to improve performance and satisfaction in organizational settings and attempts to emphasize both theory and practice. It covers a wide range of topics, from work motivation, morale, and productivity to leadership and organizational effectiveness, from small groups to large, multinational corporations. The classical Hawthorne studies initiated in 1925 constitute the specific historical root of organizational psychology. Among the principles demonstrated by these experiments was the finding that changes in the productivity of workers could not be explained simply as a function of objective factors such as physical and working conditions. Subjective factors such as morale, leadership, employees' attitudes toward the company, and social relationships were important in understanding work behavior.

The field of organizational psychology is also influenced by the changing societal view of the nature of work (and other contextual environmental factors) and of the responsibility of organizations for the quality of work life of their employees (McCormick & Ilgen, 1985; Wilpert, 1995). Organizational psychology overlaps with personnel psychology, which focuses on individual differences, selection, and assessment. New areas of inquiry include the design and evaluation of training programs, performance appraisal, the measurement of employee morale and job satisfaction, and organizational diagnosis and assessment. Organizational psychology has many sub-areas. Among them are job satisfaction, work attitudes, career development, work motivation, group process, group dynamics, leadership behavior, and organizational decision making, culture, change, and development.

WORK ATTITUDES AND CAREER DEVELOPMENT

Because individual processes are important to an understanding of organizational psychology, work attitudes, job satisfaction, and attributions are extensively studied in relation to the organizational context. The work attitudes often reflect employees' reactions to jobs, groups, leaders, and the whole organization, and often guide work behavior. Job satisfaction has been the primary area in which attitudes have been examined over the years. Locke's (1976) taxonomy of job satisfaction includes the work itself, pay, promotion, recognition, work conditions, benefits, supervision, coworkers, customers, and family. A related factor is attribution. Attributions of internal causes (e.g., ability and effort) and external causes (e.g., task difficulty and luck) are influenced by available information, beliefs, and motivation. The attributions that people make regarding the causes of task performance may have significant effects on their work behavior in organizations. Most people also exhibit different managerial problem-solving styles, according to whether sensation or intuition dominates and whether feeling or thinking methods are used in evaluation information. Organizational psychology research reveals that people tend to integrate the four psychological functions in solving problems in varying situations. Obviously, several dimensions of job satisfaction and attribution determine an employee's overall satisfaction; therefore, multiple indicators should be used in measuring job satisfaction. The two standardized scales of job satisfaction are the Job Descriptive Index and the Minnesota Satisfaction Questionnaire.

The study of occupational choice and career development is an important area in organizational psychology. Schein (1980) identified three basic career patterns in organizations: engineering-based careers, with needs for challenging opportunities for higher earnings and advance; scientific-professionally–based careers, oriented more toward the intrinsic challenges of tasks; and pure professional careers. Studies show that both employees' prior orientation and their subsequent occupational socialization affect the values of career development. Holland's (1973) career theory described six dimensions of the patterns between personal orientations and occupational environments: realistic, intellectual, social, conventional, enterprising, and artistic. Super and Hall's (1978) developmental theory suggests six major stages for occupational choice: exploration, reality testing, experimentation, establishment, main-

tenance, and decline. Career identification is formed on the basis of organizational characteristics and the individual's self-concept.

WORK MOTIVATION

Work motivation is a principal area of organizational psychology, with three general categories of motivation theories: need-motive-value theories, cognitive-choice theories, and self-regulation–metacognition theories (Kanfer, 1990). The need-motive-value theories attempt to explain motivational factors in terms of stable disposition such as personality, need structure, and values. Among these theories are Maslow's (1954) need hierarchy theory and Alderfer's (1969) existence-relatedness-growth theory. Some intrinsic motivation theories focus on higher-order motives, such as Deci's (1975) cognitive evaluation theory and Hackman and Oldham's (1980) job characteristics theory, which concentrates on how job and organizational events affect task interest and perceptions of personal control as critical psychological states in work behavior. Adams's (1963) equity theory deals with cognitive and social exchange relationships based on the feelings of how fair the employee is treated compared with others. Other well known theories in this category include Herzberg's (1966) motivator-hygiene theory and McClelland's (1961) achievement motivation theory.

The cognitive-choice theories focus on the cognitive process involved in choice. Vroom's (1964) valence-instrumentality-expectancy theory represents the framework of those theories that emphasize the perceived probability of successful performance given certain effort. Weiner's (1986) three-dimensional attribution theory (locus, stability, and controllability) emphasizes motivational influence of attributions on behavior. Wang's (1986) attributional model of motivation demonstrates that the goal structures (individual vs. team) of the work system affect the attributional patterns, which in turn largely determine the worker's subsequent affect, expectation, and work motivation.

The self-regulation–metacognition theories emphasize the motivational processes in goal-directed behavior. Locke's goal-setting theory intends to increase task efficiency and effectiveness by specifying the goal attributes and desired outcomes (Locke & Latham, 1984).

GROUP PROCESS AND GROUP DYNAMICS

The studies on group process and group dynamics are significantly influenced by the pioneering work of Lewin (*Resolving Social Conflicts,* 1948, and *Field Theory in Social Science,* 1951). Variables such as group norms, group pressure, intergroup conflicts, group leadership styles (democratic vs. authoritarian), group cohesiveness, and interpersonal communication were carefully studied. Moreno's sociometric method is a popular technique for group assessment and regrouping practice; it is also used for measuring group cohesiveness, which is often defined as forces that lead an individual to remain in or leave a given group. Group cohesiveness is considered a significant factor in group effectiveness. One useful framework for understanding workgroup behavior is the Harvard model, which describes group behavior in terms of two systems (external and internal systems behaviors), three components (activities, interactions, and sentiments), and the relationship among background factors, required behavior, emergent behavior, and consequences (Lawrence & Seiler, 1965).

Group decision making is one of the major topics in group psychology. There are two lines of research in this area: a social psychological approach, dealing with role perception, participation, power sharing, and groupthink factor; and a cognitive approach, emphasizing goal structures, creative problem solving, cognitive resource use, uncertainty assessment, information distribution, and decision support. Another aspect of group dynamics is intergroup behaviors. Goal conflicts, resource sharing, task relations, and substitutability are found to be the principal factors affecting intergroup relationships.

LEADERSHIP AND ORGANIZATIONAL DECISION MAKING

Leadership is considered a process of influencing group activities toward the achievement of goals. It is the product of interactions among leaders, subordinates, and organizational goals. The sources of leadership power include legitimate power, reward power, coercive power, referent power, and expert power. The effective use of power relies on the match between leadership styles and situations. There are three kinds of leadership models in organizational psychology. The traits models focus on the important personality traits responsible for leadership success, but they neglect the crucial influence of the leader's behavior and various situations on leadership effectiveness. The behavioral models suggest that the relationship between leaders and their subordinates determine the effectiveness of the leadership, and that certain leadership behaviors are important for the accomplishment of group and organizational goals. Ohio State University's leadership studies, begun in the late 1940s, resulted in the two-dimensional model of leader behavior: consideration (oriented toward good job relationships) and initiating structure (oriented toward formal standards and rules of performance). However, these models paid much attention to the relationship but little to the effects of the specific situations and, therefore, failed to establish a systematic relationship between leadership behavior and organizational performance.

Contingency models of leadership, in contrast, emphasize the compatibility among contingency characteristics of leaders, subordinates, groups, and organizational situations. Fiedler's contingency model is among the important leadership theories; the model has three contingency variables: leader-member relations, task structure, and leader position power, which in combination create eight situations. The model shows the effectiveness of either relationship-motivated leadership or task-motivated leadership among different situations (Fiedler & Chemers, 1974). Furthermore, Fiedler's (1986) cognitive resources theory examines how situational variables such as interpersonal stress, group support, and task complexity determine whether a leader's intelligence and experience enhance group performance (Yukl & Van Fleet, 1992). Other main contingency models are House's (1971) path-goal model and Vroom and Yetton's (1973) normative model. A related active topic in organizational psychology is the assessment of leadership, the popular measures of which consist of two dimensions: the task- and relation-oriented leadership styles, and the performance and maintenance styles. A useful approach to leadership assessment is a multilevel evaluation involving supervisors, coworkers, subordinates, and the leaders themselves.

Organizational decision making is important in organizational psychology. Simon (1976) regarded administrative decision making as a process of information processing and examined human rationality within the limits of a psychological environment using the concept of bounded rationality. Heller and Wilpert (1981) adopted a new approach and used influence-power-sharing as a core variable for understanding competence use and managerial success in organizational decision making.

ORGANIZATION DEVELOPMENT

An important aspect of organizational psychology is the rapidly growing field of organization development (OD), which includes human-process interventions, technostructural interventions, and human resource management interventions. Many OD techniques, such as organizational diagnosing, sensitivity training, group consultation, managerial grid, and team training, have been developed for the purpose of moving organization members toward higher morale and better organizational performance. Their ultimate aim is to improve the total organizational system. Other aspects of organization development and change include job redesign for higher task variety; better task identity; more meaningful and stimulating tasks; the development of organizational structures that permit better distribution of influence, power, and information; and the design of more equitable systems of rewards. A major approach to organization development is action research, which focuses on planned change as a cyclical process involving close cooperation between organizational members and psychologists. It usually includes diagnosis for problem identification, feedback to key members or groups, joint diagnosis and planning for change actions, and evaluation after action (Huse & Cummings, 1985). Several recent studies suggest three OD strategies that have proved to be effective: (a) expertise strategy, focusing on the strengthening of training in knowledge, competence, and skills necessary among employees for higher performance; (b) systems strategy, emphasizing the improvement of management systems' networking for information sharing, communication, and more adaptable organizational structure; and (c) participation strategy, facilitating the high involvement of various groups and employees at all organizational levels in the planning, designing, and implementation of new objectives of production and technological change (Wang, 1993). Technological innovation, another area of research in organizational psychology, is closely related to organization development. A significant approach of organization development and technological innovation is the sociotechnical model that was originally developed from the studies at the Tavistock Institute of Human Relations in London. The sociotechnical model focuses simultaneously on the technical system and the social system, emphasizing the interaction and fit between those two systems in achieving organizational objectives.

Given the rapid development of international corporations and multinational joint ventures, the cross-cultural psychology approach is becoming more and more popular in the study of organization psychology. Wang (1993) suggested adopting a cross-cultural–socioeconomic perspective to understand organizational behavior and culture in the context of the world's economic, social, and technological development. Under the changes in contemporary firms and their competitive environments, organizational psychology research has shifted from corporatist organizations to organizing with the use of key topics such as emerging employment relations, performance management, self-management, and organizational learning (Rousseau, 1997).

REFERENCES

Adams, J. S. (1963). Toward an understanding of inequity. *Journal of Abnormal and Social Psychology, 67,* 442–436.

Alderfer, C. P. (1969). An empirical test of new theory of human needs. *Organizational Behavior and Human Performance, 4,* 142–175.

Deci, E. L. (1975). *Intrinsic motivation.* New York: Plenum.

Fiedler, F. E., & Chemers, M. N. (1974). *Leadership and effective management.* Glenview, IL: Scott, Foresman.

Hackman, J. R., & Oldman, G. R. (1980). *Work redesign.* Reading, MA: Addison-Wiley.

Heller, F. A., & Wilpert, B. (1981). *Competence and power in managerial decision making.* Chichester, UK: Wiley.

Herzberg, F. (1966). *Work and the nature of man.* Cleveland, OH: World.

Holland, J. L. (1973). *Making vocational choices: A theory of careers.* Englewood Cliffs, NJ: Prentice-Hall.

Huse, E. F., & Cummings, T. G. (1985). *Organization development and change.* St. Paul, MN: West.

Kanfer, R. (1990). Motivation theory and industrial and organizational psychology. In M. D. Dunnetter & L. N. Hough (Eds.), *Handbook of industrial and organizational psychology* (2nd ed., Vol. 1, pp. 75–170). Palo Alto, CA: Consulting Psychologists Press.

Lawrence, P. R., & Seiler, J. A. (1965). *Organizational behavior and administration.* Irwin-Dorsey.

Lewin, K. (1948). *Resolving social conflicts.* New York: Harper.

Lewin, K. (1951). Intention, will, and need. In D. Rapaport (Ed.), *Organization and pathology of thought* (pp 95-153). New York: Columbia University Press.

Locke, E. A. (1976). The nature and cause of job satisfaction. In M. D. Dunnette (Ed.), *Handbook of industrial and organizational psychology.* Chicago: Rand McNally.

Maslow, A. H. (1954). *Motivation and personality.* New York: Harper & Brother.

Mellers, B. A., Schwartz, A., & Cooke, A. D. J. (1998). Judgment and decision making. *Annual Review of Psychology, 49,* (pp. 447-477).

McClelland, D. C. (1961). *The achieving society.* Princeton, NJ: Van Nostrand.

McCormick, E. J., & Ilgen, D. R. (1985). *Industrial and organizational psychology* (8th ed.). Englewood Cliffs, NJ: Prentice-Hall.

Rousseau, D. M. (1997). Organizational behavior in the new organizational era. *Annual Review of Psychology, 48,* (pp. 515-546).

Schein, E. H. (1980). *Organizational psychology* (3rd ed.). Englewood Cliffs, NJ: Prentice-Hall.

Simon, H. A. (1976). *Administrative behavior.* New York: Macmillan.

Super, D. E., & Hall, D. T. (1978). Career development: Exploration and planning. In M. R. Rosenzweig & L. W. Porter (Eds.), *Annual Review of Psychology* (Vol. 29). pp. 333-372.

Taylor, R. N. (1992). Strategic decision making. In M. D. Dunnette & L. M. Hough (Eds.), *Handbook of industrial & organizational psychology* (2nd ed., Vol. 3, pp. 961-1007). Palo Alto, CA: Consulting Psychologists Press.

Vroom, V. H. (1964). *Work and motivation.* New York: Wiley.

Vroom, V. H., & Yetton, P. W. (1973). *Leadership and decision making.* Pittsburgh, PA: University of Pittsburgh Press.

Wang, Z. M. (1986). Worker's attribution and its effects on performance under different work responsibility systems. *Chinese Journal of Applied Psychology, 1*(2), 6–10.

Wang, Z. M. (1993). Psychology in China: A review dedicated to Li Chen. *Annual Review of Psychology, 44,* 87–116.

Weiner, B. (1980). *An attributional theory of achievement, motivation and emotion.* New York: Springer-Verlag.

Wilpert, B. (1995). Organizational behavior. *Annual Review of Psychology, 46,* pp. 59-90.

Yukl, G., & Van Fleet, D. D. (1992). Theory and research on leadership in organizations. In M. D. Dunnette & L. M. Hough (Eds.), *Handbook of industrial and organizational psychology* (2nd ed. Vol. 5, pp. 147-197). Palo Alto, CA: Consulting Psychologists Press.

Z. M. Wang
Zheijiang University, China

APPLIED RESEARCH
HAWTHORNE EFFECT
INDUSTRIAL PSYCHOLOGY
WORK EFFICIENCY

OSGOOD, CHARLES EGERTON (1916–1991)

Charles Osgood received the AB degree from Dartmouth College and the PhD degree from Yale in 1945. He then served as research associate for the U.S. Office of Scientific Research and Development, where he worked on the training of B-29 gunners. Following World War II, he joined the faculty of the University of Illinois and became professor of psychology and director of the Institute of Communication Research. In 1960 he received the Distinguished Scientific Contribution Award from the American Psychological

Association. He was elected president of the American Psychological Association in 1963.

Osgood's experimental research centered around the role of meaning within the context of learning theory. To do so, he developed the Semantic Differential Method, which has been applied to the analysis of attitudes, attitude change, personality structure, clinical diagnosis, vocational choice, consumer reactions to products and brands, and the role of meaning within different cultures. The technique was described in *The Measurement of Meaning*. The Semantic Differential consists of a quantitative procedure for measuring connotations of any given concept—it involves ratings and a variety of statistical techniques involving factoral analysis.

Many psychologists believe that Osgood's technique is a useful tool for exploring many of the higher mental processes in human beings. He published *Method and Theory in Experimental Psychology* in 1953.

STAFF

OVERMIER, JAMES BRUCE

Bruce Overmier was born in New York on August 2, 1938 (James Bruce Wheelwright, later adopted). He received a BA in chemistry from Kenyon College, an MA from Bowling Green State University in general psychology, and a PhD in experimental psychology at University of Pennsylvania in 1965. He is professor of psychology (Graduate Faculties of Psychology, Neuroscience, Psychoneuroimmunology, and Cognitive Science) at the University of Minnesota. He has held postdoctoral fellowship awards from National Science Foundation (NSF) (for study of comparative physiology at Queen Mary College, London, England), National Academy of Sciences (to Nencki Institute of Experimental Biology, Warsaw, Poland), Fogarty Center (to University of Bergen, Bergen, Norway), James McKeen Cattell Foundation (to Cambridge University), Fulbright-Hayes (to Marine Biological Institute, Kotor, Yugoslavia), and Norwegian Marshall Fund and later Norwegian Research Council (to University of Bergen). In 1990, he received an honorary Doctor of Science degree from Kenyon College. In 1999, he won the Quad-L Award in Psychology from the University of New Mexico.

Overmier was appointed Assistant Professor of Psychology at the University of Minnesota in 1965, Associate Professor in 1968, and Professor in 1971. He also has held appointment as Professor II at the University of Bergen (Norway) since 1992. Overmier was a licensed psychologist in Minnesota from 1976 to 1994. Overmier has held term teaching appointments at University of Hawaii (U.S.), Kenyon College (U.S.), Universitet i Bergen (Norway), Kansei Gakuin University (Japan), and Universidad de Seville (Spain), as well as visiting research appointments to University of Newcastle (Australia). He served as a National Research Society Sigma Xi Distinguished National Lecturer from 1999 to 2001.

Overmier's research spans specialties of learning, memory, stress, psychosomatic disorders, and their biological substrates. This research has been carried out with a variety of species of laboratory animals (fish, birds, mammals) and with human client volunteers (with Down syndrome, Korsakoff's syndrome, or Alzheimer's disease). The laboratory animals serve as models for various forms of human dysfunction and the development of therapies (e.g., "learned helplessness" first reported and named by Overmier and Seligman, 1967, and popularized as a model for depression, psychosomatic dysfunction, and posttraumatic stress syndrome). Overmier has authored more than 170 refereed research articles, book chapters, and books in his specialties. This research was funded by NSF and the National Institute of Mental Health.

Overmier has been a member and chair of the National Academy of Science's United States National Committee for Psychology (1991–2000); a member of the board of directors of American Psychological Society (APS) (1994–97); and a member of the Council of Representatives of American Psychological Association (APA) (1987–90; 1995–97). He has served as president of the Midwestern Psychological Association (1988–89), president of APA Division of Physiological and Comparative Psychology (1990–91), president of APA Division of Experimental Psychology (1992–93), and president of the Pavlovian Society (1996–97); in addition, he served both as secretary-treasurer (1981–83) and on the board of governors of the Psychonomic Society (1983–88). Overmier has also served as deputy secretary-general of the International Union of Psychological Science (1993–96), and is currently a member of both the Union's Executive Committee (1996–2000) and the board of directors of APA (1999–2001).

Overmier has been editor of the journal *Learning and Motivation* (1973–1976); associate editor of *American Psychologist* (1994–present) and *International Journal of Psychology* (1994–1998); and consulting editor or editorial board member of numerous other journals (e.g., *Journal of Experimental Psychology,* 1971–74; *Journal of Experimental Psychology: Animal Behavior Processes,* 1988–2000; *Physiological Psychology,* 1982–1985; *Behavioural Brain Research,* 1979–84). He has also served on research national advisory panels (1976–1995) for NSF and NIMH.

Overmier continues to teach undergraduate and graduate students and to engage in further research at University of Minnesota. Occasionally, Overmier publishes with his wife, Judith Ann Overmier, who is professor of library and information science at University of Oklahoma. Their most recent work is a CD-ROM reference tool on resources in international psychology. They have one daughter, Larisa Overmier Somsel.

STAFF

OXYTOCIN

Oxytocin is a peptide hormone and neuromodulator with a range of physiological and psychological effects related to reproduction and social behavior. Oxytocin is produced predominantly in the hypothalamus and is projected to the posterior pituitary for release into circulation, where it acts as a hormone. Oxytocin released into circulation plays important roles in regulating both lactation and the progression of labor. Oxytocin is the most uterotonic substance known, and pitocin, a synthetic oxytocin, is widely used by physicians to stimulate the progression of labor. Nipple stimulation during nursing stimulates synchronous firing of hypothalamic neurons via a reflex arch, resulting in the pulsatile release of oxytocin from the mother's pituitary gland. This elevation in oxytocin stimulates milk ejection by causing myoepithelial cells in the mammary gland to contract.

Oxytocin is also projected to sites within the central nervous system where it acts as a neuromodulator to affect emotionality and behavior. Oxytocin receptors are found in discrete limbic brain areas known to regulate behavior. Most of our understanding of the role of central oxytocin is derived from animal studies, and therefore the findings may or may not be relevant to humans.

REPRODUCTIVE BEHAVIOR

In animal models, central oxytocin facilitates female sexual behavior, or receptivity. Receptivity in rodents is regulated primarily by the sequential actions of ovarian estrogen and progesterone. Estrogen increases both oxytocin synthesis and the numbers of oxytocin receptors in regions of the hypothalamus involved in the regulation of sexual behavior. Oxytocin injections into the hypothalamus of estrogen-primed female rats facilitate female sexual behavior, while oxytocin antagonists block this behavior. Once mating occurs, vaginocervical stimulation results in a release of oxytocin into the plasma. Oxytocin may also play a role in sexual performance in males. For example, oxytocin levels in the cerebrospinal fluid are elevated after ejaculation in male rats, and oxytocin injections decrease the latency to ejaculation. Oxytocin also stimulates the occurrence of spontaneous, non-contact penile erections in male rats. The role of oxytocin in human sexuality is unclear; however, plasma oxytocin levels increase during sexual arousal and peak at orgasm in both men and women.

SOCIAL MEMORY

Animals living in social groups must be able to recognize familiar individuals. Several studies have suggested a role for oxytocin in the formation or expression of social memory. In rodents, social memory is based primarily on olfactory cues and can be quantified by measuring the decrease in olfactory investigation after repeated exposure to the same individual. Low doses of oxytocin enhance the formation of social memory in rats. Higher doses of oxytocin result in an amnestic effect. Mice lacking a functional oxytocin gene fail to recognize individuals even after repeated exposure, but display normal social memory after a single injection of oxytocin. Vasopressin, a peptide hormone structurally related to oxytocin, is also involved in social recognition. It is not known whether oxytocin plays a significant role in social memory for species in which individual recognition is not based on olfactory cues.

SOCIAL ATTACHMENT AND AFFILIATION

Strong social attachments are essential for successful reproduction in mammals. Oxytocin is involved in the formation of social attachments between mother and offspring, and in monogamous species, between mates. In many species, virgin females fail to display nurturing behavior toward infants of others, but females display extensive maternal care for their own offspring beginning mo-

ments after giving birth. Virgin rats receiving oxytocin injections into the brain display nurturing behavior toward pups, while interfering with oxytocin transmission interferes with the normal onset of maternal care in parturient dams. Once initiated, blocking oxytocin transmission does not interfere with maternal behavior, suggesting that oxytocin is important for the initiation, but not the maintenance, of maternal behavior. In sheep, oxytocin is released in the brain within 15 minutes of delivery of the lamb. Infusion of oxytocin into the brain of an estrogen-primed ewe elicits full maternal responsiveness within 30 s. Furthermore, vaginocervical stimulation in an estrogen-primed ewe, which causes the central release of oxytocin, also elicits full maternal responsiveness. Oxytocin also appears to facilitate the selective bond between the mother and her offspring, probably through an olfactory recognition mechanism. Ewes will allow their own lamb to suckle while rejecting other lambs. Stimulating oxytocin release during exposure to an unfamiliar lamb stimulates the ewe to bond with that lamb even if she has previously bonded with her own lamb. It is unclear whether oxytocin significantly influences the mother-infant bond in humans, although correlational studies suggest that endogenous oxytocin does influence personality traits in postpartum women. For example, women who give birth by cesarean section have fewer oxytocin pulses during breast-feeding than those who give birth vaginally, and are less likely to describe themselves during the postpartum period as exhibiting a calm personality or high levels of sociality. In mothers delivering by cesarean section, oxytocin levels are correlated with the degree of openness to social interactions and with calmness.

Like the bond between a mother and infant, strong social attachments are formed between mates in monogamous species. Prairie voles are a monogamous species of rodent and have been extensively studied as a model for understanding the neural basis of monogamy. In the prairie vole, oxytocin plays a role in formation of the bond of the female for the male, but not of the male for the female. Infusion of oxytocin into the brain of a female prairie vole even in the absence of mating results in the formation of a pair bond. Comparative studies using closely related monogamous and non-monogamous species have found that species differences in distribution of oxytocin receptors in the brain are associated with species differences in social organization. Oxytocin also enhances nonsexual affiliative behaviors. For example, experiments examining the effects of central oxytocin on social interaction in rodents have shown that oxytocin increases the time spent in physical contact with other individuals. There is speculation that central oxytocin may underlie the reinforcing nature of positive social interactions.

The role of oxytocin in human social relationships remains to be determined. Sex in humans may play a role in strengthening the emotional attachments between partners, and vaginocervical stimulation, nipple stimulation, and orgasm, each components of human sexuality, facilitate oxytocin release.

ANXIETY

Oxytocin reduces the physiological reaction to stressful situations. Lactating animals and humans exhibit a clearly decreased response to stressors. Lactating rats show an attenuated elevation in stress hormone in response to white noise, compared to virgins. Infusion of oxytocin in virgin rats also dampens the elevation of stress hormones in response to stress, suggesting that the increased oxytocin released during lactation may be acting to buffer the individual from environmental stressors. Oxytocin also has anxiolytic effects in behavioral assays of anxiety, such as the elevated plus maze.

Oxytocin has been reported to increase grooming of the upper body and genitals, and yawning in rats.

Oxytocin is not known to be directly involved in any psychiatric disorders; however, some interesting correlations have been reported. Autism is a disease characterized by, among other symptoms, deficits in social attachment in humans. One study has found that autistic children have decreased levels of plasma oxytocin compared to age-matched control children. Another study reported elevated oxytocin levels in some patients with obsessive-compulsive disorder (OCD). OCD is characterized by compulsions to perform certain acts repeatedly, such as hand-washing or other grooming behaviors.

SUGGESTED READING

Insel, T. R., Young, L., & Wang, Z. (1997). Central oxytocin and reproductive behaviours. *Reviews of Reproduction, 2,* 28–37.

Engelmann, M., Wotjak, C. T., Neumann, I., Ludwig, M., & Landgraf, R. (1996). Behavioral consequences of intracerebral vasopressin and oxytocin: Focus on learning and memory. *Neuroscience and Biobehavioral Reviews, 20,* 341–358.

Carter, C. S. (1998). Neuroendocrine perspectives on social attachment and love. *Psychoneuroendocrinology, 23,* 779–818.

Uvnäs-Moberg, K. (1998). Oxytocin may mediate the benefits of positive social interaction and emotions. *Psychoneuroendocrinology, 23,* 819–835.

L. J. YOUNG
Emory University

HORMONES AND BEHAVIOR

P

PAIN

Pain is defined by the International Association for the Study of Pain as "an unpleasant sensory and emotional experience associated with actual or potential tissue damage, or described in terms of such damage." Characterized as such, pain is a theoretical construct encompassing both the phenomenology of the sensory experience, with its associated cognitive, emotional, and behavioral components; and the neuronal substrates and processes that are proposed to subserve it. Nociception, on the other hand, is operationally defined as an empirically-derived response provoked by a tissue-damaging stimulus. Although many of our current concepts of pain perception are derived from the study of nociception, it should be noted that the study of pain cannot be reduced simply to the study of nociception. Nonetheless, in the past several decades, we have learned much, particularly with regard to the neurophysiology and neuropharmacology of nociception, which bear directly on our understanding of the subjective experience of pain and on our attempts to remedy the human misery associated with it.

The neural circuitry responsible for processing and projecting nociceptive information was the major focus of much of the initial research in this area. In this regard, it has been shown that while there is no single discrete anatomical pathway mediating pain, the conscious perception of pain is associated with activity in ascending somatosensory systems that, when preferentially stimulated, produce activation of specific brain areas relevant to pain perception (Willis, 1989). Similarly, descending pathways, termed "pain modulatory pathways," have been described as those that originate in the brain and project to the spinal cord, and that, when stimulated, produce inhibition of nociception (Fields & Basbaum, 1994). Thus, it ought to be possible to stimulate various structures in the nervous system and to modulate or diminish the pain signal and thereby alter the perception of pain; and, indeed, this is the case. This concept provides the scientific basis for the therapeutic treatment of chronic pain with electrophysiologic techniques, such as implantable stimulators, usually targeted at the spinal cord or deep brain regions (Krainick & Thoden, 1994; Young & Rinaldi, 1994).

Similarly, advances in the understanding of the neuropharmacology of nociception have yielded insights with direct application to the clinical management of pain. Morphine and other opiates have played an historic role as highly effective analgesics and continue to be mainstays of pain treatment today, particularly in the management of acute and malignant pain. In addition to the exogenously-administered opiate drugs, many endogenous opioid peptides have been discovered, several of which are involved in nociception, most notably in the spinal cord and in the periaqueductal gray region of the brain (Fields & Basbaum, 1994). In addition to the opioids, the important role that serotonin and norepinephrine neurotransmitter systems play in the descending pain modulatory pathways has led to the recognition that many drugs not previously characterized as analgesics have antinociceptive properties (Galer, 1995; Leijon & Boivie, 1991). Antidepressants and anticonvulsants, in particular, have been shown to have therapeutic benefits in the treatment of chronic pain, separately and apart from their other pharmacologic actions such as their effects on mood. These observations have expanded the therapeutic armamentarium significantly and increased the opportunities for pharmacologic therapy in the treatment of chronic pain. In fact, the ever expanding list of potentially useful drugs of different pharmacologic classes, with different mechanisms and sites of action within the nervous system, makes rational polypharmacy an option in the situation where monotherapy has proven inadequate.

One of the most provocative findings emanating from recent research is the observation that nociceptive circuitry is modifiable by experience (Hoffert, 1989). In this regard, both immediate and long-term changes indicative of neural plasticity have been demonstrated at all levels of the nervous system—central, peripheral, and autonomic. A potential role for neural plasticity in generating and maintaining pain has been suggested. Perhaps most striking in this regard is the demonstration that, under proper conditions, the preferred pathway subserving nociception can be changed to an alternate projection pathway, providing an explanation for the unpredictable results obtained with ablative procedures aimed at providing pain relief by destroying the ascending conduction pathways. Thus, it is likely that the phenomenon of neural plasticity itself may participate in the perpetuation of many forms of chronic pain, such as neuropathic pain, and that a better understanding of the mechanisms subserving plasticity may lead to better treatments for the most intractable forms of pain.

In parallel to the observations that neuronal circuitry can be modified by experience, and with an eye toward more immediate therapeutic application, is the fact that both operant and classical conditioning have been shown to be capable of modifying the association between nociception and pain perception (Fordyce, 1976; Hoffert, 1989). In the clinical setting, it is readily apparent that many psychological factors, such as prior experience, affective state, and situational context, all influence an individual's perception of pain and resultant behavior. In this regard, pain behavior, like any behavior, is subject to modification by the application of learning theory principles, and it should come as no surprise that successful pain management programs oftentimes include behavioral therapy as an adjunct to medical treatment. The goal in cognitive-behavioral therapy in the context of pain management is to decrease maladaptive attitudes and behaviors, increase activity, and decrease pain-associated anxiety and depression. Behavioral therapy is commonly used in conjunction with biofeedback and relaxation therapy, which help to make the individual mentally and physically relaxed and aware of the physiological processes that can be brought under voluntary control. As an adjunct to appropriate medical therapy, psychological interventions can enhance function and add much to the quality of life of an individual living with chronic pain.

In summary, it should be apparent from the foregoing that although a putative pathway carrying information about painful stimuli from the periphery to the brain was theorized to exist by Descartes as long ago as the 17th century, most of our current concepts regarding nociception and pain perception have been derived in only the past two decades. It is now clear that rather than being conveyed by a simple discrete neuroanatomical pathway, pain is conveyed and perceived by somewhat specialized systems that are mutable by experience, both on the cellular and behavioral levels. Similarly, although the treatment of pain has proved challenging, the notion that adequate pain relief in many conditions is unattainable has begun to give way to a multidisciplinary treatment approach that combines behavioral, pharmacologic, and physiologic treatment strategies in a rational way.

REFERENCES

Fields, H. L., & Basbaum, A. I. (1994). Central nervous system mechanisms of pain modulation. In P. D. Wall & R. Melzack (Eds.), *Textbook of pain* (3rd ed.). Edinburgh: Churchill Livingstone.

Fordyce, W. E. (1976). *Behavioral methods for chronic pain and illness.* St. Louis: C. V. Mosby.

Galer, B. S. (1995). Neuropathic pain of peripheral origin: Advances in pharmacologic treatment. *Neurology, 45* (Suppl. 9), S17–S25.

Hoffert, M. J. (1989). The neurophysiology of pain. In R. K. Portenoy (Ed.), *Neurologic clinics: Pain, mechanisms and syndromes.* Philadelphia: W. B. Saunders.

Krainick, J.-U., & Thoden, U. (1994). Spinal cord stimulation. In P. D. Wall & R. Melzack (Eds.), *Textbook of pain* (3rd ed.). Edinburgh: Churchill Livingstone.

Leijon, G., & Boivie, J. (1991). Pharmacological treatment of central pain. In K. L. Casey (Ed.), *Pain and the central nervous system.* New York: Raven.

Willis, W. D. (1989). The origin and destination of pathways involved in pain transmission. In P. D. Wall & R. Melzack (Eds.), *Textbook of pain* (2nd ed.). Edinburgh: Churchill Livingstone.

Young, R. F., & Rinaldi, P. C. (1994). Brain stimulation for relief of chronic pain. In P. D. Wall & R. Melzack (Eds.), *Textbook of pain* (3rd ed.). Edinburgh: Churchill Livingstone.

S. E. DeRossette

ENDORPHINS/EUKEPHALINS
PAIN: COPING STRATEGIES

PAIN: COPING STRATEGIES

From an early age, virtually everyone has experience with brief, relatively mild pain caused by cuts, insect bites, minor burns, bruises, toothaches, stomachaches, and routine medical and dental procedures. In addition to these relatively minor painful experiences, some individuals also will experience acute pain from major trauma, surgery, and invasive medical procedures. Others may even experience persistent pain such as chronic back pain, headaches, or pain secondary to chronic illness such as arthritis. Whenever a person is confronted with a painful situation, there are demands or requirements placed on that individual for certain responses. For example, a child receiving an injection must hold his or her arm still while a needle is inserted into the arm. Individuals spontaneously react in these situation and use various strategies to deal with pain and the demands of the situation.

COGNITIVE COPING STRATEGIES

Mental strategies or ways to use thoughts or imagination to cope with pain are usually called cognitive coping strategies. Distraction involves thinking about other things to divert attention from pain. Distraction can be internal such as imagining a pleasant scene or external such as focusing on a specific aspect of the environment. Reinterpreting pain sensations is imaging that the pain is something else such as numbness or a warm feeling. Calming self-statements refers to statements that one might tell oneself to provide comfort or encouragement (e.g., "I know I can handle this"). Ignoring pain is denying that the pain exists. Wishful thinking, praying, or hoping involves telling oneself that the pain will go away some day by faith, an act of God, or something magical. Fear and anger self-statements are statements one might tell oneself that promote fear or anger such as "I am afraid I am going to die." Catastrophizing refers to the use of negative self-statements and overly pessimistic thoughts about the future (e.g., "I can't deal with the pain"). Cognitive Restructuring refers to a process of recognizing negative thoughts and changing them to more realistic and rational thoughts.

BEHAVIORAL COPING STRATEGIES

Overt things that a person might actually do to cope with pain are called behavioral coping strategies. Increasing behavioral activity involves actively engaging in activities such as reading or visiting with friends to stay busy and unfocused on pain. Pacing activity involves taking regular planned rest breaks to avoid overdoing and experiencing increases in pain. Isolation refers to withdrawing from social contact to cope with pain. Resting refers to reclining in bed or on the couch. Relaxation involves attempting to decrease physiological arousal by remaining calm and relaxing muscles. Relaxation also is sometimes referred to as a physiological coping strategy, because it may include direct physical benefits.

Some coping strategies are effective and facilitate good adjustment, whereas other strategies are ineffective and may promote additional pain and suffering. Although intuitively certain strategies appear effective and others seem ineffective, empirical studies are needed to demonstrate the relationship between coping strategies and adjustment. This is especially important, because some strategies are effective in one situation but not the next, or for one person but not another.

CHRONIC PAIN

Most individuals probably begin to develop strategies for coping with pain from an early age and from exposure to relatively minor painful experiences. Yet the research in this area has progressed almost backward, with initial studies focusing on coping strategies used by chronic pain populations such as patients with chronic back pain or pain secondary to disease (e.g., arthritis and sickle-cell disease).

One of the first instruments designed to assess pain coping strategies systematically was the coping strategies questionnaire (CSQ) developed by Rosensteil and Keefe (1983). The CSQ measures the frequency with which individuals use various cognitive and behavioral coping strategies to deal with pain. Research using the CSQ with chronic pain patients has found that pain coping strategies can be reliably assessed and are predictive of pain, psychosocial adjustment, and functional capacity. Chronic pain patients who are high on catastrophizing and perceived inability to control and decrease pain have higher levels of depression and anxiety and overall physical impairment. Chronic pain patients who take a more active approach to managing pain by using a variety of cognitive and behavioral strategies have been found, in at least some studies, to have better functional adjustment (i.e., remain more active in work and social activities). These results have been replicated across several research laboratories and with several populations of chronic pain patients (chronic back pain, headaches, osteoarthritis, rheumatoid arthritis, and sickle-cell disease).

Taken together, the studies with chronic pain populations have generally concluded that although there seems to be some positive effects due to active coping efforts, negative thinking appears to be a more potent adverse influence on adjustment. Also, longitudinal studies have shown that coping strategies measured at one point in time are predictive of adjustment at follow-up. Thus maladaptive copers may continue to be at risk for future adjustment problems.

STABILITY AND CHANGE IN COPING STRATEGIES

Because of the significance of coping style in adjustment to chronic pain, researchers have attempted to determine whether the strategies used by individuals to cope with pain tend to be stable or change over time.

Two approaches have been used to study this issue. The first approach has been to compare coping strategies assessed during a baseline assessment to coping strategies measured at follow-up (e.g., 1 year later) with no systematic intervention occurring between the two assessment periods. Results have shown that without intervention, coping strategies are relatively stable over time, suggesting that some individuals persist in ineffective coping efforts. This stability in coping style appears to be unrelated to changes in disease severity. That is, although disease severity may lessen, this does not automatically translate into improved coping efforts, and even if there is an increase in disease severity over time, this does not necessarily mean that there will be further deterioration in adjustment. Although coping tends to be relatively stable, individuals who do become more and more negative in their thinking may experience even further deterioration in functional capacity and psychosocial adjustment over time.

The second approach to examining changes in pain coping strategies in chronic pain patients has been intervention studies. These studies have attempted to improve pain coping by training individuals in cognitive and behavioral pain coping skills. These studies have shown that with intervention, pain coping can be im-

proved, and improvements in pain coping will translate into improvements of psychosocial and functional adjustment. In one study, Keefe and colleagues (1990) trained a group of osteoarthritic knee pain patients to use relaxation, imagery, distraction, cognitive-restructuring, and pacing activity. Compared with a control group, trained subjects had lower levels of pain and psychological disability. Furthermore, individuals in the pain coping skills group who had greatest positive change in their coping strategy use (i.e., increased perceived effectiveness) had the most improvements in physical abilities. Similar findings have been reported across several types of pain problems.

Taken together, these results suggest that without intervention, the strategies an individual uses to cope with chronic pain are relatively stable over time. Change in pain coping is possible, however, and cognitive-behavioral approaches appear to provide an effective means to train individuals with various chronic pain problems to use more effective coping strategies.

ACUTE PAIN

Acute pain may result from events ranging from minor experiences to pain secondary to surgery or invasive procedures. As with chronic pain, when an individual is confronted with acute pain, he or she spontaneously reacts and uses various strategies to cope. Because acute pain situations are often also stressful and anxiety provoking, coping strategies used in these situations often include both strategies to deal with pain and to deal with anxiety.

Among the earliest attempts to examine coping strategies used in acute pain situations were studies that described preoperative and postoperative adults as either active or avoidant copers. Active copers were considered persons who approached the painful stimulus (i.e., surgery) by seeking out information, dealing with it rationally, and using cognitive strategies to cope. Avoidant copers (or those high on denial) were those who preferred not knowing information about their surgery or medical procedure and actually became anxious and experienced more pain when provided with information. Conclusions based on these early studies are limited however, because studies often attempted to categorize subjects into one of these patterns of coping based on informal interviews of questionable reliability.

More recently, systematic measures for assessing pain coping strategies in acute pain situations have been developed. Butler and colleagues developed the cognitive coping strategy inventory (CCSI) for use with postoperative pain populations. The inventory consists of subscales that are similar to dimensions found to be important in the measurement of chronic pain coping (i.e., catastrophizing, attention diversion, and imaginative inattention). Items, however, are more relevant to the acute pain experience. Research using the CCSI has found that this questionnaire is reliable and valid, and coping strategies used by postoperative patients to deal with pain are related to recovery. For example, adults who are high on catastrophizing have higher levels of pain and functional disability after surgery.

CHILDHOOD PAIN

The investigation of coping strategies in children confronting painful experiences is a relatively new area of research. In contrast to the work with adults in which questionnaires are primarily used to assess pain coping, most studies with children use interviews and observational methods to examine pain coping strategies.

Interview studies have used both open-ended and semistructured formats to gather information on how children experience pain and what they do in response to it. Ross and Ross (1984), e.g., interviewed a large sample of school-age children and asked them about the strategies that they used to cope with pain. Some of the children had chronic diseases such as sickle-cell disease or hemophilia, but most had no major medical problems and responded in regard to their coping with minor pain (e.g., cuts and bruises). Responding to open-ended questions, few children reported using self-initiated strategies to cope with pain. Of the small proportion that reported using strategies, distraction, thought stopping, and relaxation were among the more commonly reported strategies.

Observational studies of children coping with pain have focused primarily on children's reactions to painful procedures such as burn therapy or cancer-related treatments (e.g., venipunctures and bone marrow aspirations). In these studies, observers record the frequency of behaviors exhibited by the child such as crying, seeking social support, information seeking, and verbal and motor resistance. Although these behaviors are usually considered a measure of distress, some of the behaviors also can be conceptualized as coping efforts exhibited by the child to manage the pain and stress of the situation.

A few recent studies have found that coping strategies could be reliably assessed using questionnaires in school-age children. Using a modified version of the CSQ that was developed for adults, Gil and colleagues (1991) found that children who engaged in negative thinking and relied passively on strategies such as resting had more adjustment problems. This pattern of coping was associated with greater reductions in school and social activity, more frequent health care contacts, and more depression and anxiety. Children who took an active approach to managing pain by using a variety of cognitive and behavioral coping strategies were more active and required less frequent health care services.

The KIDCOPE developed by Spirito, Stark, and Williams (1988) is a questionnaire that has been designed specifically to assess coping strategies used by children to deal with stressful situations. The child identifies a recent stressful event to provide a context for responding to the coping strategy items. Given that pain is a common problem identified by children with medical problems, the KIDCOPE can be a useful instrument to assess pain coping strategies, especially because it is relatively brief and simple to complete.

Child Age and Sex

Although there appear to be almost no major differences in coping between girls and boys, differences in coping strategy use have been found across different ages. Older children tend to have more coping skills in their repertoire, especially more cognitive coping skills. Some data suggest that older children with chronic pain secondary to disease may rely more on negative thinking and passive coping strategies as they get older. By adolescence, some of their maladaptive coping patterns may become entrenched and resistant to change.

Parents

The relationship of the parent to coping and adjustment in children also has been a recent target of study. A number of studies have evaluated the effects of parent presence versus absence on child coping during painful procedures. Most of these studies have shown that although children exhibit less overt distress when their parents are absent, they may, physiologically and psychologically disturbed by their parents' absence and merely inhibiting their behavioral reaction. Thus, rather than removing the parents, researchers may need to investigate which behaviors of the parent are related to effective versus ineffective coping by children during painful procedures.

Coping strategies used by parents to cope with their own (the parent's) pain also may be related to adjustment in children with pain problems. One study (Gil et al., 1991) found that parents who took an active approach to managing their own pain had children who remained more active during episodes of sickle-cell pain. Furthermore, there appear to be significant relationships between pain coping strategies in parents and in their children, suggesting that children might learn how to cope with pain, in part, by observing their parents reactions.

CLINICAL IMPLICATIONS

Coping skills training is now a regular part of most comprehensive approaches to chronic pain management. Multidisciplinary pain programs now often include groups or individual sessions in which patients are trained to use active coping skills and cognitive restructuring techniques to manage pain. Although this type of approach is not routine for the management of most acute pain problems, there is a growing recognition for the need to train coping strategies to those undergoing medical procedures. Perhaps the area that has received the most attention has been in preparing children for surgery or for repeated invasive medical procedures such as burn therapy or cancer-related treatments. Although this is usually not done until after the child has developed a significant problem coping with pain, some clinicians are beginning to recognize the need to help prepare children to cope with painful experiences before they become oversensitized.

REFERENCES

Gil, K. M., Williams, D. A., Thompson, R. J., & Kinney, T. R. (1991). Sickle cell disease in children and adolescents: The relation of child and parent pain coping strategies to adjustment. *Journal of Pediatric Psychology, 16,* 643–663.

Keefe, F. J., Caldwell, D. S., Williams, D. A., Gil, K. M., Mitchell, D., Robertson, C., Martinez, S., Nunley, J., Beckham, J., & Helms, M. (1990). Pain coping skills training in the management of osteoarthritic knee pain: A comparative study. *Behavior Therapy, 21,* 49–62.

Rosenstiel, A. K., & Keefe, F. J. (1983). The use of coping strategies in low back pain patients: Relationship to patient characteristics and current adjustment. *Pain, 17,* 33–40.

Ross, D. M., & Ross, S. A. (1984). Childhood pain: The school-aged child's viewpoint. *Pain, 20,* 179–191.

Spirito, A., Stark, L. J., & Williams, C. (1988). Development of a brief coping checklist for use with pediatric populations. *Journal of Pediatric Psychology, 13*, 555–574.

SUGGESTED READING

Gil, K. M. (1984). Coping with invasive medical procedures: A descriptive model. *Clinical Psychology Review, 4*, 339–362.

Peterson, L. (1989). Coping by children undergoing stressful medical procedures: Some conceptual, methodological, and therapeutic issues. *Journal of Consulting and Clinical Psychology, 57*, 380–387.

K. M. GIL
University of North Carolina at Chapel Hill

FEAR
INTERNALIZATION
PAIN

PANIC DISORDER

EPIDEMIOLOGY AND COURSE OF PANIC DISORDER

Panic disorder (PD; with and without agoraphobia) is a debilitating condition with a lifetime prevalence of approximately 1.5% (American Psychiatric Association, 1994). Studies have demonstrated that this prevalence rate is relatively consistent throughout the world. Approximately twice as many women as men suffer from PD. Although PD typically first strikes between late adolescence and the mid-30s, it can also begin in childhood and in later life. While data on the course of PD are lacking, PD appears to be a chronic condition that waxes and wanes in severity. Consequences of PD include feelings of poor physical and emotional health, impaired social functioning, financial dependency, and increased use of health and hospital emergency services.

ASSESSMENT OF PANIC DISORDER

As defined in the fourth edition of the Diagnostic and Statistical Manual of Mental Disorders (American Psychiatric Association, 1994), the essential feature of PD is the experience of recurrent, unexpected panic attacks. A panic attack is defined as a discrete period of intense fear or discomfort that develops abruptly, reaches a peak within ten minutes and is accompanied by at least four of the following thirteen symptoms: shortness of breath, dizziness, palpitations, trembling, sweating, choking sensation, nausea/abdominal distress, depersonalization, paresthesias (numbness/tingling), flushes/chills, chest pain, fear of dying, fear of going crazy, or doing something uncontrolled. To warrant the diagnosis of PD, an individual must experience at least two unexpected panic attacks followed by at least one month of concern about having another panic attack. The frequency of attacks varies widely and ranges from several attacks each day to only a handful of attacks per year.

The vast majority of PD patients seeking treatment present with agoraphobia. Agoraphobia is the experience of anxiety in situations where escape might be difficult or where help may not be immediately available should a panic attack occur. Common agoraphobic situations include airplanes, buses, trains, elevators, being alone, or being in a crowd. As a result of the anxiety experienced in these situations, individuals often develop phobic avoidance resulting in a constricted lifestyle. The severity of agoraphobia ranges from mild to severe.

NEUROBIOLOGY OF PANIC DISORDER

Biological theorists conceptualize PD as a psychiatric condition that stems from an underlying biological dysfunction.

Genetics

One line of evidence for a biological etiology of PD comes from studies that demonstrate that panic tends to run in families. These studies have found that approximately one-half of all PD patients have at least one relative with PD, first-degree relatives of PD patients are approximately five times more likely to develop PD than first-degree relatives of normal controls, and that PD and agoraphobia with panic attacks are more than five times as frequent in monozygotic twins than in dizygotic co-twins of patients with PD (Woodman & Crowe, 1995). However, because of possible confounds caused by environmental influences, other studies are needed to provide further evidence for a genetic etiology of PD.

Neurotransmitter Theories

Biological theorists attempt to provide an indirect link between PD and specific neurotransmitter systems by assessing the effects of drugs on these neurotransmitter systems. Specifically, they attempt to demonstrate that drugs used to treat panic increase availability of a specific neurotransmitter or its metabolite, while drugs that induce panic decrease availability of the same neurotransmitter. An association may also be established by demonstrating that antipanic drugs decrease availability of a specific neurotransmitter while panic-provoking drugs increase availability of the same neurotransmitter. Neurotransmitters commonly implicated in the etiology of PD include norepinephrine, serotonin, and gamma-aminobutyric acid (GABA; Papp, Coplan, & Gorman, 1992).

Respiratory Physiology Theories

Respiratory physiology theories, another source of support for a biological etiology of PD, propose that panic attacks may be caused by a dysfunctional respiratory system. Several theories suggest that hyperventilation may be causally related to panic attacks. During hyperventilation, more carbon dioxide is exhaled than produced, thus lowering carbon dioxide levels in the body. To compensate for the reduction in respiratory rate caused by hyperventilation, patients experience a host of symptoms including shortness of breath, dizziness, trembling, and palpitations. Hyperventilation theorists propose that PD patients are chronic hyperventilators who acutely increase breathing during stress, leading to episodes of panic. An alternative hyperventilation model suggests that the fear of having a panic attack gives rise to somatic symptoms, which lead to increased fear, hyperventilation, and so on, until a full-blown panic attack occurs. Though plausible, neither of these theories is sufficient to fully account for the etiology of PD.

A more recent formulation by Klein and colleagues proposes that the essential disturbance in PD may be a dysfunctional suffocation monitor (Klein, 1993). Through evolution, a highly sensitive "alarm system" has developed to detect high carbon dioxide levels that indicate that the organism is in danger of suffocation. Klein suggests that in PD patients, this suffocation threshold is pathologically lowered. The PD patient's suffocation monitor is thus hypersensitive to carbon dioxide. As a result, the brain's suffocation monitor incorrectly signals a lack of oxygen, and thus triggers a false suffocation alarm. He hypothesizes that since PD patients believe they are suffocating, they experience shortness of breath and thus begin hyperventilating in order to keep carbon dioxide levels well below the suffocation threshold. Empirical support for carbon dioxide hypersensitivity in PD has come from studies that suggest that following carbon dioxide inhalation, patients with PD exhibit a more rapid increase in respiration than normal controls and other psychiatric patients. However, the false suffocation alarm hypothesis is yet to be empirically tested.

PSYCHOLOGICAL THEORIES OF PANIC DISORDER

Several proposed psychological theories of PD are supported by empirical data. This suggests that psychological factors are central to the etiology and maintenance of PD. In fact, many biological findings can be explained within these psychological theories. Findings that (a) psychological interventions alleviate panic attacks; (b) psychological treatments block laboratory-provoked attacks; and (c) psychological factors mediate laboratory-provoked attacks suggest that any valid theory of PD must include both biological and psychological factors.

Psychodynamic Models

According to Freud's early formulation, pathologic anxiety occurs when unacceptable libidinal thoughts and desires break through into consciousness. In a subsequent formulation, Freud suggested that anxiety leads to repression instead of the other way around. A panic attack, then, is a neurotic symptom that results when memories of past events are inadequately repressed. Freud also suggested that the phobic behavior exhibited by anxious patients may result from their fear of having panic attacks.

Modern psychoanalytic theorists suggest that panic attacks develop when defense mechanisms are unable to control unconscious fantasies linked to infantile fears. A newer psychodynamic formulation proposes that PD is an interaction between a patient's temperament and environmental factors. According to this model, PD patients enter the world with an inborn physiologic reactivity that may develop into a psychological vulnerability for PD. This psychological vulnerability may be influenced by such things as a decrease in feelings of safety, physiological changes associated with feelings of loss of control, or an increase in negative emotions such as anxiety, anger, or shame; and this vulnerability may ultimately result in an initial panic attack.

Although psychodynamic formulations are interesting, there is a lack of research data to validate these proposed concepts. Since many of these theories propose unconscious etiologies for PD, the proposed hypotheses may be difficult to test directly. Therefore, researchers need to develop measures to test these concepts without presuming their existence solely on the presence or absence of panic symptoms.

The Cognitive Model

The cognitive model of PD proposes that panic attacks occur when individuals perceive certain somatic sensations as dangerous and interpret them to mean that they are about to experience sudden, imminent disaster (Clark, 1986). For example, individuals may develop a panic attack if they misinterpret heart palpitations as signaling an impending heart attack. The vicious cycle culminating in a panic attack begins when a stimulus perceived as threatening creates feelings of apprehension. If the somatic sensations that accompany this state of apprehension are catastrophically misinterpreted, the individual experiences a further increase in apprehension, elevated somatic sensations, and so on, until a full-blown panic attack occurs.

PD patients report having thoughts of imminent danger during their panic attacks and also report that these thoughts typically occur after they notice specific bodily sensations. These facts provide convincing support for the cognitive model of panic disorder. Other evidence in support of this model is provided by the finding that, while laboratory-provoked attacks lead to similar physiological sensations in PD patients and normal controls, only PD patients who catastrophically misinterpret these sensations go on to develop panic attacks. Furthermore, only patients who develop panic attacks following laboratory administration of a panic-inducing substance report fears of going crazy or losing control. Further support for the cognitive model can be derived from studies demonstrating that panic attacks can be alleviated with cognitive techniques that challenge catastrophic misinterpretations.

Critics contend that the cognitive model does not explain why PD patients continue to misinterpret these somatic sensations despite the fact that their catastrophic predictions do not come true. However, since PD patients avoid or escape situations in which panic attacks are likely to occur, they may never truly learn that their panic attacks will not lead to catastrophes.

TREATMENT OF PANIC DISORDER

Psychotherapy, specifically cognitive-behavioral therapy (CBT), and pharmacotherapy have both been shown to be effective treatments for PD (Wolfe & Maser, 1994). CBT consists of a number of treatment elements including psychoeducation, monitoring of panic, cognitive restructuring, anxiety management skills training, and in vivo exposure. Support for the efficacy of CBT for PD treatment is provided by extensive studies yielding high-quality data.

Four classes of medications have been shown to be effective in the treatment of PD. These medications are selective serotonin reuptake inhibitors, tricyclic antidepressants, benzodiazepines, and monoamine oxidase inhibitors. Studies demonstrate that medications from all four classes have similar efficacy. The choice of medication for a patient depends on a consideration of possible side effects, medication cost, and other clinical circumstances.

Studies that examine the effectiveness of combining CBT and antipanic medication compared to each modality separately have thus far been inconclusive. However, conventional clinical wisdom implies that a combination is at least equivalent to either modality alone.

REFERENCES

American Psychiatric Association. (1994). *Diagnostic and statistical manual of mental disorders* (4th ed.). Washington, DC: Author.

Clark, D. M. (1986). A cognitive approach to panic. *Behaviour Research and Therapy, 24,* 461–171.

Klein, D. F. (1993). False suffocation alarms, spontaneous panics, and related conditions. *Archives of General Psychiatry, 50,* 306–317.

Papp, L. A., Coplan, J., & Gorman, J. M. (1992). Neurobiology of anxiety. In A. Tasman & M. B. Riba (Eds.), *Review of psychiatry,* (Vol. 11, pp. 307–322). Washington, DC: American Psychiatric Association Press.

Wolfe, B. E., & Maser, J. D. (Eds.). (1994). *Treatment of panic disorder: A consensus development conference.* Washington, DC: American Psychiatric Association Press.

Woodman, C. L., & Crowe, R. R. (1995). The genetics of panic disorder. In G. Asnis & H. M. van Praag (Eds.), *Panic disorder: Clinical, biological, and treatment aspects* (pp. 66–79). New York: Wiley.

W. SANDERSON
K. L. MULLER
Rutgers University

ANXIETY
CATHARSIS
FEAR
LIFE EVENTS

PARADIGMS

Paradigms are rules or regulations that set boundaries and direct actions toward accomplishing a goal successfully (Barker, 1992, p. 32). Kuhn (1970), a scientific historian, focused the attention of the scientific world on paradigms; he believed paradigms fit only the physical scientific world. Paradigms in action amount to a basic set of ideas or concepts that direct an individual's behavior, thereby setting parameters for the individual's standard way of working, or progressing toward a goal. This pattern becomes an individual's way of doing something or solving a problem.

Paradigms are found in every culture. Norms within every culture govern the boundaries of accepted behavior and become the proper way of doing things. When pattern changes occur, thus deviating from the established operating norms of any given situa-tion, Barker (1992, p. 37) referred to this as "a paradigm shift . . . a change to a new game, a new set of rules."

In every generation, changes have been initiated by nonconformists who took risks to make paradigm shifts, because paradigms equal conformity and paradigm shifts create confusion. A simple example of a paradigm shift is when a person requests pie instead of the usual cake for a birthday; breaking from the custom of a birthday cake is a paradigm shift.

Within Western culture, many paradigm shifts have occurred. During the early 1900s, the Wright brothers created a paradigm shift with their invention of the airplane. Traditionalists believed that if God wanted humans to fly, we would have wings. Paradigm shifts led to vast changes in communications after the 1940s. Telephones went from cranking the box on a party line to single-party lines, worldwide calling, car phones, cellular phones, cordless phones, 800 numbers, and so forth. Each improvement marked a paradigm shift. Subsets of the paradigm concept include a range from challengeable to unchallengeable, from theories, models, and standards to frames of reference, ideologies, rituals, and compulsions (Barker, 1992, p. 35).

FAMILY INSTITUTION

Before the 1940s, a small percentage of women were in the job market, mostly doing office-type work. The basic paradigm before World War II was that women belonged at home with the children and the men were the breadwinners. At the time, this was an acceptable way of life. By 1950, a paradigm shift occurred. More women were entering the professional world. Many women entered the labor market so the family could have "extras," but later the second income became a necessity to survive the economic crunch.

RELIGION

Many changes have taken place in religious practices, for example, in the Roman Catholic Church since Vatican II. Some changes were saying the Mass in the vernacular, the concept of healing of reconciliation, one hour of fasting before receiving communion, fewer statues, face-to-face confession, and increased lay ministries. Such changes met considerable resistance. Ritzer (1975), in his interpretation of Kuhn's original work, stated that "the paradigm that emerges victorious is the one that is able to win the most converts." As new concepts gain more followers, the resistance to paradigm changes slows down and acceptance emerges.

COGNITIVE DEVELOPMENT

Some presently accepted theories of cognitive growth and development that were originally paradigmatic are those by Erik Erikson, Sigmund Freud, Jean Piaget, and Lev Vygotsky. Another paradigm concerning intelligence is mentioned by Woolfolk, A. E. (1993, pp. 111–116), based on the theories of Alfred Binet, Charles Spearman, L. L. Thurstone, J. P. Guilford, Howard Gardner, Robert Sternberg, and many more. Each presents guidelines and boundaries in methodology, standards, models, and procedures, and each specialty is under the whole umbrella of intelligence.

EDUCATION

As the needs of the society change, the educational process must change with it, thereby creating a paradigm shift. According to Drucker (1989), traditional education was rather terminal. However, today, because of continuing rapid change in technology, education cannot terminate at the end of degree completion. Continuing education is required because of paradigm shifts. Every employing institution becomes teacher and an educational facility as well as a place of employment. Drucker (1989, p. 252) stated, "That major changes are ahead for schools and education is certain—the knowledge will demand them and the new learning theories and technologies will trigger them."

TECHNOLOGY

The word *paradigm* is used in all aspects of life because all facets of life have certain boundaries or parameters. Paradigms related to technology are changing and being accepted rapidly in this highly technological age. Frequently, the changes are so rapid that the paradigm effect does not fully occur because new paradigms are continually being adopted. Our society, as well as the rest of the world, has come a long way from the days of Thomas S. Kuhn's original concept of paradigms.

Naisbitt (1984) stated that our lives are being transformed by the acceptance of the paradigm shift as well as by the necessity of change in order to survive as a social institution. The paradigm shift indirectly mentioned by Naisbitt has taken place much more rapidly than anticipated because of the rapid advancements in technology. Peters (1988, p. 518) stated that "integrity has been the hallmark of the superior organization through the ages . . . today's accelerating uncertainty gives the issue new importance."

CONCLUSION

Barker (1992, p. 36) stated, "the interrelationship of all these paradigms is crucial to the success and longevity of any culture or organization." Some paradigms are accepted more rapidly than others. If the need is great for a change, the paradigm shift will emerge quickly.

Paradigm shifts have occurred throughout the centuries, since the beginning of humankind. As new concepts and ideas are born, paradigm shifts will continue to occur in order to meet human needs.

REFERENCES

Barker, J. A. (1990). *Future edge.* New York: William Morrow.

Drucker, Peter F. (1989). *The new realities.* New York: Harper & Row.

Kuhn, T. S. (1970). *The structure of scientific revolution.* Chicago: University of Chicago Press.

Naisbitt, J. (1984). *Megatrends.* New York: W. A. Warner Communication Company.

Peters, T. (1988). *Thriving on chaos.* New York: Alfred A. Knopp.

Ritzer, G. (1975). *Society: A multiple paradigm science.* Boston: Allyn & Bacon.

Woolfolk, A. E. (1993). *Educational psychology.* Boston: Allyn & Bacon.

P. A. CARICH
University of Missouri, St. Louis

INFORMATION PROCESSING

PARADOXICAL COLD OR WARMTH

Chronic cold agglutinin disease is an unusual form of autoimmune hemolytic anemia, characterised by severe acrocyanosis and exacerbation of haemolysis during cold exposure. The exact prevalence of the disease in various parts of the world is not known, but in Scandinavia there are probably 12 to 15 cases per million (Berentsen, Bø, Shammas, Myking, & Ulvestad, 1997).

The autoantibodies of chronic cold agglutinin disease are monoclonal IgM molecules directed against erythrocyte surface antigens. They react with highest affinity at low temperatures (0–4°C) and are therefore called cold agglutinins. However, they may also react at temperatures up to 37°C, depending on the antibody thermal amplitude. As the temperature in the peripheral circulation of the skin decreases during cold exposure, cold agglutinins bind to the erythrocytes and thereby induce acrocyanosis and other clinical symptoms of intravascular hemagglutination. Cold agglutinins are also able to bind and activate complement, a multimolecular system with cytolytic capacity. Due to a concomitant binding and activation of complement during cold agglutinin's binding to erythrocytes, the patients also suffer from anemia. The anemia is of hemolytic type and is caused by intravascular complement-mediated hemolysis.

In most patients with chronic cold agglutinin disease, the condition was previously termed "idiopathic" or "primary," to distinguish it from the rare, so-called secondary cases in which lymphoma could be identified as the cause of the autoimmune phenomenon. However, evidence has been provided that most, if not all, idiopathic or primary cases represent a clonal B-cell lymphoproliferative disease (Berentsen et al., 1997). This clonal lymphoproliferation can be demonstrated by flow-cytometric immunophenotyping in almost all cases and by histomorphological examination of the bone marrow biopsy in about half of the patients. The clonal, premalignant, or low-grade malignant B lymphocytes produce a monoclonal IgM identical to the cold agglutinin responsible for the hemolysis and clinical symptoms.

Recently, we described a patient with classic chronic cold agglutinin disease who experienced paradoxical hemolytic episodes at elevated body temperatures (Ulvestad, 1998). His hemolytic episodes were initially associated with cold exposure, but with advancing disease cold-induced hemolysis ceased and was replaced by a hemolytic disposition during febrile infections. Following this observation, we looked for similar phenomena in a series of 15 patients with chronic cold agglutinin disease. By examining their medical records we found that five of them had a paradoxical increase in hemolysis during febrile infections (Berentsen et al., 1997; Ulvestad, Berentsen, Bø, & Shammas, in press).

Preliminary clinical and experimental studies seem to provide an explanation to this paradoxical cold- and warmth-induction of hemolysis in patients with chronic cold agglutinin disease (Ulvestad, 1998; Ulvestad et al., 1999). In our series of 15 patients, serum levels of the complement fraction C3 was decreased in 9 patients and C4 was decreased in 11 patients. The C4 was below detection level in 7 patients, including the 5 patients who had experienced paradoxical hemolysis according to their medical records. Total hemolytic activity (CH50) was measured to assess the functional capacity of the patient's complement system to lyse erythrocytes. Six patients had a reduced CH50. After the serum of one complement-depleted patient was reconstituted with complement from donor serum, an increased hemolytic activity was observed.

These findings indicate that the binding of monoclonal cold agglutinin to the patient's erythrocytes and the subsequent complement binding and activation result in a chronic complement depletion in at least some of the patients. The complement depletion is probably a limiting factor to the cold-induced, complement-mediated hemolysis, and can in a few patients lead to a decrease in cold-induced hemolysis with advancing disease. During febrile infection, production of complement will be induced as part of the so-called acute phase-response. The increased production of complement is probably responsible for the paradoxical exacerbation of hemolysis during febrile illness in patients with chronic cold agglutinin disease.

Serum complement concentrations will also increase if patients with cold agglutinin disease are transfused with plasma-containing blood products. It may therefore be still more important in these patients than in others that transfusions, when necessary, are given as blood component therapy to avoid infusion of allogenic plasma.

REFERENCES

Berentsen, S., Bø, K., Shammas, F. V., Myking, A. O., & Ulvestad, E. (1997). Chronic cold agglutinin disease of the "idiopathic" type is a premalignant or low-grade malignant lymphoproliferative disease. *APMIS, 105,* 354–362.

Ulvestad, E. (1998). Paradoxical haemolysis in a patient with cold agglutinin disease. *European Journal of Haematology, 60,* 93–100.

Ulvestad, E., Berentsen, S., Bø, K., & Shammas, F. V. (in press). On the clinical immunology of chronic cold agglutinin disease. *European Journal of Haematology.*

S. Berentsen
E. Ulvestad

PARADOXICAL INTERVENTION

Paradoxical interventions are psychotherapeutic tactics that seem to contradict the goals they are designed to achieve. For example, a therapist may prescribe that clients have an unwanted symptom deliberately or restrain them from changing. In the classic definition of a therapeutic double-bind or paradox, "an injunction is so structured that it (a) reinforces the behavior the patient expects to be changed, (b) implies that this reinforcement is the vehicle of change, and (c) thereby creates a paradox because the patient is told to change by remaining unchanged" (Watzlawick, Beavin, and Jackson, 1967, p. 241).

References to resolving problems with paradoxical interventions appear as early as the eighteenth century. In this century, Dunlap applied the technique of "negative practice" to problems such as stammering and enuresis. Rosen (1953), through "direct psychoanalysis," encouraged psychiatric patients to engage in aspects of their psychosis in order to prevent relapse, and Frankl (1960) used paradoxical intention to help his patients revise the meaning of their symptoms. The most influential literature on therapeutic paradox, however, derives from Bateson's 1952–1962 project on communication. Bateson, Jackson, Haley, Weakland, and others explored the role of paradoxical "double-bind" communications in resolving as well as creating problems. Influenced by systemic/cybernetic ideas and by the work of master-hypnotist Milton Erickson, descendants of the Bateson project such as Haley, Weakland, Watzlawick, Fisch, and Selvini-Palazzoli and colleagues went on in the 1970s to develop family therapy models with paradox as a central feature. Around the same time, Frankl's paradoxical intention technique was adopted by behavior therapists who demonstrated its usefulness with specific symptoms such as insomnia, anxiety, urinary retention, and obsessions.

Although paradoxical interventions have been associated historically with particular theoretical frameworks, the current literature tends to treat them as techniques that can be applied and explained apart from the models in which they were developed. Indeed, paradoxical interventions cut across theoretical boundaries insofar as paradoxical elements can be found in virtually all schools of psychotherapy (Seltzer, 1986). Nevertheless, there are striking differences in how therapists of different theoretical orientations use paradoxical interventions. In comparing cognitive-behavioral and strategic-systemic approaches—the two frameworks most akin to therapeutic paradox—one finds that behavior therapists use "paradoxical intention" to interrupt within-person exacerbation cycles, while strategic-systems therapists use a wider variety of paradoxical interventions and more often focus on between-person (family) interaction. Another difference is that behavior therapists make their rationale explicit, while strategic therapists typically do not. In behavioral applications of paradoxical intention, for example, the therapist teaches the client to adopt a paradoxical attitude, explaining, for example, how the client's intention to force sleep is actually exacerbating the problem, and why a paradoxical intention to stay awake might make sleep come easier. The *intention* here is clearly the client's, not the therapist's, and the client is expected to do (or at least try to do) what he or she is told. In strategic applications, however, the therapist sometimes expects a patient or family to do the opposite of what is proposed, and in this sense the therapist's intention is paradoxical. In contrast to the openly shared, educational rationale of a behavior therapist, strategic therapists attempt to maximize compliance (or defiance) by framing suggestions in a manner consistent (or deliberately inconsistent) with the clients' own idiosyncratic world view (Fisch, Weakland, & Segal, 1982).

TYPES AND APPLICATIONS

Several schemes for classifying paradoxical interventions have been offered in the literature (Rohrbaugh, Tennen, Press, & White, 1981; Seltzer, 1986). Of the many types, the most commonly used are symptom prescription and restraint from change. Variations of these two techniques—asking clients to engage in the behavior they wish to eliminate or restraining them from changing—have been applied in both individual and family therapy. However, nearly all controlled studies of therapeutic paradox have involved symptom prescriptions with individuals. Based on these studies, Shoham-Salomon & Rosenthal (1987, see below) reported that outcome largely depends on how these interventions are administered.

Most paradoxical interventions involve some combination of prescribing, reframing, and positioning. *Prescribing* means telling people what to do (giving tasks, suggestions, and so on) either directly or indirectly. For example, a therapist might ask a patient to have a panic attack deliberately or prescribe that an overinvolved grandmother take full responsibility for a misbehaving child, expecting she will back off and let the mother take charge. *Reframing* involves redefining the meaning of events or behavior in a way that makes change more possible. Although reframing resembles interpretation, its goal is to provoke change rather than provide insight—and the accuracy of redefinition is less important than its impact. Thus, Haley described a case in which a wife became more sexually responsive after her frigidity was reframed as a way of protecting the husband from the full force of her sexuality, and Selvini-Palazzoli, Cecchin, Prata, and Boscolo (1978) pioneered the use of "positive connotation," a technique for changing dysfunctional family patterns by ascribing noble intentions to both the identified patient's symptom and the behaviors of family members that support it. *Positioning* is a term for altering the therapist's own role, or potential role, in a problem-maintaining system. Prescribing, reframing, and positioning are interwoven, with each at least implicit in any paradoxical strategy or intervention. Thus, prescribing that someone be deliberately anxious reframes an involuntary symptom as controllable; reframing problem behavior as a protective sacrifice carries an implicit (paradoxical) prescription not to change; and warning against dangers of improvement sometimes helps reverse or neutralize a therapist's role in a problem cycle.

Applications of paradox tend to be most varied and complex in marital and family therapy. In one case, where the focus was on reversing family members' well-intentioned but self-defeating attempt to solve a problem, a therapy team coached the relatives of depressed stroke victim to encourage him by discouraging him (Fisch et al., 1982). In another case, a therapist asked a depressed husband to pretend to be depressed and asked his wife to try to find out if he was really feeling that way. For extreme marital stuckness, a therapist may recommend paradoxical interventions such as prescribing indecision about whether a couple should separate. The most dramatic examples of paradox with families come from the early work of the Milan team (Selvini-Palazzoli et al., 1978). After complimenting a severely obsessional young woman and her parents for protecting each other from the sadness associated with the death of a family member several years earlier, the team prescribed that the family meet each night to discuss their loss and suggested that the young woman behave symptomatically whenever her parents appeared distraught.

Clinical reports describe successful applications of paradoxical intervention with a wide variety of problems including anxiety, depression, phobia, insomnia, obsessive-compulsive disorder, headaches, asthma, encopresis, enuresis, blushing, tics, psychosomatic symptoms, procrastination, eating disorders, child and adolescent conduct problems, marital and family problems, pain, work and school problems, and psychotic behavior (Seltzer, 1986). Paradoxical strategies appear least applicable in situations of crisis or extreme instability, such as acute decompensation, grief reactions, domestic violence, suicide attempts, or loss of a job, but there have been too few controlled studies to list indications and contraindications with any degree of certainty.

While some authors advocate reserving paradoxical approaches for difficult situations where more straightforward methods have not succeeded or are unlikely to succeed, paradoxical strategies are too diverse for this to make sense as a blanket rule. For example, paradoxical symptom prescription could reasonably be a first line of approach for involuntary symptoms like insomnia that to some extent are maintained by attempts to stave them off.

CHANGE PROCESSES

Explanations of how and why paradoxical interventions work are as diverse as the interventions themselves. Behavioral, cognitive, and motivational processes—alone and in combination—have been proposed to explain change in both individuals and families. At the individual level, a behavioral account of why symptom prescription helps involuntary problems such as insomnia, anxiety, and obsessive thinking is that, by attempting to have the problem, a patient cannot continue in usual ways of trying to prevent it, thus breaking an exacerbation cycle. Cognitive explanations of the same phenomena emphasize that symptom prescription redefines the uncontrollable as controllable, decontextualizes the problem, and in a fundamental way alters the symptom's meaning. A third, rather different change mechanism has been suggested for situations where clients appear to defy or oppose a therapist's directive. Here the client presumably rebels to reduce psychological reactance, a hypothetical motive state aroused by threats to perceived behavioral freedom (Brehm & Brehm, 1981).

Not surprisingly, explanations of how paradoxical interventions promote change at the family-systems level are more diverse and more abstract. Some paradoxical interventions are assumed to interrupt problem-maintaining interaction cycles between people (Fisch et al., 1982), and some, like positive connotation, presumably operate by introducing information into the system or by changing the meaning of the symptom and the family interaction that supports it (Selvini-Palazzoli et al., 1978). Motivational explanations of systems-level change suggest that paradoxical interventions work by activating relational dynamics such as "compression" and "recoil" (Stanton, 1984) or by creating disequilibrium among systemic forces aligned for and against change (Hoffman, 1981).

Some theories of paradoxical intervention attempt to combine or integrate various change processes. For example, Rohrbaugh and colleagues (1981) proposed a compliance-defiance model distinguishing two types of paradoxical interventions. Compliance-based symptom prescription is indicated (a) when an "unfree" (involuntary) symptom like insomnia is maintained by attempts to stave it off, and (b) when the potential for reactance is low (i.e., when clients are unlikely to react against attempts to influence them). Defiance-based interventions, on the other hand, work because people change by rebelling. These are indicated when clients view the target behavior as relatively "free" (voluntary) and when the potential for reactance is high.

Another model of therapeutic paradox originally proposed by Watzlawick et al. (1967) incorporates behavioral and cognitive explanations of change. The therapeutic double-bind—a directive to deliberately engage in involuntary symptomatic behavior—is a mirror image of the pathogenic "be spontaneous" paradox. The only way to obey such a directive is by disobeying it. According to Watzlawick et al. (1967), two possible consequences follow: If the client is not able to produce the symptom on demand, he or she will show less of the problem; if the client does produce the symptom, it will be with a greater sense of mastery and control. In this way clients are "changed if they do and changed if they don't." If the symptomatic behavior itself does not change, at least the client's perception of it changes—and as Raskin and Klein put it, behaviors over which one has control might be sins, but they are not neurotic complaints. Studies by Shoham-Salomon and her colleagues provide empirical support for this "two paths to change" model.

EFFICACY

When paradoxical interventions are part of a broader therapeutic strategy, their specific contribution to clinical outcome is difficult to evaluate. Nevertheless, dramatic and seemingly enduring effects on individuals and families have been documented in numerous clinical reports and case studies and in qualitative literature reviews (Seltzer, 1986).

Controlled experimental studies of paradoxical interventions with individual clients have yielded mixed results. Two independent meta-analytic reviews (Hill, 1987; Shoham-Salomon & Rosenthal, 1987) indicate that paradoxical interventions compared favorably to no-treatment control conditions, but comparisons to nonparadoxical treatments have been equivocal. Whereas Hill's (1987) meta-analysis found paradox to be superior, Shoham-Salomon and Rosenthal (1987) found that the overall effect of paradoxical interventions was as large (but no larger than) the average effect size of psychotherapy in general. Research also suggests that some forms of paradoxical intervention may be more effective than others. In Shoham-Salomon and Rosenthal's (1987) meta-analysis, the effect sizes of two positively connoted symptom prescriptions were significantly greater than those of other, nonparadoxical treatments or of symptom prescriptions that did not include a positive frame. Paradoxical interventions were most effective when the therapist either reframed the symptom positively before prescribing it (for example, praising a depressed client's tolerance for solitude or her willingness to sacrifice for the good of others), or explained the paradoxical intention (exacerbation-cycle) rationale in a way that defined the client as not "sick" but "stuck." In a recent study directly testing the importance of positive connotation, Akillas and Efran found that socially anxious men improved more when a prescription to be anxious was presented with a positive

frame (rationale) than when it was not. This supports the view that symptom prescriptions work best when they aim to alter the meaning a client attributes to the symptom.

Research on paradoxical interventions is not without limitations. For example, meta-analytic results must be interpreted cautiously because stringent inclusion criteria may compromise the clinical or ecological validity of conclusions. Moreover, as noted above, research in this area has focused almost exclusively on symptom prescription with individuals. There have been too few controlled studies to summarize the efficacy of other forms of therapeutic paradox (restraint from change, for example) or of applications with interactional systems and families.

ETHICAL ISSUES

As the popularity of paradoxical therapy increased during the 1980s, concern also grew about ways in which these techniques can be misused. Strategic applications in which therapists do not make their rationale for particular interventions explicit to clients have been criticized as manipulative and potentially harmful to the client-therapist relationship. And in analogue studies, observers of therapy vignettes have rated symptom prescription as less acceptable than straightforward behavioral interventions, even when these vignettes portrayed paradoxical interventions as more effective.

Defenders of strategic therapy, on the other hand, argue that good therapy is inherently manipulative and that therapeutic truth-telling can be not only naive but discourteous. Responsible therapists of all persuasions agree that paradox should not be used for the shock value or power it promises. Encouraging a symptom or restraining people from changing can be disastrous if done sarcastically or from a sense of frustration ("There's the window—go ahead and jump!"). It is also significant that therapists like Haley, Weakland, Palazzoli, and Hoffman, who pioneered the use of paradoxical methods, now give them less emphasis, even therapists well-versed in strategic methods find the term "paradoxical" confusing, inaccurate, and overly loaded with negative connotations. Of particular concern is that the term "paradoxical intervention," cut loose from its theoretical and clinical moorings, is too easily seen as a "quick fix" or a gimmick.

Three guidelines may decrease the potential for misusing paradoxical interventions: First, define behavior positively. When prescribing a symptom or restraining change, avoid attributing unseemly motives to people (like needing to control, resist, or defeat one another), ascribe noble intentions not only to the symptom but to what other people are doing to support it. Second, be especially cautious with challenging or provocative interventions. When restraining clients from change, for example, it is safer to suggest that change may not be advisable than to predict it will not be possible. Finally, have a clear theoretical formulation of how the problem is being maintained and how a paradoxical intervention may help to change that. The most important guideline for paradoxical (or any other) intervention is having a coherent rationale for using it.

REFERENCES

Brehm, S. S., & Brehm, J. W. (1981). *Psychological reactance: A theory of freedom and control.* NY: Academic.

Fisch, R., Weakland, J. H., & Segal, L. (1982). *The tactics of change.* San Francisco: Jossey-Bass.

Hill, K. A. (1987). Meta-analysis of paradoxical interventions. *Psychotherapy, 24,* 266–270.

Hoffman, L. (1981). *Foundations of family therapy.* New York: Basic.

Rohrbaugh, M., Tennen, H., Press, S., & White, L. (1981). Compliance, defiance, and therapeutic paradox: Guidelines for strategic use of paradoxical interventions. *American Journal of Orthopsychiatry, 51,* 454–467.

Seltzer, L. F. (1986). *Paradoxical strategies in psychotherapy: A comprehensive overview and guide book.* New York: Wiley.

Selvini-Palazzoli, M., Cecchin, G., Prata, G., & Boscolo, E. L. (1978). *Paradox and counterparadox.* New York: Aronson.

Shoham-Salomon, V., & Rosenthal, R. (1987). Paradoxical interventions. A meta-analysis. *Journal of Consulting and Clinical Psychology, 55,* 22–28.

Stanton, M. D. (1984). Fusion, compression, diversion, and the workings of paradox: A theory of therapeutic/systemic change. *Family Process, 23,* 135–168.

Watzlawick, P., Beavin, J., & Jackson, D. D. (1967). *Pragmatics of human communication.* New York: Norton.

SUGGESTED READING

Frankl, V. E. (1991). Paradoxical intention. In G. E. Weeks (Ed.), *Promoting change through paradoxical therapy* (pp. 99–110). New York: Brunner/Mazel.

Haley, J. (1973). *Uncommon therapy: The psychiatric techniques of Milton H. Erickson, MD.* New York: Norton.

Haley, J. (1987). *Problem-solving therapy* (2nd ed.). San Francisco: Jossey-Bass.

Hunsley, J. (1993). Treatment acceptability of symptom prescription techniques. *Journal of Counseling Psychology, 40,* 139–143.

Madanes, C. (1980). Protection, paradox, and pretending. *Family Process, 19,* 73–85.

Omer, H. (1981). Paradoxical treatments: A unified concept. *Psychotherapy: Theory, Research, and Practice, 18,* 320–324.

Raskin, D., & Klein, Z. (1976). Losing a symptom through keeping it: A review of paradoxical treatment techniques and rationale. *Archives of General Psychiatry, 33,* 548–555.

Shoham, V., & Rohrbaugh, M. (1997). Interrupting ironic processes. *Psychological Science, 8,* 151–153.

Weeks, G. R. (1991). *Promoting change through paradoxical therapy.* New York: Brunner/Mazel.

V. SHOHAM
M. J. ROHRBAUGH
University of Arizona

COGNITIVE THERAPY
FACTITIOUS DISORDERS
INTERNALIZATION
PSYCHOTHERAPY

PARADOXICAL SLEEP

Paradoxical sleep is a sleep stage characterized physiologically by a lack of muscle tone, rapid eye movements (REMs), and an awake cortical electroencephalographic (EEG) pattern. The paradox is the disparity between the alert EEG pattern, which implies that the person is awake or nearly so, and the indications that the person is actually more deeply asleep than at other times (difficulty in arousing, reduced muscle tone).

The term "paradoxical sleep" was introduced in a 1967 *Scientific American* article on the states of sleep by French researcher Michel Jouvet. Jouvet used the term to describe a period of apparent sleep in cats in which they exhibited high levels of neural activity with completely relaxed neck muscles. In humans, such periods are characterized by rapid eye movements, and sleep researchers use the term "REM sleep" with human subjects but "paradoxical sleep" with animals, because many species do not exhibit eye movements.

REM or paradoxical sleep is just one of several stages through which a sleeping organism passes during a sleep bout. One way to categorize the major stages is into REM sleep and non-REM (NREM) sleep. Four stages are usually distinguished in NREM sleep, labeled Stages 1 to 4, with each stage representing progressively deeper sleep. Stages 3 and 4 are collectively called slow-wave sleep (SWS), because the EEG waves are slower than in Stages 1 and 2.

REM sleep is associated with erections in males and vaginal moistening in females, as well as with reports of dreaming. In males at least, the genital changes are not necessarily associated with sex-related dreaming. Dreams also have been reported in SWS, but they are more frequent in REM sleep and generally more elaborate.

Studies of people awakened from REM sleep have answered several questions about dreaming. For example, apparently all normal humans dream, even though many people claim that they do not. When such professed nondreamers are awakened during REM sleep, they usually report dreams, although their dreams may be less vivid than those of people who usually remember their dreams upon awakening. Another observation that has been made is that dreams last about as long as they seem to, to the dreamer.

A number of studies have attempted to determine the function of REM sleep by subjecting volunteers to its deprivation. What generally happens is that subjects awakened during each REM stage and kept awake for several minutes increase their attempts at REM sleep and develop mild, temporary personality changes. Studies of paradoxical sleep-deprivation in animals reveal similar increased attempts at REM sleep and some general disturbances, none of which answer the question of what function REM sleep plays.

According to one explanation, sleep is an adaptive mechanism developed to conserve energy at night when food-gathering would be difficult for a diurnal animal. However, the evolution of many animals has resulted in regular patterns of locomotor activity, thought to occur approximately every 2 hours, during which food gathering and other activities related to survival might occur. If this 2-hour cycle continued around the clock, the animal's sleep would be periodically interrupted. Thus, in order to get a full night's sleep *and* continue with the 2-hour activity cycle, the animal enters a period of paradoxical sleep in which only the brain awakens.

Another possibility is that REM or paradoxical sleep is important for strengthening memories. Studies have shown that humans and other mammals increase REM sleep periods following a new learning experience, and that without this increase, memory deficits result. However, some have suggested that REM sleep performs just the opposite function, purging useless information from memory. It has also been suggested that infants spend an inordinate amount of time in REM sleep because such sleep is associated with the development of the brain. About all we can say at this time is that the number of disparate explanations indicates that we really do not know much about the causes and functions of paradoxical sleep.

B. M. THORNE
Mississippi State University

RAPID EYE MOVEMENT (REM) SLEEP
SLEEP

PARAMETRIC STATISTICAL TESTS

Parametric statistical tests, as opposed to nonparametric or distribution-free tests, are based on various assumptions regarding the characteristics, properties, and form of the distributions of populations from which the data are drawn. A large number of statistical tests are included among the parametric tests, primarily hypothesis-testing procedures derived from the general linear model. These include both univariate and multivariate statistical tests: the *t* test; univariate and multivariate analysis of variance and covariance (including repeated measures); Pearson product-moment correlation; simple and multiple regression (and variants including logistic regression); Hotelling's T^2; discriminant function analysis; canonical correlation; and multivariate set correlation. All other factors being equal, parametric statistical tests are more powerful than their nonparametric alternatives. However, it is more for their versatility than for their power that parametric tests have become the most common tools in behavioral research.

The principal assumptions on which univariate parametric tests are based include independence of the observations, normality of the underlying distributions, homogeneity of variance across groups (for multiple group procedures), continuity of measurement, and equality of intervals of measurement. Additional assumptions may be required for some parametric procedures, such as linearity of regression (Pearson correlation, simple and multiple regression), homogeneity of regression slopes (univariate and multivariate analysis of covariance), and sphericity (univariate and

multivariate repeated measures). The principal assumptions for multivariate statistics include independence of the observations, multivariate normal distributions for all dependent variables, and homogeneity of the variance-covariance (dispersion) matrices across groups.

In principle, when assumptions are violated, the significance level (*p* value) associated with a statistical test result may be seriously in error, increasing either Type I or Type II error rates. However, under many circumstances, univariate statistics seem to be quite robust to violations of assumptions. One exception is the violation of the assumption of independence, which is always serious. Robustness may also be compromised under certain conditions, such as when two or more assumptions are violated simultaneously, when sample sizes are very small, when sample sizes are unequal, or when one-tailed significance tests are used. When violation of assumptions is a concern, various remedial techniques can be employed, including data transformations (e.g., square root, arcsine, log) or the use of alternative, specialized analytical procedures (e.g., Welch's *t'* test, generalized estimating equations, nonparametric statistics). The assumptions underlying repeated measures procedures appear to be more restrictive than for univariate tests. Consequently, repeated measures procedures may not be as robust as univariate tests. Although not as much research has been conducted as for univariate procedures, multivariate statistical tests appear to be robust to violation of assumptions under many commonly occurring circumstances.

J. S. ROSSI
University of Rhode Island

PARANOIA

Paranoia has existed as a concept in Western thought since the ancient Greeks coined the word from *para*, meaning "beside," and *noia*, meaning "the mind." Although it often is used as a general word for madness, the verbal form of the word, *parano-so*, means "to think amiss," and thus it differs in implication from other words for madness, such as *mania*, which refers to emotional frenzy. It was not used by Hippocrates, concerned with physically caused disorders, but by philosophers and playwrights, concerned with the workings of the *psyche*, or mind.

In 1783, *paranoia* was brought into English by William Cullen, a Scottish neuropathologist, who followed the German use of the word as a general term for madness. In 1818, the term was applied to a specific syndrome, also called *Verrücktheit*, by Heinroth, and it was established by Emil Kraepelin in the 1896 and later editions of his textbook as the name of a major psychosis, distinct from manic-depressive illness and dementia praecox (schizophrenia). Kraepelin described paranoia as a system of insidiously developed and unshakeable delusions of persecution, jealousy, or grandeur involving religion, inventions, or eroticism, all accompanied by clear and orderly thinking, willing, and acting, and sometimes by hypochondriacal complaints. Usually permanent, it could also be acute and curable.

Sigmund Freud used the Kraepelinian classification of paranoia with considerable frequency in his own diagnoses, classifying it as a psychosis of defense against unacceptable and repressed thoughts and feelings, homosexual in nature, which were then projected onto other people. The most famous case of paranoia he analyzed was of Joseph Schreber, a former judge and president of the Dresden, Germany senate.

Other early investigators of paranoia and related disorders included Adolf Meyer, who saw the development of paranoia as a gradual transformation of the personality; Eugen Bleuler, who classified paranoia as a type of schizophrenia; and Ivan Pavlov, who suggested that paranoia represents abnormal signal transmission, which increases the elaboration and stability of the conditioned reflex. Later investigators included Norman Cameron, who distinguished between paranoia and paranoid states; Theodore Millon, who has described paranoid personality in detail; Swanson, Bohnert, and Smith, who authored a text on paranoid disorders from a psychodynamic viewpoint; Aubrey Lewis, who wrote a brief history of the use of the words *paranoia* and *paranoid* and concluded that they referred only to a symptomatic, toxic, or schizophrenic condition; Kenneth Colby, who developed a computer simulation of paranoid processes, based on the perception of statements as malevolent rather than benevolent or neutral; and George Winokur, who, in his presidential address to the American Psychopathological Association in 1977, replaced the term *paranoid disorders* with *delusional disorder*, declaring that it was useless to continue to explore the fine points of delusional illnesses, and that patients referred to as paranoid have nothing more or less than a delusion.

Investigations of paranoid and delusional disorders greatly increased in the 1980s. A 1981 issue of the *Schizophrenia Bulletin* included articles by Peter Magaro, K. S. Kendler and K. L. Davis, and W. W. Meissner, that showed, respectively, significant differences between paranoid and schizophrenic persons in cognitive style, in genetic and biochemical makeup, and in the formation of personality, thus laying to rest the old contention that paranoia should be subsumed under schizophrenia. Other notable investigators have included Alistair Munro, who described a spectrum of paranoid disorders and suggested that they may not be rare and are treatable.

Meanwhile, the *DSM* series both reflected and shaped developments in the field, going from relatively simple entries in the first two editions to a complex one in *DSM-III* (1980), in which the criteria for diagnosis included persecutory or jealous delusions, grandiosity, anger, ideas of reference, isolation, and suspicion. The types included paranoia per se, shared paranoid disorder (*folie a deux*), and acute paranoid disorder.

In *DSM-III-R* (1987), however, Winokur's position became the official one for diagnosis, and paranoid disorders were reduced to delusional disorder with a persistent, nonbizarre delusion as the sole criterion. Types of the disorder were traditionally labeled erotomanic, grandiose, jealous, and persecutory and a somatic type was added as well as a residual category, with the former distinguishable from body dismorphic disorder or hypochondriasis only by the patient's degree of conviction that something was wrong with his or her body.

Furthermore, the shared type of paranoid disorder was renamed and reclassified as induced psychotic disorder, and the acute type as "psychotic disorder not otherwise classified (atypical psychosis)." Paraphrenia—a mild disorder of later life long described as exhibiting characteristics of both paranoia and schizophrenia—continued to be excluded as an official diagnosis. However, the much-used categories of paranoid schizophrenia and paranoid personality disorder remained at least temporarily in the official manual.

In the wake of these changes, research on delusions increased, and has generally indicated that they are not readily defined, measured, or separated from other psychological phenomena, particularly strong emotions. Their content appears to be situation dependent, while the attributional style characteristic of them is relatively stable.

Despite the divergences in the history of paranoid or delusional disorders, it is possible to find a core concept running through the official definitions and descriptions, and the theoretical and research literature: paranoia (delusional disorder) is a mental disorder characterized by the presence of persistent nonbizarre delusions of persecutory, grandiose, or other self-referential content, not caused by other mental or organic disorders. Social and marital functioning may be impaired, while nondelusional intellectual and occupational functioning may be satisfactory.

To this must be added the reason why the disorder should be of considerable concern: excessively self-defensive or aggressive and violent behaviors related to the delusions may occur.

Numerous important issues remain for investigation. In regard to the *DSM* series, these issues include the following: the appropriateness and sufficiency of the new nomenclature and criterion, and further possible revisions; the retaining or deleting of the somatic type of delusional disorder; the content of delusions in non-Western cultures; and the possible classification of types of the disorder according to differences other than content.

Issues for research include the role of emotion in delusion formation and as a determinant of related behaviors; the possible influence of other psychological and physiological factors as well as cultural and other environmental factors in the formation and expression of delusions; the epidemiology of delusional or paranoid disorders and the frequency, intensity, and duration of delusional beliefs and related behaviors in normal populations and in special groups of normal populations. Issues in regard to theory primarily concern the relationship of delusional or paranoid disorders to each other, including shared or induced and acute forms, drug-induced forms, paranoid schizophrenia, and paranoid personality. Finally, issues in regard to intervention include: the development or refinement of instruments for the assessment of these disorders; effective modes of treatment, particularly the use of psychoactive drugs and various kinds of psychotherapy, separately or in combination; the course and prognosis of the disorders, with and without treatment; and possible means of prevention.

SUGGESTED READING

Lewis, A. (1970). Paranoia and paranoid: A historical perspective. *Psychological Medicine, 1*, 2–12.

Magaro, P. A. (1981). The paranoid and the schizophrenic: The case for distinct cognitive style. *Schizophrenia Bulletin, 7,* 632–631.

Munro, A. (1982). Paranoia revisited. *British Journal of Psychiatry, 141,* 344–349.

Scheuer, A. D. (1991). A reconceptualization of paranoia: Applications for research, classification, and intervention. Doctoral dissertation, University of Hawaii.

Winokur, G. (1977). Delusional disorder (paranoia). *Comprehensive Psychiatry, 18*(6), 511–621.

A. D. SCHEUER
University of Hawaii

HALLUCINATIONS
MANIC-DEPRESSIVE ILLNESS
PARANOID PERSONALITY
PSYCHOANALYSIS

PARANOID PERSONALITY

This well-known syndrome is described in the *Diagnostic and Statistical Manual* (*DSM-III*) (American Psychiatric Association, 1980) as exhibiting a pervasive and unwarranted suspiciousness and mistrust. Viewed by others as guarded, secretive, and devious, paranoids foster these perceptions by their tendency to question the loyalty of others, and search for hidden motives in their behavior, and by expecting to be tricked or duped. They "make mountains out of molehills," are argumentative, and are always ready to counterattack at the slightest hint of potential threat or criticism. Stubborn and defensive, they are rigid in the views they hold, and are unwilling to compromise their position. Not only is there a mistrust of others, but there is a vigilant resistance to external influences and an ever-present fear of losing the power of self-determination. The inclination to misinterpret incidental actions and statements as signifying deception or malevolence borders on the irrational, yet falls short of being a full-fledged delusional system. They display minimal affect, and are described by others as "cold" and lacking in humor. From their perspective, paranoids take pride in being objective, rational, and unemotional. Quickly disposed to be critical of others, they are unusually sensitive to criticism directed at them.

Historically the term *paranoia* can be traced back more than 2,000 years in the medical literature. Magnan (1886) alluded to premorbid paranoid personality traits in his text, but it was not until the 1913 eighth edition of Kraepelin's (1904/1899) *Lehrbuch* that the concept of a paranoid personality was explicitly formulated. In his diagnostic summary, Kraepelin notes: "This patient feels himself on every occasion unjustly treated, the object of hostility, interfered with, oppressed. The patient is difficult to get on with, is fault-finding, makes difficulties everywhere . . . boasts of performances, considers self superior to surroundings, makes special claims."

Despite the seminal role Freud played in explicating the symptom picture of the paranoid disorder, he did not construct a basis for either the development or structure of a paranoid character type. His disciple Abraham (1921) set forth a psychoanalytic framework for this personality pattern in his rendition of the "anal-character." Menninger (1940) elaborated this connection in his study of character disorders, formulating the relationship as follows: "The character traits of the anal expulsive period are chiefly those of megalomania and suspiciousness. The individual who . . . makes unwarranted claims upon his own abilities, but is inclined to attribute his failure to . . . rivals is [fixated] in the anal expulsive period . . . [and] closely related to the paranoid character."

Approaching this personality from the perspective of constitutional theorists, Sheldon and colleagues (1940) wrote of the paranoid "temperament component" as an inclination to "fight against something" and to be antagonistic and resentful of others. The following criteria were derived from a biosocial-learning, rather than a psychoanalytic or constitutional model. They were drafted by Theodore Millon in his role as diagnostic theorist to the *DSM-III* personality committee.

1. Vigilant mistrust (e.g., exhibits edgy defensiveness against anticipated criticism and deception; conveys extreme suspicion, envy, and jealousy of others).

2. Provocative interpersonal behavior (e.g., displays a disputatious, fractious, and abrasive irritability; precipitates exasperation and anger by hostile, deprecatory demeanor).

3. Tenacious autonomy (e.g., expresses fear of losing independence and power of self-determination; is grimly resistant to sources of external influence and control).

4. Minidelusional cognitions (e.g., distorts events into personally logical but essentially irrational beliefs; embellishes trivial achievements to accord with semigrandiose self-image).

5. Persecutory self-references (e.g., construes incidental events as critical of self; reveals tendency to magnify minor and personally unrelated tensions into proofs of purposeful deception and malice).

REFERENCES

Abraham, K. (1927/1921). Contributions to the theory of the anal character. In *Selected papers on psychoanalysis.* London: Hogarth.

American Psychiatric Association. (1980). *Diagnostic and statistical manual of mental disorders* (*DSM-III*). Washington, DC: Author.

Kraepelin, E. (1904/1899). *Psychiatrie. Ein Lehrbuch für Studierende und Aerzte. Achte, vollstandig umgearbeitete Auflage. II. Band. Klinische Psychiatrie.* Leipzig, Germany: J. Barth.

Magnan, V. (1886). *Leçons cliniques sur les maladies mentales.* Paris: Battaille.

Menninger, K. (1940). Character disorders. In J. F. Brown (Ed.), *The psychodynamics of abnormal behavior.* New York: McGraw-Hill.

Sheldon, W. H., Stevens, S. S., & Tucker, W. B. (1940). *The varieties of human physique.* New York: Harper.

T. MILLON
University of Miami

DIAGNOSTIC & STATISTICAL MANUAL (DSM-IV) PERSONALITY DISORDERS

PARAPSYCHOLOGY

Parapsychology is the scientific study of "psi," the generic term for the various types of "psychic" phenomena that can be studied empirically. Basically two forms of psi are distinguished: (a) extrasensory perception (ESP); and (b) psychokinesis (PK). Extrasensory perception is the ability to acquire information shielded from the senses. It can be time-displaced, in that the information may relate to past events (retrocognition) or future events (precognition). Traditionally ESP is further classified into telepathy and clairvoyance. In telepathy, the information or target is a thought in someone else's mind; in clairvoyance, it is an external event or object. Psychokinesis is the ability of the mind to affect external systems outside the sphere of its motor activity.

In the popular media, the term *parapsychology* is often used to refer to all kinds of unexplained phenomena—UFOs; astrological, palm, and tarot-card readings; "Big Foot"; the Bermuda Triangle; and ghosts and spirits. But the Parapsychological Association, an international professional society of scientists engaged in parapsychological research, limits the primary emphasis of the field to psi research alone.

BACKGROUND

The belief in psychic phenomena is as old as recorded human history. Dodds (1971) discusses some interesting cases of psychic phenomena in antiquity. An excellent historical and scholarly account of the paranormal prior to World War I is that by Brian Inglis (1977). Even in contemporary industrialized societies, psychic experiences are reported to be widespread. A random survey by the National Opinion Center of the University of Chicago revealed that a significant majority of Americans thought that they had experienced one or more psychic events in their lives (Greeley & McCready, 1975).

Along with belief there has also been persistent skepticism, the basis for which appears to be twofold. First, the phenomena are sporadic and elusive. Contrary to some claims, no one seems to be able to exercise absolute control and produce the phenomena on demand. Second, the phenomena, if genuine, have always appeared to defy natural explanation and to conflict with common-sense assumptions concerning the way we interact with our environment. When confronted with stories of divination that appeared to be genuine, Cicero told his brother Quintus: "In trying to prove the truth of the auguries you are overturning the whole system of physics" (Inglis, 1977, p. 61). In a similar vein, psychologist Donald Hebb (1951) declared: "I do not accept ESP for a moment,

because it does not make sense." He admits: "My own rejection of his [Rhine's] views is—in a literal sense—prejudice" (Hebb, 1951, p. 45).

Evidence for psi is of two kinds—qualitative and quantitative. Qualitative psi comprises those events that have a naturalistic basis and includes episodes of spontaneous psychic occurrences in everyday life (e.g., premonition of an impending catastrophe) and field manifestations such as poltergeist disturbances (technically, recurrent spontaneous psychokinesis, or RSPK). Quantitative evidence for psi is, of course, the evidence obtained in laboratory settings under controlled conditions and evaluated statistically.

Systematic collection of spontaneous psychic experiences began almost a century ago under the sponsorship of the London-based Society for Psychical Research (SPR) established in 1882. Gurney and colleagues published a two-volume classic in 1886 entitled *Phantasms of the Living;* it contains several hundred cases which, after due screening, met specific criteria of authenticity set by the investigators to safeguard against the pitfalls of human testimony (Sidgwick, 1975/1886). These investigators claimed that their authenticated cases provided *prima facie* evidence for psi.

The most extensive collection of spontaneous experiences is the U.S. collection of Rhine (1961) of some 15,000 cases. This collection, now housed at the Institute for Parapsychology in Durham, N.C., is based on a philosophy somewhat different from that of the SPR collection. The Rhine collection did not involve any effort to authenticate the cases. Its purpose was not to prove the existence of psi, but only to see whether the cases would throw any light on the psi process and thus generate fruitful hypotheses for laboratory testing.

Parapsychologists generally recognize the weakness of case material as evidence of psi. The authors of *Phantasms* were themselves quick to admit: "Our conviction that the supposed faculty of supersensuous impression is a genuine one is greatly fortified by a body of evidence of an experimental kind—where the conditions could be arranged in such a way as to exclude the chances of error that beset the spontaneous cases" (Sidgwick, 1975/1886, p. 7).

The early experimental work at SPR was largely concerned with thought transference, or telepathy. The most interesting of these experiments were carried out by Sidgwick and colleagues (1889) to test the possibility of telepathy under hypnosis. In France, Pierre Janet also carried out experiments to test the possibility of inducing hypnosis at a distance. It was reported (Gurney, 1888) that not only was it possible to induce telepathy by hypnosis at a considerable distance, but on occasions the hypnotist was able to influence the behavior of the subject telepathically. Highly successful experiments on telepathic induction of hypnosis were also reported by the Russian physiologist Vasiliev (1963).

In France, the seed of experimental parapsychology was sown by Charles Richet (1975/1923), Nobel prize-winning physiologist. He carried out ESP tests using playing cards and obtained significant results with subjects who were not known to be particularly psychic. To Richet also goes the credit for being the first to apply the calculus of probability to ESP results.

In the United States, William James was closely associated with the founding of the U.S. counterpart of the SPR, the American Society for Psychical Research (ASPR). While James's major contribution to psychical research lay in his defense of objective and free inquiry into psychic phenomena, his own investigations of Mrs. L. E. Piper, a famous Boston medium, convinced him of the reality of telepathy. For a comprehensive review of James's contribution to psychical research, see Murphy and Ballou (1969/1960).

The first serious attempt to study psi experimentally in the United States was made by Coover (1975/1917) during the period from 1912 to 1917 at Stanford University. Coover's conclusion was that his results failed to support the hypothesis of telepathy. His critics pointed out, however, that Coover's control condition (in which the subjects attempted to guess the face of playing cards without an agent transmitting them) was in fact a clairvoyance test and that the combined results did support the ESP hypothesis (Thouless, 1935). Among other early experiments in American universities were those by Troland (1929) and Estabrooks (1927) at Harvard University. Estabrooks's experiments are of special interest because, in the last series, when the agent and the subject were kept in separate rooms, the scores dropped significantly below what would be expected by chance. Such significantly below-chance scores were later identified and labeled as *psi-missing* by Rhine.

DUKE EXPERIMENTS: SYSTEMATIC RESEARCH

The publication of Estabrooks's results of experimental telepathy coincided with Rhine's arrival at Duke University in 1927 to work with William McDougall, who had a long-standing interest in psychical research. Writing fifty years after this event, Brian Mackenzie notes that the scientific stage of parapsychology began "with the founding of the Parapsychology Laboratory at Duke University in 1927, or perhaps with the first major output of this laboratory, Rhine's *Extrasensory Perception* in 1934" (Mackenzie, 1977, p. 28). As historians Mauskopf and McVaugh (1980) point out, this research monograph provided the paradigm for experimental parapsychology. It gave "a shared language, methods and problems" (McVaugh & Mauskopf, 1976) and constituted "a radical innovation and a high potential for elaboration" (Allison, 1973, p. 39).

Rhine set out to answer, by means of mathematically indisputable evidence, the question of the occurrence and range of ESP. For this purpose, he developed materials and methods that would permit easy controls and precise measurement. He used a specially designed deck of cards, which came to be known as "ESP cards." It is a deck of five cards, each group of five bearing one of the following symbols: circle, plus sign, three wavy lines, square, or star. Using these cards, Rhine tested a number of Duke students and discovered eight good subjects. Together they made a total of 85,724 trials and obtained 24,364 hits, or 7,219 in excess of chance expectation. These results clearly ruled out chance as an explanation (Rhine, 1973/1934).

Among his ESP experiments, the Pearce-Pratt series is the best known (Rhine & Pratt, 1954). In this experiment, Hubert Pearce, a student at Duke Divinity School, was the subject and J. G. Pratt was the experimenter. There were four subseries. Subseries A, C, and D were done with a distance of 100 yards between the subject and the experimenter. In subseries B, the distance was 250 yards.

Working in two separate buildings, the subject and experimenter synchronized their watches and set an exact time for the start of the experiment. The experimenter randomly chose a deck of ESP cards from several available to him, shuffled it well, and gave it a final cut. He then picked the top card, placed it face down on a book, and allowed it to remain there for one minute. At the end of the minute, he picked the next card, and so on, until he was through with all the cards. The subject, working in his cubicle in the library, attempted to identify the targets, minute by minute, and recorded his responses. Both the subject and experimenter kept their independent records in duplicate and gave one set to Rhine for his independent checking. In a total of 74 runs of 25 trials, Pearce obtained 188 hits in excess of what might be expected by chance. The probability of obtaining such a result by chance is less than 10^{-22}.

Rhine and his co-workers also carried out extensive experiments to test the possibility of psychokinesis, in which the subjects' task was to mentally influence falling dice to land with a desired face up. Controls to eliminate the artifacts of skilled throwing and dice bias were provided. After nine years of testing, Rhine claimed that he had sufficient evidence in support of PK. A significant aspect of the evidence came from an unexpected finding, a chronological falling off in the hit rate. The records of 18 independent experiments showed a highly significant tendency for the upper-left-hand quarter of the record page to show the highest percentage of hits and the lower-right-hand quarter, the lowest. This distribution of hits relating to chronological declines in scoring is labeled "quarter distribution" (QD) (Rhine & Humphrey, 1944).

Soon after convincing themselves that psi is real, Rhine and his associates set out to determine whether psi is constrained by such physical variables as size and shape of the targets, and by space and time. Having discovered no such restrictions, they moved on to relate psi to psychological variables. Notably Stuart (1947) and Humphrey (1946a, 1946b) at the Duke Laboratory and Schmeidler at the City College of New York (Schmeidler, 1960; Schmeidler & McConnell, 1958) pioneered in the study of personality and ESP correlation.

Some Confirmations

In 1940 Rhine and associates published *Extrasensory Perception after Sixty Years,* which reviewed all experimental reports on ESP published between 1882 and 1939 and dealt with a variety of criticisms of them. Of the 145 studies, 82 gave results that would be considered significant by the statistical criterion generally adopted in psychological literature. Since 1940 several hundred successful psi experiments have been reported. A majority of these have been published in the *Journal of Parapsychology* founded in 1937 by Rhine and McDougall.

Space does not allow the mention of a significant number of the successful psi experiments. Special note, however, may be made of the following: Pratt and Woodruff (1939); experiments by Ryzl and others with a Czechoslovakian subject, Pavel Stepanek (Pratt, 1973); the Musso and Granero (1973) experiment in Argentina; the experiments with Harribance by Roll and Klein (1972); the Kanthamani and Kelly (1974) experiments with Delmore; and the experiments of Schmidt (1969, 1973) using a random number generator (RNG).

The last of these have added importance in that they employed fully automated procedures advocated by critics and have since been replicated by several other investigators. Through the use of a radioactive source, strontium-90, the Schmidt machine generates random decisions as to which of four lights will be illuminated. The subject's task is to guess which lamp will light next and to press the corresponding button. When the subject pushes the button, it triggers the random lighting of one lamp and the subject has immediate feedback as to whether or not the guess was correct. The machine automatically records both the target and the guess. The RNG was extensively tested in control trials and found not to deviate from randomness. In another study, Schmidt, using essentially the same equipment, substituted for the RNG a prerecorded sequence of random numbers taken from the Rand tables. In both experiments, the results were highly significant.

PROCESS-ORIENTED RESEARCH

Researchers convinced of the reality of psi have turned their attention to studies that may throw light on the psi process. These studies are important for several reasons: (a) any evidence in support of certain lawfulness of psi would also be evidence in support of its existence; (b) since much of the skepticism is prompted by the manifest bizarreness of psi, understanding of its relationship with other and better understood phenomena may lessen intellectual resistance to its acceptance; and (c) significant understanding of the process will provide the basis for obtaining a measure of control, or at least a degree of predictability and replicability. Indeed there has been some progress.

Personality and ESP

Eysenck (1967) hypothesized that, if ESP is an ancient and primitive form of perception, extraverted subjects who are in a lower state of cortical arousal should do better in ESP tests than introverts because conditions of high cortical arousal would be unfavorable to ESP. A fairly comprehensive review of the relevant literature in parapsychology convinced Eysenck that extraverts did perform better in ESP tests than introverts. Later Kanthamani and Rao (1972) reported the results of four series of experiments that lent further support for an ESP-extraversion relationship. The ESP test involved blind matching of ESP cards and the extraversion scores were derived from Cattell's High School Personality Questionnaire. In the pilot study, the extraverts obtained significantly higher scores than introverts and the combined results of the three confirmatory series were highly significant in favor of extraverts. The extraverts tended to score more hits than expected by chance, whereas the introverts tended to psi-miss significantly—that is, to score significantly less than what is expected by chance. A recent review by Sargent (1981) revealed significant confirmations of a positive relationship between ESP and extraversion. Out of 53 ESP-extraversion correlations reported in English-language journals, 17 are significant and positive, one is significantly negative, and 35 are at chance.

Another personality relationship explored somewhat extensively in relation to ESP test scores is neuroticism. In the sense of "maladaptive behavior caused either by anxiety or defense mechanisms against anxiety," neuroticism scores tended generally to correlate negatively with ESP scores. Eight studies gave significant results in that direction and none in the opposite direction. As Palmer (1978) pointed out, in 20 out of 26 nonsignificant experiments, less neurotic subjects scored higher than more neurotic subjects.

Belief and ESP

Belief in the possibility of ESP seems to be related to ESP scoring. The pioneer in this area of research, Gertrude Schmeidler, divided her subjects into "sheep," those who believed in the possibility of ESP, and "goats," those who rejected such a possibility. She found that sheep generally tended to obtain more hits than goats. For example, in the group tests 1,157 subjects made 250,875 ESP card guesses. The sheep averaged 5.10 successful guesses (hits) in a run of 25 trials whereas the goats averaged 4.93 hits per run. The difference in the two means, though small, is highly significant statistically (Schmeidler & McConnell, 1958).

Following Schmeidler, several other investigators utilized the sheep-goat dichotomy in their research. Palmer (1971) published a review of the sheep-goat studies and found that in 13 out of the 17 experiments that employed standard methods and analyses, the sheep obtained better scores than the goats. Six of these 13 achieved statistical significance. None of the four with opposite results were significant.

Psi and Sensory Noise Reduction

Most of the traditional procedures of psychic development emphasize the importance of reduced attention and awareness to sensory input. The practice of yoga, for example, is an exercise in concentration believed to enable the practitioner to reduce attention to external sensory stimulation and intensify internal awareness. Yogic practice is also believed to help develop one's psychic abilities. Parapsychologists have experimented with a variety of procedures designed to enhance internal awareness and reduce external attention. These include Ganzfeld stimulation, hypnosis, relaxation, and meditation.

Charles Honorton and his co-workers carried out a series of tests for ESP when the subjects were in a Ganzfeld condition. Ganzfeld is a homogeneous visual field that provides the subjects with uniform visual input. The subjects generally report a sensation of being immersed in a "sea of light," and of disorientation. The occurrence of "black-out" periods is also reported (Honorton, 1977).

In the first experiment involving this testing technique, Honorton and Harper (1974) tested 30 volunteer subjects. Each subject received 35 minutes of Ganzfeld stimulation. At a randomly determined time during this period, an agent in another room viewed the contents of a randomly selected View-Master reel and attempted to influence the subject's ongoing mentation. The experimenter, located in a separate room between the subject's and sender's, recorded the subject's mentation report via an intercom. At the end of the 35-minute period, the experimenter showed the subject four View-Master reels, one of which the sender had viewed during the session. The subject and the experimenter did not know at the time which of the four was the target reel. The subject was then asked to rank-order the reels in relation to their correspondence with his mentation report. Not only were the results statistically significant overall, but also the qualitative correspondences between the reports and the reels were quite striking.

Since the publication of Honorton and Harper's report, a large number of experiments utilizing the Ganzfeld procedure have been carried out. The most extensive were by Carl Sargent (1980) at the Cambridge University. A recent review of published and unpublished Ganzfeld-ESP studies (Blackmore, 1980) shows that in 18 of the 31 published reports, significant evidence for psi was obtained. If all the published and unpublished studies are combined, 50% of the studies have achieved statistical significance beyond the 5% level.

Similar results are also reported when other procedures to reduce noise from sensory systems are employed, as in hypnosis, relaxation, and meditation. A review by Honorton (1977) shows that of the 42 studies using hypnosis, 22 gave significant evidence of ESP. Ten out of 13 studies involving relaxation and 9 out of 16 with meditation yielded significant psi results. Rao and his colleagues (1978) reported three series of experiments with 59 subjects having various degrees of proficiency in yoga and meditation. The subjects were tested on a forced-choice and a free-response ESP test before and after they meditated for at least one half hour. The results of both yielded independently significant differences between pre- and postmeditation scores.

Considering the legendary elusiveness and annoying unpredictability of psi, the number of successful experiments that involved procedures for sensory noise reduction is indeed encouraging. Another reason for hope of better control is that the rationale behind them is consistent with traditionally held beliefs concerning the development of psi abilities. There appears to be a thread running through these studies, though they are diverse in the techniques of eliciting and measuring psi. In this context, it is worthwhile to note that Ganzfeld stimulation is reported to increase electroencephalogram (EEG) alpha activity (Avant, 1965). Meditation and relaxation have a similar effect on the subject's EEG.

Several studies in parapsychological literature have attempted to relate EEG alpha activity to ESP scoring. These studies suggest that psi is related to alpha abundance as well as alpha frequency shifting from the pretest to posttest periods, indicating that some kind of noneffortful or relaxed attention may be basic in the psi process (Rao & Feola, 1979). Alpha abundance indicates a relaxed state, and an increased alpha frequency suggests an attentive state. Das and Gastant (1957) reported that the yogins they tested showed an accelerated alpha rhythm during their "deepest" state of meditation. In this context, we should also note the distinction William James made between effortful and involuntary attention, a distinction that has since been independently assumed by some EEG researchers (Oswald, 1957).

PSI-MISSING AND THE DIFFERENTIAL EFFECT

Psi-missing is the misdirecting of psi, which results in a significant avoidance of the target the subject is consciously attempting to hit. As mentioned earlier, the subjects in Estabrooks's distance series showed such a tendency. Since then, psi-missing has been observed in numerous studies. Only after a certain amount of experimentation has the meaningfulness of psi-missing become apparent, even though the statistical significance of negative deviations was obvi-

ous from the outset. Rhine (1952, 1969) suggested "negative motivation and systematic cognitive error both operating unconsciously" as possible explanations for psi-missing. It was observed that subjects with negative attitudes toward psi tend to psi-miss. Situations that cause frustration and boredom and those that create conflict in the subject's mind are also associated with psi-missing. These findings support the negative motivation hypothesis. On the other hand, the case of consistent missing (Cadoret & Pratt, 1950), in which the subject consistently mistakes or confuses one target symbol with another (i.e., responding with *star* when the target is *circle*), fits better with the systematic-cognitive-error hypothesis.

In much of the process-oriented research, psi-missing occurs in one form or another. It would appear that a successful strategy to obtain psi, especially among unselected subjects, is one that involves a method of separating hitting and missing. In the attitude-ESP studies, for example, the combined results of sheep and goats do not deviate from chance. It is the difference between the two groups that is statistically significant. Again, the combined scores of extroverts and introverts are at chance, but extroverted subjects tend to score significantly above chance in ESP tests, whereas introverted subjects tend to do the opposite to almost the same degree. Even in experiments exploring psi-conducive states such as meditation, there is often a tendency for the subjects in the control condition significantly to psi-miss (Rao et al., 1978). All these findings raise questions as to whether there is not some fine balance in nature between hitting and missing that serves a self-obscuring function for psi, and at the same time such findings challenge researchers to explore and control the conditions that give rise to positive and negative scoring.

One of the more frequently observed psi effects is the tendency for subjects to score differentially when tested under two contrasting conditions, such as two types of targets or two kinds of response modes. Rao (1965) surveyed the literature bearing on this question and labeled it the "differential effect." For example, in one of Rao's studies (Rao, 1962) he used for targets both ESP cards and cards individually prepared with symbols that were emotionally relevant to the subject. The difference in the rate of scoring between the two sets of targets was statistically significant. In another extensive study, the subjects were given an ESP test just before and soon after they appeared for an interview that assessed their suitability for a job or a course they wished to join. The results gave evidence of missing in the preinterview tests and hitting in the postinterview tests (Sailaja & Rao, 1973).

Psi-missing in general, and the differential effect in particular, point to the bidirectional nature of psi. It is because of its bidirectionality that psi appears elusive and unreliable. For the same reason, any hope of achieving predictability will lie in an understanding of the mechanisms involved in psi's apparent self-obscuring process.

THEORIES OF PSI

It is often said that parapsychology has no paradigm of its own and that its data conflict *prima facie* with the paradigm of what Kuhn (1970) calls "normal science." This does not mean, however, that there is any lack of theorizing in the field. In fact, there is a plethora of theories of varying degrees of plausibility, but none acceptable to most in the field. For a comprehensive discussion of the theories in parapsychology see Rao (1977).

The primary thrust of parapsychological theorizing so far has been directed toward explaining how psi may function in a manner relatively unaffected by space-time limitations (Rao, 1966). Some theorists have felt it necessary to postulate new entities, such as the "shin" that can transcend time and space, or new media, such as the "collective unconscious" that enable an individual to interact with the environment independently of the sensory-motor system. These theories represent what may be considered a vitalistic model. A few theorists have expressed the hope that an extension of the principles of the physical sciences will suffice to explain psi. A third, the acausal model, does away with the notion of interaction between the subject and the target. The best known theory in this category is Jung's concept of synchronicity, which postulates a noncausal linking of two events in a meaningful way (Jung & Pauli, 1955).

Two influential theoretical attempts that have generated meaningful research in recent years are described in R. G. Stanford's writings and in what are referred to as observational theories of psi. Stanford (1974, 1974b) first proposed a model, which he called "psi-mediated instrumental response" (PMIR). This was later revised and labeled the "conformance behavior model" (Stanford, 1977). According to this model, the nervous system or the brain is a complex and sophisticated random event generator (REG). The ESP subject (or the experimenter), insofar as there is a wish or need to succeed in the test, is a "disposed system." A disposed system is contingently linked to an REG under circumstances that are favorable, such that the outputs of the latter fulfill the dispositions of the former. When such conformance behavior manifests, we have ESP. Stanford argues that his theory is more than a mere description and that it has important testable implications.

The observational theories of psi make use of quantum physics; the best known is by Walker (1975). Walker's theory, an extension of his theory of consciousness, is based on the concept of hidden variables in quantum mechanics. Hidden variables are postulated to reconcile the demands of deterministic and stochastic conceptions of the development of the state vector. These hidden variables are conceived to be essentially inaccessible to physical measurement and to function independently of space-time constraints.

The possibility that observation may elicit a particular state of physical system from several possible ones suggests, according to Walker, that the observers of the process are not independent of the system, and that they are linked with each other insofar as they must agree on the final state of the system. The linking or "coupling" is maintained by the hidden variables via the "will" channel. Since the hidden variables are "nonlocal," they are capable of coupling observers separated by distance and time. In telepathy, "the will of the subject and the experimenter act together to select the particular state into which the system is collapsed" (Walker, 1975, p. 10). This means that a successful outcome in a telepathic trial is achieved by the hidden variables. Channeled through the will of the experimenter, the subject, and perhaps the agent, these variables cause a collapse of the state vector, which results in an identical call-target state, that is, a hit. In other words, what is affected is the

quantum mechanical process in the brain of the subject. The same process accounts for clairvoyance, because in both clairvoyance and telepathy there is no message transmitted in the usual sense but "a future state is being selected." Psychokinesis is explained as a process wherein the will (the hidden variables) of the subject/experimenter determines the collapse of the state vector for a physical system at the quantum level with macroscopically diverse potential states.

CRITICISM

While a major problem for parapsychologists is the difficulty in finding a paradigm, their critics find one with ease that readily gives them a number of *ad hoc* hypotheses to explain away the "alleged" psi phenomena. If the world is what we think it is, parapsychological events ought not occur. Therefore, any claim for psi, if examined thoroughly, would be found to involve some kind of error or fraud. It is not surprising, then, that the publication of Rhine's results was followed by a series of criticisms—some methodological and specific, and others theoretical and general. These were summarized by Rhine and colleagues (1940). The major methodological criticisms were: (a) that the shuffling of the cards might not have been random; (b) that the subjects could have obtained sensory cues from the backs of the cards; (c) that the experimenter or the agent could have unconsciously whispered; (d) that the experimenter could have committed recording errors that bias the results; and (e) that the statistical methods employed might have been faulty. While these criticisms may be valid in rejecting some of the results, it is extremely difficult to conceive how any of these could account for the results of such experiments as the Pearce-Pratt experiment. These criticisms, however, were useful in that they helped to bring into parapsychological research a methodological rigor that drew praise from nonparapsychologists.

One of the most biting criticisms of psi was that published in *Science* by Price (1955). Price agreed that some ESP experiments cannot be explained away by "clerical and statistical errors and unintentional use of sensory cues," but since ESP is incompatible with scientific theory, these results must be attributed to "deliberate fraud or mildly abnormal conditions" on the part of those reporting them. Price's verdict was that it is more probable that the best of psi results are the result of "a few people with the desire and the ability artfully to produce false evidence for the supernatural" (Price, 1955, p. 363). The basis for Price's rejection of psi is David Hume's argument against miracles: There can be no miracles that defy natural law. If a claim is made for a phenomenon that conflicts with established laws, it is much more parsimonious to assume error or fraud on the part of the claimant than the reality of that phenomenon.

Notwithstanding the fact that Price (1972) later withdrew his accusation and apologized to Rhine, much of the criticism of psi research still emphasizes the possibility of fraud on the part of the subject or the experimenter. With this perspective, Hansel (1980) has critically examined a number of parapsychological experiments and concludes that "it is unlikely that ESP exists" (p. 314) and that "close examination of the most spectacular findings in parapsychology . . . invariably points to some form of trickery as an alternative to ESP" (p. 308). Other critics such as Hyman (1981) and Truzzi (1980), while asserting that the existence of psi has not been proved, reject Hansel's approach as unwarranted. Hyman characterizes Hansel's position as "a dogmatism that is immune to falsification" (Hyman, 1981, p. 39). Truzzi holds that investigation of psi is legitimate even if psi turns out to be unreal. Among other recent critical books on parapsychology are those by Marks and Kammann (1980) and by Alcock (1981).

Parapsychologists have responded by pointing out that the critics excel in attacking the weak experiments while ignoring the strong ones. Critics such as Hansel are convincing, they argue, in suggesting the *possibility* of cheating but not its *probability*. No experimental situation is such that fraud can be made impossible. Given time and imagination, it will always be possible to find something that might be considered at a later date to be a weak spot. For similar reasons, British sociologists Collins and Pinch (1979) concluded that fraud as a counter-hypothesis to ESP is essentially non-falsifiable.

The claims and criticisms in psi research raise interesting questions for the sociology and philosophy of science—how we do science and what constitutes evidence. The critical questions raised against parapsychology are quite uncommon in other sciences. The critics' justification is that parapsychology makes extraordinary claims and thus they are right to demand extraordinary evidence. To the extent that psi phenomena are difficult to replicate and harmonize with the rest of our knowledge of the universe, the demand for better and more evidence is likely to continue. Demanding such evidence is not the same as denying credibility to past research.

SUMMARY

Parapsychological research is pursued currently by more than 100 scientists whose academic credentials and scientific training are comparable to those of workers in other areas of science. They have accumulated impressive results that would be regarded as completely convincing if they were in a more conventional field. But parapsychology continues to be controversial, and its findings are suspect. This state of affairs would seem to be a consequence of the apparent elusiveness and nonpredictability of psi phenomena and their perceived incompatibility with the so-called "established laws." Therefore, greater acceptance of the field will be contingent on improved replicability on one hand, and better integration with the related areas on the other. Admittedly a more adequate understanding of the phenomena is required, and the indications are that the field is moving in that direction. Psi researchers have claimed marginal replicability for the phenomena; their process-oriented research appears to converge toward the idea that sensory noise reduction procedures may heighten sensitivity to psi detection.

REFERENCES

Alcock, J. E. (1981). *Parapsychology: Science or magic?* New York: Pergamon.

Allison, P. D. (1973). *Sociological aspects of innovations: The case of parapsychology.* Unpublished master's thesis, University of Wisconsin.

Avant, L. (1965). Vision in the Ganzfeld. *Psychological Bulletin, 64,* 245–258.

Blackmore, S. (1980). The extent of selective reporting on ESP Ganzfeld studies. *European Journal of Parapsychology, 3,* 213–219.

Cadoret, R. J., & Pratt, J. G. (1950). The consistent missing effect in ESP. *Journal of Parapsychology, 14,* 244–256.

Collins, H. M., & Pinch, T. J. (1979). The construction of the paranormal: Nothing unscientific is happening. In R. Wallis (Ed.), *On the margins of science: The social construction of rejected knowledge.*

Coover, J. E. (1975/1917). *Experiments in psychical research.* New York: Arno Press.

Das, N. N., & Gastant, H. (1957). Variations de l'activite electrique du cerveau, du coeur et des muscles squilettiques au cours de la meditation et de l'extas yogigue. In *Conditionnement et reactivite en electroencephalographie.* Paris: Masson.

Dodds, E. R. (1971). Supernormal phenomena in classical antiquity. *Proceedings of the Society for Psychical Research, 55,* 189–237.

Estabrooks, G. H. (1927). *A contribution to experimental telepathy.* Boston: Boston Society for Psychical Research.

Eysenck, H. J. (1967). Personality and extrasensory perception. *Journal of the Society for Psychical Research, 44,* 55–71.

Greeley, A. M., & McCready, W. C. (1975). Are we a nation of mystics? *New York Times Magazine,* January 26.

Gurney, E. (1888). Recent experiments in hypnotism. *Proceedings of the Society for Psychical Research, 5,* 3–17.

Gurney, E., Myers, F. W. H., & Podmore, F. (1975). Phantasms of the living. In E. M. Sidgwick (Ed.), *Phantasms of the living: Cases of telepathy printed in the Journal of the Society for Psychical Research during thirty-five years.* New York: Arno Press.

Hansel, C. E. M. (1980). *ESP and parapsychology: A critical reevaluation.* Buffalo, NY: Prometheus Books.

Hebb, D. O. (1951). The role of neurological ideas in psychology. *Journal of Personality, 20,* 39–55.

Honorton, C. (1977). Psi and internal attention states. In B. B. Wolman (Ed.), *Handbook of parapsychology.* New York: Van Nostrand Reinhold.

Honorton, C., & Harper, S. (1974). Psi-mediated imagery and ideation in an experimental procedure for regulating perceptual input. *Journal of the American Society for Psychical Research, 68,* 156–168.

Humphrey, B. M. (1946a). Success in ESP as related to form of response drawings. I. Clairvoyance experiments. *Journal of Parapsychology, 10,* 78–106.

Humphrey, B. M. (1946b). Success in ESP as related to form of response drawings. II. GESP experiments. *Journal of Parapsychology, 10,* 181–196.

Hyman, R. (1981). Cold reading: How to convince strangers that you know all about them. In K. Frazier (Ed.), *Paranormal borderlands of science.* Buffalo, NY: Prometheus Books.

Inglis, B. (1977). *Natural and supernatural.* London: Hodder & Stoughton.

Jung, C. G., & Pauli, W. (1955). *The interpretation of nature and the psyche: Synchronicity and the influence of archetypal ideas on the scientific theories of Kepler.* New York: Pantheon.

Kanthamani, B. K., & Rao, K. R. (1972). Personality characteristics of ESP subjects. III. Extraversion and ESP. *Journal of Parapsychology, 36,* 190–212.

Kanthamani, H., & Kelly, E. F. (1974). Awareness of success in an exceptional subject. *Journal of Parapsychology, 38,* 355–382.

Mackenzie, B. (1977). Three stages in the history of parapsychology. Presented at the Quadrennial Congress on History of Science, Edinburgh.

Marks, D., & Kammann, R. (1980). *The psychology of the psychic.* Buffalo, NY: Prometheus Books.

Mauskopf, S. M., & McVaugh, M. R. (1980). *The elusive science: Origins of experimental psychical research.* Baltimore: Johns Hopkins University Press.

McVaugh, M., & Mauskopf, S. H. (1976). J. B. Rhine's extrasensory perception and its background in psychical research. *Isis, 67,* 161–189.

Murphy, G., & Ballou, R. O. (1969/1960). *William James on psychical research.* New York: Viking Press.

Musso, J. R., & Granero, M. (1973). An ESP drawing experiment with a highscoring subject. *Journal of Parapsychology, 37,* 13–36.

Oswald, I. (1957). The EEG, visual imagery and attention. *Quarterly Journal of Experimental Psychology, 9,* 113–118.

Palmer, J. (1971). Scoring in ESP tests as a function of belief in ESP. Part I: The sheep-goat effect. *Journal of the American Society for Psychical Research, 65,* 373–408.

Palmer, J. (1978). Extrasensory perception: Research findings. In S. Krippner (Ed.), *Advances in parapsychological research II: Extrasensory perception.* New York: Plenum.

Pratt, J. G. (1973). A decade of research with a selected ESP subject: An overview and reappraisal of the work with Pavel Stepanek. *Proceedings of the American Society for Psychical Research, 30,* 1–78.

Pratt, J. G., & Woodruff, J. L. (1939). Size of stimulus symbols in extrasensory perception. *Journal of Parapsychology, 3,* 121–158.

Price, G. R. (1955). Science and the supernatural. *Science, 122,* 359–367.

Price, G. R. (1972). Apology for Rhine and Soal. *Science, 175,* 359.

Rao, K. R. (1962). The preferential effect in ESP. *Journal of Parapsychology, 26,* 252–259.

Rao, K. R. (1965). The bidirectionality of psi. *Journal of Parapsychology, 29,* 230–250.

Rao, K. R. (1966). *Experimental parapsychology: A review and interpretation.* Springfield, IL: Thomas.

Rao, K. R. (1977). On the nature of psi. *Journal of Parapsychology, 41,* 294–351.

Rao, K. R., Dukhan, H., & Rao, P. V. K. (1978). Yogic meditation and psi scoring in forced-choice and free-response tests. *Journal of Indian Psychology, 1,* 160–175.

Rao, K. R., & Feola, J. (1979). Electrical activity of the brain and ESP: An exploratory study of alpha rhythm and ESP scoring. *Journal of Indian Psychology, 2,* 118–133.

Rhine, J. B. (1973/1934). *Extrasensory perception* (Rev. ed.). Boston: Humphries.

Rhine, J. B. (1952). The problem of psi-missing. *Journal of Parapsychology, 16,* 90–129.

Rhine, J. B., & Humphrey, B. M. (1944). The PK effect: Special evidence from hit patterns: I—Quarter distributions of the page. *Journal of Parapsychology, 8,* 18–60.

Rhine, J. B., & Pratt, J. G. (1954). A review of the Pearce-Pratt distance series of ESP tests. *Journal of Parapsychology, 18,* 165–177.

Rhine, J. B., Pratt, J. G., Stuart, C. E., Smith, B. M., & Greenwood, J. A. (1966). *Extrasensory perception after sixty years.* Boston: Humphries. (Original work published 1940)

Rhine, L. E. (1961). *Hidden channels of the mind.* New York: Sloane.

Richet, C. (1975). *Thirty years of psychical research.* New York: Arno Press. (Original work published 1923)

Roll, W. G., & Klein, J. (1972). Further forced choice ESP experiments with Lalsingle Harribance. *Journal of the American Society for Psychical Research, 66,* 103–112.

Sailaja, P., & Rao, K. R. (1973). *Experimental studies of the differential effect in life setting.* New York: Parapsychology Foundation.

Sargent, C. L. (1980). *Exploring psi in the Ganzfeld.* New York: Parapsychology Foundation.

Sargent, C. L. (1981). Extraversion and performance in "extrasensory perception" tasks. *Personality and Individual Differences, 2,* 137–143.

Schmeidler, G. R. (1960). *ESP in relation to Rorschach test evaluation.* New York: Parapsychology Foundation.

Schmeidler, G. R., & McConnell, R. A. (1958). *ESP and personality patterns.* New Haven, CT: Yale University Press.

Schmidt, H. (1969). Precognition of a quantum process. *Journal of Parapsychology, 33,* 99–108.

Schmidt, H. (1973). PK tests with a high-speed random number generator. *Journal of Parapsychology, 37,* 105–118.

Sidgwick, S., Sidgwick, E. M., & Smith, G. A. (1889). Experiments in thought transference. *Proceedings of the Society for Psychical Research, 6,* 128–170.

Stanford, R. G. (1974a). An experimentally testable model for spontaneous psi events. I. Extrasensory events. *Journal of the American Society for Psychical Research, 68,* 34–57.

Stanford, R. G. (1974b). An experimentally testable model for spontaneous psi events. II. Psychokinetic events. *Journal of the American Society for Psychical Research, 68,* 321–356.

Stanford, R. G. (1977). Are parapsychologists paradigmless in psi-land? In B. Shapin & L. Coly (Eds.), *The philosophy of parapsychology 1976.* New York: Parapsychology Foundation.

Stuart, C. E., Humphrey, B. M., Smith, B. M., & McMahan, E. (1947). Personality measurements and ESP tests with cards and drawings. *Journal of Parapsychology, 11,* 118–146.

Thouless, R. H. (1935). Dr. Rhine's recent experiments on telepathy and clairvoyance and a reconsideration of J. E. Coover's conclusions on telepathy. *Proceedings of the Society for Psychical Research, 43,* 24–37.

Troland, L. T. (1929). *The principles of psychophysiology* (Vol. 1). New York: Van Nostrand.

Truzzi, M. J. B. (1980). Rhine and pseudo-science: Some Zetetic reflections on parapsychology. In K. Ramakrishna Rao (Ed.), *J. B. Rhine: On the frontiers of science.* Jefferson, NC: McFarland.

Vasiliev, L. L. (1963). *Experiments in mental suggestion.* Church Crookham, England: Institute for the Study of Mental Images.

Walker, E. H. (1975). Foundations of paraphysical and parapsychological phenomena. In L. Oteri (Ed.), *Quantum physics and parapsychology.* New York: Parapsychology Foundation.

K. R. RAO
Duke University

COMMUNICATION PROCESS
PSEUDOPSYCHOLOGY
RESEARCH METHODOLOGY

PARASYMPATHETIC NERVOUS SYSTEM

The parasympathetic nervous system (PNS) is one division of the autonomic nervous system, which controls the function of organs and glands in the body (the efferent portion) and senses changes in these visceral systems (the afferent portion): the other autonomic division is the sympathetic nervous system (SNS). The neurons that comprise the efferent PNS arise from either the cranial nerves that exit from the brain stem and spinal cord, or from the sacral portion of the spinal cord. Thus, this system is sometimes referred to as the craniosacral division. Cranial parasympathetic fibers innervate the viscera of the head, neck, chest, and upper abdomen, including the upper portions of the gastrointestinal (GI) tract. The sacral parasympathetic fibers innervate the lower GI tract and other organs of the pelvis.

The anatomy of the efferent autonomic innervation of each organ or gland includes preganglionic neurons, which exit the brain or spinal cord, and postganglionic neurons, which directly inner-

vate the target organ. A ganglion (plural ganglia) is comprised of the cell bodies of the postganglionic neurons and is the region where the pre- and postganglionic neurons communicate with one another. In the PNS, the preganglionic fibers exiting the brain or spinal cord extend across relatively long distances in the body before reaching the ganglion. Typically, ganglia are found very near or even in the wall of the target organ or gland. Thus, the postganglionic neurons are very short, since they extend only from the ganglion to the target.

The neurotransmitter released by the axon terminals of the preganglionic neurons is acetylcholine. Acetylcholine acts on cholinergic receptors of the nicotinic subtype, which are found on the dendrites and cell bodies of the postganglionic neurons. The neurotransmitter released by the postganglionic neurons onto the target organ or gland is acetylcholine, which activates muscarinic-type cholinergic receptors on target organs and glands. Afferent autonomic fibers reaching the central nervous system run alongside the same nerves carrying efferent autonomic fibers. The visceral afferents comprise a relatively large proportion of the total number of fibers, perhaps 50% or more, in the parasympathetic nerves. Afferent autonomic fibers provide sensory information about the state of an organ, such as distension of the bladder, and also relay signals of pain. It has been hypothesized that the parasympathetic afferents relay mostly information about the state of the viscera for purposes of regulation, but play a minimal role in pain sensation.

The organs and glands controlled by the efferent PNS typically receive input from both divisions of the autonomic nervous system, a phenomenon referred to as dual innervation. When organs receive innervation from both autonomic divisions, the activity in the two divisions often produces opposite effects on the organ. For example, the heart rate is controlled by both autonomic divisions. Increased activity in the parasympathetic division decreases heart rate, and decreased activity increases heart rate. Conversely, increased activity of the sympathetic division increases heart rate, whereas decreased activity decreases heart rate. Thus, each of the two divisions are capable of bidirectionally influencing the rate at which the heart beats.

When the body is at rest, many of the organs of the body are conserving or actively storing metabolic resources for later use, a process known as anabolism. Often during such states, activity in the parasympathetic system is high relative to periods when the organism is mobile, challenged, and/or distressed. For example, during rest or relatively low levels of bodily activity, digestion of food is a priority for the body. Increased parasympathetic activation enhances digestion by producing increased motility and blood flow, and increases the secretion of digestive fluids such as acid and enzymes into the gastrointestinal tract. When an organism requires metabolic energy to maintain activity above resting levels, for example in response to a stressor or with physical exertion, activation of the parasympathetic system tends to decrease at the same time that activation of the sympathetic system tends to increase. At very high levels of metabolic need, parasympathetic activation of some organs may cease altogether. In general, humans operate somewhere between these two extremes of inactivity and high energy mobilization, and in these cases, parasympathetic effects on the organs and glands will be intermediate and tuned to the specific needs of each organ system.

In addition to the tendency for the two autonomic branches to operate in a reciprocal fashion under extremes of activity, the two autonomic divisions can operate non-reciprocally and independently. Thus, although a typical pattern of autonomic control consists of the reciprocal activation of one autonomic division accompanied by a decrease in activity in the other division, this is not the only pattern of response that can occur. The two autonomic divisions can have uncoupled effects on a target organ, with increased or decreased activity in one autonomic division in the absence of any change in the other division. Alternatively, the two branches can exert coactivational effects, such that there are simultaneous increases or decreases in activity in both autonomic divisions. The existence of the nonreciprocal patterns means that one cannot measure function in one autonomic division and, on that basis alone, infer the activation level in the other division.

SUGGESTED READING

Berntson, G. G., Cacioppo, J. T., & Quigley, K. S. (1991). Autonomic determinism: The modes of autonomic control, the doctrine of autonomic space, and the laws of autonomic constraint. *Psychological Review, 98,* 459–487.

Loewy, A. D., & Spyer, K. M. (1990). *Central regulation of autonomic function.* New York: Oxford University Press.

K. S. QUIGLEY
Pennsylvania State University

AUTONOMIC NERVOUS SYSTEM
CENTRAL NERVOUS SYSTEM
SYMPATHETIC NERVOUS SYSTEM

PARENT-CHILD RELATIONS

When individuals become parents through pregnancy, adoption, or step-parenting, they find themselves facing a disequilibrium that requires a great deal of adaptation. The parents want to develop a strong bond with their infant or child, but they still want to maintain a healthy marital relationship and adult friendships, and possibly to continue their careers. Prospective parents often ask themselves what they will be like as parents, and examine their experiences as children to see if they want to adopt a different strategy than their parents did. Parents also ask how this new being will change their lives. A new baby places restrictions on marital partners that did not previously exist; no longer will they be able to go to a movie on a moment's notice, and money likely will not be as readily available for trips, nights on the town, and so forth. If the wife has a career, she wonders how the infant will change her vocational life. She may ask, "Will it harm the baby to put her in a day care center during the first year of her life? Will I be able to find responsible baby sitters?"

More fathers have become sensitized to the important role they play in the child's development. Studies of human fathers and their infants confirm that many fathers can act sensitively and responsively with their infants (Parke & Sawin, 1980) and that infants form attachments to both their mothers and fathers at roughly the same age (Lamb, 1977). In both humans and primates, adult male behavior toward infants appears to be highly flexible and adaptive. Probably the strongest evidence of the plasticity of male caretaking abilities is derived from studies in which the males from primate species notoriously low in male interest in offspring are forced to live with infants whose female caretakers are absent. Under these circumstances, the adult males show considerable competence in rearing the infants (Parke & Suomi, 1981).

In virtually all of the investigations of fathers and infants (one exception being Field, 1978), mothers have been the primary caretakers, and fathers have had minimal caretaking responsibilities. Field (1978) found that the primary caretaking fathers resembled primary caretaking mothers in their tendencies to smile and vocalize imitatively, but acted as secondary caretaking fathers in their tendency to play games and poke at the infants. In a more elaborate study of nontraditional families, Michael Lamb and colleagues (in press) interviewed 51 couples in Sweden during pregnancy, and later observed them interacting with their 3-month-olds. Since 1974, Swedish parents have been given nine months (recently increased to 12) of paid parental leave after delivery, and the government has gone to great lengths to encourage them to take advantage of this arrangement. Half of the parents had chosen to follow the shared parenting arrangement (the nontraditional parents) and the other half followed the traditional arrangement of the father working and the mother staying home and taking care of her infant. One of the most intriguing results in Lamb's Swedish study is the manner in which the parents differentiated between sons and daughters. Like traditional mothers and fathers studied in the United States (Lamb, 1977; Parke & Sawin, 1980), the traditional Swedish parents interacted preferentially with sons. By contrast, the nontraditional Swedish parents interacted preferentially with their daughters. Lamb suggests that possibly because of their concern that their daughters are traditionally accorded less attention than sons, the nontraditional parents not only eliminated this trend, but reversed it with both mothers and fathers being responsible for this reversal. Nonetheless, whether a parent was a mother or a father differentiated the parents' behavior more noticeably than whether they were a traditional or nontraditional family. For example, fathers were much less socially active with their infants than were mothers, regardless of family type.

RECIPROCAL SOCIALIZATION AND SYNCHRONY IN PARENT-INFANT RELATIONSHIPS

Bell (1979) reviewed a number of studies related to caretaker effects on children and suggested that the effects may have been caused by the child's behavior as much as by the caretaker's. For example, researchers often discover a relation between authoritarian discipline and the child's aggression. However, aggression on the part of the child may elicit the parent's authoritarian discipline to begin with, perhaps just as easily as the discipline can increase aggression. The fact that parents differ widely in sensing the needs of their infants is one of the remarkable discoveries of the past decade. Some quickly note their child's moods and periods of distress and act to comfort the infant. This is called *synchrony*. Others may not notice the need for action or may be slow to respond. This is called *asynchrony* (Schaffer, 1977). In the psychoanalytic perspective, synchrony will generate a sense of trust in the infant; asynchrony will breed distrust. Learning theory stresses the presence or absence of clear reward contingencies. Synchrony marks the presence of clear rewards; asynchrony denotes the absence of contingent rewards. Clear contingencies make learning easier.

Recently a group of researchers in infant development at the University of Wisconsin (Donovan et al., 1978) demonstrated that mothers' synchrony with their infants' needs prompts physiological responses and that these biological indices predict how mothers rate the temperament of their infants. Thirty-two middle-class mothers, each of whom had a 3-month-old infant, were shown short videotape sequences of an unknown infant (also 3 months old) alternately smiling and crying. As mothers viewed the video scenes, the experimenters measured the women's heart rate and skin conductance, both good indicators of attention and level of arousal. The investigators also gave each mother a questionnaire that asked them to characterize their own infant's temperaments. The mothers who described their infants as "difficult" responded less sensitively to the infants on the videotapes.

Thus either the mother may learn very quickly (within three months in this case) to respond differently to a "difficult" than to an "easy" infant, or the infant's temperament may partially stem from the way in which the child is handled by the mother. It is likely that these findings show evidence of both effects. Not only should the reciprocal nature of parent-child relations be considered when we are interested in explaining the child's social behavior, but the entire system of interacting individuals in the family should be considered when we evaluate the child's development.

THE FAMILY AS A SYSTEM

As a social system, the family can be thought of as a constellation of subsystems defined in terms of generation, gender, and role (Feiring & Lewis, 1978). Divisions of labor among family members define particular subunits, and attachments define others, each family member being a participant in several subsystems, some dyadic, some polyadic.

As fathers become recognized as important socialization agents, it has become obvious that we should be studying more than two-party social interactions (Lamb, 1976). Children interact with more than one parent or adult most days of their lives, yet we know very little about how parents serve each other as sources of support as well as sources of dissatisfaction. One attempt to understand the link between spouse relationships and parent-infant relationships was conducted by Frank Pederson and his colleagues (1977). They believe that the three dyadic units of interaction— mother-father, mother-child, father-child—are interrelated. Using the husband-wife relationship as a point of reference, they set out to investigate the connections among family members. Forty-one

families were observed on three separate occasions at home, with separate observations of husband-wife and parent-infant dyads. The infants were first-born 5-month-old middle-class boys and girls.

The first hypothesis investigated was that positive interaction between the husband and wife, such as smiling and affection, would be positively linked with the expression of positive affect toward the infant by each parent. The results: There was little relationship between measures of positive husband-wife interaction and their positive interaction with the infant. However, when negative social interaction between the husband and wife was observed (e.g., verbal criticism, blame), it was strongly linked to the negative affect shown by the father toward the infant. These findings suggest that the family is a network of interacting individuals functioning as a system.

One subsystem of the family system that merits special attention is the husband-wife support system. Since many mothers now work, skills, as well as self-esteem, may emanate from this system and later may be elaborated in other contexts. But a major function of family relations, from early childhood through adolescence, seems to be the provision of a basis for environmental exploration. Exploratory activity then brings the child into contact with many different social objects, among which are other children. Through interaction with these associates, the child's own competencies in communication and role taking are extended. These associations also result in the direct acquisition of a constellation of unique attitudes and affects—each essential to social adaptation.

Belsky (1981) developed an organizational scheme of the family system that highlights the possible reciprocal influences that marital relations, parenting, and infant behavior/development may have on each other. As can be seen by following the arrows in Figure 1, these three aspects of the family system may have both direct and indirect effects on each other. An example of a direct effect is the influence of the parent's behavior on the child, while an example of an indirect effect is how the relationship between spouses mediates the way a parent acts toward the child. Sometimes such indirect effects are labeled *second-order effects* by child development researchers.

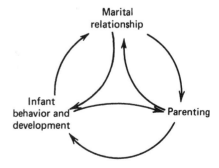

Figure 1.   A scheme for integrating the disciplines of family sociology and developmental psychology during the infancy years. From J. Belsky, Early human experience: A family perspective. (*Developmental Psychology,* 1981, *17,* p. 6. Copyright 1981 by the American Psychological Association. Reprinted by permission of the author.)

REFERENCES

Bell, R. Q. (1979). Parent, child and reciprocal influences. *American Psychologist, 34,* 821–826.

Belsky, J. (1981). Early human experience: A family perspective. *Developmental Psychology, 17,* 3–23.

Donovan, W. A., Leavitt, L. A., & Bailing, J. D. (1978). Maternal physiological response to infant signals. *Psychopsio, 15,* 68–74.

Feiring, C., & Lewis, M. (1978). The child as a member of the family system. *Behavioral Science, 23,* 225–233.

Field, T. (1978). Interaction patterns of primary versus secondary caretaking fathers. *Developmental Psychology, 14,* 183–185.

Lamb, M. E. (1977). Father-infant and mother-infant interaction in the first year of life. *Child Development, 48,* 167–181.

Lamb, M. E., Frodi, A. M., Hwang, P., Frodi, M., & Steinberg, J. (in press). Attitudes and behavior of traditional and nontraditional parents in Sweden. In R. Emde & R. Harmon (Eds.), *Attachment and affiliative systems: Neurobiological and psychobiological aspects.* New York: Plenum.

Parke, R. D., & Sawin, D. B. (1980). The family in early infancy: Social interactional and attitudinal analyses. In F. Pederson (Ed.), *The father-infant relationship: Observational studies in a family context.* New York: Praeger.

Parke, R. D., & Suomi, S. (1981). Adult male-infant relationships: Human and nonhuman primate evidence. In K. Immelmann, G. Barlow, M. Main, & L. Petrinovitch (Eds.), *Behavioral development: The Bielefeld interdisciplinary project.* New York: Cambridge University Press.

Pederson, F. A., Anderson, B. J., & Cain, R. L. (1977, March). *An approach to understanding linkages between the parent-infant and spouse relationships.* Presented at the meeting of the Society for Research in Child Development, New Orleans.

J. W. Santrock
University of Texas

CHILD ABUSE
DIVORCE
PARENTAL STYLE

PARENTAL STYLE

Parents have a legal and moral duty to rear their children. This includes providing for their sustenance and well-being, as well as their social, ethical, and personal development. In order to fulfill this responsibility, parents have to find ways to convey their principles, expectations, and regulations. Thus, the goal of parenting is to raise confident and satisfied children who can function independently and contribute to the welfare of society. Through the ages, parents have struggled with the level of direction needed to help their children successfully proceed through the developmental rites of passage to adulthood.

Rousseau (1767/1952) commented about reciprocity of rights and responsibilities between parents and children in what he called the basic social contract. He maintained that children should obey their father only as long as they needed him for their preservation. However, once children became independent, both father and child were released from their responsibilities to one another. In this patriarchal view, children were considered the property of the father. Fathers had the supreme right to command blind obedience. In addition, religious doctrine mandated parents to make their children God-fearing subjects by requiring them to submit to religious commandments and "to honor thy mother and father." Thus, an authoritarian style of parenting was purported to be the optimal method for transferring the philosophy and practices of the parents to the children.

In the 1900s, psychoanalytic premises stressed attention to children's instinctive needs. Autocratic childrearing practices were viewed as contributing to the anxiety of children by precipitously and abruptly addressing their psychosexual developmental needs. Instead, a philosophy of parental permissiveness was seen as the optimal method in order to follow the wisdom of the unconscious. Humanistic theorists such as Carl Rogers promoted a philosophy that viewed children as innately and intuitively growth-oriented. Furthermore, child rights advocates argued that youngsters have the same rights as adults in order to be self-determining. Thus, parents were inundated by ideologies to practice a laissez-faire, nonintrusive approach with their children.

Dreikurs and Grey (1968), students of Adler, adopted a democratic position of parenting that forged a middle ground of parental authority. They stressed that children should be encouraged to balance freedom with responsibility. The combination of teaching children both freedom and responsibility placed new challenges on the task of parenting. Parents no longer had an either/or solution of tyranny or indulgence, but needed to encourage children creatively through natural and logical consequences. Democratic parents used problematic behaviors as opportunities to teach their children to be more socially conscious. For instance, a temper tantrum can be handled by a "time-out" strategy and a subsequent discussion about how to handle disappointment.

BENEFITS OF AUTHORITATIVE PARENTING

Baumrind's research of more than 30 years supported the benefits of a rational approach to parenting that fostered child development through an artful balance of control with responsiveness. The underpinnings of this research began with Lewin's study of authoritarian, democratic, and laissez-faire social climates' effects on aggressive behavior (Lewin, Lippitt, & White, 1939). Baumrind (1971) refined these concepts in her study of successful and unsuccessful childrearing practices. Initially, she articulated three parental styles of handling authority: authoritative, authoritarian, and permissive. Later, she added a fourth category of parental style called rejecting-neglecting, or parents who were unengaged.

In cluster and factor analyses, Baumrind (1989) identified demandingness and responsiveness as the two major modalities in the parenting process. *Demandingness* correlates with parental at-

	RESPONSIVENESS	
	High	Low
DEMANDINGNESS High	Authoritative	Authoritarian
Low	Permissive	Unengaged

Figure 1.   Parental Styles

tributes that provide appropriate direction and control. Demanding parents can be confrontive even if a polemic position results in open conflict. Confrontation is contrasted with coercive approaches that demand power without reason. Confrontation of the problem behavior (versus intimidating the child) can result in resolution and negotiation of conflict, which enhances the child's rational internalization, self-esteem, and communication skills. Parents who insist that children embrace individually appropriate levels of responsibility, or high maturity demands, promote higher levels of prosocial behaviors and academic competence. Parental monitoring activities that provide an orderly and safe environment were also found to promote various prosocial behaviors. Monitoring is contrasted with the creation of an intrusive environment that constricts the child's appropriate level of exploration and autonomy. Finally, firm control is necessary to demonstrate parents' convictions of appropriate behaviors. Reinforcement, logical consequences, and rational punishment teach children desirable values, attitudes, and behaviors.

The preceding attributes of parental authority are insufficient alone to raise healthy, confident, and competent children. Parents who demonstrate *responsiveness* establish a loving environment that is accommodating and sensitive to the child's needs. Children who experience affective warmth from a parent develop feelings of object permanence and feel securely attached and bonded to their environment. These children become attuned to the demands of the parent and are more prone to be cooperative than children with a cold or uninvolved parent. Cognitive responsiveness refers to a parenting strategy that encourages children to express their point of view, especially during a disciplinary encounter. This increases the child's communication abilities and sense of social responsibility. Reciprocity is the extent that parents listen and respond to the needs and feelings of the child. Parents sensitively attuned to the child's motivational system can use reciprocity to uncover "win-win" solutions in the intergenerational dialogue. Parents who are responsive model prosocial communications to the child and produce children who authentically desire harmony with their parents.

Authoritative parents, who are high in both responsiveness and demandingness, remain receptive to the needs of the child for attachment and autonomy, but take responsibility for firmly guiding the actions of the child. This combination has been proven to promote self-actualization, academic competence, abstinence from tobacco and alcohol, moral development, social competence, self-reliance and many other desirable characteristics in children.

Authoritarian (autocratic) parents are high in demandingness, but low in responsiveness. They set absolute standards for their children and require unchallenged obedience and submission to parental authority. These parents frequently believe in the adage "spare the rod, spoil the child." They often are punitive in order to back up their authority. Their children show greater levels of depression and aggression, and less spontaneity, self-esteem, and creativity.

Permissive (indulgent) parents are high in responsiveness, but low in demandingness. These parents put few demands on their children, usually accept their children's impulses, and tend to avoid conflict. Since they abhor conflict, they frequently engage in very inconsistent disciplinary actions. They prefer to treat their children as peers, rather than children requiring guidance. Their children have shown to be immature, maintain poor boundaries, and have lower levels of internalization, impulse regulation, and academic achievement.

Unengaged (neglectful-rejecting) parents are low in both demandingness and responsiveness. These parents are preoccupied with their own lives and are largely uninvolved with their children. Of all the parental styles, they produce children with the most severe problems because their children are forced to fend for themselves or depend too greatly on their peer group for support. These children have greater levels of emotional indifference, detachment, impulsivity, drug use, psychopathology, behavioral problems, and poor academic performance.

CULTURAL CONSIDERATIONS

Baumrind's early research began by measuring mostly middle-class, Caucasian children who were being raised by one or both parents. Nonetheless, much of the research holds that authoritative parenting works best across cultural, racial, gender, and socioeconomic factors and family structure. Therefore, authoritative caregiving can be effective for childrearing despite any obstacles within the relationship between caregiver and child. However, Baumrind (1995) cautioned that the blend of demandingness and responsiveness is dependent upon the social and cultural context of the child. Brofenbrenner (1982/1979) agreed that the optimal balance of freedom and control depends upon the level of stability of the larger society. Due to the massive change of the family's ecology, he suggested that there is a greater need for structure in the modern family. More specifically, Kohn (1977) stated that African American parents often used authoritarian methods to instill obedience and authority in their children and to help them adapt to a bicultural reality of minority status in the American culture. In addition, caregivers need to be more vigilant in a high-crime, inner-city neighborhood than in a tranquil rural environment. Thus, parenting does not occur in isolation of the context. Although authoritative parenting has been shown to be more effective across cultures, there are many exceptions in the literature. Caution must be used to differentiate what works within different cultures.

Similarly, there have been different gender implications of parenting styles. The authoritarian approach emanates from a masculine manner of handling authority, whereas authoritative parenting is much more compatible with female development and feminine use of authority. Gilligan's (1982) research proved that girls respond much better to a consensual approach so that they can discover their own voice as opposed to blindly accepting a cultural mandate of female development. Studies have indicated that daughters respond twice as favorably than sons to authoritative parents.

CONCLUSION

Research on parental styles strongly favors an authoritative approach, which blends a flexible balance of demandingness and responsiveness with each child's passage through the developmental process. This approach provides the nurturance, safety, protection, respect, and responsive limits (Pesso, 1973) that children need to realize their optimum potential as healthy, confident, and vital members of society. Parents or other caregivers need to model the socially acceptable behaviors that they demand of their children. However, parents need to adapt the mixture of demandingness and responsiveness to the mixture of the idiosyncrasies of the child, culture, and context. For instance, children with attention-deficit/ hyperactivity disorder require greater demands for structure. Also, some parents of Pacific Island cultures are more able to emphasize responsive behaviors than their parental counterparts in urban America. Therefore, the blend of parental styles must be influenced by the child's idiosyncratic developmental process in specific cultural contexts.

REFERENCES

Baumrind, D. (1971). Current patterns of parental authority. *Developmental Psychology Monographs, 4* (no. 1, part 2).

Baumrind, D. (1989). Rearing competent children. In W. Damon (Ed.), *Child development today and tomorrow* (pp. 349–378). San Francisco: Jossey-Bass.

Baumrind, D. (1995). *Child maltreatment and optimal caregiving in social contexts.* New York: Garland.

Brofenbrenner, U. (1982/1979). *The ecology of human development.* Cambridge, Massachusetts: Harvard University Press.

Dreikurs, R., & Grey, L. (1968). *Logical consequence: A new approach to discipline.* New York: Meredith.

Gilligan, C. (1982). *In a different voice: Psychological theory and women's development.* Cambridge: Harvard University Press.

Kohn, M. L. (1977). *Class and conformity: A study in values* (2nd ed.). Chicago: University of Chicago Press.

Lewin, K., Lippitt, R., & White, R. K. (1939). Patterns of aggressive behavior in experimentally created social climates. *Journal of Social Psychology, 10,* 271–299.

Pesso, A. (1973). *Experience in action.* New York: New York University Press.

Rousseau, J. J. (1952). *The social contract.* Chicago: University of Chicago, Great Books. (Original work published in 1754)

R. A. HABER
University of South Carolina

HUMAN DEVELOPMENT
MORAL DEVELOPMENT

PARKINSON'S DISEASE

Parkinson's disease is a chronic degenerative disorder of the central nervous system. The disease usually begins slowly, with only a few apparent symptoms. Because the onset is slow and the population affected is elderly, symptoms are frequently disregarded as consequences of the aging process.

ETIOLOGY

The etiology is unknown. The epidemiological profile includes the facts that: (a) it is a disease of the elderly; (b) first symptoms are usually noted in the 60s; and (c) males are affected slightly more often than females. It has been noted that the neurotransmitter dopamine normally stored in the cells of the substantia nigra tissue in the brain are greatly depleted in Parkinson's disease. The reason is unclear.

CLINICAL MANIFESTATIONS

Because symptoms develop slowly, years may pass before the diagnosis is made. The disease is progressive, so that eventually the patient's ability to perform the activities of daily living and other independent functions is reduced. Manifestations may include:

1. Muscle rigidity associated with slowness of voluntary movement, with the muscles feeling stiff and requiring much effort to move and the trunk of the body tending to stoop forward.

2. A masklike face with the patient appearing to stare straight ahead and assuming an expressionless look with the eyes blinking less frequently than normal.

3. Tremors of the upper extremities, including activity of the thumb and fingers resulting in a characteristic "pin-rolling movement" when the hand is motionless (resting tremors).

4. Resting tremors of the foot, lip, tongue, and jaw.

5. Rigidity or rhythmic contractions on passive stretching of the muscles in the arms (cogwheel phenomenon).

6. Restlessness, including a compelling need to walk about constantly.

7. Disturbances in freeflowing movement that result in jerky and uncoordinated movements.

8. General weakness and muscular fatigue with slow initiation of movement for purposeful acts.

9. Frequent muscle cramps of the legs, neck, and trunk.

10. A weak voice, resulting in a monotonic whispering speech pattern.

11. A loss of postural reflexes which results in difficulty in maintaining balance.

12. Inability to sit erect.

13. Walking in a stooped-over position with small shuffling steps, frequently accelerating almost to a trot.

14. Mental depression related to an abnormal physical appearance, a weakened voice (which affects communication), and a frequent tendency to withdraw from normal interaction because of self-consciousness and embarrassment.

15. Common autonomic manifestations that include drooling (due to decreased frequency of swallowing), oily skin, excessive perspiration, constipation, and urinary hesitation and frequency.

MANAGEMENT

Management is directed toward control of the symptoms of the disease with drug therapy, supportive therapy and maintenance, and a physiotherapy program. Although there is no known treatment that either temporarily or permanently will stop the process of degeneration of the basal ganglia in the brain, drug therapy offers an effective method for relieving the symptoms. A comprehensive physiotherapy program is helpful in retarding the rate of disability. The need for surgery is rare because drug therapy is adequate. Most patients manage well at home with an effective drug program that often allows maintenance of a normal lifestyle.

SUGGESTED READING

Adams, R. M., & Victor, M. (1977). *Principles of neurology.* New York: McGraw-Hill.

Winter, A. (April, 1978). Clinical highlights: Some important clinical features of the tremors of Parkinsonism. *Hospital Medicine,* 98–99.

R. T. GIUBILATO
Thomas Jefferson University

ALZHEIMER'S DISEASE
CENTRAL NERVOUS SYSTEM
NEUROCHEMISTRY

PARTNER ABUSE

"Partner abuse" is a very broad term, typically referring to three diverse types of abusive behaviors that one or both partners perpetrate against the other: physical, sexual, and psychological. Physical abuse includes behaviors ranging in severity from those that are unlikely to result in injury (e.g., pushing and grabbing) to those that are life-threatening (e.g., choking, kicking, and beating). Sexual abuse refers to any undesired sexual contact that is psychologically or physically coerced. The definition of psychological abuse is particularly broad, encompassing behaviors that range from insulting or swearing at a partner, to threatening a partner, to engaging in jealous behaviors, to isolating a partner from friends and family. The multiplicity of types and severity of abusive behaviors encompassed by the term "partner abuse" led to the development of typologies of men who engage in partner abuse (Holtzworth-Munroe & Stuart, 1994). For instance, batterers are partner-abusive men who use physical aggression repeatedly and/or use physical aggression to control, intimidate, and instill fear in their partners. (Jacobson & Gottman, 1998).

Because of the greater research emphasis on physical abuse than psychological and sexual abuse, physical partner abuse is the focus herein.

PREVALENCE

Partner abuse is one of the most common forms of violence in our society. The 1975 and 1985 National Family Violence Surveys (Straus & Gelles, 1990), revealed that approximately 12% of married or cohabiting men and women in the United States engage in physical aggression against a partner annually. The lifetime prevalence of such aggression is approximately 28%. Further, approximately 3 to 5% of these men and women engage in life-threatening, physically assaultive behaviors annually. In a clinical sample of couples seeking marital therapy, up to 71% of couples report that one or, most typically, both partners have engaged in physical partner aggression in the past year (Cascardi, Langhinrichsen, & Vivian, 1992). Moreover, some form of physical aggression characterizes a substantial percentage of dating and courtship relationships (Pirog-Good & Stets, 1989). In most cases, particularly when the aggression is mild to moderate, partner abuse is bilateral. That is, both partners engage in physically aggressive behaviors. However, in the authors' experience, in relationships in which women are severely abused and often injured, men are much more likely to be abusers than women are, and women's aggression is often in self-defense. Although the previous statistics reflect rates in the United States only, partner abuse is currently recognized as an important international problem (Walker, 1999).

EXPLANATORY FRAMEWORKS AND RISK FACTORS

Several explanatory frameworks have been developed to elucidate the causes of partner abuse. Feminist accounts identify partner abuse as a product of a patriarchal (male-dominated) society. Violence in the home is viewed as one of many expressions of gender-based power inequality in society (Yllo, 1993). Psychological accounts identify partner abuse, particularly severe partner abuse, as manifestations of the interaction between individual personality traits or pathology and other risk factors such as marital discord and alcohol abuse (O'Leary, 1993). In support of this account, research has demonstrated that men who engage in partner abuse often have characteristics suggestive of personality disorders (Hamberger & Hastings, 1988). Sociological accounts identify position in the social structure as an important causal factor in partner abuse. Substantial research linking variables associated with position in the social structure (e.g., poverty, age, and race) to partner abuse provides support for this explanatory framework (Gelles, 1993). Numerous other social, psychological, and biological factors, such as self-esteem, witnessing violence as a child, relationship discord, and alcohol abuse are associated with increased risk for partner abuse perpetration, and may be causally related to such abuse (Hotaling & Sugarman, 1986).

CONSEQUENCES

The physical, psychological, and social consequences of partner abuse, particularly physical abuse, are costly, especially for women. Although women engage in physically aggressive behaviors against a partner at approximately the same rate as men, they are significantly more likely to sustain injuries as a result of such abuse (Cascardi, et al., 1992). In fact, aggression by a partner is one of the most common causes of death for young women, claiming roughly 2,000 lives annually (Browne & Williams, 1993). Victimization by a partner also puts women at increased risk for various psychological problems, such as depression, low self-esteem, and self-blame (Cascardi & O'Leary, 1992). Further, psychological abuse, which is more prevalent than physical abuse, can exact a toll as great as or greater than physical abuse.

PSYCHOLOGICAL AND LEGAL INTERVENTIONS

A variety of psychological interventions, particularly psychoeducational and therapy groups for men (and occasionally women) who abuse their partners, are currently utilized (Caesar & Hamberger, 1989). Various legal interventions, including arrest, prosecution, and restraining orders, are also used to manage this problem. For severely abused women, support groups for women are commonly used along with legal advocates, shelters, social service agencies, and individual therapeutic interventions. For women and men in less severely abusive relationships or relationships in which both the male and female engage in physically aggressive behaviors, couple or marital therapy-based interventions designed specifically to reduce psychological and physical aggression can be useful (O'Leary, Heyman, & Neidig, 1999). Partner abuse is clearly a multi-determined problem that is influenced by psychological and social factors. In turn, this problem requires multifaceted interventions including legal, psychological, social, and medical approaches.

REFERENCES

Browne, A., & Williams, W. R. (1993). Gender, intimacy, and lethal violence: Trends from 1976 through 1987. *Gender and Society, 7,* 78–98.

Caesar, P. L., & Hamberger, L. K. (Eds.). (1989). *Treating men who batter: Theory, practice, and programs.* New York: Springer.

Cascardi, M., Langhinrichsen, J., & Vivian, D. (1992). Marital aggression: Impact, injury, and health correlates for husbands and wives. *Archives of Internal Medicine, 152,* 1178–1184.

Cascardi, M., & O'Leary, K. D. (1992). Depressive symptomatology, self-esteem, and self-blame in battered women. *Journal of Family Violence, 7,* 249–259.

Gelles, R. J. (1993). Through a sociological lens: Social structure and family violence. In R. J. Gelles & D. R. Loseke (Eds.), *Current controversies on family violence* (pp. 31–46). Newbury Park, CA: Sage.

Hamberger, L. K., & Hastings, J. E. (1988). Characteristics of abusive men suggestive of personality disorders. *Hospital and Community Psychiatry, 39,* 763–770.

Holtzworth-Munroe, A., & Stuart, G. L. (1994). Typologies of male batterers: Three subtypes and the differences among them. *Psychological Bulletin, 116,* 476–497.

Hotaling, G. T., & Sugarman, D. B. (1986). An analysis of risk markers in husband to wife violence: The current state of knowledge. *Violence and Victims, 1,* 101–124.

Jacobson, N., & Gottman, J. (1998). *When men batter women.* New York: Simon & Schuster.

O'Leary, K. D. (1993). Through a psychological lens: Personality traits, personality disorders, and levels of violence. In R. J. Gelles & D. R. Loseke (Eds.), *Current controversies on family violence* (pp. 7–30), Newbury Park, CA: Sage.

O'Leary, K. D., Heyman, R. E., & Neidig, P. H. (1999). Treatment of wife abuse: A comparison of gender-specific and couples approaches. *Behavior Therapy, 30,* 475–505.

Pirog-Good, M. A., & Stets, J. E. (Eds.). (1989). *Violence in dating relationships: Emerging social issues.* New York: Praeger.

Straus, M. A., & Gelles, R. J. (Eds.). (1990). *Physical violence in American families.* New Brunswick, NJ: Transaction.

Walker, L. E. (1999). Psychology and domestic violence around the world. *The American Psychologist, 54,* 21–29.

Yllo, K. A. (1993). Through a feminist lens: Gender, power, and violence. In R. J. Gelles & D. R. Loseke (Eds.), *Current controversies on family violence* (pp. 47–62), Newbury Park, CA: Sage.

J. A. SCHUMACHER
K. D. O'LEARY
State University of New York, Stony Brook

SPOUSE ABUSE

PASSIVE-AGGRESSIVE PERSONALITY

The *Diagnostic and Statistical Manual of Mental Disorders,* (*DSM-III*) (American Psychiatric Association, 1980) stresses as the prime characteristic of these personalities their resistance to the demands by others for adequate performance. Ostensibly those with this disorder express a form of covert aggression through their behavior, evident in such actions as procrastination, stubbornness, forgetfulness, and inefficiency. Beyond their contrariness and disinclination to do things that others expect of them, they are also characterized by a capricious impulsiveness, an irritable moodiness, and a grumbling, discontented, sulky, unaccommodating, and fault-finding pessimism. Often anguished and discontented, these personalities are generalized and perennial in their complaints, never satisfied either with themselves or with others. Even in the best of circumstances, they seem to go out of their way to see the "dark lining in the silver cloud." An intense conflict appears to exist within them between being dependent and being self-assertive, resulting in ever-present ambivalence and persistently erratic moods. Personal relationships are also fraught with wrangles and disappointments, provoked repeatedly by their characteristic complaining and negative, fretful behaviors.

Emil Kraepelin, in the eighth edition of his *Lehrbuch,* published in 1913, noted a variant of the cyclothymic disposition that closely parallels contemporary descriptions of the passive-aggressive personality, specifically their "special sensitiveness to the cares, troubles and disappointments of life." Another variant shows "an extraordinary fluctuating emotional equilibrium and is strongly affected by all experiences, often in an unpleasant way." Schneider (1950/1923) came close to the mark in his description of what was then labeled "ill-tempered depressives." He summarized their prime features as being morose, cantankerous, irritable, nagging, spiteful, pessimistic, and malicious. The prime psychoanalytic theorist of character types, Wilhelm Reich, applied the label "masochist" to personalities possessing a marked tendency to obstruct others through their passively provocative behaviors. Reich (1972/1945) referred to their chronic feeling of suffering, their tendency to complain, and their desire to inflict pain upon and to debase both themselves and others. Approaching this personality pattern also from a psychoanalytic framework, Menninger (1940) described the so-called "oral-sadistic melancholiac": "He is inclined to blame the world for everything unpleasant which happens to him . . . he is cantankerous, contemptuous, petulant . . . perpetually discontented, moody." Horney (1959/1940) notes the intense dependency conflicts in this personality, those between weakness and strength, between merging and self-assertion, and between self-contempt and pride. Notable to her is this personality's way of expressing hostility, that of suffering, being helpless, and viewing oneself as victimized. Conceiving of these personalities in terms of the "activeness" of their ambivalence, rather than the "passiveness" of their aggression, Millon (1969) proposed a biosocial-learning framework for this disorder. The following diagnostic criteria were enumerated as a guide to this syndrome:

1. Labile affectivity (e.g., is frequently irritable and displays erratic moodiness; reports being easily frustrated and explosive).

2. Behavioral contrariness (e.g., frequently exhibits passively-aggressive, petulant, and fault-finding behaviors; reveals gratification in demoralizing and undermining the pleasures of others).

3. Discontented self-image (e.g., reports feeling misunderstood, unappreciated, and demeaned by others; is characteristically pessimistic, disgruntled, and disillusioned with life).

4. Deficient regulatory controls (e.g., expresses fleeting thoughts and impulsive emotions in unmodulated form; external stimuli evoke capricious and vacillating reactions).

5. Interpersonal ambivalence (e.g., assumes conflicting and changing roles in social relationships, particularly dependent acquiescence and assertive independence; uses unpredictable and sulking behavior to provoke edgy discomfort in others).

REFERENCES

American Psychiatric Association. (1980). *Diagnostic and statistical manual of mental disorders* (3rd ed.). Washington, DC: Author.

Menninger, K. (1940). Character disorders. In J. F. Brown (Ed.), *The psychodynamics of abnormal behavior.* New York: McGraw-Hill.

Millon, T. (1969). *Modern psychopathology.* Philadelphia, PA: Saunders.

Reich, W. (1972/1945). *Character analysis* (3rd ed.). New York: Orgone Institute Press.

Schneider, K. (1950/1923). *Psychopathic personalities.* London: Cassell.

T. MILLON
University of Miami

DIAGNOSTIC AND STATISTICAL MANUAL (DSM-IV)
PERSONALITY DISORDERS

PATIENT COMPLIANCE

Compliance with recommendations for medications and other medical regimens is essential to successful health care. *Compliance* has been defined as the extent to which patients follow prescribed regimens (Haynes, Taylor, & Sackett, 1979). The term *adherence* has been proposed as an alternative to *compliance,* because its meaning is more consistent with recent views of patients as active participants in their health care rather than passive recipients of services (e.g., O'Brien, Petrie, & Raeburn, 1992). *Compliance* is used in the present article because it is still most frequently used (Roter, Hall, Merisca, Nordstrom, Cretin, & Svarstadt, 1998).

Medication compliance requires a complex set of patient behaviors. Noncompliant patients may fail to take prescribed medication at all, take fewer or more than the prescribed number of doses, take doses at wrong times, or incorrectly combine medications. Patients are sometimes classified as noncompliant if they are less than 100% compliant, but an 80% level is often considered as the threshold for noncompliance (O'Brien et al., 1992). Patients may be intentionally noncompliant, for example to avoid side-effects (Cooper, Love, & Raffoul, 1982). They may also be unintentionally noncompliant for several reasons. They may want to comply, but are unable to do so because of barriers such as affordability, or they may be inadvertently noncompliant because they do not understand or remember how to take medication.

MEASUREMENT

Compliance measures should be unobtrusive, objective, and practical (Park & Jones, 1997). Patient self-report is commonly used but often underestimates noncompliance compared to more objective measures (Dunbar-Jacob, Burke, & Puczynski, 1995). Pill counts are more objective but also underestimate noncompliance (Park & Jones, 1997). Biological measures (e.g., blood assays) tend to be obtrusive and often do not provide an accurate picture of compli-

[1]Preparation of this article was supported by NIA grants R01 AG12163 and R01 AG13936.

ance behavior. Microelectronic monitoring is relatively unobtrusive, objective, and can provide a fine-grained picture of compliance behavior (Park & Jones, 1997).

EXTENT AND CONSEQUENCES OF NONCOMPLIANCE

Estimates of noncompliant patients range from 30 to 60% for a variety of patients, diagnoses, and treatments (e.g., Rogers & Bullman, 1995). Noncompliance reduces health outcomes by lowering drug efficacy and producing drug-related illness due to incorrect doses or drug combinations (e.g., Col, Fanale, & Kronholm, 1990). Because noncompliance is often not monitored by physicians, it can distort assessment of treatment efficacy for patients as well as assessment of new drugs in clinical trials (Dunbar-Jacob et al., 1995).

THEORIES OF NONCOMPLIANCE

Several social-behavioral theories have been used to explain noncompliant behavior, including the Health Belief Model (Strecher & Rosenstock, 1997), the Common Sense Model (Leventhal, Leventhal, Robitaile, & Brownlee, 1999), and self-efficacy theory (Bandura, 1997). Park and colleagues (e.g., Park, Hertzog, Leventhal, Morrell, Leventhal, Birchmore, Martin, & Bennett, 1999; Park & Jones, 1997) have attempted to integrate psychosocial approaches with cognitive theory. They propose that noncompliance is influenced by the patient's representation of illness and treatment, cognitive variables such as working memory, and external aids. Such multifactor models may help identify components of successful compliance. For example, patients must understand how to comply, accept and adopt the task as relevant, develop an adherence plan that integrates information for all medications, and then implement the plan, including remembering to take the medication (Morrow & Leirer, 1999).

PREDICTORS OF NONCOMPLIANCE

Illness and Treatment Variables

Noncompliance tends to increase with regimen complexity, such as an increase in the number of medications or times per medication, perhaps because these regimens conflict with patients' schedules (Ascione, 1994). Noncompliance varies with symptoms (O'Brien, et al. 1992) and medication side effects (e.g., Haynes, et al., 1979). It is more prevalent for chronically ill patients, in part because such patients tend to have multiple illnesses (e.g., German, 1988). Noncompliance may be more influenced by chronically ill patients' representations of illness than by objective factors (e.g., Leventhal, et al., 1999). Psychosocial research has focused on relationships between beliefs and noncompliance. For example, perceived benefits of treatment and severity of illness are more important predictors of medication noncompliance than of preventative behaviors (Strecher & Rosenstock, 1997).

Patient Variables

There is little evidence that noncompliance varies with gender, socioeconomic, or ethnic factors, although research is limited (e.g., Dunbar-Jacob et al., 1995). Noncompliance relates primarily to education and cognitive ability. For example, older adults' com-

prehension of medication information is predicted by education level (Diehl, Willis, & Schaie, 1995). Less educated patients tend to have lower health literacy, defined as the ability to understand basic information related to medication and other services. Lower health literacy also predicts poorer health outcomes and less utilization of services (Gazmararian, Baker, Williams, Parker, Scott, Green, Fehrenbach, Ren, & Koplan, 1999). Older adults' noncompliance is a critical problem because they are a growing segment of the population, they tend to use more health services than other age groups, and they may be more vulnerable to the consequences of noncompliance (e.g., Ascione, 1994). Older patients often recall less health information (Morrell, Park, & Poon, 1989). Recent studies with electronic monitoring find increased noncompliance among adults over age 75, in part because of cognitive declines (Morrell et al., 1997; Park et al., 1992). These studies also find higher noncompliance for middle-aged than for young-old adults (age 65–74; Morrell et al., 1997; Park et al., 1999). Noncompliance for middle-aged adults may reflect busy lifestyles that interfere with prospective memory (Park et al., 1999). Higher levels of compliance among young-old adults, on the other hand, may reflect the fact that they have sufficient cognitive ability to develop adherence plans as well as health representations that support compliance. The latter point is consistent with evidence that self-efficacy beliefs predict compliance (e.g., Lorig, Seleznick, Lubeck, Ung, Chastain, & Holman, 1989).

Provider-Patient Communication

Patient satisfaction and compliance relate to task-oriented communication behaviors by physicians, such as amount of information provided, as well as to partnership-building behaviors, such as more positive and less negative talk (Hall, Roter, & Katz, 1988). They also relate to a participatory style that involves patients (Hall et al., 1988). Patient-provider relationship may be especially important for compliance by chronically ill elders (e.g., German, 1988).

REDUCING NONCOMPLIANCE

There are few intervention studies with rigorous designs, such as randomized control trials (Haynes, McKibbon, & Kanani, 1996; Roter et al., 1998). Nonetheless, the literature suggests the importance of several approaches for reducing noncompliance. Cognitive approaches focus on simplifying the compliance task and eliminating comprehension and memory failures that produce unintentional noncompliance (Haynes, Wang, & Gomes, 1987; Park & Jones, 1997). Psychosocial approaches focus on intentional noncompliance.

Cognitive Approaches

The relationship between noncompliance and regime complexity suggests that one way to improve compliance is to simplify the regimen by reducing or synchronizing times for multiple medications (Ley, 1997). Reducing medication times has been found to reduce noncompliance (Baird et al., 1984).

Sensorimotor barriers can be mitigated by simple interventions. Large print on labels compensate for visual declines, and easy-to-open containers address reduced dexterity due to arthritis or other conditions (Ascione, 1994; Morrow, Leirer, & Sheikh, 1988). Comprehension and memory problems are addressed by improving instructions on container labels and pamphlets accompanying prescriptions. Improvements have targeted instruction content (e.g., complete information), language (e.g., explicit, simple words and sentences), format (e.g., list versus paragraph), and organization (Hartley, 1999; Ley, 1997; Morrow et al., 1988; Morrow & Leirer, 1999). Instructions can also take advantage of patient knowledge. Both older and younger patients possess schemas for organizing medication information, and they better remember instructions that follow these schemas (Morrow & Leirer, 1999). Icons or pictures address problems related to limited education and literacy (e.g., Morrow & Leirer, 1999). Noncompliance is reduced by improved medication packaging (e.g., Wong & Norman, 1987), calendars, or other aids that help patients organize medications into an adherence plan (e.g., MacDonald, MacDonald, & Phoenix, 1977), and by pill organizers if they are correctly loaded (Park & Jones, 1997). Noncompliance is also improved by automated telephone messages that support patients' prospective memory and symptom-monitoring (e.g., Tanke & Leirer, 1994).

Improving provider-patient communication can reduce noncompliance. Teaching communication skills to physicians, such as asking for information during history-taking, improves patient recall and health outcomes. Similarly, teaching patients to ask questions and provide information also improves health outcomes (e.g., Stewart, 1995). These gains may reflect increased patient satisfaction as well as memory (Hall et al., 1988; Ley, 1997).

Psychosocial Approaches and Patient Education

Educational programs based on psychosocial approaches focus on intentional noncompliance. There is some evidence that such interventions improve compliance by targeting belief-based barriers such as perceived vulnerability to illness and benefits and costs of treatment (Janz & Becker, 1984; Strecher & Rosenstock, 1997). Such benefits may occur for reasons in addition to influencing specific beliefs, such as increased patient knowledge or self-efficacy (e.g., Lorig et al., 1989).

Other Interventions

Several methods attempt to shape compliance behavior, including behavioral contracting (Haynes et al., 1979), feedback (Kruse, Rampmaier, Ullrich, & Weber, 1994), and financial incentives (Giuffrida & Torgerson, 1997). Noncompliance is reduced by increasing social support, which may reflect the influence of significant others on patients' prospective memory, health beliefs, or self-efficacy (Park & Jones, 1997).

Because interventions often contain multiple components, it is difficult to identify why noncompliance is reduced. At the same time, more intensive or comprehensive interventions are more likely to reduce noncompliance (Haynes et al., 1996; Roter et al., 1998), perhaps by addressing multiple components of noncompliance for each patient or by helping a wider range of patients.

CONCLUSIONS

Although there are many compliance studies, relatively few have adequately measured compliance. Thus, little is known about successful compliance or how and why noncompliance occurs (Dunbar-Jacob et al., 1995; Park & Jones, 1997). Nonetheless, there is a consensus that noncompliance remains a pervasive health care problem (e.g., O'Brien et al., 1992). Challenges for future research include the following: First, there is a need for intervention research based on a comprehensive model that addresses both intentional and unintentional compliance (cf. Park & Jones, 1997). Second, a complex, patient-based approach is needed, including profiles of noncompliant patients so that providers can better recommend suitable methods for specific noncompliance conditions. This "tailoring" strategy may be the most cost-effective way to address noncompliance. In addition to reducing noncompliance, it is important to initiate successful compliance, because it may be easier to first establish accurate compliance than to modify existing practices (Dunbar-Jacob et al., 1995). Finally, research should focus on implementing interventions within existing health delivery systems once efficacy has been demonstrated in clinical trials.

REFERENCES

Ascione, F. (1994). Medication compliance in the elderly. *Generations, 18,* 28–33.

Baird, M. G., Bentley-Taylor, M. M., Carruthers, S. G., Dawson, K. G., Laplante, L. E., & Larochelle, P. (1984). A study of the efficacy, tolerance, and compliance of once-daily versus twice-daily metoprolol (Betaloc) in hypertension. *Clinical and Investigative Medicine, 7,* 95.

Bandura, A. (1997). Self-efficacy and health behaviour. In A. Baum, S. Newman, J. Weinman, R. West, & C. McManus (Eds.), *Cambridge handbook of psychology, health, and medicine* (pp. 160–162). Cambridge: Cambridge University Press.

Col, N., Fanale, J. E., & Kronholm, P. (1990). The role of medication noncompliance and adverse drug reactions in hospitalizations of the elderly. *Archives of Internal Medicine, 150,* 841–845.

Cooper, J. W., Love, D. W., & Raffoul, P. R. (1982). Intentional prescription nonadherence (noncompliance) by the elderly. *Journal of the American Geriatrics Society, 30,* 329–333.

Diehl, M., Willis, S. L., & Schaie, W. (1995). Everyday problem solving in older adults: Observational assessment and cognitive correlates. *Psychology and Aging, 10,* 478–491.

Dunbar-Jacob, J., Burke, L. E., & Puczynski, S. (1995). Clinical assessment and management of adherence to medical regimens. In P. M. Nicassio & T. W. Smith (Eds.), *Managing chronic illness: A biopsychosocial perspective* (pp. 313–349) Washington, DC: American Psychological Association.

Gazmararian, J. A., Baker, D. W., Williams, M. V., Parker, R. M., Scott, T. L., Green, D. C., Fehrenbach, S. N., Ren, J., & Koplan, J. P. (1999). Health literacy among Medicare enrollees in a managed care organization, *Journal of the American Medical Association, 281,* 545–551.

German, P. S. (1988). Compliance and chronic disease. *Hypertension, 11,* II56–II60.

Giuffrida, A., & Torgerson, D. (1997). Should we pay the patient? A review of financial incentives to enhance patient compliance. *British Medical Journal, 3,* 703.

Hall, J. A., Roter, D. L., & Katz, N. R. (1988). Meta-analysis of correlates of provider behavior in medical encounters. *Medical Care, 26,* 657–675.

Hartley, J. (1999). What does it say? Text design, medical information, and older readers. In D. C. Park, R. W. Morrell, & K. Shifren (Eds.), *Processing of medical information in aging patients* (pp. 233–248). Mahwah, NJ: Erlbaum.

Haynes, R. B., McKibbon, K. A., & Kanani, R. (1996). Systematic review of randomized trials of interventions to assist patients to follow prescriptions for medications. *Lancet, 348,* 383.

Haynes, R. B., Taylor, D. W., & Sackett, D. L. (1979). *Compliance in health care.* Baltimore, MD: Johns Hopkins University Press.

Haynes, R. B., Wang, E., & Gomes, D. M. (1987). A critical review of interventions to improve compliance with prescribed medications. *Patient Education and Counseling, 10,* 155–166.

Janz, N. K., & Becker, M. H. (1984). The health belief model: A decade later. *Health Education Quarterly, 11,* 1–47.

Kruse, W., Rampmaier, J., Ullrich, G., & Weber, E. (1994). Patterns of drug compliance with medications to be taken once and twice daily assessed by continuous electronic monitoring in primary care. *International Journal of Clinical Pharmacology and Therapeutics, 32,* 452–457.

Leventhal, E. A., Leventhal, H., Robitaile, C., & Brownlee, S. (1999). Psychosocial factors in medication adherence: A model of the modeler. In D. C. Park, R. W. Morrell, & K. Shifren (Eds.), *Processing of medical information in aging patients* (pp. 145–166). Mahwah, NJ: Erlbaum.

Ley, P. (1997). Recall by patients. In A. Baum, S. Newman, J. Weinman, R. West, & C. McManus (Eds.), *Cambridge handbook of psychology, health, and medicine* (pp. 315–317). Cambridge: Cambridge University Press.

Lorig, K., Seleznick, M., Lubeck, D., Ung, E., Chastain, R. L., & Holman, H. R. (1989). The beneficial outcomes of the arthritis self-management course are not adequately explained by behavior change. *Arthritis and Rheumatism, 32,* 91–95.

MacDonald, E. T., MacDonald, J. B., & Phoenix, M. (1977). Improving drug compliance after hospital discharge. *British Medical Journal, 2,* 618–621.

Morrell, R. W., Park, D. C., Kidder, D. P., & Martin, M. (1997). Adherence to antihypertensive medications across the life span. *The Gerontologist, 37,* 609–619.

Morrell, R. W., Park, D. C., & Poon, L. (1989). Quality of instructions on prescription drug labels: Effects on memory and comprehension in young and old adults. *The Gerontologist, 29,* 345–354.

Morrow, D. G., & Leirer, V. O. (1999). Designing medication instructions for older adults. In D. C. Park, R. W. Morrell, & K. Shifren (Eds.), *Processing of medical information in aging patients* (pp. 249–265), Mahwah, NJ: Erlbaum.

Morrow, D. G., Leirer, V. O., & Sheikh, J. (1988). Adherence and medication instructions: Review and recommendations. *Journal of the American Geriatric Society, 36,* 1147–1160.

O'Brien, M. K., Petrie, K., & Raeburn, J. (1992). Adherence to medication regimens: Updating a complex medical issue. *Medical Care Review, 49,* 435–454.

Park, D. C., Hertzog, C., Leventhal, H., Morrell, R. W., Leventhal, E., Birchmore, D., Martin, M., & Bennett, J. (1999). Medication adherence in rheumatoid arthritis patients: Older is wiser. *Journal of the American Geriatrics Society, 47,* 172–183.

Park, D. C., & Jones, T. R. (1997). Medication adherence and aging. In A. D. Fisk & W. A. Rogers (Eds.), *Handbook of human factors and the older adult* (pp. 257–287). San Diego, CA: Academic Press.

Park, D. C., Morrell, R., Freske, D., & Kincaid, D. (1992). Medication adherence behaviors in older adults: Effects of external cognitive supports. *Psychology and Aging, 7,* 252–256.

Rogers, P. G., & Bullman, W. R. (1995). Prescription medication compliance: A review of the baseline of knowledge. A report of the National Council on Patient Information and Education. *Journal of Pharmacoepidemiology, 2,* 3.

Roter, D. L., Hall, J. A., Merisca, R., Nordstrom, B., Cretin, D., & Svarstatd, B. (1998). Effectiveness of interventions to improve patient compliance: A meta-analysis. *Medical Care, 36,* 1138–1161.

Stewart, M. A. (1995). Effective physician-patient communication and health outcomes: A review. *Canadian Medical Association Journal, 152,* 1423–1433.

Strecher, V. J., & Rosenstock, I. M. (1997). The health belief model. In A. Baum, S. Newman, J. Weinman, R. West, & C. McManus (Eds.), *Cambridge handbook of psychology, health, and medicine,* (pp. 113–116). Cambridge: Cambridge University Press.

Tanke, E. D., & Leirer, V. O. (1994). Automated telephone reminders in tuberculosis care. *Medical Care, 32,* 380–389.

Wong, B. S. M., & Norman, D. C. (1987). Evaluation of a novel medication aid, the calendar blister-pak, and its effect on drug compliance in a geriatric outpatient clinic. *Journal of the American Geriatrics Society, 35,* 21–26.

D. G. MORROW
University of New Hampshire

PAUL, GORDON L. (1935-   )

Gordon L. Paul, an American behavioral scientist and clinical psychologist, is one of the leading clinicians, researchers, and theoreticians in the mental health field. A committed scientist/practitioner, Paul is noted for his outstanding contributions to clinical research methods and program evaluation. His contributions to the understanding, assessment, and treatment of the most extensive as well as the most severe emotional, behavioral, and mental problems have been especially noteworthy. He is a practicing licensed psychologist and certified health-service provider with supervisory experience in both inpatient and outpatient settings.

Widely respected as a consultant on mental health research, services, and system operations, he has also been actively involved in university teaching at the graduate and professional levels.

The son of Ione Hickman (Perry) and Leon Dale Paul, Paul was born on September 2, 1935 in Marshalltown, IA, where he attended public schools and graduated from high school in 1953. He and Joan Marie Wyatt were married on December 24, 1954. Their marriage produced two sons, Dennis Leon and Dana Lee; a daughter, Joni Lynn (Fredrickson); and six grandchildren (Andrew, Sara, and Lonni Fredrickson; Alexandra, Gordon II, and Joseph Paul).

During his youth Paul performed for ten years as a professional musician, including four years with the US Navy (1954–58). Music and psychology were his undergraduate majors, with mathematics and business as minor areas of study. He received the Bachelor of Arts degree ("with highest honors") in 1960 from the University of Iowa, Iowa City, after previously attending Marshalltown Junior College in Marshalltown, IA (1953–54), the US Naval School of Music in Washington DC (1954–55), and San Diego City College in San Diego, CA (1955–57). Paul was inducted into Phi Beta Kappa and Chi Gamma Iota honor societies at the University of Iowa. Master's (1962) and doctoral (1964) degrees ("with distinction") were earned following graduate study in clinical and physiological psychology at the University of Illinois at Urbana-Champaign. He completed postdoctoral training at the Veterans Administration Medical Center in Palo Alto/Menlo Park, CA and at Stanford University in Palo Alto, CA (1964–65).

Returning to the University of Illinois at Urbana-Champaign as a faculty member in the graduate clinical program in 1965, Paul remained there for 15 years, twice receiving the Award for Excellence in Graduate Training. A supervising psychologist at the University Psychological Clinic, he also served as director of the Psychosocial Rehabilitation Units (1968–73) and as director of the Clinical-Research Unit (1973–84) at the Adolf Meyer Mental Health Center in Decatur, IL. Since 1980, when he was awarded the Hugh Roy Cullen and Lillie Cranz Cullen Distinguished Chair in Psychology, Paul has been a member of the graduate faculty and supervising clinical psychologist at the University of Houston in Houston, TX. He has maintained a private practice in clinical and consulting psychology since 1964.

Paul has been a member of or advisor to numerous review and policymaking groups at regional, state, and national levels. He has addressed more than 200 professional organizations, universities, and mental health agencies internationally and throughout the United States. His memberships in advocacy groups on behalf of people who suffer from severe emotional, behavioral, and mental problems and disabilities include the National Alliance for the Mentally Ill and the Mental Health Association. Among Paul's elected positions are president of Section 3, Division 12, of the American Psychological Association (1972–73) and fellow status in the American Psychological Association, including Divisions 12 (Clinical) and 25 (Behavior Analysis), the Association for Clinical Psychosocial Research, the American Psychological Society, and the American Association of Applied & Preventive Psychology.

In addition to his extensive public service, Paul has served on the editorial boards of seven major professional journals. These include the *Journal of Behavior Therapy and Experimental Psychiatry,*

Journal of Abnormal Psychology, Schizophrenia Bulletin, and *Journal of Psychopathology and Behavioral Assessment.* He has also been a frequent consulting editor for 19 journals, including the *Journal of Applied Behavior Analysis, Psychological Bulletin, Psychosomatic Medicine, Psychophysiology, Journal of Consulting & Clinical Psychology, Archives of General Psychiatry, Psychiatric Services, Journal of Nervous and Mental Disease, Psychological Assessment, American Psychologist,* and *Current Directions in Psychological Science.*

Paul's research program has led to many awards and significant recognition for methodological contributions and for development of cost-effective assessment and treatment procedures. His early publications on clinical research methodology and the assessment and treatment of anxiety-related problems became "citation classics" (*Science Citation Index* and *Social Science Citation Index*). Many "expert listings" have noted his accomplishments. Among these listings are Paul's inclusion as one of the "100 Most Outstanding Clinical Psychologists in the USA" in *The Clinical Psychologist* (1975) and as one of "327 Best Mental Health Experts" (among 37 experts for schizophrenia) in *Good Housekeeping* (1994).

The 1964 Creative Talent Award in the Field of Development, Counseling, and Mental Health, from the American Institute for Research, provided early recognition of Paul's clinical research. Paul received several more formal awards in later years. These include the 1977 Distinguished Scientist Award of the Society for a Science of Clinical Psychology (Section 3, Division 12, American Psychological Association), a Mental Health Association Research Award (1985), Commendation of Accomplishments by the Houston Mayor and City Council (1993), and the Distinguished Scientific Contributions to Clinical Psychology Award of the American Psychological Association, Society of Clinical Psychology (1999).

Paul's early methodological contributions and research on anxiety contributed to new understanding and effective psychosocial treatment procedures for the most extensive problems in the mental health field. These early and continuing works were among those that formed the foundation for the evidence-based practice movement in psychology. Paul's clinical research has been at the forefront of those demonstrating the utility of psychosocial principles for the understanding and effective nonpharmacological treatment of problems ranging from "anxiety disorders" through "schizophrenia."

Although his earliest work focused on outpatient problems, the clinical research group led by Paul for more than 30 years has primarily focused on mental health service systems and the very severe, chronic problems associated with psychoses. This work has resulted in science-based psychosocial training procedures that provide effective and cost-efficient treatment to hospitalized mental patients who were previously thought to be untreatable. In addition to a treatment program that works for previously untreatable mental patients, the Social-Learning Program, Paul's clinical-research group has developed a comprehensive new approach to assessment and monitoring of patient, staff, and program functioning in residential and inpatient treatment settings. Reviewers have likened the development of the new technology,

The Computerized TSBC/SRIC Planned-Access Observational Information System, as akin to the development of the cloud chamber in physics and the electron microscope in biology, in which "the technical gain may be a difference in kind, not merely a difference in degree."

REFERENCE

Lieberman, H. J. (1987). Assessments contribution to social revolution: Comments of a consumer on the residential assessment methodology of Gordon Paul and colleagues. In D. R. Peterson & D. B. Fishman (Eds.), *Assessment for decision* (pp. 204–213). New Brunswick, NJ: Rutgers University Press.

STAFF

PAVLOV, IVAN PETROVICH (1849–1936)

Ivan Petrovich Pavlov was the eldest of 11 children. He learned about hard work and responsibility at an early age. In 1860, Pavlov entered a theological seminary, but in 1870 he changed his mind and went to the University of St. Petersburg to study animal physiology. He received his degree in 1875, started medical training, studied in Germany, and returned to St. Petersburg to begin a long career in physiological research. He earned his doctorate in 1883 from the Military Medical Academy. In 1891, he was appointed director of the Department of Physiology at the Institute of Experimental Medicine in St. Petersburg, and in 1897, he became a professor at the university. In 1904, his research work on the primary digestive glands was recognized with the Nobel prize.

Pavlov's research also concerned nerves of the heart and studies of the higher nerve centers of the brain. His methodology for the research, and his greatest scientific achievement, was conditioning, a technique that significantly influenced the development of psychology. Pavlov's research became a model and standard for objectivity and precision. In his controlled experiments, he studied the formation of conditioned responses, reinforcement, extinction, spontaneous recovery, generalization, discrimination, and higher order conditioning (all applied concepts to learning and association in psychology). Pavlov's most important writings were *The Work of the Digestive Glands* and *Conditioned Reflexes.*

Pavlov's work was a cornerstone for the development of behaviorism, in which the conditioned reflex is so important. John B. Watson took the conditioned reflex as the basic unit of behavior and made it the building block of his program of behaviorism. The conditioned response was used during the 1920s, in the United States, as the foundation for learning theories, thus generating further research and theory.

N. A. HAYNIE

PEABODY PICTURE VOCABULARY TEST

The Peabody test is presented in a 175-page booklet, with each page containing four illustrations of common objects such as toys, kitchen appliances, and animals. The test is administered as follows: The examiner says the stimulus word (for example, "candle"). The subject is asked to point to or otherwise indicate the correct answer. The range of this test is considerable. However, the pictures are not spaced at psychologically meaningful intervals. That is, for one mental year (or the equivalent) there may be only two plates at one level, whereas for another mental year there may be as many as a dozen. The subject receives a total score in terms of correct replies, which can be converted to a standard score, a percentile, and, if one wishes, an IQ.

The Peabody test has considerable versatility as well as range. Even retarded children like and can function on this test. It can be viewed as a test of general intelligence on the basis of the argument that (keeping environmental conditions constant) children who are inherently brighter are more likely to do well on this test than children who are not as bright. The test comes in two forms. Validity and reliability levels are considered acceptable for individual clinical use, and this test is frequently employed in combination with other tests, such as the Wechsler-Bellevue tests and the Stanford-Binet.

SUGGESTED READING

Dunn, L. M., & Dunn, L. M. (1981). *Peabody picture vocabulary test—revised: Manual for forms L and M.* Circle Pines, MN: American Guidance Service.

A. SIMPKINS
University of Hawaii

INTELLIGENCE MEASURES
NONVERBAL INTELLIGENCE TESTS

PEAK EXPERIENCES

The discoverer of peak experiences, Abraham Maslow (1968/1962), described them as rare, exciting, oceanic, deeply moving, exhilarating, elevating experiences that generate an advanced form of perceiving reality, and are even mystic and magical in their effect upon the experimenter. Lowry reflects the attitude and enthusiasm of the humanistic psychology that Maslow lathered, suggesting, "There is really no way of succinctly conveying the richness, the spirit, the *je ne sais quoi* of Maslow's writings on the subject of peak experience" (Lowry, 1973, p. 51).

THE 19 CHARACTERISTICS

Maslow's concept of "self-actualizing" and of Being Cognition was sometimes used interchangeably with peak experiences. The 19 characteristics found in the original paper (Maslow, 1959) constitute perhaps the best available description of that oceanic, positive experience.

Those most pertinent may be summarized as follows: There is an experience of wholeness, of unity, and in the perceptual process, the person attends fully. The perceptions are richer. Subjects asked to report such experiences select love experiences; mystic, aesthetic, and creative experiences; and insight experiences. There is a disorientation in time and space—the person loses sight of the present environment. It is a positive experience; never an evil or negative one. The self-actualized person lives comfortably with polarities. The person at the peak is godlike, particularly in the complete, loving, uncondemning, compassionate, and perhaps amused acceptance of the world and of the person. The peak experience chases away fear and there is a healthy childishness in the person's behavior.

POSITIVE EXPERIENCE

Maslow paid less attention to the entire range of positive experience but acknowledged the existence of "foothill" or lesser, yet still positive, experiences making their own contribution to the self-actualizing personality. Seven categories are often used to describe the positive experiences: divine experience, conquest of a skill, excitement, human relationships, beauty, earned success, and completion. Supporting the propositions of Maslow as well as positive experience theory, studies by Puttick (1964) and by Privette (1964) show a "childlike sense of humor" as being characteristic of self-actualizing persons. While Maslow concentrated almost exclusively on the peak positive experience, Lynch (1968) studied both sides of the continuum, intense positive and intense negative experience. He found that only a third of the experiences reported were positive. This suggests that the general pattern is for one to leave untapped a greater share of life's joyful intensities.

OTHER PEAK-EXPERIENCE RESEARCHERS AND THEORETICIANS

Many humanistically oriented, and even some behavioral psychologists found peak experiences quite researchable. The literature shows the response to Maslow's propositions to be quite varied. A large number of theoretical and philosophical questions were raised. For example, is the peak experience a new level of consciousness? Is it valid?—The latter is a question that Lowry answers uncertainly.

But experience of any kind has not been welcome in U.S. psychological laboratories. Maslow (1966/1956) argued, along with others, for a "respectable place for experiential data," and Day (1974) saw the peak experience as related to Platonic essences. Beulka (1976) enthusiastically welcomed the peak experience as having a grounding in Talmudic lore. Phenomenology as the study of perceptual data in contrast to objective data is the true home of the peak experience. Rosenblatt and Bartlett (1976) found a relationship of peak experience to two major phenomenological concepts—paradoxical intention and intentionality, and Armor (1969) supported the position that the peak experience constitutes "a transcendence of the usual form of consciousness common to all mankind."

Psychology became divided into three forces with the growth of humanistic psychology, behaviorism, and psychoanalysis. Blanchard (1969) has presented some common ground, suggesting that the peak experience can lead to self-fulfillment or self-destruction. He also sees a sense of adventure in the peak experience.

PEAK EXPERIENCES IN EDUCATION AND THE ARTS

Maslow suggested that the two easiest ways of triggering peak experiences were through classical music and sex. He argued for an intrinsic education, by which he meant "learning to be a human being in general, and second, learning to be this particular human being" (Maslow, 1971, p. 170). Beyond music itself as a trigger for the peak experience, Maslow was enthusiastic about rhythm exercises, athletics, and dancing. He asserted, "The love for the body, awareness of the body and a reverence of the body—these are clearly good paths to peak experiences" (Maslow, 1971, p. 176). However, he also saw the possibility of mathematics education as peak producing, adding wryly, ". . . of course there are mathematics teachers who have devoted themselves to preventing this" (Maslow, 1971, p. 178).

Support for some of these propositions was not slow in coming in the form of empirical studies. "Experience" had long before been rejected by objectivistic psychology. Yet when it returned in the form of peak and positive experience, there was no rush to eliminate it, even though objectivists remain skeptical—but respectful. Responding to Maslow's challenge to education, Wilgenbusch (1980) saw the possibility of developing Maslow's call for a human potential in teacher education.

Researchers in music also answered the Maslovian call. Pennington (1973) developed a quantitative measurement of the peak experience in music. Pafford (1970) asked 400 students to read an autobiographical description of a peak experience and then asked them if they had had a similar one. Pafford reports a significant correlation between such an admission and an active interest in creative writing, painting, music, and poetry.

For Privette's study of the transcendent, positive, and peak experiences, a musician describes being carried away by his own performance on the trumpet as each of the performers in a band took turns improvising. The trumpeter reported that he was conscious only of his own music and his self; it was not until the experience was almost all over that he realized the dancing had stopped and all had gathered around to listen to his improvisations. The empirical data and the case studies reported lend credibility to the relationship between art and peak experience.

THE DRUG EXPERIENCE

Early in his descriptions of the peak experience, Maslow permitted himself to consider drug experiences as possibly having some similarity to the peak experience. However, he clearly rejected this as reported in a later paper by Hardeman (1978). Maslow is quoted as saying, "I would certainly be very wary about the possibilities of drug induced peak experiences. Peak experiences that really change the person come about where they are earned . . . as the result of a year of sweating on a psychoanalytic couch" (Hardeman, 1979, p. 24).

Nevertheless, a sizable literature has grown up around the use of dipropyltryptamine (DPT) with terminal cancer patients. For example, Richards (1975) reported that in 15 of 34 subjects the drug resulted in a peak experience, and that testing and interviewing by therapists supported the probability of reduced stress in those patients. However, two social workers who rated "blind" before and after the drug therapy did not judge the patients to be any different after the therapy. On the other hand, Klavetter and Mogar (1967) reported a study in which subjects given LSD for a 14-month period indicated positive changes. It appears that at best the issue of the presumed similarity of drug and peak experiences must remain in doubt.

A FURTHER EMPIRICAL STUDY

The issue of the researchability of Maslow's contributions became of more and more consequence as both behaviorism and humanistic psychology grew in popularity. Studies cited previously demonstrate that empirical studies have not been neglected in the exploration of the validity of the peak experience. Wuthnow (1978) has reported on perhaps the most ambitious effort so far. His team used a stratified sample of 1,000 persons representative of all those aged 16 or over living in the five counties that constitute the San Francisco-Oakland area. Forty professional interviewers conducted the one-hour interviews. Reports of having had certain peak experiences were made by 88% of the subjects. "High peakers" were most likely to feel that their lives were meaningful. Nonpeakers were more likely to hold materialistic values. High peakers also were more likely to be concerned about social problems.

REFERENCES

Armor, T. (1969). A note on the peak experience and a transpersonal psychology. *Journal of Transpersonal Psychology, 1,* 47–50.

Beulka, R. P. (1976). Setting the tone: The psychology-Judaism dialogue. *Journal of Psychology and Judaism, 1,* 3–13.

Blanchard, W. H. (1969). Psychodynamic aspects of the peak experience. *Psychoanalytic Review, 56,* 87–112.

Day, J. L. (1974). *Platonic essences utilized as models for Maslow's peak experiences.* Unpublished doctoral dissertation, U.S. International University.

Hardeman, M. A. (1978). A dialogue with Abraham Maslow. *Journal of Humanistic Psychology, 19,* 23–28.

Klavetter, R. E., & Mogar, R. E. (1967). Peak experiences: Investigation of their relationship to psychedelic therapy and self-actualization. *Journal of Humanistic Psychology, 7,* 171–177.

Lowry, R. J. (1973). *A. H. Maslow: An intellectual portrait.* Monterey, CA: Brooks/Cole.

Lynch, S. (1968). *Intense human experience: Its relationship to openness and self concept.* Unpublished doctoral dissertation, University of Florida.

Maslow, A. H. (1959). Cognition of being in the peak experiences. *Journal of Genetic Psychology, 94,* 43–66.

Maslow, A. H. (1966/1956). *Psychology of science.* New York: Harper & Row.

Maslow, A. H. (1968/1962). *Toward a psychology of being.* New York: Van Nostrand Reinhold.

Maslow, A. H. (1971). *The farther reaches of human nature.* New York: Viking.

Pafford, M. K. (1970). Creative activities and "peak" experiences. *British Journal of Educational Psychology, 40,* 283–290.

Pennington, J. S. (1973). *The musical peak experience* (doctoral dissertation, Ohio State University, 1972). *Dissertation Abstracts International, 34*(2-A), 601–602.

Privette, P. G. (1964). *Factors associated with functioning which transcends modal behavior.* Unpublished doctoral dissertation, University of Florida.

Puttick, W. H. (1964). *A factor analytic study of positive modes of experiencing and behaving in a teacher college population.* Unpublished doctoral dissertation, University of Florida.

Richards, W. A. (1975). *Counseling, peak experiences and the human encounter with death: An empirical study of the efficacy of DPT-assisted counseling in enhancing the quality of life of persons with terminal cancer.* Unpublished doctoral dissertation, Catholic University of America.

Rosenblatt, H. S., & Bartlett, I. (1976). Some phenomenological aspects of the peak experience. *Southern Journal of Educational Research, 10,* 29–42.

Wilgenbusch, N. (1980). *Maslow's concept of peak experience education: Impossible myth or possible mission?* Flat River, MO: Mineral Area College. (ERIC Document Reproduction Service no. ED 199 250)

Wuthmow, R. (1978). Peak experiences: Some empirical tests. *Journal of Humanistic Psychology, 18,* 59–76.

SUGGESTED READING

Hallaq, J. H. (1977). Scaling and factor analyzing peak experiences. *Journal of Clinical Psychology, 33,* 77–82.

Landsman, T. (1974). The humanizer. *American Journal of Orthopsychiatry, 44,* 345–352.

Maslow, A. H. (1954). *Motivation and personality.* New York: Harper & Brothers.

Ravizza, K. (1977). Peak experiences in sport. *Journal of Humanistic Psychology, 17,* 35–40.

T. LANDSMAN
University of Florida

EMOTIONS
TRANSPERSONAL PSYCHOLOGY I AND II

PEARSON, KARL (1857–1936)

Called the founder of the science of statistics, Karl Pearson made contributions of major importance to the development of the biological, behavioral, and social sciences. His application of mathematical and statistical methods to the study of biological problems, particularly evolution and genetics, ranks among the great achievements of science.

An exceptionally brilliant student, Pearson was graduated with honors in mathematics from Cambridge University, where he also studied physics, philosophy, religion, and law (he was admitted to the bar). His motto was the basic theme of his life: "We are ignorant; so let us work." While a professor of applied mathematics at the University of London, he published works on elasticity and on the philosophy of science, before coming under the influence of Sir Francis Galton, who helped to shape Pearson's subsequent career. Mainly as a result of reading Galton's *Natural Inheritance* (1889), he became a devoted disciple and personal friend of the great man, and his career was set on the course that led to the development of statistical theory and methods suited to dealing with the problems posed by Galton's work on human variation, heredity, and eugenics. Inspired by Galton's ideas, Pearson stated that "real knowledge must take the place of energetic but untrained philanthropy in dictating the lines of feasible social reform." Galton's great influence on Pearson is attested to by the latter's devoting almost 20 years to writing a four-volume biography, *The Life, Letters, and Labours of Francis Galton* (1914–1930). In 1904, Pearson was appointed the first director of the Galton Laboratory at the University of London, and was the first professor to occupy the Chair of Eugenics, which Galton had endowed with a gift of £45,000.

Pearson's many statistical contributions are now a standard part of the research methodology of the behavioral and social sciences. They include mathematical formulations of types of frequency distributions, measures of skewness and kurtosis, curve fitting, the standard deviation σ, the "chi-square" test, the contingency coefficient, the product-moment correlation coefficient r; biserial, multiple, tetrachoric, and nonlinear correlation, and derivation of the probable errors and sampling distributions of a variety of statistics, published in Pearson's *Tables for Statisticians and Biometricians* (1914). He also invented principal components analysis, a forerunner of factor analysis later developed by Charles Spearman. Few scientists have contributed a more useful and enduring legacy than did Pearson.

A. R. JENSEN
University of California at Berkeley

PEDIATRIC PSYCHOLOGY

Pediatric psychology exists at the intersection of developmental psychology, health psychology, and child psychopathology. The term was originally developed by Logan Wright in 1967 when he defined a pediatric psychologist as "any psychologist dealing primarily with children in a medical setting that is non-psychiatric in nature." *The Journal of Pediatric Psychology* defines pediatric psychology as "an interdisciplinary field addressing the full range of physical and mental development, health and illness issues affecting children, adolescents and families" (Roberts et al., 1988).

The need for this area of psychology was first articulated in 1930 by John Anderson, a pediatrician. The first psychologist to suggest a marriage of psychology and pediatrics was Kagan (1965), with Wright's 1967 paper in the *American Psychologist* being credited as formally marking the birth of the field. The Society of Pediatric

Psychology, formed in 1968, is Section 5 of Division 12 of the American Psychological Association.

Pediatric psychology differs from child psychology in that the point of intervention usually is medical rather than psychiatric. Much of the work in pediatric psychology occurs in university medical centers, but the field has spread gradually from tertiary care sites to community hospitals as well as primary care settings of private medical groups and individual practices.

The need for this field results from the increasing successes of pediatric medicine as well as a growing sophistication of both pediatrics and psychology. As physicians are able to save more children (and thus decrease mortality), morbidity increases. Progress in medicine has transformed many formerly fatal illnesses to chronic diseases. Thus there is a growing population of children who must cope with residual distress, prolonged or chronic treatments, and the sequelae of treatment. Each such child lives in a matrix of family, health care systems, educational system, and community, all affected by the child's physical and psychological health status.

A factor in the growth of pediatric psychology is that medicine has found the biomedical model of illness to be too simplistic. The biopsychosocial model is now shared by medicine and psychology. Pediatricians, especially, have come to appreciate that behavioral, psychological, and social issues must be addressed to effectively treat disease. Currently research has shown that over half of visits to a pediatrician involve behavioral or academic questions (Roberts & Wright, 1982), two-thirds of children admitted to a pediatric ward could benefit from a psychiatric consultation (Stocking et al., 1972), and that children with multiple hospital admissions are more likely to have psychiatric symptoms, learning problems, or conduct disorders (Quinton & Rutter, 1976).

In almost all circumstances the pediatric psychologist functions as a member of a treatment team. The role played by the psychologist can be adjunctive, consultative, or as an equal member of the team.

SERVICES PROVIDED BY PEDIATRIC PSYCHOLOGISTS

Psychological Evaluation
In the context of the medical setting not only do psychological factors need to be evaluated, but consideration must be given to the child's medical status, its impact on the child's behavior, its psychological impact, and the requirements of treatments and their impact on the child. Relevant family factors which need to be assessed include social and financial resources, health beliefs, changes in the family due to the illness, and the family's view of the illness. Health care system variables are relevant, including availability of care and patient and family functioning within the system, as well as variables in the larger sociocultural environment (i.e., the culture's view of a particular diagnosis such as AIDS.)

Improvement of Compliance
A frequent role of the pediatric psychologist is to help the patient achieve medical compliance. While compliance is an issue in all of medical psychology, pediatric psychology often deals with patients who do not understand the necessity for their treatment and may

be experiencing developmental needs for achieving independence that are counter to the need to comply. In this role, the psychologist can be thought of as an agent of the medical system acting for the benefit of the patient.

Pain Control

Psychologists possess a number of skills that provide an alternative or adjunct to pharmacologic pain control. Relaxation training, biofeedback-assisted relaxation, and hypnosis can be used to provide pain prophylaxis. In children, pain-induced behaviors may be ambiguous (such as irritability, withdrawal, or regression). As behavioral experts, pediatric psychologists can work with health care workers so that pain can be recognized and treated in the most appropriate and effective manner.

Treatment of Psychogenic Illness

Physicians are frustrated and frequently made angry when patients present psychologically "caused" illnesses. The physician knows the illness has no organic base and has few tools to help the patient who is clearly in distress. Patients are usually equally convinced of the "reality" of their illness and also become angry and frustrated when their distress is ignored or denigrated. When the physician views the psychologist as a member of the health care team, the patient's confidence in the system and its ability to recognize and treat their distress is confirmed.

Identification and Treatment of Psychologic Factors Impacting Health and Illness

The psychologist works with the physician as a member of a team in providing complete health care. In this role, the psychologist provides assessment and treatment that can be catalytic in its effect on efficacy of medical treatment. The pediatric psychologist may also deal with child and/or family adjustment to illness as well as helping improve management of the child in the hospital.

Ethicist and Child Advocacy

Medical advances have brought with them complex ethical issues. The pediatric psychologist is in a unique position to help the medical system as well as the patient and the family. In instances such as deciding whether to continue treatment, helping the medical system understand the psychological impact of its treatment, or recognizing the more subtle forms of abuse or neglect, the pediatric psychologist is able to fulfill a need met by no other person within the system.

Educate

Because pediatric psychology is a new field, its services and roles may not be known to potential users. Thus each consultation should be viewed as an opportunity to educate other members of the system (Russo, 1987). In this way a wider service network can be created, benefiting both patients and the health care system.

Research

Any new scientific field must prove itself not only through service but through research. Psychologists are trained as scientists as well as practitioners, the only professional in the medical system bene-

fiting from this particular training model. Thus, psychologists bear the responsibility of increasing the knowledge base of pediatric psychology.

A number of personal skills are demanded of the pediatric psychologist. First there must be an understanding of personal and professional stimulus values because pediatric psychologists frequently work with people who have no mental health problems per se but still require services. A pediatric psychologist must possess a high frustration tolerance as referrals are sometimes received with no preparation to patient or parents, or referrals are made as the patient is about to leave the hospital, or there may be failure to acknowledge the psychologist's expertise, and occasionally there may be failure of other professionals to carry out recommendations. The pediatric psychologist must avoid professional fanaticism in treatment teams. Others within treatment teams such as nurses, social workers, and physiotherapists hold different conceptual models that must be acknowledged and understood. There must be a tolerance for an unpredictable work schedule with need for services occurring emergently. The psychologist often works with hostile patients, who may be unable to understand their need for referral to and treatment by a psychologist. He or she must also be able to work with diverse data sets, with information coming from a variety of sources, demanding various levels of sophistication and knowledge to use them efficiently. Working as a member of a team within the medical setting also requires acceptance of dependance on other professions and an ability to empathize with the medical providers' perspectives, needs, and stresses. Finally, the pediatric psychologist must be able to work with the physically ill.

Training is a most important issue within pediatric psychology. Periodic conferences are held by the Society of Pediatric Psychology specifically to develop training standards. Four areas of knowledge have been defined as necessary for the competent practice: basic psychology, clinical psychology, developmental psychology, and health psychology. Training in the 1990s is almost always obtained at the internship or postdoctoral level, although several graduate programs in pediatric psychology do exist. A directory of available practica, internships, and fellowships is available through the Society of Pediatric Psychology.

REFERENCES

Kagan, J. (1965). The new marriage: Pediatrics and psychology. *American Journal of Diseases of Children, 110,* 272–278.

Quinton, D., & Rutter, M. (1976). Early hospital admissions and later disturbances of behavior: An attempted replication of Douglas' findings. *Developmental Medicine and Child Neurology, 18,* 447–459.

Roberts, M., LaGreca, A., & Harper, D. (1988). Another stage of development. *Journal of Pediatric Psychology, 13,* 1–5.

Roberts, M. C., & Wright, L. (1982). The role of the pediatric psychologist as consultant to pediatricians. In J. Tuma (Ed.), *Handbook for the practice of pediatric psychology* (pp. 251–289).

Stocking, M. et al. (1972). Psychopathology in the pediatric hospital: Implications for community health. *American Journal of Public Health, 62,* 551–556.

Wright, L. (1967). The pediatric psychologist: A role model. *American Psychologist, 22,* 323–325.

SUGGESTED READING

Journal of Pediatric Psychology.

Magreb, P. R. (1978). *Psychological management of pediatric problems* (Vols. 1 & 2). Baltimore: University Park Press.

Roberts, M. C., & Walker, C. E. (Eds.). (1989). *Casebook of child and pediatric psychology.* New York: Guilford.

Routh, D. K. (Ed.). (1988). *Handbook of pediatric psychology.* New York: Guilford.

Tuma, J. M. (Ed.). (1987). *Handbook for the practice of pediatric psychology.* New York: Wiley. (Original work published 1982)

Wright, L., Schaefer, A. B., & Solomons, G. (1979). *The encyclopedia of pediatric psychology.* Baltimore: University Park Press.

J. S. HOFFMAN
Honolulu, Hawaii

CHILD ABUSE
CHILD PSYCHOLOGY
EMOTIONAL CONTAGION
PAIN: COPING STRATEGIES
RELAXATION TRAINING
SOMATOPSYCHICS

PEDOPHILIA

Pedophilia (from the Greek, meaning "love of children") is a psychosexual disorder essentially characterized by the act or fantasy of engaging in sexual activity with prepubertal children as a repeatedly preferred or exclusive method of achieving sexual excitement (*Diagnostic and Statistical Manual III,* 1980). That is, unlike most adults who prefer other consenting adults as sexual partners, the pedophiliac is repeatedly or exclusively drawn to children for sexual excitement and satisfaction. Pedophiliac sexual activities may vary in intensity and include stroking the child's hair, and, when initiated by a male, holding the child close while covertly masturbating, manipulating the child's genitals, encouraging the child to manipulate his, and, less frequently, attempting intromission. Youngsters of any age up to puberty may be the object of pedophiliac attention; force seldom is employed.

Compared with most other paraphilias or "sexual deviations," there is more research available on the characteristics manifest in this particular disorder. Perhaps this situation is understandable, in that pedophilia is viewed as an outrage by society, can result in obvious psychological damage to the victim, frequently leads to the arrest of the pedophiliac, and consequently creates an incarcerated group that can be readily studied. On the basis of what has been found empirically, pedophiliacs typically know the children they molest—neighbors, family, friends, relatives (Gebhard et al., 1965).

The first episode may be prompted by the child's innocent uninhibited display of affection, especially if the predisposed adult is affected by alcohol, loneliness, or an unhappy marriage. From this point, the activities may go on for weeks, months, or even years until they are discovered, as when the child tells the parents.

While the disorder occurs predominantly in males, instances of pedophilia in females have been reported. Moreover, about twice as many pedophiliacs are oriented toward opposite-sexed children as are oriented homosexually; a smaller percentage are attracted to either boys or girls. Pedophiliac individuals range in age from adolescence through the 70s, with a significant percentage in their mid- to late-30s. Further, there is some evidence that etiological factors in this disorder may vary quite a bit, depending upon the age of the offender (Mohr et al., 1964). For example, some adolescent pedophiliacs are sexually inexperienced with persons of their own age and may thus prefer the less psychologically threatening sexual outlet that children can provide. Those in their mid-30s more often manifest other kinds of maladjustments, including alcoholism, which are frequently associated with the aberrant sexual act. Older pedophiliacs often suffer from feelings of loneliness and isolation, and may reach out via sexual activity with a child for some kind of intimate human contact.

Other research has further bolstered the position that persons who commit pedophiliac offenses fall into a variety of categories (Cohen et al., 1969; Rossman, 1973). By far the most common category contains psychologically immature offenders—individuals with chronic difficulties in relating to persons of their own age and who thus are sexually comfortable only with children. In most cases, these individuals know the child in question. A second category contains persons who impulsively regress to pedophilia under stress. Acting impulsively, this type of offender is usually not acquainted with the victim. A third category is comprised of men who have had powerful early sexual experiences with young boys (e.g., in reformatories) and have never progressed sexually much beyond that point. These pedophiliacs are typically callous and exploitative in their sexual behavior, and tend to frequent cheap film theaters and other areas to seek out vulnerable children. A final category consists of antisocial personalities who prey upon children in quest of new sexual thrills. Not infrequently, the pedophiliac behavior in this instance is motivated by both aggressive and sexual components, with the child often being physically harmed during the sexual act.

Other investigators have noted additional severe psychopathology in some pedophiliac offenders (e.g., alcoholism, schizophrenia, organic mental disorders) in which lowered inhibitory controls appeared to underlie the sexual act. Thus the dynamics entering into pedophilia may vary significantly from person to person. Although the various tragic acts of pedophilia may be equal in the eyes of society, the motives contributing to such actions may be complex and varied indeed.

REFERENCES

American Psychiatric Association. (1980). *Diagnostic and statistical manual of mental disorders* (3rd ed.). Washington, DC: Author.

Cohen, M., Seghorn, T., & Calmas, W. (1969). Sociometric study of the sex offender. *Journal of Abnormal Psychology, 74,* 249–255.

Gebhard, P. H., Gagnon, J., Pomeroy, W., & Christenson, C. (1965). *Sex offenders: An analysis of types.* New York: Harper & Row.

Mohr, J., Turner, R., & Jerry, M. (1964). *Pedophilia and exhibitionism.* Toronto, Canada: University of Toronto Press.

Rossman, P. (1973). The pederasts. *Society, 10,* 28–32, 34–35.

D. J. ZIEGLER
Villanova University

LONELINESS
PERSONALITY DISORDERS
SEXUAL DEVIATIONS

PEER INFLUENCES

High-quality relationships are important for all aspects of the development and well-being of children and adolescents. Traditionally, the relationships between children and adults have been viewed as the most important vehicle for ensuring effective socialization and development. Child-child relationships have been assumed to be, at best, relatively unimportant and, at worst, unhealthy influences. Such views were mistaken. Prominent theorists such as Freud, Mead, Piaget, Erickson, Kohlberg, and many others have argued that high-quality peer relationships are essential for an individual's development and well-being, and hundreds of research studies have validated their views.

The research on peer influences may be divided into three eras (Ladd, 1999). In the 1930s, social scientists tended to study the nature of children's peer groups and the association between children's characteristics and their positions in peer groups. In the 1970s and 1980s, social scientists tended to study the impact of peer relationships on long-term development and adjustment. Numerous longitudinal studies have demonstrated that poor peer relations during childhood are a major predictor of later deviance such as delinquency and psychopathology. In the 1990s, social scientists tended to focus on the effects of children's behavior on the formation and maintenance of peer relationships, the origins of children's social skills and skill deficits, and the affective and physiological correlates of children's peer competence and relationships.

Peer relationships with a wide age range of other children or adolescents are a critical element in human development and socialization. Young people must acquire competencies, attitudes, values, and perspectives in encounters with peers, and they must also occupy a comfortable niche within their peer culture. Compared with interaction with adults, interactions with peers tend to be more frequent, more intense, and more varied throughout childhood and adolescence. Specific research studies supporting the statements in this article may be found in Johnson (1980), Johnson and Johnson (1999), Ladd (1999), and Bukowski, Newcomb, and Hartup (1996).

INFLUENCES ON VALUES, ATTITUDES, PERSPECTIVES, AND SOCIAL COMPETENCIES

In their interactions with peers, children directly learn attitudes, values, skills, and information unobtainable from adults. The way in which ingroup messages are phrased, the nature of clothing and hairstyles, the accepted music, what is enjoyable or distasteful, what competencies need to be practiced and developed, and how to react to adult authority are largely based on peer influences. The socializing importance of peers does not end during adolescence. Friends and colleagues have a critical impact on one's values, attitudes, perspectives, and social competencies throughout a person's life.

Prosocial and Antisocial Behavior

Interaction with peers provides support, opportunities, and models for prosocial or antisocial behavior. Peers provide both the norms, models, and motivation for engaging in prosocial actions and the opportunity for doing so. If peers promote prosocial actions such as honesty, altruism, cooperation, and respect for individuals, individuals will tend to engage in such behavior. It is while interacting with peers that a person has the opportunity to help, comfort, share with, take care of, and give to others. Without peer interaction, many forms of prosocial values and commitments might not be developed. There is a solid and established link, furthermore, between prosocial behavior and peer acceptance.

Whether or not adolescents engage in problem or transition behaviors such as the use of illegal drugs, sexual intercourse, and delinquency is related to their perceptions of their peers' attitudes toward such behaviors. If individuals perceive their friends as disapproving of such actions, they will tend not to engage in them. The widescale rejection of a person by peers, furthermore, tends to promote antisocial actions by the child, such as instrumental and impulsive aggressiveness, disruptiveness, and other negatively perceived behavior.

Impulsiveness

Children frequently lack the time perspective needed to tolerate delays in gratification. But as they develop and are socialized, the focus on their own immediate impulses and needs is replaced with the abilities to take longer time perspectives and to view their individual desires from the perspectives of others. Peers provide expectations, directions, models, and reinforcements for learning to control one's impulses.

Aggressive impulses provide an example. While instrumental aggression aimed at achieving selfish ends may be correlated with peer rejection, aggressive or rough play may have developmental benefits. Peer interaction involving such activities as rough-and-tumble play is important in helping children learn to master aggressive impulses. Rough play promotes the acquisition of a repertoire of effective aggressive behaviors and helps establish necessary regulatory mechanisms for modulating aggressive affect. Children who are unusually timid in the presence of an attack have often lacked exposure to rough play with peers.

"Perspective-Taking" Ability

Children learn to view situations and problems from perspectives other than their own through interactions with their peers. Changes in perspective are critical competencies for cognitive and social development. They have been related to a number of important characteristics, including the ability to present and comprehend information, to constructively resolve conflicts, to willingly disclose personal information, to help group problem solving, and to display positive attitudes toward others in the same situation. All psychological development may be described as a progressive loss of egocentrism and an increase in ability to take wider and more complex perspectives. Primarily through interaction with one's peers, egocentrism is lost and increased "perspective-taking" ability is gained.

Autonomy

Autonomy is the ability to understand what others expect in any given situation and to be free to choose whether or not to meet their expectations. In making decisions about which behavior is appropriate, autonomous people tend to consider both their internal values and the expectations of other people, and then to respond in flexible and appropriate ways. Autonomy is the result of the internalization of values derived from previous caring and supportive relationships (internalized values provide guides for appropriate behavior and self-approval) and the acquisition of social skills and social sensitivity (which provide accurate understanding of others' expectations for one's behavior). Peer relationships have a powerful influence on the development of values, social skills, and social sensitivity and on the internalization of the acceptance and support that form the basis for self-approval. Children with a history of isolation from or rejection by peers often are inappropriately other-directed. They conform to group pressures even when they believe the recommended actions are wrong or inappropriate.

Loneliness

Children need constructive peer relationships to avoid the pain of loneliness. While adults can provide certain forms of companionship, children need close and intimate relationships with peers with whom they can share their thoughts, feelings, aspirations, hopes, dreams, fantasies, joys, and pains. Peer rejection and peer victimization predict loneliness and its accompanying emotional distress.

Identity

Throughout infancy, childhood, adolescence, and early adulthood, a person moves through several successive and overlapping identities. The physical changes involved in growth, the increasing number of experiences with other people, one's increasing responsibilities, and one's general cognitive and social development all cause changes in self-definition. The final result is a coherent and integrated identity. In peer relationships, children become aware of the similarities and differences between themselves and others, they experiment with a variety of social roles that help them integrate their own sense of self, they clarify their attitudes and values and integrate them into their self-definition, and they develop a frame of reference for perceiving themselves.

Coalitions

For humans, banding together creates survival value against enemies and environmental problems. In childhood, most people make friends and form attachments. Coalitions are formed that provide help and assistance not only during childhood and adolescence, but throughout adulthood as well. This instinct for coalitions is sometimes formalized through organizations such as fraternities and sororities that bring young adults together for mutual benefit.

Aspiration, Productivity, and Psychological Health

In both educational and work settings, peers have a strong influence on productivity and aspirations. Supportive relationships with peers are related to achievement and to academic competence. Peer rejection predicts school absenteeism, grade retention, and adjustment difficulties. The more one's peers value academic excellence and the higher their academic aspirations, the more likely one is to achieve and to seek out opportunities for higher education.

Psychological Health

The ability to maintain interdependent, cooperative relationships is a primary manifestation of psychological health. Poor peer relationships in elementary school predict psychological disturbance and delinquency in high school, and poor peer relationships in high school predict adult pathology. The absence of friendships during childhood and adolescence seems to increase the risk of mental disorder. Peer rejection predicts loneliness and emotional distress while friendships and peer acceptance are related to socioemotional adjustment. Children adapt better to stressful situations when in the presence of friends or familiar peers. Peer victimization exists when children are exposed to abusive processes that promote cognitive-affective states such as insecurity, mistrust, or fearfulness. It forces children into the roles of aggressors and victims. Peer victimization is linked with a number of adjustment difficulties during childhood, including anxiety, loneliness, depression, and school maladaptation.

PROMOTING POSITIVE PEER RELATIONSHIPS

Unfortunately, many modern schools, families, and other institutions are not structured in ways to foster healthy peer relations among children and adolescents. While it was possible in earlier eras to take for granted many constructive aspects of peer relationships, this is definitely not the case in the present time. Contemporary children have fewer occasions for peer interaction than did previous generations. Fostering constructive peer relationships may be one of the most important challenges facing parents, educators, and other adults who wish to promote healthy development and effective socialization in children.

To promote positive peer relationships, children should first have continuous opportunities to cooperate with peers and occasionally engage in competition. Second, children should receive specific training in the skills needed to build and maintain positive relationships, such as conflict resolution and peer mediation. Being skilled in resolving conflicts may be especially important for constructive peer relationships. Third, the norms of caring, support, encouragement, assistance, reciprocity, and so forth should be established. The rights and responsibilities of collaborators and friends should be clear. Fourth, a set of civic values needs to be taught and inculcated. Those values include commitment to the common good and to the well-being of others, a sense of responsibility to contribute one's fair share of the work, respect for the efforts of others and for them as people, behaving with integrity, caring for others, compassion when others are in need, and appreciation of diversity.

REFERENCES

Bukowski, W., Newcomb., A., & Hartup, W. (Eds.). (1996). *The company they keep: Friendship in childhood and adolescence.* New York: Cambridge University Press.

Johnson, D. W. (1980). Importance of peer relationships. *Children in Contemporary Society, 13,* 121–123.

Johnson, D. W. (2000). *Reaching out: Interpersonal effectiveness and self-actualization* (7th ed.). Boston: Allyn & Bacon.

Johnson, D. W., & Johnson, R. (1999). *Learning together and alone: Cooperative, competitive, and individualistic learning* (5th ed.). Boston: Allyn & Bacon.

Ladd, G. (1999). Peer relationships and social competence during early and middle childhood. *Annual Review of Psychology* (Vol. 50, pp. 333–359). Palo Alto, CA: Annual Reviews.

D. W. JOHNSON
R. T. JOHNSON
University of Minnesota

ADOLESCENT IDENTITY FORMATION
AFFECTIVE DEVELOPMENT
BONDING AND ATTACHMENT
DEVELOPMENT OF HUMAN SOCIAL BEHAVIOR
MIDDLE CHILDHOOD

PENFIELD, WILBER GRAVES (1891–1976)

Educated in the United States, Wilbur Graves Penfield moved to Canada in 1928 and became a Canadian citizen in 1934. After receiving a medical degree, he specialized in neurology and neurosurgery. His experience as a clinician and researcher at various institutions in America and Europe was extensive and varied. As a member of the faculty of McGill University in Montreal, Penfield founded the Montreal Neurological Institute, which he directed until his retirement in 1960. He remained active to the end of his life as a lecturer, consultant, and writer. He was editor, author, or coauthor of six books on the nervous system, and the author of a book of essays, a biography (of Alan Gregg), and two historical novels. His last book, *The Mystery of the Mind,* is a venture into a critical study of the mind/brain relationship.

Among Penfield's numerous contributions, the most outstanding were the development of neurosurgical treatment of certain forms of epilepsy; a better understanding of the functional organization of the human cerebral cortex; and the discovery that electric stimulation of certain parts of the cortex in human subjects can evoke vivid memories of past life experiences, a kind of "flashback" of earlier life events.

Penfield's theory of the mind/brain relationship, based on his experience as a neurosurgeon and brain investigator, is original and provocative. He refused to equate mind with the brain activity and did not preclude the possibility of the survival of the mind after brain death. Penfield (1975, p. 89) once stated: "Whether the mind is truly a separate element or whether, in some way not yet apparent, it is an expression of neuronal action, the decision must wait for further scientific evidence." In a preceding paragraph, however, he wrote: "It is obvious that science can make no statement at present in regard to the question of man's existence after death, although every thoughtful man must ask that question."

H. MISIAK
Fordham University

PERCEPTUAL DISTORTIONS

Distortions of perception are of three kinds: those coming from within the individual, those due to the medium between the person and the stimulus object, and those attributable to properties of the object itself.

THE INDIVIDUAL

Perceptual distortions from within the individual might arise from properties of the individual, as insanity or personality factors, or from temporary induced states, as from drugs. These lines from Samuel Taylor Coleridge's *Kubla Khan* might describe an induced state:

> *Beware! Beware!*
> *His flashing eyes, his floating hair!*
> *Weave a circle round him thrice,*
> *And close your eyes with holy dread,*
> *For he on honey-dew hath fed,*
> *And drank the milk of Paradise*

Coleridge claimed that the poem came to him in an opium dream, though literary critics dispute this. Huxley (1970/1954) described vivid perceptual experiences from taking mescaline—perhaps the most talented description of drug effects; many perceptual effects have been documented from a variety of drugs. The painter Vincent van Gogh was confined to an institution for mental illness, but can the powerful effects of such paintings as "The night cafe" or "The Starry Night" be ascribed to the effects of a psychosis on a talented artist? Edvard Munch seemed to document hysteria in the painting "The Scream" ("a personal confession of schizoid fears," according to Reinhold Heller), but does the painting show what he saw? Perhaps our own perceptual responses are as interesting as the art. In a more experimental vein, the McGill studies by Bexton (1956), Heron (1956), and others observed perceptual hallucinations in individuals subjected to prolonged perceptual isolation. Bonding or attachment between individuals seems to be responsible for Wittreich's (1961) or Dion and Dion's (1976) subjects seeing loved ones of normal size in a distorted room. Values, needs, and personality factors, along with isolation, drugs, and mental disturbance, may all result in perceptual distortions, though they are sometimes difficult to investigate experimentally.

THE MEDIUM

The 16th-century Spanish painter El Greco produced elongated paintings that have been said to be the result of visions, madness, or astigmatism. While permanent enough, astigmatism would be a medium effect, although critics agree that El Greco's paintings represent his personal style, not an astigmatism.

Aniseikonic glasses distort the retinal image without harming the focus. Ames (1961) described many distortions produced by them. Wittreich and his colleagues (1961) found that perceived body distortions from the aniseikonic glasses were less for girls than for boys. A number of prism experiments, starting in the 1890s with the classical inverted image studies by Stratton, have been reviewed by Rock (1966) and by Welch (1978). The nature of prismatic effects, and adaptation to them is complex, allowing no simple conclusion.

Water, as are optical lenses, is a distorting visual medium—from the water and also from the diver's face mask that produces size and distance distortion. Welch (1978) and Ross (1974) have reviewed such studies.

Sound suffers many distortions that depend on the medium. Divers breathe helium or nitrogen and may sound like "Donald Duck," a squeaky type of speech that is hard to understand. The Doppler effect is a distortion produced by an approaching sound, as from a siren on an ambulance, that suddenly drops as the vehicle passes. Echoes sound different depending on the angle from which they bounce off an object. Auditory mirages in the open environment can make sounds appear to come from more than one direction.

THE STIMULUS OBJECT

Perceptual distortions from the object itself include the well-known visual illusions where objects may appear to be different than their true size or length. Auditory, tactual, and taste illusions are also important.

Pirenne (1970) showed visual distortions produced by photographing objects from a fixed point. Columns of equal size may appear so elliptical as to look egglike. He illustrates in detail the famous Pozzo painting on the ceiling of the church of St. Ignazio in Rome. It looks correct and three dimensional only when viewed from one position; a view from a different place exposes the deception and makes the picture look deformed.

Perceptual distortions produced by the subject, the medium, or the stimulus object reveal many fascinating perceptual problems. But Coleridge was wrong. The "milk of Paradise" is not opium or

any other drug, but, as every thinking person knows, the study of perception.

REFERENCES

Ames, A. (1961). Aniseikonic glasses. In F. P. Kilpatrick (Ed.), *Explorations in transactional psychology.* New York: New York University Press.

Bexton, W. H., Heron, W., & Scott, T. H. (1956). Effects of decreased variation in the sensory environment. *Canadian Journal of Psychology, 10,* 13–18.

Dion, K. L., & Dion, K. K. (1976). The Honi phenomenon revisited: Factors underlying the resistance to perceptual distortion of one's partner. *Journal of Personality and Social Psychology, 33,* 170–177.

Heller, R. (1973). *Edvard Munch: The scream.* New York: Viking.

Heron, W., Doane, B. K., & Scott, T. H. (1956). Visual disturbances after prolonged perceptual isolation. *Canadian Journal of Psychology, 10,* 1318.

Pirenne, M. H. (1970). *Optics, painting and photography.* Cambridge, England: Cambridge University Press.

Rock, I. (1966). *The nature of perceptual adaptation.* New York: Basic Books.

Ross, H. E. (1974). *Behaviour and perception in strange environments.* London: Allen & Unwin.

Stratton, G. M. (1897). Vision without inversion of the retinal image. *Psychological Review, 4,* 341–360.

Welch, R. B. (1978). *Perceptual modification: Adapting to altered sensory environments.* New York: Academic.

Wittreich, W. J. (1959). Visual perception and personality. *Scientific American, 200*(4), 56–60.

Wittreich, W. J., Grace, M., & Radcliffe, K. B., Jr. (1961). Three experiments in selective perceptual distortion. In F. P. Kilpatrick (Ed.), *Explorations in transactional psychology.* New York: New York University Press.

R. D. WALK
George Washington University

PERCEPTUAL ORGANIZATION

For most psychologists, the topic of perceptual organization means Gestalt psychology. Kurt Koffka's *Principles of Gestalt Psychology,* published in 1935, is a treatise whose message was that perception is organized. Koffka inveighed against the "constancy hypothesis," the notion that sensations have one, and only one, meaning. The chick picks the larger of two pieces of grain even though the larger one is further away and so projects a smaller image on the eye than the nearer one. Many experiments were cited to show that children, animals, and adults pick relationally, that they respond to the total situation. He wrote: "Things look as they do because of the field organization . . . processes organize themselves under the prevailing dynamic and constraining conditions" (Koffka, 1953/1935, pp. 98, 105).

Koffka was summarizing a generation of Gestalt research that began about 1910 with Max Wertheimer and Wolfgang Köhler. Gestalt was a revolt against introspection or the notion that the way to study perception was to analyze the perceptual stimulus into elementary, meaningless sensations. Gestalt psychology also minimized the role of learning or experience in perception.

The Gestalt psychologists formulated rules related to perceptual organization that are still relevant. They noted that the perceptual field is composed of the figure or object of attention and of a background—figure and ground. They formulated figure-ground principles and principles of perceptual grouping. For example, things close together or proximal are grouped; similar things are grouped; things that move together or have a "common fate" are grouped. Also included is a principle of good continuation or of continuing natural meaningful lines. These are, in brief, proximity, similarity, common fate, and good continuation, and they are examples of grouping principles relevant in a wide variety of contexts. The Gestaltists also noted that organization is spontaneous. If we see a row of equally spaced dots, we tend to see them as groups despite their equal distance from each other. This spontaneous organization, even when none exists in the stimulus pattern itself, shows the power of the tendency toward organization.

The Gestalt psychologists also believed in the primacy of the third dimension—that the third dimension is not constructed out of experience, but all perceptual organization is three-dimensional. They believed that perception is natural and innate, not dependent on complex learning processes. This contrasts with the view of Hermann von Helmholtz (19th century), who believed that perception was constructed out of elementary sensations.

Since 1935, the study of perceptual organization has been aided by many technical advances. Computers can build complex perceptual stimuli; oscilloscopes can present complex patterns; speech and other complex sounds (such as bird songs) can be analyzed with a sound spectrogram; a speech synthesizer can present complex speech stimuli; and the motion picture, the tape recorder, and the television camera are instruments for research.

A minor recurring theme is the debate over whether perception is a direct process, as compared with a more constructed process based on cognitive processes. The Gestalt psychologists took a more direct approach, Helmholtz a more cognitive one. Gibson (1966, 1979) has a post-Gestalt direct approach and he describes the perceiver as actively responding to the invariant relations in the environment. Hochberg (1978) and Gregory (1970) take more constructionist positions.

PICTURE PERCEPTION

One problem with picture perception as it relates to perceptual organization is whether the two-dimensional projection of a scene shown in a picture can be naturally decoded by the observer. Must we learn to see pictures? Are some pictures better than others?

The two extremes on this issue usually cited are those of Goodman (1968), who holds that pictures are cultural products ("almost any picture may represent almost anything"), and of Gibson (1954,

1960, 1971), who defended the view that literal projection is the only way for a picture to be drawn ("the artist . . . uses projective geometry, of necessity"). Research has focused on special populations of limited experience with pictures outside the Western tradition, such as animals, natives of primitive cultures, and children. In many respects, the Gibsonian position is upheld in that ordinary photographs of objects can easily be interpreted by natives of non-pictorial cultures, by some animals, and by children. But spatial projection in pictures does not completely uphold the Gibsonian view. Four-year-old children pick as the best picture one with literal perspective, but adults picked a more modified perspective in one study, while in another study neither school children nor adults accepted a literal perspective view. We have apparently learned to pick as representative a picture with some modification of literal perspective. These issues have been discussed by Hagen and Jones (1978) and by Walk (1981).

Arnheim (1974) applies Gestalt principles to artistic representations. He also views artistic representations as conceptual, citing the ease with which impressionist painters, regarded as unnatural in their day, are now totally accepted. Gombrich (1961) may seem closer to a direct Gibsonian view in his celebration of the use of projective geometry in pictorial representation, but he also allows for conceptual factors in his stress on the importance of schemata in representations.

EVENT PERCEPTION

A perceptual event takes place over time. Research on event perception has revealed an amazing capability of the visual system to organize in a minimum of time. The research also agrees with the Gestalt claim that natural perception is three-dimensional.

Let us suppose you took a wire coat hanger, elongated it, then bent it in half twice. If a strong light were to project its shadow onto a translucent screen, you would see a mass of lines. If the wire mass were rotated, you would see a three-dimensional tangle of wires—no longer a flat, meaningless mass, but its true form. This is known as the *kinetic depth effect.* In another demonstration, a large square is shrunk to the size of a smaller square, but the observer does not see a large square shrinking in size. Rather, the square seems to recede from the observer, and, as it gets larger, to approach the observer. The square shrinks and expands in a two-dimensional plane but the observer's nervous system seems to prefer the three-dimensional interpretation. In a study by Schiff and colleagues (1962), a small round shadow expanded in size until it filled the screen, a phenomenon labeled *looming,* and on seeing this, monkeys ducked and withdrew. Bower and colleagues (1970) found that young infants would withdraw from an optically presented shadow that expanded, a demonstration of the early appearance in humans of this adaptive response to looming.

Johansson (1978), a pioneer in event perception research, has described such research. Individuals were fitted with small flashlights in a dark room and photographed during movement. A person who looked at these lights as a static pattern might describe a "Christmas tree." But only two or three frames of motion picture film were required to identify a person walking. Cutting and Proffitt (1981) describe how such an abstract pattern is sufficient for identification of the sex of the walker. They also describe their search for the invariants that underlie this discrimination, for which they posit a "center of moment" around which the walker moves that is higher in women than in men.

Event perception research shows the natural perception of events that stretch out in time. It supports the primitiveness of three-dimensional perception. The center-of-moment hypothesis may help describe the underlying structure of complex perceptual organizations.

MOTION PICTURES

The perception of motion pictures has interesting problems of perceptual organization. The motion picture must reproduce the motion from the living environment in a realistic way, and it must tell a story that is compelling and imaginative. Hochberg and Brooks (1978) discuss many of the perceptual problems of the film medium. Sequential action means cutting from scene to scene, close-ups, distance shots, different angles. Bad cutting can mean perceptual and conceptual jumpiness and unintended motion effects. Some effects are immediate, but many are conceptual, depending on the rate of the story. The context is of overriding importance in deciding the meaning of a scene; a man with a neutral facial expression might appear satisfied, sad, or religious, depending on the previous scenes. Because many conceptual factors enter into film making, we cannot interpret a film in a direct perceptual manner on the basis of the immediate action taking place. The film maker, often with an identifiable style, dwells the camera on a small detail, views the scene from many close and far perspectives, and skips rapidly over parts of less importance, all in the interest of the conceptual task of building a dramatic narrative. The camera also captures the transformations under motion discussed previously. The abstract motion of people walking, running, dancing, resting, arguing, fighting, loving, pleading; of joy and grief; the characteristic motion patterns of babies, children, adolescents, adults, the aged; of males and females—all of these characteristic motions might well be portrayed with Johannson's points of light, "invariances under transformation," that are interpreted as fairly direct perceptual experiences. Thus the film medium is a direct perception of action and a contextual construction of a larger unit, illustrating both Gibsonian and Helmholtzian principles.

MUSIC PERCEPTION

Music tends to be grouped by frequency, the higher frequencies separately from the lower. In competition of frequencies into each ear, the tendency for right-handed people is to hear high frequencies in the right ear (which projects to the left or speech hemisphere) and lower frequencies in the left ear, projecting to the right or more spatial hemisphere. This is the perceptual experience even though it is contrary to the physical stimulus relationships. If a musical series is played with ascending and descending scales so that one ear receives an ascending note and the other ear a descending note, subjects hear two melodies, a higher one and a lower one, and also tend to hear higher frequencies in one ear and lower ones in the other. Deutsch (1975) calls these "musical illusions," and they illustrate the strong tendency for proximity in frequency of tones to

prevail, of high tones grouped together and lower tones grouped together. "Good continuation" would allow the subject to follow the ascending series and the descending one, but grouping by pitch prevails.

Another type of grouping is based on timbre. Subjects easily group similar melodies played by different instruments.

Subjects recognize a melody played in a different key. None of the individual notes are the same, but the relationships are preserved. This is transposition. Many musical relationships are built around this basic phenomenon and its relations. Octave generalization refers to the perceptual equivalence of notes an octave apart, and in Western music tones an octave apart have the same name. It is found even in animals. Octave generalization is so strong that some musicians may recognize the note of a piece, but not the correct octave. Contour is a form of transposition. It means, in essence, the general relationships of a melody; interval sizes may vary and the general ups and downs are there, though not exactly. Dowling (1982) describes the development of such discriminations by children and adults. Untrained listeners can tell the general contour of a melody, but they have difficulty with new materials. The effect of musical training is to help in the recognition of interval differences. Training helps in applying the whole tonal scale system with its relationships, especially to new information.

Music has a certain accent or beat that is intersensory; the rhythm has kinesthetic and visual as well as auditory components. People organize equal unaccented beats into spontaneous groups; this is termed *subjective organization.* The related visual phenomenon with a matrix of equally separated squares was mentioned before.

SPEECH PERCEPTION

The acoustic stimulus for speech perception is perceived categorically. A speech signal of many variations is perceived as one sound. The analogy is to the color spectrum where physical wavelengths vary continuously from 400 to 700 millimicrons, but we perceive discrete bands of color—red, green, blue, yellow.

Advances in technology produced the spectrogram and the speech synthesizer. The spectrogram is a visual record of speech sounds with high frequencies on the top and low frequencies at the bottom, and duration graphed from left to right. A typical speech sound, such as a *ba,* has three formants or concentrations of sound energy: two fairly low, around 700 and 1,200 hertz, respectively, and one fairly high, around 2,400 hertz. The *ba* consonant is represented by a slight change from low to a little higher in the second and third formants. A *pa* is almost exactly the same as a *ba* except for a slight initial hesitation, a delay in *voice onset time.* The first formant (lowest sound) begins prior to or simultaneously with the higher formants in a voiced consonant such as *b,* whereas the first formant is delayed relative to the higher ones in *p.* If you pronounce it, you can feel the difference. The relation between the first formant and higher ones can be manipulated continuously with the speech synthesizer. Yet the ear hears only a change from *b* to *p;* this is *categorical perception.* Interestingly, different languages use different regions of the *b-p* continuum. English speakers hear an abrupt transition from *b* to *p* as voice onset time is varied, French speakers hear a more gradual transition, and Thai speakers hear three sounds, a *b,* a *p,* and a *pʰ* sound. Categorical perception of speech shows a number of different ways of perceiving, depending on one's experience.

Silence is important in integrating our speech percepts. The function of small segments of silence is to provide emphasis, to produce stoplike consonants. Increasing the fricative duration (as in *shh*) also helps produce stop consonants. A word stream initially heard as *gray ship* becomes *gray chip* if the sound interval after *gray* is increased. Increasing the length of the *sh* sound and increasing the silent interval makes the percept *great ship.* Silence helps to organize speech perception.

Speech perception is influenced by vision, an intersensory effect. McGurk and MacDonald (1976) showed that a speaker mouthing one sound while the voice spoke another made for a compromise. The sound *ba* while the speaker mouthed *ga* would be heard as *da.* The auditory sound was heard easily by itself, but the sight of a speaker mouthing a conflicting sound provided the compromise. Children were not as affected as adults, and thus the visual-audition effect must be based on experience.

INTERSENSORY RELATIONS

Perceptual organization extends to the relationships among the senses. Infants can recognize that a felt shape is equivalent to one they have seen. This is, in Gibson's words, a cross-modal invariant, in that shape properties are recognized easily in two modalities, touch and vision. In infants, it cannot be based on experience. A dramatic demonstration of cross-modal equivalence without prior experience comes from an experiment by White and colleagues (1970). Blind adults learned to use a device that translates a visual pattern into impulses delivered to vibrators on their back. An approaching visual object loomed large, and more and more vibrators were activated. Some blind subjects ducked to this looming tactual object, a real example of cross-modal equivalence in a second sense modality, the tactual one, where objects cannot loom. This is a dramatic demonstration of the unity of the senses.

Unity of the senses means that the senses respond similarly to qualities perceived by more than one modality, and Marks (1978) has described research that crosses sense modalities. He points out linguistic relations between the senses that are celebrated in poetry. An Egyptian love poem of 1200 B.C. still sounds contemporary:

> *The sound of your voice is sweet,*
> *full like the taste of dark wine.*

Nevertheless the senses do have differences, even when the information is also available to another modality. Vision is the spatial modality *par excellence* and the blind are handicapped relative to the blindfolded sighted on tasks where spatial references from the environment are helpful. The deaf are not as good at lip reading as hearing persons are, apparently because of stored auditory information, though both deaf and hearing people do develop phonetic codes. We conclude that perceptual organization may be organized across modalities, as in cross-modal recognition in infants, without

experience, but some aspects of modality discrimination are dependent on experience with the other modality. This is another demonstration of the importance of both direct perception and constructed perceptual processes.

ALARM SYSTEMS

The organization of the alarm system for audition and that for olfaction have some interesting similarities. Alarm calls used by small birds are high-pitched sounds that begin gradually. Such a call is very difficult to localize. Both the species that makes the call and many other species hear the alarm, and all can take cover from a predator, such as a diving hawk. But mating calls are more specific. They permit individual identification of a species, and the short clucks and chirps are easy to locate. Olfactory pheromones used by insects to signal alarm show great similarities whereas sex pheromones are narrowly specific and highly potent. The broadness of the alarm system as contrasted with the specificity of the sex attractant system is a remarkably similar principle of organization in two different modalities.

CONCLUSIONS

Post-Gestalt understanding of the principles of perceptual organization has ties with the earlier Gestalt work, but it is best understood as a different focus on similar problems. Research on speech perception, event perception, music perception, and olfaction, and with sensory substitution systems is representative of research based on technology not available to the Gestaltists. Nevertheless the central Gestalt theme, that of the natural organization of all perceptual processes, is strongly upheld.

REFERENCES

Arnheim, R. (1974/1966/1954). *Art and visual perception: A psychology of the creative eye.* Berkeley & Los Angeles: University of California Press.

Bower, T. G. R., Broughton, J. M., & Moore, M. K. (1970). Infant responses to approaching objects: An indicator of response to distal variables. *Perception and Psychophysics, 9,* 193–196.

Cutting, J. E., & Proffitt, D. R. (1981). Gait perception as an example of how we may perceive events. In R. D. Walk & H. L. Pick, Jr. (Eds.), *Intersensory perception and sensory integration.* New York: Plenum.

Deutsch, D. (1975). Musical illusions. *Scientific American, 233*(4), 92–104.

Dowling, W. J. (1982). Melodic information processing and its development. In D. Deutsch (Ed.), *The psychology of music.* New York: Academic.

Gibson, J. J. (1954). A theory of pictorial perception. *Audio-Visual Communication Review, 1,* 3–23.

Gibson, J. J. (1960). Pictures, perspective and perception. *Daedalus, 89,* 216–227.

Gibson, J. J. (1966). *The senses considered as perceptual systems.* Boston: Houghton Mifflin.

Gibson, J. J. (1971). The information available in pictures. *Leonardo, 4,* 27–35.

Gibson, J. J. (1979). *The ecological approach to visual perception.* Boston: Houghton Mifflin.

Gombrich, E. H. (1961). *Art and illusion: A study in the psychology of pictorial representation.* Princeton, NJ: Princeton University Press.

Gregory, R. L. (1970). *The intelligent eye.* New York: McGraw-Hill.

Hagen, M. A., & Jones, R. K. (1978). Cultural effects on pictorial perception: How many words is one picture really worth? In R. D. Walk & H. L. Pick, Jr. (Eds.), *Perception and experience.* New York: Plenum.

Hochberg, J. E. (1978). *Perception* (2nd ed.). Englewood Cliffs, NJ: Prentice-Hall.

Hochberg, J. E., & Brooks, V. (1978). The perception of motion pictures. In E. C. Carterette & M. Friedman (Eds.), *Handbook of perception* (Vol. 10). New York: Academic.

Johansson, G. (1978). Visual event perception. In R. Held, H. W. Leibowitz, & H.-L. Teuber (Eds.), *Handbook of sensory physiology* (Vol. VIII). Berlin: Springer-Verlag.

Marks, L. (1978). *The unity of the senses: Interrelations among the modalities.* New York: Academic.

McGurk, H., & MacDonald, J. (1976). Hearing lips and seeing voices. *Nature, 264,* 746–748.

Schiff, W., Caviness, J. A., & Gibson, J. J. (1962). Persistent fear responses in Rhesus monkeys to the optical stimulus of "looming." *Science, 136,* 982–983.

Walk, R. D. (1981). *Perceptual development.* Monterey, CA: Brooks/Cole.

White, B. W., Saunders, F. A., Scadeen, L., Bach-y-Rita, P., & Collins, C. C. (1970). Seeing with the skin. *Perception and Psychophysics, 7,* 23–27.

SUGGESTED READING

Deutsch, D. (1978). The psychology of music. In E. C. Carterette & M. P. Friedman (Eds.), *Handbook of perception* (Vol. X). New York: Academic.

Hagen, M. A. (Ed.). (1980). *The perception of pictures* (2 vols.). New York: Academic.

Kubovy, M., & Pomerantz, J. R. (1981). *Perceptual organization.* Hillsdale, NJ: Erlbaum.

Liberman, A. M. (1982). On finding that speech is special. *American Psychologist, 37,* 148–167.

Liberman, A. M., & Studdert-Kennedy, M. (1978). Phonetic perception. In R. Held, H. W. Leibowitz, & H.-L. Teuber (Eds.), *Handbook of sensory physiology* (Vol. 8). Berlin: Springer-Verlag.

Marler, P. (1972). The drive to survive. In National Geographic Society, *The marvels of animal behavior.* Washington, DC: National Geographic Society.

Millar, S. (1981). Cross-modal and intersensory perception and the blind. In R. D. Walk & H. L. Pick, Jr. (Eds.), *Intersensory perception and sensory integration.* New York: Plenum.

O'Connor, N., & Hermelin, B. (1981). Coding strategies of normal and handicapped children. In R. D. Walk & H. L. Pick, Jr. (Eds.), *Intersensory perception and sensory integration.* New York: Plenum.

Pick, A. D. (1979). Listening to melodies: Perceiving events. In A. D. Pick (Ed.), *Perception and its development: A tribute to Eleanor J. Gibson.* Hillsdale, NJ: Erlbaum.

Strange, W., & Jenkins, J. J. (1978). Role of linguistic experience in the perception of speech. In R. D. Walk & H. L. Pick, Jr. (Eds.), *Perception and experience.* New York: Plenum.

Teuber, M. L. (1974). Sources of ambiguity in the prints of Maurits C. Escher. *Scientific American, 231*(1), 90–104.

Wilson, E. O. (1963). Pheromones. *Scientific American, 208*(5), 100–115.

R. D. WALK
George Washington University

PERCEPTUAL DISTORTIONS

PERFORMANCE TESTS

Performance tests require overt, active responses, such as motor or manual behaviors. Such tests frequently measure motor coordination, speed, or perceptual or motor skills. Because of their usual de-emphasis on language skills, performance tests have proven useful in the assessment of the physically handicapped, particularly the deaf. A common performance test is a typing test that measures how quickly and accurately one can type. A nonperformance measure of typing might ask multiple-choice questions about typewriter parts, positions of the keys, or selection of font, but would not include actual typing performance.

One of the earliest and most popularized performance tests is the Sequin formboard, designed for assessment and sensorimotor training of the mentally retarded. This test requires that ten differently shaped pieces be placed into correspondingly shaped holes; for example, the round peg must be placed in the round hole. More complex formboards also have been developed. Another classic performance test, the Kohs Block Test, developed in 1923, requires subjects to copy patterns by placing cubes with differently colored sides together. The Porteus Maze Test, originally developed in 1914 as a measure of foresight and planning ability, contains sets of mazes graded in difficulty. These early tests, and others like them, continue to be used on IQ tests, such as the Stanford-Binet and Wechsler tests.

The Wechsler intelligence tests produce three IQ scores: verbal, performance, and full-scale. The full-scale IQ is a combination of verbal and performance subtests, and the performance subtests require subjects to perform tasks such as assembling puzzles, forming blocks into patterns, and arranging pictures in a logical sequence. Analyses of the profile or pattern of the subtest and the verbal and performance IQ scores frequently are performed to provide descriptions of cognitive strengths and weaknesses and insight into possible localization of brain dysfunction and personality factors. For example, sociopaths and people with left-hemisphere damage are believed to tend to score higher on performance than on verbal items.

Performance tests have been used extensively by the military (for example, flight training simulators to measure pilots' skills) and business (for example, typing tests). In nonacademic settings, performance tests, when obviously related to job skills, generally are acceptable to those being tested for hiring, placement, retention, or promotion considerations. Academic settings also use performance tests; for example, tests of penmanship and oral reading and writing skills (based upon assessing "work samples").

Although performance tests frequently have greater face validity, nonperformance paper-and-pencil tests remain the most commonly used test format. The paper-and-pencil tests, when administered to people sufficiently experienced in this format, can provide measurements that are valid, less expensive, and more conducive to group testing.

SUGGESTED READING

Anastasi, A., & Urbina, S. (1997). *Psychological testing* (7th ed.). Upper Saddle River, NJ: Prentice Hall.

Kaplan, R. M., & Saccuzzo, D. P. (1997). *Psychological testing* (4th ed.). Pacific Grove, CA: Brooks/Cole.

M. J. ALLEN
California State University, Bakersfield

BLOCK DESIGN TEST
WECHSLER INTELLIGENCE TEST

PERL, EDWARD ROY (1926-   )

Edward Roy Perl was born on October 6, 1926, in Chicago, the son of a surgeon with a strong interest in scientific discovery. As a schoolboy he became fascinated by electrical phenomena and electronic devices, constructing various pieces of equipment. He was an active radio amateur while in grammar school. He finished high school and the first part of college at the University of Chicago. Volunteering in the U.S. Navy in 1943, he was assigned to an officer training program (V-12) at the University of Illinois at Urbana-Champaign and subsequently began medical school in that program at the University of Illinois in Chicago. His first exposure to research on the nervous system came through Lazlo Meduna a psychiatrist working at the Illinois Neuropsychiatric Institute (INI) who introduced Perl to the encephalographers Fredrick and Irna Gibbs. He learned the elements of electroencephalography from the Gibbses in his first year of medical school. Subsequently, he was attracted to experimental neurophysiology by Elwood Henneman, a postdoctoral fellow working in Warren S. McCulloch's laboratory at the INI. While a medical student, Perl worked in the Department of Physiology to devise an electronic device for in-

stantaneously measuring chest capacitance as a novel method for beat-by-beat measurement of cardiac output; this led to his first scientific publication (with Whitehorn) and was the basis of his MS dissertation (1951). Perl was a visiting student (1948) at the Harvard Medical Service of the Boston City Hospital, where, after receiving the MD degree in 1949, he served as an intern in internal medicine (1949–1950). With encouragement by Henneman, a postdoctoral position was arranged after the internship with Vernon Mountcastle in the Department of Physiology at The Johns Hopkins University School of Medicine. After 2 years at Johns Hopkins (1950–1952), Perl was called to active duty as a medical officer in the U.S. Army and assigned to the Walter Reed Army Medical Center. At Walter Reed he did experimental electroencephalography and cerebral electrophysiological studies that led to his first publications in neuroscience.

Upon discharge from the Army in 1954, Perl took an appointment as an assistant professor in the Department of Physiology at the Upstate Medical Center of the State University of New York in Syracuse where he was promoted to associate professor in 1957. In 1957 he moved to the Department of Physiology of the University of Utah in Salt Lake City. He became a professor at Utah in 1964, serving as acting chairman on two occasions. In 1971 he moved to North Carolina as professor and chair (1971–1989) of the Department of Physiology at the University of North Carolina at Chapel Hill (UNC-CH) where he was named Sarah Graham Kenan Professor in 1983. He directed the neurobiology program at UNC-CH from 1973 to 1978. Currently he directs an active research laboratory in the Department of Cell and Molecular Physiology at UNC-CH.

Perl has been a visiting professor at several universities both within and outside the United States: Faculté des Sciences, Paris, France (1965 and 1980); the Department of Physiology at UCLA (1968); Université d'Aix-Marseille, Faculté des Sciences, Marseille (1970); Department of Physiology, Monash University, Victoria, Australia (1974); the Department of Neurosciences, Centro de Investigacion y de Estudios Avanzados del Instituto, Politecnico Nacional, Mexico City, Mexico (1977); College de France, Paris (1982 and 1985); and the Department of Physiology, Nagoya University School of Medicine (1986).

Among other honors and recognition, Perl is a fellow of the American Academy of Arts and Sciences (1992) and of the Association for the Advancement of Science (1955). He is an honorary member of the Japanese Physiological Society (1997) and of the International Association for the Study of Pain (1999). In 1991 he received the Bristol-Myers Squibb Award for Distinguished Research on Pain. In 1997 he received a Distinguished Alumni Award from the University of Illinois and the degree Doctor Honoris Causa from The Semmelweis University of Medicine (Budapest, Hungary). In 1998 he was given the Gerard Prize of the Society for Neuroscience for Outstanding Contributions to Neuroscience.

Perl is a neuroscientist whose major scientific contributions have involved electrophysiology, often in combination with histological or histochemically-based analyses. Attracted to neuroscience as a college and medical student by the Gibbses, McCulloch, and Henneman, his principal training in the field came from Vernon B. Mountcastle as a fellow in the Department of Physiology at The Johns Hopkins University School of Medicine. His first neuroscience studies utilized electroencephalography and responses of the cerebral cortex to sensory input. Subsequently, his work focused on reflex and somatosensory mechanisms of the mammalian spinal cord associated with fine-diameter peripheral afferent fibers. He is widely recognized for pioneer efforts in the documentation of the existence of nociceptors (pain receptors) as specific subsets of primary afferent fibers, for seminal studies on the distribution of nociceptor terminations in the spinal cord, and for first evidence of the selective excitation of neurons in the superficial laminae of the spinal dorsal horn by nociceptors. His investigations also first called attention to sensitization of nociceptors as an important feature underlying the sensory aspects of pain. This body of research, published in the late 1960s through the early 1980s, provided strong evidence for specific neural mechanisms underlying nociception and pain and thereby challenged alternative views. Subsequently, Perl's attention turned to the functional organization of superficial laminae of the spinal cord (marginal zone—lamina I; substantia gelatinosa—lamina II) and synaptic mechanisms operating therein. Among these latter studies were early efforts in establishing roles played by glutamate and purinergic substances as synaptic mediators in the superficial dorsal horn region. Recent work has focused on phenotypic changes in nociceptors as a consequence of partial denervation and the possible role of adrenergic receptor up-regulation as the basis of the development of pathological sensation induced by adrenergic substances. Several of his experimental designs have introduced novel technologies.

Perl also contributed importantly to neuroscience through leadership in the formation of the Society for Neuroscience. He organized the survey that led both to the formation and to the form of the Society, drafted the initial by-laws, and was its acting president during the Society's initial year. He has served as a member of the editorial boards of several physiology and neuroscience journals and as a reviewer for others. He has been on numerous National Institutes of Health review panels and was a member of the National Board of Medical Examiners from 1968 to 1980. He served on several committees for the National Academy of Sciences, including acting as chair of the Research Briefing Panel on Pain, Committee on Science, Engineering, and Public Policy.

STAFF

PERLS, FREDRICK (FRITZ) (1893–1970)

Fredrick Perls studied at the University of Freiburg, and received the MD degree at the University of Berlin. In 1926, he became an assistant to Kurt Goldstein at the Institute for Brain-Injured Soldiers. His association with Goldstein gave him the idea of the *gestalt* or "whole," which he later incorporated into his own method of psychotherapy. He studied with and was psychoanalyzed by well-known analysts William Reich, Karen Horney, and Otto Fenichel. When Hitler came to power, Perls left Germany for Holland in 1933. In 1946, he came to the United States, where he founded the New York Institute for Gestalt Therapy. His first book, *Gestalt Therapy,* was published in conjunction with Ralph Hefferline and Paul Goodman. Other books included *Gestalt*

Therapy Verbatim (1969) and his autobiography, *In and Out of the Garbage Pail,* published in the same year.

His major contribution to psychology was the development of a new method of psychotherapy, which he named Gestalt therapy. It was both an outgrowth and a rejection of psychoanalysis. Perls accepted the psychoanalytic concept that behavior disorders are the result of unresolved conflicts arising from a person's past. These conflicts must be discovered and "worked through." On the other hand, he stressed the "here and now" in a more humanistic approach that emphasized responsibility, freedom, and an active attempt to "become." His therapy also made use of "acting out" as vividly as possible. This could involve screaming, kicking, yelling, and crying. In this way, the client could confront inner feelings, take responsibility, and learn to control them, and in this way unify these feelings and actions into a new whole (gestalt) and learn to live an open and honest life.

Perls's therapy stressed a rather authoritarian role on the part of the therapist. Feelings and candor were emphasized rather than reason. Those humanistic therapists who have preferred a gentler, more acquiescent role on the part of the therapist have criticized Perls's method as inappropriate for proper human growth.

R. W. LUNDIN
Wheaton, Illinois

PERSONAL CONSTRUCT PSYCHOLOGY

Personal construct psychology (PCP) represents a coherent, comprehensive theory of personality that has special relevance for psychotherapy. Originally drafted by Kelly in 1955, PCP has been extended to a variety of domains, including organizational development, education, business and marketing, and cognitive science. However, its predominant focus remains the study of individuals, families, and social groups, with particular emphasis on how people organize and change their views of self and world in the counseling context.

At the base of Kelly's theory is the image of the person-as-scientist, a view that emphasizes the human capacity for meaning-making, agency, and ongoing revision of personal systems of knowing across time. Thus, individuals, like incipient scientists, are seen as creatively formulating *constructs,* or hypotheses about the apparent regularities of their lives, in an attempt to make them understandable, and to some extent predictable. However, predictability is not pursued for its own sake, but is instead sought as a guide to practical action in concrete contexts and relationships. This implies that people engage in continuous extension, refinement, and revision of their systems of meaning as they meet with events that challenge or invalidate their assumptions, propelling their personal theories toward greater adequacy.

Kelly formally developed his theory through a series of corollaries, which can be broadly grouped into those concerned with the process of construing, the structure of personal knowledge, and the social embeddedness of our construing efforts. At the level of process, PCP envisions people as actively organizing their perceptions of events on the basis of recurring themes, meanings attributed to the "booming, buzzing confusion" of life in an attempt to render it interpretable. By punctuating the unending flow of experience into coherent units, people are able to discern similarities and differences of events in terms that are both personally significant and shared by relevant others. At the level of structure, PCP suggests that meaning is a matter of contrast—an individual attributes meaning to an event not only by construing what it is, but also by differentiating it from what it is not. For example, a given person's unique description of some acquaintances as "laid-back" can only be fully understood in the context of its personal contrast—say, "ambitious" as opposed to "uptight." At a broader level, individuals, social groups, and whole cultures orient themselves according to (partially) shared constructs such as "liberal vs. conservative," "pro-life vs. pro-choice," and "democratic vs. totalitarian," which provide a preferred basis for self-definition and social interaction. Especially important in this regard are core constructs, frequently unverbalizable meanings that play critical organizing roles for the entirety of our construct systems, ultimately embodying our most basic values and sense of self. Finally, at the level of the social embeddedness of our construing, PCP stresses both the importance of private, idiosyncratic meanings and the way in which these meanings arise and seek validation within relational, family, and cultural contexts.

To a greater extent than other "cognitively" oriented theories of personality and psychotherapy, PCP places a strong emphasis on emotional experiences, which are understood as signals of actual or impending transitions in one's fundamental constructs for anticipating the world. For example, individuals might experience threat when faced with the prospect of imminent and comprehensive change in their core structures of identity (for example, when facing dismissal from a valued career or abandonment by a partner they counted on to validate a familiar image of themselves). Alternatively, people might experience anxiety when confronted with events that seem almost completely alien and uninterpretable within their previous construct system. This attention to the delicate interweaving of meaning and affect has made PCP an attractive framework for contemporary researchers and clinicians concerned with such topics as relational breakdown, trauma, and loss, all of which can fundamentally undercut one's assumptive world and trigger a host of significant emotional and behavioral responses.

As an approach to psychotherapy, PCP stresses the importance of the therapist making a concerted effort to enter the client's world of meaning and understand it from the inside out, as a precondition to assisting with its revision. In this way the therapist does not assume to be an expert who guides clients toward a more rational or "objectively true" way of thinking. Instead, he or she works to help clients recognize the coherence in their own ways of construing experience, as well as their personal agency in making modifications in these constructions when necessary. At times the therapist prompts the client's self-reflection by making use of various interviewing strategies such as the laddering technique to help articulate core constructs, or narrative exercises such as self-characterization methods, as a precursor to experimenting with new ways of construing self and others. Such changes may be further fostered by the creative use of in-session enactment, fixed role therapy (in which clients try out new identities in the course of daily life), and other psychodramatic techniques.

A unique feature of PCP is its extensive program of empirical research, conducted by hundreds of social scientists around the world. Most of this research has drawn on repertory grid technique (see entry in this encyclopedia), a flexible method for assessing systems of personal meanings, which has been used in literally thousands of studies since Kelly first proposed it. By providing visual and semantic maps of an individual's construct system and how it applies to important facets of one's life (e.g., relationships with friends, partners, and family members), grids have proven useful in both clinical and research settings. Among the many topics investigated using this method are the body images of anorexic clients; the ability of family members to understand one another's outlooks; children's reliance on concrete versus abstract construing of people; and the degree of commonality of work team members in their construing of common projects.

Finally, it is worth emphasizing that PCP, despite its status as the original clinical constructivist theory, remains a living tradition that continues to attract scholars, researchers, and practitioners from a broad range of disciplines. More than many theories, it has established a sizable following and annual conferences outside of North America, with vigorous programs of training, research, and practice in countries as diverse as Australia, Germany, Spain, and the United Kingdom. As it has grown in influence, it has also begun to be integrated with other, more recent "postmodern" traditions of scholarship, including other constructivist, social constructionist, and narrative therapy approaches. While these various perspectives differ in some respects, each draws attention to the way in which personal identity is constructed and transformed in a social context. Likewise, each focuses on the role of language in defining reality, and each suggests a collaborative role for the psychotherapist attempting to assist clients with the problems of living.

SUGGESTED READING

Fransella, F. (1996). *George Kelly.* Thousand Oaks, CA and London: Sage.

Journal of Constructivist Psychology. Philadelphia & London: Taylor & Francis.

Kelly, G. A. (1955). *The psychology of personal constructs.* New York: Norton.

Neimeyer, R. A., & Mahoney, M. J. (Eds.). (1995). *Constructivism in psychotherapy.* Washington, DC: American Psychological Association.

Neimeyer, R. A. & Neimeyer, G. J. (Eds.). (1990–2000). *Advances in Personal Construct Psychology* (vols. 1–5). Greenwich, CT: JAI Press.

R. A. Neimeyer
University of Memphis

S. K. Bridges
Humboldt State University

REPERTORY GRID TECHNIQUE

PERSONALITY ASSESSMENT

The measurement of personality traits has been an important function of clinical psychologists for many decades. Personality is not a matter to be guessed at or to be estimated by untried, unscientific, and unreliable methods. Rather it is an area that has been diligently investigated by psychologists with the result that proved and respected methods of assessing personality have been developed that are widely recognized and respected as having value far beyond the casual methods used during the prescientific era.

PURPOSES OF PERSONALITY ASSESSMENT

Determination of Responsibility in Legal Matters

It is difficult to answer the question of whether a person charged with some criminal offense should be held responsible for that offense or the person is suffering from a mental disease or defect that precludes such responsibility. In making such determinations, courts rely heavily on psychologists who use measurement tools to determine whether the person can understand reality the way an ordinary person does, can think logically and rationally, and if he or she can plan and organize behavior in such a way as to be held responsible. The use of psychological tests to measure personality is considered fairly objective and thus more reliable than more subjective means of appraisal. A particularly knotty problem is that of "malingering." Sometimes an offender will attempt to feign mental illness to escape punishment for a crime. The public is suspicious of the ability of mental health professionals to detect such deception. The use of psychological tests, however, certainly enhances the capacity of professional teams to make accurate decisions. For example, the Minnesota Multiphasic Personality Inventory (MMPI) has special scales that detect test-taking attitudes and will indicate if someone is exaggerating symptoms. Also, projective tests such as the Rorschach are difficult to fake because most people do not have the necessary technical knowledge to give the right answer to provide a particular diagnostic impression to the skilled psychological examiner. Thus, the psychologist often proves to be a key person in some close decisions.

Determination of Suitability for Child Custody

A very difficult matter to decide is to which parent a child should be awarded where there is disagreement. Courts would like to have a parent who is responsible, nurturant, patient, and stable, and obviously everyone tries to appear so when applying for child custody. However, psychologists, with their sophisticated means of appraisal, may be able to determine more accurately than others whether someone really does have good parental characteristics or is just pretending. For example, stories that the parent makes up on the Thematic Apperception Test (TAT) might be viewed as demonstrating the kind of needs and behaviors typical of the story teller. Since some of the scenes deal with child-parent interactions, information concerning the parental style of the person taking the test can be inferred. The content of Rorschach responses and the method by which the person taking the test deals with blot characteristics, such as shading and color, will be further evidence concerning the emotional depth of the person relative to warmth and nurturance. In addition, personality inventories such as the Bem Sex Role Inventory (BSMRI) reveal whether one attributes desirable parental characteristics to oneself. The combination of self-report and indirect evidence is particularly useful in making determinations in borderline cases.

Vocational Choices for Individuals Seeking Counseling

The question of what occupation to choose is crucial for all persons since it will determine to a large extent their general feeling of competence and adequacy. Through personality assessment, it is possible to determine whether one is better suited for a sedentary or an active occupation, or for work involving close contact with people, with more structured and formal contact, or perhaps with no contact at all. Many persons claim that they are interested in person-related occupations because of the social pressures to be gregarious and sociable, and to engage in service to others. However, if they are basically solitary, seclusive individuals, such a choice may result in the person being unsuccessful and unhappy. On the other hand, a person who has strong interpersonal needs and requires the presence of others will probably be dissatisfied in an occupation that involves working alone. But self-report about such matters is limited by the amount of accurate information people have about themselves, which is often incomplete. By using indirect psychological tests such as projective methods and empirically derived inventories, it is possible to obtain a more objective appraisal of an individual's basic social orientation. This information might then be added to information from other tools of vocational counseling, such as interest tests, aptitude tests, and tests of ability, to help in making this crucial life decision.

Planning Psychotherapeutic Intervention

There are many different kinds of psychotherapies and not all are equally suited to everyone. Through assessment of personality, it can be predicted that some people will respond well to introspective techniques that lead to insight, that others may most benefit from individual record-keeping and behavioral assignments. The chance of succeeding in the strategy used is enhanced by trying to match the person to the method. Although some psychotherapists start out as doctrinaire based on the orientation they received during their professional training, they soon learn that no one approach works equally well with all clients. Most psychotherapists become increasingly eclectic with the passage of time. They try to develop appropriate strategies for each client as early in the therapeutic process as possible so that the client can proceed with dispatch to a more effective and happy existence. Measurement of personality can result in at least preliminary matching of the client to the therapeutic strategy of choice.

LEVELS OF PERSONALITY ASSESSMENT

Terms in general use are of little significance to psychologists. For instance, it is sometimes said that a person has a "lot of personality" or has "no personality." This is not a meaningful concept to psychologists, since they consider personality a complex of factors rather than a single dimension for which a certain quantity can be present. Other terms, such as "colorful personality," simply describe an individual who is dramatic, and tends to act out feelings.

The measurement of the personality is probably one of the most difficult and complex tasks. It can be measured at several distinct levels.

The Behavioral-Public Role

Most persons who come to the attention of psychologists have been referred because of characteristics that impinge unfavorably upon others. For example, many people are involuntarily committed to hospitals not so much because of "mental disease," but because of abrasive and obnoxious behavior that other people cannot tolerate. Also, many children are brought to child guidance clinics because their parents or teachers cannot deal with their disruptive behavior. Similarly, when families appear for therapy, often one or more of them are there unwillingly, at the insistence of the others who find their behavior intolerable. Thus the personality assessment program must include some observations of behavior, either naturalistic or contrived, as this often is the area in which the trouble arose. Social workers characteristically have been aware of this level of personality, as are individuals in daily contact with hospitalized persons, such as nurses and nursing assistants. Psychologists and psychiatrists, however, sometimes tend to rely excessively upon the self-report and symbolic levels, and they probably need to be more aware of the importance of this level as well.

Conscious Self-Concept

Obviously any personality assessment program must include some information provided by the individual that is based upon conscious views of the self. The most common method for obtaining this kind of information is the clinical interview. Another is the personality inventory, such as the MMPI. Personality inventories have the added advantage of being scored in such a way as to predict many kinds of behavior that previously were shown to have high correlations with test behavior. Undue reliance upon the medical model of prescribing for people rather than involving them as collaborators might produce a lack of attention to this level. Practitioners who believe that unconscious motives tend to preempt conscious ones also believe that it is not worthwhile to pay attention to what an individual says in a self-analysis. However, it would be perilous to ignore this level since it is the one upon which most decisions are made by most people. Not allowing the person being examined to discuss his or her own view of the difficulties is patronizing and not in line with the collaborative model of intervention.

The Private-Symbolic Level

To comprehend the personality totally, most psychologists include some measure of the individual's fantasies, inner life, or unconscious. The most common method of doing this is through the administration of projective tests such as the Rorschach or TAT.

PRESENT STATUS OF PERSONALITY ASSESSMENT

It is hoped that the preceding has given the reader some idea of the scope of the field of personality assessment. The field is expanding as more uses for the assessment of personality are being found. Methods need to be quick and more efficient than those used in the past, as befits an expanding population.

Psychologists often form the apex of a pyramid in which they supervise paraprofessionals who supervise volunteers. Therefore, personality assessment methods need to be simplified, with only the interpretation remaining complex. This would tend to maximize the professional time of the skilled psychologist, who thus can be of greater service to a greater number of people who need objective feedback concerning their personality characteristics.

The psychological journal that deals most directly with the field described is the *Journal of Personality Assessment.* Over the years, there have been more studies using objective methods of personality assessment than those using projective methods. There has been an increasing emphasis on self-administered tests and computerized scoring and prediction of behavior. Generally the field of personality assessment seems still to be expanding. The number of articles being submitted continues to increase, and the number of assessment areas being tapped continues to multiply. It would appear that the field of personality assessment continues to be a major function of clinical psychologists, and is developing technically and demonstrating increasing sophistication with the use of modern technology.

SUGGESTED READING

Dahlstrom, W. G., Welsh, G. S., & Dahlstrom, L. E. (1972). *An MMPI handbook:* Vol. I. *Clinical interpretation.* Minneapolis: University of Minnesota Press.

Dahlstrom, W. G., Welsh, G. S., & Dahlstrom, L. E. (1975). *An MMPI handbook:* Vol. II. *Research developments and applications,* Minneapolis: University of Minnesota Press.

Rabin, A. I. (Ed.). (1981). *Assessment with projective techniques.* New York: Springer.

W. G. KLOPFER

INTERVIEWING (SELECTION)
PROJECTIVE TECHNIQUES
TESTING METHODS

PERSONALITY DISORDERS

Numerous attempts have been made to specify definitive criteria for distinguishing normal personalities from personality disorders. Central to an understanding of this distinction is the recognition that normality and pathology, as they relate to personality, are relative concepts, arbitrary points on a continuum or gradient. Not only is personality so complex that certain spheres of functioning will operate adaptively while others do not, but environmental circumstances change such that behaviors that prove suitable at one time will fail to be so at another. The Task Force responsible for developing the 1980 version of the *Diagnostic and Statistical Manual* of *Mental Disorders,* (3rd ed.) (American Psychiatric Association, 1980) acknowledged that personality disorders represented syndromes that were "fuzzy at the edges." These disorders not only shade imperceptibly into the ordinary problems of everyday life but, in contrast with other clinical syndromes, have few clearly delineated symptoms or distinguishing signs to serve as identifying, no less definitive markers.

Certain nonsymptomatological features do distinguish personality disorders from other clinical syndromes. Most notable are the pervasiveness and duration of their clinical signs. To elaborate, the characteristic traits that typify the disorders of personality tend to be enduring; they often are evident by childhood or adolescence and persist as notable features throughout the individual's life span. Further, they are expressed in a wide variety of settings, displaying themselves across the broad landscape of significant life situations—in social, occupational, and family contexts. This durability and omnipresence, rather than the specificity of particular behaviors, serve to distinguish personality disorders from other clinical states.

Note should be made of several criteria that help in differentiating personality "traits" from personality "disorders." Although the behaviors that comprise traits either underlie or are identical to those comprising disorders, certain features aid in distinguishing between them. First, disorders are usually, but not invariably, associated with feelings of subjective distress. Second, the disordered individual employs interpersonal styles and coping strategies, few in number, but adaptively inflexible—that is, both practiced rigidly and imposed upon situations for which they are ill suited. Third, the behaviors that characterize disorders are often, in themselves, pathogenic. That is, they foster vicious circles by perpetuating and intensifying preexisting difficulties—for example, possessing a coping style that leads one to restrict opportunities for new learning, to misconstrue essentially benign events, and to provoke reactions from others that reactivate earlier problems. Fourth, disorders are noted by their tenuous stability, that is, their fragility, lack of resilience, and, in general, ready vulnerability to even minor conditions of subjective stress or social tension.

Eleven personality disorders comprise the list promulgated in *DSM-III.* They are presented here sequentially in terms of their increasing severity according to guidelines formulated by Kernberg (1975) and Millon (1981):

Dependent personality.   This passive pattern of relating to others is characterized by a helplessness and clinging behavior, by compliance and lack of initiative, and by a search for attachments in which one can lean entirely on the leadership of others for affection and security.

Histrionic personality.   This style is characterized by a lability of affect, by capricious and demonstrative behaviors, by an active solicitation and manipulation of others to gain attention, and by an insatiable and indiscriminate search for approval and stimulation.

Narcissistic personality.   This pattern is noted by an air of egocentric self-assurance and a pretentious superiority, by a tendency benignly to exploit others for one's own advantage, and

by immature fantasies and a careless disregard for the rights of others.

Antisocial personality.   This individual is mistrustful of others, seeks autonomy and retribution for what are seen as past injustices, displays irritability, impulsiveness, and aggressiveness, and often engages in socially irresponsible behavior.

Compulsive personality.   Characterized best by their inability to express feelings, by their rigid conformity to authority and regulations, these individuals appear joyless, value self-discipline, and are perfectionistic and overly organized.

Passive-aggressive personality.   Noted by a pervasive, if passive, resistance to meeting the expectations that others have of them, this type voices ambivalent feelings toward most matters, and vacillates between social deference and conformity at one time, stubborn negativism at another, and guilt and contrition, the next.

Schizoid personality.   This style is typified by a social passivity, by minimal emotional and affectionate needs, a general listlessness and apathy, and a marked deficiency in both the capacity for and interest in maintaining warm and empathic human relationships.

Avoidant personality.   This actively detached type reflects a pattern of social pan-anxiety and interpersonal mistrust, an alienation and devaluation of self and, despite longings for acceptance and affection, a pervasive hypersensitivity to potential derogation and humiliation.

Borderline personality.   An advanced or dysfunctional pattern, this disorder is characterized by intense endogenous moods, an ambivalence or lack of clarity regarding self-identity and significant relationships, and recurring periods characterized by simultaneous feelings of rage, love, and guilt toward others.

Paranoid personality.   Here is seen a vigilant mistrust of others, an edgy defensiveness against anticipated criticism, a pervasive and usually unwarranted suspiciousness and expectancy of deception, a provocativeness, and a tenacious insistence on maintaining one's personal autonomy.

Schizotypal personality.   This poorly integrated and dysfunctional type exhibits a variety of behavioral eccentricities, introduces personal irrelevancies into thought and communication, often appears self-absorbed, and displays either an ever-present air of anxious wariness or a total flattening of affect.

REFERENCES

American Psychiatric Association. (1980). *Diagnostic and statistical manual of mental disorders* (3rd ed.). Washington, DC: Author.

Kernberg, O. F. (1975). *Borderline conditions and pathological narcissism.* New York: Aronson.

Millon, T. (1981). *Disorders of personality: DSM-III, Axis II.* New York: Wiley-Interscience.

T. MILLON
University of Miami

AVOIDANT PERSONALITY
BORDERLINE PERSONALITY
DEPENDENT PERSONALITY
HISTRIONIC PERSONALITY
NARCISSISTIC PERSONALITY
PARANOID PERSONALITY
PASSIVE-AGGRESSIVE PERSONALITY
SCHIZOID PERSONALITY
SCHIZOTYPAL PERSONALITY

PERSONALITY THEORIES

Many illustrious names in psychology and psychiatry have been associated with personality theory. Some were clinicians who gleaned their theoretical insights from their therapeutic work, including Sigmund Freud, Carl Jung, Alfred Adler, Karen Horney, Erich Fromm, Harry Stack Sullivan, Erik Erikson, and Rollo May. Some, such as Gordon Allport and Raymond Cattell, obtained their findings from the research laboratory. And some engaged in both clinical work and research, including Henry Murray, George Kelly, Abraham Maslow, and Carl Rogers.

These differing methodologies have often been a source of controversy. Research-oriented psychologists have decried the seemingly untestable concepts, and the lack of quantification, which pervade theories derived from the clinical setting. In turn, laboratory research has been criticized as artificial and frequently trivial. Yet while both approaches have undeniable weaknesses, both have unique strengths as well, and both have contributed significantly to our understanding of the human personality.

In essence, a theory of personality is a set of unproved speculations about aspects of human behavior. Established facts are often lacking in scientific work, but theories offer guidelines that serve in the absence of more precise information.

To this end, the personality theorist devises a variety of interrelated terms and concepts (*constructs*). Ideally these constructs should satisfy several criteria. A good personality theory provides convenient descriptions, establishes a framework for organizing substantial amounts of data, and focuses attention on matters of greater importance. It also explains the phenomena under study, offering answers to such significant questions as the causes of individual differences in personality and why some people are more disturbed than others. The theory should also generate predictions, so that it may be evaluated and improved (or, if necessary, discarded). Finally, a valuable theory usually leads to important practical applications. It facilitates control and change of the environment, by bringing about better techniques of parenting, education, or psychotherapy.

Theoretical constructs (such as the Freudian id, ego, and superego) are not undeniable truths, nor are they concrete entities. They are concepts created (or adopted) by the theorist better to describe, explain, predict, and control human behavior. Thus any theory of personality represents but one possible way of interpreting and understanding psychological phenomena. Some prominent psychologists prefer to remain wedded to a single theory, convinced that it is superior to all others. But it would seem sound to conclude that every major theory has significant virtues as well as defects, and that those who understand and utilize constructs from a variety of personality theories will have available many more conceptual tools (and a more flexible approach) for unraveling the mysteries of human behavior.

HUMAN NATURE

Personality is a comprehensive construct, and motivation is a fundamental aspect of behavior. Thus most theories of personality are in part theories of motivation, and make crucial (albeit often quite different) assumptions about the basic nature of human beings.

The Quality of Human Motives

Many personality theorists have been intimately concerned with a challenging, if perhaps untestable, issue: Is human nature inherently malignant or benign?

At the most negative extreme is psychoanalysis, which assumes that our powerful innate drives include incest and destructiveness. Since society will not tolerate such threats to its existence, it inevitably comes into conflict with the individual; and since the demands of society are conveyed through the parents and then internalized by the child at an early age, these conflicts eventually become intrapsychic. Freudian theory thus posits a rather pessimistic definition of mental health: the ability to resolve our inescapable inner conflicts by channeling our drives away from inborn illicit wishes, and into less satisfying but more socially acceptable forms of behavior (sublimating them).

At the other extreme are theories that assume that our innate potentialities are wholly positive, and that we all have the capacity and the desire to develop them in constructive ways. These benign drives do not conflict with societal demands, so compromising them through sublimation is unnecessary. Thus to Adler, Horney, and Rogers, mental health consists of trying to satisfy our innate desires and psychopathology occurs only if and when this healthy drive toward self-realization (actualization, self-perfection) is blocked by external social forces, notably pathogenic parenting. Horney and Rogers likewise regard much of intrapsychic conflict as a pathological (and evitable) clash between healthy wishes that misguidedly have been repressed, and the conscious but self-defeating goals that have replaced them. Adlerian theory rejects the idea of intrapsychic conflict altogether, concluding instead that the conscious and unconscious are invariably united in the service of one's chosen life goals.

Between these extremes are theorists who attribute to humans both malignant and benign drives. Jung assumes that some of our unconscious motives are indeed dark and frightening, while others can serve as wellsprings of creativity that will guide us toward constructive solutions to our problems. Maslow posits a weak inherent tendency toward positive growth and benevolence, which the far more powerful forces of learning and culture all too easily can convert into hatred and destructiveness. Allport theorizes that we all possess deeply rooted selfish and irrational tendencies, together with the inherent potential to outgrow this unreason and become mature, considerate adults. Fromm concludes that every human being has the capacity for love and responsibility toward others, but that fulfilling this potential is extremely difficult because we all begin life as wholly self-centered (narcissistic) infants. Erikson has modified psychoanalytic theory by attributing to people important constructive motives actively supported by society, such as preserving a sense of individuality and inner wholeness (identity) and striving to master the environment in socially approved ways.

The Dynamics of Human Motives

Freudian theory posits that activated drives create a state of tension or excitation, experienced as unpleasant. The basic objective of all human behavior is to achieve pleasure and avoid pain, and we accomplish this by taking action that will reduce our drives and restore a state of equilibrium. Sullivan also concludes that a fundamental goal is to reduce inner tensions. However, Murray argues that we are motivated by the desire to achieve the pleasure that accompanies the reduction of needs, rather than some homeostatic or vegetative end state where no drives are active. We therefore readily learn to postpone eating or sex in order to develop greater levels of tension and make the subsequent drive reduction still more enjoyable, and we bemoan the loss of these drives if some accident or disease should deprive us of them.

Many theorists have taken exception to the drive-reduction model of motivation, pointing out that numerous tension-increasing activities are highly rewarding in their own right: curious exploration, acquiring an admired skill or level of competence, increasing one's understanding of the world or oneself, pursuing new adventures. Thus Maslow espouses a dualistic theory of motivation wherein we do seek to reduce some drives, such as hunger, thirst, safety, and obtaining love and esteem from others (deficiency motives), while other drives include the pleasurable tension-increasing activities described, the unselfish and nonpossessive giving of love to others, and the fulfillment of one's positive inner potentials and capacities (growth motives). Allport agrees that we need to reduce such drives as hunger, thirst, oxygen deprivation, and the need for sleep, but concludes that drive reduction is not a major determinant of adult behavior. Instead, mature individuals may well maintain or even increase levels of tension to achieve relatively distant goals. Furthermore, most adult motives become independent in purpose (functionally autonomous) of their childhood or adolescent origins, with what was originally a means to an end (e.g., going to sea to earn a living) becoming an end in itself. Allport is perhaps the only major personality theorist who contends that the motives of children and adults differ significantly in kind, rather than in degree.

Freud posits that all mental (and physical) behavior is determined by prior causes (psychic determinism). However, most other theorists (e.g., Jung, Adler, Sullivan, Allport, Murray, Rogers, Maslow, May) conclude that behavior must also be understood in terms of its purpose or goal (teleology). Personality is not merely shaped by the past, but also by our intentions and expectations for the future.

There is general agreement among personality theorists that some degree of human motivation is unconscious, and cannot readily be called to mind. Thus most would regard "know thyself" as a highly desirable goal, albeit a difficult and challenging one.

The Catalog of Human Motives

Yet another controversy concerns the specific content of human motivation. Both the number and the kinds of human motives have been hotly disputed—but there is also some agreement, as the following list indicates:

Freud.   Sexuality (which includes the whole range of erotic, pleasurable experience), destructiveness.

Jung.   Hunger, thirst, sexuality, power, activity, creativity, feeling that one's life has meaning (as through religion), becoming one's true self by uniting the various opposites that comprise the human personality through some middle path (individuation), and other drives that are difficult to identify because instinctual behavior is easily confused with conscious motives.

Adler.   Seeking to overcome the feelings of inferiority that inevitably result from our helplessness as infants—all of us have the innate potential to do so by striving to master our formidable environment in ways that promote the common good (social interest). Inherited instincts play no role in determining human behavior, as we actively and deliberately select our life goals and the means of achieving them.

Horney.   An innate drive to develop our positive, unique potentialities in constructive ways (self-realization).

Fromm.   Organic drives such as hunger, thirst, sex, and defense through fight or flight that bind us inextricably to the animal kingdom, and that contrast sharply with such nonorganic and uniquely human drives as the need for others, the need to master our environment, the need to feel that "I am I" (identity), and the need for a personal philosophy that establishes our values and guides our behaviors accordingly.

Sullivan.   The need for others; the need to reduce anxiety; the need to reduce such drives as hunger, thirst, oxygen deprivation, sex, elimination of bodily wastes, and sleep; the need to be tender to one's offspring. Personality exists, and can be studied, only through its interpersonal manifestations.

Erikson.   Sexuality; destructiveness; the need to achieve a sense of individuality, inner wholeness, and continuity (identity); the need to master our environment; the need to develop mutually enhancing relationships with other people.

Allport.   Instinctual drives that we strive to reduce, including hunger, thirst, oxygen deprivation, and sex; cognitive drives that are relatively independent of biological drives, and that may involve maintaining or even increasing levels of tension; the need for a unifying philosophy that gives meaning to one's life, and affords some answer to such tragic problems as suffering and death. Motives vary so much from one individual to another that it is impossible to explain personality in terms of a few universal drives.

Murray.   The need for abasement, achievement, affiliation, aggression, autonomy, overcoming failure (counteraction), defending against assault or blame (defendance), deference, dominance, being seen and heard (exhibition), avoiding pain and harm (harm-avoidance), avoiding humiliation (infavoidance), nurturance, order, play, rejecting others, sensuousness (sentience), sex, succorance, and understanding events and the problems of life.

Kelly.   Kelly is the only major personality theorist who explicitly rejects motivational constructs as unnecessary. However, he implicitly assumes that we all need a sense of order and predictability in our dealings with the external world.

Rogers.   An innate tendency to develop our wholly positive capacities and potentials in constructive ways (actualization); a need for positive regard from others, especially such significant others as parents.

Maslow.   Deficiency motives that involve drive reduction, such as hunger, thirst, safety, and obtaining love and esteem from others; growth motives that involve pleasurable tension increases, including curiosity, creativity, and competence. Human motives are too complicated and interrelated to be explained in terms of separate and distinct drives, and are therefore organized by Maslow in a hierarchical model wherein one level remains relatively unnoticed and unimportant until lower levels have been satisfied: physiological needs (lowest), safety, belongingness and love, esteem, self-actualization (highest).

May.   The need to exist in the world into which we are born, and to achieve a conscious and unconscious sense of ourselves as an autonomous and distinct entity (Dasein, or being-in-the-world). Dasein comprises three simultaneous and interrelated modes: physiological and physical; social; and the psychological realm of one's self, potentials, and values.

Cattell.   Food, mating, gregariousness, parental protectiveness, curious exploration, security, self-assertion, narcissistic sex, pugnacity, acquisitiveness; perhaps also appeal, rest, constructiveness and creativity, self-abasement, disgust, and laughter. The basic elements of the human personality can be identified best through the statistical technique of factor analysis.

Pessimistic Freudian theory has little trouble explaining healthy behavior: Proper parenting nudges the reluctant child along the road to effective sublimations and socially acceptable satisfactions. Similarly, those who posit a partly or wholly optimistic view of human nature can readily explain psychopathology and destructiveness. Adler theorizes that pathogenic parental behaviors, such as pampering and neglect, create the belief that external obstacles and personal weaknesses cannot be overcome through one's best efforts (inferiority complex). The child now strives for superiority to the environment in cowardly and harmful ways, ones that emphasize evading problems instead of attacking them and taking advantage of other people rather than social interest. Horney concludes that parents who are themselves neurotic behave in pathogenic ways determined by their own needs (e.g., overprotectiveness, overindulgence, humiliation, and derision), thereby causing the child to become so profoundly anxious as to abandon the healthy quest for self-realization in favor of an all-out drive for safety. Rogers theorizes that the child abandons its healthy innate desires when parents who are misguided (although not necessarily neurotic) influence it in other directions, and make their love and positive regard conditional on obedience. Fromm and Erikson conclude that human destructiveness occurs when such healthy motives as identity and mastery are frustrated: It is not the result of illicit instincts, but rather is "the outcome of unlived life."

This theoretical adroitness might lead one to question the importance of motivational constructs. In actuality, however, such assumptions do exert a profound effect on the remainder of the theory. For example, Freud recommends not allowing the child too much (or too little) gratification, so as to prevent the illicit wishes from becoming dominant. On the other hand, Adler and others stress that the child's healthy needs must be fully satisfied, and inveigh against the kinds of parental behaviors that block such gratification. Also, as we have seen, the specific benign motives attributed to us differ from theorist to theorist. Thus conclusions and recommendations regarding matters of major importance cannot be divorced from—and are in fact determined by—the theorist's particular view of human nature.

THE STRUCTURE OF PERSONALITY

Some theorists have sought to depict the complicated, often contradictory, aspects of personality by devising appropriate structural constructs. Thus Freud refers to our "seething cauldron" of irrational, amoral, and unconscious innate motives as the id; to the more rational, partly conscious, problem-solving, and self-preservative aspect of personality as the ego; and to our partly conscious, learned standards of right and wrong as the superego. Erikson and Murray also utilize these three constructs, but define them somewhat differently. Erikson attributes greater strength and autonomy to the ego, and less to the id. Murray assumes that the id includes both destructive and constructive instincts, such as creativity.

Jung's model of the psyche is particularly chaotic, with different components capable of gravitating between consciousness and unconsciousness, or even fusing into a single entity. The personal and conscious aspect of personality is called the ego, and represents the center of one's awareness and feelings of identity. The collective and conscious aspect, the persona, is the protective facade that enables us to meet the demands of society while concealing our true inner nature. The personal unconscious includes material not within our awareness because it has been forgotten, repressed, or perceived subliminally, as well as our primitive and guilt-laden characteristics. And the collective unconscious, a major and controversial Jungian construct, consists of a storehouse of latent predispositions to apprehend the world in particular ways (archetypes) inherited from our ancestral past.

Other theories focus upon the self as a primary structural construct. For example, Rogers concludes that we all try to actualize those abilities and goals that we perceive as our own. Ideally this learned and conscious self-concept remains consistent with our healthy innate desires and capacities. But it is all too easy to abandon our organismic drives in order to satisfy parental conditions for love and positive regard, and to accept the incorrect evaluations of ourselves that these significant others establish for us. The self-concept then becomes a distorted guideline that clashes with our true wishes (and makes it difficult even to recognize them), with this inner schism producing anxiety, confusion, and even psychopathology. Sullivan also stresses the importance of our self-perceptions, including both the desirable "good me" and the reprehensible "bad me." The more intense the anxiety we experience at an early age, the more rigid and extensive is this self-system, and the more resistant we are to change—even the positive change and flexibility necessary for constructive growth.

In contrast to the preceding theorists, Allport does not draw a clear distinction between motivational and structural constructs. He defines personality in terms of some 4,000 traits, such as friendliness, ambition, cleanliness, enthusiasm, seclusiveness, shyness, and talkativeness. Every personality is a unique collection of personal traits, although a given culture does evoke roughly similar modes of adjustment that permit comparisons among different people (common traits). Allport also posits an ego- or self-like construct, the proprium, which includes eight distinctively personal aspects of experience (e.g., the bodily self, continuing self-identity, self-esteem, the self-image). Cattell has used factor analysis to reduce Allport's lengthy list of traits, emerging with 16 presumably more fundamental temperament and ability traits.

Not all personality theorists regard structural constructs as necessary, or even desirable. Adlerian theory has little need of them, since it conceptualizes conscious and unconscious as a unified whole. Horney, although emphasizing the importance of intrapsychic conflict, does not consider it feasible to adopt a structural schema of personality. To May, attributing emotions and behaviors to abstract structural constructs is misleading and depersonalizing. And Fromm concludes that psychology is better off without the restrictive influence of concepts such as the id, ego, and superego. These theorists warn that, despite often-stressed cautions, structural constructs are likely to become reified. Continuous usage may well produce the belief that we all have (say) an id, ego, and superego and this will make it more difficult to dispense with constructs that lose their utility in light of subsequent discoveries, a not unlikely occurrence in view of our relatively limited knowledge of the human personality.

Amid these various controversies, however, there is at least one island of agreement. The defense mechanisms that Freud attributes to the ego (e.g., denial of reality, displacement, fantasy, projection, rationalization, reaction formation) have been accepted and incorporated into virtually every theory of personality, if at times with some changes in terminology and in the underlying rationale. Adler posited similar mechanisms, which he labeled "safeguarding tendencies."

THE DEVELOPMENT OF PERSONALITY

Freud's view of human nature is reflected in his approach to personality development, which he defines in terms of psychosexual stages. During the first five to six years of life, particular regions of the body become both the child's primary source of pleasure and the main focus of conflict with the parents: first the oral stage (mouth and lips, feeding), followed by the anal stage (anus, toilet training), and then the phallic stage (penis or clitoris, Oedipus complex). Development ideally should culminate in the genital stage, characterized by effective sublimations and realistic enjoyments. But if the child meets with excessive gratification or frustration during a pregenital stage, personality development to some extent will become fixated at that stage, and adult behavior will be influenced accordingly. (For example, anal fixation is typified by miserliness, stubbornness, and orderliness.) Some degree of fixation is probably inevitable but strong fixations interfere markedly with healthy functioning, and make it more likely that an adult will regress to childish behaviors in the face of severe stress or frustration.

Freudian theory regards personality development as virtually complete by about the age of 6 years, a contention that has evoked considerable opposition. Erikson argues that personality continues to change throughout one's life, and posits eight epigenetic psychosexual stages that range from infancy to age 50 and beyond. Each stage is characterized by a specific psychosocial crisis brought on by increasing physiological maturity, and by correspondingly greater demands by the parents and society, and each should result in the emergence of a particular ego quality, if personality development is to proceed successfully. For example, the crisis of the first (oral-sensory) stage is learning to trust (or mistrust) other people and this crisis is successfully resolved if the child develops an enduring belief that its most fervent wishes are attainable (hope). Sullivan, who regards developmental psychology as the key to understanding human behavior, agrees that significant changes in personality occur during later childhood and adolescence. He posits seven epochs through which personality may develop, ranging from infancy to adulthood, with each epoch representing an optimal time for certain innate capacities to reach fruition. Thus premature attempts to train the child before it is organismically ready to demonstrate the expected behaviors will end in failure, while training that is postponed too far beyond the ideal time is likely to prove inadequate. Although the specific stages enumerated by Erikson and Sullivan have been disputed, modern psychologists generally share their belief that periods beyond early childhood (e.g., adolescence) play an important role in the development of the human personality.

The majority of personality theorists have rejected the idea of developmental stages. They prefer to concentrate on the goals of personality development (e.g., Jungian individuation, Adlerian socially interested striving for self-perfection, Horneyan self-realization, Rogerian actualization, Maslowian self-actualization), and to caution against those parental pathogenic behaviors that will prevent the child from reaching this ideal.

Character Typologies

Freud is by no means the only theorist who has devoted some attention to personality types. Jung describes individual differences in personality in terms of two dimensions: the typical way in which we apprehend external stimuli (thinking, feeling, sensation, or intuition), and whether we characteristically attend more to the external environment (extraversion) or to our own subjective world (introversion). There is an innate tendency for one aspect of each dimension to become dominant, which must be realized for personality development to be successful. Fromm refers instead to the desirable productive orientation, typified by a love of life, rational thought, and work that benefits oneself and others. He contrasts this ideal with such undesirable (nonproductive) characteristics as the receptive orientation (seeking to be protected and nurtured by others), the exploitative orientation (obtaining satisfaction through force or cunning), the hoarding orientation (miserliness, compulsive orderliness, obstinacy), the marketing orientation (trying to fashion an exterior facade that will be coveted on the social market, even at the cost of repressing one's own needs for identity and self-realization), authoritarianism, conformity, narcissism, destructiveness, and compulsive strivings for power.

In contrast to the preceding theorists, Adler opposes the use of character typologies. Instead he argues that we all develop our own particular style of life. To be sure, this may involve such undesirable character traits as selfishness, arrogance, vanity, jealousy, avarice, hostility, and helplessness; or it may include healthy characteristics such as social interest, cheerfulness, optimism, sympathy, and genuine modesty. But every personality is at least somewhat unique, and the aforementioned terms are used solely because our language lacks sufficient precision to describe all of the subtle nuances that distinguish one human being from another. Allport agrees that every personality is unique, and that Adler's construct of the style of life is preferable to any character typology.

Criteria of Mental Health

Freud's definition of mental health consists of two characteristics, the ability to love and the ability to work. Allport posits six criteria, including a unifying philosophy that gives purpose to one's life, self-extension to such meaningful spheres of human endeavor as one's marital partner and work, the capacity for loving relationships free of crippling possessiveness and jealousy, emotional security and self-acceptance, and accurate self-insight. To Rogers, the fully functioning person responds to innate needs and desires rather than to self-denying external standards, enjoys total self-acceptance, forms successful interpersonal relationships, and is fully and spontaneously open to the experience of each moment. And Maslow posits some 15 characteristics of the self-actualizing (fully human) person, such as a more accurate perception of reality, greater acceptance of self and others, greater spontaneity and self-knowledge, a greater need for privacy, greater creativity, greater social interest, deeper and more loving interpersonal relationships, and greater autonomy and resistance to enculturation. Adler's criterion of mental health is *Gemeinschaftsgefühl* (social interest), and he argues that all human failures, such as criminals and psychotics, have a fatal lack of social interest in other people.

PERSONALITY THEORIES: CONTRIBUTIONS AND CRITICISMS

Personality theorists have applied their constructs and principles to numerous important areas, often with considerable success: the interpretation of dreams, the causes and dynamics of psychopathology, psychotherapy, education, work, religion, literature, and even such specific issues as prejudice and the reports of flying saucers. Many specific constructs enjoy widespread acceptance, including unconscious processes, "Freudian slips" (parapraxes), the defense mechanisms, narcissism, resistance, transference, anxiety, introversion, extraversion, inferiority complex, superiority complex, lifestyle, body language, compensation, intrapsychic conflict, identity crisis, traits, need for achievement, self, self-esteem, self-hate, and self-actualization. Thus personality theory has provided a wealth of invaluable insights that have contributed substantially to our understanding of human behavior.

The course of personality theory has also been demarcated by major constructs that have been rejected by most modern psychologists, such as Freud's metaphysical and unmeasurable concept of libido (psychic energy). Given the essentially speculative nature of personality theory, however, such failures are to be expected. The essence of theoretical work is to posit, evaluate, and revise, discarding those constructs that ultimately prove to be useless or that fade in the light of new discoveries. A cogent criticism would be that not enough constructs have been discarded by the theorists who created them. Personality theorists have been far too free with neologisms, and have often duplicated each other's concepts without any apparent knowledge of having done so. This may be due to a genuine conviction that one's own theory is different, to an ignorance of the views of other theorists, or to a misunderstanding of others' true positions—whatever the reason, it represents a serious waste of time and effort.

The inability of personality theorists to resolve the most fundamental of issues (e.g., the nature of human motivation) may lead one to question the merits of this field of endeavor. But it must be recognized that it is difficult to study subject matter that is capable of thought, lying to others, and even self-deception, and arrive at truly significant conclusions. Despite the difficulties, the creative and broad scope of thought reflected in theories of personality represents an essential adjunct to the typically narrow findings of modern empirical research, and it offers rich rewards to anyone seeking to describe, explain, predict, or alter the behavior of human beings.

SUGGESTED READING

Adler, A. (1957/1927). *Understanding human nature.* Greenwich, CT: Fawcett.

Adler, A. (1962/1931). *What life should mean to you.* New York: Capricorn Books.

Adler, A. (1969/1929). *The science of living.* New York: Anchor Books.

Allport, G. W. (1955). *Becoming: Basic considerations for a psychology of personality.* New Haven, CT: Yale University Press.

Allport, G. W. (1961). *Pattern and growth in personality.* New York: Holt, Rinehart & Winston.

Cattell, R. B., & Kline, P. (1977). *The scientific analysis of personality and motivation.* New York: Academic.

Ellenberger, H. F. (1970). *The discovery of the unconscious: The history and evolution of dynamic psychiatry.* New York: Basic Books.

Ewen, R. B. (1980). *An introduction to theories of personality.* New York: Academic.

Freud, S. (1962/1923). *The ego and the id.* New York: Norton.

Freud, S. (1964). New introductory lectures in psychoanalysis. In J. Strachey (Ed.), *The standard edition of the complete psychological works of Sigmund Freud.* (pp. 7–184). London: Hogarth. (Original work published 1933)

Freud, S. (1968/1900). The interpretation of dreams. In *The standard edition of the complete psychological works of Sigmund Freud* (Vols. 4–5). London: Hogarth.

Freud, S. (1968/1916). Introductory lectures on psychoanalysis. In *The standard edition of the complete psychological works of Sigmund Freud* (Vols. 15–16). London: Hogarth.

Freud, S. (1969/1940). *An outline of psychoanalysis* (Rev. ed.). New York: Norton.

Fromm, E. (1957/1951). *The forgotten language: An introduction to the understanding of dreams, fairy tales, and myths.* New York: Grove Press.

Fromm, E. (1965/1941). *Escape from freedom.* New York: Avon Books.

Horney, K. (1945). *Our inner conflicts: A constructive theory of neurosis.* New York: Norton.

Horney, K. (1950). *Neurosis and human growth: The struggle toward self-realization.* New York: Norton.

Jung, C. G. (1963/1961). *Memories, dreams, reflections.* New York: Pantheon.

Jung, C. G. (1972/1917–1928). *Two essays on analytical psychology.* Princeton, NJ: Princeton University Press.

Jung, C. G. (1976). *Psychological types.* Princeton, NJ: Princeton University Press. (Original work published 1921)

Jung, C. G. (Ed.). (1968). *Man and his symbols.* New York: Dell. (Original work published 1964)

Kelly, G. A. (1955). *The psychology of personal constructs.* New York: Norton.

Maslow, A. H. (1968/1962). *Toward a psychology of being.* New York: Van Nostrand Reinhold.

Maslow, A. H. (1970/1954). *Motivation and personality* (2nd ed.). New York: Harper & Row.

May, R. (1969). *Love and will.* New York: Norton.

May, R., Angel, E., & Ellenberger, H. F. (Eds.). (1967/1958). *Existence: A new dimension in psychiatry and psychology.* New York: Touchstone Books.

May, R. (Ed.). (1981/1969/1961). *Existential psychology.* New York: Random House.

Murray, H. A., et al. (1938). *Explorations in personality.* New York: Oxford University Press.

Roazen, P. (1976/1975). *Freud and his followers.* New York: Meridian.

Rogers, C. R. (1961). *On becoming a person.* Boston: Houghton Mifflin.

Rogers, C. R. (1977). *Carl Rogers on personal power.* New York: Delacorte.

Sullivan, H. S. (1968/1953). *The interpersonal theory of psychiatry.* New York: Norton.

R. B. EWEN
Miami, Florida

ANALYTICAL PSYCHOLOGY
HORNEY'S THEORY
PERSONAL CONSTRUCT PSYCHOLOGY
PSYCHOANALYSIS
SULLIVAN'S INTERPERSONAL THEORY

PERSONALITY TYPES

Typal categorization is one of the oldest ways of distinguishing individuals with respect to personality differences. Numerous typologies have been proposed by philosophers, writers, psychiatrists, and psychologists. In these typologies individuals have been classified in terms of social behavior, pathology, modes of imagery, values, interests, attitudes, and various features of biological constitution assumed to be related to temperament. It is likely that every personality variable that has captured much interest on the part of psychological theorists has been incorporated into a typology at some time. So pervasive is this approach to human personality that a comprehensive catalog of all known typologies would be difficult to compile. There is much overlap among typologies, however, and it is possible to recognize a small number of polarities that recur extensively.

Most of the people who create typologies have a strong interest in achieving an understanding of people as total entities, and they assume that personality is characterized by a fair amount of enduring structure. The popularity of typologies can be understood in light of the fact that they offer an economical way of summarizing complex configurations of variables—a way of characterizing the whole person in terms of a small number of very broad categories. The critics of typological description, on the other hand, have long contended that the simplicity of the typology leads to inaccuracy, that the typal categories are artificial, and that the distinctive features of the individual are lost when he or she is lumped together with many other people who have distinctive qualities of their own. Critics have also argued that no extant typology can claim to capture a truly basic set of categories, since each one reflects the special interest of its creator. They have also contended that every typology assumes that relevant trait distributions are bimodal—that people tend to have either a lot of the trait central to a given type or little of that trait. Most psychological traits, of course, are distributed unimodally, with relatively few people lying at the extremes that correspond to typal categories. In short, people do not fit neatly into types.

In response, it can be argued that every astute typologist knows that people vary quantitatively in psychological traits and that only a few people fit typal categories well. The type has to be understood as an ideal form or a point of reference that is useful for describing and understanding individuals to the extent that they approximate it. It has often been recommended that typal categories be replaced with trait dimensions. Thus, William Sheldon (Sheldon, Stevens, Tucker, 1940) sought to convert physique types to dimensions of physique, while Gordon Allport and Philip Vernon (Allport, Vernon, & Lindzey, 1931/1960) constructed questionnaire scales to measure the variables central to Edouard Spranger's (1920/1928) value types. A number of investigators have devised scales to measure quantitatively the components of Carl Jung's (1921/1976) typology. This kind of work can yield more accurate description, but it does not represent a fundamental shift in our mode of conceptualizing. The typal category continues to serve implicitly as a point of reference when we move to dimensional trait measurement, since we tend to interpret a scale score by reference to an image of the (perhaps nonexistent) individual who scores at the extreme on the scale.

It should be noted that the imprecision of the typology is bound up with its simplicity. In principle, it is possible to achieve a high degree of descriptive precision with a typology, provided we are willing to sacrifice simplicity. To achieve both comprehensiveness and precision, we could cross-classify individuals by a large number of very specific dichotomous variables. We could thereby derive complex typal categories that would be more univocally descriptive than any combination of scale scores resting on the same set of information.

The oldest known system of personality typing is the astrological system devised by ancient observers of the sky. The principal feature of this system is a set of twelve patterns or types that correspond to twelve signs of the zodiac. Another ancient typology that has received attention for centuries is based on the ideas of Hippocrates. In the fifth century B.C.E. he identified four basic humors of the body—blood, phlegm, yellow bile, and black bile. He believed that imbalances of the four humors caused many diseases and also affected temperament. Claudius Galen, who lived in the second century A.D., is usually credited with developing a four-fold typology of temperaments based on the humors. The types are sanguine, phlegmatic, choleric, and melancholic. Galen claimed that each results from the relative predominance of one of the humors. While the humoral doctrine can no longer be taken seriously, Galen's types have continued to interest psychologists, and they have been reinterpreted by such theorists as Wilhelm Wundt, Ivan Pavlov, and Hans Eysenck.

The idea that temperament is related to physique also has a long history, and most of the typologies that presuppose this relationship were influenced by another contribution of Hippocrates. He described two contrasting physical types—*habitus apoplecticus* (which is relatively thick, strong, and muscular) and *habitus phthisicus* (relatively thin, delicate, and weak). A number of related typologies appeared during the 19th and early 20th centuries. Giacinto Viola (1933) called the types "macrosplanchnic" and "microsplanchnic" and developed a morphological index that makes use of several bodily measurements.

Early in the 19th century, Leon Rostan of France introduced a three-fold variant of the typology, calling the types digestive, muscular, and respiratory-cerebral. This scheme was subsequently adopted and modified by several German theorists. Early in the 20th century, the psychiatrist Ernst Kretschmer (1922/1925) called the three types pyknic, athletic, and asthenic (later called leptosomic). He also added a fourth type, the dysplastic, which manifests an inconsistent mixture of the components of the three basic types.

Kretschmer observed that psychiatric patients with dementia praecox (schizophrenia) tend to be of the asthenic type—they tend to be relatively thin or of linear build. Manic-depressive patients, on the other hand, were more likely to be pyknic—rounder in form with more fatty tissue. He argued that, with respect to personality, there were two psychotic types, the schizoid (expressed in schizophrenia) and the cycloid (expressed in manic-depressive psychosis). He also surmised that within the normal population one could distinguish two corresponding non-pathological types, the schizothymic (characterized by introversion, sensitivity, and seriousness) and the cyclothymic (with a more outgoing disposition, greater affectivity, and a tendency toward mood swings). He contended that pyknic individuals tend to be cyclothymic, while asthenic, athletic, and dysplastic individuals tend to be schizothymic. Kretschmer's work provided a foundation for the later work in this country of William Sheldon (Sheldon et at., 1940; Sheldon & Stevens, 1942), who favored abandonment of a typology as such. Instead, Sheldon advocated the use of a somatotype, in which three numerals (each based on a seven-point scale) are used to express an individual's standing on three components of physique. He found

evidence for three corresponding components of temperament, which he also sought to measure.

The typologies noted thus far rest on an analysis either of cosmic events or of properties of the body, but typologies of a more strictly psychological nature also have a long history. An example is the enneagram (Riso, 1987). It was promoted by the spiritual seeker and occult teacher George Gurdjieff, but it had been introduced several centuries earlier, and its origin is obscure. It consists of nine personality types—three that emphasize feeling, three that emphasize doing, and three that emphasize relating. The types are said to be interrelated in ways that govern the sequence the individual will follow in the case of either personal growth or deterioration. The enneagram has enjoyed some popularity in recent years, but it has received little serious attention from psychologists.

People have often been classified in terms of their basic motives, interests, or values. An early typology of this sort was offered by Plato (1973). Plato regarded the human soul as possessing three basic principles or components. One is concerned with appetites, or with the love of eating, drinking, sensual pleasure, or money. A second is concerned with passion or spirit. It may be expressed as courage, pugnacity, power, ambition, or a quest for honor. The third is the philosophic, reasoning element, which underlies the love of knowledge or learning. There are three personality types, which differ with respect to the relative prominence of these components. One class of individuals seeks wealth or gain, another seeks honor, and a third seeks truth or wisdom. Each type has its own evaluative criteria, but Plato considered the third type, the philosopher, to be the most highly developed and the best qualified to rule the state.

Early in the 20th century, a related six-fold typology was suggested by the German psychologist Edouard Spranger (1920/1928). He classified people in terms of their preference for any of six possible evaluative attitudes—their preferred ways of experiencing meaning or value. The cognitive attitude, which ascribes significance to ideas as such, is emphasized by individuals of the theoretical type. The other attitudes (and their corresponding types) were called economic, aesthetic, religious, social, and political. The economic, political, and theoretical types correspond roughly to Plato's three types.

Other typologists have proposed hierarchical schemes in which each type represents a level or stage of development. The typologist's own value system is usually evident in the order assigned to the types. A 19th century example would be the three types described by Søren Kierkegaard (1944/1957). At the lowest stage is the aestheticist. Such an individual is open to many forms of experience, but tends to be lost in the immediacy of his or her sensations or thoughts and denies the reality of personal decision. At the next level is the ethical individual, who accepts the responsibility of making decisions and chooses to live by duty but is bound by established ethical laws. At the highest level is the religious individual, who accepts full responsibility for individual choice. Such an individual declares independence from society and established rules and seeks through dependence on God to make choices that coincide with divine will.

A schema presented by Otto Rank (1929/1945) is similar in its rejection of societal conformity. The first of three adult types is the normal individual, who accepts the majority will as his or her own and is adjusted to the surrounding society. At a higher level, though maladjusted, is the neurotic, who rejects societal standards but has nothing with which to replace them. The neurotic takes a step in the direction of independence, but the third type, the creative individual, succeeds in expressing a personal will. Like Kierkegaard's religious type, this individual acts independently and creatively and experiences unity of purpose.

Kierkegaard's typology represents one Christian view of stages of development toward an ideal relationship between the individual and the divine. Hindu thought stresses the importance of recognizing the illusion of individuality and moving beyond it. Sri Aurobindo (1970), a major Hindu spiritual leader of the 20th century, has provided a developmental typology in which the highest level is the gnostic individual, who is fully identified with the universal self, the spiritual ground common to all being, rather than with the individual ego. Many other hierarchical typologies are possible, since every developmental theory that postulates stages of development provides a foundation for typal classification. The Freudian theory of psychosexual development is an obvious example, for it has long been a common practice for psychoanalytic writers to categorize people in terms of the pregenital stages at which they are fixated.

One form of typology that is still more common is dichotomous classification, in which two types are viewed as alternative ways of experiencing or dealing with the world. Dozens of such typologies have been proposed, and many of them have in common a distinction between inward and outward tendencies. These tendencies have commonly been labeled "introversion" and "extraversion," but they may be construed in terms of interest, attention, the content of experience, the mode of expression, or the locus of the strongest determinants of action and experience. Given the variety of ways in which inner-outer contrasts can be formulated, there have been many disputes regarding the equivalence of different typologies that assume this basic form.

The best known typology involving introversion and extraversion is that of Carl Jung (1921/1976), who regarded these as two fundamental alternative attitudes. He believed each of us has a constitutional predisposition toward one or the other. According to Jung, these two attitudes operate in combination with four basic psychic functions—two rational, or judgmental, functions (thinking and feeling), and two irrational, or perceptual functions (sensation and intuition). Each of us tends to favor one of the four functions in conscious adjustments, and this is designated the superior function. A second function, the auxiliary function, tends to be used in combination with the superior function. If the superior function is a rational function, the auxiliary will be irrational; if the former is irrational, the latter will be rational. There are altogether sixteen possible combinations of a dominant attitude, superior function, and auxiliary function. Jung assumes that everyone uses both attitudes and all four functions in some way; the attitude and functions that are less developed or favored by a given individual simply tend to operate with less conscious control.

Of the dichotomous typologies proposed by philosophers, two have been widely employed by people of other disciplines. One is the contrast between the Apollonian and Dionysian styles of life

proposed by Friedrich Nietzsche (1956). The Apollonian individual favors control, balance, and restraint and is oriented toward inner images of beauty, while the Dionysian favors unrestrained experience and expression. The other typology was proposed by William James (1907), who distinguished two kinds of philosophers. He characterized the tender-minded philosopher as rationalistic, intellectualistic, idealistic, optimistic, religious, free-willist, monistic, and dogmatic, and the tough-minded type as empiricist, sensationalistic, materialistic, pessimistic, irreligious, fatalistic, pluralistic, and skeptical. James argued that underneath the opposing philosophic positions lay two opposing temperaments, and others have found it easy to apply these types to people in other walks of life.

Two major dichotomies proposed for psychiatric classification have also been widely influential. One was Emil Kraepelin's (1899/1904) typology of the psychoses, involving a major division between manic-depressive psychosis and dementia praecox (later known as schizophrenia). The other was a comparable division proposed by Pierre Janet (1894, 1903) for the psychoneuroses, the major categories being hysteria and psychasthenia. It has often been suggested that both these dichotomies represent pathological versions of extraversion and introversion. Kretschmer's concepts of cyclothymia and schizothymia represent an effort to identify the normal variants of the psychotic categories, and they are not strictly equivalent to extraversion and introversion in all senses of these terms. Many diagnostic categories are now employed by psychiatrists, and the elaborate system used in contemporary practice constitutes a more comprehensive typology than either Kraepelin or Janet envisioned.

Typal concepts are often invoked to encompass trait constellations that allegedly predispose the individual to a particular medical or social condition. Examples are the authoritarian personality in the case of ethnic prejudice (Adorno, Frenkel-Brunswik, Levinson, & Sanford, 1950), type A in the case of coronary heart disease, and addictive personality. For many such concepts, research fails to reveal either a coherent trait pattern of the sort hypothesized or a reliable association between that pattern and the focal condition. If our primary aim is to identify coherent patterns of traits that consistently appear together in many individuals, we can seek them through analysis of large sets of measured psychological traits. There are many possible quantitative methods that can be used to derive taxonomies (Bolz, 1972). Thus far, none has yielded a classification of personality types that has won wide acceptance.

REFERENCES

Adorno, T. W., Frenkel-Brunswik, E., Levinson, D. J., & Sanford, R. N. (1950). *The authoritarian personality.* New York: Harper.

Allport, G. W., Vernon, P. E., & Lindzey, G. (1960). *Study of values.* Boston: Houghton Mifflin. (Original work published 1931)

Aurobindo, S. (1970). *The life divine.* Pondicherry, India: Sri Aurobindo Ashram.

Bolz, C. R. (1972). Types of personality. In R. M. Dreger (Ed.), *Multivariate personality: Contributions to the understanding of personality in honor of Raymond B. Cattell* (pp. 161–206). Baton Rouge: Claitor's Publishing.

James, W. (1907). *Pragmatism: A new name for some old ways of thinking.* New York: Longman Green.

Janet, P. (1894). *L'etat mental des hysteriques.* Paris: Rueff.

Janet, P. (1903). *Les obsessions et la psychasthenie.* Paris: Alcan.

Jung, C. G. (1976). *Psychological types.* Princeton, NJ: Princeton University Press. (Original work published 1921)

Kierkegaard, S. (1957). *Either/or.* Princeton, NJ: Princeton University Press. (Original work published 1944)

Kraepelin, E. (1904/1899). *Psychiatrie. Ein Lehrbuch für Studierende und Aerzte. Achte, vollstandig umgearbeitete Auflage. Band II. Klinische Psychiatrie.* Leipzig: J. Barth. (Original work published 1899)

Kretschmer, E. (1925). *Physique and character: An investigation of the nature of constitution and of the theory of temperament.* London: Paul, Trench, Trubner. (Original work published 1922)

Nietzsche, F. W. (1956). *The birth of tragedy and the genealogy of morals.* Garden City, NY: Doubleday.

Plato. (1973). *The republic and other works.* Garden City, NY: Anchor.

Rank, O. (1945). *Will therapy and truth and reality.* New York: Knopf. (Original work published 1929)

Riso, D. R. (1987). *Personality types: Using the enneagram for self-discovery.* Boston: Houghton Mifflin.

Sheldon, W. H., & Stevens, S. S. (1942). *Varieties of human temperament: A psychology of constitutional differences.* New York: Harper.

Sheldon, W. H., Stevens, S. S., & Tucker, W. B. (1940). *The varieties of human physique.* New York: Harper.

Spranger, E. (1928). *Types of men.* Halle, Germany: Niemeyer. (Original work published 1920)

Viola, G. (1933). *La constituzione individuale.* Bologna, Italy: Cappeli.

R. W. COAN
University of Arizona

PERSONALITY ASSESSMENT
PHRENOLOGY
TYPE A PERSONALITY
TYPE B PERSONALITY

PERSONNEL EVALUATION

Personnel evaluations are formalized practices that provide information about the job performance of employees. Evaluations serve two general purposes—administrative and developmental. Administrative purposes are served to the extent that the evaluations are used to make personnel decisions about such things as salary increases, job assignments, promotions, and selection for training program participation. Developmental uses serve employees by providing information about their performance on the job and also information that can guide planning for future career roles.

The development of instruments and practices involves at least three major classes of processes and choices: the specification of the performance criteria, the development of performance evaluation measures, and the choice of evaluators.

PERFORMANCE CRITERIA

The quality of any personnel evaluation system depends upon the identification of the major dimensions of performance on the evaluated jobs. These dimensions must be relevant to successful and unsuccessful performance on the job. For example, if one were evaluating the performance of a bank teller, the dimensions of interpersonal interaction with customers, the ability to balance the drawer at the end of the day, and the ability to "interact" with the central computer through individual terminals might represent some of the dimensions of the job on which evaluations should be based. Collectively, the set of dimensions makes up the criteria, and the criteria are identified through job analyses.

Criteria can be classified in many different ways. However, psychologists think in terms of two general classes, with the second of these further subdivided. The first classification labels criteria as objective or subjective. Objective criteria are usually part of the records kept on employees and, for the most part, are quite straightforward. Subjective criteria are usually based on some individual's evaluation of the employee's performance. Subjective criteria can be further divided into trait-related and behavior-related criteria. Examples of trait-related criterion dimensions are friendliness, honesty, aggressiveness, ambition, helpfulness, and dedication. Behavior-related criteria would be similar to those described in the bank teller example—relationships with customers and knowledge and accuracy of transactions when working with equipment on line with the central computer.

Psychologists almost always favor the use of objective criteria plus subjective ones that are behaviorally oriented. However, when the total evaluation is taken into account and it is necessary to compare employees across a wide variety of different types of jobs, the use of behaviorally based evaluations is more difficult. Also, some critical dimensions of work are subjective by nature—for example, cooperation, customer satisfaction, and teamwork.

PERFORMANCE MEASURES

Once criteria for job performance have been identified, the next task is to construct measures of them. Objective criteria, by their very nature, usually have standards for measurement. For subjective measures of performance, evaluation scales must be developed. Such development requires constructing scales that are reliable, valid, unbiased, and as free as possible from contamination.

A variety of scaling procedures and practices exist for scale construction. The perfect evaluation scale, or even one that clearly stands out above the rest, has eluded experts. However, this difficulty should not imply that there have not been some major advances in evaluating subjective measures of job performance. Critical behaviors that have been identified by job incumbents and scaled according to importance for effective job performance work well.

EVALUATORS

Because of the hierarchical nature of most organizations in which supervisors are responsible for the work of their subordinates, most performance evaluations are done by employees' immediate supervisors. It is also common for the next higher level of supervision to endorse the evaluations. In spite of this practice, there is no reason to believe that supervisors are in the best position to provide the evaluation. In fact, work with peer ratings—ratings obtained from others at a level parallel to the employee—shows that peers are excellent sources of evaluation and are often better sources than supervisors. Obviously, the person completing the evaluation must be quite familiar with the dimensions being evaluated. Since so much work today goes on with other people and in teams, performance evaluations called "360-degree feedback" are frequently completed by superiors, peers, and subordinates. These evaluations are primarily for helping the employee see how others see him or her, and not for administrative purposes such as raises or promotions.

PROCESS CONCERNS

Up until the mid-1970s, psychologists working in the area of performance appraisal concentrated nearly all of their efforts on the development of performance rating scales and the procedures for using these scales. It was assumed that evaluators had well-formed notions about performance and that the primary goal was to develop rating scales in a way that would formulate the raters' judgments into an accurate appraisal. In the past few years, psychologists have recognized that evaluation development is not that simple. It is commonly believed that few additional improvements can be accomplished through scale construction alone. It is now time to turn attention to the evaluation process as a whole.

One of the most important aspects of this process is the recognition that the evaluator is faced with a person-perception problem that requires the perception, memory, and recall of events related to employees. From this perspective, it is necessary to understand how people perceive others, how they retrieve information about others from memory, how the performance evaluation procedure requires them to record their evaluation, and the use to which the ratings will be put. Finally, in addition to looking at the evaluator, more attention must be paid to the characteristics of the performance setting. Although performance evaluations are important to psychologists who develop evaluation systems and to the employees who deserve fair and thoughtful evaluations, the appraisal process may be just another task that must be completed by a certain deadline for a manager with many other responsibilities. More attention needs to be paid to the situations in which appraisals take place so that conditions can be established that will increase the probability that accurate evaluations will result. Again, the recent trend is to be more aware of situational constraints affecting personnel evaluation systems.

SUGGESTED READING

Ilgen, D. R., Barnes-Farrell, J. L., & McKellin, D. B. (1993). Performance appraisal processes research in the 1980s: What has it contributed to appraisal in use? *Organizational Behavior and Human Decision Processes, 54,* 321–368.

Landy, F. L., Zedeck, C., & Cleveland, J. (Eds.). (1983). *Performance measurement and theory.* Hillsdale, NJ: Erlbaum.

Latham, G. P., & Wexely, K. N. (1983). *Increasing productivity through performance appraisal.* Reading, MA: Addison-Wesley.

D. R. ILGEN
Michigan State University

JOB ANALYSIS
JOB EVALUATION
PERSONNEL SELECTION

PERSONNEL SELECTION

Staffing organizations requires making decisions about people. In every organization, decisions must be made concerning whom to hire, to promote, to transfer, to terminate, to lay off, and, probably less frequently, to demote. In discussing why selection decisions must be made and why it is difficult to make accurate decisions, Guion (1976) states, "It is an appropriate policy to hire those who will work well and dependably at the tasks they are paid to perform. Unfortunately, however, one cannot describe or measure job performance before it occurs."

Much organizational effort is involved in making selection decisions. Included, according to Schneider (1976), are human resource planning, recruitment of personnel, choosing appropriate methods for making the decisions, and research on selection procedures.

HISTORY

Selection decisions have been made throughout history. Usually the judgments of people about other people have sufficed, and the development of a science of personnel selection is relatively new. Its antecedents evolved in the latter part of the 19th century with the work, as described by Peterson (1926), of Francis Galton, J. M. Cattell, Alfred Binet, and others on the measurement of individual differences.

The first applications of measurement principles in selecting people for occupations came early in the present century and are described by Burtt (1942). Around 1911, Hugo Munsterberg developed a test for railway motormen and compared scores obtained on the test with records of performance in carrying out the work. Subsequently he developed tests for telephone operators and related their scores to progress in training for the job. Somewhat later, the Bureau of Salesmanship Research was established at the Carnegie Institute of Technology and studies were made to improve the selection of sales personnel.

During World War I, psychologists working with the armed services developed the first tests that could be administered to large groups of people. The screening of nearly two million recruits on their intellectual abilities ensued. Following the war, the availability of large-scale testing made possible the expanded use of tests for selection purposes. The testing industry, exemplified by the founding of the Psychological Corporation, came into being. Guion (1976) credits Freyd (1923) with the first published statement of principles for properly using tests in selecting people for occupations.

Much research on personnel selection took place during the 1920s and 1930s. Included were many advances in the use of statistical procedures. World War II stimulated research on selection, with large numbers of psychologists either joining or being employed by the armed services to carry out this work. Following the war, several books described what had been accomplished (e.g., Flanagan, 1948). Psychologists also continued their interest in personnel selection. Several books and many articles were published reporting studies and discussing issues pertaining to the subject.

With the passage of the Civil Rights Act of 1964 came challenges to traditional practices for selecting personnel. Psychologists began to examine the impact of selection procedures on the employment of minorities, women, and other groups protected by law. The background for the issues raised and the subsequent history have been described by Miner and Miner (1978).

SELECTION METHODS

Undoubtedly the use of psychological tests in personnel selection has received more attention from psychologists than have other methods available for this purpose. Other methods are used, however, and have been subjected to considerable investigation.

As noted by Guion (1976), interviewing is the most widely used method for making selection decisions. Studies by psychologists, however, raise doubts as to its reliability and validity for this purpose. Periodically, reviews of research on interviewing have been published. Schmitt concludes his review by stating: "There is not much in the research of the last half dozen years to bolster the confidence of a personnel interviewer concerned with the reliability and validity of his decisions. There is a good deal of evidence concerning the influence of variables which may make his decisions less reliable and valid" (Schmitt, 1976, p. 97).

Despite his pessimism, however, Schmitt offers suggestions for improving the interviewing process and for conducting further research on interviewing.

Unlike interviewing, a relatively subjective process, psychological tests are standardized and are objectively scored. They are designed to measure characteristics of individuals, such as abilities (knowledge, aptitudes) and personality attributes (temperament, interests, values). Many are paper-and-pencil instruments, easy to administer and score, and relatively inexpensive. Though often costly to design, literally hundreds of tests have been published and are reviewed periodically in *The Mental Measurements Yearbook* (e.g., Buros, 1978).

Some tests are work sample tests. They are designed to directly measure abilities required in a particular job or occupation and are samples of functions found in diverse kinds of occupations. The cost of developing such tests may be high. Administering and scoring the tests also may be costly; for some, equipment must be maintained. With some exceptions, therefore, the use of work sample tests tends to be limited.

Many studies have been made of psychological tests as methods for making selection decisions, demonstrating that scores on tests are predictive of job performance. Among reviews are those by Ghiselli (1973) and by Asher and Sciarrino (1974).

The notion that a person's past behavior is indicative of future behavior is the basis for a method used in selecting people referred to as biographical information or, briefly, as biodata. The method, as traced by Owens (1976), originated with the application forms on which job applicants are asked to furnish information concerning educational background, work experience, marital status, home ownership, and so forth. Statistical analyses demonstrated that many items correlated with aspects of subsequent job performance. Refinements led to questionnaires using multiple-choice formats.

Biodata questionnaires must be designed for the occupation for which they are to be used. Large samples of job applicants are required. Furthermore, the questions asked eventually become outdated. Development and maintenance costs thus tend to be high. That the investment can be worthwhile, however, is indicated by Thayer (1977), who relates the history of over 50 years of use of biodata by the life insurance industry in selecting sales personnel. As noted by Owens, the utility of the method in predicting job performance has been demonstrated by studies conducted in many settings.

Projective techniques, exemplified by the well-known Rorschach ink blot test, were designed by psychologists for use in psychodiagnosis (Sundberg, 1977). A psychologist trained in their interpretation is required because of the diversity of responses to the deliberately ambiguous stimuli. As a consequence, the application of projective techniques to the selection of personnel has been limited. Their use in the selection of managerial personnel, however, has been documented by Kingslinger (1966) and research with one technique, an incomplete-sentence test, on the motivation to manage is described by Miner (1977).

Psychodiagnosis is not, of course, limited to projective techniques. Many methods are used for this purpose. Sundberg (1977) describes the variety of methods and identifies the approaches used as personality assessment (also referred to as individual assessment). Since World War II, individual assessment has been widely used, though not well documented, in personnel selection.

A psychologist may use only one method—a lengthy interview, for example—or a variety of methods, including ability tests, personality tests, projectives, and an interview. The psychologist then reviews the information obtained and evaluates the suitability of the applicant for the position in question.

The process is essentially a judgmental one, and generally is quite costly. As a consequence, it tends to be restricted to managerial and other higher level occupations. Because of the nature of the process, including the confidentiality of reports to client organizations, research on its utility in predicting job performance has been limited. Despite the absence of supporting data, however, many organizations have faith in it and continue to use it.

Another procedure for making selection decisions, also essentially judgmental, is the Assessment Center method. In this case, several assessors are used. This method focuses on the use of simulations, which are exercises in which the behaviors of applicants are observed. Examples, including the leaderless group discussion and the in-basket exercise, are described by Crooks (1977).

Though the history of the method dates back to the 1930s, its popularity has been relatively recent. As described by Moses and Byham (1977), the Assessment Center method is used for selecting managers, salespersons, high school principals, FBI agents, engineers, police officers, firefighters, and persons for many other occupations.

The assessors may be psychologists, but usually are persons familiar with the occupation for which selection decisions are to be made. It is essential that the assessors be thoroughly trained. Though the process is judgmental, it is standardized for a given occupation and is based on analysis of its requirements. Careful observation of behavior is required of the assessors, who must prepare accurate reports for presentation to all members of an Assessment Center staff. The staff considers all of the information obtained on each applicant in making its evaluations of suitability for employment, promotion, or other personnel action.

Application of the method tends to be costly, though cost varies considerably depending on the length of the assessment, number of assessors involved, and other factors. Consequently its use tends to favor, but is not limited to, higher level occupations. Psychologists have contributed greatly to the development of the Assessment Center method and seek to ensure its proper use. For example, "Standards and ethical considerations for assessment center operations: December, 1978" was issued by the Task Force on Assessment Center Standards chaired by Joseph Moses. Many studies of the method have been made, both of the process and of its utility in predicting job performance. A number of the studies have been reviewed by Huck (1977). Though its utility has been demonstrated, research to improve the method is being conducted.

RESEARCH

The development of a science of personnel selection requires research. Furthermore, applications of selection methods frequently require that studies be made to evaluate their utilities. Many aspects of selection are thus involved, including validity and validation, job analysis, job performance measurement, selection practices, and recruiting.

Validity and validation are a primary concern of psychologists using selection methods. All selection decisions are predictions of future behavior, and all involve error. People who subsequently fail may be accepted for employment, whereas those who would have succeeded if accepted may be rejected. The aim is to minimize selection error.

The traditional approach used to accomplish this purpose is known as criterion-related validation. Typically, an analysis of the job or occupation is made to ascertain its requirements. From the information obtained, a measure of job performance is developed. In addition, hypotheses are formulated with respect to the behavioral characteristics required for success in the occupation. A sample of applicants for the job or a sample of incumbent employees is selected and administered selection procedures designed to measure the hypothesized characteristics. The subsequent or current performance of each person in the sample is then measured, and scores on the selection procedures for each are statistically related to the measure or measures of performance. The results of the statistical analysis provide an estimate of the error in prediction. The higher the relationship obtained, the lower is the prediction error.

The criterion-related validation approach can lead to inaccurate estimates of prediction error. The sample of applicants or job incumbents may not be representative of the applicant population or the number of people in the sample may be insufficient. The measure(s) of job performance may be inaccurate. Commonly used supervisory ratings of performance, for example, can be unreliable or biased. Extraneous influences may distort the performance measure(s). In conducting validation research, psychologists seek to control these and other sources of potential inaccuracy in obtaining estimates of prediction error.

In addition to validation research, psychologists devote much effort to research on selection practices. Such studies are directed at improving the methods used. The focus is on the processes involved, for example, writing test questions that are easily understood.

Many methods for making job analyses have been developed. Though research on the methods and their applications has been less extensive than research on selection procedures, much has been accomplished. McCormick (1979) has described much of this research.

The measurement of job performance poses many difficulties. As noted, inaccurate measurement of job performance can invalidate criterion-related validation research. The issues involved are complex.

Recruitment of people to staff an organization is both external to the organization, when personnel new to the organization are to be hired, and internal, when promotions and transfers are involved. Relatively little research has been devoted to this aspect of personnel selection, even though a proficient selection system is partially dependent on recruiting the caliber of people required to maintain an effective organization. In recent years, more attention has been paid to this aspect of personnel selection. It is exemplified by the research of Wanous (1977).

ISSUES

Debates over the validity of selection procedures are common. Limitations of the traditional criterion-related approach to determining the validity of selection methods have been noted, and alternative approaches have gained both professional and legal recognition. They are referred to as *content validity* and *construct validity.* Along with criterion-related validity, both are included in the *Principles for the Validation and Use of Personnel Selection Procedures* issued by the Division of Industrial and Organizational Psychology of the American Psychological Association and in the *Uniform Guidelines on Employee Selection Procedures* (1978) adopted by the Equal Employment Opportunity Commission, Civil Service Commission, U.S. Department of Justice, and U.S. Department of Labor.

Content validity refers to the relevance of the tasks, items, and other aspects of a selection method. Whether, for example, the questions asked in a job knowledge test are representative of the knowledge a person must have to perform the work properly is a matter of content validity. In contrast, construct validity is theory oriented. To establish the construct validity of a selection procedure, a psychologist seeks evidence to support or refute hypotheses on which the method is based. Both approaches to determining the validity of a selection procedure focus on the method rather than on the criterion of job performance and the relationship of the selection procedure to the criterion as does criterion-related validity.

As discussed by Guion (1977), both content and construct validity approaches to establishing the validity of a selection procedure are controversial. He notes that validity refers to inferences from scores or ratings derived from a selection method rather than from its construction. Thus the very existence of content validity can be questioned. Construct validity requires a series of investigations, laborious to undertake, that require well-established methodologies.

Related to issues concerning the validities of selection procedures are issues with respect to bias, especially of psychological tests, criticized as being "culturally biased" and discriminatory to minorities. These criticisms arise from the fact that minority groups tend to obtain lower scores on many tests, paper-and-pencil ability tests in particular. Attempts have been made to develop "culture-free" tests, but have not been successful. Psychologists have conducted many studies to ascertain whether tests are biased against minorities when used in vocational selection. Debate over the results of such studies has been lengthy. As summarized by Linn (1978), many psychologists conclude that ability tests are predictive of job performance for minorities as well as for nonminorities, and therefore are not biased against minorities.

Whether the use of ability tests in personnel selection is fair, however, raises issues that pertain to how tests are used in selection. Several models of test fairness, described and discussed by Dunnette and Borman (1979), have been devised and evaluated. Objections have been raised with respect to each of the models. The issues have been reviewed by Novick and Ellis (1977).

While debates over bias and fairness in the use of ability tests for selection purposes have taken place largely among psychologists, legal issues have emerged that involve not only psychologists, but also many persons outside of the profession. These issues stem from the passage of the Civil Rights Act of 1964, which permits employers to use professionally developed ability tests as long as they do not use them to discriminate against minorities, women, and other groups protected by law. A series of guidelines on personnel selection have been issued by federal enforcement agencies, and many court decisions have been rendered that bear directly on the use of selection procedures. Among these are two U.S. Supreme Court decisions, namely, Griggs et al. v. Duke Power Company (401 U.S. 424, 1971) and Albemarle Paper Company v. Moody (402 U.S. 405, 1975). The first decision, often referred to as a "landmark" decision, specifies that where selection procedures have an "adverse impact" on the employment of protected groups, the employer must establish that the procedures are "job related" and a "business necessity." The second decision supported and clarified the first decision. The history of these legal matters and their impact on selection procedures has been reviewed by Miner and Miner (1978) and summarized by Novick (1981) and by Bersoff (1981).

Another legal action that has had implications for selection procedures is one that involved tests for upgrading. In this instance, a labor union sought access to the tests and to the scores of employees. The case was heard finally by the U.S. Supreme Court. By a five to four decision, the court upheld the employer's position, thus protecting the security of the tests and the confidentiality of the scores obtained by employees. The case is discussed by Roskind (1980).

Psychologists for many years have been aware that many ethical issues must be considered in personnel selection. Ethical issues are, however, complex, and are not easily resolved through the issuance of ethical guidelines. London and Bray (1980) discuss the need for research on how to resolve ethical issues when standards are not provided.

VALIDITY GENERALIZATION

The assumption that selection procedures are specific to each situation and thus must be proved valid for each situation has long concerned psychologists involved in personnel selection. Not only are validation efforts costly, but often they are not feasible, especially when using the criterion-related approach favored by many psychologists. Furthermore, as long as situational specificity must be assumed, selection research remains a technology rather than a science. The need to develop methods leading to general principles or laws governing selection procedures and the history of efforts to invent such methods is discussed by Guion (1976).

A renewed interest, with specific reference to the use of ability tests in selection, has led to many studies seeking to establish the generality of such tests for a number of occupations. This research and the results obtained are summarized by Schmidt and Hunter (1981). Statistical methods have been devised for correcting sources of error in previously conducted studies using criterion-related designs. The sources of error corrected, a total of seven referred to as "statistical artifacts," include small sample sizes, criterion unreliability, and restrictions in score ranges. From the results of their studies, Schmidt and Hunter (1981, p. 1128) concluded, "Professionally developed cognitive ability tests are valid predictors of performance on the job and in training . . . in all settings." As might be expected, the sweeping conclusions reached by Schmidt and Hunter, and their colleagues, along with the methods used in arriving at them, have been the subject of considerable controversy. For example, Tenopyr (1981) notes that supervisory ratings, which may be biased, were the performance criteria in most of the studies on which the conclusions are based. Nevertheless, interest in the topic has been marked.

The implications of research on validity generalization for employers who wish to use ability tests in selecting employees are clear. Acceptance, professional and legal, of methods for establishing the validity of tests without requiring validation studies for each situation would relieve employers of costly, and frequently not feasible, research. The employer, using appropriate job analysis methods, would be required only to demonstrate the comparability of jobs in his or her organization to those for which validity has been established.

REFERENCES

American Psychological Association. (1978). Report of the task force on the role of psychology in the criminal justice system. *American Psychologist, 33,* 1099–1113.

Asher, J. J., & Sciarrino, J. A. (1974). Realistic work sample tests: A review. *Personnel Psychology, 27,* 519–533.

Bersoff, D. N. (1981). Testing and the law. *American Psychologist, 36,* 1047–1056.

Buros, O. K. (Ed.). (1978). *The eighth mental measurements yearbook.* Highland Park, NJ: Gryphon Press.

Burtt, H. E. (1942). *Principles of employment psychology.* New York: Harper.

Crooks, L. A. (1977). The selection and development of assessment center techniques. In J. L. Moses & W. C. Byham (Eds.), *Applying the assessment center method.* New York: Pergamon.

Dunnette, M. D., & Borman, W. C. (1979). Personnel selection and classification systems. In M. R. Rosenzweig & L. W. Porter (Eds.), *Annual Review of Psychology, 30,* 477–525.

Flanagan, J. C. (Ed.). (1948). *The aviation psychology program in the Army Air Forces: Report no. 1.* Washington, DC: U.S. Government Printing Office.

Freyd, M. (1923). Measurement in vocational selection: An outline of research procedure. *Journal of Personnel Research, 2,* 268-284, 377–385.

Ghiselli, E. E. (1973). The validity of aptitude tests in personnel selection. *Personnel Psychology, 26,* 461–477.

Guion, R. M. (1976). Recruiting, selection, and placement. In M. D. Dunnette (Ed.), *Handbook of industrial and organizational psychology.* Chicago: Rand-McNally.

Huck, J. R. (1977). The research base. In J. L. Moses & W. C. Byham (Eds.), *Applying the assessment center method.* New York: Pergamon Press.

Kingslinger, H. S. (1966). Application of projective techniques in personnel psychology since 1940. *Psychology Bulletin, 66,* 134–149.

Linn, R. L. (1978). Single-group validity, differential validity, and differential prediction. *Journal of Applied Psychology, 63,* 507-512.

London, M., & Bray, D. W. (1980). Ethical issues in testing and evaluation for personnel decisions. *American Psychologist, 35,* 890–901.

McCormick, E. J. (1979). *Job analysis: Methods and applications.* New York: Amacom.

Miner, J. B. (1977). Motivational potential for upgrading among minority and female managers. *Journal of Applied Psychology, 62,* 691–697.

Miner, M. G., & Miner, J. B. (1978). *Employee selection within the law.* Washington, DC: Bureau of National Affairs.

Moses, J. L., & Byham, W. C. (1977). *Applying the assessment center method.* New York: Pergamon.

Novick, M. R. (1981). Federal guidelines and professional standards. *American Psychologist, 36,* 1035–1046.

Novick, M. R., & Ellis, D. D. (1977). Equal opportunity in educational and employment selection. *American Psychologist, 32,* 306–320.

Owens, W. A. (1976). Background data. In M. D. Dunnette (Ed.), *Handbook of industrial and organizational psychology.* Chicago: Rand-McNally.

Peterson, J. (1926). *Early conceptions and tests of intelligence.* New York: World Book.

Roskind, W. (1980). DECo. v. NLRB and the consequences of open testing in industry. *Personnel Psychology, 33,* 3–10.

Schmidt, F. L., & Hunter, J. E. (1981). Employment testing: Old theories and new research findings. *American Psychologist, 36,* 1128–1137.

Schmitt, N. (1976). Social and situational determinants of interview decisions: Implications for the employment interview. *Personnel Psychology, 29,* 79–101.

Schneider, B. (1976). *Staffing organizations.* Santa Monica, CA: Goodyear.

Sundberg, N. D. (1977). *Assessment of persons.* Englewood Cliffs, NJ: Prentice-Hall.

Tenopyr, M. L. (1981). The realities of employment testing. *American Psychologist, 36,* 1120–1127.

Thayer, P. W. (1977). Somethings old, somethings new. *Personnel Psychology, 30,* 513–524.

SUGGESTED READING

Arvey, R. D. (1979). *Fairness in selecting employees.* Reading, MA: Addison-Wesley.

Tenopyr, M. L., & Oeltjen, P. D. (1982). Personnel selection and classification. In M. R. Rosenzweig & L. W. Porter (Eds.), *Annual Review of Psychology, 33,* 581–618.

Thorndike, R. L. (1949). *Personnel selection: Test and measurement techniques.* New York: Wiley.

D. L. GRANT
Roswell, CTA.

EMPLOYMENT TESTS
INDUSTRIAL PSYCHOLOGY
JOB SATISFACTION
OCCUPATIONAL ADJUSTMENT

PETERSEN, ANNE C.

Anne C. Petersen is the senior vice president for programs at the W. K. Kellogg Foundation of Battle Creek, MI. As a senior member of the executive staff, she provides overall leadership for programming, including the development of effective programming strategies, teamwork, policies, philosophies, and organization-wide systems to accomplish the programmatic mission of the Foundation—helping people to help themselves. The implementation of strategic and innovative philanthropic approaches that obtain significant results for people and communities has been a particular emphasis of her work. She also is responsible for human and financial resources as well as planning and reviewing all program areas.

Previously, Petersen was nominated by the US President and confirmed by the US Senate as the deputy director and chief operating officer of the National Science Foundation (NSF), then a $3.6 billion federal research agency with 1,300 employees, based in Washington, DC. She worked closely with the National Science Board, the National Science and Technology Council, White House officials, and senior NSF management on national science policy. NSF is the only federal agency responsible for supporting nonmedical research and education in all fields of science and engineering, through grants to more than 2,000 institutions nationwide. At NSF she worked especially on enhancing public understanding of science and capitalizing on the synergy between research and education, among other priorities.

Before joining NSF, Petersen was vice president for research and dean of the Graduate School at the University of Minnesota. She was professor of adolescent development and pediatrics. As the first research vice president, she developed university partnerships with industry and the policies to support this work. Other priorities were facilitating interdisciplinary research and increasing the effectiveness of graduate programs, especially for students of color.

Petersen was the first dean of the College of Health and Human Development, and professor at the Pennsylvania State University. As dean she reached the five-year strategic planning goals for research funding and student enrollments within two years. Earlier she was department head of an interdisciplinary department, Human Development and Family Studies, at Penn State. Through her efforts, the department was recognized one of the top few departments in the university.

Early in her career, Petersen was on the faculty at the University of Chicago and headed the Laboratory for the Study of Adolescence at the Michael Reese Hospital and Medical Center. She also developed a funded training program for interdisciplinary clinical research on adolescence. At the same time, she was associate director for the health program at the John D. and Catherine T. MacArthur Foundation. She helped develop this program as the foundation was establishing itself.

Petersen's funded research focused on adolescent biopsychosocial development and mental health, and resulted in more than a dozen books and nearly 200 articles on these topics as well as gender issues, physical health, higher education, research methods, and science policy. She developed three measures of development in adolescence that are still in use for research purposes. Her work on puberty is often cited; she was a leader in noting and demonstrating scientifically the importance of considering the influence of biological change on psychological and social changes in adolescence. Her research on adolescent depression was also pioneering, testing hypotheses for the increased risk for depression among girls. She has presented frequently at scientific meetings, academic conferences and symposia, and public lectures. Her work has been recognized with many lectureships, awards, and honors.

Among her service roles, Petersen chairs a board of the National Academy of Sciences (NAS) on Behavior, Cognition, and Sensory Sciences, and serves on a NAS/Institute of Medicine (IOM) Adolescent Forum. She has served previously as chair or member of other NAS or IOM groups. She has served as reviewer and in editorial roles for several journals. Petersen has been a member or chair of numerous funding panels for federal agencies and private foundations. She has also served on several boards and advisory groups for scientific organizations, nonprofit associations, and corporations. She was a founding member of the Society for Research on Adolescence, and also served as president and council member. She is the past president of Developmental Psychology, American Psychological Association and of the division on Human Development of the American Educational Research Association. Petersen is a fellow of the American Association for the Advancement of Science, the American Psychological Association, and the American Psychological Society, and was elected to the Academy of Behavioral Medicine Research. She has won other awards and honors including election as a member of the Institute of Medicine, National Academy of Sciences.

Petersen holds a bachelor's degree in mathematics, a master's degree in statistics, and a doctorate in measurement, evaluation, and statistical analysis from the University of Chicago, IL. She is a native of Little Falls, MN.

STAFF

PETERSON, DONALD R. (1923-   )

Peterson received the BA, MA, and PhD (1952) degrees from the University of Minnesota, where he was most strongly influenced by P. E. Meehl but also studied under D. G. Paterson, S. R. Hathaway, K. E. Clark, H. Gough, D. Harris, statistician A. Treloar, and philosopher H. Feigl. Following receipt of the PhD, he accepted a position in the psychology department at the University of Illinois, Urbana-Champaign, where he taught a wide range of subjects from introductory psychology to advanced seminars in personality, behavior disorders, and clinical assessment. At Illinois, he followed his dissertation research on the diagnosis of subclinical schizophrenia with studies that confirmed Meehl's contentions about the superiority of actuarial over clinical modes of prediction and provided a basis for predicting outbreak of florid schizophrenic symptoms among psychiatric outpatients initially diagnosed under various nonpsychotic labels, most commonly psychoneuroses or character disorders. He soon formed collaborative affiliations with R. B. Cattell, with whom he published a series of studies on personality structure in children; H. C. Quay, with whom he published research on children's behavior disorders and juvenile delinquency; and W. C. Becker, his main partner in studies of parent-child relationships. On a Fulbright scholarship, he conducted research on parent-child relationships in Sicily, which he published with G. Migliorino of the University of Palermo.

The trait-based research with which he began yielded some useful outcomes. His finding that a small number of group factors produced more stable results than the large numbers of factors typically examined by Cattell and others was one of the discoveries that led to the "big five" conceptions of personality structure that were commonly accepted in following years. The publication that described his behavior problem checklist became a "citation classic," and a revised version developed primarily by Quay became widely used as a research instrument and as a clinical screening device for children's behavior problems in the schools. However, close study of correlations among conceptually comparable factor scores across different data modes (e.g., ratings, questionnaire responses, and objective tests) consistently showed very low levels of correspondence. Correlation coefficients typically hovered around .30.

In the 1960s, these and other considerations led Peterson to question the value of most research on traits, to emphasize the force of situational influences on behavior in natural settings, and to insist on interactional perspectives in the study of personal dispositions and social process. His book, *The Clinical Study of Social Behavior* (1968), summarized those views. While Peterson was formulating his ideas, W. Mischel was independently arriving at similar conclusions. Mischel's influential book, *Personality and Assessment,* was also published in 1968. Peterson treated the main argument that occupied Mischel's entire book in a single chapter and went beyond to propose a scientifically grounded clinical psychology, one procedurally composed of multimethod strategies for assessment and change at individual, group, and organizational levels.

In 1963, Peterson became director of the psychological clinic at the University of Illinois and in 1964 was appointed director of the department's PhD program in clinical psychology. During those same years, APA's committee on the scientific and professional aims of psychology, with 24 distinguished scientists, scientist-practitioners, and practitioners as members and K. E. Clark as chair, concluded that the hybrid scientist-practitioner programs in which all American clinical psychologists had been educated up to that time were doing neither part of their combined jobs effectively. The modal number of publications by graduates of the research-oriented programs was (and still is) zero; graduates who entered careers of practice were often scorned by faculty and felt ill-prepared for the challenges of professional work. The committee recommended the creation of programs specifically designed to prepare students for careers of professional service and award of a professional degree, the Doctor of Psychology (PsyD) degree, upon completion of graduate studies. Scientist-practitioner programs leading to the PhD were to be continued, with preparation for careers of scholarly research emphasized more strongly than before. With the support and active participation of L. G. Humphreys, who had been a member of the "Clark committee" and was then head of the Illinois psychology department, Peterson organized the first PsyD program in the United States, admitting the first class of students in 1968.

In ensuing years, Peterson focused his scholarly research on interaction process in marital relationships. Among other consequences, this led to collaboration with H. Kelley, E. Berscheid, and others in a book, *Close Relationships* (1983). Peterson's interest in

behavior disorders continued. From 1970 to 1972 he served as editor of the *Journal of Abnormal Psychology.* But his concern for integrity in the education of professional psychologists remained a dominant passion. In 1975, he became first dean of the Graduate School of Applied and Professional Psychology at Rutgers University, the first university-based professional school to award the PsyD degree. From that time on, most of his publications were concerned with education and training for the practice of psychology. Discontinuation of the Illinois PsyD program, which ultimately became a poor fit with the predominant emphasis on research in the Illinois psychology department, along with continuing growth of PsyD programs in small colleges and free-standing professional schools, required special efforts to maintain the scholarly quality of practitioner programs. Peterson contributed to these efforts as a founding officer (1976) and president (1980–1983) of the National Council of Schools and Programs of Professional Psychology, member (1978–1980) and chair (1980) of the APA Committee on Accreditation, member (1980) of the executive board of the Council on Postsecondary Accreditation, and persistently through his writings. His major papers on professional education in psychology are presented in *Educating Professional Psychologists: History and Guiding Conception* (1997). Among other honors, he received the APA award for distinguished contributions to professional psychology as a professional practice in 1983 and the APA award for distinguished career contributions to education and training in psychology in 1989.

D. R. PETERSON
Rutgers University

PHENYLALANINE

Phenylalanine is an essential hydrophobic aromatic amino acid. The term "essential" in this context means that the amino acid cannot be synthesized endogenously and must be obtained through diet. A common amino acid in proteins, phenylalanine is the immediate precursor of tyrosine, a nonessential amino acid from which catecholamine neurotransmitters are made (Figure 1).

PHENYLALANINE METABOLISM

Phenylalanine not used in protein synthesis is oxidized to tyrosine by the enzyme tyrosine hydroxylase (Figure 2). This reaction requires a cofactor, tetrahydrobiopterin (BH_4), which is synthesized de novo from guanosine triphosphate. In the reaction, BH_4 is converted to quinonoid dihydrobiopterin, which is reduced back to BH_4 by dihydropteridine reductase. This recycling pathway serves the important function of maintaining the BH_4 cofactor.

HYPERPHENYLALANINEMIA

Hyperphenylalaninemias are inborn disorders of phenylalanine metabolism. Normally, about 25% of phenylalanine is used for protein synthesis and the remaining 75% is converted to tyrosine. Hydroxylation of phenylalanine is the principal pathway for phenylalanine runout from body fluids. If this process is impaired,

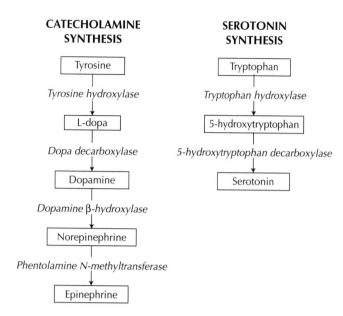

Figure 1. Catecholamine and serotonin biosynthetifc pathways. Enzymes are in small italicized type.

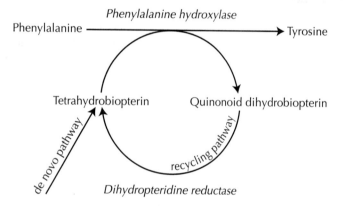

Figure 2. Phenylalanine metabolism. Enzymes are in small italicized type. Reprinted with permission from Baumeister & Baumeister (1998). Dietary treatment of hyperphenylalaninemia. *Clinical Neuropharmacology 21(1)*, 18–27.

continued input of phenylalanine from diet and endogenous sources (i.e., peptide turnover) causes the concentration of phenylalanine in plasma to rise. Impairment of hydroxylation can result from a defect in phenylalanine hydroxylase or, less frequently, in one of the enzymes involved in BH_4 synthesis or recycling. Phenylketonuria (PKU) is a type of hyperphenylalaninemia caused by a marked deficiency of phenylalanine hydroxylase that results in a plasma phenylalanine level of > 16.5 mg/dl. Phenylalanine hydroxylase deficiencies that produce a lesser elevation of phenylalanine are called non-PKU hyperphenylalaninemias.

Clinical Manifestation

Marked elevation of phenylalanine is associated with clinical manifestations most notably involving the central nervous system. Untreated or late-treated PKU usually results in a host of neurologic sequelae including severe mental retardation, seizures, and behavioral (e.g., self-mutilation, aggression, and hyperactivity) and psychiatric (e.g., depression and mania) disorders. A consistent neuropathologic finding is abnormalities in cerebral white matter revealed by magnetic resonance imaging. Persons with non-PKU hyperphenylalaninemia appear to have few clinical manifestations, although recent neuroimaging studies have identified abnormalities in this group.

Recent research has elucidated the relation between genotype and clinical manifestations in the hyperphenylalaninemias. These disorders have an autosomal recessive mode of inheritance. More that 300 distinct mutations of the gene that encodes phenylalanine hydroxylase (located on chromosome 12) have been identified. Severity of the genetic mutation of both alleles correlates with severity of the biochemical and cognitive phenotypes. The presence of a mild mutation on one allele is protective. Intelligence quotient scores tend to be lower when the mutation on both alleles is severe, than when one is severe and the other mild. Nevertheless, there is wide variation of IQ within genotype groups due to other influences, such as inherited intellectual disposition and the timing, effectiveness, and duration of treatment.

Aberrant behavior in PKU may be related to neurotransmitter deficiencies. Concentrations of dopamine and serotonin in cerebrospinal fluid have been found to be reduced in persons with hyperphenylalaninemia, and both of these neurotransmitters have been implicated in deviant behaviors, sometimes severe (e.g., self-mutilation), that often occur in untreated PKU. The cause of the neurotransmitter deficit is not established, though reduced synthesis is implicated. Two possible bases for reduced synthesis are (a) decreased transport of precursor amino acids to sites of neurotransmitter synthesis due to competition with phenylalanine for transporters; and (b) diminished activity of hydroxylase enzymes. Although in PKU phenylalanine hydroxylase is defective, this alone does not appear to reduce catecholamine synthesis, because in the absence of phenylalanine hydroxylase activity tyrosine becomes an essential amino acid and its intake in diet is normally adequate. However, in hyperphenylalaninemias caused by impaired BH_4 synthesis or recycling, activities of tyrosine, tryptophan, and phenylalanine hydroxylase are all diminished because all three enzymes require the BH_4 cofactor. Reduction in tyrosine and tryptophan hydroxylation does interfere with neurotransmitter synthesis.

Treatment

Nervous system damage in PKU is thought to result from phenylalanine toxicity. Recent evidence indicates that the concentration of phenylalanine in the brain is a more important indicator of neurologic risk than is concentration in blood. Dietary restriction of phenylalanine shortly after birth lowers plasma and brain phenylalanine and prevents major neurologic sequelae. Because early detection and treatment are essential, screening for PKU at birth is now routine in the United States and many other nations. In the past it has been customary to ease dietary restrictions in school-age children on the assumption that the brain is less vulnerable at this time. However, mounting evidence that this practice is associated with behavioral, cognitive, and neurologic deterioration indicates a need to maintain the restricted diet into adolescence or longer. There is evidence that some neurotoxic effects of phenylalanine in persons who were treated early but later removed from diet and in persons never treated early are reversible to some extent by late initiation of a phenylalanine-restricted diet.

Treatment of disorders of BH_4 synthesis or recycling (which are relatively rare) requires additional measures. In these disorders, catecholamine and serotonin neurotransmitters are deficient even when phenylalanine is controlled because BH_4 is a required cofactor for tyrosine and tryptophan hydroxylase. Treatment with L-dopa and 5-hydroxytryptophan, the immediate precursors of dopamine and serotonin, is necessary to correct deficiencies in these neurotransmitters.

Maternal PKU

Children who do not have hyperphenylalaninemia but who are born to affected women who do not maintain dietary restrictions during pregnancy can suffer various teratogenic effects of phenylalanine, including mental retardation, microcephaly, growth retardation, and heart malformations. This condition is called maternal PKU. Control of blood phenylalanine by maternal dietary restriction from conception to birth is associated with improved fetal outcome. About 90% of infants born to PKU mothers not maintained on the phenylalanine-restricted diet during pregnancy are severely affected. It has been estimated that without proper maternal control of phenylalanine, the benefits of infant screening and treatment for PKU will be erased in one generation.

SUGGESTED READING

Baumeister, A. A., & Baumeister, A. A. (1998). Dietary treatment of destructive behavior associated with hyperphenylalaninemia. *Clinical Neuropharmacology, 21,* 18–27.

Guttler, F., Azen, C., Guldberg, P., Romstad, A., Hanley, W. B., Levy, H. L., Matalon, R., Rouse, B. M., Trefz, F., Platt, L., Ullrich, K., Waisbren, S. E., Friedman, E. G., de la Cruz, F., & Koch, R. (1999). Relationship between genotype, biochemical phenotype, and cognitive performance in the maternal phenylketonuria collaborative study. *Pediatrics, 104,* 258–262.

Scriver, C. R., Kaufman, S., Eisensmith, R. C., & Woo, S. L. C. (1995). The hyperphenylalaninemias. In C. R. Scriver, A. L. Beaudet, W. S. Sly, & D. Valle (Eds.), *The metabolic bases of inherited disease* (7th ed.). New York: McGraw-Hill.

A. A. BAUMEISTER
Louisiana State University

PHENYLKETONURIA (PKU)

Phenylketonuria (PKU) is a rare genetic metabolic disorder (about 1 in 16,000 births in the United States) in which the incomplete oxidation of an amino acid (phenylalanine) can lead to brain damage and severe mental retardation. It is caused by the absence of the enzyme phenylalanine hydroxylase, normally found in the liver. Phenylalanine is a naturally occurring amino acid important for optimal growth in infants and for nitrogen equilibrium in adults. It is found in many common foods, including milk. However, when phenylalanine builds up to an extremely high level, it is converted into a toxic acid (phenylpyruvic acid), which can be detected in the urine. Symptoms of PKU are usually absent in the newborn period. Later, mental retardation becomes the most important symptom. The majority of untreated phenylketonurics show mental retardation, usually severe. They tend to have lighter skin, hair, and eyes than unaffected family members. Many neurologic symptoms and signs, especially affecting reflexes, occur. Both petit and grand mal epileptic seizures are common in older children. Also common are hyperactivity, psychotic states, and an unpleasant body odor caused by the presence of phenylacetic acid in the urine and sweat (Turner & Helms, 1979).

The devastating effects of PKU can be avoided through the administration of tests (e.g., Guthrie test) to determine whether a newborn infant shows proper metabolism of phenylalanine. If not, the child can be placed on a special diet, low in phenylalanine, to prevent a buildup of this chemical to dangerous levels. The phenylalanine intake of the child must be limited so that the essential amino acid requirement is met, but not exceeded. This allows normal growth and development, but prevents accumulation of phenylalanine in the blood. Monitoring of the child and the child's plasma phenylalanine levels is required. Treatment must be initiated during the first days of life to minimize mental retardation. Treatment started after 2 to 3 years of age may be effective only in controlling extreme hyperactivity and seizures. Some authorities feel that treatment may be terminated when myelination of the brain is complete, at about 5 years of age, while others believe it should be continued for life. Early and well-maintained treatment makes normal development possible and avoids central nervous system involvement.

REFERENCES

Turner, J. S., & Helms, D. B. (1979). *Life span development.* Philadelphia, PA: Saunders.

J. L. ANDREASSI
City University of New York, Baruch College

DOWN'S SYNDROME
MENTAL RETARDATION
SEX CHROMOSOME DISORDERS

PHEROMONES

Pheromones can be broadly defined as chemical signals that pass between organisms of the same species and have an inherent communicatory function. Pheromones appear to have originated in the earliest life forms and continue to serve as the primary means of communication in many species, including most terrestrial and aquatic invertebrates, fishes, and mammals with nocturnal habits. The ways in which organisms employ pheromones are as diverse as their life histories. While some species possess a single pheromone system, others may employ numerous systems with overlapping functions. Pheromones are notorious for their potency and specificity—qualities that are often attributed to their being detected by specialized components of the olfactory system. Few pheromones have been definitively identified, with the exception of many of those used by insects, and the chemical composition of pheromones appears highly varied. Further, identified pheromones have frequently been found to be mixtures of relatively common compounds. The defining characteristic of pheromones, therefore, lies in the intrinsic ability of recipients to recognize them, and not in their chemical identity per se, although the latter may also be notable.

Pheromones are most appropriately characterized by their actions. Generally, the actions of pheromones are species-specific, although this is not always the case. Pheromones may have behavioral and/or physiological effects. Pheromones with significant behavioral effects often are termed "releasers"; those with physiological effects are called "primers." Releasers are the best known and include sex pheromones, aggregation pheromones, territorial pheromones, and alarm pheromones. Sex pheromones are used by many terrestrial, aquatic, and aerial species in locating and selecting mates. Some of these cues are remarkably potent; for example, male moths may be attracted to the odor of females located hundreds of meters away. Similarly, male dogs respond to the scent of bitches in heat nearly a kilometer upwind, and male goldfish detect female sex pheromones at concentrations ranging down to 1 gram in 3 billion liters of water.

Aggregation about pheromones are used by many species to bring individuals of the same species together. Examples include unicellular slime molds that are forming fruiting bodies, migrating lampreys locating spawning rivers based on the odor of larval conspecifics that they contain, and insects swarming. In contrast, many terrestrial mammals, such as antelopes and badgers, use territorial pheromone marks to keep individuals of the same species apart and maintain optimal spacing. Alarm pheromones are also commonly used by both terrestrial and aquatic organisms. For example, when injured, many fish release alarm pheromones ("Schreckstoff") from their skin. Because of their potency and specificity, releaser pheromones are frequently used in the management of unwanted nuisance species, particularly insects.

Priming pheromones are also employed by a wide variety of species, and their actions may be dramatic. For example, unidentified urinary odors of male mice serve to advance puberty in juvenile females (Vandenburgh effect), while female urinary odors have the opposite effect. Pregnant rodents will abort pre-implantation embryos if exposed to the odor of a male that is not the father of their young (the Bruce effect). Male goldfish and carp synchronize their endocrine cycles with those of ovulatory females by detecting hormonal sex pheromones released by the latter. Among the honeybees, development of future queens is influenced by pheromonal signals circulating within the hive. Just as evolution has favored organisms that develop chemosensory systems that detect cues of behavioral importance, it has also frequently led to development of conspecific cues that mediate physiological synchrony.

As one might expect, the biochemical nature of pheromones varies enormously among species. It is best understood amongst the insects, but about a dozen vertebrate pheromones have also been clearly identified. Pheromones frequently appear to be composed of molecules (or more often, sets of molecules) that originally served other, related functions. A good example of such an unspecialized system is that of the goldfish and its relatives, which use common hormonal products as sex pheromones. In some instances, considerable specialization may have occurred, presumably when donors derive benefit from signal production. For instance, many insects and ungulates possess specialized pheromone glands that produce large amounts of molecular blends, the release of which they control. A well-known example of such a system is that of the noctuid moths, whose sex pheromones are precise species-specific mixtures of up to seven simple fatty acids and related acetates, aldehydes, and alcohols. Among mammals, only two (single-component) pheromones have been clearly identified (one in the pig and one in the elephant), and most mammalian pheromones appear to be complex mixtures whose actions are subtle and hidden within the body odor of the donor.

Regardless of whether they are specialized, pheromonal signals generally have chemical characteristics that complement the ecological needs of the species in question. Thus, alarm and sex pheromones in terrestrial insects are frequently composed of low molecular weight, volatile compounds that spread and fade quickly. Interestingly, elephants use some of the same volatile cues as moths do for ephemeral sex signals. Fish often use relatively small and highly-soluble conjugated steroids as sex pheromones. Hyenas, on the other hand, have evolved to use high molecular weight compounds as territorial marks that last for months in the hot sun. In rodents, marking pheromones appear to take the form of a large stable protein known as a major urinary protein (MUP), which is bound to a smaller ligand and is long-lived.

Biological responses associated with pheromonal exposure are attributable to specializations in the nervous systems of the receiving animals. Many striking parallels are beginning to emerge between how invertebrates and vertebrates process pheromonal information. For instance, peripheral sensitivity to pheromones is often sexually dimorphic in both invertebrates and vertebrates. Also, in both instances, processing of pheromonal information appears to be closely associated with specialized but well-defined component(s) of their olfactory systems. Pheromones have proven useful in exploring how olfactory information is processed, from receptor-ligand interactions to the mechanisms that drive specific behaviors in the central nervous system.

Pheromones are detected by olfactory receptor neurons concentrated in a sensory epithelium in the nose or mouth of vertebrates and on sensory hairs located on the antennae of invertebrates such as moths and lobsters. Pheromones appear to bind with receptor proteins (which have yet to be fully elucidated) on the surface of these neurons and then project to specialized regions of the antennal lobe (invertebrates) or olfactory bulb (vertebrates). While single-unit recording has shown pheromonally-sensitive receptor neurons in insects to be tuned to a narrow range of pheromone compounds, molecular and electrophysiological techniques now suggest that a specific type of receptor neuron, the microvillar cell, mediates many pheromone responses in vertebrates and is likely to be narrowly tuned.

There are also strong similarities between invertebrates and vertebrates in the organization of neurons that receive and process pheromonal information from receptor neurons in the insect olfactory lobe and in the fish and mammalian olfactory bulb. In male moths, axons from olfactory receptor neurons project to a specialized subset of glomeruli, the macroglomerular complex (MGC) located in the lobe. Well-defined connections among the MGC glomeruli give male moths the remarkable ability to discriminate precise species-specific mixtures and perform specific flight maneuvers millisecond by millisecond. Although less well understood, specific mapping of olfactory receptor neurons also appears to occur in the vertebrate olfactory bulb. In fish, this mapping appears to occur in medial regions of the olfactory bulb. The situation appears even more complex for terrestrial vertebrates, including mammals, which have a dual olfactory system comprised of the main olfactory epithelium and the vomeronasal organ (VNO) located in the roof of the mouth. Although both systems may mediate pheromone responses in older, experienced animals (e.g., pigs and rabbits), the VNO appears to be the primary system for discriminating pheromones and is needed by naïve rodents to respond to priming cues. The VNO appears highly specialized; in rodents the VNO possesses only microvillar receptor neurons that project to a specific set of mitral (output) cells of the accessory olfactory bulb (AOB). The AOB then projects subcortically to the hypothalamus, where it excites neurosecretory cells to release reproductive hormones when stimulated by primer pheromones.

Although responsiveness to pheromones is fundamentally instinctual, some chemical signals associated with kin and mate recognition appear to be learned. For example, honeybees learn to recognize surface hydrocarbon mixtures on the bodies of nest mates, whom they will then allow to enter the nest. Young mice will imprint on the odor type of their parents (which appears to be closely associated with the Major Histocompatability Complex [MHC]) and will avoid it later in life when choosing mates. Also, adult female mice learn the odor of males during mating and distinguish it from that of other males in the Bruce effect. The latter phenomenon has proven to be an interesting model system for investigating olfactory memory.

If we are like other mammals, it is probable that many behavioral and physiological aspects of human biology are influenced by pheromones, but as yet none of these are conclusively demonstrated or identified. Presently, it seems doubtful that we have a functioning VNO. However, there are suggestions that, as in mice, human mate-choice may be influenced by the smells associated with the MHC system, with people choosing partners with a different MHC profile. We can be most confident about the role of pheromones in menstrual synchrony, which occurs among women living in close proximity, although the specific compounds are not yet known. With the advent of new molecular techniques and the means to visualize neural activity in vivo, our understanding of pheromone function and identity is expected to advance rapidly in the new millennium.

SUGGESTED READING

Johnston, R. E., Müller-Schwarze, D., & Sorensen, P. W. (Eds.). (1999). *Advances in chemical signals in vertebrates.* New York: Kluwer.

Sorensen, P. W., Christensen, T. A., & Stacey, N. E. (1998). Discrimination of pheromonal cues in fish: Emerging parallels with insects. *Current Opinion in Neurobiology, 8,* 458–467.

Vandenbergh, J. G. (1999). Pheromones, Mammals. In E. Knobil & J. D. Neill (Eds.), *Encyclopedia of Reproduction* (Vol. 3). New York: Academic Press.

Wyatt, T. D. (2001). *Pheromones and animal behaviour: Communication by smell.* Cambridge: Cambridge University Press.

P. W. SORENSEN
T. D. WYATT
University of Minnesota

ANIMAL COMMUNICATION

PHILOSOPHY OF PSYCHOTHERAPY

Psychotherapy is often considered to be an applied science consisting of a compendium of techniques or approaches validated by empirical research. Alternately, it is viewed as an art form requiring a creative, intuitive, and individualistic approach to clients and their problems. However, psychotherapy can also be regarded as influenced in a fundamental way by broader philosophical underpinnings that transcend its scientific, human engineering, or artistic dimensions. Examples of some of these domains are: (a) our possessing a priori categories of understanding that are part of therapeutic work, such as certain assumptions about reality, and underlying narrative structures; (b) the inevitability of value-laden issues in therapy; (c) the presence of societal and cultural influences on the practice of psychotherapy, and the effect of psychotherapy on the terms in which people in our society view themselves; and (d) the importance of regarding clients as having ethical and legal standing as well as being free agents, quite apart from their status as the objects of scientific understanding and healing (Messer & Woolfolk, 1998; Woolfolk, 1998). This article will take up each of these areas in turn.

A PRIORI CATEGORIES OF UNDERSTANDING

Every intellectual endeavor has a starting point prior to empirical investigation. Without the ontologies and conceptual categories that are prior to experience we could not organize the world into objects and events. When we look at the world, we do so through particular lenses or conceptual schemes that influence what we see. Philosophical analysis is a tool for making the properties of these lenses explicit, helping us to understand the concepts that underlie our thinking.

One aspect of the philosophical and cultural a priori is referred to by contemporary philosophers as the background. It contains the taken-for-granted knowledge and norms that are implicit in our practical and theoretical activities. For example, our clients have a certain cultural background, which we most often share. To understand how much we take this common cultural understanding for granted, one ought to imagine the practice of psychotherapy in a different culture—say, Japan. When individuals seek psychotherapy in Japan, it is frequently not to reduce their own distress, which is the norm in Western culture, but because they believe they possess traits that may cause discomfort to others (Bankart, 1997). With such clients, who are not imbued with such Western ideals as individualism, autonomy, and self-realization, the entire project of psychotherapy is viewed very differently. What one means by such therapeutic goals as interpersonal effectiveness and emotional maturity are no longer so obvious and straightforward.

Consider, too, as an example of the background, the contrasting narrative themes underlying different forms of treatment, which often go unrecognized. One typology of narratives describes four such visions or viewpoints: romantic, tragic, ironic, and comic (Frye, 1957). From the romantic viewpoint, life is an adventure or quest, a drama of the triumph of good over evil, virtue over vice, and light over darkness. It idealizes individuality and authentic self-expression. The romantic vision underpins humanistic approaches to psychotherapy, which stress the value and possibilities for spontaneity, authenticity, and creativity. The ironic vision, in contrast, encompasses an attitude of detachment and suspicion, of keeping things in perspective, and of recognizing the fundamental ambiguity and mystery of every issue that life presents. Whereas behavioral and cognitive therapists tend to take client complaints at face value, and humanistic therapists accept most client feelings as authentic expression, psychoanalytic therapists are more likely to look for hidden meanings, paradoxes, and contradictions. This puts them more squarely in the ironic mode.

The tragic vision is an acceptance of the limitations in life—not all is possible, not all is redeemable, not all potentialities are realizable. The clock cannot be turned back, death cannot be avoided, human nature cannot be radically perfected. Many aspects of psychoanalysis fall within the tragic vision. Individuals are determined by events of their early childhood, which are subject to repression and are beyond their conscious purview. The outcome of psychoanalytic treatment is not unalloyed happiness or all obstacles overcome, but rather the fuller recognition and acceptance of what one's struggles are about, and the conditions and limitations of life. By contrast, within the comic vision, the direction of events is from bad to better or even best. Obstacles and struggles are ultimately overcome. Harmony and unity, progress and happiness prevail. Cognitive-behavioral therapy holds out the promise of finding greater happiness through the application of scientific principles of healing, while humanistic approaches emphasize the substantial possibility for gratification. These underlying visions profoundly affect both the process and desired outcomes of these different forms of treatment.

PSYCHOTHERAPY AND VALUES

Virtually all of the innovators who made significant contributions to psychotherapy, such as Freud, Rogers, Wolpe, Perls, and Beck, considered themselves to be discoverers of morally neutral, scientific knowledge, and viewed psychotherapy as an objective application of that knowledge to the goal of psychological health. By contrast, philosophical analysis helps us to see how values often establish (albeit covertly) the criteria for intervention, influence patterns of therapeutic exploration, and promote standards for client

conduct. For example, a man comes to a therapist announcing that he is considering leaving his wife for a much younger, recently married woman, and wants help making the decision. A therapist operating within the values of liberal, secular individualism would stress the happiness and contentment of the individual above all else and above all others, encouraging him to explore the issue in these self-directed (some might say selfish) terms. One who holds to communitarian values might be more inclined to address how the client's decision to leave his wife will cause others to suffer, such as spouses, children, and other family members. Yet another therapist, hewing to religious values such as the sanctity of marriage, might emphasize the psychological and moral consequences of breaking marital vows. Despite claims to the contrary, there is no value-free psychotherapy.

THE INTERSECTION OF PSYCHOTHERAPY WITH SOCIETAL AND CULTURAL WORLDVIEWS

The institution of psychotherapy is a significant source of, and influence on, contemporary customs, values, and worldviews, and is constantly incorporating them in its purview (Messer & Wachtel, 1997; Woolfolk, 1998). For example, all societies need mechanisms that establish which behavior is to be promoted and which is to be proscribed. Although we most often think of clinicians as healers, they also function as agents of social control. The clinician is granted responsibility for many bizarre, incapable, or destructive individuals whom the rest of society will not or cannot tolerate.

Psychotherapy and its related theory and language are also cultural phenomena that have affected how people think about themselves. For example, laypeople refer to Freudian slips, defenses, guilt complexes, conditioned responses, existential angst, identity crises, or discovering their true selves—all terms related to the activity of psychotherapy. Similarly, when they explain their problems in terms of childhood occurrences such as parental neglect or harsh criticism, repressed memories, or learned associations, they demonstrate that psychotherapy is far more than a scientific or technical endeavor. Its language constitutes the very belief systems that people employ to make sense of their lives.

THE CLIENT AS A PERSON WITH AGENCY

In addition to understanding and treating clients based on science, psychotherapists must recognize that each of their clients has legal and ethical standing as a person. In discussing with clients the scheduling of appointments, setting of fees, establishing of therapeutic goals, or assessment of whether the benefits of a course of therapy are commensurate with its costs, the ground rules come from ethics and practical reason, not from science. Psychotherapists regard clients in these discussions not as objects of science, but as parties to a contract, as free agents, as consumers with the prerogative to decide and choose.

In summary, psychotherapy is not only a scientific, medical, or technical enterprise but is undergirded by philosophical assumptions, many of which are covert. Given its role as a guide for living, psychotherapy is influenced by the prevailing sociocultural milieu, its customs and values. In turn, psychotherapy has had a profound effect on our very definition of who and what we are and that to which we aspire.

REFERENCES

Bankart, C. P. (1997). *Taking care: A history of Western and Eastern psychotherapies.* Pacific Grove, CA: Brooks/Cole.

Frye, N. (1957). *Anatomy of criticism.* Princeton, NJ: Princeton University Press.

Messer, S. B., & Wachtel, P. L. (1997). The contemporary psychotherapeutic landscape: Issues and prospects. In P. L. Wachtel & S. B. Messer (Eds.), *Theories of psychotherapy: Origins and evolution.* (pp. 1–38). Washington, DC: American Psychological Association Press.

Messer, S. B., & Woolfolk, P. L. (1998). Philosophical issues in psychotherapy. *Clinical Psychology: Science and Practice, 5,* 251–263.

Woolfolk, R. L. (1998). *The cure of souls: Science, values and psychotherapy.* San Francisco: Jossey-Bass.

S. B. MESSER
R. L. WOOLFOLK
Rutgers University

EXISTENTIALISM PSYCHOTHERAPY

PHOBIAS

A phobia is an irrational fear. Phobias may manifest as fears of specific animate or inanimate objects, such as fear of snakes (ophidiophobia); fear of a defined group or class of people (xenophobia, fear of foreigners; androphobia, fear of men); fear of impending or anticipated occurrences (astrophobia, fear of lightning; school/test phobia, fear of school or of exams); or a fear of virtually anything else that one can imagine. The following are a few of the other major phobias frequently reported in the clinical literature:

	Fear of
Acrophobia	High places
Agoraphobia	Going out of the house
Claustrophobia	Closed spaces
Cynophobia	Dogs
Cypridophobia	Venereal Disease
Electrophobia	Electricity, especially getting a shock
Genophobia	Sex
Gynophobia	Women
Hodophobia	Traveling
Hydrophobia	Water
Hypnophobia	Sleep
Kakorrhaphiophobia	Failure
Mysophobia	Dirt
Pathophobia	Disease
Thanatophobia	Death

The objective assessment of any fear typically is open to debate regarding the extent and circumstances under which real dangers are posed by the feared object or event. Two criteria, unrelated to the appraisal of potential danger, differentiate phobias from rational, non-neurotic fears.

First, phobias have an obsessive nature. A phobic individual is often compelled to dwell on the feared thing far more than is necessary under the objective circumstances. Phobic thinking may take the form of fantasies, such as a thanatophobe fantasizing about his or her funeral or imagining over and over what the dying moment will be like. Characteristically these types of phobic fantasies combine fear with a sense of fascination, almost pleasure, as images of the object or scenarios of the event cause a trepidation and trembling much as one might experience on a scary amusement ride. The fantasy itself may produce a sense of "relief" in that it allows momentary mastery over the fearfulness.

A second characteristic that differentiates a phobia from a realistic fear concerns the way in which anxiety is handled. A phobia typically produces so high a level of anxiety that it is immobilizing, preventing the person from acting in a way that could prove effective in alleviating the anxiety. Whereas a rational fear will frequently precipitate behaviors designed to protect one from a danger, phobias often place their victims in more danger, either by temporarily paralyzing them in awe-struck inactivity, or by compelling them to confront the danger in an unproductive manner. For example, a person with a normal (nonphobic) fear of swimming in the ocean might learn to become a good swimmer and learn ocean safety rules as a protection against the surprises of tides and undercurrents. A person with a phobic dread, on the other hand, might not learn to swim at all and, in a dangerous situation near water, might panic and drown, immobilized by anxiety.

Still there is often a marginal line between a rational fear, anxiety, and a phobia. A person suffering from general anxiety and malaise may go through days unable to do anything; may be listless, lethargic, unable to act or make decisions—all without exhibiting a specific phobia. One may, in other words, be phobic toward life itself, dreading everything from the mundane to the unusual. Although this is more commonly referred to as anxiety hysteria or neurasthenia, in many ways it parallels the phobic reaction. What delineates the diagnostic criterion between a phobic fear and generalized anxiety is not always agreed upon, but seems to depend on the concreteness of the feared object or event.

CAUSES OF PHOBIAS

There is no single universal explanation of the etiology of phobias. Psychologists generally elucidate the cause of a phobia according to the theory of personality development, behavior, or clinical practice to which they subscribe. It is generally agreed, however, that some phobias may have direct events preceding their onset and others may not. For example, a person caught in a terrible hotel fire may develop a case of pyrophobia (fear of fire), but of the hundreds of people trapped in the hotel at the same time, the majority will not become phobic. The terrifying event then is not in itself sufficient to account for the phobia.

This kind of event is called the precipitating trauma or traumatic event, and may or may not be viewed as the direct cause of the phobia, depending on the theoretical orientation of the psychologist making the judgment. A behavioral psychologist would place more emphasis on the importance of this event than would a psychoanalyst or rational-emotive therapist. Three chief models of phobia then, are the psychoanalytic, the behavioral, and the cognitive.

The Psychoanalytic Model

Freud categorized phobia as part of the constellation of symptomatic neuroses he called "anxiety hysteria" (*Angsthysterie*), which also includes conversion hysteria. A phobia is an expression of repressed sexual fantasies, usually of an Oedipal nature, in conflict with defenses mustered to help contain these feelings. Typically the phobic object, like a symbol in a dream, represents a compromise between an unconscious fear and its defenses, which, when analyzed, reveal the primordial nature of the conflict.

Freud's famous case of Little Hans (1910) offers his most detailed discussion of phobia. Hans had developed a fear of large animals, especially horses, soon after witnessing a large horse falling (the "precipitating trauma"). This generated into an agoraphobic response, rendering Hans unable to leave his house. Analysis of the child's unconscious, by Freud and the boy's father, revealed the causes of the phobia, which, expressed in the nomeclature of psychoanalysis, involved castration anxiety, murderous Oedipal wishes against his father, and aggressive-erotic fantasies about his parents. These fears were countered by the defenses of repression, displacement, and projection—whereby Hans forgot his primitive traumatic memories (repression), saw the horse as his father (displacement), and imagined that the horse wanted to hurt him (projection). Thus the unconscious conflict that embodies the energy of repressed rage against the father emerges in the guise of the phobia.

The Behavioral (Social Learning) Models

The behavioral, or social learning explanations of phobia focus on how an individual learns an inappropriate anxiety-evoking response to a stimulus that was initially neutral, or unexciting. There are three main paradigms used: classical conditioning, operant conditioning, and modeling.

The etiology of a phobia was the subject of investigation in one of the first major experiments in behavioral psychology, still a landmark decades after publication. John B. Watson and Rosalie Rayner induced a phobia in Albert, an 11-month-old boy, by using the classical conditioning model associated with Pavlov and his eponymous dog. First they observed Albert's natural fondness for small furry animals. Clearly he was not phobic. Then, whenever Albert reached out to touch the rodent, the experimenters emitted a loud, frightening noise. During several trials, they paired this neutral, conditioned stimulus (CS)—the rat—with the fear-evoking, unconditioned stimulus (UCS), the noise. In time, the boy came to experience fear whenever he saw the rat, even when the noise was no longer emitted. This had become his conditioned phobic response (CR), the result of pairing the previously neutral stimulus (rat) with the unconditioned stimulus (loud noise). Soon thereafter, he developed a phobia for all furry objects, apparently generalizing the fear of the rat to these other objects as well (Watson & Rayner, 1920).

According to the operant conditioning paradigm of B. F. Skinner, phobias develop not only from adventitious, or even intentional, pairing of stimuli, but also from a person's intentional, voluntary operations on the environment, and the consequences of these operations (or reinforcers). If certain voluntary behaviors become associated with highly unpleasant and anxiety-evoking consequences, they are capable of developing into a phobic reaction.

The modeling (observational learning) paradigm, developed extensively by Albert Bandura, suggests that phobias are learned—at least in part—by direct exposure to the anxieties and irrational fears of another, especially one to whom we feel connected, or feel a certain empathic attachment (Bandura, 1965, 1968). With this paradigm, neither pairing of stimuli nor reinforcement is required; mere exposure is enough. A 2-year-old who sees his mother screaming at the sight of a dog running through the backyard may develop a fear of dogs as he perceives, learns, experiences, and feels along with her at that terrified moment.

Most behavioral psychologists today are not so naive or dogmatic as to believe that a single, linear conditioning paradigm can itself explain the etiology of all phobias. Increasingly we find bold lines of dynamic insight fused with multiple facets of behavioral models. In a clinical description, typical of eclectic behavioral explanations, Garvey andHegrenes (1966, p. 172) explain the history of a 10-year-old boy's school phobia in this way:

Jimmy had an intense fear of losing his mother, illustrated by his fantasies about the various kinds of harm that could happen to her. . . . Thus "losing mother," which can be conveyed verbally in various ways, was a danger signal eliciting a fear response. (More precisely, a danger signal elicits certain responses from which the presence of fear may be inferred. These responses . . . are usually thought to be physiological; for example, changes in heart rate, galvanic skin response, etc.) When this danger signal was repeatedly paired with a neutral stimulus such as school (as the mother often did by telling Jimmy that, "One of these days when you come home from school, I won't be here"), "school" eventually became a conditioned stimulus capable of eliciting conditioned responses, namely the physiological responses associated with "loss of mother" and consequently, fear. Finally, when this fear became too intense, Jimmy refused to go to school. . . . By staying home his fears were diminished, and since fear reduction is thought to be reinforcing, the avoidance response (not going to school) was strengthened.

This spectrum of clinical insights—from psychoanalysis, classical conditioning, modeling, and operant conditioning theory—elucidates through a behavioral lens the question of what causes a phobia.

The Cognitive Model

The cognitive model may be behaviorally oriented or dynamically oriented. Both orientations bring to bear, in explaining the causes of a phobia, the person's cognitions with learning paradigms. The cognitive-behavioral explanation views thinking as a mediating process between stimulus and response. A phobia develops when the individual's thinking results in distortions that cause certain types of inappropriate responses (combining anxiety and fear with avoidance behavior) to what are really nondangerous stimuli.

The cognitive-dynamic view of phobia, represented by Albert Ellis' rational-emotive therapy (RET), extends this further by dissecting and clarifying the thinking processes involved in the distortion. In growing up, Ellis suggests, we are taught to think and feel certain connections about ourself, others, and things in the world.

Connections that are associated with the idea of "This is good" argues Ellis (1958), become positive human emotions, such as love or joy, while those associated with the idea that "This is bad" become negative emotions, colored with painful, angry, or depressive feelings. A phobia is an illogical and irrational connection, associating "This is bad" or "This is dangerous" with things that really are not. The difference between the rational-emotive point of view and the psychoanalytic is that in RET the patient's thinking is said to be distorted because of early-life cognitive—as opposed to strictly emotional—confusions. It is not suggested that later in life he or she is "traumatized" or "fixated" at this early thinking. As with any thinking, it can be changed by logic and reasoning—an important implication for therapeutic practice of RET.

Other Explanations

Because of its universality and high incidence, phobia and its causes have been a constant subject of lively debate and speculation by almost all the seminal thinkers of contemporary social and psychological theories or systems. Hence the range of explanations is widespread.

Existential thinkers, such as Rollo May and Victor Frankl, view phobia as a reflection of the alienation, powerlessness, and meaninglessness in modern life, a consequence in part of industrialization and impersonalization. Other humanistic psychologists, such as Abraham Maslow, see phobia as they do neurosis in general, as a failure in personal growth, a thwarting of the possibilities of human potential.

Some theorists have focused on the physiological and genetic aspects of phobia. Edward O. Wilson, founder of the science of sociobiology, for example, sees phobia as a remnant of our genetic evolution. "In early human history," Wilson says, "phobias might have provided the extra margin needed to insure survival" (Wilson, 1978, p. 70).

TREATMENT OF PHOBIA

Partisans of each of the theories discussed use techniques and methods of treating phobia consistent with what they accept as its cause. Psychoanalysts, believing it to be a product of repressed memories hidden under layers of defense, use free association, dream analysis, and interpretation to strip away the layers and get to the core of the conflict. Then, through a catharsis—a sudden emotionally charged freeing of the repressed—the patient can overcome the phobia and recover. Freud also suggested that patients suffering from phobia should be exposed directly to the feared object, something that is central to contemporary behavior therapies.

Behavioral psychologists have developed an impressive armamentarium of techniques for treating phobia. Two of the widely used paradigms are systematic desensitization and flooding.

Systematic desensitization is a form of classical conditioning in which anxiety-evoking stimuli are paired with inhibitory responses, either through imagination (vicarious desensitization) or in real-life situations (in vivo desensitization). This method, developed by Joseph Wolpe, asks the patient to discuss in detail with the therapist the components of his or her fear with the goal of con-

structing a hierarchical list of anxiety-evoking stimuli in order of intensity. These stimuli are then dealt with one at a time, in order, until the one that evokes the most anxiety is no longer capable of generating anxiety. For example, let us say a patient has a fear of driving a car. A hierarchy may be constructed of: (a) getting into the car; (b) starting the engine; (c) releasing the brake; (d) putting it into "drive;" (e) pulling out of the parking spot, and so on. Every time the patient thinks of the current item in the heirarchy, he or she is relaxed and made to feel comfortable by the therapist. Then, the next item, more anxiety evoking, can be introduced and desensitized. Ultimately the stimulus (the phobic-related thought) will fail to elicit the anxiety it once did.

Flooding (or implosive therapy) is a modified form of classical conditioning. As with systematic desensitization, it may be conducted vicariously or in vivo. Flooding "is a method of treating phobias by rapid exposure in real life to the feared object or situation, maintaining maximum tolerable anxiety until it begins to diminish, then continuing closer and closer exposure until the patient or client is comfortable in the situation which was previously feared" (Curtis, 1976). While it is considered a rapid method and effective, at least in the short term, it does expose the patient to high levels of anxiety, levels that some consider too high and possibly dangerous.

The process of rational-emotive therapy is characterized by the therapist's communication (often highly dramatic) to the patient of the distortions in his or her thinking. This is much like a teaching technique and is, in fact, geared toward helping the patient learn about how illogical thinking leads to illogical and phobic behavior patterns.

All four methods—psychoanalysis, systematic desensitization, implosive therapy, and rational-emotive therapy—claim high rates of cure. Empirical evidence tends to support this, at least insofar as comparison with disorders such as depression and schizophrenia are concerned.

REFERENCES

Bandura, A. (1965). Influence of models reinforcement contingencies on the acquisition of imitative responses. *Journal of Personality and Social Psychology, 1,* 589–595.

Bandura, A. (1968). Modelling approaches to the modification of phobic disorders. In R. Porter (Ed.), *The role of learning in psychotherapy.* London: Churchill.

Curtis, G., Nesse, R., Buxton, M., Wright, J., & Lippman, D. (1976). Flooding in vivo as a research tool and treatment method for phobias: A preliminary report. *Comprehensive Psychiatry, 17,* 153–160.

Freud, S. (1957). The antithetical meaning of primal words (1910). In *The standard edition of the complete psychological works of Sigmund Freud* (Vol. 11). London: Hogarth.

Garvey, W. P., & Hegrenes, J. R. (1966). Desensitization technique in the treatment of school phobia. *American Journal of Orthopsychiatry, 36,* 147–152.

Watson, J. B., & Rayner, R. (1920). Conditioned emotional reactions. *Journal of Experimental Psychology, 3,* 1–14.

Wilson, E. O. (1978). *On human nature.* Cambridge, MA: Harvard University Press.

G. S. BELKIN
Brown University

ANXIETY
PERSONALITY DISORDERS

PHONEME

Linguistic analyses have traditionally represented the forms of speech in terms of phonemes. The word *cat,* for instance, can be represented by a sequence of three phonemes: /k/, /æ/, and /t/. Changes in the phonemic construction of a word will result in a different word, or a nonsense word. For example, reordering the phonemes in *cat* can produce other words, such as *act* (/ækt/) or *tack* (/tæk/), whereas replacing the /k/ with a /p/ results in a new word, *pat.* Words like *cat* and *pat* that differ in the identity of a single phoneme are referred to as minimal pairs, and provide a useful source of evidence for defining the phonemic inventory for a language. In an alphabetic language such as English, the phonemic nature of speech is made explicit by the close correspondence between letters and the phonemes they represent. Logographic languages (e.g., Chinese) do not share this correspondence; instead, characters are used to represent whole words.

A further division of speech sounds is possible, into subphonemic units called phonetic features. The representation of a phoneme consists of a set of phonetic features, which capture the similarities and differences between groups of phonemes. For example, the difference between the phonemes /t/ and /k/ is largely due to the difference in the place of closure created by the tongue touching the roof of the mouth. The same contrast is found between /d/ and /g/, and between /n/ and /ŋ/ (the final phoneme in "ring"). This contrast can be represented by one or more place of articulation features.

It is important to realize that the abstract notion of a phoneme obscures a great deal of variation in the form of speech. The context in which a phoneme is uttered has a strong effect on the way in which it is articulated, and this results in a wide variation of acoustic forms all being termed as the same phoneme. Similarly, the discrete sequences of symbols in a phonemic transcription do not properly represent the temporal structure of the speech waveform, in which information about different phonemes is spread across time and overlaps. A critical issue in the psychological study of speech is whether mental representations of speech reflect the diversity and detail of the speech waveform or the abstractness and simplicity of the phonemic transcription.

PHONEMES IN SPEECH PERCEPTION

It is clear that some aspects of the organization of speech sounds in perception correspond to phonemic categories. It is possible to create artificial continua using recorded speech or a speech synthesizer in which the extremes correspond to two typical phonemes.

Typically adults will show categorical perception of these continua; that is, they will find it difficult to discriminate between two sounds on a continuum that would be classed as the same phoneme, but will find it relatively easy to discriminate between two sounds that cross a phoneme boundary. Infants as young as one month old show similar discontinuities in their perception of these continua. In fact, early in development, infants are able to discriminate between speech sounds that are allophonic in their language (i.e., phonetically distinct members of the same phoneme category) but are different phonemes in other languages. This ability is lost in the first year of life, as the infant becomes familiar with the phonemes of his or her native language.

One possible conclusion to be drawn from these studies of infant speech perception is that people are born with an innate universal phonemic inventory, from which the contrasts relevant to the child's native language are consolidated. However, various nonhuman species such as chinchillas and macaque monkeys have also shown categorical perception of some phonemic contrasts. So what is innate may in fact be more physical aspects of the auditory system, which provide a basis for discrimination between some sounds but not others. Through this view, the phonemic systems of languages have evolved in order to take advantage of these abilities and deficits.

Although categorical perception of phonemes is found from infancy, it is less clear how aware people are of these units. Alphabetic languages lend themselves to a phonemic decomposition of speech by the literate adult. This makes the conscious manipulation and decomposition of speech (such as deciding what the initial phoneme of "spin" might be) a relatively simple task. However, for verbally proficient illiterate adults and for speakers of nonalphabetic languages, this is not the case. It seems that the existence of the phoneme as a unit at a conscious level relies more or less on explicit teaching through learning to read alphabetic scripts.

The phoneme has been proposed as the initial unit of classification in speech perception at a subconscious level. The assumption is that words are identified by comparison between this representation and stored phonemic representations of words. However, the lack of context-invariant characteristics for many phonemes has weakened this proposal, and other models have been suggested in which speech is mapped onto larger units (e.g., the syllable) or smaller units (e.g., acoustic features) before searching the lexicon for a matching word. The matching process between the speech waveform and the mental lexicon has also been proven to be sensitive to a wide range of subtle changes in the forms of words, suggesting that very little acoustic detail is discarded during the recognition of spoken words. Currently, there is no consensus on the importance of the phoneme unit in spoken-word recognition.

PHONEMES IN SPEECH PRODUCTION

There is greater agreement among psycholinguists about the role of the phoneme in speech production. Most current models assume that words are selected according to the conceptual requirements of the speaker, and then the phonemes making up that word are selected for articulation, possibly with reference to a store of known syllables. Originally, these models relied on data from speech errors in order to define the units involved in production. Errors are not common in natural speech, but when they do occur many of them involve substitutions, anticipations, or perseverations of phonemes. In the case of spoonerisms, the substitution results in sequences that correspond to real words (e.g., "you have hissed all the mystery lectures" instead of "you have missed all the history lectures"). These phonemic errors will often preserve the syllabic information related to the phonemes involved, such that syllable-initial phonemes are unlikely to end up at the end of another syllable. Phonemic similarity and whether or not the change would produce a real word are also influential factors in defining the likelihood of a speech error. In the last few years, such error data have been augmented by more sophisticated techniques that allow error-free speech production to be studied. These techniques have been particularly useful in mapping out the time course of the various processes in speech production.

G. GASKELL
University of York, United Kingdom

SPEECH DEVELOPMENT

PHOTORECEPTORS

Photoreceptors are sensory nerve cells, specialized for the task of translating the absorption of light into electrical signals, which are the language of the nervous system. Photoreceptors have reached the physical limits of light detection and can register the absorption of a single light quantum. On the other hand, our eye can adapt its sensitivity to light levels a billion-fold higher.

The interior surface of the vertebrate eye chamber is covered by the retina, which is part of the central nervous system. It contains the light-sensitive photoreceptors as well as neurons that process the photoreceptor information before it is relayed to the brain by the retinal ganglion cells. The retina is inverted—that is, the light must fall through all retinal layers until it reaches the photoreceptors (Figure 1). Two types of photoreceptors can be distinguished: The rods are responsible for vision in dim light, the cones for daylight and for color vision. Photoreceptors each have a cell body with a nucleus, an axon that forms synapses with other neurons in the retina, and an inner segment that contains the machinery for routine cellular metabolism. Photoelectrical transduction takes place in a highly specialized cell compartment, the outer segment, which contains photopigment molecules, all biochemical components for the signal amplification, and the ion channels needed to generate the electrical response.

PHOTOTRANSDUCTION

The ion channels in the outer segment are opened by intracellular messenger molecules, cyclic guanosine monophosphate (cGMP; Yau & Baylor, 1989; Finn, Grunwald, & Yau, 1996). In the dark, the cGMP concentration in the outer segment is high, the channels open, and Na^+ and Ca^{2+} ions flow through these open channels

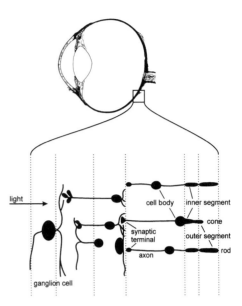

Figure 1. Section through the eye and the retina, showing different retinal cell types.

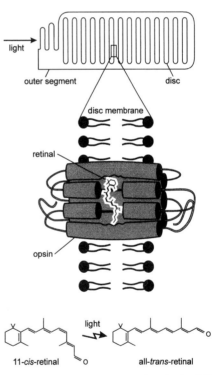

Figure 2. The rod outer segment contains hundreds of discs with millions of rhodopsin molecules.

into the cell, thereby adjusting the membrane voltage to around -30 mV. At this membrane potential, the photoreceptor releases transmitter molecules at its synaptic terminal. A network of retinal neurons processes this information and relays it to the brain, where it is interpreted as "dark."

Rod outer segments are effective light-catchers. They contain a stack of flat, hollow membrane compartments, called discs (Figure 2). The photopigment rhodopsin is found in high concentration within the disc membranes. A single rod photoreceptor may con-

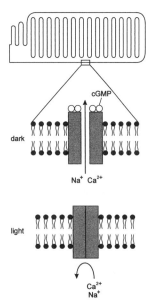

Figure 3.   In the dark, ions enter the outer segment through the cGMP-gated channels in the plasmamembrane. Upon illumination, channels close and the influx ceases.

tain up to 2,000 discs, with altogether 100 million rhodopsin molecules. Rhodopsin consists of a protein part (the opsin), which is inserted into the disc membrane, and a light-absorbing part (the aldehyde form of vitamin A, retinal; see Figure 2). Retinal can exist in different forms. The folded 11-cis form of retinal is bound within the opsin molecule. Absorption of a light quantum causes the 11-cis retinal to switch to the elongated all-trans form, which induces a conformational change in the rhodopsin molecule—that is, it becomes activated. Light-activated rhodopsin is capable of activating protein molecules called transducin, which in turn activate a third protein class, the phosphodiesterase. The activated phosphodiesterases destroy cGMP molecules. As a consequence, the cGMP concentration falls rapidly and the cGMP-dependent ion channels close. As fewer positive ions flow into the cell, the membrane voltage becomes more negative and less transmitter is released at the synapse (Yau, 1994). This information is processed further and is finally interpreted by the brain as "light."

SENSITIVITY AND ADAPTATION

One light-activated rhodopsin molecule may activate up to 3,000 transducin molecules, each of which can activate one phosphodiesterase molecule. Each phosphodiesterase can cleave up to 2,000 cGMP molecules per second. With this high amplification, the absorption of one light quantum could result in the destruction of around one million cGMP molecules. This closes so many channels that the membrane voltage changes measurably. Rods can detect a single light quantum. With brighter light, more cGMP is destroyed, more channels close, and the voltage can reach -70 mV.

Photoreceptor adaptation is only incompletely understood. The internal messenger Ca^{2+} is very important (Kaupp & Koch, 1992). The internal Ca^{2+} concentration is high in the dark, when Ca^{2+} ions enter the outer segment through the cGMP-gated chan-

nels, but drops rapidly when the channels close upon illumination. Ca^{2+} binding proteins in the outer segment serve as Ca^{2+} sensors and relay the change in Ca^{2+} concentration to their target enzymes, to adjust their activity. One consequence is the activation of the enzyme guanylyl cyclase, which increases cGMP production. Furthermore, the light response becomes truncated. At low Ca^{2+} concentration, light-activated rhodopsin is shut off by the proteins rhodopsin kinase and arrestin, so that fewer transducin molecules are activated. The gain of the cascade becomes smaller—that is, the cell becomes less sensitive and its operating range increases. Many more adaptive mechanisms in the retina are postulated. Some originate in the retinal network, some follow a circadian rhythm.

PSYCHOPHYSICS

Cone photoreceptors function in a manner similar to that of rods, but are less sensitive. The human retina contains three types of cones with different opsins. They form the basis for color vision, because they differ in their sensitivity to light of different wavelengths. Mutations in the cone opsins may result in abnormal color vision. Visual acuity and color vision are best in the central retina, the so-called fovea, where cones are densely packed. Only in the fovea is the information of each cone cell transmitted separately from others to the brain. In contrast, in the peripheral retina, many photoreceptors converge onto one postsynaptic cell; hence resolution is lower. In most vertebrate retinae, the rods are more numerous (120 million in a human eye) than the cones (6 million per eye). The fovea is night-blind, because it does not contain rods.

Vertebrate photoreceptors show slow light responses. Dark-adapted rods may need two hundred ms. to build up the light response, which can last up to a second. This time is needed for the high signal amplification. Light-adapted rods and cones are faster, but their light response still lasts 20 to 50 ms. Our photoreceptors cannot resolve more than 50 events per second; therefore, pictures in movies are fused in our perception and we see a continuous motion. In comparison, photoreceptors of many insects would need more than 200 pictures per second for fusion.

OTHER PHOTORECEPTORS

The pineal organ of the brain, which is involved in the generation of circadian rhythms, developed from photoreceptors similar to those found in the retina. In many non-mammalian vertebrates, such as fish, the pinealocytes contain photopigments and are light-sensitive, while those of mammals are not. The parietal eye, as found on the skull of some lizards, is another light-sensitive brain structure and may even have an optical apparatus. A great variety of photoreceptors has evolved in the animal kingdom. Not only do photoreceptors of invertebrates differ in their morphology from those of vertebrates, but also their signal transduction seems to involve different biochemical pathways that are not fully elucidated at present.

REFERENCES

Yau, K.-W., & Baylor, D. A. (1989). Cyclic GMP-activated conductance of retinal photoreceptor cells. *Annual Review of Neuroscience, 12,* 289–327.

Finn, J. T., Grunwald, M. E., & Yau, K.-W. (1996). Cyclic nucleotide-gated ion channels: An extended family with diverse functions. *Annual Review of Physiology, 58,* 395–426.

Yau, K.-W. (1994). Phototransduction mechanism in retinal rods and cones. *Investigations in Ophthalmology and Visual Science, 35,* 9–32.

Kaupp, U. B., & Koch, K.-W. (1992). The role of cGMP and Ca^{2+} in vertebrate photoreceptor excitation and adaptation. *Annual Review of Physiology, 54,* 153–175.

F. MUELLER
Forschungszentrum Juelich GmbH, Germany

COLOR VISION
EYE

PHRENOLOGY

Phrenology, now an outmoded theory of personality, originated with the speculations of the physician-anatomist Franz Joseph Gall (1758–1828). Intrigued by a personal inference that individuals with bulging or prominent eyes had good memories, Gall began to look for personality correlates of other features such as broad foreheads, prominent jaws, and so on. Ultimately, he focused his attention primarily on the brain and skull and founded what he called the new science of craniology. Knowledge of the brain and nervous system at that time was vestigial at best. In consequence, much of Gall's early work in his theory included the development of new techniques of dissection, perfection of the construction of brain and skull models, and the amassing of a unique collection of skulls. The superb quality of this supporting anatomical work gave Gall great credibility when he first presented his ideas to the medical community.

Gall's basic belief was that mental functions are located in the brain, and that their exercise and perfection would lead to localized brain development. This, in turn, would lead to appropriate enlargement of the related areas of the surrounding skull. Thus, by a very close scrutiny of the skull and its various prominences, one could obtain a detailed, individualized diagnosis of an individual's personal qualities and characteristics. He was thus the first researcher to postulate what has come to be known as localization of brain function—a precursor of modern neuropsychology in which physiological measures of brain and nervous system activity are correlated with psychological observations.

Around 1800, Spurzheim (1776–1823), a pupil of Gall, joined him on a lecture tour to espouse the new science of phrenology (a term never used by Gall). A dynamic and convincing lecturer, Spurzheim changed the emphasis to stress mostly the detection of the presence of positive faculties and their modifiability by means of strategic training. The approach to "reading bumps" became less akin to medical diagnosis and more to quackery and fortunetelling. Correspondingly, phrenology lost its popularity and acceptance by medical groups, but simultaneously became popular with the general public.

SUGGESTED READING

Davies, J. D. (1955).

Spurzheim, J. G. (1827).

Winkler, J. K., & Bromberg, W. (1939).

M. E. REUDER

PSEUDOPSYCHOLOGY

PHYSICAL ATTRACTIVENESS

Physical attractiveness has been defined as: "That which represents one's conception of the ideal in appearance; that which gives the greatest degree of pleasure to the senses" (Hatfield & Sprecher, 1986, p. 4). Beginning with Darwin (1971), anthropologists have long tried to discover universal standards of attractiveness. One must know what various peoples consider sexually appealing, if one is to predict the course of sexual selection and, ultimately, human evolution. Darwin's painstaking observations finally convinced most scientists that culture sets the standard, and thus it was futile to search for universals. Any lingering hopes of identifying sweeping standards were shattered in Ford and Beach's (1951) landmark survey of more than 200 primitive societies. They, too, failed to find any universal standards of sexual allure.

Recently, however, sociobiologists have revived hopes that more sophisticated sociobiological theory and research techniques may finally enable scientists to pinpoint some aesthetic universals. In one promising study, Langlois and Roggman (1990) found evidence that the Greek's golden mean may serve as the standard of appeal. The authors assembled photographs of the faces of men and women. Using video and computer techniques, they generated a series of composite faces (truly average men and women). They found that composites were more attractive than any individual face.

Other sociobiologists have tested the hypothesis that men and women prefer faces that, in a sense, have it all—faces that combine the innocence of childhood with the ripe sexuality of the mature. Early ethnologists observed that men and women often experience a tender rush of feeling when they view infantile "kewpie doll" faces—faces with huge eyes, tiny noses and mouths, and little chins. Other authors e.g., proposed that men and women should be aroused by faces that possess features associated with maturity, especially lush, adult sexuality (for example, thick hair, dewy skin, and full lips) or mature power (for example, high cheekbones or a firm jaw and chin). Most recent evidence finds that people like faces that possess both assets: large eyes, a small nose, full lips, and a strong jaw and chin (Cunningham, Barbee, & Pike, 1990). Whether these preferences will turn out to be universal is not yet known. Historians (Banner, 1983) remind us that, in any society, standards of beauty often change at a dizzying rate.

EVIDENCE THAT PEOPLE ARE BIASED IN FAVOR OF THE PHYSICALLY ATTRACTIVE

Scientists find that most people, most of the time, are biased in their reactions to good-looking versus unattractive people. This discovery is certainly not new. The Greek philosopher Sappho contended that "what is beautiful is good." Today's scientists, however, have come to a little better understanding of just how, where, when, and why physical appearance is important. There seem to be four steps in the stereotyping process:

1. Most people know that it is not fair to discriminate against the unattractive (they would be incensed if others discriminated against them).

2. Privately, most people take it for granted that attractive and unattractive people are different. Generally, they assume that what is beautiful is good and what is unattractive is bad.

3. Most people treat good-looking and average people better than they treat the unattractive.

4. As a consequence, a self-fulfilling prophecy occurs. The way people are treated shapes the kinds of people they become. (Hatfield & Sprecher, 1986, p. 36).

There is evidence that people do perceive attractive and unattractive people differently (see Hatfield & Sprecher, 1986; Bull & Rumsey, 1988; for encyclopedic reviews of this research). In a classic experiment, researchers (Dion, Berscheid, & Hatfield, 1972) showed college men and women yearbook photographs of men and women who varied markedly in appearance and asked them their first impressions of the students. Young adults assumed that handsome men and beautiful women possessed many virtues. They assumed that the good-looking people were more sociable, outgoing, poised, interesting, exciting, sexually responsive, kind, nurturant, modest, strong, and sensitive; and that they were warmer and had better characters than their homely peers. Good-looking people were also expected to have more fulfilling lives. Students predicted the good-looking people would be happier, have more successful marriages, find better jobs, and live more satisfying lives. On only one dimension were young adults not prejudiced about good looks; they did not expect attractive people to make naturally good parents.

Observers recognize that good looks might have a dark side. For example, Dermer and Thiel (1975) asked college students to rate college women who varied greatly in attractiveness. In general, subjects assumed that attractive and average women possessed more appealing personalities and were more socially skilled than unattractive women. In this study, however, researchers also documented some ugly truths about beauty. Subjects expected attractive women to be more vain and egotistical, more bourgeois (i.e., materialistic, snobbish, and unsympathetic to oppressed peoples), and less committed to their marriages (more likely to have extramarital affairs or to request a divorce) than homely women. Similar results have been secured by Eagly and her colleagues (1991).

Not only do people think that attractive people are special, but they also treat them that way (Bull & Rumsey, 1988; Hatfield & Sprecher, 1986). Teachers award good-looking grade school, high school, and college students with better grades than their less attractive counterparts for the same work. Executives are more likely to hire and promote good-looking men and women and to pay them more. Clinicians spend more time with good-looking clients;

they get better care and do better in therapy. Unattractive people are more likely to be judged mentally ill. Attractive law-breakers are less likely to get caught, less likely to be reported to the authorities, less likely to be found guilty, and even if convicted, are less likely to receive strict sentences. Good-looking people are less likely to be asked to help others, but more likely to receive assistance if they ask for help or are in trouble. Finally, society's biases ensure that good-looking men and women have a marked advantage at every stage of an intimate relationship. Attractive people have an easier time with meeting potential dates and mates and with attracting more appealing dates and mates; and they end up with better dating and marital relationships. They have an advantage in sustaining these relationships. If things go wrong, they find it easier to start anew.

There are some limits to peoples' preferences for and biased treatment of the most attractive people, of course. Some types of people seem to care more about looks than do others: Traditional men and women seem to care more about looks than do the less traditional; and men seem to care more about another's looks than do women. People care more about looks in some situations than in others. Appearance seems to matter most when people are getting acquainted; later on, other things—intelligence, personality, and so forth—become more important. Appearance matters more in romantic settings than in such settings as employment or other more social situations.

What effect does such stereotyping have on men and women? The evidence is mixed (Bull & Rumsey, 1988; Hatfield & Sprecher, 1986). Good-looking and unattractive people are not as different as people assume them to be. Self-esteem and self-concept are positively related to how good-looking people think they are, but not to their actual appearance. The personalities of the attractive and unattractive differ only slightly, if at all. A few studies (have found that the good-looking) are slightly more inner-directed, more assertive, more likely to seek success, and possess more fear of failure than do others. Other studies have failed to replicate these results.

Attractive and unattractive people do seem to differ in one respect. Good-looking people appear to be more confident in romantic and social situations and to possess more social skills. People expect good-looking people to be charming; they treat them that way, and as a consequence, good-looking people become more socially skilled. This self-fulfilling aspect of physical attractiveness was demonstrated in a study by Snyder, Tanke, and Berscheid (1977). Men and women at the University of Minnesota were recruited for a study on the acquaintance process. First, men were given an instant snapshot and biographical information about the person in the photo. In fact, the snapshot was a fake; it depicted either a beautiful or a homely woman. Men were asked their first impressions of the woman. Those who believed they had been assigned a beautiful partner expected her to be sociable, poised, humorous, and socially skilled. Those who thought they had been assigned to an unattractive partner expected her to be unsociable, awkward, serious, and socially inept. Such prejudice is not surprising; it is known that good-looking people make exceptionally good first impressions.

The next set of findings, however, was startling. Men were asked to get acquainted with their partners via the telephone. Male expectations had a dramatic impact on the way they talked to their partners during the telephone call. That, in turn, created a correspondingly great impact on the response of the women. Men, of course, thought they were talking to a beautiful or homely woman; in fact, the women on the other end of the line varied greatly in appearance, although most were probably average in looks. Nonetheless, within the space of a telephone conversation, the women became what the men expected them to be. After the telephone conversation, judges listened to tapes of the woman's portion of the conversation and tried to guess what the women were like just from that conversation. Women who had been talked to as if they were beautiful, soon began to sound that way. They became unusually animated, confident, and socially skilled. Those who had been treated as if they were unattractive soon began acting withdrawn, unconfident, and awkward. The men's prophecies had been fulfilled.

How did this happen? When the men's portions of the conversation were analyzed, it was found that those men who thought they were talking to a beautiful woman were more sociable, sexually warm, interesting, independent, sexually permissive, bold, outgoing, humorous, and socially skilled than the men who thought they were talking to a homely woman. The men assigned to an attractive woman were also more comfortable, enjoyed themselves more, liked their partners more, took the initiative more often, and used their voices more effectively. In brief, the men who thought they were talking to a beautiful woman tried harder. Undoubtedly, this behavior caused the women to try harder, too. If the stereotypes held by the men became reality within the ten minutes of a telephone conversation, one can imagine what happens when people are treated well or badly over a lifetime. In fact, researchers have found some evidence that the attractive are in fact unusually socially skilled and experienced.

The evidence makes it clear that good-looking people have an advantage over unattractive people in life. However, a careful analysis of existing data makes it clear that the emphasis of research should be on unattractive people. If the relationship between appearance and a host of other variables—self-esteem, happiness, job opportunities, dating and popularity—are examined, it is soon discovered that the relationship between appearance and advantage is not a monotonically decreasing one. The data make it evident that extremely attractive people have only a small advantage over their more ordinary peers. Average-looking people have a real advantage over the unattractive or the disfigured.

REFERENCES

Banner, L. W. (1983). *American beauty.* Chicago: The University of Chicago Press.

Bull, R., & Rumsey, N. (1988). *The social psychology of facial appearance.* New York: Springer-Verlag.

Cunningham, M. R., Barbee, A. P., & Pike, C. L. (1990). What do women want? Facialmetric assessment of multiple motives in the perception of male facial physical attractiveness. *Journal of Personality and Social Psychology, 59,* 61–72.

Darwin, C. (1871). *The descent of man, and selection in relation to sex.* New York: Appleton.

Dermer, M., & Thiel, D. L. (1975). When beauty may fail. *Journal of Personality and Social Psychology, 31,* 1168–1176.

Dion, K., Berscheid, E., & Hatfield, E. (1972). What is beautiful is good. *Journal of Personality and Social Psychology, 24,* 285–290.

Eagly, A. H., Ashmore, R. D., Makhijani, M. G., & Longo, L. C. (1991). What is beautiful is good, but . . . : A meta-analytic review of research on the physical attractiveness stereotype. *Psychological Bulletin, 110,* 109–128.

Ford, C. S., & Beach, F. A. (1951). *Patterns of sexual behavior.* New York: Harper & Row.

Hatfield, E., & Sprecher, S. (1986b). *Mirror, mirror: The importance of looks in everyday life.* Albany, NY: SUNY Press.

Langlois, J. H., & Roggman, L. A. (1990). Attractive faces are only average. *Psychological Science, 1,* 115–121.

Snyder, M., Tanke, E. D., & Berscheid, E. (1977). Social perception and interpersonal behavior: On the self-fulfilling nature of social stereotypes. *Journal of Personality and Social Psychology, 35,* 656–666.

SUGGESTED READING

Cash, T. F. (1995). *What do you see when you look in the mirror?* New York: Bantam Books.

Bull, R., & Rumsey, N. (1988). *The social psychology of facial appearance.* New York: Springer-Verlag.

Hatfield, E., & Sprecher, S. (1986b). *Mirror, mirror: The importance of looks in everyday life.* Albany, NY: SUNY Press.

E. HATFIELD
R. L. RAPSON
University of Hawaii

HALO EFFECT
PYGMALION EFFECT
STEREOTYPING

PIAGET, JEAN (1896–1980)

Piaget published his first scientific paper at the age of 10, and received his doctorate in 1917, at the age of 21, from the University of Neuchatel, in his research studies on mollusks. After working in a psychology laboratory in Zurich, he went to Paris and to Geneva, where he studied the psychology of thought and was appointed professor of psychology in 1940. In 1952, he was named professor of child psychology at the Sorbonne in Paris. He was actively involved in UNESCO and in educational activities in Switzerland.

Piaget's major interest was in intellectual or cognitive behavior throughout childhood and adolescence. His field was genetic epistemology—the examination of the formation of knowledge itself, that is, of the cognitive relations between subject and objects. Piaget studied the relationships that are formed between the individual as knower and the world he or she endeavors to know.

The two most important concepts of genetic epistemology are

functional invariants and *structures.* Functional invariants are cognitive processes that are inborn, universal, and independent of age: accommodation, assimilation, and organization. Structures are defined as intellectual processes that change with age. Piaget's structures are identified in the developmental stages of the period of sensorimotor intelligence, the period of preoperational thought, the period of concrete operations, and the period of formal operations.

The structure for the sensorimotor period (birth to 2 years of age) is circular reaction, a simple sensorimotor adaptive response to a specific stimulus, repeated a number of times. The principal structures of preoperational thought (ages 2 to 6 years) are egocentrism (sees only his or her own point of view), centration (attention to only one feature of a situation), and irreversibility (inability to reverse direction of thinking once started). During the period of concrete operations (ages 6 to 11 years), the main structural concept is grouping, a system of classification. It is a coherent and organized symbolic system of thinking with assimilation and accommodation in balance; intellectual adaptation takes place. In formal operations (ages 11 to 15), a lattice-group structure performs scientific reasoning with hypotheses, predictions, and the testing of these. It is a network of ideas in which everything is related to everything else. The balancing of cognitive growth patterns is called the equilibration process; it is the assimilation of new cognitive structures without destroying the existing structure (Nordby & Hall, 1974).

Piaget's early books were based on observations and experiments done with his two daughters. Four volumes appeared between 1926 and 1930 on thought processes and conceptualizations in children. In the 1950s, he published *The Psychology of Intelligence* and *The Origins of Intelligence in the Child.*

N. A. HAYNIE
Honolulu, Hawaii

PIAGET'S THEORY

Between 1960 and 1980, a theory of intellectual development, formulated by Swiss biologist and philosopher Jean Piaget (1896-1980) dominated, and continues to influence, psychological thought about the development of the child's thinking, particularly logical thinking. The theory maintained that logical thought undergoes a series of fundamental changes such that the later ways of thinking are dependent upon, yet qualitatively distinct from, the earlier ones, and that thinking always moves in the direction of greater logical consistency. His subsidiary theories treated the development of moral judgment, perceptual development, the development of images, and memory development.

GENETIC EPISTEMOLOGY

Piaget sought to make a contribution to genetic epistemology, a discipline originally formulated by the American psychologist Baldwin that draws upon philosophy, psychology, logic, biology, cybernetics, and structuralism. It treats all factors that bear on the questions: What is knowledge? From whence does it come? What conditions make it possible? Piaget's focus was on the development of knowledge within each life span, as well as the historical development of knowledge within the culture, particularly Western scientific cultures. Genetic epistemology, as seen by Piaget, attributed the development of knowledge and intelligence within the individual, and within the culture, to the same developmental and basically biological mechanisms and principles.

Piaget's position was that of constructivism, which holds that the fundamental categories and structures of our minds are not given a priori, but are constructed by us in the course of development through evolving systems by which we act on and transform the environment and our own minds. The succeeding levels or stages are always reformulations or reconstructions of the preceding way of acting on the world and validating knowledge, and they are always more consistent and more coherent than the preceding way.

THE EPISTEMIC SUBJECT

Piaget's theory of intellectual development is about an idealized person, the epistemic subject, the pure knower who has no individual characteristics—no personality, sex, motivation (other than to know), culture, or nationality. The description of the child's competence to solve a logical problem tells us what the child can do if no other factors are present to mitigate the performance. In his later works, Piaget considered what procedures the child actually followed in solving problems and how these procedures or strategies utilized the child's competence. While the epistemic subject understands and knows events, the psychological subject succeeds in any number of tasks, often without any understanding of his success. In fact, the lag between success on a task and understanding the task is the typical finding.

The subject matter that the epistemic subject knows is restricted to those truths that are necessarily true. For example, when $A = B$ and $B = C$, not only is it true that $A = C$, but it is necessarily true, it must be the case, and it could not possibly be otherwise. We know this, or deduce this, without any need to measure or empirically compare A and C in any way. At its core, Piaget's theory is about how we construct the truths we take to be necessary truths—the truths that have to be as they are and could not conceivably be different from what they are.

THE CLINICAL METHOD

In virtually all of Piaget's research, the child is seen individually, given some materials or apparatus to manipulate, and questioned about what he or she did in a relaxed clinical attitude—with the questions tailored to the child's responses. What the child says or believes about what was done is important, but great emphasis also is placed upon what the child actually does, how the problem is tackled, what errors the child makes, and so forth. Invariably the child is asked to think about a common childhood event, such as flattening a clay ball or playing marbles, in a new way, or to consider a new possibility in an ordinary childlike task, such as lining sticks up in order by their lengths. The tasks or problems set for the children are usually designed to reveal the structure of the child's reasoning about some significant epistemological question—the nature of causality, necessity, implication, time, or space, and so forth.

THE STAGES OF INTELLECTUAL DEVELOPMENT

Over the sixty or so years during which Piaget published parts of his theory, there were continuous revisions in its details. The result was that all he claimed, and all that subsequent empirical research supports, is a general outline or skeleton of a theory, one full of gaps and claims modified by others. Even with respect to the number of stages of intellectual development, there was some variation in his work from time to time, but most accounts set forth four main stages—the *sensorimotor stage* (0–2 years), with six substages; the *preoperational stage* (2–7 years), with two substages; the *concrete operational stage* (7–12 years), with two substages; and the *formal operational stage* (12 years and up). Within each stage and substage, Piaget frequently distinguished three levels: failure, partial success, and success. In the final versions of the theory, development was viewed not as linear progression through fixed age-related stages, but as an unending spiral in which the differentiated forms and content at one level are reworked, restructured, integrated, or synthesized at the higher levels of the spiral.

Sensorimotor Stage

The six substages of this stage yield the principal accomplishments of the construction of coordinated movements, representation, and intentionality. A specific tangible accomplishment is the construction of the permanent object, now thought to occur earlier than Piaget's initial formulation.

Preoperational Stage

During this stage, the children discover a number of additional functional regularities, truths, and associations about the environment. Their thinking, however, is distinguished by surprising limitations. It seems captivated by only one aspect of a situation, often their own point of view (egocentrism), to the exclusion of other dimensions or perspectives. Preoperational thought, besides being centered on a single salient feature of an event, seems to flow in sequences of simple juxtaposition rather than sequences of logical implication or physical causality.

Concrete Operational Stage

The errors of the preoperational stage are corrected subsequently, but not uniformly or all at once. The solutions to the problems are domain-specific, worked out separately for the various domains of problems. For example, the notion of invariance is acquired sequentially and separately for the domains of number, length and mass, area, weight, time, and volume.

Formal Operational Stage

Here the child is able to consider several possibilities and to vary all but one in an analysis of a physical event. The ability to vary, mentally and hypothetically, all but one of the possible aspects of a situation means that form can be considered and manipulated apart from its content and that reality can be subjugated to possibility.

FUTURE WORK

The problem of novelty and spontaneity in thought, a core issue in the theory, remained unsolved by Piaget's theory. How does new knowledge arise out of a cognitive structure that did not, in any discernible way, contain the new knowledge? By what mechanism does new knowledge emerge, and how does it come to be seen as necessarily linked to other knowledge? These problems, of course, endure in all developmental theories of intellectual development, not just Piaget's.

F. B. MURRAY
University of Delaware

LEARNING THEORIES

PICK'S DISEASE

Pick's disease, considered a subtype of frontal lobe dementia, is a relatively rare and possibly heritable progressive neurodegenerative disorder appearing 10 to 20% as often as Alzheimer's disease. Duration of the disease from diagnosis to death is 5 to 10 years (Tissot, Constantinidis, & Richard, 1985). The disease typically affects individuals between the ages of 45 and 65 years (Hodges, 1994). In Pick's disease patients, brain imaging and autopsy examinations characteristically display progressive frontotemporal lobar atrophy. Due to clinical overlap with other cortical dementias, neuropathologic confirmation is required to establish a definitive diagnosis of Pick's disease.

NEUROPATHOLOGY OF PICK'S DISEASE

Neuropathologic changes associated with Pick's disease include atrophy of the anterior portion of the frontal lobe and a characteristic atrophy of the anterior portion of the superior temporal gyrus (anterior to the central sulcus) with preservation of the posterior portions of that gyrus. The parietal and occipital lobes are generally spared. The atrophy leaves the gyri with a knife-edge appearance. The lateral ventricles, particularly the frontal horns, are dilated due to the atrophic changes. There is also a characteristic severe loss of the granular neurons that comprise the dentate gyrus of the hippocampal complex. Subcortical structures in which neuronal loss occurs include the basal ganglia, amygdala, nucleus basalis of Meynert, substantia nigra, and locus ceruleus (Hof, Bouras, Perl, & Morrison, 1994; Hansen, 1994). Brainstem and cerebellar areas with connections to the cortex are also typically involved (Braak, Arai, & Braak, 1999; Dickson, 1998). In contrast to severely abnormal computed tomography or magnetic resonance images, electroencephalographic recordings are usually normal.

Neuropathologic features of Pick's disease include severe cerebral cortical neuronal loss, Pick bodies, and ballooned neurons (Pick cells; Giannakopoulos et al., 1996). Pick bodies are intracytoplasmic argyrophilic neuronal inclusions composed of straight filaments, microtubules, and occasional paired helical filaments (similar to those in Alzheimer's disease neurofibrillary tangles; Hof et al., 1994). Although there is some neuronal loss in the nucleus basalis of Meynert, cortical levels of choline acetyltransferase are not reduced in Pick's disease as they are in Alzheimer's disease.

COGNITIVE CHANGES IN PICK'S DISEASE

Clinical manifestations of Pick's disease reflect the distribution of neuropathological changes. Cognitive deficits typically follow alterations in personality and behavior. Behavior changes may include disinhibition, impulsivity, apathy, and decreased initiative. Patients may begin to exhibit inappropriate social behaviors and neglect personal responsibilities. Emotional changes vary and can include depression, anger, mania, irritability, or lability. Patients commonly lack insight into their behavioral and personality changes. Due to severe atrophy of the frontal lobes, patients with Pick's disease have marked impairments in planning and organizing complex activities, set-shifting, judgment, sequencing, and sustaining attention. Their inability to sustain attention and organize activities can give a misleading impression of memory impairment. However, patients generally have preserved memory function, evident by cue-enhanced immediate memory and information retrieval abilities. Patients with Pick's disease may have language disturbances characterized by echolalia and perseveration, reduced production of speech, use of stereotyped phrases, and late mutism. Articulation, syntax, and phonology are generally preserved. General intelligence, orientation, perceptual skills, and visuospatial abilities are often intact. In addition, sensory, motor, and reflex functions remain normal through most of the disease (Mendez, Selwood, Mastri, & Frey, 1993; Hodges, 1994; Mendez et al., 1996).

COMPARISON OF PICK'S AND OTHER NEURODEGENERATIVE DISEASES

As cognitive and behavioral performance progressively deteriorate, it becomes increasingly difficult to differentiate Pick's disease from other cortical dementias such as Alzheimer's disease and necessitates neuropathologic confirmation (Arnold, Hyman, & Van Hoesen, 1994). Pick's disease causes extensive atrophy and gliosis throughout the frontal lobe and anterior temporal lobe, most prominent in cortical layer three. Pick bodies are most evident in the insula and inferior temporal cortex. Loss of hippocampal dentate gyrus granular neurons with relatively preserved pyramidal neurons is characteristic of Pick's disease, while in Alzheimer's disease there is early loss of hippocampal pyramidal neurons with preservation of the dentate gyrus neurons. Nearly three-quarters of Pick's disease patients display early personality changes and behaviors such as roaming, hyperorality, and disinhibition, while less than one-third of Alzheimer's disease patients have such symptoms. These behaviors correlate with the greater frontal and temporal lobe damage in Pick's disease.

In addition to the clinical overlap of Pick's disease with Alzheimer's disease, the neuropathologic features of Pick's disease overlap with those of frontal lobe dementia, primary progressive aphasia, corticobasal degeneration, and multisystem atrophy. Because of the neuropathologic similarities, these latter disorders have been grouped together under the heading "Pick's complex."

Attempts have been made to differentiate Pick's disease from progressive supranuclear palsy and corticobasal degeneration (Feany et al., 1996). All three disorders have abnormalities of cortical and subcortical regions; however, Pick's disease has more cortical involvement, progressive supranuclear palsy has more subcortical damage, and corticobasal degeneration has equal cortical and subcortical pathology. The three disorders all have significant pathology in the substantia nigra, subthalamic nucleus, and locus ceruleus. However, Pick's disease has greater numbers of ballooned neurons than the other diseases; corticobasal degeneration can be distinguished by numerous neuropil threads in gray and white matter and neurofibrillary tangles in the globus pallidus; and progressive supranuclear palsy has numerous tangles in the globus pallidus with few neuropil threads or ballooned neurons. Thus, although there are significant overlaps, neuropathologic changes are relatively distinct for each disorder, suggesting separate pathophysiologic entities.

REFERENCES

Arnold, S. E., Hyman, B. T., & Van Hoesen, G. W. V. (1994). Neuropathologic changes of the temporal pole in Alzheimer's disease and Pick's disease. *Archives of Neurology, 51,* 145–150.

Braak, E., Arai, K., & Braak, H. (1999). Cerebellar involvement in Pick's disease: Affliction of mossy fibers, monodendritic brush cells, and dentate projection neurons. *Experimental Neurology, 159,* 153–163.

Dickson, D. W. (1998). Pick's disease: A modern approach. *Brain Pathology, 8,* 339–354.

Feany, M. B., Mattiace, L. A., & Dickson, D. W. (1996). Neuropathologic overlap of progressive supranuclear palsy, Pick's disease and corticobasal degeneration. *Journal of Neuropathology and Experimental Neurology, 55,* 53–67.

Giannakopoulos, P., Hof, P. R., Savioz, A., Guimon, J., Antonarakis, S. E., & Bouras, C. (1996). Early-onset dementia: Clinical, neuropathological and genetic characteristics. *Acta Neuropathologica, 91,* 451–465.

Hansen, L. (1994). Pathology of the other dementia. In R. D. Terry, R. Katzman, & L. Bick (Eds.), *Alzheimer disease* (pp. 172–173). New York: Raven.

Hodges, J. R. (1994). Pick's disease. In A. Burns & R. Levy (Eds.), *Dementia.* London: Chapman & Hall. 739–752

Hof, P. R., Bouras, C., Perl, D. P., & Morrison, J. H. (1994). Quantitative neuropathologic analysis of Pick's disease cases: Cortical distribution of Pick bodies and coexistence with Alzheimer's disease. *Acta Neuropathologica, 87,* 115–124.

Mendez, M. F., Selwood, A., Mastri, A. R., & Frey, W. H. (1993). Pick's disease versus Alzheimer's disease: A comparison of clinical characteristics. *Neurology, 43,* 289–292.

Mendez, M. F., Cherrier, M., Perryman, K. M., Pachana, N., Miller, B. L., & Cummings, J. L. (1996). Frontotemporal dementia versus Alzheimer's disease: Differential cognitive features. *Neurology, 47,* 1189–1194.

Tissot, R., Constantinidis, J., & Richard, J. (1985). Pick's disease. *Handbook of Clinical Neurology, 2,* 233–246.

J. A. TESTA
University of Oklahoma

AGING: PSYCHOLOGICAL & BEHAVIORAL CONCOMITANTS
ALZHEIMER'S DISEASE
PARKINSON'S DISEASE

PINEL, PHILIPPE (1745–1856)

At the beginning of the nineteenth century, France became the first country to initiate reforms involving more humane care for those people identified as insane. At that time, Pinel was one of the leading physicians in Paris. In 1792, he was appointed superintendent of the hospital, La Bicêtre. There the inmates were chained up in dungeons as if they were wild beasts, and frequently were put on display for those curious enough to pay a small fee to view them.

Pinel made a personal plea to the Revolutionary Commune to unchain some of the inmates and allow them to see the light of day. They were put under the care of physicians who shared his humane attitude, and were allowed to live in sunny rooms, and even to walk about on the grounds of the hospital. All of this was an "experiment." Pinel could have lost his head if it had been a failure, but in many cases the results were nothing short of miraculous. In his *Treatise on Insanity,* Pinel described the behavior of the patients. One case was that of an English officer who had been chained for 40 years. When he tottered out, on legs weak from lack of use, into the sunny day, he exclaimed, "Oh, how beautiful!" Pinel also made a plea for more humane treatment of the insane, who, at that time, were regarded by many as wicked and possessed by demons. He set forth an alternative, naturalistic explanation, which related disturbed behavior to some possible malfunction of the brain.

Pinel was later transferred to the hospital called Salpêtière, where he instituted similar reforms with equal success. He was succeeded by Jean Esquirol, who continued such reforms throughout many parts of France.

R. W. LUNDIN
Wheaton, Illinois

PITUITARY

The name "pituitary" was applied to the small gland beneath the brain's hypothalamus in the early 17th century because of the mistaken notion that the structure made phlegm—hence the term "pituitary," which literally means "snot gland." Hypophysis is a less colorful name for the pituitary.

For descriptive, embryological, and functional reasons, the pituitary is divided into two lobes: the anterior lobe or adenohypophysis, and the posterior lobe or neurohypophysis. The structure is connected to the hypothalamus by the infundibulum or hypophyseal stalk. A schematic drawing of the pituitary is shown in Figure 1.

ANTERIOR LOBE OR ADENOHYPOPHYSIS

Because of its role in the control of other endocrine glands, the pituitary is often called the master gland of the body. This designation is more appropriately applied to the pituitary's anterior lobe

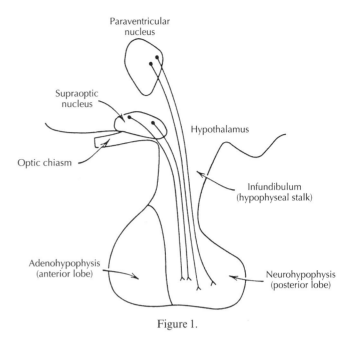

Figure 1.

than it is to the posterior lobe, as the adenohypophysis manufactures and secretes hormonal substances that regulate the body's most important glands (e.g., the adrenal glands, the thyroid gland, the gonads). In fact, the prefix "adeno-" means gland.

The anterior lobe of the pituitary arises from skin cells from the roof of the mouth, and the surgical approach to the pituitary is through the roof of the mouth, giving one a better appreciation of the gland's location in the head. Although it is not in direct neural contact with the brain, the activities of the adenohypophysis are regulated by the hypothalamus, which secretes neurochemicals called releasing factors that travel to the anterior lobe through a system of blood vessels.

The releasing factors regulate the secretion of anterior lobe hormones such as somatotropin, thyrotropin, adrenocorticotropin, lactogenic hormone, and the gonadotropins. Each will be discussed briefly.

Somatotropin (STH) is a growth-promoting hormone and, in fact, is sometimes called growth hormone. Its presence at appropriate developmental periods is essential for normal growth.

Thyrotropin (TSH, or thyroid-stimulating hormone) acts on the thyroid gland to promote the synthesis, storage, and release of the thyroid's hormone, thyroxine. Thyroxine is involved in the regulation of the body's metabolism.

Adrenocorticotropin (ACTH, or adrenocorticotropic hormone) stimulates the production and release of hormones by the adrenal cortex (the adrenal glands are above the kidneys). ACTH triggers the release of glucocorticoids (e.g., cortisol), which are important in carbohydrate metabolism and in the body's resistance to stress. ACTH itself is released in response to physical or emotional stress.

Lactogenic hormone (LTH, or prolactin) acts on the mammary glands to promote milk secretion. Prolactin is also important for the display of parental behaviors in vertebrates.

The gonadotropins have different names and effects, depending on the organism's sex. For example, luteinizing hormone (LH) is necessary for ovulation in females. In males, LH acts on cells in the testes to cause them to produce testosterone.

POSTERIOR LOBE OR NEUROHYPOPHYSIS

The posterior lobe of the pituitary, or the neurohypophysis, is physically connected to the hypothalamus and merely stores and secretes substances manufactured by two hypothalamic nuclei: the supraoptic and the paraventricular. The supraoptic nuclei make vasopressin, which is also known as antidiuretic hormone (ADH). ADH acts primarily on the kidneys to reclaim water that would otherwise be lost through urination. Lack of ADH causes diabetes insipidus, a disorder characterized by excessive drinking and urination.

The paraventricular nuclei manufacture oxytocin, which is a smooth muscle-stimulating hormone. Oxytocin plays an important role in inducing the contractions of the uterine walls during the birth process (i.e., labor pains). In addition, it is required for the release of milk in response to suckling. Oxytocin's role in males is not known.

B. M. THORNE
Mississippi State University

ANTERIOR PITUITARY GLAND

PITUITARY DISORDERS

The pituitary gland is a small body, about the size of a pea, and weighs about one-half gram. It lies at the base of the brain and is connected to the hypothalamus, an important brain structure, by a stalk. The pituitary is actually two separate glands, anterior and posterior pituitary, each with its own secretions. Almost all pituitary secretions are controlled by the hypothalamus (Guyton, 1977). The anterior pituitary secretes six important hormones and the posterior secretes two hormones important for human functioning. The anterior pituitary hormones include: (a) the growth hormone, which promotes growth; (b) adreno corticotropin (ACTH), which controls secretions of another gland, the adrenal cortex; (c) thyroid-stimulating hormone (TSH), which controls the rate of secretion of thyroxine, a thyroid gland hormone; (d) prolactin, which promotes mammary gland development and milk production; (e) follicle-stimulating hormone (FSH); and (f) luteinizing hormones (LH). The last two are both important in reproductive activities. The two hormones secreted by the posterior pituitary are the antidiuretic hormone, which controls the release of body fluids, and oxytocin, which promotes labor contractions. Disorders in growth hormone secretion can be either in the direction of over- (hyper-) or under- (hypo-) secretion. Hyposecretion in childhood leads to dwarfism. A child aged 10 may have the body of a child of 4 or 5; and the same person at age 20 may have the physical development of a child of 7 or 10. In the past decade, human growth hormone, obtained from cadavers, has made it possible for children who undersecrete to grow relatively close to normal height. Hypersecretion of growth hormone prior to adolescence can lead to gigantism, in which a person can reach a height of eight to nine feet. Gigantism is often caused by a tumor of the pituitary gland, which, if diagnosed, can be treated by gamma irradiation.

When hypersecretion of growth hormone occurs in the postadolescent period, the person does not grow taller, but the bones enlarge. This produces a condition known as "acromegaly," in which bone enlargement occurs in bones of the nose, the lower jawbone, the forehead, the hands, and the feet. Among treatment methods that have proved effective are radiotherapy, proton-beam therapy, and removal of the pituitary gland.

Overproduction of ACTH can lead to Cushing's disease. The face and body become puffy because of excess fat deposits; acne and excess facial hair growth also occur. Removal of the adrenal glands or pituitary gland is a possible treatment. Undersecretion of ACTH can cause Addison's disease, which is characterized by apathy, anemia, low blood pressure, muscle weakness, and a bronze skin coloring.

An excess of TSH produces symptoms of hyperthyroidism, which include intolerance to heat, increased sweating, muscular weakness, nervousness, extreme fatigue but inability to sleep, and hand tremors. An undersecretion of TSH results in hypothyroidism, the symptoms of which include sleeping 14 to 16 hours a day, muscular sluggishness, slow heart rate, mental apathy, and increased weight. If not detected in infants, hypothyroidism can lead to cretinism, a severe form of mental retardation. Thyroid extract is used to treat hypothyroidism, and antithyroid drugs such as propylthiouracil can combat hyperthyroidism. The undersecretion of FSH and LH interferes with reproductive functions. In the male, the FSH stimulates sperm production and androgens; in the female, it stimulates growth and maturation of egg cells by the ovaries, as well as the release of estrogens (Guyton, 1977).

Vasopressin, also known as antidiuretic hormone (ADH), acts to decrease water secretion by the kidneys. Thus a lack of ADH would result in excessive urine production, and an excess would cause urinary retention. Oxytocin is another hormone secreted by the posterior pituitary. It causes contraction of the pregnant uterus. Oxytocin also promotes release of milk from the breast into the nipple. An excess of oxytocin would lead to excessive uterine contractions in a pregnant female, whereas an undersecretion might inhibit contractions, causing prolonged periods of labor.

REFERENCES

Guyton, A. C. (1977). *Basic human physiology.* Philadelphia, PA: Saunders.

J. L. ANDREASSI
City University of New York, Baruch College

CENTRAL NERVOUS SYSTEM
NEUROCHEMISTRY
PITUITARY

PLACEBO

The term "placebo" is derived from the Latin for "placate" or "please." Some of the earliest definitions of placebo are in Quincy's *Lexicon* (1787), "a commonplace method or medicine" ("or" may have been a typographical error intended to be "of") and in Hooper's *Medical Dictionary* (1811), "an epithet given to any medication adopted more to please than benefit." A more comprehensive definition has been given by Shapiro (1968) as "any therapy (or that component of any therapy) that is deliberately used for its nonspecific psychologic or physiologic effect, or that is used for its presumed effect on a patient, [symptom or illness] but which, unknown to patient and therapist, is without specific activity for the condition being treated."

THE UBIQUITOUS PLACEBO

Patients have always been soothed by medicines that do not work physiologically. None of the medicines used by Hippocrates or Galen, for instance, would be found on the shelves of the modern drugstore. Two of the most "effective" medicines of medieval times were theriac powder, an ancient concoction of 30 to 60 ingredients including ground Egyptian mummy and viper flesh, and the legendary bezoar stone made from the gallstones of goat. Most folk medicine is based on the placebo. For example, the copper bracelet widely worn to ward off arthritic pain has no known physiological effects. The files of the Federal Drug Administration are full of once-new miracle drugs that have mysteriously become ineffective over the years. Indeed, it has become clinical lore to use a new drug while it still works.

The placebo response has been documented in pharmacological studies related to adrenal gland secretion, angina pain, blood cell counts, blood pressure, cold vaccine, common cold, cough reflex, fever, gastric secretion/motility, headache, insomnia, measles vaccine, oral contraceptives, pain (acute and chronic), pupil dilation/constriction, rheumatoid arthritis, vasomotor function, vitamins, warts, and so on. Placebo medication has inhibited gastric acid secretion, bleeding ulcers, and has mimicked the effects of amphetamine, ipacac, and LSD, as well as most psychoactive drugs. It has reduced adrenocorticol activity and serum lipoproteins. It has been used in drug withdrawal studies as a substitute for morphine and Talwin injections. Placebo side effects mimic active medication side effects and show standard pharmacological properties, such as dose-response curves.

Placebo effects are not limited to pharmacological agents, and have been well documented in studies of psychotherapy, acupuncture, hypnosis, and behavioral treatments for insomnia and pain (without in any way implying that these procedures do not have specific as well as documentable nonspecific effects). Such surgical and dental procedures as ligation of mammary arteries for angina pain (in which electrocardiac changes were found with sham surgery) and bruxism have been shown to be only placebo effects.

There is a dearth of placebo-controlled studies on the plethora of over-the-counter medications, nutritional herbs and other health supplements and new treatments, the majority of which will eventually turn out to be no different from powerful placebos. Much of alternative medicine involves treatments for which the patient/consumer and the therapist/supplier both believe in their efficacy. It may turn out that these mutual expectations and faith in the treatment's efficacy is the primary therapeutic ingredient.

There are several theories about the mechanisms underlying placebo effects. These include discussions of the role of anxiety, conditioning, endorphins, experimenter bias, and suggestion. None of these theories have strong empirical support, and the role of belief and expectation in mediating the placebo response seems to have the most validity and empirical support.

The placebo response has been viewed as a nuisance variable in methodological studies. It can have powerful positive therapeutic effects. It can just as easily have powerful negative therapeutic effects called the *nocebo* effect. Due to negative expectations an otherwise healthy person may show medical symptoms when he or she first learns what side effects may occur and what are the symptoms of the disease. Psychosomatic symptoms and the iatrogenic effects of informed consent and medical procedures, as well as Australian Aborigine bone pointing and South American voodoo death, are examples of powerful nocebo effects.

THE PLACEBO EFFECT IN DOUBLE-BLIND TRIALS

The placebo response is best known as a methodological control procedure in pharmacological studies. Medication is given double-blind, so that neither the patient nor the researcher/clinical observer knows whether a real medication or a placebo has been administered. It has generally been considered as a nuisance variable methodologically, and the ideal but impossible goal of research studies has been to attempt to eliminate its effect. Because of the reactive nature of all research, the effects of the interpersonal doctor-patient relationship, and the drug-giving ritual, the expectation is communicated that relief of symptoms is imminent. Logically, the double-blind method is a good illustration of the classic method of differences underlying the scientific method. Under double-blind conditions, the maximized placebo response is subtracted from the active medication effect, leaving the net medication effect.

There are a number of methodological difficulties with the classic double-blind procedure, particularly in the so-called crossover design. Even in double-blind studies, either the observer or the patient may break the code (because of side effects or attribution of symptoms) and recognize which agent has been given. To prevent this from occurring, active placebos may be employed in which substances are used that mimic the side effects of the active drug. It is incumbent upon the researcher to collect impressionistic data from both patient and observer concerning which agent they believe was administered. These perceptions often influence the patients' responses more than their drug/placebo status. There are studies in which the investigator's guess about whether a patient has received drug or placebo is more correlated with the results than whether the patient in fact received drug or placebo. Unless these interactions are evaluated, the success of the double-blind integrity cannot be evaluated. In treatment studies in which the placebo effect is atypically low compared to an active treatment, it is likely that the blind code was inadvertently broken by the many cues determining a patient's response. In spite of these and other limitations, the placebo control is still the method of choice in evaluating the specific effects of new pharmacological agents.

CLINICAL SIGNIFICANCE OF PLACEBO

Beecher (1959) was perhaps the first to document systematically that the placebo response can be a powerful therapeutic agent. In his classic studies of pain, Beecher reviewed 15 double-blind studies ($N = 1082$) of morphine treatment of postoperative pain. He reported that 35 percent of these patients experienced levels of pain reduction comparable to those patients given a standard injection of morphine. In 11 subsequent studies ($N = 908$), a strong placebo effect was found in 36 percent of patients (Evans, 1981). Beecher's 35 percent clinical efficacy fails to recognize that even a standard dose of morphine was effective in only about 70 percent of patients in these studies. An index of placebo efficiency, derived by comparing the effectiveness of placebo with the effectiveness of morphine, indicates that placebo was 56 percent as effective as morphine in these studies. Similarly, Evans reported that, in averaging available double-blind studies since Beecher's review, placebo is about 55 percent as effective as aspirin, Darvon compound, codeine, and Zomax. These consistencies imply that the placebo response is proportional to the assumed efficacy of the treatment itself. In an early double-blind study, the then-new antipsychotic drug chlorpromazine was about 55 percent as effective as placebo in each of the seven years studied, but the effectiveness of chlorpromazine and of placebo was reduced proportionally each year. The effectiveness of the placebo in year one was much higher than the effectiveness of chlorpromazine in year seven of the study.

Clearly the placebo effect has powerful therapeutic implications if the mechanisms involved can be understood and applied clinically in a positive manner. The placebo response is apparently mediated in all treatment contexts by expectancy, anxiety reduction, and cues that emanate from the subtleties of doctor-patient relationship. Studies have shown that the placebo response is not related to suggestibility, gullibility, conformity, or related traits.

CLINICAL APPLICATIONS OF PLACEBO

Under what circumstances, if any, should placebos be actively prescribed? Most physicians admit that they have occasionally used placebos knowingly, but less than their colleagues, particularly those in other specialties. This unfortunate negative view of the placebo denies the significance of the doctor-patient relationship. Some critics argue that placebos are inherently unethical because deception is involved. From the point of view of the patient's contract with the physician to get better, any prescription or treatment, even if it is nonspecific, that may achieve a positive clinical goal is reasonable. Indeed, it may be unethical to deny the patient a treatment that may well be effective, inexpensive, and relatively safe.

The placebo has a number of potential clinical applications. First, it involves mechanisms that, once understood more efficiently, will lead to more rational methods of treatment in medicine and behavioral medicine. Placebo may also be a powerful diagnostic tool. For example, anesthesiologists may use placebo nerve blocks for diagnostic purposes. Unfortunately, there is a tendency for wrong conclusions to be drawn. Some physicians have learned to equate response to a placebo diagnostic test with the belief that the symptom (e.g., pain) is psychological and nonorganic. From the patient's point of view, there is no such thing as psychological pain. Rather, viewed in a positive light, successful placebo response indicates that the patient has the resources to manipulate and control symptoms at some level. (Of course, issues of secondary gain, depression, and the like in direct symptom removal must be handled carefully therapeutically.) A positive placebo will often predict a positive therapeutic outcome. In many cases, the nonspecific placebo effects and the specific treatment effects are interactive and cumulative. The two components cannot be separated in an individual's response to treatment. In addition, placebos sometimes can be used as an alternative to medications as a substitute for potentially dangerous drugs, and as an aid in withdrawal from active or addictive medication.

The placebo effect is a significant part of the total treatment context. The nature of the doctor-patient relationship and the expectations of treatment and cure that are communicated in this context provides the basis for powerful nonspecific therapeutic interventions. By harnessing the power of the placebo, it is possible to develop more rational treatment modalities in many areas of medicine and therapy.

REFERENCES

Beecher, H. K. (1959). *Measurement of subjective responses.* New York: Oxford.

Evans, F. J. (1981). The placebo response in pain control. *Psychopharmacology Bulletin, 17,* 72–76.

SUGGESTED READING

Brody, H. (1977). *Placebos and the philosophy of medicine.* Chicago: University of Chicago Press.

Evans, F. J. (1974). The power of the sugar pill. *Psychology Today, 7,* 55–59.

Frank, J. (1973). *Persuasion and healing.* Baltimore: Johns Hopkins University Press.

Shapiro, A. K. (1960). A contribution to the history of the placebo effect. *Behavioral Science, 5,* 398–450.

Wall, P. (1994). The placebo and the placebo response. In P. Wall & R. Melzack (Eds.), *Textbook of pain* (3rd ed.). Edinburgh, Scotland: Churchill Livingstone.

White, L., Tursky, B., & Schwartz, G. E. (1985). *Placebo: Theory, research, and mechanisms.* New York: Guilford.

F. J. EVANS
The Reading Hospital, PA

BEHAVIORAL MEDICINE
DOUBLE BLIND RESEARCH
EXPECTANCY THEORY
HYPNOSIS
PAIN
PSYCHOPHARMACOLOGY
SELF-FULFILLING PROPHECY

PLANNED SHORT-TERM PSYCHOTHERAPY

Although occasional references to short-term psychotherapy appeared prior to the inauguration of the community mental health movement in the early 1960s, serious examination of brief psychotherapies began at the same time that mental health professionals recognized the importance of serving the mental health needs of the entire community. Time-limited psychotherapy was thought to be a strategy that had the potential for helping greater numbers of clients in the community.

The literature on planned short-term psychotherapy has increased exponentially since then, and there are now more than 150 books and 4,000 published papers on that topic. No school of psychotherapy has been unaffected by this literature. There are now numerous descriptions and outcome studies of planned short-term individual and group approaches to psychodynamically oriented, cognitively and behaviorally oriented, solution-focused, and strategic psychotherapies with both children and adults in both inpatient and outpatient settings.

This growing literature has had a profound impact on the funding and practice of psychotherapy primarily because of its consistent evidence that planned short-term psychotherapies, often as short as a single interview, generally appear to be as effective as time-unlimited psychotherapies, virtually regardless of client characteristics, treatment duration, or therapist orientation. Furthermore, almost identical findings have been reported for short-term inpatient psychiatric care. Perhaps no other finding has been reported with greater regularity in the mental health literature than the apparent equality of time-limited and time-unlimited psychotherapy in terms of its clinical effect.

Health economists concerned about the alarming increase in the cost of medical care could hardly have been expected to ignore the evidence that, in the case of psychotherapy at least, longer is rarely better. Indeed, were it not for the consistent evidence of the effectiveness of planned short-term psychotherapy, the writings in this field might have ended up simply as a footnote in the ongoing history of psychotherapy. What seems to be happening in the practice of psychotherapy parallels what is happening in general health services. Treatment has become shorter rather than longer; is taking place increasingly in outpatient rather than inpatient settings; and is less, rather than more, invasive.

Planned short-term psychotherapy is not simply less of time-unlimited psychotherapy. Rather, the practice of planned short-term psychotherapy rests on four fundamental principles uniquely associated with it that distinguish it from traditional time-unlimited approaches. Furthermore, evidence suggests that training in these principles and their application improves the clinical effectiveness of therapists.

First, recent research has consistently found that improvement during an episode of psychotherapy is negatively accelerated—very rapid at first, then slowing significantly. Accordingly, therapists who are interested in making the best use of time take advantage of the initial period of rapid improvement by keeping episodes of therapy as short as possible while at the same time encouraging clients to return for additional brief therapeutic episodes when they are needed. Although traditionally-trained psychotherapists tend to think that when a client returns to treatment it is a sign that

the initial treatment episode was a failure (an assertion for which there is no empirical evidence), planned short-term psychotherapy is designed to be intermittent—multiple individual brief treatment episodes within an ongoing therapeutic relationship.

Second, brief psychotherapy is especially empowering to the therapist. The evolution from time-unlimited to planned short-term psychotherapy results in a fundamental change in the role of the therapist—from a passive one, in which the gradual deconstruction of conflict is observed, to a more active one, in which the therapist takes a more directive stance in helping plan every aspect of the clinical episode. Planned short-term psychotherapy requires an active collaboration between client and therapist in establishing therapeutic goals, conducting the therapeutic episode, and bringing it to an agreed-upon conclusion.

Third, in contrast to traditional time-unlimited psychotherapies that place unique therapeutic importance on the face-to-face clinical contact, planned short-term psychotherapies assume that the time between clinical contacts and after the conclusion of a clinical episode has significant therapeutic potential. Accordingly, the therapeutic episode is designed to use the time between sessions planfully and to start a therapeutic process that can continue after the face-to-face contacts have been brought to an end. Small changes during the treatment episode may be all that is required to start a process that will lead to significant and long-lasting clinical improvement.

Short-term psychotherapists look to the time between sessions as a potentially valuable occasion for work to be done by the client—keeping a log or a diary, establishing a schedule, having a conversation with a specific person on a specific topic, writing, reading, or rewarding oneself. An episode of psychotherapy is thought of as starting, rather than completing, the change process. In addition, numerous empirical studies have also identified the so-called "sleeper effect," evidence that the effects of psychotherapy continue, and often increase, long after the therapeutic episode has been concluded. One way that planned short-term psychotherapists build on this sleeper effect is to include a planned follow-up contact into the therapeutic episode. Such posttreatment contacts not only create a unique opportunity to evaluate the consequences of their work, but appear to extend the life and the effectiveness of therapeutic interventions.

Fourth, time-conscious therapists think of each client contact as a self-contained unit, an opportunity to accomplish a significant, focused piece of clinical work so that additional contacts may not be necessary. A therapeutic episode is thus thought of as a series of single sessions. In contrast to traditional psychotherapists who tend to underestimate how helpful they can be to people in brief periods of time, therapists who practice planned short-term psychotherapy believe that virtually all clients can be helped and can be helped relatively quickly, regardless of diagnosis or problem severity. The psychological climax of every interview is intended to be a skillful intervention—a well-timed interpretation, a carefully-considered activity plan designed to modify undesired behavior, or a proposal whose goal is to change interpersonal interaction.

There are numerous cases, of course, when psychotherapy needs to be extended in order to achieve satisfactory results. These instances can rarely be predicted in advance, however, and mental health professionals are learning to make time available to treat clients who need longer-term psychotherapy by making sure that all their clients receive only the psychotherapy they need, but no more.

For more than 35 years the empirical literature has underlined the remarkable efficacy of planned short-term psychotherapy. The theoretical literature is equally impressive in helping put these new clinical practices in a conceptually rich and historically revered context. Mental health professionals, while properly insisting on avoiding undertreatment, are beginning to accept the affirmation of their effectiveness in brief periods of time and are increasingly alert to avoiding overtreatment as well.

SUGGESTED READING

Bloom, B. L. (1997). *Planned short-term psychotherapy: A clinical handbook* (2nd ed.). Boston, MA: Allyn & Bacon.

B. L. BLOOM
University of Colorado

PSYCHOTHERAPY
PSYCHOTHERAPY TECHNIQUES

PLATO (427–347 B.C.)

Plato was born to parents from old, aristocratic Athenian families. He had political ambitions but became disillusioned with politics and abandoned them after the forced suicide of Socrates. Plato left Athens, and traveled to Megara, Syracuse, and Tarentum, before returning to Athens. Here he founded the Academy, which continued until 529 A.D. Plato's influence on Western thought has been inestimable, extending to metaphysics, epistemology, ethics, politics, mathematics, and several branches of natural science.

Plato's psychological views were not presented in a systematic form but may be found scattered through the dialogues. As a philosopher, Plato valued above all the life of reason, which could put humans in touch with timeless essences, permanent and exact. These stood in sharp contrast to the temporary and imprecise appearances revealed by sense perception. Thus there is in Plato a dualism of things known through the senses and Ideas and Forms known through reason. It is the Ideas that are real, for they are absolute, permanent, and perfect. While reason is capable of grasping Ideas, and therefore of gaining true knowledge, the senses can yield only opinion at best.

If knowledge cannot be obtained through the senses, it must be intuited through a higher power, the mind or soul. Some passages in the dialogues make it appear that for Plato the soul was immaterial and immortal and totally different in principle from the body, but it is possible that he was simply using fable, myth, and metaphor to stress the point that the soul as the virtue and dignity of human beings (a Socratic view) was to be most highly esteemed. Greek doctrines of soul were generally naturalistic, but most classical scholars have regarded Plato as an exception, a Greek dualist who divided a human being into material body and immaterial

soul. Plato did speak of the transmigration of souls and probably was influenced by Pythagorean and Orphic mystery views.

For Plato the body was a hindrance to the soul in the acquisition of knowledge, and sight and hearing were inaccurate witnesses. Plato, as a rationalist, appeared quite ready to abandon the body and the senses for the unimpeded activity of the soul capable of handling absolute being. Plato argued that all knowledge is recollection and that we have carried it with us from an earlier existence. In the *Meno*, Socrates questions an untutored slave boy in such a way as to demonstrate that the boy knows geometry even though he had been unaware that he possessed the knowledge. It seemed obvious that the knowledge must be attributed to acquaintance before birth. This is the essence of Plato's famous reminiscence doctrine.

Plato spoke of the soul as a unity, but he also described it as having three aspects: reason, located in the head; spirit or courage, located in the chest; and appetite, located in the abdomen. While Plato exalted reason, he was keenly aware of the irrational element in people that frequently gives rise to conflict. Reason is analogous to the charioteer who has trouble controlling an unruly and headstrong horse (appetite) but little difficulty with a fine, spirited animal (spirit). Reason must serve as a guide, producing harmony in the soul and leading appetite and spirit toward goals that reason alone understands.

Plato favored rational, deductive science over the empirical and inductive. Yet while he did not formulate a coherent or systematic psychology, he did develop, on the basis of astute observation, a variety of psychological descriptions and theories. These extended from the special senses, through imagination, memory, desire, sleep and dreams, feeling and understanding, to thinking and reasoning.

P. E. LICHTENSTEIN

PLAY DEVELOPMENT

Mark Twain defined work as whatever a body was obliged to do and play as whatever a body was not obliged to do. Play is activity for its own sake and can be viewed, relative to children, as what they do when allowed to freely choose activity.

Play is a vehicle for learning that enables a child to grow cognitively, socially, physically, and emotionally. It is more than simply "a child's work," as within the context of play the child learns about interrelationships and is afforded the means to become an effective participant.

The development of play proceeds through stages that coincide with the child's cognitive and social development. Children initially pass through a period of solitary play, in which play is independent of activities of others and there is minimal communication. Parallel play is characterized by children playing beside, but not really with, each other. Cooperative play, the most complex form of play, occurs when children engage in organized activities, where leadership and elaborate social roles are assumed. The opportunity for a child to experiment through play is considered essential for normal development.

Sex differences are noted in the cognitive, social, and physical aspects of play. Regardless of age, boys tend to be more overtly aggressive than girls. Entrance into male groups is easier to achieve but harder to sustain; entrance to female groups is more difficult to attain but more long lasting once achieved. Considerable sex differences across ages are seen in the social and physical requirements of play choice.

There are numerous theoretical approaches to play development, and these are generally more elaborate and explanatory than supportive experimental findings.

One predominant theory approaches play as the developmental opportunity to practice cognitive and social skills representational of the more stringent demands that will be made at later ages. This developmental theory of play encourages varied, early, and controlled childhood experiences as precursors of optimum development.

The recapitulation theory conceptualizes play as an evolutionary link between the child and all biological and cultural stages that have preceded human beings on the phylogenetic scale. Human kings, the most complex of biological and social animals, require a longer time for the young experimentally to master the various demands imposed by the environment.

Observation, interpretation, and structuring of a child's play are methods of understanding the unique manner in which a child communicates with and perceives the world. Such approaches utilize play as a therapeutic method for treating behavioral or emotional disorders of children.

Basic to all theory and practice, play is a primary means by which children learn about the cognitive, social, and physical expectations of later life through symbolic/representational activity. The opportunity to engage in varied play experiences is necessary, but not sufficient, for a child to achieve maximum potential.

SUGGESTED READING

D'Heurle, A. (1979). Play and the development of the person. *The Elementary School Journal, 79,* 225–234.

Ellis, M. J. (1973). *Why people play.* Englewood Cliffs, NJ: Prentice-Hall.

Ellis, M. J., & Scholtz, G. J. L. (1978). *Activity and play of children.* Englewood Cliffs, NJ: Prentice-Hall.

Levy, J. (1978). *Play behavior.* New York: Wiley.

Sutton-Smith, B. (1980). Children's play: Some sources of play theorizing. In K. H. Rubin (Ed.), *New directions for child development—children's play.* San Francisco: Jossey-Bass.

Wolfgang, C. H., & Sanders, T. S. (1981). Defending young children's play as the ladder to literacy. *Theory Into Practice, 20,* 116–120.

A. THOMAS
New York University School of Medicine

EARLY CHILDHOOD DEVELOPMENT
INFANT PLAY BEHAVIOR

PLAY THERAPY

The term "play therapy" is employed in at least two different ways to describe child psychotherapy. First, the term sometimes refers to particular clinical approaches that centrally emphasize children's play as a means of therapeutic communication and as a modality in which children's problems can be solved (e.g., Bromfield, 1992; Ciottone & Madonna, 1996; Kaduson & Schaefer, 1997; McMahon, 1992; Schaefer, 1993; Singer, 1993). Second, the term "play therapy" is employed more generally to describe diverse approaches to individual child psychotherapy, insofar as such approaches rely on children's play as a mode of communication. In fact, most child therapists employ play (Johnson, Rasbury, & Siegel, 1997), although they differ about whether play is considered central or relatively incidental to the process of change. Such differences of opinion depend upon therapists' theoretical orientations and upon the children's ages and their problems.

Various forms of play are useful in child psychotherapy. Even simple practice play (e.g., bouncing a ball) can help a child relax and become comfortable with the therapist. In addition, games with rules (e.g., checkers) can be used to teach a child about fair play (e.g., Gardner, 1993a). Symbolic or pretend play, however, is especially important for psychotherapy, because such play expresses children's experiences beyond their limited capacity to verbally explain themselves.

Symbolic play entails engaging in one activity with one object for the purpose of representing a different activity and a different object. Thus, a child might jump about while holding a broomstick, playing "horsie," in order to represent a cowboy riding a horse. Symbolic play can involve toys (e.g., dolls or action figures) or sociodramatic scenes in which children join together to enact stories. Symbolic play represents and communicates children's personal viewpoints about real events as well as their wishes, fears, and other personal reactions to those events (e.g., Bretherton, 1989; Ciottone & Madonna, 1996; Johnson et al., 1997; Schaefer, 1993). For example, children would not play "horsie" unless they were familiar with the possibility of riding horses and had some feelings about the matter. In fact, researchers find that children are especially likely to symbolically enact events and wishes that have aroused their anxiety as well as their wishes (Watson, 1994). Symbolic play is "often so revealing of the child's otherwise hidden wishes and percepts [that it] can open the inner world of the child to the therapist" (Coppolillo, 1987, p. 228).

Beyond providing therapists with information about the child, therapeutic orientations that place a very central value on play propose that engaging in symbolic play is inherently "curative." Symbolic play sometimes provides children with an avenue to actually resolve the anxiety and dilemmas that are expressed symbolically (Bretherton, 1989; Ciottone & Madonna, 1996; Schaefer, 1993; Watson, 1994). In part, play might relieve by allowing a symbolic expression of experiences that would be too threatening to express directly (Johnson et al., 1997; Watson, 1994). Moreover, while playing, children are "in charge," and they experience the relief of being active and in control, in contrast to the powerlessness they ordinarily experience in threatening situations (Coppolillo, 1987; Erikson, 1977; Sarnoff, 1976; Schaefer, 1993). Moreover, some authors propose that children can construct new ways of coping with their dilemmas when they miniaturize or "model" dilemmas symbolically (e.g., Erikson, 1964, 1977; Watson, 1994).

Client-centered and existential therapists permit considerable uninterrupted play in therapy (Axline, 1947; Ellinwood & Raskin, 1993; Moustakas, 1953). These therapists presume that play is therapeutic insofar as it occurs in the context of an accepting, clarifying, and confidential therapeutic relationship. They believe it is the relationship that allows children to fully express their subjective experiences and impressions. Although not necessarily accepting this unique emphasis on the therapeutic alliance, all approaches to child therapy presume that the quality of the relationship is important (Shirk & Saiz, 1992).

In contrast to emphasizing the benefits of unimpeded play, other therapists actively intervene while the child is playing. For example, psychodynamic therapists intervene by providing children with interpretations about the meanings of the wishes, fears, and ways of coping that are represented symbolically (Coppolillo, 1987; Singer, 1993). Such interpretations are intended to help children to understand and express their experiences not only symbolically, but also consciously. More conscious understanding can permit more adaptive ways of coping. Moreover, some therapists emphasize the need to explicitly interpret relationships between actual traumatizing events and the repetitive play through which some children symbolize such traumas (Silvern, Karyl, & Landis, 1995).

Other therapeutic approaches grant play a somewhat incidental role, not a central one. For example, play can be an adjunct to cognitive-behavioral therapy that has a primary goal of teaching new cognitions about the social world and new ways of coping with emotions and with social interactions. Kendall and Braswell (1993) suggested that playing out problematic social interactions can reveal children's perspectives and point to any problematic cognitions that should be corrected. Knell (1993) proposed a cognitive-behavioral approach to play therapy in which therapists structure the child's play, which is integrated into educational techniques such as modeling, role-playing, and reinforcement of adaptive thoughts and behavior.

Whatever the particular approach, play therapy is ordinarily conducted in a therapeutic playroom. To facilitate the therapy process, the playroom is ideally equipped with a variety of materials that are suitable for children of different ages and backgrounds. Materials should be sufficiently varied to encourage enacting diverse themes and personal issues (Johnson et al., 1997). Unstructured materials include items such as sand, water, and clay; they are intended to allow maximum freedom of self-expression. Structured materials include items such as cars, puppets, and dolls. Therapists often introduce such toys to elicit play about particular themes that deal with feelings, attitudes and conflicts in family or peer relationships (Johnson et al., 1997). For example, therapists often introduce two doll houses into the playroom for children who are adjusting to having two homes after adoption or divorce (e.g., Kuhli, 1993). Similarly, toy medical equipment might be introduced to children who are facing a medical procedure (Oremland, 1993).

Instead of focusing on toys, many therapists have adopted the "mutual storytelling" technique that was introduced by Gardner (1971, 1993b). The therapist begins to tell a story that raises a ther-

apeutic issue; the client finishes the story while the therapist suggests adaptive outcomes.

Although play therapy has traditionally been employed with diverse emotional and behavioral disorders, in recent years several specialized approaches have been developed for particular life problems. As examples, specialized approaches have been developed for children who have been sexually abused (Ciottone & Madonna, 1996; McMahon, 1992), children who have been otherwise traumatized (Silvern et al., 1995; Webb, 1991), children who are undergoing frightening medical procedures (Oremland, 1993), and children with developmental or physical handicaps (Hellendoorn, van der Kooij, & Sutton-Smith, 1994).

Moreover, in recent years, the use of play has been extended beyond its traditional role in individual psychotherapy to other treatment modalities. For example, play techniques have been integrated into family therapy (Gil, 1994). Additionally, school-based programs train socially disadvantaged children to engage in symbolic play with the intention of preventing developmental, psychological, and school problems (Hellendoorn et al., 1994). Furthermore, play has been integrated into many parent training approaches (Foote, Eyberg, & Schuhmann, 1998; Strayhorn, 1994). Although the goals of parent training are typically to improve childrearing and discipline, empirical findings have revealed that it is more effective to initially establish play interactions between children and parents than to immediately focus on discipline skills (Foote et al., 1998).

Since there are many approaches to child psychotherapy, it is important for parents to inquire about therapists' orientations and practices. By itself, the term "play therapy" reveals little about the characteristics of the treatment.

REFERENCES

Axline, V. M. (1947). *Play therapy.* Boston: Houghton Mifflin.

Bretherton, I. (1989). Pretense: The form and function of make-believe play. *Developmental Review, 9,* 393–401.

Bromfield, R. (1992). *Playing for real.* New York: Penguin.

Ciottone, R. A., & Madonna, J. M. (1996). *Play therapy with sexually abused children.* Northvale, NJ: Aronson.

Coppolillo, H. P. (1987). *Psychodynamic psychotherapy of children.* Madison, WI: International Universities Press.

Ellinwood, C. G., & Raskin, J. J. (1993). Client-centered/humanistic psychotherapy. In T. R. Kratochwill & R. R. Morris (Eds.), *Handbook of psychotherapy with children and adolescents* (pp. 264–375). Boston: Allyn & Bacon.

Erikson, E. (1964). Toys and reasons. In M. Haworth (Ed.), *Child psychotherapy* (pp. 3–11). New York: Basic.

Erikson, E. (1977). *Toys and reasons.* New York: W. W. Norton.

Foote, R., Eyberg, S., & Schuhmann, E. (1998). Parent-child interaction approaches to the treatment of child behavior problems. In T. H. Ollendick & R. J. Prinz (Eds.), *Advances in clinical child psychology* (Vol. 20; pp. 125–143). New York: Plenum.

Gardner, R. A. (1971). *Therapeutic communication with children: The mutual storytelling technique.* New York: Science House.

Gardner, R. A. (1993a). Checkers. In C. E. Schaefer & D. M. Cangelosi (Eds.), *Play therapy techniques* (pp. 247–262). Northvale, NJ: Aronson.

Gardner, R. A. (1993b). Mutual storytelling. In C. E. Schaefer & D. M. Cangelosi (Eds.), *Play therapy techniques* (pp. 199–209). Northvale, NJ: Aronson.

Gil, E. (1994). *Play in family therapy.* New York: Guilford.

Hellendoorn, J., der Kooij, R., & Sutton-Smith, B. (Eds.) (1994). *Play and intervention.* Albany, NY: State University of New York Press.

Johnson, J. H., Rasbury, W. C., & Siegel, L. J. (1997). *Approaches to child treatment: Introduction to theory, research, and practice.* Boston: Allyn & Bacon.

Kaduson, H. G., & Schaefer, C. E. (1993). *101 favorite play therapy techniques.* Northvale, NJ: Aronson.

Kendall, P., & Braswell, L. (1993). *Cognitive-behavioral therapy for impulsive children* (2nd ed.). New York: Guilford.

Kuhli, L. (1993). The use of two houses in play therapy. In C. E. Schaefer & D. M. Cangelosi (Eds.), *Play therapy techniques* (pp. 63–68). Northvale, NJ: Aronson.

Knell, S. M. (1993). *Cognitive-behavioral play therapy.* Northvale, NJ: Aronson.

McMahon, L. (1992). *The handbook of play therapy.* London: Tavistock/Routledge.

Moustakas, C. (1953). *Children in play therapy.* New York: Ballantine.

Oremland, E. K. (1993). Abreaction. In C. E. Schaefer (Ed.), *Therapeutic powers of play* (pp. 143–165). Northvale, NJ: Aronson.

Sarnoff, C. (1976). *Latency.* New York: Aronson.

Schaefer, C. E. (1993). What is play and why is it therapeutic? In C. E. Schaefer (Ed.), *Therapeutic powers of play* (pp. 1–15). Northvale, NJ: Aronson.

Shirk, S., & Saiz, C. C. (1992). Clinical, empirical and developmental perspectives on the therapeutic relationship in child psychotherapy. *Development and Psychopathology, 4,* 713–728.

Silvern, L., Karyl, J., & Landis, T. (1995). Individual psychotherapy for traumatized children of abused women. In E. Peled, P. G. Jaffe, & J. L. Edelson (Eds.), *Ending the cycle of violence: Community responses to children of battered women* (pp. 43–76). Thousand Oaks, CA: Sage.

Singer, D. G. (1993). *Playing for their lives.* Toronto: The Free Press.

Strayhorn, J. M. (1994). Psychological competence-based therapy for young children and their parents. In C. W. LeCroy (Ed.), *Handbook of child and adolescent treatment.*

Webb, N. B. (1991). *Play therapy with children in crisis.* New York: Guilford.

Watson, M. W. (1994). *Children at play: clinical and developmental approaches to representation and meaning: The relation between anxiety and pretend play.* New York: Oxford University Press.

SUGGESTED READING

Buchsbaum, H., Toth, S. L., Clyman, R. B., Cicchetti, D., & Emde, R. N. (1992). The use of a narrative story stem technique with maltreated children: Implications for theory and practice. *Development and Psychopathology, 4,* 603–625.

Schaefer, C. E., & Cangelosi, D. M. (Eds.). (1993). *Play therapy techniques.* Northvale, NJ: Aronson.

Wachtel, E. F. (1994). *Treating troubled children and their families.* New York: Guilford.

L. SILVERN
B. M. BAUGHAN
University of Colorado, Boulder

CHILD PSYCHOLOGY
PLAY
PLAYDEVELOPMENT

POLAND, PSYCHOLOGY IN

Psychological concepts and observations can be found in many Polish philosophical, pedagogical, and literary writings appearing before the 18th century. In the 19th century, several works were published that discussed psychological problems from the empirical viewpoint. The same viewpoint characterized the book considered the first textbook of psychology written in Polish, *The Philosophy of the Human Mind* (1821) by Jan Sniadecki, a philosopher, mathematician, and astronomer well versed in British empirical philosophy. In the second part of the 19th century, Polish intellectuals interested in psychology studied elsewhere, especially under Wilhelm Wundt, Franz Brentano, and Théodule Ribot. They became acquainted with experimental psychology, which they subsequently promoted in their country; one of the most active of these was Julian Ochorowicz (1850–1917).

THE FORMATIVE YEARS

Ochorowicz, who received his doctorate at Leipzig in 1874, was the first to lecture in Poland on psychophysics and psychophysiology, at the University of Lvov (1880–1887). In his systematic psychology, he combined the principles of Wundtian experimental psychology with concepts of French psychiatry. He was the first to point out the need for an international congress of all psychologists. His efforts were successful, and the First International Congress of Psychology convened in Paris in 1889. The scope of Ochorowicz's writings was varied, and included such subjects as the theory of evolution, criminology, psychopathology, hypnotism, and suggestion. William James was interested in Ochorowicz and read his books in French. One of his books was translated into English as *Mental Suggestion* (1887).

The earliest centers of psychological research and teaching were the Jan Kazimierz University in Lvov and the Jagiellonian University in Cracow, where the first psychological laboratories were established (1901 and 1903). Soon the University of Warsaw also became an influential center for psychology. Its laboratory, organized in 1910, was later expanded into a psychological institute. The heads of these centers—Kazimierz Twardowski (1866–1938), Wladyslaw Heinrich (1863–1957), and Edward Abramowski (1868–1918)—were the true builders and leaders of Polish psychology in the first decades of the 20th century.

Of these three leaders, the most respected and influential was Twardowski, founder of the first Polish psychological laboratory and professor at Lvov for 43 years. A student of Franz Brentano in Vienna, he also worked in Wundt's laboratory and studied under Carl Stumpf in Munich. For Twardowski, psychology was a science of mental life studied through introspection, resembling Brentano's psychological system, but strongly emphasizing precise logical analysis of psychological concepts. Polish psychological terminology owes much to Twardowski, who, because of his knowledge of German, French, and English, was able to express in Polish the meaning of psychological terms developed in other countries. Several generations of psychologists were taught by Twardowski.

Heinrich, in Cracow, was first and foremost an experimentalist. After his studies under Richard Avenarius in Zürich, he introduced experimental and physiological psychology in Cracow in 1897, and founded and directed the first Polish Institute of Experimental Psychology—which, for a long time, was the principal center of experimental research. He was an advocate of a psychology completely free from any philosophical bonds and based solely on experimentation and objective methodology. Abramowski had close contacts with French and Swiss scholars. He studied in Geneva, where he worked with Edouard Claparède. His early interest was the psychological foundation of sociology. He presented his ideas on this subject in a book in French, *Les Bases Psychologiques de la Sociologie* (1897). His experimentation on memory, subconscious phenomena, and particularly on will, won him recognition in Europe. Another Warsaw psychologist, who too became known in other European countries, was Jan W. Dawid (1859–1914). An early promoter of educational psychology, he was the author of an intelligence test for children (1911), which antedated the Binet test. This test was used extensively in Poland for almost 50 years. Dawid was the father of Polish psychometrics, which has remained one of the strongest fields in Polish psychology.

The problems studied and the methods used by Polish psychologists at the turn of the century, and after, were identical to those in other countries. The character of Polish psychology for the first 40 years of the 20th century was similar to that of most European psychology: introspectionistic, mentalistic, associationistic, and functional. However, the country's research facilities and resources were severely limited. Poland, from the end of the 18th century until 1918, was partitioned and occupied by Austria, Germany, and Russia. With the exception of the Austrian-occupied territory, Polish cultural life and the use of the Polish language were greatly suppressed. Therefore, psychology did not have the necessary conditions and freedom for normal growth and expansion. The area of psychology that traditionally has received the strongest support in Poland, because it was essential for the survival and development of the nation, was educational psychology, together with developmental psychology. Both fields usually have been linked together. It

is thus not surprising that the first Polish psychological journal was devoted to educational and developmental psychology, *Przeglad Pedagogiczny* (Pedagogical Review, 1882). Later another journal was devoted to these fields, *Chowanna, Educational Psychology* (in Polish), published in 1881 by a philosopher and psychologist, Henryk Struve, was probably the first book on educational psychology in any language, and is proof of an early interest in this field in Poland.

BETWEEN TWO WORLD WARS (1918–1939)

After Poland regained its political independence in 1918, psychology enjoyed more favorable conditions for development. Departments of psychology were established at the newly created universities—Lublin, Poznan, Warsaw (Free University), and Wilno. Psychology also was taught at teachers' training schools, secondary schools, and other educational institutions. General and educational psychology were the main subjects of teaching and research, but other branches were also represented in the academic curricula, such as psychometrics, psychophysiology, and social psychology.

Among the psychologists of the interwar period, the most influential—largely because of his textbooks—was Wladyslaw Witwicki (1878–1947), a professor at Warsaw University. Respected as an excellent teacher and eloquent speaker, he was also a prolific author. Witwicki was drawn more toward introspective, theoretical, and philosophical analyses than to laboratory investigations, whose value he nevertheless recognized. Experimental laboratory approach was represented by Stefan Blachowski (1889–1963), a long-time director of the Psychology Institute at Poznan University. He received his doctorate at the University of Göttingen, and later studied under Twardowski in Lvov. His experimental investigations dealt with sensations, perception, and learning. One of his major achievements was the founding and editorship of the leading psychological quarterly *Kwartalnik Psychologiczny*. International in character, it printed articles of foreign contributors in English, French, and German. For several years, Blachowski served on the editorial board of the American *Psychological Abstracts*.

Leaders in educational and developmental psychology were Stefan Baley (1885–1952) in Warsaw and Stefan Szuman (1889–1972) in Cracow. Both had medical degrees. Some facets of Baley's work were similar to Piaget's investigations on the development of children's thinking and speech. He initiated several innovative projects related to school psychology, psychological counseling, mental hygiene, forensic psychology, and care of prison inmates. Baley's greatest accomplishment was his *Educational Psychology* (in Polish, published posthumously in 1958), a synthesis of Polish and foreign investigations on the psychological foundation of educational theory and practice. Particular emphasis in this book was placed on the psychology of teaching. Szuman also carried out studies on the development of children's thinking, speech, emotions, and artistic creativity. Using questionnaires, diaries, and personal letters, Szuman and his collaborators surveyed views on the philosophy of life among Polish youth. Szuman's studies and theories generated a great deal of research and publication.

AFTER 1945

During World War II (1939–1945), Polish psychology, like the Polish nation itself, suffered heavy losses. Psychology departments were inactive, their laboratories and libraries destroyed or plundered. Many psychologists were imprisoned or lost their lives. As soon as the war ended, the reconstruction of the universities and scientific institutions began and proceeded at a rapid pace. The prewar departments of psychology were restored and new ones added in several new universities, at Gdansk, Lodz, Lublin, Torun, and Wroclaw.

Postwar psychology retained its prewar character and followed the former patterns of activity, but paid more attention to mental testing and practical applications in education, clinics, and industry. This type of psychology was not in harmony with the communist model of psychology. Labeled by the Marxists as "bourgeois," it was subjected to sharp attacks. When Soviet psychology—soon after the observance of the 100th anniversary of Ivan Pavlov's birth (1949)—was reorganized to conform to the teachings of Pavlov and postulates of the Communist party, Poland had to follow the Soviet model. As a consequence, psychological clinics, vocational guidance centers, and laboratories in industrial psychology were closed, and psychologists were forbidden to administer mental tests. The teaching of psychology in secondary schools was abolished. Specialization in psychology at the universities was no longer possible. Courses in psychology were offered only to students who planned to become school teachers. Psychologists who did not follow the Marxist line were barred from teaching and official positions, could not publish their works, and were not allowed to travel abroad. Psychology was almost completely cut off from Western psychology and its literature.

This period ended in 1956, when the annual convention of the Polish Psychological Association rejected ideological restrictions on research and practice. As the restrictions ceased and contacts with the West were restored, psychology gradually regained its former standing as science and profession. Nevertheless, the Marxist viewpoint had to be respected, and psychology's philosophical and methodological framework had to remain consistent with Marxism. Appointments to academic key positions had to be approved by the Communist party. While some psychologists actively promoted the Marxist viewpoint in their teaching, writing, and research, the majority stayed aloof from political activities, maintaining a strictly objective empirical attitude with respect to psychological issues of the day.

Educational and Developmental Psychology

Psychologists after the Stalinist era were eager to expand their field, and were receptive to new ideas and novel areas of psychological inquiry. Among the popular and active fields were educational psychology, psychometrics, and clinical psychology. Investigations concentrated particularly on learning and its disabilities, mental hygiene, vocational guidance and selection for special training, individual differences, and factors determining normal growth and development. A relatively new area of research was opened, the psychology of teaching, which included such topics as personality of the teacher, teacher-pupil interaction, and pupil interaction in and outside the classroom. Although the Poles showed a great deal of ingenuity and independence, the influence of Piaget, as well as that of some contemporary Soviet educational psychologists, was discernible. The organ of educational psychology is a bimonthly journal, *Psychologia Wychowawcza* (*Educational Psychology*). Each issue contains, in addition to articles and book reviews, resumés in Polish of articles that have appeared in U.S. educational and developmental journals.

Psychometrics

The testing movement, which started and flourished in interwar Poland, gained further momentum after World War II. Suppressed for a time, as indicated before, the movement resumed with renewed vigor. The tests were and are constructed for the needs of schools, vocational guidance, hospitals, and courts, and especially for clinical practice. The construction and use of tests has been coordinated by the Psychometric Laboratory of the Polish Academy of Sciences. Psychometrics was the principal activity of many psychologists. They examined all the standard tests used in other countries (mostly in the United States) and adapted them for their purposes. Engaged in these activities was Mieczyslaw Choynowski, at one time the head of the Psychometric Laboratory, whose contributions to psychometrics have been substantial. He spent some time in the United States, visiting testing centers and contacting prominent specialists in psychometrics.

Clinical Psychology

Of all the applied fields, clinical psychology is now the most popular specialty. Its focus is, according to the generally accepted concept elaborated by Andrzej Lewicki (1909–1973) and his associates, "disturbances of adjustment." Most clinical psychologists work with psychiatrists in mental hospitals, mental health clinics, and penal institutions. Clinical psychology was supported and helped by a prominent psychiatrist, Kazimierz Dabrowski (1902-1980), who in 1935 organized the Institute of Mental Hygiene in Warsaw. After the war, Dabrowski revived the institute, and in addition opened the Higher School of Mental Hygiene, whose aim was to train clinical psychologists. In 1965, Dabrowski migrated to Canada, where he promoted his own original psychotherapeutic system of "positive disintegration." According to him, disintegration of personality can have a positive and beneficial effect on personality and its growth. This system, which found a substantial number of followers in North America, was expounded by Dabrowski in several books, such as *Personality-Shaping Through Positive Disintegration* (1967) and *Mental Growth Through Positive Disintegration* (1970).

A specialty not well known to Western psychology is defectology. This term is applied to the borderland of clinical psychology and education of the handicapped. Its concern is directed to individuals who are deaf, blind, socially maladjusted, suffer from speech disorders, or are chronically ill. The task of the psychologist is to evaluate the developmental potentialities and rehabilitative possibilities of the patient and to design special training, school curricula, and methods of rehabilitation. The aim of defectology is to make the individuals active and independent, and to ensure them as rich a personal and social life as possible.

Physiological Psychology

Research in this field has always existed in Poland but has not attained prominence. This is true because of the structure of psychology departments at Polish universities, which relegated such studies to the biology departments. Examples of publications that were classified as contributions to physiological psychology were *Psychology of Animals* and *Psychology of Apes* (both in Polish, 1946), by an outstanding biologist, Jan Dembowski (1889–1963). The most significant achievements of international renown were made by Jerzy Konorski, M.D. (1903–1973) and his co-workers. After having discovered a new type of conditioned reflex, which later became known in the United States as operant behavior or instrumental conditioning, Konorski conducted many experiments to determine the neurophysiological mechanism of this reflex. He devoted his life to the study of not only conditioning, but other brain/behavior relations as well. His writings, especially his book *The Integrative Activity of the Brain* (1968), were well received in the United States.

PRESENT STATUS

Psychology in Poland is a vibrant and popular discipline that attracts many young people. The departments of psychology at various schools receive more applications for admission each year than they can accommodate. In 1980, there were about 5,000 psychologists. There are four psychological periodicals, and several other journals publish articles written by psychologists. The national psychological organization, founded in 1948, has 1,500 members and 17 local branches. National conventions of the Polish Psychological Association are held every second year. Governmental legislation regulates the professional status of psychologists.

All fields of psychology are represented, but the most popular branches are clinical, educational, and industrial psychology, in that order, indicating that psychology in Poland is clearly service oriented. In a socialist state, psychology is expected to be particularly sensitive to the social and individual needs of the nation, and therefore should give priority to the programs that would satisfy these needs and serve the interests of the country. Education and mental health care are at the top of this list.

The influence of American psychology is predominant in Poland. American psychological literature is widely read and discussed, and outstanding textbooks are promptly translated into Polish. The knowledge of current Western psychology is thorough and deemed indispensable in the training of psychologists.

There have been numerous and lively exchange programs between Poland and the United States. The Fulbright exchange program has proved particularly beneficial to both countries. Under this program, American psychologists have visited Poland, given lectures, presided at seminars, and offered regular academic courses, usually at the graduate level, and many eminent Polish psychologists visited U.S. psychological centers and established contacts with them. Scores of young people from Poland studied and conducted research at U.S. universities. Polish psychologists, on their part, are eager to inform Americans about their progress and attainments. Their books and journal articles often include re-

sumés in English. In 1970, a special journal in English was initiated, *Polish Psychological Bulletin,* to inform the Anglo-American psychological community about psychological activities in Poland.

The contributions made to American psychology by many Polish-born and Polish-trained psychologists who have made the United States their home are also worthy of mention. They have shared their talents and achievements with their adopted country. There are no statistics available, but a relatively large group of Polish-born psychologists have gained prominence and influence within U.S. psychology.

REFERENCES

Konorski, J. (1970/1967). *Integrative activity of the brain: An interdisciplinary approach.* Chicago: University of Chicago Press.

H. MISIAK
Fordham University

POLICE PSYCHOLOGY

The origins of American police psychology have been traced back to at least 1916, when Terman attempted to use the then-current Stanford-Binet test, First Edition, to identify "good" prospective police officers in California. His research indicated officers are likely to require a minimum IQ of 80 to adequately perform job duties. Few published contributions to police psychology ensued until the mid-twentieth century, when psychologists began to offer services to various local, state, and federal law enforcement organizations.

Precipitated by the advancements of police psychologists in the 1960s and 1970s, especially those of Reiser (1972) and his associates, a rapidly growing interest developed in providing psychological services to law enforcement agencies. Given the considerable growth during the past dozen years, police psychology is likely to be one of the principal directions of forensic and clinical psychological practice as we enter the third millennium.

WHAT IS IT?

Psychological services for law enforcement frequently involves new applications of traditional clinical and industrial-organizational psychological services. Police psychology is a specialty subsection of forensic psychology. Police psychology is the interface between the behavioral sciences and law enforcement.

Police psychological services are generally grouped into two categories: employee services and organizational services. Employee-oriented services generally recognize the employee as the client. Employee assistance services include counseling and assessment requested by the employee. Organizational services recognize the agency as the client and include preemployment psychological evaluations, fitness-for-duty evaluations, and management consultations. Hybrid services (such as crisis counseling) have developed which are both employee-oriented and organizational in nature. Crisis counseling may be requested and organized by the agency, but agency administrators have limited access to the process (Super, 1999). Police psychologists may provide services as agency employees or as contractual consultants, depending on the specific needs and resources of the agency.

Assessment

Approximately one-third of police psychologists assist in the selection of recruits for police training and in the selection of trainee graduates for positions in law enforcement. Psychologists conduct fitness-for-duty evaluations of police officers who have been in stressful or physically debilitating interactions while on the job. Psychologists have also participated in the assessment procedures for advanced placements and promotions within the law enforcement community (Blau, 1994).

Psychological assessment techniques, including interviews, objective personality tests, intelligence tests, and in vitro video-based assessment have been used to assist in the selection of law enforcement officers, corrections officers, and special police team members (SWAT, hostage negotiation, undercover agents, child protection specialists, and so forth). The three approaches commonly used in preemployment psychological evaluation include: (a) selection of the best suited applicants; (b) screening out of undesirable applicants; and (c) a combination of the two (Blau, 1994; Super, 1999).

Intervention

Psychologists provide therapeutic services for police officers who are under stress, such as grief counseling for police officers and families. The need for counseling may stem from officers who are injured or killed in the line of duty. Police psychologists provide family counseling, counseling services for the children of police officers, and drug and alcohol counseling. Police psychologists assist in establishing peer counseling teams within the law enforcement agency (Kurke & Scrivner, 1996). Some psychologists offer psychoeducational evaluations for officers' children to address issues which may peripherally affect the officer's ability to discharge sworn duties.

Operations. Psychologists may be requested to provide operational services, including investigative hypnosis, investigative strategies when working with mentally disturbed suspects, hostage negotiation, and offender psychological profiling (Blau, 1994; Reese & Solomon, 1996). Although the above services are frequently viewed by laypersons as being at the core of what police psychologists do, these types of services generally represent a small part of professional activity.

Training. Psychologists provide training in police academies on such topics as offenders, stress recognition and prevention, proper methods of addressing irate citizens' complaints, cultural diversity, interviewing techniques, interpersonal skills, effective communication, impulse control, suicide prevention and intervention, and group behavior. Psychologists provide continuing education for police officers who must earn a specified number of credits every several years to maintain their sworn status. Continuing education topics may range from the psychology of driving to stress inoculation.

Strategic Planning

Generally, law enforcement has been reactive rather than proactive to crime. Modern law enforcement administrators are becoming increasingly more proactive by attempting to address prospective community needs, employing new applications of psychological services, and attempting to address changing community needs. This is at the heart of strategic planning. Psychologists, primarily industrial and organizational psychologists, have been providing strategic planning consultations to police management with increasingly more regularity during the mid and late 1990s. Sensitivity and restraint training is an area which has recently been explored.

Research

One of the most important and most overlooked contributions by police psychologists is research involving the development of local norms, base rates, and predictive effectiveness (Super, 1999). Project funding has become more available as law enforcement administrators become more aware of the potential cost-benefits of research (Blau, 1994).

WHY IS THIS DEVELOPING NOW?

Police departments are currently being pressed to acquire accreditation. Accreditation is one method of demonstrating an agency's efficiency and modernization. As of 1999, the Commission on Accreditation for Law Enforcement Agencies (*CALEA*) has accredited 457 local agencies throughout the United States. There are approximately 17,000 local police agencies in the United States. Many of these will seek accreditation to participate in lower-cost risk management insurance plans. Accreditation requires departments to provide various psychological services, including preemployment psychological assessment, fitness-for-duty assessment, and assessment for hostage negotiations and SWAT team applicants. In the near future, accreditation guidelines are likely to require the availability of psychologists, on staff or as consultants, to respond to postcritical incident stress situations.

One of the agency administrator's greatest incentives for seeking psychological services is to decrease the probability of costly litigation against the department. Psychologists are helpful in selecting those people who will do the best possible job as law enforcement officers. Ongoing counseling and training by psychologists help those already working to maintain job skills and emotional stability in a stressful work setting.

WHAT'S NEXT?

Division 18 (Public Service) of the American Psychological Association (APA) has a Police Psychology and Public Safety subsection. Starting in about 1989 with 20 or so members, in 1999 there were approximately 252 members, including 3 fellows and 22 students in this subsection. Standards for preemployment psychological evaluations and fitness-for-duty evaluations have been developed and are under ongoing revision as new techniques emerge and as new applications of psychology to law enforcement arise. Several graduate institutions have begun to offer courses in police psychology.

REFERENCES

Blau, T. (1994). *Police psychology: Behavioral science services for law enforcement.* New York: Wiley.

Kurke, M., & Scrivner, E. (Eds.). (1996). *Police psychology in the 21st century.* Hillsdale, NJ: Erlbaum.

Reese, J. T., & Solomon, R. M. (Eds.). (1996). *Organizational issues in law enforcement.* Washington, DC: US Department of Justice, Federal Bureau of Investigation.

Reiser, M. (1972). *The police department psychologist.* Springfield, IL: Thomas.

Super, J. T. (1999). Forensic psychology and law enforcement. In A. Hess & I. Weiner (Eds.), *The handbook of forensic psychology,* (2nd ed., pp. 409–439). New York: Wiley.

SUGGESTED READING

Reese, J. T., & Scrivner, E. (Eds.). (1994). *The law enforcement family: Issues and answers.* Washington, DC: US Department of Justice, Federal Bureau of Investigation.

T. H. BLAU
J. T. SUPERS

FORENSIC PSYCHOLOGISTS: ROLES AND ACTIVITIES
FORENSIC PSYCHOLOGY
PSYCHOLOGY AND THE LAW

PORTEUS, STANLEY DAVID (1883–1972)

Stanley David Porteus, after a decade as a school teacher in Victoria, studied at the Melbourne Educational Institute and the University of Melbourne. During this period, he was superintendent of special schools in Melbourne. In 1919, he became director of research of the Psychological Laboratory at the Training School at Vineland, NJ. He moved to the University of Hawaii in 1922, where he was professor of clinical psychology and director of the psychological and psychopathic clinic. From 1948 until his death, he held the titles *emeritus.*

In 1929, Porteus led an expedition to northwest Australia, and another expedition to the Kalahari Desert of South Africa in 1934. He published two books on Hawaii and two novels—one about early Australia and the other concerning Archibald Campbell's voyage around the world in the early nineteenth century.

Porteus began his best known work in psychology while at the Vineland Training School. In 1915, he published his Porteus Maze Test as a supplement to Henry H. Goddard's 1909 translation of Alfred Binet's intelligence tests. The printed mazes on which the proper path was drawn with a pencil were used in the diagnosis of mental retardation. In particular, they were designed to measure

foresight and planning capacity. As soon as the subject made an error by entering a cul-de-sac or crossing a line, the maze was removed and a second trial given. The mazes were graded in difficulty from age 3 to adult. Since the mazes could be administered without verbal instructions and had no time limits, they were widely used in unusual circumstances. One adaptation was for cerebral-palsied children. The mazes were included in Grace Arthur's 1930 Point Scale of Performance Tests.

The technical quality of the Porteus Mazes restricts them to research use only. No information on consistency upon reexamination (reliability) is available and the comparison groups for the scores are inadequately described. Porteus himself stated that the utility or validation was far less than satisfactory.

In his other research, Porteus reported on cross-cultural abilities, particularly with African and Hawaiian groups. He also published articles on mental changes after psychosurgery, such as a bilateral prefrontal lobotomy.

C. S. PEYSER
The University of the South

POSTTRAUMATIC STRESS DISORDER IN ADULTS

DEFINITION OF PTSD

Posttraumatic stress disorder (PTSD) is an extreme psychobiological reaction to a traumatic event characterized by profound disturbances in cognitive, behavioral, and physiological functioning. The diagnosis is applied when an individual has experienced, witnessed, or been confronted with an event involving perceived or threatened loss of life, serious injury, or loss of physical integrity and which evoked fear, helplessness, or horror. This may include military combat, sexual or physical assault, motor vehicle accidents, and major disasters.

The DSM-IV symptoms of PTSD are organized under three clusters: 1) reexperiencing (e.g., intrusive thoughts, nightmares, flashbacks, and psychophysiological reactivity to reminders of the trauma); 2) avoidance and emotional numbing (e.g., avoiding stimuli associated with the trauma, and inability to experience a full range of emotions); and 3) hyperarousal (e.g., hypervigilance, exaggerated startle response, and sleep disruption). By definition, these symptoms must persist for more than one month and produce clinically significant distress or impairment.

PREVALENCE AND ETIOLOGY OF PTSD

Estimates of the prevalence of lifetime PTSD in the general adult population range from 1% to 12% (see Fairbank, Schlenger, Saigh, & Davidson, 1995). The probability of developing the disorder after exposure to a traumatic event depends largely on the nature and severity of the event; the highest rates have been observed in individuals exposed to military combat (30%; Kulka et al., 1990) and rape (49%; Breslau et al., 1998).

The relationship between trauma exposure and the development of PTSD is also mediated by a number of psychosocial and individual difference variables. Psychosocial risk factors for the development of PTSD include: family history of psychiatric illness, childhood trauma or behavior problems, and the presence of psychiatric symptoms prior to the trauma (see Fairbank et al., 1995). A number of individual difference variables also play a role in the etiology of the disorder. For example, the rate of PTSD in women, after controlling for trauma exposure, is approximately twice as high as the rate for men (Breslau et al., 1998). Personality traits may influence rates of trauma exposure or mediate the development of symptoms after exposure. For example, certain traits have been identified as possible liabilities for PTSD (e.g., introversion and neuroticism; Breslau, Davis & Andreski, 1995) while others appear to represent resilience factors (e.g., hardiness; King, King, Fairbank, Keane & Adams, 1998). To explain the gender differences in PTSD prevalence, some authors have reflected upon the types of traumatic events to which men and women are differentially exposed. Men are more likely to be exposed to moving vehicle accidents, while women are more likely to be exposed to sexual assault. Different types of events do evoke differential rates of PTSD (see Breslau et al., 1998).

ASSESSMENT OF PTSD

A comprehensive clinical assessment of PTSD should include administration of structured diagnostic interviews, self-report psychometrics, and an evaluation of trauma across the lifespan. Several structured interviews are available, and the Clinician-Administered PTSD Scale for the DSM-IV (Blake et al., 1990) and the PTSD module of the Structured Clinical Interview for the DSM—IV (First, Spitzer, Gibbon, & Williams, 1997) have become standards in the field. Self-report instruments can also assist in diagnosis or provide efficient, low-cost methods for research and screening purposes. Of these, several were constructed specifically for assessing PTSD (e.g., Mississippi Scale for Combat-Related PTSD; PTSD Checklist; PTSD Diagnostic Scale). Others were devised using existing items from major inventories such as the Minnesota Multiphasic Personality Inventory and the Symptom Checklist-90. Finally, instruments such as the Potential Stressful Events Interview and the Traumatic Stress Schedule are used to evaluate trauma across the lifespan. Virtually all of the available diagnostic measures of PTSD and self-report instruments possess excellent psychometric properties.

TREATMENT OF PTSD

Treatment for PTSD typically involves the use of psychotherapy, pharmacotherapy, or both. Of the psychotherapies, exposure-based approaches (e.g., systematic desensitization, flooding, prolonged exposure, imaginal and in vivo exposure, and implosive therapy) have received the most attention and empirical support to date (Keane, 1998). The common feature of each is the practice of gradually exposing the therapy client to trauma-related cues to desensitize and extinguish the accompanying conditioned emotional and physiological reactions. The therapeutic mechanism is generally conceptualized within the framework of classical conditioning; repeated exposure to trauma-related cues (e.g., trauma-related images evoked from memory) in the absence of the feared negative consequences (e.g., the trauma itself) reduces the conditioned fear, anxiety, and avoidance characteristics of PTSD.

A second promising category of empirically-validated treatments for PTSD is cognitive therapy. This approach is designed to identify and modify dysfunctional trauma-related beliefs and to teach specific cognitively-based coping skills. The procedure may also involve tasks that include an element of exposure, such as writing or describing the trauma to uncover trauma-related cognitions.

The third psychotherapy approach is anxiety management, variously referred to as relaxation training, stress inoculation, or biofeedback training. This approach does not focus on the trauma itself, but is instead geared toward teaching an individual the requisite skills for coping with stress, often via the use of relaxation. For this reason, anxiety management is often an adjunctive treatment to trauma-focused treatments.

Few controlled studies have directly compared treatments for PTSD. One recent study compared prolonged exposure, cognitive restructuring, combined exposure and cognitive restructuring, and relaxation training treatment (Marks, Lovell, Noshirvani, Livanou, & Thrasher, 1998). The authors reported that prolonged exposure and cognitive restructuring were each therapeutic when used alone; the effects were not additive when used together, but all three were more effective than relaxation. A more recent study compared prolonged exposure to stress inoculation and to their combination (Foa et al., 1999). All three active treatments were equally effective and better than a waitlist control group. There were some distinct advantages accorded to the prolonged exposure group.

Pharmacological treatment of PTSD is primarily designed to treat symptom clusters of PTSD, rather than the entire syndrome or any underlying physiological dysregulation. Several classes of antidepressants have been found to be modestly effective, including monoamine oxidase inhibitors, tricyclics, and selective-serotonin reuptake inhibitors (SSRIs; Yehuda, Marshall, & Giller, 1998). The SSRIs are currently the first choice of psychopharmacological treatment for PTSD.

REFERENCES

Blake, D. D., Weathers, F. W., Nagy, L. N., Kaloupek, D. G., Klauminset, G., Charney, D. S., & Keane, T. M. (1990). A clinician ratings scale for assessing current and lifetime PTSD: The CAPS-1. *Behavior Therapist, 18,* 187–188.

Breslau, N., Kessler, R. C., Chilcoat, H. D., Schultz, L. R., Davis, G. C., & Andreski, P. (1998). Trauma and posttraumatic stress disorder in the community. The 1996 Detroit area survey of trauma. *Archives of General Psychiatry, 55,* 626–632.

Breslau, N., Davis, G. C., & Andreski, P. (1995). Risk factors for PTSD-related traumatic events: A prospective analysis. *American Journal of Psychiatry, 152,* 529–534.

Fairbank, J. A., Schlenger, W. E., Saigh, P. A., & Davidson, J. R. T. (1995). An epidemiologic profile of Posttraumatic Stress Disorder. In M. J. Friedman, D. S. Charney, & A. Y. Deutch (Eds.), *Neurobiological and clinical consequences of stress: From normal adaptation to PTSD*. Philadelphia: Lippin-cott-Raven.

Foa, E. B., Dancu, C. V., Hembree, E., Jaycox, L. H., Meadows, E. A., & Street, G. (1999). A comparison of exposure therapy, stress inoculation training, and their combination for reducing posttraumatic stress disorder in female assault victims. *Journal of Consulting and Clinical Psychology, 67,* 194–200.

First, M. B., Spitzer, R. L., Gibbon, M., & Williams, J. B. W. (1997). *Structured Clinical Interview for DSM-IV Axis I Disorders—Clinician Version (SCID-CV)*. Washington, DC: American Psychiatric Press.

Keane, T. M. (1998). Psychological and behavioral treatments for post-traumatic stress disorder. In P. E. Nathan & J. M. Gorman (Eds.), *A guide to treatments that work* (pp. 398–407). New York: Oxford University Press.

King, L. A., King, D. W., Fairbank, J. A., Keane, T. M., & Adams, G. A. (1998). Resilience-recovery factors in post-traumatic stress disorder among female and male Vietnam veterans: Hardiness, postwar social support, and additional stressful life events. *Journal of Personality and Social Psychology, 74,* 420–434.

Kulka, R. A., Schlenger, W. E., Fairbank, J. A., Hough, R. L., Jordan, B. K., Marmar, C. R., & Weiss, D. (1990). *Trauma and the Vietnam War generation: Report of findings from the National Vietnam Veterans Readjustment Study*. New York: Brunner/Mazel.

Marks, I., Lovell, K., Noshirvani, H., Livanou, M., & Thrasher, S. (1998). Treatment of posttraumatic stress disorder by exposure and/or cognitive restructuring: A controlled study. *Archives of General Psychiatry, 55,* 317–325.

Yehuda, R., Marshall, R., & Giller, E. L., Jr. (1998). Psychopharmacological treatment of post-traumatic stress disorder. In P. E. Nathan & J. M. Gorman (Eds.), *A guide to treatments that work* (pp. 377–397). New York: Oxford University Press.

M. W. Miller
J. M. Pierce
T. M. Keane
Boston Department of Veterans Affairs Medical Center
Boston University School of Medicine

ANXIETY
FEAR
STIMULUS GENERALIZATION

POWER: STRATEGIES AND TACTICS

Power refers to the ability to make decisions that have an important impact and that involve others (Greenberg & Baron, 2000; McClelland, 1970, 1975; Winter, 1973). Often, power involves controlling the behavior of others, although many times those others voluntarily accept the directives of power holders without feeling any loss of independence. In everyday language, power refers to getting one's way, to having "clout." Many people are socialized to distrust power, to feel that only evil and manipulative individuals are interested in acquiring it, and to feel that they themselves should avoid places where powerful people congregate. In reality, power is like fire. It can be used for good intentions, and it can be used to pursue evil goals. Power and the strategies and tactics that go along with it may be viewed as a tool to further the goals people set for themselves (Brislin, 1991).

Some individuals want to be associated with powerful people. Assume that an individual is one of four junior executives in line for a promotion to the senior executive ranks. Each of the four candidates has a sponsor at the vice presidential level in the large organization. Each individual wants his or her sponsor to have power to implement the promotion to the higher level in the organization.

THE ROLE OF PERSONALITY IN POWER

Some people are more interested in acquiring power than others; the most effective power-holders possess a combination of motives. Four such motives or aspects of personality are (McClelland, 1975): (a) the need for *power*, which refers to the desire to have an impact on the lives of others; (b) the need for *achievement*, which refers to the desire to set and work toward goals, such as starting a new business or inventing a new computer technology; (c) the need for *affiliation*, which refers to the desire to be with and to interact pleasantly with others; and (d) *impulse control*, which refers to the ability to set aside any of the previous motives when required by the demands of the social situations in which individuals find themselves.

Leaders tend to be average to high in the power motive, which should be higher than the affiliation motive. There must be limits to powerholders' need for affiliation because they will inevitably make decisions that cause unhappiness among some people. On the other hand, there must be some affiliation motive or else power holders run the risk of becoming tyrants who have no concern for the impacts of their decisions on others (Kipnis, 1976). The achievement drive of power holders must be high enough that they set reasonable goals, but not so high that personal efforts to pursue the goals becomes paramount in their lives. Power holders do not necessarily do all the work to accomplish their goals themselves: They take steps to ensure that *others* do the work necessary to attain the goals. One reason that first-rate inventors or entrepreneurs sometimes become poor company presidents is that different motives are called for in different stages of a complex organization's development. To invent a new technology or to start a new business, a high achievement drive is necessary. If the technology or business is extremely successful, the power motive becomes necessary to manage the efforts of others involved in organizational efforts such as accounting, finance, research and development, legal matters, manufacturing, marketing, and so forth.

Impulse control is the ability to keep any one motive in check, or more informally, to say no to oneself. When attached to the power motive, impulse control leads to the ability not to use clout when the social situation calls for restraint. For example, a power holder might be tempted to use his or her power and shout at a secretary, fire a manager, or make a hasty decision about organizational expansion. With the desirable quality of impulse control, a leader can resist the temptation to use power and can think about the long-term disadvantages of giving in to temptations.

USING POWER

The power motive alone is no guarantee of success. Individuals must combine this motive with other ones for a proper balance among power, achievement, affiliation, and impulse control. Individuals must also learn a number of strategies and tactics for the successful use of power (Brislin, 1991; Fang, 1999; Yukl & Falbe, 1998). Although some of these strategies and tactics have a dark or manipulative side, many involve sensitivity to others, cooperative interaction, and the pursuit of goals that are often formulated in a democratic manner. When used in this positive manner, the intelligent and sensitive use of power can become part of effective leadership. Individuals without a power motive can become quite sophisticated about power; often, they learn that they need some knowledge of it to pursue their goals and that they are placed at a disadvantage if they avoid power and power holders. For example, a university professor who wants a new course of study introduced in the department may find that even if he or she is uninterested in power it may be necessary to know about it. Professors frequently learn that they must understand power to work through curriculum committees, deans, and boards of regents, not to mention through rival professors who have other plans for the limited resources that plague efforts to expand departmental offerings.

A strategy reflects careful planning about one's future because it refers to complex sets of behaviors (e.g., resource and network development and developing the image of a winner) that will have many positive implications in the pursuit of power. *Tactics,* on the other hand, refer to more specific behaviors useful at a certain time and place in the pursuit of specific goals (e.g., sending up trial balloons or providing firsthand experiences). Brislin (1991) developed an extensive list of both strategies and tactics useful in the acquisition and use of power; examples of each follow.

SOME STRATEGIES IN THE ACQUISITION AND USE OF POWER

Developing a Network and Exchanging Favors

Power is an aspect of relationships among people, and most powerful individuals have cordial interactions with a wide variety of others. Although one image of a power holder may be that of a deranged monarch ordering people to commit drastic deeds, reminiscent of a bad Hollywood movie influenced by Machiavelli, power holders are most often cordial people who communicate well with others (Kotter, 1982). This is especially true in a democracy, in which various institutional supports such as the legal system, unions, and the media enable people to complain about the callous behavior of leaders. Cordial relations with others are necessary because no one person has all the skills or knowledge needed to develop and implement complex projects. Assume, for example, that two executives want to suggest the development of a new product line. They must convince power holders, necessitating communication skills. They must research the present marketplace, necessitating knowledge of survey methods, finance, production, and accounting. They must make predictions about the eventual con-

sumption of the products, demanding knowledge of distribution systems. In addition, legal concerns will be raised at many steps in the planning process. No two people can possess all this knowledge. The two will have to integrate the efforts and talents of others.

These efforts will be much easier if the two executives know many other people who are part of a circle of acquaintances or a network (Nahavandi & Malekzadeh, 1999). These others may be old classmates, members of other departments within the same organization, people met through community activities or social gatherings, and so forth. People in one's network are not necessarily friends with whom one shares emotions. Rather, people in a network are useful to each other because they exchange favors. If people cease to be useful to one another, they each drop out of the other's network (Triandis, Brislin, & Hui, 1988; Triandis, 1995), although they may reenter into a network relationship later if they become mutually useful again.

The exchange of favors occurs in a manner similar to that described by Cialdini (1993). One member of a network knows tax law. He or she exchanges a few key pieces of advice with a lawyer who knows which terms found in advertising can be considered part of the public domain. Another person is especially knowledgeable about the ways that senior executives want proposals presented to them. He or she can exchange this information with another in the expectation that help will be forthcoming on the design of a survey instrument to measure market demands. People who are knowledgeable about organizational developments through active participation in the grapevine can exchange information learned for a variety of favors. There is a sense of obligation in the exchange of these favors: One is expected to receive and to give. One who does not return favors is simply dropped from network membership and finds him- or herself out of various information loops that keep people up to date regarding developments in their organizations. Network development and maintenance may seem cold and unfeeling, and yet people must be able to exchange favors with others if they are to develop complex projects and if they are to keep themselves informed about goings-on in large organizations. Many power holders know hundreds of people with whom they can exchange favors, but they cannot become deeply involved in the emotional lives of all them. Becoming comfortable with network development is necessary to becoming more sophisticated about the nature of power in decision making.

Resource Development

To become an active participant in networks, the individual must have a resource that becomes the source of the favors he or she can offer. Seven categories of resources have been identified in the analysis of power (Brislin, 1991; Foa, 1971): money, status, information, services, love and sex, goods, and the time and energy people can devote to various projects (Csikszentmihalyi, 1999). Money may be the most easily understandable of the resources, because funds are almost always needed to start and maintain projects. Furthermore, most people have competed for funds at some point (e.g., for a scholarship or a new project in school or church) and so are aware of the power that access to money can bring. Money also represents one aspect of unfairness in the pursuit of power: Chil-

1226 POWER: STRATEGIES AND TACTICS

dren who grow up with wealth and are heirs to it have an advantage. Without the advantage, providing services (e.g., volunteer activities within the community) can earn access. Individuals might ask themselves, "Where do influential people in my community meet?" Such places differ from city to city but may include the support guild for the opera or symphony, the blood bank, youth sports, clubs, political action groups, college alumni organizations, and so forth. There individuals can exchange their services (e.g., editing a newsletter or volunteering for committee work) for access to the influential people, with the eventual possibility of calling on these people for favors. Another possibility for the nonwealthy is information. Individuals might make a point of developing knowledge about information that everyone needs to know at some point but that is not easily or widely available. Candidates include tax law, statistics, computer technology, and how to make effective presentations to the general public. At times, the information can be the names and unlisted phone numbers of influential people in one's network, as long as these people are not so widely known as to be easily accessible to everyone.

Developing a Positive Image and Becoming a Winner

People are better able to communicate with and integrate the talents of others if they have the positive image of a winner. A winner is someone with the reputation for being successful, for being able to get things done, and for being able to set and to achieve goals. When people have a reputation for getting things done (Brislin, 1991), others want to become attached to them. In developing this positive image, Weick (1984) suggests that people be aware of the strategy known as small wins. Instead of setting goals so ambitious that people run the risk of failure and thus becoming known as losers, Weick suggests that people divide projects into a set of winnable steps. As people achieve success in attaining these steps, they develop good reputations. A positive reputation allows them access to resources that in turn permit them to set the next, somewhat more ambitious goal. Because one aspect of human nature is that others like to be associated with winners more than with losers, people who achieve success in their winnable goals will attract individuals willing to become involved in future efforts. With these additional resources and colleagues, more work can be done along the route to the accomplishment of ambitious goals. A subtle aspect of this strategy is that the key people may want to keep their eventual goals a secret and to behave as if each of the smaller steps is the only objective they have at any one time. If the eventual goal becomes widely known, that will become the focus of the attention of others, and a failure to attain it will tarnish reputations. If the smaller, more attainable goals are in the forefront, the key people can claim success as each is achieved.

For example, an assistant professor in a psychology department may want to introduce a multicourse curriculum aimed at increasing sensitivity to cultural, ethnic, racial, and gender issues. If he or she proposes such a program as the first action, the plan may be turned down because of budget restrictions and because the program does not include the concerns of certain powerful and tenured professors. Instead, the professor might propose a set of steps, keeping the eventual goal to himself or herself. He or she might develop a unit on race or gender and integrate it into the current introductory, social, or developmental course. If the class has 30 students, 5 of them may be good public speakers. The professor could ask each of these students to prepare a short presentation on a concept in psychology that has been informed by the study of race or gender and have these students present their ideas in a departmental colloquium. Influential professors may receive a personal invitation. After this experience, the assistant professor can propose a new course and can later suggest that other courses be added as enrollment figures demonstrate the demand. With success achieved in these steps, the assistant professor becomes known as a winner and his or her likelihood of finding support for the more ambitious goal is increased.

SOME TACTICS IN THE ACQUISITION AND USE OF POWER

As mentioned earlier, tactics are specific and identifiable behaviors that allow people to gain the support of others and to deal with opposition to their proposals (Fang, 1999; Yukl & Falbe, 1998).

Leaks and Trial Balloons

One of the facts individuals learn as they become more sophisticated about power is that there will be opposition to almost any proposal. Psychologists wanting more public funding of health care will find themselves unsupported by lawyers who want programs that provide legal services for the poor. Members of both these professions will find that others disagree about priorities. Educators will argue that a higher priority should be put on school facilities and teacher salaries; social workers will argue for increases in the food stamp program and in aid for dependent children. Even when all these proposals are widely recognized as worthwhile, people will find opposition from others who think that one is a higher priority than another in an era of tight budgets. Or they will find that other groups have the same goals, such as health care, but are proposing a different set of plans to address the same issues.

The case for any one person's proposal can be strengthened if the exact arguments of the opposition are clear. If probable criticisms are known, special attention can be given to countering them in the proposal. The criticisms can sometimes be identified through the use of leaks and trial balloons (Smith, 1988). Using leaks, people communicate some key ideas in their proposals without attaching their names to them. If opponents respond to the leaks, the reasons for criticism can be addressed in the actual proposal that has names attached to it. On issues of public policy, leaks can often be supplied to newspaper reporters who attribute the proposed ideas to unnamed community leaders. In organizations, ideas with an anonymous source can sometimes be put on the grapevine. This can be done by sharing the ideas with an active grapevine participant with a reputation for not revealing sources. Another way is to leave unsigned memos around the photocopy machine, as if someone were trying to make copies but forgot to take the original off of the machine. Later, users of the machine read the memo (human nature) and put the ideas into the grapevine.

Trial balloons are similar to leaks, but the sources of ideas are usually attached to any communication with others. The ideal trial balloon contains the essence of a proposal but is presented in such a way that it can be disavowed if necessary. Furthermore, the potential of a disavowal has to be thought through so that it can be done in a manner that does not damage the image of powerholders. In national politics, trial balloons can be launched by a *former* cabinet officer or other former high ranking official. The official appears on a political talk show and says that the administration is considering a policy change. If the later response from political commentators and elected representatives is favorable, then the president can later introduce the formal proposal. If the response is highly unfavorable, the current administration can disavow the ideas by saying that they are not being considered and that the former official was simply stating the ideas of a private citizen.

Sophisticated executives such as vice presidents of universities know they will occasionally appear foolish after sending up trial balloons that had been cleared at the highest administrative levels. If the public response to the proposals is highly negative, the university president will disavow knowledge of the proposals and will state that the lower ranking officials were speaking on their own and were exercising one of the great hallmarks of academic freedom.

Clear Images and Firsthand Experiences

When one communicates with others to enlist their support, one's messages should contain clear images that will remain in the memories of others. People are exposed to so much information through newspapers, television, magazines, and interpersonal exchanges that they can easily be overwhelmed. Potential power holders who want attention paid to their proposals must compete for people's attention. One tactic is to personalize the message. If a proposal calls for a new leukemia treatment center at the state hospital, communications that stress how many individuals will benefit may compete poorly with the many general statements the intended listeners hear everyday. If the communication stresses the benefits to one specific leukemia victim who is described in a way that appeals to people's long-term memories, then more support for the proposal may be forthcoming. For example, a young girl named Michelle could be described as one who had to give up her position on the neighborhood baseball team because of leukemia. The communication could then stress the help that could be given to Michelle "and all the other children like Michelle afflicted with this dread disease." Virtually all newspaper and television reports on community events include face-to-face interviews with someone involved. Journalists long ago discovered that the personalization of news stories increases attention.

Clear images can often be conveyed through firsthand experiences (Elms, 1972; Pettigrew, 1998). People who become involved in firsthand experiences develop clear memories because their own actions and observations become part of their image of a policy issue. Firsthand experiences have more impact than secondhand stories about an issue because people become actively involved, can ask questions that reflect personal concerns, and can reflect on others' responses to their concerns. To continue with the previous example, potential supporters could be given a tour of the current hospital facilities. There, they would meet several children carefully chosen for their attractiveness and articulateness. The people seeking support should stress that the prognosis for some of these children is good as long as modern medical treatment is readily available. The potential supporters would be encouraged to see for themselves that these children could receive much better treatment if the proposal could be implemented.

Sandboxes and Boogeymen

Some tactics are useful for dealing with opposition to proposals. One is to give the opponents a so-called sandbox, or a seemingly important task that has no long-term implications for policy development in an organization. The opponents become so busy playing in the sandbox that they leave the power holders alone. This is a common tactic found on university campuses. Department chairs sometimes find themselves faced with an angry group of students who are opposing a policy change that will add more required courses. The chair then asks the students to do a study on the types of courses that university alumni have found most helpful both in job searches and career development. The students may busy themselves with this important-sounding study, but in actuality the department chair can make recommendations for required courses whatever the results of the study. If the chair finds that the study results are consistent with his or her recommendations, then the study can be included in any formal proposal. If the chair finds that the study supports the students' recommendation for no new courses, then the study can be dismissed. Favorite reasons for the latter action include sample sizes too small, sampling biases, and the fact that the students had insufficient time for a definitive study.

Appealing to boogeymen is another tactic to deal with an opposition. Children learn about boogeymen as the source of severe punishment for not sharing their candy with friends or for behaviors that are interpreted as slights by other children. When applied to adult interactions, boogeymen are vague sources of power, not clearly visible, to which a power holder can appeal. Returning to the assistant professor and the coursework proposals, an unsympathetic department chair can say something like, "Sharon, I'm all for it, but the board of regents just wouldn't go for this in these budget-conscious times." In actuality, the chair has only the vaguest idea of how the board of regents would react. But by appealing to the boogeymen regents, the chair hopes to distract the assistant professor from her goals.

It is not recommended that people use sandboxes and boogeymen, because of the negative ethical implications. Rather, these tactics are discussed so that the reader will recognize them when used by the opposition. At times, such tactics can be countered. If one knows that a sandbox task is being proposed, he or she might say, "I appreciate your efforts to get me involved. I wonder, however, if my talents would be better used in task more related to the proposal." If one thinks that boogeymen are being called on, he or she might say, "I appreciate your pointing that out. Which regents do you think I could approach face to face to convince them of the proposal's quality?" Even if unsuccessful in changing the assignment or obtaining names, one will often communicate that he or she is sophisticated about the use of power, and that clever tactics should not be used against him or her. Power holders may conclude that one knows what is going on and that one should be taken seriously in the future.

BECOMING MORE SOPHISTICATED

Some people learn quite early about power as part of their socialization when they see their lawyer or politician parents participating in networks, exchanging favors, developing complex plans, and working on strategies and tactics. Others do not have access to the application of power when they are young and must learn about it as adults. One way to become more sophisticated is to participate in voluntary community activities. In addition to developing a network, people can observe the processes of coalition formation, effective communication of ideas, creation of a winning image, and so forth (Brislin, 1991). A further possibility is to obtain a seat on the community activity's budget committee. No matter what proposal for the use of money is put forward, it is guaranteed that someone will prefer another use. In observing how successful people use skills, strategies, and tactics to push forward their preferred plans, careful observers can learn a great deal about power's use. They can also learn that the most sophisticated approach is to not view power as an end in itself. Rather, power should be looked on as a tool to be used in compassionate and intelligent leadership.

REFERENCES

Brislin, R. (1991). *The art of getting things done: A practical guide to the use of power.* New York: Praeger.

Cialdini, R. (1993). *Influence: Science and practice* (3rd ed.). New York: HarperCollins.

Csikszentmihalyi, M. (1999). If we are so rich, why aren't we happy? *American Psychologist, 54,* 821–827.

Elms, A. (1972). *Social psychology and social relevance.* Boston: Little, Brown.

Fang, T. (1999). *Chinese business negotiating style.* Thousand Oaks, CA: Sage.

Foa, U. (1971). Interpersonal and economic resources. *Science, 171,* 345–351.

Greenberg, J., & Baron, J. (2000). *Behavior in organizations* (7th ed.). Upper Saddle River, NJ: Prentice-Hall.

Kipnis, D. (1976). *The powerholders.* Chicago: University of Chicago Press.

Kotter, J. (1982). What effective general managers really do. *Harvard Business Review, 60*(6), 157–167.

McClelland, D. (1970). The two faces of power. *International Affairs, 24*(1), 29–47.

McClelland, D. (1975). *Power: The inner experience.* New York: Irvington.

Nahavandi, A., & Malekzadeh, A. (1999). *Organizational behavior: The person-organization fit.* Upper Saddle River, NJ: Prentice-Hall.

Pettigrew, T. (1998). Intergroup contact theory. *Annual Review of Psychology, 49,* 65–85.

Smith, H. (1988). *The power game: How Washington works.* New York: Random House.

Triandis, H. (1995). *Individualism and collectivism.* Boulder, CO: Westview.

Triandis, H., Brislin, R., & Hui, C. H. (1988). Cross-cultural training across the individualism-collectivism divide. *International Journal of Intercultural Relations, 12,* 269–289.

Weick, K. (1984). Small wins: Redefining the scale of social problems. *American Psychologist, 39,* 40–49.

Winter, D. (1973). *The power motive.* New York: Macmillan.

Yukl, G., & Falbe, C. (1998). Influence tactics in upward, downward, and lateral influence attempts. *Journal of Applied Psychology, 75,* 132–140.

R. W. BRISLIN
College of Business Administration, University of Hawaii

ACCULTURATION
APPLIED RESEARCH
LEADERSHIP STYLES
SOCIAL EXCHANGE THEORY
SOCIAL INFLUENCE

PRAISE

Praise is defined as warm approval. The term implies both information about the correctness of an action, and a positive evaluation of the action. It is commonly accepted that praise has an effect on behavior. It is one of the most frequently used reinforcers in a variety of settings.

Most research on praise has been conducted in school settings and has concerned the variables that contribute to the effectiveness of praise as a reinforcer. In general, praise is most effective with students in the lower grades. At these grade levels, it is particularly effective with students of low ability and those from low socioeconomic backgrounds. In their book on *Classroom Management,* Daniel and O'Leary conclude that praise is most effective when it is contingent only on the desired behavior, refers to the specific behavior, and is credible.

Researchers in the field of attribution theory note that praise affects the attributions of our own and others' ability. Low ability is attributed to individuals who are praised for success, but receive neutral feedback for failure. High ability is attributed to individuals who are criticized for failure, but receive neutral feedback for success (Meyer et al., 1979).

A number of psychologists and educators, including John Holt, Maria Montessori, Jean Piaget, and Donald Tosti, suggest that praise is harmful to the educational process. They argue that praise interferes with intrinsic motivation, and hence has a negative effect on the student's learning in the long run. There is empirical support for this thesis. In a review of studies of praise, Eden (1975) concluded that inappropriate praise lowers motivation. Students who expect no extrinsic rewards for good work seem to respond negatively to praise or other extrinsic motivation.

Praise is an example of a common-sense construct that is found to be more complex than generally supposed when it is subjected to empirical research. Praise is not universally effective; it is effective in certain situations when delivered in certain ways. The research on praise has enabled teachers and others to use praise effectively rather than haphazardly.

REFERENCES

Eden, D. (1975). Intrinsic and extrinsic rewards and motives. *Journal of Applied Social Psychology, 5,* 348–361.

Meyer, W. U., Bachmann, M., Biermann, U., Hempelmann, M., Plöger, F. O., & Spiller, H. (1979). The informational value of evaluative behavior: Influences of praise and blame on perceptions of ability. *Journal of Educational Psychology, 71,* 259–268.

SUGGESTED READING

Brophy, J. (1981). Teacher praise: A functional analysis. *Review of Educational Research, 51,* 5–32.

R. A. Shaw
Brown University

REWARDS AND INTRINSIC INTEREST
SCHOOL LEARNING

PRECOCIOUS DEVELOPMENT

Precocity refers to an earlier than expected maturation level. The term is often used to refer to untimely ripeness or premature fruiting. A child who is described as precocious has developed more and earlier than expected for a child that age.

Early development can be general or specific in its manifestation. General precocity refers to a child advanced in numerous areas: intellectual, social, and physical. Specific precocity is more often the case, and this typically does not present any adverse conditions for the child. However, precocity symptomatic of biological untimeliness is often pathological in that the biological patterns are highly regulated by genetic composition. Any deviations in biological development tend to produce distortions in physical structure. Females who display precocious puberty develop pubic hair, breast enlargement and contour, and menses at very young ages. Males who display precocious puberty show signs of hirsutism or virilization. Recent studies have suggested that nutritional and body composition may influence the development of reproductive competence in mammals. Witchel, Arslanain, and Lee (1999) reported no significant relationships between circulating gonadotropin and leptin concentrations. This is important because prior assumptions held that leptin concentrations communicated nutritional status to the neuroendocrine reproductive axis (Heger, Partsch, Peter, Blum, Kiess, & Sippell, 1999). Individuals with neurodevelopmental disabilities are more at risk for premature sexual development when compared to children without a neurodevelopmental disability (Siddiqi, Van Dyke, Donohue, & McBrien, 1999). This has been reported for Williams syndrome (Cherniske, Sadler, Schwartz, Carpenter, & Pober, 1999). An interesting case study involving monozygotic twin females both with neurofibromatosis type I (nf1) found that the sister with optic pathway glioma developed precocious puberty, but the sister without the optic pathway glioma did not (Kelly, Sproul, Heurta, & Rogol, 1999). While precocious puberty is often found in nf1 patients, it is almost always associated with the optic pathway glioma.

Another type of a specific biological precocity involves premature "old age," in which the young sufferers actually die from symptoms of old age (rapid deterioration of the body and its organs, etc.). Precocity of cognitive functions has been reported on in the literature for centuries. For example, J. S. Mill is said to have learned Greek by the age of 3.

While precocious puberty and aging are more clearly biologically traced, it is difficult to discern whether precocious cognitive development is a result of biological factors or environmental influence.

REFERENCES

Cherniske, E. M., Salder, L. S., Schwartz, D., Carpenter, T. O., & Pober, B. R. (1999). Early puberty in Williams syndrome. *Clinical Dysmorphia, 8*(2), 117–121.

Heger, S., Partsch, C. J., Peter, M., Blum, W. F., Keiss, W., & Sippell, W. G. (1999). Serum leptin levels in patients with progressive central precocious puberty. *Pediatric Research, 46*(1), 71–75.

Kelly, T. E., Sproul, G. T., Heurta, M. G., & Rogol, A. D. (1999). Discordant puberty in monzygotic twin sisters with neurofibromatosis type 1 (nf1). *Clinical Pediatrics, 37*(5), 301–304.

Siddiqi, S. U., Van Dyke, D. C., Donohue, P., & McBrien, D. M. (1999). Premature sexual development in individuals with neurodevelopmental disabilities. *Developmental Medical Child Neurology, 41*(6), 392–395.

Witchel, S. F., Arsinian, S., & Lee, P. A. (1999). Leptin concentrations in precocious puberty or untimely puberty with and without GnRH analogue therapy. *Journal of Pediatric Endocrinology & Metabolism, 12*(6), 839–845.

R. A. Leark
Pacific Christian College

EARLY CHILDHOOD DEVELOPMENT
HUMAN DEVELOPMENT
LIFE-SPAN DEVELOPMENT

PREJUDICE AND DISCRIMINATION

Although often employed interchangeably by lay persons and the media, the terms *prejudice* and *discrimination* possess distinct meanings for most social scientists. The former denotes the possession of *negative attitudes* of a particular kind regarding members of a specific group or category; the latter is the term applied to the *negative actions* that result from prejudicial attitudes and that are directed against the targets or victims of prejudice. Someone who is prejudiced may, in certain situations, practice discrimination.

More specifically, social scientists view prejudice as the possession of negative attitudes targeted at members of some particular group (religious, racial, ethnic, political)—attitudes that give rise to negative or unfavorable evaluations of individuals seen as belonging to that group. The perception that one belongs to a certain group is the precipitating factor in prejudicial feelings—not the actual attributes or behaviors of the person being judged. Prejudiced individuals may fall victim to errors in the processing and recall of information regarding the objects of their negative feelings. Such individuals will, over time, come to think of their "targets" in a certain way, and effectively will filter out or ignore information inconsistent with or contrary to what they have come to believe about those targets.

As an attitude, prejudice is seen as having a tripartite nature, as possessing cognitive, affective, and behavioral components.

A person's beliefs and expectations regarding a particular group constitute the cognitive component of the prejudicial attitude. The term *stereotypes* has come to designate networks or clusters of such beliefs and expectations. The basis of all stereotypes is the that all those who belong to a specific category or group—ethnic, religious, racial, political, or any other classification—manifest similar behaviors and possess similar attitudes. The widespread application of stereotypes largely ignores human differences and individual differences.

Individuals who are prejudiced against specific groups will tend to experience intense negative feelings when they come into contact with these groups, either directly or indirectly. The affective component of the prejudicial attitude comes into play here, with profound negative emotional feelings tending to accompany cognitive reactions to objects of prejudice.

The behavioral component of prejudice has engendered the most research interest. Here the concern is the tendency of prejudiced individuals to act in a negative manner toward targets of their prejudice. When such tendencies become manifest in overt behavior, discrimination is said to occur. Numerous constraints upon behavior that may be operating in everyday situations may prevent existing prejudicial feelings from being transformed into discriminatory behavior. If such obstacles are not present in a given instance, however, the prejudicial thought or tendency can find expression in the behavioral act, which may vary in intensity from the lowest level, mere social avoidance, to acts of extreme violence, or even genocide.

The magnitude of the social problem represented by prejudice and discrimination, along with the waves of social concern they have engendered, have given rise to a subset of new terminology. *Tokenism* refers to a form of subtle discrimination marked by a tendency on the part of prejudiced individuals to behave in an overtly positive, accommodative manner toward the objects of their prejudice when such behavior extracts little cost or involves minimal effort. What makes tokenism such a potentially destructive force is that it can be used to rationalize discriminatory behavior at higher levels of social significance: To act in a group's behalf in some small way today may excuse one from making more substantial concessions or sacrifices at some later date. Other terminology that has appeared in response to the increasing research emphasis on questions involving prejudice and discrimination includes *sexism* and *ageism.* The former refers to prejudicial attitudes held toward females or males as a group; the latter signifies prejudicial attitudes directed against the elderly as a group. Both terms embrace not only beliefs and feelings held regarding the target groups, but discriminatory tendencies as well.

The attitudinal nature of prejudice has generated measurement research modeled after much of the attitude literature. The cognitive, affective, and behavioral components of prejudice have all been the object of research directed at assessing the nature and extent of prejudice in the population at large. The cognitive or belief component of prejudice, the assessment of stereotypes, is generally tapped through a trait-selection procedure. Individuals are given a list of ethnic, religious, racial, and political categories and a list of traits, and are asked to note which traits are associated with which group(s). Information on the affective or feeling component of prejudice is generally derived through the use of attitude scales engineered to measure the level of an individual's positive or negative feelings toward specific groups. Respondents may be provided with a list of polar adjectives and asked to rate certain groups accordingly; or they may be given a series of statements pertaining to one or another group and asked to indicate the level of their agreement or disagreement (a Likert-type scale). The *social distance scale* is an important tool in research into the behavioral component of prejudice. Subjects are presented with a series of hypothetical relationships between themselves and members of specific groups. The series of items represents increasing levels of closeness or intimacy between respondents and members of various groups (ranging from residing in the same country at the lowest level to intermarriage at the highest level), with the subjects being asked to indicate, for a given group, their willingness to accept individuals from that group into a given level of intimacy.

F. L. DENMARK
Pace University

AGGRESSION
ANDROGYNY
ATTITUDES
ETHNOCENTRISM
SCAPEGOATING
STEREOTYPING

PREMARITAL INTERVENTION

One of the most important developments in the field of marriage over the past decade has been an increase in the understanding of the factors that predict marital success. Using this new knowledge, researchers have developed programs to help couples stay happy and prevent marital distress and divorce. Most often, such preventive efforts take place in the context of premarital intervention (Stanley, Markman, St. Peters, & Leber, 1995). The term "intervention" is preferable to "counseling" since the former is conceptually consistent with the preventive framework.

THE NEED FOR INTERVENTION

Most adults seek a long-term relationship in marriage. This is not surprising, since marriage is good for the mental and physical health of spouses (e.g., Lillard & Waite, 1995). Numerous studies have shown that, overall, married people have lower rates of mental health problems, better physical health, and longer life spans than do unmarried people. In addition, growing up in a home with two stable and happy parents is probably one of the best protective factors for children against a wide variety of mental, physical, educational, and peer-related problems (Markman, Halford, & Lindahl, in press).

However, not all marriages are associated with these positive outcomes. Despite the fact that marital divorce rates have decreased throughout the 1980s and into the 1990s, couples marrying for the first time continue to face a projected 40 to 50% lifetime chance of divorce (U.S. Bureau of the Census, 1992, p. 5). Countless other couples never divorce but remain in distressed and/or abusive relationships (Notarius & Markman, 1993).

Importantly, marriages that become distressed are associated with numerous mental and physical health problems, including depression, especially in women, and alcoholism, especially in men (see Halford & Bouma, 1997, for a review). In fact, living under conditions of high levels of marital conflict constitutes a major risk factor for both the parents and children involved (Coie et al., 1993; Grych & Fincham, 1990). While initial investigations focused on the negative effects of divorce, recent studies have suggested that the destructive conflict that often precedes divorce is more damaging to parents and their children (Markman, et al., in press). Thus, a major goal of psychologists is to help couples stop their marriages from becoming distressed, thereby avoiding this array of negative consequences and instead continuing to reap the physical and psychological benefits of a healthy marriage.

THE CASE FOR PREVENTION

Since the divorce rate skyrocketed in the 1960s and 70s, the dominant mode of intervention with couples has been marital therapy, initiated after the marriage has become distressed. This type of intervention, however, has been shown to have some significant limitations. Although marital therapists are able to achieve success comparable to that from other forms of intervention, they are typically not able to move distressed couples into the nondistressed or happy range—even with the best of treatment protocols or counseling efforts (Halford, 1998).

Thus, since psychologists and marital therapists are not able to recreate the positive characteristics of marriages once they have deteriorated, perhaps the best way to help promote successful marriages is to help happy couples stay happy. To do so, the field must intervene at the beginnings of relationships. Research has shown that divorce is most likely to occur in the first 7 to 10 years of marriage (Glenn, 1998), and that how couples interact and manage conflict during this early critical period is strongly related to risk for future marital failure (Clements, Stanley, & Markman, 1998;

Gottman, Coan, Carrere, & Swanson, 1998; Matthews, Wickrama, & Conger, 1996). Thus, prevention programs for couples have received increasing attention as viable ways to reduce relationship distress and divorce.

PREVENTION PROGRAMS

The field of prevention science identifies three broad types of prevention programs: universal, selected, and targeted. Applied to prevention with couples, *universal* prevention programs are open to all couples in a specific population, usually defined by developmental stage (e.g., couples planning marriage, preparing to have their first child, etc.). *Selected* programs are designed for couples who are at higher risk for problems, such as couples with at least one partner who experienced parental divorce, aggression, or alcoholism. *Targeted* programs are aimed at couples who are already showing early signs of distress (e.g., first time low-level aggression). Here, we will focus on universal and selected programs that are designed to keep happy couples happy, since targeted programs are essentially early-treatment rather than preventive programs.

Universal or selected prevention programs for couples have typically focused on assessment and awareness of self and partner, enhancing knowledge for decision making, and development of interpersonal skills (Silliman, Stanley, Coffin, Markman, & Jordan, in press). Two key preventive strategies are raising protective factors and lowering risk factors for marital distress and divorce. Protective factors, or factors that increase the chance that couples will do well over time, include friendship between spouses (e.g., Markman, Stanley, & Blumberg, 1994), interpersonal support (e.g., Pasch & Bradbury, 1998) and mutual dedication (Stanley & Markman, 1992). A potent risk factor linked with increased chance of marital failure is negative communication (e.g., Clements, Stanley, & Markman, 1998; Gottman, 1994). Thus, preventive interventions often aim at increasing or enhancing these protective factors as well as teaching skills to help couples avoid risk factors for relationship distress.

Programs do vary, however, by the techniques they emphasize. Specifically, Relationship Enhancement (Guerney, 1977) focuses on empathy-building and communication skills. Couple Communication is a communication skills training program, including self- and other-awareness exercises (Miller, Wackman, & Nunally, 1976). Some recently developed programs focus on active listening and empathy (e.g., Long, Angera, Carter, Nakamoto, & Kelso, 1999).

One of the most extensively researched programs is PREP (Prevention and Relationship Enhancement Program), which aims at lowering risk factors through in-depth skills training in conflict management, and raising protective factors by teaching couples how to protect the positive elements in marriage (e.g., Markman, Stanley, & Blumberg, 1994). PREP is an empirically-based, short-term, psychoeducational program that is delivered in roughly one to six sessions, lasting anywhere from 6 to 16 hours. Couples receive the intervention in group format, where they listen to lectures and presentations and watch videotapes of various forms of destructive and constructive ways of handling marital conflict. The couples then work with trained coaches to learn the skills taught in the program. Other researchers are developing a program that uses much of the material from PREP, but focuses more strongly on promoting enrichment of the relationship (e.g., CARE; Rogge & Bradbury, 1999).

DO PREVENTION PROGRAMS WORK?

Perhaps the best known research effort in this area involves the implementation of PREP and its variations. Results clearly indicate that couples can learn the skills taught in the program and maintain the use of these skills for up to 15 years after the program ends. Further, in two of the major studies on PREP, the program is associated with substantially lower divorce and/or breakup rates up to five years following intervention (see Stanley et al., 1999). For example, in a long-term follow-up of the German version of the program, PREP intervention couples had a divorce rate of 4%, while control couples who received alternative premarital intervention or no intervention had a divorce rate of 24% (Hahlweg, Markman, Thurmaier, Engl, & Eckert, 1998).

Similarly, evaluations of Relationship Enhancement (RE) have found gains in communication skills, disclosure, and empathy for RE participants over those participating in control groups (Avery, Ridley, Leslie, & Milholland, 1980; Heitland, 1986). However, other studies have not shown sustained gains in disclosure or in problem-solving skills (Ridley & Bain, 1983; Ridley, Avery, Harrell, Leslie, & Dent, 1981). In a review of studies on Couples Communication, Wampler (1990) found that couples showed strong gains in quality of communication following participation, but that these gains diminished over time.

There are problems in interpreting the results of these studies, including nonrandom assignment (in some cases) and selection effects. However, there is no doubt that the field has made great strides in offering to couples, while they are still happy, the benefits of research and theory that enable them to increase their odds of having a successful marriage.

PREVENTION IN THE COMMUNITY: REACHING OUT

Despite the promise of enhancing marital success and preventing divorce through the use of empirically based premarital interventions, the vast majority of couples marrying today do not benefit from these programs. Since most couples do not typically interact with the mental health professionals who administer the research-based programs, not many couples are being informed about and/or trained in skills proven to protect and enhance marriages. In fact, prevention efforts will likely be unsuccessful in reaching couples at risk for mental health and relationship problems, if the field keeps targeting mental health professionals to train and to deliver these programs. Mental health professionals are not trained in prevention, typically do not share prevention ideology, and cannot earn a living delivering prevention programs even if they do care about prevention goals. Furthermore, most couples will not seek out mental health professionals for any service, let alone prevention services. For example, it is estimated the 90% of couples who divorce will never have seen a marital therapist (Markman et al., in press).

People will, however, turn to other help providers. In particular, scientists in divorce prevention in the United States have viewed re-

ligious organizations as central in the dissemination of divorce prevention efforts (Stanley et al., 1995; Stanley, 1997). This is logical, given that roughly 75% of marriages take place in churches or synagogues and that such agencies—particularly the Catholic Church—have historically advocated premarital education. Furthermore, this messenger is close to the couple on many important dimensions (ethnicity, religion, proximity). Even this premarital intervention in religious institutions has been transformed over the last 25 years; generally, religious institutions, which have traditionally offered educational forums and information sessions for couples, are shifting to embrace more research-oriented approaches to divorce prevention. One such research-based prevention program, PREP (mentioned earlier), is now being effectively administered to engaged couples in religious organizations (ROs) by their clergy (Stanley et al., 1999).

In other marriage-saving movements (e.g., McManus, 1996), one community-oriented approach involves the mentoring of engaged or newly-married couples by successful or resilient, older couples in the church. Although these latter premarital counseling efforts do not typically adopt researched prevention programs such as PREP, they often incorporate the use of reliable and valid premarital inventories developed by marital and family researchers (e.g., Olson, Fournier, & Druckman, 1986) to aid in identifying couples at risk for divorce within their congregations (for a review of valid premarital inventories, see Larson et al., 1995).

FUTURE DIRECTIONS

Many couples are likely to have a successful marriage and have less need for premarital intervention than do higher risk couples. Therefore, more recent efforts have been focused on such couples—for example, those who as children experienced conflict and divorce in their families or those whose parents suffered mental or physical health problems (see the work of Halford et al., in Australia). Moreover, a program will be helpful to the extent that it is available at low or no cost in a community setting, with an agenda that fits the developmental stage of the couple. The program should be offered in an appropriate setting and needs to be contextualized to the ethnic and cultural background of the couple. It would also be helpful if components were added to deal with the specific needs of the couple (e.g., dealing with work stress, parenting issues, health-related problems, retirement adjustments, etc.). Another avenue through which prevention efforts may be effectively and broadly channeled is the media. Such efforts might range from more structured home video adaptations of programs like PREP, to take-home messages from popular TV and radio shows, magazines, and books (Sanders, 1999).

In general, prevention efforts will likely succeed when they are offered by organizations and people that couples naturally have contact with and already trust. In these settings, services are normalized, educational, inexpensive (if not free), and relatively brief, accommodating a large number of couples and families.

REFERENCES

Avery, A. W., Ridley, C. A., Leslie, L. A., & Milholland, T. (1980). Relationship enhancement with premarital dyads: A six month follow-up. *American Journal of Family Therapy, 3,* 23–30.

Clements, M. L., Stanley, S. M., & Markman, H. J. (1998). *Prediction of marital distress and divorce: A discriminant analysis.* Manuscript submitted for publication.

Coie, J., Watt, N., West, S., Hawkins, J., Asarnow, J., Markman, H., Ramey, S., Shure, S., & Long, B. (1993). The science of prevention: A conceptual framework and some directions for a national research program. *American Psychologist, 48,* 1013–1022.

Glenn, N. D. (1998). The course of marital success and failure in five American 10-year marriage cohorts. *Journal of Marriage and the Family, 60,* 569–576.

Gottman, J. M. (1994). *Why marriages succeed or fail.* New York: Simon & Schuster.

Gottman, J. M., Coan, J., Carrere, S., & Swanson, C. (1998). Predicting marital happiness and stability from newlywed interactions. *Journal of Marriage and the Family, 60,* 5–22.

Grych, J., & Fincham, F. (1990). Marital conflict and children's adjustment. *Psychological Bulletin, 108,* 267–290.

Guerney, B. G., Jr. (1977). *Relationship enhancement.* San Francisco: Jossey Bass.

Halford, K. (1998). The ongoing evolution of behavioral couples therapy: Retrospect and prospect. *Clinical Psychology Review, 18,* 613–633.

Halford, K., & Bouma, R. (1997). Individual psychopathology and marital distress. In K. Halford & H. J. Markman (Eds.), *Clinical handbook of marriage and couples intervention* (pp. 291–321). New York: Wiley.

Hahlweg, K., Markman, H. J., Thurmaier, F., Engl, J., & Eckert, V. (1998). Prevention of marital distress: Results of a German prospective longitudinal study. *Journal of Family Psychology, 12,* 543–556.

Heitland, W. (1986). An experimental communication program for premarital dating couples. *The School Counselor, 34,* 57–61.

Larson, J. H., Holman, T. B., Klein, D. M., Busby, D. M., Stahmann, R. F., & Peterson, D. (1995). A review of comprehensive questionnaires used in premarital education and counseling. *Family Relations, 44,* 245–251.

Lillard, L. A., & Waite, L. J. (1995). 'Til death do us part: Marital disruption and mortality. *American Journal of Sociology, 100,* 1131–1156.

Long, E. C., Angera, J. J., Carter, S. J., Nakamoto, M., & Kelso, M. (1999). Understanding the one you love: A longitudinal assessment of an empathy training program for couples in romantic relationships. *Family Relations, 48,* 235–242.

Markman, H., Halford, K., & Lindahl, K. (in press). The nature of marriage. In A. Kazdin (Ed.), *The Encyclopedia of Psychology,* American Psychological Association. Oxford University Press.

Markman, H. J., Stanley, S. M., & Blumberg, S. L. (1994). *Fighting for your marriage: Positive steps for preventing divorce and preserving a lasting love.* San Francisco: Jossey Bass.

Matthews, L. S., Wickrama, K. A. S., & Conger, R. D. (1996). Predicting marital instability from spouse and observer reports of marital interaction. *Journal of Marriage and the Family, 58,* 641–655.

McManus, M. J. (1996). The marriage-saving movement. *The American Enterprise, 7,* 28–35.

Miller, S., Wackman, D. B., & Nunally, E. W. (1976). A communication training program for couples. *Social Casework, 57,* 9–18.

Notarius, C., & Markman, H. J. (1993). *We can work it out: Making sense of marital conflict.* New York: Putnam.

Olson, D. H., Fournier, D., & Druckman, D. H. (1986). *PREPARE.* Minneapolis: PREPARE/ENRICH.

Pasch, L. A., & Bradbury, T. N. (1998). Social support, conflict, and the development of marital dysfunction. *Journal of Consulting and Clinical Psychology, 66,* 219–230.

Ridley, C. A., Avery, A. W., Harrell, J. E., Leslie, L. A., & Dent, J. (1981). Conflict management: A premarital training program in mutual problem solving. *American Journal of Family Therapy, 9,* 23–32.

Ridley, C. A., & Bain, A. B. (1983). The effects of a premarital relationship enhancement program on self-disclosure. *Family Therapy, 1,* 13–24.

Rogge, R. D., & Bradbury, T. N. (1999, November). *Expanding beyond conflict: Moving from preventing erosion to promoting enrichment.* Paper presented at the Annual Convention of the Association for Advancement of Behavior Therapy, Toronto.

Sanders, M. (1999, November). *Advances in disseminating empirically-based family prevention programs.* Paper presented at the Annual Convention of the Association for Advancement of Behavior Therapy, Toronto.

Silliman, B., Stanley, S. M., Coffin, W., Markman, H. J., & Jordan, P. L. (in press). Preventive interventions for couples. In H. Liddle, D. Santisteban, R. Levant, & J. Bray (Eds.), *Family psychology intervention science.* Washington, DC: American Psychiatric Association.

Stanley, S. M. (1997). What's important in premarital counseling? *Marriage and Family: A Christian Journal, 1,* 51–60.

Stanley, S. M., Bradbury, T. N., & Markman, H. J. (In press). Structural flaws in the bridge from basic research on marriage to interventions for couples: Illustrations from Gottman, Coan, Carrere, and Swanson (1998). *Journal of Marriage and the Family.*

Stanley, S. M., & Markman, H. J. (1992). Assessing commitment in personal relationships. *Journal of Marriage and the Family, 54,* 595–608.

Stanley, S. M., Markman, H. J., St. Peters, M., & Leber, D. (1995). Strengthening marriages and preventing divorce: New directions in prevention research. *Family Relations, 44,* 392–401.

Stanley, S. M., Markman, H. J., Prado, L. M., Olmos-Gallo, P. A., Tonelli, L., St. Peters, M., Leber, B. D., Bobulinski, M., Cordova, A., & Whitton, S. (1999). *Short term effects of premarital training in a religious, community based sample.* (Manuscript submitted for publication)

U.S. Bureau of the Census. (1992). Marriage, divorce, and remarriage in the 1990's (Current Population Reports, 23–180). Washington, DC: U.S. Government Printing Office.

Wampler, K. S. (1990). An update of research on the Couple Communication Program. *Family Science Review, 3,* 21–40.

S. Hartman
S. Whitton
H. Markman
S. Stanley
University of Denver

MARRIAGE COUNSELING

PREMORBID ADJUSTMENT

Premorbid adjustment refers to those characteristics of a person's interpersonal, academic, and occupational functioning that were evident prior to the onset or initial diagnosis of a mental disorder. The term is most commonly referred to in the literature on schizophrenia, but the concept is applicable to all mental disorders. Interest in premorbid adjustment grew out of a developmental model of psychopathology in which symptoms are understood as one of the consequences of failure to cope with various developmental tasks.

CONCEPTUAL ISSUES

Several issues related to the concept of premorbid adjustment remain unresolved. First, because few (if any) longitudinal studies have been published, it is not clear exactly what impaired premorbid adjustment indicates. Since ratings of premorbid adjustment are based on retrospective reports, completed at varying intervals after the onset of the disorder, questions remain about the degree to which ratings are indicative of precursors of a specific disorder, evidence of nonspecific precursors, or early evidence of the disorder itself (Strauss, Klorman, & Kokes, 1977). Second, conceptualizations of premorbid adjustment vary considerably, from single dimensional models to models of complex incremental developmental processes with multiple interactive components. Current consensus is that premorbid adjustment scales should incorporate age-appropriate norms for different developmental stages and a multidimensional structure that includes demographic, social relations, leisure activities, academic and work history, and affective expression variables (Strauss et al., 1977).

MEASURES OF PREMORBID ADJUSTMENT

The Elgin Prognostic Scale (EPS; Wittman, 1941) was the first major scale that measured dimensions of premorbid adjustment. The revised EPS includes estimates of personality patterns, rate of onset of symptoms, precipitating events, presenting symptoms, duration of psychosis, and body build (Becker, 1956). Validity studies indicate that the EPS is effective in predicting the extremes of outcome among schizophrenic patients (i.e., very good or very poor). However, individual EPS items such as heterosexual contact, range of interests, marital status, and duration of psychosis are correlated with outcome, for most patients, at about the same level of the total score of the EPS (Burstein, Adams, & Chapman, 1974).

Phillips (1953) devised an ordinal prognostic scale that included three parts: a) premorbid history, b) precipitating factors, and c) signs of the disorder. Subscale measures of the intensity of involvement in personal relationships, level of sexual maturity, and the capacity to assume social responsibility showed the highest correlations with outcome. Harris (1975) developed an abbreviated form of the PMH scale to avoid problems of item redundancy and to eliminate item measures of information that was often not available in case records. Reliance on rehospitalization as an outcome measure and the high correlation between PMH scores and marital status are limitations of evidence for the validity of the PMH.

Ullmann & Giovannoni (1964) developed a self-report questionnaire to measure premorbid functioning in order to avoid the inconsistencies in the information available in hospital records. The scale includes 24 true-false biographical questions that are based on developmental conceptualizations. However, researchers have reported that patients have difficulty reading the items, frequently misinterpret questions on the scale, and may bias their answers to manipulate their environment (Magaro, 1968). A complicating factor relevant to all scales is that premorbid adjustment is difficult to rate because the life history events on which most scales are based are often part of a distant past that is difficult to reliably ascertain and rate.

The Premorbid Adjustment Scale (PAS) was developed to evaluate the degree of achievement of developmental goals in four major areas during several periods of life before the onset of schizophrenia: social accessibility-isolation, peer relationships, ability to function outside the nuclear family, and capacity to form intimate sociosexual ties (Cannon-Spoor, Potkin, & Wyatt, 1982). The PAS has been found to be useful in identifying patients likely to become chronically hospitalized.

In 1961 Zigler and Phillips published the Social Competence Scale (SCS), intended to serve as a prognostic instrument that would be broadly applicable to the general population. The SCS appears to be a valid measure of social competence in the general population (McCreary, 1974).

Strauss and Carpenter (1977) proposed the use of a multidimensional premorbid measure: (1) frequency of social contacts, (2) percentage of time employed, (3) severity of symptoms, and (4) amount of time spent out of hospital during follow-up. The Strauss-Carpenter Prognostic Scale includes items to rate level of useful work; social class; social relationships; heterosexual relationships; quality of treatment facilities used; family history of psychiatric hospitalization; age of onset of symptoms; action problems; flat affect; duration of previous hospitalization; time since first occurrence of psychotic symptoms; presence of thought disorder, delusions, and hallucinations; presence of depression, hypomania, or mania; and presence of precipitating events. Two- and five-year follow-up of patients using multidimensional outcome criteria indicated that the most efficient predictive outcome formula was based on the simple sum of three predictors: previous hospitalizations, previous social contacts, and previous employment. Please refer to Kokes, Strauss, and Klorman (1977) for a more comprehensive review of these and other premorbid adjustment measures.

SUMMARY

Ratings of premorbid adjustment are a useful way to reduce heterogeneity within diagnostic groups and can contribute to our understanding of general psychopathology. The lack of a standardized definition of premorbid adjustment across instruments has hampered progress in the identification of the relationships between premorbid status, symptoms, and outcome. A standard scale to measure outcome would facilitate research; but theoretical issues remain obstacles to the development of such an instrument. Finally, it is the consensus of most experts that the term "premorbid adjustment" should be replaced with a broader concept of prior social functioning (Keith & Buchsbaum, 1978).

REFERENCES

Becker, W. C. (1956). A genetic approach to the interpretation and evolution of the process-reactive distinction in schizophrenia. *Journal of Abnormal and Social Psychology, 53,* 229–236.

Burstein, A. G., Adams, R. L., & Chapman, L. J. (1974). Prognosis in schizophrenia. *Journal of Nervous and Mental Disease, 159,* 137–140.

Cannon-Spoor, E. H., Potkin, S., & Wyatt, R. (1982). Measurement of premorbid adjustment in chronic schizophrenia. *Schizophrenia Bulletin, 8,* 470–484.

Harris, J. G. (1975). An abbreviated form of the Phillips Rating Scale of Premorbid Adjustment in schizophrenia. *Journal of Abnormal Psychology, 84,* 129–137.

Keith, S. J., & Buchsbaum, S. (1978). Workshop on factors related to premorbid adjustment. *Schizophrenia Bulletin, 4,* 252–257.

Kokes, R. F., Strauss, J. S., & Klorman, R. (1977). Measuring premorbid adjustment: The instruments and their development. *Schizophrenia Bulletin, 3,* 186–213.

Magaro, C. P. (1974). A validity and reliability study of the process-reactive self-report scale. *Journal of Consulting and Clinical Psychology, 32,* 482–485.

McCreary, C. P. (1974). Comparison of measures of social competency in schizophrenics and the relation of social competency to socioeconomic factors. *Journal of Abnormal Psychology, 83,* 124–129.

Phillips, L. (1953). Case history data and prognosis in schizophrenia. *Journal of Nervous and Mental Disease, 117,* 515–525.

Strauss, J. S., & Carpenter, W. T. (1977). Prediction of outcome in schizophrenia: III. Five-year outcome and its predictors. *Archives of General Psychiatry, 34,* 159–163.

Strauss, J. S., Klorman, R., & Kokes, R. F. (1977). Premorbid adjustment in schizophrenia: Part V. The implications of findings for understanding research and application. *Schizophrenia Bulletin, 3,* 240–244.

Ullmann, L., & Giovannoni, J. (1964). The development of a self-report measure of the process-reactive continuum. *Journal of Nervous and Mental Disease, 138,* 38–42.

Wittman, P. (1941). Scale for measuring prognosis in schizophrenic patients. *Elgin State Hospital Papers, 4,* 20–33.

Zigler, E., and Phillips, L. (1961). Social competence and outcome in psychiatric disorder. *Journal of Abnormal and Social Psychology, 63,* 264–271.

G. D. Shean
College of William and Mary

PRESCRIPTION PRIVILEGES

Some might argue that prescription privileges are a natural extension of present laws already on the books (e.g., California) that "establish that psychologists should be knowledgeable about psychopharmacological effects of populations at risk and are encouraged to seek additional education in the area of geriatric pharmacology" (Ch. 1539 of the statutes of 1990). Also, in Hawaii, State House Resolution 334–90 recommended a series of roundtable discussions dealing with Hawaii's unserved mental health needs and included "the possibility of allowing appropriately trained psychologists to prescribe psychotropic medications . . . under certain conditions" (Slife & Rubenstein, 1992). Even more recently, in December 1998, the legislature in the territory of Guam passed a measure giving psychologists the right to prescribe under the supervision of psychiatrists. There are currently about 16 psychologists in Guam. In 1998, legislation for prescription privileges was in process (pending or about to be introduced) in seven states, and an additional 25 state associations had established task forces to work toward this aim according to DeLeon, Sammons, and Fox (1998). Graduate schools in several states have begun to provide psychopharmacology training, as have some private organizations. A special section of *Professional Psychology: Research and Practice* edited by Esteban Olmedo included, among others, such topics as the pursuit of prescription privileges (Cullen & Newman, 1997), the Department of Defense psychopharmacology demonstration project (see also APA, 1991), and the practicality of predoctoral prescription training for psychologists (1997). Gutierrez and Silk (1998) published a review of the psychological literature on prescription privileges for psychologists which cited over 40 references. There appears to have been considerable activity in this arena since Slife and Rubenstein's *Taking Sides* (1992) listed prescription privileges as one of ten new controversial issues leading to spirited debates.

Psychologists are not newcomers to the arena of physical interventions. Jansen and Barron (1998) in reviewing this topic asserted that biofeedback techniques, alarm bells for bed-wetting, galvanic skin responses, and polygraph assessments are examples of physical interventions already used by psychologists. Direct involvement of physical interventions by psychologists have included behavior management procedures with children. The American Psychological Association's task force on physical interventions had two reports on this topic. In 1986, the task force concluded that research and clinical training must take account of physical interventions by psychologists, including psychopharmacology. Jansen and Barron pointed out that even though psychologists have been active in the development of physical interventions, they have been automatically excluded from giving medications because they do not have the title of physician. They agreed that medication providers must have adequate training, but some psychologists question whether the "right" training is permitted to some professions whereas others are denied that training. DeLeon (1990) noted that development of model curricula in psychopharmacology was the subject of a special retreat of the American Psychological Association's Board of Professional Affairs in 1989. That board gave high priority to the consideration of psychopharmacological interventions by psychologists to meet the public's need. Smyer (1992) summarized the reasons for including psychopharmacology in the curriculum for psychologists who work with older adults. Older adults have significant contact with psychotropic medications (as well as with prescription medications in general), and he emphasized that psychopharmacological agents are useful in treatment of mental disorders of older adults. He also noted that psychopharmacology is a principal factor in the treatment of the mentally ill elderly. Smyer did not take a stand on prescription privileges as such, but he outlined content areas important for curriculum and practicum experiences and included psychologists' interactions with prescribers as a suggested topic in geriatric psychopharmacology. In 1995, the Council of Representatives of the American Psychological Association adopted a resolution which favored prescription privileges for psychologists.

MEETING SOCIETY'S NEEDS—THE PUBLIC POLICY PERSPECTIVE

DeLeon, Fox, and Graham (1991) argued that prescription privileges for psychologists are necessary and essential to meet the needs of quality care for the mentally ill and to deal with the problems of excessive medication for the elderly. They noted that 28 states, as of 1991, permit nurse practitioners to prescribe and that optometrists can prescribe in all 50 states. Overall, it is the power of the individual states to determine which health practitioners have prescriptive authority. Physician-extenders (nurses, nurse practitioners, physicians assistants, etc.) require supervision by physicians to prescribe, while health practitioners such as dentists, optometrists, and podiatrists are usually given independent status without physician supervision.

At the federal level, psychologists have legally prescribed medications within the Indian Health Service. Jennings (1988), director of Mental Health Programs at the Santa Fe, NM Indian Hospital, wrote, "the single compelling warrant for prescription privileges is desperate need for services, desperate need to add another agent to psychology's therapeutic armamentarium that may contribute to the relief of human suffering. . . . Privileges granted to psychology are not seen as a threat either to income or professional territory" (p. 2). The Department of Defense (Sammons and Brown, 1997) authorized a demonstration pilot project permitting military psychologists to receive training to administer some psychotropic medications. Ten psychologists have completed this program.

To underscore the societal value of administering psychotropic drugs by psychologists, DeLeon, Fox, and Graham (1991) pointed out that more than half of outpatient mental health visits are conducted by general medical practitioners and that nursing home residents are often medicated using drugs designed to treat mental disorders despite the fact that most of these elderly patients are not mentally ill.

On the other side of the age continuum, there is widespread discussion among professionals as to the justification for medicating children. DeLeon, Folen, Jennings, Willis, and Wright (1991) indicated that proper diagnosis is crucial in using medications for children with attention-deficit/hyperactivity disorder but that they may not be necessary with other psychological disorders. A policy implication raised by these authors has to do with whether medications are sometimes prescribed for children whose parents are not able to manage their child's behavior. It is possible that the primary concern is not the child's activity level but rather the parents' inability to cope with their child. Evaluating the stress level of the parent may lead to a productive course of action without necessarily subjecting children to medications. The authors pointed out that further research regarding the effects of medications on adolescents and mentally retarded youth is needed. Clinical child psychologists need to know more about the efficacy of psychoactive drugs with children and the general area of psychopharmacology. The authors emphasized that the power to prescribe also is the ability to use medications judiciously or not at all, depending on the circumstances. In a report chaired by Barkley and colleagues (1990) on the role of clinical child psychologists, it was argued that because child psychologists are already participants in decisions to medicate children they should be familiar with child psychopharmacology.

No discussion on prescription privileges would be complete without citing objections to psychologists prescribing drugs. Breggin's *Toxic Psychiatry* (1991) is noteworthy in this regard. Breggin argued that the administration of drugs by psychiatrists is a political and financial issue encouraged by the "Psychopharmacological complex" that "pushes biological and genetic theories, as well as drugs, on the society" (p. 408). He argued that psychiatry as a profession must discontinue its financial collaboration with drug companies and must not make inaccurate claims regarding genetic and biological causes of mental illness. Breggin insisted that love, understanding, and psychotherapy are the answers to psychiatric problems. His concerns revolve around the addictive and damaging aspect of drugs, especially if the patient has not been apprised in advance of the effects and consequences of psychotropic medications. Breggin also took to task psychologists who advocate prescription privileges. He noted that some psychologists have become envious of the status accorded to psychiatrists and states that drug companies are sponsoring and funding seminars at meetings of psychologists to discuss the advantages of prescription privileges.

Fox (1988) suggested that prescription privileges for psychologists is in the public interest because the research training of psychologists makes them uniquely competent to evaluate the effects of medications. Furthermore, the good of society would be advanced because psychologists with prescription privileges would find it easier to work with nonpsychiatric physicians. A physician who is not a psychiatrist may choose not to use certain medications for the treatment of emotional disorders or may not be familiar with the overall course of many emotional disorders. Fox suggested that many physicians prefer working with a psychologist rather than a psychiatrist, and many physicians would probably have little difficulty in letting a nonmedical practitioner who was knowledgeable about mental disorders prescribe appropriate medications. Fox argued that it may not be wise for psychologists to restrict their roles, as restrictions ultimately diminish their ability to be helpful to their patients.

POLITICAL AND IDENTITY CONSIDERATIONS

DeNelsky (1991) pointed out that efforts to obtain prescription privileges would involve psychology in a full-scale war with psychiatry. Jancin (1989) reported that when DeLeon, at the meeting of the American Psychiatric Association, predicted that psychologists will eventually gain prescription privileges, there was "fussing and fuming" by the psychiatrists. Kingsbury (1992b), a psychologist who is also a psychiatrist, claimed that psychiatry is currently less interested in psychotherapy while continuing to stay up to date on psychopharmacology. He argued that psychopharmacology is primarily medical, has little to do with psychological principles, and does not really belong within the armamentarium of psychologists. Arthur Shechet (pers. comm., 1990), worried that psychology would be merged with psychiatry in the public's mind, noted that psychology's move to seek prescription privileges would be opposed not only by psychiatry but by the entire American Medical Association. Barron (1989) analyzed the prescription privileges effort as a "me-too" effort to imitate the powerful (M.D.) father figure. Handler (1988) insisted that clinical psychology has advanced because it is different from psychiatry, in that psychologists are more broadly trained in contrast to the "biologically reductionistic model of mainstream medicine" (p. 45). Handler zeroed in on a central argument: Psychologists focus on the self, and it is the relationship between the therapist and the patient that produces more self-control. He maintained that searching for the meaning of symptoms may be more important than the symptoms themselves. Handler stated that there may be times that medications are necessary. However, he objected to medications as the central change agents, because patients can learn more about themselves without medications and "have a more meaningful growth experience" (p. 48). He asked for a clear distinction between those who practice psychotherapy as opposed to those whose primary orientation is biological and, therefore, excludes psychotherapy. He cautioned that failing to stand up for one's professional identity and distinctiveness may be equivalent to giving up one's birthright. Brentar and McNamara (1991b) disagreed. They do not believe that prescription privileges represent a loss of identity, and argued that psychology as a field is evolving and prescription privileges is a possible step. They suggested that there are often objections to changing the status quo and that psychologists may be waiting for empirical evidence before there is full support for changes in the field.

Fox (1989) recognized that psychology might have to decide on the best time to use its limited resources to seek changes such as prescription privileges. He suggested, however, that timing is not the real issue at stake but the right of a profession to decide its direction. Fox insisted that it is the job of psychologists to decide their own fate rather than having other professions decide what the boundaries of psychology should be.

May and Belsky (1992) speculated that prescription privileges are just another step toward the medicalization of psychology. They see this as too narrow a focus and believe that the problems of the elderly, the chronically mentally ill, and other underserved groups are social problems. One possible solution could be obligatory service for professionals in underserved areas, instead of awarding prescription privileges to psychologists. The use of primary prevention would further psychology, and this should be the next frontier instead of prescription privileges. They suggested that prescription privileges could be handled more effectively by those who already have at least some track record (e.g., the nursing profession).

The medicalization of psychology is addressed in detail by DeNelsky (1991). He suggested that psychiatry made a decision about twenty years ago to medicalize its status. Rather than increasing its growth, psychiatry has not increased its share of the mental health market. Instead, it appears that the general public has accepted psychology as a mental health discipline, and psychologists are currently the largest group of doctoral-level mental health providers in this country. Perhaps, DeNelsky suggested, this has come about because psychology is distinctly different from psychiatry. Moving to prescription privileges, he warned, is likely to reduce the distinction and might affect psychology adversely. Kingsbury (1992a) agreed that psychotherapy training for psychiatrists has diminished and that psychology is probably the acknowledged leader in the field of psychotherapy.

Brentar and McNamara (1991b) cautioned about the assumption that psychiatrists have given up on psychotherapy as a treatment method. This might be true in public settings in which funding limitations have placed restrictions on psychosocial interventions. In the private sector, however, they contend that psychiatrists are still quite active in providing psychotherapy either by itself or in addition to psychotropic medications.

DeNelsky (1991) and Kovacs (1988) raised concern about energy expenditures. If prescription privileges were to become a major priority for psychology, other efforts (e.g., hospital privileges, minimum mental health benefits, and so on) might well take a backseat. On the other hand, some might argue, prescription privileges might actually facilitate hospital privileges, as hospital administrators might prefer giving privileges to those who can provide a full range of services.

Prescription privileges require changes in licensing laws. Whenever changes are made in licensing laws, these laws are opened to a variety of changes. Some of them are not wanted by the various professions affected. DeNelsky suggested this could constitute a major political risk. Because there is no unanimity on the topic of prescription privileges, potential efforts to change licensing laws could be divisive. DeNelsky recognized that all psychologists would not be mandated to seek such privileges, but he did note that there would be pressures on those without such privileges to obtain them.

MARKETING ISSUES

Fox (1988) argued that the development of specialized medical treatment programs have mushroomed, even though psychologists do offer such treatments independently. He cited the growth of hospital-based treatment programs for alcoholism, pain management, and behavior disorders of children as examples. Characteristically, these programs do not use psychologists as equal or autonomous partners. DeNelsky (1991) agreed that this may well be true, but cites figures that show that psychiatry has actually been losing its market share over the past five years for outpatient visits of patients. Figures on this topic fluctuate, however, depending on changing standards of reimbursement for inpatient versus outpatient treatment.

A major concern of psychologists has been the topic of access to hospital patient populations. This includes the ability to admit and discharge patients, enhanced clinical privileges for psychologists working in medical settings, and obtaining full medical staff membership with vote. Some progress along these lines has occurred, but Boswell and Litwin (1992) noted that less than 6% of hospital-affiliated psychologists have obtained admission or discharge privileges and only 16% have obtained full medical staff memberships. These authors surveyed 582 hospital-affiliated licensed psychologists who responded to an earlier questionnaire by these authors. They noted that, in the original survey, 49% either strongly disagreed or disagreed with the statement that prescription privileges should be adopted as an advocacy position of the American Psychological Association, whereas 27% strongly agreed or agreed with that position. The remaining 24% were unsure. A resurvey of these groups indicated that more than 33% of the respondents had changed their position on this topic. For example, of the respondents who were unsure last year, 45% remained unsure but 30% now agreed or strongly agreed, while 25% now disagreed or strongly disagreed. Shifts also occurred in those groups who had previously taken a position for or against prescription privileges. Overall, the authors stated about 35% of the respondents had changed their minds on this topic even though the overall number of psychologists who supported or approved prescription privileges had not changed. The authors also emphasized that the percentage of psychologists responding to their survey was only 31% of the total original sample, and they cautioned readers not to overgeneralize their data. Nevertheless, this study suggests that prescription privileges continues to be a controversial issue even among hospital-based psychologists.

In their discussion, these authors noted that one important issue raised by those surveyed is whether or not prescription privileges will result in maintaining distinctiveness from psychiatry and whether or not the credibility of psychologists will be affected. Advocates of prescription privileges do not believe credibility or distinctiveness will be influenced whereas opponents believe otherwise.

TRAINING ISSUES

Brentar and McNamara (1991a) discussed three types of training models that could provide psychologists with the competence needed to begin prescribing psychotropic medications. The first is postdoctoral intensive training for psychologists wishing to become competent. A second would be a continuing education model, using workshops or seminars, that could provide intensive training and updating for individuals already trained. The third model would incorporate relevant training into existing graduate programs, a difficult and expensive venture that would also lengthen an already long graduate training program. The authors suggested that interdisciplinary training with institutions that already have training programs in place might be a solution. Thus, schools of optometry, nursing, or osteopathic medicine could be sites at which psychologists would be trained. This, of course, would be a problem for students at graduate schools in more remote areas where affiliation with other training programs might not be available.

As to the content of training programs, there are clear differences of opinion as to what is needed. Some, like Fox (1988), argued that training should be similar to that received in medical school courses such as neuroanatomy, physiology, endocrinology, biochemistry, and clinical pharmacology. On the other hand, Brentar and McNamara (1991a) noted that some state boards of optometry use a 30-hour training program to certify optometrists to prescribe relevant ocular medications.

The training at the Uniformed Services University of the Health Sciences consists of a 2-year effort, with didactic training occurring in the first year and hands-on supervised training at a major medical treatment center in the second year, according to DeLeon (1992a). He emphasized that the entire topic of prescription privileges is basically an educational concern. The Nova University School of Psychology program to train psychologists in psychopharmacology has been developed. It includes a didactic component after which trainees observe, gather patient information, and eventually recommend medications for the patient to a psychiatrist. This program is designed for psychologists with earned doctorates in psychology who possess sufficient prior relevant knowledge as determined by the director of training.

Jennings (1988) described the qualifications and experiences necessary to provide limited prescription privileges at the Indian Health Service Hospital. Requirements include at least one year of postdoctoral experience in assessment and treatment. Prior training must include familiarity with laboratory tests designed to assess patients who will be given psychoactive drugs, knowledge within the area of compliance with medications, and clinical psychopharmacology coursework, which must be clearly documented. At least six months of prior experience must include physician oversight.

Although this is clearly a postdoctoral effort, many psychologists suggest that training programs for prescription privileges would eventually need to be included within predoctoral settings. DeNelsky (1991) argued that the time required for psychologists to complete the doctoral degree would have to be extended and psychological training would be basically changed.

Fox, Schwelitz, and Barclay (1992) described a proposed curriculum designed to produce psychologists capable of functioning as limited practice prescribers similar to dentists and podiatrists. These psychologists can prescribe medications within their area of expertise and are not subject to physician oversight. The curriculum requires an undergraduate knowledge base in biology, chemistry, and preparation for graduate level courses in biochemistry, physiological and biological aspects of drug interaction, current topics in psychopharmacology, clinical psychopharmacology and therapeutics, professional and ethical issues in psychopharmacology, clinical psychopharmacology laboratory, chemical dependency, neuropsychology and laboratory, and psychopathology. This comes to a total of 39 credit hours. He pointed out that at his institution, students already take 21 of the 39 credit hours proposed in this new curriculum.

It should be noted that the interest in training has become the concern of graduate students. In 1999, Hanson and colleagues raised concerns related to undergraduate education as well as concerns about future graduate education in psychology. She points out that the curriculum currently endorsed by APA is designed for professionals who are fully trained and licensed. Nevertheless, undergraduates may want to think about tailoring their curriculum to consider eventual prescription privileges. On the graduate level, Hanson suggests there may be some concerns that adding additional courses might compromise the unique skills and identity of graduate students. She points out, however, that the ultimate goals are to train psychologists who, in addition to their training, can also prescribe psychotropic medications. Furthermore, she points out that one compelling reason to seek prescription privileges is to serve underserved groups (e.g., the elderly, Native Americans, and those living in rural areas).

FINANCIAL CONCERNS, PROFESSIONAL LIABILITY, AND OVERMEDICATION

Piotrowski (1989) speculated on what would happen if psychologists were successful in gaining prescription privileges. One possible concern might be whether all practicing psychologists would have to share in the financial burden of increased malpractice premiums. Fox (1989) stated that it is a common practice in other professions to stipulate that one will not perform certain procedures or will restrict one's practice in specified ways. Those who choose not to administer medications should not be required to pay for the increased costs involved. Thus, surgeons pay higher premiums than do family practitioners, and anesthesiologists pay higher premiums than do pediatricians.

Aside from financial concerns, the overall issue of risk for psychologists increases dramatically with the obtaining of prescriptive authority. Imagine the depressed patient for whom drugs are appropriately prescribed but who misuses the prescription to make a suicide attempt. In addition, professionals are often faced by patients who are insistent on obtaining medications to deal with troubling psychological symptoms.

There is a considerable amount of varying opinions about the topic of prescription privileges. Most psychologists agree that some patients do benefit from medications for their psychological problems. Many psychologists would even concur that some patients with severe psychological problems need psychotropic medications. Some of those psychologists also believe that providing medications is the domain of medicine and psychiatry, and that psychology should stick to psychotherapy.

There are those who argue that there are many underserved patient populations in this country who receive little, if any, psychosocial treatment and who are overmedicated. The perception, at times confirmed by psychiatrists (Kingsbury, 1992b), that psychotherapy is not a major focus within psychiatry has been noted. Because psychologists are well-trained in research and are competent in offering psychosocial interventions (psychotherapy), they might be in a better position to use both prescription privileges and psychotherapy in the treatment of patients, as they are the least likely to overmedicate. These psychologists take the position that prescription privileges, similar to hospital privileges, are natural extensions of psychological practice, are in the best interests of the public, and in effect represent sound public policy. They argue that issues concerning training, malpractice insurance, changes in licensing laws, third-party reimbursements, hospital privileges, and so on are real but secondary issues.

CONCLUSION

Opinions on this topic have appeared in letters to the editor of the *APA Monitor* and are heard in discussions with clinical psychologists. Clearly, there are public policy, training, and marketing issues involved in the controversial area of prescription privileges for psychologists. As of 1999, however, the overarching issues appear to focus on political and identity concerns. Currently, a significant number of psychologists believe that a battle with psychiatry will result in a more widespread war with organized medicine, which might not be in the best interest of organized psychology. Others worry about being viewed as "junior psychiatrists." They express concern that winning the prescription privileges war will result in the medicalization of psychology. Included here is the fear that confidence in psychosocial treatment modalities offered by psychologists will diminish, because some members of the public will be afraid that they will receive drug treatments from psychologists and thus will turn to other professionals (social workers, counselors, ministers) for psychological interventions. On the other hand, some psychologists are concerned that more patients will turn to them for a quick fix via medications rather than taking the more arduous path of psychotherapy.

There are responses to these concerns. Psychologists are already involved in physical interventions, although these may not be high-profile when compared with prescription privileges. To argue that psychologists rely exclusively on nonphysical interventions is simply not true. In addition, as Fox (1989) noted, psychology is not exclusively a mental health discipline because it deals broadly with behavior change in such areas as health, interpersonal functioning, learning, vocational functioning, and rehabilitation. Psychology impacts, among others, families, the able elderly, the physically handicapped, and those with learning disabilities, be they children or adults. Psychology has made major strides in the area of neuropsychology and in health psychology. Prescription privileges can be seen as one more step in the education and training of psychologists to be helpful to society. For those who argue that some psychologists will misuse these privileges because of status, greed, or other reasons, the truth is that there will always be unscrupulous individuals in all professions. There is no evidence that prescription privileges will increase the number of unscrupulous providers.

The argument that prescription privileges should not be allowed because they would fundamentally change the nature of psychology is probably the core argument. Many psychologists believe that prescription privileges should never be permitted because they violate the fundamental tenets of psychology. Nevertheless, a sizable majority of psychologists do believe that some patients need psychotropic medications at some time in their lives. It should be noted that the Task Force on Psychologists' Use of Physical Interventions did define the practice of psychology as including both physical and psychological interventions (Jansen and Barron, 1988). Fox (1989) pointed out that the use of such physical interventions should occur within the context of improving the quality of services, within the competence of the provider, and in the service of consumer welfare.

REFERENCES

American Psychological Association (1991). DOD prescription privileges training program continues. *Practitioner, 5,* 5.

Barkley, R., Conners, C., Barkley, A., Gadow, K., Gittleman, R., Sprague R., & Swanson, J. (1990). Task force report: The appropriate role of clinical child psychologists in the prescribing of psychoactive medications for children [Monograph]. *Journal of Clinical Child Psychology, 19*(Suppl.), 1–38.

Barron, J. (1989). Prescription rights: Pro and con. *Psychotherapy Bulletin, 24,* 22–24.

Boswell, D., & Litwin, W. (1992). Limited prescription privilege for psychologists: A 1-year follow-up. *Professional Psychology: Research and Practice, 23,* 108–113.

Breggin, P. (1991). *Toxic psychiatry.* New York: St. Martin's Press.

Brentar, J., & McNamara, J. (1991a). The right to prescribe medication: Considerations for professional psychology. *Professional Psychology: Research and Practice, 22,* 179–187.

Brentar, J., & McNamara, J. (1991b). Prescription privileges for psychology: The next step in its evolution as a profession. *Professional Psychology: Research and Practice, 22,* 194–195.

Cullen, E. A., & Newman, R. (1997). In pursuit of prescription privileges. *Professional Psychology: Research and Practice, 28*(2), 101–106.

DeLeon, P. H. (1990). The medication debate: Hawaii's legislature acts. *Register Report,* 9–11.

DeLeon, P. H. (1992a). National health insurance—Alive and doing well. *Register Report, 18,* 4–6.

DeLeon, P. H. (1992b). Prescription privileges: Our educational systems become involved. *The Independent Practitioner, 12,* 27–29.

DeLeon, P. H., Folen, R., Jennings, F., Willis, D., & Wright, R. (1991). The case for prescription privileges: A logical evolution of professional practice. *Journal of Clinical Child Psychology, 3,* 254–267.

DeLeon, P. H., Fox, R., & Graham, S. (1991). Prescription privileges: Psychology's next frontier? *American Psychologist, 46,* 384–393.

DeLeon, P. H., Sammons, M. T., & Fox, R. E. (1998). Prescription privileges. *Missouri Psychologist, 1,* 225–229.

DeNelsky, G. (1991). Prescription privileges for psychologists: The case against. *Professional Psychology: Research and Practice, 22,* 188–193.

Fox, R. E. (1988). Prescription privileges: The implication for the practice of psychology. *Psychotherapy, 25,* 501–507.

Fox, R. E. (1989). Some practical and legal objections to prescription privileges for psychologists. *Psychotherapy in Private Practice, 6,* 23–39.

Fox, R. E., Schwelitz, F., & Barclay, A. (1992). A proposed curriculum for psychopharmacology training for psychologists. *Professional Psychology: Research and Practice, 23,* 216–219.

Gutierrez, P. M., & Silk, K. R. (1998). Prescription privileges for psychologists: A review of the psychological literature. *Professional Psychology: Research and Practice, 29*(3), 213–222.

Handler, L. (1988). Monkey see, monkey do: The prescription-writing controversy. *The Clinical Psychologist, 41,* 44–48.

Hanson, K. M., Louie, C. E., Van Male, L. M., Pugh, A. O., Karl, C., Muhlenbrook, L., Lilly, R. L., & Hagglund, K. J. (1999). Involving the future: The need to consider the views of psychologists-in-training regarding prescription privileges for psychologists. *Professional Psychology: Research and Practice, 30*(2), 203–208.

Jancin, B. (1989, June). Say psychologists will win prescribing privileges fight. *Clinical Psychiatry News,* p. 1.

Jansen, M., & Barron, J. (1988). Introduction and overview: Psychologists' use of physical interventions. *Psychotherapy, 25*(4), 487–491.

Jennings, F. (1988). *Psychologists and prescription privileges.* Unpublished manuscript.

Kingsbury, S. (1992a). Some effects of prescribing privileges. *American Psychologists, 47,* 426–427.

Kingsbury, S. (1992b). Some effects of prescribing privileges. *Professional Psychology: Research and Practice, 23,* 3–5.

Kovacs, A. (1988). Shall we take drugs? Just say no. *Psychotherapy Bulletin, 23,* 8–11.

May, W., & Belsky, J. (1992). Response to "Prescription privileges: Psychology's next frontier?" of the siren call: Should psychologists medicate. *American Psychologist, 47,* 427.

Piotrowski, C. (1989). Prescription privileges: A time for some serious thought. *Psychotherapy Bulletin, 24,* 16–18.

Rupert, P. W., Kozlowski, N. F., Hoffman, L. A., Daniels, D. D., & Piette, J. M. (1999). Practical and ethical issues in teaching psychological testing. *Professional Psychology: Research and Practice, 30*(2), 209–214.

Sammons, M. T., & Brown, A. B. (1997). The Department of Defense psychopharmacology demonstration project: An evolving program for postdoctoral education in psychology. *Professional Psychology: Research and Practice, 28,* 107–112.

Smyer, M. (1992, April). *Psychopharmacology: An essential element in educating clinical psychologists for working with older adults.* Paper presented at the National Conference on Clinical Training in Psychology: Improving Psychological Services for Older Adults, Washington, DC.

Slife, B., & Rubenstein, J. (Eds.). (1992). *Taking sides.* Guilford, CT: Dushkin.

N. ABELES
Michigan State University

BEHAVIORAL MEDICINE
MEDICAL MODEL OF PSYCHOTHERAPY
PSYCHOPHARMACOLOGY

PRIBRAM, KARL H.

Karl Pribram earned both his BS and MD degrees from the University of Chicago. After spending a year at the University of Tennessee where he was instructor in surgery, Pribram moved to Jacksonville, FL. There he practiced neurosurgery and began a brain research program at the Yerkes Laboratory for Primate Biology. He later briefly succeeded K. Lashley as director of the Laboratory. After receiving his certification by the American Board of Neurological Surgery in 1948, Pribram received an appointment as lecturer in the department of physiology at Yale University, where he spent his next ten years. During this period, he also served as director of research at the Institute of Living, a mental hospital in Hartford, CT. In 1958 he was awarded a Fulbright fellowship to work at Cambridge University in England and another to work at the Center for Advanced Studies in the Behavioral Sciences, where he coauthored the influential book *Plans and the Structure of Behavior* with G. Miller and E. Galanter. While at the Center, Pribram was offered a joint appointment of professor in the departments of psychology and psychiatry at Stanford University, where he spent the next thirty years, having been awarded a lifetime research career award from NIH. On becoming professor emeritus at Stanford and certified by the Board of Medical Psychotherapists, he accepted the James P. and Anna King University Professor Chair at Radford University in Virginia, where he directs the Center for Brain Research and Informational Sciences. In 1999, he was appointed distinguished research professor at Georgetown University.

Pribram is widely known for his work in neurophysiology, neuropsychology and neurophilosophy through his publication of about 100 data papers and 200 reviews and theory papers. He is the recipient of numerous awards, among them the Lifetime Contribution Award from the Board of Medical Psychotherapists, the Award for Original Contributions to Philosophy from the International Society of Research and Philosophy, and an award from the Society of Biological Psychiatry. In 1999 Pribram was honored as the first recipient of the VIZE 97 Prize awarded by the President of the Czech Republic, Vaclav Havel; the Computing Anticipatory Systems Award from the Liege meetings in Belgium, and the Noetic Medal of Consciousness Research.

Pribram is the author of *Plans and the Structure of Behavior* (with Miller and Galanter), *Languages of the Brain, Freud's Project Reassessed* (with M. Gill), and a more recent book entitled *Brain and Perception: Holonomy and Structure in Figural Processing* (1991). In 1992, he was awarded an honorary PhD by the University of Montreal. In 1996, Pribram was awarded an honorary doctorate in philosophy by the University of Bremen. Additionally, Pribram has hosted and edited the proceedings of the annual Appalachian Conferences on Behavioral Neural Dynamics held in Radford, VA, in 1992, 1993, 1994, 1995 and 1996, and a conference on Brain, Cognition, and Communication held at Georgetown University in 1999. The Georgetown meeting inaugurated Georgetown's Institute for Cognition and Computation and commemorated Pribram's eightieth birthday.

STAFF

PRIMACY AND RECENCY EFFECTS*

When humans are presented with a list of items to remember, they usually remember those items which occurred at the beginning and end of the list better than those items which occurred in the middle. The capacity to remember these early list items better than the middle items is known as the *primacy* or *priority effect,* whereas the ability to learn items later in the list more quickly than items in the middle of the list is referred to the *recency* or *finality effect* (Raffel, 1936; Welch & Burnett, 1924). These memory phenomena were first described by Bigham (1894, see also Smith, 1896) over one hundred years ago and have been studied extensively in humans ever since. In fact, these memory effects have played an important role in many theories of human learning and memory function (Anderson & Bower, 1972; Crowder, 1989, Glanzer & Cunitz, 1966).

THEORETICAL EXPLANATIONS

The most promising explanations of the primacy and recency phenomena appear to be those that postulate the formation of the contextual or configural associations (Hintzman, Block, & Summers, 1973; Wells, 1974). The configural association theory proposes that a compound stimulus is represented by a conjunction of the simple elements of a compound, such that exposure to one of the elements of the compound may allow access to the entire representation (i.e., the configural association). In list-learning memory tasks, the spatiotemporal relationships between stimuli and their position in the list require the formation and activation of these configural associations, particularly for early items. The simple associative process, on the other hand, requires only that the associative strength of the stimulus be of sufficient magnitude in order for recognition of an item at the end of the list (i.e., the item most recently seen) to occur. Therefore, the primacy effect is thought to be mediated by the formation of con-

*The opinions and assertions contained in this report are the private views of the author and are not to be construed as official or as reflecting the views of the Army or the Department of Defense. In conducting the research described in this report, the investigators adhered to the Animal Welfare Act and the *Guide for the Care and Use of Laboratory Animals,* NIH Publication No. 86–23.

figural associations, and the recency effect is believed to be mediated by the "trace" (simple) associations. Consequently, tasks dependent upon the formation and activation of configural associations are thought to require more effort than tasks dependent upon simple associations. It should be noted that attempts to describe the primacy and recency effects in terms of retroactive and proactive interference, trace strengths, or sequential-associations (Hull, Hovland, Ross, Hall, Perkins, & Fitch, 1940; McGeoch & Irion, 1952) have not been successful (Ebenholtz, 1963; Young, 1959).

Evolutionary Convergence

Humans, nonhuman primates, and infraprimates all display primacy and recency memory effects. For instance, in addition to the numerous studies demonstrating the presence of the primacy and recency memory effects in humans under a wide variety of testing conditions (e.g., Dong, 1972), the primacy and recency effects have been observed in a chimpanzee with a test of free recall of Yerkish primate words (Buchanan, Gill, & Braggio, 1981) and in squirrel monkeys and rhesus monkeys tested on a serial probe recognition task (e.g., Castro & Larsen, 1992; Sands & Wright, 1980a). Similarly, primacy and recency effects have been reported in rats tested on a spatial recognition memory task (DiMattia & Kesner, 1984), in rabbits tested using a habituation-learning paradigm (Wagner & Pfautz, 1978), and in pigeons trained on a serial probe recognition task (Santiago & Wright, 1984). From an evolutionary perspective, these data indicate that humans, nonhuman primates, and infraprimates possess similar learning and memory processes.

Separate Memory Processes

There are four lines of evidence that support the general hypothesis that the primacy memory effect and recency memory effect are mediated by distinct memory processes: behavioral, developmental, anatomical, and neuropharmacological (Craik, 1970; Glanzer & Cunitz, 1966; Waugh, 1960).

BEHAVIORAL EVIDENCE

Decreasing the interstimulus interval (the amount of time between the presentation of one item in the list and the next item in the list) diminishes the primacy effect without affecting the recency effect. This finding was reported in both humans and nonhuman primates (Cook, Wright, & Sands, 1991; Intraub, 1980). Conversely, increasing the retention interval (the time between the last item in the list and the memory test) decreases the recency effect, without affecting the primacy effect (Wright, Sands, & Santiago, 1984). That the primacy and recency memory effects can be dissociated by these changes in behavioral testing procedures is consistent with the theory that separate memory mechanisms are involved.

DEVELOPMENTAL EVIDENCE

In both human and nonhuman primate memory development, the recency effect is observed prior to the primacy effect (Hagen, Joneward, & Kail, 1975; Matzke & Castro, 1998). Children between the ages of two and four readily display a recency effect but did not reveal a primacy effect until six years of age, even when encouraged to engage in rehearsal (Hagen et al., 1975). In nonhuman

primates (rhesus monkeys), the processes mediating the recency affect are present at 21 months of age, but the primacy affect did not emerge until 35 to 47 months of age (Matzke & Castro, 1998). Thus, the primacy and recency memory effects are developmentally dissociated, suggesting separate memory systems with different developmental time courses.

ANATOMICAL EVIDENCE

In both humans and infraprimates, the presence of the primacy effect, but not the recency effect, has been shown to depend on the integrity of the hippocampal formation (Kesner, 1985). For example, epileptics who underwent hippocampectomy displayed an attenuated primacy effect when presented with a list of 30 words to remember, while the recency effect remained unaffected (Milner, 1978). Similarly, hippocampally damaged rats tested on an eight-arm radial maze showed a disrupted primacy effect and an unaltered recency effect (Kesner & Novak, 1982).

NEUROPHARMACOLOGICAL EVIDENCE

From a neuropharmacological viewpoint, the integrity of the cholinergic system is important for the establishment of the primacy effect, but not the recency effect. Cholinergic receptor antagonists have been shown to disrupt the primacy but not the recency effects in humans examined on an immediate recall test of 12 words (Hinrichs, Mewaldt, Ghoneim, & Berie, 1982; Richardson, Frith, Scott, Crow, & Cunningham-Owens, 1984) and in nonhuman primates evaluated on a serial probe recognition task (Castro, 1997). Alzheimer's patients with disrupted cholinergic function also displayed no evidence of a primacy effect when given a recall test of 12 unrelated words, yet they still showed a robust, albeit lowered, recency effect (Miller, 1971). The GABA-benzodiazepine system, however, is more involved in mediating the recency effect than the primacy effect. For instance, diazepam has been shown in nonhuman primates to disrupt the recency effect, while only minimally affecting the primacy effect (Castro, 1995).

REFERENCES

Anderson, J. R., & Bower, G. H. (1972). Recognition and retrieval processes in free recall. *Psychological Review, 79,* 97–123.

Bigham, B. (1894). Memory. *Psychological Review, 1,* 453–461.

Buchanan, J. P., Gill, T. V., & Braggio, J. T. (1981). Serial position and clustering effects in a chimpanzee's "free recall." *Memory and Cognition, 9,* 651–660.

Castro, C. A. (1995). Primacy and recency effects in Rhesus monkeys (Macaca mulatta) using a serial probe recognition task: I. Effects of diazepam. *Psychopharmacology, 119,* 421–427.

Castro, C. A. (1997). Primacy and recency effects in rhesus monkeys (Macaca mulatta) using a serial probe recognition task: II. Effects of atropine sulfate. *Behavioral Neuroscience, 111,* 676–682.

Castro, C. A., & Larsen, T. (1992). Primacy and recency effects in nonhuman primates. *Journal of Experimental Psychology: Animal Behavior Processes, 18,* 335–340.

Cook, R. G., Wright, A. A., & Sands, S. F. (1991). Interstimulus interval and viewing time effects in monkey list memory. *Animal Learning and Behavior, 19,* 153–163.

Craik, F. I. M. (1970). The fate of primary memory items in free recall. *Journal of Verbal Learning and Verbal Behavior, 9,* 143–148.

Crowder, R. G. (1989). Modularity and dissociations in memory systems. In H. L. Roediger III & F. I. M. Craik (Eds.), *Varieties of memory consciousness* (pp. 271–294). Hillsdale, NJ: Erlbaum.

DiMattia, B. V., & Kesner, R. P. (1984). Serial position curves in rats: Automatic versus effortful information processing. *Journal of Experimental Psychology: Animal Behavior Processes, 10,* 557–563.

Dong, T. (1972). Probe versus free recall. *Journal of Verbal Learning and Verbal Behavior, 11,* 654–661.

Ebenholtz, S. M. (1963). Serial learning: Position learning and sequential associations. *Journal of Experimental Psychology, 66,* 353–362.

Glanzer, M., & Cunitz, J. (1966). Two storage mechanisms in free recall. *Journal of Verbal Learning and Verbal Behavior, 5,* 351–360.

Hagen, J. W., Joneward, R. H., & Kail, R. V. (1975). Cognitive perspectives on the development of memory. In H. W. Reese (Ed.), *Advances in child development and behavior, Vol. 10* (pp. 57–101). New York: Academic.

Hinrichs, J. V., Mewaldt, S. P., Ghoneim, M. M., & Berie, J. L. (1982). Diazepam and learning: assessment of acquisition deficits. *Pharmacology, Biochemistry and Behavior, 17,* 165–170.

Hintzman, D. L., Block, R. A., & Summers, J. J. (1973). Contextual associations and memory for serial position. *Journal of Experimental Psychology, 97,* 220–229.

Hull, C. L., Hovland, C. I., Ross, R. T., Hall, M., Perkins, D. T., & Fitch, F. B. (1940). *Mathmatico-deductive theory of rote learning.* New Haven, CT: Yale University.

Intraub, H. (1980). Presentation rate and the representation of briefly glimpsed pictures in memory. *Journal of Experimental Psychology: Human Learning and Memory, 6,* 1–12.

Kesner, R. P. (1985). Correspondence between humans and animals in coding of temporal attributes: Role of hippocampus and prefrontal cortex. *Annals of the New York Academy of Sciences, 444,* 122–136.

Kesner, R. P., & Novak, J. M. (1982). Serial position curve in rats: Role of the dorsal hippocampus. *Science, 218,* 173–175.

Matzke, S. M., & Castro, C. A. (1998). Primacy and recency effects I Rhesus monkeys (Macaca mulatta) using a serial probe recognition task: III. A developmental analysis. *Developmental Psychobiology, 32,* 215–224.

McGeoch, J. A., & Irion, A. L. (1952). *The psychology of human learning.* New York: Longmans.

Miller, E. (1971). On the nature of the memory disorder in presenile dementia. *Neuropsychology, 9,* 75–81.

Milner, B. (1978). Clues to the cerebral organization of memory. In P. Buser & A. Rougeul-Buser (Eds.), *Cerebral correlates of conscious experience* (pp. 139–153). Amsterdam: Elsevier.

Raffel, G. (1936). Two determinants of the effect of primacy. *American Journal of Psychology, 48,* 654–657.

Richardson, J. T. E., Frith, C. D., Scott, E., Crow, T. J., & Cunningham-Owens, D. (1984). The effects of intravenous diazepam and hyoscine upon recognition memory. *Behavioural Brain Research, 14,* 193–199.

Sands, S. F., & Wright, A. A. (1980a). Primate memory. Retention of serial list items by a rhesus monkey. *Science, 209,* 938–940.

Santiago, H. C., & Wright, A. A. (1984). Pigeon memory. Same/different concept learning, serial probe recognition acquisition, and probe delay effects on the serial-position function. *Journal of Experimental Psychology: Animal Behavior Processes, 10,* 498–512.

Smith, W. G. (1896). Studies from Harvard psychological laboratory. *Psychological Review, 3,* 21–31.

Waugh, N. C. (1960). Serial position and the memory-span. *American Journal of Psychology, 73,* 68–79.

Wagner, A. R., & Pfautz, P. L. (1978). A bowed serial-position function in habituation of sequential stimuli. *Animal Learning & Behavior, 6,* 395–400.

Welch, G. B., & Burnett, C. T. (1924). Is primacy a factor in association-formation? *American Journal of Psychology, 35,* 396–401.

Wells, J. E. (1974). Strength theory and judgments or recency frequency. *Journal of Verbal Learning and Verbal Behavior, 22,* 219–223.

Wright, A. A., Sands, S. F., & Santiago, H. C. (1984). Monkey memory: Same/different concept learning, serial probe acquisition, and probe delay effects. *Journal of Experimental Psychology: Animal Behavior Processes, 10,* 513–529.

Young, R. K. (1959). A comparison of two methods of learning serial associations. *American Journal of Psychology, 72,* 554–559.

C. A. CASTRO
Walter Reed Army Institute of Research

MEMORY
NEURAL MECHANISMS OF LEARNING

PRIMARY MOTOR CORTEX AND PRIMARY SOMATIC SENSORY CORTEX

The primary motor cortex and the primary somatic sensory cortex represent two principal components of sensory motor integration implemented in the brain. Motor cortex has a fundamental function to control voluntary movements, whereas somatic sensory cortex receives and analyzes tactile, joint, and muscle sensory inputs, sometimes in relation to voluntary movement. From classical perspectives, motor cortex functions as the final waystation for already-processed movement commands, relaying signals from premotor cerebral cortical sites to the spinal cord. Similarly, somatic sensory cortex has often been viewed as a pipe to relay subcortical inputs to higher-order cortical sites for further processing. Recent evidence indicates more complex and crucial roles for primary motor cortex and primary somatic sensory cortex in processing motor and somatic sensory information.

PRIMARY MOTOR CORTEX

In the past two decades, new concepts have emerged about the function and role of motor cortex in movement control. Instead of resembling an automatic "piano-player" superimposed upon spinal cord output, motor cortex now appears to have significant functions beyond controlling movement to involve movement planning, motor learning, and motor cognition. The neural substrate for these higher-order functions of motor cortex likely relates to the distributed and plastic anatomical and functional organization within motor cortex.

Motor Cortical Organization

Motor cortex has three functional subdivisions, one each for the upper limb, the lower limb, and the head and neck. Output from neural elements within these subdivisions, either individual neurons or circuits, yields the motor commands that elaborate voluntary movement. Previous notions concerning organizing principles of motor cortex indicated a somatotopic pattern that resembled a distorted but recognizable body shape—the homunculus—represented upon the surface of the motor cortex. Each major subdivision also appeared to have an orderly proximal-to-distal arrangement of its component parts. A functional consequence of the homuncular arrangement could imply dedication of specific neural elements, such as a cortical column, to controlling one body part, perhaps a finger.

Recent evidence suggests that the neural elements in motor cortex subdivisions do not have a regular and organized somatotopic pattern. Using the motor cortex arm representation as an example, neurophysiological and neuroimaging data now indicate a widely distributed, multiple and overlapping representation of the fingers, wrist, elbow, and shoulder in the motor cortex arm area. Thus, neural circuits in motor cortex having functional connections with the fingers are intermingled, and perhaps shared, with comparable circuits for the wrist, elbow, and shoulder. Intermingling of functional representations does not appear to extend beyond the major motor cortex subdivisions of the head, arm, and leg. Instead, integration of, for example, hand and head movements likely occurs at other cortical, subcortical, or spinal sites. The distributed and shared functional organization of motor cortex can provide for flexibility and enormous storage capacity.

Motor Cortex Plasticity and Cognition

Motor function has nearly infinite flexibility, ranging from capabilities to learn new simple or complex tasks to recover from CNS damage. Changes in motor cortex internal processing and motor cortex output likely contribute to behavioral flexibility. Indeed, it became apparent nearly one hundred years ago that motor cortex output could exhibit flexibility. These early observations indicated that the functional coupling of single motor cortex sites could exhibit plasticity. The flexibility of motor cortex output appears to depend, in part, upon behavioral or physiological context. For example, setting oneself to move or receiving more somatic sensory input can yield differing motor cortex output, even though the peripheral motor system has not changed. These effects may be explained by changes in central set by neural facilitation of motor cortex networks. Though motor cortex representations are flexible, there remain limits on such flexibility. In the normal brain, arm sites retain functionality related to arm movements, and the same stability occurs for head and leg sites. Nevertheless, the form and functionality of motor cortex output appears to depend on local interactions and synaptic inputs.

Possibly related to its flexible output, motor cortex appears to have an important role in adapting and learning motor skills. Motor representations in motor cortex of humans exhibit modification following short-term or long-term experience. Repeating a finger movement alters motor cortex representations rapidly, sometimes within five or ten minutes. Learning a movement sequence changes the amount of functional activation in motor cortex or the coupling between motor cortex and target structures in the spinal cord. Motor cortex patterns also change when humans learn to associate arbitrary visual signals with already known motor skills; a simple example would be braking a car for a blue light. The association between the blue light and the act of braking is new, but both the stimulus and the movement are known.

Neural substrates in motor cortex may provide the basis for motor learning. Plasticity occurs between sites interconnected with internal, or horizontal, connections in motor cortex. Many of these horizontal connections exhibit short- and long-term synaptic plasticity. Blockade of motor cortical synaptic plasticity reduces behavioral manifestations of motor learning or motor cortex output shifts. Further, learning a new motor skill appears to leave a memory trace in the synaptic organization of local circuits of motor cortex. The coupling of functional studies on motor cortex relationships to motor learning and the new findings on synaptic reorganization of motor cortex suggest the motor cortex does have an important role in skill acquisition.

A motor cortex capacity in learning suggests roles for motor cortex in other higher-order functions, including cognition. Neurons in motor cortex have functional relationships with movement planning and appear to code for abstract movement features such as direction, movement goal, and target position. Most importantly, activity of motor cortical neurons occurring during cognitive activities can be uncoupled from observable movements or neuronal excitability occurring within motor portions of the spinal cord. In humans, mental rehearsal of movements activates motor cortex, again without observable movements.

PRIMARY SOMATIC SENSORY CORTEX

The primary somatic sensory cortex receives detailed sensory information about the skin, muscle, and joints from subcortical relay stations. It has four anatomically distinguishable subdivisions that separately process sensation related to skin surface deformations or deep joint and muscle sensations. Each somatic sensory cortex subzone has a complete representation of the body surface in a distorted homuncular shape similar to that occurring in motor cortex. Differing from motor cortex, the representation of the body surface in somatic sensory cortex has greater regularity, with little overlap among circuits processing somatic sensory input from nearby body parts. Somatic sensory cortex has a columnar organization, such that neurons aligned vertically process that same type of somatic sensory stimulus impinging on the same point of the body surface. The processing occurring in the vertical columnar units appears to have a role in converting sensory data into perceptions of stimulus velocity, texture, and form. Thus, somatic sensory cortex, like motor cortex, does not function solely as a passive conduit between lower and higher centers, but has local processing units. Somatic sensory cortex relays locally processed information laterally to other body part representations within somatic sensory cortex and to motor and association areas of the cerebral cortex.

Representation of the body surface in somatic sensory cortex exhibits plasticity following injury or experience. Denervation of peripheral somatic sensory input by nerve injury or pathological changes deprives cortical zones of crucial inputs. The withdrawal of input to somatic sensory cortex can yield unresponsive zones, but more commonly neighboring body representations in somatic sensory cortex appear to expand into the denervated cortical territory. Thus, a functional expansion occurs. Analogous expansions or reorganizations occur in relation to experience. Repetition of sensory-based actions, either related or unrelated to associative tactile learning, can yield expansion of body representations of the appendage used repetitively into adjacent representations.

In summary, primary motor cortex and primary somatic sensory cortex have complete and complex representations of the body. These two areas represent the major cortical output and input structures for sensory motor integration. Motor and somatic sensory cortex do not function as simple purveyors of already-processed motor commands (motor cortex) or of unprocessed somatic sensory inputs. They have key roles as higher-order information processing structures and participate in many aspects of sensory motor integration.

SUGGESTED READING

Buonomano, D. V., & Merzenich, M. M. (1998). "Cortical plasticity: From synapses to maps." *Annual Review of Neuroscience, 21,* 149–86.

Kaas, J. H. (1997). Topographic maps are fundamental to sensory processing. *Brain Research Bulletin, 44,* 107–12.

Sanes, J. N., & Donoghue, J. P. (2000). Plasticity and primary motor cortex. *Annual Review of Neuroscience, 23,* 393–415.

J. N. SANES
Brown University

PRIMARY SOMATOSENSORY CORTEX

PRIMARY PREVENTION OF PSYCHOPATHOLOGY

Primary prevention involves efforts to reduce the future incidence of emotional disorders and mental conditions in populations of persons not yet affected. The efforts are proactive. Primary prevention sometimes is directed at high-risk groups, or at groups approaching high-risk situations or potential life crises. Programs in primary prevention may involve the reduction of organic factors contributing to psychopathology, efforts to reduce avoidable stress, the building of competencies and coping skills, the development of improved self-esteem, and the enhancement of support networks and groups.

The logic of investing in efforts at primary prevention is supported in several ways. First, the incredible imbalance between the number of people suffering emotional distress and those with mental disorders makes it impossible for individual interventionists to reach those needing help, and this gap is difficult to bridge. For example, in the United States, it is estimated by various sources who have conducted careful epidemiological studies that about 15% of the population is afflicted with "hard core mental disturbances," and an even larger group each year undergoes severe life crises resulting from stresses such as marital disruption and divorce, the death of a loved one, or involuntary unemployment. Individual professional mental health services are reported by the President's Commission on Mental Health (1978) as being available only to some 7 million people. This is the total annual number served with at least one visit to a mental health facility or mental health professional practitioner. Obviously only a very small proportion of persons undergoing mental and emotional disturbances is being seen by a mental health professional. People take their emotional problems to general medical practitioners (where they are likely to get a prescription for a mild tranquilizer), or to members of the clergy, or simply to neighbors or friends. Even if one takes all of these other helpers into consideration, a majority of persons with emotional problems still receives little or no help. To complicate this problem further, the President's Commission on Mental Health (1978) found large groups within the society to be inappropriately served. These groups include members of minority groups, the physically handicapped, the mentally retarded, children and adolescents, and women. In summary, the mental health system, relying as it does on individual therapy, whether physical or psychological, is a long way from supplying enough help to those in need. Groups at highest risk for every kind of mental and emotional pathology (such as migrant farm workers) are least likely to have any help available; groups affluent and sophisticated about psychological services, but not severely affected, are the ones most likely to receive psychotherapeutic services. This continuing disparity buttresses the historic public health view: No mass disorder afflicting humankind is ever brought under control or eliminated by attempts at treating the afflicted individual or by attempts at producing large numbers of individual practitioners.

Most of the enormous improvement in the health and increasing longevity of members of our society has come about as a result of the successful application of the methods of primary prevention within the field of public health. Public health prevention methods are relatively simple and straightforward. They involve "finding the noxious agent" and taking steps to eliminate it or neutralize it; or "strengthening the host," which really means finding methods of building up the resistance of people against the noxious agent; or "preventing transmission," keeping the noxious agent from reaching the host. These effective methods of reducing the incidence of the great plagues that have afflicted humankind over the centuries resulted from the medical insight developed in the latter years of the 19th century, which held that each disease has a specific cause. Once the cause had been identified, steps could be taken to eliminate it or protect the host from contracting it. Thus we have seen the gradual elimination of typhoid fever, tuberculosis, polio, and smallpox, to name just a few diseases that have gradually disappeared.

During the early enthusiasm for the application of public health methods in the field of mental disorder, it seemed just a matter of time until these "mental illnesses" could also be brought under control and eliminated. Indeed the success of psychiatry early in the 20th century in identifying the cause of general paresis as resulting from untreated syphilis, and the discovery of the role of vitamin deficiency in the development of pellagral psychosis, served both to support and sustain the hope that each mental illness gradually would yield the secret of its causation, thus leading to effective methods of treatment and prevention. But as time has passed, it has gradually become apparent that most of the so-called mental illnesses may not have a specific and unique cause. And as the psychiatric nomenclature has continued to embrace more and more conditions that clearly do not represent true illnesses (school phobias, marital disruption, learning disabilities, substance abuse, and so on), it is increasingly clear that separate physical causes will not be found for each psychiatric label.

While there are helpful analogies between the strategies for the prevention of physical illness and the prevention of mental conditions, there are also dangers. It is easy to accept the psychiatric position that the mental conditions to be prevented are also illnesses/diseases with specific physical causes that can be discovered and eliminated. As a matter of fact, relatively few genuine and specific causes of mental diseases have been established, and they represent only a small fraction of the conditions with which we are concerned.

We must recognize that a high level of stress-causing conditions (such as powerlessness, unemployment, sexism, marital disruption, loss of support systems) can cause any of several patterns of emotional disruption (such as depression, alcoholism, anxiety, hypertension). In brief, there is a nonspecific relation between causes and consequences.

If our purpose is to reduce the incidence of the different conditions or compulsive lifestyles we refer to as mental disorders, is there any way to think about organizing our prevention efforts? The following is a formula that may be helpful:

$$\text{Incidence} = \frac{\text{Organic factors} + \text{Stress}}{\text{Competence} + \text{Self-esteem} + \text{Support networks}}$$

To succeed in preventive efforts is to reduce the incidence of the various forms of emotional disturbance. There are several strategies for accomplishing that purpose: The first of these is to prevent,

minimize, or reduce the number of organic factors. The more an organic factor can be reduced or eliminated, the smaller the resulting incidence will be. To give specific examples:

1. Reduction of the amount of brain damage resulting from lead poisoning or from accidents reduces the resulting mental conditions.

2. Prevention of damaged genes from developing into damaged individuals (after amniocentesis, aborting a fetus with chromosomal abnormalities) prevents the birth of a retarded or brain-damaged infant.

3. Provision of medication to reduce hypertension lowers the incidence of brain injury resulting from strokes.

4. Improvement of the circulation of blood to the brain reduces the rate of later cerebral arteriosclerosis.

A second strategy that is obvious from the formula involves the reduction of stress. Here relationships become more complex. No longer are there such clear cause-and-effect relationships as were observed in the discussion of organic factors. Stress takes many forms. Reducing stress requires changes in the physical and social environment. Environmental stress situations involve a whole complex of interacting variables. Some forms of social stress are a product of deeply ingrained cultural values and ways of life not easily susceptible to change. Stress may result from low self-esteem that becomes a kind of self-fulfilling prophecy. Women and members of ethnic minorities, who learn from earliest childhood that their sex or race is seen as inferior, grow up with lower self-esteem, which may be exceedingly difficult to change. Preventive efforts take the form of public education, changes in the mass media, and the reshaping of pervasive value systems. Clearly such efforts encounter the angry resistance of the power forces that get real benefit from the values being criticized.

An area of major research investigation in recent years has been the relationship between stressful life events and the onset of both physical illness and mental disturbance. Studies report correlations between severity of life stresses and the probability of the appearance of specific illnesses in the future. Statistically significant relationships have been found between the stresses of life change and diseases such as tuberculosis, heart attacks, accidents, leukemia, and diabetes. High life stress has been repeatedly associated with subsequent mental and emotional disturbances. Being part of a strong support network reduces the risk of exposure to stress.

Techniques for protecting individuals against high stresses, or providing ways of reducing and mitigating the effects of such stressful situations, might be expected to reduce the incidence of both physical and mental problems. Working with high-risk groups likely to undergo significant stress might be significant to prevention (Joffe & Albee, 1981).

Another area of intervention relevant to the reduction of the incidence of emotional disorder involves efforts at increasing self-esteem, support systems, and the competence of people to deal with life's problems, particularly problems of social interactions, and the development of a wide range of coping skills. In this area, recent research indicates that children can be taught social and cognitive skills that increase their ability to deal with the problems of living, which, as a consequence, reduces the incidence of frustration and emotional disturbance (Bond & Rosen, 1980; Kent & Rolf, 1979).

The model described by the formula obviously has shortcomings. Often intervention results in changes in all areas. For example, training in a sport may involve regular practice with resulting improvement in physical coordination, bodily health, musculature, circulation, and a sense of physical well-being. At the same time, the subject may experience a reduction of stress as he or she burns up energy in physical activity; meanwhile improvement in competence in performing the physical requirements of the sport may increase self-confidence and self-esteem. Thus improvement occurs at all levels.

Ultimately many prevention efforts will require societal change through political action (Joffe & Albee, 1981). For this reason, the struggle to redistribute power as a strategy for the prevention of psychopathology has only begun.

REFERENCES

Bond, L., & Rosen, J. (Eds.). (1980). *Primary prevention of psychopathology: Competence and coping during adulthood.* Hanover, NH: University Press of New England.

Joffe, J. M., & Albee, G. W. (1981). *Prevention through political action and social change. The primary prevention of psychopathology* (Vol. V). Hanover, NH: University Press of New England.

Kent, M. W., & Rolf, J. E. (Eds.). (1979). *Primary prevention of psychopathology: Promoting social competence in children* (Vol. 4). Hanover, NH: University Press of New England.

President's Commission on Mental Health. (1978). *Report to the President from the President's Commission on Mental Health* (Vols. 1–4). Washington, DC: U.S. Government Printing Office.

G. W. ALBEE
Florida Mental Health Institute

HOT LINE SERVICES
PSYCHOTHERAPY

PRIMARY SOMATOSENSORY CORTEX

The somatosensory cortex was defined in earlier human studies as the cortical region the stimulation of which provoked subjective somatosensory experiences. It was defined in various other mammals as the cortical region where somatosensory-evoked potentials were recorded after stimulation of the periphery. The cortical areas involved in the somatosensory processing are distributed widely in the parietal lobe, the postcentral gyrus, posterior parietal regions, and lateral regions. They form a connected network with serial (hierarchical) and parallel cortico-cortical connections. Among them, the primary somatosensory cortex (or the first somatosensory cortex [SI]) is defined as the area where the shortest-latency, evoked potentials are recorded after stimulation of the periphery. It receives direct and strongest projections from the thalamic ventrobasal complex—specific relay nuclei mainly for the dorsal column-lemniscal system that conveys innocuous somatosensory signals from the periphery.

ANATOMY

The SI of primates is composed of four different cytoarchitectonic areas of Brodmann: areas 3a, 3b, 1, and 2 in the postcentral gyrus. The thalamic ventrobasal complex projects mainly to areas 3a and 3b. Sensory signals from deep tissues—muscles or joints—project mainly to area 3a, while those from the superficial tissues—skin or intra-oral mucous membrane—project mainly to area 3b. Areas 1 and 2 receive fewer projections from the thalamic ventrobasal complex and instead receive cortico-cortical projections from areas 3a and 3b and some additional projections from the thalamic association nuclei. All the four cytoarchitectonic subdivisions of SI have connections to the second somatosensory cortex (SII) in the lateral regions (see Jones, 1986; Burton & Sinclair, 1996).

SOMATOTOPIC REPRESENTATION OF THE BODY SURFACE

It is generally accepted that the sensory cortex is characterized with topological and orderly representation of the receptor sheet. In the primary somatosensory cortex of the primate, the oral cavity, face, hand, arm, trunk, leg, and foot are represented somatotopically along the lateral-medial axis of the postcentral gyrus. Penfield and Boldrey (1937) invented a homunculus to describe such an arrangement. The somatotopic representation of the body over the cortical surface was demonstrated in various other mammals by recording evoked potentials. The cortical tissue devoted to each body-part representation is not even. That part of the body which is exaggerated differs among animals. In primates, the cortical region devoted to the representation of the oral cavity, face, hand, or foot is much larger compared to that for the trunk or proximal limbs (see Burton & Sinclair, 1996).

HIERARCHICAL PROCESSING IN THE FINGER REGION

Modern microelectrode techniques to record single neuronal activity in awake animals enabled scientists to analyze detailed organization of the enlarged cortical finger representation in the monkey (Burton & Sinclair, 1996). In the finger region of area 3b in the monkey, functionally unique parts of fingers (i.e., tips, ventral glabrous surfaces, and dorsal surfaces) are represented separately, forming different subdivisions of area 3b. In areas 1 and 2, progressive interphalangeal or interdigital integration takes place along the rostro-caudal axis of the postcentral gyrus; thus, receptive fields of neurons in areas 1 and 2 become larger, covering more than one phalange of a finger, or more than one finger. The interdigital integration is more remarkable in the ulnar fingers than in the radial ones. There are unique types of neurons in areas 1 and 2 with selectivity to specific features of stimulus, such as the direction of a moving stimulus; the presence of an edge or rough surface; those that are activated better or solely by the monkey's active hand movements, including reaching; or those facilitated or inhibited by attention. Diversity in the receptive field of cortical neurons was pointed out also in conjunction with a cortical column (a perpendicular array of neurons). There are a number of additional observations in favor of serial hierarchical processing.

The integration proceeds to combine information from the bilateral sides in the higher stages of hierarchical processing: A substantial number of neurons with bilateral or ipsilateral receptive fields are found in the caudalmost part (areas 2 and 5) of the postcentral finger region (Iwamura, Iriki, & Tanaka, 1994). Bilateral integration is seen also in other body parts. The bilateral receptive fields are large and the most complex types found in this gyrus. The distribution of the bilateral receptive field neurons roughly corresponds to that of callosal connections in this gyrus.

PLASTIC CHANGES IN THE REPRESENTATION OF FINGERS

After extensive training to use three fingers together, there emerged in area 3b of owl monkey neurons with multidigit receptive fields, which were never seen in untrained animals (Wang, Merzenich, Sameshima, & Jenkins 1995). Blind persons who use three fingers together to read Braille frequently misperceive which of the fingers actually touches the text. In these subjects an expansion and dislocation of SI hand representation were found by magnetic source imaging technique (Sterr et al., 1998). The representation area of fingers measured by magnetic source imaging increased in the left hand in string players possibly as the result of extensive training (Elbert, Pantev, Weinbruch, Rockstroh, & Taub, 1995).

ATTRIBUTES OF TACTILE PERCEPTION REPRESENTED IN CORTICAL ACTIVITY

Cortical activities representing spatio-temporal patterns of tactile skin stimulation such as flutter-vibration, motion, direction, length, velocity of tactile stimulus, surface texture, spatial form, and so on, have been studied (see Burton & Sinclair, 1996). DiCarlo, Johnson, and Hsiao (1998) found that 94% of area 3b neurons in the finger region contained a single central excitation, as well as regions of inhibition located on one or more sides of the excitatory center. It was thus indicated that area 3b neurons act as local spatio-temporal filters and may contribute to form and texture perception.

CORTICAL REPRESENTATION OF PAIN

Single-cell recordings in the monkey established that nociceptive pathways project to area 3b and 1 of the primary somatosensory cortex. Pain has a sensory component in addition to its strong emotional component, and is processed by multiple distributed cortical loci. The SI cortex is involved in the sensory-discriminative aspect of pain, especially stimulus localization, while intensity may be coded by multiple cortical areas (see Treede, Kenshalo, Gracely, & Jones, 1999).

REFERENCES

Burton, H., & Sinclair, R. (1996). Somatosensory cortex and tactile perceptions. In L. Kruger (Ed.), *Touch and pain,* (pp. 105–177). London: Academic.

DiCarlo, J. J., Johnson, K. O., & Hsiao, S. S. (1998). Structure of receptive fields in area 3b of primary somatosensory cortex in the alert monkey. *Journal of Neuroscience, 18,* 2626–2645.

Elbert, T., Pantev, C., Wienbruch, C., Rockstroh, B., & Taub, E. (1995). Increased cortical representation of the fingers of the left hand in string players. *Science, 270,* 305–307.

Iwamura, Y., Iriki, A., & Tanaka, M. (1994). Bilateral hand representation in the postcentral somatosensory cortex. *Nature, 369,* 554–556.

Jones, E. G. (1986). Connectivity of the primate sensory-motor cortex. In E. G. Jones & A. Peters (Eds.), *Cerebral cortex, sensory-motor areas and aspects of cortical connectivity* (Vol. 5). New York: Plenum.

Penfield, W., & Boldrey, E. (1937). Somatic motor and sensory representation in the cerebral cortex of man as studied by electrical stimulation. *Brain, 60,* 389–443.

Sterr, A., Muller, M. M., Elbert, T., Rockstroh, B., Pantev, C., & Taub, E. (1998). Changed perceptions in Braille readers. *Nature, 391,* 134–135.

Treede, R.-D., Kenshalo, D. R., Gracely, R. H., & Jones, A. K. P. (1999). The cortical representation of pain. *Pain, 79,* 105–111.

Wang, X., Merzenich, M. M., Sameshima, K., & Jenkins, W. M. (1995). Remodelling of hand representation in adult cortex determined by timing of tactile stimulation. *Nature, 378,* 71–75.

Y. IWAMURA
Toho University, Japan

PRIMATE BEHAVIOR

Since the order *Primates* includes some 200 species ranging in size from less than 100 g to more than 100 kg, in habitat from the tropical rain forest to hot desert to mountain and temperate climates that include heavy snow cover for most of the winter months, in social group sizes from two to hundreds, and in both nocturnal and diurnal activity patterns, uniformity of behavior within the order is not to be expected. There are, however, some similar physical, growth, sensory, motor, and hence behavioral characteristics that many possess, so that some patterns of behavioral similarity can be discerned.

One such characteristic of primates is that in general they are born as singletons, so that they usually do not have an age-comparable sibling either as a companion or as a competitor during the growth period. The infant is not without attention, however, for the newborn of many species attracts the interest of other adult and semiadult females and of other juveniles of both sexes. Moreover, primates generally have a long infancy and adolescence—several years in many species; therefore, dependence on the mother is close and protracted. During this time, the male protects the helpless, burdened mother. Intimate bonds are thus established between them that last throughout life. Such bonds serve to maintain family integrity and to provide information essential to the deterrence of intrafamilial breeding. The long juvenile period affords the youngster the opportunity to learn the rules of social stratification and of communication, to acquire information about the environment (e.g., water-hole locations, home range limits, and nest construction, if it is customary for the species to make one), and to acquire physical skills needed in later life.

Another characteristic of many primates is versatility of posture and locomotion, particularly among the simians and apes. Because of its prehensile hands, the infant can travel with the mother by clinging to her fur. The infant may ride on her back or cling to her chest or to her groin. The adult or infant may walk on all fours, walk upright using the hands to transport objects, climb tree trunks, or swing from branch to branch (brachiation). Not all species engage in all these activities, but many perform more than one habitually. With this postural and locomotory competence, many primates are equally skilled in the trees or on the ground. Oddly, however, most primates do not take to water eagerly, even though it is known that some, and perhaps many, species can swim (the great apes probably excepted), even from the age of 1 or 2 days.

Many primates possess opposable thumbs that can press against the pads of the fingers. Prehensile toes and, in a few South American species, prehensile tails add to the primate's capability for handling and maneuvering objects. This skill enables these animals to move about on the ground or in the trees while carrying objects or picking fruit, or regulating the activities of an infant.

Higher primates, particularly chimpanzees, can use tools, which they construct to reach and rake in objects that otherwise would be out of reach (or to insert into termite nests and then extract in order to eat the termites adhering to them).

The sensory capacities of primates are not distinguishably superior to those of other animals, although most primate species possess color vision that is similar, but apparently not identical, to that of humans with normal color vision; it seems to be like that of persons who are color-weak.

The most outstanding characteristic of the primates is the upper limit, in some species, of their capacity for cognitive achievement. They have the ability to internally represent and modify informational input, which allows them to respond to a signal after it has disappeared, to recognize a sign whose value (meaning) changes from one circumstance to another, to identify a stimulus—say a sphere, haptically (by active touch) after they have been shown it (cross-modal transfer). South American monkeys readily climb a pole to reach food and chimpanzees have invented ladders. Other cognitive activity includes the use of symbols as means of communication. Whether or not this activity demonstrates the use of language in the human sense is a matter of some dispute; nevertheless, skill levels such as these have not even been approached by nonprimate species.

Ethologists have taught that much of the behavior of lower animals is regulated by genetic factors rather than by learning. Experiments in which closely related but behaviorally distinct species are interbred reveal that the behavior patterns of the offspring correspond to expectations based on Mendelian laws of inheritance. Such genetic experiments, along with isolation experiments in which the behaviors appear on schedule despite the fact that learning is prevented, show the importance of such instinctive (inherited) behaviors in the life economy of the animals. Yet, at least

in the domain of reproductive behavior, studies of the few higher primates that were raised isolated from others of their species (macaques and apes) show that reproduction behavior is devastated, a fact that indicates the dominance of learning over instinct in this domain. Other activities such as nest building, which predominantly are genetically expressed in lower animals, may be mainly acquired through experience, perhaps at a very early age. It has been established, for example, that chimpanzees born in the forests of Africa built nests when given "suitable" materials even many years after they were imported to the laboratory or zoo. Laboratory-born animals, in contrast, merely played with the same materials. The chimpanzees were imported as babies, and it is inconceivable that they actually constructed a nest in Africa. It is clear that not only did they learn the rudiments of nest building by observation, but they learned the principles of nest building rather than the specifics of it, because the "suitable" materials consisted of shredded paper, shredded wood, pine straw, tree branches, and lengths of rope, quite unlike the intact trees in which their mothers made their nightly nests.

A. J. RIOPELLE
Louisiana State University

ETHOLOGY
HERITABILITY
INSTINCT

PRIMING

Priming is a long-term memory phenomenon that produces increased or decreased efficiency of processing repeated stimuli, typically words, pictures, or ideas. Most long-term memory tasks comprise three phases: (a) a study phase in which stimuli are encoded; (b) a retention interval in which an unrelated task is performed; and (c) a test phase in which memories of the encoded stimuli are retrieved. Retrieval can be measured either as a conscious recollection of the study-phase stimuli, or as a nonconscious change in processing speed, processing accuracy, or response bias accrued to the recently studied material. Retrieval tasks that require conscious and deliberate reconstruction of the study-phase experience are referred to as explicit, direct, or declarative. Retrieval tasks that require no reference to the study-phase experience are referred to as implicit, indirect, or procedural (Richardson-Klavehn & Bjork, 1988).

Priming memory is revealed on implicit tasks. In the test phase of a priming memory experiment, the subject is asked to perform a task that is ostensibly unrelated to the study-phase task but, in actuality, requires repeated processing of studied stimuli and new processing of unstudied stimuli. In some tasks, processing of the identical study-phase stimuli is required (identity or direct priming). In other tasks, processing of stimuli that are *related* to the study-phase stimuli is required (indirect priming). Priming memory is calculated as the difference in performance between repeated versus new stimuli, which reflects memory acquired in the study phase and retrieved in the test phase.

Priming memory has been measured on a variety of different implicit tasks. For example, seeing the word STORK or a picture of a stork in a study phase makes people in a test phase quicker to identify that word or picture when it is presented in complete form (naming tasks), in partial form (degraded naming tasks), or very briefly in time (perceptual identification tasks). Seeing the word STORK in a study phase makes people in a test phase quicker to decide whether STORK is an example of a bird (category-exemplar verification tasks). Seeing the word STORK in a study phase makes people in a test phase more likely to produce that word when asked to complete three letters (STO___) into the first word that comes to mind (word-stem completion tasks), to add letters so as to make a fragment (S_ _ R _) into a real word (word-fragment completion tasks), to say the first word that comes to mind that goes with the word BABY (word-association tasks), or to provide examples of birds (category-exemplar production tasks).

Priming is not limited to previously known items or well-known associations between items (e.g., BIRD-STORK). Priming has been demonstrated using novel items such as nonsense pseudowords (e.g., BLURK; or nonrepresentational line patterns and designs). Further, priming for new associations has been shown by presenting unrelated pairs of words together in a study phase (e.g., TABLE-PRIDE, WINDOW-POTATO, MOUNTAIN-PRIDE), and then comparing test-phase priming for identical pairs (TABLE-PRIDE) versus recombined pairs (WINDOW-STAMP). People show greater priming for the identical than the recombined pairs, thereby demonstrating priming for a novel association between two words created by their random pairing in a study phase.

Priming is not a unitary memory phenomenon. Any given task invokes multiple cognitive mechanisms that drive multiple kinds of priming. For example, a functional dissociation between tasks that invoke primarily perceptual or conceptual processes in priming has been demonstrated in studies with young subjects. Perceptual priming tasks draw upon processes concerned with the visual, auditory, or tactile form of a target stimulus. These tasks yield priming that is maximal when stimuli are analyzed for perceptual features at study and at test, and diminished by study-test changes in perceptual features (e.g., auditory-to-visual modality and word-to-picture notation). By these criteria, certain priming tasks are considered primarily perceptual (Roediger & McDermott, 1993), including word and picture identification, lexical decision, picture and word naming, degraded picture and word naming, word-fragment completion, word-stem completion, and anagram solution. Conceptual priming tasks draw upon processes concerned with the content or meaning of a target stimulus. These tasks yield priming that is maximal when stimuli are analyzed for conceptual features at study and test, and insensitive to study-test changes in perceptual features. By these criteria, certain priming tasks are considered largely conceptual, including word association, category-exemplar production, and fact completion (Roediger & McDermott, 1993).

Neuropsychological and neuroimaging studies have begun to reveal the neural mechanisms supporting priming memory. Amnesic patients with focal bilateral damage to mesial-temporal or diencephalic structures have normal levels of priming memory for the very materials they cannot recall or recognize (Gabrieli et al., 1994). Priming memory is also intact in patients with progressive damage to subcortical nuclei due to Parkinson's disease (without dementia; Bondi & Kaszniak, 1991) and Huntington's disease (Heindel, Salmon, Shults, Walicke, & Butters, 1989). Thus, the neural substrate supporting priming memory does not appear to include limbic, diencephalic, or subcortical circuits.

Studies of patients with Alzheimer's disease (AD) have suggested which neural substrates may underlie priming memory (Fleischman & Gabrieli, 1998). AD is characterized by degeneration of mesial-temporal structures, which, as in focal amnesia, results in profoundly impaired recall and recognition. Unlike focal amnesia, AD is additionally characterized by progressive and selective damage to association neocortices, which causes deficits in multiple cognitive domains as well as reduction or failure of some kinds of priming memory. These findings suggest that the association neocortex may be the critical neural substrate underlying priming memory.

Some kinds of priming memory remain robust in AD, and the pattern of preservation and loss in priming parallels the regional distribution of neuropathological change that occurs in the disease. Posterior cortical regions are relatively preserved early in the course of AD (e.g., Damasio, Van Hoesen, & Hyman, 1990), and so is perceptual priming (e.g., Fleischman et al., 1995); while anterior cortical regions are damaged in AD (e.g., Damasio, Van Hoesen, & Hyman, 1990), and conceptual priming is impaired (e.g., Monti et al., 1996). These AD findings converge with recent findings from neuroimaging activation studies (e.g. Blaxton et al., 1996); and focal lesion studies; (e.g Gabrieli, Fleischman, Keane, Reminger, & Morrell, 1995); that have demonstrated a posterior cortical locus for visual perceptual priming and have implicated regions of left frontal cortex (Gabrieli, Desmond, Demb, & Wagner, 1996) and left frontal and temporal cortex (Blaxton et al., 1996) in conceptual priming.

Priming as a long-term memory phenomenon independent of conscious forms of long-term memory is a relatively recent discovery. Initial studies date back 25 to 30 years, but the most intensive research in the area has been done only in the past ten years. These empirical and theoretical analyses of priming have contributed valuable information regarding the functional neuroarchitecture of normal human memory. Neuropsychological and neuroimaging analyses of priming form essential components of this scientific effort, and promise to extend our clinical understanding of how human memory changes in the face of aging and neurological disease.

REFERENCES

Blaxton, T. A., Bookheimer, S. Y., Zeffiro, T. A., Figlozzi, C. M., Gaillard, W. D., & Theodore, W. H. (1996). Functional mapping of human memory using PET: Comparisons of conceptual and perceptual tasks. *Canadian Journal of Experimental Psychology, 50,* 42–54.

Bondi, M. W., & Kaszniak, A. W. (1991). Implicit and explicit memory in Alzheimer's disease and Parkinson's disease. *Journal of Clinical and Experimental Neuropsychology, 13,* 339–358.

Damasio, A. R., Van Hoesen, G. W., & Hyman, B. T. (1990). Reflections on the selectivity of neuropathological changes in Alzheimer's disease. In M. F. Schwartz (Ed.), *Modular deficits in Alzheimer-type dementia* (pp. 83–99). Cambridge, MA: MIT Press.

Fleischman, D. A., & Gabrieli, J. D. E. (1998). Repetition priming in normal aging and Alzheimer's Disease: A review of findings and theories. *Psychology & Aging, 13,* 88–119.

Fleischman, D. A., Gabrieli, J. D. E., Reminger, S. L., Rinaldi, J. A., Morrell, F., & Wilson, R. S. (1995). Conceptual priming in perceptual identification for patients with Alzheimer's disease and a patient with right occipital lobectomy. *Neuropsychology, 9,* 187–197.

Gabrieli, J. D. E., Desmond, J. E., Demb, J. B., & Wagner, A. D. (1996). Functional magnetic resonance imaging of semantic memory processes in the frontal lobes. *Psychological Science, 7,* 278–283.

Gabrieli, J. D. E., Fleischman, D. A., Keane, M. M., Reminger, S., & Morrell, F. (1995). Double dissociation between memory systems underlying explicit and implicit memory in the human brain. *Psychological Science, 6,* 76–82.

Gabrieli, J. D. E., Keane, M. M., Stanger, B. Z., Kjelgaard, K. S., Corkin, S., & Growdon, J. H. (1994). Dissociations among structural-perceptual, lexical-semantic, and event-fact memory systems in Alzheimer, amnesic and normal subjects. *Cortex, 30,* 75–103.

Heindel, W. C., Salmon, D. P., Shults, C. W., Walicke, P. A., & Butters, N. (1989). Neuropsychological evidence for multiple implicit memory systems: A comparison of Alzheimer's Huntington's and Parkinson's disease patients. *The Journal of Neuroscience, 9,* 582–587.

Monti, L. A., Gabrieli, J. D. E., Reminger, S. L., Rinaldi, J. A., Wilson, R. S., & Fleischman, D. A. (1996). Differential effects of aging and Alzheimer's disease on conceptual implicit and explicit memory. *Neuropsychology, 10,* 101–112.

Richardson-Klavehn, A., & Bjork, R. A. (1988). Measures of memory. *Annual Review of Psychology, 39,* 475–543.

Roediger, H. L., & McDermott, K. B. (1993). Implicit memory in normal human subjects. In H. Spinnler & F. Boller (Eds.), *Handbook of neuropsychology* (Vol. 8, pp. 63–131). Amsterdam: Elsevier.

D. A. Fleischman
Rush-Presbyterian St. Luke's Medical Center

DECLARATIVE MEMORY
MEMORY
PROCEDURAL MEMORY

PRINCE, MORTON (1854–1929)

Morton Prince was one of the early American pioneers in the study of abnormal psychology. Shortly after receiving the MD degree, he became a follower of S. Weir-Mitchell, who had developed a "rest cure" for a disorder characterized by psychological weakness called neurasthenia. He then studied in Paris and became acquainted with the famous French physician, Pierre Janet, who had developed a theory of abnormal behavior in which certain symptoms were an expression of a *dissociation* or splitting-off from the normal organization of the personality. Thus Prince became a member of the school of "dissociation" and applied the concept later to his study of the multiple personality. He also was attracted to Freud's idea of a dynamic psychology, according to which the bases of human conduct are to be found in drives or instincts.

In 1905, Prince founded the *Journal of Abnormal Psychology* and became its first editor. He encouraged the publication of clinical and experimental studies of abnormal behavior in this journal, and, in fact, admonished American psychologists of the time for ignoring that area of psychology. In 1927, he founded the Psychological Clinic at Harvard.

He is best known for *The Dissociation of a Personality,* in which he described the biography of a multiple personality. Sally Beauchamp had three distinct personalities, which alternated with each other. These he characterized as the saint, the devil, and the woman. Two of the personalities had no knowledge of the existence of the others, except from what they were told. Thus each of these had complete amnesia for the others, so each was dissociated from the others. The third had knowledge of the existence of the other two and thus existed in a *coconscious* manner (a term invented by Prince). The significance of the work lay in the fact that it was the first extensive record of a multiple personality and laid the foundation for further study of this unusual condition.

R. W. Lundin
Wheaton, Illinois

PRISONER'S DILEMMA

The prisoner's dilemma is the name given to an interpersonal game extensively investigated by social psychologists interested in social conflict and its resolution. "Game" in this sense refers to a social situation involving interdependent decision making; that is, a situation in which each party's welfare depends not just on what he or she does, but rather on the combination of responses made by the two parties. Game theory as a formal mathematical discipline categorizes interpersonal games into zero-sum (or constant-sum) games, games of coordination, and mixed-motive games. Zero-sum games are situations of complete competition between the parties—any decision combination that one party prefers is disliked by the other. Coordination games are situations in which the possible decision combinations are given exactly the same preference ordering by both parties, and are often called games of complete cooperation. Mixed-motive games involve both competitive and cooperative elements. The prisoner's dilemma game is the best known mixed-motive game in psychology.

Games are usually presented in normal (or matrix) form in social psychology. Figure 1 represents a simple two-person, two-choice game, where each of the two parties has two choice alternatives, and each party's welfare depends upon the resultant

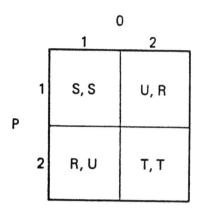

Figure 1.   A game matrix.

combination of choices. The letters entered into the matrix represent payoffs to the two parties for each choice combination. The letter on the left side of each cell represents the payoff to the party whose choices are labeled on the vertical axis (*P*); the letter on the right side of each represents the payoff to the person whose choice alternatives are labeled on the horizontal axis (*O*). A game meets the minimal criteria for a prisoner's dilemma if the following conditions are met for both parties: $U < T < S < R$ (criteria from mathematical game theory are more rigorous). The game is based on an analogy attributed to the mathematician A. W. Tucker. The analogy involves two prisoners held by the police for a crime. The police separate the two prisoners, and inform each that if he will give evidence against the other, he can go free. The prisoners are aware that if only one gives evidence, the other will receive the maximum penalty, say 20 years; but if both give evidence, each will receive a moderate sentence, for example, 10 years. However, if neither gives evidence, each will be tried on a minor charge, with a penalty for each of a fine and less than a year in prison. Each would prefer to go free, but if both give evidence, both will go to jail for years. On the other hand, opting for the minor charge by refusing to give evidence may in fact result in the most severe penalty if the other gives evidence. Refusing to give evidence is defined as a cooperative response, since both must do so for the choice to yield mutually beneficial payoffs. Giving evidence may be seen as competitive—as an effort to obtain the best outcome for oneself at the expense of the other, or as defensive, in an effort to thwart the competitive intention of the other. Experimental subjects who have played this game typically make competitive choices despite the collectively poor payoffs this strategy yields. Its extensive use by experimental social psychologists is attributable to its obvious parallels with recurrent problems of conflict, such as arms races.

SUGGESTED READING

Pruitt, D. G., & Kimmel, M. J. (1977). Twenty years of experimental gaming: Critique, synthesis, and suggestions for the future. *Annual Review of Psychology, 28,* 363–392.

Rapoport, A., & Cbammah, A. M. (1965). *Prisoner's dilemma: A study in conflict and cooperation.* Ann Arbor, MI: University of Michigan Press.

W. P. SMITH
Vanderbilt University

CONFLICT MEDIATION
COOPERATION/COMPETITION

PRIVILEGED COMMUNICATIONS

The privacy of communication between a client and a psychologist is critical to the client's willingness to disclose personal information in a therapy or an evaluation setting. Clients may avoid therapy and evaluation, or not discuss matters of personal intimacy in such situations, if they are not certain that such personal disclosures will be kept private. Lack of protection of the client's communication, therefore, may preclude the maximum benefits of the relationship.

There are two major concepts that address the issue of privacy of communication between client and psychologist (Shah, 1969). The first, confidentiality, is dealt with in the ethical standards of mental health professions (e.g., American Psychological Association, "Ethical principles of psychologists") and holds that psychologists and others have the ethical responsibility not to reveal, except in certain special situations (e.g., a danger to someone), the disclosures of clients. The principle of confidentiality has been upheld in judicial and legislative actions of some states. The principle does not, however, protect client-psychologist communications from being revealed when the latter is a witness in a court action.

The second concept is that of privileged communication. Most states have established statutes that prevent psychologists from being forced to testify concerning information disclosed by the client in the professional relationship, except under certain conditions (Foster, 1980). Most states also cover physicians in their privileged communication statutes, while some also have laws that cover psychiatrists specifically, and some cover social workers. Privileged communication statutes are legislative products of the states. No federal law grants the client-psychologist relationship a communication privilege.

The privilege—that is, the choice as to whether information will be made public—belongs to the client. This explicitly provides that no professional covered by a privileged communication statute has the legal right to reveal information independently of the client's consent. Should a client wish to have the information revealed, the psychologist is obligated to comply. In certain cases (e.g., competency hearings), a judge may deny the privilege whenever the evidence revealed by the professional is likely to be in the best interests of the client or of society (Swoboda et al., 1980).

A breach of confidentiality may not be a breach of privilege but a breach of privilege is always a breach of confidentiality (Siegel, 1979). Privileged communication is, therefore, a narrower concept than confidentiality. It is specific to the judicial process and not relevant to communication with other professionals, parents, and so forth, as are the constraints of confidentiality.

The types of privilege granted to clients in their communications with mental health professionals vary among jurisdictions. Some statutes give psychologists the same privilege as attorneys. Others identify the privilege as identical to that granted to physicians, whereas some have a specific privilege granted to psychologists and others to psychotherapists. One issue unique to mental health is whether professional contact occurred. Clients are not usually concerned about keeping the fact that they have consulted an attorney private, while they might well wish to keep private the fact that they have consulted a psychologist. Therefore, a client of a psychologist often may need greater protection under the law than a client of an attorney (Foster, 1980).

Criteria for exercise of the communication privilege often require licensure or certification of the psychologist and clarity of a professional relationship between client and psychologist. That is, the statute applies only if the person involved in the litigation is one with whom the psychologist has had a clear professional relationship. Information that the psychologist obtains outside the relationship is usually not protected (DeKraai & Sales, 1981).

A related issue pertains to which other people are covered in privileged communication statutes. If psychologists are entitled to a statutory privilege, but secretaries and other personnel are not, the privilege is virtually worthless, because such personnel have, of necessity, some access to confidential information (Jagim et al., 1978). A similar situation occurs in group therapy. If group members' communications are not protected from revelation by other members, clients may be justifiably cautious about discussing intimate personal matters, even if the client-therapist relationship is protected. This, potentially, limits the gains of group therapy. Some states include in their statutes secretaries, psychological assistants, other clients, and any person associated with mental health treatment. However, most do not.

There are times when individuals other than the client may assert or waive the communication privilege. Legal guardians and representatives of deceased clients often are accorded the same privilege as the client. In some jurisdictions, the psychologist may assert the communication privilege if the client neither waived nor asserted it (DeKraai & Sales, 1981).

There is a delicate balance between the individual's right to privacy, society's interests, and the necessity for revelation in court proceedings (Nye, 1980). Many states have dealt with these issues by describing exceptions to the privilege. One exception in several states exists whenever a judge believes that the importance of the proceeding outweighs that of the client's privacy. Others limit the privilege to civil actions, or exclude specific crimes (e.g., homicide, rape, child abuse) from the privilege. Danger to another individual is also used in some states as an exception to the communication privilege. In some states, a psychologist is not obligated to keep a client's communications privileged if the client files a legal complaint of malpractice against the psychologist. The privilege is waived in some states when clients use their own mental condition as a part of their claims, as in an insanity defense, or when examination of a client is ordered by the court. The final major exception included in some privileged communication statutes is when the professional determines that the client is in need of hospitalization for a mental disorder (DeKraai & Sales, 1981).

The existing privileged communication statues, therefore, vary as to which professionals are covered, the basis of the privilege, and the exceptions to the privilege. They are similar in that they all provide the protection to the relationship, grant the privilege to the client, and are not absolute.

REFERENCES

American Psychological Association. (1977). *Ethical standards of psychologists.* Washington, DC: Author.

De Kraai, M. B., & Sales, B. D. (1981). *Privileged communication of psychologists.* Lincoln, NE: De Kraai & Sales.

Foster, L. M. (1980). State confidentiality laws: The Illinois act as model for new legislation in other states. *American Journal of Orthopsychiatry, 50,* 659–665.

Jagim, R. D., Wittman, W. D., & Noll, J. O. (1978). Mental health professionals: Attitudes toward confidentiality, privilege, and third-party disclosure. *Professional Psychology, 9,* 458–466.

Nye, S. (1980). Patient confidentiality and privacy: The federal initiative. *American Journal of Orthopsychiatry, 50,* 649–658.

Shah, S. A. (1969). Privileged communications, confidentiality, and privacy. *Professional Psychology, 1,* 56–59.

Siegel, M. (1979). Privacy, ethics and confidentiality. *Professional Psychology, 10,* 249–258.

Swoboda, J. S., Elwork, A., Sales, B. D., & Levine, D. (1980). Knowledge of and compliance with privileged communication and child-abuse-reporting laws. *Professional Psychology, 11,* 714–721.

T. S. BENNETT
Brain Inquiry Recovery Program

LAW, PSYCHOLOGY AND PROFESSIONAL ETHICS

PROBABILITY

Probability theory is important to psychology because it is the foundation upon which statistics are based, and statistics are the tools for conducting empirical research. To the extent that the idea of statistical significance is based on notions of chance and probability, it may be said to have a very long history indeed. It seems clear, for example, that gambling, the throwing of dice ("astragali" and "tali"), and randomization mechanisms such as the drawing of lots are very ancient—if not prehistorical—practices. To be sure, these notions were quite vague by modern standards. In fact, what is perhaps most surprising is that even the simplest sort of probability calculus was not invented until relatively recent times. Why this did not take place much earlier is a matter of some mystery and controversy.

BRIEF HISTORICAL OVERVIEW

Systematic work leading to a formal appreciation of probability did not begin until around 1650. It was at this time that the idea of relative frequencies and the likelihood of particular events, based on gathered data, began to take hold. The primary motivation for the study of probability at this time (besides gaming) was the establishment of actuarial tables based on local death records (Bills of Mortality), which recorded not only numbers of deaths but also causes of death. These records were initially compiled to keep track of the progress of the Black Death, which began to afflict London late in the 16th century. In a sense, then, the origin of modern statistics and probability theory can be seen as a result of the plague, an idea undoubtedly consonant with the feelings of many students beginning the study of statistics and probability.

John Graunt (1620–1674) was the first to organize mortality records for the purpose of making probabilistic inferences (primarily with respect to population trends) based on actual proportions and relative frequencies of events. For example, he argued in reasonably modern terms that one need not fear dying insane ("a Lunatick in Bedlam") because the odds against it were quite high (about 1500:1). About the same time, on the continent, gambling and the analysis of games of chance provided the basis for further development of probability theory in the work of Blaise Pascal (1623–1662), Pierre Fermat (1601–1665), Christian Huygens (1629–1695), and, somewhat later, Jacob Bernoulli (1654–1705). This work saw the first development of a true mathematical foundation or theory of probability. Early in the 18th century, work on the binomial distribution was begun, first by Bernoulli and later by Abraham de Moivre (1667–1754). Bernoulli at this time also developed the theorem that eventually became known as the Law of Large Numbers, probably one of the most important events in the development of probability theory as it relates to statistical testing. The work of Pierre Simon de Laplace (1749–1827), a French mathematical astronomer and mathematician, was also especially significant. His two main treatises on the theory of probability and the "laws of chance," published in 1812 and 1814, provide the main bases upon which probability theory is founded. In these works, Laplace postulated seven general principles of the calculus of probabilities. This work led eventually to the development of the method of least squares, the law of errors, and the normal distribution, notably by Laplace, Carl Friedrich Gauss (1777–1855), and others early in the 19th century.

One of the first practical applications of this work outside the realm of gaming was in the area of astronomy. The general problem was the necessity of fitting observations to theoretical distributions in order to be able to reject discrepant observations. When astronomers became concerned with errors of measurement early in the 19th century, they eagerly seized upon the contemporary work of Gauss. Because it is the oldest of the exact sciences, it is perhaps ironic that astronomy was the first to systematically apply the principles of probability. Particularly interested in the work of Gauss was the Prussian astronomer Friedrich Wilhelm Bessel (1784–1846), who in 1818 devised the concept of the probable error, a precursor of the standard deviation and comparable, in modern terms, to a 50% confidence interval. Thus, many of the ingredients necessary for the development of statistical tests and statistical inference—probabilistic inference, distribution theory, methods of least squares, and the probable error—were all present before 1850.

Extension of the use of the probable error from astronomy to the biological and social sciences was first proposed by the Belgian astronomer and mathematician Lambert Adolphe Quetelet (1796–1874). Before Quetelet, it is fair to say that the word "statistics" retained its original meaning, referring primarily to descriptive data about the state, or so-called political arithmetic. Quetelet was the first to envision the utility of combining statistics with the theory of probability and so develop a social science based on the Law of Large Numbers described by Bernoulli and others. The most famous example of Quetelet's work was his description of the frequency distribution of the heights of 100,000 French army conscripts. He noted that the distribution closely followed the normal curve described by Laplace and Gauss, and he was able to compute its probable error. Using this information, Quetelet calculated the number of conscripts expected in each of the height categories and compared these to the observed numbers. He found that the number of conscripts in the lowest category, just below the minimum height requirement, considerably exceeded the expected number, while the observed frequency in the category just above the cutoff was deficient by the same amount. He ascribed the discrepancy to fraud, asserting that such an occurrence could not have arisen through measurement error.

Quetelet's work greatly influenced the subsequent work of Francis Galton (1822–1911), and through Galton, had great impact on the founders of modern statistics early in the 20th century, including Karl Pearson (1857–1936) and Ronald Fisher (1890–1962). The influence of Quetelet's work was substantial because it was the first to present the principles of probability in terms accessible to non-mathematicians and to suggest specific applications for probability theory beyond the evaluation of measurement error in the physical sciences. Quetelet expounded the view that social phenomena were subject to quantitative laws just as physical phenomena obeyed the laws of Newton and Kepler. He believed that the fusion of statistics and probability could reveal the underlying laws of nature governing human behavior, leading ultimately to his concept of *l'homme moyen,* the average man. Such a view fit nicely the contemporary mechanistic philosophy that resulted from the scientific revolution of the 17th century, the legacy of Newton and Descartes. Ironically, the mechanistic view was shortly to fall in the physical sciences, but it became the dominant force in the developing science of human behavior and, of course, remains so today.

CLASSICAL DEFINITION OF PROBABILITY

Suppose an event E can occur in M ways and fail to occur in N ways. Under the condition that M and N are equally likely to occur, the probability of success (i.e., that the event will occur) is:

$$p = \Pr\{E\} = M/(M + N)$$

The probability of failure (i.e., that the event will not occur) is:

$$q = \Pr\{\text{not } E\} = M/(M + N)$$

Hence:

$$p + q = M/(M + N) + N/(M + N) = 1$$

and

$$q = 1 - p$$

The addition theorem states that if two or more events are mutually exclusive (i.e., the occurrence of one prevents the occurrence of the other), the probability that either one of them or any combination of them will occur is the sum of their probabilities:

$$\Pr \{E_1 + E_2\} = \Pr \{E_1\} + \Pr \{E_2\}$$

The multiplication theorem states that if two or more events are independent (i.e., the occurrence of one is not dependent upon the occurrence of the other), the probability that the events will occur simultaneously or in succession is the product of the individual probabilities:

$$\Pr \{E_1 \times E_2\} = \Pr \{E_1\} \times \Pr \{E_2\}$$

SAMPLING WITH AND WITHOUT REPLACEMENT

An important concept in the application of the principles and theorems of probability is that of sampling with replacement and sampling without replacement. In sampling with replacement, the likelihood of an event remains constant for all events because the occurrence of any particular event does not affect the likelihood of that event's happening again. In sampling without replacement, the occurrence of a particular event precludes the possibility of that event's happening again because the specific case is not replaced. In sampling with replacement, the addition and multiplication theorems are usually applied. In sampling without replacement, the probability situation is considerably altered and the probability distribution assumes the form and properties of a mathematical distribution known as the hypergeometric distribution.

PROBABILITY DISTRIBUTIONS

Frequency distributions encountered in statistics are generally considered to be probability distributions, that is, in a general form of $(p + q)^n$. Although a probability distribution is discrete, it smooths out to a reasonable approximation of a continuous distribution as sample size (n) becomes increasingly large, that is, as $n \to \infty$. If $p = q = .5$, then as $n \to \infty$, the probability distribution, as first shown by Bernoulli in the early 19th century, approximates the normal curve. Hence, it assumes the properties of normality. Specifically, the distribution becomes symmetric, mesokurtic, and asymptotic. Hypothesis testing in statistics rests heavily on these properties, especially that of being asymptotic. In this context, asymptotic refers to the property of the normal distribution of approaching (but never equal to) zero in the limit at the extreme ends of the distribution. Thus, the normal probability distribution ranges theoretically from $-\infty$ to $+\infty$. Standards for rejecting the null hypothesis have been established on the basis of such a distribution.

STANDARDS FOR REJECTION OF H_0

By convention, the minimum level for rejection of H_0 is set at the 5% probability level, referred to as the .05 level of significance. Also, conventionally, two other significance levels have been established. These are the 1% and the 0.1% probability levels. These rejection levels are denoted by the Greek letter α and are usually referred to as alpha levels. In rejecting the null hypothesis, the experimenter concludes, on the basis of appropriate statistical tests, that the probability that the observed findings could have re-

sulted from chance occurrence rather than from actual causes is less than the specified α level. For example, for the 5% level, rejection of the null hypothesis is denoted as $p < .05$. It is important to note, however, that conclusions drawn on the basis of hypothesis testing are entirely dependent, in the final analysis, on probability statements derived from distributions that are asymptotic. Hence p can never be 1.00 or .00. Therefore, all conclusions drawn from the application of statistical methods to empirical data are probabilistic in nature. They may appear to be quite convincing on the basis of the magnitude of the probabilities associated with rejecting (or accepting) H_0. However, there is always a margin of error associated with the statistical decision to reject or not reject H_0. Thus, one can never be absolutely certain of—and it is in principle impossible to prove—an hypothesis. Although the foregoing argument applies specifically to the normal probability distribution, the same is of course true for tests based on other statistical distributions, such as the t and χ^2 distributions, as well as multivariate probability distributions.

J. S. ROSSI
P. F. MERENDA
University of Rhode Island

CONFIDENCE INTERVALS
SAMPLING
STATISTICS IN PSYCHOLOGY

PROCEDURAL MEMORY

DEFINING MEMORY
Howard (1994) concluded:

Memory is learning that sticks; when learning occurs, new synapses forms, old synapses are strengthened or both. These new or strengthened connections are the new learning. . . . With continued use, the hippocampal cells extend the storage of the new learning to the cerebral cortex, which then becomes the primary location of long-term memory (storage and retrieval). . . . Herein lies the home of procedural memory. . . . When a new learning chunk reaches the cerebral cortex, it apparently is stored for the long-term. . . . The hippocampus is a kind of broker that binds memory until the cortex takes over and becomes its handler.

Gazzaniga (1988) reports that memory occurs not just in the brain, but throughout the nervous system. In animal research, animals with no hippocampus can remember remote items but not recent items, which is the normal condition.

Memory appears to be fully developed by 8 years of age. At that point, we remember an average of one bit of information out of every 100 we receive. There is some debate about the relation of memory to IQ, but Howard (1994) concludes that there is no direct relationship between IQ and memory. Howard also posits that it is not sufficient to learn a new concept, skill, or body of information:

One must convert it into long-term memory (procedural memory resides in long-term memory. In other words, if you take the time to read a book or article on how to be a better listener, you probably will not remember the skills or concepts unless you practice three strategies. Minninger (1984) has categorized all the many memorization gimmicks into these: intend, file, and rehearse. This approach has been around for some time. Erasmus wrote in 1512, "Though I do not deny that memory can be helped by places and images, yet the best memory is based on three important things: namely study [rehearse], order [file], and care [intend]." Intend to remember something. That is, don't assume that it will just stick after exposure; you need to make a point of wanting to remember it. File it by organizing and playing with it in your own special way. And rehearse it, or practice it, as a way of showing that you intend to remember it. Do it and say it repeatedly. These three generic strategy types are the means by which short-term memory is converted to long-term memory.

PROCEDURAL MEMORY (LONG-TERM MEMORY)

Procedural memory is akin to long-term memory. Benjamin and colleagues (1990) concluded that we should "think about the enormous capacity of long-term memory. There are a vast number of items stored for later use such as song titles, poetic expressions and traces of home-life." Thus, long-term memory has two important features: the lasting nature of the stored information and the great size of the repository.

Tulving (1972) made a distinction between two types of information stored in long-term memory. The first type of long-term memory relates to specific events in one's life and functions as a sort of autobiographical reserve. This type of memory is called episodic memory. Examples of episodic memory include the night of your high school graduation, your whereabouts at noon yesterday, and what time you got out of bed this morning. Because episodic memory is difficult to verify, it is difficult to study. A second type of information in the long-term memory is concerned with general knowledge, and is referred to as semantic memory. Semantic memory is knowledge of such items as the formula for computing the area of a circle, the role played by Harriet Tubman in the Underground Railroad, and the lifetime batting average of Babe Ruth. Each of these events is impersonal, with no definite reference to the self. Because semantic memory is easily verified, it has been a popular topic among memory researchers.

Tulving (1985) has updated his theory and now distinguishes among three memory systems. Along with episodic and semantic memory, he considers procedural memory to be a separate information system. Procedural memory basically involves the formation and retention of habits. In this regard, procedural memory is concerned with S-R (stimulus-response) connections. As a rule, cognitive processes are not at work in this memory system, which is present in both animals and humans. An example of procedural memory is serving a tennis ball. You are not consciously aware of each individual movement, nor are you actively thinking about how to combine the movements. You just toss the ball and swing, and depending on your past memory experience, you either render a polished delivery or a "hack."

REFERENCES
Gazzaniga, M. S. (1988). *Mind matters: How mind and brain interact to create our conscious lives.* Boston: Houghton-Mifflin.

SUGGESTED READING
Bartlett, F. C. (1932). *Remembering.* Cambridge, England: Cambridge University Press.

Bolles, E. B. (1988). *Remembering and forgetting:* An inquiry into the nature of memory. New York: Walker.

Miller, G. A. (1956). *The magical number seven, plus or minus two: Some limits on our capacity for processing information. Psychological review, 63,* 81–97.

Simon, H. (1969). *Sciences of the artificial.* Cambridge, MA: MIT Press.

N. J. Cohen
Behavioral Sciences Dept.
Bowie State University

FORGETTING
MEMORY

PROCEDURAL SKILL LEARNING

Procedural skill, psychomotor skill, and technical skill are terms used interchangeably to describe the performance of a manual task that requires a motor act or movements. The term "procedural skill" is more frequently used to describe a medical procedure. These procedures can vary in scope and complexity from the simple application of a plaster of Paris cast to the performance of a technically challenging surgical procedure.

PSYCHOMOTOR DOMAIN AND LEARNING THEORY

There are three traditional domains of learning: cognitive, affective, and psychomotor. The psychomotor domain describes a hierarchy of learning specific to psychomotor skills. Although most individuals have the capability to learn a skill, some will have a greater ability than others. *Trait ability* describes a natural ability that is inherent to the individual and unmodifiable. This is differentiated from *skill ability,* which is more specific to a motor task and may be modified and improved through the use of an educational strategy (Singer, 1972).

When learning a motor act, there are various sensory inputs that, if correctly interpreted and referenced against the original movement, represent useful feedback and will result in the correction and improvement of performance (Adams, 1987; Schmidt, 1975). For this sensory information to become useful feedback or *knowledge of results,* it must be perceived correctly by the learner. Knowledge of results is required to learn, correct, and improve the performance of a motor action. In these theories of motor learning, knowledge of results or feedback describes perceptual information rather than third-party observer feedback. Although this individual sensory feedback is necessary to learn motor skills, learning is likely further augmented by timely expert observer feedback.

PROCEDURAL SKILL LEARNING PROGRAMS

Procedural skill learning requires both a cognitive and a psychomotor phase. In the cognitive phase, the learner understands the context of the procedure, including indications, contraindications, and other relevant information. The second phase of learning a motor skill, the psychomotor phase, begins with visualization and verbalization, both of which require opportunities to see and describe the procedure from start to finish. The most important components of learning in the psychomotor phase involve practice with both correction and reinforcement. In order for practice to be effective and efficient, expert observer feedback is necessary.

When considering issues of procedural skill learning and competence, the educational setting must be considered. There are essentially two practice settings for procedural skill learning. The first is artificial and includes the use of models, cadavers, and computers. Unfortunately, artificial settings have not been developed for many procedures. In addition, excessive costs may limit the use of an artificial setting for procedural skill learning. The second setting for practice uses real patients in a real clinical environment. Patient and physician anxiety, the sensation of crossing tissue planes, and working in a bloody field are difficult to reproduce. The problem with incorporating real practice into a procedural skill educational program is the difficulty in guaranteeing consistent clinical educational opportunities. In addition, there are obvious concerns related to the learning curve and the potential for patient morbidity when procedures are being learned using real patients.

PROCEDURAL SKILL COMPETENCE

Practice is commonly identified as the most important component of motor skill learning, and it is assumed that "practice makes perfect." However, there are numerous variables that influence the goal of achieving procedural skill competence.

The concept of clinical competence is complex and controversial. Newble (1992) defined competence as "the mastery of a body of relevant knowledge and the acquisition of a range of relevant skills." Therefore, psychomotor skills are a component of a broader concept of clinical competence. Miller (1990) described competence within the context of a pyramidal hierarchy from the most basic level of knowledge, in which the student "knows, knows how, shows how" and then "does" the procedure independently in clinical practice. Miller's conception of competence represents a continuum from "safe" or "functionally adequate" to a level of "skill mastery." The level of competence expected of a second-year medical student will differ from that expected of a clerk, resident, or staff physician. Educators should therefore create objectives that predefine expectations for this continuum of procedural skill competence.

Expectations of competence should also consider variations in the learner's skill ability as well as issues of procedure-specific skill competence. Frequently, competence is defined by self-assessment in absolute terms or represented by the number of exposures to a particular procedure. Although the number of procedures performed (n) is important, it cannot be considered the sole measure of competence. Variations in the skill abilities of learners make it inappropriate to assume that the performance of a fixed number of procedures will lead to skill competence. Whenever possible, objective evaluation tools should be used to assess the achievement of competence. With such a tool, n becomes more flexible as a component of competence rather than an end point.

PROCEDURAL SKILL MAINTENANCE

Once skill competence has been achieved, the issue of skill maintenance becomes relevant. The factor most commonly associated with skill maintenance is again n, the frequency with which the procedure is performed. Although evaluation tools are considered useful as a measure of an educational program's success, the ultimate measure of competence is improved patient outcome.

There are many variables that influence outcome, such as the appropriateness and effectiveness of the procedure in question. However, the skill with which the procedure is performed is obviously important. For example, coronary artery bypass surgery is an effective means of treating critical ischemic heart disease when patients are selected appropriately. However, assuming appropriate patient selection, the results and patient outcomes for bypass surgery may still vary from one institution to another. One of the major reasons cited for this variance is operator skill, which is directly attributed to the volume of cases performed (n; Tu & Naylor, 1996).

Motor learning theory supports the need for sensory feedback to learn a psychomotor skill. Procedural skill programs should emphasize third-party expert observer feedback in their educational methodology. The achievement of procedural skill competence requires a number practice opportunities (n). However, n may vary from one individual to another and, therefore, competence is best measured by objective evaluation.

REFERENCES

Adams, J. A. (1987). Historical review and appraisal of research on the learning, retention and transfer of human motor skills. *Psychological Bulletin, 101,* 41–74.

Miller, G. E. (1990). The assessment of clinical skills/competence/performance. *Academic Medicine, 65*(9 Suppl), S63–7.

Newble, D. I. (1992). Assessing clinical competence at the undergraduate level. *Medical Education, 26*(6), 504–511.

Schmidt, R. A. (1975). A schema theory of discrete motor skill learning. *Psychological Review, 82*(4), 225–260.

Singer, R. N. (1972). *The psychomotor domain: Movement behaviors.* Philadelphia, PA: Lea & Febigor.

Tu, J. V., & Naylor, C. D. (1996). Coronary artery bypass mortality rates in Ontario: A Canadian approach to quality assurance in cardiac surgery. Steering Committee of the Provincial Adult Cardiac Care Network of Ontario. *Circulation, 94*(10), 2429–2433.

G. KOVACS
Dalhousie University

PROFESSIONAL ETHICS

Ethics are standards that govern personal and professional conduct. In psychology and related professions, principles of ethical behavior and judgment are typically developed for the protection of consumers of services, professionals, organizations, research subjects, the profession, and society as a whole.

Ethical standards may be organized around the person or group to whom the professional is responsible (e.g., "Code of ethics" of the National Association of Social Workers) or around broad classifications of principles (e.g., the American Psychological Association, "Ethical principles of psychologists"). In either case, standards are usually general guidelines for making determinations about ethical actions both before and after they occur, rather than sets of rules for every possible professional action. When professional organizations, such as the American Psychological Association (APA) develop standards of ethics, adherence to the standards is often held as one of the conditions of membership. The standards then become a basis for the adjudication of issues of alleged unethical conduct.

Systems of ethical principles are based on the goals, objectives, and fundamental values of the profession. They do not carry the weight of civil or criminal law, but may serve as guidelines for developing legislation or for determining whether accepted standards of practice have been violated in civil liability proceedings. Ethical principles are usually rewritten periodically to reflect the development of the profession, changes in the standards of society as a whole, or the results of judicial proceedings.

The APA's first formal ethical standards were published in 1953, and have since undergone several revisions. The principles cover several broad areas of professional conduct.

The first area, "responsibility," emphasizes that psychologists should be extremely sensitive to the potential outcomes of their professional actions. Psychologists are expected to analyze carefully the consequences of activities such as research, teaching, and applied service. They are responsible for clarifying their own professional relationships, presenting information objectively, and recognizing their obligations to others. It is not sufficient to rely on benevolent intent in evaluating one's actions. Rather, the actual outcome must be considered and applied with integrity to one's judgment of appropriate professional conduct.

The principle of "competence" stresses that psychologists must engage in professional activity only in those areas for which they clearly have the ability, knowledge, training, and experience. Inherent in this principle is that psychologists both recognize and communicate accurately to others their areas of competence and the limitations of their skills. Psychologists are expected to obtain both information and supervision in any activity before engaging in that activity professionally. The rapid progress of psychology demands that education of psychologists be an ongoing process to keep them abreast of such progress. This principle also recognizes that psychologists may have personal problems that interfere with professional effectiveness and explicitly requires that they seek assistance from others or refrain from activities with which such problems interfere.

The principle of "moral and legal standards" requires psychologists to acquaint themselves with standards of behavior in the community and to apply this information to the development of their own systems of personal and professional values and conduct. Knowledge of legal issues relevant to professional conduct is essential. Consideration of the values and rights of others is expected to govern professional activities, as is an awareness of the possibility that one's actions may potentially interfere with those of other members of the profession.

The principle governing "public statements" specifies ways of presenting an individual's or organization's professional qualifications, affiliations, and functions. Specific types of information that can be provided to the public are delineated and psychologists are expected to limit their communications to clear descriptions of products and services. The utmost care must be taken not to mislead others or to make statements that cannot be supported by research or practice. Psychologists are specifically mandated to correct any misleading statements made about them by others.

The principle of "confidentiality" is essential to effective psychological practice. Information communicated to psychologists in the context of professional relationships must not be communicated to anyone else in any manner without the consent of the person concerned, unless there is some clear danger to that person or others. Records also must be kept confidential by psychologists.

The principle concerned with the "welfare of the consumer" is designed to protect the rights of those who use psychological services. Psychologists are expected to assist in safeguarding the consumer's interests by dealing fairly in making financial arrangements for services, in providing only those services that benefit the client, and in clarifying the nature of multiple commitments to individuals and organizations. Psychologists are expected to respect the freedom of consumers to participate in any procedure. This principle specifically proscribes sexual intimacies with clients.

The principle concerned with "professional relationships" emphasizes the obligations of psychologists in dealing with other professionals. Psychologists are expected to consider the needs and abilities of other professionals and to secure the best possible services for clients. This principle specifies the procedure for assigning credit for contributions to publications and for dealing with possible ethical violations.

The principle governing the use of "assessment techniques" requires psychologists to observe relevant standards for such techniques (American Psychological Association, *Standards for Educational and Psychological Tests*), to maintain the security of the techniques, and to prevent their misuse. Psychologists are expected to respect the client's right to know the results of assessments and their interpretation.

The principle concerned with "research with human participants" is so complex as to require a lengthy separate publication (American Psychological Association, *Ethical Principles in the Conduct of Research with Human Participants*). Ethical conflict is sometimes unavoidable in that the value of the research must be weighed against any potential risk to participants. Research that deceives participants or may cause physical or mental harm requires special care. Research participants must be informed as fully as practicable before and after the research, and must clearly know that they may choose not to participate or to withdraw at any time, with no adverse consequences.

The final principle covers the "care and use of animals." Animal research subjects are to be treated humanely and in a manner that complies with existing laws. Larson (1982) discusses the difficulties involved in meeting requirements of legal and ethical conduct, while trying to do meaningful research with animals.

These areas of ethical concern illustrate the types of issues with which psychologists and other professionals are concerned. It is clear that the emphasis is on protecting those with whom psychologists work. This emphasis helps to protect psychologists as well, by providing a framework in which to practice and the backing of a consensus of one's colleagues. In addition, it militates against intrusion from outside the profession.

Several major problems exist in developing and adhering to ethical standards. One is that there are widely varying methods for dealing with clients, many of which do not have clear standards of application. Second, the behavior of those seeking psychological services is often in conflict with societal expectations and the psychologist has responsibilities to both. A third problem is that of integrating the goals and values of the profession with those of society, as defined by statutory and case law. Yet another is that of psychologists in nonpsychological settings (e.g., business), where different organizational standards apply. These are but a few of the many problems involved in developing clear ethical guidelines.

There are several groups of clients for whom judgments about ethical practice are particularly difficult for psychologists. Mentally retarded people constitute one group which, by virtue of its members' lack of ability to make their own effective decisions, places an extra burden of care on the psychologist. Allen and Allen (1979) have addressed some of the ethical issues with retarded populations. With such populations, psychologists are often placed in a position of considerable power in making such decisions as where clients will live, under how much control, and how their time will be used. At the same time, retarded clients must be accorded the same consideration as other clients and the decision-making process often includes other responsible parties, such as parents and courts.

A second group that requires special ethical consideration by virtue of inadequate self-protection skills comprises children. Children are particularly vulnerable to violations of their rights because these rights are limited under the law. Glenn (1980) discusses major ethical problems involved in child treatment. Psychologists are often in a position where they must assert the rights of the child, even beyond the requirements of the law. A common situation where this is true is one in which a parent has legal right of access to information concerning the child, but the psychologist believes this is not in the child's best interest. It is essential that providers of psychological services to children be especially cognizant of local laws and clarify the situation for all concerned prior to beginning treatment.

Family treatment also raises unusual ethical issues. Fox (1976) has discussed a variety of ethical problems in working with families, as have Hines and Hare-Mustin (1978). Confidentiality is difficult to maintain, as therapists frequently find themselves in a position of communicating with some family members outside the family treatment setting, and these communications, even though they may be helpful to the family, must be kept confidential. Another problem arises when families become involved in treatment that originally involved a single family member. The ethical issues here are to clarify the question of which person is the client and to resolve mixed loyalties. Finally, families provide ready contexts for psychologists to potentially act out their own personal problems.

Therapy groups present special ethical problems in that members of such groups are bound only by their own moral standards and not by formal ethical or legal standards. Therefore, group members may behave in a potentially harmful way toward other members or may fail to keep information confidential. These difficulties require the psychologist to exercise extra care in protecting every client in the group.

Another group that creates difficult ethical issues consists of clients who use insurance coverage to pay for psychological services. Psychologists, to receive insurance payments, must communicate some information about the client (e.g., diagnosis, rationale for treatment, number of sessions) to the insurance company. That information is, therefore, no longer confidential.

It is evident that ethical principles do not resolve all problems encountered by psychologists. Exceptions to typical ethical judgment situations occur with changes in psychological theory and practice. Integration of societal and professional values with legal requirements and the unique needs of individuals is an ongoing process.

Ethical principles therefore, are not static sets of rules, but rather are guidelines within which individual psychologists must still make continuous judgments in the best interests of all those concerned. While no set of principles will ever eliminate all unethical behavior, continued refinement of the principles has established a firm basis for ethical psychological behavior.

REFERENCES

Allen, D. F., & Allen, V. S. (1979). *Ethical issues in mental retardation.* Nashville, TN: Abingdon.

American Psychological Association. (1973). *Ethical principles in the conduct of research with human participants.* Washington, DC: Author.

American Psychological Association, American Educational Research Association, and National Council on Measurement in Education. (1974). *Standards for educational and psychological tests.* Washington, DC: Author.

Fox, R. E. (1976). Family therapy. In I. B. Weiner (Ed.), *Clinical methods in psychology.* New York: Wiley.

Glenn, C. M. (1980). Ethical issues in the practice of child psychotherapy. *Professional Psychology, 11,* 613–773.

Hines, P. M., & Hare-Mustin, R. T. (1978). Ethical concerns in family therapy. *Professional Psychology, 9,* 165–171.

Larson, C. C. (1982). Animal research: Striking a balance. *APA Monitor, 1,* 12–13.

T. S. BENNETT
Brain Inquiry Recovery Program

CRISIS INTERVENTION
PRIVILEGED COMMUNICATIONS

PROGRAM EVALUATION

To evaluate a social program requires knowledge of the program's purpose and performance, and criteria against which they can be compared. Program evaluation research uses the tools of inquiry from the social sciences to investigate social programs, decide upon appropriate performance criteria, and assess program effectiveness. Its purpose is to aid rational decision making about social programs by consumers, program administrators, and policy makers.

Program evaluation research is most typically applied to sponsored activities implemented through an identifiable organizational structure with designated staff, appropriate facilities, defined budget, and so forth. In principle, program evaluation research might be applied to any such program though, in practice, its domain has been almost exclusively human service programs. For example, some areas of major activity are education, health care, mental health, social service, employment, housing, criminal justice, and rehabilitation.

Program evaluation research was applied to many of the New Deal programs of the Franklin D. Roosevelt era (Chapin, 1947), but it was catapulted forward during the 1960s under the influence of the "Great Society" programs of Lyndon Johnson (Williams, 1971). In that period, the federal government sponsored massive programs to eliminate poverty, reduce urban decay, and improve the education of minorities and the economically disadvantaged. Evaluation requirements were written into much of the supporting legislation and numerous evaluation studies were commissioned to assess new program alternatives and, in some cases, to win political acceptance for new proposals. Not until the 1970s, however, was program evaluation research consolidated as a defined field of endeavor complete with its own professional organizations, conferences, and journals. Concurrently it attained increased institutionalization with the establishment of training programs in various universities and the addition of permanent program evaluation staff in many federal and state agencies.

The backdrop for the rise of program evaluation research was a progressive transformation of the U.S. economy from a predominantly industrial base to a service base (Bell, 1976). Since 1969, more than 60% of both the gross national product and the labor force has been devoted to service-related activities; by 1979, the proportion was 70%. Furthermore, the greatest recent growth has been in the area of human services (in contrast to personal services)—particularly health, education, and government itself. The human services portion of the federal budget alone has more than doubled since the 1960s, and state and local budgets have shown similar trends. Thus, whereas social programs had been largely local, small scale, and often voluntary efforts early in the century, in recent times they have become a massive subsystem of the society.

Basically, the program evaluation movement represents the development of information systems to provide feedback to program administrators, program sponsors, policy makers, and consumers about the performance of public-sector human service programs. As the number, extent, and complexity of such programs have increased, so too have governmental demands for more information about their effectiveness and for more tools with which to control them. Program evaluation research has grown up first as an offshoot of applied social research and policy analysis, and then as a fully rooted specialty area in its own right.

APPROACHES AND TECHNIQUES

Program evaluation research does not constitute a unified field. It has no conceptual or methodological paradigm and only a few agreed-upon principles and practices. The community of evaluation researchers is united more by common purpose than by common method. The intellectual structure of the enterprise is not formed of consistent interlocking concepts, but comprises a miscellaneous assortment of ideas and methods from which a researcher picks and combines, depending upon personal preferences and the particular application at hand. Glass and Ellett (1980) identified no fewer than seven different conceptions of program evaluation, each with its own methods, themes, and advocates.

The watershed distinction among the varieties of approaches to program evaluation research is between those with predominant emphases on "evaluation" and those who stress "research." The evaluation perspective recognizes that to judge the value of a program adequately, all aspects of the program that contribute to its worth must be investigated. This includes goals, outcome, personnel, organizational structure, budget, morality, and need. Such a broad investigation, however, strains the capability of conventional social science methodology, at least the more rigorous requirements for tight experimental designs and validated quantitative measurement. Within the program evaluation perspective, therefore, there has been a steady growth in the application of broader, more flexible, if less definitive, methods. For example, anthropological and ethnographic techniques (often called "naturalistic"), which rely heavily on interviews, first-hand observations, and key informants, have attracted considerable attention (Guba & Lincoln, 1981). Such approaches permit what has been called "responsive" evaluation—that is, investigation of the particular concerns held by program decision makers and consumers and timely reporting of the results to make them optimally useful (Stake, 1975). In this mode, the program evaluator is largely a practitioner-consultant in the service of a particular client program.

The research perspective views its task as determining in the most methodologically sound fashion possible, whether a social program actually produces the effects expected. In this perspective, social programs are viewed as instances of organized social engineering intended to accomplish specific results. This cause-and-effect conception is quite compatible with the social science methodology of controlled experimentation and quantitative measurement, which has evolved to study causal connections in social phenomena. The "social experimentation" approach associated with Donald Campbell and his colleagues, for example, is typical of the program research perspective (Campbell, 1969; Riecken & Boruch, 1974). In this approach, randomized experiments and quasi-experiments to test the effects of social programs are advocated. Properly done, such experimental comparisons provide relatively unequivocal estimates of the impact of the social program on the alleged beneficiaries and thus answer a central evaluation question: "Did the program have the desired effect?" Program research approaches, however, also seek to build a body of useful generalizations regarding social problems and effective social intervention—practical theory resulting from a research orientation toward social programs. In this mode, the program evaluator is primarily a researcher testing a hypothesis about program effects.

Most actual program evaluation research represents some combination of the program evaluation perspective and the program research perspective. Reported program evaluations generally incorporate some sort of comparative research design in an attempt to assess the effects of the program on recipients as compared with nonrecipients. The comparison groups often are not randomized experimental and control groups, however, and methodological practices in this area have been criticized (Bernstein & Freeman, 1975). On the other hand, it is also quite common for evaluators to attempt to be responsive to the needs and interests of program administrators by including in their study an investigation of program operations and activities, costs, staff, and other factors related to the service delivery and the program organization itself, often referred to as the "process" component of the evaluation. Such investigation not only provides program managers with information that can be used to improve the program, but also indicates how completely the program is implemented, a requisite condition for any effects to appear.

In addition to the relative extremes of controlled experimentation and qualitative ethnographic study, several other specific program evaluation techniques are worthy of mention. For instance, the issue of whether a program is appropriate to the needs of a community, a catchment area, or a clientele occasionally arises. For such situations, a set of techniques known collectively as "needs assessment" has been developed (Warheit et al., 1974). Community or key informant surveys, records of existing service agencies, and analyses of social indicators (e.g., census data) are the most frequent components. Alternatively it may be questionable that the program is itself an appropriate candidate for evaluation research. "Evaluability assessment" provides a formal program definition and a specification of the evaluation approaches, if any, that might be appropriate (Rutman, 1980). Another specialized technique is a benefit-cost analysis, adapted from economics (Levin, 1975). Its purpose is to monetarize the benefits of a program and compare them with the costs of various alternative programs or program implementations. Finally, there is a variety of management-oriented approaches that are distinguished by their applicability to the operational decisions that program administrators confront. Decision analysis applies statistical decision theory in support of management decision making in the face of uncertainty (Edwards et al., 1975). Goal-attainment monitoring and generically similar procedures systematize program goals and establish information feedback systems that routinely inform program managers of progress toward those goals (Attkisson et al., 1978).

As numerous evaluation studies in a particular program area accumulate, they provide a valuable archive of information about contrasting program approaches and overall effects. One subspecialty of program evaluation research, known as "meta-analysis," addresses itself to the problem of integrating studies and identifying the broad patterns of results that emerge. At the simplest level, this consists only of collecting the relevant reports and tallying the results in summary form. Studies that use quantitative measures and comparative research designs, however, lend themselves to a more sophisticated approach. Glass (1981) has pioneered the technique of representing the effects of such programs in a common metric so that all eligible studies can be compared and aggregated. The results of this procedure are twofold. First, it permits an overall assessment of the extent to which a certain type of social intervention has beneficial effects on the recipients, aggregated over all implementations and clients. Second, it permits a detailed analysis of the characteristics of the programs (and the supporting research) associated with more and less successful outcomes. In this way, broader generalizations about social programs can be constructed that transcend the idiosyncracies of individual implementations.

ORGANIZATIONAL ASPECTS

During the 1970s, program evaluation research began to consolidate as an organized field of specialization. Various professional organizations were founded, most notably the Evaluation Research Society and Evaluation Network, and less formal evaluation groups were formed within several existing professional organizations. Professional journals devoted exclusively to program evaluation research and related issues arose more or less concurrently (*Evaluation, Evaluation Review, Evaluation and Program Planning*), and others have since appeared (*Educational Evaluation and Policy Analysis*). Additional systematization of the evaluation literature was provided with the two-volume *Handbook of Evaluation Research* (Guttentag & Struening) and the periodic *Evaluation Studies Review Annual* published by Sage. With this increased academic identity came training programs designated specifically for program evaluation research, largely as an area of specialization within a conventional social science program. By 1979, a survey commissioned by the Evaluation Research Society was able to identify more than 60 such training programs throughout the United States, almost all at the graduate level.

Despite its increased disciplinary identity, program evaluation remains a multidisciplinary endeavor in terms of the primary affiliations of its practitioners. The membership of the Evaluation Research Society, for example, represents over 30 different disciplines. Furthermore, no discipline predominates, though most members are social scientists. Thus, program evaluation research remains a bridging discipline—a varied but identifiable collection of concepts and methods spanning the traditional social sciences and the world of social programs and the problems they address.

REFERENCES

Attkisson, C. C., et al. (Eds.). (1978). *Evaluation of human service programs.* New York: Academic.

Bell, J. E. (1976). A theoretical framework for family group therapy. In P. J. Guerin (Ed.), *Family therapy: Theory and practice* (pp. 129–143). New York: Gardner Press.

Bernstein, I. N., & Freeman, H. E. (1975). *Academic and entrepreneurial research: The consequences of diversity in federal evaluation studies.* New York: Russell Sage Foundation.

Chapin, F. S. (1947). *Experimental designs in sociological research.* New York: Harper.

Edwards, W., Guttentag, M., & Snapper, K. (1975). A decision-theoretic approach to evaluation research. In M. Guttentag & E. L. Struening (Eds.), *Handbook of evaluation research* (Vol. 1). Beverly Hills, CA: Sage Publications.

Glass, G. V., & Ellett, F. S. (1980). Evaluation research. *Annual Review of Psychology, 31,* 211–228.

Glass, G. V., McGaw, B., & Smith, M. L. (1981). *Meta-analysis in social research.* Beverly Hills, CA: Sage.

Guba, E. G., & Lincoln, Y. S. (1981). *Effective evaluation.* San Francisco: Jossey-Bass.

Guttentag, M., & Struening, E. L. (Eds.). (1975). *Handbook of evaluation research* (Vols. 1, 2). Beverly Hills, CA.: Sage.

Levin, H. M. (1975). Cost-effectiveness analysis in evaluation research. In M. Guttentag & E. L. Struening (Eds.), *Handbook of evaluation research,* Vol. 2. Beverly Hills, CA: Sage.

Riecken, H. W., & Boruch, R. F. (Eds.). (1974). *Social experimentation: A method for planning and evaluating social intervention.* New York: Academic.

Rutman, L. (1980). *Planning useful evaluations: Evaluability assessment.* Beverly Hills, CA: Sage.

Stake, R. E. (Ed.). (1975). *Evaluating the arts in education: A responsive approach.* Columbus, OH: Merrill.

Warheit, G. J., Bell, R. A., & Schwab, J. J. (1974). *Planning for change: Needs assessment approaches.* Rockville, MD: National Institute of Mental Health.

Williams, W. (1971). *Social policy research and analysis: The experience in the federal social agencies.* New York: American Elsevier.

M. W. LIPSEY
Vanderbilt University

APPLIED RESEARCH
CRITICAL INCIDENT TECHNIQUE
MEASUREMENT
OBSERVATIONAL METHODS
ORGANIZATIONAL DIAGNOSIS

PROGRESSIVE MATRICES (RAVEN'S)

Developed by British psychologist J. C. Raven and first published in 1938, the *Progressive Matrices* (PM) tests measure the ability to educe relationships among figural elements contained in a matrix. Items employ either a complete pattern from which a piece has been removed, or figural elements placed in discrete rows and columns, with one element missing. The missing element must be selected from six or eight answer choices presented. These tests re-

portedly assess the ability to perceive and think clearly, minimizing the influences of verbal communication and past experience (Raven et al., 1976). Some psychologists consider PM to be a relatively pure measure of Spearman's g.

Administration may be either individually or in groups, and requires 30 to 45 minutes. Percentile rank norms, based upon English standardization samples, are available for the various editions by 6-month intervals, ages 3½ to 14, and thereafter by 1- or 5-year intervals. Users are advised to complement PM with one of Raven's vocabulary scales (Mill Hill or Crichton) to obtain a complete assessment of intellectual functioning. Generalizability of the norms to non-European cultures appears questionable (Anastasi, 1982).

REFERENCES

Anastasi, A. (1982). *Psychological testing* (5th ed.). New York: Macmillan.

Raven, J. C. (1960). *Guide to the standard progressive matrices.* London: Lewis.

Raven, J. C., Court, J. H., & Raven, J. (1976). *Manual for Raven's progressive matrices and vocabulary scales.* London: Lewis.

G. J. ROBERTSON
Wide Range, Inc.

INTELLIGENCE MEASURES
NONVERBAL INTELLIGENCE TESTS
PSYCHOMETRICS

PROJECTIVE TECHNIQUES

Explorations in Personality by Henry Murray, published in 1938, referred to "projection tests." In the same year, Lawrence Frank, in a privately circulated memorandum, used the term *projective methods* (followed by his paper on "Projective method for the study of personality" in 1939). Horowitz and Murphy, also in 1938, published an article on "Projective methods in the psychological study of children." Not until later did the terms "projective methods" and "projective techniques" become interchangeable.

Over the years, *projection* has been defined rather narrowly. As one of the standard defense mechanisms described by psychoanalysts, it evokes the psychopathological connotation of this process seen in paranoia and paranoid behavior. It refers to the attribution of one's own unacceptable thoughts, feelings, and characteristics to other persons. Actually Freud himself considered projection a much broader process. "But projection is not especially created for the purpose of defense, it also comes into being where there are no conflicts" was his comment in *Totem and Taboo.* He points out the general tendency for the projection of "inner perceptions to the outside" and its importance in shaping our view of the outside world.

Originally Frank (1939) described a projective technique as "a method of studying the personality by confronting the subject with a situation to which he will respond according to what the situation means to him." In addition to this rather broad description, Frank

(1948) subsequently indicated that a projective technique "evokes from the subject what is in various ways expressive of his private world and personality process." Many other definitions have been proposed. Their common denominator may be contained in the following propositions:

1. Projective techniques present relatively ambiguous stimuli to the examinee.

2. The techniques are "response-free" in the sense that there are no right or wrong responses and the examinee is free to give whatever responses appear suitable.

3. Responses are interpreted as reflecting central personality tendencies and affective states.

4. The obtained records are also viewed, in varying degrees, as reflections of the cognitive processes and personality style of the subject.

Since projection is such a ubiquitous process that characterizes a good deal of human experience, particularly perceptual and expressive behavior, a great many situations may facilitate this process, which, in turn, may be interpreted. Projective "techniques" or projective "tests" present a standard set of stimuli under specified conditions so that the responses obtained are attributable primarily to personality differences. Thus projection of personal needs and styles may be seen in much of human behavior and so interpreted, but only a limited number of methods or situations qualify for the designation of projective tests or techniques.

Some of the currently listed projective techniques date back to an era when the term was unknown. For example, the *word association* method originally employed in Wundt's laboratory, and subsequently used in the clinical setting by Jung, is retrospectively adopted as the "first projective technique." The subject is presented with a standard series of words and is asked to respond to each word with the first association (word) that comes to mind. Thus the stimuli and instructions are fairly standard, but the freedom of the subject to respond is considerable. Both content and style (Rapaport et al., 1946) are interpreted clinically. Psychometric refinements of the technique involve response lists based on a normative sample that allow the computation of the deviation of a given response from the available norm.

The best known projective technique is the Rorschach test. In his 1921 monograph *Psychodiagnostiks,* Hermann Rorschach introduced his "perceptual diagnostic" test, which consists of ten inkblots—five chromatic and five achromatic. The examinee's task is to respond with an interpretation of these unstructured visual stimuli. Although Rorschach referred to his inkblots as *Zufallsformen* or accidental forms (i.e., unstructured), the accumulated evidence indicates that those standard stimuli initiate associations that are common to a great many people. The inkblots are not "meaningless," but reflect a shared meaning among respondents. For this reason, Rorschach referred to his method as a perceptual-diagnostic experiment rather than as a test of imagination.

Perhaps second in popularity is the Thematic Apperception Test (TAT), first introduced by Morgan and Murray in 1935 and subsequently elaborated in *Explorations in Personality* (Murray, 1938). The TAT is a picture-story test, consisting of 20 pictures with alternatives for some of them, for women and men, girls and boys. Most of the pictures are of clearly recognizable people of different ages and both sexes in some form of interaction or relationship. The pictures are sufficiently structured to present a considerable range of situations that may be related to many important facets of a person's life. Examinees are asked to make up a story about each picture, to "describe what is happening at the moment, what the characters are feeling or thinking," what "led up to the event shown in the picture," and what the "outcome" will be. The subject's task is, in some ways, rather more complex than in the Rorschach task, which involves reporting immediate single percepts. The TAT requires the construction of a story with a past, present, and future. In interpreting the stories, stress is placed on dominant "themas"—the interaction between drives and the environment. A number of scoring methods have developed, extended, and modified some of the original interpretive approaches proposed by Murray and his associates. Clinicians often use particular cards of the TAT series to explore some specific area of concern that the pictures are expected to evoke. The research use of TAT in the study of the achievement motive by McClelland and co-workers (1948) is well known.

Still another illustration of a projective method is the *sentence completion technique.* This is a relatively structured verbal method whereby sentence stems or incomplete sentences are presented to the examinee, who is instructed to finish them as quickly as possible. The partial sentence presented limits the degrees of freedom of the respondent much more than the other methods do. Also the respondent has a much clearer awareness of the meaning of the responses. On the Rorschach, or even the TAT, respondents are not aware to what extent their "private worlds" are projected into their productions. In the case of sentence completion, the situation is much different in this respect, approaching the conditions of a questionnaire or a structured interview. There is, however, greater freedom or greater choice of responses than in the other mentioned methods of investigation and diagnosis. Many forms of the sentence completion tests are available. Some are especially designed to investigate particular areas of interest, by employing stems that are expected to evoke a specific content. Generally the method investigates attitudes in the areas of family, sex, guilt, anxiety, and so on. Some specific forms, such as the ones designed by Loevinger and her co-workers (1970), attempt to assess formal and abstract variables, such as levels of ego development, rather than more concrete areas of concern.

Projective drawings, doll play, and story completion, as well as adaptations of the Rorschach (e.g., the Holtzman inkblot method) and the TAT (Children's Apperception Test) models, are some of the methods that have further expanded the field of projective techniques. Numerous other adaptations and "tailor-made" methods have also been published.

Over the years, projective techniques have often been attacked by scientifically oriented critics. They have questioned the reliability and validity of the techniques employed. Literally thousands of research studies with the Rorschach, TAT, and other methods have been published during the past four decades. Some unique research design problems had to be faced. Much of the research supports the reliability of the Rorschach (Exner, 1978) and some of the other methods. But a good deal of the field remains controversial despite the continued evidence of the clinical usefulness of the methods.

REFERENCES

Exner, J. E. (1978). *The Rorschach: A comprehensive system. Vol. 2: Current research and advanced interpretations.* New York: Wiley Interscience.

Frank, L. K. (1939). Projective methods for the study of personality. *Journal of Psychology, 8,* 389–413.

Frank, L. K. (1948). *Projective methods.* Springfield, IL: Thomas.

Horowitz, R., & Murphy, L. B. (1938). Projective methods in the psychological study of children. *Journal of Experimental Education, 7,* 133–140.

Loevinger, J., & Wessler, R. (1970). *Ego development.* San Francisco: Jossey-Bass.

McClelland, D. C., & Atkinson, J. W. (1948). The projective expression of needs. 1. The effect of different intensities of the hunger drive on perception. *Journal of Psychology, 25,* 205–222.

Morgan, C. D., & Murray, H. A. (1935). A method for investigating fantasies: The Thematic Apperception Test. *Archives of Neurology and Psychiatry, 34,* 289–306.

Murray, H. A. (1938). *Explorations in personality: A clinical and experimental study of fifty men of college age.* New York: Oxford.

Rapaport, D., Gill, M., & Schafer, R. (1946). *Diagnostic psychological testing: The theory, statistical evaluation and diagnostic application of a battery of tests* (Vol. 2). Chicago: Year Book Publishers.

Rorschach, H. (1949/1921). *Psychodiagnostics.* New York: Grune & Stratton.

A. I. RABIN
Michigan State University

**HOUSE-TREE-PERSON TEST
RORSCHACH TECHNIQUE
SENTENCE COMPLETION TESTS
THEMATIC APPERCEPTION TEST**

PSEUDODEMENTIA

The American Psychiatric Association's *Diagnostic and Statistical Manual of Mental Disorders,* Fourth Edition, describes dementia as an organic mental syndrome characterized by global impairment in memory severe enough to interfere with the ability to work or carry out social activities. Memory loss in dementia can be associated with faulty judgment, a tendency to avoid new tasks, and problems with impulse control. Friends and family may also note personality changes. *DSM-IV* generally assumes that dementia has an underlying organic cause.

For dementia to be diagnosed, there must be evidence of impairment in short-term as well as long-term memory. In addition, one of the following must be present: (1) impairment in abstract thinking as noted, for example, by impaired performance in such tasks as defining words and concepts and finding similarities and differences in related words; (2) impaired judgment; (3) other impairments of higher cortical functioning, which can include problems in carrying out language or motor functions; and (4) changes in personality.

If no findings point to an organic basis for dementia, the manual advises that an organic cause can still be assumed if no other factors can be found as causative agents. Pseudodementia refers to nonorganic factors that can account for symptoms of dementia. Initially, this condition was named depressive pseudodementia under the assumption that depression will cause cognitive symptoms, including memory impairments. Swihart and Pirozzolo (1988) pointed out that pseudodementia as a diagnostic category is not clearly defined, explaining that characteristic features of pseudodementia include reversibility of memory and other intellectual impairments once the nonorganic disorder has been accurately diagnosed and treated. In contrast, dementia is not reversible and is usually progressive, even though there may be long, plateau-like periods.

Most often, pseudodementia occurs in individuals over the age of 50, although it can occur at any age. LaRue, Dessonville, and Jarvik (1985) noted that 30% of individuals may be incorrectly classified. Some individuals improve without treatment, whereas others respond to treatment for depression. Although it is often difficult to apply clinical criteria to differentiate between demented and depressed individuals, there have been a number of attempts to do so. In pseudodementia, memory loss for recent events is about the same as for distant events (demented patients often have greater memory loss for recent events). Pseudodemented patients' emotional reactions (coping, affective state, concern about disability, and general complaints) tend to be emphasized in contrast to demented patients, and previous psychological problems are more frequently reported, though the ability to concentrate may be relatively intact. Overall, performance on neuropsychological assessment tasks may be more variable, with a greater likelihood of "don't know" answers as opposed to "near misses." Most authorities agree that pseudodementia is especially difficult to diagnose. Furthermore, this diagnosis has not been demonstrated to be conclusive, and is often based on an overall pattern of diagnostic signs and the overall clinical history of the patient rather than on specifically pertinent symptom constellations.

The previously cited authors suggested that pseudodementia represents a consciousness-raising diagnosis that encourages health service providers to be cautious in making a diagnosis of dementia, because this often results in termination of active treatment attempts. Swihart and Pirozzolo (1988) pointed out that just because dementia is eventually irreversible, efforts at treating demented patients should not cease.

Zarit and Zarit (1998) discuss pseudodementia under the rubric of the association of dementia and depression. They suggest, along with other authorities, that it is not accurate to assume that pseudodementia is reversible, though it is always important to evaluate potential reversible elements. Starkstein and Robinson (1993) emphasize the impact of depression on cognitive functioning and go on to speculate that perhaps there is a different mechanism operating for patients with left-side brain lesions as opposed to right-side lesions. They found that patients with right hemisphere lesions with depression do not show the same cognitive impairments that patients with left hemisphere lesions do.

While depression has been noted as an important determinant in the diagnosis of pseudodementia, other conditions may produce nonorganic memory impairments. Individuals diagnosed as suffering from chronic schizophrenia or other psychotic disorders may have memory dysfunctions. Most often, the clinical history for such individuals is sufficient to rule out a dementing process. Malingering (deliberately falsifying symptoms for some material gain) can also result in a diagnosis of pseudodementia or dementia, but clinical history, overall patient symptoms, and careful psychological testing should minimize diagnostic dilemmas. Finally, the diagnosis of factitious disorder (the intentional production of symptoms without any evident outside incentives) could be consistent with pseudodementia. Psychological and neuropsychological assessment is helpful in making a differential diagnosis.

Among the major organic mental disorders other than dementia that produce memory impairment, *DSM-IV* lists delirium and amnestic disorders. In delirium, a major notable factor is the reduced ability to maintain attention. There is often a reduced level of consciousness so that patients have difficulty keeping awake. Sleep disturbances, perceptual problems (e.g., hallucinations or misinterpretations), confusion, and disorientation, may also be present. The problems with short-term and long-term memory also exist for individuals diagnosed with amnesia. However, in contrast to dementia, there is usually no impairment of abstract thinking, no personality change, and no other problems in higher mental functions among amnestics.

There is a lack of consensus for the diagnosis of pseudodementia. Salzman and Gutfreund (1986) stated that pseudodementia is neither pseudo nor dementia. They insisted that it is a genuine impairment of memory secondary to depression without impairment of other mental processes. They believe it is helpful to differentiate patients both on the basis of mood and cognitive functions as well as on age. They used a four-category descriptive system, starting with the young-old (under the age of 80) who are mildly to moderately depressed. Then come the young-old who are severely depressed followed by the old (older than age 80) who are mildly to moderately depressed; they are followed by the old who are severely depressed. These authors contended that the assessment of memory loss as a function of depression is relatively easy for the first group and increasingly difficult for the other three groups. In their opinion, the over 80 and severely depressed groups may not be amenable to accurate assessment.

The importance of distinguishing between depression and dementia in the elderly is vital. Very often, Salzman and Gutfreund (1986) state, physicians will prescribe antidepressant medications if they suspect that a patient may be depressed. Although this may be helpful for younger patients, it may be less than helpful for older patients, because antidepressant medications may be toxic for the elderly and, almost paradoxically, the chemical nature of some of the antidepressant drugs may in (itself) produce memory impair-

ment. Every effort should be made to differentiate dementia from pseudodementia, recognizing that neither dementia nor pseudodementia are clearly defined categories and that the assessment of pseudodementia is fraught with great difficulties, especially for those over 80 who are severely depressed.

REFERENCES

LaRue, A., Dessonville, C., & Jarvik, L. F. (1985). Aging and mental disorders. In J. Birren & K. W. Schaie (Eds.), *Handbook of the psychology of aging*. New York: Van Nostrand Reinhold.

Salzman, C., & Gutfreund, J. (1986). Clinical techniques and research strategies for studying depression and memory. In L. Poon (Ed.), *Handbook for clinical memory assessment of older adults*. Washington, DC: American Psychological Association.

Starkstein, S. E., & Robinson, R. G. (1993). *Depression in neurologic disease*. Baltimore: The Johns Hopkins University Press.

Swihart, A., & Pirozzolo, F. (1988). The neuropsychology of aging and dementia: Clinical issues. In H. A. Whitaker (Ed.), *Neuropsychology studies of nonfocal brain damage: Dementia trauma* (pp. 1–60). New York: Springer-Verlag.

Zarit, S. H., & Zarit, J. M. (1998). *Mental disorders in older adults: Fundamentals of assessment and treatment*. New York: Guilford.

N. ABELES
Michigan State University

ALZHEIMER'S DISEASE
CENTRAL NERVOUS SYSTEM DISORDERS
DEPRESSION
LATE LIFE PSYCHOSIS

PSEUDOPSYCHOLOGY

Work that superficially or deceptively resembles psychology can range from that of subprofessional quality to outright quackery. Some pseudopsychology is a benign and entertaining pastime, but other forms can be harmful.

Professional and scientific psychology requires controlled observations under precisely specified, repeatable conditions. To the extent that its work depends on casual observation, anecdotes, and testimonial evidence, it is subprofessional or unscientific. When claims are made for rapid, large change in behavior (particularly with minimal expenditure of money and personal effort), the appropriate label is "quackery."

Why does pseudopsychology persist? One answer is that there is a handsome profit to be made in alleviating anxiety. Who does not want to acquire a charming personality or a perfect memory easily? A related answer is the tendency to accept flattery uncritically. Very few charlatans criticize the individual. The few instances of the success of the pseudopsychology are remembered but the many failures are forgotten. Some pseudopsychologies depend on the human tendency toward categorical, stereotyped thinking.

Given the diversity of approaches to psychology, it is difficult precisely to distinguish developing subfields of psychology from borderline pseudopsychology. Whether memory can be transferred from one organism to another (Carney, 1978; Miller & Holt, 1977) or whether primates can acquire language (Sebeok & Umiker-Sebeok, 1980) is currently unclear, yet these are legitimate areas of research. Events such as voodoo death appear to exist, but the mechanisms are little understood.

EXAMPLES OF PSEUDOPSYCHOLOGY

The following examples of pseudopsychology, although they have some supporters, are without any currently demonstrable evidence of value.

Astrology

According to many astrologists, not only is an individual's basic temperament related to the moment of birth, but divination of future events is based on the current pattern of stars and planets. The popularity of astrology is seen in the frequent publication of horoscopes in newspapers. There even is a book of horoscopes for dogs.

Specific contemporary criticisms of astrology include the fact that the moment of birth rather than that of conception is chosen as the focal point and astrology's failure to revise calculations in accordance with developments in modern astronomy.

Numerology

Although there have been extremely complex numerology systems such as the cabalistic, the usual practice comes from Pythagoras. In one common system, letters of one's name are converted into numbers by the simple code A = 1, B = 2, and so on. The digits in this number are then added, repeating if necessary, until a single digit is obtained and interpreted. For a daily prediction of events for an individual, the digits of the date of birth and the day in question are also added. Other systems take the number derived from the name and relate it to various principles or deities.

Color Preference

From the earliest times, color has symbolized various natural phenomena: red for fire, gold for sun, white for moon, green for crops. One recent practice is to ask the individual to rank 10 color chips in order of preference; without any research basis, it is claimed that the subject's personality can be deduced from the ranking (Lee, 1972).

Phrenology

In this eighteenth- and nineteenth-century movement, popularized by Franz Gall and Johann Spurzheim, it was hypothesized that various human traits were associated with specific parts of the brain. Individuals with strong tendencies purportedly had enlargements of the corresponding brain area; these areas were detected by examining the shape of the skull. Between 30 and 40 faculties, such as benevolence and acquisitiveness, were identified.

Contemporary research indicates that the traits usually identified in phrenology are not closely associated with any special brain area (Watson, 1981). In addition, the shape of the skull does not correspond to the contours of the brain.

Physiognomy

From the most ancient times, personality has been related to physical appearance. Basic body structure was used for personality predictions by people from Hippocrates of Cos to William Sheldon. Fat people are said to be jolly; tall, thin people are viewed as quiet thinkers. Research evidence indicates that the modest relationship between personality and physique is better explained by learning and social stereotypes than heredity (Anastasi, 1958).

Other physiognomic variants include analysis of the shape of the head and face, by the Swiss mystic John Lavater; detection of criminality, by the Italian psychiatrist Cesare Lombroso; and the measurement of personality by ranking preferences in photographs of people, by the Swiss psychiatrist Lipot Szondi (Lubin, 1953). One minor variant of physiognomy interpreted personality by the location, shape, and color of moles on the body.

Palmistry

Divination using the hands is found in two forms. The more common, chirosophy, relates the lines on the palm to personality and fate. One method considers the dominant hand to indicate "natural" tendencies while the nonpreferred hand shows learned traits and the inclination to follow the natural traits. Chirognomy uses the shape of the hand and fingers, the way the fingernails are cut, and mannerisms in holding and moving the hands.

Graphology

The slant, size, letter formation, and other characteristics of handwriting are stated to be related to personality. Analysts disagree as to whether the signature or a sample of "casual" writing is more revealing. Handwriting analysis is more popular in Europe than in the United States. Research indicates too slight a relationship between personality and handwriting for practical prediction (Holt, 1965; Nevo, 1986).

Skilled students of questioned documents are quite capable of determining, with a high degree of probability, whether or not the same individual wrote or printed two passages, but that is all.

Cold Reading

"Cold" refers to lack of prior information about the client. The soothsayer first builds rapport by describing past events, and then moves to prediction. The technique, described by William Gresham (1949), involves placing the individual in one of seven categories, beginning with standard statements for the category, and modifying comments according to the subtle cues of the subject's body language and facial expression.

A number of props may be used: playing or Tarot cards, dice, dominoes, tea leaves, a pendulum, a divining rod, a Ouija board, or a crystal ball. Palmistry and graphology are sometimes performed as cold readings.

Parapsychology

Clairvoyance is the instantaneous awareness of an event without the usual means of obtaining the knowledge. Telepathy is communication between two individuals without the use of obvious links. Precognition is the foretelling of future events in specific detail. Collectively these three phenomena are referred to as extrasensory perception (ESP). Psychokinesis (PK) is the manipulation of physical objects via thought.

Even the best research designed to demonstrate the phenomena of ESP and PK is characterized by lack of adequate controls (Hansel, 1980). Rhine and others have complained that stricter research standards are asked of parapsychology than of other areas, but selective stringency is entirely appropriate. Many instances of fraud are documented ("Psychokinetic fraud," 1974). The more unlikely the event, the more convincing must be the evidence.

In some circumstances, particularly with PK, most psychologists are unable to design proper controls: A skilled prestidigitator is needed. With adequate controls, ESP disappears; its adherents often claim that a hostile environment prevents the phenomenon. Individuals claiming to have PK usually refuse to perform with a magician present. As Martin Gardner (1981) notes, occult demonstrations fail on television talk shows where the host has a background in magic. Professional magicians apparently have moved objects and bent items such as spoons and keys under conditions in which others claim to do so by occult powers. Skilled legerdemain is fascinating entertainment; it is unfortunate that some conjurers insist on claiming mystical sources for their abilities.

Therapautic Touch

In the early 1970s Dolores Krieger, PhD, Professor of Nursing at New York University, and her mentor, Dora Kunz, a natural healer, developed Therapeutic Touch (TT). A scientific base is claimed for TT. The explanation for TT involves adjustment of a "universal life force energy" that flows in all living organisms, thus creating an energy field around the body that can be detected by the practitioner (and the aura-detecting Kirlian photography). The original TT is non-contact; it appeared to one observer as if a mime were pretending to give a massage to a real person.

In 1996 Emily Rosa, for her 4th grade science project, demonstrated that under blind control conditions practitioners of TT were unable to determine which of their hands was closer to the investigator's hands [coin toss determined the hand; 44% correct judgments in contrast with chance accuracy of 50%]. With additional data collection the next year the study [21 practitioners, 280 total trials] was published in the *Journal of the American Medical Association*. Also, accuracy was unrelated to number of years (1 to 21) experience with TT.

The Pentagon awarded a grant in excess of $350,000 to researchers at the University of Alabama in Birmingham to study TT in burn patients. After finding no difference between the TT and "sham" treatment control groups for those of the 131 who completed the study, the major conclusion in the Final Progress Report was "The greatest lesson learned from this process is that the inclusion of a true control group in addition to a sham and treatment group is required because a strong placebo effect occurs from the special attention given to patients in the 'sham' treatment" (Turner, 1996). Unlike Emily Rosa, the UAB researchers failed to see that their data strongly suggest that the only impact of TT is placebo.

While it can still reasonably be claimed that TT has not been tested on a wide variety of medical problems (this lack of good research—in contrast with a plethora of anecdotes—after almost three decades is a serious deficiency on the part of those taking money as TT practitioners), the identical results obtained by the initially neutral Emily Rosa and the strongly pro-TT researchers at UAB suggest the likelihood of any meaningful impact of TT to be minuscule, hence its inclusion here.

Demonology, Witchcraft

In the fourteenth and fifteenth centuries, the most common explanation of bizarre behavior was possession by demons. Later, in the early colonial days, the witch was considered to have consciously sold the soul to the devil in exchange for the powers.

Dream Analysis

Freud wrote about "fixed symbols," features of dreams that meant the same thing for all individuals. Umbrellas and pencils were said to be male sexual symbols, coming out of water was birth, tooth extraction was castration or abortion. Freud's notion of fixed symbols is now considered erroneous (Mosak, 1955). Although many within a culture may use a common symbol, humans are too unique automatically to apply an interpretation without regard to individual differences.

In the hands of a trained clinician, dream analysis is a useful tool, which points to a person's traumas, anxiety, and wishes. But it is the individual's hopes or expectations for the future that are discerned in some dreams, rather than simple prediction of the future.

REFERENCES

Anastasi, A. (1958). *Differential psychology* (3rd ed.). New York: Macmillan.

Carney, R. E. (1978). Reactions of planarians after cannibalization of planarians exposed to four stimulus combinations. *Journal of Biological Psychology, 20,* 44–49.

Gardner, M. (1981). *Science: Good, bad, and bogus.* Buffalo, NY: Prometheus.

Gresham, W. L. (1949). Fortune tellers never starve. *Esquire, 32*(5). In N. H. Pronko (Ed.), *Panorama of psychology.* Belmont, CA: Brooks/Cole.

Hansel, C. E. M. (1980). *ESP and parapsychology: A critical reevaluation.* Buffalo, NY: Prometheus.

Holt, A. G. (1965). *Handwriting in psychological interpretations.* Springfield, IL: Thomas.

Lee, S. G. (1972). Review of the Lüscher Color Test. In O. K. Buros (Ed.), *The seventh mental measurements yearbook.* Highland Park, NJ: Gryphon.

Lubin, A. (1953). Review of the Szondi Test. In O. K. Buros (Ed.), *The fourth mental measurements yearbook.* Highland Park, NJ: Gryphon.

Miller, B. E., & Holt, G. L. (1977). Memory transfer in rats by injection of brain and liver RNA. *Journal of Biological Psychology, 19,* 4–9.

Mosak, H. H. (1955). Language and the interpretation of "sexual" symbolism. *Journal of Consulting Psychology, 19,* 108.

Nevo, B. (Ed.). (1986). *Scientific aspects of graphology: A handbook.* Springfield, IL: Thomas.

Psychokinetic fraud. (1974, September). *Scientific American, 231*(3), 68, 72.

Sebeok, T. A., & Umiker-Sebeok, J. (Eds.). (1980). *Speaking of apes: A critical anthology of two-way communication with man.* New York: Plenum.

Watson, W. C. (1981). *Physiological psychology: An introduction.* Boston: Houghton Mifflin.

SUGGESTED READING

Christopher, M. (1970). *ESP, seers, and psychics.* New York: Crowell.

Gilovich, T. (1991). *How we know what isn't so: The fallibility of human reason in everyday life.* New York: Free Press.

Wolman, B. B. (Ed.). (1979). *Handbook of dreams: Research, theories, and applications.* New York: Van Nostrand Reinhold.

C. S. Peyser
University of the South

EXTRASENSORY PERCEPTION
PARAPSYCHOLOGY
PHRENOLOGY
SUPERSTITION

PSYCHIATRIC SOCIAL WORK

Social work is a complex, diverse, and somewhat amorphous profession. The diversity of the tasks assumed by social workers requires an equally diverse knowledge base, one to which virtually all of the social and behavioral disciplines contribute. This knowledge is shaped to fit the mission of the profession and the needs of the clients it serves. Thus understanding social work requires not only knowledge about its technologies, but also about the function of the profession.

DEFINITION

The use of the phrase "psychiatric social worker" is anachronistic. It predates 1955 when various professional social work groups, including the American Association of Psychiatric Social Workers, merged to form the National Association of Social Workers (NASW). The continued use of the term is understandable, however, in view of the diversity of roles, training, fields of practice, and approaches found among those titled "social worker."

Social workers include people with no special training as well as those holding degrees ranging from the associate to doctoral level. The untrained are largely, but not exclusively, employed by large public agencies. Until 1974, when the Council on Social Work Education (CSWE) began to accredit baccalaureate programs, the professional social worker was considered to be one who had earned the master's degree from an accredited school of social work. Issues concerning the differentiation between the BA degree and the MA or MSW degree have been a matter of debate within the profession since that time.

There is also considerable diversity in the roles and expertise of social workers. The majority of professional social workers are trained and employed to work with individuals, families, and small groups for the purpose of resolving psychosocial problems. This branch of social work is contemporarily referred to as clinical social work, direct practice, or social treatment. Other social workers specialize, by training and practice, in designing and implementing social policy, working with communities, administering agencies and programs, and conducting research.

Diversity within fields of practice and population groups also exists. Clinical social workers can be found in such settings as mental health, medical, school, child welfare, family service, public welfare, corrections, and industry. A growing number of social workers are in private practice. Some specialize with particular populations, such as children or the elderly. Others specialize in work with particular problems, such as mental illness, disabilities, or addictions. The generic nature of clinical social work education enables social workers to translate their skill from one agency to another and among differing populations.

There is considerable confusion in the minds of the public about what a social worker is. The problem of defining one is somewhat more complex than the problem the blind men encountered in describing the elephant. They at least had a common term for the object of their observations. The phrase *psychiatric social worker* should probably be abandoned for something more generic, such as clinical social worker, because the education and skill do not differ across settings. And perhaps *clinical social worker* should be reserved for those who hold a master's degree in social work to minimize our identity problems.

Regardless of the appropriate labels, psychiatric social workers are employed in mental health settings, usually hold a master's degree in social work, and are expert in social treatment (working with individuals, families, and small groups). Their education provides them with the following kinds of knowledge and skill:

1. An understanding of the common human needs of clients regardless of the setting in which they are encountered or the problem they present.

2. Knowledge about the effects of the help-giving systems as well as those systems in which the client interacts.

3. Knowledge about cultural diversity.

4. Knowledge about the environment with respect to both its effects on the individual and the alteration of it.

5. Knowledge about social welfare policy, programs, and resources and how to obtain them.

6. Commitment to the underclass.

7. Ability to intervene with a range of problems, settings, and clients.

8. Research skills.

The role that social workers play in the delivery of mental health services can be demonstrated by examining the professional affiliation of those who staff mental health facilities. In 1974, 17% of the professional care staff in inpatient and outpatient, private and public mental health facilities were social workers (Taube, 1974). This is in contrast to psychiatrists and psychologists who, respectively, represented 14% and 11% of the full-time professional staff. Among such facilities, private mental hospitals hired the smallest percentage of social workers (3%) and outpatient clinics, the largest (26%). In 1976, approximately 31,200 social workers were employed in mental health facilities as compared with 14,950 clinical psychologists. The total number of psychiatrists during the same year was 24,432 (*Health Resources Statistic: 1976–1977,* pp. 150, 233, 247). Assuming that staffing patterns adequately reflect service, social workers provide more mental health care than psychiatrists or psychologists do.

HISTORY

The profession of social work has its roots in what was referred to as charity work or friendly visiting. The purpose of these efforts was to provide for the "worthy poor." Social Darwinism and the Protestant Ethic were in flower and poverty was thought to result from individual deficiencies. Thus it was important to weed out those whose poverty resulted from their own immorality (such as excessive drinking) and to provide for those deemed the "worthy poor," the victims of circumstance. Part of the function of the friendly visitor was investigation and another part was to help the poor master their own difficulties. The Settlement House movement, which began in the 1880s, also influenced social work. Young professionals were attracted to reside among the poor and they produced a number of publications that informed a wide audience about the conditions of poverty. A goal of the Settlement House workers was to help people in the neighborhoods organize to solve social problems.

A number of forces coincided in the late 19th century that shifted the focus somewhat from the scientific dispensing of charity to social reform. The charity organizers and the Settlement House workers had learned a great deal about the causes of poverty—subsistence wages, child labor, unsafe working conditions, and so on—and had promulgated this information to the middle and upper classes. A number of economic depressions marked the last decade of the 19th century, and many were awakened to the fact that people were unemployed through no fault of their own. Finally, the accumulation of wealth in the last half of that century was so great that many were convinced that the nation was at its apex and the job was preservation. The objects of concern for preservation ranged from the national forests to the country's children. The progressive era had begun. It was characterized by concern for economic and social reform, the emergence of the profession of social work, and the development of numerous special interest groups.

This brief description of the formative years of social work includes some of the currents that remain a part of the profession. Among them are concern for the basic survival needs of people, a tension between counseling and social reform, a concern for families and about the environments of the needy, and conflicting traditions of fact gathering, social control, and client advocacy. These divergent urges are of some consternation to the profession, and perhaps to educators in particular, as they struggle to define the needed curricular content. Since social work is largely the manifestation of society's altruism, and since social problems are unlikely to disappear but rather to transmogrify, depending on the economic and political conditions of the country, it is likely that the tensions will continue. Perhaps the strains are functional in that their continuous, side-by-side existence allows various postures to achieve preeminence as needed.

APPROACHES TO INTERVENTION

From approximately the 1930s until sometime during the 1960s, clinical social workers were immersed in what is often referred to in histories of social work as the psychoanalytic deluge. It is difficult to understand the virtually universal acceptance of Freudian theory. During the early decades of the century, social work was striving to achieve professional status. It has been suggested that psychoanalytic theory, in vogue at that time, provided an intellectual base for the infant profession. Also, as previously described, social workers ply their trade in many different settings and Freudian psychology seemed to offer a generic base applicable to all of them.

During the 1960s, research into the effectiveness of social work was begun and the findings were disappointing. This decade also brought renewed interest in civil rights and poverty. These forces led many social workers to question the usefulness of the psychoanalytic approach in helping individuals, and, in fact, the validity of devoting so much of our attention and resources to social treatment when so much hardship resulted from the social and economic structure. As a result, an increasing number of social workers turned their attention to social reform (a group that still represents a small percentage of all social workers, however) and the clinical social workers began to develop, examine, and use approaches other than the dominant psychoanalytic one. At this writing, it is likely that every articulated approach to intervention is used at least occasionally by at least a few social workers. Only the predominant ones and those unique to social work are described here.

Psychosocial casework (Hamilton, 1940; Hollis, 1964) has its roots in the 1930s and is frequently referred to as the diagnostic approach. As this title implies, it emphasizes diagnosis, and diagnosis is formulated in terms of psychoanalytic theory. The approach is characterized by a fairly lengthy assessment phase during which facts are gathered for the purpose of accumulating a psychosocial history. The object of this endeavor is to understand the nature and dynamics of the client's personality from the analytic viewpoint. Attention to the environment or situation of the client is extolled, as it is in most approaches developed by social workers. However, as it lacks a theory or a conceptualization of environments and a technology for intervening with them, this aspect of the approach has at best taken a back seat. Support and insight are the tools by which weak egos are bolstered and conflicts are resolved. There seems to be a difference between the psychosocial approach as written and as it has been employed. The various authors that have contributed to it over the years acknowledge the importance of the environment as a causal factor and as an arena for intervention.

They do not assume that treatment will always be lengthy. Nevertheless, the power of the approach lies in its psychoanalytic base, and that is what has been absorbed by students and implemented by practitioners. The stance of the practitioner of this approach is the aloof or objective one; treatment tends to be long, change efforts are directed at the internal dynamics of the client, and these dynamics are understood in terms of states of awareness, psychic structures, energy, and defenses.

The *functional* model of practice (Robinson, 1930) was developed during the 1930s. In this approach, casework is seen as a process by which specific social services are delivered within the context of an enabling relationship. The helping process is emphasized, especially the aspects of initiating, sustaining, and terminating it. The function of the agency provides the focus for work and assessment or diagnosis is related to the client's use of service. The functional approach is employed by a very small percentage of social workers but many of its principles have influenced more recent scholarly contributions.

The *problem-solving* approach (Perlman, 1957) to casework evolved in the late 1950s. The differences between it and the psychosocial approach seem minor in light of the more recent changes but bordered on heretical at the time. The four major concepts within this approach are person, problem, process, and place. The process refers to that which occurs between social worker and client and the place refers to the agency in which help is offered. The stress on the last three variables differentiates this approach from the psychosocial one. In addition, the theoretical viewpoint emphasizes ego psychology and the work of John Dewey. In other words, the coping capacities of the individual are given more recognition.

Task-centered casework (Reid & Epstein, 1972) is also a problem-solving approach. The differences between it and Perlman's articulation of problem solving are dramatic, however. In this approach, the focus clearly shifts from the person to the problem. The target problem(s), that which is to be altered, is identified by the client rather than by the worker's assessment of personality deficits. Assessment is focused on the problem, the conditions that describe it, its frequency, duration, or severity—rather than on the person. This approach is a planned, short-term one. Intervention consists of helping the client engage in activities or tasks designed to reduce or eradicate the target problem. Task-centered casework is not founded on a theory of personality, but on empirical findings about the nature of intervention: the drop-out rate; the improvement in early phases of treatment; and the effectiveness of short-term treatment. This approach is the only one developed by social workers that has been demonstrated to be effective in a number of controlled research investigations.

A number of approaches based on *systems* theory have evolved (Goldstein, 1973; Pincus & Minahan, 1973). The ready acceptance of this framework for thinking is undoubtedly the promise it offers for a conceptual view of the environment. In these approaches, assessment consists of examining the various overlapping systems that might be causing or maintaining the problem. These approaches open up the question of who or what is to be changed and who is to do the changing. For example, problems experienced by children in a classroom might be the result of the teacher's behav-

ior. It might be determined that the most effective way to alter the behavior of the teacher is by bringing pressure to bear on the principal, and that this would be accomplished most effectively by organizing the parents of the children in that classroom. This example illustrates another attribute of models for intervention that are based on systems theory, and that is their generic quality. During the 30 or so years of the psychoanalytic deluge, methods for intervention in social work were categorized as casework, group work, and community organization. This division was unsatisfactory because it was often necessary for the social worker who was expert in one of these areas to utilize skills from another arena. The systems approach provides a framework that encompasses all of the methods.

The newly emergent *ecological* perspective (Germain & Gitterman, 1980) is a variant on systems approaches. In this approach, stress is attributed to a lack of reciprocity between the individual and the environment. The adaptive capacities of clients are supported and environmental pressures are alleviated. One of the major advances explicated in the ecological approach is the recognition that most problems are neither solely the result of individual deficiencies nor of the social order.

Three other recent additions to our interventive tools are *empirical clinical practice* (Jayaratne & Levy, 1979), *behavioral* models, and *eclectic* approaches (Mullen, 1978; Tolson, 1981). All of them are reflections of the profession's increasing concern for accountability. The single-case designs utilized in empirical clinical practice models have provided a means to examine the effectiveness of intervention. Adaptations of the $N = 1$ design are being developed to meet the kinds of problems presented to social workers, many of which do not readily lend themselves to repeated measurement. The eclectic models are conceptual tools for selecting the most effective interventions from a variety of approaches. Finally, behavioral procedures, described elsewhere, are being used increasingly by social workers.

The use of *family treatment* was evident from the inception of social work (Sherman, 1981). It was not until the late 1950s, however, that models for intervening with families were articulated. The various approaches to family treatment have generally evolved from the work of interdisciplinary teams, which included social workers, psychiatrists, and psychologists, among others. Most work with families, regardless of the profession of the practitioner, tends to be eclectic. Social workers, like other helping professionals, employ the structural approach, communication and Bowenian theory, and psychodynamic and behavioral approaches.

Social group work, a method that consists of working with a small number of individuals collectively, emerged during the Settlement House movement. Like the Settlement House workers, group workers are an interdisciplinary lot. Early group work efforts were related to issues of social reform and concrete or physical problems. It was not until the 1940s that group work began to be used to help the emotionally troubled. The specific purpose and functions of social group work remain a matter of debate. Education, social reform, recreation, prevention, and therapy compete as *raisons d'être,* probably because "work with groups is generic to all types of issues and actions" (Wilson, 1976, p. 38). Distinctions between various models for working with groups are not as clear-cut as those that exist among casework models. The same differences in emphasis do exist, however. Thus, paralleling the casework models, models for social group work have been developed around the following orientations: psychosocial, functional, systems, task centered, and problem solving. Distinctions among these approaches have been described.

REFERENCES

Germain, C. B., & Gitterman, A. (1980). *The life model of social work practice.* New York: Columbia University Press.

Goldstein, H. (1973). *Social work practice: A unitary approach.* Columbia, SC: University of South Carolina Press.

Hamilton, G. (1951/1940). *Theory and practice of social casework* (Rev. ed.). New York: Columbia University Press.

Health resources statistics 1976–1977. US Department of Health, Education, and Welfare, Public Health Services. Office of Health Research, Statistics, and Technology. National Center for Health Statistics.

Hollis, F., & Woods, M. E. (1981/1964). *Casework: A psychosocial therapy* (3rd ed.). New York: Random House.

Jayaratne, S., & Levy, R. L. (1979). *Empirical clinical practice.* New York: Columbia University Press.

Mullen, E. J. (1978). The construction of personal models for effective practice: A method for utilizing research findings to guide social interventions. *Journal of Social Service Research, 20,* 45–63.

Perlman, H. H. (1957). *Social casework: A problem-solving process.* Chicago: University of Chicago Press.

Pincus, A., & Minahan, A. (1973). *Social work practice: Model and method.* Itasca, IL: Peacock.

Reid, W. J., & Epstein, L. (1972). *Task-centered casework.* New York: Columbia University Press.

Robinson, V. P. (1930). *A changing psychology in social case work.* Philadelphia, PA: University of Pennsylvania Press.

Sherman, S. N. (1981). A social work frame for family therapy. In E. R. Tolson & W. J. Reid (Eds.), *Models of family treatment.* New York: Columbia University Press.

Taube, C. A. (1974). *Staffing of mental health facilities U.S.* Washington, DC: U.S. Department of Health, Education, and Welfare, Public Health Service; Alcohol, Drug Abuse, and Mental Health Administration, National Institute of Mental Health, Series B (no. 8).

Tolson, E. R. (1981). Conclusions: Toward a metamodel for eclectic family practice. In E. R. Tolson & W. J. Reid (Eds.), *Models of family treatment.* New York: Columbia University Press.

Wilson, G. (1976). From practice to theory: A personalized history. In R. W. Roberts & H. Northen (Eds.), *Theories of social work with groups.* New York: Columbia University Press.

E. R. TOLSON
University of Washington

PSYCHOANALYSIS

The term *psychoanalysis* is used in three ways: (a) to designate a loosely knit body of *ideas on the nature of the human mind,* in particular, personality development and psychopathology; (b) to describe a *technique of therapeutic intervention* in a range of psychological disturbances; and (c) to designate a *method of investigation.* All were originated during the last decades of the 19th century by the Viennese-Jewish physician, Sigmund Freud (1856–1939), whose revolutionary discoveries brought a new level of self-awareness and, for better or for worse, a permanently altered image of humankind. All three bodies of thought have been evolving, branching, and proliferating since their inception. This evolution has issued in an increasingly comprehensive and broad usage of the term psychoanalysis by therapists and scientists, and in folk wisdom. Doubtless Freud was one of those great thinkers who "disturb the sleep of the world."

Usually, though not always, shifts in psychoanalytic theory have had rapid and visible consequences for clinical work. Psychoanalysis, as therapy, in its inception regarded as its central task the uncovering of pathogenic memories; this gave way to the search for fantasies, and with the theoretical shift away from "instincts and their vicissitudes" to the discerning of configurations of characteristically adaptive patterns of human relationships and of work, in a particular society. Least spelled out, as psychoanalysis commences its second 100 years, are the technical implications for therapy and for social change of the most comprehensive psychoanalytic theory extant.

A survey of psychoanalysis brings into relief the implicit observation—increasingly validated in studies of the creative process in the natural, as well as in the social, sciences—that all discoveries issue in part from the psychological struggles of the discoverer (anonymous, 1970). This includes Freud, as well as those who broke from him and those who extended his vision. Powerful personal motives in each life history, as well as the historical moment, are determinants in the particular piece of reality, psychological or physical, seized by *any* discoverer.

THE FIRST PHASE

Freud, the "first psychoanalyst," made his monumental discoveries in the context of a threefold crisis—in therapeutic technique, in the conceptualization of clinical experience, and in a personal crisis. All three crises were, in essence, one, and were the necessary dimensions of discovery in psychology. Erikson writes in *Insight and Responsibility:* "A man, I will submit, could begin to study man's inner world only by appointing his own neurosis that angel with whom he must wrestle and whom he must not let go until his blessing, too, has been given" (Erikson, 1964, p. 23).

As that other great 19th-century reviser of the human image, Charles Darwin, had used the Galapagos Islands as his laboratory, so the neurologist Freud, much influenced by Darwin, used his consulting room. The "dominant species" under investigation, at first (1889) by means of the techniques of hypnosis, were mainly Victorian women diagnosed as suffering from hysteria. Freud, while still a medical student, had been deeply impressed by the work of internist Joseph Breuer, who was using hypnosis for therapy. His later observations of the work of neurologists A. A. Liebault, H. Bernheim, and J. Charcot in France, who were also using hypnosis—fundamentally an interpersonal relationship in an altered state of consciousness—confirmed his impression that this therapeutic technique offered better results than the then-fashionable electrotherapy. Unlike his colleagues, however, he became convinced that the source of difficulty ("forgotten mental contents") had not simply been "split off" but had been "pushed out" of, or "dragged down" from, immediate awareness by powerful *motivational* forces. This was a critical turn: to bring into focus the human psychological capacity to defend against pain. At first Freud called this process *defense,* and later *repression,* stating early that, "The theory of repression is the cornerstone on which the whole structure of psychoanalysis rests." From the start, Freud underscored that repression is "not a premise, but a finding."

Freud's initial discovery of a level of mentation, which is not accessible to immediate awareness, but which, nonetheless, has observable effects on behavior and on experience, rests on this dynamic concept; it antedates, however, his first use of the word, "psycho-analysis" in 1896. His innovation is a good example of what Thomas Kuhn has described as the development of a new paradigm. It stood in contrast to the view of his first collaborator (in the "hypnotic-cathartic method"), Breuer, who theorized that there was a simple absence of communication between what he called a "hypnoid" mental state and waking consciousness. He assumed, moreover, that, in such a hypnoid mental state, a real trauma—for example, a girl's seduction by her father—had occurred and had been "forgotten." Indeed, Breuer's first classic patient, Anna O., recalled under hypnosis her disgust upon seeing a lap-dog drink out of a glass. After what the patient called this "chimney-sweeping," that is, the recall in hypnosis, her hitherto inexplicable terror of drinking water from a glass vanished.

For a time, Freud tried to allow the older, more physiological theory to exist side by side with his new model until "observation showed me always and only one thing" (Freud, 1957/1914). He became totally convinced that the "splitting off" of mental contents—often "converted" into symptoms—was deeply motivated in his cases of hysteria and was not simply an absence of communication between mental states. He was convinced, moreover, that the inaccessibility of some mental contents resulted from the development of some ill-defined "energies" designed to keep them out of awareness. Of far greater significance for him than the etiology of hysteria was his growing conviction that *similar defensive processes were part of the psychology of ordinary normal human beings* as well who, though they might be free of symptoms, did make slips of the tongue, tell jokes, and have dreams.

During this first phase (pre-1896), Freud came to the bold, and then bitterly contested, conclusion that the etiology of hysteria was psychological and not "neurological." Moreover, he took very seriously Breuer's casual comment that nervous disorders are always *secrets d'alcove* (marriage bed), Charcot's that in these cases it is always "la chose genitale," and Chrobak's famous prescription for a woman suffering from acute anxiety, "Penis normalis, dosim repetatur!" Freud began to develop the hypothesis that there are three major determinants in hysteria: a *psychological trauma,* a *conflict of affects,* and a *disturbance in the sphere of sexuality.* He was accumulating clinical evidence for this position from these early studies of hysteria, where the trauma was believed to be the outcome of an actual seduction. Stubborn symptoms frequently disappeared with the "catharsis" of recalling a painful memory (the "abreaction of strangulated affect") and Freud published, with Breuer as senior author, two papers: in 1893, "On the psychical mechanism of hysterical phenomena: Preliminary communication," and in 1895, the classic "Studies on hysteria," which explicated the conviction that the psychological "lesion" lay in the forgotten painful *reality event.*

The Psychoses of defence was published in 1896. This paper is actually the beginning of psychoanalysis, although Freud had not yet coined the word. The theory of this first phase collapses when Freud discovered, to his dismay, that his patients' reports of infantile seduction were not necessarily reports of actual experiences, but of fantasies. As a result, what he saw as "reality experience" lost its central position and only slowly regained it in the course of the next half-century. The center of interest, both in theory and therapy, shifted from the reality experience to the processes whereby the fantasies had come into being. This line of thought initially led Freud to an exploration of instinctual drives and their vicissitudes, a period sometimes described as that of "id-psychology," roughly 1900–1914.

THE SECOND PHASE

The second phase of psychoanalytic inquiry began with Freud's discarding of the formal techniques of hypnosis and the introduction of his method of "free association": his patient, supine on a couch, was instructed by him—sitting behind on a chair—simply to say freely anything and everything that came to mind, without conscious censorship. For an hour, five or six times a week, the psychoanalyst would "decode" these associations and, in pursuit of curative insight, interpret their meanings to the patient. This fundamental rule of the earliest *therapeutic intervention* was called by Freud "psycho-analysis." It is the technique prescribed both for the training of, and use by, "classical" or "orthodox Freudian" psychoanalysts. It was also Freud's prime method of investigation. Anecdotal evidence suggests that, in his clinical work, Freud was often empathic, spontaneous, and supportive, and did not restrict himself to detached interpretations of the warded-off "instincts" in these "free associations."

However, for purposes of inquiry into the workings of the mind, he used this method on the assumption that if conscious censorship is voluntarily suspended, the inner resistance—the concept is used as in electricity, not as in willful stubbornness—will lessen, thus permitting the emergence into awareness of "repressed" material or, at least, of its derivatives. In this way, the psychoanalyst is afforded many fragments of the jigsaw puzzle, which, taken together, compose the picture of the nature of the painful conflict of those affects that, defensively, have had to be repressed. It is remarkable how early in his thinking there appeared some of Freud's key concepts, such as *defense* (of which repression is a special case), *resistance,* and, soon, *transference:* the idea that a pattern of desires, fears, conflicts, loves, hates, and associated defenses may be transferred, usually unconsciously, from one significant interpersonal relationship in one's history to another. So powerful had this phenomenon of transference been in one of Breuer's female cases that he had fled in panic, leaving this stormy terrain entirely to Freud. Over a period of 100 years, these basic discoveries have been incorporated into the everyday thinking of most of the civilized world.

Freud, early on, decided that the theory of psychoanalysis was an attempt to account for "two striking and unexpected facts of observation," namely, the "facts of transference and resistance." He declared that any line of investigation that takes these two facts as the starting point of its work has "a right to call itself psychoanalysis even though it arrives at results other than my own." He refers here simultaneously to a therapeutic technique and to a method of inquiry.

It was the method of free association, especially in the decoding of dreams, that Freud used, first in his intrepid pained and epochal self-analysis, and later in his classic case of "Dora," the first detailed psychoanalytic case history to be published (1905). In this case, Freud demonstrated not only the clinical uses of dream interpretation, but the giant theoretical advances he had made in his classic *Interpretation of Dreams* (1900), regarded by him as his most important theoretical work.

By this time, the simple notion of "sexuality" as the source of conflict had been broadened to include all physical pleasure as well as the "tender emotions" (affection, love), and the term *psychosexual* had appeared.

The conditions of dreaming (i.e., sleep, when the muscular apparatus is "disconnected") provided a golden opportunity in Freud's self-analysis to study the difference between logical thought processes ("secondary thought process") and illogical—condensed, for example, or displaced—processes ("primary thought process") as in dreams, jokes, and poems.

From the beginning, Freud sought to put his general theory of the human mind "on psychological ground" and to free this theory from the constraints of the biology and neurology of his time. Indeed, despite the often dramatic successes of the hypnotic-cathartic "talking cure" in the first phase of his work (a phase with which many people, including clinicians, end their acquaintance with psychoanalysis), Freud increasingly believed that his discoveries might be ultimately more influential in general science than as a mode of therapy.

Even in the earliest phase, while exploring therapeutic techniques, his conviction was growing that he was discovering in the human psyche new forces "equal in dignity" to the physical and chemical forces inherent in matter. Freud was endowed, first and foremost, with a passion—as he wrote to his idealized "listener," the biologist Wilhelm Fliess—to learn ". . . the origin and nature of humanity: how did human beings come to be what they are; and what in effect are they?" He wanted to answer such questions far more than to pin down the specific etiology and therapy of the hysterias.

In this second phase of psychoanalysis, begun around 1897 and ending in 1923, Freud vigorously pursued not only the questions of "instincts and their vicissitudes" (1915), but also the central problem of the possible source for that dynamic (defensive-repressive) force that regularly—in patients and in normal people—keeps certain painful mental contents from awareness. As early as 1905, he was discussing "ego-functions" as "ego-instincts." He thought of these as "instinctual drives" whose main function, in the interest of survival, was to defend against painfully conflicted affects. Here was an adumbration of the later (1923) idea of the tripartite structural division of the human psyche into the anthropomorphized *id* (instincts), *ego* (executive functions), and *superego* (conscience or ideals).

THE THIRD PHASE

Between 1900 and 1923, the psychoanalytic movement expanded organizationally, theoretically, and clinically, and experienced as well its major secessions. Once Freud had recovered from the shock that the pathogenic repressed memories were not necessarily of actual events but of fantasies, an entire range of a child's subjective experience—not simply infantile sexuality—opened up.

In the early days of psychoanalysis, an address on the sexual factor in hysteria to the Vienna Society for Psychiatry and Neurology had been met by cold silence and a "void which formed itself about me," a void sometimes filled with "expressions of scornful or pitying superiority." However, the years directly following the publication of Freud's seminal *Interpretation of Dreams* (1900) and what he called "my book on jokes," *Jokes and Their Relation to the Unconscious* (1905), brought "a number of young doctors" to learn and to teach not only a theory of pathology and a technique of therapy, but also some of the basic laws governing human thought processes. The miraculous natural experiment of their own nightly dreams, and those of their patients, were often at the heart of the discussions among the handful of doctors who began to meet in Vienna every Wednesday evening in the fall of 1902.

Unconscious thought processes—not so easy to study in the normal stable state of waking consciousness, where the frontiers of the ego are safeguarded—more readily yielded their secrets by way of the regular event of dreaming. In his *Interpretation of Dreams,* Freud pursued the universal inclination of dreams to "form fresh unities" out of disparate elements "which in our waking thoughts we should certainly have kept separate" (condensation). Or, again, that an element that was of no consequence in the dream thoughts "appears to be the clearest" and thus the most important feature of the manifest dream (or vice versa), he called displacement. In this "Kingdom of the Illogical," as Freud called it, these *condensations, displacements,* and *symbolizations* characterize a kind of thinking in which laws of formal logic have no place: This is the language and syntax of poetry, myth, magic, mysticism, and psychosis—the awesome *primary process.* This primary process systematized by Freud is in contrast to the more familiar *secondary process,* which *is* governed by laws of logic. This will later be linked by him to the "reality principle."

Not long after the publication of the *Interpretation of Dreams,* a communication came from a well-known psychiatrist, Eugen

Bleuler, then head of the famous public mental hospital in Zurich (the Burghölzli); and, after a visit to Freud by Dr. Max Eitingon, the assistant physician at the Burghölzli, Dr. Jung initiated a meeting (Salzburg, 1908) "which brought together friends of psychoanalysis" from Vienna, Zurich, and a few other places. Here Freud could present his venture into psychoanalytic "characterology": a paper on "Character and anal erotism."

In the face of what was still a "very emphatic repudiation," Freud was grateful for the support of the Zurich School of Psychiatry, and in particular for Jung's exploration of the psychoanalytic technique with schizophrenia. Bleuler's and Jung's attempts to apply psychoanalytic concepts to the therapy of psychoses were less important to Freud than the fact that his new friends were reporting the same basic psychological processes in schizophrenia as he had seen in the hysterias, dreams, and jokes, and the psychopathology of everyday life. The general psychological theory was taking shape.

Despite this interest in Zurich in his work, Freud continued to be largely ignored and regarded with suspicion, disdain, and active hostility by the few medical colleagues in Vienna who acknowledged his existence. It was not until 1909 that he was offered a first real opportunity to speak in public about his creation, "psychoanalysis"; this was at Clark University in Worcester, MA The American psychologist G. Stanley Hall, encouraged by the earlier interest taken by William James—the first American to take notice of Freud, invited him to present the results of his earlier investigation on hysteria.

On this occasion, appreciated by Freud as momentous for his work, he credited Breuer for having brought "psycho-analysis" into existence by his work on hysteria in the 1880s. Five years later, regretting the disproportionate credit he had given Breuer, Freud said, "It is one thing to give utterance to an idea once or twice in the form of a passing aperçu and quite another to mean it seriously . . . and to win it a place among accepted truths." By 1914, Freud reported the "very great triumph" of finding that direct observation of young children had confirmed "my statements about infantile sexuality," which had earlier been founded "almost exclusively" on the findings of analysis in adults.

In 1920, an underestimated and little-read 90-page volume appeared, *Beyond the Pleasure Principle,* in which Freud sketched the fundamental outlines for a keystone concept: It is the "repetition-compulsion," he wrote, that stands "beyond the pleasure principle."

In 1923, Freud's *Das Ich und Das Es* appeared, which was published in English as *The Ego and the Id,* and which crowned the third phase of psychoanalysis.

The routine translation of the word *Ich* (which in German literally means "I") as "ego" has encouraged a great deal of theoretical obfuscation. It has probably delayed the consolidation of an organismic and psychosocial concept of the "self," or "self-identity," or of "I-ness," while encouraging an anthropomorphic and reified concept, called "the ego." In the tripartite structural point of view, the ego mediates between drives (id), conscience (superego), and as yet vaguely defined, social realities.

In *The Ego and the Id,* Freud discussed the character and the evolution of the ego (the self, the I). He argued that when a person has to give up an "object" (i.e., a relationship), there ensues a mod-

ification within the "I" that can be described only as a *reinstatement* of that object as, for example, in melancholia. "The exact nature of this substitution," he writes, "is as yet unknown to us" (Freud, 1962/1923). He speculates that the "taking in" of this lost person makes the giving up easier; indeed, *this identification may be the sole condition for such giving up of a relationship.* In the theoretical language of this period: ". . . the sole condition under which the *id can give up its objects."*

In the early phases of development, he concludes, the I is a *precipitate of abandoned relationships* and contains a record of past choices. Sometimes, the alteration in character occurs before the object has been given up, thus conserving the relationship. If these object identifications become "unduly intense and incompatible with one another, a pathological outcome will not be far off," as in multiple personalities. Here, then, is the precursor of the later psychoanalytic theory of object relations, of splitting, of psychosocial development, and of identity elements constituting the adult personality.

In therapeutic application of the theory of *The Ego and the Id,* the psychoanalyst, said Freud, notices that when the patient approaches repressed material "his associations fail," and "we then tell him that he is dominated by a resistance." The patient may be unaware of this resistance, although it emanates from the ego. This observation led Freud to the final abandonment of the idea that neuroses are a simple conflict between the conscious and the unconscious. Instead, he pursued the train of thought begun several years earlier in his *Beyond the Pleasure Principle* and concluded from his understanding of the structural conditions of the mind that the conflict is between the organized ego (partly unconscious) and what is repressed and dissociated from it.

Of central importance in the functional importance of the ego is the fact that control over the approaches to motility devolves upon it. Thus, in relation to the id (*das ES* = the it)—roughly the repository of all instinctual drives—the ego is "like a man on horseback who has to hold in check the superior strength of the horse." The often-forgotten difference is that "the rider seeks to do so with his own strength while the ego uses borrowed forces."

The conceptual shortcoming of this early picture of the relation of drives and ego lay in that the ego is seen still, more or less, as the helpless rider of the id horse and is "obliged to guide it where it wants to go." There is little room in it for the experience of willing or choosing. Moreover, although some independent developmental roots are attributed to this ego, there is as yet no evolving and systematic (epigenetic) ground plan of a biopsychosocial nature.

Not until 1926 did Freud repudiate the idea that the ego (defensive, executive, and adaptive functions) is totally subservient to the id (drives). In *Inhibitions, Symptoms and Anxiety,* he detailed the processes whereby the ego initiates *defense* by way of the *signal of anxiety* and becomes increasingly able, in the course of development, to turn the passively experienced anxiety into a kind of active anticipation. In this new use, the ego makes use of the pleasure principle in pursuing its own ends, has a range of defenses and is ultimately concerned with *reality relationships;* therefore, it curbs instinctual drives when action prompted by them would lead into reality danger. He retained here, however, the central role of sexual and aggressive instinctual drives.

Freud discussed the development of the ego ideal and the superego—roughly the conscience or an unconscious sense of guilt—only as a defensive internalization, an identification with the father by a male child, adding in a footnote, "Perhaps it would be safer to say 'with the parents,'" and acknowledging the "constitutional bisexuality of each individual." The ego ideal and superego are derivates of ego functioning and are seen at this time as the normal resolution of the Oedipus complex: When the male child perceives his father as the obstacle to the carrying out of his (forbidden) desires toward his mother, the ego brings in this reinforcement (thus the term *superego*) to help in carrying out the repression "by erecting this same obstacle within itself." The more intense the original conflict, the more exacting later on is the domination of the superego over the ego—in the form of conscience or perhaps of an unconscious sense of guilt.

In the concepts of superego and ego ideal, Freud was supplying forces to represent what he called, "the higher, moral spiritual side of human nature." Thus it becomes the complex task of ego functioning to mediate—and to provide a delaying action—between the peremptory demands from the drives (id), these moral or spiritual restraints (superego), and the real world. "Religion, morality and a social sense," wrote Freud, "were originally one and the same thing."

In *Ego and the Mechanisms of Defence,* Anna Freud (1946/1937) recommended full study of the mental structures, id, ego, and superego, and described the familiar nine defenses previously discussed by Freud in scattered works: repression, regression, reaction formation, isolation, undoing, projection, introjection, turning against the self, reversal, and, adding a significant tenth, sublimation (the displacement of instinctual aims). She listed four additional defense mechanisms: denial, restriction of the ego, identification with the aggressor, and a form of altruism. Freud had credited Alfred Adler with originating many of these defense mechanisms. Clearly, in clinical work, interpretations of "resistance" and "transference" were now increasingly directed to the ways in which the ego defends against the drives. Anna Freud pointed out that "the odium of analytic unorthodoxy" no longer attaches to the study of the ego. Although the primacy of instinctual wishes remains, the focus has shifted toward ego psychology.

The issue of orthodoxy includes the secessions of Adler in 1911, Jung in 1913, Otto Rank in 1924, and Sandor Ferenczi in 1927.

Jung (1875–1961)

In 1906, Freud, then almost 50, received as a gift Jung's account of his word-association experiments, highly sympathetic to psychoanalysis. In this experimental psychopathology, Jung introduced the *complex* as a link between an affect and an idea. It is clear from his letter of thanks, the first of a seven-year correspondence, that Freud was deeply grateful, and eager to maintain contact with this young (Jung was 31), non-Jewish Swiss physician who held an important post in a prestigious psychiatric clinic in Zurich, far from a hostile Vienna. Freud was always concerned lest psychoanalysis remain "a Jewish affair."

During the seven years (1906–1913), over the protests of the leading Viennese (mostly Jewish) psychoanalysts such as Adler and Wilhelm Stekel, Jung became the recognized political leader of the movement and Freud's heir apparent. Freud, convinced of the importance of establishing a broad base of adherents, saw to it that Jung became president of the Association and editor of its chief periodical, the *Jahrbuch.* Adler withdrew in 1911, to be followed a couple of years later by Stekel.

The turning point between Freud and Jung came in 1912 when, instead of organizing their annual international psychoanalytic congress, Jung accepted an invitation to lecture at Fordham University in New York, a Jesuit school. Ernest Jones had refused to go on the ground of its being an "unsuitable venue for a discussion of psychoanalysis." Freud had already begun to be unhappy at the direction of Jung's thought into religion, mysticism, and mythology, finding his thinking confused. In *Totem and Taboo* (1912), Freud stressed the *parallel* in the psychology of children, primitives, and neurotics, not the inherited continuity from prehistory. Moreover, Freud regarded Jung's transfer to clinical data from "far-off" fields unwarranted and antitherapeutic. Direct reports from Jung's former patients persuaded Freud that the basics of psychoanalysis (resistance and transference) were being neglected in favor of fuzzy discussions of "archetypes" and "the collective unconscious." Jung's forays into theory were inward, to the "night side of the eye," as Adler's would be outward, toward social reality. From the start, Jung had found Freud and his circle "peculiar," and had had great difficulty with the concepts of psychosexuality, preferring to think of instinctual drives in more metaphorical terms. In 1913, convinced that Jung had renounced the fundamental tenets of psychoanalysis, Freud wrote to his intimate friend, the Hungarian Ferenczi, "Jung is crazy; but I don't really want a split." But the split had already occurred.

Jung's enterprise, using active imagination, would be called, *analytical psychology,* and from 1913 on, his thought returned to the materials of his first book, written in 1902, *On the Psychology and Pathology of So-called Occult Phenomena.*

Adler (1870–1937)

The Viennese psychoanalysts—all rivals for Freud's favor—banded together to protest Freud's elevation of Jung to a position of leadership. The most prominent rebel was Adler, of whom Freud had held a high opinion in the early years. By 1910, Freud was convinced that both Adler, a socialist, and Stekel would "soon end up by denying the existence of the unconscious." This judgment was provoked by Adler's early interests in what later became "ego strivings" in the psychoanalytic literature. Freud had thought well of the lively and forceful Adler's book on the role of defective organs in personality development, and of his observations on character formation. Nonetheless Adler's single-minded focus on the psychological effects of organ inferiority (he is best known for the "inferiority complex") was the source of Freud's concern that Adler would soon deny the hard-won territory of the existence of unconscious mental processes and daimonic drives, a terrain for which Freud thought Adler had little gift.

Adler claimed priority for the conception of the unity of the neuroses and for a dynamic view of them; Adler saw the aggressive drive as the source of energy when people compensate for their inferiorities. During 1910 and 1911, Adler's elaboration of this position precipitated the break with Freud. Adler began to write about *feelings* of inferiority, especially in the child who feels weak and insignificant; to this ("feminine") sense of weakness the crucial reaction is "masculine protest," that is, compensating with strength.

By the time Freud placed the aggressive instinct within the death instinct (Thanatos) as opposed to the life instinct (Eros) (1920, 1923), Adler was no longer concerned with instincts. He considered the aggressive drive and the will to power as central means of defense and adaptation. In this, Adler anticipated by many years the developments in clinical ego psychology and the significant work of such "culturalists" as Erik Erikson, Harry Stack Sullivan, Karen Horney, and Erich Fromm, who questioned the primacy of instinctual forces. Freud granted in 1914 that Adler had indubitably brought "something new to psychoanalysis—a contribution to the psychology of the ego. . . ," adding, ". . . and then expected us to pay too high a price for this gift by throwing over all the fundamental theories of analysis" (Freud, 1957, p. 61).

THE FOURTH PHASE

Adaptation and Psychosocial Development

By the mid-1930s, Freud's dimly implied conception of the ego's relative autonomy from drives—and its integrative functions—had been made explicit by Nunberg (1931) and Waelder (1936). Ten years earlier, Freud, in *Group Psychology and the Analysis of the Ego*, had begun to address the issues of the outside (social) reality, commenting, ". . . from the very first, individual psychology is at the same time social psychology." However, there remained a conspicuous theoretical gap regarding precisely *what* the ego was supposed to integrate and/or execute, as well as *how* this occurs. Toward the end of the decade, two psychoanalysts—widely separated geographically and in modes of thought—began to address this central problem. Neither Heinz Hartmann (1894–1970) nor Erikson (1902–1994) had, however, a clear awareness of the other's work on adaptation.

Hartmann, with some Jewish ancestry, was reared in a typically nonreligious "enlightened" family of nonobserving Zwinglian Swiss Protestants, the basic belief system resting on rational education. He was born and schooled in Vienna; an undergraduate interest in the natural sciences and in pharmacology soon changed to medicine and psychiatry at the University of Vienna. He worked at the Psychiatric and Neurologic Institute and at the Vienna Psychoanalytic Institute until the Nazi occupation of Austria in 1938. Cultivated, formal, scholarly, and personally distant, he developed an interest in 19th-century scientific methodology and emphasized the necessity that psychoanalysis become a "natural" science.

In 1939, Hartmann published an essay, "Ego psychology and the problem of adaptation," in which he emphasized "those processes and working methods of the mental apparatus which lead to *adapted achievements.*" Clearly this was a topic for which the psychoanalytic method of investigation—employed exclusively with persons who had failed in this department—was ill-suited for data collection. He suggested that functions such as perception, intention, object comprehension, thinking, language, motor development, and learning, evolve substantially apart from instinctual conflicts. He called this, "a conflict-free ego sphere," adding that instinctual drives alone do not guarantee survival and that we must assume mediation by an *innate* ego apparatus if the infant is to adapt to the average expectable

environment. The growth, for example, of perception or of locomotion is not necessarily caught up in erotic or aggressive conflict. Hartmann managed, however, to avoid challenging Freud's instinct theory by stating that these adaptive achievements are the outcome of "neutralized instinctual energies."

Anna Freud has reported that when she first brought her work on the defensive functions of the ego to the Vienna Psychoanalytic Society in 1936, Hartmann had contrasted his own view with hers to show that "the ego at war with the id" was far from the whole story. She says, "This was news to me which I was not yet ready to assimilate." These early discussions of the ego's executive functions of defense and adaptation, which adumbrate object-relations theory and self-psychologies, worked toward, and yet stopped far short of, the systematic attention to the ego's role in the relationship of individuality and communality. They stopped short also of integrating soma, psyche, and ethos.

Hartmann's mode of thought was logical and abstract; he never, for example, cited clinical material in the exposition of his ideas. Son of a leader in adult education for working people and of a sculptress mother, Hartmann developed a keen sense both for ethical values and for conflict-free energies. However, his characteristic mode of thought set the tone after Freud's death for the development of ego psychology: theoretical, holding affect at a safe distance, and paying scant attention to the essential role of human connectedness—as it unfolds in the life cycle—and of creative strengths in the epigenesis of all biopsychosocial development. Absent also was a radically interdisciplinary perspective; the average expectable environment was that of Western civilization in the late 19th and early 20th centuries.

By 1936, the basic theoretical tenets of psychoanalysis were being woven into American psychiatry by Harry Stack Sullivan (1892–1949). In continuous contact with Yale anthropologist Edward Sapir and Chicago sociologist Harold Lasswell, he had been engaged for several years in building bridges between a psychoanalytic American psychiatry and the social sciences. These interdisciplinary discussions on culture and personality ran parallel to psychoanalyst Erikson's concurrent exchanges at Harvard with anthropologists such as Margaret Mead, Gregory Bateson, Ruth Benedict, and Scudder Mekeel. Although for a brief span (1936-1939) Sullivan and Erikson overlapped in New Haven (Sullivan made frequent journeys from New York City), their interdisciplinary work—stemming from the Freudian revolution—developed independently and quite differently. They shared essentially what Sullivan termed Freud's "postulate of the unconscious" plus an emphasis on the social (interpersonal) view of human interests.

Sullivan, an Irish-American Catholic, only child of a humble farm family, was early aware of his sense of the Irish as an oppressed, enslaved, and exploited people, persecuted for religious belief, and a people whose self-esteem had been eroded for 3 centuries. The destruction of self-esteem became a central problem for Sullivan and—because of his psychoanalytic inquiry into the schizophrenic process—he has been called the "theorist of the lonely." Attracted by a lecture in 1926 given by Freud's disciple Ferenczi, Sullivan maintained a "dialogue" with Ferenczi by way of psychiatrist Clara Thompson, whom he sent to Budapest to study with Ferenczi so she could teach him what she had learned. Ferenczi, known as the "haven of lost cases," inspired Sullivan's ideas about homosexuality and schizophrenia. In 1928, when Thompson first went to Budapest, Ferenczi had already introduced into his psychoanalytic work the idea that patients "needed to be accepted and loved if they were to get well," a piece of unorthodoxy to prove fatal to his relationship with Freud, who found this approach "needy" and childish.

The importance of the therapist's contribution to the transaction with a patient (countertransference) had been mentioned only glancingly by Freud (1910, 1915). Sullivan, following Ferenczi's lead, stated in his first published paper that Freud's great contribution, was the "postulate of the unconscious," adding by 1937, "the crying need is for observers who are growing observant of their observing." Under the influence of William Alanson White and the Swiss Adolph Meyer's psychobiology, Sullivan moved decisively away from the orthodoxies of psychoanalysis and into an "American" psychiatry, with Freud's postulate of the unconscious as the groundwork and interpersonal relations (roughly equivalent to object relations) as the superstructure. In contrast to Freud's view of the ego's defensive functions as intrapsychic, Sullivan saw "security operations" as an interpersonal activity and anxiety as originating in *interpersonal* transactions. Sullivan's controversial body of work, discounted by some as an insufficiently generalized projection of his own personality warp (he led a deviant and troubled existence and was hospitalized on at least one occasion for a psychotic episode) has provided significant bridges between psychoanalysis, American psychiatry, and the social sciences in the period between 1921 and 1940.

Sullivan's direct influence on psychoanalytic thought in the United States extended during the 1930s and 1940s to many of the refugee European psychoanalysts who were fleeing Nazi persecution. Karen Horney (1885–1952), for example, shared his emphasis on the social (interpersonal) and, in preference to genetic interpretation, she put the "here and now" at the center of therapy adumbrating the 1960s and 1970s when clinical workers such as Merton Gill, Irwin Hoffmann, and Robert Langs made this a central tenet of the analysis of transference. She shared also Sullivan's downgrading of instinct theory and sexuality and, along with Erikson, though less systematically, saw people configurationally. Self-esteem is a significant item for Horney, and she discusses neurosis as simultaneously a disturbance in human relationships and (later) as a disturbance as "in relation to the self." With Erikson, she rejected Hartmann's concept of adaptation to an average expectable environment. Her main concern, however, beyond female psychology, was not theory but therapy. The two were, in essence, one concern, as she turned her attention to self-image and character structure as conditioned by social organization. The security operations that humans evolve are adaptive, she argued, as well as defensive.

By 1941, Horney ran afoul of the American Psychoanalytic Association and, in direct competition with it, founded the American Institute for Psychoanalysis. Much encouraged in this by psychoanalysts Fromm and Wilhelm Reich, she later read Fromm out of her organization, oddly enough, on grounds of his nonmedical training.

Erikson (1902–1994)

Probably the most influential, and certainly the most widely read, of psychoanalysts since Freud, Erikson has significantly moved beyond Freud while stating that his "ancestry" lies in clinical psychoanalysis. His revitalization of the Freudian tradition stems essentially from his systematic attempt to comprehend the simultaneous interweaving and evolution of the workings of the body, the psyche, and the society over the entire life cycle and into the sequence of generations. Cutting across all of the life stages are his concerns for evolving world views or belief systems and their relation to each psychosocial crisis as well as to ethical development.

From the start, Erikson showed a clear awareness of the foundations in evolving psychoanalytic theory for a new view of the role of *psychosocial reality relationships* in adaptation—almost synonymous, in fact, with the concepts of interpersonal transactions and object relations. His biopsychosocial model provides a locus for the various theories of object relations (Fairbairn, Winnicott, etc.) as well as for the emerging self-systems and self-psychologies (Sullivan, Jacobson, Hartmann, Kohut). All of these bodies of observation had for many years remained outside the theoretical scope of psychoanalytic ego psychology. Clinicians were, of course, using these ideas all along.

Erikson's theory, like much of Freud's, ranges widely over phenomenological (clinical, developmental, historical) propositions without systematically differentiating among them. Thus the conceptual status of this psychoanalytic theory of biopsychosocial development is as yet not entirely clear. Nonetheless it provides the first giant step since Freud's early discoveries toward integrating body, mind, and social organization.

SUMMARY

While the term *psychoanalysis,* as investigative mode, therapy, and theory, is on the wane outside of psychoanalytic circles, the fundamentals of the Freudian revolution—as well as the post-Freudian revisions—since the late 19th century have been progressively incorporated into the mainstream not only of psychology and psychiatry, but also of the social sciences, the humanities, education, and history:

1. The postulate of a *level of mentation, not accessible to immediate awareness,* but which has observable effects on experience and on behavior.

2. The concept of *psychological defense against pain,* which drives mental contents from awareness and seeks alternative solutions.

3. The *biopsychosocial and epigenetic view* that, from the start to the end of the life cycle (and into the sequence of generations), the "I" and the "We" (self-identity and group identity) are a product of the *simultaneous evolution of the body, the mind, and the society.*

4. The concept that, *along with the human propensity for conflict, there stands the potential for creative synthesis* in the service not only of survival but of genuine adaptation.

5. That beyond the pleasure principle stands repetition-compulsion, which means *the persistent effort to master actively that which has been (painfully) passively experienced.*

On the assumption that a decisive step has been taken by the Freudian revolution toward an interpenetration of the psychological, the technological, and the political in the human order, a contemporary biopsychosocial theory permits the investigation of not only innovations in therapy, but also alternative modes of conflict-resolution within individuals, interpersonally and collectively. Planetary survival may depend on the judicious use of such applied psychoanalysis.

REFERENCES

Erikson, E. H. (1964). *Insight and responsibility.* New York: Norton.

Freud, A. (1946/1937). *The ego and mechanisms of defense.* New York: International Universities Press.

Freud, S. (1915). The unconscious. In J. Strachey (Ed.), *Standard edition of the complete psychological works of Sigmund Freud* (Vol. 14). London: Hogarth.

Freud, S. (1953/1920). Beyond the pleasure principle. In *The standard edition of the complete psychological works of Sigmund Freud* (Vol. 19). London: Hogarth.

Freud, S. (1957/1912). Totem and taboo and other works. In *The standard edition of the complete psychological works of Sigmund Freud* (Vol. 13). London: Hogarth.

Freud, S. (1957/1914). On narcissism: An introduction. In *The standard edition of the complete psychological works of Sigmund Freud* (Vol. 14). London: Hogarth.

Freud, S. (1960/1921). *Group psychology and the analysis of the ego.* New York: Bantam Books.

Freud, S. (1962/1923). *The ego and the id.* New York: Norton.

Freud, S. (1968/1900). The interpretation of dreams. In *The standard edition of the complete psychological works of Sigmund Freud* (Vols. 4, 5). London: Hogarth.

Freud, S. (1968/1905). Jokes and their relation to the unconscious. In *The standard edition of the complete psychological works of Sigmund Freud* (Vol. 8). London: Hogarth.

M. BRENMAN-GIBSON
Harvard Medical School

EGO DEVELOPMENT
ERIKSONIAN DEVELOPMENTAL STAGES
HORNEY'S THEORY
NARCISSISTIC PERSONALITY
OEDIPUS COMPLEX
PSYCHOANALYTIC STAGES
SULLIVAN'S INTERPERSONAL THEORY

PSYCHOANALYTIC STAGES

Psychoanalytic stages, or psychosexual stages, are stages of psychosexual development postulated by Freud to account for personality development. Based on the assumption that early child-hood experiences importantly shape adult personality, social experiences at each stage presumably leave some permanent residue in the form of attitudes, traits, and values acquired at that stage. Further, it is assumed that a certain amount of sexual energy (libido) is present at birth and thereafter progresses through these psychosexual stages. More specifically, Freud theorized that the central theme running through personality development is the progression of the sex instinct through four universal stages—oral, anal, phallic, and genital. A period of *latency* intervenes between the latter two psychosexual stages but, strictly speaking, it is not a stage. Freud assigned crucial significance to the first three of these stages, termed *pregenital* stages, in the formation of adult character structure.

THE ORAL STAGE

During the oral stage of psychosexual development, which lasts approximately throughout the first year of life, the primary erogenous zone is the mouth. Through activities associated with the mouth—sucking, swallowing, biting—infants experience their first continuous source of pleasure, and thus the mouth region becomes a focal point of rudimentary psychosexual satisfaction. Fixation in the oral-aggressive phase (enter teeth), characterized by biting and chewing activities, may result in a "bitingly" sarcastic, argumentative, and hostile adult personality. From the psychoanalytic perspective, then, there is little wonder why people experience serious difficulties in giving up such activities—ultimately their psychological roots can be traced back to the first year of life.

THE ANAL STAGE

During the second and third years of life, the primary erogenous zone is the anus. Children at this stage are thought to derive considerable pleasure from temporary retention of feces (i.e., permitting, minor pressure to be exerted against the lower intestine and anal sphincter) or expulsion of feces (i.e., immediate tension reduction). With the onset of parentally controlled toilet training, however, the child's pleasures in this regard encounter the stiff opposition of social restraints, and various fixations may occur. Reflecting the assumption of the importance of early childhood experience in personality formation, Freudians believe that such an approach to toilet training forges the way for the development of adult productivity and creativity.

THE PHALLIC STAGE

The genitals become the primary erogenous zone during the phallic stage of psychosexual development, which extends from the fourth through the fifth years of life. During this stage, children can be observed examining their sex organs, masturbating, and showing interest in matters pertaining to birth and sex. But perhaps more importantly, this period of life serves as the stage on which the most critical psychological drama of childhood is played out—the Oedipus complex. Freud theorized that every child unconsciously wishes to possess the opposite-sexed parent and simultaneously dispose of the same-sexed parent.

Freud believed that the boy experiences intense conflict over his incestuous desires toward the mother, and that he fears retaliation from the father for such desires. Specifically, the small boy fears that the father will discover his sexual desires and retaliate by cutting off the boy's penis.

The little girl during the phallic stage is depicted as discovering that, unlike her father, she lacks a penis. Immediately following this anatomical discovery, the girl wishes she had one—a desire which, in psychoanalytic theory, is called *penis envy.* Penis envy in girls is roughly equivalent psychologically to castration anxiety in boys and, together, penis envy and castration anxiety are known as the castration complex in Freudian theory.

Failure to resolve the Oedipus conflict and unresolved Oedipal feelings lie at the root of many psychological disorders when viewed from the perspective of psychoanalytic theory. As the Oedipus complex becomes resolved, the child is presumed to move into a period of latency (lasting approximately from age 6 to 12) in which the sex instinct remains relatively dormant and psychic energy is redirected into nonsexual activities, such as school and athletics.

THE GENITAL STAGE

With the onset of puberty, genital sexuality is reawakened and the genital stage of psychosexual development, extending from puberty until death, begins. During the genital stage, narcissistic strivings become fused with, and largely transformed into, the seeking of heterosexual relationships involving mutual gratification. Thus the adult genital personality type, the successful end product of psychosexual development in psychoanalytic theory, is characterized by capacity for mature heterosexual love, responsible concerns beyond the self, and productive living in society.

SUGGESTED READINGS

Freud, S. (1920). *A general introduction to psychoanalysis* (J. Riviere, Trans.). New York: Washington Square Press.

D. J. ZIEGLER
Villanova University

DEVELOPMENTAL STAGES
PSYCHOANALYSIS

PSYCHOLINGUISTICS

Even though the psychological study of language is rather old, psycholinguistics, a discipline specifically devoted to the psychological implications of language, is relatively new. It is generally agreed that its birth took place during a seminar at Cornell University in the summer of 1953, where a group of psychologists and linguists met to examine the approaches to language of linguistics, learning psychology, and information-processing theory (Osgood & Sebeok, 1954). But the main impulse that helped to constitute psycholinguistics and to make it popular came from a completely different direction. For years, psychologists had been busy trying to conciliate structural linguistics with theories of learning using the

techniques of word association, left-to-right analysis of sentences, and the statistical interpretation of frequency and order of words in speech. Cornell's seminar represented the peaking of this tendency just when it was about to be profoundly altered by the appearance of Noam Chomsky's linguistic theory.

THE IMPACT OF CHOMSKY'S THEORY

In his *Syntactic Structures,* Chomsky (1957) pointed out some of the inadequacies of the then-current approach. The speaker of any language can produce and understand an unlimited number of grammatically correct sentences and can decide whether any given sentence is grammatically correct, even if it is unfamiliar. This means, according to Chomsky, that human beings have the innate capacity to create grammatically correct sentences and that this capacity does not come from previous experience.

Underlying the surface structure of a spoken language is a deep structure of rules permitting the generation of all possible grammatically correct sentences. Some of these rules are specific to a given language, but there are also basic rules common to all languages and one can speak of a "general grammar" closely linked with the structure of the mind and with human nature and its biological foundations. Because of this "natural" quality of the general grammar, and the fact that a child possesses a Language Acquisition Device (LAD) that enables the analysis of the linguistic productions heard in accordance with formal rules, the child develops linguistic competence. Thus Chomsky's theory is nativistic and directly opposed to the empirism professed by behaviorists, and even by the mainstream of contemporary psychology. In spite of this opposition, or perhaps because of it, his ideas have had a great impact and in the 1960s dominated the field of psycholinguistics.

The rapid expansion of Chomsky's psycholinguistics coincided with what has been termed a change of paradigm in psychological science, the shift of many psychologists from behaviorism to cognitivism. The connection between Chomskian linguistics and cognitive psychology has been accepted by Chomsky (1968), who describes linguistics as "a particular branch of cognitive psychology."

NEW TRENDS

The growing interest of psychology in all aspects of language soon surpassed Chomsky's formulations and it became increasingly more difficult to keep syntactic considerations apart from the meaning of the sentence and its functions in a communicative context.

The change has been especially noticeable in the study of the acquisition of language in childhood. For Chomsky, language is fundamentally innate and its development in the child depends on an internal dynamic, and thus it might be assumed that Chomsky's psycholinguistics would not be concerned with the study of child language. In fact, the opposite is true. Some psychologists, inspired by Chomsky, set about the task of proving that children, from their first utterances, have a set of consistent rules that explain all their verbal productions, and that this initial grammar evolves according to an internal logic until it coincides with adult grammar. Taking into account the fact that the study of child language has been traditionally descriptive, or interested only in explaining the origin and meaning of words, the new approach proved encouraging and productive. A series of books appeared that changed the current ideas about language in childhood, particularly as to grammatical structure (Menyuk, 1969; McNeill, 1970; Bloom, 1970; Slobin, 1971; Brown, 1973). But the limitations of the new approach soon became evident also. In accordance with their theoretical views, observers of child language considered only the linguistic productions of children and neglected the gestures and actions accompanying the child's words. Not surprisingly, researchers have gradually abandoned methodological limitations to place the verbal language of children in its real context, a behavioral and communicative situation.

Something similar has been taking place in psycholinguistics. Besides the codification processes and the formal rules of syntax, psycholinguistics deals at present with the physiological basis of language, the possibilities of verbal communication between animals, the functions of language in behavior, the relationship between language and thought, and the problems of meaning.

In doing this, psycholinguistics is no longer limited by the linguist seeing language as a set of formal rules, but views language in all its complexity. As the dependency on linguistics decreases, the term *psycholinguistics* loses its reason for being and the old denomination, *psychology of language,* is resumed.

REFERENCES

Bloom, L. (1970). *Language development: Form and functions in emerging grammars.* Research Monograph 59. Cambridge, MA: MIT Press.

Brown, R. W. (1973). *A first language: The early stages.* Cambridge, MA: Harvard University Press.

Chomsky, N. (1957). *Syntactic structures.* The Hague: Mouton.

Chomsky, N. (1968). *Language and the mind.* New York: Harcourt, Brace & World.

McNeill, D. (1970). *The acquisition of language: The study of developmental psycholinguistics.* New York: Harper & Row.

Menyuk, P. (1969). *Sentences children use.* Cambridge, MA: MIT Press.

Osgood, E. C., & Sebeok, T. A. (Eds.). (1954). *Psycholinguistics: A survey of theory and research problems.* Bloomington: Indiana University Press.

Slobin, D. I. (1971). *The ontogenesis of grammar.* New York: Academic.

SUGGESTED READING

Garman, M. (1990). *Psycholinguistics.* New York: Cambridge University Press.

Paivio, A. I. Begg. (1981). *Psychology of language.* Englewood, NJ: Prentice Hall.

Steinberg, D. (1996). *An introduction to psycholinguistics.* London: Longman.

M. Siguan
Barcelona, Spain

BILINGUALISM
COMMUNICATION PROCESSES
LANGUAGE DEVELOPMENT

PSYCHOLOGICAL ASSESSMENT

Psychological assessment is considered one of the most important functions in applied psychology. In psychological assessment the practitioner uses observation, interviews, and psychological tests to gain information about client's personality characteristics, symptoms, and problems in order to arrive at practical decisions about their behavior. In the assessment study the practitioner identifies the main sources of a client's problems and attempts to predict the likely course of events under various conditions.

Mental health patients may present with behavioral, emotional, or physical discomforts that are often difficult for a clinical practitioner to understand initially. Usually, in mental health settings a clinical psychologist attempts to understand the nature and extent of the patient's problem by a process of inquiry that is similar to the way a detective might approach a case by collecting evidence and using inductive and deductive logic to focus on the most likely factors. Assessment of mental disorders is usually more difficult, more uncertain, and more protracted than it is for evaluation of many physical diseases. Yet, early assessment of mental health problems is extremely important in clinical practice—no rational, specific treatment plan can be instituted without at least some general notion of what problems need to be addressed.

In order for psychological assessment to proceed effectively, the person being evaluated must feel a sense of rapport with the clinician. The assessor needs to structure the testing situation so that the person feels comfortable. Clients need to feel that the testing will help the practitioner gain a clear understanding of their problems, to understand how the tests will be used, and to understand how the psychologist will incorporate test results in the clinical evaluation.

What does a clinician need to know in psychological assessment? First, of course, the problems must be identified. Are they of a situational nature; that is, have they been precipitated by some environmental stressor, or are the problems more pervasive and long-term? Or is it perhaps some combination of the two? Is there any evidence of recent deterioration in cognitive functioning? How long has the person had the symptoms and how is he or she dealing with the problem? What, if any, prior help has been sought? Are there indications of self-defeating behavior or low self-esteem, or is the individual using available personal and environmental resources? Following are several important areas to be considered in a psychological assessment.

PERSONAL HISTORY

It is important to have a basic understanding of the individual's history and development, family history (whether the person has relatives with a history of mental illness), intellectual functioning, personality characteristics, and environmental pressures and resources. For example, how does the person characteristically respond to other people? Are there excesses in behavior present, such as eating or drinking too much? Are there notable deficits, for example in social skills? Does the person show any inappropriate behavior?

PERSONALITY FACTORS

Assessment needs to include a description of any relevant long-term personality characteristics. Has the person behaved in deviant or bizarre ways in particular situations; for example, in circumstances requiring submission to legitimate authority? Do there seem to be personality traits or behavior patterns that predispose the individual to behave in maladaptive ways across a broad range of situations? Does the person tend to become dependent on others to the point of losing his or her identity? Is the person able to accept help from others? Is the person capable of accepting appropriate responsibility for others' welfare? Such questions are necessarily at the heart of many assessment efforts.

SOCIAL SITUATIONS

It is also important to evaluate the social contexts in which the individual functions. What environmental demands do they face? What emotional support or special stressors exist in the person's life?

The diverse information about the individual's personality traits, behavior patterns, and environmental demands must be integrated into a consistent and meaningful picture often referred to as a dynamic formulation, because it describes the current situation and provides hypotheses about what is driving the person to behave in maladaptive ways. The clinician should try to arrive at a plausible explanation; for example, a reason why a normally passive and mild-mannered man suddenly flew into a rage and became physically abusive toward his wife. The formulation will allow the clinician to develop hypotheses that might explain the client's future behavior. What is the likelihood that the person would get worse if the problems are left untreated? Which behaviors should be the initial focus of change, and what treatment methods are likely to be most efficient in producing this change? What changes might reasonably be expected if the person were provided a particular type of therapy?

Clients who are being assessed in a clinical situation are usually highly motivated to be evaluated and usually like to know the results of the testing. They usually are eager to give some definition to their discomfort. In many situations it is important to incorporate information from a medical evaluation in the psychological assessment in order to rule out physical abnormalities that may be causing or contributing to the problem.

Clinical assessment attempts to provide a comprehensive picture of an individual's psychological functioning and the stressors and resources in his or her life situation. In the early stages of the process, the assessment psychologist attempts to obtain as much information about the client as possible—including present feelings, attitudes, memories, demographic facts, important formative life events—and trying to fit the diverse pieces together into a meaningful pattern. Starting with a global technique, such as a clinical interview, clinicians may later select more specific assess-

ment tasks or tests. The following procedures are some of the methods that may be used to obtain the necessary data.

THE ASSESSMENT INTERVIEW

The assessment interview is usually the initial and often the central information source in the assessment process. This is usually a face-to-face interaction in which information about various aspects of a patient's situation, behavior, past history characteristics, and personality is acquired. The initial interview may be relatively open in format, with an interviewer deciding about his or her next question based on the client's answers to other ones, or it may be more structured so that a planned set of questions is followed. In structured interviewing the clinician may choose from a number of possible interview formats whose reliability has been established in research. The structured interviewing approach is likely to be more reliable but may be less the spontaneous than the free-response interview.

Clinical interviews can be subject to error because they rely upon human judgment to choose the questions and process the information. The assessment interview can be made more reliable by the use of rating scales that serve to focus inquiry and quantify the interview data. For example, the person may be rated on a three-, five-, or seven-point scale with respect to suicide potential, violence potential, or other personality characteristics depending upon the goals of the assessment.

THE CLINICAL OBSERVATION

One of the most useful assessment techniques that a clinician has for gaining patient-relevant information is direct observation. Observation can enable the clinician to learn more about the person's psychological functioning; for example, personal hygiene, emotional responses, and such pertinent behaviors as depression, anxiety, aggression, hallucinations, or delusions. Clinical observation is probably more effective if conducted in the natural environment (such as classroom or home); however, it is more likely to take place upon admission or in the clinic or hospital ward.

Clinical observation can provide more valuable information in the clinical situation if it is objectively structured; for example, the use of structured rating scales helps maintain objectivity. The most useful rating scales are those that enable a rater to indicate not only the presence or absence of a particular behavior but also its prominence. Standard rating scales can provide a quantifiable format for rating clinical symptoms. For example, the Hamilton Anxiety Rating Scale (Hamilton, 1959) specifically addresses behavior related to the experience of intense anxiety and has become almost the standard for assessing anxiety states. Observations made in clinical settings by trained observers can provide behavioral data useful in ongoing clinical management of patients; for example, to focus on specific patient behaviors to be changed.

PSYCHOLOGICAL TESTS

Psychological tests are standardized sets of procedures or tasks for obtaining samples of behavior. A client's responses to the standardized stimuli are compared with those of other people having comparable demographic characteristics, usually through established test norms or test score distributions. Psychological tests are useful diagnostic tools for clinical psychologists in much the same way that blood tests or X-ray films are useful to physicians in diagnosing physical problems. In all these procedures, problems may be revealed in people that would otherwise not be observed. The data from tests allow a clinician to draw inferences about how much the person's psychological qualities differ from those of a reference norm group, typically a sample of "normal" persons. Psychological tests have been developed to measure many psychological attributes in which people vary. Tests have been devised to measure such characteristics as coping patterns, motive patterns, personality factors, role behaviors, values, levels of depression or anxiety, and intellectual functioning.

Two types of psychological tests are typically incorporated in psychological assessments in clinical practice—intelligence tests and personality tests.

Intelligence Tests

In many cases it is important to have an evaluation of the person's level of intellect functioning. The clinician can assess intellectual ability with a wide range of intelligence tests. For example, if the patient is a child, the Wechsler Intelligence Scale for Children-Revised (WISC-III) or the current edition of the Stanford-Binet Intelligence Scale might be used for measuring the child's intellectual ability. For measuring adult intelligence, the Wechsler Adult Intelligence Scale-Revised (WAIS-III) is the most frequently used measure.

Individually administered intelligence tests—such as the WISC-R, WAIS-III, and the Stanford-Binet—are labor-intensive and typically require 2 to 3 hours to administer, score, and interpret. The information obtained about the cognitive functioning of patients, however, can provide useful hypotheses about the person's intellectual resources and capability of dealing with problems.

Personality Tests

The clinician would likely employ several tests designed to measure personal characteristics. Personality tests are of two general types—projective and objective tests.

PROJECTIVE TECHNIQUES

Projective techniques are unstructured tasks; for example, the clinician might use ambiguous stimuli, such as incomplete sentences which the person is asked to complete. The individual's responses to these ambiguous materials are thought to reveal a great deal about their personal problems, conflicts, motives, coping techniques, and personality traits. One important assumption underlying the use of projective techniques is that the individual (in trying to make sense out of vague, unstructured stimuli) tends to "project" their own problems, motives, and wishes into the situation, because they have little else on which to rely in formulating their responses to these materials. Projective tests are considered to be valuable in providing clues to an individual's past learning and personality. The three most frequently used projective tests are the Sentence Completion Test, the Thematic Apperception Test

(TAT), and the Rorschach. Due to space considerations this article will examine only the Rorschach and the TAT.

The Rorschach test was developed by the Swiss psychiatrist Rorschach in 1911. The test uses ten inkblot pictures to which the person is instructed to look at each card and tell "what it looks like or reminds you of." After the initial responses to all the cards are recorded, the examiner then goes back through the responses to determine "what about the inkblot made it look the way it did." Once the responses are obtained, the clinician must then interpret what they mean—this normally involves scoring the protocol according to a standard method in order to determine what the responses mean. The most widely used and reliable scoring system is the Exner Comprehensive System (Exner, 1993). The indexes resulting from the scoring summary are then employed to explore the literature to determine the meaning of the responses. Experience with the instrument is extremely important in arriving at useful hypotheses about clients.

The Thematic Apperception Test (TAT) was introduced in 1935 by Morgan and Murray as a means of studying personality traits. The TAT uses a series of pictures about which a subject is instructed to create stories. The content of the pictures is highly ambiguous as to actions and motives, so that people tend to project or attribute their own conflicts and worries into their stories. Interpretation of the stories is impressionistic. The interpreter reads the constructions and rationally determines what potential motives as behavioral tendencies the respondent might have in "seeing" the pictures in the ways they did. The content of the TAT stories is thought to reflect the person's underlying traits, motives, and preoccupations.

Projective tests, like the Rorschach and TAT, can be valuable in many clinical assessment situations, particularly in cases where the task involves obtaining a comprehensive picture of a person's personality makeup. The great strengths of projective techniques are their unstructured nature and their focus on the unique aspects of personality. However, this is also a weakness, because their interpretations are subjective, unreliable, and difficult to validate. In addition, projective tests typically require a great deal of time to administer and advanced skill to interpret. The clinician must also employ more objective tasks in order to put the client's symptoms and behavior in an appropriate perspective.

Objective Personality Scales—The MMPI-2 Objective tests are *structured* in that they use questions or items that are carefully phrased. In giving alternative responses as choices, they provide a more controlled format than projective instruments and thus are more amenable to more quantifiable response analysis, which in turn enhances the reliability of test outcomes. The most widely used of the major structured inventories for personality assessment is the Minnesota Multiphasic Personality Inventory (MMPI), now known as the MMPI-2 after a revision in 1989 (Butcher, Dahlstrom, Graham, Tellegen, & Kaemmer, 1989). It is described here because it is the most widely studied test in this class of instruments, and because in many ways it is the most successful of the class.

The MMPI was introduced for general use in 1943 by Hathaway and McKinley. Today, it is the most widely used personality test for both clinical assessment and psychopathologic research in the United States and is the assessment instrument most frequently taught in graduate clinical psychology programs. Moreover, translated versions of the MMPI-2 are widely used internationally (Butcher, 1996). The MMPI-2 consists of 567 items covering topics ranging from physical symptoms and psychological problems and social attitudes. Normally, subjects are encouraged to answer all of the items either *true* or *false*.

The MMPI-2 is interpreted using scoring scales that have been devised to measure clinical problems. The MMPI clinical scales were originally developed by an empirical item selection method. The pool of items for the inventory was administered to a large group of normal and several quite homogeneous groups of clinical patients who had been carefully diagnosed. Answers to the items were then analyzed to see which ones differentiated the various groups. On the basis of these findings, the clinical scales were constructed, each consisting of the items that were answered by one of the patient groups in the direction opposite to the predominant response of the normal group. This method of item selection, known as empirical keying, produced scales that were valid in predicting symptoms and behavior. If a person's pattern of true/false responses closely approximate that of a particular group, such as depressed patients, it is a reasonable inference that he or she shares other psychiatrically significant characteristics with the group— and may in fact be functioning "psychologically" like others in that group.

Each of these clinical scales measures tendencies to respond in psychologically deviant ways. Raw scores of a client are compared with the scores of the normal population, many of whom did (and do) answer a few items in the critical direction, and the results are plotted on the standard MMPI-2 profile form. By drawing a line connecting the scores for the different scales, a clinician can construct a profile that shows how far from normal a patient's performance is on each of the scales. The Schizophrenia scale, for example, is made up of the items that schizophrenic patients consistently answered in a way that differentiated them from normal individuals. People who score high (relative to norms) on this scale, though not necessarily schizophrenic, often show characteristics typical of the schizophrenic population. For instance, high scorers on this scale may be socially withdrawn, have peculiar thought processes, may have diminished contact with reality, and in severe cases may have delusions and hallucinations.

One extremely useful feature of the MMPI-2 is that it contains a number of scales to evaluate test-taking attitudes. It includes a number of validity scales to detect whether a patient has answered the questions in a straightforward, honest manner. For example, there is one scale that detects lying or claiming extreme virtue and several scales to detect faking or malingering. Extreme endorsement of the items on any of these measures may invalidate the test.

The MMPI-2 is used in several ways to evaluate a patient's personality characteristics and clinical problems. The traditional use of the MMPI-2 is as a diagnostic standard. The individual's profile pattern is compared with profiles of known patient groups. If the client's profile matches a particular group, information about patients in this group can suggest a broad descriptive diagnosis for the patient under study. A second approach to MMPI interpretation is

referred to as content interpretation. This approach is used to supplement the empirical interpretation by focusing on the content themes in a person's response to the inventory. For example, if an individual endorses an unusually large number of items about depression, a clinician might well conclude that the subject is preoccupied with low mood.

APPLICATIONS OF CLINICAL ASSESSMENT

Assessment in Mental Health Settings

Most clinical assessment is undertaken in medical, psychiatric, or prison settings to evaluate the mental health status of people with problems. The practitioner would administer, score, and interpret the battery of tests, usually at the beginning of the clinical contact, and develop an integrated report. The report would likely focus on such tasks as developing mental health treatment plans (Beutler & Berran, 1995).

Psychological Assessment in Forensic or Legal Cases

One of the fastest-growing applications of psychological tests involves their use in evaluating clients in court cases. Psychological tests have been found to provide valuable information for forensic evaluations—particularly if they contain a means of assessing the person's test-taking attitudes (such as the MMPI-2, which contains several measures that provide an appraisal of the person's cooperativeness or frankness in responding to the test items). Many litigants or defendants in criminal cases attempt to present themselves in a particular way (for example, to appear disturbed in the case of an insanity plea or impeccably virtuous when trying to present a false or exaggerated physical injury), their motivations to "fake good" or "fake bad" tend to result in noncredible test patterns.

Because of their scientific acceptability, well-known psychological tests, such as the WAIS-III and MMPI-2, are widely accepted by courts as appropriate assessment instruments. In order for a test to be allowed into testimony, it must be shown to be an accepted scientific standard. The primary means of assuring that tests are appropriate for court testimony is that they are standardized and are not experimental procedures (Ogloff, 1995). Psychological assessments in court cases can provide information about the mental state of felons on trial, to assess the psychological adjustment of litigants in civil court cases, and to aid in the determination of child custody in divorce cases.

Psychological Tests in Personnel Screening

The use of personality tests in employment screening has a long tradition; actually, the first formal use of a standardized personality scale in the United States was implemented to screen out World War I draftees who were psychologically unfit for military service (Woodworth, 1920). Today, personality tests are widely used for personnel screening in occupations that require great public trust. Some occupations, such as police officers, airline flight crews, fire fighters, nuclear power plant workers, and certain military specialties, require greater emotional stability than most other jobs. Maladaptive personality traits or behavior problems in such employees can result in public safety concerns. For example, someone who behaves in an irresponsible manner in a nuclear power plant control room could significantly endanger the operation of the facility and the surrounding community. The potential for problems can be so great in some high-stress occupations (e.g., air traffic controllers) that measures need to be taken in the hiring process to evaluate applicants for emotional adjustment.

Personnel screening for emotional stability and potentially irresponsible behavior requires a somewhat different set of assumptions than clinical assessment. One assumption is that personality or emotional problems, such as poor reality contact, impulsivity, or pathological indecisiveness, would adversely affect the way in which a person would function in a critical job. Psychological tests should not be the sole means of determining whether a person is hired. Psychological tests are more appropriately used in the context of an employment interview, a background check, and a careful evaluation of previous work records.

SUMMARY

Psychological assessment is one of the most important and complex activities undertaken by clinical psychologists. The goals of psychological assessment include identifying and describing the individual's symptoms; possible causes and severity of the problem; as well as exploring the individual's personal resources, which might be valuable in the decisions to be made.

A broad range of psychological assessment methods is used for gathering relevant psychological information for clinical decisions about people. The most flexible assessment methods are the clinical interview and behavior observation. These methods can provide a wealth of clinical information. Psychological tests are used to measure personality by employing standardized stimuli for collecting behavior samples that can be compared with other individuals through test norms. Two different personality testing methods have been employed: projective tests, such as the Rorschach, in which unstructured stimuli are presented to a subject, who then "projects" meaning or structure on to the stimulus, thereby revealing "hidden" motives, feelings, and so on; and objective tests, or personality inventories, in which a subject is required to read and respond to itemized statements or questions. Objective personality tests usually provide a cost-effective way of collecting personality information. The MMPI-2 provides a number of clinically relevant scales for describing abnormal behavior. Psychological tests are widely used for making clinical decisions in mental health settings, forensic applications, and personnel screening for positions that require emotionally stable employees.

REFERENCES

Beutler, L. E., & Berran, M. R. (1995) (Eds.). *Integrative assessment of adult personality.* NY: The Guilford Press.

Butcher, J. N. (1996). *International adaptations of the MMPI-2.* Minneapolis: University of Minnesota Press.

Butcher, J. N., Dahlstrom, W. G., Graham, J. R., Tellegen, A., & Kaemmer, B. (1989). *Minnesota Multiphasic Personality Inventory-2 (MMPI-2): Manual for administration and scoring.* Minneapolis: University of Minnesota Press.

Exner, J. (1993). *The Rorschach: A comprehensive system* (Vol. 1). New York: Wiley.

Hamilton, M. (1959). The assessment of anxiety states by rating. *British Journal of Medical Psychology, 32,* 50–55.

Morgan, C. D., & Murray, H. A. (1935). A method for investigating fantasies. *Archives of Neurology and Psychiatry, 34,* 289–306.

Ogloff, J. (1995). The legal basis of forensic application of the MMPI-2. In Y. S. Ben-Porath, J. R. Graham, G. C. N. Hall, R. D. Hirschman, & M. S. Zaragoza (Eds.), *Forensic applications of the MMPI-2.* Thousand Oaks, CA: Sage.

Woodworth, R. S. (1920). *The Personal Data Sheet.* Chicago: Stoelting.

J. N. BUTCHER
University of Minnesota

BENDER GESTALT
CYNICAL ASSESSMENT
DIAGNOSTIC & STATISTICAL MANUAL
INTELLIGENCE MEASURES
PERSONALITY ASSESSMENT
PROJECTIVE TECHNIQUES
QUESTIONAIRES
RORSCHACH
STRONG-CAMPBELL INTEREST INVENTORY
THEMATIC APPERCEPTION TEST

PSYCHOLOGICAL ASSESSMENT, HISTORY OF

The term *psychological assessment,* as employed in contemporary psychology, encompasses all of the varied methods utilized in the psychological evaluation of individuals, groups, and environments. These techniques cover a wide spectrum of approaches and include tests, rating scales, interview schedules, and direct observational procedures. The field of psychological assessment is a major subdiscipline in contemporary psychology, and is represented by numerous books and journals and by several professional societies. Assessment occupies a central place in clinical psychology, organizational psychology, education, and other applied areas. It also plays a crucial role in such basic scientific areas as personality psychology, social psychology, and developmental psychology.

Contemporary methods of assessment did not arise fullblown, but were developed from a long historical background. An awareness of this background can enhance one's understanding and appreciation of the current and future scene in assessment. For convenience of exposition, the history of psychological assessment can be divided into three major periods. First came the long centuries preceding the emergence of scientific assessment, which to a considerable degree prepared the way for later rapid development of the field. Second came the period from the latter part of the nineteenth century to the middle of the twentieth century, during which the foundations of scientific assessment were laid down. Finally, there have been numerous recent advances that, taken together, frame a third division in the history of assessment, from about 1950 to the present.

PRECURSORS OF SCIENTIFIC ASSESSMENT

It is plausible to assume that members of the human species, at or very shortly after the emergence of *Homo sapiens,* engaged to some degree in the psychological evaluation of their fellows. Certain traits, such as bravery, leadership, tenderness, and cooperation were of crucial importance in the survival of human groups, and early men and women doubtless assessed their acquaintances very carefully, if not always consciously, along these and other pertinent lines.

Historical Background

The two chief methods of assessment in the ancient world—both of which had tremendous influence for centuries, and indeed to some extent still do—were astrology and physiognomy. From the earliest times, the relative positions of the planets as they moved across the heavens were interpreted by many persons as harbingers of future events. Our interest here is in horoscopic astrology; that is, descriptions of and predictions for individuals based on the position of the planets at the time of their births. The most important ancient work on horoscopic astrology was the *Tetrabiblos,* written in the second century AD by Claudius Ptolemaeus. Personal astrology had the advantage as an assessment device of being carried out without ever seeing the person being evaluated, provided one knew the assessee's day, and preferably hour, of birth. The disadvantage of horoscopic astrology is that it is totally invalid (though this was not always apparent). Despite this latter reality, ancient astrology ushered in two important developments in the dawning process of systematic psychological assessment: It required and stimulated the development of a vocabulary and primitive taxonomy for the description of human personalities, and it fostered the development of a class of experts considered to have special knowledge and skill in personal or psychological assessment.

The other major ancient approach to assessment was physiognomy, or the art of understanding personality from the observation of an individual's physique, including styles of movements and gestures. Physiognomy was an advance from astrology in that its underlying rationale had at least some validity, though the ancient practitioners wildly exaggerated and grossly misinterpreted the relations between body and character—for example, if a person can be conceived to look like a certain animal, then that person has the psychological characteristics of that animal. The major early work in this area was *Physiognomics,* once attributed to Aristotle but now considered to have been written by others associated with the Peripatetic school.

Both horoscopic and physiognomic assessment, often intermixed with humoral conceptions—which also derived from the ancient Greek world—were popular and respected throughout the medieval and Renaissance periods. In 1575, during the later Renaissance, the first systematic statement of the need for psychological assessment in human affairs appeared in a Spanish book by Juan Huarte titled *Examen de Ingenios para las Ciencas,* later translated into various languages (in English as *The Tryal of Wits*). Huarte argued that since different people have different talents ("wits"), and since different occupations require different skills, it would be desirable to have experts ("Triers") go about the state examining youths, so that appropriate matches could be made between persons and positions. The signal features of Huarte's work were its emphasis on individual differences and its assumption that these are, in principle, measurable.

These two notions appeared even more explicitly in two brief treatises in 1691 and 1692 by Christian Thomasius. This early German philosopher theorized that personalities differ along four major dimensions: sensual pleasure, ambition, greed, and rational love. He developed rating scales for evaluating individuals on these dimensions and published the first quantitative data on actual individuals in the entire history of psychology. He even proposed a primitive conception of reliability of measurement. His insights were quite premature in the long perspective of history, however, and had little influence.

The later eighteenth century saw a strong revival of uncritical physiognomic approaches to the reading of human character, stimulated largely by Johann Lavater's *Physiognomische Fragmente.* In the early nineteenth century the new trend in assessment was phrenology. This conception pioneered by Franz Joseph Gall and popularized by Johann Christoph (Caspar) Spurzheim and others, held that specific mental functions are centered in particular regions of the brain, and that an individual's values on these functions can be assessed by examining the contours and external topography of the individual's skull. Though completely invalid, and viewed suspiciously even in its heyday, phrenology nevertheless to some degree pioneered and popularized the ideas of individual assessment, quantitative measurements, written reports, and efforts to evaluate test validity.

Another nineteenth-century series of events that influenced the later development of assessment was the case of the "wild boy of Aveyron" and its aftermath. This boy, discovered in a wooded area in France, seemed to lack all evidence of civilization. Jean Gaspard Itard attempted, with little success, to train the child in the ways of society, but eventually decided that he was mentally defective. However, his assistant Edouard Seguin became interested in the training of feebleminded children. He invented a formboard—the Seguin Formboard—which for a time was widely employed in the evaluation of mentally deficient children.

Transition to Scientific Assessment

In the later part of the nineteenth century, Francis Galton began the movement to scientifically based assessment. Galton, a cousin of Charles Darwin, was particularly interested in individual differences. His classic book, *Inquiries into Human Faculty and Its Development* (1883), presented a wealth of empirical data on a variety of human attributes and powers, including imagery, associations, and sensory capacities. Galton had a passion for observing, measuring, and counting, and was primarily responsible for introducing a quantitative emphasis into assessment. As a result of this interest he developed a statistic for indicating the relationship—or co-relation—between variables. In the hands of Galton's disciple Karl Pearson, this measure was developed into the now familiar Pearsonian coefficient of correlation, which serves as the primary statistical tool of assessment. In his wide-ranging research, Galton introduced the ideas of surveys and questionnaires, but his main reliance was on laboratory techniques such as reaction time, visual acuity, color discrimination, and immediate memory.

Though Galton had employed the term "test" in a similar way as its modern sense, the word became more clearly established in the assessment lexicon in James McKeen Cattell's important 1890 article, "Mental Tests and Measurements." Cattell was an American who had spent some time in Galton's laboratory. The 1890s saw a number of other prescient advances in systematic assessment. In 1891 Hugo Munsterberg, in Germany, published a list of tasks (e.g., naming colors) that he had used in evaluating the intellectual capacities of children. In the same year, at Columbia University, Cattell began an ongoing research project in which a variety of sensorimotor tasks, patterned after those of Galton but more extensive, were administered annually to college freshmen in order to determine the tests' abilities to predict college grades. A number of other American psychologists were also becoming interested in mental tests, and in 1895 the American Psychological Association—itself only three years old—set up a committee (with Cattell as chairman) to encourage cooperation among the various university laboratories in the standardization and collection of mental test data. In 1896 in Germany, Hermann Ebbinghaus developed a completion technique (filling in of blanks in prose material) to assess mental fatigue in children; and in the same year Lightner Witmer, at the University of Pennsylvania, founded the first psychological clinic, which involved intensive assessment of children. These various developments indicate that by the turn of the century the preliminaries were over, and that the foundation had been prepared for a concerted scientific approach to psychological assessment.

THE FOUNDATIONAL PERIOD

Intelligence Assessment

The breakthrough to a reasonable degree of accuracy in assessment was made in the area of intelligence. There had long been both popular and academic interest in the concept of intelligence—though not always by this name—since it has always been obvious on a commonsense level that people differ markedly among themselves on mental quickness, acuity, and capacity. In 1900 the general hope among psychologists, following the lead of Galton and Cattell, was that mental capacity could be assessed by measuring what were then assumed to be its underlying sensorimotor constituents—reaction time, visual and auditory acuity, aspects of memory and perception, and so on. These hopes, however, were seriously undermined when a detailed report on the results of Cattell's study at Columbia to predict college results by sensorimotor tests, performed by Clark Wissler in 1901, was largely negative.

An alternative approach developed in Paris proved to be more successful. This approach was based on the idea of presenting to the subject a variety of tasks requiring different levels of intelligence. In October 1904, the Minister of Public Instruction in Paris appointed a commission to examine the education of retarded children. This highlighted the need for improving methods for determining which children should be assigned to special schools. In order to help with such decisions, Alfred Binet and Theodore Simon, in 1905, put together a scale consisting of 30 items ranging in difficulty (e.g., 1—coordination of head and eyes in following a lighted match; 30—distinguishing between abstract terms). This can be considered the first successful intelligence test. It was followed by a more elaborate 1908 scale, which consisted of 58 tests, and these were grouped by the age levels (ages 3 through 13) at which most children were expected to succeed. In 1911, prior to Binet's untimely death, a further revision appeared, based on more extensive normative data.

Reactions to the Binet-Simon scales were positive and widespread (Goodenough, 1949); it was evident that they helped to fill a perceived need in elementary education and in work with the mentally retarded. In America two psychologists took the lead in advancing the assessment of intelligence. Lewis M. Terman's 1905 dissertation had been based on a comparison of "bright" and "stupid" boys. Henry H. Goddard translated the 1908 and 1911 Binet scales into English, and they became even more widely used. There were several other translations, but the one which had the largest impact—this in fact was more than a translation, but rather was an extensive revision—was that made by Terman, who was then at Stanford, in 1916. This test, known as the Stanford-Binet, shortly became the standard against which all other tests were evaluated. One reason for the immediate popularity of this test was its application of the concept of the intelligence quotient (IQ). In 1911, Stern had suggested that a child's mental age—determined by the level of tests that the child passes—might be divided by the child's chronological age to give a quick picture of mental capacity. This ratio, when multiplied by 100, is the idea of the IQ.

It was recognized very early that, despite the dominance of the Binet-like tests, they had certain limitations. One of these was that they were hardly applicable to children with very limited verbal skills. Accordingly, there was a strong effort to develop performance scales, or tests in which intelligence could be inferred from manipulative responses. One of these, the Seguin Formboard, was noted above. A number of others, including the Porteus Maze Test, the Kohs Block Design test, and the Goodenough Draw-a-Man test, were all developed, with considerable success, early in the twentieth century.

The next problem faced by test makers interested in the measurement of intelligence was an efficient method of assessing a large number of persons on a single occasion. Arthur S. Otis, who was associated with Terman at Stanford, was the preeminent early leader in this endeavor. His pencil and paper instrument became the model for the Army Alpha Test, which was administered to American recruits in the first World War.

In 1937, Terman, in collaboration with Maude A. Merrill, brought out a new revision of the Stanford-Binet. There remained, however, a serious need for a highly valid, individual test of intelligence designed specifically for adults. Such a test could not utilize the mental age concept, since mental growth does continue into adulthood. The answer was the Wechsler-Bellevue Intelligence Scale, published in 1939. This test, which included separate verbal and performance parts, was developed by David Wechsler, who was then the chief psychologist at the Bellevue Psychiatric Hospital in New York, and who earlier had been a student of Cattell. Wechsler later improved his test for adult intelligence, and also constructed tests for children.

Throughout much of this period, particularly in the 1920s and 1930s, the concept of the IQ, as measured by the better tests, tended to be viewed by many psychologists as of unimpeachable validity, and as reflective of innate and unchanging human capacity. By the 1940s, however, considerable evidence had accumulated that measures of IQ are influenced, at least to some degree, by environmental factors.

Personality Assessment

Two of Cattell's students, Robert S. Woodworth and Edward L. Thorndike, contributed in major ways to the field of assessment. Woodworth's chief service in assessment—he was best known as an experimental and motivational psychologist—was in the development of the first personality inventory, called the Personal Data Sheet, which was used in the first World War to help identify unstable American soldiers. Though information-gathering questionnaires had been utilized earlier by Galton, Woodworth's 116-item (example: Do you feel sad or low-spirited most of the time?) was the first to be framed as a test, developed on an empirical basis, and designed to yield a definite score. It was the forerunner of numerous other inventories devised during the next two decades (Goldberg, 1971), of which the most popular was probably the Bernreuter Personality Inventory. Though many of the inventories were directed toward the assessment of maladjustment, by the 1930s some were designed to measure specific personality traits.

Most of these early inventories are now of only historical interest, but one—the Minnesota Multiphasic Personality Inventory, or MMPI, first introduced in 1943, turned out to have amazing utility and longevity, and was translated into numerous foreign languages. This inventory, by Starke Hathaway and Jovian McKinley, was designed specifically for use in the assessment of psychopathological dimensions.

The Rorschach Inkblot Test consists of 10 cards showing colored prints of inkblots. The subject, responding imaginatively, indicates what the blots, or part of blots, might represent. Several earlier authors, including Binet, had conceived that inkblots might be employed to measure imaginativeness, but Hermann Rorschach, a Swiss psychiatrist, was the first to create a useable inkblot test in 1921, based on the assumption that the subject "projects" himself or herself into the responses, thus revealing pertinent personality data.

The Thematic Apperception Test (TAT) consists of a group of pictures, not all of which are typically utilized with a subject, to which the subject responds by telling a story stimulated by the picture. Again, the assumption is that the person necessarily reveals his or her main personality themes in the contents of the stories. This test, based in part on Henry A. Murray's theory of personality was introduced in 1935 by Christiana D. Morgan and Murray.

Other Early Developments

Another important area of assessment which received considerable attention during the period under review was the measurement of interests. Though there had been several earlier rudimentary moves toward interest assessment, the first systematic (though very limited) inventory was devised by Bruce Moore in 1921. The major development in this area was made by Edward K. Strong, who may have been influenced by Thorndike, his professor at Columbia who had himself done some earlier research in the area. In 1927, Strong, who was then at Stanford with Terman, published his Vocational Interest Blank (Campbell, 1968), the ancestor of all later interest scales.

Another significant focus on assessment was in educational achievement. Thorndike was influential in stimulating development in this area, and the Stanford Achievement Tests, devised by Terman and others, were widely utilized.

Still another field enjoying basic development during the 1920s and 1930s was the assessment of particular abilities, or aptitudes. Among the pioneers here were Clark L. Hull (later famous for his learning theory), Donald G. Paterson, John G. Darley, and Walter Bingham.

This brief survey has necessarily passed over a number of seminal instruments developed during the period under review. These include the Bender Visual-Motor Gestalt test (for brain injury); the Army General Classification Test (used in World War II), and the Downey Will-Temperament tests.

Scientific assessment is based on a sophisticated statistical underpinning as much as on test instruments themselves. The rapid development of psychometric theory, including basic conceptions of reliability, validity, and factor analysis, was spurred by such statisticians as Pearson, Charles Spearman, L. L. Thurstone, and J. P. Guilford, and was fundamental to overall progress in assessment.

RECENT AND CURRENT TRENDS

The measurement of intelligence has continued to attract scientific attention. In addition to intense theoretical examination, improved tests for the assessment of intelligence have been developed. These include a revision and update of the classical Stanford-Binet (Thorndike, Hagen, & Sattler, 1986), and new editions of the Wechsler series, including the Scale for Children and the form for adults (Wechsler, 1997). Several new intelligence tests have appeared; perhaps the most prominent of these is the Kaufman Assessment Battery for Children (K-ABC; Kaufman & Kaufman, 1983).

It became increasingly evident that in some instances the validity of intelligence tests was adversely affected when used with disadvantaged or culturally different persons. The result was the development of techniques to circumvent this problem; one such instrument is the System of Multicultural Pluralistic Assessment (SOMPA; Mercer & Lewis, 1978), a broad assessment approach that includes parental interviews.

Objective questionnaire tests have continued to flourish, and numerous new specialty tests, designed to apply to a wide range of human characteristics, have been constructed. These include a variety of aptitude, achievement, and interest tests, millions of which are administered annually, especially in school and vocational settings. The available tests for psychopathology and personality are much too numerous to be listed here, but several of the more prominent ones may be noted. The MMPI, known in its new version as the MMPI-2 (Butcher, Dahlstrom, Graham, Tellegen, & Kaemmer, 1989), continues to be the most widely employed objective clinical instrument. The popular California Psychological Inventory, originally constructed in 1957, was recently revised and updated (Gough & Bradley, 1996).

While objective questionnaires are still typically administered in a pencil and paper format, the development of computer-assisted test administration has been a major achievement of recent decades. Another new advance has been to supplement classical test construction methodology with item response theory. These two advances together have made possible a new objective test technology known as adaptive testing. In this procedure, the items administered to a subject are not all set in advance, but are determined by his or her responses to earlier items.

Projective tests are not used as widely as they formerly were, though the Rorschach has been considerably reinvigorated by a newer interpretive system (Exner 1993). An important new trend has been the employment of structured interviews, following the adaptive methodology noted above, especially in the evaluation of psychopathology. An additional major area of development in the last half of the twentieth century has been the design of sophisticated instruments for neuropsychological assessment. Still another important trend is the perspective termed behavioral assessment (Nelson & Hayes, 1986), which tends to eschew traditional methods of assessment in favor of direct observation of subjects.

It is obvious, both intuitively and on the basis of empirical research, that human behaviors are determined not only by the characteristics of the behaving person—as assessed by the methods reviewed above—but also by the features of the situation or environment in which the behavior occurs. It is therefore noteworthy that a number of new techniques for assessing certain environments are now available.

At the present time, psychological assessment, having descended from remote and unheralded beginnings, has become a large and flourishing enterprise, with numerous tests and procedures available for evaluating a wide variety of psychological functions. Assessment occupies a major place in the overall discipline of psychology, and its services are increasingly sought by the larger society, especially in the areas of education, industry, and public health. A number of new tests and procedures are in the process of development, and can be expected to improve and enlarge the field of assessment in the years ahead.

REFERENCES

Butcher, J. N., Dahlstrom, W. G., Graham, J. R., Tellegen, A., & Kaemmer, B. (1989). *Minnesota Multiphasic Personality Inventory-2; Manual for administration and scoring.* Minneapolis: University of Minnesota Press.

Cattell, J. M. (1890). Mental tests and measurements. *Mind, 15,* 373–381.

Campbell, D. P. (1968). The Strong Vocational Interest Blank: 1927–1967. In P. McReynolds (Ed.), *Advances in psychological assessment* (Vol. 1, pp. 105–130). Palo Alto, CA: Science and Behavior Books.

Exner, J. E., Jr. (1993). *The Rorschach: A comprehensive system: Vol 1. Basic foundations* (3rd ed.). New York: Wiley.

Galton, F. (1883). *Inquiries into human faculty and its development.* London: Macmillan.

Goodenough, F. L. (1949). *Mental testing: Its history, principles, and applications.* New York: Rinehart.

Gough, H. G., & Bradley, P. (1996). *California Psychological Inventory Manual* (3rd ed.). Palo Alto, CA: Consulting Psychologists Press.

Kaufman, A. S., & Kaufman, N. L. (1983). *Kaufman Assessment Battery for Children: Administration and scoring manual.* Circle Pines, MN: American Guidance Service.

Mercer, J. R., & Lewis, J. F. (1978). *System of Multicultural Pluralistic Assessment.* San Antonio: Psychological Corporation.

Nelson, R. O., & Hayes, S. C. (1986). *Conceptual foundations of behavioral assessment.* New York: Guilford.

Thorndike, R. L., Hagen, E. P., & Sattler, J. M. (1986). *The Stanford-Binet Intelligence Scale, Fourth Edition: Guide for administering and scoring.* Chicago: Riverside.

Wechsler, D. A. (1997). *Wechsler Adult Intelligence Scale: Third Edition.* San Antonio: Psychological Corporation.

SUGGESTED READING

Dahlstrom, W. G. (1985). The development of psychological testing. In G. A. Kimble & K. Schlesinger (Eds.), *Topics in the history of psychology* (Vol. 2, pp. 63–113). Hillsdale, NJ: Erlbaum.

DuBois, P. (1970). *A history of psychological testing.* Boston: Allyn & Bacon.

Edwards, A. J. (1971). *Individual mental testing: Part I. History and theories.* San Francisco: Intext Educational Publishers.

Goldberg, L. R. (1971). A historical survey of personality scales and inventories. In P. McReynolds (Ed.), *Advances in psychological assessment* (Vol. 2, pp. 293–336). Palo Alto, CA: Science and Behavior Books.

McReynolds, P. (1986). History of assessment in clinical and educational settings. In R. O. Nelson & S. C. Hayes (Eds.), *Conceptual foundations of behavioral assessment* (pp. 42–80). New York: Guilford.

P. McReynolds
University of Nevada

PSYCHOLOGICAL HEALTH

All psychotherapeutic systems have a view of human nature, a concept of disease etiology and a vision of psychological health (Shapiro, 1983). The intention of therapy is to work toward the vision of psychological health as defined by each particular orientation. In Allport's words, it is the "ought or should toward which every counselor, therapist, and healer should seek" (Allport, 1955).

The vision of psychological health as defined by each approach is predicated upon and consistent with its view of human nature. These views can be understood as paradigms, or "world hypotheses" (Kuhn, 1970; Schwartz & Russek, 1997) from which professionals operate in pursuing their work. While such paradigms are necessary to make sense out of our lives and work, they can also be limiting. For example, psychology has traditionally been pathology-based, viewing psychological health as the mere absence of symptoms (e.g., *DSM-IV,* 1994). This paradigm has resulted in little investigation into positive psychological health.

Reflecting a dissatisfaction with pathology-based clinical and mental health classifications, some researchers are developing—and empirically investigating—models of positive health (Walsh & Shapiro, 1983; Schwartz, 1990; Ickovics & Park, 1998; Tedeschi, Park, & Calhoun, 1998). There has also been an increasing interest in non-Western approaches to psychological health. These investigations suggest that elimination of pathology may give us the concept of the "average" or "normal" rather than a concept of true positive or "optimal" psychological health. This paradigm shift regarding health is reflected by Seligman (1998), president of the American Psychological Association (APA), in his assertion that there has been too great a focus on what makes people sick rather than what makes people well. The buffers of disease and disability are at least in part based on human strengths and competencies. Further, psychological health may need to be seen as interconnected with and part of a larger view of "health" in general. For example, in the original constitution of the World Health Organization in 1946, a view of health evolved which was stated in positive terms: "Health is a state of complete physical, mental, and social well-being and is not merely absence of disease or infirmity."

FIVE VIEWS OF HUMAN NATURE AND PSYCHOLOGICAL HEALTH

Becoming aware of and making explicit our views of psychological health can illuminate how traditional models may limit our ability to understand health, and also allow for a broadening of the paradigm. In order to move toward the intention of a more systemic approach to psychological health it is first important to understand the models or hypotheses about human nature, summarized in Table 1.

Biomedical Approach

View of Human Nature   The biomedical paradigm, which guides modern medicine and psychiatry, views human nature as determined in large part by our biological/physiological processes. An example can be seen in the biomedical approach to depression. Assessment leads to a precise diagnosis for which an organic cause is identified (e.g. lack of serotonin), then a treatment specific to the pathology is prescribed (e.g., SSRI—selective-serotonin reuptake inhibitor).

Goal of Therapy   The goal of therapy is to alleviate undesired symptoms via medication, restore biochemical homeostasis, and thereby achieve "psychological health."

Psychodynamic Approach

View of Human Nature   Psychodynamic psychology, pioneered by Freud, views behavior as a product of competing instincts, needs, and impulses. Different analytic schools disagree about the exact nature of these needs. Freud himself postulated several theories from sex and survival, to love and aggression, and finally life and death. Regardless of orientation, they all subscribe to the same basic premise: namely, that man is unconscious or alienated from the basic aspects of his "self." As Freud noted, "man is lived by unknown and uncontrolled forces" (Freud, 1923) that originate in the "amoral" id. Since these mental forces are unconscious, a person is not fully aware of how they manifest; and the result of the conflict is called neurosis or "mental illness."

Goal of Therapy   From a psychodynamic view of human nature, psychological health is achieved by uncovering the repressed facets of the self in order to evolve an accurate and acceptable self-image. The psychodynamic therapist listens for connections made between "the patient's current thoughts and feelings and his or her past experiences—sometimes very early ones—with the knowledge that many of these experiences have been 'forgotten' or repressed and can only be seen in their current, often disguised or distorted manifestation" (Usher, 1993). The therapist's task is "to make the unconscious conscious, to recover warded off memories, and over-

Table 1.   Comparison and Contrast of Five Schools of Psychotherapy

Subject	Biomedical	Psychodynamic	Cognitive-Behavioral	Humanistic-Existential	Transpersonal
View of Human Nature	Primarily biological/ physiological processes.	Ruled by unconscious amoral id.	Blank slate. Determined by environmental stimuli, or cognitive representations of stimuli.	Innately self-actualizing (H). Existence precedes essence (E).	Interconnected. Capable of going beyond ego identity.
Goal of Psychotherapy	Normalize chemical imbalances.	To make the unconscious conscious, "where id was, ego shall be."	Competently respond to environment. Reinterpret illogical cognitions.	Foster self-actualization (H). "Choices" create authentic self (E).	Go beyond identification with limited ego. See interconnection with others and world.

come infantile amnesia" (Greenson, 1968). Therefore, psychological health according to the psychodynamic view is achieved when repressed desires, fears, and depressions are made conscious and brought under control. "Where id was, ego shall be" (Freud, 1961, pp. 57–58).

Behavioral/Cognitive-Behavioral Approach

View of Human Nature   The cognitive-behavioral approach views human nature as a *tabula rasa,* a blank slate. The individual is not motivated by the intrapsychic forces of ego and id, but instead by environmental stimuli and social interactions (or cognitive representations of the two). Therefore, psychological maladjustment is a likely sequelae from maladaptive learning, reinforcement patterns, or cognitive distortions.

Goal of Therapy   A cognitive-behavioral approach (Ellis, 1962; Beck, 1976; Meichenbaum, 1977) teaches clients to identify and reinterpret the illogical notions that underlie their distressing symptoms. Since cognitions, feelings, and behaviors are causally interrelated, cognitive-behavioral approaches alter the maladaptive cognitions in an attempt to bring about behavioral and affective change. Psychological health is achieved when maladaptive patterns (cognitive and behavioral) are recognized and changed, consequently alleviating undesired symptoms.

Humanistic/Existential Approach

View of Human Nature   The humanistic/existential approach views the individual as controlled by neither a "genetic" amoral id nor by external stimuli. The humanistic approach instead views the individual as constantly changing or "becoming," with the capacity for full conscious awareness. "The organism has one basic tendency in striving—to actualize, maintain, and enhance the experience of the organism" (Rogers, 1951). The existential approach argues that there is no "innate" self-actualizing nature; in other words, existence precedes essence, and therefore a person must "create" his or her authentic self (Yalom, 1980). The unhealthy person from the humanistic/existential viewpoint is one who restricts the task of openly discovering and making sense of his or her existence, turns away from the responsibility of creating choices, and fails to relate with others and the world authentically in the present moment.

Goal of Therapy   The goal of humanistic/existential therapy is to foster self-actualization, allowing the client to assume full responsibility for developing his or her identity. Ultimately, this entails authentically encountering the human environment, the inevitability of isolation and mortality, and realizing that if one cannot choose one's fate, one can nevertheless choose one's own attitude toward it. As May (1969) notes, realizing that "we are our choices [does not] change the fate, but it greatly changes the person."

Transpersonal Approach

View of Human Nature   The transpersonal approach views human nature as having an impulse towards ultimate states that are positive and motivated by values which transcend the self (Maslow, 1962, 1969; Sutich, 1969; Walsh & Vaughan, 1994). Further, the transpersonal approach sees humans as having an interconnected "essence," as wholes within larger wholes (Shapiro & Schwartz, in press).

Goal of Therapy   From the transpersonal tradition, the goal of therapy is to extend the identity or sense of self beyond the "narrow self" so that individuals realize their connection with others and the world. The qualities of the healthy person include realizing the limits of ego identity, developing compassion, opening to peak experiences, and being aware of unitive consciousness, ultimate values, and meaning.

TOWARD A MORE SYSTEMIC APPROACH TO PSYCHOLOGICAL HEALTH

Each of the above traditions created a different view of human nature and psychological health. A problem arises, however, when each tradition feels it has the one and only true view of psychological health. Therefore, it may be appropriate in our current state of knowledge to move toward the intention of a more systemic approach to psychological health. For example, Wilber (1977) proposes that each of the major schools of psychology is fairly accurately addressing the issues and pathologies of particular developmental levels. Therefore, each is true for that level but is only explaining a part of the spectrum or whole of human development. As a result, the many conflicting definitions of psychological health resonate with the Sufi story of four blind men who examined an elephant in four places. The elephant was thought to be a rope, a snake, the wings of a bird, or the bark of the tree, depending on whether the man felt the tail, the trunk, the ears, or the skin. Any complete view of psychological health needs to integrate the unique vantage offered by each tradition by maximizing health on the physical, mental, and social level as suggested by the World Health Organization's multilevel definition. In addition, a "spiritual" dimension that addresses the ultimate issues of value, meaning, and our human place in the cosmos may also be an important aspect.

Such a multilevel, systemic view of psychological health is complementary, rather than exclusive. For example, a comprehensive treatment plan for depression may include addressing biochemical imbalances (biomedical), learning coping strategies to handle environmental stressors (behavioral), interpreting cognitive distortions (cognitive), overcoming lack of trust in oneself (humanistic), examining unconscious intrapsychic conflict (psychodynamic), and exploring ultimate spiritual questions (transpersonal). Depending on the patient, an intervention open to all levels may be helpful in increasing psychological health (Wilber, 1977, 1996; Schwartz & Russek, 1997; Shapiro & Astin, 1998; Shapiro & Schwartz, 2000).

Thus, a more comprehensive view of psychological health may best be achieved by honoring the viewpoint of each tradition. Such an integration of the above views of psychological health would encompass the biomedical through the transpersonal. It would include the traditional measures such as positive affect, life satisfaction, positive sense of control, self-determination, and self-acceptance. It would also extend the criteria to include sensitivity to the body and its needs (i.e., physical well-being), increased depths of relationships (i.e., interpersonal well-being), purpose in life, personal growth, self-actualization, and realizing the limits of ego identity (i.e., existential/spiritual well-being) (Jahoda, 1958; Ryff, 1989). Clearly, more research is needed to help evolve a systemic, multilevel, and integrative definition of psychological health. Such knowledge has the potential to considerably augment both clinical practice and even society at large.

REFERENCES

Allport, G. W. (1955). *Becoming: Basic considerations for a psychology of personality.* New Haven, CT: Yale University Press.

American Psychiatric Association (1994). *Diagnostic and statistical manual of mental disorders* (4th ed.). Washington, DC: Author.

Beck, A. (1976). *Cognitive therapy and the emotional disorders.* New York: International Universities Press.

Ellis, A. (1962). *Reason and emotion in psychotherapy.* New York: Stuart.

Freud, S. (1923). *The ego and the id.* New York: W. W. Norton.

Freud, S. (1961). *Civilization and its discontents.* New York: W. W. Norton.

Greenson, R. (1968). *The technique and practice of psychoanalysis* (Vol. 1). New York: International Universities Press.

Ickovics, J. R., & Park, C. L. (1998). Paradigm shift: Why a focus on health is important. *Journal of Social Issues, 54*(2), 237–244.

Jahoda, M. (1958). *Current concepts of positive mental health: A report to the Staff Director, Jack R. Ewalt.* New York: Basic Books.

Kuhn, T. S. (1970). *The structure of scientific revolutions.* Chicago: University of Chicago Press.

Maslow, A. (1962). *Toward a psychology of being.* New York: Van Nostrand.

Maslow, A. (1969, Spring). The farther reaches of human nature. *Journal of Transpersonal Psychology,* V. L, no. 1, p. 4.

May, R. (Ed.). (1969). *Existential Psychology.* New York: Random House.

Meichenbaum, D. (1977). *Cognitive behavior modification: An integrative approach.* New York: Plenum.

Rogers, C. R. (1951). *Client-centered therapy.* Cambridge, MA: Houghton Mifflin.

Ryff, C. D. (1989). Happiness is everything, or is it? Explorations on the meaning of psychological well-being. *Journal of Personality and Social Psychology, 57*(6), 1069–1081.

Schwartz, G. E. (1990). Psychobiology of repression and health: A systems approach. In J. Singer (Ed.), *Repression and dissociation: Implication for personality, theory, psychopathology and health* (pp. 337–387). Chicago: University of Chicago Press.

Schwartz, G. E., & Russek, L. G. (1997). The challenge of One-Medicine: Theories of health and eight "World Hypotheses." *Advances: The Journal of Mind-Body Health, 13*(3), 7–23.

Seligman, M. (1998, April 29). *Opening Remarks (Testimony).* Congressional Briefing on Prevention. Washington, DC: US Congress.

Shapiro, D. H. (1983). A content analysis of Eastern and Western, traditional, and new-age approaches to psychotherapy, health, and healing. In D. H. Shapiro & J. A. Astin (Eds.), *Control therapy: An integrated approach to psychotherapy, health, and healing.* New York: Wiley.

Shapiro, D. H., & Astin, J. A. (1998). *Control Therapy: An Integrated Approach to Psychotherapy, Health, and Healing.* New York: Wiley.

Shapiro, S. L., & Schwartz, G. E. (2000). The role of intention in self-regulation: Toward intentional systemic mindfulness. In P. Pintrich, M. Boekaerts, & M. Zeidner (Eds.), *Handbook of Self-Regulation* (pp. 253–273). New York: Academic Press.

Sutich, A. J. (1969, Spring). Some considerations regarding transpersonal psychology. *Journal of Transpersonal Psychology,* 18.

Tedeschi, R. G., Park, C. L., & Calhoun, L. G. (Ed.). (1998). *Posttraumatic growth: Positive changes in the aftermath of crisis.* Mahwah, NJ: Erlbaum.

Usher, S. F. (1993). *Introduction to psychodynamic psychotherapy techniques.* New York: International Universities Press.

Walsh, R. N., & Shapiro, D. H. (1983). *Beyond health and normality: Explorations of exceptional psychological well-being.* New York: Van Nostrand.

Walsh, R. N., & Vaughan, F. (Eds.). (1994). *Paths beyond ego.* Los Angeles: Tarcher.

Wilber, K. (1977). *Spectrum of consciousness.* Wheaton, IL: Quest.

Wilber, K. (1996). *Brief history of everything.* Boston: Shambhala.

World Health Organization (1946). Original constitution. In G. C. Stone, F. Cohen, & N. E. Adler (Eds.), *Health Psychology.* San Francisco: Jossey-Bass.

Yalom, I. D. (1980). *Existential psychotherapy.* New York: Basic.

D. H. SHAPIRO
University of California, Irvine

C. SANTERRE
S. L. SHAPIRO
University of Arizona

J. A. ASTIN
University of Maryland School of Medicine

BEHAVIORAL MEDICINE
COMMUNITY PSYCHOLOGY
HEALTH & PSYCHOLOGY
MENTAL ILLNESS: EARLY HISTORY
PRIMARY PREVENTION OF PSYCHOTHERAPY
PSYCHOANALYSIS

PSYCHOLOGICAL SCIENCE

Psychological science is concerned with the application of scientific method and principles to the study of a set of questions that traditionally have been categorized as psychological in nature. It also is the body of theories and facts about the questions and issues that have emerged from this process. Psychological science is different from mere philosophical speculation about psychological questions. It also is different from the so-called self-help literature that deals in an intuitive way with problems of living. Psychological science requires empirical observation and experimental verification of its speculations, that are often cast as, and considered to be, scientific theories. Defined in this way, psychological science is the discipline of all but a few university departments of psychology.

PSYCHOLOGICAL VS. COGNITIVE SCIENCE

Because of the development in the past quarter century of the multidisciplinary program called cognitive science, we must make further distinctions. Cognitive science, called the "mind's new science" by Gardner (1992), represents a coalition of approaches that includes aspects of the disciplines of psychology, linguistics, philosophy, neuroscience, computer science, and anthropology. Some observers would use "psychological science" as the name of the basket concept, naming specific psychologists whose expertise is in the several focus areas. Because that battle is lost, however, we are faced with a problem: how to differentiate cognitive science from psychological science per se. Pending further developments, for the time being we can conceptualize psychological science as a science dealing with traditionally psychological questions, a science with its own methodology and a philosophy that resists the reduction of psychological questions to brain processes. They must be understood in their own context, on their own terms. Some would argue that psychological processes are based upon emergent properties and functions of the intact functioning organism that require their own set of assumptions and logic. Whether ultimately true or not, such a stance defines a set of issues that can mark off psychological science as a separate and distinct domain of cognitive science.

PSYCHOLOGICAL QUESTIONS

Psychological questions, at least historically, deal somehow with mental processes and conscious experience or awareness of one's existence and the world in which one exists, a concept that is closely related to mind. Going back to antiquity, humans have speculated about the nature of mind, of the relationship of mind to the world in which they live, of the relationship of mind to the body of which it is a part, of the nature of knowledge and how it is acquired, and of the relationship between mind and human action. Down through the ages, such philosophical speculation constituted a major focus of such notable thinkers as Plato and Aristotle and of a range of philosophers following the Renaissance, including Descartes, Hobbes, Locke, Berkeley, and Kant. Of these, Kant is remembered for his insistence that there could be no science of psychology. This opinion was based on his belief that mental events were not measurable, and thus there could be no mathematical analysis or description of them. Furthermore, according to Kant, mental events were brief and subject to distortion by the observa-

tion process itself, and mental events could not be produced by experimental means; they had their own existence and obeyed their own laws and whims. There simply could not be a science dealing with such an unmanageable and even nonphysical subject matter.

PSYCHOLOGY AND SCIENCE

The development of psychological science required the emergence of a sophisticated view of science and then a demonstration of the capability of the scientific method to be relevant to psychological questions. These requirements seem to have been satisfied around the middle of the nineteenth century, at which time many of Kant's objections appear to have been surmounted by methodological advances leading to pertinent discoveries in physiology. If a date must be provided for the birth of psychological science, perhaps it would be 1874, the year that Wundt's *The Principles of Physiological Psychology* was published. The preface to this work begins with this remarkable statement: "This work which I here present to the public is an attempt to work out a new domain of science."

THE BEGINNINGS

Partly in response to the shortcomings of Wundt's introspective procedure, and partly as an outgrowth of early successes in animal psychology, another methodological approach, the behaviorist movement, emerged in the first half of the twentieth century. In part, behaviorism has been seen as an outgrowth of what has been called functionalistic psychology, with a concern for explaining the function of mind and how mind could be implicated in the coping behavior of the human as well as other animals. But it soon seemed apparent that human and animal behavior could be studied in their own right. The behaviorist approach, as enunciated by Watson in 1913, was "a purely objective experimental branch of natural science. . . . Introspection forms no essential part of its methods" (p. 158). Mind and conscious experience were ruled out as topics of scientific investigation because they were not directly observable. Behaviorism, at least in the United States, became a dominant force in psychology and formed the basis for a substantial portion of research publications from 1920 through 1960.

CURRENT PSYCHOLOGICAL SCIENCE

Modern-day cognitive psychology emerged when psychology was nearly 100 years old, and today is almost synonymous with experimental psychology. Cognitive psychology's subject matter returns to questions of mind, but not in the form conceptualized by Wundt. Rather than examining the nature of conscious experience from the perspective of the observer of that experience, cognitive psychology focuses on theoretical mental processes as they are manifested in observable measures such as accuracy and response time. In this approach, specific characteristics of mental processes are hypothesized, and the observable consequences of assumptions about the characteristics are derived. Experiments are conducted then to determine whether or not the hypothesized consequences occur, with a positive result bolstering confidence in the power of the theoretical assumptions. This form of experimentation has, as its empirical base, observable responses made by the experimental subject, responses that depend on the activities of the hypothesized processes under investigation. From this perspective, cognitive psychology can be viewed as a return to an earlier view about the subject matter of psychological investigation but with the adoption of the sophisticated and objective methodology of behaviorism. Psychology's focus is not currently on the structure of conscious experience. Rather it is focused on the tasks of identifying and explicating the processes that are involved in attention, memory, pattern recognition, linguistic behavior (speaking, listening, and reading), thinking, problem solving, and associated problems.

The history of psychological science from its beginnings in the laboratory of Wundt to the present day reveals a great broadening of its concern. Wundt's experimental procedures were generally limited to the question of identifying the elements of the structure of mind conceptualized as conscious experience. The behavioristic movement substituted a concern with the functioning of animal and human organisms interacting with an environmental context. Present-day cognitive psychology has returned to questions of mental activity but with a different goal than that of Wundt. Along the way, psychology adopted a number of methodologies and procedures that extended its scope, and it grew by encompassing a number of areas related to its main goal. Psychology adopted the analytic methodology of statistics and in many areas was able to harness mathematical models to augment its growing methodological armament. The methods and goals of psychological science were applied to a wide variety of psychological questions and in a variety of settings. Today, the introductory textbook in psychology displays a wide array of applications of the methodology of psychological science, ranging from basic subfields of psychology such as perception, learning, cognition, social psychology, and personality to such topics as drug abuse, mental illness, and gender differences, for all of which our knowledge has been extended through psychological science.

REFERENCES

Gardner, H. (1985). *The mind's new science: A history of the cognitive revolution.* New York: Basic.

Watson, J. B. (1913). Psychology as the behaviorist views it. *Psychological Review, 20,* 158–177.

Wundt, W. (1874). *Grundzüge der physiologischen Psychologie.* Leipzig: Englemann.

A. Boneau
George Mason University

DOUBLE BLIND RESEARCH
RESEARCH METHODOLOGY
SCIENTIFIC METHOD

PSYCHOLOGY AND THE COURTS

The metaphor of a courtship has been used to describe the historical and developing relationship between law and psychology. The growth of the discipline of psychology has led to new psychological knowledge and a variety of related treatments, and these, in turn, have provided the courts with new options and perspectives in dealing with its most vexing cases: the alleged "mentally ill," whose behavior is disturbing, potentially harmful, and seemingly inexplicable; the alleged "criminally insane," whose conduct violates the law, yet whose culpability is questioned; the so-called "juvenile delinquent," who defies supervision and limits, yet who needs both; and the alleged "incompetent," who needs paternalistic protection and relief in certain spheres of functioning, yet who protests benevolent interventions.

Historically this courtship began in the classical age of the 17th and 18th centuries, when human beings of reason began to confine those who were unreasonable in hospitals (Hôpital Général), leprosariums, Zuchthäusern, workhouses, and asylums that dotted the European landscape. The guardian and gatekeeper of these semijuridical structures was the physician. The purposes of confinement were mixed: to punish, to treat, to make the inhabitants diligent, work, repent, and recant their madness, and accept society's normative and reasonable standards. As the historian Michel Foucault (1973) notes, the physician was society's authorized emissary to madness; the relationship between reasonable and unreasonable people would now be conducted through the physician, and thus "through the abstract universality of disease."

The courts' courtship of psychology coincided, in good part, with their own shift in emphasis—moving increasingly from retribution to rehabilitation, from punishment to treatment. The words of Justice Stewart, speaking for the Supreme Court in *Robinson v. California,* are illustrative: "But, in the light of contemporary human knowledge a law which made a criminal offense of such a disease (mental illness) would doubtless be universally thought to be an infliction of cruel and unusual punishment in violation of the Eighth and Fourteenth Amendments . . . Even one day in prison would be a cruel and unusual punishment for the 'crime' of having a common cold." This trend and shift in goal, as one of its repercussions, has led the courts to turn increasingly to the mental health practitioners ". . . to furuish the requisite rehabilitative formula." Kittrie (1971) characterizes this courtship of law and psychology as the "Therapeutic State."

Psychologists, psychiatrists, psychotherapists, mental health professionals, and behavioral scientists of varying stripes have generally been responsive to these overtures. "And why not?" as Leifer (1964) asks. "They have everything to gain and nothing to lose by it. In exchange for helping the court out of its difficulty, the psychiatrist's own claim to scientific status is underwritten by the courts." London (1964), takes note of the rise in respectability accorded the therapist: Formerly the therapist was regarded as an eccentric on the fringes of medicine, "mumbling arcane obscenities"; but now therapists have risen "from relative obscurity to chairs of eminence and couches of opulence in the finest universities and neighborhoods in the Western World."

Currently the psychological expert enters the courtroom, is accorded "expert witness" status, and is typically asked to render *clinical judgment* regarding specific questions as they relate to a *specific* individual: Is the defendant competent to stand trial? Was the defendant criminally insane at the time of the act? Is the individual currently dangerous to self or others? Is the person mentally ill? Is the person in need of treatment? And should the person be involuntarily committed to a mental hospital? In addition, a newer trend is discernible that promises even more psychologists in the courtroom. Loftus and Monahan (1980), in "Trial by data," note that in addition to the traditional "clinical judgment" testimony, behavioral scientists are now taking the stand to present *research expertise* that relates *generally* to a variety of matters and groups of individuals, such as eye witness judgments; cross-racial accuracy; jury size, selection, and deliberation findings; brain chemistry and functioning; and mind/brain interactions.

It may be said that this courtship has led to marriage; but contention, confusion, and questions remain. Lawyers are questioning the validity of the psychologists' clinical judgments, as the article by Ennis and Litwack (1974), provocatively entitled, "Psychiatry and the prescription of expertise: Flipping coins in the courtroom," indicates. Psychiatrists, most notably Thomas Szasz (1977), raise the question of whether these experts are masquerading in the costume of benevolence. Historians, legal scholars, philosophers, ethicists, psychiatrists, and psychologists are asking questions about paternalism and the limits of benevolence. As Rothman (1978) asks, "Where should the authority of the caretaker leave off and the rights of the cared-for begin?"

Finkel (1980) has written, "It is, unfortunately, an all too common sight today for patients to enter the courtroom seeking relief from their healers as well as from their disorders; and therapists, formerly the defenders of mental health, now have to defend themselves and their practices." The "rights of mental patients" increasingly are being discussed, written about, and litigated within the wedded disciplines. Rights to treatment, rights to refuse treatment, and the right to be different are being weighed against society's right to protect and improve itself. The "balance point" has not always been easy to find.

For the healer "to heal thyself," and for blind justice to see, self-examination is required. There is the need to examine and question psychologists' assumptions, motivation, perspective, and language, along with their treatment practices and their judgments. If this "unwholesome collusion" or "conspiracy of success" that has wedded psychology to the courts is to be made right, psychologists must look more closely and deeply at its roots, and their own involvement.

At the core of many controversies lies the concept of mental illness or one of its variations, such as mental disease or psychopathology. Fingarette (1972) notes that the term *mental disease* has been a key element in all of the insanity tests adopted by federal and state courts. And it continues to be the central element in statutes relating to grounds for involuntary commitment, yet the status of the concept of mental illness remains very much in doubt. Is it a medical concept, an analogy, or a myth?

Psychiatry's 19th-century roots in medicine, in neurology in particular, coupled with the often naive materialism of that age, led to the conviction that mental disease was at bottom a physical disease; and some breakthroughs, notably the connecting of the disorder general paresis to the disease of syphilis, fueled the conviction and fed the promise that the physical causes would soon be discovered. But the early promises proved empty, as when no or-

ganic impairment, brain lesion, or anatomical or physiological connection could be found for many mental disorders, of which hysteria was a prime, early example.

In the 20th century, the concept of mental illness is being used more as a metaphor, or analogy, or parallel than as a synonym for an actual physical disease. "Mental illness" is now *like* a "physical illness," as "mental breakdown" is *like* a "physical breakdown." However, problems with this parallel crop up when a closer examination of the analogy is made: Significant differences emerge between mental and physical disorders in terms of onset; etiology; symptoms; impact on areas of mental, emotional, social, and occupational functioning; responsiveness to treatment; and cure rates. Szasz (1960) views mental illness as "problems in living"; in this view, he widens, if not abandons, the medical context of disorders in favor of one that involves social, legal, ethical, moral, and political factors. The courts, however, in the absence of any judicial definition of mental disease, continue to rely on psychiatric and psychological expertise to define a concept that cannot be defined, simply or purely, in medical, psychiatric terms. This point, and the related problems of language and perspective, will become clearer by using as one example the legal question of insanity.

Fingarette (1972) writes, "When the criminal law asks questions concerning mental disease and insanity, it is concerned with the defendant's mental capacities *with respect to the law*. In whatever way this concern is precisely formulated, it is one that by its very nature cannot be cast in purely psychiatric categories." It will not do, for example, for the psychological expert to announce that the person has some psychiatric disorder (e.g., schizophrenia) listed in the *Diagnostic and Statistical Manual* (e.g., *DSM-III*), as this mental illness is not equivalent to "insanity." And from the psychological or psychiatric perspective, the legal term *insanity* makes no sense in psychiatric terms. The different languages, legal and psychiatric, derive from differing approaches—the moralistic and punitive approach of the law, on the one hand, and the scientific, rehabilitative approach of psychiatry, on the other. The *dualistic* language of law speaks of "moral responsibility," "will," and "intent," while the allegedly *deterministic* language of psychology speaks of "unconscious motivation," "lack of ego control," and "schizophrenia." The two disciplines, both seeking common ground, often come into conflict.

When psychological experts take the stand to testify at an involuntary commitment hearing, for example, they are often asked to render a judgment regarding mental illness, and a prediction regarding "dangerousness." These judgments and predictions are typically based on interviews (a mental status exam) and psychological testing. But upon critical cross-examination, questions about the psychologist's methods and inferences, their validity and reliability, and the psychologist's accuracy and "expertness" come to the foreground. The psychological expert, through a technical language that employs such terms as "repression," "defense mechanism," "ego," and "id," draws a portrait that may help illuminate the seemingly bizarre and unintelligible behavior of the alleged mentally ill. The portrait may provide a coherent, intelligible accounting of the behavior such that the seemingly purposeless actions of the defendant are now shown to be purposeful, though not necessarily rational. But to speak of "purposes," to explain actions in terms of the defendant's thoughts, motives, fears, and emotions, the expert uses teleological and mentalistic concepts not entirely dissimilar to the language of the law and the lay public. The expert just "does it better"—more skillfully weaving an explanation where the courts and lay people found none.

The psychologist's skill, particularly in the area of treatment, has wedded the courts to mental health professionals with the thread and hope that therapy will set the courts and allegedly mentally ill free from their respective disorders. The promise has not yet panned out. Involuntary treatment and hospitalization have not been effective remedies, and their failures have led patients back to the courts, where they assert their right to treatment, or to be free. More potent treatments, such as drugs, electroconvulsive therapy (shock treatment), behavior modification, and psychosurgery, also led patients back to the courts, this time asserting their right to refuse treatment. Therapists and patients, the community and the courts, find themselves entangled and confused as never before.

Disentanglement does not necessarily mean divorce. A separation may be healthy in order for psychologists to analyze their practices, ethics, and conceptions, their language and intents. A separation may also provide the time to examine what each can do well, what promises each can keep and cannot keep, and what each may reasonably expect from the other. Psychology and law can relate, do relate, and, in some sense, must relate. The search goes on, through action and reflection, for that sane, common ground.

REFERENCES

Ennis, B. J., & Litwack, T. R. (1974). Psychiatry and the presumption of expertise: Flipping coins in the courtroom. *California Law Review, 62,* 693–752.

Fingarette, H. (1972). *The meaning of criminal insanity.* Berkeley, CA: University of California Press.

Finkel, N. J. (1980). *Therapy and ethics: The courtship of law and psychology.* New York: Grune & Stratton.

Foucault, M. (1973). *Madness and civilization: A history of insanity in the age of reason.* New York: Vintage Books.

Kittrie, N. N. (1971). *The right to be different: Deviance and enforced therapy.* Baltimore: Johns Hopkins University Press.

Leifer, R. (1964). The psychiatrist and tests of criminal responsibility. *American Psychologist, 19,* 825–830.

Loftus, E., & Monahan, J. (1980). Trial by data: Psychological research as legal evidence. *American Psychologist, 35,* 270–283.

London, P. (1964). *The modes and morals of psychotherapy.* New York: Holt, Rinehart & Winston.

Rothman, D. (1978). Introduction. In W. Gaylin, I. Glasser, S. Marcus, & D. Rothman (Eds.), *Doing good: The limits of benevolence.* New York: Pantheon.

Szasz, T. S. (1977). *Psychiatric slavery.* New York: Free Press.

SUGGESTED READING
Cowen, E. L. (1973). Social and community interventions. *Annual Review of Psychology, 24,* 423–472.

Ennis, B. J., & Emery, R. D. (1973). *The rights of mental patients.* New York: Avon.

Finkel, N. J. (1976). *Mental illness and health: Its legacy, tensions, and changes.* New York: Macmillan.

Goldstein, A. S. (1967). *The insanity defense.* New Haven, CT: Yale University Press.

Monahan, J. (Ed.). (1976). *Community mental health and the criminal justice system.* New York: Pergamon.

Robinson, D. N. (1973). Therapies: A clear and present danger. *American Psychologist, 28,* 129–133.

Schofield, W. (1964). *Psychotherapy: The purchase of friendship.* Englewood Cliffs, NJ: Prentice-Hall.

N. J. FINKEL
Georgetown University

COMPETENCY TO STAND TRIAL
EXPERT TESTIMONY
FORENSIC PSYCHOLOGY
LAW, PSYCHOLOGY AND
PUNISHMENT

PSYCHOLOGY AND THE LAW

The field of psychology and law first began to develop within the last century and is currently in its greatest period of growth and expansion. Psychologists have become increasingly involved with legal issues, both in research and in practice, and the field of psychology and law has expanded rapidly in recent years. This growth is evidenced by the publication of numerous books and the creation of book series in psychology and law, and of journals and periodicals specifically targeted toward psychology and legal issues; by the establishment of such specialized professional associations as the American Psychology-Law Society (AP-LS), the psychology and law division of the American Psychological Association (APA), the American Academy of Forensic Psychology, and the American Board of Forensic Psychology; and by the development of educational and internship experiences (Bersoff, 1999). In addition, many graduate schools have developed degree programs in which a specialization or concentration in psychology and law can be obtained, and a number of universities have established joint psychology and law degree programs in which both a PhD and a law degree are obtained (Bersoff, 1999; Bersoff et al., 1997). The following provides an overview of the major areas in which psychologists in the field of psychology and law are engaged.

EXPERT WITNESS

Psychologists have for some time now been recognized in most courts as experts in a variety of criminal and civil issues and in class action suits with respect to mental patient and prisoner rights. The legal status of psychologists in the courtroom was first established in *Jenkins v. United States* (307 F.2d 637, 1962). (Many of the areas of expertise are discussed later.)

Though heavily criticized at first (see Ennis & Litwack, 1974; Szasz, 1963), the use of psychologists and other mental health professionals as experts to assist the court in making legal decisions has gained greater acceptance in the past few decades. Perhaps one of the most articulate critics of this practice was the late Judge David Bazelon. With respect to mental health issues such as competency and responsibility, Bazelon objected to the way in which experts communicated the findings of their evaluations to the court. He was particularly concerned with the tendency of experts to testify in conclusory terms, rather than to testify simply on the substance of the evaluation. Bazelon (1975) stated, "Psychiatrists have never been able to understand that conclusory labels and opinions are no substitute for facts derived from disciplined investigation. . . . [An opinion] is only as good as the *investigation,* the *facts,* and the *reasoning* that underlie it" (p. 181). The APA Task Force on the Role of Psychology in the Criminal Justice System recommended that, "since it is not within the professional competence to offer conclusions on matters of law, psychologists should resist pressure to offer such conclusions" (Monahan, 1980, p. 9). Currently, it is considered good professional practice to leave the ultimate legal issue for the court to decide rather than to offer a conclusory opinion on the matter (Melton, Petrial, Poythress, & Slobogin, 1997).

There is little doubt that an expert witness can have a major impact on a legal decision. In the area of competency to stand trial, for example, there is nearly certain court acceptance of the evaluator's conclusion (Hart & Hare, 1992; Roesch & Golding, 1980). The potential power and influence of experts have led some mental health professionals to call upon those experts to set limits on their own testimony and to examine the effects of their power on the individual, the courts, and society (Robitscher, 1978).

A number of articles and books have appeared in recent years to help experts prepare for and cope with cross-examination (e.g., Brodsky, 1999; Ceci & Hembrooke, 1998; Poythress, 1980). These resources provide excellent information on the role of the expert witness and include descriptions of possible rebuttal tactics to cross-examination questions, including numerous references and examples of how the expert can respond. Less helpful, at least in terms of helping an expert to testify in a fair manner, are manuals such as the ones by Ziskin and Faust (1988; see also Ziskin, 1995); this book is a guide for lawyers on how to attack psychological and psychiatric testimony. While many of the criticisms discussed by Ziskin and Faust are quite legitimate, their suggested strategy often relies on attempts to make the expert appear foolish or unscholarly by focusing on, for example, a particular test item from a battery of tests administered to the client. Out of context, a particular item may appear absurd, but the court or jury may not be made aware that a conclusion would never be made on the basis of a single test-item response.

RISK ASSESSMENT

The assessment of risk for violence is an area in psychology and law that has undergone a type of paradigm shift, represented by a change in terminology and in the way we think about and assess the issue of violence prediction. In the past, this area involved the *pre-diction of* dangerousness and violence. Currently, it involves the assessment of *risk for* violence. This paradigm shift resulted from the recognition of a number of difficulties associated with the prediction of dangerousness, one of the more prominent of which was the relative inability of psychologists—or of any mental health professional—to predict accurately dangerousness or violence (Monahan, 1981). In fact, the APA Task Force on the Role of Psychology in the Criminal Justice System (Monahan, 1980) had as one of its recommendations:

Psychologists should be extremely cautious in offering predictions of criminal behavior for use in imprisoning or releasing individual offenders. If a psychologist decides that it is appropriate in a given case to provide a prediction of criminal behavior, he or she should clearly specify (a) the acts being predicted, (b) the estimated probability that these acts will occur during a given time period, and (c) the factors on which the predictive judgment is based. (pp. 11–12)

A major reason for such cautionary statements is that violent behavior was considered to be a low base-rate event, which makes accurate predictions exceedingly difficult (Meehl & Rosen, 1955). Countless empirical studies had consistently shown error rates in predicting dangerousness to be exceedingly high. In 1981, Monahan published a widely influential book entitled *Predicting Violent Behavior: An Assessment of Clinical Techniques,* which delineated some of the difficulties encountered in conducting good research in the area of the prediction of violence. The research that has since followed from Monahan's recommendations (1981, 1984, 1988) has been methodologically superior to previous research, with results that are directly applicable to improved clinical assessment. Furthermore, the base rates in some specific populations, such as violent offenders, is sufficiently high to make predictions feasible.

The change from the prediction of dangerousness to the assessment of risk involves thinking about and assessing those factors that will increase or decrease the probability that an individual will become violent in the future. Instead of attempting to make a prediction about a particular individual (and whether he or she is dangerous), the focus changed to an examination of those situational and dispositional factors that would increase or decrease the probability that a particular individual will become violent. Several risk-assessment instruments have been developed to guide evaluators through a consideration of particularly important and empirically-derived variables (see Boer, Hart, Kropp, & Webster, 1997; Kropp, Hart, Webster, & Eaves, 1995; Webster, Douglas, Eaves, & Hart, 1997; Webster, Harris, Rice, Cormier, & Quinsey, 1994).

EYEWITNESS IDENTIFICATION AND TESTIMONY

The reliability and validity of eyewitness identification and eyewitness testimony constitute an area in which psychologists often serve as researchers and expert witnesses, both in criminal and in civil cases. Involvement as an expert witness has increased substantially in recent years, spurred on by the publication of two major books in the late 1970s (Loftus, 1979; Yarmey, 1979) and numerous articles since that time. Much research has been conducted and numerous articles and books written about the fallibilities of eyewitnesses (see Wells, 1997; Wells & Loftus, 1984; Wells et al.,

1998). The research tends to show that the identification of suspects by eyewitnesses is often unreliable (Wells, 1993), and in addition, that an individual's memory of an event can be altered in numerous ways (e.g., through fabrication, forgetting, and even more subtle means). For example, Loftus (1993) has shown that even the way in which a question is asked can alter an individual's response.

The research findings on eyewitness identification and eyewitness testimony have not been without scrutiny. The validity of some of the research findings on eyewitness behavior has been questioned, particularly with respect to the limited theoretical integration of the findings and the lack of demonstrated generalizability to real-life witness situations due to heavy reliance on laboratory research (Wells, 1993). Some researchers have made attempts to address these criticisms by making the experimental situations more realistic (e.g., Malpass & Devine, 1980).

The research on eyewitness testimony and eyewitness identification has recently taken a step beyond simply describing and identifying problems with eyewitnesses. Much of the research has begun to focus on how to remedy the problems associated with eyewitness identification and testimony so as to decrease the potential negative impact on the effective functioning of the criminal justice system. Wells and colleagues have developed a series of recommendations to be used by law enforcement officials when conducting lineup and photo-spread procedures (Wells et al., 1998). In addition, a number of the prominent researchers in this field joined together to form the National Institute of Justice's Technical Working Group for Eyewitness Evidence, and have recently published a manual entitled *Eyewitness Evidence: A Guide for Law Enforcement* (1999).

JURY RESEARCH

Social scientists in the field of psychology and law have been called upon to serve as trial consultants and are often involved in the selection of jurors in both criminal and civil trials. They have conducted surveys of communities to determine demographic composition, attitudes about the defendant, or key issues involved in a particular case, such as the appropriateness of capital punishment or the influence of pretrial publicity. Social scientists, however, have sometimes gone beyond simply ensuring that a jury represents a fair cross-section of a community, by attempting to select jurors who would be biased in favor of a particular outcome. The ethical and legal implications of social science's involvement in juror selection have been debated, of course. Opponents have argued that such selection is costly, is biased against indigent and other defendants who are unable to afford social scientists, and could be used as easily to provide jurors in favor of the prosecution as it could for the defense (Berman & Sales, 1977).

Perhaps the most persuasive argument against social science's involvement in jury selection is that there is little empirical support for the idea that the composition of the jury is a major factor influencing the verdict. In fact, there is considerable evidence that the verdict is based more on the evidence presented than on demographic characteristics of the jury (Fulero & Penrod, 1990) or on characteristics of the defendant, such as attractiveness (Kalven & Zeisel, 1966), although research on the influence of defendant

characteristics has produced conflicting results (Loftus & Monahan, 1980).

A recent review of the body of literature on jury research that has been conducted over the past two decades indicated that a relatively large proportion of this research has focused on questions related to witness performance and litigation strategies, and that a somewhat smaller proportion has focused on evaluation of evidence; capital punishment, death qualification, and other sentencing; juror characteristics; offender, plaintiff, and offense characteristics; criminal defense strategies; and judicial instructions (Nietzel, McCarthy, & Kern, 1999). These authors identified four areas of research that constitute "major jury research controversies," as each area has mixed results, a sizeable literature, important practical implications, and potential social policy ramifications. These four areas are: the relationship between attitudes toward the death penalty and verdicts or evaluations of evidence; the effects of judicial instructions on understanding and behavior; the influence of expert testimony by mental health professionals on verdicts and decision making; and the influence of certain litigation strategies on verdicts and decision making (see Nietzel et al., 1999).

One of the most prominent criticisms of jury research is that the conclusions have been based on simulated jury situations rather than on actual juror behavior (Nietzel et al., 1999). A recent review of the literature indicated that empirical studies of real jurors or juries were relatively rare (Nietzel et al., 1999); however, some research on real juries is being conducted (e.g., Heuer & Penrod, 1994; Vidmar, 1994). Although well-conducted simulation studies can teach us about real-life jury phenomena, a trend toward greater methodological realism is evident in the literature, and the continuation of this trend has been encouraged (Nietzel et al., 1999).

COMPETENCY AND RESPONSIBILITY

Several types of competency are relevant to and centrally involve psychologists interested in legal issues. One of the most prominent, "competency to stand trial," is a legal term that refers to procedures allowing for the postponement of the trial of defendants who are determined to be incompetent (i.e., not able to communicate properly with their attornies and/or to participate fully in their own defenses; see Roesch, Zapf, Golding, & Skeem, 1998, for a review). Other types of criminal competencies include competence to waive Miranda warnings, competency to plead guilty, and competency to be executed. Civil competencies that are relevant to the field of psychology and law include competency to make treatment decisions, competency to participate in research, and testamentary capacity, to name but a few.

Grisso has written extensively about the assessment of different competencies in adults (1986; Grisso & Appelbaum, 1998a) and juveniles (Grisso, 1998a). In addition, Grisso has been involved in the development of a number of instruments to assess different competencies (see Grisso, 1986, 1988, 1998b; and see Grisso & Appelbaum, 1998b). In 1986, Grisso coined the term "forensic assessment instruments," and since that time there has been a move toward the development of these instruments to assist evaluators in assessing the criteria required by a defendant for competency to stand trial (e.g., Everington, 1990; Golding, 1993; Golding, Roesch, & Schreiber, 1984; Poythress et al., 1999; Roesch, Zapf, Eaves, & Webster, 1998). Perhaps one of the most extensive competency research and development initiatives is that of the MacArthur Foundation Research Network on Mental Health and the Law. The end result of the MacArthur Network's research initiative was the development of two competency assessment instruments: the MacArthur Competence Assessment Tool—Criminal Adjudication (MacCAT-CA; Poythress et al., 1999) and the Mac-Arthur Competence Assessment Tool—Treatment (MacCAT-T; Grisso & Appelbaum, 1998b).

The competence of mental patients and prisoners to consent to treatment as well as to participate in research is a matter of some concern and debate (Grisso & Appelbaum, 1998a). For a long time in the history of our treatment of such individuals, the issue of consent was not even considered. It was assumed that commitment to a mental hospital or sentence to a prison gave the institutional authorities the right to treat individuals in whatever manner those authorities deemed appropriate. This view was challenged in the courts, and several decisions held that institutionalized persons do indeed have a right to refuse treatment (Winick, 1997).

The issue of criminal responsibility involves determining the appropriateness of a defense of insanity for criminal defendants. Although state laws vary, the basic philosophy is that to convict a person who is charged with a crime, he or she must be considered responsible for his or her criminal behavior. That is, the criminal behavior must have been a product of free will. If a defendant's behavior was not a product of free will, then he or she should not be held responsible for the crime (see Golding, Skeem, Roesch, & Zapf, 1998, for a review of criminal responsibility). There have been several variations on the requisite criteria for a defense of insanity (e.g., Perlin, 1994; Steadman et al., 1993). Currently, the modal insanity defense criteria involve either formulations of the American Law Institute (ALI) or restricted versions of the traditional M'Naghten test. The American Law Institute, Section 4.01, proposed the legal test that: "A person is not responsible for criminal conduct if at the time of such conduct as a result of mental disease or defect he lacks substantial capacity either to appreciate the criminality (or wrongfulness) of his conduct or to conform his conduct to the requirements of law." The M'Naghten test stipulates that a person is not responsible for his or her actions if "laboring under such a defect of reason, from disease of the mind, as not to know the nature and quality of the act, or, did not know it was wrong." Defendants found not guilty by reason of insanity are technically acquitted of their crimes, but most states automatically confine these defendants to an institution for an indefinite length of time.

Since the much-publicized trial of John W. Hinckley, Jr., who was found not guilty by reason of insanity (NGRI) after his attempt to kill President Ronald Reagan in 1981, a great deal of court reform and legislative revision with regard to the insanity defense has occurred. Three states have abolished the insanity defense altogether, and others have instituted alternatives such as "diminished responsibility" and "guilty but mentally ill" (GBMI) provisions. These alternatives allow for a finding of guilt but a reduction in either the seriousness of the charge or the severity of the punishment if mental disorder was determined to have influenced the criminal act.

Since mental illness is the basis of the insanity defense, mental health professionals have been heavily involved in assessments of defendants' mental states. Psychiatrists and psychologists often testify on the issue and make recommendations concerning the defendant's responsibility. As in the case of competency to stand trial, forensic assessment instruments (e.g., Rogers, Wasyliw, & Cavanaugh, 1984) and semi-structured protocols (e.g., Melton et al., 1997) have been developed to assist evaluators in assessing mental state at the time of an offense.

TREATMENT

A frequent role of psychologists is one of providing a variety of treatments to individuals in both the mental health and criminal justice systems. Issues surrounding the provision of these services are considered separately for each system.

In mental health, the concept of a right to treatment has received a great deal of attention. A number of legal decisions have established the right of mental patients in institutions to a certain minimum standard of treatment. These decisions have done much to advance the treatment of mental patients, although they have been criticized for not going far enough. For example, *Wyatt v. Stickney* (325 F. Supp. 781, 1972) ordered that a mental hospital must have a certain professional-to-patient ratio; that patients must have individual treatment plans; and that patients had the right to refuse certain treatments. The decision did not specify standards with respect to the nature or potential effectiveness of the treatments. If a treatment is not likely to be effective or does not have to be given in an institution, then the establishment of a right to such treatment is a hollow victory.

Two of the most significant changes in mental health were the reform of civil commitment statutes and deinstitutionalization. Psychologists who provide treatment either in institutions or outpatient settings are affected by these changes and, in fact, were sometimes instrumental in achieving reform. With regard to civil commitment, the involuntary commitment of individuals to mental hospitals was made more difficult. Persons who are simply mentally ill can no longer be routinely committed. Rather, there must be evidence that they may become dangerous to themselves or to others; and, because of the increasing availability of psychotropic medications that serve to reduce psychotic symptoms, many long-term patients have been released from the mental hospitals. Finally, many more patients were discharged from institutions as a result of deinstitutionalization. The long-term impact of these changes was not as substantial as the reformers had hoped. While the changes in the commitment laws and deinstitutionalization did substantially reduce the number of patients in mental hospitals, the impact of these reforms was such that many of these chronically mentally-ill individuals are now living homeless on the streets or have become entangled in the criminal justice system (see Teplin, 1984; 1991) and are not getting the mental health services they require.

In the criminal justice system, mental health professionals are involved with treating three types of populations: those mentally disordered offenders who have not yet been adjudicated and, therefore, are at the pretrial stage; those mentally disordered offenders who have been adjudicated and have been incarcerated in either a correctional or a forensic facility; and those non-mentally ill individuals who have been incarcerated. Each of these three groups will be discussed separately.

In the majority of cases, individuals who are mentally ill are seen by mental health professionals at the pretrial stage for either an evaluation of competency to stand trial or an assessment of mental state at the time of the offense. Statues regarding the treatment of these offenders vary from state to state. Generally, mental health professionals are more involved with assessment of mental state and competency in this population of individuals than with treatment. Those individuals who are found by the court to be incompetent to stand trial are usually remanded to a forensic facility for treatment to restore competency. Once an incompetent individual is restored to competency, the court then proceeds with his or her trial.

The treatment of those mentally disordered offenders who have already been adjudicated usually occurs within the context of a secure mental health facility (forensic facility) or a special unit or wing within a prison or jail. Those mentally disordered defendants who were adjudicated to be insane are usually sent to a forensic facility where they are legally required to undergo mental health treatment (see Heilbrun & Griffin, 1999, for a review of some of these programs). Those mentally disordered defendants who were adjudicated as guilty and incarcerated are sent to jail or prison, where they may or may not receive mental health treatment. Unfortunately, jails and prisons typically offer little in the way of mental health treatment (Roesch, Ogloff, Zapf, Hart, & Otto, 1998) and, as a result, individuals who require treatment (and who are willing and able to consent to treatment) do not always receive it. Steadman, McCarty, and Morrissey (1989) conducted a national survey of jail mental health services and found that their emphases were problem identification and administering medication. The majority of programs offered some type of drug or alcohol service, but psychological counseling was available in less than half of the jails surveyed. Some researchers have argued that pretrial jail facilities are highly appropriate places for mental health interventions (Ogloff & Roesch, 1992), as this is the entry point into the criminal justice system for many offenders. Screening programs at pretrial facilities allow those individuals who are in need of mental health treatment to be identified. The critical component involved in confirming that individuals who are in need of treatment actually receive the appropriate services is a mechanism whereby these individuals can be followed, first, through the different components of the criminal justice system, and then, especially, upon release, to ensure continuity of care (see Steadman et al., 1989; Ogloff & Roesch, 1992). Steadman(1992) used the term "boundary spanners" to characterize those individuals who fulfill this role and who are able to cross over the boundaries of the separate systems and ensure that the needed services are being provided.

The appropriateness of treatment as applied to non-mentally ill criminal populations has been questioned, as has the effectiveness of such treatment. Throughout the 1980s and 1990s, the ideology behind the criminal justice system in the United States has shifted toward an attitude of "incapacitation through incarceration"

(Barr, 1992, cited in Wrightsman, Nietzel, & Fortune, 1998) and away from rehabilitation. With more offenders being incarcerated for longer periods of time and with the prevailing ideology of the criminal justice system, the jails and prisons in the United States are extremely populated; and, as a result, it has become difficult to provide treatment programs that effectively target specific offending behavior and reduce recidivism. In addition, some have questioned whether it is even possible to treat criminal behavior. Research has focused on attempting to determine what types of treatment work best for which types of offenders and crimes (see Kratcoski, 1989, and Lester, Braswell, & Van Voorhis, 1992, for reviews).

THE IMPACT OF PSYCHOLOGY

Has psychological research and theory had an impact on the legal system? It undoubtedly has, but the exact degree to which it has is unknown. That the courts have cited psychological research in some of their decisions and have allowed the APA to submit amicus briefs, which are objective, non-partisan summaries of the literature on a specific topic, suggests that psychological research is having some impact on the legal system. The influence of any social science data on policy decisions is often indirect, and it is rare that a single study, or even an entire body of research, would dictate a legal decision or policy. It is possible that legal and policy decisions are made quite independently of data, with confirming research being used to make the decision appear more scientific and disconfirming research being ignored. Furthermore, as Monahan (1980) points out, the same body of research can be used to support two very different policies. He uses the example of prediction research to show how the findings can be used to support either greater or lesser use of prisons.

While social scientists typically do not have control over the way in which their data are applied, there is little doubt that empirical data can be useful in legal decision-making (Roesch, Golding, Hans, & Reppucci, 1991). Tanke and Tanke (1979) suggested that to have a greater impact, "social scientists must (a) identify empirical questions relevant to judicial decisions, (b) consult with legal experts to develop experimental research and criticism designed to produce information relevant to legal issues, and (c) present such information in a manner that is timely and merits acceptance by the judicial process" (p. 1134). In addition, Zapf and Roesch (1999) have argued that in order to adequately disseminate psychological research that may have an impact on the legal system, psychologists need to publish more of their research findings in a format that is familiar to (and in resources that are easily accessible to) legal professionals. That is, they need to publish in legal journals and periodicals as well as in psychological ones.

CONCLUSIONS

The preceding reviewed a number of issues in which psychologists have become involved in the legal arena. In the coming years, psychologists are likely to continue to increase their involvement, and, potentially, their impact. From an empirical perspective, research addressing a number of questions arising out of legal decisions or procedures will continue to be necessary in order to expand and refine the field. The continued effects of deinstitutionalization, greater external validity of jury decision-making studies, the effectiveness and appropriateness of treatment of offenders, the issues of consent and the right to refuse treatment, and the ability to accurately assess risk for violence are but a few of the important questions that need to be addressed continually in the form of empirical research.

REFERENCES

Bazelon, D. L. (1975). A jurist's view of psychiatry. *Journal of Psychiatry and Law, 3,* 175–190.

Berman, J., & Sales, B. D. (1977). A critical evaluation of the systematic approach to jury selection. *Criminal Justice and Behavior, 4,* 219–240.

Bersoff, D. N. (1999). Preparing for two cultures: Education and training in law and psychology. In R. Roesch, S. D. Hart, & J. R. P. Ogloff (Eds.), *Psychology and law: The state of the discipline* (pp. 375–401). New York: Kluwer Academic/Plenum.

Bersoff, D. N., Goodman-Delahunty, J., Grisso, J. T., Hans, V. P., Poythress, N. G., & Roesch, R. G. (1997). Training in law and psychology: Models from the Villanova conference. *American Psychologist, 52,* 1301–1310.

Boer, D. P., Hart, S. D., Kropp, P. R., & Webster, C. D. (1997). *Manual for the Sexual Violence Risk—20: Professional guidelines for assessing risk of sexual violence.* Burnaby, BC: Mental Health, Law, and Policy Institute, Simon Fraser University.

Brodsky, S. L. (1999). *The expert expert witness: More maxims and guidelines for testifying in court.* Washington, DC: APA.

Ceci, S. J., & Hembrooke, H. (Eds.). (1998). *Expert witness in child abuse cases: What can and should be said in court.* Washington, DC: APA.

Ennis, B. J., & Litwack, T. R. (1974). Psychiatry and the presumption of expertise: Flipping coins in the courtroom. *California Law Review, 62,* 693–752.

Everington, C. T. (1990). The Competence Assessment for Standing Trial for Defendants with Mental Retardation (CAST-MR): A validation study. *Criminal Justice and Behavior, 17*(2), 147–168.

Fulero, S. M., & Penrod, S. D. (1990). Attorney jury selection folklore: What do they think and how can psychologists help? *Forensic Reports, 3,* 233–259.

Golding, S. L. (1993). *Interdisciplinary Fitness Interview-Revised: A training manual.* State of Utah Division of Mental Health.

Golding, S. L., Roesch, R., & Schreiber, J. (1984). Assessment and conceptualization of competency to stand trial: Preliminary data on the Interdisciplinary Fitness Interview. *Law and Human Behavior, 8,* 321–334.

Golding, S. L., Skeem, J. L., Roesch, R., & Zapf, P. A. (1998). The assessment of criminal responsibility: A historical approach to a current controversy. In I. B. Weiner & A. K. Hess (Eds.), *Handbook of forensic psychology* (2nd ed., pp. 379–408). New York: Wiley.

Grisso, T. (1986). *Evaluating competencies: Forensic assessments and instruments.* New York: Plenum.

Grisso, T. (1988). *Competency to stand trial evaluations: A manual for practice.* Sarasota, FL: Professional Resource Exchange.

Grisso, T. (1998a). *Forensic evaluation of juveniles.* Sarasota, FL: Professional Resource Press.

Grisso, T. (1998b). *Instruments for assessing understanding and appreciation of Miranda rights.* Odessa, FL: Psychological Assessment Resources.

Grisso, T., & Appelbaum, P. S. (1998a). *Assessing competence to consent to treatment: A guide for physicians and other health professionals.* New York: Oxford University Press.

Grisso, T., & Appelbaum, P. S. (1998b). *MacArthur Competence Assessment Tool for Treatment (MacCAT-T).* Sarasota, FL: Professional Resource Exchange.

Hart, S. D., & Hare, R. D. (1992). Predicting fitness to stand trial: The relative power of demographic, criminal, and clinical variables. *Forensic Reports, 5,* 53–65.

Heilbrun, K., & Griffin, P. (1999). Forensic treatment: A review of programs and research. In R. Roesch, S. D. Hart, & J. R. P. Ogloff (Eds.), *Psychology and law: The state of the discipline* (pp. 241–274). New York: Kluwer Academic/Plenum.

Heuer, L., & Penrod, S. (1994). Juror notetaking and question asking during trials: A national field experiment. *Law and Human Behavior, 18,* 121–150.

Kalven, H., & Zeisel, H. (1966). *The American jury.* Boston: Little, Brown.

Kratcoski, P. C. (1989). *Correctional counseling and treatment* (2nd ed.). Prospectus Heights, IL: Waveland.

Kropp, P. R., Hart, S. D., Webster, C. D., & Eaves, D. (1995). *Manual for the spousal assault risk assessment guide* (2nd ed.). Vancouver, BC: The British Columbia Institute Against Family Violence.

Lester, D., Braswell, M., & Van Voorhis, P. (1992). *Correctional counseling* (2nd ed.). Cincinnati: Anderson.

Loftus, E. F. (1993). Psychologists in the eyewitness world. *American Psychologist, 48,* 550–552.

Loftus, E. F., & Monahan, J. (1980). Trial by data: Psychological research as legal evidence. *American Psychologist, 35,* 270–283.

Malpass, R. S., & Devine, P. G. (1980). Realism and eyewitness identification research. *Law and Human Behavior, 4,* 347–358.

Meehl, P. E., & Rosen, A. (1955). Antecedent probability and the efficiency of psychometric signs, patterns, or cutting scores. *Psychological Bulletin, 52,* 194–216.

Melton, G. B., Petrila, J., Poythress, N. G., & Slobogin, C. (1997). *Psychological evaluations for the courts: A handbook for mental health professionals and lawyers* (2nd ed.). New York: Guilford.

Monahan, J. (Ed.). (1980). *Who is the client?: The ethics of psychological intervention in the criminal justice system.* Washington, DC: APA.

Monahan, J. (1981). *Predicting violent behavior: An assessment of clinical techniques.* Beverly Hills, CA: Sage.

Monahan, J. (1984). The prediction of violent behavior: Toward a second generation of theory and policy. *American Journal of Psychiatry, 141,* 10–15.

Monahan, J. (1988). Risk assessment of violence among the mentally disordered: Generating useful knowledge. *International Journal of Law and Psychiatry, 11,* 249–257.

National Institute of Justice, Technical Working Group for Eyewitness Evidence (1999). *Eyewitness evidence: A guide for law enforcement.* Washington, DC: Author.

Neitzel, M. T., McCarthy, D. M., & Kern, M. J. (1999). Juries: The current state of the empirical literature. In R. Roesch, S. D. Hart, & J. R. P. Ogloff (Eds.), *Psychology and law: The state of the discipline* (pp. 23–52). New York: Kluwer Academic/Plenum.

Ogloff, J. R. P., & Roesch, R. (1992). Using community mental health centers to provide comprehensive mental health services to jails. In J. R. P. Ogloff (Ed.), *Psychology and law: The broadening of the discipline* (pp. 241–260). Durham, NC: Carolina Academic Press.

Perlin, M. (1994). *The jurisprudence of the insanity defense.* Durham, NC: Carolina Academic Press.

Poythress, N. G. (1980). Coping on the witness stand: "Learned responses" to "learned treatises." *Professional Psychology, 11,* 139–149.

Poythress, N. G., Nicholson, R., Otto, R. K., Edens, J. F., Bonnie, R. J., Monahan, J., & Hoge, S. K. (1999). *The MacArthur Competence Assessment Tool—Criminal Adjudication (MacCAT-CA).* Odessa, FL: Psychological Assessment Resources.

Robitscher, J. (1978). The limits of psychiatric authority. *International Journal of Law and Psychiatry, 1,* 183–204.

Roesch, R., & Golding, S. L. (1980). *Competency to stand trial.* Urbana: University of Illinois Press.

Roesch, R., Golding, S. L., Hans, V. P., & Reppucci, N. D. (1991). Social science and the courts: The role of amicus curiae briefs. *Law and Human Behavior, 15,* 1–11.

Roesch, R., Ogloff, J. R. P., Zapf, P. A., Hart, S. D., & Otto, R. (1998). Jail and prison inmates. In N. N. Singh (Ed.), *Comprehensive clinical psychology: Vol. 9. Application in diverse populations.* New York: Elsevier.

Roesch, R., Zapf, P. A., Eaves, D., & Webster, C. D. (1998). *The fitness interview test* (rev. ed.). Burnaby, BC: Mental Health, Law, and Policy Institute, Simon Fraser University.

Roesch, R., Zapf, P. A., Golding, S. L., & Skeem, J. (1998). Defining and assessing competency to stand trial. In I. B. Weiner & A. K. Hess (Eds.), *Handbook of forensic psychology* (2nd ed., pp. 327–349). New York: Wiley.

Rogers, R., Wasyliw, O. E., & Cavanaugh, J. L. (1984). Evaluating insanity: A study of construct validity. *Law and Human Behavior, 8,* 293–303.

Steadman, H. J. (1992). Boundary spanners: A key component for the effective interactions of the justice and mental health systems. *Law and Human Behavior, 16,* 75–87.

Steadman, H. J., McCarty, D. W., & Morrissey, J. P. (1989). *The mentally ill in jail: Planning for essential services.* New York: Guilford.

Steadman, H. J., McGreevy, M. A., Morrissey, J., Callahan, L. A., Robins, P. C., & Cirincione, C. (1993). *Before and after Hinckley: Evaluating insanity defense reform.* New York: Guilford.

Szasz, T. S. (1963). *Law, liberty, and psychiatry.* New York: Macmillan.

Tanke, E. D., & Tanke, T. J. (1979). Getting off a slippery slope: Social science in the judicial process. *American Psychologist, 34,* 1130–1138.

Teplin, L. A. (1984). The criminalization of the mentally ill: Speculation in search of data. In L. A. Teplin (Ed.), *Mental health and criminal justice* (pp. 63–85). Newbury Park, CA: Sage.

Teplin, L. A. (1991). The criminalization hypothesis: Myth, misnomer, or management strategy? In S. A. Shah & B. D. Sales (Eds.), *Law and mental health: Major developments and research needs* (pp. 149–183). Rockville, MD: US Department of Health and Human Services.

Vidmar, N. (1994). Making inferences about jury behavior from jury verdict statistics: Cautions about the Lorelei's Lied. *Law and Human Behavior, 18,* 599–619.

Webster, C. D., Douglas, K. S., Eaves, D., & Hart, S. D. (1997). *HCR-20: Assessing risk for violence* (version 2). Burnaby, BC: Mental Health, Law, and Policy Institute, Simon Fraser University.

Webster, C. D., Harris, G. T., Rice, M. E., Cormier, C., & Quinsey, V. L. (1994). *The violence prediction scheme: Assessing dangerousness in high risk men.* Toronto, ON: Centre of Criminology, University of Toronto.

Wells, G. L. (1993). What do we know about eyewitness identification? *American Psychologist, 48,* 553–571.

Wells, G. L. (1997). Eyewitness identification. In D. Faigman, D. Kaye, M. Saks, & J. Sanders (Eds.), *Modern scientific evidence: The law and science of expert testimony* (pp. 451–479). St. Paul, MN: West.

Wells, G. L., & Loftus, E. F. (1984). *Eyewitness testimony: Psychological perspectives.* New York: Cambridge University Press.

Wells, G. L., Small, M., Penrod, S. J., Malpass, R. S., Fulero, S. M., & Brimacombe, C. A. E. (1998). Eyewitness identification procedures: Recommendations for lineups and photospreads. *Law and Human Behavior, 22,* 603–647.

Winick, B. J. (1997). *The right to refuse mental health treatment.* Washington, DC: APA.

Wrightsman, L. S., Nietzel, M. T., & Fortune, W. H. (1998). *Psychology and the legal system.* New York: Brooks/Cole.

Yarmey, A. D. (1979). *The psychology of eyewitness testimony.* New York: Free Press.

Zapf, P. A., & Roesch, R. (1999). *Evaluations of competency: Guidelines for legal professionals.* Manuscript submitted for publication.

Ziskin, J., & Faust, D. (1988). *Coping with psychiatric and psychological testimony* (4th ed., Vols. 1–3). Los Angeles: Law and Psychology Press.

Ziskin, J. (1995). *Coping with psychiatric and psychological testimony* (5th ed., Vols. 1–3). Los Angeles: Law and Psychology Press.

R. ROESCH
Simon Fraser University

P. A. ZAPF
University of Alabama

COMPETENCY TO STAND TRIAL
EXPERT TESTIMONY
EYEWITNESS TESTIMONY
FORENSIC PSYCHOLOGY
PSYCHOLOGY AND THE COURTS

PSYCHOLOGY OF MUSIC

The first book specifically devoted to the psychology of music was *Tonpsychologie* by Carl Stumpf in 1883. In this book, he presented his theory of consonance and dissonance in music. He believed that tones played simultaneously and that tended to fuse together were judged to be consonant.

The field of the psychology of music has been defined in a number of different ways. Seashore, in his *Psychology of Music,* wrote about the "musical mind," which could respond to the elements of sound. The mind also possessed certain innate aptitudes or talents, which, with proper nurturing, could enable the person to be a proficient artist. There were, of course, variations in the degrees of these talents. More recently, Farnsworth in *The Social Psychology of Music* and Lundin in *An Objective Psychology of Music* have thought in more behavioral terms. Basically, people deal with a variety of perceptual, discriminative, affective, or motor responses to musical stimuli.

THE DIMENSIONS OF TONE

From a physical standpoint, a sound wave has various properties, such as frequency (number of cycles per second), intensity (amount of pressure on the ear), quality (the shape of the wave created by overtones), and duration (how long the tone is sounded). On the psychological or behavioral dimension, one responds to frequency in terms of *pitch,* that is, how high or low the tone is judged to be. In *loudness,* the concern is with how strong or weak the tone is. *Timbre* relates to the quality of the sound. Thus with some experience one may discriminate among the sounds of different musical instruments: flute, oboe, strings, brass, and so forth. The duration of the tone refers to time in music, whether the tone is short or long.

The human ear can respond to frequencies from about 20 to 20,000 hz and is most sensitive to tones in ranges of 2,000 to 4,000 hz. Thus both pitch and loudness are dependent on both frequency and intensity, and are not simple correlates of each other.

Rhythm must also be taken into account as one of the basic components of music. It consists of various patterns of tones in terms of how long they are played and which are accented (greater loudness). A march rhythm would typically be heard in terms of loud-soft-loud-soft (/-/-) or a waltz rhythm in terms of loud-soft-soft (/—). Rhythmic units are not haphazard, but are organized in regular and orderly patterns. The psychological aspects of rhythm involve both perceptual and motor responses. One hears the pattern or, if playing a musical instrument, creates the rhythm.

Another area of concern to psychologists of music involves the kinds of emotions and feelings that occur upon listening to or playing various kinds of music. These reactions can be measured by changes in physiological functions, such as heart rate, blood pressure, breathing, or the galvanic skin response. Also, a person can make a verbal report as to what is being felt: joy, sadness, exhilaration, triumph, and so on. In one experiment, Dreher found that musical people showed greater affective responding when listening to music than did nonmusical people, when this activity was measured on the psychogalvanometer. In a number of experiments, Hevner constructed an adjective circle on which subjects could check which terms characterized how they felt when listening to a variety of musical selections. She found that music performed at a fast tempo tended to be judged as happy and exciting, whereas slow music tended to be rated as calm, dignified, and tender. Furthermore, selections in which high pitches were stressed were described as happy and sprightly and those at low pitches tended to be judged as sad or majestic. Music that stressed strong beats in the rhythmic pattern were described as dignified and vigorous; the smoother flowing rhythms were described as happy and playful.

The rise and fall of affective judgments (pleasant to unpleasant) upon frequent hearings of various selections tend to vary with the nature of the composition, as well as the number of repetitions of a selection. So-called popular music rises rapidly in affective value with repetition, and then rapidly declines. For the musically educated, works of the great masters may rise more slowly in value at first, but continue to increase with repetition. More modern dissonant and atonal music tends to have generally less affective value, except for the most sophisticated musical listeners.

Farnsworth reported in *The Social Psychology of Music* a number of studies involving musical taste of professional musicians and musicologists drawn from surveys made of members of the American Society of Musicology. He found that musical tastes tended to be quite stable over the years. Bach and Beethoven were judged the most eminent composers in all four surveys, Mozart, Haydn, Handel, Schubert, and Wagner were always judged in the top 10, although there were some minor shifts in their positions from one survey to another.

What constitutes musical ability or talent? Psychologists such as Seashore have maintained that musical ability consists of many separate talents, which may or may not be related. These would include the ability to make fine discriminations in pitch, loudness, timbre, time, rhythm, and tonal memory. Mursell, in his *Psychol-*

ogy of Music, has taken a more holistic approach, indicating that musical talent involves an integration of different abilities.

The heredity-environment issue also applies to musical talent. Most researchers tend to agree that musical appreciation is strictly acquired. When the concern is with talent for performing or composing, disagreements arise. Seashore has taken a strong hereditary stand. Those stressing the importance of heredity cite certain lineages, such as the Bach family. Others who stress the important influence of environment would cite certain great composers, such as Haydn, who did not come from musical families.

Like measures of intelligence, a variety of standardized tests of musical aptitude are currently available. Although they have some predictive validity, in general, their predictions have not been as successful as those of intelligence tests. The best of the current tests include Seashore's Measures of Musical Talents, which measure degrees of discrimination for various auditory sensory capacities. The Drake Musical Aptitude Tests involve measures of musical memory and the ability to keep time. Wing's Standardized Tests of Musical Intelligence, developed in England, measure musical memory, tonal movement, tonal discrimination, and musical appreciation. The Gordon Musical Aptitude Profile tests for tonal imagery (melody and harmony), rhythmic imagery, and musical sensitivity.

Other areas of interest to psychologists of music include measures of musical performance and the effects of music on industrial production, as well as in offices and music therapy. There is experimental evidence that music can have positive effects. Music is used in occupational therapy where patients in mental hospitals can play or can perform together in bands, orchestras, and choruses. Listening to music can alter some emotional behaviors. For example, stimulating music, such as marches and lively dances, can have stimulating effects on the depressed, whereas calm music can help relieve excitement and anxiety. There is strong evidence that music generally aids the digestive processes. A number of universities have instituted both undergraduate and graduate programs in which the participants are trained in the proper use of music therapy.

REFERENCES

Farnsworth, P. R. (1969). *The social psychology of music* (2nd ed.). Iowa City: State University of Iowa Press.

Lundin, R. W. (1967/1953). *An objective psychology of music.* New York: Ronald Press.

Mursell, J. L. (1937). *The psychology of music.* New York: Norton.

Seashore, C. E. (1938). *The psychology of music.* New York: McGraw-Hill.

Stumpf, C. (1983). *Tonpsychologie* (2 vols.). Leipzig: Hirzel.

SUGGESTED READING

Davies, J. B. (1978). *The psychology of music.* Stanford, CA: Stanford University Press.

Michel, D. E. (1976). *Music therapy.* Springfield, IL: Thomas.

R. W. LUNDIN
Wheaton, IL

PSYCHOLOGY AND PHILOSOPHY

PSYCHOLOGY AND PHILOSOPHY

Concerns that are now typically part of contemporary psychology (What is the nature of the mind? What causes human happiness? How do humans come to believe or know?) were, until the end of the nineteenth century, part of the concerns of philosophers. In the latter part of the nineteenth century, investigators (e.g., Wundt) took an experimental approach to these questions, and contemporary psychology was born. Although empirical and experimental methods allow psychologists to address questions commonly outside the scope of philosophy (e.g., what is the incidence of depression?), philosophical concerns surround these empirical pursuits. Wittgenstein said, "In psychology there are experimental methods and conceptual confusion." Thus, one "philosophical" pursuit within scientific psychology is the analytic philosopher's metric: conceptual explication.

NATURALIZED EPISTEMOLOGY

Arguably, the central philosophical problem within psychology is the problem of knowledge. Psychologists want to gain and use knowledge, and seek to construct epistemologically sound methods for doing so. Thus, the question of which method(s) can be used to gain knowledge about a particular subject matter is of central concern in contemporary psychology. It is central for three reasons: (a) scientific psychology has made slow progress and it is difficult not to at least partially blame this on the limitations of its research methods; (b) the phenomena studied by psychologists may be sufficiently different from the phenomena studied by other natural scientists that the wholesale adoption of the methods of natural science to psychology may be inappropriate; and (c) psychology empirically investigates learning, or the acquisition of knowledge, and therefore may provide indigenous naturalized epistemologies. The latter point is endorsed not only by psychologists but also by prominent philosophers such as Quine and Popper.

FOLK PSYCHOLOGY

Folk psychology is a nebulous collection of prescientific theories and implicit intuitions regarding human behavior. That is to say, we often explain behavior by invoking prescientific terms such as "want," "believe," "desire," and so on. Presumably, such terms are meaningful to the lay person and scientist alike. Philosophical interest in this phenomenon varies and is a function of the degree to which we believe we are able to translate such terms into the more rigorous lexicography of science. In the absence of a clear translation (reduction) into scientific terminology, we face the unenviable task of describing, for example, a belief. Those who point to the irreducibility of terms such as "belief" often cite the doctrine of intentionality to bolster their position. According to the doctrine of intentionality, the vernacular of folk psychology is first-person, or subjective, in nature and as such is not amenable to third-person scientific accounts. On the other side of the debate are those who argue that our intuitions regarding subjectivity and first-person qualitative experience are confused and lacking in real proof.

PHILOSOPHY OF MIND

Otherwise known as the mind/body problem, the problematic nature of this field of inquiry is typically traced to Descartes' (in)famous articulation of substance dualism (though both Plato and Aristotle weighed in on the issue). Two broadly construed solutions have been proposed to the mind/body problem: dualism and monism. Though the mind/body problem has changed significantly since Descartes' time, being construed now as the problem of consciousness, the various "solutions" to this problem, as stipulated by thinkers throughout history, still address the fundamental issue at hand.

Substance dualism is the thesis that there is an essential difference between minds (mental phenomena) and bodies (physical phenomena); mind is an essentially thinking substance and body is an essentially extended substance. Given this bifurcation of reality into two separate and unconnected domains, subsequent thinkers have developed theories aimed at ameliorating the difficulties associated with our common sense intuition that the mind and body do, in fact, interact. Psychophysical interactionism stipulates that bodily (brain) states cause corresponding mental states which, in turn, are capable of causally insubstantiating subsequent bodily states. Epiphenomenalism is the thesis that bodily (brain) states cause corresponding mental states, but that these mental states are causally ineffective at bringing about subsequent bodily states. As such, epiphenomenalism is a one-way interactionism: body to mind, but not the other way around. Psychophysical parallelism avoids the problem of interaction altogether by claiming that mental and physical states run parallel to one another, like two clocks each showing the same time, but do not interact.

Monism is the thesis that all of the objects of reality are of one kind. As such, monism is the explicit denial of the dualistic claim that mind and body are essentially different. Given our predilection toward discussing the topic in terms of the "mental" and the "physical," monistic theories are devoted to describing how one of these terms is reducible, or identical, to the other. Idealism is a kind of monism that states "all things are essentially mental or, at least, depend upon the mind for their existence." Materialism is a kind of monism that states "all things are physical" or that the mind just *is* the brain. Phenomenalism is a less popular variety of monism that stipulates that all empirical statements (including, but not limited to, statements about mental and physical states) are reducible to actual or possible phenomenal appearances. In general, any monistic theory that reduces both mind and body to another more fundamental reality or substance is labeled a dual aspect theory.

FREE WILL AND DETERMINISM

As psychological explanations of human behavior become more precise, belief in free will becomes more difficult to entertain. One who maintains that "humans are free agents" claims (at least implicitly) that (a) our psychological understanding of the causes of human behavior underdetermines the actual range and complexity of observed behavior and (b) no future scientific advances will eventuate in a theory that adequately accounts for the full range of human behavior. Those who adopt a deterministic position need not necessarily claim that current psychological theory does, in

fact, account for the entire range of human behavior. Rather, the determinist need only stipulate that such an all-embracing scientific account of human behavior is possible.

W. O'DONOHUE
A. LLOYD

**MIND/BODY PROBLEM
MONISM/DUALISM**

PSYCHOLOGY: HISTORY

Psychology has roots in philosophy, mythology, medicine, physiology, physics, and astronomy among other subjects, and these have influenced its history in complex and often indirect ways. About the turn of the 20th century the pioneer German psychologist Hermann Ebbinghaus (1850–1909) noted that "psychology has a long past, but only a short history" (Boring, 1950). The "long past," in which the philosophical roots of psychology gave rise to questions and speculations concerning the nature of the universe and of humanity itself, stretches back thousands of years. However, the "short history" of psychology as an independent scientific discipline, in which empirical methods were systematically applied to obtain knowledge about humans and their behavior, ranges only from the mid-19th century to the present.

It is difficult to judge the beginning of the recorded history of psychology. One of the earliest known documents dealing, in part, with psychological issues is the Edwin Smith Surgical Papyrus, named for the first Westerner who owned it (Breasted, 1930). This Egyptian document, which dates back to perhaps 3000 B.C., describes behavioral effects of head injuries, and the brain and its convolutions; its surgeon-author may have recognized in a primitive way that the brain controls behavior—a notion that became lost for thousands of years (Cadwallader, Cadwallader, & Semrau, 1974). Documents from Babylonia and other ancient civilizations also show a concern with what today would be called psychology.

The Western tradition in psychology is generally acknowledged to have originated in about the fifth century B.C. in Greece, a civilization to which so much of Western thought and history can be traced.

EARLY GREEK PHILOSOPHERS
Cosmologists

Greek cosmologists were concerned with the general question "What is the nature of the universe?" In attempting to answer this question they developed ways of conceptualizing their subject matter that would be reexplored numerous times as science and psychology developed. These included reduction to elements, emphasis on changes or processes, the importance of the order or arrangements of the elements, and attempts to understand nature in quantitative terms (Heidbreder, 1933).

Thales (c. 640–546 B.C.) was among the first to seek an explanation of nature within nature itself rather than resorting to external means such as mythology. He believed that water was the ultimate reality and that from it all other things were derived. Democritus (c. 460–362 B.C.) presented a more advanced cosmology by proposing that the universe was made of atoms, small particles of matter that moved in lawful ways. As a part of the universe, humans were also composed of atoms, including body atoms and soul atoms.

Heraclitus (c. 500 B.C.) believed that fire was the basis of the universe, but emphasized as its central characteristic the constantly changing nature of the universe. He believed that there were no solid or stable elements; the only reality was change. In noting that one could not step into the same stream twice and that "everything flows," he emphasized processes and change rather than things as the ultimate reality.

Anaxagoras (c. 500–428 B.C.), dissatisfied with simple reduction to elements as a means of explanation, proposed considering not only the elements themselves but also their arrangement or pattern to explain the cosmos. Pythagoras (c. 580–497 B.C.) argued that the universe could best be understood through numbers and thus provided one of the earliest applications of quantitative methods in gaining knowledge of the world.

Sophists

In contrast with the cosmologists, the Sophists believed that attempts to discover the nature of reality were essentially futile and turned instead to more practical concerns. They became teachers of philosophy, treating rhetoric and dialectic as skills to be learned and applied in everyday Greek life.

Socrates

As early philosophers struggled to explain the world and thus to know it, the question "How can we know?" arose, and philosophers became concerned with the validity of knowledge and with distinguishing between knowledge acquired through the senses and knowledge gained through reason (Watson, 1978). During this time of conflicting points of view between cosmologists and Sophists, Socrates (469–399 B.C.) influenced the history of philosophy in yet another direction.

Most of what is known about Socrates comes from the dialogues written by his pupil Plato (427–347 B.C.). Socrates, through the use of skillful questions (the "Socratic method"), led his students to question the most basic of their ideas and to employ reason to reveal truth and expose contradictions. Among those of his beliefs most influential in the later development of philosophy and psychology was his assertion that, while it is futile to inquire into the nature of the cosmos, it is possible to obtain knowledge of the self through reason and thus to discover one's duty and to live a virtuous life. To "know thyself" was a theme central to his teachings.

Plato

In the writings of Plato can be found numerous concepts that have profoundly influenced the development of philosophy. Plato formulated a distinction between what today is referred to as mind and body, distinguishing between *ideas* revealed by reason, and *things* revealed by the senses. Ideas can be perfect, but their concrete representations are ever changing and imperfect. Thus, according to Plato, there is a world of ideas of which the "real" world

revealed by the senses is only an imperfect copy. In addition to a distinction between mind and matter, Plato wrote on the "soul" and its powers, and on the importance of individual differences in fitting the abilities of men to their duties in the ideal state.

Aristotle

Plato's greatest pupil was Aristotle (384–322 B.C.), considered by some to be the first psychologist because—unlike Plato, whose psychological concepts are dispersed throughout his writings—Aristotle was the first to develop a systematic psychology and to organize some of his writings into treatises on psychological subjects. Both a philosopher and a scientist, Aristotle wrote extensively on all the areas of scientific interest of his time.

Aristotle's *De Anima* ("On the soul") was the first systematic treatise on psychology. In it he gave a view of the relationship of mind and matter differing from that of Plato. For Aristotle it was a question of the relationship between matter and form, with neither able to exist apart from the other. For example, marble was matter to the statue, while the statue was the realization of the form in marble. Aristotle discussed the senses and their functions, and classified the external senses into what has become the traditional way of viewing them: sight, hearing, smell, taste, and touch.

Aristotle's treatise *De Memoria et Reminiscentia* ("On memory and recollection") has had enormous influence on the development of psychology. The single most influential concept came to be known as association, which, through connecting ideas as they are experienced, enables their later retrieval as memories. Aristotle stated that association is a lawful process based either on contiguity (events experienced together will be remembered together), or on similarity or contrast. The concept of association has provided the nucleus for many 20th-century theories of learning, although theorists have disagreed widely concerning exactly *what* is associated—ideas, images, physical movements, stimuli and responses, or other aspects of behavior.

THE RISE OF CHRISTIANITY

Aristotle represented the height of Greek naturalism, with its unity of psyche, or soul, and body, and the combination of observation and reason to achieve knowledge. With the advent of Christianity, the evolution of psychology entered a new era in which naturalistic views yielded to *super*natural ones. The soul was no longer simply an aspect of the body's functioning, but came to be viewed instead as a separate entity, a spirit independent of the laws of nature governing the physical body. One consequence for psychology was the development of a dualistic view of mind and body. Another consequence was the development of the view that humans were different, and thus separate, from animals because of their eternal soul.

Plotinus

The concept of the soul as separate from the body was influenced by Plotinus (205–270 A.D.), who reworked some of Plato's concepts so that they were in harmony with Christian views. Whereas Plato had written of perfection occurring only in the world of ideas, Plotinus believed that humans should try to become as perfect as possible, so as to achieve the independence of the soul from the body.

While Plato had believed the soul was within the body, Plotinus believed it to be incorporeal, with soul and body united but never fused. The soul functioned in perceiving the world of the senses, in reflecting, and was conscious of itself.

Augustine

Believing that one must have faith in order to know, Augustine (354–430 A.D.) believed that introspection, or examination of one's inner feelings, provided a means of knowing the soul. This self-examination—an approach that was to reappear in a greatly modified way in scientific psychology—was, together with revelation, the means of achieving truth. Augustine believed that the soul provided a representation of the Holy Trinity through its three functions of reason, memory, and will. His concern for the nonmaterial world and his reliance on introspection led to his abandonment of objective science as a means of achieving knowledge, which, because of his great influence, impeded the progress of science (Watson, 1978).

THE DARK AND MIDDLE AGES

From the time of Augustine to Thomas Aquinas (1225–1274), little advance was made in the development of psychology. The Dark Ages, extending approximately from the fifth until the tenth centuries, were a time of decline for science and culture. The writings of Plato and Aristotle were largely lost to the Western world but eventually were restored by way of Eastern culture, which underwent a rise in power and influence even as the West declined. Not until the 12th and 13th centuries, and the founding and rise to prominence of great universities such as Paris and Oxford, did an active search for knowledge resume. Works of the Greek philosophers were translated from Arabic and again introduced into the West.

Aquinas

After becoming familiar with the works of Aristotle, Thomas Aquinas attempted to recapitulate Aristotle's ideas, which were pagan and naturalistic, within a Christian framework. Reason, which had been but one function of the body to Aristotle, became transmuted by Thomas Aquinas into the Christian soul, which lacked physical substance. Thus a dualistic view of mind and body, viewing them as two entities, became full-fledged, giving rise to the so-called "mind/body problem" that was to occupy so many later philosophers.

THE RENAISSANCE AND THE RISE OF MODERN PHILOSOPHY

The Renaissance in Europe occurred approximately from the mid-15th to the beginning of the 17th century. The invention of the printing press in 1450 sparked its beginning. Voyages of exploration took place, such as those of Columbus (1451–1506). In 1543 Nicolaus Copernicus (1473–1543) published the view that the center of our planetary system was the sun rather than the earth. Other influential events included the research and discoveries of Galileo (1564–1642) in astronomy, the discovery of the circulation of the blood in 1628 by William Harvey (1578–1657), and the use of the microscope by Anton van Leeuwenhoek (1632–1723) to discover,

in 1674, the existence of microorganisms. Each of these events, as well as many others, involved the use of empirical methods to gain knowledge, relying primarily on observed events rather than on conclusions based on logic but not supported through observed evidence. This shift in methodology was to have a profound effect on the development of a scientific psychology. However, prior to the direct application of scientific method to psychological concerns, there was a period in which philosophers again posed questions concerning human nature as, within the context of the Renaissance, modern philosophy arose.

Although philosophers considered and wrote on many problems within and beyond psychology, several problems can be singled out as having had great influence on the history of psychology: the *mind/body problem,* which dealt with how the now-separated mind and body were related to each other; *empiricism,* which saw sense perception as the source of our knowledge; and its counterpart, *nativism,* which held that some of our ideas and modes of perception were innate rather than acquired through the senses; and *associationism,* which considered what and how many the laws of association might be. Throughout the writings of the modern philosophers can be found variations of concepts introduced by the ancient Greek cosmologists and philosophers.

Descartes

The first of the great modern philosophers was René Descartes (1596–1650). In his *Discourse on Method* (1637) he approached the question of the source of knowledge by holding, as did others before him, that one can know truth through reason. He presented rules of procedure for distinguishing between truth and falsity and, in asking himself what he could be certain of without doubt, he established his first principle of truth in the statement "I think, therefore I am."

In his *Passions of the Soul* (1649), Descartes approached problems more directly psychological in nature. Among his most influential formulations were his mechanistic view of man and his interactionist solution to the mind/body problem. Influenced by the operation of moving machines or automata, and particularly by the elaborate fountains in the palace gardens of his day, in which pressing a hidden pedal activated the flow of water and caused a figure, such as a statue of Neptune, to move, Descartes viewed the human body as a machine, and therefore predictable in its behavior. The flow of animal spirits regulated the movements of muscles, much as the flow of water in the fountains regulated their actions. Ultimately such functions were regulated by the soul, which was separate from the body but interacted with it at a very specific point, the pineal gland. This point of interaction was chosen because, unlike other parts of the brain which were duplicated on each side, there was but one pineal gland, providing a point at which separate images of the two eyes or other senses could be united before arriving at the soul.

Leibnitz

A different solution to the mind/body problem was proposed by Gottfried Wilhelm von Leibnitz (1646–1716) in his theory of the monad, which, reminiscent of the elements of Democritus, he conceived to be an indestructible and immutable point of force that acted in preestablished harmony with other monads. Although there were mind monads and body monads, there could be no interaction between them because of their immutability. Mind and body acted in parallel, without interaction, and thus parallelism was formulated as a solution to the mind/body problem.

In considering the source of knowledge, Leibnitz likened the mind to a block of marble in which veins and patterns suggested that one figure rather than another should be carved, thus proposing that the mind was not a blank tablet but was instead predisposed to certain ideas. Leibnitz also pointed out that one can be influenced by perceptions of which one is not consciously aware. Using the roar of the sea as an example, Leibnitz asserted that while we hear the roar rather than the little noises of each wave, nevertheless each little wave affects us to some extent—a view anticipating the concept of sensory threshold.

Locke

Whereas Descartes had viewed reason as the route to truth, John Locke (1632–1704) popularized the empiricist view that the only source of knowledge was what could be learned from sense experience. While reason could be used to organize what was in the mind, nothing could be there that had not first gone through the senses.

In his *Essay Concerning Human Understanding* (1690), Locke argued vociferously against the existence of innate ideas, and against Leibnitz's notion that the mind could be influenced by stimuli of which it was unaware. For Locke the mind began as void of all characters and came to be filled through perception and reflection, assertions in which Locke echoed Aristotle. As evidence, Locke noted that a child was not born with ideas but acquired them only gradually. The nature and variety of experience determined the scope of mental contents.

Locke has in a way been canonized for coining the expression "the association of ideas" in a section of his *Essay* in which he wrote of ideas that have a "natural correspondence and connection one with another," and of ideas connected through "chance or custom"—notions similar to Aristotle's laws of association through similarity and contiguity.

For Locke, the distinction between things and ideas was expressed through his comparison between primary qualities, which were inherent in external objects and included characteristics such as form, motion, and number, and secondary qualities that could be experienced only in the mind as sensations, such as color, sound, and taste.

Psychology was profoundly influenced by Locke's denial of innate ideas and corresponding insistence on experience as the source of knowledge, and by his discussion of the association of ideas. He did not originate these conceptualizations, but his persuasive eloquence did much to embed them into the scholarly discussions of his day.

Berkeley

In his *Essay Toward a New Theory of Vision* of 1709, George Berkeley (1685–1753) argued against an innate ability to judge distance. Instead, he argued that distance perception involved cues such as the previously learned sizes of intermediate objects, as well as the association of particular distances with sensations arising from the

positions of the muscles moving the eyes. Berkeley was thus influential in developing arguments against innate ideas and in recognizing the role of association.

James and John Stuart Mill

In his *Analysis of the Phenomena of the Human Mind* of 1829, James Mill (1773–1836) argued for a view that mental experiences could be analyzed into two sorts of mental elements, sensations and simple ideas, which are joined by association to form more complex mental phenomena. The important idea for psychology was that analysis of complex mental events could yield an understanding of them through identifying their simpler elements. Thus complex ideas such as the idea of a wall could be broken down into simpler ideas of brick and mortar, together with ideas of position and quantity. James Mill saw complex ideas resulting from the straightforward combination of single ideas—a kind of mental mechanics—whereas his son John Stuart Mill (1806–1873) proposed a kind of mental chemistry, in which mental elements combined in such a way that the result was not a simple equivalent of the sum of the parts.

Although the writings of Locke, Berkeley, and others proposed empirical views concerning the source of knowledge, and while careful observation was instrumental in many of the conclusions reached, these philosophers did not achieve a science of the mind. What they did achieve was to lay a foundation of issues and questions that would later be investigated more directly in psychology's early laboratories. However, before this could happen, methodologies of scientific investigation first had to develop in other disciplines.

SCIENTIFIC ROOTS OF PSYCHOLOGY

By the mid-19th century enormous advances had occurred in a number of the sciences. The scientific revolution had already begun to have profound effects on Western culture and especially on academic culture. Although the observational sciences—especially astronomy, gross anatomy, and the classifying aspects of sciences such as systematic biology—had long been steadily making order out of nature's once seeming chaos, the 19th century's widespread adoption of the experimental approach led to profound advances in chemistry, physics, and physiology. This success led, in turn, to the introduction of the experimental approach into psychology, transforming it, during the second half of the 19th century, from a branch of speculative philosophy to an independent, experimental science.

In *A History of Experimental Psychology,* E. G. Boring identified a number of developments, primarily within the experimental physiology of the first half of the 19th century, that provided conceptual and methodological underpinnings for the development of experimental psychology.

Physiology of the Nervous System

Discoveries relating to the nature and organization of the nervous system included the discovery in 1780 of the electrical nature of the nerve impulse by Luigi Galvani (1737–1798); the discovery in 1811 by Sir Charles Bell (1774–1842) of the distinction between sensory and motor nerves; the argument in 1826 by Johannes Müller (1801–1858) that the sensory nerve fibers were divided into five kinds, one for each of the five senses; and the measurement of the speed of the nerve impulse in 1850 by Hermann L. F. von Helmholtz (1821–1894), who found it to be far slower than previously believed, and thus amenable to experimental investigation and measurement.

Localization of Function within the Brain

This issue was to some extent popularized by the spurious assertions of Franz Joseph Gall (1758–1828), who founded the movement of phrenology, which held that each mental function had its own area within the brain, and that excessive activity in any function could bring about an enlargement of the brain and thus of the skull. Such enlargements were thought to be detectable and thus to provide indices of personality and other traits.

Attempts to combat the doctrine of phrenology were influential in stimulating legitimate attempts to determine the localization of function within the brain, such as those of Pierre Flourens (1794–1867), who systematically extirpated parts of animal brains to determine their functions. In 1832 Marshall Hall (1790–1857) reported the results of experiments concerning the distinction between voluntary and involuntary movement, stimulating the study of reflex action. In 1861 Paul Broca (1824–1880) discovered the localization in the human brain of a center for speech, and in 1870 G. Fritsch and E. Hitzig discovered the localization of motor functions in the cerebral cortex.

The Personal Equation

From another realm of science, astronomy, came the discovery of individual differences in the ability of observers to note the precise time at which a star crossed the transit point when observed through a telescope. These discrepancies—referred to as the personal equation—stimulated studies of reaction time and were important in the later development of mental chronometry, or the measurement of the time required by mental processes.

Sense Physiology

Studies of sense physiology provided another route to the study of psychological experiences. The physical study of optics and acoustics stimulated research on the physiologies of corresponding sense organs. Discoveries of laws of color mixture, for example, stimulated investigations into the nature of color vision and the eye as an optical system.

Psychophysics

Although the study of sight and hearing received the greatest attention, the investigations of touch by the German physiologist Ernst H. Weber (1795–1878) were of particular importance. In studies of the ability to discriminate differences in the weights of objects by lifting and comparing them, Weber found that the just noticeable difference (today known as the j.n.d.) between two weights could be expressed as a ratio. This important step in the history of psychology applied quantitative methods to what was essentially a psychological problem—discrimination between stimuli.

Another German, Gustav Theodor Fechner (1801–1887), saw in Weber's research an implication which led to the establishment of psychology as an independent science. In his *Elements of Psychophysics,* Fechner argued that one could determine the relationship between the mental and physical worlds by carefully measuring the physical stimulus on the one hand, and on the other hand observing the consequences of the stimulus on the observer's mental experience. To accomplish this, Fechner established psychophysical methods of measurement known today as the method of limits, the method of constant stimuli, and the method of average error. Furthermore, he developed mathematical equations for describing relationships found in the resulting data. Thus "psychophysics" was born, and one might well take the publication date of Fechner's *Elements,* 1860, as that by which to date psychology's emergence as a science.

WUNDT AND THE "NEW" PSYCHOLOGY

While Fechner showed the way for psychology to be a science, it took another German, Wilhelm Wundt (1832–1920), to make the approach widely recognized. Wundt might well be called the first modern psychologist, in that he "turned out" many of the early PhD students and wrote the first important textbook of the "new" psychology, as experimental psychology came to be called, the *Principles of Physiological Psychology.* In 1879 Wundt established a laboratory of psychology at the University of Leipzig, making Leipzig the intellectual Mecca of psychology.

In the theoretical foundations set forth by Wundt, and in the problems studied in the Leipzig laboratory, many of the themes from the philosophical and scientific roots of psychology reappear. Reminiscent of Locke's distinction between primary and secondary qualities, Wundt distinguished between mediate experience, such as the physical response of the body to stimuli like light and sound waves, and immediate experience, such as the psychological sensations of color and tone. Immediate experience, or consciousness, was the subject matter of psychology, whose goals included the analysis of consciousness into elements (which included the classes of sensations and feelings), and determining how the elements were connected, a process in which association was postulated to play a vital role. Wundt assumed a parallel relationship between the physical, mediate experience of the body, and the mental, or immediate experience of consciousness since, for Wundt, the brain did not cause consciousness but acted parallel to it. Mental elements were discovered and examined through the processes of trained introspection and experimentation. The Leipzig laboratory explored problems such as light and its effect on the retina, visual contrast, color and color blindness, afterimages, the perception of tone, discrimination of loudness and determination of auditory thresholds, estimation of time intervals, and the study of reaction times.

In many of his experiments Wundt employed numerous instruments. Some such as the tuning fork—a device which, when tapped, produced a clear tone at a particular frequency—were borrowed from physics or physiology. Others were designed or adapted by Wundt or those who worked with him. The reliance of Wundt and others on such instruments led critics of the "new" psychology to refer to it as "brass-instrument" psychology. Despite such criticism, however, the new psychology spread rapidly from Leipzig not only to other European universities but throughout the world as well. One of the earliest countries to import the Fechnerian-Wundtian experimental psychology was the United States. Psychological laboratories based on the new psychology were established at Harvard, Johns Hopkins, Yale, Cornell, and other American universities; by the turn of the century, most major American universities had established psychology laboratories.

Structuralism

Although the Cornell laboratory of Edward Bradford Titchener (1867–1927) was by no means the first in the United States, it was for a time one of the most influential. Having studied with Wundt, Titchener incorporated many of Wundt's theoretical formulations into his own psychology, which has been called structuralism because it dealt with the elemental structure, rather than the function, of consciousness (Heidbreder, 1933). Titchener set out with great zeal to establish psychology as the scientific study of consciousness, and *only* of consciousness, and was opposed to any area of inquiry being labeled as psychology if it did not fall within a very narrow range of subject matter and employ the methods of introspection and experimentation. While Titchener contributed much to the development of a tradition of experimental rigor in American psychology, his dogmatic stance stimulated much opposition.

OTHER SCHOOLS OF PSYCHOLOGY

The experimental psychology of Wundt and those who followed him was soon challenged by other points of view, both in the United States and in Europe. These differed according to how psychology was defined, what methods were proposed for its study, and what theoretical assumptions shaped the questions to be asked, the investigations to be undertaken, and the explanations of results obtained.

James

William James (1842–1910) made his major contribution to psychology in his *Principles of Psychology* (1890). His psychology is far too broad to be summarized succinctly, however, the polarity of his point of view, relative to that of Wundt, can perhaps best be illustrated by his discussions of consciousness. While the Wundtian (and later the Titchenerian) perspective viewed consciousness as something to be analyzed, much as the physicist analyzes matter into its components, James argued for considering the *utility* of consciousness in pursuing goals and in discovering means to attain them. He illustrated this by comparing the attraction of iron filings to a magnet with the attraction of Romeo to Juliet. If a card is placed between the filings and the magnet, the filings "will press forever against its surface without it ever occurring to them to pass around its sides." Romeo, however, can employ consciousness to overcome the obstacle of a wall by scaling it or finding some other route to Juliet. James argued against what he considered to be an artificial analysis of consciousness into discrete, static, and universal elements by noting that consciousness was personal, always

changing, flowing in a continuous stream, and selective, choosing from among the many stimuli that bombarded it. Just as Heraclitus had long before noted that one could not step into the same stream twice, James noted that one could never experience the same sensation (or element) twice, since each sensation modified the brain in some way—an illustration of his interactionist view of mind and body.

In his *Principles* James raised far more questions than he answered, and many of them remain the focus of continued investigation (MacLeod, 1969).

Functionalism

The pragmatic psychology of William James, together with the evolutionary theory of Charles Darwin (1809–1882), prepared the way for the development of the school of functionalism, which viewed psychological functions or processes as adaptations to the environment. One of the founders of functionalism, John Dewey (1859–1952), in his 1896 paper on the reflex arc concept in psychology, pointed out that when a child, attracted to a flame, placed a finger in it and then quickly withdrew it, not only did the reflex arc (along sensory and motor nerves) serve an adaptive purpose in minimizing injury, but also the child's perception of the flame itself, and thus of the environment, was altered in a way that would affect future responses to the flame stimulus. Thus, argued Dewey, it was artificial merely to analyze reflexive actions into elemental (sensory and motor) components without considering the *functional* significance of the entire process.

Another founder of functional psychology was James Rowland Angell (1869–1949), who, in his 1907 paper on the province of functional psychology, articulated functionalism's concern with the study of the usefulness of consciousness, in contrast with the study of mental elements. As it developed, functionalism addressed a far broader range of problems than did the structural school, including animal and child psychology, psychological testing and individual differences, and problems of abnormal psychology, in addition to memory and learning.

Ebbinghaus

The concept of association was empirically explored in diverse ways. Ebbinghaus pioneered the experimental study of human memory, inventing the nonsense syllable (e.g., RIT, ZAK) to solve the problems of uniformity and prior familiarity with materials to be learned. With himself as his subject, Ebbinghaus learned lists of nonsense syllables and then tested the strength of the associations thus formed by measuring their recall. His most famous finding was that, when the amount of material forgotten is examined as a function of time since original learning, the greatest forgetting occurs shortly after learning; subsequently, forgetting tapers off at a much more gradual rate. Ebbinghaus did not attempt to explain his findings, which have become understandable only in the light of contemporary discussions of information processing and the distinction between short-term and long-term memory.

Pavlov

Whereas Ebbinghaus explored associations among verbal stimuli, the Russian physiologist Ivan Petrovich Pavlov (1849–1936) pioneered the experimental study of physiological responses associated to environmental stimuli. For much of his early career Pavlov had investigated processes of digestion, for which he received the Nobel prize in 1904. While studying the functioning of saliva in digestion, Pavlov noticed that dogs secreted saliva before being given meat, when they first saw the meat or heard someone approaching to feed them. Realizing that the innate reflex of salivating to food had become associated to environmental stimuli through being contiguously paired with them, Pavlov launched extensive laboratory explorations into the phenomenon of "conditioned" reflexes. Over some 30 years Pavlov, together with many collaborators, investigated the circumstances under which innate reflexive responses (unconditioned responses such as salivation) to appropriate stimuli (unconditioned stimuli such as food) became associated with, or conditioned to, previously neutral stimuli (conditioned stimuli such as the sound of a bell or the flash of a light) and thus became conditioned reflexes.

Thorndike

Studies of association in animals were carried out from a rather different perspective by Edward Lee Thorndike (1874–1949), who in 1898 published results of experiments in which cats learned to escape from puzzle boxes. To escape, the hungry animal had to learn to pull a string, press a lever, or perform some other action that resulted in the box's door opening so that nearby food could be obtained. In the beginning the animal made many irrelevant movements such as clawing the box. However, after a number of trials such errors were eliminated, as the animal formed an association between the interior of the puzzle box and the movements needed to escape from it. Based on such studies of trial-and-error learning, Thorndike formulated the Law of Effect, which stated that, within a particular situation, an act leading to satisfaction will be more likely to recur. This was the earliest systematic formulation of the role of reward in learning, a concept central to most modern theories of learning.

Behaviorism

Association was also a fundamental concept in the psychology of John Broadus Watson (1878–1958), who founded the school of behaviorism. In contrast with Titchener's structuralism, which emphasized the analysis of consciousness into its elements, and the more broadly defined functionalism, which sought to determine the role of consciousness as an adaptive mechanism, behaviorism, as formulated by Watson, relied only on directly observable behavior for its data. In his 1913 article "Psychology as the behaviorist views it," which became known as the behaviorist's manifesto, Watson ruled out introspection and the study of consciousness (which could not be studied directly) and proposed instead a mechanistic view of man in which the goals of psychology were the prediction and control of behavior in humans and animals alike.

As Watson's ideas developed, he gave a central role to association. Principles of conditioning were applied in accounting for the transition from the simplest of behaviors, unlearned and present at birth, to the far more complex behaviors of the adult. Emotions were considered to be bodily reactions to specific stimuli. In his experiments with an infant who came to be known as Little Albert,

Watson demonstrated that an unlearned fear of a loud noise could, through conditioning, come to be evoked by a previously unfeared white rat, thus providing a model for the development of the emotions. Speech was also believed to be acquired by conditioning, and Watson viewed thinking as subvocal speech. Personality he viewed as the constellation of an individual's habit systems, or complex groupings of conditioned responses; depending upon the individual, these might range from religious to patriotic to parental.

Together with his emphasis on learning as the basis of most behavior, Watson espoused an environmentalist viewpoint that virtually denied the influence of heredity in shaping behavior. Behaviorism's combination of learning principles, environmentalism, and objective methodology (investigating only what could be directly observed) made it one of the most influential points of view in subsequent decades.

Gestalt Psychology

In Germany in 1910, Max Wertheimer (1880–1943), began exploring a perceptual problem which led him to question then current views concerning the combinations of sensory elements as the basis of conscious experience. When a tachistoscope—a device for visually displaying stimuli with carefully timed exposures—was used to display two lines, separated by a brief interval of time, the subject saw one line moving from one place to another, rather than two lines simultaneously or successively. Wertheimer named this illusion of apparent movement the Phi Phenomenon. Its essential characteristic was that the movement was clearly a product of the observer rather than the stimulus, since no actual movement took place. Such an experience could not be accounted for by a mosaic of sensory elements combined in some way.

Wertheimer, together with Wolfgang Köhler (1887–1967) and Kurt Koffka (1886–1941), pointed out other perceptual phenomena that illustrated how actual experience did not conform to the physical stimulus. For example, a table top is seen as rectangular even though, when viewed from any position other than directly above it, the image projected on the retina is not at all rectangular. These and other examples led to the assertion that perception of such phenomena has a kind of totality or form or Gestalt that would be destroyed if attempts were made to analyze it (Heidbreder, 1933).

Gestalt studies of perceptual grouping explored the principles by which the perceived world is organized. For example, a series of dashes such as — — — is perceived not simply as six dashes but as three *pairs* of dashes. Köhler conducted experiments with apes (Köhler, 1925) in which he found they could achieve swift, insightful solutions to problems such as moving boxes to reach bananas hanging from the ceiling of a cage. Such insightful solutions were in sharp contrast with the more gradual trial-and-error solutions observed by Thorndike with his puzzle boxes. Gestalt psychologists believed that trial-and-error learning occurred when the animal could not perceive all the parts of the problem. In contrast, an insightful solution could occur if the parts of the problem were perceived in a new relationship with one another. Gestalt psychologists explored numerous other problems which, while diverse, shared a concern with the manner in which the organization of experience defied artificial attempts to break it down into smaller units.

Psychoanalysis

While academic psychology was developing in laboratories, a clinical approach to the mind was being developed in Austria by Sigmund Freud (1856–1939). To a large extent, laboratory psychology was concerned with the conscious mind, its elements or processes, or with behavior that was directly observable and thus accessible to study. Freud became concerned with the unconscious mind and in particular with the role of unconscious motivation.

Psychoanalysis did not come into being as a fully developed discipline, nor was it a single discipline. It became a method for investigating the mind; a means of providing therapy for certain emotional disturbances, primarily neuroses; and a theory of personality.

The first significant publication in the development of psychoanalysis was *Studies on Hysteria* (1895), which Freud wrote with Joseph Breuer, a medical colleague. It included case studies of patients exhibiting hysterical symptoms (resulting from psychological causes, rather than physical ones such as disease or nerve damage) that had been alleviated when the patients had been induced to express their feelings either under hypnosis or through talking about them. This book contained the nucleus of one of Freud's major ideas: that feelings of which the patients were consciously unaware could nevertheless affect their behavior through expression as hysterical symptoms.

In 1900 *The Interpretation of Dreams* was published, containing Freud's analyses of his own dreams and developing concepts such as manifest (obvious) and latent (disguised or hidden) dream content, and the meaning of dream symbols in relation to the unconscious mind. Next, in *The Psychopathology of Everyday Life* (1901) Freud described how unconscious processes interfered with conscious activities through phenomena such as slips of the tongue. In other publications he developed his ideas concerning the development of the personality in psychosexual stages, the structure of the personality in id, ego, and superego, and the dynamics of the personality as an energy system. Freud's genius in applying concepts of unconscious motivation to account for such superficially dissimilar phenomena as hysterical paralysis, dream content, and slips of the tongue, among others, made psychoanalysis the most influential view of personality in the 20th century.

Freud had a number of followers and associates, several of whom disagreed with him about some aspects of psychoanalysis and eventually founded their own traditions. In contrast with Freud's stress on man's biological nature and the unconscious mind, Alfred Adler (1870–1937) stressed man's social nature and believed that the conscious side of personality was more important. Adler objected to Freud's emphasis on sexuality, and proposed compensation for inferiority as a major mechanism shaping personality.

Carl Gustav Jung (1875–1961) also followed Freud for several years, but objected to what he considered to be Freud's dogmatically narrow sexual interpretation of libido, the basic energy of life. Jung broke with Freud to pursue studies of his own concepts including the collective unconscious, introversion-extroversion, and the role of myth and religion in personality. Jung did not deny the importance of sexuality, but believed it should be placed within a far broader context than did Freud.

PSYCHOLOGY BEYOND THE SCHOOLS

Psychology as it existed in the decades immediately preceding and following the turn of the 20th century can be fairly described as having been dominated by the issues and points of view put forth by the various schools just described. However, it would be misleading to imply that all issues of a psychological nature could be neatly categorized as falling within the province of one or another school, or that the only major contributors were those who "founded" schools.

Evidence of this can be found, for example, in the collection of papers entitled *The First Century of Experimental Psychology,* edited by Eliot Hearst, which describes the historical development of a number of psychological problems such as comparative psychology and ethology, and developmental psychology, that have reached far beyond particular schools and have often had important contributions made by now obscure psychologists.

As psychology matured, it was inevitable that schools of psychology, adhering to particular points of view and headed by a relatively small number of individuals, should give way both to numerous derivative theories and to more eclectic research centers, as the numbers of psychologists increased. As psychology grew in scope as a discipline, the major approaches—structuralism, functionalism, associationist approaches to learning, behaviorism, Gestalt psychology, and psychoanalysis—met quite different fates.

The structural psychology of Wundt and Titchener, with its attempted definition of elements of consciousness through introspection, eventually disappeared as a discipline because it turned out to rely on fruitless lines of investigation, faulty premises, and a far too narrow scope of allowable questions. Functionalism lost its definition as a separate school, but functionalist problems became a mainstay of American psychology as concepts of adaptation and adjustment to the environment through learning and other mental processes became widely investigated. Many of the concepts of Gestalt psychology were integrated into the general data base of psychology, particularly the psychology of perception. In addition, Gestalt concepts of organization were extended to the theory and study of personality and social psychology.

The use of association—particularly association by contiguity—as the central concept of a theory of learning was expanded by later theoreticians, although this was sometimes in contradictory terms. For example, Clark Hull (1884–1952) proposed a theory stressing the importance of reinforcement in learning, whereas Edwin Guthrie (1886–1959) argued that contiguity alone between stimulus and response was sufficient for learning to occur.

Of all the schools, behaviorism has remained closest to the goals of its founder, but Watson's basic mechanism of stimulus-response conditioning has largely been supplanted by the operant conditioning of B. F. Skinner, who focused attention on behavior as a function of the contingencies, or schedules, under which rewards are obtained.

Psychoanalysis has spawned a number of derivative points of view. Although traditional Freudians have staunchly adhered to Freud's essential framework, the neo-Freudians such as Karen Horney (1885–1952) have accepted some Freudian concepts but have also given a greater role to social factors in personality development.

In experimental psychology the influence and cohesion of the separate schools flourishing in the early part of the 20th century, as well as the broad systems of psychology which they spawned, and which applied the same theoretical framework to a wide spectrum of issues, gave way to ever narrower theories. These have gradually evolved into a proliferation of what might be termed "mini-theories," combining data and hypotheses about single problems or issues. Along with this has come a proliferation of psychological journals, frequently devoted to publishing research dealing with one area of psychology. Despite this specialization, however, there is ample evidence that the issues which occupied early philosophers and experimenters, such as whether behavior is learned or innate, or how and where functions are localized within the brain, are still very much alive, as seen for example in the study of identical twins or the comparison of right and left hemispheres of the brain.

SOURCE MATERIALS IN THE HISTORY OF PSYCHOLOGY

The history of psychology can be approached in a number of ways. This account has focused selectively on presenting a general framework summarizing the contrasting conceptions of psychology that have shaped its history. A detailed chronology of events and landmarks in the history of psychology can be found in William Sahakian's *History of Psychology,* as can a bibliographic listing of the major reference works on the history of psychology, and excerpts from primary sources. Additional excerpts, organized around particular problems, are included in Diamond's *The Roots of Psychology.* References for primary sources can be found in R. I. Watson's *Eminent Contributors to Psychology.* Articles on the history of psychology appear in the *Journal of the History of the Behavioral Sciences,* published since 1965. Bibliographies of recent publications on the history of psychology are from time to time published in the *Newsletter* of the Division of the History of Psychology (Division 26) of the American Psychological Association. The Archives of the History of American Psychology at the University of Akron (Ohio) provide a repository for published and unpublished papers, correspondence, notes, and apparatus of American psychologists. Additional information concerning the locations of historical manuscripts and papers can be found in Sokal and Rafail's *A Guide to Manuscript Collections in the History of Psychology and Related Areas.*

Much remains to be learned about the history of psychology; this brief account can serve only to highlight major historical trends that continue to influence the issues of contemporary psychology. However, virtually any area or problem of today's psychology has historical roots, if care is taken to search for them. It is to be hoped that modern psychologists will study the history of their science, both to appreciate the contributions of their predecessors and to understand more fully the psychology of the present day.

REFERENCES

Aristotle. (1941). De memoria et reminiscentia (On memory and reminiscence). In R. McKeon (Ed.), *The basic works of Aristotle.* New York: Random House.

Berkeley, G. (1948/1910). Essay toward a new theory of vision (1709). In A. A. Luce & T. E. Jessop (Eds.), *The works of George Berkeley, Bishop of Cloyne.* Toronto: Nelson.

Boring, E. G. (1957/1950/1929). A history of experimental psychology (2nd ed.). New York: Appleton-Century-Crofts.

Breasted, J. H. (1930). *The Edwin Smith Surgical Papyrus.* Chicago: University of Chicago Press.

Cadwallader, T. C., Cadwallader, J. V., & Semrau, L. (1974). *Examination of the interpretation that the principles of neural control and brain localization were recognized.* Presented at the meeting of the History of Science Society, Norwalk, CT.

Descartes, R. (1955/1911). Discourse on the method of rightly conducting the reason (1637). In E. S. Haldane & G. R. T. Ross (Eds.), *The philosophical works of Descartes* (Vol. 1). New York: Dover.

Descartes, R. (1955/1911). The passions of the soul (1649). In E. S. Haldane & G. R. T. Ross (Eds.), *The philosophical works of Descartes* (Vol. 1). New York: Dover.

Diamond, S. (Ed.). (1974). *The roots of psychology: A sourcebook in the history of ideas.* New York: Basic Books.

Fechner, G. T. (1960). *Elements of psychophysics.* New York: Holt, Rinehart & Winston. (Original work published in 1860)

Freud, S. (1968/1900). The interpretation of dreams. In *The standard edition of the complete psychological works of Sigmund Freud* (Vols. 4, 5). London: Hogarth.

Freud, S. (1968/1901). The psychopathology of everyday life. In *The standard edition of the complete psychological works of Sigmund Freud* (Vol. 6). London: Hogarth.

Freud, S., & Breuer, J. (1953/1895). Studies on hysteria. In *The standard edition of the complete psychological works of Sigmund Freud* (Vol. 2). London: Hogarth.

Hearst, E. (1979). *The first century of experimental psychology.* Hillsdale, NJ: Erlbaum.

Heidbreder, E. (1933). *Seven psychologies.* New York: Appleton-Century.

James, W. (1890). *The principles of psychology.* New York: Henry Holt.

Kohler, W. (1925). *The mentality of apes.* London: Routledge & Kegan Paul.

Locke, J. (1965/1690). *An essay concerning human understanding.* London: Dent.

MacLeod, R. B. (1969). *William James: Unfinished business.* Washington, DC: American Psychological Association.

Mill, J. (1967/1829). *Analysis of the phenomena of the human mind.* New York: Kelley.

Sahakian, W. S. (Ed.). (1968). *History of psychology: A source book in systematic psychology.* Itasca, IL: Peacock.

Sokal, M. M., & Rafail, P. A. (1982). *A guide to manuscript collections in the history of psychology and related areas.* Millwood, NY: Kraus International.

Watson, J. B. (1913). Psychology as the behaviorist views it. *Psychological Review, 20,* 158–177.

Watson, R. I. (1974–1976). *Eminent contributors to psychology.* New York: Springer.

Wundt, W. (1897). *Principles of psychology,* Leipzig: Engelmann.

SUGGESTED READING

Boring, E. G. (1942). *Sensation and perception in the history of experimental psychology.* New York: Appleton-Century.

Brennan, J. F. (1982). *History and systems of psychology.* Englewood Cliffs, NJ: Prentice-Hall.

Bringmann, W. G., & Tweney, R. D. (Eds.). (1980). *Wundt studies: A centennial collection.* Toronto: Hogrefe.

Dennis, W. (Ed.). (1948). *Readings in the history of psychology.* New York: Appleton-Century-Crofts.

Fancher, R. E. (1979). *Pioneers of psychology.* New York: Norton.

Gilgen, A. R. (1982). *American psychology since World War II: A profile of the discipline.* Westport, CT: Greenwood Press.

Klein, D. B. (1970). *A history of scientific psychology: Its origins and philosophical backgrounds.* New York: Basic Books.

Leahey, T. H. (1980). *A history of psychology: Main currents in psychological thought.* Englewood Cliffs, NJ: Prentice-Hall.

Misiak, H., & Sexton, V. S. (1966). *History of psychology: An overview.* New York: Grune & Stratton.

Murphy, G., & Kovach, J. K. (1972/1949). *Historical introduction to modern psychology* (3rd ed.). New York: Harcourt Brace Jovanovich.

Nordby, V. J., & Hall, C. S. (1974). *A guide to psychologists and their concepts.* San Francisco: Freeman.

Rieber, R. W., & Salzinger, K. (Eds.). (1977). The roots of American psychology: Historical influences and implications for the future. *Annals of the New York Academy of Sciences, 291.*

Roback, A. A. (1952). *History of American psychology.* New York: Library Publishers.

Robinson, D. N. (1976). *An intellectual history of psychology.* New York: Macmillan.

Schultz, D. (1981/1975). *A history of modern psychology* (3rd ed.). New York: Academic.

Viney, W., Wertheimer, M., & Wertheimer, M. L. (1979). *History of psychology: A guide to information sources.* Detroit, MI: Gale Research.

Watson, R. I. (1979). *Basic writings in the history of psychology.* New York: Oxford University Press.

Woodward, W. R., & Ash, M. G. (Eds.). (1982). *The problematic science: Psychology in the nineteenth century.* New York: Praeger.

F. M. CAULDLE
College of Staten Island

BEHAVIORISM
EMPIRICISM
FUNCTIONALISM
GESTALT PSYCHOLOGY
LOGICAL POSITIVISM
PHILOSOPHY AND PSYCHOLOGY
PHRENOLOGY
STRUCTURALISM

PSYCHOMETRICS: NORMS, RELIABILITY, VALIDITY, AND ITEM ANALYSIS

Researchers in the field of psychometrics generally consider quantitative data from a quantitative perspective. Such data normally emerge from test responses, although they may come from a wide variety of measurement instruments. Two divisions might be identified within psychometrics: theoretical and applied psychometrics. Psychometric theory (as portrayed by Nunnally, 1978, and Lord, 1980) provides researchers and psychologists with mathematical models to be used in considering responses to individual test items, entire tests, and sets of tests. Applied psychometrics is the implementation of these models and their analytic procedures to test data (e.g., Thorndike, 1982).

The four areas of psychometric consideration include norming and equating, reliability, validity, and item analysis. Thus, each of these four categories has both theoretical formulations and actual procedures to be performed in estimating the usefulness of a test in a specific instance.

NORMING AND EQUATING

Both norming and equating procedures relate to developing test-score reporting systems. Norming tests is part of test standardization and generally involves administering the examination to a representative sample of individuals, determining various levels of test performance, and translating the raw test scores to a common metric. Two scoring models are generally used in norming: linear transformations and nonlinear transformations. Linear transformations change the mean and standard deviation of the raw test scores, but maintain all other aspects of the raw score distribution; the relative positions of examinees are unchanged. The purpose of linear transformations is typically to provide test results on scales with which psychologists are familiar and, hence, to increase the amount of information and meaning carried in a score. Common scales, for example, with their means and standard deviations (respectively), are standard or z scores (0.00, 1.00), t scores (50, 10; used with the MMPI), IQ scales (100, 15 [Wechsler] or 16 [Stanford Binet]), and the College Entrance Examination scale (500, 100).

Three nonlinear transformations are common; these include normalization transformations, percentile equivalents, and developmental norms. Normalization transformations fit the test score distribution to a normal curve while maintaining the original rank-ordering of the examinees. Percentile equivalents express each score as the proportion of examinees falling at or below that test score. Developmental norms are converted scores that express test performance relative to normal development, typically considering either years of age or schooling. Age equivalents such as mental age describe test performance in terms of behavior typical for children of various ages; grade equivalents are commonly used on educational achievement tests and express scores in terms of performance typical of school grade. Age and grade equivalent scores are often used in educational and clinical contexts; but, although they have descriptive value, they have extreme psychometric and interpretative problems (see Anastasi & Urbina, 1997; Thorndike, 1982).

Tests are sometimes equated when there are numerous forms of the same test. Although all forms should measure the same attribute with equal precision, raw scores from different forms invariably have varying percentile equivalents. Equating brings all forms to a common scale (see Kolen & Brennan, 1995, for a comprehensive introduction). Four basic equating strategies exist. In the first, each test form is administered to an equivalent (e.g., randomly sampled) group of examinees, and scores on the various forms are adjusted so that equal scores have equal percentile ranks (the same proportion falling at or below the score). In a more costly and more precise method, all examinees take all forms of the test, and equations are used to estimate the score equivalencies among the various forms. A third, frequently used method involves the administration of a common test or fraction of a test to all examinees. This common assessment serves as a bridging test that permits all measurements to be placed on a single scale; on many multi-form examinations, a few anchor items are placed on each form to serve as the bridging test. (Descriptions of each of the previous three methods are found in Angoff, 1971, and Thorndike, 1982). A final method of test-equating employs a relatively recent family of models of test scores called item response models (IRTs). The Rasch model is a useful and relatively simple IRT model; it permits scaling of tests and test items using methods presumably independent of the population from which the test data emerge. These methods are explained by Hambleton, Swaminathan, and Rogers (1991); Lord (1980); Thorndike (1982); and Wright and Stone (1979).

Norming and equating have taken on new importance with recent advents in testing, one of which is the greatly increased use of tests to make pass-fail decisions. These tests are frequently referred to as criterion-referenced tests and have been required by states as minimum competency examinations to warrant adequate skills for high school graduation, and as certification examinations to permit entry into various occupations and professions. The determination of a passing mark for each of these examinations is a norming decision, and employing multiple forms of examinations to make these decisions indicates equating.

At the turn of the millennium, one change in standardized testing is rapidly impacting both norming and equating: the use of computer-adaptive tests (Drasgow & Olson-Buchanan, 1999; Wainer, 1990). Such test are administered by computer; a test taker's responses to initial questions affect the questions administered subsequently, with the aim of reducing testing time with a level of accuracy similar to that of paper-and-pencil standardized tests. The computer programs that control the administration of such tests need to make estimates of test-taker ability after each response, so that an appropriate next question is administered. Many in educational and certification testing believe that the future of standardized testing involves computer-adaptive administration.

RELIABILITY

Both reliability and validity refer to the generalizability of test scores—the determination of which inferences about test scores are reasonable (Cronbach, Gleser, Nanda, & Rajaratnam, 1972). Reliability concerns inferences made about consistency of measurement. Consistency is defined by tradition as a family of rela-

tionships: temporal stability, similarity among tests proposed to be equivalent, homogeneity within a single test, and comparability of assessments made by raters. A procedure called the test-retest method is used to establish the reliability of a test by administering the test and then waiting a short period (e.g., 2 weeks) before administering the same test again to the same group. The two sets of scores are then compared to determine how similar they are. In the alternate-forms method, two parallel measures are developed and both are administered to a sample of examinees. Both of the previous methods use the correlation coefficient between the two sets of measurements as the reliability coefficient, an index that ranges from 0.00 to 1.00 and denotes the percentage of test variance that is reliable. Using raters essentially as parallel forms is called interrater reliability and is often relied upon when expert judgments are needed.

Each of the previous procedures flows from what has been called the classical or parallel testing model of reliability (Campbell, 1976; Nunnally, 1978). In this model, each test score is perceived as the sum of two independent components: true score and error. A true score may be thought of either as perfect measurement of the attribute in question were such assessment possible, or as the average of an infinite number of testings. Error is defined as randomly occurring deviation from the true score. Because error is random, it correlates neither with itself nor with true score. Under these conditions, it follows that when two sets of purportedly parallel measurements are correlated with one another, the resultant correlation coefficient is equal to the proportion of the individual differences resulting from the test that are due to true score differences—statistically, the ratio of true score variance to the variance of obtained scores. The classical model does not specify whether the parallel measurements may be made at the same time, or how equivalent parallel measurements need to be.

An alternate model to the parallel testing model is the domain sampling model. This model requires that a test constructor must define the universe of behaviors of interest. If it were possible to measure an individual on all aspects of the universe, the resultant performance would equal that individual's universe score. Reliability is then defined as the ability of the given test to predict that universe score. This model allows psychometricians to estimate the reliability of tests under the condition that items or tests are essentially randomly selected from the population of possible items or tests. Among the reliability estimation procedures that emanate from this model are various internal consistency formulations. These procedures estimate the correlation between the test and the universe from the average correlations between items on the test. Among these formulae are Coefficient Alpha (for all tests), various Kuder-Richardson formulae (for items scored correctly or incorrectly), and the Hoyt ANOVA approach, which is equivalent to Coefficient Alpha. Under this model, reliability is maximized by including as many items as possible (and thus a large sample of the population of items) and by having items that intercorrelate highly with one another. Campbell (1976) and Stanley (1971) describe these approaches more fully.

A third model, the generalizability model (Cronbach et al., 1972; Stanley, 1971) is a step beyond the domain sampling model;

it assumes that one may generalize over both similar and dissimilar conditions. Thus, in the domain sampling model, a researcher may estimate the reliability between two PhD-level psychologists, whereas in the generalizability model, the researcher could estimate the extent to which one may generalize from a PhD-level psychologist to a psychiatrist, a social worker, and so on. Thus, one can generalize from one set of test scores or observations to another set collected at a different time or under somewhat different conditions. Clearly, generalizability bridges the gap between reliability and validity.

VALIDITY

Validity refers to the quality with which a measurement procedure permits the desired inferences. Because psychologists make a number of different kinds of inferences using tests and measurements, there have traditionally been several kinds of validity: predictive validity, content validity, and construct validity. Predictive validity has been used to assess the ability of measurement devices to infer success on the job or in advanced education. Typically, the predictive measure is correlated with some quantified assessment of job or school success, called a criterion. Thus, tests used for admission to graduate or professional schools are frequently correlated with grades at that school (Geisinger, 1982). The resultant correlation coefficient is called the validity coefficient. Psychometricians often adjust these coefficients—for example, when the range of criterion scores is narrow or when the criterion is unreliable (see Cronbach, 1971; Messick, 1989; or Thorndike, 1982). Sometimes researchers do not wait to collect criterion data; when these data are collected at essentially the same time as the predictor, the study is said to be a concurrent validity study. Furthermore, since a single instrument is often unable to predict a criterion as well as would be desired, multiple predictors are used, often with the statistical procedure of multiple regression (this procedure weights the various predictive tests to achieve maximal prediction of the criterion). A methodology has also been developed to insure that predictions from tests do not favor one group or bias another. In general, findings of such differential validity have been quite rare.

When the purpose of a test is to assess mastery of skills within some behavioral domain, content validity is often involved. The content validity of a test is typically judged by how well the domain has been covered. Such judgments are generally made by those who are expert in the test domain. Careful and detailed description of the domain prior to test construction, and implementation of procedures to insure adequate sampling from all aspects of the domain, are critical for content validity.

In recent years, it has become accepted that construct validity subsumes predictive and content validity (Geisinger, 1992; Messick, 1989). The critical question asked with construct validity is: How well does a given test measure the trait(s) it is supposed to be measuring? The construct validity of a test is rarely determined by a single study; rather, it is the gradual accumulation of evidence that provides conclusions regarding construct validity. For example, experts may make judgments regarding the nature of the test and the relationship of test tasks to the construct in question.

More empirical procedures, however, are normally employed. For example, a test may be correlated with other measures that seem to measure the same attribute (evidence of convergent validity); experimental procedures that purportedly affect the trait may be implemented and their effect upon the test scores studied; or groups that would appear to differ on the attribute can be tested and their scores compared. It is also important to demonstrate that tests do not correlate with variables with which they should not correlate; discriminant validity is demonstrated by low correlations in such studies. Clearly, procedures implemented to insure content validity and predictive validity research may be used as part of the evidence needed for the construct validation of an instrument. Anastasi and Urbina (1997) provide a good introduction to the logic of construct validity, and Messick (1989) a rather complete summarization.

One part of validity, as acknowledged by many test theorists (e.g., Messick, 1989), relates to test fairness. If a test is valid, then it should not lead to scores that differ inappropriately among groups as divided by various racial, ethnic, or sexual lines, among others. Considerable effort has been advanced over the past 25 years to help psychologists and others develop and use psychological measures fairly (Sandoval, Frisby, Geisinger, Scheunemann, & Grenier, 1998).

ITEM ANALYSIS

The present discussion includes only an overview of item analysis procedures; detailed descriptions are found in Henrysson (1971) or Thorndike (1982). In general, most item analysis procedures either (a) look at the number of examinees answering the item correctly and incorrectly; (b) correlate individual items with other variables; or (c) check items for bias. The proportion of examinees answering an item correctly is (perhaps inappropriately) called the item difficulty. A means of improving items is to check the proportion of subjects who select each option of a multiple-choice item; computing the mean test score of individuals selecting each option is also useful. Such procedures check that options appear plausible to naive examinees while not appearing correct to the most knowledgeable. Selecting items that correlate highly with total test score maximizes internal consistency reliability in a test; selecting items that correlate highly with an external criterion maximizes predictive validity. A descriptive analog of these correlations is known as the item characteristic curve—typically, a graph that plots the proportion of examinees answering a question correctly against their total test scores (or some other estimate of their ability levels). For effective items, these graphs are positively ascending lines that do not descend as ability increases. The last set of item analysis procedures presented here, those concerned with item bias, attempt to identify items that are differentially difficult for various groups. Such item bias has come to be called differential item functioning (Cole & Moss, 1989; Holland & Wainer, 1993), indicating that the item operates differently for different groups. In other words, these procedures control for overall differences in tested ability and then search for items that are differentially difficult for minority groups. The aim is that by elimination of these items from subsequent forms of the test, the test will be made fair. At present, these procedures are being subjected to initial scrutiny and are of yet undetermined value.

CONCLUSION

Although this presentation has of necessity avoided numerical concepts, psychometrics *is* a quantitative discipline, as a perusal of the references will demonstrate. The aim of the four quantitative concepts presented in this entry is to improve the quality of data in psychology. Item analysis procedures are generally employed in test construction and refinement, with the purpose of selecting items to maximize a test's utility. The use of norms makes test scores communicate information more effectively; equating tests makes scores from varying forms of the same examination comparable. In general, the value of any psychological measuring device is defined by its validity, and the reliability of a measurement procedure limits the validity of the device (in that when individual differences on a test are due to random fluctuation, any correlations with that instrument would generally be considered to be randomly based as well). Thus, psychometrics is a discipline that employs numbers, but it is also a discipline that evaluates itself quantitatively.

REFERENCES

Angoff, W. H. (1971). Scales, norms, and equivalent scores. In R. L. Thorndike (Ed.), *Educational measurement* (2nd ed., pp. 508–600). Washington, DC: American Council on Education.

Anastasi, A., & Urbina, S. (1997). *Psychological testing* (7th ed.). Upper Saddle River, NJ: Prentice Hall.

Campbell, J. P. (1976). Psychometric theory. In M. D. Dunnette (Ed.), *Handbook of industrial and organizational psychology* (pp. 185–222). Chicago: Rand McNally.

Cole, N. S., & Moss, P. A. (1989). Bias in test use. In R. L. Linn (Ed.), *Educational measurement* (3rd ed., pp. 201–220). New York: American Council on Education/Macmillan.

Cronbach, L. J. (1971). Test validation. In R. L. Thorndike (Ed.), *Educational measurement* (2nd ed., pp. 443–507). Washington, DC: American Council on Education.

Cronbach, L. J., Gleser, C. C., Nanda, N., & Rajaratnam, N. (1972). *The dependability of behavioral measurements.* New York: Wiley.

Drasgow, F., & Olson-Buchanan, J. B. (Eds.). (1999). *Innovations in computerized assessment.* Mahwah, NJ: Lawrence Erlbaum.

Geisinger, K. F. (1982). Marking systems. In H. E. Mitzel (Ed.), *Encyclopedia of educational research* (5th ed., Vol. 3, pp. 1139–1149). New York: Macmillan and Free Press.

Geisinger, K. F. (1992). The metamorphosis in test validation. *Educational Psychologist, 27,* 197–222.

Hambleton, R. K., Swaminathan, H., & Rogers, H. J. (1991). *Fundamentals of item response theory.* Newbury Park, CA: Sage.

Henrysson, S. (1971). Gathering, analyzing, and using data on test items. In R. L. Thorndike (Ed.), *Educational measurement* (2nd ed., pp. 130–159). Washington, DC: American Council on Education.

Holland, P. W., & Wainer, H. (Eds.). (1993). *Differential item functioning.* Hillsdale, NJ: Erlbaum.

Kolen, M. J., & Brennan, R. L. (1995). *Test equating: Methods and practices.* New York: Springer.

Lord, F. M. (1980). *Applications of item response theory to practical testing problems.* Hillsdale, NJ: Erlbaum.

Magnusson, D. (1966). *Test theory.* Reading, MA: Addison-Wesley.

Messick, S. (1989). Validity. In R. L. Linn (Ed.), *Educational Measurement* (3rd ed., pp. 13–104). New York: American Council on Education/Macmillan.

Nunnally, J. C. (1978). *Psychometric theory* (2nd ed.). New York: McGraw-Hill.

Sandoval, J., Frisby, C. L., Geisinger, K. F., Scheunemann, J. D., & Grenier, J. R. (Eds.). (1998). *Test interpretation and diversity.* Washington, DC: American Psychological Association.

Stanley, J. C. (1971). Reliability. In R. L. Thorndike (Ed.), *Educational measurement* (2nd ed., pp. 356–442). Washington, DC: American Council on Education.

Thorndike, R. L. (1982). *Applied psychometrics.* Boston: Houghton Mifflin.

Wainer, H. (Ed.). (1990). *Computer adaptive testing: A primer.* Hillsdale, NJ: Erlbaum.

Wright, B. D., & Stone, M. H. (1979). *Best test design.* Chicago: MESA.

K. F. Geisinger
Le Moyne College

CLUSTER ANALYSIS
CULTURAL BIASES IN TESTS
ITEM ANALYSIS
STATISTICS IN PSYCHOLOGY

PSYCHONEUROIMMUNOLOGY

For many decades, a considerable number of psychologists believed that they had "solved" the so-called "mind/body problem" by concluding that all mental events could be reduced to physical events occurring in the brain. This was a reaction to earlier philosophical speculation that one set of laws governed mental events, while another set governed physical events. More recently, however, psychologists have began to realize that both the division of mind and body and the reduction of mind to body were socially constructed notions that began to lose their utility as advances in the neurosciences began to favor models that illustrated the identity of mind and body, or at least the close interaction of the two processes. In fact, Pert (1986) proposes that the more that is known about neurotransmitters, the more sense it makes to speak of "bodymind" than to use such traditional terms as "mind" and "body."

DEFINITION

One of the most important events in reframing traditional ideas of mind and body has been the development of psychoneuroimmunology (PNI), a term coined by Ader (1981), although the concept was presaged by Salk (1961) when he included the immune system along with genetic, behavioral, and neurological systems in his interfactoral model of disease. Clinical illustrations date back as far as 1896, when Mackenzie provoked cold symptoms in an allergic patient by means of an artificial rose. Some writers have commented on the difficulty in identifying the neural links between the brain and various component parts of the immune system, although at the cellular level there appears to be a definite relationship between the nerve cells and the immune system cells. Furthermore, the two cell lines diverge very early in embryogenesis, and the immune system probably evolved before the nervous system and was initially only an internal regulating network.

PNI is the study of behavioral-neural-endocrine-immune system interactions. It emerged from the realization that the immune system does not operate autonomously, as had been supposed by those who conceptualized it as a closed system, driven by challenges from foreign substances (antigens) and regulated by soluble products produced and released by soluble products produced and released by immune cells (e.g., lymphokines, cytokines, monokines) which serve both to communicate between immune cells both locally and at distant sites, and to control the progress of the immune response. Although antigens do initiate immune responses, and cytokines (e.g., interleukin-1) do regulate immune processes, data demonstrate that there are bidirectional communication pathways between the immune system and central nervous system (CNS), with each providing important regulatory control over the other (Maier, Watkins, & Fleshner, 1994).

THE IMMUNE SYSTEM

The general function of the immune system is to identify and eliminate antigens—foreign materials such as pathogenic microorganisms (bacteria, viruses), fungi, parasites, tumors, and toxic chemicals—that contact or enter the body. Components of the immune system are also capable of identifying and destroying mutant cells that have undergone alterations associated with malignancy, and of directing responses against donated organs and similar agents. It also acts as a regulatory, repair, and surveillance infrastructure, preventing its components from turning against each other, and assisting in tissue repair after injury. The immune system is composed of specialized cells that originate in the bone marrow, mature, and are sequestered in such organs as the thymus, spleen, lymph nodes, and peripheral lymphoid organs. From these organs, the specialized cells are released into the blood, and may return to these organs from the blood.

Identification of specific types of cells became possible with the development of monoclonal antibodies, or molecules that adhere to specific receptors found on the cells. Monoclonal antibodies can be tagged with fluorescent markers so that they can be identified and counted by a method called flow cytometry. The most important cells in the immune system are the leukocytes or white blood cells, of which there are three major categories: granulocyte cells,

monocytes (called macrophages when they mature and enter tissue), and lymphocytes. The latter are predominantly of two types: B (bone marrow) cells comprise the humoral arm of the immune response, being responsible for the production and secretion of antibodies, highly specific molecules (immunoglobulins) that recognize and combine with their target antigens, ultimately being destroyed by phagocytes. There are three general types of T (thymus) cells: Cytotoxic T cells are capable of destroying target cells; the natural killer or NK cell destroys virally infected cells and certain types of tumors; helper T cells enhance the immune response. Helper T cells are the primary target of the human immunodeficiency virus (HIV). Some immune cells secrete soluble factors, interleukins or lymphokines (if the cell is a lymphocyte), which provide communication between different cells in the immune system.

Immune function can require global alterations involving the entire organism as well as local processes (e.g., selective rapid multiplication of T cells in a lymph node in response to a detected antigen). Only the CNS can orchestrate such widespread outcomes in a coordinated fashion. Thus, the CNS must be able to exert control over some aspects of the immune response. Conversely, in order to accomplish this function, the CNS must receive information about events in the body, such as an infectious agent that has penetrated the skin, and the status of the immune processes. Thus the immune system exerts control over the neural function, and the CNS exerts control over the immune system. These neural-immune interactions permit psychological events to enter the matrix; if neural processes regulate immune processes, then potentially they can impact behavior, emotion, and cognition. PNI, then, studies these complex interactions between neural, immune, endocrinal, and behavioral processes.

TWO BRANCHES

One way of describing how the immune system achieves these ends is to divide it into two branches, each with different active agents and assignments. One branch can be referred to as the antibody-mediated or humoral subsystem, which operates through the bloodstream by means of antibodies produced by B cells. When activated by a foreign intruder or antigen, B cells produce any of five known types of antibodies, generally taking five days to do so. For example, type IgE tends to increase during stress and is responsible for allergic reactions. If house dust or pollen is injected into the skin of a person sensitive to those substances, there might be an immediate reddening and swelling caused by previously-produced antibodies going into action. If inhaled, wheezing or sneezing might occur as the result of histamines or other substances being released that are secondary to the antigen-antibody reaction (Solomon, 1990). The affected cell appears to secrete substances that affect the original signaling, completing a loop.

The action of B cells in the antibody-mediated subsystem is influenced by T cells and by macrophages, which belong to the immune system's other branch, the cell-mediated subsystem; they produce "messenger" substances (e.g., cytokines, lymphokines, monokines) that influence other immune cells. A tumor cell can be attacked by macrophages after being covered with antibodies—or can be killed directly by NK cells. Helper T cells facilitate the functions of the killer T cells and the B cells. As a result, innate immune mechanisms operate as a first line of defense against invading pathogens; those that escape are attacked by specific immune responses, which might be delayed if the proper antibodies have not yet been developed.

In addition to autonomic nervous system activity, the immune system is influenced by neuroendocrine outflow from the pituitary. Indeed, two pathways link the brain and the immune system: the autonomic nervous system (ANS) and neuroendocrine outflow by way of the pituitary gland. Both routes provide biologically active molecules capable of interacting with cells of the immune system. Neurotransmitters released from these nerves diffuse to act at distant sites, further extending the potential for neural-immune interactions. Lymphocytes, macrophages, and granulocytes possess receptors for these neurotransmitters. All immunoregulatory processes take place within a neuroendocrine environment that is sensitive to the influence of the individual's perception of events in the external world and the body's response to them. Because lymphocytes bear receptors for various hormones and neuropeptides, the cellular interactions that mediate humoral and cellular immune responses can be modulated by the neuroendocrine environment in which these immune responses occur.

MEMORY AND CONDITIONING

The capacity for memory is found in both the immune system and the CNS, as are the use of neurotransmitters and their capacities for adaptation, defense, and communication at a distance (i.e., "cell traffic"); perhaps these similarities facilitate the linkage of the two systems. The immune system has innate, nonspecific functions; the skin prevents entry of pathogens, acidity limits bacterial growth, mucus contains substances that can destroy bacterial cell walls, macrophages can engulf microorganisms they contact. NK cells, the first line of defense against tumorous cells and cells infected by viruses, are innate killers, in the sense that they do not have to learn by prior exposure or be programmed in order to do their work. But the immune system also has specific acquired immunity functions which are not innate. The underlying basis for the memory of the cells involved in the immune system's acquired functions is a change in their specific composition and their corresponding antigen-specific products.

A laboratory example of CNS involvement in the modulation of immunity is the classical Pavlovian conditioning of antibody- and cell-mediated immune responses. When a distinctly flavored drinking solution (the conditioned stimulus) is paired with injection of an immunosuppressive drug (the unconditioned stimulus), the subsequent antibody response is attenuated in conditioned animals reexposed to the conditioned stimulus (see Ader & Cohen, 1991, for a review). Therefore, in Pavlovian terms, an antigen can be thought of as an unconditioned stimulus that elicits an immune response. The demonstration of conditioned modulation of immunity in humans (Smith & McDaniels, 1983) suggests that these data may have clinical implications, assisting the understanding of how immune activity can decrease as a result of exposure to stimuli that are not ordinarily immunosuppressive. For example, Bovjberg and colleagues (1990) found that women who had undergone a number of chemotherapy treatments for ovarian cancer displayed immunosuppression after simply being brought back to the hospital for an additional treatment.

The cell-mediated and the antibody-mediated subsystems constantly interact with each other and with the nervous and endocrine systems. The antibody-mediated subsystem provides an instant reaction against toxic, viral, and bacterial foreign proteins; in addition, it is responsible for transfusion reactions against incompatible blood types when they occur. The cell-mediated subsystem is concerned with fighting virus-infected cells and foreign or abnormal cells. When a transplant reaction occurs, it is a result of the cell-mediated immune response. Cell-mediated immunity also is responsible for delayed types of allergy or hypersensitivity. For example, a person sensitive to tuberculin as a result of exposure to tuberculosis will develop an area of reddening and hardness of the skin a day or so after the injection within the skin (Solomon, 1990).

BIDIRECTIONAL PATHWAYS

Pathways between the brain and immune system are bidirectional; the CNS and the immune system form a directional interacting set of processes, each regulating the other. Activation of the immune system is accompanied by changes in hypothalamic, autonomic, and endocrine processes. Immune system activation increases the firing rate of neurons in the hypothalamus as the time of peak antibody production. Sympathetic activity, indexed by noradrenaline turnover, is increased in the spleen and the hypothalamus, and some immune responses, including those initiated by viral infections, are associated with dramatic increases in blood levels of adrenocorticotropic hormone (ACTH) and corticosterone. Such data indicate that signals generated by an activated immune system are being received and acted upon by the CNS.

Pathways between the endocrine system and the immune system are also bidirectional. Neural or lymphocyte-derived cytokines contribute to the interacting feedback mechanisms regulating the hypothalamic-pituitary-adrenal axis and its target organs by triggering the corticotropin-releasing factor or stimulating (e.g., by growth hormones) and inhibiting (e.g., prolactin) production of pituitary hormones. The potential interactions between neuroendocrine and immune processes is further shown by observations that immune cells activated by immunogenic stimuli are capable of producing neuropeptides (Ader, Cohen, & Felten, 1995).

Endogenous opioids (morphine-like peptides) and catecholamines are found in the brain and periphery and are subject to hypothalamic influences. They also are part of the body's response to stressful experiences, exerting immunomodulatory effects. There are several different opioid peptides, including beta-endorphin, which is released from the pituitary gland, and methionine enkephalin, released from the adrenal glands. Several mechanisms of their influence on immune function have been elucidated. The release of catecholamines, when stimulated with injections of epinephrine, results in redistribution of lymphocytes into circulation; in addition, injections of norepinephrine have been shown to increase NK cell activity.

PSYCHOSOCIAL FACTORS

Animal and human studies implicate psychosocial factors in the predisposition to and initiation (and progression) of various pathophysiological processes; for example, infectious, bacterial, allergic, autoimmune, and neoplastic diseases that involve alterations in immunological defense mechanisms. The chain of psychophysiological events has not yet been firmly established, but changes in several components of antibody- and cell-mediated immunity have been associated with naturally occurring and experimentally induced behavioral and emotional states. Several reports describe immune alterations associated with bereavement and depression (for a meta-analysis, see Herbert & Cohen, 1993). Clinical depression is associated with an increased number of circulating neurophils and a decreased number of NK cells, T and B lymphocytes, and helper and suppressor/cytotoxic T cells. Changes in humoral and cell-mediated immunity are associated with the affective responses to other losses, such as marital separation, divorce, Alzheimer's caregiving, battle-task vigilance in humans, and separation experiences in nonhuman primates. Changes in immune function also accompany less severe stressful experiences. For example, the level of distress in medical students during examination periods is greater than during control periods, and there are transient impairments in several parameters of immune function at such times—and the degree of the student's loneliness can moderate the immune reactions (for a review, see Kiecolt-Glaser, 1999). Furthermore, different stressors produce different immune (and ANS) reactions.

The association between stressful life experiences and changes in immune function does not establish a causal link between stress, immune function, and disease; such a chain of events has not yet been definitively established. However, major links between these systems have been described, and a new understanding of interactive biological signaling has begun. PNI encompasses studies on the effects of stress on immune functioning, the nature of the stressor as an experimental variable, and the ability of the organism to cope with stress. It studies the interactions of the body's central nervous system (in both its neurological and its psychological aspects) and the body's immune system, such as the role of the nervous system in regulating immune system functions and the ways in which stress and distress affect the nervous system. Many of the bodily effects of stress are produced by glucocorticoids—steroid hormones, which are released from the adrenal cortex, leading to synthesis by the hypothalamus of corticotropin.

Deficiencies in the immune system may increase the organism's susceptibility to infection or allow mutant cells to divide and become malignant. An overactive immune system may end up failing to differentiate between body cells and foreign cells and start attacking itself, giving rise to the so-called autoimmune diseases (e.g., rheumatoid arthritis, hyperthyroidism, lupus, HIV/AIDS). There is some evidence that these conditions may be linked to psychosocial stressors, and with overproduction or underproduction of particular hormones (e.g., Dorian & Garfinkel, 1987). However, the specific mechanisms are unknown, and the complexities and breadth of the interactions have yet to be elucidated.

The direction, magnitude, and duration of stress that induce alterations of immunity (and subsequent susceptibility to disease) are probably influenced by several interacting factors:

- quality and quantity of stressful stimulation,
- ability of an individual to cope effectively with stressful events,
- quality and quantity of immunogenic stimulation,
- sample time and component of immune system studied,
- environmental background including social support, and
- such host factors as age, gender, and nutritional state.

RESEARCH ISSUES

Some of the neurological structures involved in the immune system are also implicated in emotional responses; as a result, painful stressors and emotional distress consistently influence the nervous system. The endocrine system produces hormones (e.g., gonadal steroids, thyroid hormones, adrenal hormones) that affect immune responses. In addition, such opioid neuropeptides as the endorphins and enkephalins can enhance the immune system's functioning. There is considerable evidence that emotions, attitudes, and negative stress can adversely affect the functioning of the immune system. There is far less evidence, however, concerning the effectiveness of psychological factors in fighting illness and enhancing immune functioning.

Evidence of the immunosuppressive effects of stress leads to the logical step of modifying the stress response as a way to potentially enhance immune function. Although the literature contains some contradictory data, promising results have been obtained from a variety of training programs. Hypnosis, biofeedback, and relaxation exercises have been successfully used to help patients control such immune responses as phagocytic, T cell, and NK cell activity. However, the lack of normative data on many immune parameters impedes understanding of the significance of many of the reported changes. In addition, other potential modifiers of the immune system (e.g., psychological health, diet, exercise) may be important interactive factors. In summary, it is clear that behavioral states can cause disease susceptibility; they can also cause endocrinal changes which can affect immune response. What is not clear is whether changes in the immune system can directly affect disease susceptibility.

PNI represents a new appreciation of the interactions between behavioral, neural, endocrine, and immune processes. There has been a paradigm shift in the attempt to understand immunoregulatory function. Discovery of the innervation of lymphoid organs and the availability of neurotransmitters for interactions with cells of the immune system have added a new dimension to the understanding of the microenvironment in which immune responses occur. Another discovery, the interaction between pituitary-, endocrine-, and lymphocyte-derived hormones (which define the neuroendocrine environment in which immune responses take place) has added another level of complexity to the analysis of cellular interactions that drive immune responses. Collectively, these observations provide the basis for behaviorally induced alterations in immune function and immunologically based changes in behavior. This new paradigm may provide an understanding of the means by which psychosocial factors and emotional states influence development and progression of infectious autoimmune and neoplastic disease. Already, there are data linking right cerebral hemisphere lesions with enhancement of T-cell function. These data yield provocative correlations with handedness and the increased incidence of early dyslexia, together with the increased incidence of autoimmune disease in left-handed individuals. In view of the central role of the neocortex in the perception and interpretation of environmental stimuli, including those associated with stressful life experiences, the immunomodulatory effects of the cerebral cortex could be an important link between psychosocial factor and alterations in immunocompetence.

In sum, the anatomical arrangements are such that the brain could control immune cells and organs in the same ways it controls other peripheral structures. However, this is a possibility, not a certainty. If the brain participates in the regulation of the immune system, then brain lesions and stimulation at some brain sites should modulate some aspects of immune responses. Several studies have confirmed this modulation, indicating that the connection between the CNS and the immune system has consequences for people's health and well-being (Maier, Watkins, & Fleshner, 1994). However, investigators must not draw blanket conclusions, such as "Stress suppresses immune functions," because most studies have measured only one aspect of immunity at one point in time with a circumscribed sample. It will take a considerable amount of research to distill general principles from the specific findings that are now available.

REFERENCES

Ader, R. (Ed.). (1981). *Psychoneuroimmunology.* New York: Academic.

Ader, R., Cohen, N. (1981). The influence of conditioning on immune responses. In R. Ader, D. L. Felton, & M. Cohen (Eds.), *Psychoneuroimmunology* (2nd ed., pp. 611–646). San Diego: Academic.

Ader, R., Cohen, N., & Felton, D. (1995). Psychoneuroimmunology: Interactions between the nervous system and the immune system. *The Lancet, 345,* 99–103.

Bovjberg, D. H., Redd, W. H., Maier, L. A., Holland, J. C., Jesko, L. M., Niedzwiecki, D., Rubin, S. E., & Hakes, T. B. (1990). Anticipatory immune suppression in women receiving cyclic chemotherapy for ovarian cancer. *Journal of Counseling and Clinical Psychology, 58,* 153–157.

Dorian, B., & Garfinkel, P. E. (1987). Stress, immunity, and illness—A review. *Biological Medicine, 17,* 393–407.

Herbert, T. S., & Cohen, S. (1993). Depression and immunity: A meta-analytic review. *Psychoanalytic Bulletin, 113,* 472–486.

Kiecolt-Glaser, J. K. (1999). Stress, personal relationships, and immune function: Health implications. *Brain, Behavior, and Immunity, 13,* 61–72.

Maier, S. F., Watkins, L. R., & Fleshner, M. (1994). Psychoneuroimmunology: The interface between behavior, brain, and immunity. *American Psychologist, 49,* 1004–1017.

Pert, C. (1986). The wisdom of the receptors: Neuropeptides, the emotions, and body-mind. *Advances: The Journal of Mind-Body Health, 3*(3), 8–16.

Salk, J. (1961). Biological basis of disease and behavior. *Perspectives in Biology and Medicine, 5,* 198–206.

Solomon, G. F. (1990). Emotions, stress, and immunity. In R. Ornstein & C. Swencionis (Eds.), *The healing brain: A scientific reader* (pp. 174–181). New York: Guilford.

Smith, G. R., & McDaniels, S. M. (1983). Psychologically mediated effect on the delayed hypersensitivity reaction to tuberculin in humans. *Psychosomatic Medicine, 45,* 65–70.

S. KRIPPNER
Saybrook Graduate School

ENDORPHINS/ENKEPHALINS
GENERAL ADAPTION SYNDROME
HORMONES AND BEHAVIOR
MIND/BODY PROBLEM
NEUROCHEMISTRY
PSYCHOSOMATIC DISORDERS

PSYCHOPATHIC PERSONALITY

"The moral and active principles of the mind are strongly perverted or depraved; the power of self-government is lost or greatly impaired and the individual is found to be incapable, not of talking or reasoning upon any subject proposed to him, but of conducting himself with decency and propriety in the business of life." Thus did the English psychiatrist Prichard define the new concept of "moral insanity" in his treatise published in 1835. The same idea is embodied in the *manie sans delire* described by the father of French psychiatry, Pinel, in 1812. In that same year the first American psychiatrist, Rush, referred to persons possessed of an "innate preternatural moral depravity." The great German systematists were concerned with accounting for that large and heterogeneous group of persons whose behavior is bizarre, perverse, or outlandish—and only in some cases immoral or antisocial—but who are neither deranged nor delusional. Koch, in 1891, organized them under the heading of "psychopathic inferiorities." In the successive editions of his influential textbook, *Psychiatrie* (1883), Kraepelin plowed and replowed the same ground but, during the span of the seventh edition (1904–1914), he employed for the first time the term "psychopathic personality" as a label for the sort of people Prichard had in mind. The German nosologists, however, were reluctant to base their classifications on criteria that are sociological, or even political; one person's antisocial psychopath might be admired from another perspective as, say, a freedom fighter. Schneider's monograph *The Psychopathic Personality,* first published in 1923, defined ten varieties of deviant personality, several of which might, but did not necessarily, predispose toward antisocial behavior.

The opposite approach was taken by Partridge in 1930, who concluded that a subgroup of the persons called psychopathic had as their dominant symptom an inability or unwillingness to conform to the demands of society, and he proposed the new term "sociopathic personality." This designation was adopted by the American Psychiatric Association in the first edition of its *Diagnostic and Statistical Manual (DSM-I)*. With the publication of *DSM-III* in 1980, however, there was a reversion to the Germanic model. "Psychopathic personality" was dropped as too general and vague; "sociopathic personality," which had never really caught on, was also discarded. In their place were defined a dozen varieties of *personality disorder*, not unlike Schneider's ten psychopathies, of which several might embrace persons hitherto called psychopathic (viz., the histrionic, narcissistic, and borderline personalities) and one, the *antisocial personality*, is more explicitly tailored to Prichard's prototype.

Unfortunately, however, there is no real evidence that there are twelve types of personality disorder rather than, say, nine or nineteen, or indeed that a typological scheme is better than a dimensional one for analyzing this problem. Moreover, it is a reasonable certainty that not all of the persons who meet the descriptive criteria for antisocial personality are etiologically or psychiatrically homogeneous. By adopting criteria that are descriptive but essentially arbitrary, *DSM-IV* has opted for diagnostic reliability at the cost of validity. It is most doubtful that summary statistics compiled on the heterogeneous individuals who meet the criteria specified for antisocial personality will ever provide real illumination of this large category. More prevalent than schizophrenics, these people are a considerably greater social burden; however labeled, they constitute an important social, forensic, and psychiatric problem.

A FAMILY OF DISORDERS

The psychiatric problem is to understand why an intelligent and rational person might persist in antisocial behaviors in the face of risks and actual punishments that would inhibit most similar impulses in a normal individual. Defined thus generally, antisocial personality can be regarded as a family of disorders, comprising at least two "genera" which are themselves divisible into "species." One genus might be labeled *sociopaths* and would include those persons of broadly normal temperament who pass through the stages of conduct disorder and delinquency into adult antisocial personality because of parental malfeasance. Although our species evolved a capacity for socialization—for acquiring a self-monitoring conscience, feelings of empathy, altruistic motivations, and a sense of communal responsibility—it appears that, like our capacity for language, this latent talent must be elicited, shaped, and reinforced during childhood. This socialization of children once was the responsibility of the extended family. Judging from the low crime rates that are characteristic of traditional societies that still live in extended family groups, most children were successfully socialized in our ancient environment of evolutionary adaptation. Most modern societies, however, entrust this function just to the child's parents and his peers and the incidence of sociopathy has risen accordingly. Especially at risk are children reared by single mothers; about 70% of adjudicated delinquents in the United States were reared without the participation of their biological fathers.

A second genus consists of persons whom we might label *psychopaths* and would include species of organic dysfunction or abnormality. Some pathologically impulsive individuals seem to have a specific defect of inhibitory control. Some hyperactive children mature into impulsive psychopaths. Other persons have tyrannical sexual hungers or explosive, uncontrollable tempers or an apparent short-circuiting of aggressive and sexual instincts. The premenstrual tension syndrome can lead some women to periodic outbursts of pathological aggressiveness. These affective disturbances appear to be constitutional in origin and would obviously predispose toward antisocial behavior.

THE PRIMARY PSYCHOPATH

A thoughtful and influential essay on the clinical characteristics of the psychopathic personality, Cleckley's *The Mask of Sanity* was first published in 1941 but evolved through several editions, the last appearing in 1985. This monograph is distinguished by a vivid literary style in which an extensive series of case histories are brought to life in such a way as to make it clear that Cleckley is referring to a distinctive species of primary psychopaths who cannot be understood in terms of any of the etiological considerations discussed briefly above. From his own assessment of his material, Cleckley formulated a list of some 16 specific attributes that his cases seem to have in common. These attributes are not all equally important and a few (e.g., "suicide rarely carried out") appear to be derivative from others. The ten or so core features can be summarized as follows.

Cleckley's psychopath, "while not deeply vicious, carries disaster lightly in each hand." He may be intelligent and often displays great charm, enhanced undoubtedly by his lack of nervousness or other neurotic manifestations. Yet he is fundamentally unreliable with a remarkable disregard for truth and seems incapable of real love or emotional attachment. His antisocial behavior often appears to be inadequately motivated. He takes needless risks, giving the appearance of poor judgment, and shows an indifference to punishment by failing to learn from unpleasant experience. He lacks genuine remorse or shame, often rationalizing his behavior or laying the blame on others. He has a "specific loss of insight" or an inability to appreciate how others feel about him or to anticipate how they will react to his outrageous conduct. And, in perhaps three cases out of four, "he" is likely to be male.

Cleckley was persuaded that this syndrome results from some deep and probably constitutional defect involving an inability to experience the normal affective accompaniments of experience. A person who is colorblind cannot appreciate how a person who is not colorblind experiences a rainbow. He might learn to simulate the comments others make about the chromatic beauties of a scene and to discriminate well enough for most purposes by remembering, for example, that "red" (whatever that means) is used as a descriptor of apples yet he might never discover himself that this aspect of his experience is qualitatively different from the norm. The Cleckley psychopath, similarly, may simply be unable to experience normal guilt, remorse, frightened apprehension, or cherishing affection. Like the raw feel of the experience of color, these emotions are inherently private and unavailable to intersubjective comparison. The primary psychopath can learn what other people say in emotional situations; his protestations of love or of regret may ring as true as those of any actor yet be equally hollow. And it is possible that his indignation if he is not believed is both genuine and, in a sense, jus-

1322   PSYCHOPATHIC PERSONALITY

tified—how can he know that other people utter such statements only at the prompting of strong emotions that he has never felt?

Another approach has been to seek to understand the primary psychopath in terms of a more focal and specific defect, one of abnormality or difference from which the other features of the syndrome might derive as consequences. In particular, it has been suggested that this type of psychopath is distinguished by nothing more exotic than a low "fear IQ". All mammals can experience fear and can learn to associate anxiety with impulses that have been punished or with other stimuli that signal danger. Some people develop conditioned fear responses much more readily than other people do and have high fear IQs. A child at the low end of this same continuum will be difficult to socialize by the usual techniques of discipline that depend so heavily upon the use of fear and punishment. He may frustrate and antagonize his parents so as to be deprived of the important experience of that prototypic love relationship (this deprivation may begin quite early if the parents are themselves psychopathic). It is possible that the average child learns to identify with others as part of a self-protective effort to predict their behavior. Being relatively unconcerned with what others might do or think, the relatively fearless child may invest less effort in this aspect of social learning. One who does not readily identify with others may not readily empathize with others nor interpret their values as required for the normal development of conscience and the capacity for guilt. Fear (and its allies shame, guilt, and embarrassment) seems to be largely responsible for preventing most of us from now and then committing some of the same misdemeanors that constitute the antisocialism of the psychopath. And the absence of fear, the happy-go-lucky insouciance that emerges when shyness, self-consciousness, guilt, and apprehension are dispelled, is a cardinal attribute of "charm". An important and paradoxical corollary of the fear IQ hypothesis is that the child at risk for psychopathy should not be considered sick or defective. His is the stock from which heroes are made. With the right sort of parenting—patient, perceptive, emphasizing rewards over punishment, consistently guiding so that the child is sure to achieve these rewards, cultivating a sense of pride and self-respect to substitute for the weak inhibitions of fear and guilt—these children may grow up to be explorers and adventurers, test pilots and astronauts of the kind that Wolf admired in his book *The Right Stuff.*

If the primary psychopath is a vehicle without the brakes of fear and guilt, there is a phenocopy for whom these brakes exist but simply fail to operate from time to time. All of us have some degree of control over our aversive emotions and can tolerate pain, face danger, or confront a stressful social situation more comfortably sometimes than others, usually when we are feeling strong and rested. This capacity for emotional control seems to be hypertrophied in some individuals who are capable for hours or days at a time to effectively inhibit fear in its various manifestations. Such persons therefore are inclined (but need not necessarily yield to the inclination) to go on psychopathic binges. They are described infrequently in the literature, chiefly in cases of multiple personality in which one "personality" is the Mr. Hyde who expresses the unfettered, hedonistic "id-impulses" of the patient. The personality dubbed "Eve Black" in the case described by Cleckley and Thigpen in *The Three Faces of Eve* is a good example. In less dramatic cases, one usually sees the patient only in his or her normal, anguished and remorseful state. Because this type of emotional control seems

usually to be associated with the similarly exaggerated control over awareness of unpleasant thoughts or memories that, in the hysteroid individual, we attribute to repression, it seems appropriate to label this episodic simulation of the true primary psychopath as hysteroid psychopathy.

Lykken showed in 1957 that the primary psychopath is slow to condition fear to warning signals, tends to ignore painful electric shock in a situation where normals learn to avoid the shock, and seems generally to be less influenced than the average person is by reactions of fear or embarrassment. These findings have been replicated and extended by other investigators, most notably by Hare in a series of studies spanning thirty years. Hare has shown, for example, that the primary psychopath displays abnormally little electrodermal arousal in anticipation of a painful shock or a loud blast of noise. In this same situation, however, the psychopath shows a higher-than-normal elevation of heart rate. Other research suggests that increased heart rate can reflect the operation of an adaptive control mechanism that attenuates central nervous system arousal and perhaps, in this situation, the impact of the anticipated shock itself. Using a startle stimulus paradigm, Patrick (1994) has shown that frightening or aversive scenes, which enhance startle responses in normal subjects, affect primary psychopaths as do attractive or interesting scenes, by reducing startle.

Family studies by Cloninger and his colleagues indicate that psychopathy fits a threshold model that posits an underlying predisposition which, above some threshold (a lower threshold for males than for females), leads to the disorder. A genetically determined fear IQ, interacting with environmental influences (the style and consistency of parenting, etc.), could constitute this underlying variable of liability to psychopathy. On the other hand, the vast majority of biological relatives of primary psychopaths are not psychopaths themselves.

REFERENCES

Cleckley, H. (1941). *The mask of sanity.* St. Louis: C. V. Mosby.

Cloninger, C. R., Sigvardsson, S., Bohman, M., & von Korring, A. (1982). *Predisposition to petty criminality in Swedish adoptees. II.*

Cross-fostering analysis of gene-environment interaction. *Archives of General Psychiatry, 39,* 1242–1247.

Hare, R. D. (1993). *Without conscience: The disturbing world of the psychopaths among us.* New York: Pocket Books.

Lykken, D. T. (1995). *The antisocial personalities.* Mawah, NJ: Erlbaum.

Patrick, C. J. (1994). Emotion and psychopathy: Startling new insights. *Psychophysiology, 31,* 415–428.

Raine, A. (1993). *The psychopathology of crime.* San Diego: Academic Press.

D. T. LYKKEN
University of Minnesota

ANTISOCIAL PERSONALITY DISORDERS
CHARACTER DISORDERS
MORAL DEVELOPMENT
PERSONALITY DISORDERS

PSYCHOPHARMACOLOGY

Although drugs have been used for centuries to induce sleep and reduce pain—for example, with alcohol and opiates—not until the 1950s did present-day psychotropic and neuroleptic drugs come into being. The word *psychotropic* derives from the Greek *psyche* (mind) and *tropikos* (turning); thus a turning or changing of the mind is the essential meaning of the term. Neuroleptic derives from the Greek *neuro* (nerve) plus *lepsis* (taking hold). Disorders from such drugs appear to be neurological in nature, primarily revealing themselves as disturbances in the central nervous system (CNS). Two early psychoactive tranquilizing agents were introduced at approximately the same period: reserpine, an alkaloid derived from the root of the *Rauwolfia serpentina* plant, and chlorpromazine, a synthetically developed phenothiazine compound. Numerous other tranquilizers followed rapidly, as the pharmaceutical companies foresaw a ready market for the use of such drugs. Principal among the additions was the glycerol meprobamate, along with various other phenothiazine compounds.

Drugs *per se* cannot cure a mental or emotional illness but evidence indicates that florid psychoses can be controlled and severe psychotic anxiety abated. Schizophrenic behavior can be managed more effectively while manic depressive states and other affective disorders, such as depressions, also frequently become responsive to appropriate medication. Debilitating anxiety, as a symptom of severe neurosis, is usually ameliorated through the administration of carefully selected and monitored tranquilizers. Effective dosages vary from one person to another since blood levels are not constant even with equal dosage and body weight. Further study and research may help to tailor drugs to meet individual needs with even greater effectiveness.

Both the function and response of neurotransmitters have gained much prominence in recent years as potential avenues for dramatic breakthroughs in the understanding and treatment of mental disorders. The metabolites of serotonin, noradrenalin, and dopamine, in particular, have been the focus of the study in depressive disorders. The metabolites for these neurotransmitters are, respectively, 5-hydroxyindoleacetic acid (5HIAA), 3-methoxy-4-hydroxy-phenylglycol (MHPG), and homovanillic acid (HVA). By understanding the functioning of the catecholamines, investigators have sought to shed new light on moods and behavior. Attempts have been made to modify or block the effects of neurotransmitters so as to alter psychological reactions and feelings related to them.

Among the several ways in which psychopharmacological agents may be classified, the following categories seem to be useful for most purposes.

ANTIPSYCHOTIC DRUGS

The most commonly used types of antipsychotic medications are aliphatics and piperazines, two phenothiazine compounds. Some piperidines are employed as well; thioridazine (Mellaril) is a familiar example. (Commercial brand names appear in parentheses.) The best known aliphatic is chlorpromazine (Thorazine). Its early and widespread usage had led to its being employed as a standard for dosage measurement for other antipsychotic drugs, in particular. For example, 100 mg of chlorpromazine is the approximate equivalent of 50 mg of promazine or 16 mg of prochlorperazine (Compazine). To study the effects of other phenothiazines in a reliable manner, dosage conversion must be made to some standard for comparison.

Mental hospitals with severely disturbed and chronically ill patient populations have employed potent piperazines; for example, fluphenazine (Prolixin) and butyrophenones, especially haloperidol (Haldol). As with many strong psychoactive drugs, they may be given orally or parenterally. When oral administration is a convenient choice, hospital patients are frequently required to take the medication in view of hospital personnel to ensure ingestion, since some patients will discard the drug after pretending to swallow it. Parenteral dosage, of course, precludes this problem.

While these drugs have been useful in controlling irrational thinking, combative/aggressive behavior, and hyperactivity, serious side effects have surfaced with increasing prominence. Articles addressing one especially disconcerting side effect, tardive dyskinesia, began to proliferate in the late 1970s. This disorder results from high dosages of neuroleptic drugs over periods of six months or more, as a rule, and appears primarily in adults and the elderly, although it can manifest itself in children as well. The body areas especially affected are the lips, jaws, eyes, arms, legs, and the trunk. Movements in these parts of the body are involuntary and irregular, and initially may be confused with Parkinsonism in adults. Protruding tongue, lip and facial contortions, eye blinking, and wide, unplanned openings of the jaws are common in the face. The fingers, wrists, and arms display both athethoid (slow, writhing movements) and choreiform (rapid, jerky but coordinated) expressions. A rocking motion of the trunk may be present also. In some adult cases, the disorder appears to become irreversible, although this unfortunate result is not likely to occur with children. Dystonia (muscle tone malfunction), akinesia (absence of movement or muscle paralysis), and akathisia (restlessness, and/or inability to sit or lie down) are frequent additional accompanying symptoms of this distressing neurological malady, which characteristically appears after discontinuance of neuroleptic drugs (Fann et al., 1980).

Among the other side effects of potent psychotropics are agranulocytosis (reduction or absence of granular cells or polymorphonuclear leukocytes); jaundicing of the skin from hepatic involvement; cardiac arrythmia or infarction, as correlates of postural hypotension; along with a heightening of glaucoma and genitourinary and intestinal distress, especially in older persons. These can be managed medically by reduction or discontinuance of the drug and through counteractive biochemical procedures.

Among the commonly used phenothiazines, and their basic dosages, are the following:

Generic Name	Commercial Name	Basic Dosage
Chlorpromazine	Thorazine	100 mg
Triflupromazine	Vesprin	25 mg
Promazine	Sparine	50 mg
Trifluoperazine	Stelazine	5 mg
Fluphenazine	Prolixin	2 mg
Prochlorperazine	Compazine	16 mg
Thiopropazate	Dartal	12 mg
Butaperzine	Repoise	10 mg
Perphenazine	Trilafon	10 mg
Thioridazine	Mellaril	100 mg

A potent drug used rather extensively in the 1950s, especially for persons in mental hospitals, was reserpine (Raudixin, Harmonyl). It has since been used much more extensively as an antihypertensive.

The butyrophenones, especially haloperidol (Haldol), came into wide usage during the late 1970s. Because allergic reactions and autonomic signs were seldom seen, together with some dramatic initial instances of diminution of psychotic symptoms, its popularity increased during this period. Its potency is indicated by the fact that its standard dosage is 1/50th that of chlorpromazine, that is, 2 mg of haloperidol is the equivalent of 100 mg of chlorpromazine. Unfortunately this is one of the drugs most likely to produce tardive dyskinesia and, therefore, must be carefully monitored and given selectively. It is probably best used with younger adults.

ANTINEUROTIC OR ANTIANXIETY DRUGS

Pharmacological agents used to control tension and anxiety may be regarded essentially as antineurotic, as opposed to antipsychotic, with the exception of depressive neuroses, which are included under affective or depressive disorders. The earliest tranquilizers for the mild to moderate mental disturbances customarily found in neurotic reactions were called antianxiety drugs because the terminology connoted a calming effect without clouding of thought processes or depression of mood. Three common types of drugs were the glycerols, meprobamates (Miltown, Equanil); deprol (which combined meprobamate with benactyzine); the benzodiazepines, chlordiazepoxides (Librium), and hydroxyzine (Atarax), a diphenylmethane derivative.

Some of these drugs are, in effect, muscle relaxants and operate on the internuncial/neurons (meprobamates) while others also work through the midbrain and reticular activating system. Since these drugs often do not require parenteral administration, most are given to the patient orally, although intramuscular and intravenous delivery is done in some cases, where necessary, with selected compounds. Several benzodiazepines have a long half-life (time necessary for drug to reach half its strength in blood levels) and, therefore, only one or two doses per diem are required. Moreover, the expression of toxic effects with these drugs can be deceiving because they may appear after several days of regular administration. Because of their structure and the metabolic activity of the minor tranquilizers, suicide is unlikely with overdose when they are taken alone. However, when mixed with alcohol or other CNS depressants, a number of these drugs may become hypotensive and result in death. Every drug will vary in effective dosage and average daily amounts of many of the antianxiety compounds are difficult to substantiate. In any event, rough estimates of average daily doses for adults are listed here for a selected number of representative drugs for each type cited:

Generic Name	Commercial Name	Basic Average Dosage
Meprobamate	Miltown, Equanil	1600 mg
Meprobamate + benactyzine	Deprol	4 tablets
Diazepam	Valium	5 mg
Chlordiazepoxide	Librium	30 mg
Oxazepam	Serax	40 mg
Flurazepam hydrochloride	Dalmane	30 mg
Hydroxyzine hydrochloride	Atarax	400 mg

Physicians and patients may justifiably feel that these dosages represent too much or too little for their particular set of experiences. The placebo effect often operates in conjunction with drug ingestion, since the mere expectation that a given amount of a drug will be effective aids the process.

ANTIDEPRESSIVE DRUGS

Affective disorders account for disturbances in mood or emotional tone and include excitability, as well as depression. Some drugs that help to control anxiety are of value in dealing with heightened emotional states, such as mania and hypomania. Ideally, then, all medications for the affective states should be grouped together. Inasmuch as anxiety-reducing agents are useful with some affective states and because depression is the leading diagnostic entity in nonpublic hospitals and second only to schizophrenia in patients treated by public hospitals (Frederick, 1980), it is more workable to view the spectrum of depressive disorders under one heading.

Antidepressants are generally classified into two principal groups, tricyclic agents and monoamine oxidase (MAO) inhibitors. There are currently some 15 such drugs on the market, four MAOs and 11 tricyclics. The latter are so named because of their benzene ring chemical structure. A few bicyclic drugs, not yet on the U.S. market, may be useful additions in the future (Hollister, 1980). Stimulants are sometimes still used to combat depression. The principal stimulants employed are amphetamines (Benzedrine), dextroamphetamine (Dexadrine), and methylphenidate (Ritalin), but, for the most part, they have given way to the tricyclics and MAOs in recent times.

The antidepressants currently marketed (1982) in the United States are listed on the following page. As with other medications, average dosages are determined roughly on the basis of body weight, with an average adult weight for the combined sexes being approximately 150 pounds. Not only may varying weights make some difference, but individual metabolic differences may also be a factor. Thus the specific averages listed were calculated from the information supplied by the pharmaceutical manufacturers (*Physicians' Desk Reference,* 1982). The antidepressants, in particular, are adjusted upward or downward to reach effectiveness over a period of several weeks.

In general, tricyclics are the antidepressants of choice because some of them are apparently quicker acting and have less likelihood of serious side effects. Each of these two types of antidepressants is proscribed or should be used with extreme caution with certain patients. Tricyclics have a sedative effect but the exact mode of their action remains unknown. There is an inhibition of the membrane pump that evokes uptake of norepinephrine and serotonin in adrenergic and serotonergic neuronal tissue. Neurotransmitter activity is thereby inhibited or reduced because of prolonged neureonal action. This is believed to be at the root of antidepressant activity. Tricyclics are contraindicated in persons already receiving MAOs. Deaths have been reported as a result of convulsions and hyperpyretic crises when administered simultaneously with MAOs. Tricyclics must be given with caution to persons with glaucoma, a history of seizures, cardiovascular disorders, and those who have had problems of urinary retention. Alcohol, barbi-

Generic Name	Commercial Name	Average Daily Dosage
Monoamine oxidase inhibitors		
Isocarboxazid	Marplan	20 mg
Phenelzine sulfate	Nardil	45 mg
Pargyline hydrochloride (HCL)	Eutonyl	25 mg
Tranylcypromine sulfate	Parnate	20 mg
Tricyclic drugs		
Amitriptyline HCl	Elavil, SK-Amitriptyline	150 mg
Nortriptyline HCl	Aventyl	75 mg
Amoxapine	Asendin	300 mg
Imipramine HCl	Tofranil, Imavate, Presamine, SK-pramine	200 mg
Desipramine HCl	Norpramine, Pertofrane	150 mg
Perphenazine and amitriptyline HCl*	Etrafon	6–75 mg*
Protriptyline HCl	Vivactil	40 mg
Doxepine HCl	Sinequan, Adapin	150 mg
Cyclobenzaprine HCl	Flexeril	30 mg
Maprotiline HCl	Ludiomil	150 mg
Trimipramine maleate	Surmontil	150 mg

*Tablets contain perphenazine 2 mg and amitriptyline HCl 25 mg each, hence a daily dosage T.I.D. equals 6 and 75 mg respectively.

turates, and other CNS depressants can have potentiating effects when taken concomitantly with tricyclics. It is probably best to try a tricyclic first before prescribing an MAO. At least one tricyclic, amoxapine, has been reported to become effective in four to seven days, in contrast with the MAOs, which customarily require two weeks or more to become effective (Friedhoff & Hekimian, 1980).

The MAOs act by increasing the amounts of serotonin, epinephrine, and norepinephrine in nervous system storage areas, and heightened concentration of monoamines in the brain stem presumably brings about an antidepressant action. They are contraindicated in combination with other antidepressants, dibenzazepines, amphetamines, narcotics, antihistamines, diuretics, sedatives, anesthetics, caffeine, alcohol, and foods containing large amounts of tyramine. Persons over 60 years of age and those with cardiovascular or hypertensive disorders are considered especially at risk. Hypertensive crises have developed following ingestion of foods of high tyramine content which includes proteins where an aging process is operative. Examples are aged cheeses, red wines, caviar, herring, sausage, sherry, and sour cream, all of which are high in tyramine. Foods with moderate amounts are dried fish, avocados, chicken liver, and canned figs. Edibles with relatively low amounts of tyramines are ripe bananas, cottage cheese, yeast, and yogurt. It is best to avoid all of these for the sake of caution, including meats prepared with meat tenderizers. When transferring the patient from one antidepressant to another, or from dibenzazepines to MAOs, time should be allowed for the previous drug to wash out of the body, which ordinarily requires a drugfree period of at least one week. Despite the potential hazards noted, when proper precautions are taken, the antidepressants can be effective in reducing debilitating depression, especially when accompanied by carefully planned psychological treatment.

LITHIUM SALTS
Lithium salts were used in Europe for several years prior to their adoption for treatment in the United States. Initially thought to be useful largely for manic states, they have been shown to be of some value for depressive states as well. Produced in the form of lithium carbonate, the primary use of lithium is probably best for states of acute mania and for long-term administration in manic-depressive conditions. Precautions for its use are especially important in persons with renal or cardiovascular disorders, individuals on diuretics, and those who are debilitated or dehydrated (where sodium is depleted). Toxicity is likely a serious consequence in such cases. Pregnant women and nursing mothers should not be given lithium because it has been shown to have adverse effects on the embryos of mammals and can appear in human milk. In depression, it presumably affects neuronal activity of the catecholamines, but its biochemical action in manic patients is still not fully understood. The drug has been widely administered over the past decade and a half because of its effectiveness with manic-depressive types.

SOPORIFICS AND HYPNOTICS
Sleep-inducing and sedative drugs were used before the new crop of psychoactive drugs came on the market. These medications are still prescribed for nighttime use when sleep is desired. While they help to exert a calming effect and control anxiety, they are usually reserved for purposes of inducing sleep rather than for daytime use. Some barbiturates are short acting and others long acting in terms of both onset of action and duration. For example, phenobarbital takes an hour or more to begin its effects and lasts up to 12 hours. Amobarbital and butabarbital take 45 minutes to an hour to act and last for a period of up to eight hours. Pentobarbital and secobarbital act within about 10 minutes and have an effect that lasts no more than four hours. It is important for persons taking drugs to understand these actions, as well as the potential side effects, so that tragic errors in judgment do not occur regarding their ingestion. One should be alert to persons inclined toward self-destruction, who should be counseled so that their cooperation is obtained. Legally the psychotherapist and/or physician is on firmer ground if he or she has discussed various aspects of medications

with the patient than if no information or warnings were offered, even in suicidal cases. Patient cooperation should always be sought.

Barbiturates can decrease the effect of hormonal preparations given to women, and of anticoagulants and the antibiotic doxycycline. They can enhance or prolong the effects of corticosteroids, MAOs, and CNS depressants, including antihistamines and tranquilizers. It is important to take cognizance of the interactions and to avoid or compensate for these processes. Derivatives of pentothal of sodium are used intravenously for narcosynthesis and anesthesia. In the latter, muscles will relax within 30 seconds following unconsciousness, and the tone of the muscles of the jaw may be used as an indicator of anesthesia. Since barbiturates can be habit forming when taken orally with some regularity, patients should be warned and counseled about this possibility.

REFERENCES

Fann, W. E., Smith, R. C., Davis, J. M., & Domino, E. F. (1980). *Tardive dyskinesia.* Jamaica, NY: Spectrum.

Frederick, C. J. (1980). The suicide prone depressive: The widening circle. In *Depression in the '80s. Lederle Laboratory/New York University Symposium. Science and Medicine.* New York.

Friedhoff, A. J., & Hekimian, L. (1980). A report on a study of rapid onset of action in a new psychotherapeutic agent. In *Depression in the '80s. Lederle Laboratory/New York University Symposium. Science and Medicine.* New York.

Hollister, L. E. (1980). Pharmacologic considerations in the treatment regimen. In *Depression in the '80s. Lederie Laboratory/New York University Symposium. Science and Medicine.* New York.

C. J. Frederick
University of California at Los Angeles

ACETYLCHOLINE
AMPHETAMINE EFFECTS
ANTABUSE
ANTIANXIETY DRUGS
ANTIDEPRESSANT MEDICATION
ANTIPSYCHOTIC DRUGS
ENDORPHINS/ENKEPHALINS
HABITUATION
MARIJUANA
NEUROCHEMISTRY
STIMULANTS

PSYCHOPHYSICS

Psychophysics is the quantitative study of the relation between stimulus and sensation or sensory response. As such, it is concerned with the following questions: (a) How much stimulation is required to produce a sensation or sensory response? (b) How much must one stimulus be changed for the change to be detected? (c) In what way or ways must a stimulus be changed to be percep-

tually equivalent to another? (d) How does the sensation or sensory response change with changes in stimulus magnitudes? Answers to these questions (among others) are provided by psychophysical methods. These consist of the three classical methods (limits, adjustment, and constant stimuli) advanced, but not originated, by Fechner (1801–1887) for use in determining thresholds, numerous suprathreshold psychophysical scaling methods used for deriving measures of sensation magnitude, and signal detection theory methods used in providing measures of basic sensory sensitivity, minimally contaminated by motivational and attitudinal biases. Although employed primarily with human subjects (traditionally called observers), several of the psychophysical methods have been adapted for studying nonhuman sensitivity.

CLASSICAL PSYCHOPHYSICS

"By psychophysics," wrote Fechner (1966/1860) in his *Elements of Psychophysics,* "I mean a theory which, although ancient as a problem, is new here insofar as its formulation and treatment are concerned; in short, it is an exact theory of the relation of body and mind." Specifically, Fechner attempted to devise a precise and quantitative way of measuring the mind by providing a measure of sensation magnitude. The idea that strong stimuli generate strong sensations and weak stimuli generate weak sensations was not new. The task was to determine how strong the corresponding sensation was for a given stimulus. Quantitative attempts to do this date back, at least, to the time of the Greek astronomer Hipparchus (160–120 BC), who invented the stellar magnitude scale categorizing visible stars into six categories from faintest (sixth magnitude) to brightest (first magnitude). This scale was subsequently found to be approximated by a logarithmic function and consequently was redefined as a logarithmic scale by the British astronomer Pogson (1829–1891). The concept of a faintest visible star suggests there may be even fainter and invisible stars. Correspondingly, other stimulus dimensions could be divided into perceptible and imperceptible parts. The concept of such a division was incorporated into psychology by Herbart (1776–1841) as the threshold (or doorway) into consciousness. The idea of a threshold was influential in Fechner's analysis.

But once into consciousness, how intense is the resulting sensation? This is the basic question of psychophysics. Fechner proposed one answer: $R = k \log (I/I_0)$. The sensation magnitude (R) in Fechner's law varies directly with the logarithm of the stimulus intensity-to-threshold (I/I_0) ratio. An alternative formulation was proposed by the physicist Plateau (1801–1883), who arrived at a power function to describe the sensation of brightness. This formulation has been advanced for other senses as well as vision by Stevens (1906–1973) in a large number of experiments and theoretical articles (summarized in his 1975 in *Psychophysics: Introduction to its Perceptual, Neural, and Social Prospects).* The general equation for Stevens' power function is $R = cI^n$, where the sensation magnitude (R) varies directly with the stimulus magnitude (I) raised to a power (n). The value of n depends upon which sense is being stimulated but is considered to be relatively constant over time and across (normal) observers. The constant (c) in the equation is determined by the measurement units used.

These two theoretical formulations—Fechner's law and Stevens' law—describe differently the way sensation magnitude changes with stimulus intensity. Although both state that R increases monotonically with stimulus intensity, different predictions are made about the amount of the increase. Much experimental work has been done using numerous psychophysical methods in an attempt to determine which fits the data better. For example, by using the method of magnitude estimation (which has the observer assign numbers proportional to the stimulus magnitudes), results consistent with Fechner's law would appear as a line when graphed in semilogarithmic coordinates, while those consistent with Stevens' law would be a line in log-log coordinates. The method of bisection, in which the observer adjusts a bisecting stimulus (I_b) to be midway in sensation magnitude between two standard stimuli (I_a and I_c), would result in a stimulus that is the geometric mean of the two standards according to Fechner's law. Stevens' law predicts

$$I_b = (I_a^n + I_c^{nb})/2)^{1/n},$$

which will always be larger (for different magnitudes of I_a and I_c) than the geometric mean. On the behavioral level, Stevens' law has generally been favored, particularly for those perceptual continua in which the power-law exponent is 1.0 or greater. For small values of n, the numerical divergence in predictions may be masked by data variability.

One difficulty with both formulations is that the R specified by each is the sensation magnitude, which is not directly measured. It is treated instead as an intervening variable, mathematically specified from the input (stimulus) side and inferred from the observer's behavior on the output (response) side. On any trial (of a psychophysical experiment) several events occur: A stimulus (S) excites a receptor, which generates an electrophysiological receptor response (R_r) stimulating the action potentials which make up a neural response (R_n), which ultimately generates the sensation (R_s) that is the basis for the behavioral response (R_b). The behavioral response may be a verbal yes or no, the adjustment of a bisecting stimulus, or a verbal numerical "estimate" of the sensation. The two laws describe the relationship between S and R_s, but the experiments deal mainly with S-R_b relationships. Various approaches have been used to validate the S-R_s relations described by each of the two laws.

Cross-modality matching is a procedure introduced by Stevens in an attempt to circumvent the use of numbers by observers. It consists of having the observer adjust the stimulus on one continuum (e.g., brightness) to match a given stimulus on a second continuum (e.g., heaviness). When the various matches are graphed in log-log coordinates, the power law predicts a line having a slope equal to the ratio of the separate exponents. Evidence in support of this prediction has been reported by Stevens. Magnitude estimation may itself be treated as an instance of cross-modality matching, with the number continuum being matched against another. How much cross-modality matching results validate the power law is unclear. Ekman ("Is the power law a special case of Fechner's law?") has shown that, if one supposes that both the subjective magnitude of a stimulus (e.g., sound) and the subjective magnitude

of numbers increase in accordance with Fechner's law, then one should have a power-law relation between them. The fact that S-R_b relationships are power functions could be attributable either to Fechner's law operating twice or Stevens' law operating once.

An alternative approach has been the electrophysiological study of receptor and neural responding. Fechner stated, "[T]he stimulus does not cause sensation directly, but via the mediation of bodily activity, which in turn is more directly related to sensation" (Fechner, 1966, p. 56). Stevens viewed the exponents in his law as representing the sensory transducer transform of stimulus energy into neural activity. Here the concern is with S-R_r and S-R_n relations. Logarithmic and power-law relationships would be consistent with Fechner's law and Stevens' law respectively. There is evidence of both, but the interpretations are not simple. A logarithmic transform at one level could be transformed again at a later point. The data, while suggestive, are not conclusive.

SIGNAL DETECTION THEORY

Motivation, expectation, and attitude are biases possessed by the observer in psychophysical threshold determinations. On trials in which no stimulus is presented ("catch trials"), "yes" responses occur (indicating perception of a nonexistent stimulus). This circumstance in signal detection theory (SDT) is called a false alarm. Correct detection of the stimulus (responding with "yes" when the stimulus is present) is termed a hit. Changes in motivation, expectation, or attitude can increase the hit rate, but at the expense of elevating the false alarm rate. Classical psychophysics attempted to keep the false alarm rate low so that false alarms could safely be ignored in threshold determinations. Signal detection theory gives equal consideration to both hit and false alarm rates in determining an alternative index of sensitivity, which is designated d'. The details for computing d' depend upon the SDT procedure used, and alternative sensitivity indices are used (e.g., percent correct).

The motivational, expectancy, and attitudinal biases are collectively treated as the observer's criterion, which is estimated from the false alarm rate. The criterion can be manipulated by changing the proportion of signal trials (and so informing the observer), by instructing the observer to be more lenient or strict, or by changing the payoffs for different decisions. When data are plotted with hit rate along the ordinate and false alarm rate along the abscissa, different levels for the observer's criterion yield different data points along what is called a receiver operating characteristic (ROC) curve. Different ROC curves are generated by different signal levels, but all points on the same ROC curve represent the same level of detectability. Thus sensory and nonsensory factors can be separately identified.

APPLICATIONS

Psychophysical theory and methods have found application not only in the analysis of basic sensitivity to stimuli but also in screening for sensory deficits (where an individual's threshold is compared with known normal values), in the design of equipment and signaling devices in engineering psychology, in the study of memory using signal detection techniques, and in the comparative evaluation of clinical diagnostic tests.

REFERENCES

Fechner, G. T. (1966). *Elements of psychophysics. Vol. I.* (D. H. Howes & E. G. Boring, Eds.; H. E. Adler, Trans.). New York: Holt, Rinehart and Winston. (Original work published 1860)

Stevens, S. S.(1975). *Psychophysics: Introduction to its perceptual, neural, and social prospects.* New York: Wiley.

SUGGESTED READING

Baird, J. C. (1997). *Sensation and judgment: Complementarity theory of psychophysics.* Mahwah, NJ: Erlbaum.

Falmagne, J.-C. (1985). *Elements of psychophysical theory.* New York: Oxford University Press.

Green, D. M., & Swets, J. A. (1966). *Signal detection theory and psychophysics.* New York: Wiley.

Macmillan, N. A., & Creelman, C. D. (1991). *Detection theory: A user's guide.* New York: Cambridge University Press.

Marks, L. E. (1974). *Sensory processes: The new psychophysics.* New York: Academic.

Stebbins, W. C. (Ed.). (1970). *Animal psychophysics: The design and conduct of sensory experiments.* New York: Appleton-Century-Crofts.

Swets, J. A. (1996). *Signal detection theory and ROC analysis in psychology and diagnostics: Collected papers.* Mahwah, NJ: Erlbaum.

G. H. ROBINSON
University of North Alabama

FECHNER'S LAW
WEBER'S LAW

PSYCHOPHYSIOLOGY

Psychophysiology is the study of mental or emotional processes as revealed through involuntary physiological reactions that can be monitored in an intact subject. It is helpful to distinguish psychophysiology from physiological psychology, which is the study of the physiological substrate of mental events. A physiological psychologist seeks to understand the neural processes that mediate psychological phenomena, through research in which the independent variables are usually physiological in nature (e.g., electrical stimulation of some center in the brain. The effects of these manipulations are studied using dependent variables that are mainly psychological, such as appetitive or avoidant behavior, emotional responding, and the like.

For the psychophysiologist, this sequence is reversed. The independent variables usually will be psychological; thus, a human subject may be asked a question, given a problem to solve, instructed to perform some task or to attend to a series of simple stimuli, be put under emotional stress, and so on. The dependent variables will be physiological changes that can be recorded peripherally either as electrical signals (e.g., brain waves, muscle potentials, the electrocardiogram) or as pressure, volume, or temperature changes (e.g., breathing movements, blood pressure, skin temperature). Rarely, the psychophysiologist might use biochemical changes in urine, blood, or sweat as dependent variables.

Psychophysiology must be distinguished also from the field of psychosomatic medicine, since workers in both fields share an interest in many of the same physiological manifestations of mental and emotional events. For the psychophysiologist, the physiological reaction is a medium that carries a message about events occurring in the mind or brain. The fact that fear can produce peripheral vasoconstriction and a rapid heart beat is of concern to the student of psychosomatic medicine who is interested in these physical reactions in their own right. It is the fear itself and the fact that cold hands and tachycardia *betoken* fear that interest the psychophysiologist.

Psychophysiology is not one of the substantive disciplines within psychology, such as psychopathology or social psychology, but rather it is a technology that might be (and has been) employed in all these disciplines. In this respect, psychophysiology is to psychology as, say, microscopy is to physiology. The psychophysiologist's formal training may be in psychology, physiology, medicine, or engineering. Because many of the phenomena studied are electrical in nature and the instrumentation is electronic, a psychophysiologist must understand at least the rudiments of electrical theory. Many psychophysiologists function adequately with minimum training in anatomy and physiology. A typical psychophysiologist will devote part of his or her professional career to improving methods of measurement or inventing new ones and the remaining time in applying this technology to some substantive problem in psychology, psychiatry, or even such diverse fields as criminology or political science. Most North American as well as many European psychophysiologists are members of the Society for Psychophysiological Research and subscribe to its journal, *Psychophysiology.*

PSYCHOPHYSIOLOGICAL MEASUREMENT

The immediate object of psychophysiological measurement is to generate an electrical signal that faithfully mimics the manner in which the physiological phenomenon being measured varies over time. Once the phenomenon has been represented as an electrical signal, it may easily be amplified or filtered; visualized as a tracing on a polygraph chart or on the face of a cathode-ray tube (CRT); recorded for later playback and analysis on a tape recorder; or fed into a computer. Some psychophysiological phenomena, such as the electroencephalogram (EEG), the electromyogram (EMG), and the electrocardiogram (ECG), are already electrical signals generated in the body, and their measurement requires only a pair of electrodes appropriately placed to pick up the biological voltage, connected to the input of an amplifier that will boost this voltage until it is strong enough to be recorded in some way. The most versatile method of recording is one that allows the original signal to be reproduced later, as a tape recording may be played back, but most psychophysiology laboratories also make a permanent visual record of the signal using an electrically driven pen that moves up and down with changes in the signal and writes on a paper chart that moves laterally. A polygraph consists of several pen motors arranged side by side, each driven by a separate amplifier, so that several separate signals may be recorded on the same time base on one chart. A polygraph with, say, four amplifiers and pen motors is said to have four channels. It is important to see that a single channel may contain numerous variables; for example, the ECG channel provides a complex analog record of the electrical events associated with the cardiac cycle. Many separate variables may be quantified from this record: the height of the P-, R-, and T-waves, the time periods between them, the time between successive R-waves (which is the reciprocal of heart rate), and so on.

Electrodes

Electrodes used in psychophysiology are junctions where the flow of electric current changes from electronic (in the wires of the external circuitry) to ionic (in the skin and other tissues). Such an interface is subject to electrochemical processes that can produce polarization. A polarized electrode acts like a high-pass filter that discriminates against slow or low-frequency changes. Relatively nonpolarizing electrodes are available, typically made of silver and coated with silver chloride. An electrode paste or electrolyte is applied between the skin surface and the electrode; the properties of this conductive paste are also important for successful recording.

Transducers

Phenomena such as pressure or temperature changes can be converted into electrical signals by means of an appropriate transducer. For example, a thermister is a device the electrical resistance of which varies reliably with temperature; by passing a weak electric current through a thermister probe and amplifying the voltage developed across it, one can produce a signal that accurately represents changes in temperature. A strain gauge, similarly, changes in resistance as it is flexed and can therefore act as the sense organ of a pressure transducer or of a device for measuring (for example) breathing movements.

Some psychophysiological phenomena that do not produce signal voltages directly may involve changes in the electrical properties of tissue and may be measured by passing an external sensing current through the tissue. The electrical conductance of the palmer skin is one example. The standard technique for measuring the skin conductance response (SCR) involves applying a constant voltage of 0.5 volt between two nonpolarizing electrodes attached to the palmer skin surface and measuring the small direct-current flow (less than 10 microamperes per square centimeter) through the tissues. A number of physiological phenomena, including blood flow, heart action, muscle contraction, and respiration, produce changes in the electrical impedance of the associated tissue; these changes may be measured by passing a weak, high-frequency (e.g., 50 kHz) sensing current through the body. These impedance techniques are infrequently used but have considerable promise for specialized applications.

Noise

The modern world is literally full of what may be thought of as electrical noise—electromagnetic emanations from television transmitters, electric motors, passing autos, fluorescent lights, and so forth—which the human body picks up as an antenna does. Bioelectric signals originating in the body, similarly, become noise when they are not the signal one wants to measure but appear nonetheless in one's recordings. Where once it was necessary to study weak signals such as the EEG in awkward and expensive shielded rooms, using ranks of storage batteries to provide power untainted by the AC mains, modern amplifiers make this task much simpler. The noise-rejecting capabilities of these amplifiers will be realized, however, only if one (and only one) low-resistance electrode connects the subject to earth or electrical ground.

Noise of biological origin, as when eye movements affect the EEG or when the ECG shows up unwanted in the electrodermal channel, requires special solutions. Sometimes reorientation of the electrodes will suffice. If the noise consists mainly of frequencies outside the bandwidth of the desired signal, a bandpass filter may provide the solution. A third approach is to measure the noise directly in a separate channel and then subtract it from the signal channel by electronic inversion and summation.

Safety

Unpleasant electric shocks are always a potential hazard in the vicinity of apparatus connected to the AC power mains. These same shocks can easily be fatal if the recipient happens to be well grounded. Subjects in psychophysiological research are almost always well grounded. It is necessary, therefore, to take sensible precautions. The voltage with respect to ground of every electrode, wire, or other conductive surface with which the subject might come into contact should be measured, and a variety of other safety measures are available.

Recorders

All modern polygraphs have standard outputs at which an amplified representation of each signal channel is available for connection to the input of a recorder or other device. Multichannel analog tape recorders are available, both reel-to-reel and cassette types, with which the information being graphically recorded by the polygraph can be electronically recorded for later playback. This makes it possible to input selected segments of the signal to a computer for analysis or to make a new polygraph recording at a different chart speed, for example. Because most psychophysiological channels will contain frequencies below the low-frequency limits of direct tape recording, these analog data recorders work on the frequency modulation (FM) principle. A carrier frequency of, say, 1,000 Hz is caused to vary in frequency in proportion to the signal and the FM carrier is recorded. The reverse process of demodulation is accomplished on playback.

Digital tape recorders are also available, usually as part of a computer installation, which can store and play back with great accuracy digital (numerical) information. To use this method, the polygraph output must pass first to an analog-to-digital (A/D) converter, which will measure the signal at specified intervals and output these measurements as a series of binary numbers. On playback, a digital-to-analog D/A converter will perform the reverse operation. Digital recording is more expensive than analog, and would normally be used as part of (or in preparation for) computer analysis of the data.

Computers

Most psychophysiology laboratories now employ small computers for on-line control of experiments and immediate analysis of data, and also for more complex subsequent analyses. Laboratory interface systems are available that make it possible to turn things on and off under computer control; to generate stimuli; to time events; and to provide data, command signals, and other information from the laboratory to the computer. The computer may present pictorial or alphanumeric information to the subject by means of a CRT display or a variety of auditory stimuli including spoken words such as "right," "wrong," and "good!", which have been digitally recorded and stored in the computer's memory. Psychophysiologists of the past have needed a working knowledge of electrical principles, physiology, and statistics, and a more than rudimentary understanding of psychology; competent psychophysiologists of the present require a working knowledge of the computer as well.

ANALYZING THE DATA

The variance of a sample of scores on some psychophysiological variable can be partitioned thus:

$$\sigma_\omega^2 = \sigma_\psi^2 + \sigma_\phi^2 + \sigma_\varepsilon^2 \tag{1}$$

where σ_ψ^2 is the variance due to individual differences in the underlying psychological variable of interest, σ_ϕ^2 is the orthogonal component of variance due to physiological differences, and σ_ε^2 represents measurement error. If skin conductance level (SCL, represented by ω) is being measured, for example, ψ might be central nervous system (CNS) arousal or energy mobilization, ϕ would reflect individual differences in the density and activity of volar sweat glands, and ε would increase with variations in the cleaning of the skin surface, in the positioning of the electrodes, in the area of skin contacting the electrolyte, and so on.

Underlying most psychophysiological measurement is the implicit assumption that ω is a monotonically increasing function—and, it is hoped, a simple linear function—of the underlying variable of interest, ψ, as in:

$$\omega = a + b\psi + \varepsilon \tag{2}$$

Using SCL again as the example, the parameter a would represent this subject's minimum SCL when sudomotor activity is zero, while b would be determined by the reactivity of the entire electrodermal system (i.e., the increase in conductivity produced by a unit increase in ψ; very similar assumptions are implicit in most psychological measurement). The problem is that the parameters a and b also vary, often within the same individual from time to time, and certainly from one individual to another. This is the variation represented by σ_ϕ^2 in Equation 1. The job of the psychophysiologist is, first, to ensure that the physiological variable chosen (ω) *is* linearly related to ψ, at least approximately, and then to try to minimize both measurement error σ_ε^2 and σ_ϕ^2 (the variance due to physiological variability, within subjects or between subjects, which also must be regarded as error variance in this context).

The Linearity Assumption

Consider an experiment in which the subject is intensely stressed at the outset, then allowed to relax and go to sleep, while skin potential level (SPL) is continuously monitored. The SPL will be fairly low under intense stress, will rise to a maximum while the subject is, say, listening to an interesting story, then will fall again to a minimum when the subject goes to sleep. These individual curves show us that SPL has an inverted U-shaped relationship to CNS arousal and is therefore a poor index of that variable. Suppose that, in the same experiment, we also measure electrodermal responses—SCRs from one hand and resistance changes or SRRs from the other. Because resistance is the reciprocal of conductance, and the responses are being elicited over widely varying levels of tonic SCL and SRL, the SCRs will be poorly correlated with the corresponding SRRs. Thus SCR and SRR cannot be equivalent indicants of the same psychological process (e.g., of the psychological impact of the stimulus). Which of the two should be used? Lykken and Venables (1971) show that there is both theoretical and empirical support for the view that conductance is more simply related to central events than is resistance.

These examples illustrate that it is important to investigate the form of the relationship between ω and ψ, that this requires experimental manipulation of ψ (remembering, as we have seen, that the parameters of the function also will vary among subjects), and that the investigation will be illuminated by whatever one knows about the physiological substrate of the variable studied.

Minimizing Extraneous Variance

Minimizing variance resulting from error of measurement is largely a matter of competent and consistent technique; the details will depend on the variable being measured. To minimize variance due to extraneous physiological differences requires a statistical correction for individual differences in the range over which the measured quantity can vary in that subject at that time (Lykken, 1972). The basic idea is to estimate the parameters a and b of Equation 2 for each individual subject and then obtain a range-corrected score for each subject thus:

$$\text{score}_{rc} = \frac{(\text{score} - min)}{max} \tag{3}$$

In the case of SCL, for example, min would be the subject's minimum SCL obtained when relaxed or asleep. The estimate of max might be obtained from that subject's maximum SCL shown under high stress. In the case of phasic changes such as the SCR, min or the minimum value is always zero. Phasic response values can therefore be range-corrected merely by dividing by an estimate of that subject's maximum response amplitude.

THE CHANNELS OF PSYCHOPHYSIOLOGY

A number of organ systems provide the psychophysiologist with a variety of (clouded) windows through which to observe mental events. This section reviews the most widely studied of these systems.

The Cardiovascular System

People have been drawing inferences about one another's mental and emotional processes from cardiovascular changes since the dawn of history, because some changes—blushing and blanching of the skin, pounding of the heart, cold hands, and the like—can be detected without instrumental assistance. The important channels are the electrocardiogram (ECG), arterial pressure, finger pulse pressure, and perhaps digital temperature. The ECG is a sequence of electrical signals generated by the busy heart muscle and radiated throughout the body. The psychophysiological variable most commonly derived from the ECG channel is heart rate (the reciprocal of the time interval between successive R-waves produced by ventricular contractions). The ECG is often fed into a device called a cardiotachometer, which electronically measures this interval, converts it to rate, and outputs a signal proportional to instantaneous heart rate. In the intact subject, blood pressure can be measured only intermittently by auscultation. A pressure cuff on the upper arm is inflated until the brachial artery is sufficiently compressed to occlude the flow of blood. With a stethoscope over the artery distal to the cuff, the pressure is gradually released until the first Korotkoff sounds are heard; these sounds are caused by the spurting of blood through the arterial occlusion during the peak of the pressure cycle, just after ventricular contraction. The first sounds mark the peak, or systolic, blood pressure. As pressure is relaxed further, the sounds wax and wane until a point is reached at which blood flow continues even at the minimum of the pressure cycle; this is the diastolic pressure.

Electronic detectors are now available to replace the ears of the skilled clinician and can measure blood pressure reliably, although their absolute accuracy may be off by several millimeters of mercury. Automatic systems for intermittently inflating and deflating the cuff have been used with some success, but the process is cumbersome and is both distracting and uncomfortable to the subject. A possibility currently being explored is that blood pressure may be reliably related to pulse transit time—that is, the time required between the initiation of the pressure pulse when the ventricles contract and the arrival of that pulse at, say, the finger. Peripheral blood flow can be detected either by a pressure transducer (a plethysmograph) on a finger or by means of a photoplethysmograph, a device in which a light is directed into the skin at an angle and the reflections detected by a photoelectric cell. The reflectance varies as blood surges in and out of the vascular bed of the dermis, yielding a signal that varies with the digital pressure pulse.

One must always remember that the heart has more important things to do than to whisper secrets to the psychophysiologist, and it is under strong homeostatic control. Heart rate and blood pressure tend to obey the Law of Initial Values, which states that the change in either variable produced by a stimulus will be correlated with the prestimulus level of that variable; a pressor stimulus will cause a smaller increase in the rate of an already racing heart than in one beating slowly and calmly.

The Electrodermal System

Compared with subdermal tissues, the skin has a relatively high resistance to the passage of electric current. In the latter part of the 19th century, it was discovered that the resistance of the thick skin of the palms and soles was extraordinarily reactive to psychological stimulation. It is known that the sweat glands in these volar regions subserve a special function: instead of helping with thermoregulation, they moisten grasping surfaces in preparation for action. Dry palmar skin is both slippery and more subject to abrasion. Neural circuits arising in the activating systems of the midbrain control volar sweating, which increases tonically with central nervous system (CNS) arousal, and which also shows wavelike, phasic increases in response to any stimulus important enough to produce an orienting response. In part because the sweat gland tubules provide a low-resistance pathway through the epidermis, the electrical resistance of the skin varies with sweat gland activity. Since, in fact, resistance varies inversely with sweating, current practice is to measure skin conductance, the reciprocal of resistance.

Skin conductance level (SCL) is lowest in a drowsy or somnolent subject, rises sharply with awakening, and rises still further during mental effort or emotional storm. Superimposed upon the tidal changes of SCL are the wavelike, phasic skin conductance responses (SCRs) to stimulation. After a latency of perhaps 1.5 seconds, conductance rises rather quickly to a peak, then returns more or less rapidly to the prestimulus level. Both the latency period and the size and shape of the SCR are affected by hand temperature; if the hand is cold, SCRs are sluggish and diminished in amplitude. The SCR amplitude seems to vary with the psychological impact of the eliciting stimulus; other things being equal, strong stimuli produce larger SCRs than do weak stimuli, but an unexpected or especially significant weak stimulus will produce a larger SCR than an expected but meaningless strong stimulus.

Probably as a result of the inward pumping of sodium ions from secreted sweat, the skin surface tends to be 10 to 80 mV (millivolts) negative with respect to the underlying tissues. As a result also of sweat gland activity, this endogenous skin potential provides a channel of information that is to some extent parallel with the skin conductance channel, but there are nonlinearities that complicate interpretation. The skin potential response (SPR) may be an increase in negativity, an increase followed by a decrease, or a monophasic wave of decreased negativity, depending on the strength of the stimulus and the prestimulus SPL. For these reasons, the modern tendency is to employ the skin conductance channel in preference to skin potential.

Electromyography

An electrode on the skin over any muscle mass, referenced against an electrode in some quiescent region such as an earlobe or over the shin, will pick up a high-frequency (100–500 Hz) signal produced by the repeated firing of hundreds of thousands of muscle fibers. This signal can be electronically integrated to yield a simpler curve representing average muscle tension. Except perhaps in deep or Stage 4 sleep, the striate muscles maintain a degree of tonus even at rest, with individual fibers firing asynchronously at a low rate. In a tense individual, this resting tonus may be quite high, either generally or in specific muscle groups. Surface electromyography provides a means of monitoring such subactive muscle tension. One common application is in relaxation training with or without biofeedback, in which some easily interpretable indicate of current muscle tension is fed back to guide the subject's efforts to achieve voluntary control.

Eye Movements and the Pupillary Response

The eyes, those portals through which the brain receives so much of its information about the external world, are also called the windows of the soul through which the psychophysiologist may see glimpses of the workings of that brain. Eye movements and the direction of gaze can be monitored by electrooculography (EOG). The eye is like a little battery with the cornea about 1 mV positive with respect to the back of the retina. If electrodes are positioned adjacent to the outer canthus of each eye, then, when both eyes are turned to the right, for instance, the electrode on that side becomes electropositive to the one on the left. Another pair of electrodes above and below one eye will record vertical eye movements. The sensitivity of the EOG is illustrated by the fact that, when subjects track a target moving sinusoidally from side to side of an oscilloscope screen, the EOG recorded on the polygraph will usually be a nearly perfect sine wave. If the target is then driven by a triangular waveform, the EOG record will reproduce this change.

The EOG has been used to study the saccadic eye movements employed in reading or in searching a visual display. It has also been used in the study of nystagmus and the smooth following movements with which the eyes track a moving target. A defect in smooth tracking performance has been shown by Philip Holzman and colleagues (1974) to be characteristic of most schizophrenic patients. This deficit appears to result from some central defect in the processing of visual information. Because it appears in schizophrenics in remission as well as in many first-degree relatives of these patients, it is now believed that visual smooth-following dysfunction may prove to be a marker for the genetic predisposition associated with that disorder.

The size of the pupil, which can vary from about 2 to about 8 mm in diameter, is regulated by the autonomic nervous system so as to tend to hold constant the intensity of light admitted to the retina. The pupil is also reactive to psychological stimulation with small (< 1 mm) but regular changes (usually dilations) following a stimulus with latencies on the order of 0.2 second. Of the various techniques that have been used for measuring these pupillary responses, the most sophisticated involves a television monitoring system using infrared illumination and automatic measurement of the image of the pupil, which yields an output signal proportional to pupil size that can be recorded on the polygraph. An accumulation of evidence (Beatty, 1982) indicates that the pupillary response measures the proportion of total cognitive processing capacity that has been invested in the analysis of the eliciting stimulus. For this reason, larger responses will be elicited by more complex stimuli or more difficult problems, by more interesting or more important stimuli, and also by those near-threshold stimuli that are detected (and thus require processing) as compared with those that escape detection. Earlier theories that pupil size varies with the attractiveness of stimuli are subsumed by the processing hypothesis; it is likely that more attractive stimuli tend to be subjected to more intensive processing. Pupillary responses to relatively simple mental tasks are larger for less intelligent subjects, suggesting that the less efficient brain must deploy a greater proportion of its resources to solve a given problem.

Electroencephalography

While the electroencephalograph (EEG) might appear to provide the most direct window of all through which to observe mental events, the electroencephalographer has been likened to a spy, prowling outside the concrete walls of a great factory complex, trying to infer from the din of noises reaching the outside what is going on within. The electrical activity of the brain is far more complex than the most elaborate manufactured computer; only a billionth part of this information is available at the brain's surface, and still less at the scalp. Since an electrode on the scalp integrates electrical activity over a considerable area of cortex, a reasonably comprehensive record of the total EEG may be obtained from about 20 electrodes distributed systematically over the head. A set of standard placements has been defined, called the International Ten-Twenty System. The complete montage will be used by clinicians looking for EEG evidence of tumors or epileptiform activity, whereas the researcher more commonly uses only one or a few EEG channels.

The most common use of the spontaneous EEG is in sleep research, in which, with additional channels recording lateral eye movements and muscle tension, it is possible to identify the stages of sleep with considerable reliability. Computer programs are available for doing a fast Fourier transform of a segment of EEG from, say, a relaxed waking subject, thus producing a spectrum or graph of the frequency content of the EEG, most of it contained in the band from zero to 20 Hz. An individual's EEG spectrum is both relatively distinctive and stable, as long as it is obtained each time under similar conditions. The spectra of monozygotic twins tend to be as similar as those of one person measured on two occasions. Though it seems reasonable to expect that the features of the spectrum, the relative amount of theta activity, the midfrequency of the alpha rhythm, and so on, ought to have interesting psychological correlates, none have as yet been reliably demonstrated.

Event-Related Cortical Potentials

Virtually any stimulus sensed by the subject will produce an effect upon the EEG; indeed, much of the apparently spontaneous EEG may be simply the composite effect of the flux of stimulation, external and internal, that continuously bombards the sensorium. To detect the effect of all but the most intense stimuli against the background of EEG activity requires repeated presentations of the stimulus, so that the immediate poststimulus segments of the EEG record can be averaged together. If 100 0.5-second EEG segments are randomly selected and then averaged, the mean will tend toward a straight line. But the 100 0.5-second segments that follow 100 presentations of, say, an auditory click will each contain the event-related cortical potential (ERP) elicited by that click, a relatively complex train of waves time-locked to the stimulus. The averaging process minimizes the random background activity and reveals the features that are consistent in each sample.

The earlier components of the ERP seem to represent earlier stages of cerebral processing. Recent evidence suggests the possibility of a relationship between the speed (latency) of these components and some basic dimension of intelligence. Later components, especially a positive wave about 300 msec poststimulus, seem to reflect the completion of a process of stimulus identification or classification. The actual latency of this wave varies with reaction time, and its amplitude varies with the information content of the stimulus; unexpected, important, or possibly memorable stimuli produce larger P300 components.

The study of the psychological correlates of components of the ERP, and the use of these data in formulating and testing models of the way in which the brain processes information, constitute one of the most active and promising areas of current psychophysiological research.

REFERENCES

Andreassi, John L. (1995). *Psychophysiology: human behavior and physiological* (3rd ed). Hillsdale, NJ: L. Erlbaum.

Beatty, J. (1982). Task-evoked pupillary responses, processing load, and the structure of processing resources. *Psychological Bulletin, 91,* 276–292.

Hasset, James (1978). *A primer of psychophysiology.* San Francisco: W.H. Freeman.

Holzman, P. S., Proctor, L. R., Levy, D. L., et al. (1974). Eye-tracking dysfunction in schizophrenic patients and their relatives. *Archives of General Psychiatry, 31,* 143–151.

Lykken, D. T. (1972). Range correction applied to heart rate and to GSR data. *Psychophysiology, 9,* 373–379.

Lykken, D. T., & Venables, P. H. (1971). Direct measurement of skin conductance: A proposal for standardization. *Psychophysiology, 8,* 656–672.

Martin, I., & Venables, P. H. (Eds.). (1980) *Techniques in psychophysiology.* New York: Wiley.

Stern, R. M., Ray, W. J., & Davis, C. M. (1980). *Psychophysiological recording.* New York: Oxford University Press.

D. T. LYKKEN

AUTONOMIC NERVOUS SYSTEM
BRAIN WAVES
CENTRAL NERVOUS SYSTEM
NEUROPSYCHOLOGY

PSYCHOSEXUAL STAGES

In Freud's (1938) personality theory, development is described in terms of stages defined by the specific expression of sexual, or libidinal, urges. Those areas of the body—the erogenous zones—that give rise to libidinal pleasure at specific ages are identified as the focus of each developmental stage. Thus the pleasure derived from sucking liquids and mouthing foods of varying consistencies and temperatures is the focus of the first developmental period, the *oral stage.* The satisfaction surrounding the retaining and expelling of feces defines the second period, the *anal stage.* The *phallic stage*

refers to the period in which the young child begins to explore the genitals and derives pleasure from their manipulation. These three stages, called the pregenital stages, span respectively, the first year of life, the second two years, and the years from three to five, roughly.

The pregenital stages are followed by a period of supposed psychosexual quiescence, the *latency period,* which lasts from the end of the phallic stage at approximately age five until the onset of puberty. During the latency period, libidinal urges are said to be repressed. Puberty, however, brings with it a resurgence of the pregenital urges, which now focus specifically on the pleasures which derive from the genital organs; the name of this final developmental period is the *genital stage.*

Libidinal urges in Freudian theory are not equatable with genital sexuality. For example, three of the psychosexual stages are "pregenital." The term *libido* is meant to define a broad concept of mental sexual energy occurring even in infancy. Nor do the stages refer only to male sexuality, despite the masculine language. For example, the phallic stage refers to the last pregenital stage of both sexes.

ORAL STAGE

The oral stage of development in Freud's theory is characterized by a need for nurturance and an acquisition of pleasure derived primarily from the process of being nurtured and centering on the main avenue of nurturance, the mouth and lips. The main sources of pleasure are first the stimulation of the lips and mouth and the sucking, mouthing, and swallowing of food, and later, pleasure is derived from the biting and chewing of food. In Freudian theory, these early gratifications are said to be the precursors of the development of later character traits. Thus, the two main sources of oral pleasure, oral incorporation and biting (seen as aggressive), may be the prototypes for later habits and personality traits. Oral incorporation as a predominant trait may lead to an "incorporative" style of living, including acquisition of material things and acquisitiveness in personal relationships. An oral aggressive style may include such behavior traits as "biting" sarcasm, "chewing out" an opponent, and spewing out an invective. Because of the dependent nature of the infant-caregiver relationship, dependency and need for approval are seen as main components of the oral character. Some evidence for this relationship has been found by Masling, Weiss, and Rothschild (1968), who studied the Rorschach responses of a group of conforming and nonconforming college undergraduates. The measure of conformity was the respondents' tendency to mimic the erroneous responses of a confederate of the experimenter in a perceptual task—the paradigm first described by Asch (1956). Masling and colleagues found that the most conforming subjects gave significantly greater "oral-dependent" responses on the Rorschach test, when compared with the least conforming subjects.

ANAL STAGE

The anal stage extends approximately from one year of age to two, and it refers to the period of a child's life in which learning bowel and bladder control is a primary task and the pleasure and pain derived from expelling and retaining feces are the main libidinal outlet. The maturation of the nervous system now allows for voluntary control of the anal sphincters. The toddler in the anal period is growing in independence and self-assertion. Freud saw the events surrounding the task of toilet training as crucial for later character formation. A child who is harshly trained and severely punished for accidents before acquiring control may express rage by defecating at will at inappropriate times or by being selfish and stingy (anal retentive). Conversely, the child who is rewarded and praised for control efforts becomes the generous (anal expulsive) and often creative individual. Overindulgence can lead to messiness and vagueness. In *Personality Theories,* Maddi summarized the traits ascribed to the anal character by earlier writers such as Freud, Fenichel, and Abraham: "Stinginess-overgenerosity, constrictedness-expansiveness, stubbornness-acquiescence, orderliness-messiness, rigid punctuality-tardiness, meticulousness-dirtiness, and precision-vagueness" (Maddi, 1972, p. 273).

PHALLIC STAGE

Between two and three years of age, the child begins more active exploration of his or her body. The locus of erotic pleasure shifts from the anus to the genitals as the young child discovers the pleasurable effects of masturbation. One of the main tenets of Freudian theory, the Oedipus complex, has its origins in this stage. Named for the mythical Greek king of Thebes who killed his father and married his mother, the Oedipus complex refers to the child's incestuous desire for the opposite-sexed parent. In the boy, the simultaneous pleasure from autoerotic activity coupled with a desire for the mother and a rivalry with his father generates anger in his father, which the boy perceives as a threat. Since the erotic pleasure emanates from the genitals, the boy assumes that the father may destroy them. Freud called this perceived threat *castration anxiety.* As a result of this fear, the boy represses his incestuous attachment to his mother and his anger to his father and identifies with his father. That is, he forms a warmer bond with his father and begins to act like him. Simultaneously, he incorporates the father's values and develops an internal set of standards, known as the superego.

The resolution of the Oedipus complex in the girl is not so clear or specific in Freudian theory. Since castration to the girl appears to be a *fait accompli,* she blames her mother, whom she sees as sharing her plight, and envies the organ of the males and his favored position and power. Freud's term for this condition was *penis envy.* The girl gradually gives up her attachment to her father and begins to identify with her mother.

GENITAL STAGE

After a period of psychosexual quiescence, termed latency, puberty brings with it a resurgence of the phallic strivings and more realistic capabilities for their expression. Once again, masturbation becomes a source of erotic satisfaction, and appears so nearly universal and urgent that Freud called this adolescent impulse *onanism of necessity.* Armed with full adult genitalia and sexual drives, the growing adolescent shifts his or her affection from parents to peers, first of the same sex (a brief homosexual phase, just

after puberty), and then of the opposite sex. In the fully integrated adult, the psychosexual urges most often find expression in activity with an opposite-sexed partner of roughly the same age. More important, these urges are no longer purely narcissistic, as they were in the pregenital stages. The psychosexual urges now extend and generalize to altruism, friendship, sharing, and loving of a more adult nature.

REFERENCES

Asch, S. E. (1956). Studies of independence and conformity: I. A minority of one against a unanimous majority. *Psychological Monographs, 70* (9, entire No. 416), 1–70.

Freud, S. (1969/1938/1935/1920). *A general introduction to psychoanalysis.* New York: Pocket Books.

Maddi, S. R. (1976/1972/1968). *Personality theories: A comparative analysis* (3rd ed.) Homewood, IL: Dorsey Press.

Masling, J., Weiss, L., & Rothschild, B. (1968). Relationships of oral imagery to yielding behavior and birth order. *Journal of Consulting and Clinical Psychology, 32,* 89–91.

J. P. McKINNEY
Michigan State University

PSYCHOANALYSIS

PSYCHOSOMATIC DISORDERS

The term psychosomatic disorder generally refers to a type of physical condition in which the etiology or course is related to significant psychological factors. A psychosomatic disorder involves a demonstrable organic pathology, such as a duodenal ulcer, or a known pathophysiological process, such as a migraine headache. These conditions usually include such disorders as rheumatoid arthritis, asthma, and essential hypertension, and are not limited to a single physiological system.

Psychosomatic disorders were not specifically listed in the fourth edition of the *Diagnostic and Statistical Manual of Mental Disorders* (*DSM-IV*), but are referred to as "psychological factors affecting medical condition," and in the ninth edition of the *International Classification of Diseases* (ICD-9) as "psychic factors associated with diseases classified elsewhere."

HISTORICAL BACKGROUND

Psychosomatic concepts have roots in ancient philosophical thoughts about mind-body relationships. Emperor Huang Ti (c. 2697–2597 BC) recorded in his *Classic of Internal Medicine* keen observations on the etiology, diagnosis, treatment, and prognosis of psychosomatic illnesses. Herbal doctors of the Babylonian-Assyrian civilization (c. 2500–500 BC) considered sin to be the source of sickness and exorcism to be the cure, with mind and body interaction being central to their concept of disease.

Socrates (496–399 BC) and Hippocrates (466–375 BC) also offered early acknowledgement of the role of mental factors in health and disease. Heinroth in 1818 first employed the word "psychosomatic," a term later popularized by German psychiatrist Jacobi. Scientific medicine achieved major progress toward the end of the nineteenth century, with an emphasis on physical disease, as a result of the discoveries in morbid anatomy, microbiology, and biochemistry. The gap between the biological and the psychological aspects of illness remained until a rapprochement began to develop in the early twentieth century, largely because of the work of Freud, Pavlov, and Cannon. Freud's elaboration of the unconscious, Pavlov's studies of the conditioned reflex, and Cannon's notion of fight and flight reactions offered important psychological concepts that stimulated the growth of the psychosomatic approach in health care.

A psychosomatic movement began in Germany and Austria in the 1920s, and many Europeans, such as Alexander, migrated to the United States, bringing along the European interest in psychosomatic disorders. In 1939, the birth of the journal *Psychosomatic Medicine,* under the editorship of Dunbar, reflected the growing interest in this field in the United States. In time, important volumes began to appear in the 1940s and 1950s, including Weiss and English's *Psychosomatic Medicine,* Alexander's *Psychosomatic Medicine,* and Grinker's *Psychosomatic Research.*

Early psychosomatic methodology consisted mainly of clinical observations. By the late 1950s, an increasing number of psychologists were engaged in laboratory and clinical psychosomatic experiments. There was a declining interest in researching psychoanalytic concepts in psychosomatic problems, while there was a growing trend toward experimental research studying human biological response to hypnotic techniques, conditioning, and sensory input and deprivation. Psychosomatic research with animals provided a large body of scientific information, with relevant implications for human physiology and clinical practice.

THEORETICAL CONCEPTS

Although Freud never mentioned "psychosomatic disorder" in his writings, he stressed the role of psychic determinism in somatic conversion hysteria. Freudian followers provided further refinement of psychoanalytic concepts vis-à-vis psychosomatic phenomena, including Dunbar's description of personality profiles (e.g., the ulcer personality, the coronary personality, and the arthritic personality), as well as Alexander's analysis of psychodynamic patterns underlying asthma, ulcers, arthritis, hypertension, and other disorders.

Important psychosomatic concepts also emerged in nonpsychoanalytic schools. Corticovisceral theory prevailed in Eastern Europe, dominated by Pavlovian neurophysiology and conditioning research. In the United States, psychological stress theory, such as Cannon's concept of bodily homeostasis, Wolff's research on the adaptive biological responses, and Selye's work on pituitary adrenal responses, formed the foundation for psychosomatic research and clinical approaches. Social or ecological concepts have also been elaborated, as in the early Midtown Manhattan Project or the more recent life-change studies by Rahe and Holmes.

TYPE OF DISEASE

In 1950, Alexander listed seven classic psychosomatic diseases: essential hypertension, peptic ulcer, rheumatoid arthritis, hyperthyroidism, bronchial asthma, colitis, and neurodermatitis. More recently, the extensive classification system of the ninth *International Classification of Diseases* provided a comprehensive list of psychosomatic disorders, including the following:

1. Psychosomatic disorders involving tissue damage, such as asthma, dermatitis, eczema, gastric ulcer, mucous colitis, ulcerative colitis, urticaria, and psychosocial dwarfism.

2. Psychosomatic disorders not involving tissue damage, such as psychogenic torticollis, air hunger, psychogenic hiccup, hyperventilation, psychogenic cough, yawning, cardiac neurosis, cardiovascular neurosis, neurocirculatory asthenia, psychogenic cardiovascular disorder, psychogenic pruritus, aerophagy, psychogenic cyclical vomiting, psychogenic dysmenorrhea, and teeth grinding. A psychosomatic syndrome can also be categorized according to the major organ systems affected.

In the following, psychological factors may be a cause or an aggravating stress that affects the course of the disorder:

1. Gastrointestinal disorders: gastric and duodenal ulcers, ulcerative colitis, anorexia nervosa, bulimia, obesity, irritable colon, spastic colitis.

2. Respiratory disorders: asthma, hyperventilation, tuberculosis.

3. Skin disorders: neurodermatitis or eczema, pruritus, urticaria, psoriasis, skin allergies, herpes.

4. Musculoskeletal disorders: rheumatoid arthritis, temporomandibular jaw syndrome, muscle contraction headache.

5. Metabolic and endocrine disorders: thyrotoxicosis, myxedema, diabetes mellitus, Addison's disease, Cushing's syndrome, parathyroid disease, hypoglycemia.

6. Gynecological and obstetrical disorders: menstrual disorders (premenstrual tension, menorrhagia, pseudocyesis), conception and pregnancy (sterility, spontaneous abortion).

7. Cardiovascular disorders: coronary artery disease, essential hypertension, congestive heart failure, vasodepressive syncope, migraine headaches, angina pectoris, arrhythmia, cardiospasm, tachycardia.

8. Hematological disorders: hemophilia.

9. Others: immune diseases, chronic pain syndrome, allergic reactions.

TREATMENT

The early roots of psychosomatic medicine consisted of psychoanalytically oriented therapies, such as those of Alexander and his associates. In more recent decades, nonanalytic psychotherapies have become more prominent. With the increasing sophistication in pharmacotherapies, psychiatrists find the use of psychotropic medications helpful, including various tranquilizers and antidepressants. Group psychotherapy is especially suitable for certain psychosomatic patients, such as those with bronchial asthma, who find relief in meeting others with similar concerns and learn to identify and verbalize significant feelings related to this condition.

In cases where psychosomatic reactions may be the result of learned patterns of behavior—for example, certain sexual dysfunctions—behavior therapy is an effective therapeutic method. One of the oldest forms of psychosomatic therapies, hypnosis, has been found to be effective in disorders such as hyperventilation, peptic ulcer, and headaches.

The recent decades have seen a rapid growth in psychologists' employment of behavior modification techniques, exercise, and relaxation therapies, such as Jacobson's progressive relaxation, Luthe's autogenic training, and biofeedback to treat headaches and other stress-related disorders. In addition, principles and methods of transcendental meditation, yoga, controlled breathing, and Morita therapy have also been used with psychosomatic disorders.

SUGGESTED READING

Kaplan, H. I., & Saddock, B. J. (1996). *Concise textbook of clinical psychiatry.* Baltimore: Williams & Wilkins.

Stoudemire, A. (Ed.). (1995). *Psychological factors affecting medical conditions.* Washington, DC: American Psychiatric Press.

W. T. TSUSHIMA
Straub Clinic and Hospital

BEHAVIORAL MEDICINE
MENTAL ILLNESS: EARLY HISTORY

PSYCHOSOMATICS

Although the term was coined in the early 19th century, "psychosomatics" was used quite differently then than it is today (Margetts, 1950). Initially it referred to problems such as phobias and obsessions that now would be labeled as clearly psychological; it was never widely used until rescued in the 1940s by Flanders Dunbar.

Today psychosomatics is defined as covering three areas (Lipowski, 1968):

1. The science of the relationships between psychological and biological events.

2. A holistic approach to medical practice that gives "equal consideration to the person who has the disease and to the disease the person has" (Henker, 1982).

3. Consultation activities where mental health professionals work with physically ill patients.

Psychosomatics, in its broadest sense, includes all interactions between behavior—thoughts, feelings, actions—and physical illness. Such relationships have been recognized for centuries. In fact, the bulk of medical treatments operated on psychological prin-

ciples until the modern era emerged in the late 19th century. Today, when new medical "miracles" appear regularly, psychosomatics serves as a reminder that diseases do not arise and run their course in a vacuum; they exist only in patients.

Physicians rarely ask for psychological help when they treat "psychosomatic" patients. Consultation liaison is a "poor relation" division in most psychiatry departments. One of the reasons for this is that the claims for the psychosomatic approach run contrary to the way in which physicians traditionally prefer to proceed—by interpreting symptoms as manifestations of disturbances in various organs. If the real trouble lies in the functioning of the whole person, traditional medical procedures tend to grind to a halt. The usual "solution" at this point is to turn to a psychological explanation. Patients are often convinced by this sequence of events that "psychological" means not really worthy of serious concern.

This tendency to diagnose by exclusion also leads professionals to label symptoms as psychosomatic when they do not know what causes them. How many women have been told that dysmenorrhea is due to "rejection of the feminine role"?

SPECIFICITY THEORIES

Modern psychosomatics began in the late 1920s and early 1930s. Since this was a time when psychoanalysis dominated clinical work in psychology and psychiatry, the psychoanalytic emphasis on etiology as the key to cure took over psychosomatics as well. This emphasis continued well into the 1950s and beyond, producing a number of theories that attempted to delineate precisely just how psychological problems could produce somatic disease. These can roughly be divided into specificity and nonspecificity theories.

A specificity theory holds that definite psychological constellations produce each psychosomatic disorder. Specificity hypotheses fall into four general groups: (a) personality specificity theory; (b) conflict specificity theory; (c) emotion specificity theory; and (d) response pattern specificity (Engelsmann, 1977).

Personality specificity theory is associated primarily with Dunbar (1943). This approach holds that definite personality traits lead to specific physical symptoms. These ideas have recently reappeared as "risk factors" said to represent predispositions to disease. Much attention has been focused, for example, on the A-type behavior pattern and the evidence linking it with coronary artery disease (Friedman & Rosenman, 1974; Thoresen et al., 1981).

Alexander and French (1948) are associated with conflict specificity theory. This theory is an extension of the psychoanalytic notion of conversion, according to which unconscious conflicts are resolved by being "converted" into somatic symptoms. Specific conflicts are said to be associated with specific diseases, although the relationship is mediated through the autonomic nervous system and does not "resolve" the conflict. These notions supposedly apply particularly well to the psychosomatic disorders, the seven diseases initially studied from this point of view: peptic ulcer, bronchial asthma, rheumatoid arthritis, ulcerative colitis, essential hypertension, thyrotoxicosis, and neurodermatitis.

All specificity theories seek to solve the "symptom choice" problem on psychological grounds. Symptom choice means simply: "Why does patient A develop asthma while patient B is hypertensive?" The emotion specificity hypothesis suggests that specific emotions lead to definite somatic changes, and eventually to particular somatic disturbances (Grace & Graham, 1952). Carruthers (1981) reviews psychophysiological evidence that provides some support for this idea. Anxiety may be distinguished from anger, for example, by the balance between adrenaline and noradrenaline acting on body tissues, with noradrenaline predominating in anger.

Response pattern specificity theory (Malmo, 1967) rests on individual differences in stress-response patterns. Gastric reactors are prone to ulcers; blood pressure reactors are prone to hypertension. These notions place symptom choice at the physiological level and anticipate, to some extent, more recent developments.

Although all the specificity approaches contribute something to an understanding of psychosomatics, none survives in its original form. Research has given partial support to all, but complete support to none.

NONSPECIFICITY THEORIES

As specificity theories began to bog down, the nonspecificity position rose in esteem. It was, in fact, incorporated into the 1952 *Diagnostic and Statistical Manual of Mental Disorders,* which contained a section labeled "Psychophysiologic disorders." The nonspecificity position maintains the etiological primacy of psychological factors in at least some cases of certain physical diseases but abandons the attempt to explain symptom choice. The explanatory burden is carried by the vaguely defined construct "organ vulnerability."

The *alexithymia* hypothesis advanced by Nemiah and Sifneos is in the nonspecificity tradition (Gottschalk, 1978). Certain people, alexithymics, find it difficult to experience or express emotions as others do. They are said to be particularly subject to psychosomatic disturbances. Although these ideas have received a good deal of attention, they remain controversial.

None of these theories have been extensively validated, although all can explain some phenomena. Psychosomatics is a complex area; multiple causation seems more likely than linear sequences. This complexity makes investigations likely to be misleading or fruitless when based on simple correlations between poorly measured psychological elements and physical symptoms. Studies of intervening events and mediating factors are necessary.

A useful organizing notion is the concept of stress (Selye, 1936). Much of Selye's work dealt with physical and chemical inputs. Modern psychophysiology extends and amplifies Cannon's work employing the psychological stress concept. The findings to date suggest the following likely conclusions: (a) Different emotions are associated with different patterns of changes. (b) There are considerable individual differences in these patterns. (c) The patterns are often such that one can begin to see that physical diseases might arise from their continuation over long periods (Christie & Mellett, 1981).

It is now so obvious that psychological events influence somatic phenomena that many experts reject Cartesian dualism altogether and think of mind and body as one. Family physicians report that 20 to 50% of their patients suffer from functional complaints.

Health care delivery researchers are beginning to reject the notion that third-party payments for psychological therapy will break the system. Instead "offset research" suggests that such financial support actually may save money by reducing the number of unnecessary patient visits to physicians—a modern version of the "apple a day." Mental health professionals specializing in behavioral medicine are demonstrating replicable results from treatment, something that has been a long time coming.

REFERENCES

Alexander, F. G., & French, T. M. (1948). *Studies in psychosomatic medicine.* New York: Ronald Press.

Carruthers, M. (1981). Field studies: Emotion and beta-blockade. In M. J. Christie & P. G. Mellett (Eds.), *Foundations of psychosomatics.* New York: Wiley.

Christie, M. J., & Mellett, P. G. (Eds.). (1981). *Foundations of psychosomatics.* New York: Wiley.

Dunbar, H. F. (1943). *Psychosomatic diagnosis.* New York: Hoeber.

Engelsmann, F. (1977). The psychologist's role in psychosomatics. *Psychosomatics, 18,* 47–52.

Friedman, M., & Rosenman, R. H. (1974). *Type A behavior and your heart.* New York: Fawcett Crest.

Gottschalk, L. A. (1978). Psychosomatic medicine today: An overview. *Psychosomatics, 19,* 89–93.

Grace, W. J., & Graham, D. T. (1952). Relationship of specific attitudes and emotions to certain bodily diseases. *Psychosomatic Medicine, 14,* 243–251.

Henker, F. O. (1982). Conflicting definitions of the term "psychosomatic." *Psychosomatics, 23,* 8–11.

Lipowski, Z. J. (1968). Review of consultation psychiatry in psychosomatic medicine, III: Theoretical issues. *Psychosomatic Medicine, 30,* 395–422.

Malmo, R. B. (1967). Physiological concomitants of emotion. In A. M. Freedman & H. I. Kaplan (Eds.), *Comprehensive textbook of psychiatry.* Baltimore: Williams & Wilkins.

Margetts, E. L. (1950). The early history of the word psychosomatic. *Canadian Medical Association Journal, 63,* 402–404.

Selye, H. (1936). A syndrome produced by diverse nocuous agents. *Nature, 138,* 32.

Thoresen, C. E., Telch, M. A., & Eagleston, J. R. (1981). Approaches to altering the type A behavior pattern. *Psychosomatics, 22,* 472–482.

H. A. STORROW
University of Kentucky

BEHAVIORAL MEDICINE
HEALTH PSYCHOLOGY
MIND/BODY PROBLEM
PSYCHOLOGICAL HEALTH
SOMATOPSYCHICS

PSYCHOSTIMULANT TREATMENT FOR CHILDREN

Psychostimulant medication has become the mainstay treatment for children with attention-deficit/hyperactivity disorder (ADHD), and is typically administered alone or more typically as part of a comprehensive treatment regimen involving some form of behavior therapy and parent training. An estimated 2.8% of youths in the United States between 5 and 18 years of age received psychostimulant treatment during the 1990s Methylphenidate (MPH and its product-name equivalent, Ritalin) is the most commonly used psychostimulant for treating children with ADHD, and is prescribed for approximately 90% of cases. The basic psychopharmacological properties and clinical usefulness of psychostimulants in treating children with ADHD is well established. Clinical trials have been conducted since the 1930s (Bradley, 1937), and over the course of the ensuing sixty years, positive treatment effects have been consistently documented for a wide range of outcome variables. These include improvements in concentration, schoolwork, learning of verbal and nonverbal information, use of study time, and behavior (including peer relationships), as well as enhanced short- and long-term memory ability and reduced impulsivity and aggression. Titrating MPH (i.e., determining correct dosage), however, has become increasingly more complex in recent years. Issues related to determining appropriate dosage and which behaviors or variables to target for intervention have been subjected to empirical scrutiny.

TITRATING PSYCHOSTIMULANTS

Several misconceptions concerning both the initial titration of and dosage effects associated with psychostimulants prevail. Popular among these is the notion that a child's gross body weight should be used to establish initial dosage parameters using a milligram of medicine per kilogram of body weight (mg/kg) ratio—the implicit assumption being that heavier children require more medicine than do lighter-weight children. Two studies have addressed this issue in recent years (Rapport, DuPaul, & Kelly, 1989; Rapport & Denney, 1997), with both reporting a lack of relationship (not even a trend) between children's body weights and clinical responses to MPH.

A more complicated issue concerns the dose-response nature of psychostimulants. For example, there is widespread belief that different behavioral domains are optimized at widely discrepant dosage levels in children. In brief, lower dosages are thought to optimize cognitive performance while higher dosages are required to optimize behavior and manageability in the classroom. Neither comprehensive literature reviews (see Rapport & Kelly, 1991) nor direct observations of children receiving psychostimulant treatment while working in classroom or laboratory environments have supported this contention. Instead, both classroom behavior and cognitive performance (including academic performance) have been found to be affected at similar dosage levels, usually within the middle to higher dosage range when using MPH (Douglas, Barr, O'Neill, & Britton, 1986; Rapport, Denney, DuPaul, & Gardner, 1994). It should be stressed, however,

that these results are based on average responses of large groups of children. The optimal dosage for a particular child must be carefully determined in the context of a controlled medication trial.

SELECTING APPROPRIATE TARGET BEHAVIORS

Most children are prescribed psychostimulants by their primary physician and seen routinely in an office setting for purposes of monitoring treatment effectiveness (including the possibility of emergent symptoms or side effects). Physicians, in turn, rely primarily on parent and teacher reports to (a) establish whether a child has shown a favorable response to the medication and (b) determine the most effective dosage. What would appear to be a relatively straightforward endeavor is in fact complicated by a number of factors. Neither children nor their parents are particularly astute at delineating positive treatment effects. Because of the relatively short behavioral life of MPH (approximately 4–5 hr from time of ingestion) and dissimilarities between the home and classroom setting (particularly the fewer cognitive demands associated with the former), parents are not ideally situated to judge treatment effectiveness. Moreover, the findings of a recent study reveal that neither initial presenting characteristics of the child (e.g., level of pretreatment hyperactivity or age) nor changes in particular behavioral domains (e.g., attention or reduced impulsivity) portend improvement in other important areas such as academic functioning (Denney & Rapport, 1999). Conversely, improved academic functioning nearly always coincides with improved behavior. The essence of this finding is that children's academic performance in the classroom should serve as the primary target for titrating psychostimulants in children. Assessment of this domain can be accomplished by using the Academic Performance Rating Scale (APRS; DuPaul, Rapport, & Perriello, 1991) or a similar instrument that provides a valid index of children's classroom academic performances.

CONCLUSIONS

The use of psychostimulants as a therapeutic regimen to treat children with ADHD remains a controversial topic. A majority of children (approximately 80%) derive clear and sustained benefit from this therapeutic modality, although most experienced clinicians and researchers concur that neither this nor any treatment regimen used alone adequately addresses the multifaceted difficulties associated with ADHD. When used, controlled medication trials across a wide dosage range are strongly recommended owing to the unique response children exhibit to psychostimulants. Outcome assessment should, at the very least, include multiple, standardized, treatment-sensitive measures across settings (home and school) throughout the duration of the clinical trials as well as at scheduled intervals thereafter to assess continuity and maintenance of treatment effects. Finally, clinical indices of improvement should ideally include measures from both the behavioral and cognitive (academic) domains, owing to the latter variable's established relationship with long-term academic achievement and adult outcome.

REFERENCES

Bradley, C. (1937). The behavior of children receiving Benzedrine. *American Journal of Orthopsychiatry, 94,* 577–585.

Denney, C. B., & Rapport, M. D. (1999). Predicting methylphenidate response in children with Attention Deficit Hyperactivity Disorder: Theoretical, empirical and conceptual models. *Journal of the American Academy of Child and Adolescent Psychiatry, 38,* 393–401.

Douglas, V. I., Barr, R. G., O'Neill, M. E., & Britton, B. G. (1986). Short term effects of methylphenidate on the cognitive, learning, and academic performance of children with attention deficit disorder in the laboratory and the classroom. *Journal of Child Psychology and Psychiatry, 27*(2), 191–211.

DuPaul, G. J., Rapport, M. D., & Perriello, L. M. (1991). Teacher ratings of academic skills: The development of the Academic Performance Rating Scale. *School Psychology Review, 20,* 284–300.

Rapport, M. D., & Denney, C. (1997). Titrating methylphenidate in children with attention-deficit/hyperactivity disorder: Is body mass predictive of clinical response? *Journal of the American Academy of Child and Adolescent Psychiatry, 36,* 523–530.

Rapport, M. D., Denney, C., DuPaul, G. J., & Gardner, M. (1994). Attention Deficit Disorder and methylphenidate: Normalization rates, clinical effectiveness, and response prediction in 76 children. *Journal of the American Academy of Child and Adolescent Psychiatry, 33,* 882–893.

Rapport, M. D., DuPaul, G. J., & Kelly, K. L., (1989). Attention-deficit hyperactivity disorder and methylphenidate. The relationship between gross body weight and drug response in children. *Psychopharmacology Bulletin, 25*(2), 285–290.

Rapport, M. D., & Kelly, K. L. (1991). Psychostimulant effects on learning and cognitive function: Findings and implications for children with attention deficit hyperactivity disorder. *Clinical Psychology Review, 11,* 61–92.

M. D. RAPPORT
University of Central Florida

ATTENTION-DEFICIT/HYPERACTIVITY DISORDER (ADHD)

PSYCHOSURGERY

Psychosurgery, by definition, implies the destruction of healthy brain tissue for the relief of severe, persistent, and debilitating psychiatric symptomatology. Its use can be traced back with early archeological evidence of trepanation in 2000 BC (Valenstein, 1980). However, the first widespread application of psychosurgical procedures to psychiatric patients began in the late 1930s, reached its peak in the 1960s, and began to decline in the 1970s (Weingarten, 1999).

In the first half of this century, the technique most frequently used for creating lesions was frontal lobotomy, wherein fibers in the frontal lobes were cut bilaterally. Initially this was accomplished by placing a cutting instrument into burr holes drilled through the skull, or through the bony orbits above the eyes, and then rotating the instrument. More precise placement of lesions became possible during the 1950s as a result of the invention of a stereotaxic instrument that held the head in a fixed position; a knife or electrode could then be lowered into the brain at a point predetermined by a set of three-dimensional coordinates as defined by a brain map or atlas. In this manner, well-localized lesions could be made. The use of knife cuts was gradually replaced by the use of electric currents or radio-frequency waves delivered through electrodes. Some neurosurgeons have also used cryoprobes, radioisotopes, proton beams, ultrasound, and thermocoagulation for this purpose (Weingarten, 1999).

Emotional changes occur in a variety of neurological disorders including epilepsy, stroke, and trauma. Clinically, it has been noted that lesions in distinctly different areas of the brain will disrupt emotional processing at different levels or stages. Therefore, a common feature shared by theories of emotional dysfunction is that multiple brain systems are involved (Gainotti, Caltagirone, & Zocolotti, 1993). The theories are broadly classified into those stressing asymmetrical contributions of the two cerebral hemispheres, and those emphasizing frontal-cortical-subcortical system connections. Thus, Bear (1986) has accented the role of the right hemisphere in emotion, because over phylogenetic development, language functions have evolved to occupy homologous left-hemisphere sites. Others (see Borod, 1993) have advanced modular models which combine concepts from lateral dominance with ideas about the brain's other axes (dorsal-ventral and anterior-posterior). Here, the right hemisphere's putative role in emotion is modified by a valence hypothesis: The right hemisphere controls negative emotions, while the left controls positive emotions. Additionally, identifiable circuit-specific behavioral aberrations can be recognized after damage to frontal-cortical-subcortical circuits, such as the "environmental dependency syndrome" (Lhermitte, 1986) and "utilization behaviors" (Lhermitte, Pillon, & Serdaru, 1986; described in the section on Central Nervous System Disorders [Frontal Lobe Dysfunction]).

In the main, psychosurgery has continuously targeted bilateral brain systems. The most effective early targets for relief of psychiatric symptoms appear to involve the medial and ventral areas of the frontal lobes. Other regions of the brain with well-defined connections to specific frontal areas have been selected as targets for psychosurgery. These connecting regions include the cingulum, the amygdala, several areas in the thalamus and hypothalamus, and anterior portions of the internal capsule (to interrupt frontothalamic projections). The term "tractotomy" refers to the interruption of fiber tracts connecting frontal areas with lower brain centers, and it has been used in the treatment of severe depression, anxiety, and Obsessive-Compulsive Disorder. Amygdalotomy has been effective in a majority of patients with aggressive behaviors associated with temporal lobe epilepsy (Jasper, Riggio, & Goldman-Rakic, 1995). Pallidotomy in patients with severe Parkinson's disease restores in some cases relatively normal motor function (see Lang & Lozano, 1998). It remains to be seen, however, how long the beneficial effects last.

Since psychosurgery most usually is performed on apparently normal brain tissue, its practice has generated considerable controversy. The National Commission for the Protection of Human Subjects of Biomedical and Behavioral Research supported several intensive investigations on the use and efficacy of psychosurgery. As indicated in a resultant report by the US Department of Health, Education and Welfare and the follow-up reports published in Valenstein's book (Valenstein, 1980), the Commission considered many pros and cons, including risks and benefits. Opponents of the use of psychosurgery have compared it to the abuses of human subjects in biomedical experiments carried out in Germany during World War II. Those in favor of psychosurgery have argued that its prohibition would rob patients of their right to effective medical treatment by limiting the scope of procedures available.

On the basis of the diverse and extensive information reviewed by the Commission, recommendations were made to the US Department of Health and Human Services (DHHS) regarding the use of psychosurgery. One recommendation encouraged DHHS to support evaluative studies of the safety and efficacy of the procedures, and two other recommendations detailed conditions for, and approval of, their limited use with institutionalized individuals. Obviously psychosurgery is a topic that involves many ethical, scientific, and legal concerns, and there is no easy resolution of the controversy associated with its use.

REFERENCES

Bear, D. M. (1986). Hemispheric asymmetries in emotional function. In B. K. Doane & K. E. Livingston (Eds.), *The limbic system: Functional organization and clinical disorders.* New York: Raven Press.

Borod, J. C. (1993). Cerebral mechanisms underlying facial, prosodic, and lexical emotional expression: A review of neuropsychological studies and methodological issues. *Neuropsychology, 7,* 445–463.

Gainotti, G., Caltagirone, C., & Zocolotti, P. (1993). Left/right and cortical/subcortical dichotomies in the neuropsychological study of human emotions. *Cognition and Emotion, 7,* 71–93.

Jasper, J. H., Riggio, S., & Goldman-Rakic, P. (Eds.). (1995). *Epilepsy and the functional anatomy of the frontal lobe.* New York: Raven Press.

Lang, A. E., & Lozano, A. M. (1998). Medical progress: Parkinson's disease. *New England Journal of Medicine, 339*(16), 1130-1143.

Lhermitte, F. (1986). Human autonomy and the frontal lobes. Part II: Patient behavior in complex and social situations: The "environmental dependency syndrome." *Annals of Neurology, 19,* 335–343.

Lhermitte, F., Pillon, B., & Serdaru, M. (1986). Human autonomy and the frontal lobes. Part I: Imitation and utilization behavior: A neuropsychological study of 75 patients. *Annals of Neurology, 19,* 326–334.

Valenstein, E. S. (Ed.). (1980). *The psychosurgery debate: Scientific, legal and ethical perspectives.* San Francisco: Freeman.

Weingarten, S. M. (1999). Psychosurgery. In B. L. Miller & J. L. Cummings (Eds.), *The human frontal lobes. Functions and disorders* (pp. 446–460). New York: Guilford.

M. OSCAR-BERMAN
P. McNAMARA
Boston University School of Medicine, and
Boston VA Medical Center

BRAIN INJURIES
NEUROSURGERY

PSYCHOTHERAPY

What is psychotherapy? Although originally defined as one-on-one sessions between a patient and a therapist with the intent of changing the inner workings of the patient's psychological life, over the last several decades psychotherapy has broadened in its formats, participants, procedures, and focus (there are now over 250 different forms of psychotherapy) so that any definition of psychotherapy must be far-ranging enough to encompass the discipline's full spectrum. What relaxation therapy, family therapy, cognitive therapy, group therapy, insight-oriented therapy, play therapy (with children), and exposure therapy—to name a few—have in common is a set of psychological or behavioral procedures, delivered by one or more therapists, designed to change the thoughts, feelings, somatic symptoms, or behaviors of one or more participants who are seeking help.

Although the practice of psychotherapy is not regulated, it is generally delivered by psychologists, psychiatrists, social workers, family therapists, psychiatric nurses, pastoral counselors, or addiction counselors. Surveys have found that 2.2 to 4.4% (depending on the city) of the United States population makes at least one visit to a mental health specialist in a six-month period (Hough, Landsverk, Karno, & Burnam, 1987). People who seek psychotherapy do so for a variety of reasons, including treatment for an ongoing psychiatric disorder (such as agoraphobia or depression), difficulty coping with recent stressful life events, or desire for more success in or satisfaction with life.

HISTORY

Psychotherapy in its modern form can be traced to Sigmund Freud in the late 19th century. Psychoanalysis was developed as a long-term treatment designed to bring to the patient's awareness repressed unconscious conflicts. Despite the large number of brands of psychotherapy today, only a few general schools have continued to be influential. The psychodynamic, or analytic, school continued to develop over the 20th century. Under the influence of Sandor Ferenczi, Otto Rank, Franz Alexander, and Thomas French, the analytic school shifted toward shorter-term treatments that included increased therapist activity. Modern psychodynamic therapy evolved in the 1970s under the influence of Malan, Mann, Sifneos, and Davanloo, who encouraged a focal treatment that explored patients' maladaptive interpersonal styles within the context of time limits. In the 80s, Luborsky and Strupp and Binder published manuals for implementing short-term dynamic psychotherapy. These treatments focus mainly on interpretating, in the context of a supportive therapeutic relationship, maladaptive relationship patterns as they influence the patient's current relationships and functioning.

Closely related to dynamic treatments, the interpersonal school was first described by Harry Stack Sullivan. Sullivan focused on interpersonal relationships as they influenced the development of the patient's personality. In 1984, Klerman, Weissman, Rounsaville, and Chevron published a manual for interpersonal psychotherapy. This treatment emphasizes the patient's current interpersonal relationships. Unlike dynamic treatments, developmental factors and maladaptive relationship patterns as they are expressed in the therapeutic relationship are not given direct attention.

Carl Rogers developed the client-centered school of psychotherapy. This approach focuses on the psychological climate created by the therapist. An environment characterized by genuine acceptance, sensitive understanding, and empathic understanding is believed to foster within the patient the ability to reorganize his or her personality. Unlike dynamic therapy, the climate of the therapeutic relationship alone is believed to foster the patient's gains.

The behavioral school of psychotherapy has also remained influential. Behavior therapy has its base in learning theory. The model postulates that symptoms are a result of learned behaviors that are subject to direct manipulation by contingency management and classical conditioning. Techniques focus on modifying behavior through positive and negative reinforcement and desensitization.

The cognitive school of psychotherapy was founded by Albert Ellis in the 1950s. In rational emotive therapy, problems are seen as a result of faulty expectations and irrational thoughts. The goal of this treatment is to teach patients to modify their thinking patterns. In 1979, Aaron Beck published a manual for cognitive therapy of depression. This treatment focuses on identifying, testing the validity of, and correcting the dysfunctional beliefs that underlie the patient's cognitions.

These types of psychotherapy are applied in both an individual and group format. In individual therapy the therapist works one-on-one with the patient, while group formats may include groups of strangers brought together to work on a specific topic, couples, or families. The family systems approach to psychotherapy focuses on each family member as coequal in importance. The therapist helps the members identify problems in the family system and to reorganize themselves as an effective family unit.

A recent trend to emphasize the common factors across the various schools of psychotherapy has paved the way for the movement towards integration of different approaches. Many practitioners find it useful to borrow techniques from multiple schools to maximize patient benefit. Cognitive and behavioral techniques are often used in conjunction and seen as important complements to each other in the therapeutic process.

Another recent trend has been toward short-term, rather than long-term, treatment. This trend has been influenced in part by research conducted on brief therapy and in part by the need to contain health care costs (i.e., most insurance companies will pay for only a limited number of sessions of psychotherapy).

RESEARCH ON PSYCHOTHERAPY

Although many are skeptical of psychotherapy as a treatment, it has been investigated in research studies more than any other medical procedure, with well over 1,000 studies of psychotherapy performed to date. Extensive reviews of the research literature have concluded that, broadly speaking, psychotherapy works; research is now directed toward the more specific question of finding out what type of psychotherapy procedure works best with identified types of patient problems or disorders, and on developing new techniques for enhancing treatment benefits. Other research examines psychotherapy as it is delivered in the community—its effectiveness, cost, and dose-response relationships. Yet another form of psychotherapy research (process studies) looks at what actually happens during psychotherapy sessions and attempts to unravel the relationship between the actions of the therapist in session and the changes in the patient.

Research on specific treatment procedures for different problems and disorders has led to recommendations about which psychotherapy procedures have sufficient empirical support. These recommendations are based largely upon the results of studies in which patients are randomly assigned to psychotherapy versus a control group (e.g., a waiting list, or a psychological or pill placebo). Specific psychotherapies have received strong empirical support as treatments of Obsessive-Compulsive Disorder, Major Depressive Disorder, Panic Disorder, Agoraphobia, and Generalized Anxiety Disorder (Chambless et al., 1996).

Studies of psychotherapy as it is practiced in the community have yielded important data on the number of treatment sessions that are necessary to help patients achieve a recovery from their symptoms. About a year of treatment (58 sessions) is needed to produce symptomatic recovery for 75% of patients (Kopta, Howard, Lowry, & Beutler, 1994). While brief psychotherapy may be of help to many, these data suggest that longer-term psychotherapy may still be needed for other patients to reach full recovery.

REFERENCES

Chambless, D., Sanderson, W. C., Shoham, V., Johnson, S. B., Pope, K. S., Crits-Christoph, P., Baker, M., Johnson, B., Woody, S. R., Sue, S., Beutler, L., Williams, D. A., & McCurry, S. (1996). An update on empirically validated therapies. *The Clinical Psychologist, 49,* 5–18.

Hough, R. L., Landsverk, J. A., Karno, M., & Burnam, M. A. (1987). Utilization of health and mental health services by Los Angeles Mexican Americans and non-Hispanic whites. *Archives of General Psychiatry, 44,* 702–709.

Kopta, S. M., Howard, K. I., Lowry, J. L., & Beutler, L. E. (1994). Patterns of symptomatic recovery in psychotherapy. *Journal of Consulting and Clinical Psychology, 62,* 1009–1016.

P. Crits-Christoph
M. B. Connolly
University of Pennsylvania

ANALYTICAL PSYCHOLOGY
ASSERTIVENESS TRAINING
BEHAVIOR THERAPY
BIBLIO THERAPY
BIOFEEDBACK
BRIEF PSYCHOTHERAPY
COGNITIVE BEHAVIOR THERAPY
COGNITIVE THERAPY
CRISIS INTERVENTION
ECLECTIC PSYCHOTHERAPY
EXPERIENTIAL PSYCHOTHERAPY
FAMILY THERAPY
GESTALT THERAPY
GROUP PSYCHOTHERAPY
IMPLOSIVE THERAPY
PLAY THERAPY
PSYCHOANALYSIS
REALITY THERAPY
RELATIONSHIP THERAPY
TRANSACTIONAL ANALYSIS

PSYCHOTHERAPY, BRIEF

The proper length of psychotherapy has been a subject for discussion since the time of Sigmund Freud. Freud himself was concerned about the length of time required for psychoanalysis and believed that as our knowledge of human personality and psychopathology was increased by means of psychoanalysis, the time required for therapy would gradually diminish. However, his expectations were not confirmed. On the contrary, it became apparent, in the United States at least, that as psychoanalysis became perfected it also increased in length.

Because of the historical importance of psychoanalysis and psychodynamic therapy in the development of psychotherapy, for many years it was a commonly held view that psychotherapy required a moderately long period of time to secure positive results. The belief was that the individual's neurotic problems developed over a period of many years and that the underlying causative factors were repressed unconscious conflicts. Consequently, it took time to treat repressed conflicts and overcome patients' resistances. Therefore, the therapist could not force therapeutic progress by being overly directive but had to play a patient and rather passive role. In fact, to proceed too quickly could be detrimental because the clients would be forced to confront their conflicts before they were ready to do so.

Psychoanalysis and psychodynamic therapy were dominant for the first half of the twentieth century and, because of their strongly held beliefs, therapy clearly was not viewed as a brief process. However, most therapists today have a different view of the psychotherapeutic process and are engaged in many different forms of brief psychotherapy, including briefer forms of psychodynamic therapy.

A number of events occurring in the 1960s led to some significant changes in the mental health disciplines in the United States. The Joint Commission on Mental Illness and Health appointed by the US Congress came up with a number of conclusions and recommendations after 5 years of study and deliberation. Among them was the view that psychoanalysis was both too expensive and time-consuming to meet the needs of the majority of people requiring psychotherapeutic services. It also was recommended that community mental health centers be set up to meet these needs, and along with this development a number of innovative programs featuring crisis intervention and brief psychotherapy were developed. Instead of long waiting lists for conventional psychotherapy, walk-in clinics and emergency clinics provided round-the-clock services with brief therapy lasting from six to ten sessions. The rationale was that treatment provided at the time of crisis would be briefer, would help the individual return to his or her previous level of functioning, and would prevent the problem from becoming chronic.

Some research reports also indicated that despite the psychoanalytic emphasis on long-term psychotherapy, the median length of therapy in outpatient clinics was from six to eight sessions. Clearly, most patients wanted their therapy to be brief, and it was apparent also that many will terminate therapy on their own after a few sessions despite the opposing views of the therapists. Gradually, over time, therapists have modified their views about the required length of therapy and more recently, other developments also have tended to emphasize and reinforce brevity in psychotherapy.

Brief therapy differs from long-term psychotherapy in a number of ways. Although no absolute number of sessions defines brief psychotherapy, most appear to be in the range of 16 to 25 sessions, although some are as brief as 1 session and some may extend to about 40 sessions. Brief therapy may be time-limited, for which a specific number of sessions or period of time is announced in advance, or there may be no specific time limit but a general time frame provided by the therapist. In this way, the client or patient has a clear idea of how long therapy is expected to last at the outset of therapy.

Brief psychotherapy is more focused than traditional psychotherapy. The various forms of brief psychodynamic therapy tend to emphasize a specific focus for therapy, although there are variations among them. Operating from a different theoretical perspective, cognitive-behavioral therapies tend to focus on specific problems or symptomatic behaviors. The role of therapists in brief psychotherapy is quite different from the more traditional therapeutic role in that to a significant degree the therapist assumes a more directive and active role.

In brief therapy, attention is focused on the patient's problems and his or her current life situation. The present becomes the focus instead of events in the distant past. The goal is to help the client with the problems that brought him or her to therapy and not with a more lofty hypothetical goal of "personality reconstruction."

Some forms of brief psychotherapy, particularly cognitive-behavioral ones, try to teach clients coping mechanisms and procedures that can be used to prevent and overcome problems in the future.

Thus the practice of brief psychotherapy differs in many respects from the traditional practice of long-term psychotherapy. The active role of the therapist, the expectations about the relative length of therapy, and the more problem-centered and specific goals of therapy appear to speed the process and to make it a more efficient approach to psychotherapy than time-unlimited approaches. In recent years a number of brief therapies have developed training manuals that facilitate research appraisals, although criticisms of an overreliance on such manuals as limiting attention to patient individuality have also been made. Most of the research on psychotherapy outcome actually has been conducted on brief therapy and, in general, positive findings have been secured. In fact, several studies have shown that brief forms of psychotherapy have secured outcomes comparable with those reported for therapies of longer duration. The growth of managed care and insurance reimbursement for therapy have also increased the emphasis on brief forms of psychotherapy.

It should also be emphasized that brief psychotherapy is not a panacea for all psychological problems, but is an effective form of therapy for anxiety disorders, moderate depression, marital problems, and related difficulties. Except for very severe cases, such as psychotic behavior and extremely disturbed cases of personality disorders, brief therapy should be the first choice for most individuals. As is true of all forms of therapy, the skill of the therapist and the motivation of the patient are important factors in the types of outcome secured in brief psychotherapy.

SUGGESTED READING

Budman, S. H., & Gurman, A. S. (1988). *Theory and practice of brief therapy.* New York: Guilford.

Garfield, S. L. (1998). *The practice of brief psychotherapy* (2nd ed.). New York: Wiley.

Hoyt, M. F. (1995). *Brief therapy and managed care: Readings for contemporary practice.* San Francisco: Jossey-Bass.

Koss, M. P., & Shiang, J. (1994). Research on brief psychotherapy. In A. E. Bergin & S. L. Garfield (Eds.), *Handbook of psychotherapy and behavior change* (4th ed., pp. 664–700). New York: Wiley.

S. L. GARFIELD
Washington University

COGNITIVE BEHAVIOR THERAPY
PSYCHOTHERAPY
TIME-LIMITED PSYCHOTHERAPY

PSYCHOTHERAPY: HISTORICAL ROOTS

Sigmund Freud, regarded as the founder of psychoanalysis and the father of 20th century psychotherapy, was well aware that psychotherapy was not something new; rather, it was the oldest profession. While Freud's theory of personality, theory of therapy, and techniques of therapy seemed revolutionary at the dawn of this century, their historical roots can be traced to far more distant times and disparate places than 19th century Vienna. The therapeutic themes of insight, catharsis, and working through—themes that we associate with Freud and more modern schools and systems of psychotherapy—are but ancient themes clothed in updated forms. By means of a historical and anthropological approach—an approach that might bring a smile to Freud himself—the current manifest forms of therapy will be unveiled and disrobed, to lay bare their latent roots.

The anthropologist Sir James George Frazer, author of *The Golden Bough,* found a group of individuals emerging from the rest of the community in the most ancient of societies. Accorded special status, these individuals were called chiefs, kings, priests, and priestesses, and served as the community's magicians, shamans, sorcerers, witchdoctors, and therapists. In *Shamanism: Archaic Techniques of Ecstasy,* the historian of religions Mircea Eliade wrote: "This small mystical elite not only directs the community's religious life but, as it were, guards its 'soul.' The shaman is the great specialist in the human soul; he alone 'sees' it, for he knows its 'form' and its destiny."

In a time before "soul" gave way to "psyche," these earliest healers performed numerous functions for both the individual and the group: they were diviners, seers, prophets, and clairvoyants; herbalists, medicine men, doctors; men and women of knowledge who knew the sacred myths and modes of therapeutic healing and wholeness; and exemplars—archetypes and prototypes of humans and what they may yet become—who stood before their fellows not unlike the Greek heroes in their time, as intermediaries between the gods and mortals, and between temporal, profane time and the sacred, transtemporal perspective.

Shamans acquired their powers typically in one of three ways: through divine communion and bestowal, as in Yakut folklore, where the shaman had a celestial wife or husband; as a received gift, often following a successful journey through, and analysis of, their own madness, or through outright inheritance from a parent shaman; and through their own industry, studying the craft over many years in an apprenticeship arrangement with other sorcerers. The Greek myth of the first therapist, Tiresias, told by the mythologist Joseph Campbell in *The Masks of God: Occidental Mythology,* reveals both the acquisition of power and its attendant dangers.

Tiresias, with staff in hand, is walking through the woods but does not see where he steps. Suddenly he and his staff stand between two snakes who are copulating. The snakes, upset by this earthly intrusion amid their heavenly union, punish Tiresias by transforming him into a woman. Tiresias wanders for seven years as a woman, until one day he comes upon those same two snakes, again copulating; this time seeing them, he consciously steps between them with his staff and is again transformed, this time back to a man, although retaining knowledge of his life in feminine form. The staff (the *axis mundi*) between the entwined snakes forms the caduceus, the symbol of medicine, and Tiresias is now ready for his first therapeutic encounter. And a tough one it is: Zeus and

Hera, king and queen of the gods, husband and wife, and brother and sister, are in an argument that neither can settle. The question is: who has more fun during intercourse, the male or the female? Zeus says the female, Hera the male. Tiresias is summoned to settle the issue that divides this heavenly couple. Tiresias answers, "The female does." Hera, angered at his answer, blinds him, but as compensation Zeus gives Tiresias the heavenly gift of foresight. While Tiresias' first attempt at marital therapy was not, by most standards, entirely successful, the blind prophet returns to the earthly landscape able to "see" what others with eyes intact, including King Oedipus, could not.

Shamans "see"—into themselves, others, the soul, and beyond. They have knowledge of both the divine and the bestial side of man. They have experienced "death," resurrection, and transformation in their own initiation rites, dying through self-analysis and returning anew. Thus they are well prepared to help others "cross the bridge" and make the "difficult passage" from one way of being to another. By knowing both the conscious and unconscious sides of the self and by doing their own therapeutic work on themselves, they become the community's sanctioned guide on this therapeutic, transcendent journey—a journey Heinrich Zimmer has called "the oldest romance of the soul."

This romantic journey has a dark side, and the portrait of this early therapist would be incomplete without mentioning it. Frazer uses words like "knave," "imposter," and "conscious deceiver," while others use terms such as "charlatan," "trickster," and "dabbler in the black arts." In light and dark forms, the therapist is perceived by the community on both personal and symbolic levels. When today's clients meet their modern therapists, these historical yet contemporary images are present, and not only in the innermost, unconscious recesses of the mind; often they are brought forward and projected (through transference) onto the therapist: the client may expect the therapist to be omniscient, omnipotent, or an outright fraud. The client may wonder whether this therapist is human, devilish, or godlike, an ally or trickster, or paradoxically both. A sampling of therapeutic techniques from distant, disparate, and current times will follow, to unveil the enduring themes of therapy and, in a modest way, unmask the therapeutic intentions that lie beneath.

"Insight" is an ancient, current, and recurrent therapeutic theme. In 1494 the German poet Sebastian Brant, author of *Das Narrenschiff* (The ship of fools), penned these lines (Zeydel, 1944, p. 58):

> For fools a mirror shall it be
> Where each his counterfeit may see.
> His proper value each would know,
> The glass of fools the truth may show.

But centuries before Brant wrote those lines, Asian shamans were employing copper mirrors to induce trance states, and at the beginning of the 19th century the philanthropist William Tuke, in founding his insane asylum, the Retreat, near York in England, placed mirrors on the walls. In 20th century offices, psychoanalysts sit out of view of the patient and serve as a blank screen, while Rogerian therapists "reflect" back the client's feelings. Psychodrama-

tists may employ a mirror technique where the protagonist steps out of the scene and watches an auxiliary ego (another individual) replay the scene just as he or she did, while group therapists who videotape the sessions may stop the tape at a key moment and replay it. All these examples illustrate, in their varying ways, the theme of insight.

Freud's early work on the problem of hysteria convinced him that, for a cure to come about, a repressed, unconscious idea must be brought into conscious awareness. Brant was similarly convinced that fools must come to see what they foolishly overlook—their own madness. For the Tungus, Khingan, and Birartchen shamans, the word for mirror, "panaptu," derived from "pana," which meant "soul" or "spirit": this connection between mirror and soul, amplified through the hypnotic trance that the mirror induced, would allow the shaman to "see" into the sick soul of the client. Menninger, in his *Theory of Psychoanalytic Technique*, makes the point that the analytic arrangement serves to promote self-visualization: against the backdrop of a black screen and analytic silence the patient's words, feelings, and motivations "echo," such that the patient now comes to "see" what formerly remained buried in the unconscious. These varied therapeutic mirrors serve a common purpose—they raise the dead, so to speak, bringing to conscious light what is missed, overlooked, unconscious, unseen.

Insights can come from a variety of sources: objects, special states, hypnosis, dreams, words, and actions. Therapists both old and new have tossed shells and coins, read books and tea leaves, and consulted Tarot and Rorschach cards in the hope of enhancing their insights. Two anthologies, Harner's *Hallucinogens and Shamanism* and Middleton's *Magic, Witchcraft, and Curing,* illustrate the use of induced states to obtain a wider perspective and greater insight.

Hypnosis, a procedure traceable to the practices of Asian shamans and brought to the West by Jesuit missionaries who mistook it for "arctic hysteria," opened an exciting and highly contentious debate that raged for over 100 years, involving such figures as Anton Mesmer (from whom we get the word "mesmerism"), Benjamin Franklin, James Braid, Hippolyte Bernheim, Jean Martin Charcot, Pierre Janet, and Sigmund Freud. It was the Manchester physician Braid who coined the word "hypnosis," derived from the Greek word for "sleep," to replace the much maligned term "mesmerism." But soon Braid himself became dissatisfied with his own term and wished to change it once again, this time to "monoeidism." Braid recognized that "hypnosis" was a misnomer because, far from being asleep, the hypnotic subject was awake as never before. Janet provides a clarifying example in his *Principles of Psychotherapy,* recounting the incident in which a pupil of Mesmer, the Marquis de Puysegur, put an eight-year-old shepherd boy named Victor into hypnotic trance. Victor entered a peculiar sleep state (somnambulism) in which he could move and speak, and spoke of things he could not possibly know! Janet writes: "This was a revelation. . . . To transform a human mind, to render it capable of seeing everything and understanding everything, of knowing everything, what a magnificent and divine undertaking! . . . In a word, men must set about to produce clairvoyant somnambulists" (Janet, 1924, p. 8).

Bernheim believed that this special condition, which created acute attention and concentration, led to a *restitutio ad integram:* in this condition, lucidity into the unconscious was greatly increased, and a process of reintegration of conscious and unconscious begins. In the language of the 20th-century hypnotherapist Milton Erickson, an idea tends to realize itself (the Law of Concentrated Attention); past experiences are revived (revivification); and, in the "mode of the unconscious," a reassociation and reorganization of ideas may come about. Hypnosis, for Erickson, helped people sidestep their own learned limitations, their frozen frames of reference and belief systems, leading to a more spontaneous opening, shifting, and closing of belief systems. Hypnosis may be likened to therapeutic trickery, where disbelief is suspended and another psychic reality is entered into; yet this trick is intended to lead the person back to the very reality that must be dealt with, but now, hopefully, the person returns with new insights, an altered perspective, and a new integration that comes from reestablishing the unconscious-conscious dialogue that had previously lapsed into silence.

Freud, in *The Interpretation of Dreams,* saw dreams as the royal road to the unconscious; through his method of dream interpretation, insight into the latent meaning of the dream could be brought to light. But Freud was not the first therapist to look for the hidden meaning in dreams. Two hundred years before Freud, the Iroquois Indians were interpreting dreams with a theory and method remarkably similar to Freud's. They conceptualized two parts of the mind: a conscious part and a primary, unconscious part. The latter represented the basic desires, which were revealed in disguised and symbolic forms in the dream. These desires, or latent wishes, needed to be recognized (brought into awareness) and then expressed (catharted). It is to this second theme of therapy—catharsis—that we next turn.

Another enduring notion regarding madness, mental illness, or abnormal behavior is that there exists within the afflicted person some corruption. The corruption might be conceptualized as a demon, spirit, pathogen, emotion, or idea. A corollary also widely accepted was that the corruption had to be purged from the system: demons were berated and the afflicted flagellated, and malevolent spirits and peccant humours were trephined (removed by holes cut in the head), as shown in Hieronymous Bosch's painting *The Cure of the Folly.* One form of purging was a sucking method used by Mestizo healers in Iquitos, Peru, by Jivaro shamans of Ecuador, and by Koskimo and Kwakiutl sorcerers in Vancouver. Therapeutic trickery was often a part of this technique: the anthropologist, Claude Lévi-Strauss (1967) reports that the Kwakiutl shaman Quesalid was trained to hide a piece of goose down in his mouth, bite his gums or tongue at the right moment, roll the down in the blood, and then, after biting into the depressed patient's stomach, spit the bloody down out and claim that the bloody worm (i.e., the corruption) had been purged. Quesalid's results were quite impressive. The therapeutic intent was not simply to deceive: many shamans recognized that patients and the community needed to see something "real" (i.e., physical), even though the shaman believed the disorder to be spiritual or psychological (i.e., nonphysical) in nature.

A very different perspective on illness was offered by Hippocrates, when Greek medicine came to replace an earlier perspective that conceived the corruption as a spirit. Zilboorg and Henry, in *A History of Medical Psychology,* quote Hippocrates: "If you cut open the head, you will find the brain humid, full of sweat and smelling badly. And in this way you may see that it is not a god which injures the body, but disease." This perspective was seen again in the 17th century, when medicine's sovereignty over psychiatric conditions was almost complete. The leading physician of that era, Thomas Sydenham (known as the English Hippocrates), still spoke of "humours" in his treatises on "Physick," but there was a subtle difference now: these physical humors were being invested with psychological and moral images such as "corrupt," "peccant," and "sinful." What remained the same was the theory of therapy—purging. As the physicians of the period confronted these diseases of the mind and disorders of the passions, they would offer emetics to cause vomiting, cathartics to loosen the bowels, blood letting to purge the taint, and sundry medicines to cause sweating and urinating, all in the hope that the pathogen would be purged.

While many hoped that these "physicks" would work, there was doubt, as Shakespeare notes in *Macbeth,* Act V, Scene iii, when Macbeth summons the doctor to administer some potion to free Lady Macbeth of her "thick-coming fancies that keep her from her rest."

> *Macbeth:* Cure her of that!
> Canst thou not minister to a mind diseased,
> Pluck from the memory a rooted sorrow,
> Raze out the written troubles of the brain,
> And with some sweet oblivious antidote
> Cleanse the stuffed bosom of that perilous stuff
> Which weighs upon the heart?
> *Doctor:* Therein the patient must minister to himself.
> *Macbeth:* Throw physic to the dogs, I'll none of it!

Eventually emotions began to replace humors, as psychology slowly emerged from medicine. Therapeutically we move from cathartics to cartharsis: the therapeutic theme endures, only the outpouring is changed. When the patient Anna O. spoke of "chimney sweeping," Josef Breuer and Freud would hear and see the therapeutic value of catharsis. For Freud, the hysteric needed to discharge the "strangulated" affect. In the patient's reexperiencing some traumatic event or fantasy, reliving the emotion as the traumatic memory comes into consciousness, the themes of insight and catharsis merge.

Freud was aware that something more was needed beyond insight and catharsis. While insight dealt with cognition and catharsis dealt with emotions, the patient's "will" had to be incorporated for this therapeutic mix to work. In 1914 Freud wrote "Working through," stressing that the patient must work at assimilating what he or she hears and at integrating these insights into everyday actions. The theme of work, of which working through is its current extension, has both historical and mythical roots.

While hard labor was Adam's punishment and penance for the Fall, it also became his therapy. In the Renaissance, madness, folly, and illness were viewed as a fall from reason, a fall from the social, moral requisites of man; work held out the therapeutic promises of redemption. In Foucault's *Madness and Civilization* (1973), treatment and punishment seemed to become fused and confused, as hospital and workhouse became indistinguishable.

When John Howard toured prisons and hospitals in the late 18th century, he found a maxim engraved on the wall of some prison-turned-hospital: "Make them diligent, and they will be honest." "Diligence" was most often translated as "work." Benjamin Rush—a signer of the Declaration of Independence, physician general to the Continental Army of the United States, and father of American psychiatry, whose face adorns the seal of the American Psychiatric Association—delivered a "Sermon on exercise" to his patients, asking, "How long will thou sleep, O sluggard?" His therapeutic directive was work.

Not everybody was happy with work. Dr. Amariah Brigham, superintendent of New York's Utica State Hospital in the 19th century, felt that it was not manual labor *per se* that was effective, rather, work is for the purpose of "engaging the attention and directing the mind." External work must promote internal work so as to increase awareness.

Insight, catharsis, and work—current and ancient themes of therapy—have awaited the therapeutic travelers on their very special journey. In historical, anthropological, and current times, therapists and clients have journeyed outward and inward to find and transcend their self. They have journeyed outward to the countryside, mountains, the water's edge, and then in, plunging into the sea and darkness to see the light. They have traveled to places such as Epidaurus, Lourdes, Canterbury, and Esalen to find their peace of mind.

Most often, however, they went inward, journeying into consciousness, dreams, their passions, and their unconscious to find the other half and be whole. In embarking on "the oldest romance of the soul," they must work for their insights and catharsis. It does not come easy. The quest is timeless and the payoff has been questioned. What endure are its themes.

REFERENCES

Campbell, J. (1964). *The masks of God: Occidental mythology.* New York: Viking Press.

Eliade, M. (1964). *Shamanism: Archaic techniques of ecstasy.* Princeton, NJ: Princeton University Press.

Frazer, J. (1963/1890). *The golden bough* (13 vols.). London: Macmillan.

Freud, S. (1957/1914). On the history of the psychoanalytic movement. In *The standard edition of the complete psychological works of Sigmund Freud* (Vol. 14). London: Hogarth.

Freud, S. (1968/1900). The interpretation of dreams. In *The standard edition of the complete psychological works of Sigmund Freud* (Vols. 4, 5). London: Hogarth.

Foucault, M. (1973). *Madness and civilization: A history of insanity in the age of reason.* New York: Vintage Books.

Harner, M. J. (Ed.). (1973). *Hallucinogens and shamanism.* London: Oxford University Press.

Janet, P. (1924). *Principles of psychotherapy.* New York: Macmillan.

Lévi-Strauss, C. (1967). The sorcerer and his magic. In C. Lévi-Strauss (Ed.), *Structural anthropology.* Garden City, NY: Anchor Books.

Menninger, K. (1964/1958). *Theory of psychoanalytic technique.* New York: Harper Torchbook.

Middleton, J. (Ed.). (1967). *Magic, witchcraft, and curing.* Garden City, NY: Natural History Press.

Zeydel, E. H. (1944). *The ship of fools by Sebastian Brant.* New York: Columbia University Press.

Zilboorg, G., & Henry, G. W. (1941). *A history of medical psychology.* New York: Norton.

SUGGESTED READING

Eliade, M. (1975/1958). *Rites and symbols of initiation: The mysteries of birth and rebirth.* New York: Harper & Row.

Fancher, R. E. (1973). *Psychoanalytic psychology: The development of Freud's thought.* New York: Norton.

Finkel, N. J. (1976). *Mental illness and health: Its legacy, tensions, and changes.* New York: Macmillan.

Frank, J. D. (1973). *Persuasion and healing.* Baltimore: Johns Hopkins University Press. (Original work published 1961)

Kopp, S. B. (1971). *Guru: Metaphors from a psychotherapist.* Palo Alto, CA: Science & Behavior Books.

N. J. FINKEL
Georgetown University

BEHAVIOR THERAPY
COUNSELING PSYCHOLOGY: HISTORY
HYPNOSIS
MENTAL ILLNESS: EARLY HISTORY
PSYCHOLOGY: HISTORY
PSYCHOTHERAPY

PSYCHOTHERAPY RESEARCH

Psychotherapy research is concerned primarily with the evaluation of the impact and process of psychological interventions for clinical disorders (e.g., depression, anxiety), problems of living (e.g., marital discord), and medical conditions (e.g., chronic pain). It is also concerned with characteristics of the client and therapist as they relate to the process and outcome of treatment. Most of the research in psychotherapy has focused on individual treatment. However, a considerable number of empirical investigations has also been conducted on couple, family, and group therapy.

PSYCHOTHERAPY OUTCOME

With regard to outcome, more than 50 years of research has shown that psychotherapy works: It is more effective than placebo, pseudo-therapies, or the absence of treatment (Lambert & Bergin, 1994). Based on the findings of controlled clinical trials (e.g., Chambless & Hollon, 1998), researchers have been able to identify a large number of empirically-supported treatments (EST) for specific clinical problems experienced by adults, adolescents, and children (see Kendall & Chambless, 1998). Most of the current EST are cognitive-behavioral treatments (CBT), in part because cognitive-behavior therapists have devoted more energy to empirically assess the outcome of their interventions than have therapists from other orientations. However, with the exception of a number of specific problems (e.g., panic disorder, phobias, childhood aggression, psychotic behaviors, health-related behaviors) for which CBT currently stands as the treatment of choice, comparative outcome research suggests that the impact of different forms of psychotherapy tends to be equivalent (Lambert & Bergin, 1994). As noted by Kopta, Lueger, Saunders, & Howard (1999), differences between therapists appear to explain more of the outcome variance than differences between treatments. Outcome research (i.e., dose-effect studies) has also demonstrated that clients' improvement tends to follow a consistent pattern across a variety of psychotherapeutic approaches, with acute distress improving faster than chronic distress, which in turn improves faster than characterological symptoms (see Kopta et al., 1999).

Although psychotherapy works, its impact has clear limitations. The efficacy of treatment for a number of clinical problems, such as personality disorders, remains to be firmly established. Although the EST movement previously mentioned demonstrates that a large number of individuals can benefit from psychotherapy when it is applied in controlled clinical trials, it is not clear how these findings may generalize to clinical practice in natural settings (cf., issue of efficacy versus effectiveness). Moreover, a number of clients terminate treatment prematurely, others do not respond to therapy, and some even deteriorate (Garfield, 1994; Lambert & Bergin, 1994). This state of affairs clearly indicates that there is room for improvement in therapy outcome. As a strategy to increase the beneficial impact of therapy, therapists have attempted to integrate, combine, or selectively prescribe techniques associated with different therapeutic orientations (Castonguay & Goldfried, 1994). With a few exceptions (see Glass, Victor, & Arnkoff, 1993), however, these integrative and/or eclectic efforts have not received considerable empirical attention.

PSYCHOTHERAPY PROCESS

Whereas outcome research focuses on whether psychotherapy works, process research investigates how it works (or why it fails to work for everyone). Researchers have studied process variables related to the therapist (e.g., competence or skills, adherence to treatment manuals, use of specific techniques or principles of change, focus of intervention, verbal and nonverbal activity, response modes, goals and intentions, expectations, emotions, self-disclosure, self-acceptance, self-congruence); to the client (e.g., aims, expectations, suitability to treatment, concerns, intentions, verbal and nonverbal activity, content of dialogue, response modes, self-exploration, emotional experience, voice quality, perception of therapist actions or intentions, identification with or internalization of the therapist, descriptions and explanations of change, openness versus defensiveness, cooperation versus resistance); to the client-therapist relationship (e.g., working alliance,

mutual influence, affiliative and disaffiliative patterns of interaction); and to the structure of treatment (e.g., duration of therapy, stages of treatment, frequency of sessions, fees, client role preparation, stability of therapeutic arrangements, use of supervision, procedures for termination). These variables have been studied either by investigating a single form of therapy or by comparing different approaches (see Arnkoff, Victor, & Glass, 1993; Beutler, Machado, & Allstetter Neufeldt, 1994; Elliott & James, 1989; Garfield, 1994; Goldfried, Greenberg, & Marmar, 1990; Greenberg & Pinsoff, 1986; Hill, 1982, 1990; Kopta et al., 1999; Orlinsky, Grawe, & Parks, 1994; Rice & Greenberg, 1984).

One goal of process research is to describe what happens during therapy. For example, several studies have shown that therapists can adhere to treatment protocols and that various forms of treatment can be differentiated based on the therapist's use of prescribed techniques (e.g., DeRubeis, Hollon, Evans, & Bemis, 1982). However, studies have also demonstrated that there are important differences between what therapists do and what they say they do (or what their theoretical orientation prescribes them to do). For example, supportive interventions (e.g., persuading the phobic client to enter the phobic situation, intellectual guidance, education, prescription of daily activities, altering interactions with significant others) have been found to be prevalent in different modalities of psychodynamic treatment, including classical psychoanalysis (Wallerstein & Dewitt, 1997). A study by Truax (1966) has also suggested that rather than being non-directive, the interventions of Carl Rogers followed a process of operant conditioning. Moreover, behavior therapists have been found to demonstrate higher levels of empathy than psychodynamic therapists (Sloane et al., 1975).

Above and beyond its purely descriptive function, another goal of process research is to identify the factors that facilitate or interfere with clients' improvement. As indicated by Orlinsky et al. (1994), a number of process variables have been positively linked with outcome. Among them, the quality of the therapeutic alliance has been shown to be the strongest predictor of improvement. According to Lambert (1992), common factors (such as the alliance) and placebo effects account for approximately 45% of the variance in therapy outcome. Process research has also provided support for the therapeutic importance of variables assumed to be unique to particular approaches. Clients' emotional experience has been frequently related to outcome in humanistic treatment (Klein, Mathieu-Coughlan, & Kiesler, 1986). Furthermore, the use of homework and other specific techniques has been linked to improvement in cognitive therapy (e.g., Burns & Nolen-Hoeksema, 1991; DeRubeis & Feeley, 1990; Feeley, DeRubeis, & Gelfand, 1999; Persons, Burns, & Perloff, 1988). On the other hand, other techniques prescribed by the cognitive therapy manual have been found to be either unrelated to outcome (e.g., DeRubeis & Feeley, 1990; Feeley et al., 1999; Jones & Pulos, 1993) or negatively associated with improvement (Castonguay et al., 1996). Similarly, the technique of transference interpretation is not always linked with positive change in psychodynamic therapy (Henry, Strupp, Schacht, & Gaston, 1994). Henry, Strupp, and colleagues (1993) have also found that along with an increased adherence to a treatment manual, psychodynamic therapists showed a higher level of disaffiliative communications (e.g., hostile messages toward clients) following a training program that was in part designed to reduce therapists' hostile interaction with difficult clients. Such disaffiliative communication patterns were associated with poor outcome in another study (Henry, Schacht, & Strupp, 1990).

It should be noted that for several authors the methods and statistical analyses typically used in process-outcome studies are not always adequate to capture the complexity of the process of change (e.g., Elliott, 1983; Hill, 1982; Russell & Trull, 1986; Stiles, 1988). For instance, correlational strategies (which assume a linear relationship between the frequency of the process variable and outcome) cannot provide information concerning the context within which a process variable takes place. Because such strategies are based on the assumption that the more one uses a therapeutic intervention the better it is for the client, correlational strategies fail to take into consideration the fact that the therapist will use an effective technique more or less frequently, based on the client's needs. The timing or appropriateness of a technique, in other words, is more important than the frequency with which it is used (Stiles, 1988). As a result, several investigators have developed new ways of conducting process research (e.g., task analysis, sequential analysis, interpersonal process recall) in order to provide contextual and finer-grained analyses of patterns of interaction between participants, especially during significant (i.e., helpful or detrimental) therapeutic episodes (Elliott, 1983; Hill, 1982, 1990; Rice & Greenberg, 1984; Russell & Trull, 1986).

CLIENT AND THERAPIST CHARACTERISTICS

Psychotherapy researchers have also been interested in examining characteristics of clients and therapists. A large number of demographic variables have been investigated (e.g., age, gender, social class, and ethnicity) but none of them appear to account for a significant part of the outcome variance (Beutler, Machado, & Allstetter Neufeldt, 1994; Garfield, 1994). Professional characteristics of therapists such as specialty (e.g., clinical psychology, social work, psychiatry), level of training, and experience have also failed to predict client improvement reliably (Beutler et al., 1994). A number of personal characteristics of both the client and therapist, however, are related to the psychotherapy process and outcome. For example, clients' psychological health has been shown to predict therapeutic benefits (Luborsky, et al., 1993). In addition, the therapist's expertness, attractiveness, and trustworthiness (as perceived by the client) have been linked with positive change (Beutler et al., 1994). Similarity between therapist and client on certain values (e.g., honesty, wisdom) is predictive of improvement, but so is discrepancy on other values (e.g., social status, friendship). Interestingly, the convergence of the client's values with those of the therapist during the course of treatment has been consistently related to positive outcome (Beutler et al., 1994).

In different forms of psychotherapy for depression, clients' pretreatment level of perfectionism has been negatively related to outcome (Blatt, Quinlan, Pilkonis, & Shea, 1995). The presence of a personality disorder also appears to be a poor prognostic for a number of Axis I disorders, such as depression, anxiety disorders, and eating disorders (e.g., Hoffart & Martinsen, 1993; Rossiter,

Agras, Telch, & Schneider, 1993; Shea et al., 1990). Related to these findings, several studies suggest that clients with interpersonal problems (e.g., hostility) have difficulty establishing a therapeutic alliance (Arnkoff et al., 1993; Kopta et al., 1999) and seem to be less responsive to both psychodynamic and cognitive-behavioral treatments than are those who do not have such difficulties (Horowitz, Rosenberg, & Bartholomew, 1993; Pincus & Borkovec, 1994). Also negatively related to outcome are the therapist's level of emotional disturbance and distress (Beutler et al., 1994). Moreover, Henry and colleagues (1990) have found that the therapist's negative introject (i.e., hostile and controlling way of relating toward self) is predictive of negative interpersonal patterns in the client-therapist relationship.

Studies have also examined whether the matching of client and therapist variables could improve the impact of therapy. Matching demographic variables has not led to significant results. A large number of studies have also investigated the potential interaction between client characteristics and types of therapy (Shoham-Salomon, 1991). With few exceptions, however, this research has led to a paucity of reliable findings. Among these exceptions is the work of Beutler and colleagues (1991), who demonstrated that clients with an externalized coping style (those who react to stress by acting out and blaming others) improved more in a symptom-oriented treatment (i.e., cognitive therapy [CT]) than did clients with an internalized style of coping (those who tend to ruminate and self-blame when confronted with stress). On the other hand, internalizing clients responded most to an insight-oriented treatment (i.e., supportive/self-directive therapy [S/SD]). Beutler and colleagues (1991) have also found that whereas clients high in reactance level (those who resist being controlled by others) fare better in a nondirective type of treatment (i.e., S/SD) than in directive forms of therapies (i.e., focused-expressive therapy and CT), clients low in reactance respond more to CT than to S/SD.

CONCLUSION

Research has offered considerable information with regard to the impact of psychotherapy, the mechanisms of change, and the characteristics of the client and therapist that are related to the outcome and process of different approaches. At this point in time, however, it is fair to say that psychotherapy research has had a limited impact on clinical practice. For example, although the current ESTs represent for many researchers the ultimate embodiment of the scientific-practitioner model, they are perceived by many clinicians as irrelevant academic efforts, if not major threats to valid clinical practice. Fortunately, efforts to bridge the gap between researchers and clinicians have begun to emerge (Newman & Castonguay, 1999). Without such a bridge, it is more than likely that future attempts to improve the effect of psychotherapy and to understand the process of change will be seriously hampered.

REFERENCES

Arnkoff, D. B., Victor, B. J., & Glass, C. R. (1993). Empirical research on factors in psychotherapeutic change. In G. Stricker & J. R. Gold (Eds.), *Comprehensive handbook of psychotherapy integration* (pp. 27–42). New York: Plenum.

Beutler, L. E., Engle, D., Mohr, D., Daldrup, R. J., Bergan, J., Meredith, K., & Merry, W. (1991). Predictors of differential response to cognitive, experiential, and self-directed psychotherapeutic procedures. *Journal of Consulting and Clinical Psychology, 59*, 333–340.

Beutler, L. E., Machado, P. P. P., & Allstetter Neufeldt, S. (1994). Therapist variables. In A. E. Bergin & S. L. Garfield (Eds.), *Handbook of psychotherapy and behavior change* (4th ed., pp. 229–269). New York: Wiley.

Blatt, S. J., Quinlan, D. M., Pilkonis, P. A., & Shca, M. T. (1995). Impact of perfectionism and need for approval on the brief treatment of depression: The National Institute of Mental Health Treatment of Depression Collaborative Research Program revisited. *Journal of Consulting and Clinical Psychology, 63*, 125–132.

Burns, D. D., & Nolen-Hoeksema, S. (1991). Coping styles, homework compliance, and the effectiveness of cognitive-behavioral therapy. *Journal of Consulting and Clinical Psychology, 59*, 305–311.

Castonguay, L. G., & Goldfried, M. R. (1994). Psychotherapy integration: An idea whose time has come. *Applied and Preventative Psychology, 3*, 159–172.

Castonguay, L. G., Goldfried, M. R., Wiser, S., Raue, P. J., & Hayes, A. H. (1996). Predicting outcome in cognitive therapy for depression: A comparison of unique and common factors. *Journal of Consulting and Clinical Psychology, 64*, 497–504.

Chambless, D. L., & Hollon, S. D. (1998). Defining empirically supported therapies. *Journal of Consulting and Clinical Psychology, 66*, 7–18.

DeRubeis, R. J., & Feeley, M. (1990). Determinants of change in cognitive therapy for depression. *Cognitive Therapy and Research, 14*, 469–482.

DeRubeis, R. J., Hollon, S. D., Evans, M. D., & Bemis, K. M. (1982). Can psychotherapies for depression be discriminated? A systematic investigation of cognitive therapy and interpersonal therapy. *Journal of Consulting and Clinical Psychology, 50*, 744–756.

Elliott, R. (1983). Fitting process research to the practicing psychotherapist. *Psychotherapy: Theory, Research, and Practice, 20*, 45–55.

Elliott, R., & James, E. (1989). Varieties of client experience in psychotherapy: An analysis of the literature. *Clinical Psychology Review, 9*, 443–467.

Feeley, M., DeRubeis, R. J., & Gelfand, L. A. (1999). The temporal relation of adherence and alliance to symptom change in cognitive therapy for depression. *Journal of Consulting and Clinical Psychology, 67*, 578–582.

Garfield, S. L. (1994). Research on client variables in psychotherapy. In A. E. Bergin & S. L. Garfield (Eds.), *Handbook of psychotherapy and behavior change* (4th ed., pp. 190–228). New York: Wiley.

Glass, C. R., Victor, B. J., & Arnkoff, D. B. (1993). Empirical research on integrative and eclectic psychotherapies. In G. Stricker & J. R. Gold (Eds.), *Comprehensive handbook of psychotherapy integration* (pp. 9–25). New York: Plenum.

Goldfried, M. R., Greenberg, L. S., & Marmar, C. (1990). Individual psychotherapy: Process and outcome. *Annual Review of Psychology, 41*, 659–688.

Greenberg, L. S., & Pinsoff, W. M. (1986). *The psychotherapeutic process: A research handbook.* New York: Guilford Press.

Henry, W. P., Schacht, T. E., & Strupp, H. H. (1990). Patient and therapist introject, interpersonal process, and differential psychotherapy outcome. *Journal of Consulting and Clinical Psychology, 58*, 768–774.

Henry, W. P., Schacht, T. E., Strupp, H. H., Butler, S. F., & Binder, J. L. (1993). Effects of training in time-limited dynamic psychotherapy: Mediators of therapists' responses to training. *Journal of Consulting and Clinical Psychology, 61*, 441–447.

Henry, W. P., Strupp, H. H., Butler, S. F., Schacht, T. E., & Binder, J. L. (1993). Effects of training in time-limited dynamic psychotherapy: Changes in therapist behavior. *Journal of Consulting and Clinical Psychology, 61*, 434–440.

Henry, W. P., Strupp, H. H., Schacht, T. E., & Gaston, L. (1994). Psychodynamic approaches. In A. E. Bergin & S. L. Garfield (Eds.), *Handbook of psychotherapy and behavior change* (4th ed., pp. 467–508). New York: Wiley.

Hill, C. E. (1982). Counseling process research: Philosophical and methodological dilemmas. *Counseling Psychologist, 10*, 7–19.

Hill, C. E. (1990). Exploratory in-session process research in individual psychotherapy: A review. *Journal of Consulting and Clinical Psychology, 58*, 288–294.

Hoffart, A., & Martinsen, E. W. (1993). The effect of personality disorders and anxious-depressive comorbidity on outcome in patients with unipolar depression and with panic disorder and agoraphobia. *Journal of Personality Disorders, 7*, 304–311.

Horowitz, L. M., Rosenberg, S. E., & Bartholomew, K. (1993). Interpersonal problems, attachment styles, and outcome in brief dynamic psychotherapy. *Journal of Consulting and Clinical Psychology, 61*, 549–560.

Jones, E. E., & Pulos, S. M. (1993). Comparing the process in psychodynamic and cognitive-behavioral therapies. *Journal of Consulting and Clinical Psychology, 61*, 306–316.

Kendall, P. C., & Chambless, D. L. (1998). Special section: Empirically supported psychological therapies. *Journal of Clinical and Consulting Psychology, 66*, 3–163.

Klein, M. H., Mathieu-Coughlan, P., & Kiesler, D. J. (1986). The experiencing scales. In L. S. Greenberg & W. M. Pinsoff (Eds.), *The psychotherapeutic process: A research handbook* (pp. 21–71). New York: Guilford.

Kopta, S. M., Lueger, R. J., Saunders, S. M., & Howard, K. I. (1999). Individual psychotherapy outcome research: Challenges leading to greater turmoil or a positive transition. *Annual Review of Psychology, 50*, 441–469.

Lambert, M. J. (1992). Psychotherapy outcome research: Implications for integrative and eclectic therapists. In J. C. Norcross & M. R. Goldfried (Eds.), *Handbook of psychotherapy integration* (pp. 94–129). New York: Basic Books.

Lambert, M. J., & Bergin, A. E. (1994). The effectiveness of psychotherapy. In A. E. Bergin & S. L. Garfield (Eds.), *Handbook of psychotherapy and behavior change* (4th ed., pp. 143–189). New York: Wiley.

Luborsky, L., Diguer, L., Luborsky, E., McLellan, A. T., Woody, G., & Alexander, L. (1993). Psychological Health-Sickness (PHS) as a predictor of outcomes in dynamic and other psychotherapies. *Journal of Consulting and Clinical Psychology, 61,* 542–548.

Newman, M. G., & Castonguay, L. G. (1999). Reflecting on current challenges and future directions in psychotherapy: What can be learned from dialogues between clinicians, researchers, and policy makers? *Journal of Clinical Psychology/In Session, 55,* 1407–1413.

Orlinsky, D. E., Grawe, K., & Parks, B. K. (1994). Process and outcome in psychotherapy—Noch einmal. In A. E. Bergin & S. L. Garfield (Eds.), *Handbook of psychotherapy and behavior change* (4th ed., pp. 270–376). New York: Wiley.

Persons, J. B., Burns, D. D., & Perloff, J. M. (1988). Predictors of dropout and outcome in cognitive therapy for depression in a private practice. *Cognitive Therapy and Research, 12,* 557–575.

Pincus, A. L., & Borkovec, T. B. (1994). *Interpersonal problems in generalized anxiety disorder: Preliminary clustering of patients' interpersonal dysfunction.* Paper presented at the meeting of the American Psychological Society, New York (June).

Rice, L. N., & Greenberg, L. S. (1984). *Patterns of change: Intensive analysis of psychotherapy process.* New York: Guilford.

Rossiter, E. M., Agras, W. S., Telch, C. F., & Schneider, J. A. (1993). Cluster B personality disorder characteristics predict outcome in the treatment of bulimia nervosa. *International Journal of Eating Disorders, 13,* 349–357.

Russell, R. L., & Trull, T. J. (1986). Sequential analyses of language variables in psychotherapy process research. *Journal of Consulting and Clinical Psychology, 54,* 16–21.

Shea, M. T., Pilkonis, P. A., Beckham, E., Collins, J. F., Elkin, I., Sotsky, S. M., & Docherty, J. (1990). Personality disorders and treatment outcome in the NIMH Treatment of Depression Collaborative Research Program. *American Journal of Psychiatry, 147,* 711–718.

Shoham-Salomon, V. (1991). Introduction to special section on client-therapy interaction research. *Journal of Consulting and Clinical Psychology, 59,* 203–204.

Sloane, R. B., Staples, F. R., Cristol, A. H., Yorkston, N. J., & Whipple, K. (1975). *Psychotherapy versus behavior therapy.* Cambridge, MA: Harvard University Press.

Stiles, W. B. (1988). Psychotherapy process-outcome correlations may be misleading. *Psychotherapy, 25,* 27–35.

Truax, C. B. (1966). Reinforcement and non-reinforcement in Rogerian psychotherapy. *Journal of Abnormal Psychology, 71,* 1–9.

Wallerstein, R. S., & DeWitt, K. N. (1997). Intervention modes in psychoanalysis and in psychoanalytic psychotherapies: A revised classification. *Journal of Psychotherapy Integration, 7,* 129–150.

L. G. CASTONGUAY
A. J. SCHUT
M. J. CONSTANTINO
Pennsylvania State University

PSYCHOTHERAPY
PSYCHOTHERAPY: HISTORICAL ROOTS

PSYCHOTHERAPY TECHNIQUES

Systems of psychotherapy number in the hundreds, ranging from Adlerian psychotherapy to Zaslow's Z-process attachment. All systems seek to change the person for the better. Some focus on overt behavior or action, some on cognitions or intellectual conceptions, and some on the affect or emotional. Whatever the relative focus, the basic agreement between a therapist and a client involves some anticipated change in the person.

Several different changes may be sought. Using overt behavior as an illustration, this change may involve: (a) an increase in a desirable behavior; (b) a decrease in inappropriate behavior; and/or (c) an existing behavior modified so that it occurs under more appropriate circumstances than at the start of therapy.

Psychotherapy systems differ markedly in *time focus*. Following the lead of Sigmund Freud, the analytic approaches tend to focus on the past. Although few today accept Freud's notion that the three critical early life events are nursing, toilet training, and the Oedipal complex, learning prior to the teen years is known to be important in personality development. Other systems, notably the behavioral ones, focus on the present. The future hopes and aspirations of the client are the major focus for Adlerian and existential approaches.

SPECIFIC TECHNIQUES

The following are specific examples of the types of techniques that therapists use to change the behaviors/cognitions/affects of clients.

Talking—Focus on the Intellect

Free association—tradition of Sigmund Freud. The therapist listens nonjudgmentally to the report of mental images in whatever order the client prefers to use. Interpretation is done at a later time.

Free association—tradition of Carl Jung. The client is asked to respond to words selected and sequenced by the therapist; responses range from a single word to a brief sentence. Both the content of the response and any delay in giving it are interpreted.

Dream analysis—tradition of Sigmund Freud. The story of the dream as recalled is the manifest content; interpretation is based on the underlying or latent content that expresses a wish. Since the wishes often involve past trauma, the person attempts to disguise the true meaning of the dream and thereby to minimize pain.

Dream analysis—tradition of Carl Jung. The underlying meaning of dreams is a recommendation of the inner Self to the conscious person. Many dreams end with a solution to a current problem. Dreams are self-correcting: If the client or therapist misinterprets the dream, the Self resends the message in a clearer form.

Dream analysis—tradition of Alfred Adler. The dream is an example of problem solving, rehearsal for future action.

Nondirective interview. This procedure is emphasized by Carl Rogers (1951). The client is asked to talk with minimal guidance from the therapist. The therapist limits comments to repeating or rephrasing the statements made and describing the degree of expressed feeling. The client is encouraged to confirm or to correct the therapist's understanding.

Imagination. In Akhter Ahsen's Eidetic Psychotherapy, the client may be asked to imagine the humiliation of failure and then the pride of success. Detailed descriptions of the feelings in both circumstances are required. The underlying message is that the client is in control and can choose the feelings of success or of failure.

Directive interview. The client is asked a fixed sequence of questions or asked to respond to a standard scale. The more restricted format is used to obtain specific information of particular interest to the therapist, such as associations with the birth process for Otto Rank.

Analysis of videotaped behavior. The client is asked to interpret the behavior shown along stipulated dimensions (facial expression, congruence of words and facial expression). The behavior segment shown is usually of the client. A variation occasionally used is to confront the client in the immediate moment: Monitors are placed in view; the therapist remotely controls the camera and focuses on various body parts.

Interpretation. Freud stated that the nonjudgmental attitude in psychoanalysis should be dropped occasionally to permit interpretation. Albert Ellis tells clients that it is not the external unfortunate happening that makes them feel rotten; rather it is the irrational catastrophizing of the event that produces the pain. Harry Stack Sullivan always couched interpretations to the severely disturbed as hypotheses that could be accepted or rejected. In the Conflict Resolution Therapy of Lakin Phillips, the therapist helps the client conceptualize the nature of the conflict beneath the problem and then asks the client to produce a solution. The solution is often role-played. As the client becomes better at analyzing situations into specific conflicts, the therapist withdraws direction. One therapist who takes considerable effort to avoid any interpretations is Rogers.

Rumpelstiltskin. The therapist occasionally can affect behavior dramatically by the "magic" of the right word or interpretive phrase. A receptive client can be vastly changed by giving a name to the core problem (Torry, 1972).

Confrontation. The therapist points out the client's failure to accept responsibility for the cure in a momentary "attack." Less general errors such as exaggeration of complaints or overgeneralization are pointed out and labeled irrational. Problems may be conceptualized as due to a faulty life script based on impossible goals, to an unreasonable desire for security, to minimizing of self-worth, or to a general misperception of life.

Humor. Various styles of humor may be used to confront the client. Exaggeration to absurdity, mimicry of self-defeating behavior, ridicule of idiotic behavior, and sarcasm carefully combined with nonvocal warmth and acceptance are used.

Contradictory messages. In Frank Farrelly's Provocative Therapy, the therapist vocally agrees with the pessimism expressed by the client but nonvocally supports the notion that the client can be helped. Further *reality testing* is encouraged by taking the client's negative statements to their logical extreme or by immediately and superficially agreeing with a statement of "I'm no good."

Telephone interview. Conversations over the telephone reduce the social cues and seem particularly useful to anxious and unstable individuals for whom a therapist is highly threatening (Grumet, 1979). Others report similar advantages to having clients "converse" at computer terminals.

Silence. Adler often folded his hands and said nothing to force the client to reconsider conclusions and motivations. Many other therapists include silence as an important technique.

Talking—Focus on the Affect

Supportive. The client is considered not to be sick but simply discouraged. The mistakes made are not fatal; one must enhance one's faith in oneself. Since the anxiety exceeds the current coping mechanisms or defenses, the therapist supports the client while the coping ability is increased.

Feeling talk. In assertiveness training, the client is taught deliberately to utter spontaneously felt emotions. When the client disagrees with what is said, this feeling must be expressed by contradicting, and even attacking, the view put forth. Deliberate use of the word I is encouraged. Sometimes a standard session with a therapist is videotaped. Then an inquirer takes the place of the original counselor and the videotape is viewed. The client is asked to stop the tape at any point where the feelings then present are recalled. Understanding is sought in the cognitive, nonverbal, and affect domains. In the Ego-State Therapy of John and Helen Watkins, the mixed emotions of the client are formalized into "multiple personalities." A description of each "ego" is made and laid on a separate chair; each ego is then given a descriptive name. Conflicts are analyzed by rearranging the pattern of chairs, by the client adopting the perspective of the chair currently occupied and talking to the ego of another chair, or by having one ego state arbitrate between two others.

Poetry. The clients express emotion by reading poems selected both by the therapist and by themselves.

Pets. The presence of pets in the office is suggested, especially for child clients. Not only are dogs an immediate source of comfort, but they can become an opening topic of conversation (Levinson, 1965).

Displacement. The client is taught to channel a desire or need into a more adaptive behavior. In Alcoholics Anonymous, for example, the supportive friendship of members replaces alcohol.

Relaxation. Progressing from the initial training in relaxation to instructions by the therapist, the client is taught exercises that may be done in any setting to reduce the level of anxiety.

Hypnosis.   Sometimes hypnosis is used as an adjunctive procedure to decrease the inhibition or censorship of anxiety-arousing material.

Emotional reliving.   Many systems stress the benefit of vivid recollection of the detail of traumas. Thomas Stampfl's Implosive Therapy, Flooding, and Arthur Janov's Primal Therapy include reliving as a central technique.

Haircut.   During an agreed period, the client must listen to a tirade on faults and errors without any attempt at a defense. In George Bach's Creative Aggression, the receiver of the "haircut" sets the time limit for the process, and may even refuse or postpone the session.

Scream.   In Daniel Casriel's New Identity Process, the client is taught to show emotion with the voice. In other systems, such as Janov's Primal Therapy, the later understanding and cognitive restructuring of the emotional outpouring are of at least equal importance with the emotional release of the actual screaming.

Talking—Focus on Rehearsal of Behavior

Fixed role.   George Kelly's technique (1955) begins with the client writing a description of the self in the third person. Another sketch is prepared, this one with at least one major alternative trait. The client is told that the true role is "going on vacation" for a fixed period, such as two weeks. During this period, the alternative role is to be adopted as fully as possible. At the end of the time, the alternative role is abandoned, but the client probably will modify the original role somewhat. A therapist in the tradition of Adler often will ask clients to behave "as if" a different role or lifestyle were theirs for the next week. Donald Meichenbaum also asks the client to behave "as if" in order to restructure the cognitive self-instructions. In the related technique of Stress Inoculation, the client rehearses coping techniques, including relaxation.

Imagination.   The client relaxes with eyes closed and then imagines a scene suggested by the therapist. In Joseph Wolpe's Systematic Desensitization, the scenes are presented in a graded series from least to most anxiety arousing. This is in direct contrast with Stampfl's Implosive Therapy, in which only the most anxiety-arousing scenes are used.

Consequences.   In the Covert Conditioning of Joseph Cautela, the client is asked to imagine the positive, negative, and neutral consequences of specific behavioral acts.

Group therapy.   Not only is group therapy an economical use of the limited number of therapists, it is ideal for clients who have difficulties involving relationships with others. The group becomes a rehearsal for the client's regular environment. It is also comforting to see that other people have anxieties. Most groups are composed of relatively homogeneous clients—the same level of vulnerability, a common problem, or a natural group.

Psychodrama.   Jacob Moreno's procedure (1946) borrows heavily from the theater. In soliloquy, the client moves and speaks about a particular life circumstance. With a double, the client portrays himself or herself, with another member of the group moving, acting, and behaving as the patient would. With multiple doubles, several other members take part, each portraying how the patient would respond to the situation at a particular point in the past or in the future. In mirror, another member of the group portrays the

client, who maintains an observer role. In role reversal, the patient portrays a significant individual (such as the mother) while another group member portrays the client.

Actively Behaving

Modeling.   Appropriate behavior is demonstrated live or on videotape, by the therapist or by others. Albert Ellis and Arnold Lazarus focus on specific skills, such as asking for a date or being interviewed for a job. Adler considered the whole relationship with the client to be a model of appropriate interpersonal contact. In Structured Learning, a situation is modeled in a group setting. Then each of the clients personalizes the situation to a real-life circumstance. Social reinforcement and feedback follow the rehearsal.

Play therapy.   The client, particularly a young child, is provided many human figures and other objects, perhaps in a sand box. As a story is acted out with figures, the therapist may ask questions about the characters and events (Axline, 1964).

Physical activity.   Activities include massage (Vegetotherapy of Wilhelm Reich, Rolfing), jogging (Ronald Lawrence), movement awareness (Feldenkrais, Dance Therapy), and physical attack with rubber bats (Bach's Creative Aggression).

Art therapy.   Drawings or other creative exercises are done. For those who have trouble communicating with others, a group mural is often constructed.

Negative practice.   Originated by Knight Dunlap, the technique asks the client to repeat the maladaptive behavior or thought to fatigue. Viktor Frankl calls this "paradoxical intention." An Adlerian therapist may ask a client to increase that which is being fought against.

Setting Factors

Transference.   The client places trust and confidence in the therapist and readily accepts the suggestions made. Rogers states that the therapist must be genuine in the therapy, must express the feelings of the moment in a positive human relationship. Jung stresses acceptance of the client with all the defects; the therapist is genuinely open in expression. In the Reevaluation Counseling of Harvey Jackins, questions are asked not to gain information, but to assure the client that the therapist is listening with interest to all statements made. In the Social Influence Therapy of John Gillis, expectations may be built by severe "initiation rites," such as shaving of heads in some drug groups, by isolation as in Primal Therapy, or by inconvenient appointment times (also see Goldstein, 1962).

Social role.   The therapist must be careful to avoid the conventions of society in giving or accepting gifts, changing appointment times, and other apparently "after-the-hour" comments. Such items may be expressions of important underlying emotions (Beier, 1966).

Triad counseling.   The sessions are conducted by the counselor but with an anticounselor or devil's advocate present in addition to the client (Pedersen, 1981). The procedure is especially helpful in overcoming the barrier of a client from a very different culture from that of the therapist.

Indirect Contact with Clients

Training parents or peers.   The intervention is designed by the professional but is executed by others naturally present in the client's environment. Training may include the "bug in the ear" with the therapist giving instructions in the immediate situation via private radio. The therapist may also arrange for particular consequences for certain behaviors in the client's environment.

Bibliotherapy.   Both self-help and professionally oriented works may have far-reaching impact.

Prevention.   The therapist consults with laypeople and paraprofessionals in the design of systems that intervene before the difficulties become major distresses. Specific examples include work with predelinquents and consultation in the job setting concerning alcohol and other drug use.

REFERENCES

Axline, V. M. (1964). *Dibs: In search of self.* New York: Houghton Mifflin.

Bach, G. R., & Goldberg, H. (1974). *Creative aggression.* Garden City, NY: Doubleday.

Beier, E. G. (1966). *The silent language of psychotherapy.* Chicago: Aldine.

Goldstein, A. P. (1962). *Therapist-patient expectancies in psychotherapy.* New York: Pergamon Press.

Grumet, G. W. (1979). Telephone therapy: A review and case report. *American Journal of Orthopsychiatry, 49,* 574–584.

Kelly, G. A. (1955). *The psychology of personal constructs.* New York: Norton.

Levinson, B. M. (1965). Pet psychotherapy: Use of household pets in the treatment of behavior disorder in childhood. *Psychological Reports, 17,* 695–698.

Moreno, J. L. (1959). *Psychodrama* (2 vols.). Beacon, NY: Beacon House. (Original work published 1946).

Pedersen, P. B. (1981). Triad counseling. In R. J. Corsini (Ed.), *Innovative psychotherapies.* New York: Wiley Interscience.

Torrey, E. F. (1972). *The mind game: Witchdoctors and psychiatrists.* New York: Bantam Books.

Torrey, E. F. (1972). What Western psychotherapists can learn from witchdoctors. *American Journal of Orthopsychiatry, 42,* 69–76.

SUGGESTED READING

Binder, V., Binder, A., & Rimland, B. (Eds.). (1976). *Modern therapies.* Englewood Cliffs, NJ: Prentice-Hall.

Corsini, R. J. (Ed.). (1981). *Handbook of innovative psychotherapies.* New York: Wiley.

Kaplan, H. I., & Sadock, B. J. (Eds.). (1971). *Comprehensive group psychotherapy.* Baltimore: Williams & Wilkins.

C. S. PEYSER
University of the South

BEHAVIOR THERAPY
BRIEF PSYCHOTHERAPY
COGNITIVE THERAPY
CRISIS INTERVENTION
PSYCHOTHERAPY
PSYCHOTHERAPY: HISTORICAL ROOTS

PSYCHOTHERAPY TRAINING

Psychotherapy training has two aspects, one concerning the models of training in graduate programs, the other focusing on the way by which psychotherapy is learned. A number of conferences and articles since the end of World War II have defined model clinical and counseling psychology training programs. These models usually invoke an image of training that weaves together basic didactic psychology along with the teaching of psychotherapy. David Shakow (1969) developed a model curriculum in which the student began clinical training concurrently with education in the basic processes (learning, motivation, research design and analysis, biological and social processes). The student's exposure to clinical work, along with basic, clinically informed research, increased as he or she progressed through the second and succeeding years of the doctoral program. One recent APA conference concentrated on lifelong learning and continuing education requirements. The conference participants studied how postdoctoral education might attend to complex skills such as psychotherapy. Regrettably, from Shakow's day to the present, these proposals have been largely ignored. Implementation is more difficult than recommendation. Manualized treatment, non-PhD programs, and psychotherapy effectiveness research are current developments that could affect psychotherapy training.

Manuals that detail psychotherapeutic treatment for defined problems are supposed to increase the effectiveness of psychotherapy in this era of managed care and attention to the so-called bottom line. For highly defined problems during research trials, manuals seem effective. However, they are far from universally accepted. They stifle the therapist's ability to explore the patient's life in the event that more important underlying problems may be stimulating the presenting complaint. Indeed Lehman, Gorsuch, and Mintz (1985) found that most presenting complaints mask the real problem for which a patient seeks treatment. In areas that are more complex, manuals are inadequate.

Psychotherapy effectiveness studies continue to show that there are salutary effects of psychotherapy. These effects seem to be related to the therapist's style and personality more than to the particular theoretical bent or persuasion of the therapist. Again influenced by managed care, recent research efforts focus on therapeutic efficacy, that is, getting the most dose-effect benefit possible to cut cost of care irrespective of the client's needs.

A growing source of clinical psychologists seems to be doctorate in psychology (PsyD) programs rather than the more traditional doctorate of philosophy in psychology (PhD) programs. While PsyD programs emphasize hands-on training at the expense of the research and basic process approach, PhD programs depend on the student's natural interest and on internship to supply the bulk of psychotherapy training. The internship provides supervised psychotherapy experiences with a variety of clients (adult, child, inpatient, and outpatient) with a variety of problems (psychosis, anxiety disorders, personality disorders, and medical conditions with psychological sequellae). Some feel that competence in psychotherapy develops only after a minimum of five years of postdoctoral clinical work, during which the student-psychotherapist can see changes in a number of patients' lives over time, and see how his or her skills can affect people.

PSYCHOTHERAPY SUPERVISION

Psychotherapy supervision is the modality by which students learn psychotherapy. Allen K. Hess (1980) summarized the models of supervision that include the supervisor in the roles of lecturer, teacher, peer, monitor, learned elder, and therapist. A number of models posit stages through which the student psychotherapist is presumed to pass. These include the demystification of psychotherapy, the acquisition of technical skills, and the beginning of mastery of complex skills and judgments, such as timing of interventions and tailoring techniques to the particular patient. Similarly, supervisors are presumed to pass through stages en route to becoming accomplished supervisors. Deborah Swain (1981) found that supervisors perceive supervisee performance along five dimensions: (a) clinical sense, exemplified by listening skills, maintaining poise, and allowing the client to make decisions; (b) preparation for supervision and psychotherapy, such as organizing materials before sessions; (c) theoretical and cognitive knowledge, as seen by relating clinical material to theoretical concepts; (d) self-awareness and appropriate disclosure, such as access to feelings about patients that can be discussed in supervision; and (e) boundary management, as shown by being on time for appointments, knowing clinic rules, and attending to record keeping. Lee Aldrich (1982) found students regard supervisors along eight stable dimensions: defensiveness, professionalism, experience as a clinician, theoretical base, experience as a teacher, appropriate interest in the supervisee's life, likableness, and able to motivate.

Recent years have seen more attention devoted to models of supervision, an emergent interpersonal theory of supervision, and qualitative research. The problem with more nomothetic and quantitative research is the small subject pool from which to draw supervisee-supervisor teams, and to which one might apply randomization to test hypotheses. Nonetheless, the qualitative research that is emerging tends to show how supervisors can help train psychotherapists.

REFERENCES

Aldrich, L. G. (1982). *Construction of a scale for the rating of supervisors of psychotherapy.* Unpublished master's thesis, Auburn University.

American Psychological Association. (1994). *Education and training beyond the doctoral degree: Proceedings of the APA conference on postdoctoral education and training in psychology.* Washington, DC: Author.

Hess, A. K. (1980). Training models and the nature of psychotherapy supervision. In A. K. Hess (Ed.), *Psychotherapy supervision: Theory research and practice.* New York: Wiley.

Lehman, R. S., Gorsuch, R. L., & Mintz, J. (1985). Moving targets: Patient's changing complaints during psychotherapy. *Journal of Consulting and Clinical Psychology, 53,* 49–54.

Shakow, D. (1969). *Clinical psychology as science and profession: A forty year odyssey.* Chicago: Aldine.

Swain, D. D. (1981). *Behaviorally anchored rating scale for recipients of psychotherapy supervision: Instrument construction.* Unpublished master's thesis, Auburn University.

A. K. HESS
Auburn University at Montgomery

CLINICAL GRADUATE TRAINING IN PSYCHOLOGY PSYCHOTHERAPY: HISTORICAL ROOTS

PUNISHMENT

As a result of early life experiences, punishment is a topic that psychologist and layperson alike find difficult to discuss in objective or neutral terms. Not long ago, corporal punishment was widely approved. Parents and teachers were told that "to spare the rod is to spoil the child." Both educational and legal systems depended upon punishment. Punishment now has fallen into some disfavor. Physical punishment is seldom employed in schools, for example. Within the family, what once was approved of as punishment may be considered "child abuse" or "spouse abuse" (Steinmetz & Strauss, 1974). And the ultimate punishment, capital punishment, is now extremely rare. But despite the trend in public attitudes towards disfavor regarding some types, punishment or potential punishment is still pervasive in the world today. As might be expected, people are questioning the use of punishment, raising issues such as: Does punishment work? When, how, and why?

WHAT IS PUNISHMENT?

There is no lack of competing definitions for punishment. *Webester's Seventh New Collegiate Dictionary* (p. 693) defines the noun *punishment* as "retributive suffering, pain, or loss," and the verb *punish* as "to inflict a penalty for the commission of (an offense) in retribution or retaliation . . . to inflict injury upon: hurt." Psychologists (e.g., Skinner, 1953) defined punishment in procedural terms, as presentation of an aversive stimulus following a response. In this case, "aversive stimulus" was defined as a stimulus that increases the probability of responses that terminate the stimulus. Solomon provided a working definition in which punishment was construed as "a noxious stimulus, one which will support, by its termination or omission, the growth of new escape or avoidance responses" (Solomon, 1964, p. 239). And Azrin and Holz proposed as a "minimal" definition, "a consequence of behavior that reduces the future probability of that behavior" (Azrin & Holz, 1966, p. 381). No one definition describes all types of punishment. Unfortunately, as a definition becomes more inclusive, it tells us less about the phenomenon. For the purposes of this discussion, punishment in most cases refers to the addition of an aversive consequence that results in a reduction of tendency to behave in a certain way.

IS PUNISHMENT EFFECTIVE?

Early works on punishment seemed to demonstrate that it was ineffective in eliminating behavior. In *Walden Two,* Skinner, speaking through the character of Frazier, wrote, "In the long run punishment doesn't reduce the probability that an act will occur" (Skinner, 1948, p. 260). However, more recent work on punishment makes it clear that punishment can suppress or eliminate behavior. How effective punishment is in accomplishing this depends upon various factors that vary from situation to situation, including characteristics of the punishing stimulus (e.g., intensity, temporal proximity, frequency, and scheduling), characteristics of the behavior being punished (e.g., whether instrumental, consummatory, instinctive, or reflexive, and whether originally established by reward or by punishment), and characteristics of the subject being punished.

Intensity of Punishment

In general, research on punishment intensity has found that the greater the intensity of the punishing stimulus, the greater is the suppression of the punished behavior. According to Azrin and Holz (1961), the intensity of punishment of behaviors previously established by reward or positive reinforcement determines whether the results are: (a) detection and arousal (i.e., no suppression of behavior); (b) temporary suppression (i.e., effects are not permanent); (c) partial suppression (i.e., only part of behavior is permanently suppressed); or (d) complete elimination of the behavior being punished. In the first case, "punishment" applied with too low an intensity actually may become a secondary reinforcer and increase rather than suppress the unwanted behavior (Solomon, 1964). In the latter case, punishment of too high an intensity may result in serious side effects and/or death.

When the behavior being punished is consummatory rather than instrumental, intensity of punishment seems to have little effect. Even punishments of relatively low intensity appear to suppress eating and sexual behaviors. Eating behaviors can be so effectively suppressed that the animal dies of starvation (Solomon, 1964).

Temporal Proximity

In general, for punishment to be maximally effective, it should follow immediately the behavior to be suppressed. While nonimmediate punishment can appear to be effective, particularly during the initial stages of punishment, the effects typically are not permanent. Immediacy of punishment appears to determine both permanence and final degree of behavior suppression (Azrin & Holz, 1966).

Manner of Introduction

How punishment is first introduced can be critical. Punishment that has been introduced at a low intensity and gradually increased over a period of time has considerably less effect than does punishment that is presented suddenly at full intensity. Adaptation to punishment can occur and reduce the effectiveness of punishment (Solomon, 1964).

Frequency and Scheduling of Punishment

In general, it appears that increased frequency of punishment results in increased effectiveness of punishment, and that continuous punishment is more effective than intermittent punishment. Given such effects of frequency and scheduling, one might expect some loss of effectiveness during any "vacation" from punishment. Azrin and Holz (1966) indicate that this is not the case, that the lapse of time *per se* does not reduce the effect of punishment. More research is needed to clarify these issues. In the child development literature, "consistency" in child rearing is generally considered desirable. Nevertheless, according to Burton, some "inconsistency in the use of disciplinary techniques is desirable for producing internalized self-control" (Burton, 1976, p. 193).

Various Characteristics of the Behavior Being Punished

Effectiveness depends upon the strength of the punished response (Solomon, 1964). The presence or absence of reinforcement of the punished response also determines how effective punishment of that response is (Azrin & Holz, 1966). Continued reinforcement of a punished behavior appears to compete and interfere with the suppression effects of punishment. Effectiveness also depends upon whether the behavior being punished was originally established by reward or by punishment. According to Solomon (1964), when the behavior punished was originally established by (or to avoid) punishment, punishment may be ineffective, or in some cases may strengthen the behavior being punished rather than eliminate it.

Subject Characteristics

There is some evidence indicating that punishment is decreasingly effective as the subject's motivation for the punished behavior increases (Azrin & Holz, 1966). Effectiveness also varies with familiarity of the subject with the punishment being used, with species, and with age and developmental stage within species of subjects (Solomon, 1964). Most of the research on punishment has been carried out on infrahuman subjects rather than human subjects. Human cognitive abilities (e.g., reasoning and imagination) can also influence effectiveness of punishment. Verbalization of rationale seems to facilitate discrimination and generalization of punishment effects in humans. Descriptive verbalization and recall of what is being punished appear to reduce the impact of time delays between behavior and punishment. In some cases, observation of punishment by humans seems to have some effects, as though the punishment were experienced vicariously. And, finally, punishment of humans appears to be most effective within a context of love (Burton, 1976).

THEORIES OF PUNISHMENT

Various theories have been used to explain how and why punishment results in a reduction of the frequency of the punished behavior. Dinsmoor (1954, 1955) explained punishment effects in terms of simple stimulus-response (S-R) principles of avoidance learning. Basically this explanation holds that punished behaviors decrease in frequency because of an increase in frequency of behaviors that compete with or interfere with the punished response. Another theory (Mowrer, 1960) explains punishment effects in terms of fear conditioning and reinforcement of whatever action or inaction eliminates or controls the fear. For a discussion and critique of these and other theories of punishment, see Dunham (1971).

Relevant Questions

Why do some subjects seem to enjoy and seek punishment? Occasionally a punishment procedure actually increases rather than decreases the frequency of the behavior being punished. As noted earlier, this can occur when the punished behavior was originally established by punishment. Azrin and Holz (1966) pointed out that other reverse effect phenomena are commonly observed in clinical psychology (e.g., masochism), criminology (e.g., self-punitiveness), and child guidance (e.g., attention getting). Sometimes a child appears to be deliberately misbehaving to get a parent to stop whatever he/she is doing to administer punishment. In such cases, it appears that the parent has paid attention to the child primarily in response to misbehavior, and has unwittingly transformed the "punishment" into reinforcement. The end result may be a situation in which punishment not only does not appear to be effective, but also in which the child or individual appears to seek more "punishment." Rather than contradict the effectiveness of punishment, such phenomena confirm the effectiveness of reinforcement.

Are there undesirable side effects that result from punishment? Experiments on monkeys (Brady, 1958; Masserman & Pechtel, 1953) clearly show that punishment can have neurotic or seemingly harmful emotional side effects. While such side effects are indeed frightening and should not be ignored, they do not appear in all experiments involving use of strong punishment (Solomon, 1964). Punishment may also result in termination of a social relationship, operant aggression directed toward the punishing agent, and/or elicited aggression against individuals who had nothing to do with the original punishment (Azrin & Holz, 1966). In the punishment process, behaviors that result in escape from the aversive situation are reinforced. For humans, this means that punishment may have a side effect of destroying a social relationship and of making further social control of the punished behavior more difficult. For example, punishment in school may result in tardiness, truancy, and/or dropping out of school. Individuals may also discover that they can eliminate a punishing stimulus by attacking its source. Thus a potential side effect of punishment is aggression directed at the punishing individual. And, finally, punishment may result in aggression directed at some innocent bystander, in some ways like the proverbial worker who comes home to kick the dog. Whether through escape or aggression, termination of social relations can be a serious side effect of punishment for humans and society.

IN SUMMARY

Punishment can be effective in reducing or eliminating undesirable behaviors. How effective a given punishment situation is depends upon various factors, including characteristics of the punishing stimulus, the behavior being punished, and the subject being punished. Potential side effects of punishment, such as termination of social relations, should be considered in any application, especially when humans are involved.

REFERENCES

Azrin, N. H., & Holz, W. C. (1961). Punishment during fixed-interval reinforcement. *Journal of the Experimental Analysis of Behavior, 4*, 343–347.

Azrin, N. H., & Holz, W. C. (1966). Punishment. In W. K. Honig (Ed.), *Operant behavior: Areas of research and application.* New York: Appleton-Century-Crofts.

Brady, J. V. (1958). Ulcers in "executive monkeys." *Scientific American, 199*, 95–103.

Burton, R. V. (1976). Honesty and dishonesty. In T. Lickona (Ed.), *Moral development and behavior.* New York: Holt, Rinehart & Winston.

Dinsmoor, J. A. (1954). Punishment: I. The avoidance hypothesis. *Psychological Review, 61*, 34–46.

Dinsmoor, J. A. (1955). Punishment: II. An interpretation of empirical findings. *Psychological Review, 62*, 96–105.

Dunham, P. J. (1971). Punishment: Method and theory. *Psychological Review, 78*, 58–70.

Masserman, J. M., & Pechtel, C. (1953). Neurosis in monkeys; A preliminary report of experimental observations. *New York Academy of Science Annals, 56*, 253–265.

Mowrer, O. H. (1960). *Learning theory and symbolic processes.* New York: Wiley.

Skinner, B. F. (1948). *Walden two.* New York: Macmillan.

Skinner, B. F. (1953). *Science and human behavior.* New York: Macmillan.

Solomon, R. L. (1964). Punishment. *American Psychologist, 19*(4), 239–253.

Steinmetz, S. K., & Strauss, M. A. (Eds.). (1974). *Violence in the family.* New York: Dodd, Mead.

SUGGESTED READING

Lester, D. (1979). Modern psychological theories of punishment and their implications for penology and corrections. *Corrective and Social Psychiatry and Journal of Behavioral Technology, Methods and Therapy, 25*(3), 81–85.

Lickona, T. (Ed.). (1976). *Moral development and behavior.* New York: Holt, Rinehart & Winston.

Walters, G. C., & Grusec, J. E. (1977). *Punishment.* San Francisco: Freeman.

J. W. ENGEL
University of Hawaii

LEARNING THEORIES
REINFORCEMENT
REWARDS

PYGMALION EFFECT

The term Pygmalion effect refers broadly to the effects of interpersonal expectations, or the finding that what one person has come to expect of another can come to serve as a self-fulfilling prophecy. These effects of interpersonal self-fulfilling prophecies have come to be called Pygmalion effects in general, but especially so when the interpersonal expectancy effects occur in an educational context.

EARLY LABORATORY EXPERIMENTS

The earliest studies were conducted with human participants. Experimenters obtained ratings of photographs of stimulus persons from their research participants but half the experimenters were led to expect high photo ratings and half were led to expect low photo ratings. In the first several such studies, experimenters expecting higher photo ratings obtained substantially higher photo ratings than did experimenters expecting lower photo ratings (Rosenthal, 1966, 1976).

To investigate the generality of these interpersonal expectancy effects in the laboratory, two studies employing animal subjects were conducted. Half the experimenters were told their rats had been specially bred for maze (or Skinner box) brightness, and half were told their rats had been specially bred for maze (or Skinner box) dullness. In both experiments, when experimenters had been led to expect better learning from their rat subjects, they obtained better learning from their rat subjects (Rosenthal & Fode, 1963; Rosenthal & Lawson, 1964).

PYMALION EFFECTS IN THE CLASSROOM

If rats became brighter when expected to by their experimenters, then it seemed not farfetched to think that children could become brighter when expected to by their teacher. Accordingly, all of the children in a study (Rosenthal & Jacobson, 1968) were administered a nonverbal test of intelligence, which was disguised as a test that would predict intellectual "blooming." The test was labeled as "The Harvard Test of Inflected Acquisition." There were 18 classrooms in the school, three at each of the six grade levels. Within each grade level the three classrooms were composed of children with above average ability, average ability, and below average ability, respectively. Within each of the 18 classrooms, approximately 20 percent of the children were chosen at random to form the experimental group. Each teacher was given the names of the children from his or her class who were in the experimental condition. The teacher was told that these children had scored on the "Test of Inflected Acquisition" such that they would show surprising gains in intellectual competence during the next eight months of school. The only difference between the experimental group and the control group children, then, was in the mind of the teacher.

At the end of the school year, eight months later, all the children were retested with the same test of intelligence. Considering the school as a whole, the children from whom the teachers has been led to expect greater intellectual gain showed a significantly greater gain than did the children of the control group (Rosenthal & Jacobson, 1968).

DOMAINS INVESTIGATED

A dozen years after the "Pygmalion in the Classroom" study was completed, the research literature on interpersonal expectancy effects had broadened to include 345 experiments that could be subsumed under one of eight domains of research: human learning and ability, animal learning, reaction time, psychophysical judgments, laboratory interviews, person perception, inkblot tests, and everyday situations. After another dozen years had gone by, the overall mean effect size of the 479 studies was found to be an r of .30. An r of that magnitude can be thought of as the effects of interpersonal expectations changing the proportion of people performing above average from 35% to 65% (Rosenthal & Rubin, 1978, 1982; Rosenthal, 1991).

THE FOUR FACTOR THEORY

A considerable amount of research has been summarized, employing a meta-analysis, suggesting how teachers may treat differently those children for whom they have more favorable expectations (Harris & Rosenthal, 1985). Table 1 summarizes these differences as four factors, two that are primary and two that are somewhat smaller in their magnitude of effect.

CURRENT RESEARCH

The most recent work, and that currently in progress, continues to examine the effects of interpersonal expectancies in an ever-widening circle of contexts. Pygmalion effects in management (Eden, 1990), in courtrooms (Blanck, Rosenthal, Hart, & Bernier, 1990; Halverson, Hallahan, Hart, & Rosenthal, 1997), in nursing homes (Learman, Avorn, Everitt, & Rosenthal, 1990), and in a variety of classrooms (Babad, 1992) are under investigation. It has

Table 1.   Summary of Four Factors in the Mediation of Teacher Expectancy Effects

Factor	Brief Summary of the Evidence
Central Factors	
1. Climate (Affect)	Teachers appear to create a warmer socio-emotional climate for their "special" students. This warmth appears to be at least partially communicated by nonverbal cues. (Estimated effect size $r = .29$)
2. Input (Effort)	Teachers appear to teach more material and more difficult material to their "special" students. (Estimated effect size $r = .27$)
Additional Factors	
3. Output	Teachers appear to give their "special" students greater opportunities for responding. These opportunities are offered both verbally and nonverbally (e.g., giving a student more time in which to answer a teacher's question). (Estimated effect size $r = .17$)
4. Feedback	Teachers appear to give their "special" students more differentiated feedback, both verbal and nonverbal, as to how these students have been performing. (Estimated effect size $r = .10$)

Note: Even the smallest effect size r listed above reflects a difference in performance levels of 55% versus 45%; the larger effect size rs listed above reflect a difference in performance levels of 64% versus 36%.

been shown that organizational effectiveness can be increased by raising leaders' expectations, that juries' verdicts of guilty can be increased by assigning them judges to instruct them who believe the defendant to be guilty, that the depression levels of nursing home residents can be reduced by raising the expectation levels of caretakers, and that teacher expectations can serve as self-fulfilling prophecies in other countries and for more than simply intellectual tasks. In all these cases the mediating variables are receiving special attention with the evidence growing rapidly that much of the mediation is occurring by means of unintended nonverbal behavior (Ambady & Rosenthal, 1992).

REFERENCES

Ambady, N., & Rosenthal, R. (1992). Thin slices of expressive behavior as predictors of interpersonal consequences: A meta-analysis. *Psychological Bulletin, 111,* 256–274.

Babad, E. (1992). Teacher expectancies and nonverbal behavior. In R. S. Feldman (Ed.), *Applications of nonverbal behavioral theories and research.* Hillsdale, NJ: Erlbaum.

Blanck, P. D., Rosenthal, R., Hart, A. J., & Bernieri, F. (1990). The measure of the judge: An empirically-based framework for exploring trial judges' behavior. *Iowa Law Review, 75,* 653–684.

Eden, D. (1990). *Pygmalion in management.* MA: Lexington.

Halverson, A. M., Hallahan, M., Hart, A. J., & Rosenthal, R. (1997). Reducing the biasing effects of judges' nonverbal behavior with simplified jury instruction. *Journal of Applied Psychology, 82,* 590–598.

Harris, M. J., & Rosenthal, R. (1985). Mediation of interpersonal expectancy effects: 31 meta-analyses. *Psychological Bulletin, 97,* 363–386.

Learman, L. A., Avorn, J., Everitt, D. E., & Rosenthal, R. (1990). Pygmalion in the nursing home: The effects of caregiver expectations on patient outcomes. *Journal of the American Geriatrics Society, 38,* 797–803.

Rosenthal, R. (1966). *Experimenter effects in behavioral research.* New York: Appleton-Century-Crofts.

Rosenthal, R. (1976). *Experimenter effects in behavioral research* (enlarged ed.). New York: Irvington.

Rosenthal, R. (1991). *Meta-analytic procedures for social research* (rev. ed.). Newbury Park, CA.

Rosenthal, R., & Fode, K. L. (1963). The effect of experimenter bias on the performance of the albino rat. *Behavioral Science, 8,* 183–189.

Rosenthal, R., & Jacobson, L. (1968). Pygmalion in the classroom. New York: Holt, Rinehart, and Winston.

Rosenthal, R., & Lawson, R. (1964). A longitudinal study of the effects of experimenter bias on the operant learning of laboratory rats. *Journal of Psychiatric Research, 2,* 61–72.

Rosenthal, R., & Rubin, D. B. (1978). Interpersonal expectancy effects: The first 345 studies: *The Behavioral and Brain Sciences, 3,* 377–386.

Rosenthal, R., & Rubin, D. B. (1982). A simple general purpose display of magnitude of experimental effect. *Journal of Educational Psychology, 74,* 166–169.

R. ROSENTHAL
University of California, Riverside

EARLY CHILDHOOD EDUCATION